BIBLE DICTIONARY

BIBLE DICTIONARY

General Editor:
G. Douglas Young, Ph.D.
Founder, Institute of Holy Land Studies, Jerusalem

Revision Editor:
James Swanson, Th.B., M.S.M.

Associate Editors:
George Giacumakis, Ph.D.
President, Institute of Holy Land Studies, Jerusalem

John R. Kohlenberger III, Th.B., M.A.

Tyndale House Publishers, Inc. • Wheaton, Illinois

All Scripture, unless otherwise noted, is
taken from the New International Version
of the Bible. Copyright © 1973, 1978,
1984 by the International Bible Society.
Used by permission of Zondervan Bible
Publishers.

Cover design by Julie Chen. Artwork from
Wood River Media, Inc. San Rafael, CA.

ISBN 0-8423-3776-8

Printed in the United States of America.

03 02 01 00 99 98
6   5   4   3   2   1

Preface to the Revised Edition

The first edition of *Young's Bible Dictionary* was highly acclaimed for its treatment of the history, archaeology, and culture of the Bible, having been assembled in Israel by resident and visiting faculty of the Institute of Holy Land Studies, Jerusalem. Its revised edition, the *Young's Compact Bible Dictionary*, has been greatly enhanced: it contains thousands of new topics and cross-references, hundreds of maps and illustrations, yet is easier to use, and thus should meet the needs of a larger audience of Bible students.

How to Use This Book

A Bible Dictionary provides biblical, historical, and theological information about Bible people and places, plants and animals, books and events, culture and background. Conveniently arranged in alphabetical order, one simply looks up the subject of interest to find instant insights.

The *Young's Compact Bible Dictionary* (*YCBD*) provides three routes to locating information.

First, the topics themselves. With more than 6,300 entries (plus "see references"—explained below), the *YCBD* is the most thorough compact Bible Dictionary available. The entry headings are based on the New International Version (NIV), currently the best-selling English translation, but reflect the vocabulary of most modern versions.

Second, the "*see*" references. Though headings are based on the NIV, the *YCBD* contains hundreds of cross-references based on the vocabulary and spelling of the time-honored King James Version (KJV). For example, LONG-SUFFERING directs the user to *see* PATIENCE, for EMMANUEL *see* IMMANUEL, for BESOM *see* BROOM. *See* references also point to large articles that treat a number of smaller concepts. For example, BABOON, KATYDID, and LOCUST all point to BEASTS; CARBUNCLE, EMERALD, and ONYX point to PRECIOUS STONES AND METALS. Within entries, *see* references identify related topics for further study. For example, CALENDAR invites the user to *see also* CHRONOLOGY and TIME; DREAM to DIVINATION, DIVINE.

Third, unique to the *YCBD*, is the Topical Index in the front of the book. This Index organizes more than 400 entries under 29 major subject headings, loosely based on the 200 series of the Dewey Decimal System. There the user can find all articles relating to such subjects as GENERAL CULTURAL & BIBLICAL BACKGROUND OF THE NT and OT, THEO-

LOGICAL SYSTEMS and TERMS, BELIEVERS' LIFE IN CHRIST, and CHRISTIAN PRACTICES.

Besides explanatory information, each article is thoroughly indexed to the Bible itself. In this way, the *YCBD* functions as a Concordance or Topical Bible. If the article cites every biblical reference to its subject (in the NIV), it ends with a dagger (†). For example, see ACZIB, ARARAT, and ELIMELECH.

Special attention has been given to the treatment of proper and place names. The *YCBD* provides information on every person in the Bible, unless this person is only mentioned in a genealogical list. Similarly, every place in the Bible is treated, unless that place is only mentioned to define a border or land allotment. Articles on proper and place names are subdivided into different individuals and locations, such as ADAM 1, a Canaanite town, and ADAM 2, the first man. Places are usually referenced with coordinates that are used to locate them on the standard Survey of Israel maps (such as those published in the *Student Map Manual* [Zondervan]).

Because the meanings of names are often used significantly in the Bible, most names have been defined in English. ABRAHAM and ABRAM are defined as "father of many" and "exalted father," a promise which became a reality because God has multiplied and preserved the Jewish people throughout the centuries. When the many technical sources used for this research do not agree on the meaning of names, the major options are cited. For example, JAAZIAH may mean either "Yahweh is strong" or "Yahweh nourishes." When a name could not be defined with certainty, such as JABBOK, JERIBAI, or KALLAI, no definition is offered. The user is strongly warned against using the meaning of names to interpret the Bible or to draw out "hidden" spiritual meaning unless the text does so specifically (as in Gen. 2:23 or 1 Sam. 25:25).

A special thanks is due to the many involved in this revision: to Dr. G. Douglas Young, Dr. George Giacumakis (his successor), and the other eleven contributors for the production of the original book; to John R. Kohlenberger III for his collaboration and companionship; to Dr. Ken Taylor who first conceived of this revision; to my friends Dr. Al Baylis, Dr. John Moore, and Dr. Ed Goodrick for reading selected articles and offering valuable suggestions; to Sandra, my lovely wife, mother of eight, and author, for typing and proofing the entire revised manuscript; to Rollie Aden and Sue Winsinger for their proofreading and suggestions; to Richard Wells, an inspiring example of Christian living, for his thoughtful suggestions when he read through the revision; to Dr. Philip Comfort, whose thorough and erudite editing was greatly appreciated.

The revision editor echoes the hope of the original editors that the volume "may assist those who desire to study the Word of God" and that this study will change each student to become more closely conformed to the Teacher, our Lord Jesus Christ.

James A. Swanson

Preface to the First Edition of "Young's Bible Dictionary"

The late Dr. G. Douglas Young, President Emeritus and Professor of Judeo-Christian Studies of the Institute of Holy Land Studies in Jerusalem, saw the need for an inexpensive, one-volume dictionary of the Bible. He secured the contributions of renowned scholars to assist in this project. As general editor he completed about three-fourths of this work prior to his death in May of 1980. Since I was Dr. Young's successor, it fell to me to bring this dictionary to completion in order for students of the Bible to have it for their use.

Up-to-date one-volume dictionaries of the Bible are few in number. Those in English from a Jerusalem, Israel milieu are almost nonexistent, and one especially prepared for the millions of evangelical laymen in particular is unique.

Likewise, the need is clear for more extensive articles in certain areas, such as those in archaeology, geography, history, and theology. These articles in this volume express the latest research in Israel and a theological viewpoint which is in conformity to the text of Scripture.

Special recognition must go to Nina Tronstein, former secretary to Dr. Young, for her tedious efforts to bring this project to light. She worked through all this material a number of times in order to produce a systematic organization of the contents. Special consideration also goes to Audrey Rosenbaum who did most of the final typing, along with assistance from Joan Hall and Marta Rios.

An expression of gratitude is in order to the twelve [original] contributors who have been most patient until the work of their efforts has actually come into print. They faithfully met their deadlines even though the publication of this volume was delayed.

May this volume assist those who desire to study the Word of God.

George Giacumakis, Jr.
Jerusalem, Israel, 1984

Contributors

G.L.A. GLEASON L. ARCHER, JR., B.A., B.D., LL.B., Ph.D.
Professor of Old Testament and Semitic Studies
Trinity Evangelical Divinity School, Deerfield, Illinois
Isaiah, Book of; Money; Pentateuch; Tabernacle; Temple

P.W.C. PHILIP W. COMFORT, B.A., M.A., Ph.D.
Senior Editor, Bible Department, Tyndale House Publishers
Tyndale House editor of this revision of *Young's Compact Bible Dictionary*
Visiting Professor, New Testament, Wheaton College, Illinois
Biblical Manuscripts

J.C.C. J. CLEMENT CONNELL, B.A., M.A.
formerly Director of Studies and Lecturer in New Testament
Exegesis, London Bible College, London, England
God, Names of; Godhead

R.D.C. ROBERT D. CULVER, A.D., B.D., Th.M., Th.D.
formerly Professor of Theology, Trinity Evangelical
Divinity School, Deerfield, Illinois
Annual Visiting Professor of Theology, Winnipeg
Theological Seminary, Winnipeg, Manitoba, Canada
Christ, Work of; Festivals; Sacrifices and Offerings; Salvation, Application of; Scripture

G.G. GEORGE GIACUMAKIS, JR., B.A., M.A., Ph.D.
Professor of History, Institute of Holy Land Studies,
Jerusalem, Israel

E.W.G. EDWARD W. GOODRICK, Th.B., B.A., M.S., D.D.
formerly Professor of Greek and Bible at Multnomah School of the
Bible, Portland, Oregon
Tongues, Gift of

D.G. DONALD GUTHRIE, B.D., M.Th., Ph.D.
Vice-principal, London Bible College, London, England
Christ, Life and Teachings of

G.W.K. GILBERT W. KIRBY, M.A.
formerly Principal and Lecturer in Practical Theology, London Bible
College, London, England
Sin

Contributors

J.R.K.   **JOHN R. KOHLENBERGER III, Th.B., M.A.**
Bible Researcher and Writer
Abortion, Decalogue, Law, Spirit

R.N.L.   **RICHARD N. LONGENECKER, B.A., Ma.A., Ph.D.**
Professor of New Testament
Wycliffe College, University of Toronto, Toronto, Ontario, Canada
Paul, Life and Teachings of; Pauline Epistles

J.B.P.   **J. BARTON PAYNE, A.B., M.A., B.D., Th.M., Ph.D.**
Late Professor of Old Testament
Covenant Theological Seminary, St. Louis, Missouri
*Assyria and Asshur; Babylon, Babylonia; Calendar; Chronology;
Egypt; Hasmoneans; Herods, The; Judges of Israel; Kings of Judah
and Israel; Maccabees; Persia; Rome, Citizen of, Rome, Roman;
Seleucids*

A.F.R.   **ANSON F. RAINEY, B.A., B.D., Th.M., M.A., Ph.D.**
Professor of Ancient Near Eastern Cultures and Semitic Linguistics
Tel Aviv University, Tel Aviv, Israel
Archaeology

H.R.T.R.   **HALVOR R. T. RONNING, B.A., B.D., M.A.**
Lecturer in Historical Geography
Institute of Holy Land Studies, Jerusalem, Israel
Geography of the Holy Land

J.A.S.   **JAMES A. SWANSON, Th.B., M.S.M.**
Bible Researcher and Editor
*Attributes of God; Bible Versions; Biblical Languages; Communion,
Views of; Existence of God; Fellowship; Giving; Hermeneutics; I Am;
Parenting; Soul; Systematic Theology; Usury*

W.B.W.   **WILBUR B. WALLIS, B.A., B.D., S.T.M., Ph.D.**
Emeritus Professor of New Testament
Covenant Theological Seminary, St. Louis, Missouri
*Acts, Book of; Gospels, The Four; Hebrews, Book of; Revelation,
Book of*

E.M.Y.   **EDWIN M. YAMAUCHI, B.A., M.A., Ph.D.**
Professor of History
Miami University of Ohio, Oxford, Ohio
Jerusalem

G.D.Y.   **G. DOUGLAS YOUNG, B.Sc., B.D., S.T.M., Ph.D.**
Late President Emeritus and Regents Professor of Judaeo-Christian
Studies
Institute of Holy Land Studies, Jerusalem, Israel

Abbreviations

Abbreviations

lit.	literally
LXX	Septuagint
MPH	miles per hour
MS	manuscript
MSS	manuscripts
Mt.	Mount
N	North
NASB	New American Standard Bible, 1960
NEB	New English Bible, 1961
NIV	New International Version, 1978
NJB	New Jerusalem Bible, 1985
NKJV	New King James Version, 1982
NT	New Testament
OT	Old Testament
P	papyri
per se	by or in itself
pl.	plural
Pss.	Psalms (plural)
RSV	Revised Standard Version, 1946
RV	English Revised Version, 1881
S	South
v.	verse
vv.	verses
W	West
ZPEB	*The Zondervan Pictorial Encyclopedia of the Bible*, Zondervan

The Books of the Bible

Ge.	Genesis	Isa.	Isaiah	Ro.	Romans
Ex.	Exodus	Jer.	Jeremiah	1Co.	1 Corinthians
Lev.	Leviticus	La.	Lamentations	2Co.	2 Corinthians
Nu.	Numbers	Eze.	Ezekiel	Gal.	Galatians
Dt.	Deuteronomy	Da.	Daniel	Eph.	Ephesians
Jos.	Joshua	Hos.	Hosea	Php.	Philippians
Jdg.	Judges	Joel	Joel	Col.	Colossians
Ru.	Ruth	Am.	Amos	1Th.	1 Thessalonians
1Sa.	1 Samuel	Ob.	Obadiah	2Th.	2 Thessalonians
2Sa.	2 Samuel	Jnh.	Jonah	1Ti.	1 Timothy
1Ki.	1 Kings	Mic.	Micah	2Ti.	2 Timothy
2Ki.	2 Kings	Na.	Nahum	Tit.	Titus
1Ch.	1 Chronicles	Hab.	Habbakuk	Phm.	Philemon
2Ch.	2 Chronicles	Zep.	Zephaniah	Heb.	Hebrews
Ezr.	Ezra	Hag.	Haggai	Jas.	James
Ne.	Nehemiah	Zec.	Zechariah	1Pe.	1 Peter
Est.	Esther	Mal.	Malachi	2Pe.	2 Peter
Job	Job	Mt.	Matthew	1Jn.	1 John
Ps.	Psalms	Mk.	Mark	2Jn.	2 John
Pr.	Proverbs	Lk.	Luke	3Jn.	3 John
Ecc.	Ecclesiastes	Jn.	John	Jude	Jude
SS.	Song of Songs	Ac.	Acts	Rev.	Revelation

Deuterocanonical Works Cited

1Macc.	1 Maccabees
2Macc.	2 Maccabees

A Topical Index

A Topical Index

A Topical Index

AARON When Aaron was three years old living in Egypt with his parents and older sister, the Egyptian princess rescued his baby brother Moses in his papyrus basket at the edge of the Nile River (Ex. 2:1-10; 7:7). Aaron grew up to become the first priest and founder of the priesthood of Israel. He made his appearance in the unfolding drama of redemption at the time of God's commission to Moses to lead the sons of Israel out of Egyptian bondage into a Promised Land. When Moses protested that he was not a good speaker, God appointed Aaron to be his prophet (*nabi*) to speak to the people in his place (Ex. 4:10-17). He was an eloquent representative, both to persuade the people of Israel that the time of their deliverance had indeed come, and to prevail upon Pharaoh to give up his bondslaves. After the Exodus, during the attack by the Amalekites, Aaron and Hur assisted Moses on the hilltop while Joshua led the fighting in the field (Ex. 17:8-13). In the incident of the golden calf, however, Aaron did not manifest the same strong character as Moses (Ex. 32:1-6). While Moses was away, on the mountain of God, Aaron allowed the people to pressure him into making the idol, bringing God's judgment on their sin.

The rich and symbolically colored clothing for Aaron's robe as high priest is described in Ex. 39; his induction into office in Lev. 8. Aaron alone, once a year, entered the Most Holy Place (Lev. 16). He was the Levite *par excellence*.

Aaron and his sons were the sacrificing priests while the Levites, Aaron's brothers, were his assistants, ministering especially in regard to the tabernacle (Nu. 3–4, 18). Aaron's sons were ordained and anointed to minister in the priest's office. The two oldest, Nadab and Abihu, died before the LORD due to transgression (Lev. 10.1-7). The priesthood continued through Aaron's two youngest sons, Eleazar and Ithamar (Nu. 3:2-4).

Neither Aaron nor Moses were allowed to enter the Promised Land because of their lack of trust in God (Nu. 20:12). Aaron died on the top of Mt. Hor at the age of 123 years (Nu. 33:39), and the nation wept for him for thirty days. In the NT the priesthood of Aaron is compared and contrasted with the priesthood of Christ (Heb. 5:4; 7:11).

AARONITES KJV for "those from the clan of Aaron" in 1Ch. 12:27; 27:17. †

AB *See* CALENDAR

ABADDON {destruction} Rev. 9:11. † *See* DEAD, ABODE OF

ABAGTHA One of seven chamberlains, a eunuch, who was sent by the Persian King Xerxes to bring Queen Vashti before him (Est. 1:10). †

ABANA 2Ki. 5:12. † *See* AMANA; DAMASCUS

ABARIM {geographical areas beyond} The mountain range just E of the Salt Sea (Dead Sea) from which Moses viewed the land given by the LORD to the sons of Israel (Nu. 27:12). The Israelites came to this in the last stage of their journey from Egypt, as given in Nu. 33:47-48 before the sons of Israel camped in the plains of Moab. Later it was associated with Lebanon and Bashan (Jer. 22:20). Its highest peak is Mt. Nebo, where Moses died (Dt. 32:49). †

ABBA [father] An Aramaic word meaning "father" which Jesus used in the Garden of Gethsemane (Mk. 14:36) and which Paul used in two notable passages on the children or sons of God (Ro. 8:15; Gal. 4:6). All three of its occurrences in the NT are in prayers addressed to God. †

ABDA [servant of Yahweh]
1. A man in charge of forced labor under King Solomon (1Ki. 4:6). †
2. One of the 284 Levites who lived in Jerusalem in the time of Nehemiah (Ne. 11:17); spelled Obadiah in 1Ch. 9:16. †

ABDEEL [servant of El] The father of Shelemiah, a member of King Jehoiakim's court (Jer. 36:26). †

ABDI [servant of Yahweh *or* my servant]
1. A member of the clan of Merari (1Ch. 6:44; 2Ch. 29:12). †
2. One of the members of the priesthood who had married foreign women in the times of Ezra (Ezr. 10:26). †

ABDIEL [servant of El] Father of Ahi, a Gadite who lived in Bashan (1Ch. 5:15). †

ABDON [servant] Name of four OT persons and a Levitical town.
1. One of the judges of Israel (Jdg. 12:13-15). †
2. The head of one of the Benjamite families living in Jerusalem in the time of David (1Ch. 8:23). †
3. A Benjamite ancestor of King Saul (1Ch. 8:30; 9:36). †
4. A trusted official of King Josiah's court (2Ch. 34:20). † *See also* ACBOR
5. A town of the tribe of Asher given to the sons of Kohath, tentatively identified with a tell (ancient mound) (165-

272) Jos. 19:28; 21:30; 1Ch. 6:74. † *See also* JUDGES OF ISRAEL

ABEDNEGO [servant of Nego *or* Nebo] *See* SHADRACH

ABEL 1. [morning mist] The second son of Adam and Eve, and a shepherd by trade. Abel was murdered by his older brother, Cain, when Abel's offering from the firstborn of his flock was accepted, while Cain's offering from the produce of the soil was not looked on with favor (Ge. 4:10, 16). He is described by the NT as a righteous man and a martyr who acted by faith in the matter of the sacrifice he offered to God (Mt. 23:35; Lk. 11:51; Heb. 11:4; 12:24). †

ABEL 2. [meadow] This word is always used in the NIV in composition with other names and places. This is to be distinguished from the name of Abel found in Ge. 4ff. In 2Sa. 20:18 Abel is short for ABEL BETH MAACAH. *See* next six references. †

ABEL BETH MAACAH, ABEL OF BETH MAACAH, ABEL BETH-MAACHA [meadow of the house of Maacah] A fortified town near Dan on the border with Lebanon (204-296). It was to this town that Joab pursued the rebellious Sheba after the attempted coup by David's son Absalom (2Sa. 20:14-22); later it was taken by Ben-Hadad, the king of Damascus (1Ki. 15:20); then by the Assyrian king Tiglath-Pileser III (2Ki. 15:29).†

ABEL THE GREAT KJV in 1Sa. 6:18 is a transliteration of the Hebrew text. It could be translated "meadow" but is more likely "stone" and is so rendered in italics in the KJV and simply rendered "large stone" by most versions.

ABEL KERAMIM [meadow of vineyards] A place (228-142) in Ammon, not far from modern Amman in Jordan, to which the judge Jephthah pursued the Ammonites (Jdg. 11:29-33). The place name is rendered "the plain of the vineyards" in the KJV. †

ABEL MAIM [meadow of waters] A variant of, or an additional name for, Abel Beth Maacah (2Ch. 16:4). †

ABEL MEHOLAH [meadow of the round dance] A town (203-197) whose location has not been exactly identified, but on the boundary of King Solomon's fifth district in the Jordan Valley (1Ki. 4:12). Gideon pursued the Midianites this far eastward (Jdg. 7:22), and it was probably the birthplace of Elisha the prophet (1Ki. 19:16). †

ABEL MIZRAIM [meadow of Egypt, mourning of Egypt] The Canaanites gave this name to the threshing floor of Atad. It was a meadow E of the Jordan River where the funeral procession of the patriarch Jacob stopped for seven days of mourning. The record makes a play on the word *abel*, which can mean either "meadow" or "mourning" (Ge. 50:11). †

ABEL SHITTIM [meadow of the acacia trees] Nu. 33:49 is the only occurrence of the full form of the name; elsewhere it is just called Shittim. † *See* SHITTIM

ABEZ *See* EBEZ

ABI [(my) father] *See* ABIJAH 6.

ABI-ALBON [(my) father is Albon] One of David's mighty men of whom nothing is known except that he was known as the Arbathite (2Sa. 23:31). †

ABIA, ABIAH 1Ch. 3:10; *cf.* Mt. 1:7. *See* ABIJAH 2. and 3.

ABIASAPH [(my) father has gathered] A descendant of the clan of Korah (Ex. 6:24). Ebiasaph is a variant spelling. † *See* EBIASAPH

ABIATHAR [(my) father gives abundance] The only son of the priest Ahimelech who escaped the slaughter of eighty-five priests by Doeg the Edomite during the time David was fleeing from King Saul (1Sa. 22:20-23; 23:6-9; 30:7; 2Sa. 8:17; 15:24-36; 17:15; 19:11; 20:25; 1Ki. 4:4; 1Ch. 15:11; 18:16; 24:6; 27:34). He joined King David and served with Zadok as high priest throughout his

reign. When he conspired to make Adonijah, David's son, the king in Solomon's place, Solomon deprived him of his priesthood and banished him to Anathoth (1Ki. 1:7, 19, 25, 42; 2:22, 26-27, 35). Jesus referred to Abiathar in Mk. 2:26 as a high priest and not to his father, Ahimelech. Several solutions have been satisfactorily offered. Consult a Bible commentary for possible solutions. †

ABIB [heads or spikes of grain] Ex. 13:4; 23:15; 34:18; Dt. 16:1. † *See* CALENDAR

ABIDA [(my) father knows] A son of Midian, and grandson of Abraham and Keturah (Ge. 25:4; 1Ch. 1:33). †

ABIDAN [(my) father is judge] The representative of the tribe of Benjamin at the census in the Sinai (Nu. 1:11; 2:22; 7:60, 65; 10:24). †

ABIDE *See* REMAIN

ABIEL [(my) father is El]
1. The father of Kish (1Sa. 9:1), and grandfather of King Saul (1Sa. 14:51). †
2. One of the famous thirty mighty men of King David (1Ch. 11:32). †

ABIEZER, ABIEZRITE [(my) father is help]
1. The collective name of the descendants of Abiezer, a clan in the Gileadite branch of the tribe of Manasseh. Gideon was a member of this clan (Jos. 17:2; Jdg. 6:11, 24, 34; 8:2, 32). †
2. One of David's mighty men from Anathoth (2Sa. 23:27; 1Ch. 11:28; 27:12). †
3. A descendant of Manasseh related to Gilead (Nu. 26:30; 1Ch. 7:18). † *See also* IEZER

ABIGAIL [(my) father rejoices *or* "cause of" joy]
1. The exceptionally wise and beautiful wife of the ill-mannered and wealthy Calebite, Nabal of Maon. When Nabal (whose name means "senseless, foolish") dealt with David in an insulting and ill-tempered way at the shearing festival, Abigail persuaded David not to avenge

himself in needless bloodshed. Later when Nabal died, David sent Abigail an offer of marriage. Abigail accepted and became David's wife along with Ahinoam of Jezreel (1Sa. 25).

2. One of David's two sisters and the mother of Amasa, a commander of David's army (1Ch. 2:16-17).

ABIHAIL [(my) father has power/ wealth, "cause of" strength]

1. A Levite of the Merarite clan (Nu. 3:35). †

2. The wife of Abishur (1Ch. 2:29). †

3. A Gadite who lived in the land of Bashan (1Ch. 5:14). †

4. Mother of King Rehoboam's wife Mahalath (2Ch. 11:18). †

5. Father of Queen Esther and uncle of Mordecai (Est. 2:15; 9:29). †

ABIHU [he is (my) father] One of the four sons of Aaron and Elisheba (Ex. 6:23). Abihu was included in the select number who witnessed the theophany at the ratification of the covenant received at Mt. Sinai (Ex. 24:1-11). Later all four sons were admitted to the priest's office, but Abihu and his brother Nadab, in the course of their ministry, did that which was not prescribed and were struck by fire and died (Lev. 10:1-3).

ABIHUD [(my) father has grandeur] A Benjamite listed as the third son of Bela (1Ch. 8:3). †

ABIJAH [(my) father is Yahweh]

1. Son of Beker of the tribe of Benjamin (1Ch. 7:8).

2. The younger son of Samuel. Abijah served as judge in Beersheba but did not follow the ways of his godly father (1Sa. 8:1-9).

3. A son of Jeroboam I who died in childhood as prophesied by the prophet Ahijah (1Ki. 14:1-18).

4. One of the descendants of Aaron representing the eighth of the twenty-four divisions made by David for purposes of temple service (1Ch. 24:10). The father of John the Baptist was a priest in this division of Abijah (Lk. 1:5).

5. The son and successor of Rehoboam as king of Judah. *See* KINGS OF JUDAH AND ISRAEL

6. Mother of King Hezekiah of Judah (2Ch. 29:1; 2Ki. 18:2), abbreviated to Abi.

7. One of the signers of the community document at Jerusalem in the days of Ezra the scribe (Ne. 10:7).

8. One of the chiefs of the priests who returned with Zerubbabel from Babylon to Jerusalem (Ne. 12:4).

ABIJAM [(my) father is the sea *or* father of the West] *See* KINGS OF JUDAH AND ISRAEL

ABILENE [meadow] The district of the tetrarchy ruled by Lysanias when John the Baptist began his public ministry (Lk. 3:1). This small mountainous region of the Ante-Lebanons was attached to the city of Abila on the bank of the Abana River NE of Mt. Hermon and NW of Damascus. †

ABIMAEL [(my) father is El] In the genealogies of Ge. 10:28 and 1Ch. 1:22, Abimael is one of the thirteen sons of Joktan, grandchildren of Eber and descendants of Shem. †

ABIMELECH [(my) father is a king, (my) father is Molech]

1. This may be a royal title of Philistine kings, as in the use of "pharaoh" by the Egyptians and "Agag" by the Amalekites. Both Abraham (Ge. 20–21), and later Isaac (Ge. 26), attempted to deceive an Abimelech, a Philistine king of Gerar (near Gaza) in the matter of calling their wives their sisters. Though the incidents are similar, the narrative assumes that two different Abimelechs are intended, possibly the father and later his son.

2. One of Gideon's sons who had his brothers murdered and himself proclaimed king by the men of Shechem. His violent reign of three years came to a dishonorable end (Jdg. 9).

3. The son of Abiathar and priest during the reign of King David (1Ch. 18:16).

4. A name designating Achish, king of Gath, in the title of Psalm 34. *See also* ACHISH; JUDGES OF ISRAEL

ABINADAB [(my) father is generous,
(my) father is Nadab]

1. A man who lived on the hill of Kiriath Jearim in the days of the Judges to
whom the men of the town entrusted the
ark of the LORD when it was returned by
the Philistines (1Sa. 7:1; 2Sa. 6:3; 1Ch.
13:7). †

2. The second oldest of David's seven
brothers. The three oldest sons of Jesse
served in Saul's army (1Sa. 16:8; 17:13;
1Ch. 2:13). †

3. One of Saul's sons who fell with his
father in the battle of Mt. Gilboa (1Sa.
31:2; 1Ch. 8:33; 9:39; 10:2). †

ABINOAM [(my) father is gracious-
ness] The father of Barak who lived
in Kedesh of Naphtali (Jdg. 4:6, 12; 5:1,
12). †

ABIRAM [(my) father is exalted]

1. A descendant of Reuben, he conspired against Moses and was destroyed
by God (Nu. 16:1, 12, 24, 25, 27; 26:9;
Dt. 11:6), poetically related in Ps. 106:17.
†

2. The firstborn son of Hiel of Bethel
(1Ki. 16:34). †

ABISHAG [(my) father strays] A great
beauty from Shunem who served as
King David's nurse and attendant during
the last days of his old age (1Ki. 1:1-4, 15).
After David's death, Adonijah's ambi-
tious request for Abishag in marriage
resulted in his being put to death (1Ki.
2:12-25) by Solomon who interpreted it
as an attempt to take the throne. †

ABISHAI [(my) father is Jesse] A fear-
less and loyal professional soldier in the
service of David. Abishai was the oldest
of the three sons of Zeruiah, David's sister. Abishai accompanied David into
Saul's military camp in a daring adven-
ture (1Sa. 26) and was present at the battle in the "field of daggers" or "field of
hostilities" near the pool of Gibeon. His
brother Asahel was killed by Abner, the
commander of Saul's army (2Sa. 2:16-
23). In the first Ammonite campaign
when Joab found it necessary to deploy
David's army on the two fronts, Joab
divided his forces, and those not under

his command he entrusted to Abishai's
leadership (2Sa. 10:7-14). In the battle of
Absalom's rebellion, the forces of David
were divided between Joab, Abishai, and
Ittai the Gittite (2Sa. 18:1-8). Abishai had
the honor of being the commander of the
mighty men of David known as the
"Thirty" (2Sa. 23:18-19). It must have
been one of the highlights of his career
when he saved the life of the king he so
faithfully served in the midst of one of
David's last battles (2Sa. 21:15-17).

ABISHALOM [(my) father is peace] A
variant name of Absalom (1Ki. 15:2, 10).
† *See* ABSALOM

ABISHUA [(my) father is salvation]

1. One of the sons of Bela, the firstborn of Benjamin (1Ch. 8:4). †

2. Son of Phinehas and father of
Bukki in the line of Levi (1Ch. 6:5, 50;
Ezr. 7:5). †

ABISHUR [(my) father is a wall]
Descendant of Judah, ancestor of David,
Abishur was the son of Shammai the
Jerahmeelite, married to Abihail (1Ch.
2:28-29). †

ABITAL [(my) father is (the) night dew]
The wife of David and mother of his fifth
son, Shephatiah (2Sa. 3:4; 1Ch. 3:3). †

ABITUB [(my) father is good] The son
of Shaharaim and his wife Hushim, in
the line of Benjamin (1Ch. 8:8-11). †

ABIUD [(my) father has grandeur] The
son of Zerubbabel and father of Eliakim;
an ancestor of Jesus Christ (Mt. 1:13). †
Abiud is the Greek form of the Hebrew
Abihud.

ABJURATION *See* OATH

ABLUTION *See* PURIFICATION

ABNER [(my) father is NER (a lamp)]
Saul's cousin and the commander of his
army (1Sa. 14:50-51). Abner introduced
David to Saul at the famous victory of
David over Goliath (1Sa. 17:55-58). He
later accompanied Saul in the senseless
pursuit of David in the wilderness (1Sa.
26). When Saul died in battle Abner supported Saul's son Ish-Bosheth as king to

rule over Israel in his father's place (2Sa. 2:8-10). Later, as a result of censure by Ish-Bosheth, Abner negotiated with the elders of Israel for a transfer of allegiance to David. At this stage Abner met a violent death by assassination at the hand of Joab who was determined to avenge his brother's death. David grieved over Abner's tragic death, wept at his funeral, and eulogized Abner as a great prince in Israel (2Sa. 3:22-39).

ABOMINATION That which is ritually or ethically abhorrent or repugnant to the LORD. Such practices and objects include: idolatry, as in the worship of Ashtoreth (Astarte) of the Sidonians or Milcom of the Ammonites (1Ki. 11:5); human sacrifice (2Ki. 16:3); divination and sorcery (Dt. 18:9-14); unclean beasts (Lev. 11:10); sexual perversion (Lev. 18:22-23); lying (Pr. 12:22); unethical business practices (Pr. 20:23); and evil motivation of the heart (Pr. 6:18, 19; Lk. 16:15).

ABOMINATION THAT CAUSES DESOLATION A phrase occurring in the book of Daniel and in the teaching of Jesus (Da. 9:27; 11:31; 12:11; Mt. 24:15; Mk. 13:14). This abomination that desolates or appalls, involving a pollution of the sanctuary of the temple in Jerusalem, apparently has reference both to the desecration by Antiochus Epiphanes in 168 B.C. and to a future desolating or appalling abomination in the end times. This teaching of Jesus has been interpreted by some as a reference to the destruction of the temple by the Roman Titus in A.D. 70 and by others as applying to the eschatological figure of the Antichrist or "man of lawlessness," which foreshadows the second coming of Christ (2Th. 2:3).

ABORTION The intentional termination of a pregnancy that results in the death of the fetus, the unborn child. Though strongly denounced by the early church fathers, this widespread practice is not mentioned in the Bible. Yet, two passages imply that the unborn child is a fully human person.

In Lk. 1:44, Elizabeth states by the Holy Spirit that the six-month-old fetus in her womb "leaped for joy" at the sound of Mary's greeting, a clearly human response. Ex. 21:23-25 describes the situation when an injury to a woman causes a premature birth. Interpreters debate whether the penalties ("life for life, eye for eye," etc.) apply only to the mother or to both mother and child. The Code of Hammurabi (ANET, 175:209-214) applies the "eye for eye" penalties to the mother, but allows a monetary fine for the child's death. The Middle Assyrian Laws (ANET, 184:50-52), more contemporary with the Mosaic law, demands a life for the life of the fetus. These laws also prescribe capital punishment for a woman who attempts her own abortion (ANET, 184:53). One could deduce that this high view of human life would be shared by the OT law, and that abortion would similarly be considered murder. However, this conclusion can only be reached by deduction and not by the direct teaching of Scripture. (J.R.K.)

ABRAHAM, ABRAM [father of many, exalted father] Called Abram until his name was changed by God to Abraham (Ge. 17:5). Together with Terah, his father, his nephew Lot, and his wife Sarai (her name was later changed to Sarah in Ge. 17:15), he left his birthplace in Ur of the Chaldeans in Mesopotamia for Haran on the Euphrates NW of Ur. After the death of his father, he left for Canaan and at Shechem (176-179) began his sojourn (Ge. 11:27-32; 12:1-7; 15:7; Ac. 7:4). After a brief stay in Egypt because of a famine in Canaan, he returned to Canaan where Lot left him for Sodom—he himself settling near Hebron (Ge. 13:1, 8-12, 18). Lot was taken by the king of Elam but rescued in the expedition which his uncle led, as a result of which Abram met and was blessed by Melchizedek, king of Salem (Ge. 14:1-16, 18-20).

As Sarai was barren she followed the ancient custom of giving a maidservant to her husband who bore him a son, Ishmael (Ge. 16). It was at this time that God once again gave his promise to Abram

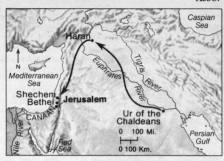

ABRAM'S JOURNEY TO CANAAN
Abram, Sarai, and Lot traveled from Ur of the Chaldeans to Canaan by way of Haran.

that he would make him the father of a great nation and give him the land as an everlasting possession, and changed his name to Abraham (Ge. 12:2; 13:14-16; 17:5-8). Several well-known stories are connected with Abraham: his intercession for Sodom and Gomorrah; the banishment of Hagar and her son Ishmael; the birth of his firstborn (by Sarah), Isaac; the call to sacrifice his son Isaac; the burial of Sarah in the cave of Machpelah (Ge. 18:16ff.; 21:1-21; 22:1-19; 23:1-20). Abraham married Keturah after Sarah's death and had a second family. He was buried in the cave of Machpelah at the age of 175 (Ge. 25:1-10). The life of Abraham is usually dated in the beginning of the second millennium B.C.

From the NT we learn that Christ was descended from Abraham (Mt. 1:1; Lk. 3:34), and that the Christians as well as the Jews thought of him as the founder of the faith and a man of great faith (Mt. 3:9; Heb. 11:8-19). Paul stated that Abraham received the promise and blessing of God by faith, that these are passed on to the Gentiles through Christ, and that those who believe in Christ are also the seed of Abraham (Gal. 3:6-9, 14, 16-18).

ABRAHAM'S SIDE (BOSOM) A figure of speech used by Jesus in the parable of Lazarus and the rich man, signifying a place or state of rest after death (Lk. 16:19-31). In Rabbinic thought, to be in Abraham's bosom (side) was to enter Paradise.

ABRAM *See* ABRAHAM

ABRONAH A place where the Israelites camped on the way to Ezion Geber after Jotbathah (Nu. 33:34-35). †

ABSALOM [father is peace] David's third son, whose name means "Father is peace," was the source of intense grief to his father. Absalom, whose mother, Maacah, was daughter of Talmia, king of Geshur, was a promising son (2Sa 14:25), but he avenged the humiliation of his beautiful sister by having David's oldest son murdered. This initiated the fulfillment of Nathan's dire prophecy about David's future (2Sa. 12:10-11; 16:20-23). Absalom fled from his father—and only after three years asylum at his mother's family home in Geshur and two more years in Jerusalem, but barred from the king's court, was Absalom allowed to see David (2Sa. 14). In the next four years Absalom plotted and executed a rebellion, driving David from Jerusalem. Absalom's death in the ensuing struggle brought forth the expression of David's deep and moving grief (2Sa. 19:1-8). He is twice called Abishalom in 1Ki. 15:2, 10.

ABSTAIN, ABSTINENCE *See* FAST, FASTING

ABYSS [unfathomable depth] *See* DEAD, ABODE OF

ACACIA *See* TREES

ACBOR [jerboa, a kind of long backlegged, long-tailed rodent that jumps on two feet]

1. The father of one of the kings of Edom (Ge. 36:38-39; 1Ch. 1:49). †

2. One of King Josiah's men sent to consult the prophetess Huldah about the "Book of the Law" found in the temple (2Ki. 22:12, 14); called *Abdon* in 2Ch. 34:20. Perhaps also an official of Jehoiakim (Jer. 26:22; 36:12). † *See* ABDON 4.

ACCAD A variant spelling of AKKAD. *See* GEOGRAPHY OF THE HOLY LAND *Akkad; see also* AKKADIAN

ACC(H)O From earliest times this was a key port (158-258) for the northern part of the land of Canaan. It is mentioned in the early Egyptian records, eighteenth and fourteenth centuries B.C. Assyrians conquered it in 701 and 640 B.C. In the third century B.C. its name was changed to *Ptolemais*, the name by which the Apostle Paul knew it (Ac. 21:7). The Arabs changed the name back again, but the Crusaders knew it as St. Jean d'Acre. Napoleon tried to conquer it in 1799 but failed, and it was held by the Turks until General Allenby's victory in 1918. The ancient tell (mound) is just E of the modern city. In biblical times Acco was in the land given to the tribe of Asher (Jdg. 1:31). It is called *Ummah* in Jos. 19:30. †

ACCOMPLISH *See* FULFILLED

ACCOUNTABILITY *See* ONE ANOTHER

ACCURSED *See* CURSE and DEVOTE

ACELDAMA *See* AKELDAMA

ACHAIA *See* GEOGRAPHY OF THE HOLY LAND

ACHAICUS {belonging to Achaia} A Christian from Corinth who visited Paul at Ephesus (1Co. 16:17). †

ACHAN {*a word play from ACHAR*, troubler} A Judahite who took for himself some of the spoils from Jericho which had been dedicated to the LORD, and was stoned. For this the LORD punished Israel by a defeat at Ai (Jos. 7:1, 18-26; 22:20). He is called Achar in 1Ch.

2:7 and the place of the stoning "the Valley of Achor" (Jos. 7:22-26). †

ACHAR {trouble} *See* ACHAN

ACHAZ {he has grasped} *See* AHAZ

ACHBOR {jerboa, a kind of long back-legged, long-tailed rodent that jumps on two feet} *See* ACBOR

ACHIM {(Yahweh) is my brother} *See* AKIM

ACHISH A king of the Philistine city of Gath in the time of David. On one occasion David fled there for refuge from Saul but had to feign madness to escape from the Philistines. On another occasion he was given asylum there (1Sa. 21:10-12, 14; 27:2-3, 5-6, 9-10, 12; 28:1, 2; 29:2-3, 6, 9; 1Ki. 2:39-40). These historical passages become the traditional backdrop of Ps. 34 (in the title called Abimelech). Achish was the leader of the Philistine armies at Gilboa where Saul and Jonathan were killed (1Sa. 31:1-6). † *See also* ABIMELECH 4.

ACHMETHA *See* ECBATANA

ACHOR {trouble} A valley near Jericho on the boundary between the tribes of Judah and Benjamin (Jos. 7:24-26; 15:7; Isa. 65:10; Hos. 2:15). Some identify it with Wadi Kelt. A curse was placed upon it which is to be lifted at Messiah's coming. † *See also* ACHAN

ACHSA {decorative anklet} *See* ACSAH

ACHSHAPH *See* ACSHAPH

ACHZIB *See* ACZIB

ACRE, A CITY *See* ACC(H)O

ACRE, A MEASURE *See* WEIGHTS AND MEASURES

ACROPOLIS {crest of city, high ground of city} A high point of the city, usually for defense and/or worship.

ACROSTIC A poetic construction taking the first letter of a line or strophe to form a word, an alphabetical order, or other codes of some kind. Lamentations 3 is an example of an alphabet acrostic composition for each line of each stanza; Pss. 9 and 10, each fourth line; Ps. 119 an acrostic for each strophe. Though disputed, some have seen the name *Yahweh* in the Book of Esther using the first letter of certain successions of letters. Though the New Testament contains no known acrostics, memory tools can be found in the genealogy of Mt. 1, using symmetry (three groups of 14, using key points of Abraham, David, the Exile). Early Christians used the memory device of "fish" from the Greek word IX-THUS, I for Jesus, X for Christ, TH for God's, U for Son, S for Savior. *See* POETRY

ACSAH [decorative anklet] The daughter of Caleb whom he gave as wife to Othniel, the conqueror of Kiriath Sepher (later called Debir). He gave her the Negev, or south land, and upper and lower springs near to the city (Jos. 15:16-17; Jdg. 1:12-13; 1Ch. 2:49). † *See* DEBIR

ACSHAPH [sorcery, witchcraft, illicit fascination] A city (158-240) in the tribal territory of Asher (Jos. 19:25). It was conquered by Joshua after it had allied itself with the king of Hazor against the Israelites (Jos. 11:1; 12:20). †

ACTS, BOOK OF Acts is the logical sequence (part two) to the Gospel narratives and was written by Luke, the author of the third Gospel. In the Acts there are a series of passages narrated in the first person, the famous "we" sections (chaps. 16, 20—21, 27—28), which show that the author was a companion of Paul and an eyewitness of many of the events he records. Probabilities within the New Testament as well as the unanimous testimony of the church point to Luke, the beloved physician, as the writer (Col. 4:14).

Two personalities are especially prominent in Acts: Peter and Paul. Peter dominates the one major division of the book (Ac. 1—12), and Paul the rest (Ac. 13—28). The events of Acts cover approximately the thirty years from the resurrection of Christ to the imprison-

ment of Paul at Rome. The outline of the book is given in Christ's own words when he said those who believe in him would be witnesses in Jerusalem, Judea, Samaria, to the uttermost parts of the world (Ac. 1:8). A series of key texts traces the major geographical frontiers the early witnesses traversed as Christianity expanded in the Roman world. Ac. 6:7 summarizes the progress to that point in Jerusalem; Ac. 9:31 carries us out to the next wider horizon of Judea, Galilee, and Samaria; Ac. 12:24 gives us the transition from the early days in Jerusalem and Judea to the advance through Antioch into the Roman world. As Paul advanced to the Aegean shores, Luke paused to summarize again with a note of progress (Ac. 16:5), and in Ac. 19:20, after the evangelization of the Aegean shores is completed, we are told "the word of the Lord spread widely and grew in power" (Ac. 19:20). Finally, when Paul reached Rome, the final note of progress concludes the book (Ac. 28:30-31).

Around the leading figure of Peter are grouped the main events of Ac. 1—12. Peter appears as the spokesman in the choice of a successor to Judas. After the miraculous demonstration of the presence of the Holy Spirit at Pentecost (Ac. 2), Peter showed that all the evidence demonstrates that Jesus is Lord and Christ (Ac. 2:36). Peter and John were instrumental in healing a lame man at the gate called Beautiful (Ac. 3—4), and in explaining events as divine testimony to Jesus Christ. To Peter it fell to rebuke Ananias and Sapphira in their attempted deceit (Ac. 5). Peter, when the apostles were forbidden to preach in the name of Christ (Ac. 5), replied, "We must obey God rather than men!" A lengthy narrative (Ac. 9—11) centering around Peter shows how God revealed his plan to include Gentiles in his church. The triumphant operation of divine power to release Peter from imprisonment (Ac. 12) is the last reference to Peter in the earlier portion of Acts, though he appears again at the Jerusalem council (Ac. 15).

Interwoven with the earlier narrative of the expansion of the church is the preparation for the wider mission of the church. Jesus had declared his purpose (Ac. 1:8). In the implementation of that purpose, Paul, the great minister for the

THE JERUSALEM COUNCIL
Some Judaizers taught that the Gentile believers had to be circumcised to be saved. Paul and Barnabas went to Jerusalem to discuss this problem with the leaders there. After the Jerusalem council, Paul and Barnabas returned to Antioch with good news.

Gentiles, was called (Ac. 9). To Peter was revealed the doctrine, in the case of Cornelius, that the Gentile was to be received into the church as a Gentile, only on condition of faith in Christ. Luke then retraced the events which led to the founding of the church at Antioch (Ac. 11:19-26). Antioch became the "advance base" of mission effort in the Roman world, so that the establishment of a strong church there, pastored by Paul and Barnabas, is of great significance in the unfolding of God's plan.

In chapter 13 the mission career of Paul began and can be conveniently summarized in the four main journeys of Paul. The first is narrated in Acts 13–14. Paul and Barnabas and party toured Cyprus, sailed N to the coast of Asia, preached at Pisidian Antioch, swung eastward to Iconium, Derbe, and Lystra, and returned to Attalia, whence they sailed to Antioch. Outstanding on this journey was Paul's address in the synagogue at Pisidian Antioch, featuring his proof from the Resurrection and OT prophecy that Jesus was the promised Messiah and the initiation of a distinctive Gentile work to which Paul had been called.

In the interval between the first and second journey, opposition to the work of Paul developed and increased. His work in Galatia was attacked, and Paul replied with the Galatian epistle. Further unrest led to the convening of the Jerusalem council with the resulting public disavowal of the doctrine and tactics of Jewish sectarians. This decision was conveyed to the Gentile churches.

At the beginning of the second journey, Paul revisited the churches established on the first journey and then moved N and W through Asia Minor to Troas near ancient Homeric Troy. From there the party sailed to Macedonia, establishing churches at Philippi and Thessalonica. After leaving Macedonia, Paul stopped briefly at Athens, delivering the famous discourse to the Areopagus. A long stay of eighteen months founded the famous but troubled church at Corinth. From there Paul wrote First and Second Thessalonians in love and encouragement to his friends at Thessalonica. Paul returned to Antioch and set out again on the third journey for Ephesus. A long ministry of over two years evangelized all Asia Minor (Ac. 19:10) and established the famous churches mentioned in the seven letters of the Revelation. From Ephesus Paul wrote First Corinthians and later, from Macedonia, Second Corinthians as he journeyed toward Corinth. During a brief third visit at Corinth (2Co. 12:14; 13:1), Paul wrote the great epistle to Rome (Ac. 20:3).

On returning to Jerusalem, Paul was accused of bringing a Gentile into the temple and was mobbed (*see* MIDDLE WALL OF PARTITION). Roman authorities intervened and kept him in custody two years at Jerusalem and Caesarea. The delays of Roman rulers compelled Paul to appeal to Caesar. No charge could be laid against Paul since he based his case wholly on the reality of

THROUGH MACEDONIA AND ACHAIA
A riot in Ephesus sent Paul to Troas, then through Macedonia to Achaia. In Achaia he went to Corinth to deal with the problems there. Afterwards, he returned to Troas, retracing his steps.

the resurrection of Christ and he called on the Roman court to take judicial notice of that well-known public event (Ac. 26:8, 23, 26). Acts 27 and 28 tell of the famous voyage and shipwreck of Paul's party and the final arrival at Rome. Luke was in Paul's company at this time and the book ends at this point. The most natural supposition is that the book was also written and published at this time.

In the two-year imprisonment which followed, some of Paul's most memorable work was done in the writing of Philippians, Ephesians, Colossians, and Philemon. Here Acts ends with a note of triumph and progress: Paul preaching and teaching with all boldness, none forbidding him.

Luke's historical work of Luke-Acts is the earliest and the only contemporary account of the beginnings of Christianity. In the fourth century, Eusebius of Caesarea wrote the first church history. In the intervening period the basic narrative of Luke and the rest of the NT was recognized by friend and foe as the authentic account of Christian beginnings. (W.B.W.)

ACZIB {deceit}

1. An important Canaanite seaport town (159-272) in the territory of the tribe of Asher N of Acco (Jos. 19:29; Jdg. 1:31). †

2. A Judahite town (145-116) in the western foothills (Shephelah) near Mareshah which according to the prophet would "prove deceptive to the kings of Israel" (Jos. 15:44; Mic. 1:14). †

A.D. Latin for "in the year of the Lord (Jesus)." The time from Jesus to the present. Non-Christians sometimes prefer the designation C.E. for "Common Era." *See* GOSPELS, THE FOUR (¶ 2.)

ADADAH A town in the S of Judah's territory (Jos. 15:22). †

ADAH {adornment}

1. The mother of Jabal and Jubal and wife of Lamech, the sixth mentioned in Adam's line (Ge. 4:19-20, 23). †

2. A Hittite wife of Esau (Ge. 36:2, 4, 10, 12, 16). †

ADAIAH {adornment of Yahweh}

1. A descendant of Levi who ministered in song in the tabernacle (1Ch. 6:41). †

2. A son of Shimei and descendant of Benjamin (1Ch. 8:21). †

3. A priest in Jerusalem, son of Jeroham (1Ch. 9:12; Ne. 11:12).†

4. Grandfather on the mother's side of King Josiah (2Ki. 22:1).†

5. Father of Maaseiah, an army officer who helped to overthrow Queen Athaliah (2Ch. 23:1). †

6. An ancestor of a Judahite of Jerusalem (Ne. 11:5). †

7. A son of Bani who married a foreigner during the exile (Ezr. 10:29). †

8. A son of Binnui who also married a foreigner in the exilic times (Ezr. 10:39). †

ADALIA One of the sons of Haman, enemy of the Jews (Est. 9:8). †

ADAM {(red) earth, *or* (ruddy) skin color)}

1. A Canaanite town (201-167) on the East bank of the Jordan River near the mouth of the Jabbok River (Jos. 3:16).

2. The first man. The story of man's being formed from the dust of the ground, made in the image of God, placed in the Garden of Eden, and given dominion over the other forms of life is

recorded in the first two chapters of Genesis. He lived 930 years (Ge. 5:3-5). A major difference in the biblical account from other creation accounts is indicated in Ge. 2:7, where the record states that which had been formed from the dust of the ground did not become animate, did not become man, a living being, until after the divine inbreathing into that which was formed from the dust. All other animal life that was made earlier was already animate, was living, had *nephesh hayah,* but man did not have it until this special type of creation (*see* SOUL).

Adam's mate likewise had a peculiar origin, made from a rib taken from man (Ge. 2:20-22). Adam and Eve were instructed by God not to eat of the fruit of the tree in the middle of the garden or they would die. However, the serpent said, "When you eat of it your eyes will be opened, and you will be like God, knowing good and evil." All humanity is physically descended from Adam and Eve (including Christ as to the flesh) and thus related. Because of this relationship, labor, pain, sin, and death passed upon all men. Represented in their father Adam, all (excluding Christ, Heb. 4:15) did sin (Lk. 3:38; Ro. 5:12; 1Co. 15:22).

ADAMAH [(red) earth] A city in the tribal area of Naphtali, vicinity of Sea of Galilee, but its exact location is not known (Jos. 19:36). †

ADAMANT *See* PRECIOUS STONES AND METALS, *Flint*

ADAMI NEKEB [the ground of piercing] (193-239) A city in the tribal area of Naphtali (Jos. 19:33). †

ADAR, MONTH [*possibly* dark, clouded] Ezr. 6:15; Est. 3:7, 13; 8:12; 9:1, 15, 17, 19, 21. † *See* CALENDAR

ADAR, PEOPLE [majestic] *See* ARD(ITES); *see also* CALENDAR, *March*

ADBEEL [(the) grief of El] One of the twelve sons of Ishmael who were princes of tribes. In the first millennium B.C., a tribe of that name was located between Canaan and Egypt (Ge. 25:13; 1Ch. 1:29). †

ADDAN *See* ADDON

ADDAR [glorious]
1. A fortress city and boundary city of the inheritance of Canaan to the Israelites, on the S border of Judah (Jos. 15:3); also called Hazar Addar (Nu. 34:4). † *See* HAZAR ADDAR
2. A son of Bela (1Ch. 8:3). The same as Ard in Nu. 26:40. † *See* ARD(ITES)

ADDER *See* BEASTS 1.

ADDI One in the genealogy of Jesus (Lk. 3:28). †

ADDICTION Devotion or surrender to a habit or substance. The Christian is to be self-controlled (1Co. 9:27; Gal. 5:22). *See* DRINK

ADDON An unidentified place in Babylonia from which some returned with Zerubbabel after the exile (Ezr. 2:59; Ne. 7:61). †

ADER [flock] *See* EDER 3.

ADIEL [adornment of El]
1. A man of the tribe of Simeon (1Ch. 4:36). †
2. The father of a priest who returned from the exile in Babylon (1Ch. 9:12; *cf.* Ne. 11:13). † *See* AZARAEL 5.
3. The father of the keeper of the treasuries of David (1Ch. 27:25). †

ADIN [voluptuous, luxurious] The head of a large family which returned from the Babylonian exile and one of the signers of Nehemiah's covenant (Ezr. 2:15; 8:6; Ne. 7:20; 10:16). †

ADINA [adorned] A leader in David's army from the tribe of Reuben (1Ch. 11:42). †

ADINO [adorned one of his] A transliteration in 2Sa. 23:8 in the LXX and the KJV, NKJV, ASV, NASB, "Adino the Eznite," translated "he wielded his spear" based on the parallel passage in 1Ch. 11:11, and is so rendered in the RSV, NIV, JB. The footnotes in many versions rightly note the Hebrew is obscure in this passage.

ADITHAIM {double (row) of adornments} An unidentified town listed with others in the northern end of the western foothills (Jos. 15:36). †

ADJURE, ADJURATION *See* OATH

ADLAI {be just} The father of one of David's herdsmen (1Ch. 27:29).†

ADMAH {(red) earth} An unidentified city in the Jordan Valley which revolted against the king of Elam and was later destroyed along with Sodom and Gomorrah (Ge. 10:19; 14:2, 8; Dt. 29:23; Hos. 11:8). †

ADMATHA {unrestrained} One of the seven princes of Media and Persia in the days of King Xerxes (Est. 1:14). †

ADMIN A variant reading adopted by the JB in Lk. 3:33. The KJV has *Aram;* ASV and NEB, *Arni;* NKJV and NIV, *Ram.* The ancient manuscripts vary greatly in this portion of Scripture.

ADMINISTRATORS *See* PRESIDENTS, PREFECT

ADNA {delight}
1. An Israelite whom Ezra induced to divorce his foreign wife after the exile (Ezr. 10:30).†
2. A priest in the days of Nehemiah (Ne. 12:15).†

ADNAH {delight}
1. An officer of King Saul who deserted to David when he was at Ziklag (1Ch. 12:20).†
2. An officer in the army of King Jehoshaphat (2Ch. 17:14).†

ADONAI *See* LORD; *See also* GOD, NAMES OF, GODHEAD 4.

ADONI-BEZEK {lord of BEZEK} A Canaanite king who had his thumbs and big toes cut off after his capture by the men of Judah, just as he had done to seventy others. He died in captivity in Jerusalem (Jdg. 1:57).†

ADONI-ZEDEK {(my) lord is righteousness} A king of Jerusalem who

made an alliance with four other kings against Joshua and the Israelites. After Joshua defeated them at Gibeon they hid in a cave at Makkedah, were discovered, killed, and buried in the cave (Jos. 10:1-28).†

ADONIJAH {(my) lord is Yahweh}
1. A son and heir to David's throne. However, one of David's other wives, Bathsheba, with the help of the priest Zadok and the prophet Nathan, secured the succession for her son Solomon (2Sa. 3:4; 1Ki.1). After the death of David, Solomon had him put to death (1Ki. 2). †
2. One of the Levites whom King Jehoshaphat sent out to teach the Law in Judah during his reforms (2Ch. 17:7-9).†
3. The head of one of the families that returned from the Babylonian captivity with Ezra and Nehemiah (Ne. 10:16). He is called Adonikam in Ezr. 2:13; 8:13; Ne. 7:18.†

ADONIKAM {(my) lord arises} Ezr. 2:13; 8:13; Ne. 7:18. † *See* ADONIJAH 3

ADONIRAM {(my) lord is exalted} He served kings David, Solomon, and Rehoboam as superintendent of the forced (vassal) labor (2Sa. 20:24; 1Ki. 4:6; 5:14; 2Ch. 10:18). Rehoboam sent him to collect tribute from the ten northern tribes that had revolted but they stoned him to death (1Ki. 12:18). In some places the Hebrew text reads *Aduram.*

ADONIZEDEC *See* ADONI-ZEDEK

ADOPTION Two clear cases of adoption, taking another's child into one's own family, are noted in the OT. Moses was adopted by Pharaoh's daughter, and Esther by Mordecai (Ex. 2:10; Est. 2:7, 15). But there is no clear evidence to show that the Israelites, in Israel, practiced adoption. In the NT, adoption is a figure of speech which expresses the relation of either the Israelites to God or individuals who have a certain type of faith to God. These are spiritual relations of sonship and not physical or creation relationships. God adopted Israel as sons (Ex. 4:22; Dt. 14:1; Ro. 9:4). He also adopts as sons all who come unto him through faith in Jesus Christ (Eph. 1:4-12; Ro. 8:14-21; Gal. 4:5). These are subject to God's control, have his Spirit dwelling within them, receive his corrective chastisement in this life, and his inheritance in the world to come (Gal. 4:6; Heb. 12:5-11; Ro. 8:23). God redeemed Israel from the bondage of Egypt and made them his sons. So God redeems from the bondage of sin all those who have faith in Christ as Savior and Lord, and ultimately by resurrection he redeems them from death itself. *See* CHRIST, WORK OF, *Redemption*; *See also* SALVATION, APPLICATION OF

ADORAIM [*possibly* pair of knolls] A city (152-101) in the tribal area of Judah and one of those fortified by King Rehoboam. Dura, an Arab village, marks the site today (2Ch. 11:9). †

ADORAM [(my) lord is exalted] *See* ADONIRAM

ADORATION, ADORE *See* PRAISE; WORSHIP

ADORNMENT *See* DRESS

ADRAMMELECH [nobility of Molech (king)]
1. A son of the Assyrian king Sennacherib who was involved in the murder of his father at Nineveh (2Ki. 19:37; Isa. 37:38).†
2. A pagan deity (2Ki. 17:31). † *See also* DEITIES 1., last ¶

ADRAMYTTIUM A seaport city in Mysia in Asia Minor. Paul sailed from Caesarea to Sidon, passed near to Cyprus, and landed at Myra in Asia Minor on a ship registered at Adramyttium (Ac. 27:2-5). †

ADRIA *See* ADRIATIC SEA

ADRIATIC SEA On Paul's shipwreck journey to Rome the ship was badly tossed on the Adriatic Sea (Adria) between Crete and Malta where it was finally wrecked (Ac. 27:27). †

ADRIEL [(my) help is El] The man to whom King Saul gave his daughter Merab as wife in spite of the fact that she

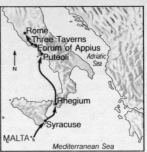
ADRIATIC SEA (Arrows show Paul's trip from Malta to Rome.)

had been earlier promised to David (1Sa. 18:19; 2Sa. 21:8). †

ADULLAM, ADULLAMITE [retreat, refuge, *possibly* (they are) just]
1. A city (150-117) in the western foothills conquered by Joshua and assigned to the tribe of Judah (Jos. 12:15; 15:35; 2Ch. 11:7; Mic. 1:15). Before the captivity in Egypt Judah had married a girl of Adullam (Ge. 38:1-2). It was one of Rehoboam's fortified towns which continued down to the Babylonian captivity and was repopulated after the return from that exile (2Ch. 11:15; Ne. 11:30). The place is perhaps best known in the phrase "cave of Adullam" from the incidents in David's life when he made it his headquarters during his flight from Saul (1Sa. 22:1ff., 2Sa. 23:13).
2. An Adullamite is one from the city of Adullam (Ge. 38:12, 20). †

ADULTERESSES *See* ADULTERY

ADULTERY In the OT adultery applied only to a woman who was either betrothed or married. Adultery was strictly forbidden and was punishable by death by stoning (Lev. 18:20; 20:10; Dt. 22:22, 24). In common with local practices in other Middle Eastern countries in antiquity, a wife suspected by her husband could be obliged to undergo a test by "the bitter water that brings a curse" (Nu. 5:13-31).

In the NT Jesus condemned not only the act itself but also one who has adulterous thoughts. It is also adultery to divorce a wife and marry another. Christians are repeatedly warned against adultery and fornication. In the NT the husband is bound by as strict a morality as is the wife (Mt. 5:27-32; Mk. 10:11-12; 1 Co. 6:9). *See also* DIVORCE

ADUMMIM {red (streaks)} An ascent or pass which went up through a wadi (steep valley) through which in antiquity passed the road from Jericho to Jerusalem. It was a part of the border between the tribes of Judah and Benjamin (Jos. 15:7; 18:17). †

ADURAM *See* ADONIRAM

ADVENT The coming of Christ. *See* CHRIST, LIFE AND TEACHINGS OF, Work of Christ 9., *Second Advent*; ESCHATOLOGY

ADVERSARY *See* DEVIL

ADVOCATE A person who is a representative of one or more individuals before another or others. Christ speaks to the Father in the believer's defense (IJn. 2:1). The Greek word *parakletos* used here is elsewhere rendered "Counselor" and is applied by Christ to the Holy Spirit (Jn. 14:16, 26). *See* GODS, NAME OF 6.

AEGEAN SEA *See* SEA, AEGEAN

AENEAS {*possibly* praise} A paralytic inhabitant of Lydda whom Peter healed, a miracle which caused all who lived in Lydda and Sharon to turn to the Lord (Ac. 9:32-35). †

AENON {spring} An unidentified place, probably in the Jordan Valley, where John baptized (Jn. 3:23). †

AEON {a segment of time, a very long time, eternity} *See* ETERNITY; TIME

AFFUSION To baptize by pouring. *See also* BAPTISM

AFRAID *See* FEAR

AGABUS A NT prophet who at Antioch predicted a famine would spread over the entire Roman world. It came in the time of Claudius. At Caesarea he predicted

the imprisonment of Paul in Jerusalem (Ac. 11:27-28; 21:10-11). †

AGAG, AGAGITE {*possibly* violent}

1. In Balaam's oracle it is said that Israel's king will be "greater than Agag." No other information is given (Nu. 24:7). †

2. An Amalekite king captured by King Saul. Saul saved his life and this was considered an act of disobedience to the LORD worse than divining. For this Saul lost his kingship (ISa. 15:8-9, 20, 32-33). †

3. Haman, who sought to destroy all the Jews at the Persian court was an Agagite (Est. 3:1, 10; 8:3, 5; 9:24). †

AGAPE {love—volitional and self-sacrifical love} *See* LOVE

AGAPE FEAST {Love Feast} *See* LOVE FEAST

AGAR *See* HAGAR

AGATES *See* PRECIOUS STONES AND METALS, Precious Stones 1., *ruby*

AGE *See* TIME

AGE-DAY THEORY *See* DAY-AGE THEORY

AGE, OLD *See* ELDER

AGEE {*possibly* fugitive} Father of one of David's mighty men (2Sa. 23:8, 11). †

AGNOSTIC One who does not know whether God exists. He may be a skeptic but is not an atheist.

AGONY A KJV, NKJV, RSV transliteration in Lk. 22:44. The Greek word is similar in sound and meaning to the English word "agony" and has the idea of "anguish," and is so translated in the NIV. Some synonyms are "pine away, torment, pain, torture, anguish, pangs."

AGORA {market place} *See* MARKET, MARKETPLACE

AGRAPHA {unwritten} The sayings of Jesus known in tradition but not found in Scripture.

AGREEMENT *See* COVENANT

AGRICULTURE *See* FARMING

AGRIPPA Ac. 25:13ff.; 26:1ff. † *See* HERODS, THE

AGUE *See* SICK, SICKNESS 4., *Fever See also* DISEASE, *Malaria*

AGUR {gatherer, *possibly* wage earner} The author of Proverbs 30 (Pr. 30:1). †

AHAB {brother of father} A false prophet condemned by the true prophet Jeremiah. He was executed by King Nebuchadnezzar of Babylon by being roasted in a fire (Jer. 29:20-23). *See also* KINGS OF JUDAH AND ISRAEL

AHARAH {brother of RAH} The third son of Benjamin (1Ch. 8:1). †

AHARHEL {brother of Rachel} A Judahite, son of Harum (1Ch. 4:8). †

AHASAI *See* AHZAI

AHASBAI {I seek refuge in Yahweh} The father of one of David's mighty men (2Sa. 23:34). †

AHASUERUS *See* XERXES

AHAVA A place in Babylonia where Ezra gathered the Jews who came back with him from the captivity in Babylon (Ezr. 8:15, 21, 31). †

AHAZ {he has grasped} One of Saul's descendants through his son Jonathan (1Ch. 8:35; 9:42). *See also* KINGS OF JUDAH AND ISRAEL

AHAZIAH {Yahweh has upheld} *See* KINGS OF JUDAH AND ISRAEL

AHBAN {brother has sageness} A Judahite of the house of Jerahmeel (1Ch. 2:29). †

AHER {another, a substitute} A man of the tribe of Benjamin (1Ch. 7:12). †

AHI {my brother, *possibly* Yahweh is (my) brother} A Gadite (1Ch. 5:15; *cf.* Ge. 46:23; Nu. 26:42). †

AHIAH *See* AHIJAH 6.

AHIAM {brother of mother} One of David's mighty men (2Sa. 23:33). †

AHIAN {little brother} A man of the tribe of Manasseh (1Ch. 7:19). †

AHIEZER {(my) brother is a help}
1. A leader of the tribe of Dan during the desert wanderings (Nu. 1:12; 2:25; 7:66, 71; 10:25). †
2. One of David's mighty men, a Benjamite, an archer and slingshot expert (1Ch. 12:3). †

AHIHUD {(my) brother has grandeur}
1. A leader of the tribe of Benjamin who helped Moses in the division of the land of Israel (Nu. 34:27). †
2. The head of a house in Benjamin (1Ch. 8:7). †

AHIJAH {(my) brother is Yahweh}
1. A descendant of Judah (1Ch. 2:25).
2. One of the mighty men of David's army (1Ch. 11:36).
3. A man who had the charge of the treasuries of the temple in David's time (1Ch. 26:20).
4. A prophet who told Jeroboam that God was going to take the kingdom from Rehoboam and give ten tribes to him (1Ki. 11:29-32). He also predicted the end of the line of Jeroboam (1Ki. 14:1-11).
5. The father of one of the kings of Israel, Baasha (1Ki. 15:27).
6. A leader under Nehemiah who set his seal to the covenant. His name is AHIAH which is a variant of AHIJAH (Ne. 10:26). †

AHIKAM {(my) brother stands} King Josiah sent him to ask the prophetess Huldah about the Book of the Law discovered in the temple (2Ki. 22:12, 14). He was also one who helped Jeremiah when his life was threatened (Jer. 26:24; 39:14; 40:5-7, 9, 11, 14, 16; 41:1-2, 6, 10, 16, 18; 43:6).

After the kingdom of Judah had been taken into captivity, his son Gedaliah was made the ruler over the people left behind and thus was the last ruler in Jerusalem at the time of the end of the kingdom (2Ki. 25:22; 2Ch. 34:20). †

AHILUD {(my) brother is born}
1. The father of one of the recorders in the reigns of David and Solomon (2Sa.

8:16; 20:24; 1Ki. 4:3; 1Ch. 18:15). †

2. The father of one of the men who had to provide food for King Solomon one month in each year (1Ki. 4:12). †

AHIMAAZ [(my) brother is fury]

1. The father of one of the wives of King Saul (1Sa. 14:50).

2. During the revolt of Absalom against his father David, Ahimaaz was one of the two who stayed at the court to keep David posted on developments there (2Sa. 15:27, 36).

3. A son-in-law of King Solomon and one of the men responsible for providing the king's food for a month each year (1Ki. 4:15).

AHIMAN [*possibly* (my) brother is a gift]

1. One of the three giants, sons of Anak, whom Caleb expelled from Hebron and was later defeated by Judahites (Jos. 15:14; Jdg. 1:10). He and his two brothers were noted by the twelve Israelites who came up to spy out the land earlier (Nu. 13:22-33). †

2. A gatekeeper of the camp of the Levites in the days of King Saul (1Ch. 9:17). †

AHIMELECH [(my) brother is king]

1. A priest at Nob who gave holy bread and the sword of Goliath to David when he was fleeing from King Saul (1Sa. 21:1-2, 8; 22:9-11, 14, 16, 20; 23:6; 30:7). When Saul heard of this he had all the priests at Nob, plus the other residents, killed for having aided David. Only one escaped, the son of Ahimelech, Abiathar (1Sa. 22:17-21). †

2. A Hittite soldier who followed David in the years he was fleeing from Saul (1Sa. 26:6). †

3. The son of the Abiathar and grandson of Ahimelech, noted above; a priest in David's reign (2Sa. 8:17; 1Ch. 18:16; 24:3, 6, 31). †

AHIMOTH [(my) brother is my support] A descendant of Levi in the line of Kohath (1Ch. 6:25). †

AHINADAB [(my) brother is willing] King Solomon's officer in charge of his food services at Mahanaim, one of twelve such officers (1Ki. 4:14). †

AHINOAM [(my) brother is pleasant]

1. One of Saul's wives (1Sa. 14:50). †

2. A wife of David and the mother of his first child, Amnon (1Sa. 25:43; 27:3; 30:5; 2Sa. 2:2; 3:2; 1Ch. 3:1). †

AHIO [(my) brother is Yahweh]

1. One of the two sons of Abinadab who drove the cart that carried the Ark from Kiriath Jearim to Jerusalem (2Sa. 6:34; 1Ch. 13:7). †

2. A Benjamite and uncle of King Saul (1Ch. 8:31; 9:37). †

3. Another Benjamite (1Ch. 8:14). †

AHIRA [(my) brother is my friend, *or* (my) brother is evil] A prince of the tribe of Naphtali during the exodus from Egypt (Nu. 1:15; 2:29; 7:78, 83; 10:27). †

AHIRAM, AHIRAMITE [(my) brother is exalted] A son of Benjamin (Nu. 26:38); perhaps the Aharah of 1Ch. 8:1. †

AHISAMACH [(my) brother is a support] A Danite and father of one of those selected to work on the building of the tabernacle (Ex. 31:6; 35:34; 38:23). †

AHISHAHAR [(my) brother was born at early dawn] A descendant of Benjamin (1Ch. 7:10). Compare the list of names in 1Ch. 8:1-40. †

AHISHAR [(my) brother is upright, *or* (my) brother has sung] One of King Solomon's officials in charge of his palace (1Ki. 4:6). †

AHITHOPHEL [*possibly* (my) brother is in the desert *or* (my) brother is foolishness] A valued counselor of David and father of one of his mighty men (2Sa. 16:23). However, when David's son Absalom revolted against his father, Ahithophel joined him, and later after the rebellion had been crushed, fearing the outcome, he hanged himself (2Sa. 15:31; 17:23).

AHITUB [(my) brother is goodness]

1. The father of one of Saul's priests (1Sa. 14:2-3).

2. The father of Zadok, David's priest (2Sa. 8:17).

3. The grandfather of Zadok, the priest of David (1Ch. 9:11). The identification and separation of several men by this name is not clear.

AHLAB {fat, fruitful, healthy} A Canaanite city, just N of Tyre (172-303), in the tribal area of Asher (Jdg. 1:31). †

AHLAI {Alas!, I wish that!}
1. One of the descendants of Judah (1Ch. 2:31). †
2. Father of one of David's mighty men (1Ch. 11:41). †

AHOAH A grandson of Benjamin (1Ch. 8:4). †

AHOHI, AHOHITE The grandfather of one of David's three mighty men (2Sa. 23:9, 28; 1Ch. 11:12, 29; 27:4). †

AHOLA, AHOLAH {she who has a tent} *See* OHOLAH

AHOLIAB {father's tent} *See* OHO-LIAB

AHOLIBAH {tent in her} *See* OHO-LAH

AHOLIBAMAH {tent of the high place}
See OHOLIBAMAH

AHUMAI A descendant of Judah (1Ch. 4:2). †

AHUZAM, AHUZZAM {possessor} A descendant of Judah (1Ch. 4:6). †

AHUZZATH {possession} An advisor of Abimelech of Gerar who visited Isaac (Ge. 26:26).†

AHZAI {Yahweh has grasped} A priest (Ne. 11:13). †

AI {the ruin, the heap}
1. Abraham encamped between Bethel and Ai and built an altar to the LORD there. The place is called *Ha'ai* in the Hebrew text, which literally means "the ruin" (Ge. 12:8; 13:3; Jos. 8–10). After Abraham's trip to Egypt he returned first to Ai. Later, at the start of the conquest under Joshua, the Israelites were first defeated there because of the disobedience of Achan, but after his punishment by the LORD, their second attempt to take it was successful. It is called Aiath and Aija also (Isa. 10:28; Ne. 11:31). Modern scholars have been identifying Bethel with Beitin (172-148) and Ai with et-Tell nearby. There are many problems with the identification, however. Some suggest that the two places should be nearer to Jerusalem and that their identity is not yet established.
2. A place that seems to be near Heshbon, E of the Jordan (Jer. 49:3).

AIAH {black kite (a type of hawk)}
1. A grandson of Seir the Horite (Ge. 36:24; 1Ch. 1:40). †
2. A parent of one of King Saul's concubines (2Sa. 3:7; 21:8, 10-11). †

AIATH {*possibly* ruin, heap} Some consider Aiath (Isa. 10:28) as another name

*ABRAM'S JOURNEY
FROM AI TO EGYPT*

for Ai. Aharoni gives it a possible second location at (175-145) (Isa. 10:28). *See also* AI

AIJA {ruin, heap} *See* AI (the city) Ne. 11:31 †; also AIAH (the person) 1.

AIJALON {(the) place of the deer}
1. A valley W and slightly N of Jerusalem (about 12 miles) that was under the control of Egypt before the Israelite conquest under Joshua. Here Joshua won an important victory when the sun stood still at Gibeon and the moon in the valley of Aijalon (Jos. 10:12). †
2. A town (152-138) within the valley by the same name. It was given to the tribe of Dan as one of the Levitical cities. They failed to conquer it and only in David's days did this take place. Solomon gave it to the tribal area of Benjamin (Jos. 19:42; 21:24; Jdg. 1:35; 1Sa. 14:31; 1Ch. 6:69; 8:13; 2Ch. 11:10; 28:18). King Rehoboam made it one of his defense cities but the Philistines took it later (2Ch. 11:10; 28:18). †
3. An unidentified town in the tribal area of Zebulun (Jdg. 12:12). †

AIJELETH SHAHAR {doe of the morning} *See* PSALMS, TITLES OF 4.

AIN {an eye(ball) *or* spring (of water)}
1. A town (212-236) on the eastern border of Israel's territory (Nu. 34:10-12). †
2. A town in the tribal area of Judah, thought by some to be near Beersheba. It was specifically named for the allotment to the Levites (Jos. 15:32; 19:7; 21:16; 1Ch. 4:32). †
3. A Hebrew word used in composition with other words. It usually means "spring of." Also written as "En" as in "En Gedi." *See* FOUNTAIN

AIN FESHKA {spring of FESHKA} *See* EN EGLAIM; SCROLLS, DEAD SEA; *see also* SALT SEA, *En Feshka*

AJAH *See* AIAH 1.

AJALON *See* AIJALON

AKAN A descendant of Esau and Seir the Horite (Ge. 36:27; 1Ch. 1:42). †

AKELDAMA {field of blood} In Ac. 1:19 it is called "Field of Blood" where Judas fell and "burst open" after his remorse over his betrayal of Jesus. Matthew records that the chief priests took the betrayal money from Judas, thirty pieces of silver, and bought the field for a place of burial for strangers. Matthew calls it "Field of Blood" but does not use the term Akeldama (Mt. 27:3-10). Suggested allusions to the Mt. 27 passage are Jer. 18:2-12; 19:1-15; 32:6-10; Zec. 11:13. Solutions to this dilemma are varied and it is best to consult a good commentary for fuller explanations. While the exact location of this field is not known, an ancient tradition places it on the southern slope of the eastern end of the Hinnom Valley, S of Jerusalem's walled city.

AKHENATON {blessed spirit of (the god) Aton} *See* EGYPT

AKIM {Yahweh is my brother} One in the genealogy of Christ (Mt. 1:14). †

AKKAD *See* GEOGRAPHY OF THE HOLY LAND

AKKADIAN A Semitic language of about 2250 B.C. from Accad in northern Babylon (Ge. 10:10).

AKKO *See* ACC(H)O

AKKUB {guard}
1. A descendant of David and Solomon who lived after the Babylonian captivity (1Ch. 3:24). †
2. One of the temple gatekeepers in the time of Nehemiah (Ne. 7:45; 11:19; 12:25; 1Ch. 9:17; Ezr. 2:42). †
3. A temple servant (Ezr. 2:45). †
4. One of those who helped the people understand the Law in the days of Ezra (Ne. 8:7). †

AKRABBIM {scorpions} *See* SCORPION PASS

ALABASTER A stone, carbonate of lime, used in ancient times for making flasks and boxes for holding perfumes and ointments. A jar of alabaster contained the ointment with which a woman anointed the head of Jesus (Mt. 26:7; Mk. 14:3; Lk. 7:37). †

An Alabaster Vase

ALAMETH [concealment] *See* ALEMETH 1.

ALAMMELECH *See* ALLAMMELECH

ALAMOTH 1Ch. 15:20. †; *See also* PSALMS, TITLES OF 10., (1)

ALCOHOL(ISM) *See* ADDICTION; DRINK

ALEMETH [concealment]
1. A descendant of Benjamin (1Ch. 7:8). †
2. A descendant of Saul and Jonathan, and also a Benjamite (1Ch. 8:36; cf. 9:42). †
3. A village (176-136) in the tribal areas of Benjamin (1Ch. 6:60; also called Almon (Jos. 21:18). †

ALEXANDER
1. Alexander the Great, King of Greece, conqueror of the East at the end of the fourth century B.C. He is not mentioned by name in the Bible.
2. The son of Simon of Cyrene, who was compelled to carry the cross of Jesus (Mk. 15:21). †

Coin of Alexander the Great

3. A member of the high priestly family before whom Peter and John were tried (Ac. 4:6). †
4. One whom made "shipwreck" of his faith and was handed over to Satan for it by Paul—perhaps the coppersmith who did Paul much harm (1Ti. 1:19-20; 2Ti. 4:14-15). †
5. One who tried to speak for the Jews during the riot in Ephesus over their god Artemis (Ac. 19:33-34). †

ALEXANDRIA A city of Egypt founded by Alexander the Great in the end of the fourth century B.C. and the home of a large Jewish community. Apparently those of this community also maintained a synagogue at Jerusalem, for some of them opposed Stephen and thus contributed to his death by stoning (Ac. 6:9-10; 7:57-58). Apollos of Alexandria helped Paul at Ephesus and Corinth (Ac. 18:24; 19:1).

ALGUM, ALGUMWOOD *See* TREES

ALIAH *See* ALVAH

ALIAN [*possibly* ascending one *or* tall] *See* ALVAN

ALIEN *See* STRANGER

ALLAMMELECH [oak of the king *or* oak of (the god) Molech] An unidentified town in the tribal area of Asher (Jos. 19:26). †

ALLEGORICAL INTERPRETATION *See* HERMENEUTICS

ALLEGORY A figurative treatment of one subject under the guise of another. An allegory is a symbolical narrative. A prime illustration is found in Gal. 4:24ff. rendered "is an allegory" (RSV), from the Greek word *allegoreo*. After NT times, extensive use was made of allegory in both Jewish and Christian circles. *See* PARABLE

ALLELUIA [you all praise! Yahweh] *See* HALLELUJAH

ALLIANCES *See* COVENANT

ALLON [oak]
1. A descendant of Simeon (1Ch. 4:37). †
2. KJV, NEB (Elon-bezanannim) in Jos. 19:33 for "oak" or "large tree" in Zaanannim.

ALLON BACUTH [oak of weeping] An unidentified place, perhaps near Bethel where the nurse of Rebekah, wife of Isaac, was buried (Ge. 35:8). †

ALMIGHTY *See* GOD, NAMES OF

ALMODAD [El is loved] One of the descendants of Shem, son of Noah (Ge. 10:26; 1Ch. 1:20). †

ALMON *See* ALEMETH 3., and BETH DIBLATHAIM; *see also* TREES, Fruit Trees, *Almond*

ALMON DIBLATHAIM [way of the double fig cakes] Somewhere in Moab, it is one of the stops in the exodus from Egypt (Nu. 33:46-47). †

ALMOND *See* TREES

ALMS The giving of alms is the voluntary giving of contributions to or for the poor. In OT times it was required and practiced even though the word is not found in the text (Dt. 15:7-11). This act came later to have very great significance, even that one could himself be forgiven by practicing it (Da. 4:27). In later Judaism and in the NT it takes on even greater importance for the observant (Ac. 3:1-3; 10:2; 24:17). It was prominent in the teaching of Jesus (Mt. 6:2-4; 25:31-40; Mk. 9:41).

ALMUG, ALMUGWOOD *See* TREES

ALOES *See* PLANTS, PERFUMES, AND SPICES

ALOTH An unknown town or district associated with Asher (1Ki. 4:16). *See also* BEALOTH

ALPHA AND OMEGA *See* GOD, NAMES OF, GODHEAD 7.

ALPHABET *See* WRITING

ALPHAEUS
1. Father of one of the apostles, James the younger (Mt. 10:3; Mk. 3:18; Lk. 6:15; Ac. 1:13). He is husband of one of the Marys, mother of James and Joseph (Joses) (Mk. 15:40; *cf.* Mt. 27:56). †
2. Father of one of the apostles, Levi, i.e., Matthew (Mt. 9:9; Mk. 2:14). †

ALTAR A place for making sacrifices to God or to pagan deities. An altar for the God of Israel had to be built from earth or from unhewn stone and could not be so high that it required steps to reach its top (Ex. 20:24-26). In early biblical times some were to commemorate the appearance of deity or to mark an important event (Ge. 12:7; Dt. 27:1-8). The horned altar was made during the time of King Solomon. It was a square pillar with horn-like protrusions at each of its upper four corners. On the horns of these special altars a part of the blood of the sacrifice was to be placed, and fugitives could claim asylum by taking hold of them (Ex. 29:12; 1Ki. 2:28). Gradually over a period of time, the altar of the temple in Jerusalem became the legal place of sacrificing.

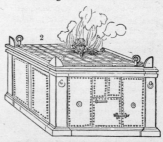

The Altar for Burnt Offerings

The Incense Altar

ALTASCHITH [(do) not destroy] *See* PSALMS, TITLES OF 3., *destroy not*

ALUSH One of the stopping places on the Exodus, somewhere in the Sinai peninsula (Nu. 33:13-14). †

ALVAH A chief of Edom descended from Esau (Ge. 36:40; 1Ch. 1:51). †

ALVAN [*possibly* ascending one, *or* tall] Ancestor of a subclan in Edom (Ge. 36:23; 1Ch. 1:40). †

AMAD An unidentified town in the tribal area of Asher (Jos. 19:26).†

AMAL [laborer, troubler] One of the descendants of Asher (1Ch. 7:35). †

AMALEK, AMALEKITES A people descended from Esau, the son of Abraham, who lived S of Judah in the desert area (Ge. 36:9, 12; Nu. 13:29). Their wars with Israel began during the Exodus where their first defeat took place at Rephidim (Ex. 17:8-16). Wars between Amalekites and Israel continued sporadically until the times of King Hezekiah (Nu. 14:45; Jdg. 3:13; 1Sa. 14:47-48; 15:7; 30:1, 17-18; 1Ch. 4:43). Moses at the command of God declared their ultimate overthrow (Ex. 17:14; Dt. 25:17-19).

AMAM An unidentified town of southern Judah (Jos. 15:26). †

AMANA A place associated with Lebanon and Hermon in SS. 4:8. Amana is a variant reading in 2Ki. 5:12. Though all versions have Abana, the ASV, RSV, NASB footnote the variant reading in 2Ki. †

AMANUENSIS *See* TERTIUS

AMARANTHINE *See* PLANTS, PERFUMES, AND SPICES, Flowering Plants 8.

AMARIAH [Yahweh has said]
1. A descendant of Levi, Kohath, and Aaron (1Ch. 6:7, 11, 52; 23:19; 24:23; Ezr. 7:3; Ne. 12:13). †
2. A chief priest in the days of King Jehoshaphat (2Ch. 19:11).
3. One of the Levites in charge of the free will offerings in the days of King Hezekiah (2Ch. 31:15). †
4. An ancestor of the prophet Zephaniah who was probably in the royal line of Judah (Zep. 1:1). †
5. One of those who had married foreign women in the time of the Babylonian captivity (Ezr. 10:42). †
6. A leading Judahite who lived in Jerusalem in the days of Nehemiah (Ne. 11:4). †
7. One of the signers of the covenant in the days of Nehemiah, perhaps also one who came up from Babylon with Zerubbabel (Ne. 10:3; 12:2). †

AMASA [(my) people are from Jesse]
1. A relative of King David who sided with Absalom when he revolted against his father (2Sa. 17:25), but whom David forgave and later set as the head of his armies in the place of Joab (2Sa. 19:13). Joab suspected him of treachery and later killed him (2Sa. 20:4-13; 1Ki. 2:5, 32; 1Ch. 2:17). †
2. A chief of the northern tribal confederacy who stood up against King Pekah when he tried to take Judean prisoners (2Ch. 28:12). †

AMASAI [(my) people are from Jesse]
1. A Levite descended from Kohath and Levi (1Ch. 6:25, 35) who assisted King Hezekiah in his reforms (2Ch. 29:12). †

2. Chief of David's Thirty, one who came to him at Ziklag (1Ch. 12:1, 18). †

3. One who blew trumpets before the ark of God in Jerusalem in the days of David (1Ch. 15:24). †

AMASHAI, AMASHSAI A priest in the days of Nehemiah who volunteered to live in Jerusalem (Ne. 11:13). †

AMASIAH [Yahweh carries a load] One of the builders for King Jehoshaphat in Judah (2Ch. 17:16).†

AMAZIAH [Yahweh is powerful]
1. A king of Judah. *See* KINGS OF JUDAH AND ISRAEL

2. A descendant of Simeon (1Ch. 4:34).

3. A Levite descended from Merari (1Ch. 6:45).

4. A priest at Bethel in the days of King Jeroboam who opposed the prophet Amos (Am. 7:10-17).

AMBASSADOR This word has the idea of an envoy, or representative for someone. An ambassador was an established concept at that time and was an appropriate word in light of the apostle's ministry of reconciliation (2Co. 5:20; *cf.* Eph. 6:20).

AMBER KJV for "glowing metal" in Eze. 1:4, 27; 8:2. Some say it is an alloy of silver and gold, but this is not certain.

AMEN [so be it] Transliteration of a Hebrew word expressing agreement, similar to the English "so be it" (Nu. 5:19-22); used also in prayers and in liturgies (Dt. 27:15-26; Ps. 106:48; Jer. 28:6). In the NT it is most frequently used in the conclusion of either a declaration of praise to God or a prayer (Ro. 11:36; 15:33; Php. 4:20). Jesus used it in the beginning of many of his statements (Jn. 5:24) where it appears as, "I tell you the truth." It appears as a name for Jesus himself in Rev. 3:14.

AMETHYST *See* PRECIOUS STONES AND METALS

AMI
A son of one of Solomon's servants (Ezr. 2:57). †

AMILLENNIALISM The belief that the millennial (1000 yr.) rule of Christ (mentioned in Rev. 20:46) is not a physical 1000-year kingdom on earth.

AMINADAB *See* AMMINADAB 1.

AMITTAI [true] The father of the prophet Jonah (2Ki. 14:25; Jnh. 1:1). †

AMMAH An unidentified hill where Joab and Abner confronted one another (2Sa. 2:24). †

AMMI [my people] *See* LOAMMI

AMMIEL [El is my kinsman]
1. The Danite representative in the twelve spies who went to spy out the land for the Israelites (Nu. 13:12). †

2. The father of Bath-shua (Bathsheba), one of David's wives and mother of Solomon (1Ch. 3:5). †

3. The father of Makir who was the protector of the last son of King Saul (2Sa. 9:4-5; 17:27). †

4. A son of Obed-Edom, one of the gatekeepers (1Ch. 26:5). †

AMMIHUD [(my) people have grandeur]
1. The name of four men, one in each of four tribes: Ephraim, Simeon, Naphthali, and Judah (Nu. 1:10, 2:18; 7:48, 53; 10:22; 34:20, 28; 1Ch. 7:26; 9:4). †

2. The father of Talmai, the king of Geshur, with whom Absalom hid out from David for three years (2Sa. 13:37). †

AMMINADAB [(my) people are generous]
1. The father-in-law of Aaron (Ex. 6:23) and an ancestor of David and Jesus Christ (Ru. 4:19; Mt. 1:4).

2. A Levite, the son of Kohath and father of Korah (1Ch. 6:22).

3. A Levite head of a family in the time of King David (1Ch. 15:10-11).

AMMINADIB KJV for "my people" or "of the people of the prince" in SS. 6:12. *See also* AMMINADAB

AMMISHADDAI [Shaddai is (my) kinsman] A member of the tribe of Dan, father of the leader of the camp of Dan following the host in the wilderness wanderings (Nu. 1:12; 2:25; 7:66, 71; 10:25). †

AMMIZABAD [(my) people have given a gift] Son of one of David's mighty thirty men (1Ch. 27:6). †

AMMON, THE CLAN [people] *See* BEN-AMMI

AMMON, THE LAND *See* GEOGRAPHY OF THE HOLY LAND

AMNON [trustworthy]
1. David's first son, Amnon, dishonored his half-sister and was murdered for his actions by his half-brother Absalom (2Sa. 3:2; 13:1-22).
2. A descendant of Judah (1Ch. 4:20).

AMOK [capable, KB] A chief of the priests who came with Zerubbabel from Babylon after the captivity (Ne. 12:7, 20). †

AMON [trustworthy]
1. The governor of Samaria in the reign of King Ahab (1Ki. 22:26).
2. A descendant of one of Solomon's servants who returned from the Babylonian captivity (Ne. 7:59). *See* KINGS OF JUDAH AND ISRAEL; *see also* DEITIES

AMON, CITY OF Translated Amon in Jer. 46:25; otherwise THEBES in the NIV. *See* THEBES

AMORITES [*possibly* hill dwellers, BDB; westerners, KB] A people who lived in the land of Amurru, W of Mesopotamia, probably in Syria and at least a part of Palestine. Some also lived in the Judean hill country, others E of the Jordan in Heshbon and Bashan (Jos. 9:10; 10:5). According to 1Ch. 1:13-14, they descended from Canaan. In the middle of the third millennium B.C., the Akkadian records of Sargon the First, and again the records of the Sumerian Gudea at about 2000 B.C., refer to campaigns against the Amorites to secure building materials. One of their important centers was the city of Mari on the Euphrates River E of Byblos and Tad-

mor. After the beginning of the second millennium B.C., they spread widely, but their empire ended with the conquest by King Hammurabi of Babylon who took Mari and scattered the people. They intermarried with Indo-Europeans, and others existed for many centuries scattered in smaller states as we have already noted. There are many references to them in the Amarna Letters from Egypt of the fourteenth century B.C.

Their language was a dialect of NW Semitic. The early kings had Semitic names even though later Horite and Hittite names were more prominent. As a buffer state, its precarious existence in this area came to an end in 1297 with the Battle of Orontes, after which it came under Hittite control until that empire too came to its end a hundred years later. References are found to them in the Bible from the patriarchal times to the time of King Solomon, at which time we find them as slaves (Ge. 15:18-21; Jos. 24:8; 2Ch. 8:7).

AMOS
1. A prophet. *See* AMOS, BOOK OF
2. A man in the lineage of Joseph, Christ's genealogy (Lk. 3:25).

AMOS, BOOK OF [burden bearer] *See* PROPHETS, BOOKS OF THE MINOR

AMOZ [strong] The father of the prophet Isaiah (Isa. 1:1).

AMPHIPOLIS [a city surrounded *or* a city conspicuous] An important trading center in Greece through which Paul passed on one of his missionary journeys (Ac. 17:1). †

AMPLIAS, AMPLIATUS A Christian at Rome, loved by Paul (Ro. 16:8). †

AMRAM, AMRAMITE [exalted people]
1. A grandson of Levi who married Jochebed, his father's sister, and became the father of Miriam, Moses, and Aaron (Ex. 6:16, 18, 20; Nu. 3:19, 27; 26:58-59; 1Ch. 6:2-3, 18; 23:12-13; 24:20; 26:23). †
2. Father of some men who had married foreign women during the Babylo-

nian captivity but who later put them away (Ezr. 10:34, 44). †

AMRAPHEL The king of Shinar who, among others, invaded patriarchal Palestine and took the goods of Sodom and Gomorrah and along with them the nephew of Abram (Abraham), Lot (Ge. 14:1, 8-9, 12). The identification with Hammurabi, king of Babylon, is not accepted by most scholars of Babylonian history. †

AMULET *See* CHARMS

AMUN *See* THEBES

AMZI {*possibly* Yahweh is my strength}
   1. A descendant of Levi (1Ch. 6:46). †
   2. A priest who served in the second temple (Ne. 11:12). †

ANAB {grape} A town (143-089) in the hill country of Judah near Hebron and Debir (Jos. 11:21; 15:50). †

ANAH A son of Zibeon, the Hivite. His daughter was one of Esau's wives (Ge. 36:2, 14, 18, 20, 24-25, 29; 1Ch. 1:38, 40-41). †

ANAHARATH A town (194-228) of the tribe of Issachar SE of Mt. Tabor (Jos. 19:19). †

ANAIAH {Yahweh responds} One who signed the covenant after the return from the Babylonian captivity and stood with Ezra when he read the Book of the Law to the people (Ne. 8:4; 10:22). †

ANAK, ANAKIMS, ANAKITES {(long) necked, tall} A people found in Palestine in the days of Joshua's conquest among whom were apparently many large people, even giants. They were also known as Rephaites and called Emites by the Moabites (Dt. 2:10-11, 21). After Joshua their remnants lived in the Philistine cities (Jos. 11:21-22).

ANALOGY OF THE FAITH The process of consulting other Scriptures to interpret unclear passages by the clear passages.

ANAMIM, ANAMITES A tribe or group descended from Mizraim (Egypt) (Ge. 10:13; 1Ch. 1:11). †

ANAMMELECH [Anat is king] 2Ki. 17:31. † *See* DEITIES

ANAN {cloud} One of the men who signed the covenant in the days of Nehemiah (Ne. 10:26). †

ANANI {Yahweh is a covering} A son of Elioenai, a descendant of King Solomon (1Ch. 3:24).†

ANANIAH {Yahweh is a covering}
   1. Grandfather of one who repaired the walls of Jerusalem after the return from the Babylonian captivity (Ne. 3:23). †
   2. A town (174-131) settled by Benjamites after the return noted above (Ne. 11:32). †

ANANIAS {Yahweh is gracious}
   1. Together with his wife, Sapphira, he was involved in a lie in the days of the early church, was rebuked by Peter, and struck down by death for the lie (Ac. 5:1-8). †
   2. One who was used to restore sight to the Apostle Paul after his conversion, and to baptize him (Ac. 9:10-17; 22:12). †
   3. A pro-Roman high priest before whom Paul was tried (Ac. 23:2; 24:1). †

ANAT {a Canaanite goddess} *See* ANAMMELECH; DEITIES

ANATH {a Semitic goddess "Anath"} Father of one of Israel's judges, Shamgar (Jdg. 3:31; 5:6).

ANATHEMA {devoted to destruction} *See* CURSE; DEVOTE, DEVOTED THING

ANATHOTH, ANATHOTHITE {plural of ANAT}
   1. A town (174-135) of Benjamin just N of Jerusalem given to the priests, also the home of Jeremiah the prophet (Jos. 21:13, 17-19). It was resettled after the Babylonian captivity (Ezr. 2:23).
   2. A grandson of Benjamin (1Ch. 7:8).

3. One of those who signed the covenant with Nehemiah (Ne. 10:19).

ANCIENT OF DAYS A title for God found only in Daniel (Da. 7:9, 13, 22). †

ANDREW [manly] *See* APOSTLES

ANDRONICUS [victor (over) man] One whom Paul refers to as a "relative" who had been in prison with him, a man outstanding among the apostles (Ro. 16:7). †

ANEM [springs] A city of refuge from the tribe of Issachar somewhere in the vicinity of Mt. Tabor (1Ch. 6:73). A parallel passage is Jos. 21:29 where the city is called En Gannim (spring of gardens). †

ANEMONE *See* PLANTS, PERFUMES, AND SPICES, Plants for Food 3., *lily*

ANER
1. An Amorite chief who was allied with Abraham against the eastern kings (Ge. 14:13, 24). †
2. An unidentified town in Manasseh which was given to the Kohathites (1Ch. 6:70). †

ANGEL [messenger] A translation given to the Hebrew word which basically means "messenger" as we know from such usages as found in Jdg. 6:35. The Greek word used to render this Hebrew word was *angelos*, which ultimately came into English as "angel." These messengers could be human or they could be superhuman agents of God. Two appeared in human form to Abraham with the LORD (Ge. 18:1-2, 22). *See also* CHERUB and SERAPHIM. They ate, were able to fight, and could be charged by God with error (Ge. 18:8; 32:1; Job 4:18). When God sent prophets to his people, angels were often intermediaries bringing messages in visions (Eze. 8:1-8). After the return from Babylon, the picture of angels in the Bible becomes much more complex—as also in the Dead Sea Scrolls. Some are found with individual names such as Gabriel (Da. 8:16; Lk. 1:19), and

Michael (Da. 12:1; Rev. 12:7). In the NT Christ refers to their existence, but they no longer are intermediaries to bring God's messages since that role is now put into the hands of Christ or the Holy Spirit (Ac. 9:5; Gal. 1:12). Because of abuses it was necessary for Paul to warn the churches against the worship of angels (Col. 2:18). There are two references to an archangel in 1Th. 4:16 and Jude 9.

One angel is called "the angel of God" (Ge. 21:17; 31:11; Ex. 14:19; Jdg. 6:20; 13:69) or "the angel of the LORD" (Ge. 16:7ff.; 22:11ff.; Ex. 3:2; 22:22ff.; Jdg. 2:14; 5:23; 6:11ff.; 13:3ff.). † Some believe this angel to be an appearance of God (theophany) or a specially commissioned high ranking angel. Many believe this to be Christ, the preincarnate Word, the second person of the Trinity.

The term "angels of the churches" in Rev. 1:20; 2:1–3:22 probably refers to the leaders of the individual churches. *See also* DEVIL; THEOPHANY

ANGEL OF THE LORD [messenger of Yahweh] *See* ANGEL, last ¶

ANGELOLOGY *See* SYSTEMATIC THEOLOGY

ANGER *See* WRATH

ANGUISH *See* AGONY

ANIAM [I am kinsman] A descendant of Manasseh (1Ch. 7:19). †

ANIM [springs] A town (156-084) in the hill country of Judah (Jos. 15:50). †

ANIMALS OF THE BIBLE *See* BEASTS

ANIMISM The veneration of physical objects in the conviction that conscious spirits are present in them.

ANISE *See* PLANTS, PERFUMES AND SPICES

ANNA [grace] A prophetess descended from the tribe of Asher, a widow of many years, who spent her time worshiping, fasting, and praying at the temple. When she saw the child Jesus, she spoke of him to all who were looking for redemption in Israel (Lk. 2:36-38). †

ANNAS [grace] For nine years a high priest in Jerusalem; the father-in-law of Caiaphas who was the high priest at the time of Jesus' arrest (Lk. 3:2; Jn. 18:13, 24). Deposed by the Romans, he was still considered high priest by the Jews (Ac. 4:6). †

ANNIHILATE *See* ANATHEMA; CURSE; DEVOTE, DEVOTED THING

ANOINT, ANOINTED The application of oil to a person or thing for healing or as a sacred rite (Ex. 30:22-33; Ps. 23:5; Mk. 6:13; Jas. 5:14). Kings, priests, and sometimes even prophets were consecrated to their offices by having oil poured on their heads (2Ki. 9:13). In the NT the prophet, priest, and king *par excellence* was Christ who is called the "Anointed One" (Ac. 4:24-28). The Hebrew word for anoint was transliterated into Greek as *messias* and then later into English as *messiah*. The usual Greek word for anointed, *christos*, came into English as "Christ." Both are applied to Jesus as titles in the N.T.

ANT *See* BEASTS 6.

ANTEDILUVIANS Those who lived before the biblical flood. *See* FLOOD

ANTELOPE *See* BEASTS 2.

ANTHOTHIJAH [Anathothite + Yahweh] A descendant of Benjamin (1Ch. 8:24). †

ANTHROPOLOGY *See* SYSTEMATIC THEOLOGY

ANTHROPOMORPHISM The giving of human form to Deity. In the Bible God is spoken of in anthropomorphic terms as a means of communicating to men the invisible (immaterial) attributes and characteristics of God who is Spirit.

ANTI-LEBANON *See* GEOGRAPHY OF THE HOLY LAND, *Ante-Lebanon*

ANTICHRIST [against Christ] In the eschatological war of the end of days, the Antichrist is the great opponent of Christ who will finally be completely defeated.

John noted that there are also many antichrists, those who deny that Jesus is the Christ (IJn. 2:18, 22; 4:3; 2Jn. 7). † *See* ABOMINATION THAT CAUSES DESOLATION

ANTILEGOMENA Disputed books in the NT Christian canon—among which Origen identified as Hebrews, James, 2 Peter, 2 and 3 John. The Homolegomena were the books of the NT canon which were not in dispute.

ANTINOMIANISM The rejection of the idea that the Christian life needs to be governed by laws. This idea ignores the fact that there is a law of Christ (Gal. 6:2). Also, Christ gave us commandments (Jn. 13:34-35).

ANTINOMY A contradiction between two apparently equal, valid principles or inferences. The doctrine of the Trinity (God is one yet three "persons") is an example of antinomy. A similar idea to antimony is one of the definitions of a paradox or an anomaly.

ANTIOCH The name of many cities which were named after the father of the founder of the Seleucid dynasty, whose dynasty was centered in Antioch of Syria. Two of these cities are noted in the NT.

1. *Antioch of Syria* on the Orontes River about fourteen miles E of the Mediterranean Sea and one of the most important centers of commerce in the Middle East. In post-NT times the Romans conquered it and made it the capital of their province of Syria, 69 B.C. Under persecution in Jerusalem many early Christians fled to Antioch and there established a thriving church to whose assistance Barnabas and Paul were sent. Here it was that the followers of Jesus were first called Christians (Ac. 11:19-26). This church at Antioch became the center of the early missionary outreach. Paul's first two missionary journeys began here (Ac. 13:1-2; 15:35-36). It was a center of the attempt to mix law and grace so vigorously opposed by Paul, which led to the council at Jerusalem of the leaders of the church

(Ac. 15; Gal. 2:11). The results of this council were delivered to Antioch in a letter.

2. *Antioch of Pisidia*, a city which bordered on the province of Pisidia, but which was actually in the province of Galatia. Paul visited it in his missionary journeys (Ac. 13:14; 2Ti. 3:11).

THE FIRST MISSIONARY JOURNEY: FROM ANTIOCH TO CYPRUS

ANTIOCHUS In intertestamental times a number of the Seleucid kings of Syria bore this name. Perhaps the best known is Antiochus IV Epiphanes (175-163 B.C.) who tried to Hellenize the Jews. This attempt failed, resulting in the Maccabean revolt that set Judea free from Syrian rule. He was not mentioned by name in the Bible, although some scholars see Epiphanes predicted in Da. 11:36.

ANTIPAS
1. One of the names of Herod the Tetrarch. *See* HERODS, THE
2. An early Christian martyr in Pergamum (Rev. 2:12-13). †

ANTIPATER *See* HERODS, THE

ANTIPATRIS A town (143-168) founded by Herod the Great at the foot of the central mountain range in Palestine between Jerusalem and the coast. Paul stayed there overnight when he was being taken as a prisoner from Jerusalem to Caesarea (Ac. 23:31). † *See also* APHEK 1.

ANTIPATRIS

ANTONIA, TOWER OF *See* TOWER

ANTOTHIJAH *See* ANTHOTHIJAH

ANTOTHITE An inhabitant of Anathoth. *See* ANATHOTH

ANUB {fruitful} A descendant of Judah (1Ch. 4:8). †

ANVIL A common tool of the metal worker, from a Hebrew word with one of its definitions "to strike, to beat" (Isa. 41:7). †

APE 1Ki. 10:22; 2Ch. 9:21. † *See* BEASTS 3.

APELLES A Christian of Rome greeted by Paul (Ro. 16:10). †

APHARSAKITES, APHARSATHCHITES KJV, NKJV transliteration in Ezr. 4:9; 5:6; 6:6. The NIV translates this word correctly as "officials," the NASB "lesser governors," JB "legates," and similarly by other versions. *See also* GOVERNOR

APHARSITES KJV for "Persian" in Ezr. 4:9, and so translated in NIV, NKJV. *See also* PERSIA

APHEK {stronghold}
1. A Canaanite town (143-168) on the edge of the Plain of Sharon which later became a Philistine base used against Israel. Josephus states that Herod built the town of Antipatris on its ruins. Today it is known as Rosh ha-Ayin (Jos. 12:18; 1Sa. 4:1; 29:1). *See also* ANTIPATRIS
2. A town located in the plain of Acco

(160-250) in the tribal area of Asher (Jos. 19:30).

3. A town (210-243) near the Sea of Galilee where King Ahab defeated the Syrians under Ben-Hadad (1Ki. 20:26-34).

APHEKAH [the fortress] An unidentified town in the hill country of Judah (Jos. 15:53).†

APHIAH A Benjamite ancestor of King Saul (1Sa. 9:1). †

APHIK *See* APHEK

APHRAH *See* BETH OPHRAH

APHSES *See* HAPPIZZEZ

APOCALYPSE [disclosure] A word commonly used as a name for the Book of Revelation.

APOCALYPTIC LITERATURE A type of literature found in the ancient world. Highly symbolic, it dealt with the future, was cosmic, and portrayed the world as a fight between good and evil (or dualistic forces). The Bible has two books that are apocalyptic: (parts of) Daniel and Revelation. Other parts of some Bible books are described by some as of this type of literature: (parts of) Joel, Amos, Zechariah. There are many noncanonical books that are apocalyptic, some before and some after the time of Christ. The Book of Enoch and Shepherd of Hermas are two. *See* SCRIPTURE, *Pseudepigrapha*

APOCRYPHA [hidden, obscure] *See* SCRIPTURE 4, *apocrypha*

APOLLONIA An unidentified town in Greece through which Paul and Silas passed en route to Thessalonica (Ac. 17:1). †

APOLLOS An Alexandrian Jew who came to Ephesus and was there instructed by Aquila and Priscilla. He preached in Achaia and later acquired a following in Corinth (Ac. 18:24, 27; 19:1; 1Co. 1:12; 3:4-6, 22; 4:6; 16:12; Tit. 3:13). Paul encouraged him to revisit Corinth (1Co. 16:12) and had asked Titus to help him (Tit. 3:13). †

APOLLYON [destroyer] Rev. 9:11. † *See* DEAD, ABODE OF

APOLOGETICS A branch of Christian theology that seeks to make a defense of the gospel against critics, and sets forth reasons to believe in the gospel. This use is not related to the common idea of "being sorry." *See* EXISTENCE OF GOD

APOSTASY [abandonment] A turning or wandering away from the tenets of one's faith. On a larger scale, it can mean "rebellion" — something which is to take place in the church before the second coming of Christ (2Th. 2:12).

APOSTATE One who leaves the Christian faith.

APOSTLES [messengers] A term applied generally, but not exclusively, in the NT to the twelve men chosen by Christ to learn of him and then to bear witness of him to the world. They were: Simon, also called Peter, and his brother Andrew; the sons of Zebedee, James and John; Philip; Bartholomew, also called Nathanael; Matthew, also called Levi; Thomas; James, son of Alphaeus; Judas, son of James, also called Thaddaeus; Simon the Zealot; and Judas Iscariot (Mt. 10:2-4; Mk. 3:16-19; Lk. 6:14-16; Ac. 1:13). Most of them were Galileans. Three were especially close to Jesus — Peter, James, and John — and were with Jesus on several key occasions: on the Mount of Transfiguration and in the Garden of Gethsemane (Mt. 17:1; Mk. 14:33). Judas Iscariot, after his betrayal of the Lord and his suicide, was replaced by Matthias (Ac. 1:26). Paul, Barnabas, and others are also called apostles (Ac. 14:14; Ro. 16:7; Gal. 1:19).

APOSTLES CREED *See* CONFESSION 2.

APOSTOLIC AGE The time covered by the authority of the apostles, extending to about the end of the first century.

APOSTOLIC FATHERS A group of Christian writers of about A.D. 150 to 200. Clement, Ignatius, and Polycarp were in this group.

APOSTOLIC SUCCESSION The belief that the authority of the apostles could be handed down to following generations by ordination or laying on of hands.

APOTHECARY *See* VESSEL

APPAIM [(a pair of) nostrils] A descendant of Judah (1Ch. 2:30-31). †

APPAREL *See* DRESS

APPEARING *See* ESCHATOLOGY

APPHIA A Christian woman to whom Paul sent greetings (Phm. 2). †

APPII, APPIUS, FORUM OF A town through which Paul passed en route to his trial in Rome, some forty miles S of Rome (Ac. 28:15). †

APPIUS, MARKET OF *See* APPIUS, FORUM OF

APPOINTED *See* ELECT, ELECTION

APPLE *See* TREES

"APPLE OF THE EYE"
1. A figure of speech in Hebrew that reads literally "(little) man of the eye." It may be translated as the "pupil," as many versions do, but is a special figure for tender care and preciousness. The KJV and NIV keep the figure (Dt. 32:10; Ps. 17:8; Pr. 7:2).
2. KJV for the Hebrew, "daughter" of the eye (La. 2:18; *cf.* Zec. 2:8). It may be best translated "pupil" but is not translated in many versions because "pupil of the eye" equals "eye." The KJV, though, may well be right in that it has the same meaning as 1.

APRON *See* DRESS

AQABAH, GULF OF *See* GEOGRAPHY OF THE HOLY LAND

AQUEDUCT [water channel] A channel for conveying water (2Ki. 18:17; Isa. 7:3; 36:2). King Hezekiah's famous conduit is known in Jerusalem to this day. His aqueduct was an underground tunnel carved out of solid rock. The Romans built channels supported where necessary by arches, as at Caesarea and elsewhere.

AQUILA [eagle] A Jew of Pontus who, with his wife Priscilla, had moved from Rome to Corinth because of the expulsion of the Jews from Rome by the emperor in A.D. 52. Paul lived with them during his ministry in Corinth, and they moved with him to Ephesus later where their house was a place of meeting for the church there (Ac. 18:2, 18-19, 26; Ro. 16:3-5; 1Co. 16:19). They instructed Apollos in the things of Christ (Ac. 18:24-26). †

AR [*possibly* city] A town of Moab, or on its border, near the Arnon River (Nu. 21:15, 28; Dt. 2:9, 18, 29; Isa. 15:1). †

ARA A descendant of Asher (1Ch. 7:38). †

ARAB [bushwhack, ambush]
1. A hill country town (153-093) in the tribal area of Judah (Jos. 15:52).
2. A desert people. *See* ARABS; GESHAN

ARABAH [desert] *See* GEOGRAPHY OF THE HOLY LAND

ARABIA *See* GEOGRAPHY OF THE HOLY LAND

ARABS [desert plateau dwellers] Originally the inhabitants of the Arabian peninsula S of Syria, particularly the inhabitants of the northern part of this area, consisting of many different tribes: Ishmaelites, Midianites, Sabeans, Hagarenes, Amalekites. They descended from Abraham by Keturah and from Ishmael. With their camels they traveled lucrative trade routes from Egypt to Babylon and all areas between (Isa. 60:6; Eze. 27:21-22). Perhaps one of the best known stories of interconnections with Israel is the visit of the Queen of Sheba to Solomon (1Ki. 10:1-13). During the period of the kings of Israel and Judah there were times of harassment by these tribes and a time when they were under tribute to Judah (2Ch. 17:11; 21:16-17; 22:1; 26:17). At least one Arab was among those who opposed the work of

Nehemiah, Geshem by name (Ne. 2:19). In the NT Paul referred to Arabia (in the Sinai) in Gal. 4:25, and noted his time spent in Arabia after his conversion. Men from Arabia were among the multitude on the Day of Pentecost (Ac. 2:11). Exactly when and from where the ancestors of the modern Arabs came to Palestine is not known with certainty. It could not have been before the end of NT times and probably not until after Roman times, which ended in the fourth century.

ARAD {wild donkey}

1. A descendant of Benjamin (1Ch. 8:15). †

2. A Canaanite city (152-069). An Israelite city (162-076). The excavations at Tell Arad have shown that the latter was unoccupied between Early Bronze and Israelite times, a gap of 2000 years. Thus archaeologists place the Canaanite city at Tell Malhata nearby, which was occupied in Middle Bronze and Late Bronze times. The army of the king of Arad (Malhata) defeated the Israelites during their exodus from Egypt (Nu. 21:1-3; 33:40). In Joshua's conquest, however, the victory went the other way (Jos. 12:14). The relatives of Moses' in-laws then lived in the area (Jdg. 1:16).

Archaeological excavations at Tell Arad conducted by Dr. Yohanan Aharoni of Tel Aviv University have uncovered the Israelite Arad, a city occupied from Solomonic times down to the end of the kingdom of Judah. One of the most fascinating parts of the excavation was the discovery of an Israelite temple founded in the earliest period and used through the times of Josiah. This temple was smaller but of the same proportions as the Solomonic temple in Jerusalem. †

ARAH {he wanders}

1. A descendant of Asher and the collective name of his descendants who came with Zerubbabel from the Babylonian captivity (1Ch. 7:39; Ezr. 2:5; Ne. 6:18; 7:10). †

2. A town or district of the Sidonians (Jos. 13:4). Also known as Mearah in some versions. The *Me* is translated "from" in the NIV. †

ARAM

1. A descendant of Asher (1Ch. 7:34).

2. One of the ancestors of Jesus, called Ram in Ru. 4:19; Mt. 1:3; Lk. 3:33.

ARAMAIC LANGUAGE *See* BIBLICAL LANGUAGES

ARAMEANS A country and a people. *See* GEOGRAPHY OF THE HOLY LAND

ARAMITESS KJV in 1Ch. 7:14. *See* ARAMEANS

ARAM GESHUR *See* GESHUR 1.

ARAM MAACAH An Aramean kingdom in the area of Bashan and Mt. Hermon, sometimes called Maacah (1Ch. 19:6). † *See* MAACAH 10.

ARAM NAHARAIM Ge. 24:10; Dt. 23:4; Jdg. 3:8; 1Ch. 19:6. † *See* EBER

ARAM ZOBAH *See* ZOBA(H)

MOUNTAINS OF ARARAT
Noah's ark touched land in the Mountains of Ararat located in present-day Turkey near the Russian border.

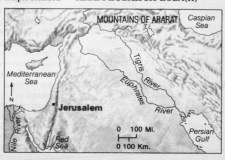

ARAN {wild goat} A descendant of Esau
(Ge. 36:28; 1Ch. 1:42). †

ARARAT A kingdom near Lake Van
called Urartu in Assyrian. The sons of
the Assyrian king Sennacherib fled there
after they had murdered their father
(2Ki. 19:37; Isa. 37:38; Jer. 51:27).
Noah's ark rested on "the mountains of
Ararat" after the Flood had receded (Ge.
8:4). Some scholars think that because
the plural "mountains" is used, the region
can be identified generally but not the
exact location. There are a number of
traditions relative to the particular location. †

ARATUS *See* SCRIPTURE 2, *The
Reliability of the Bible*

ARAUNAH {strong} The Jebusite
owner of a threshing floor on Mt.
Moriah which was bought by David,
where he brought the Ark of the Covenant and built an altar (2Sa. 24:16ff.;
1Ch. 21:15ff.), and where Solomon later
built the temple (2Ch. 3:1). In the Hebrew text he is also called Ornan. (See
the footnote in 1Ch. 21:15, NIV.) †

ARBA {four} The father of Anak and
founder of the city of Kiriath Arba, later
called Hebron (Jos. 14:15; 15:13; 21:11). †

ARBATHITE {person from ARABAH}
Identifies the place of origin of Abi-
Albon, one of David's thirty mighty
men. He was from Beth Arabah or from
the Arbah itself (2Sa. 23:31; *cf.* 1Ch.
11:32).

ARBITE A native of the town Arba
(2Sa. 23:35). †

ARCH *See* CORNERSTONE, *capstone*

ARCHAEOLOGY {study of ancient
things}
1. History and Philosophy of Archaeology
   a. The Scope of Archaeology in
the past
   b. The Scope of Archaeology
Today
2. Materials of Archaeology
   a. Inscriptions
   b. Architecture

c. Small Objects, Pottery
d. Weapons, Coins, Metals
e. Clothing
3. Periods of Time
   a. The Periods Described
   b. Dating Methods
4. History of Research
   a. 18th Century
   b. 19th Century
   c. 20th Century
5. Methods of Archaeology
   a. Vertical Cut Method
   b. The Three-Dimensional Method
6. Philosophy of Archaeology
   a. The Purpose of Archaeology
   b. The Subjective Nature of Interpretation

1. *History and Philosophy.* Archaeology is the scholarly investigation of past
human life, especially as it is revealed
through relics, i.e., material objects that
have survived from ancient times.

a. The word *archaeology* is derived
from the Greek *archaio* and *logos*, i.e.,
the orderly arrangement of facts regarding ancient things. During the Hellenistic Age, the term was used in the sense
of "antiquarian lore," "ancient legends,"
"history." For example, Josephus' famous
history of the Jews called the *Antiquities*
in English, was called *Ioudaikes ar-
chaiologias*. The term came to be used
by scholars in the eighteenth century to
mean all study of antiquity. In that
broadest sense, it was applied to areas
that today might be limited to physical
anthropology on the one hand or to art
history and linguistics on the other.

The emphasis on everyday life as the
legitimate study of archaeology can be
seen in nineteenth-century works on biblical and Jewish antiquities based on the
written documents. The biblical and Tal-
mudic references to buildings, utensils,
rituals, food stuffs, and agriculture were
collected systematically and studied
philologically like any other cultural or
historical subject.

b. Today "archaeology of the Near
East" is a specialty in its own right.
Within this field there is what many call
"biblical archaeology." One cannot

divide the fields of study very easily because some parts of the Bible deal with adjacent countries such as Egypt, Mesopotamia, Iran, and others. From a logical point of view, the archaeology of Palestine (Eretz Israel) is a special area of study which greatly overlaps but is not necessarily the equivalent of biblical archaeology. The legitimacy of the latter term has recently been brought into question. It is best to admit that the Bible, the most extensive written document to survive from the ancient Near Eastern World, deals a great deal with the life of Israel and its neighbors. Therefore, it is reasonable and desirable that the material side of Israelite and contemporary cultures be clarified by archaeological research. Such investigations will be seen to have a legitimacy of their own, however, apart from their connection with biblical tradition.

More complex today is the question of where archaeology belongs in the range of academic disciplines. It will often be found associated with anthropology in the framework of the social sciences. This is especially true of prehistoric archaeology, particularly in the New World, in the Western Hemisphere, and also the islands of the Pacific. On the other hand, archaeology that began with an interest in the Old World, mainly classical Greece and Rome and the Near East, was closely associated with the literary and linguistic research in those fields. Thus, archaeology became a branch of biblical and ancient Near Eastern studies. This placed archaeology within the humanities. The same overlapping occurs, therefore, as in the field of history, which partakes of both the social sciences and the humanities. Furthermore, new applications of the natural sciences are being utilized every year in the analysis of archaeological materials. Fortunately, modern archaeology now benefits from the current ecological concern. The total environment of ancient man is studied in all its facets. He is seen as not only a military and political entity but also as a social being who was influenced by and who influenced his physical surroundings. As will be seen below in the discussion of the philosophy of the discipline, archaeology is a combination of all three fields, though the final interpretation of any given mass of materials must be conducted in terms of the human value judgments of the investigators. In that sense, it is more a part of the humanities, even though statistical studies and scientific analyses may be utilized.

2. *Materials*. During the Renaissance the classical authors received new attention along with the objects of Graeco-Roman art. With the campaign by Napoleon to the Middle East, the Western world became aware of the vast monumental culture of Egypt. The learned men who accompanied the French army in 1799 recorded surface remains, such as pyramids, temples, and tombs. Other explorers began to bring back to Europe their reports, drawings, and tracings of buildings, ruins, inscriptions, and other objects. In addition, the study of life in the Muslim countries of the nineteenth century became a special object of interest, and many parallels to aspects of biblical culture were discerned. The materials that attracted the interest of scholars varied greatly.

a. Inscriptions, especially the hieroglyphs and cuneiform, became a focus of research for many specialists. The texts in these scripts were usually found on "archaeological" objects, such as stelae, statues, temple walls, bas-reliefs; and their decipherment can legitimately be called archaeological research. The Phoenician script, first discovered in statues from Malta, was also decoded in the early nineteenth century, thus providing the key to later finds of Hebrew inscriptions from Palestine.

b. Architecture naturally has become a major field of archaeological research because in some countries, such as Greece and Egypt, there were major buildings, mainly temples, which survived the ravages of time. They can be excavated and at least partially reconstructed. Monumental tombs also provide details of an architectural nature, the abodes of the dead being built in a manner analogous to those of the living. With the advance of excavation technique, interest has been attracted to the badly ravaged remains of architecture found buried beneath the ruins of subsequent cities. Fortifications, including the earthen ramparts (a wall-like ridge) used to create city mounds, gate complexes, postern gates, and other innovations have come to light. Public and private buildings are often preserved only in their stone foundations, the brick superstructure having been obliterated by the action of nature and of man. Even the flimsy dwelling of primitive man can sometimes be retrieved by careful excavation of the traces in the soil, postholes, and other perishable details leaving traces in the ground.

Decorative aspects of architecture such as wall paintings and sculptured columns belong, in one sense, to the study of ancient art. Their connections with minor glyptic and miniature painting are often the subject of special study.

c. Small objects cover a wide range of human activity. The most widespread of all is pottery. From the time of ceramic utensils (Neolithic pottery, see below), man has used and broken vast amounts of pottery. It has been demonstrated that techniques of manufacture and styles of design and decoration underwent a development throughout the ages. The classification of these details according to their chronological appearance was made possible by comparisons with similar finds in Egypt where the vessels came from datable tombs. Thus, there are certain features such as styles of burnishing and painting, shapes of rims and bases, and others, which are now identifiable as belonging to particular periods in the country's history. Even sherds bearing such recognizable characteristics can be used as a rough indication for dating. Nevertheless, the pottery chronology holds good only for major periods in most cases. Refinements for shorter phases of time, such as the centuries of the Judean monarchy, are far from satisfactory.

d. Weapons are another class of artifacts requiring special study. The objects found in excavations can be compared to representations in Assyrian and Egyptian art. When metals are involved, modern technology is helping to analyze the alloys used, and geologists are searching for the sources of the original ore. Metal objects of agricultural and other domestic use receive similar treatment. For the later periods coins comprise a valuable category of metal finds, often with datable inscriptions.

Personal ornaments often appear in tombs and, on occasion, in stratified excavations. Since a large percentage of such items were imports from neighboring cultures, they are of special value for chronological and cultural relationships. Ivory plaques carved as furniture decorations have also been found. Their study is an important aspect of ancient art in Eretz-Israel and its cultural ties with Phoenicia and Egypt.

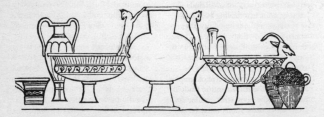

Ancient Egyptian Bowls and Vases

Coin of Maximian Commemorating Oppression against Christians

Coin of Diocletian Commemorating Oppression against Christians

Coin of Constantine Commemorating the First Official Recognition of Christianity

e. Only in the dry climate of the desert was it possible for items of clothing to be preserved. Finds of that nature have occurred in caves of the Judean Desert and Northern Sinai. In Egypt, however, an abundance of cloth samples from various periods has been recovered along with whole plants and other organic materials.

Special skills have been developed, mostly by trial and error, for the recovery and preservation of small finds. Care must be taken in removing them from the ground (after exact recording of the find spot), sometimes by using wax, plaster, or other preservatives. Then comes the stage of cleaning, particularly the metal objects, and repair when possible. The objects must be drawn and photographed after which the real scientific study begins. Comparisons with similar finds from other excavations must be made and conclusions drawn. The richest source for details of everyday life from which to deduce parallels for finds in Eretz-Israel is Egypt, where most phases of everyday life are amply illustrated by pictures, captions, and even the objects themselves, marvelously preserved.

3. *Periods of Time.* Archaeology deals only with the remains of human life while geology, of course, treats the whole history of the earth's crust. Historians refer to the ages of most-ancient man as the Paleolithic (Old Stone), Mesolithic (Middle Stone), and Neolithic (New Stone) Ages. They date the Old Stone Age in the Pleistocene (or Glacial) period, i.e., the last million years of the earth's existence. During that time, prehistoric man was a hunter and food-gatherer. In the New Stone Age, belonging to the Holocene (or Recent) Epoch, since about 9000 B.C., man became a food producer, cultivating cereals and domesticated animals. He began to use pottery about 6000 B.C.

a. For Eretz-Israel, one may say that the Proto-historic period begins with the Chalcolithic Age, about 5000-3200 B.C., when copper tools were used alongside stone. The Early Bronze Age (3200 to 2200) corresponds to the Old Kingdom of Egypt and the Sumerian and Akkadian periods of Mesopotamia. Written texts are absent in the Levant (*see* LEVANT) except for the rich archive recently discovered at Elba in northern Syria. When the last of the Early Bronze city states were destroyed, the country was largely given over to a seminomadic culture in which only temporary settlements of a flimsy nature were established (Middle Bronze I, really an intermediate period). By about 2000 B.C. the city-state regime of the Levant was reestablished and the predominant ethnic elements seem to have been Amurrite (Amorite). This was the Middle Bronze Age proper (Middle Bronze IIA). By about 1800 B.C. the life of the area is illuminated by the archives from Mari on the Euphrates. The Late Bronze Age, when some historical texts finally shed light on the land of Canaan (the central and southern Levant), extends from about 1550 to 1200 B.C. With the introduction of iron tools, we enter the Iron Age, when the historical/ethnic names can be used with more facility. The Israelite period from 1200 to 586 B.C. is followed by Babylonian rule until 539 when the Persian period begins. The Hellenistic Age is inaugurated by Alexander's conquests in 331, and the Roman period can be counted from Pompey's arrival in 63 B.C. The latter extends to A.D. 323.

b. The calculations for dating the above-mentioned periods are based on various lines of evidence. The earliest periods, especially those of prehistory, are derived from geological evidence and also from carbon 14 tests on organic materials preserved in excavations. The earlier historic periods are defined in terms of relationships with the chronology of Egypt which is at least partly anchored in astronomical observations. There are some similar tie-ins with the chronology of Mesopotamia. The relative absence of datable inscriptions in the Levant make the establishment of solid historical/cultural contacts with Egypt most imperative.

Technically, the remains of medieval and early modern times also fall within the scope of the antiquities laws in most Middle Eastern countries, including Israel. Thus, one finds archaeologists active in the study of those later periods as well. At many sites, one must first deal properly with the later remains, for otherwise the earlier remains and their degree of preservation (or disturbance) cannot be adequately understood.

Biblical archaeology covers such a wide range of these interests that one may find scholars in that field working on everything from prehistoric to medieval materials and sites.

4. *History of Research*. Modern archaeological research developed out of Western man's curiosity about himself and his world. During the Renaissance, attention was drawn to the artistic works of classical Greece and Rome; but with the Age of Enlightenment, scholars took an active interest in the physical world. Throughout the centuries there had been

pilgrims visiting the Holy Land and its sacred sites, but the solid scholarship in geographical study like that of the church fathers (Eusebius and Jerome) was not renewed until the eighteenth century.

a. The first excavations in ancient ruins were conducted at the two Roman cities destroyed by Vesuvius in A.D. 79, beginning at the seaport of Herculaneum (in 1738) and later in the main city of Pompeii (1748). However, it was the campaign of Napoleon in 1799 that opened up the Near East to Western scholars. The staff of learned men that accompanied him brought back an abundance of information about the antiquities and the natural history of Egypt and the Levant. The first modern map (1:100,000) of the Palestine coastal plain was produced.

b. During the first thirty years of the nineteenth century, there were some pioneer explorers such as Seetzen and Burckhardt. They copied Greek inscriptions, noted archaeological remains on the surface, and recorded many Arabic names of places and geographical features. It was clear from their reports that names from the Bible and other ancient sources were still preserved.

After the conquest of the land by Mohammed Ali in 1831, the more stable social conditions that ensued encouraged further serious exploration by Westerners. In 1838 Robinson and Smith made their landmark trip across the Sinai and around southern Palestine recording the locations and names of dozens of places. Their memories provided the first scientific and geographical description of the land and their compass readings were the basis for Kieppert's map which held the field for many years. Robinson and Smith made a second trip fifteen years later to complete their survey. Meanwhile, other travelers, such as Porter and Thompson, continued to explore other parts of the country and to furnish the Western world with information about the life and customs of the land. The increase of influence by the colonial powers within the Ottoman Empire and the use of steamships contributed to an increase in tourism and travel by clergy-men and scholars.

More intensive scientific exploration began in earnest after the Crimean war. The Palestine Exploration Fund was established in 1865 and fielded teams to explore Sinai and to excavate in Jerusalem. During the 1870s their team made the first complete map of Western Palestine using modern methods of surveying and cartography (map making). They and other scholars associated with the Palestine Exploration Fund, Clermont-Ganneau, Warren, Wilson, and others, recorded antiquities all over the country and contributed studies on special biblical and historical topics.

In Mesopotamia, explorers such as Botta and Layard had proved in the 1830s and 1840s that the large mounds (*tells* in Arabic) contained the remains of ancient cities. They were recovering impressive monuments in stone for their respective national museums. In Egypt, teams of scholars made epigraphic surveys of inscriptions and wall reliefs, and individual excavators, such as Mariette, brought to light the remains of ritual installations as well as statuary and other funerary remains. But in Palestine, not all scholars had learned the lessons of Mesopotamia. Conder, head of the Palestine Exploration Fund Survey, denied that the tells (mounds) were the sites of ancient towns. In general, archaeology was concerned with surface remains: temples, churches, burial caves, pillars, and other architectural pieces. Warren and the American Selah Merill, among others, were already contending that the tells were the real deposits of ancient remains from the Old Testament period. The controversy raged until it was finally settled by the excavations of Flinders Petrie at Tell el-Hesi in 1890.

During the nineteenth century books on archaeology were also written by philologists (language specialists). The details of everyday life as described in the Bible and the Talmud were assembled in a systematic manner. The various terms were treated linguistically and the texts were analyzed. Very little was as yet available from the material finds of field research to illustrate the points raised by such philological studies.

c. The great turning point was with Flinders-Petrie's work at Tell el-Ḥeṣi in 1890. He worked for six months and demonstrated that the mounds of Palestine were built of layers of debris deposits during the various building and destruction phases in the life of the settlement. He showed that the artifacts within the respective layers changed in style with the progress of the ages, from the more primitive to the more advanced. This was especially true of the pottery both in terms of manufacture and decoration. Henceforth, excavations were conducted at other sites, such as Macalister at Gezer (190-209) and Sellin and Watzinger at Jericho (190-809). Attention was paid to the ceramic evidence, the sherds within the debris. There was yet no agreement as to the proper dating of many pottery styles. On the other hand, careful attention to the architectural remains and their associated soils was initiated by Reisner and Fisher during three years at Samaria (190-810).

Only after World War II was there any agreement achieved in pottery chronology. This was done especially by the great University of Chicago effort at Megiddo from 1925 to 1936, the reports of which are still basic to all architectural and ceramic interpretation in Palestinian archaeology. Though the expedition suffered somewhat by changes in its leadership, its massive achievements, removing several strata of that most important site and publishing them handsomely, have hardly been surpassed to this day. At the same time, Albright conducted a parallel endeavor on a much smaller scale at Tell Beit Mirsim from 1926 to 1932. He was first in print with his pottery chronology and thus earned the credit as the man who brought order out of chaos in ceramic chronology. His site was also dug with fairly careful stratigraphic and architectural control and his publications are lucid and trustworthy. In spite of certain excusable errors in interpretation, the Tell Beit

Mirsim excavation is still basic to understanding the discipline.

During the 1930s there were several major expeditions. Beth-Shan was excavated by the University of Pennsylvania from 1921 to 1933, but its publication was only partial. Starkey began work in a very systematic fashion at Tell ed-Duweir in 1932 but was murdered by Arab villagers in 1938 on the eve of the uprising against the mandate authorities. A new joint expedition was launched at Samaria and Garstang renewed work at Jericho. In pre- and Proto-history, there were expeditions to the Carmel caves and to Tuleilat el-Ghassul, respectively.

Surface exploration was begun E of the Jordan by Glueck during the 1930s. In the previous century there were partial efforts made, but the region in its entirety had not been thoroughly covered or even mapped properly. Glueck sought, with only relative success, to apply the method of pottery dating to surface surveys. His work pointed the way to more sophisticated work in the post World War II period.

After the Israel War of Independence in 1948, work was renewed mainly by Israeli expeditions in Israel and by American, French, and British teams in Jordan and the West Bank. A leading figure in these efforts was K. Kenyon, whose work at Jericho helped to solve some of the questions left unanswered by Garstang, particularly with regard to its destruction in the middle of the millennium. Other expeditions, led by less experienced personnel, began to adopt her stratigraphic methods. In a way this was healthy, but unfortunately, the Kenyonist doctrinaire attitude to certain dogmas of interpretation became even more extreme among her followers. Her work at Jerusalem in the 1960s only served to muddle most of the major problems troubling the students of that city's history.

Meanwhile, a more practical application of stratigraphic excavation was developing among the Israeli excavators. The great expedition to Hazor (actually a group of excavations directed by experienced scholars each in a separate area, coordinated by Y. Yadin) provided them an opportunity to establish methods of recording that utilized the lessons learned by Teisner and Fisher with the pottery analysis of Albright and the Megiddo publications. Henceforth, the archaeologists of the Hazor team branched out to major excavations in various parts of the country: Aharoni to Ramat Rahel (170-127) and Arad, Amiranto Arad and Tell en-Najila, Dothan to Ashdod, and Yadin to Masada. The nationwide and even municipal archaeological departments were busy rescuing antiquity sites from the threat of modern land development. Government departments of antiquities in all Levantine countries continued the work of the former mandated authorities of Britain and France.

Survey was also continued, especially by a nationwide effort in Israel. Foreign teams are now working intensively in Jordan. Hundred of sites are being recorded, placed under the protection of the antiquities law, and settlement patterns from various historic and prehistoric periods are being studied. Modern cartographic methods are also making it easier to do archaeological and ecological studies.

5. *Methods of Archaeology.* Various techniques have been developed over the years for the uncovering and recording of ancient deposits. Considerable controversy has arisen with regard to methods of excavation although the opposing schools are doing basically the same kind of work. After the major developments of the late nineteenth and twentieth centuries (in which there was recognition of the architectural and cultural layers and the analysis of ceramics and other artifacts by chronological periods), further refinements were made in the post World War I period.

a. M. Wheeler had developed the study of the debris deposit, his "geology of the site," with emphasis on vertical-sections cut through the soil and recorded in drawings. He was thus able to define more clearly such features as foundation trenches for walls, associated floors, intrusive pits, and others. His chief disciple, K. Kenyon, brought his method to the Near East. However, this approach was also accompanied by certain tenets of interpretation which diverge from reality—for example, that a floor should be dated by the sherds under it and in its makeup rather than by the pottery vessels found *in situ* (i.e., in its natural location) on it. The recording produced by holders of this view are somewhat clumsy in that each layer of soil is treated as a locus (a specific site) even when it may represent only a passing phase—for example, a wind deposit during a period of abandonment. The vertical sections between excavation areas are often left in place through a sequence of several strata thus hampering the elucidation of whole structural complexes such as rooms and buildings. Pottery restoration is also hindered when part of a room is not excavated since parts of various vessels may remain in the balks. Defenders of the Wheeler-Kenyon method may thus fall into a trap. They may become servants of a system instead of making the system serve them.

b. Stratigraphy is, in fact, a three-dimensional feature of the antiquity site. The occupation levels are built on the ruins of the predecessors and pits, foundation trenches cut through the deposits below. Stubs of older walls are often incorporated into later structures and soil containing earlier artifacts was used to fill in constructing floors and other features in the latest stratum. Potsherds from earlier periods thus work their way up in a mound and later sherds work their way downward. For that reason, dating should be based on whole vessels *in situ* wherever possible.

Recording must also be designed to cope with the three-dimensional situation. Vertical sections in the five-meter (16.4 by 16.4 feet) squares preserve only one dimension of the deposits. The photographs, taken constantly during the excavation process, give a realistic dimension to the structures and other features, especially when a person is included as a human measuring stick. But the most accurate record is that on the horizontal plane, the draftsmen's accurate scale plan of the area, with recorded levels for floors, walls, and other features. Artifacts must be recorded in their exact position both by depth and area. The finds are related to their feature (pit, floor, etc.), the feature to its structure or structures, and these later are then associated with all other such features that were contemporary on the site. Prose descriptions of each locus and of each occupational level (consisting of all the loci that originally came into existence during the same period) serve to fill in the picture.

6. *Philosophy of Archaeology.* Methods of excavation and other research will naturally be shaped to suit the goals of the project. The attitude of the investigator to archaeological research determines his goals and thus his methods.

a. First and foremost, archaeology should devote itself to the material way of life of ancient man. Only when actual epigraphic finds are made can it be said that the excavation is producing *historical* information. Too often the archaeologist has assumed that his goal was to excavate the history of the site. The method chosen is that of excavating a narrowly restricted area "to get the sequence" of occupation levels. Though sometimes necessary, such a method is destructive of the real occupation features that played a role in the life of the inhabitants. It is better to uncover larger areas, logical assemblages of loci that together will illustrate the character of the occupation in its respective phases. The sequence will also be obtained, but not at the expense of spatial stratigraphy.

b. Interpretation of archaeological information, even when it includes many laboratory reports and even the most careful and objective recordings, is still a subjective affair. Though the objects found have an objective reality, their meaning as witnesses to life on the site can only be grasped by the exercise of human judgment. For example, two major activities in the past, public building works in times of prosperity and brutal destruction in times of war, usually leave their traces in the ruins of an ancient site. However, the dating of such features as structures and destruction levels depends upon some precise link with known historical events. In even the best of cases, that essential link between material finds and historical or even ethnic factors is tenuous in Palestinian archaeology. This is due to the paucity of written materials discovered in stratified contexts. Recently there has been some criticism of the "biblical" archaeologist for being too bound up with his philological (literary) and historical studies to do objective work in the field. If anything, the "biblical" archaeologist has given too much credence to the "objectivity" of his material finds at the expense of sound historical analysis apart from mere archaeological evidence. *One must work in the two disciplines separately and then exercise the utmost caution when trying to link them up*. Most archaeologists' historical syntheses are highly tentative at best.

For the time being, it is better to concentrate on elucidating the material culture reflected at a particular site along with its chronological development. Every modern excavation should be coordinated with a level regional survey as well as geological and other investigations aimed at archaeometric evaluations. The cultural analysis of artifacts and the social organization reflected in the layout of the site play a dominant role in this interpretation. All these factors together may then be placed in the framework of the known historical details and an attempt at synthesis be made. (A.F.R.)

ARCHANGEL [ruling angel] 1Th. 4:16; Jude 9. † *See* ANGEL

ARCHELAUS [ruler of people] Mt. 2:22. † *See* HERODS, THE

ARCHER *See* ARMS AND ARMOR

ARCHEVITES *See* ERECH

ARCHI, ARCHITE *See* ARKITE, ARKITES

ARCHIPPUS A Christian of Colossae to whom Paul refers as "our fellow soldier" (Col. 4:17; Phm. 2). †

ARCHITECTURE *See* ARCHAEOLOGY; HOUSE; TABERNACLE; TEMPLE

ARCTURUS KJV for an astronomical constellation, in Job 9:9; 38:32. In the NIV and most versions rendered as the "Bear." †

ARD(ITES) [humpbacked] A grandson of Benjamin who is also called Addar. His descendants were known as Ardites (Ge. 46:21; Nu. 26:40; Jos. 15:3; 1Ch. 8:3). †

ARDON [humpbacked] A descendant of Judah and Caleb (1Ch. 2:18). †

ARELI(ITES) A son of Gad and founder of the family of the Arelites (Ge. 46:16; Nu. 26:17). †

AREOPAGITE *See* AREOPAGUS

AREOPAGUS [hill of the Greek god, Ares]
1. A limestone hill that is NW of the Acropolis within sight of the Parthenon in Athens, connected by a sloping area. The hill reaches 380 ft. high and overlooks the ancient marketplace. The foot of the Acropolis is but 100 yds. away, and the Parthenon was easily viewed from this location. In the first century A.D., the Council of Areopagus met in the Agora, *Stoa Basileios. See also* MARS HILL
2. The name of a group (council) of learned people in Athens who on one occasion met to hear Paul. In these meetings of the Areopagus the judges of Athens conducted court, examined candidates, and appointed lecturers. Paul was taken before them to explain his message (Ac. 17:16ff.). (In Ac. 17:22, the Areopagus most certainly refers to the council and not the geographical location because of the words "in the midst," KJV, "in the meeting," NIV.) *See also* MARS HILL

ARETAS [virtuous] The dynastic name of the kings of Nabatea. One is mentioned in the NT, probably Aretas IV, the father-in-law of Herod the Tetrarch, whose governor at Damascus tried to seize Paul (2Co. 11:32). †

ARGOB [mound]

1. A region which included sixty fortified cities in Bashan which was conquered by and became the tribal area of one-half of Manasseh (Dt. 3:4, 13-14; Jos. 13:29-30; 1Ki. 4:13). †

2. A man killed by Pekah (2Ki. 15:25), in many versions. † The NEB, RSV omit the reading "Argob and Arieh" as an addition to the Hebrew text, mentioned in a footnote. The JB also omits, using an ellipsis, with no footnote. †

ARIANISM The view that Christ is the highest created being but not "very God of very God, begotten not made." This heresy was condemned at the Council of Nicea in A.D. 325.

ARIDAI One of Haman's sons (Est. 9:9). †

ARIDATHA One of Haman's sons (Est. 9:8). †

ARIEH See ARGOB 2.

ARIEL [lioness of El]

1. A man of Israel with Ezra in Babylon (Ezr. 8:16). †

2. A symbolic name given to the city of Jerusalem by Isaiah, in which he compares Jerusalem with the area of the altar in the temple (Isa. 29:1-2, 7). †

ARIMATHEA The unidentified hometown of one called Joseph, who took possession of the body of Jesus after the Crucifixion and buried it in a tomb which he had prepared for himself (Mt. 27:57; Mk. 15:43; Lk. 23:51; Jn. 19:38). †

ARIOCH

1. One of the kings in the confederacy which plundered Sodom and Gomorrah (Ge. 14:1, 9). †

2. The executioner of King Nebuchadnezzar of Babylon (Da. 2:14-15, 24-25). †

ARISAI One of Haman's sons (Est. 9:9). †

ARISTARCHUS [best ruler] A Macedonian traveling companion of Paul who was later also one of his fellow prisoners (Ac. 19:29; 20:4; 27:2; Col. 4:10; Phm. 24). †

ARISTOBULUS [best adviser] A Christian at Rome (Ro. 16:10). †

ARK [box]

1. Noah's ark. A ship of wood built by Noah about the size of a light cruiser which had three stories and a door on one of its sides. It housed Noah and his family, seven pairs of every kind of clean animal and one pair of every unclean (Ge. 6:11-22).

2. The Ark of the Covenant of the LORD; also called Ark of the Testimony, Ark of the LORD, and Ark of God (Dt. 10:8; Ex. 25:22; 1Sa. 3:3). It is described in Ex. 25:10-22. It was covered by a gold lid called an atonement cover. Bezalel was the master craftsman who worked under the direction laid down by Moses (Ex. 37:1-9). In it were kept the two tablets of stone on which were inscribed the Ten Commandments, a gold jar of manna, and beside it a copy of the book of the Law (Dt. 31:26; Heb. 9:4). The whole was housed in the Most Holy Place of the tabernacle (Ex. 26:34). The Ark, under the charge of the Kohathites, went with the Israelites during the years of wandering in the Exodus. It was at the head of the people as they crossed the Jordan and was put in a sanctuary at Shiloh (Nu. 3:29-32; Dt. 31:9; Jos. 3:11, 17; 1Sa. 1:3; 3:3). It was taken by the Philistines to Ashdod, moved to Gath and Ekron, and later returned by them to Beth Shemesh from which place it came eventually to Jerusalem in the days of David by way of Kiriath Jearim, finally to be placed in the Most Holy Place in the temple built by Solomon (1Sa. 5:1, 8, 10; 7:1; 2Sa. 6:2-3, 17; 1Ki. 8:1, 6). Since the destruction of the first temple, the Ark has been lost.

3. A chest for keeping money and valuables. The money was gathered for

the repairs to the temple (2Ki. 12:9-11; 2Ch. 24:8-11). This was a box beside the Ark of the Covenant, used for keeping gold (1Sa. 6:8, 11, 15).

4. A mummy box for a dead person (Ge. 50:26).

ARK OF THE COVENANT *See* ARK 2.

ARKITE An inhabitant of a village on the border between Ephraim and Benjamin. David's friend Hushai was one (Jos. 16:2; 2Sa. 16:16; 17:5). *See also* ARKITES

ARKITES
1. A group of people descended from Canaan who originated in the area of Sidon (Ge. 10:17; 1Ch. 1:15).

2. Jos. 16:2. *See* ARKITE

ARM Often used as a figure of speech in the Bible to mean power or strength. An outstretched arm of the LORD shows tremendous strength. An arm might mean "army" in certain contexts.

ARMAGEDDON The location of the "battle on the great day of God Almighty" (Rev. 16:16). † The word translated means "Mount Megiddo." In the great valley below the ancient city of Megiddo many famous battles of antiquity were fought and hence many consider the word Armageddon to refer to an eschatological battle that will be fought in that valley, the Valley of Jezreel. *See also* GEOGRAPHY OF THE HOLY LAND

ARMAGEDDON: the Great Battle to be fought in the plain between Megiddo and Jezreel

ARMENIA *See* ARARAT

ARMINIANISM This view is at odds with Calvinism. This view holds that: 1. The decree of salvation applies to all who believe in Christ and persevere in the faith. 2. Christ died for all men. 3. The Holy Spirit must help people do truly good things, like believing in Christ for salvation. 4. Men can resist God's saving grace. 5. It is possible for those who are Christians to fall from grace. Arminianism believes that God elects by foreknowledge, not sovereign choice. John Wesley followed Arminius's beliefs.

ARMINIUS A Dutch Reformed theologian (1560-1609) opposed to Calvin's theology.

ARMLET A band worn on the upper arm as distinct from a bracelet which was worn on the lower arm. They were considered items of luxury (Nu. 31:50).

ARMONI [(one) born in the dwelling tower, the palace] A son of Saul who, with his brother and five of the grandchildren of Saul, were given to the Gibeonites by David. They were hanged by the Gibeonites (2Sa. 21:8). †

ARMOR-BEARER The leaders were accompanied into the battle by young men who bore their implements, whether shield, spears, or arrows, and who gave the *coup de grace* (the death blow) to fallen enemies (1Sa. 17:7; 2Sa. 18:14-15; Jdg. 9:54).

ARMORY *See* ARMS AND ARMOR; WAR

ARMS AND ARMOR In defense the body was covered with a helmet, a coat of mail or breastplate, and greaves (leg armor) of bronze. A shield or buckler was carried. Offensive weapons consisted of the sword, spear or javelin, sling, bows and arrows, battering rams.

Helmets were often nationally distinctive, but no description of an Israelite one exists. Some were made of bronze (1Sa. 17:5, 38). The word is also used in both testaments, figuratively, of salvation (Isa. 59:17; Eph. 6:14). Greaves were of leather or metal and protected the legs both front and back from ankle to knee. Goliath wore greaves of bronze (1Sa. 17:6).

Shields or bucklers were probably leather strips fastened over a wooden frame. They were either round or oval in shape. Some were covered with bronze, and even gold (Ps. 35:2; Jer. 46:3; 1Ki. 14:26-27). The shield too was used symbolically, for divine protection, salvation, and faith (Ps. 3:3; 18:2; Eph. 6:16).

Swords were of at least three types. One was of a short two-edged variety carried by all the foot soldiers (Jdg. 3:16; 1Sa. 25:13). A second was long handled and sickle-shaped. The third type was a long straight-edged sword of iron. In the Bible the sword is also used symbolically of war and destruction. In the NT it symbolizes the penetrating power of the word of God (Eph. 6:17; Heb. 4:12).

The spear, lance, or javelin was a weapon of offense (Jos. 8:18; Job 41:29). Some were heavy, long, and tipped with flint or metal, while others were lighter and designed for throwing rather than jabbing (1 Sa. 18:11; 1Ki. 18:28).

The bow and arrow were used in longer range offensive actions by the archers. Bows were made of a strong elastic wood or were of the composite type made of alternating layers of wood and horn glued and bound together. The strings were of gut from one of several animals. The arrows were made of reeds, or light wood, and feathers, and were usually tipped with flint or metal. Arrows were kept in quivers usually carried by the armor-bearer.

The sling was of two thongs of leather braided cords with a pocket between them for the smooth, rounded stone. The stone was fired by whirling the apparatus round and round the head and then suddenly releasing one of the thongs (1Sa. 17:40, 49; 2Ch. 26:14). Each army had special corps of slingers and the Benjamites seemed to have been specialists (1Ch. 12:2). "Machines" were also used. These consisted of catapults and battering rams. The former slung arrows or large stones (2Ch. 26:15). The latter were either simple beams of great

length, sometimes metal-tipped, and housed in a protective tower mounted on wheels (2 Sa. 20:15; Eze. 4:2). They are noted in Eze. 4:2 and were possibly used in 2Sa. 20:15.

The axe, war club, hammer, and deadly weapons were also used by the warrior for close-range fighting (Pr. 25:18; Jer. 46:22; 51:20; Eze. 9:2).

ARMY In earliest times able-bodied men were expected to bear arms and support their chief. The men were called to arms by a messenger or the ram's horn (Jdg. 6:35; 1Sa. 13:3). Conscription (the "draft") seems to have started with the monarchy under the first king, Saul (1Sa. 14:52). By David's time the army was arranged in twelve parts of 24,000 each, with each part serving one month each year (1Ch. 27:1). Males twenty years old and over were liable for service (Nu. 1:3). Something of the organization is reflected in Nu. 2:33; Dt. 20:5-9; 24:5; 2Ch. 25:5). The men received no pay but all did share in the booty (1Sa. 30:24-25). The first mechanized units appear in the Israel of King Solomon with his chariots (1Ki. 4:26). The army units consisted of families, thousands, hundreds, fifties, and tens. Commanders and officers are mentioned without further detail (1Ch. 27:1).

ARNAN A descendant of David (1Ch. 3:21). †

ARNI *See* ARAM 2.

ARNON A river which flows into the Sea of Arabah, (the Salt or Dead Sea) near its middle on the E, separating Moab and Ammon (the Amorites) and, later, the tribes of Reuben and Gad (Nu. 21:13; Dt. 3:16).

AROD *See* ARODI

ARODI {humpbacked} A son of Gad, whose descendants were known as Arodites (Ge. 46:16; Nu. 26:17). †

AROER, AROERITE {juniper}
1. A city (228-097) on the northern bank of the Arnon gorge on the southern border of the kingdom of Sihon king of

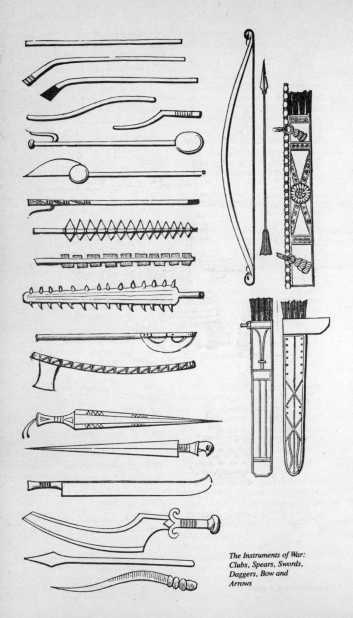

The Instruments of War:
Clubs, Spears, Swords,
Daggers, Bow and
Arrows

Ancient Forms of Armor

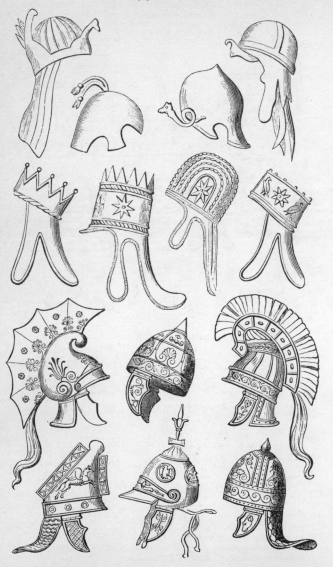

*Shield and Spears:
A Greek Soldier; Roman
Soldiers*

the Amorites (Nu. 32:33), and later in the tribal area of Reuben. Later it was fought over by the Moabites and the Syrians (Jos. 12:2; Dt. 3:12; 2Ki. 10:33); also mentioned in the Moabite Inscription.

2. A town (148-062) in the territory of Judah near Beersheba (1Sa. 30:28).

3. *See* PLANTS, PERFUMES, AND SPICES, Miscellaneous Plants 13., *Aroer*

AROMA That which affects the sense of smell favorably, otherwise an odor, or mere smoke. This is true in both the literal and figurative senses (Nu. 15:3; Jn. 11:39; Isa. 65:5).

AROMATICS *See* PLANTS, PERFUMES, AND SPICES

ARPAD, ARPHAD A city of Syria which fell to the Assyrians in the middle of the eighth century B.C. and was used as a warning to Israel by the Assyrians to submit to them (2Ki. 18:34; 19:13; Isa. 10:9; 36:19; 37:13; Jer. 49:23). †

ARPHACHAD *See* ARPHAXAD

ARPHAXAD A son of Shem and ancestor of Abraham; probably also a tribal group (Ge. 10:22, 24; 11:10-13; 1Ch. 1:17-18, 24; Lk. 3:36).†

ARRABON *See* SEAL

ARROGANCE *See* PRIDE

ARROW *See* ARMS AND ARMOR

ARTAXERXES A Persian king, son of Xerxes, who reigned from 465 to 424 B.C. He permitted both Ezra and Nehemiah to return with groups to rebuild the temple and the walls of Jerusalem (Ezr. 4:7-8, 11, 23; 6:14; 7:1, 7, 11-12, 21; 8:1; Ne. 2:1; 5:14; 13:6). †

ARTEMAS [(given by) Artemis] A companion of Paul (Tit. 3:12). †

ARTEMIS A goddess (Ac. 19:24, 27-28, 34-35). † *See* DEITIES

ARTIFICER *See* CRAFTSMEN

ARTILLERY KJV for "weapons" (1Sa. 20:40). *See* ARMS AND ARMOR

ARUBBOTH, ARUBOTH An unidentified site perhaps in the Plain of Sharon near Socoh (1Ki. 4:10). †

ARUMAH [lofty] A city (180-172) near Shechem (Nablus) where Abimelech lived for a time (Jdg. 9:41). †

ARVAD, ARVADITES A leading Phoenician city (229-473) N of Byblos and an important maritime center (Ge. 10:18; 1Ch. 1:16; Eze. 27:8, 11). †

ARZA When King Baasha of Israel was drinking in Arza's house, he was murdered by Zimri who took Israel's throne (1Ki. 16:9). †

ASA [*possibly* healer, BDB; myrtle, KB]
1. A Levite son of Elkanah (1Ch. 9:16).
2. *See* KINGS OF JUDAH AND ISRAEL.

ASAHEL [El has made]
1. A nephew of David and brother to Joab (2Sa. 2:18-32; 3:30). He was one of David's mighty men (2Sa. 23:24), but was killed by Abner (1Ch. 2:16; 11:26; 27:7).
2. A Levite instructor in the Law in the time of Jehoshaphat (2Ch. 17:8). †
3. A temple overseer in the time of Hezekiah (2Ch. 31:13). †
4. A contemporary of Ezra (Ezr. 10:15). †

ASAHIAH *See* ASAIAH 4.

ASAIAH [Yahweh has made]
1. A descendant of Simeon (1Ch. 4:36). †
2. A descendant of Levi who helped David bring the Ark to Jerusalem (1Ch. 6:30; 15:6, 11). †
3. A returnee from the captivity in Babylon (1Ch. 9:5). †
4. A servant of King Josiah in the group that went to inquire of the prophetess Huldah about the book of the Law discovered by Hilkiah (2Ki. 22:12, 14; 2Ch. 23:20). †

ASAL *See* AZEL

ASAPH [gatherer]
1. One of David's musicians, a descendant of Levi, who with his family

after him played and sang in the service of music before the Ark (lCh. 15:17; 16:4-5). One hundred and twenty-eight of these singers came back from Babylon with Zerubbabel and resumed their duties in the second temple (Ezr. 2:41; 3:10). Twelve Psalms are entitled "A Psalm of Asaph" (Pss. 50, 73-83).

2. The father of a recorder in the days of King Hezekiah (2Ki. 18:18).

3. A keeper of the king's forest who was instructed to help Nehemiah to secure lumber (Ne. 2:8).

4. One whose descendants were gatekeepers in the days of David (lCh. 26:1).

ASAREEL, ASAREL A descendant of Judah (lCh. 4:16). †

ASARELAH One of David's temple musicians; also called Jesarelah (lCh. 25:2). |

ASCENSION While the word is not used, the concept of the ascension of Christ is clear from the several passages which note that he "ascended" to the Father (Jn. 20:17; Eph. 4:8). *See* CHRIST, WORK OF 6.

ASCENTS, SONG OF *See* SONG OF ASCENTS

ASCETICISM The practice of strict self-denial for personal and spiritual reasons.

ASENATH [(belonging to) the goddess Neith] A daughter of Potiphera, priest of On, and the wife of Joseph (Ge. 41:45, 50; 46:20). †

ASER KJV in Lk. 2:36; Rev. 7:6. *See* ASHER

ASH, ASHES *See* FULLER; RED HEIFER; SACRIFICES AND OFFERINGS

ASH TREE KJV for "pine" (Isa. 44:14). *See* TREES

ASHAN [smoke] An unidentified town in the tribal area of Judah and Simeon which became a Levite city (Jos. 15:42; 19:7; lCh. 4:32; 6:59). †

ASHARELAH *See* ASARELAH

ASHBEA [abundance] *See* BETH ASHBEA

ASHBEL, ASHBELITE(S) [possibly a form of "man of BAAL," BDB; having a long upper llp, KB] A son of Benjamin, the clan of Ashbel (Ge. 46:21; Nu. 26:38; lCh. 8:1). †

ASHCHENAZ *See* ASHKENAZ

ASHDOD *See* AZOTUS; PHILISTINE CITIES

ASHDODITES Inhabitants of Ashdod.

ASHDOTH PISGAH [slopes of PISGAH] *See* PISGAH

ASHER, ASHERITE(S) [Happy One!] A son of Jacob (Ge. 30:13) and founder of the tribe with that name, located on the seacoast N of the Carmel range and W of the Jezreel Valley.

ASHERAH, ASHERIM, ASHEROTH *See* DEITIES

ASHHUR [possibly darkness, dawn, BDB; a Babylonian goddess, KB] A son of Caleb (lCh. 2:24; 4:5). †

ASHIMA 2Ki. 17:30. † *See* DEITIES

ASHKELON *See* PHILISTINE CITIES

ASHKENAS *See* ASHKENAZ

ASHKENAZ A people and country on the upper Euphrates near Armenia (Ge.10:3; lCh. 1:6; Jer. 51:27). †

ASHNAH Two towns in the western hills of Judah between Eshtaol and Hebron (Jos. 15:33, 43). †

ASHPENAZ [guest] Chief of court officials at Babylon in the time of Nebuchadnezzar (Da. 1:3). †

ASHRIEL *See* ASRIEL

ASHTAROTH

1. Plural of Ashtoreth. *See* DEITIES

2. The capital of Og, king of Bashan, a city (243-244) inhabited by giants (Rephaites) (Dt. 1:4; Jos. 9:10; 12:4, 13:12). After the Israelite conquest, this city was in the tribal area of Manasseh (Jos. 13:31), one of the Levitical cities (lCh. 6:71). †

ASHTEROTH KARNAIM [ASHER-OTH of the pair of horns, (two peaks?)] Where Kedorlaomer and the kings with him defeated the Rephaites (Ge. 14:5). † *See* KARNAIM

ASHTORETH *See* DEITIES

ASHURBANIPAL [Ashur creates a son] *See* ASSYRIA, the last ¶

ASHURBANIPAL Ezr. 4:10. † *See* AS-NAPPER; OSNAPPAR

ASHURI, ASHURITES A group over which Abner made Ish-Bosheth, Saul's son, the king (2Sa. 2:9). † *See* GESHUR, GESHURITES 2.

ASHURNASIRPAL, ASHURNASIR-PAL II *See* ASSYRIA, ¶ 3., *Ashur-nasir-pal*

ASHVATH [possibly wrought iron] A descendant of Asher (1Ch. 7:33). †

ASIA A geographical location and generally in NT times a Roman province, occupying roughly the western one-fourth of Asian Turkey (Ac. 2:9; 6:9; 16:6; 19:10, 22, 26-27; 20:4, 16, 18; 21:27; 24:19; 27:2; Ro. 16:5; 1Co. 16:19; 2Co. 1:8; 2Ti. 1:15; 1Pe. 1:1; Rev. 1:4). † In the Bible, this is not the same as the Far East (i.e., China). *See* GEOGRAPHY OF THE HOLY LAND

ASIARCHS [rulers of the Roman Province of Asia] Translated in the NIV "the officials of the province" in Ac. 19:31. †

ASIEL [El has made] A descendant of Simeon (1Ch. 4:35). †

ASKELON *See* ASHKELON

ASLEEP A word sometimes used to denote death (1Co. 11:30; 15:6; 1Th. 4:13). *See* SLEEP

ASNAH [possibly thornbush, BDB; he who belongs to (the god) Nah, IDB] His sons were a special class of temple servants who returned from Babylon with Zerubbabel (Ezr. 2:50). †

ASNAPPER *See* OSNAPPAR

ASP *See* BEASTS 1., *Cobra, Serpent, Snake, Viper*

ASPATHA [possibly given from a sacred horse] One of the sons of Haman (Est. 9:7). †

ASPERSION *See* SPRINKLE

ASRIEL, ASRIELITE(S) A descendant of Manasseh, a clan of Asriel (Nu. 26:31; Jos. 17:2; 1Ch. 7:14). †

ASS *See* BEASTS 4., *Donkey*

ASSARION *See* MONEY

ASSEMBLY *See* AREOPAGUS; CHURCH; MARKET, MARKET-PLACE; SYNAGOGUE

ASSHUR A son of Shem who gave his name to a country, Assyria (Ge. 10:22). *See* ASSYRIA

ASSHURIM, ASSHURITES A group descended from Dedan who was a grandson of Abraham by Keturah (Ge. 25:3). †

ASSIR [prisoner]
1. A son of Korah (Ex. 6:24; 1Ch. 6:22). †
2. A son of Ebiasaph (1Ch. 6:23, 37). †
3. KJV, NKJV in 1Ch. 3:17 for "the captive" in most other versions.

ASSOS A seaport town to which Paul walked from Troas (Ac. 20:13-14). †

ASSUAN *See* SYENE

ASSUR *See* ASSYRIA

ASSURANCE *See* SALVATION, APPLICATION OF, *Perseverance*

ASSYRIA AND ASSHUR Among the five sons of Shem was Asshur (Ge. 10:22), from whom came the Assyrian people. In their highland territory in northern Mesopotamia (*see* GEOGRAPHY OF THE HOLY LAND), they developed as rugged shepherds (Na. 3:18). But their culture began under the Hamite Nimrod (Ge. 10:11) from the S; Sumerians settled in Assyria in about 2900 B.C. and Sargon of Akkad included it in his Semitic Empire of 2400. Language and religion, except for the national god Asshur, were thus borrowed from others; but the Assyrians proved to be good organizers, disciplined and warlike, similar to the Romans in later history. Puzur-Ashur I (2100) first assumed the kingship; but while Assyria developed commercial colonies as far as Cappadocia, it remained generally under the control of Babylon.

Assyrian independence came under Ashur-uballit I in 1375. The greatest of the early Assyrians, however, was Tiglath-Pileser I, who brought order and empire to the Near East from his capital city of Asshur, 1115 on. He twice captured Babylon, conquered to the Black Sea, and took as far S as Arvad on the Mediterranean. He rehearsed, indeed, the Sargonid conquests of the eighth and seventh centuries. Of his immediate successors, only Ashur-rabi III showed strength, in 1000 B.C. he conquered to the NE corner of the Mediterranean but just missed contact with his contemporary David, who had advanced to the Euphrates.

Assyria experienced a century of power under four monarchs from 884 to 782 B.C. Ashur-nasir-pal II (884-859) was one of the most hideous figures of all history—cruel, but a powerful soldier directing his Assyrian bowmen. He took Carchemish and as far as Lebanon; and it is possible that Omri of Israel may have paid him tribute (876 B.C.). Shalmaneser III (859-824), after various campaigns, reached Qarqar, N of Hamath on the Orontes in 853 B.C. Syria, Israel under Ahab, and others held him off in a great battle. But in 841 (*see* CHRONOLOGY) he ravaged the Syrian country; and Jehu of Israel paid him tribute, as depicted on the "black obelisk." Shamshi-Adad V (824-811) was not in the west but did break Babylon. Adad-nirari III (811-782) overran Syria in 803; and, because of the Assyrian intervention, Jehoahaz of Israel was able to defeat Damascus in three battles (2Ki. 13:5). Weak kings followed in Assyrian Nineveh from 782 to 745, under one of whom Jonah the prophet, an advisor to Jeroboam II of Israel (793-753), won an audience as he could not have before or after, perhaps in connection with the solar eclipse of 763 (Jnh. 3:5).

In 745 a general Pulu (biblical "Pul" (2Ki. 15:19), revolted and put an end to the dynasty of Tiglath-Pileser I. Significantly, he assumed the title Tiglath-Pileser III (1Ch. 5:26); and under him and his successors, the Sargonids, Assyria rose to even greater heights than it had known under his namesake. Azariah of Judah headed a western confederacy to oppose him but was defeated in 743. Menahem of Israel and Rezin of Damascus, though not Azariah himself, who escaped, were forced to pay heavy tribute to Assyria (2Ki. 15:19). In seeming retaliation Rezin and Pekah of Israel attacked Azariah's grandson Ahaz of Judah, who foolishly appealed to Nineveh for help (16:7). Tiglath-Pileser marched to Gaza in 734, took three-and-a-half Israelite tribes of Gilead and Galilee captive in 733 (15:29), and de-

THE ASSYRIAN
EMPIRE
The Assyrian empire
extended from
the Persian Gulf, across
the Fertile Crescent, and
south to Egypt. Shalmaneser III extended the
empire toward the Mediterranean Sea by conquering cities as far
west as Qarqar. Tiglath-pileser extended the
empire south into Syria,
Israel, and Judah.

stroyed Damascus in 732. He died in 727, to be succeeded by Shalmaneser V, who took Samaria just before his death in 722 (17:36); and Sargon II deported the remaining six-and-a-half Israelite tribes (v. 18), replacing them with the foreign "Samaritans" (vv. 24–41; *cf.* Ezr. 4:2, 10; Isa. 7:8).

Hezekiah of Judah was left to face Assyria. He twice submitted before the attacks of Sargon in 720 and 711, only to revolt upon the accession of his rash son Sennacherib (705-681), in defiance of Isaiah's warnings (Isa. 22:8-14; 30:1-7). Sennacherib advanced, and in 701 Hezekiah lost much of Judah and was forced to pay a heavy fine (2Ki. 18:13-16). Yet when the Assyrian broke his truce, demanded further surrender, and went on to blaspheme the God of Israel (Isa. 36:15, 20), God sent his angel, who struck down 185,000 of the Assyrian army in one night (by plague?) and accomplished a deliverance for his people that ranks second only to their crossing of the Red Sea 750 years before (Isa. 37:36).

Hezekiah's son Manasseh gave up the independence that had been so dearly won by submitting to Esarhaddon (681-669) in 675 as the latter prepared to attack Egypt. He was later taken captive by Ashurbanipal (669-626), perhaps after the eastern revolts of 652-648 (2Ch. 33:11). But this was Israel's last contact with Assyria. The later Sargonids had overextended themselves. After 628 Scythian barbarians flooded over the once great Assyrian Empire (*See* SCYTHIANS); and Nineveh itself fell to the combined forces of Media and Babylon in 612, just as the prophets Balaam and Nahum once predicted (Nu. 24:24; Na. 3:1, 19). (J.B.P.)

ASSYRIAN LANGUAGE *See* ASSYRIA

ASTAROTH *See* ASHTAROTH

ASTARTE *See* DEITIES 2., *Ashtoreth, Ashtaroth*

ASTROLOGERS *See* DIVINATION, DIVINE

ASTROLOGY *See* DIVINATION, DIVINE

ASUPPIM KJV for "(house) of stores" in 1Ch. 26:15, 17.

ASWAN Eze. 29:10; 30:6. † *See* SEVENEH; SYENE

ASYLUM *See* CITY OF REFUGE

ASYNCRITUS Ro. 16:14. †

ATAD [thornbush] A place not precisely identified (Ge. 50:10-11). †

ATARAH [circlet, wreath] The wife of one of the descendants of Judah (1Ch. 2:26). †

ATAROTH [circlets, wreaths]
1. A town (213-109) given to and built by the tribe of Gad in the former area of Sihon, king of the Amorites (Nu. 32:3, 34).†
2. A town in the territory of the descendants of Joseph (Jos. 16:2, 7). †
3. Jos. 16:5. *See* ATAROTH A(D)-DAR
4. 1Ch. 2:54, KJV, "Ataroth house of Joab." *See* ATROTH BETH JOAB

ATAROTH A(D)DAR [wreaths of grandeur] A city on the border between Benjamin and Ephraim (Jos. 16:5; 18:13). †

ATER One or more persons who came back from the Babylonian exile with Zerubbabel. One seems to have been the head of the clan, another a gatekeeper, another a signer of the covenant with Nehemiah (Ezr. 2:16-42; Ne. 7:21, 45; 10:17). †

ATHACH An unidentified town in southern Judah where David sent some of the plunder from Ziklag (1Sa. 30:30). †

ATHAIAH [possibly (the) superiority of Yahweh] A descendant of Judah who lived in Jerusalem (Ne. 11:4). †

ATHALIAH [possibly Yahweh is exalted, BDB; oldest of Yahweh, KB]
1. *See* KINGS OF JUDAH AND ISRAEL.

2. A descendant of Benjamin (1Ch. 8:26).

3. One who came up with Ezra from Babylon (Ezr. 8:7).

ATHANASIAN CREED *See* CONFESSION

ATHANASIUS The champion against Arianism; he lived from A.D. 296 to 373.

ATHARIM [*traditionally* way of the spies] A trade route in the Negev (Nu. 21:1). †

ATHEISM The conviction that there is no God. Early Christians were accused of atheism because they did not believe in the Roman polytheistic gods.

ATHENS, ATHENIANS The capital of the Greek state of Attica with a long and illustrious history. Here Paul presented his case to the Areopagus (Ac. 17:15-22; 18:1). *See* AREOPAGUS

ATHLAI [*possibly* Yahweh is exalted, BDB; oldest of Yahweh, KB] A Jew who divorced his foreign wife in the time of Ezra (Ezr. 10:28). †

ATHLETE One who competed in various events, including running, wrestling, and boxing. This included vigorous training (1Ti. 4:7-8). The spiritual life of the Christian is often compared to competing in a contest (2Ti. 2:5). The Christian athlete runs and trains to win an imperishable crown (1Co. 9:25). The idea is used figuratively to picture a team striving together for the cause of Christ (Php. 1:27; 4:3). *See* CROWN

ATONEMENT *See* CHRIST, WORK OF

ATONEMENT, DAY OF *See* CALENDAR and FESTIVALS

ATONEMENT, LIMITED The belief that Christ died only for the chosen or elect.

ATONEMENT, UNLIMITED The belief that Christ died for the elect and nonelect.

ATONEMENT, VICARIOUS The belief that Christ was a satisfactory, substitutionary sacrifice for sinners.

ATROTH [circlets, wreaths] *See* following entries

ATROTH BETH JOAB [circlets, folds of the house of Joab] A descendant of Judah (1Ch. 2:54). †

ATROTH SHOPHAN [circlets, folds of SHOPHAN] An unidentified town in the region of Moab E of the Jordan (Nu. 32:35). †

ATTAI

1. A descendant of Judah. His father was an Egyptian slave (1Ch. 2:35-36). †

2. A descendant of Gad who joined David at Ziklag (1Ch. 12:11).†

3. A son of King Rehoboam of Judah (2Ch. 11:20). †

ATTALIA A seaport town in the Roman province of Pamphylia, from which Paul sailed to Antioch at the end of his first missionary journey (Ac. 14:25-26). †

ATTIRE *See* DRESS

ATTRIBUTES OF GOD The attributes of God are a categorization of some of the characteristics that God possesses. This list is not exhaustive but representative of some of God's personality traits.

1. *Omnipresent*. God is everywhere present, free of limits of space or time (Isa. 40:12ff.).

2. *Omniscient*. God is all knowing — past, present, future. God knows both actual and potential (Isa. 40:13-14; Ps. 139:1-6; Heb. 4:13).

3. *Omnipotent*. God is all powerful; he can do anything he wishes to do in alignment with his character (Ps. 115:3; Jer. 32:27; 1Ti. 6:15-16). He has the sovereign right to rule (Ro. 9:19).

4. *Spiritual*. God is in essence nonmaterial, nonphysical. He is Spirit (Jn. 4:24).

5. *Immutable*. God never changes. God is not evolving, devolving, getting better or worse. His perfection does not change (Mal. 3:6; Jas. 1:17).

Jumping or Leaping

Discus Throwing

Wrestling

Boxing

Ancient Greek Horse Race

Ancient Greek Chariot Race

Ancient Greek Foot Race

Ancient Greek Torch Race

6. *Unity.* God is indivisible—i.e., he cannot be broken into parts (Dt. 6:4). Note that this attribute does not change the biblical fact that God is three "persons." Jesus is God (Jn. 1:1). The Holy Spirit is God (Ac. 5:3-4). The Father is God (Eph. 1:3). *See also* TRINITY

7. *Moral Attributes.* There are many traits of God in the Scripture that deal with his moral character, both stated plainly (i.e., Ex. 34:6-7) and stated in the context of how God deals with his saints in the Scripture stories. In the study of these, the Christian can especially find strength and courage to deal with life's trials. To name a few, the LORD is compassionate, gracious, patient, holy, just, abounding in love, wise, understanding, just, faithful, holy (Ex. 34:6-7; Da. 2:20; 1Jn. 4:8; Rev. 4:8; Gal. 5:22). (J.A.S.)

AUGURY *See* DIVINATION

AUGUSTINE OF HIPPO A bishop of N Africa (about A.D. 400), considered by many to be the greatest theologian of the early church. His voluminous writings include *The City of God.*

AUGUSTUS {reverend, holy} The name conferred by the Roman senate on the emperor of Rome around the time of the birth of Jesus (Lk. 2:1). Herod built Caesarea and Caesarea Philippi in his honor. †

AUL *See* AWL

AUTHORIZED VERSION A term to signify a version of the Bible is endorsed by church or state. Though other versions have been "authorized" (i.e., the

Great Bible in 1539, about seventy-five years before the 1611 KJV), the King James Version (KJV) is known as the Authorized Version (AV). *See* BIBLE, VERSIONS OF

AUTHORITY OF THE BIBLE *See* SCRIPTURE

AUTHORITY, SUBJECTION TO The Christian view of authority is that God is the Creator of rulers and their governments (Pr. 21:1; Col. 1:16; 1Pe. 3:22). Therefore, Christians are to be subject to them (Ro. 13:1; Tit.3:1). Government exists for punishing wrong doing (1Pe. 4:12-19). At times when Christ's direct commission (Mt. 28:19-20), is forbidden, God, not man, must be obeyed (Ac. 5:29). Christ is the highest authority (Eph. 1:21; Col. 2:10).

AUTOGRAPH The original manuscript of a writing.

AVA *See* AVVA

AVE MARIA A Latin term for "Hail, Mary."

AVEN {evil power, uncanny things, wickedness}
1. A place in the kingdom of Damascus referred to as "Valley of Aven" (Am. 1:5). †
2. *See also* BETH AVEN.

AVENGER OF BLOOD Often in primitive societies, and in the Mosaic Law as well, a murderer was to be killed by the avenger of blood who was the nearest relative of the murdered. The OT makes a clear distinction between manslaughter and willful murder, however. One accused of the former could flee to a city of refuge and be safe until the judges heard his case. The entire procedure is carefully prescribed in Nu. 35:9-34.

AVIM, AVIMS, AVITES *See* AVVIM, AVVITES

AVITH An unidentified Moabite town, residence of the king (Ge. 36:35; 1Ch. 1:46). †

AVOIDANCE Sometimes the Christian is to fight a good fight of faith, other times he is to keep away from those who cause divisions (Ro. 16:17) and turn away from godless chatter (1Ti. 6:20; 2Ti. 2:16, 23; Tit. 3:9).

AVVA A city from which the Assyrian king brought people to Samaria after he removed captives from the latter. These were among those who intermarried, and the Samaritans were the result (2Ki. 17:24). † It is possibly connected with Ivvah. *See* IVVAH

AVVIM A town of Benjamin (Jos. 18:23). †

AV(V)ITES
1. The inhabitants of the area near Gaza who were destroyed and replaced by the Philistines (Dt. 2:23; Jos. 13:3). †
2. A people living in Samaria after the prisoner exchange policy of the Assyrian king at the time of the captivity of the ten tribes; their gods were Nibhaz and Tartak (2Ki. 17:31). †

AWL A small tool for boring mentioned in connection with the practice of permanently enslaving an individual (Ex. 21:6; Dt. 15:17).†

AX, AXE *See* ARMS AND ARMOR

AXLETREES KJV for "axle" in many versions (1Ki. 7:32-33). † *See also* WHEEL

AYYAH A town of Ephraim (1Ch. 7:28). GAZA in KJV, NEB; AZZAH in the ASV; AZZAH footnoted in NASB; AYYAH in the NIV, JB, NKJV, RSV. The differences come from a textual decision whether to read the middle letter of the name as the Hebrew letter "yodh" or "zayin." †

AZAL *See* AZEL 2.

AZALIAH {Yahweh is keeping in reserve} A scribe in the days of King Josiah (2Ki. 22:3; 2Ch. 34:8). †

AZANIAH {Yahweh has listened} A descendant of Levi who signed the covenant with Nehemiah (Ne. 10:9). †

AZARAEL, AZAREEL, AZAREL
{El has helped}

1. A Benjamite who joined David at
Ziklag (1Ch. 12:6). †

2. A musician at the temple (1Ch.
25:18). †

3. A leader in the tribe of Dan in
David's day (1Ch. 27:22).†

4. A man who married a foreign
woman during the Babylonian captivity
(Ezr. 10:41). †

5. A priest in Nehemiah's day (Ne.
11:13). †

6. A musician in Nehemiah's day (Ne.
12:36). †

AZARIAH {Yahweh has helped}

1. 2Ki. 14:21; 15:1ff.; 1Ch. 3:12. † *See*
KINGS OF JUDAH AND ISRAEL

2 and 3. Two descendants of Judah
(1Ch. 2:8, 38-39). †

4. A priest, a high official in Solomon's time (1Ki. 4:2). †

5. One over the officers in Solomon's
time (1Ki. 4:5). †

6, 7, and 8. Three Levites in the time
of David (1Ch. 6:9-11, 14, 36; Ezr. 7:1,
3). †

9. A prophet in the days of King Asa
who urged reforms (2Ch. 15:18). †

10. A son of King Jehoshaphat (2Ch.
21:2). †

11 and 12. Two commanders of
hundreds who helped the priest Jehoiada
to overthrow Queen Athaliah and put
Joash on the throne. The second may be
the same as 3 above (2Ch. 23:1). †

13. The high priest in King Uzziah's
day who rebuked the king for assuming
a priestly prerogative (2Ch. 26:16-20). †

14. A chief of Ephraim who supported the prophet Oded in not allowing
the Israelites to keep captives of Judah
taken in a battle (2Ch. 28:12). †

15. Father of a Levite who helped in
the cleansing of the temple in the days of
King Hezekiah (2Ch. 29:12; 31:13). †

16. A Levite who was involved in the
cleansing of the temple as in 15 above
(2Ch. 29:12). †

17. A high priest in the days of King
Hezekiah (2Ch. 31:10).†

18. One of the builders of the wall in

the time of Nehemiah (Ne. 3:23-24). †

19. One who came up from the
Babylonian captivity with Zerubbabel
(Ne. 7:7). He is called Seraiah in Ezr.
2:2. †

20. One who helped the people understand the Law in the time of Ezra (Ne.
8:7). †

21. One who signed the covenant
with Nehemiah (Ne. 10:2). †

22. One who was in the dedication
procession at the completion of the
building of the walls by Nehemiah (Ne.
12:33). †

23. A leader who called Jeremiah the
Prophet a liar because of the message he
brought (Jer. 43:2). †

24. The Hebrew name of Abednego,
one of Daniel's three friends in Babylon
(Da. 1:6-7, 11, 19; 2:17). †

AZARIAHU An NIV rendering in
2Ch. 21:2 for AZARIAH (the second
mentioned in the verse) in many versions. Though not the traditional transliteration, it is a better rendering of the
Hebrew pronunciation. †

AZAZ {strong} A descendant of Reuben
(1Ch. 5:8). †

AZAZEL {goat removed} On the Day of
Atonement two goats were selected.
Aaron as the high priest was instructed
to cast lots for them to see which one was
to be sacrificed and which one was to be
driven out into the wilderness bearing
the sins of the people. The latter was the
goat for Azazel (Lev. 16:7-26). There are
a number of conjectures as to the interpretation of this word, but that it was
intended as an object lesson for the people to remind them of the removal of their
sin is clear.

AZAZIAH {Yahweh is strong}

1. A descendant of Ephraim (1Ch.
27:20). †

2. A Levite temple musician (1Ch.
15:21). †

3. An officer in charge of the contributions and tithes in the days of King
Hezekiah (2Ch. 31:13). †

AZBUK Father of a Nehemiah (not the leader and author of the book) who worked on the restoration of the walls in Nehemiah's days (Ne. 3:16). †

AZEKAH [*possibly* hoe (the ground)] A city (144-123) in the western foothills (shephelah) taken by Joshua and allocated to the tribe of Judah in the buffer area between Judah and the Philistines (Jos. 10:10-11; 15:35; 1Sa. 17:1). Just E of Azekah, David vanquished the giant Goliath. It was one of the last cities to hold out against the Babylonian invaders as is also interestingly confirmed by the Lachish Letters of archaeological fame (Jer. 34:7). Judeans still lived there after the Babylonian captivity (Ne. 11:30; 2Ch. 11:9). †

AZEL [noble]

1. A descendant of Saul and Jonathan (1Ch. 8:37-38; 9:43-44).
2. An unidentified place in Zec. 14:5, in the NIV, ASV, NASB; AZAL in the KJV, NKJV; ASAL, NEB. The RSV translates it not as a proper name but a word of proximity, "side." The JB uses the LXX transliteration "Jasol."

AZEM *See* EZEM

AZGAD [strong is Gad] The head of a family that came back from the Babylonian captivity with Zerubbabel and signed the covenant with Nehemiah (Ezr. 2:12; 8:12; Ne. 7:17; 10:15). †

AZIEL 1Ch. 15:20. † *See* JAAZIEL

AZIZA [powerful] One who put away his foreign wife in Ezra's day (Ezr. 10:27).†

AZMAVETH [strong one of death, ISBE; camel fodder, a plant of the plumose family, KB]

1. One of David's mighty men (2Sa. 23:31; 1Ch. 11:33). †
2. A Benjamite whose son joined David at Ziklag, perhaps the same as 1 above (1Ch. 12:3). †
3. A descendant of Saul who came back from the Babylonian captivity (1Ch. 8:36; 9:42). †
4. An official in charge of the treasury in David's day, perhaps the same as 1 above (1Ch. 27:25). †
5. A village (174-137) resettled after the Babylonian captivity (Ne. 12:29); also called Beth Azmaveth (Ne. 7:28). †

AZMON [strongly (built body)] A town (085-010) on Judah's southern border not far from the "Wadi of Egypt" (Nu. 34:4; Jos. 15:4). †

AZNOTH TABOR [*possibly* peaks of TABOR] A city (186-237) in the tribal area of Naphtali (Jos. 19:34).†

AZOR [help] A descendant of Zerubbabel in the ancestry of Jesus (Mt. 1:13-14). †

AZOTUS The same as OT Ashdod (Jos. 13:3; Ac. 8:40). † *See* PHILISTINE CITIES

AZRIEL [El is (my) help]

1. A leader of that part of the tribe of Manasseh which stayed E of the Jordan (1Ch. 5:24). †
2. A descendant of Naphtali (1Ch. 27:19). †
3. The father of one whom King Jehoiakim commanded to burn the scroll that Jeremiah dictated to Baruch (Jer. 36:24-27). †

AZRIKAM [(my) help arises]

1. A descendant of David through Solomon (1Ch. 3:23). †
2. A descendant of Saul through Jonathan (1Ch. 8:38; 9:44).†
3. A Levite who returned from the Babylonian captivity (1Ch. 9:14; Ne. 11:15). †
4. The commander of King Ahaz's palace (2Ch. 28:7). †

AZUBAH [abandonment]

1. A wife of Caleb (1Ch. 2:18-19). †
2. The mother of King Jehoshaphat of Judah (1Ki. 22:42; 2Ch. 20:31). †

AZUR *See* AZZUR

AZZAH *See* AYYAH; GAZA

AZZAN [strong] A descendant of Issachar (Nu. 34:26). †

AZZUR [help]

1. A signer of the covenant with Nehemiah (Ne. 10:17). †

2. Father of the false prophet Hananiah in the days of King Zedekiah and the prophet Jeremiah (Jer. 28:1). †

3. Father of one of the leaders of the people in the days of the prophet Ezekiel (Eze. 11:1). †

B

BAAL(S) {master, owner, lord} The word *Baal* means "lord" or "husband." It is also the name of a deity. Hence names compounded with Baal mean the owner, the lord of, or the particular Baal deity worshiped in that place after which the place gets its name.

1. An unidentified city in Simeon, perhaps the Baalath Beer (Ramah in the Negev) of Jos. 19:8; 1Ch. 4:33.

2. A descendant of Reuben (1Ch. 5:5).

3. A descendant of Benjamin (1Ch. 8:30).

4. *See also* DEITIES.

BAALAH {feminine of BAAL}

1. An alternate name for the town of Kiriath Jearim (159-135) on the border between Judah and Benjamin (Jos. 15:9). The Ark of the Covenant, lost to the Philistines in battle in the days of the priest, Eli, eventually was returned by way of Beth Shemesh to Kiriath Jearim (1Sa. 6:21; 7:1), from which place, also called Baalah of Judah, King David brought it to Jerusalem (2Sa. 6:2); also called Kiriath Baal (Jos. 15:60).

2. A location on the border of the tribe of Judah near Jabneel called Mt. Baalah (Jos. 15:11).

3. One of the most southerly towns on the border of the tribe of Judah, in the Negev (Jos. 15:10), also belonging to the tribe of Simeon called Balah and Bilhah (Jos. 19:3; 1Ch. 4:29).

BAALATH {feminine of BAAL} A town (129-138) in the original tribal area of Dan, later rebuilt by Solomon for grain storage (Jos. 19:44; 1 Ki. 9:18; 1Ch. 4:33; 2Ch. 8:6). † *See also* BAAL(S) 2.

BAALATH BEER {BAAL of the well} Jos. 19:8. † *See* BAAL(S) 2.

BAAL-BERITH {lord of a covenant} *See* DEITIES

BAAL GAD {lord of good luck} An unidentified town at the foot of Mt. Hermon taken in the conquest by Joshua (Jos. 11:17; 12:7; 13:5). †

BAAL HAMON {lord of HAMON, *or* possessor of abundance} The unidentified site of one of Solomon's vineyards (SS. 8:11). †

BAAL-HANAN {BAAL is gracious}

1. King of Edom (Ge. 36:38-39; 1Ch. 1:49-50). †

2. The tender of David's olive and sycamore trees (1Ch. 27:28). †

BAAL HAZOR The place near Ephraim (177-153) where Absalom's servants killed Amnon (2Sa. 13:23ff.). †

BAAL HERMON A site in the area of the half of the tribe of Manasseh whose allotment was E of the Jordan (Jdg. 3:3; 1Ch. 5:23). †

BAALI KJV for "my master" (Hos. 2:16). *See also* BAAL(S)

BAALIM *See* BAAL(S) 4.

BAALIS {*possibly* son of delight, *or* BAALS (plural)} A late king of Ammon (Jer. 40:14). †

BAAL MEON A city in Moab that was rebuilt by the Reubenites after the conquest by Joshua, but retaken by the Moabites in the ninth century and its destruction prophesied; also called Beon, Beth Baal Meon, and Beth Meon (Nu. 32:3, 38; Jos. 13:17; 1Ch. 5:8; Jer. 48:23; Eze. 25:9).

BAAL OF JUDAH *See* BAALAH 1.

BAAL PEOR *See* DEITIES

BAAL PERAZIM {lord of making a breech, breaking through} A place whose exact location is unknown but where David defeated the Philistines. Perhaps the Mt. Perazim of Isa. 28:21; 2Sa.5:18-20; 1Ch. 14:11. †

BAAL SHALISHAH An unidentified place from which food was brought to Elisha and his school of prophets, where it was multiplied to feed a large number (2 Ki. 4:42-44). †

BAAL TAMAR {BAAL of the palm tree} A place from which the attack of Gibeah was launched in the battle between Israel and the men of Benjamin (Jdg. 20:33). †

BAAL-ZEBUB {lord of the flies} 2 Ki. 1:23, 6, 16. † *See* DEITIES

BAAL ZEPHON {lord of the North}
1. An unidentified place in Egypt near where the Israelites camped just before crossing the Red (Reed) Sea (Ex. 14:2, 9; Nu. 33:7). †
2. *See* DEITIES

BAANA {son of affliction}
1 and 2. Two of Solomon's officers who provided food for the king, one from the Megiddo area and the other from Asher (1 Ki. 4:12, 16). †
3. Father of a Zadok who worked on the walls with Nehemiah (Ne. 3:4). †

BAANAH {son of affliction}
1. One who with his brother murdered Saul's son Ish-Bosheth and was on that account executed by David (2Sa. 4:2ff.). †
2. Father of one of David's mighty men (1Ch. 11:30; 2Sa. 23:29). †
3. One of the important returnees with Zerubbabel from the Babylonian captivity (Ezr. 2:2; Ne. 7:7; Ne. 10:27). †

BAARA {passionate (burning) one} One of the divorced wives of a descendant of Benjamin (1Ch. 8:8). †

BAASEIAH An ancestor of the temple singer Asaph (1Ch. 6:40). †

BAASHA *See* KINGS OF JUDAH AND ISRAEL

BABEL
1. Part of the kingdom of Nimrod, son of Cush, son of Ham, son of Noah, a mighty hunter (Ge. 10:10). In some versions it is called Babylon.
2. The word has two interpretations: from *bab ili* (gate of god) or from *balal* (confusion) — the name of the city where men tried to build a tower with its top in the heavens, where God confused the existing single language of man into many

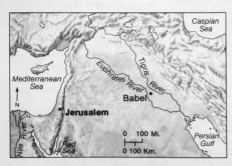

THE TOWER OF BABEL
The plain between the Tigris and Euphrates rivers provided a good location for the tower of Babel.

and then scattered mankind over the face of the earth (Ge. 11:19). (A word play could have been intended, in which the writer used both *bab ili* and *balal* to suggest that the self-effort of obtaining a "gateway to godhood" leads to "confusion.")

BABOON *See* BEASTS 3.

BABYLON, BABYLONIA [gate of god(s)] The history of Babylon in Mesopotamia commences with the kingdom of the Hamite Nimrod, three generations after the Flood (Ge. 10:10). Soon thereafter it became the site of the "ziggurat" or temple-tower of Babel, mankind's attempt at self-glorification which God frustrated by the introduction of differing languages (Ge. 11:78). The very name comes from *balal* "to confound" (Gen. 11:9), though the Babylonians preferred to derive it from the Akkadian, *bab ili,* meaning "gate of god."

During the third millennium B.C., the center of Mesopotamian power shifted southward, first to various Sumerian city-states (biblical Shinar) for the two centuries following 2400 to the Semitic Empire of Sargon I of Akkad, and then again from 2100-2000 to Sumer. In its renaissance under the Third Dynasty of Ur on the Persian Gulf, it was the home of Abraham before his call to Canaan (Gen. 11:28-31; *See also* CHRONOLOGY).

Sumuabu founded the First, or Amorite, Dynasty of Babylon, 1850-1550 B.C. Hammurabi (1728-1686), the sixth king, took Sumer and held to the North. He made Babylonian, in the Sumerian character, an international language and is best known for his law code, certain elements of which find parallels in the Pentateuchal codes that God revealed to Moses some two and a half centuries later. The modern, lower dating for Hammurabi makes it impossible to equate him, as was once done, with the Amraphel of Shinar (Ge. 14), whose hostile contact with Abraham preceded the year 2000 *(see* CHRONOLOGY). About 1550 a Hittite raid destroyed Babylon. Barbarian Kassites invaded

and held power until about 1180 B.C. Dynasty II of Isin then produced Nebuchadnezzar I (in Hebrew text also spelled Nebuchadrezzar), who showed great power but finally lost out before 1100.

Assyrian intervention characterized Babylon for centuries, until the rise of Naponassar (747-735 B.C.) marked the beginning of a new era, with struggles for independence. Marduk-pal-iddina II of Chaldea (biblical Merodach-Baladan) held the throne in Babylon from 721 to 710 and conspired with Hezekiah of Judah against Assyria (Isa. 39:12), so that the prophet Isaiah announced a future exile of the Jews to this same Babylon (39:67; 48:20). Sargon II of Assyria, however, proceeded to drive out Marduk-pal-iddina and personally took the throne of Babylon in 709.

Following the decline of Assyrian strength, Nabopolassar, (626-605 B.C.), a native Babylonian, rose to power in Chaldea. Pushing northward he held all Babylonia by 616. He allied himself with Cyaxares the Mede and advanced to the final attack on Nineveh in 612, thus founding the Neo-Babylonian empire. At Carchemish in 605, Neco II of Egypt (see 2Ch. 35:20-24) was routed by the armies of Nabopolassar under his son Nebuchadnezzar (Jer. 46:2). (Nebuchadrezzar is rendered as Nebuchadnezzar consistently in the NIV. Some occurrences are footnoted as "Hebrew Nebuchadrezzar.") Nebuchadnezzar proceeded to occupy Judah and all the West (2Ki. 24:7). The prophet Jeremiah then spoke of seventy years of Babylonian domination of the Near East (Jer. 25:11; 29:10); and Daniel described Babylon as "the head of gold," the first of the four great empires that would climax in the Rome of NT times (Da. 2:37-38; *cf.* 7:4).

Succeeding to his father's throne, Nebuchadnezzar II (605-562)was faced by continuous unrest and revolt in Judah, which led to the four deportations of the divinely ordained Babylonian exile: in 605, only Daniel and a few other noble hostages (Da. 1:13; 2 Ch. 36:6-7); in 597, King Jehoiachin, Ezekiel, and 10,000 of the leaders of the people (2Ki. 24:12-14); in 586, King Zedekiah and the main body of the people, after the final destruction of Jerusalem (25:8-11); and in 582, some 745 others who were left after the murder of Gedaliah, the governor for the remnant (2Ki.25:25; Jer. 52:30). Israel grieved by the waters of Babylon (Ps.137), but God promised recompense for the empire's wanton cruelties (Jer. 50-51). Meanwhile, Nebuchadnezzar built huge fortifications and the "hanging gardens of Babylon," which were one of the seven wonders of the ancient world. His power led to a form of insanity, "lycanthropy," described in Da. 4.

Amil-Marduk (biblical Evil-Merodach), 562-560 B.C. granted certain honors to the captive Jewish king, Jehoiachin (2Ki. 25:27-30), and was succeeded by Nergal-shar-usur (biblical Nergal-Sharezer), 560-556, who had been an officer of Nebuchadnezzar at the destruction of Jerusalem (Jer. 39:3, 13). Soon thereafter the religious and commercial powers in Babylon diverted the throne to a wealthy scholar, Nabunaid, who was faced by increasing unpopularity. After 552 these powers appointed Nebunaid's son Belshazzar as regent. In October of 539 the armies of Cyrus the Persian attacked the Babylonians under Belshazzar at Opis, defeated them, and received the submission of the city of Babylon without further fighting. Daniel interpreted the handwriting on the wall against Belshazzar, and that night the cit-

adel was taken and he was slain (Da. 5).

Babylon continued on as one of the Persian capitals (Ezr. 6:1), but gradually decreased in importance. When Peter fled from Herod Agrippa I in A.D. 44 (Ac. 12:17), he may have taken residence in Babylon (1 Pe. 5:13), unless this last is merely a symbolic name for Rome as the corresponding harlot city of that day (cf. Rev. 17:36; 18). (J.B.P.)

BABYLONISH *See* BABYLON, BABYLONIA

BACA {balsam tree, *or* weeping} A valley noted in Ps. 84:6. † (It is possible that this word is a variant spelling of the Hebrew word meaning "to weep."

BACHRITES *See* BEKER

BACKSLIDE

1. A nonbiblical term that describes a lessening of one's commitment to Christ. When one is not pressing on to the goal of the high calling of Christ (Php. 3:13-15), one's attitude and actions can regress to the point of carnal living (to walk as mere men, 1Co. 3:3) instead of living as a mature Christian. *See* CARNAL; FLESH

2. The NIV translates a word for "apostasy" or forsaking of the LORD (Jer. 2:19; 3:22; 14:7; 15:6; Eze. 37:23).

BADGER KJV for "goats," (RSV) and "sea cows," (NIV). *See* BEASTS 9.

BAHURIM, BAHARUMITE {young men} Bahurim is an unidentified town between Jerusalem and Jericho, probably nearer Jerusalem. Both Shimei

THE BABYLONIAN EMPIRE
(Arrows show exile route of Judah.)

(who cursed David) and Azmaveth (one of David's mighty men who is called a Baharumite and a Barhumite) came from there (2Sa. 3:16; 16:5; 19:16; 23:31; 1Ch. 11:33; 1Ki. 2:8). Jonathan hid from Absalom in Bahurim (2Sa. 17:18ff) †

BAJITH A KJV transliteration in Isa. 15:2 (Bayith, ASV), rendered "house" or "temple" in most versions. The RSV revocalizes the Hebrew to "daughter." The NEB similarly translates "people."

BAKBAKKAR A Levite who returned from Babylonian captivity (1Ch. 9:15). †

BAKBUK [gurgling (sound coming out of a bottle)] The father of some of the men who returned from the Babylonian captivity (Ezr. 2:51; Ne. 7:53). His name may be onomatopoeic (i.e., his name, repeated over and over, sounds like the action of a gurgling sound out of a vessel). †

BAKBUKIAH [Yahweh pours out]
1. A leading Levite among the returnees from the Babylonian captivity (Ne. 11:17; 12:9). †
2. A temple officer after the return (Ne. 12:25). (Some identify him with number 1.) †

BAKEMEATS KJV for "baked goods" (Ge. 40:17).

BALAAM [possibly BAAL (lord) of the people, BDB; possibly the clan brings forth, IDB; devourer, glutton, KB]
A man from Mesopotamia summoned by Balak, king of Moab, to come and curse the Israelites as they were entering Palestine from Egypt. An angel met him on his journey to Palestine and ordered him to bless, not curse, which he did (Nu. 22–24). The incident of Balaam's donkey seeing the angel before his master did is found in Nu. 22:21ff. Later, the Israelites killed Balaam after he had tried to involve them in idolatry (Nu. 31:8; *cf.* Jude 11; Rev. 2:14).

BALAC *See* BALAK

BALADAN [god (Merodach) gives a son] The father of one of the kings of Babylon (2Ki. 20:12; Isa. 39:1). † *See*

BABYLON, BABYLONIA; *see also* MERODACH BALADAN

BALAH *See* BAALAH 3.

BALAK [devastator] The king of Moab who tried to get Balaam to curse the Israelites (Nu. 22–24; Rev. 2:14; Jude 11).

BALANCE *See* WEIGHTS AND MEASURES

BALM *See* PLANTS, PERFUMES, AND SPICES

BALSAM *See* PLANTS, PERFUMES, AND SPICES, Miscellaneous Plants 12., *Balsam tree*

BAMAH [high location (for cultic worship)] The word is transliterated only in Eze. 20:29 where the prophet is making a play on words; elsewhere it is translated "high place" (Jer. 32:35).

BAMOTH [high locations (for cultic worship)] One of the stops of the Israelites E of the Jordan during their Exodus wanderings (Nu. 21:19-20). †

BAMOTH BAAL [high locations (for BAAL worship)] An unidentified site E of the Jordan where Balak took Balaam to try to get him to curse Israel. Later it was in the tribal area of Reuben (Nu. 22:41; Jos. 13:17). It is called simply Bamoth in Nu. 21:19. †

BAN *See* DEVOTE, DEVOTED

BAND KJV for a company or detachment of soldiers (Mt. 27:27; Jn. 18:3; Ac. 10:1; 27:1). A cohort was one-tenth of a legion, about 600 men.

BANI [descendant]
1. One of David's thirty mighty men (2Sa. 23:36, KJV).
2. A man of Judah who returned from the exile in Babylon (1Ch. 9:4).
3. An ancestor of one of David's temple singers and a descendant of Levi (1Ch. 6:46).
4. One or several Levites in Jerusalem in the days of Nehemiah (Ne. 3:17; 8:7; 10:13-14).
5. An ancestor of men who married foreign women during the Babylonian captivity (Ezr. 10:29).

BANK, BANKER *See* MONEY;
MONEY CHANGER

BANNER This was an ensign or "sign"
or "signal" that was for military and tribal
identification and rallying (Nu. 2:2; Ps.
74:4). A similar word is translated "standard" in Nu. 2:3ff. Another similar word
is found in Ex. 17:15; Isa. 31:9; 49:22.
This is not a "flag," but a pole with a con-
figuration or symbol, often an animal
figure (Nu. 21:8). A banner identifies the
group it represents. Many ancient cultures had these banners.

BANQUET *See* FEAST

BAPTISM A word transliterated from
the Greek word *baptisma* with various
meanings during different periods of
time and with a variety of groups: bap-
tisms in pre-Christian times, that of
John, that of Jesus, and finally that of the
church. The word itself appears in the
NT but not in the OT. The Greek translators of the OT use it three times. The
one clear context is 2Ki. 5:14, where
Naaman the leper "dipped" himself in the
Jordan River and was made clean. While
this word, being Greek, is not used in the
OT, the concept of washing with water
for cleansing is clear in Lev. 15:8; 17:15-
16. Both sprinkling of the water and
washing were used, or perhaps they were
used together (Nu. 19:17-19). In the times
before Christ, proselytes were baptized,
washed, as a part of the initiatory rites
into the community. This practice was
found also at the Dead Sea Scroll community.

John's baptism added something new,
an emphasis on personal repentance
from sin. It may also have been an initiatory rite to the believing community, but
it now involves personal activity in
repentance and dedication to a new life
(Lk. 3:3, 10-13).

The baptism of Jesus was by John but
there was a difference. It was not for
repentance from sin; it was to "fulfill all
righteousness" (Mt. 3:13-15). Jesus was
approaching the age of thirty and ready
to begin his ministry (Lk. 3:21, 23). At
the beginning of his ministry, the high
priest and his sons were washed. Later,
priests began their service the same way
at the age of thirty (Ex. 29:4; Nu. 4:3).
Christ came as the High Priest and his
ministry was inaugurated in the traditional manner by washing with water.

The church's baptism was linked with
repentance and with admission to the
community of the church. A mature individual recognizing the fact that he or
she was a sinner, believing in Jesus
Christ as Savior and Lord, and having
confessed this before men, was given the
rite of baptism as a sign of spiritual
cleansing and purification and admission to the church. Circumcision was
given to sons of the faithful in OT times
and baptism was given to all infant children of the faithful from earliest NT
times. Those who hold this latter position base it in measure on Col. 2:11-12.
Many believe in adult baptism only. It is
not a rite that regenerates the one to
whom it is applied but is merely an outward sign that one has professed his faith
in Christ and obedience to him and thus
is ingrafted into Christ and partakes of
all his benefits (Ro. 6:15; 1Pe. 3:21-22).
See articles below.

**BAPTISM, COVENANTAL VIEW
OF** In this idea, baptism has in the New
Covenant the same position that circumcision had in the Old Covenant. Baptism
is a sign of partnership in the New Covenant. So then, only adults who believe
and children of parents who believe are
to be baptized.

BAPTISM, INFANT Normally the
practice of effusion or sprinkling water
upon an infant. To some this is a sacrament bringing salvation to the infant. To
others it is a covenantal duty of the parents. To others it is a dedication of the infant to God by the parents. The practice
is not directly taught in the Scripture, but
some see inferences in the practices of
the Old Covenant (circumcision) and the
NT with respect to household salvation
(Ac. 16:31).

BAPTISM OF JESUS *See* CHRIST,
LIFE OF

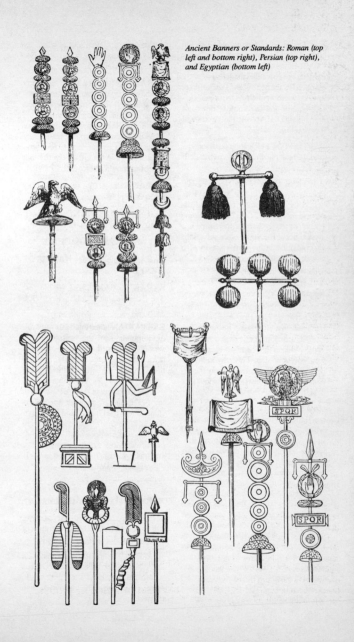

Ancient Banners or Standards: Roman (top left and bottom right), Persian (top right), and Egyptian (bottom left)

BAPTISM OF THE DEAD On the basis of one interpretation of 1Co. 15:29, this procedure was practiced by the Marcionites and Novatianists. It is currently practiced by the Mormons. The Bible reference is problematic as to its exact interpretation and the context does not demand that the Apostle Paul endorsed this practice.

BAPTISM OF FIRE John purifies with water, Christ purifies with fire (Mt. 3:11-12; Lk. 3:16-17). *See* FIRE

BAPTISM OF THE HOLY SPIRIT Promised in Mt. 3:11; Mk. 1:8; Lk. 3:16, occurring at Pentecost, this is a fulfillment of Joel 2:28-32 (Ac. 2:16-21). Some teach that the baptism of the Spirit is a special act of the Spirit after salvation, accompanied by a manifestation of a charismatic gift. Others understand 1Co. 12:13 as stating that all regenerate persons have undergone this baptism.

BAPTISMAL REGENERATION The teaching that baptism results in the regeneration of the one who is baptized—usually based upon Jn. 3:5 and Tit. 3:5. Some believe that Ac. 2:38 could indicate that baptism secures the forgiveness of sins. Those who do not believe this see baptism as simply the appeal to God for a clear conscience (1Pe. 3:21-22).

BAR {son} The Aramaic equivalent of the Hebrew word *ben* and Greek *huios* which is "son." Examples of this word used with others are as follows: Barsabbas, Bartholomew, Bar-Jesus, Bar-Jonah, Bartimaeus. The word often has the same idea in both testaments—that "son of" means one of a particular class of people. "Son of encouragement" means one who is of the class of those who encourage, i.e., an encourager. Compare also sons of thunder (Mk. 3:17), sons (subjects) of the kingdom (Mt. 8:12), sons of the evil one (Mt. 13:38), son of hell (Mt. 23:15), son (man doomed) of destruction (2Th. 2:3), son (man) of peace (Lk. 10:6), sons (people) of the age (Lk. 20:34). Jesus as the Son of God (and Son of Man) is an exception

to this idiom. Jesus was not merely "godly," he was God's actual Son. *See* SON, SONSHIP

BARABBAS {son of a father, *possibly* son of a rabbi (teacher)} An insurrectionist against the Romans imprisoned for his sedition. During the trial of Jesus before the Roman procurator, Pilate asked the assembled crowd whether they wanted him to give amnesty to Barabbas or to Jesus, and the crowd elected that Barabbas should go free (Mt. 27:17, 21).

BARACHEL {El blesses} *See* BARAKEL

BARACHIAH, BARAKIAH {Yahweh blesses} *See* BEREKIAH

BARACHIAS *See* BARACHIAH

BARAK {lightening} *See* JUDGES OF ISRAEL

BARAKEL, BARACHEL {El blesses} The father of one of Job's friends (Job 32:2, 6). †

BARBARIAN Some think this word onomatopoeic; i.e., the imitation of a sound. This word, repeated over and over *(bar . . . bar . . . bar)*, was (to the listener) like the unintelligible sounds of someone speaking a foreign (not Greek) language. Hence the word in the NT means a language not understandable to the Greek mind, or someone not of the Greek culture. A barbarian was looked down upon as an uncultured, primitive savage. *See*, for example, Ro. 1:14 ("non-Greek," NIV) and 1Co. 14:11 ("foreigner," NIV).

BARBER'S Eze. 5:1.

BARHUMITE *See* BAHURIM

BARIAH {*possibly* board, bar; fugitive, ISBE; descendant, KB} A descendant of David (1Ch. 3:22). †

BAR-JESUS {son of Joshua} A magician and false prophet on the island of Cyprus whom Paul declared the Lord would strike with temporary blindness; also called Elymas (Ac. 13:5-12).

BAR-JONA [son of Jonah, *or* son of John] Mt. 16:17; Jn. 1:42; 21:15-17 † *See* BAR

BARKOS [son of (pagan god) KOS] Father of some who returned from the Babylonian captivity (Ezr. 2:53; Ne. 7:55). †

BARLEY *See* PLANTS, PERFUMES, AND SPICES, Plants for Food 1.

BARN *See* STOREHOUSE

BARNABAS [son of comfort] A native of Cyprus who sold his property and gave the proceeds to the apostles in Jerusalem (Ac. 4:36-37), and later encouraged the Christians in Jerusalem to receive Paul as one of them (Ac. 9:26-29). It was Barnabas who brought Paul to the work at Antioch and later accompanied him on his missionary journey (Ac. 11:22-30; 12:25; 13:13). Together they were at the Jerusalem Council where policy concerning Gentile converts was established (Ac. 15:1-2, 12). He parted company with Paul over John Mark, but both continued on missionary journeys. Paul speaks well of him later, although nothing more is known of his activities (Ac. 15:36-40; 1Co. 9:6; Col. 4:10).

BARREL KJV for a "jar" that could hold solid food or liquid. A wooden slated barrel was not the object in mind according to the original language, but rather a clay vessel. *See* POTTER, POTTERY

BARREN To be barren was a condition of a sterile, infertile, childless, or over-aged woman in the Bible. Fertility was an act of the LORD (Ge. 16:12; 21:1; 1Sa. 1:5). To not be barren was to be fruitful and a sign of the LORD's blessing.

BARSABAS, BARSABBAS [son of Sabbath, *or* son of Saba]
   1. The defeated candidate in the casting of the lot to replace Judas among the twelve apostles; also known as Justus and Joseph (Ac. 1:23). †
   2. One chosen by the Jerusalem Council to go with Paul to the brethren in Antioch, Syria, and Cilicia with the message of the Council; also called Judas (Ac. 15:22). †

BARTHOLOMEW [son of Talmai] *See* APOSTLES

BARTIMAEUS [son of Timai *or* son of uncleanness] A blind beggar of Jericho who was healed by Jesus (Mk. 10:46-52). †

BARUCH [be blessed]
   1. The secretary of Jeremiah to whom the prophet dictated (Jer. 36:26, 32). This writing so angered the king that he ordered it burnt, but Jeremiah redictated it, and it is apparently an unidentified part of the book of Jeremiah (Jer. 36). He accompanied Jeremiah on his exile to Egypt after the start of the Babylonian captivity of Judah (Jer. 43:6-7).
   2. One of the builders of the walls of Jerusalem in the days of Nehemiah (Ne. 3:20), and perhaps one of the signers of the covenant with him (Ne. 10:6).
   3. Father of one of the dwellers in Jerusalem after the return from the Babylonian captivity (Ne. 11:5).

BARUCH, BOOK OF *See* SCRIPTURE

BARZILLAI [(made) of iron]
   1. A Gileadite from E of the Jordan who befriended King David when he was fleeing from Absalom. David on his deathbed instructed his son Solomon to show loyalty to his descendants (2Sa. 17:27-29; 1Ki. 2:7). His descendants also came back from the Babylonian captivity (Ezr. 2:61).
   2. The father of one of King Saul's sons-in-law (2Sa. 21:8).

BASEMATH, BASHEMATH, BASMATH [fragrant]
   1 and 2. One of the wives of Esau (Ge. 26:34; 36:3).
   3. A daughter of King Solomon (1Ki. 4:15).

BASHAN [fertile stoneless land] *See* GEOGRAPHY OF THE HOLY LAND

BASHAN-HAVOTH-JAIR *See* HAV(V)OTH JAIR

BASIN, BASON *See* BOWL; LAVER; SACRIFICES AND OFFERINGS

BAT *See* BEASTS 7.

BAT, A NAME When used with a name this represents the Hebrew word for "daughter," also spelled Bath as in Bathsheba. It can mean a daughter in the familial sense or be figurative for one who belongs to a certain class of people (e.g., Mal. 2:11 "daughter of a foreign god"). *See* APPLE OF THE EYE 2.

BATH, A MEASURE *See* WEIGHTS AND MEASURES

BATH, A NAME *See* BAT, A NAME

BATH, BATHING Apart from the cases of the daughter of Pharaoh bathing in the river, and Bathsheba the wife of Uriah the Hittite bathing on the rooftop (Ex. 2:5; 2 Sa. 11:2), bathing as we know it in the twentieth century is not discussed in the Bible. However, it was a common practice to wash the dusty feet of guests (Ge. 18:4; SS. 5:3; Lk. 7:44). And in NT times washing hands before eating was a ritual (Mt. 15:2, 20). *See* PURIFICATION

BATH RABBIM {daughter of a multitude} The name of a city E of the Jordan (SS. 7:4). †

BATHSHEBA {seventh daughter, *or* daughter of an oath} The wife of Uriah the Hittite whom David saw bathing on her rooftop. David committed adultery with her and had her husband killed so that later he could marry her. Nathan the prophet was sent by God to rebuke David for his adultery and murder. Their first child died, but the future King Solomon was the second (2Sa. 11–12; 1Ch. 3:5).

BATHSHUA {*possibly* daughter of opulence, BDB} A Canaanitess who bore three sons to Judah (1Ch. 2:3). †

BATTERING RAMS *See* ARMS AND ARMOR

BATTLE *See* ARMS AND ARMOR; WAR

BATTLE-AX *See* ARMS AND ARMOR

BATTLE-BOW *See* ARMS AND ARMOR

BATTLEMENT *See* PARAPET

BAV(V)AI *See* BINNUI 2.

BAYITH *See* BAJITH

BAYTREE *See* PLANTS

BAZLITH, BAZLUTH A temple servant in the days after the return from the Babylonian captivity (Ne. 7:54; Ezr. 2:52). †

BDELLIUM *See* PRECIOUS STONES AND METALS 14., *Resin*

BEALIAH {Yahweh is Lord} A Benjamite who joined David when he was fleeing from Saul (1Ch. 12:5). †

BEALOTH {*fem. pl. of* BAAL} An unidentified town in Judah (Jos. 15:24). † *See* ALOTH

BEAM A large piece of timber used to support the roof of a building (1Ki. 6:9-10). In the parable traditionally associated with the "mote and beam in the eye," the NIV renders these words as "speck and plank" (Mt. 7:35). In the case of the weaver's rod (beam), it is the bar on which the warp was bound in the loom (1Sa. 17:7).

BEANS *See* PLANTS, PERFUMES, AND SPICES, Plants for Food 2.

BEAR *See* BEASTS 8.

BEARD Carefully groomed hair on the face was a sign of manly vitality. Its neglect was a sign of mental derangement (1Sa. 21:13; 2Sa. 19:24). While in mourning, men either cut off or plucked out the beard (Jer. 41:5). To cut off a man's beard was to humiliate him (2Sa. 10:4-5). The Israelites were forbidden to cut the hair at the sides of their heads (Lev. 19:27), and later the hair around their temples was grown long, as do the Orthodox Jews of today.

BEARING OF CHILDREN *See* PARENTING

BEAST, THE In Revelation there are two fiends. These devilish creatures ravish the earth during the Tribulation.

1. This creature rises from the sea (13:1-8), also known as the Abyss (11:7), from where evil comes. The harlot rode it (17:3-17). Anyone with its mark will receive God's wrath (14:9, 11; 15:2; 19:19-20). The final destiny of the Beast is eternal punishment (20:10).

2. Another wild creature or monster comes up from the earth, which is the same as the false prophet (13:11-18).

BEASTS

1. *Cobra, Serpent, Snake, Viper.* These reptiles breathe air, are vertebrates, and crawl on the belly or creep on short legs (1Ki. 4:33; Ro. 1:23). The serpent is an elongated, limbless reptile with scales (Ge. 3:14; Pr. 30:19). Synonymous with the words *serpent* or *snake* are the viper and the cobra, all poisonous (Ge. 49:17; Dt. 32:33; Ps. 140:3; Pr. 23:32; Isa. 11:8).

2. *Antelope, Deer, Doe, Gazelle, Ibex, Mountain Sheep, Roe Deer.* These are among the clean animals (Dt. 14:4-5). (Note: "clean" animals are animals that could be eaten by the Jews; "unclean" animals were not allowed to be eaten by the Jews.) The doe is parallel to gazelle in SS. 2:7 and is probably a synonym. The doe is mentioned in Pr. 5:19, where it is a synonym for deer. While there are many varieties and species

known today, and while many doubtless existed in biblical times, the clearest analogy for the modern reader is to forms of deer and wild sheep.

Gazelle (or Ariel)

Ibex

Antelope

3. *Ape, Baboon.* Monkeys probably from India, probably not the large animals known by those terms today (1Ki. 10:22).

4. *Bull, Camel, Cattle, Cow, Donkey, Mule, Goat, Heifer, Herds, Horse, Ox, Sheep.* The domesticated clean animals were cattle or herds and flocks. Cattle and herds refer to the larger animals: cow, ox, bull, and their heifers. The word *flock* covers the smaller animals, the sheep and goats. The donkey, mule, and the horse were unclean; the former two were the work animals, while the latter was used in war. The camel too was among the unclean animals but was very

useful in the Palestinian country as a beast of burden whose hair was used for making cloth. Certain types could cover 150 miles in a day or carry a load of 400 pounds. *See also* FOAL

Ancient Egyptian Horse

5. *Coney* (Rock Badger), *Rabbit, Rat, Sea Cow.* All are unclean animals. The coney is a small-hoofed animal much like the rabbit in size. It lives in rocky areas and is totally unlike the animal called "badger" in modern times (Lev. 11:29; Dt. 14:7; Ps. 104:18). From the sea cow came the skin for the cover of the tabernacle (Ex. 36:19).

Rock Badger

6. *Ant, Bee, Chameleon, Cricket, Flea, Fly, Frog, Gecko, Gnat, Grasshopper, Hornet, Katydid, Lizard, Leech, Locust, Maggots, Moth, Scorpion, Skink, Slug, Spider, Worm.* While the group covers different phyla there is one characteristic they have in common: they are small. On reptiles, see following and also number 1 on previous page. The others in this group are arachnids, insects, or reptiles. The *frog* is a tailless, leaping amphibian and is noted mostly in the incidents of the ten plagues in Egypt (Ex. 8:1-15). The *spider* and the *scorpion* are arachnids. The former have

in common that they spin webs. In the Bible this is a symbol of frailty (Job 8:14). There are many species of both the spiders and the scorpions. Scorpions are characterized by the curved stinging tail (Dt. 8:15). Among the insects are the clean ones, the *katydid* (a type of grasshopper), *locust, grasshopper,* and *cricket* (Lev. 11:22; Ps. 78:46). These have worm-like larvae which are unclean and are called *maggots* or *worms* (Job 25:6). The *leech* is mentioned in Pr. 30:15; *moth* in Job 4:19; Ps. 39:11; Isa. 51:8; Mt. 6:19-20. Since the moth is an insect that consumes cloth, it is used in association with the consumption of wealth. The *flea* is a jumping wingless insect, referred to in 1Sa. 24:14. References to the *fly* are mostly in connection with the account of the ten plagues in Ex. 8:21-31. The word *gnat* may refer to the gnat as we know it, or to the mosquito or sand fly. It, too, is used mostly in connection with the ten plague account (Ex. 8:16-18). With one exception the *bee* and *hornet* are noted for their stinging feature (Dt. 1:44; 7:20). The exception is in the case of Jdg. 14:8 where honey is mentioned in connection with the insect that produces it.

Locust

Reptiles not discussed in number 1 include the *chameleon, gecko, skink,* and several kinds of *lizards* (the great lizard, the wall lizard, the monitor lizard). They are all unclean. The first lizard could change colors. The second is an animal of rather uncertain character, perhaps a reptile. The *skink* was a harmless smooth-scaled lizard; it has a long tail and usually short legs (Lev. 11:29-30). They are all unclean animals. The *slug* is mentioned in Ps. 58:8. *See also* MOLE

7. *Bat.* A nocturnal flying mammal which because it flies is listed with birds (unclean birds) in Lev. 11:19.

8. *Bear, Dog, Fox, Hyena, Jackal, Leopard, Lion, Wolf, Weasel.* All are carnivorous mammals (Isa. 11:7; Jdg. 15:4; Mt. 8:20; Isa. 34:14; Ps. 63:10; Isa. 11:6; Jer. 13:23; Hab. 1:8; Jdg. 14:5; Ps. 7:2; Jn. 10:12; Jer. 5:6; Lev. 11:29). The *dog* is a domesticated carnivorous mammal (Ex. 11:7). It is also used as a term of contempt for a man, especially an enemy—in the expression "dead dog" (Rev. 22:15).

9. *Behemoth, Dragon, Leviathan, Rahab, Monster of the Deep, Sea Cow.* The *behemoth* mentioned in Job 40:15 is thought by some to be the hippopotamus or the elephant. In early extrabiblical literature it is a name for one of the mythical monsters. *Leviathan, rahab,* and the *monster of the deep* are all undefined sea monsters (Job 3:8; 7:12; 26:12; Ps. 74:13-14; 89:10; Job 3:8; Isa. 27:1). In some verses they seem to be mythological only, while in others some of them would seem to have been real also. For *dragon, see* DEITIES and DEMONS. *Sea cows* are called *badgers* in the KJV. Their skin was used to cover the tabernacle.

10. *Boar, Hedgehog, Pig.* The former, a wild swine or pig, is noted in Ps. 80:13. There are many references to the latter in both Testaments (Lev. 11:7; Mt. 8:30; Isa. 66:3).

BEATITUDES [divine favor] A word which is used to refer to the teachings of Jesus that begin with "Blessed are" in Mt. 5:3-12 and Lk. 6:20-23.

BEBAI [child] The father of some who returned from the Babylonian captivity (Ezr. 2:11; 8:11; 10:28; Ne. 7:16; 10:15). †

BECAME THE FATHER OF *See* SEED

BECHER *See* BEKER

BECHORATH, BECORATH [firstborn] A descendant of Benjamin and ancestor of King Saul (1Sa. 9:1). †

BED The common man in biblical times could not afford a bed in the modern sense of that word. He slept on the ground wrapped in his outer cloak or on some sort of mat on the floor (Ex. 22:26-27; Ac. 5:15). Simple beds were known and are probably reflected in 2Sa. 17:28 and 1Sa. 19:15. Beds as luxury items are referred to frequently—decked with tapestries, perfumed with spices, inlaid with ivory, and with headboards (Am. 6:4; Pr. 7:16-17; Ge. 47:31). Guests at a banquet, at least in Roman times, reclined on beds or couches arranged around the banqueting table and this was probably what took place at the first Lord's Supper (Jn. 13:23).

BEDAD [solitary] Father of one of the kings of Moab (Ge. 36:35; 1Ch. 1:46). †

BEDAN
1. A descendant of Manasseh (1Ch. 7:17). †
2. A variant name of BARAK from KJV, NKJV, ASV, NASB (footnote) in 1Sa. 12:11. The NIV, RSV, NEB, JB have *Barak* based on ancient manuscripts. *See* BARAK

BEDEIAH One who married a foreign woman during the captivity in Babylon (Ezr. 10:35). †

BEE *See* BEASTS 6.

BEELIADA [BAAL knows] A son born to David in Jerusalem, also known as Eliada (2Sa. 5:16; 1Ch. 14:7). †

BEELZEBUB [lord of the flies] *See* DEITIES and DEVIL

BEELZEBUL A better transliteration of the Greek in the NASB and JB for *Beelzebub* in most other versions.

BEER [cistern, well]
1. A stopping place for the Israelites during their exodus from Egypt, on the border of Moab (Nu. 21:16).
2. The place to which Jotham fled from Abimelech (Jdg. 9:21).

BEER, A DRINK *See* DRINK

BEERA {cistern, well} A descendant of Asher (1Ch. 7:37). †

BEERAH {cistern, well} A descendant of Reuben captured by the Assyrian king Tiglath-Pileser (1Ch. 5:6). †

BEER ELIM {cistern, well of ELIM} An unidentified town in Moab (Isa. 15:8). Possibly BEER 1. †

BEERI {(my) cistern, well}
1. The Hittite father of one of Esau's wives (Ge. 26:34). †
2. The father of the prophet Hosea (Hos. 1:1). †

BEER LAHAI ROI {well that belongs to the Living One seeing me} An unidentified site in the Negev where the angel appeared to Hagar when she was fleeing from Sarah (Ge. 16:14). Isaac and Rebecca met and later settled there (Ge. 24:62; 25:11). †

BEEROTH, BEEROTHITE(S) {cisterns, wells} A city (167-136) of Gibeon and later Benjamin. Saul's murderers and Joab's armor-bearer came from there (Jos. 9:17; 18-25; 2Sa. 4:2; 23:37). Some of its inhabitants came back from the Babylonian captivity (Ezr. 2:25).

BEERSHEBA A town (134-072) originally in the tribal area of Judah and later assigned to Simeon, called "the well of the oath" or "the well of the seven" (Jos. 15:28; 19:2; Ge. 21:22-32). Many ruins from the end of the fourth millennium B.C. exist in the region of modern Beersheba, but the tell (ancient mound) Sheba of antiquity was not yet occupied in the days of the patriarchs. The Beersheba of those days had no king. The patriarchs sacrificed to God somewhere in the area in a place they called Beersheba (Ge. 21:33; 46:1). The phrase "from Dan to Beersheba" was the standard for describing the limits of Palestine (Jdg. 20:1). It was the site of a religious sanctuary in the days of the kings of Judah (Am. 5:5). The largest horned altar yet discovered indicates the existence

of a temple altar, but nothing remains of the temple itself. It was still occupied even after the return from the Babylonian captivity (Ne. 11:27). Persian and Roman remains have been excavated on the site.

BE ESHTARAH, BEESH-TERAH A city in the tribal area of Manasseh E of the Jordan given to the Levites (Jos. 21:27). † *See* ASHTAROTH (1Ch. 6:71)

BEEVES *See* BEASTS 4., *Cattle*

BEG, BEGGAR To beg or to ask alms was an accepted practice in biblical times. Cases appear in both Testaments: (Ps. 109:10; La. 4:4; Mk. 10:46; Lk. 18:35; Ac. 3:2).

BEGAT, BEGET KJV for "became the father of." *See* SEED

BEGOTTEN *See* FIRSTBORN

BEHEAD *See* PUNISHMENT

BEHEMOTH *See* BEASTS 9.

BEHOLD A common interjection in the OT and NT in many versions. The Greek word is an imperative from the word "to see." But it is best understood from the OT that this word has no visual connotation. This word calls the reader's attention to what follows.

BEKA, BEKAH *See* WEIGHTS AND MEASURES

BEKER {young male camel}
1. A son of Benjamin (Ge. 46:21).
2. A descendant of Ephraim; also called Bered (Nu. 26:35; 1Ch. 7:68; 7:20). †

BEL {Babylonian deity BEL} *See* DEITIES

BEL AND THE DRAGON *See* SCRIPTURE, *Apocrypha*

BELA, BELAH, BELAITE(S) {swallower, devourer}
1. A king of Edom (Ge. 36:32).
2. Benjamin's first son, with a clan (Ge. 46:21; Nu. 26:38).
3. A descendant of Reuben who lived E of the Jordan (1Ch. 5:8).
4. Another name for the city of Zoar.

Its king was involved in the battle at Sodom and Gomorrah (Ge. 14:2, 8).

BELIAL {wicked, without use} In the OT the word is translated wicked men, troublemakers, or scoundrels (Dt. 13:13; 1Sa. 2:12; 10:27; 1Ki. 21:10). The word is used in 2Co. 6:15 to designate the opposite of Christ—just as darkness is the antithesis of light.

BELIAR A variant reading of Belial in 2Co. 6:15. See footnote of the NIV. *See* BELIAL

BELIEVE A synonym for "to have faith." In OT times when a man believed God, it was accounted to him for righteousness (Ge. 15:6; Hab. 2:4). In NT times righteousness and eternal life are given to those who believe in Jesus as Son of God, Savior, and Lord (Jn. 3:15-16, 18, 36; 1Jn. 4:5-12; 2Pe. 3:18). *See* FAITH, FAITHFUL

BELIEVER One who believes or has tenacious faith in Christ, a Christian.

BELL Small bells of gold alternated with other ornaments on the lower part of the high priest's robe (Ex. 28:33-35). There is a reference to "bells of the horses," which is even less revealing as to the nature of these bells (Zec. 14:20).

BELLOWS An important part of the blacksmith's workshop and that of the refiner. The word is found in Jer. 6:29, but the concept is also clear in Isa. 54:16. These were leather bags fastened to wooden or ceramic nozzles which were operated either by hand or by treading with the feet.

BELLY *See* EMOTIONS

BELOVED A word related to *agape*; it is a warm, cherishing term for "dear friend" or "friend that is loved" (1Jn. 2:7).

BELSHAZZAR {(pagan god) BEL protect the king} The last Chaldean king to reign over Babylon. He reigned as coregent with his father Nabonidus, who is sometimes called the last king. He is called son of Nebuchadnezzar in the Bible, but in that context the word *son*

is used in one of its normal Semitic usages of "descendant" (Da. 5:2, 30-31). *See also* BABYLON, BABYLONIA

BELT *See* DRESS

BELTESHAZZAR {protect his life} *See* DANIEL 4.

BEMA *See* SEAT, JUDGMENT

BEN A Hebrew word for "son." See the articles below for names with BEN in composition. *See* BAR for figurative use. *See* SON, SONSHIP

BEN-ABINADAB {son of ABIN-ADAB} A son-in-law of King Solomon who was in charge of collecting his food in the area of Naphoth Dor (1Ki. 4:11). †

BENAIAH {Yahweh has built}
1. One of David's mighty men, who also supported Solomon for the throne and killed Joab (2Sa. 23:20; 1Ki. 1:38; 2:28-31).
2. Another of David's mighty men who later was one of King Solomon's officers (2Sa. 23:30; 1Ch. 27:14).
3. A descendant of Simeon (1Ch. 4:36).
4. One of David's musicians, a Levite (1Ch. 15:18).
5. One who was to blow the trumpet before the Ark in David's day (1Ch. 15:24).
6. The grandfather of Jahaziel through whom God spoke of victory over Moab to King Jehoshaphat (2Ch. 20:14).
7. An overseer in the reign of King Hezekiah (2Ch. 31:13).
8, 9, 10, and 11. Men who married foreign wives during the Babylonian captivity (Ezr. 10:25, 30, 35, 43).
12. Father of one of the princes who gave evil counsel to men of Jerusalem, and died for it (Eze. 11:1-2, 13).

BEN-AMMI {son of my people} Grandson of Lot and founder of the Ammonites (Ge. 19:38). †

BEN-DEKER {son of DEKAR (pierces)} An officer of King Solomon (1Ki. 4:9). †

BENE-BERAK [sons of BARAK (lightning)] A town (133-160) in the original tribal area of Dan (Jos. 19:45). †

BENEDICTION *See* BLESS, BLESSING

BENE-JAAKAN [*possibly* son of JAAKAN] A stop in the wilderness wanderings of the Israelites during the exodus from Egypt (Nu. 33:31-32). †

BENEVOLENCE, DUE KJV for "marital duty," i.e., the obligation of conjugal acts (1Co. 7:3). *See also* MARRIAGE

BEN-GEBER [son of strength] One of King Solomon's twelve food collectors, in the area of Ramoth-Gilead (1Ki. 4:13). †

BEN-HADAD [son of HADAD (pagan storm god)] The name of three kings of ancient Syria at Damascus.

1. Ben-Hadad I captured parts of Israel from its king, Baasha, at a time when Baasha was at war with King Asa of Judah (1Ki. 15:18-21).

2. Ben-Hadad II, son of Ben-Hadad I, who was defeated by Ahab of Israel, forced to give back the territory his father had seized from Israel, and to give certain commercial rights (1Ki. 20:1-34). Later, they were allies against the Assyrians at Qarqar but soon fought again with one another (1Ki. 22:1-36).

3. Ben-Hadad III was the son of the servant Hazael of Ben-Hadad II who had usurped his master's throne (2Ki. 8:7-15; 13:3). Jehoash, king of Israel, defeated him and forced him to return all the territories captured from Israel (2Ki. 13:25).

BEN-HAIL [son of strength] A prince sent by King Jehoshaphat to teach in Judah (2Ch. 17:7). †

BEN-HANAN [son of grace] A descendant of Judah (1Ch. 4:20). †

BEN-HESED [son of HESED (loyal love)] One of King Solomon's food-collecting officers in Judah (1Ki. 4:10). †

BEN HINNOM [son of HINNOM] A man whose name was given to a valley immediately W of the ridge on which the city of Jerusalem was built (Jer. 19:2, 6). It is from this name that the term Gehenna eventually arose.

BEN-HUR [son of HUR] King Solomon's food collector in the area of the hill country of Ephraim (1Ki. 4:8). †

BENINU [our son] One of the Levites who signed the covenant with Nehemiah (Ne.10:13). †

BENJAMIN, BENJAMITE [son of (the) right hand, BDB; southerner, KB]

1. The last son of Jacob and second by Rachel. Born in sorrow and pain just before Rachel died, she called him Ben-Oni ("son of my sorrow"), but Jacob later named him Benjamin (Ge. 35:16-18). Founder of one of the twelve tribes (Jdg. 21:1). The relationship in Egypt with his older and full brother Joseph is beautifully narrated (Ge. 42–45).

2. A descendant of Benjamin (1Ch. 7:10).

3. One who married a foreign wife during the Babylonian captivity (Ezr. 10:32).

4. A builder of the walls with Nehemiah (Ne. 3:23).

BENO [his son] A descendant of Aaron who served in the priesthood (1Ch. 24:26-27). †

BEN-ONI *See* BENJAMIN 1.

BEN-ZOHETH [son of ZOHETH] A descendant of Judah (1Ch. 4:20). †

BEON A place E of the Jordan where the tribes of Gad and Reuben resided (Nu. 32:15). †

BEOR

1. The father of Balaam, who failed to curse Israel as he was requested (Nu. 22:56).

2. Father of a king of Edom (Ge. 36:32).

BERA The king of Sodom defeated in the battle of the kings (Ge. 14:2). †

BERACAH [blessing]

1. A descendant of Benjamin who joined David at Ziklag (1Ch. 12:3). †

2. A valley near Bethlehem which got its name from King Jehoshaphat's blessing the LORD there (2Ch. 20:26). †

BERACAH, VALLEY OF *See* BERACAH

BERACHIAH *See* BEREKIAH

BERAIAH [Yahweh creates] A descendant of Benjamin (1Ch. 8:21). †

BEREA(N) A city in Macedonia not far from Thessalonica where Paul's message met with success (Ac. 17:10-14; 20:4). †

BERECHIAH *See* BEREKIAH

BERED [*possibly* freezing rain]

1. An unidentified site in the wilderness of Shur (Ge. 16:14). †

2. A descendant of Ephraim (1Ch. 7:20). †

BEREKIAH [Yahweh blesses]

1. A son of Zerubbabel (1Ch. 3:20).

2. The father of Asaph the singer (1Ch. 6:39).

3. A Levite who returned from Babylon (1Ch. 9:16).

4. A Levite doorkeeper for the Ark (1Ch. 15:23).

5. A prince in Ephraim at the time of King Pekah (2Ch. 28:12).

6. A builder of the walls with Nehemiah (Ne. 3:4).

7. Father of the prophet Zechariah (Zec. 1:1; Mt. 23:35).

BERI A descendant of Asher, and his descendant (1Ch. 7:36).†

BERIAH

1. A son of Asher (Ge. 46:17). His descendants are called Beriites in Nu. 26:44.

2. Son of Ephraim (1Ch. 7:23).

3. A descendant of Benjamin who lived in Aijalon (1Ch. 8:13).

4. A descendant of Levi (1Ch. 23:10).

BERITE Normally understood as a son of Bichri, or possibly Becher (2Sa. 20:14). †

BERIITE(S) *See* BERIAH 1.

BERITH *See* EL-BERITH

BERNICE [victorious] The oldest daughter of Herod Agrippa I and sister of Herod Agrippa II. She was married to her uncle; after his death, she had an incestuous relationship with her brother. She was with this brother and Governor Festus in Caesarea when Paul's case was heard there (Ac. 25:13, 23; 26:30).†

BEROEA Berea in RSV.

BERODACH-BALADAN *See* MERODACH-BALADAN

BEROTHAH A city on the boundary of the land, in the prophetic account by Ezekiel (Eze. 47:16).†

BEROTHAI A Syrian city (257-372) captured by David; also called Cun in 2Sa. 8:8. † *See also* CUN

BERYL *See* PRECIOUS STONES AND METALS

BESAI [in secret council of Yahweh, KB] One who returned with Zerubbabel from the Babylonian captivity (Ezr. 2:49; Ne. 7:52). †

BESEECH *See* EXHORTATION

BESODEIAH [in secret council of Yahweh] The father of one who worked with Nehemiah to repair the Old Gate of Jerusalem (Ne. 3:6). †

BESOM *See* BROOM

BESOR A brook, wadi, or ravine that runs from near Beersheba to the sea near Gaza (1Sa. 30:9-10, 21). †

BESTIALITY Forbidden sexual relations with an animal, worthy of death in the Old Covenant (Lev. 18:23; 20:15).

BETAH *See* TEBAH 1.

BETEN [womb, bowels] A town (160-241) in the lot of the tribe of Asher (Jos. 19:25). †

BETH

1. The second letter in the Hebrew alphabet. In English transliteration it can

have a hard *b* or a soft *v* sound, depending on phonetic rules.

2. A transliteration of the Hebrew word for *house*. A house may be a literal abode, or figuratively a family or dynasty (Ac. 16:31). *See also* HOUSE

BETHABARA {site (house) of ABARAH (depression)} A KJV, NKJV rendering in Jn. 1:28. Most other versions read "Bethany," based on earlier and a great diversity of Greek manuscripts.

BETH ANATH {house of ANAT} A town (190-289) in the tribal area of Naphtali (Jos. 19:38; Jdg. 1:33). †

BETH ANOTH {house of ANATH (plural)} A town (162-107) in the tribal area of Judah (Jos. 15:59). †

BETHANY {*possibly* site (house) of ANY (Ananiah) *or* poor ones *or* unripe figs)}

1. A town just over a mile E of Jerusalem, where the home of Mary, Martha, and Lazarus was located. Jesus spent much time there, and it was there that he raised Lazarus from the dead (Mt. 26:6; Mk. 11:1; Jn. 12:1).

2. A place where John the Baptist baptized, east of the Jordan (Jn. 1:28). This is not the hometown of Lazarus. It is currently not identified. *See* BETHABARA

BETHANY
Jesus often visited Bethany to see his friends Mary, Martha, and Lazarus. He spent much of his last week in Bethany.

BETH ARABAH {house of ARABAH (desert plain)} A town (197-139) near Jericho on the border between Judah and Benjamin (Jos. 15:6, 61; 18:18, 22). †

BETH-ARAM *See* BETH HARAM, BETH HARAN

BETH ARBEL {house of ARBEL} A town (229-218) destroyed by Shalman (Hos. 10:14). †

BETH ASHBEA {house of ASHBEA} An unidentified town where a family of linen workers lived (1Ch. 4:21). †

BETH AVEN {house of idolatry} A town (175-141) near Ai and Michmash on Benjamin's border, on the edge of the Judean wilderness (Jos. 7:2; 18:12; 1Sa. 13:5; 14:23). Translated this means "house of wickedness." A symbolic name for Bethel which means "house of God" (Hos. 4:15; 5:8; 10:5). †

BETH AZMAVETH {strong of death, ISBE; house of AZMAVETH (camel fodder, a plant of the plumose family), KB} Men from this town came up from the Babylonian captivity, perhaps identical with Azmaveth (174-137) (Ne. 7:28). †

BETH BAAL MEON {house of BAAL MEON} A city (219-120) E of the Jordan allocated to the Reubenites (Jos. 13:17). †

BETH BARAH {house of BARAH (the river ford)} An unidentified site near the Jordan River, a staging area in Gideon's fight against the Midianites (Jdg. 7:24). †

BETH-BEIRI, BETH BIRI {den (house) of BIRI (a lioness)} A city in Simeon (1Ch. 4:31). † *See* BETH LEBAOTH

BETH CAR {site (house) of a lamb} An unidentified site to which the Israelites pursued the Philistines after one of their battles (1Sa. 7:11). †

BETH DAGON {temple (house) of DAGON (pagan god)}

1. A town (134-156) in the tribal area of Asher (Jos. 19:27). †

2. An unidentified town in the lowlands of Judah (Jos. 15:41). †

BETH DIBLATHAIM [house of DIB-LATHAIM] A city (228-116) in Moab (Nu. 33:46; Jer. 48:22), perhaps also Almon Diblathaim. †

BETH EDEN [house of EDEN] Probably the Bitadini of the Assyrian records. The "people of Eden" came from there. A city-state near the Euphrates (2Ki. 19:12; Eze. 27:23; Am. 1:5). †

BETH EKED [house of EKED] An unidentified place between Samaria and Jezreel (2Ki. 10:12, 14). †

BETHEL, BETHELITE [site (house) of El]

1. A town (172-148) generally thought to be at modern Beitin. Questions have been raised since Bethel is said to be twelve miles N of Jerusalem according to the *Onomasticon* of Eusebius, while Beitin is farther. Ai is located near the biblical Bethel. Abraham built an altar between these two towns (Ge. 12:8). Jacob's dream happened there (Ge. 28:10ff.). In the Israelite invasion Joshua captured its king (Jos. 12:9), and it was assigned to the tribal area of Benjamin (Jos. 18:22). The Ark of God was there for some time in the days prior to the monarchy (Jdg. 20:26-27). Because it was the site of a strategic road intersection, it had great importance in the days of the kings of Judah and Israel. When the ten tribes split off from the two, Jeroboam set up a statue of a golden calf in the temple he built there (1Ki. 12:28-31). The prophets cried against his idolatry (1Ki. 13:1-2; 2Ki. 10:29), and only after the fall of Samaria was the temple destroyed (2Ki. 23:15-20). It was reoccupied after the return from Babylon (Ezr. 2:28).

2. A town in the tribal area of Simeon also known as Betheul and Bethuel (Jos. 19:4; 1Ch. 4:30).

BETH EMEK [site (house) of EMEK (the valley)] A city (164-263) in the tribal area of Asher (Jos. 19:27). †

BETHER KJV, NKJV, NASB, ASV for a possible translation "rugged hills" in the RSV, NIV. Another possibility is "cinna-mon" and is so rendered in the NEB, SS. 2:17. The JB switches two Hebrew letters and revocalizes the Hebrew to read "covenant."

BETHESDA [site (house) of mercy] A pool in Jerusalem where invalids came for healing (Jn. 5:23). †

BETH EZEL [site (house) of EZEL (nearby)] A town probably in Judah (Mic. 1:11). †

BETH GADER [site (house) of GADER (of a stone hedge)] A town in the tribal area of Judah (1Ch. 2:51). †

BETH GAMUL [site (house) of recompence] A city (235-099) of Moab (Jer. 48:23). †

BETH GILGAL [site (house) of Gilgal] One of the towns from which the singers came at the time of the dedication of Nehemiah's rebuilt wall (Ne. 12:29). † *See* GILGAL

BETH-HACCEREM *See* BETH HAKKEREM

BETH HAGGAN [site (house) of HAGGAN (the garden)] King Ahaziah fled in this direction (178-207) from Jehu (2Ki. 9:27). †

BETH HAKKEREM [site (house) of HAKKEREM (the vineyard)] A town (170-127) of Judah perhaps at the site of modern Ramat Rachel, S of Jerusalem (Ne. 3:14; Jer. 6:1). †

BETH HARAM, BETH HARAN A town (214-136) and a valley in which the town was located E of the Jordan in the tribal area of Gad (Nu. 32:36; Jos. 13:27). †

BETHHOGLA, BETH HOGLAH [site (house) of HOGLAH (partridge)] A Benjamite city (197-136) in the Jordan Valley (Jos. 15:6; 18:19-21). †

BETH HORON [site (house) of HORON (ravine, hollow)] Reference is made (Jos. 10:10; 16:3, 5) to "going up to Beth Horon," to "Lower Beth Horon" (158-144), and to "Upper Beth Horon" (160-143). The road of the ascent of Beth

Horon was from the earliest times the main road up into the hill country from the coast at Joppa (modern Yaffo). The road passed between two Beth Horons and thus it and the two cities were of extreme importance militarily. After the battle at Gibeon, Joshua pursued the kings down this road as did King Saul the Philistines later (Jos. 10:10-11; 1Sa. 13:18). It was still important in Hellenistic, Roman, and Crusader times. The two towns were in the tribal area of Ephraim on the southern border (Jos. 16:3; 18:13). King Solomon fortified these cities, but in the time of the divided monarchy they were in Israel (2Ch. 8:5; 25:13).

BETH JES(H)IMOTH {site (house) of JESHIMOTH (desolation)} A town (208-132) in Moab taken by the Israelites and assigned to the tribal area of Reuben (Nu. 33:49; Jos. 12:3; 13:20). It had been retaken by the time of the prophet Ezekiel (Eze. 25:9). †

BETH LE APHRAH *See* BETH OPHRAH

BETH LEBAOTH {house of BIRI (the lioness)} An unidentified town in the tribal area of Judah-Simeon called Beth Biri in 1Ch. 4:31, and Lebaoth in Jos. 15:32; 19:6. †

BETHLEHEM {site (house) of food; *possibly* temple (house) of Lakhmu (pagan deity)}
1. A city (169-123) in the tribal area of Judah near which the patriarch Jacob's wife Rachel was buried and from which King David came (Ge. 35:19; 1Sa. 16:1, 18). It was a Philistine stronghold through the days of King Saul and into David's days also (2Sa. 23:16). King Rehoboam of Judah built up towers of defense there (2Ch. 11:6). It was still inhabited by Jews after the return from the Babylonian captivity (Ezr. 2:21), and was the birthplace of Jesus Christ, prophesied by Micah and recorded in the Gospels (Mic. 5:2; Mt. 2:5; Lk. 2:4).
2. Bethlehem (168-238) in the tribal area of Zebulun in the N (Jos. 19:15).

BETHLEHEM
Caesar's decree for a census of the entire Roman Empire made it necessary for Joseph and Mary to leave Nazareth, their hometown, and travel the 70 miles to Bethlehem, the city of David.

BETH-LEHEM-JUDAH *See* BETH-LEHEM 1.

BETH MAACAH {house of MAACAH} The same as Abel Beth Maachah (2Sa. 20:14-15).

BETH MARCABOTH {site (house) of MARCABOTH (chariots)} An unidentified city in the tribal area of Simeon (Jos. 19:5; 1Ch. 4:31). †

BETH-MEON *See* BETH BAAL MEON, BAAL MEON

BETH MILLO {site (house) of MILLO (fill of dirt)}
1. An unidentified site near the ancient city of Shechem (Jdg. 9:6, 20). †
2. King Joash's officials assassinated him at "Beth Millo, on the road down to Silla" (2Ki. 12:20). †

BETH NIMRAH {*possibly* site (house) of NIMRAH (spotted leopard), BDB; house of a basin of clear, limpid water, KB} A town (210-146) in the tribal area of Sihon, king of Heshbon, on the E side of the Jordan (Nu. 32:36; Jos. 13:27). † *See* NIMRAH

BETH OPHRAH {site (house) of OPHRAH (dust)} The people of Samaria and Jerusalem are told to mourn in this city by the prophet Micah (Mic. 1:10). †

BETHPALET *See* BETH PELET

BETH PAZZEZ {site (house) of PAZ-ZEZ (scattering)} A town in the tribal area of Issachar (Jos. 19:21). †

BETH PELET {site (house) of PELET (escape)} A town in the tribal area of Judah near the border with Edom (Jos. 15:27). After the return from the Babylonian captivity, it was again occupied (Ne. 11:26). †

BETH PEOR {site (house) of PEOR} A city in the tribal area of Reuben E of the Jordan. The Israelites during their exodus from Egypt camped near there, and Moses was buried nearby (Jos. 13:20; Dt. 3:29; 4:46; 34:6). †

BETHPHAGE {site (house) of unripe figs} A village near Bethany and Jerusalem known in the Bible only from the references to it connected with the triumphal entry of Jesus to Jerusalem (Mt. 21:1; Mk. 11:1; Lk. 19:29). †

BETH-PHELET *See* BETH PELET

BETH RAPHA {site (house) of RAPHA (healing)} An unidentified site in the tribal area of Judah (1Ch. 4:12). †

BETH REHOB {site (house) of RE-HOB (main street, market)} An unidentified town in the upper Jordan Valley where inhabitants fought against David and were defeated (Jdg. 18:28; 2Sa. 10:6). †

BETHSAIDA {site (house) of fishing} The town of Philip, Andrew, and Peter on the northern shore of the Sea of Galilee. Jesus healed a blind man there (Mk. 8:22), and later denounced the city for its unbelief (Mt. 11:21).

BETH SHAN, BETH SHEAN {site (house) of SHAN (repose)} A city (197-212) long inhabited by man because of the warmth of its climate and the abundance of water. From the fourth millennium to about 1500 B.C. it was settled first by nomads and then by Canaanites. It was an important Egyptian fortress city for a time and was followed by Canaanite and then Philistine occupancy.

The Philistines placed the body of Saul on the city wall after they defeated Israel and killed the king. David finally captured it and it became important during Israelite times (Jos. 17:16; Jdg. 1:27; 1Sa. 31:10; 1Ki. 4:12). In NT times it was a Roman city called Scythopolis, one of the cities of the Decapolis.

BETH SHEMESH(ITE) {temple (house) of SHEMESH (pagan sun god)}
1. A city (147-128) located at the northern end of the western foothills (Shephelah) with a history going back to the fourth millennium B.C. It was in the area allocated to the tribe of Dan, but they were unable to drive its inhabitants out. This was the Ark's first stop when it was making its journey back from its Philistine captivity (Jos. 15:10; 1Sa. 6:9ff.). It is called Ir Shemesh or "sun city" (Jos. 19:41). Solomon made it an administrative center, but later King Ahaz lost it to the Philistines who held it until the Babylonians destroyed it in the sixth century.
2. A city (181-271) in the tribal area of Naphtali from which the Israelites were not able to drive out the natives but upon whom they put forced labor (Jos. 19:38; Jdg. 1:33).
3. A town (199-232) in the tribal area of Issachar (Jos. 19:22).

BETH SHITTAH {site (house) of SHITTAH (acacia trees)} An unidentified town in the Valley of Jezreel to which Gideon chased the defeated Midianites (Jdg. 7:22). †

BETH TAPPUAH {*possibly* site (house) of TAPPUAH (apricot) *prunus armeniaca*, IDB; (apple tree) *pyrusmalus*, BDB, ISBE, KB} A city (154-105) in the tribal area of Judah; also called Tappuah (Jos. 15:53; 1Ch. 2:43). †

BETH TOGARMAH {site (house) of TOGARMAH} *See* TOGARMAH

BETHUEL {man of El}
1. *See* BETHEL 2.
2. The father of Rebekah and nephew of Abraham (Ge. 22:23).

BETHUL *See* BETHEL 2.; BETHUEL

BETHZATHA The RSV and JB rendering based on a different Greek reading in Jn. 5:2. Most other major versions have "Bethesda."

BETH ZUR, BETHZUR A city (159-110) in the tribal area of Judah. Rehoboam fortified it, and it was still inhabited after the return from the Babylonian captivity (Jos. 15:58; 1Ch. 2:45; 2Ch. 11:7; Ne. 3:16). Here Judas Maccabeus defeated the Greek army under commander Lysias. Today it is called Beit Sur. †

BETONIM [pistachio nuts] A town (217-154) in the tribal area of Gad (Jos. 13:26). †

BETRAYAL To hand someone over into the enemies' possession is a betrayal. It is a sign of the end times that there will be betrayal (Mt. 24:10). Judas was the one who double-crossed Jesus for 30 shekels (Mt. 26:14-16; *cf.* Ex. 21:32; Zec. 11:12).

BETROTH To promise in marriage. *See* MARRIAGE

BETTING *See* LOT 3.

BEULAH [married] KJV, NIV for "married" (Isa. 62:4).

BEWARE *See* WATCH

BEYOND THE JORDAN *See* PERAEA

BEZAI
1. Head of a family that returned from the Babylonian captivity with Zerubbabel, (Ezr. 2:17; Ne. 7:23). †
2. One who signed the covenant with Nehemiah (Ne. 10:18). †

BEZALEEL, BEZALEL [in the shadow of El]
1. The chief architect of the tabernacle, a worker in wood, metal and precious stones (Ex. 31:1ff.).
2. An Israelite who married a foreign woman during the days of the Babylonian captivity (Ezr. 10:30).

BEZEK After the death of Joshua, it was here (187-197) that the men of Judah and Simeon defeated the Canaanites and Perizzites, and here Saul mustered the men for the battle to deliver Jabesh Gilead (Jdg. 1:4-5; 1Sa. 11:8-11). †

BEZER [(metallic) ore, *or* place of refuge]
1. A descendant of Asher (1Ch. 7:37).
2. A city (235-132) in the tribal area of Reuben E of the Jordan, which became a city of refuge (Dt. 4:43; Jos. 20:2, 8).

BIBLE *See* SCRIPTURE

BIBLE VERSIONS
ANCIENT VERSIONS
Aramaic Targums. As the Hebrew language became more remote to the common people, Aramaic was used to explain or paraphrase what the Scriptures meant. This was then put in written form.

Septuagint (LXX). The story is told in "The Letter to Aristeas" that in Egypt seventy (or seventy-two) translated the Hebrew Scriptures into Greek. This version, abbreviated "LXX," was often used by the NT authors. This version is often the bridge between Hebrew thought and the NT. There were other OT translations in Greek: Aquila's, Symmachus's and Theodotion's.

Old Latin. These are versions of the OT and NT prior to Jerome's Vulgate. The OT was based on the LXX, not the Hebrew Old Testament.

Vulgate. In A.D. 383 Eusebius Hieronymus, known today as Jerome, was asked to make a revision of the Old Latin versions, both OT and NT.

Old Syriac. A dialect of Aramaic, from the second century.

Peshitta was new Syriac from the fourth century A.D.

Coptic. A later form of Egyptian (from the hieroglyphic) developed in the Christian Era, written in the Greek alphabet. *Sahidic* and *Bohairic* are later dialects.

Gothic. Ufilas in about A.D. 375 translated the Scripture into Gothic (a Germanic tribe).

Miscellaneous. Armenian, Georgian,

Ethiopic, Slavonic, Arabic, Persian, Frankish, and many other translations were made throughout church history.

ENGLISH VERSIONS

1. Wyclif to the King James.

Wyclif's. The first English Bible, completed in 1382. John Pyrvey was credited with a complete revision in 1388. For 150 years this book was widely used and was the only Bible that was complete. It was an extremely literal rendering of the Latin Vulgate.

Tyndale's. In 1525 his NT was based on the Greek text and hence, according to his opponents, in "error" with the Vulgate rendering. He was a competent scholar. A great deal of KJV NT follows the Tyndale version. He completed only a portion of the OT. He was found guilty of heresy and put to death by strangling.

Coverdale's. In 1535 translated by Myles Coverdale, actually a revision of Tyndale's work.

Matthew's. In 1537 a revision of Tyndale's version by one pen named Thomas Matthew (actually John Rogers).

Taverner's Bible. A revision of Matthew's Bible by Richard Taverner.

The Great Bible. In 1539 a revision was made of the Matthew's Bible by Coverdale, supported by Cromwell. It was called the Great Bible because of its size. It became a popular version with the laity.

Geneva Bible. In 1560 this was a revision of the Great Bible with Tyndale's clear influence, but closer attention in the OT to the Hebrew text. This was the version used by the Pilgrims, John Bunyan, and King James himself.

Bishop's Bible. In 1568 this was the revision of the Great Bible by Bishops, not nearly as popular as the Geneva Bible.

Douai-Rheims. In 1609 a Roman Catholic version.

King James Bible. In 1611 King James sanctioned a new version to be made. Forty-seven scholars were commissioned to do the work. This version was to have no marginal notes (the Reformer's notes were sometimes too radical for the status quo) and was to be used in all the churches of England only in time of divine service. The Bishop's Bible was to be the basis of the work. Though not accepted for the first 50 years, this version has endured over the centuries to the present day. *See* AUTHORIZED VERSION

2. Some committee-made versions after the King James Bible.

The English Revised Version, the ERV, 1881. A committee work by 51 to 65 British and American scholars, who made as few changes as possible to the KJV while yet being true to the original. All changes were to be made by two-thirds majority vote.

The American Standard Version, the ASV, 1901. This was the American rendition of the 1881 version.

The Revised Standard Version, the RSV, 1946. This is a revision of the KJV, 1881, and 1901 versions. The New Revised Standard Version (NRSV), 1990, is a revision of the RSV.

The New American Standard Bible, the NASB, 1960. This was a revision, done by 58 translators, of the ASV, 1901.

The New English Bible, NEB, 1961. A completely new translation made by joint church committees from England, Scotland, and Ireland. A revision is to be published in the 1990s.

The Jerusalem Bible, the JB, 1966; (New Jerusalem Bible, 1985). An English adaption of the French *La Bible de Jerusalem.* A unique feature of this version is the rendering of the divine name of God as "Yahweh," instead of the usual "the LORD."

The New International Version, NIV, 1978. This version is a completely new translation, a trans-denominational effort by 115 translators in conjunction with the New York International Bible Society.

The New King James Version, NKJV, 1982. This is a partial revision of the KJV, done by 119 "translators," who removed some archaic word forms while maintaining essentially the same original text of the KJV.

TANAKH A single volume published

in 1985. This is a work of the threefold Jewish canon of Scripture, known to Christians as the OT. Fourteen translators and editors were involved over the last three decades in producing this work. (J.A.S.)

BIBLICAL CRITICISM *See* CRITICISM

BIBLICAL INTERPRETATION *See* HERMENEUTICS

BIBLICAL LANGUAGES Three primary languages comprise the Bible's writings. The OT was written primarily in Hebrew, and in certain verses and passages in Aramaic. The NT was written in Greek. The Bible also reflects (through loan words) the words, phrases, place names, and persons from many ancient cultures.

1. HEBREW LANGUAGE

Except for those passages listed under Aramaic Language, the OT was written in Hebrew. It is from the NW Semitic group of languages, akin to Ugaritic, Phoenician, Moabite, Edomite.

There are twenty-three consonants used in today's script. Some of the consonants can also be used as a kind of vowel. The vowel patterns were developed later in history to preserve the pronunciation of earlier times. There were three systems of vocalization developed, two with the vowels above the line, the Babylonian and Palestinian. The Tiberian system has the vowels under the line, also known as the Masoretic system. Most Hebrew texts today have the latter system. This form of vowel marking is sometimes the "culprit" behind differences in the pronounciation of some names and places (and spellings in English versions). This has also been the cause of several variant readings in various Hebrew manuscripts.

The Hebrew script does not look at all familiar to the Western eye; yet once the system is learned, it is certainly no less regular than the English language. The distinction that Hebrew is a "concrete" and "descriptive" language while Greek (in the NT) is an "abstract" language is an artificial distinction that is often repeated, yet without merit.

2. ARAMAIC LANGUAGE

A N Semitic language which was introduced to Syria and Mesopotamia by the Arameans. It became the *lingua franca* of the entire area until it was superseded by Greek after the conquest of Alexander the Great in the end of the fourth century B.C. As the Arameans were successful traders, their language as well as their trade went with them. The earliest extant inscriptions in this language go back to the ninth century B.C. It existed in a number of dialects and was written in a number of differing scripts; for example, the dialect and script of the brief passages of Aramaic in the Bible (Ezr. 4:8–6:18; 7:12-26; Jer. 10:11; Da. 2:4–7:28). In the NT a number of Aramaic words are also found (Mk. 5:41; 7:34; 15:34). It is probable that Jesus usually spoke this language, and sometimes also both Greek and Hebrew. Especially among some Middle East Christians, there is a debate as to whether the NT was written originally in Greek, Hebrew, or Aramaic. The last is the least likely.

3. GREEK LANGUAGE

The NT was written entirely in Greek. The biblical Greek of the NT was known as Koine (common) Greek of the day. At the turn of this century, discoveries of extrabiblical Greek gave new insights into the nature of biblical Greek. Some of the grammar and structure are common, yet much of the significant vocabulary and theological ideas (and some grammatical features) are from OT Hebrew. The Septuagint was a bridge between these two testaments. The language of biblical Greek has 24 vowels and letters, and many of the forms and sounds are familiar to the Western eye. A common misconception is that God choose Greek because it was a language with no ambiguity. Yet the language of the NT has ambiguities. The important thing is that the Greek language was *adequate* to communicate God's truths. (J.A.S.)

BIBLICAL MANUSCRIPTS

1. Old Testament Manuscripts
   a. Dead Sea Scrolls
   b. Masoretic Manuscripts
   c. Versions (See BIBLE VERSIONS)

2. New Testament Manuscripts
   a. Papyrus Manuscripts
   b. Major Uncial Manuscripts
   c. Versions (See BIBLE VERSIONS)

1. OLD TESTAMENT MANUSCRIPTS

a. The *Dead Sea Scrolls* are manuscripts that were found in caves W of the Dead Sea in 1947 and in subsequent years. The community that produced the scrolls lived in Qumran. The place is known today as Khirbet (ruin of) Qumran, two miles N of an oasis called Ain Feshka or En Feshka. The Dead Sea Scrolls consist of manuscripts containing portions of all the OT books except Esther. The largest portions come from the Pentateuch (especially Deuteronomy—25 manuscripts), the major Prophets (especially Isaiah—18 manuscripts), and Psalms (27 manuscripts). The Dead Sea Scrolls also consist of portions of the Septuagint, Targums, and Apocryphal fragments; a commentary on Habakkuk; and secular documents about the Qumran society. The Qumranic documents date between the third century B.C. and the first century A.D. The secular documents are of extreme importance because they shed much light on a period of Israel's history for which not too much written material exists. Prior to the discovery of the Dead Sea Scrolls, scholars possessed extant portions of the OT text in the Nash Papyrus (discovered in 1902, containing the Ten Commandments, dated around the second century B.C.), the Cairo Genizah Fragments (dated between the sixth and ninth centuries), and various Masoretic manuscripts (dated from the ninth century and later). Thus, the Dead Sea Scrolls are a very valuable tool for OT textual criticism.

b. *Masoretic Manuscripts* are those manuscripts produced by European Jewish scribes who, between the sixth and tenth centuries A.D., worked carefully to preserve the OT text as they transmitted it from copy to copy. (The Hebrew word *masora* means "that which is transmitted"; hence, the name—Masoretic Manuscripts.) Some of the more important Masoretic Manuscripts are the Cairo Codex of the Prophets (A.D. 895), containing the Prophets; the British Museum Codex Oriental 4445 (ninth/tenth century), containing a large portion of the Pentateuch; the Leningrad Codex of the Prophets (A.D. 916), containing the Major Prophets; the Leningrad Codex (A.D. 1008/9), having the complete OT text; and the Aleppo Codex (A.D. 900-925), originally containing the entire OT text but now with a quarter of its text missing—lost sometime during the days Israel was being founded as a state.

2. NEW TESTAMENT MANUSCRIPTS

a. *Papyrus Manuscripts.* During the past 100 years over ninety papyri fragments containing portions of the NT have been discovered in Egypt. Many of these manuscripts date between the second and fourth centuries; they, therefore, provide early testimony to the NT text. Some of the most important NT papyri are the Oxyrhynchus Papyri, the Chester Beatty Papyri, and the Bodmer Papyri. The Oxyrhynchus Papyri were discovered by Grenfell and Hunt in the ancient rubbish heaps of Oxyrhynchus, Egypt; this site yielded volumes of papyrus fragments containing all sorts of written material (literature, business and legal contracts, letters, etc.) in Koine Greek, as well as nearly thirty manuscripts containing portions of the NT. Some of the more noteworthy papyri are P1 (Matt. 1), P5 (Jn. 1, 16), P13 (Heb. 2-5, 10-12), and P22 (Jn. 15-16). The Chester Beatty Papyri (named after one of the owners, Chester Beatty) were purchased from a dealer in Egypt during the 1930s by Chester Beatty and by the University of Michigan. The three manuscripts in this collection are very early and contain a large portion of the NT text. P45 (third century) contains portions of all four Gospels and Acts; P46 (c. 200) has almost all of Paul's Epistles and Hebrews; and P47 (third century) contains Revelation 9–17. The Bodmer Papyri (named after the owner, M. Martin Bodmer) were purchased from a dealer in Egypt during the 1950s and 1960s. The three important papyri in this collection are P66 (c. 175, containing almost all of John), P72 (third century, having all of 1 and 2 Peter and Jude), and P75 (c. 200, containing large parts of Luke 3–John 14). The NT papyri have been very helpful in shaping modern editions of the Greek NT.

b. *Major Uncial Manuscripts.* Among the thousands of extant manuscripts having portions of the NT or the entire NT text, there are several noteworthy uncial manuscripts. (They are called "uncial" because the lettering was done with capital letters, as opposed to "minuscule" manuscripts—those written with small letters and/or in cursive. For the most part, uncial manuscripts date before the seventh century.) Two of the most important uncial manuscripts are Codex Sinaiticus and Codex Vaticanus. Codex Sinaiticus was discovered by Constantin von Tischendorf in St. Catherine's Monastery situated at the foot of Mt. Sinai. It dates around A.D. 350, contains the entire NT, and provides an early and fairly reliable witness to the NT autographs. Codex Vaticanus had been in the Vatican's library since at least 1481, but it was not made available to scholars (like Tischendorf and Tregelles) until the middle of the nineteenth century. This codex, dated slightly earlier than Sinaiticus, has both the OT and NT in Greek, excluding the last part of the NT (from Heb. 9:15 to the end of Rev.) and the Pastoral Epistles. For the most part, scholars have commended Codex Vaticanus for being one of the most trustworthy witnesses to the NT text. Other noteworthy uncial manuscripts are Codex Alexandrinus (fifth century, displaying nearly all of the NT), Codex Ephraemi Rescriptus (a fifth-century document containing

a large portion of the NT—partially erased and written upon with the sermons of St. Ephraem—later deciphered by the painstaking efforts of Tischendorf and the use of chemicals), Codex Bezae (a fifth-century manuscript named after Theodore Beza, its "discoverer," containing the Gospels and Acts and displaying a text quite different from the manuscripts mentioned above), and the Freer Codex (a fifth-century manuscript housed in Washington D.C., Smithsonian Institute, containing the Gospels). These manuscripts have been very instrumental in the formation of critical editions of the Greek NT. (P.W.C.)

BIBLIOLATRY The worship of the Bible, as opposed to the God of the Bible. Note, though, that all that is known about the Christian God comes from the Bible. To believe his Word is true, authoritative, and without error is not necessarily bibliolatry.

ΚΑΙΟΜΟΛΟΓΟΥΜε
ΝωϹΜΕΓΑΕϹΤΙΝ
ΤΟΤΗϹΕΥϹΕΒΕΙΑϹ
ΜΥϹΤΗΡΙΟΝΟϹΕ
ΦΑΝΕΡωΘΗΕΝϹΑΡ
ΚΙ·ΕΔΙΚΑΙωΘΗΕΝ
ΠΝΙωΦΘΗΑΓΓΕΛΟΙϹ
ΕΚΗΡΥΧΘΗΕΝΕ
ΘΝΕϹΙΝΕΠΙϹΤΕΥ
ΘΗΕΝΚΟϹΜω·
ΑΝΕΛΗΜΦΘΗΕΝ
ΔΟΞΗ

Codex Sinaiticus, showing 1 Timothy 3:16, which in this manuscript reads, "And confessedly great is the mystery of godliness: who was manifested in flesh, justified in spirit, seen by angels, proclaimed among nations, believed [on] in the world, taken up in glory."

Codex Alexandrinus, showing Acts 20:28, which in this manuscript reads, "Take heed to your-selves and to all the flock, among which the Holy Spirit has made you overseers, to shepherd the church of the Lord [other manuscripts read "God"], which he purchased with his own blood."

Codex Vaticanus, showing Psalm 1:1-3.

BIBLIOLOGY *See* SYSTEMATIC THEOLOGY

BICHRI, BICRI [first born] The father of Sheba who mounted an unsuccessful revolt against King David (2Sa. 20:1-22). †

BIDKAR [son of DEKER (piercing)] The military aide of Jehu before the latter became king (2Ki. 9:25). †

BIER A portable framework for the transport of the dead before burial (2Sa. 3:31; 2Ch. 16:14; translated "coffin" in Lk. 7:14).

BIG-BANG THEORY A theory of how the universe as we now know it came into being, with all matter concentrated in one place, superdense. As a result of an explosion, matter became spread throughout what is now the universe, which is continuing to expand. The big-bang theory is also known as the superdense-state theory. This theory cannot explain the axiom that "something cannot come from nothing." Even this superdense particle could not have eternally existed. A God-created universe is still the best explanation for the origin of the world.

BIGTHA A eunuch of King Xerxes in Susa (Est. 1:10). †

BIGTHAN, BIGTHANA One of the officers of the Persian King Xerxes who plotted against his monarch and was killed for it (Est. 2:21-23; 6:2). †

BIGVAI

1. One who returned with Zerubbabel from the Babylonian captivity (Ezr. 2:2).

2. One who signed the covenant with Nehemiah (Ne. 10:16).

BIKATH AVEN *See* AVEN 1.

BILDAD [Bel (pagan deity) has loved] One of Job's friends (Job 2:11; 8:1; 18:1; 25:1; 42:9). †

BILEAM [(a gift) brought to the people] A city of refuge in the tribal area of Manasseh (1Ch. 6:70). †

BILGAH, BILGAI [gleam, smile]

1. A priest in David's time (1Ch. 24:14). †

2. A priest who returned from the Babylonian captivity with Zerubbabel (Ne. 12:5, 18); also called Bilgai in Ne. 10:8. †

BILHAH

1. *See* BAALAH 3.

2. Rachel's maidservant who became a concubine of her husband, Jacob, and bore Dan and Naphtali. Later her stepson Reuben also had relations with her (Ge. 29:29; 30:58; 35:22).

BILHAN

1. A Horite chief (Ge. 36:27; 1Ch. 1:42). †

2. A descendant of Benjamin (1Ch. 7:10). †

BILSHAN [their BEL (lord)] A leader who returned with Zerubbabel from the Babylonian captivity (Ezr. 2:2; Ne. 7:7). †

BIMHAL [son of circumcision] A descendant of Asher (1Ch. 7:33). †

BINDING AND LOOSING *See* KEY, KEY OF THE KINGDOM

BINEA A descendant of Saul and Jonathan (1Ch. 8:37; 9:43). †

BINNUI [a son]

1. Father of a priest in Ezra's temple (Ezr. 8:33). †

2. One who worked on the city wall after the return from the Babylonian captivity (Ne. 3:18, 24; 10:9); also called Bavvai in some Hebrew manuscripts. †

3. Ancestor of some who returned from the captivity with Zerubbabel; also called Bani (Ezr. 2:10; Ne. 7:15). †

4 and 5. One who married a foreign wife during the Babylonian captivity and the ancestor of such a one (Ezr. 10:30, 38). †

6. A Levite who came back from the captivity with Zerubbabel (Ne. 12:8). †

BIRDS It is important to note that often the exact identity of the bird species is not known (*see* IBIS for a sampling of unclean birds in Lev. 11:14ff.).

1. *Bat.* A mammal that flies, and for that reason is listed with birds.

2. *Cock, Hen, Rooster* (Mt. 26:34; Pr. 30:31; Mt. 23:37). Their eggs were used for food (Job 6:6; Lk. 11:12). The crowing of a cock is mentioned in one significant incident—Peter's denial of Jesus (Mt. 26:34, 74-75).

3. *Cormorant.* One of a family of large sea birds that feed on fish; it is mentioned in the passages where the unclean birds are listed—the birds that observant Jews could not eat (Lev. 11:13-19; Dt. 14:12-18).

Cormorant

4. *Dove, Partridge, Pigeon, Quail, Swift, Thrush, Turtledove.* Birds not

found in the list of unclean animals. The *Dove, Turtledove,* and *Pigeon* were used in making sacrifices. The word translated "dove" is loosely applied to a number of smaller species of pigeon. It is used to symbolize innocence and purity (Lev. 1:14; 14:22). The *Partridge* was hunted in the mountains (1Sa. 26:20), and the *Quail,* which seems to be a small type of *Partridge,* appears in the account of the feeding of the Israelites in the wilderness wanderings (Ex. 16:13; Nu. 11:31). The *Swift* and *Thrush* are noted in Isa. 38:14.

quite likely the ostrich. Some were tall, wading birds with long bills, necks, legs, and wings. What we may know of most of them (not those with varieties) may be learned from any standard dictionary or encyclopedia on birds. Some are water birds, of course, and others are birds of prey on land. Special mention of the *Eagle* and *Falcon* may be seen in Dt. 28:40; 32:11; Job 28:7; 39:26; Eze. 17:3; Pr. 30:17. The *Hoopoe* has a head crest of erectile plumes and a long, curved bill.

Kite

Rock Dove

Osprey (or Fishhawk)

Partridge

5. *Eagle, Falcon, Gull, Hawk, Heron, Hoopoe, Black and Red Kites, Osprey, Owl, Stork, Vulture, Black Vulture.* All of these are unclean birds—it was forbidden to eat them. They are all listed as such in Lev. 11:13-19 and Dt. 14:12-18. The precise identification of some of these birds in modern terminology is uncertain. There are six varieties of *Owls* listed: *Little, Horned, Screech, Great, White, Desert.* One of these is

6. *Ostrich.* A large desert bird that inhabits waste places.

It is described as a swift runner, faster than a horse, and lays its eggs in the open; it is an unclean bird (Job 39:13-18).

7. *Peacock.* In the NIV translated twice "baboons" and once as "ostrich" (1Ki. 10:22; Job 39:13).

8. *Raven.* An unclean bird (Lev. 11:15). In the OT some of its features are used for illustrations: the black locks of hair, its nesting in lonely places, its be-

ing fed by God (SS. 5:11; Isa. 34:11; Ps. 147:9). Jesus used the ravens to illustrate God's provision (Lk. 12:24). It was a raven that was sent out first from Noah's ark (Ge. 8:7). Elijah was fed by them (1Ki. 17:4-6).

9. *Sparrow.* The Hebrew word rendered "sparrow" (Ps. 84:3) is often translated "bird" or "fowl" in the Bible. This bird was commonly sold in the market (Lk. 12:6-7).

10. *Swallow.* A bird noted for its swift flight (Pr. 26:2), often used in parallel with the sparrow (Ps. 84:3). The meaning of the Hebrew word in contemporary terminology is not certain.

BIRSHA {disagreeable in taste} The king of Gomorrah (Ge. 14:2). †

BIRTH *See* SWADDLING CLOTHES

BIRTHDAY Specific celebrations of birthdays are mentioned for the Pharaoh of Egypt and King Herod Antipas, but not in general (Ge. 40:20; Mt. 14:6; Mk. 6:21).

BIRTHRIGHT The portion of the inheritance of the firstborn son (Dt. 21:17). The inheritance was divided into portions, with the firstborn receiving two portions or a double portion. Esau sold his birthright to Jacob (Ge. 25:29-33); it could be lost by misconduct (1Ch. 5:1). *See* INHERITANCE

BIRTHSTOOL *See* STOOL

BIRZAITH, BIRZAVITH {well of olive oil} A descendant of Asher (1Ch. 7:31). † /

BISHLAM {son of SHALOM (peace)} An officer of the Persian king who was opposed to the rebuilding of Jerusalem (Ezr. 4:7). †

BISHOP *See* OVERSEER

BIT *See* BRIDLE

BITHIAH {*possibly* worshiper of Yahweh, BDB; (female pagan god) queen, KB} A daughter of Pharaoh who married a Jew (1Ch. 4:18). †

BITHRON {gully} KJV, NIV, NKJV, ASV in 2Sa. 2:29. The RSV renders as "forenoon," NASB, NEB, JB "all morning." The NIV notes this can mean "ravine" or "morning."

BITHYNIA A region in NW Asia Minor where Paul and Timothy wished to go but were forbidden by the Spirit (Ac. 16:7). *See also* 1Pe. 1:1. †

BITTER HERBS *See* PLANTS, PERFUMES, AND SPICES

BITTER WATERS *See* JEALOUSY, WATER OF

BITTERN *See* BIRDS 5., *owl* (NIV)

BIZIOTHIAH, BIZJOTHJAH A town in the tribal area of Judah in the south (Jos. 15:28). † This can be vocalized in the Hebrew as "and her daughters" (i.e., surrounding villages) and is so translated in both an ancient version and the NEB. Every major modern English version transliterates this word, contra NEB, and gives no footnote with "and her daughters" as an alternative rendering.

BIZTHA One of the eunuchs of the Persian king Xerxes (Est. 1:10). †

BLACKSMITH A general word for craftsman in iron, a forger of items both for domestic use and warfare (1Sa. 13:19; Isa. 44:12; 54:16).

BLAINS KJV for a festering sore related to a boil (Ex. 9:9-10). *See* SICK, SICKNESS 1.

BLASPHEMY {speak reviling} Dishonoring and reviling the name, work, or being of God by word or deed. It is sometimes translated "cursed" or "profaned" (1Ki. 21:10, 13; Isa. 52:5; Eze. 20:27; 36:20). Death by stoning was the penalty (Lev. 24:16). *See* CURSE

BLASPHEMY AGAINST THE HOLY SPIRIT To speak evil of the Holy Spirit, a sin referred to by Jesus in Mt. 12:31; Mk. 3:28-29; Lk. 12:10. To attribute the works of Christ, done in the power of the Holy Spirit, to Satan is not forgiven. This was likely not a single occurrence but an ongoing process of hardening of the heart toward Christ. Christ offers forgiveness to all who ask. To ask the question in concern of your relationship to Christ, "Have I committed the unpardonable sin?" shows that you have not. Peter denied Christ, yet continued in the faith (Jn. 18:15).

BLASTUS [sprout (of a vine, branch)] A trusted personal servant of Herod Agrippa who acted as an intermediary for the people of Tyre and Sidon (Ac. 12:20). † *See* CHAMBERLAIN

BLEMISH *See* SICK, SICKNESS

BLESS, BLESSING The word *bless* and its derivatives in both Testaments are synonyms for the word *happy* (Ge. 30:13). In the Beatitudes it has this meaning in Mt. 5:3-12. It also denotes thanks to God (Mt. 26:26). To bless someone is to ask divine favor on that one (Ps. 129:8). Blessings are gifts from God or man. In Jos. 15:19 the Hebrew word is translated "special favor."

The blessing given to the firstborn was highly coveted and not to be revoked. To be given the blessing was to receive a position of power and favor (Ge. 27:1ff.). Jacob gives out the blessings in Ge. 49:1ff., and Moses the tribes (Dt. 33:1ff.). Note that Reuben and Simon and Levi were not given the blessing of the firstborn for their deeds; rather Judah was. *See also* FIRSTBORN

BLESSING, THE CUP OF The cup of thanksgiving (NIV). *See* LORD'S SUPPER

BLINDNESS Blindness in the Bible is often thought to be caused by sin (Ex. 4:11; Jn. 9:2). It is a punishment for evil—by God (Ge. 19:11; Ac. 13:11) and by man (Jdg. 16:21). It was a sign of disgrace to have your eye gouged out (1Sa. 11:2). In Semitic hyperbole (exaggeration), Jesus said it is preferable to self-induce blindness than to continue in sin (Mt. 5:29). *See also* DISEASE; SICK, SICKNESS

BLOOD In the OT the picture presented is of life in the blood and the blood itself was life. It could not be eaten, and it was the blood that made atonement (Ge. 9:46; Lev. 17:11, 14; Dt. 12:23). "Whoever sheds the blood of man, by man shall his blood be shed." The offering of blood was part of the ritual of atonement so that when the sacrifice was killed its blood had to be poured out on the altar (Ex. 24:8; 29:12, 16, 20; Lev. 16:15-16, 27).

In the NT it was the blood of Jesus Christ that made the atonement, which means that his death was considered a sacrifice, and the blood was poured out to make the atonement. Life is in the blood; there can be no remission of sin without its being shed. Therefore, it required the death of a lamb without blemish or defect to make the sacrifice in OT times. That is why Christ is called both sinless and the Lamb of God (Heb. 9.11-14, 22; 10:19; 1Pe. 1:19; 1Jn. 1:7). *See* LIFE

BLOOD, AVENGER OF *See* AVENGER OF BLOOD

BLOOD, FIELD OF *See* AKELDAMA

BLOOD, ISSUE OF *See* DISEASE

BLOODGUILT *See* AVENGER OF BLOOD

BLOODY SWEAT *See* DISEASE

BLUE *See* COLORS

BOANERGES [sons of thunder] A nickname of the Zebedee brothers (Mk. 3:17). † For the meaning of "son of" *see* BAR

BOAR *See* BEASTS 10.

BOAST *See* PRIDE

BOAT *See* SHIP

BOAZ
1. A Bethlehemite who married Ruth the Moabitess after the death of her husband. From the descendants of this union came King David and Jesus (Ru. 4:1-10, 18-21; Mt. 1:5-6). *See* MARRIAGE, *kinsman-redeemer*; RUTH
2. The name of one of the two bronze

pillars that stood in the vestibule of Solomon's temple (1Ki. 7:15-22).

BOAZ AND JACHIN *See* TEMPLE

BOCHERU *See* BOKERU

BOCHIM *See* BOKIM

BODY *See* FLESH

BODY OF CHRIST
1. The corporal body of Christ that died on the cross (Mt. 27:59; Jn. 2:21; Heb. 10:10).
2. The mystical body of Christ, *See* COMMUNION, VIEWS OF.
3. The church of Christ referred to as the body of Christ, stressing unity (Ro. 12:5; 1Co. 12:13, 27; Eph. 1:23; 2:16; 3:6; 4:4, 12, 16; 5:30; Col. 1:18-24; 2:19; 3:15).

BODY LIFE *See* ONE ANOTHER

BOHAN {thumb, big toe} A son of Reuben; his stone (landmark) was on the border between Judah and Benjamin (Jos. 15:6; 18:17). †

BOIL *See* SICK, SICKNESS

BOKERU {his first born} descendant of Jonathan (1Ch. 8:38; 9:44). †

BOKIM {weepings} An unidentified site near Gilgal where men wept (*bokim*) because of Israel's disobedience to God (Jdg. 2:15). †

BONDAGE *See* SLAVE, SLAVERY

BONDMAID, BONDMAN, BOND-SERVANT, BONDWOMAN *See* SLAVE

BONES In the OT often a synonym for "body" (Ps. 42:10). The dry bones of Ezekiel's vision represent the scattered Israelites in exile, and their coming together represents the regathering and coming to life again of Israel (Eze. 37). It was required that no bone of a sacrificial animal could be broken. In the NT the fact that no bone of Jesus was broken in his death was considered the fulfillment of prophecy, as he was the sacrifice (Ex. 12:46; Ps. 34:20; Jn. 19:36). *See also* FLESH

BOOK A scroll of vellum or parchment (treated animal skins). A modern bound book of pages (codex) is not the same form as an ancient book. *See* PAPYRUS; PARCHMENT; SCROLL; WRITING

BOOK OF LIFE An ancient register for the cities' population (Ps. 69:28; Isa. 4:3). A heavenly register of the heavenly citizens who possess everlasting life (Da. 12:1; Lk. 10:20; Php. 4:3; Heb. 12:23; Rev. 13:8; 17:8; 20:15; 21:27). *See also* SCROLL

BOOTH A crude temporary shelter for man or animal to keep off the sun (Ge. 33:17; Jnh. 4:5). This cover was probably made out of interwoven branches (Ne. 8:15). It was a special festival shelter at the harvest feast, as a reminder of the Exodus by their forefathers (Lev. 23:42; Ne. 8:14ff.).

BOOTHS, FEAST OF *See* CALENDAR and FESTIVALS 6.

BOOTY *See* PLUNDER

BOOZ *See* BOAZ

BOR ASHAN {pit of smoke} An unidentified site to which David sent part of the plunder after his return to Ziklag from fighting the Philistines (1Sa. 30:30). †

BORN AGAIN The term Jesus said in Jn. 3:3. It can also be translated "born from above." It is also a theological phrase generally referring to the act of regeneration through the Holy Spirit (Tit. 3:5). *See* BAPTISM; GOD, NAMES OF; GODHEAD 6., *Holy Spirit*

BORN OF GOD *See* CHRIST, WORK OF

BORN OF THE SPIRIT *See* BAPTISM; GOD, NAMES OF; GODHEAD 6., *Holy Spirit*

BORROW, BORROWING *See* DEBT

BOSCATH *See* BOZKATH

BOSOM, ABRAHAM'S *See* ABRAHAM'S SIDE

BOSOR *See* BEOR 1.

BOSSES KJV for "strong" in reference to the center of a shield (Job 15:26, NIV).

BOTCH *See* SICK, SICKNESS 1., *Boil*

BOTTLE *See* POTTER, POTTERY; FLASK; VESSEL; WINESKIN

BOTTOMLESS PIT *See* DEAD, ABODE OF, *Abyss*

BOUNDARY STONES Stones could be markers of boundaries (Jos. 15:6; 18:17) and it was forbidden to remove them (Dt. 19:14; Pr. 22:28).

BOW THE KNEE *See* WORSHIP

BOW, OF BOAT Ac. 27:30, 41. *See* SHIP

BOW, WEAPON *See* ARMS AND ARMOR

BOWELS *See* EMOTIONS

BOWL These vessels could be made of gold or other metal, but the vast majority were made of baked clay. Some were glazed and some painted. It is by the glazing and painting on bowls and sherds (broken pieces of these vessels) that archaeologists date some of the strata in their excavations. *See* ARCHAEOLOGY; POTTER, POTTERY; VESSEL

BOWLS OF WRATH *See* REVELATION, *Chaps. 15-19*

BOX The Hebrew word is also translated "chest," "horn," and "flask" (1Sa. 6:8; 2Ki. 9:1; 1Ki. 1:39). The woman who anointed Jesus had an ointment-filled alabaster box (jar) (Mt. 26:7).

BOXING *See* ATHLETE

BOX-TREE KJV for "cypress" in Isa. 41:19. *See* TREES

BOZEZ {oozy place} One of the two steep cliffs which were landmarks near Michmash (1Sa. 14:4-5). †

BOZKATH {"swollen," elevated spot} An unidentified site in Judah (Jos. 15:39; 2Ki. 22:1). †

BOZRAH {enclosure (for sheep), fortress}
1. A city (289-214) in Moab E of the Jordan (Jer. 48:24).
2. An important Edomite city (208-016) at the junction of the Kings Highway and the Way of Shur (Isa. 63:1). Its destruction was foretold in Jer. 49:13.

BRACELET A common adornment worn on the lower arm by both men and women, made of gold in the case of luxury but usually of iron, silver, or glass (Ge. 24:47; Eze. 16:11). *See* ORNAMENTS

BRAMBLE *See* PLANTS, PERFUMES, AND SPICES, Spiny Plants

BRANCH A number of different Hebrew words are translated into English as *branch* (Ge. 40:10; Ex. 25:33; Jer. 11:16). Some are used figuratively in the sense of "offspring" or even "head," and some designate the messianic King who is to come (Job 15:32; Isa. 9:14; 11:1; Jer. 33:15). In the NT it is frequently used to refer to disciples. Christ is the vine, and the disciples are the branches (Jn. 15:5).

BRASEN *See* BRONZE; PRECIOUS STONES AND METALS 1.

BRASS, BRASSWORKER KJV for "bronze." Brass is an alloy of copper and zinc; bronze is an alloy of copper and tin. *See* BRONZE; PRECIOUS STONES AND METALS 1.

BRAZEN SEA *See* SEA, MOLTON

BRAZEN SERPENT *See* SERPENTS, FIERY

BREAD A basic staple in the diet of ancient Israel usually made from wheat or barley. It was made by being ground in a mill and rubbed between two stones or by being beaten in a mortar with a pestle and then kneaded in a kneading-trough. Unleavened bread was baked immediately after grinding without the use of yeast, and it was this bread that was used at Passover and during the Feast of Unleavened Bread. It could be baked as small cakes (like modern pancakes) on a griddle placed over a fire (Lev. 2:5), on hot coals (1Ki. 19:6), or in an oven (Lev. 2:4). Archaeologists have discovered numerous ovens, circular in shape. The fire was built inside the circular clay oven; and when the clay walls were hot, the wet dough would be stuck on the hot clay sides until it dropped off when cooked. Bread was baked by both women and men (Ge. 40:16; Jer. 37:21). In the NT Christ presents himself as the "bread of life" (Jn. 6:35). He who believes in Christ is said to partake of this "heavenly bread" and will live forever (Jn. 6:50-51). *See* OVEN

BREAD, SHEW *See* SHOWBREAD, SHEWBREAD

BREAKFAST *See* MEALS

BREAKING OF BREAD *See* COMMUNION, VIEWS OF; LORD'S SUPPER

BREASTPIECE Its exact structure and composition are unknown, but it was a part of the high priest's garment, made of the best of fabrics (Ex. 28:15) and was attached to the ephod by four golden rings (*see* EPHOD). On it were two jewels, each one bearing on it the name of six of the tribes of Israel. The Urim and the Thummim were in it, and the high priest would bear these and the names of the tribes before the LORD when he entered the Holy Place (Ex. 28:29-30). *See* URIM AND THUMMIM

BREASTPLATE *See* ARMS AND ARMOR

BREATH *See* GOD, NAMES OF, GODHEAD 6.

BREECHES *See* DRESS, *Undergarments*

BRETHREN OF THE LORD Brothers of Jesus: James, Joseph, Simon, and Judas (Mt. 13:55). It is significant that "his brothers" did not believe in him until after his resurrection (Jn. 7:1, 3-5; Ac. 1:14), and that they are distinguished from the apostles (1Co. 9:5).

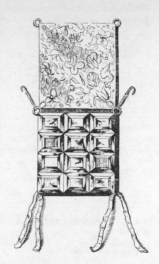

The High Priest's Breastpiece

BRIBE The giving of a gift intended to influence the recipient in his exercise of a legal duty (1Sa. 8:3). Bribery was prohibited in Israel (Ex. 23:8).

BRICK Bricks were a common building material in the ancient world. The bricks could be quite durable if dried in the sun, but kilning was also practiced. Straw or vegetable matter made the bricks stronger and of better consistency. Bricks came in all different sizes, but generally Near Eastern bricks were larger than a commonly perceived fireplace brick of today (Ge. 11:3; Ex. 5:7-19). *See* POTTER, POTTERY

BRIDE, BRIDECHAMBER KJV for "bridegroom" (Mt. 9:15; Mk. 2:19; Lk. 5:34).

BRIDE OF CHRIST A expression for the church (2Co. 11:2; Rev. 19:7; 21:2, 9; 22:17).

BRIDECHAMBER *See* MARRIAGE

BRIDLE, BIT As we know them today, these were also used in biblical times.

The words are used both in a literal and figurative sense (Ps. 32:9; Isa. 30:28).

BRIER *See* PLANTS, PERFUMES, AND SPICES, Spiny Plants

BRIMSTONE The word rendered *brimstone* in some versions is translated in the NIV as "sulphur," usually found in volcanic areas. The destruction of Sodom and Gomorrah was by fire and sulphur (Ge. 19:24, 28), which could have resulted from a volcanic eruption or even an earthquake that released sulfuric gases that killed the people. "Fire and brimstone"(burning sulphur) as a method of divine punishment is also found in Rev. 14:10; 19:20.

BRONZE An alloy or mixture of copper and tin. Brass is a mixture of copper and zinc, which was not used in biblical times. Bronze has also a reference to hardness (Lev. 26:19), or obstinacy in sin (Isa. 48:4-5).

BROOK Several Hebrew words are so translated into English. One is a perennial stream, brook, or river as we know it (Ps. 42:1). The others are what are called in the Middle East *wadis*, which are stream beds, dry except immediately after rain (Dt. 2:13; 2Sa. 15:23).

BROOM Broom is mentioned in Isa. 14:23. It is implied in other passages (Mt. 12:44). For broom tree or broom bush, *See* PLANTS, PERFUMES, AND SPICES, Miscellaneous Plants 2.

BROTHER *See* SISTER

BROTHER-IN-LAW, DUTY OF *See* MARRIAGE

BUBASTIS *See* PI BESETH

BUCKET OR PAIL *See* PITCHER; POTTER, POTTERY

BUCKLER *See* ARMS AND ARMOR

BUDDHISM An Eastern religion founded by Siddhartha Gautama (about 566-486 B.C.). Buddhist teaching rests on four "excellent truths":

1. All existence involves suffering.

2. Suffering can be ended if desire is conquered.

3. There is an eightfold path to the conquering of desire.

4. This path consists of right views, intentions, speech, action, livelihood, effort, mindfulness, and concentration. The goal of the Buddhist is to escape from the chain of reincarnations to nirvana, where there is cessation of desire. Buddhism and Christianity differ on many basic concepts of who God is and how to relate to him. Self-effort is Buddhistic; Christ's effort for us is Christian. *See also* REINCARNATION

BUILD UP *See* EDIFICATION

BUKKI [proved of Yahweh, BDB; mouth (gurgle sounds) of Yahweh, ISBE]

1. The representative of the tribe of Dan in the dividing of the land of Canaan (Nu. 34:22). †

2. A descendant of Aaron (Ezr. 7:4; 1Ch. 6:5, 51). †

BUKKIAH [proved of Yahweh] A Levite leader of the temple musicians (1Ch. 25:4, 13). †

BUL *See* CALENDAR

BULL, BULLOCK *See* BEASTS 4.

BULRUSH *See* PLANTS, PERFUMES, AND SPICES, Flowering Plants 5.

BUNAH A descendant of Judah (1Ch. 2:25). †

BUNNI

1. A Levite who was with Ezra when the law was read (Ne. 9:4). †

2. One who sealed the covenant with Nehemiah (Ne. 10:15). †

3. Another leader (Ne. 11:15). † *See* BANI

BURDEN KJV for "utterance, the Word of the LORD." *See* ORACLE

BURIAL To the Israelite, burial was very important. Not to be buried was a curse (Ps. 79:3; Isa. 14:18-20). After death the eyes were closed by a relative or friend, and the body was washed, anointed, wrapped in linen with a special cloth over the head, and placed in a room of the house until the time of interment (burial), which usually took place on the same day (Ge. 46:4; Mk. 16:1; Mt. 27:59; Jn. 11:44; Ac. 9:37). Friends followed the bier to the grave or tomb (2Sa. 3:31; Jdg. 8:32). *See also* CAVE

The only biblical allusion to Egyptian embalming concerns Joseph's bones (Ge. 50:2-3, 26; Jos. 24:32). He probably was mummified. The Israelites did not practice this elaborate process.

BUSH *See* PLANTS

BUSHEL *See* WEIGHTS AND MEASURES

BUSINESS *See* OCCUPATIONS AND PROFESSIONS; TRADE

BUTLER *See* CUPBEARER

BUTTER KJV for "curds" or "curdled milk" (NIV). *See* FOOD

BUY *See* RANSOM; REDEEMER; REDEEMING THE TIME

Ancient Jewish Funeral Procession

BURNING *See* FIRE

BURNING BUSH A bush that burned but was not consumed, in which the angel of the LORD appeared (Ex. 3:2-3; Dt. 33:16; Mk. 12:26). This was a crucial event in the life of Moses and was where God revealed his personal name. *See* ANGEL; GOD, NAMES OF; GODHEAD 2.; MOSES

BURNT OFFERING *See* SACRIFICES AND OFFERINGS

BURNT SACRIFICE *See* SACRIFICES AND OFFERINGS

BUZ [contempt]
1. A nephew of Abraham (Ge. 22:21). †
2. A descendant of Dan (1Ch. 5:14). †
3. A place (Jer. 25:23). †

BUZI [contempt] The father of the prophet Ezekiel (Eze. 1:3). †

BUZZARD *See* BIRDS 5.

BYBLOS *See* GEBAL

BYSSUS *See* LINEN

BYWAYS KJV for "winding paths" (Jdg. 5:6).

C

CAB *See* WEIGHTS AND MEASURES

CABBON An unidentified site in Judah in the western foothills (Jos. 15:40). †

CABUL
1. A town in the tribal area of Asher (Jos. 19:27). †
2. A part of the tribal area of Naphtali which Solomon gave to Hiram, king of Tyre, but which he refused to accept (1Ki. 9:13; cf. 2Ch. 8:2). †

CAESAR The family name of a series of Roman emperors: Octavius (Augustus), Tiberius, Caligula, Claudius, and Nero. They were all related in some way to Julius Caesar and bore his name. Later the term became a title by which the emperor of Rome was designated. *See* EMPEROR; ROME

CAESAREA A coastal city NW of Jerusalem built by Herod the Great on the site of an earlier Phoenician port, also of major importance in NT times. After Herod, it became the capital of the Roman province of Palestine. Here Herod Agrippa I was struck with blindness (Ac. 12:19-23). An inscription bearing the name of Pontius Pilate was discovered there by archaeologists. An early Christian, Philip, lived there (Ac. 8:40; 21:8). It was the home of the centurion Cornelius who sent for Peter (Ac. 10:1ff). Paul was in prison there for two years before being sent on to Rome (Ac. 24:27; 27:1-2).

CAESAREA PHILIPPI One of the main sources of the water of the river Jordan comes out of the rocks at the foot of Mt. Hermon, which in antiquity had the name Paneas after the Roman god Pan. Herod the Great built a temple there and his son Philip enlarged the city, naming it after the Roman emperor Tiberius Caesar. Jesus visited the city with his disciples (Mt. 16:13; Mk. 8:27). †

CAIAPHAS A son-in-law of the high priest Annas, who was appointed to his post by the Romans (Jn. 18:13). He made the statement, "It is better for you that one man die for the people than that the whole nation perish" (Jn. 11:49-50). After Jesus' arrest and appearance before Annas, he was taken to Caiaphas, who sent him onto Pilate (Jn. 18:28-29). He also sat on the trial of Peter (Ac. 4:6). *See* CHIEF PRIESTS; PRIESTS

CAIN {metal worker, BDB and KB; brought forth, acquired—Ge. 4:1} The first son of Adam and Eve, a tiller of the soil, who killed his brother Abel—being jealous because God received Abel's offering but not his own (Ge. 4:1-8). (Most sources say his name in the Hebrew comes from a root that means "metal worker, iron smith," or possibly a noun, "spear." The writer of Genesis used a similar sounding root to a word play: "to get, to acquire.") *See* KAIN

CAINAN {worker in iron, metal worker} An ancestor of Jesus (Lk. 3:36-37; cf. Ge. 10:24; 11:12 in the LXX). † *See* KENAN

CALAH [strength, vigor] A city of Mesopotamia founded by the hunter Nimrod (Ge. 10:11-12). †

CALAMUS *See* PLANTS, PERFUMES, AND SPICES

CALCOL One of the wise men of whom it is said that Solomon was wiser (1Ki. 4:31; 1Ch. 2:6). †

CALDRON The English translation of several words used for cooking pots (1Sa. 2:14).

CALEB [dog, BDB; the snappish, warding off, KB] One of the twelve spies sent by Moses to spy out the land of Canaan, and one of two who brought back a good report. For this he was promised entrance into the Land of Canaan while all the others of his age died in the wilderness. Joshua gave him Hebron, and in turn Caleb gave Debir to his daughter and son-in-law (Nu.13:2ff.; 14:24; Jos. 14:13ff.; 15:15ff.). A variant Hebrew spelling is Kelubai (1Ch. 2:9).

CALEB-EPHRATAH 1Ch. 2:24. *See* EPHRATAH 2.

CALENDAR A calendar is a system of reckoning time, with special references to the limits and subdivisions of the year. Throughout its history, biblical Israel based its calendar upon solar years with their changing seasons. Thus the very name for year in Hebrew, *shana*, means "change," in contrast with Egypt's system of a slowly shifting date for New Year's.

Originally, "the end of the year" seems to have occurred after the fall harvest in September or October (Ex. 23:16; 34: 22); but from the Exodus onward, Passover (spring) marked "the first month of the year" (Ex. 12:2). Israel later returned to the fall (as in the modern "Jewish New Year's"), yet the Mosaic month numbering was retained, so that, paradoxically, the regnal years of the Judean kings began in their seventh month. In 2Ki. 22:3, for example, an event in Josiah's eighteenth year is followed (2Ki. 23:23) several months later by a Passover (first

Month	Modern Equivalent	Canaanite	Babylonian	Reference	Sacred Feasts
1	April (or late March)	Abib	Nisan	Ex. 13:4 Neh. 2:1	14th day, Passover; 15-21, Unleavened Bread
2	May	Ziv	Iyyar	1 Kgs. 6:1	
3	June		Sivan	Esth. 8:9	6, Pentecost (Weeks, or Harvest)
4	July		Tammuz		
5	August		Ab		
6	September		Elul		
7	October	Ethanim	Tishri	1 Kgs. 8:2	1, Trumpets (Rosh Hashanah—New Year's Day); 15-21, Tabernacles (Booths, Ingathering)
8	November	Bul	Marcheshvan	1 Kgs. 6:38	
9	December		Kislev	Neh. 1:1	25, Dedication—Hanukkah (Lights)
10	January		Tebeth	Esth. 2:16	
11	February		Shebat	Zech. 1:7	
12	March		Adar	Ezra 6:15	14-15, Purim

month) in the same eighteenth year.

The year was divided into months, with designations that indicated the seasons: Abib, "new grain" (Lev. 2:14) for instance, refers to the initial month of spring when the barley ripened (Ex. 23:15; Dt. 16:1). Similarly the "Gezer Calendar," found in 1908, preserves in the scratched writing of a tenth century B.C. schoolboy the agricultural operations throughout the twelve months, starting in the fall. The Hebrew names for month are *hodeshyerah*, which mean "new moon" and suggest lunar months that began with the first appearance of the new moon (Ge. 1:14; Ps. 104:19). Yet the true lunar month consists, approximately, of an awkward 29½ days, so that in its earliest records (Moses' writings in Genesis), perhaps due to Egyptian influence, each month has thirty days (Ge. 8:3-4 compares with 7:11; see also Nu. 20:29 and Dt. 34:8 compared with Dt. 21:13). Then, by adding either five or six days at the end of a year, or a thirteenth month inserted every several years, Israel's calendar continued to reflect the true solar year. But Israel soon shifted back into lunar months of either twenty-nine or thirty days, so that the first of every month was a new moon feast, and Passover's fourteenth day fell at full moon (Ps. 81:3).

The Bible reflects three different ways of naming the months. From early times, descriptive Canaanite names were used, though only four are mentioned in the Bible; from the time of Moses onward, the months were simply numbered starting in the spring; and after the exile, Syro-Babylonian names were adopted. These are as follows, in accordance with Israel's feasts: Each month was divided into weeks of seven numbered days, which ran consecutively, irrespective of the months. The Sabbath, or seventh day, might thus fall on any day of the month, though at Christ's crucifixion it seems to have coincided with Passover on the fourteenth of Nisan (Jn. 19:31), which was indeed the case on April 7, A.D. 30. (J.B.P.) *See* CHRONOLOGY; GOSPELS, THE FOUR (¶ 2.); TIME

CALF *See* BEASTS; RED HEIFER

CALF, GOLDEN Three golden calves are noted. One was made by Aaron and the other two by Jeroboam I of Israel. These were all idolatrous and condemned (Ex. 32, 1Ki. 12.28-29). *See* DEITIES; IDOL, IDOLATRY

CALLS, CALLED

1. To call on the name of the LORD is to worship him (Ge. 13:4). To call on the name of Christ results in salvation (Ro. 10:12-14; 1Co. 1:2; 2Ti. 2:22).

2. To be called is to be a believer (Ro. 1:3; 8:28; 11:29; 1Co. 1:24, 26; Gal. 1:15; 1Th. 2:12; 2Th. 2:14; 1Pe. 2:9; 5:10). It is a calling to freedom, hope, and a pure life, which believers are to strive to be worthy of (Gal. 5:13; Eph. 1:18; 4:4; 1Th. 4:7; 2Th. 1:11; 2Ti. 1:9; 1Pe. 1:15). Some see this calling as an irresistible act of God; others see the calling as an invitation to be accepted or rejected. *See* ELECT, ELECTION; SALVATION, APPLICATION OF

CALNEH, CALNO [all of them]

1. An unidentified city in Mesopotamia founded by Nimrod (Ge. 10:10; cf. Eze. 27:23). †

2. An unidentified Syrian city (Am. 6:2; Isa. 10:9). †

CALVARY KJV for "skull," based on the Latin version in Lk. 23:33. *See* GOLGOTHA

CALVIN, JOHN A Reformer (1509-1564) who gave the Reformed faith its most comprehensive and methodical statement through his *Institutes of the Christian Religion*.

CALVINISM The beliefs of John Calvin. The term is applied particularly to the doctrine of election, according to which God autonomously chose some for salvation not because of any worthiness or even foreseen belief, but simply by his free will. Arminianism is an opposing view.

CAMEL *See* BEASTS 4.

CAMEL'S HAIR *See* DRESS; JOHN THE BAPTIST

CAMON *See* KAMON

CAMP

1. It appears that in nomadic days men pitched their tents in a circle around their cattle and sheep for protection, and this was their encampment. Out of this grew other types of protective encampments such as that around the tabernacle during the wilderness wanderings of the Israelites in their exodus from Egypt. Three tribes pitched their tents on each of the four sides of the central rectangular area in which the tabernacle was pitched. In an inner circle about the tabernacle were the four major groups of the Levites, as in Numbers 2–3.

2. Sometimes to camp or encamp is to go to war (Jos. 11:5; Jdg. 7:1). *See also* WAR

CAMPHIRE *See* PLANTS, PERFUMES, AND SPICES, Flowering Plants 3., *Henna*

CANA [reed] A NT town usually identified with a village on the edge of Nazareth, but more probably with a ruin approximately eight miles farther N called Khirbet Kana. Here Jesus performed his first miracle, changing water into wine, and from here he healed a nobleman's son living in Capernaum (Jn. 2:1-11; 4:46). This was Nathanael's village (Jn. 21:2). †

CANAAN, CANAANITES [land of purple, *hence* merchant, trader] A Canaanite, as far as the Bible is concerned, is a Hamitic descendant of Canaan, cursed in Ge. 9:24-25. Though variously explained as to why Canaan and not Ham is cursed, this curse explains why the Canaanites were detestable to the Israelites (sons of Shem) in later Bible history, in the time of Joshua and even later. The area of Canaan was the whole of the territory W of the Jordan (Nu. 33:51). The boundary is more specific in Ge. 10:19. The sons of Canaan are mentioned in Ge. 10:15, and many of the same are listed in Ex. 3:8; Dt. 7:1; and elsewhere. *See* CONQUEST OF CANAAN and GEOGRAPHY OF THE HOLY LAND

CANAANITE, SIMON THE KJV based on transliterating a similar word in the Greek in Mt. 10:4. Lk. 6:15 and Ac. 1:13 call the apostle "the Zealot." Therefore commentators have concluded that the word translated "Canaanite" in Mt. 10:4 is probably an Aramaic word transliterated into Greek, which means "zealot." It is not related in meaning to the Canaanite in the preceding article. *See* APOSTLES

CANANAEAN An ASV, RSV rendering of "Zealot" in Mt. 10:4. *See* CANAANITE, SIMON THE

CANDACE A queen of Ethiopia whose treasurer was baptized by Philip (Ac. 8:26ff.). †

CANDLESTICK *See* LAMP, LAMPSTAND

CANE *See* PLANTS, PERFUMES, AND SPICES

CANKER KJV for "gangrene" (2Ti. 2:17). *See* SICK, SICKNESS

CANKERWORM KJV for "locust in larvae stage," translated in the NIV usually as "young locust." *See* BEASTS 6.

CANNEH An unidentified town named with Haran and Ashur (Eze. 27:23), possibly connected with Calneh. †

CANON The group of books recognized as authoritative by the church.

CANONIZATION The process in the Roman Catholic church for attributing sainthood to a person.

CANTICLES *See* SONG OF SOLOMON, BOOK OF

CAPERNAUM [village of Nahum] A town on the northern shore of the Sea of Galilee where Jesus spent much time. It is even called his own town on one occasion (Mt. 9:1). Here Jesus healed the servant of a Roman centurion (Mt. 8:5ff.); it was the home of Matthew, a tax collector who became an apostle (Mt. 9:9). Here he healed Peter's mother-in-law and performed many other miracles of healing (Mt. 8:14-15; 9:1ff.; Jn.

4:46ff.). Here too he gave his address to the multitude on the day after the feeding of the 5,000 (Jn. 6:24ff.). For their unbelief he predicted the ruin of the city (Mt. 11:23-24).

CAPERNAUM: The site of Jesus' early Galilean ministry—after he left Nazareth and was baptized in Bethabara.

CAPHTOR, CAPHTHORIM, CAPHTORITES The country or area from which the Philistines came (Jer. 47:4; Am. 9:7). Because of the close connections between Egypt and Crete (called Keftiu) that go back into the third millennium B.C., it is thought by some that the Philistines come from Crete (the Kerethites of Eze. 25:16) and that this is Caphtor. Others think that the term *Caphtor* covers a wider coastal area in Asia Minor from which the Philistines came in the general movement of the Sea Peoples toward the end of the second millennium B.C. At least it is clear from the different kinds of headgear of the Philistine soldiers that they were not all from one group.

CAPITAL An ornamental decorative item on the tops of pillars usually of massive size—Doric, Corinthian, Ionian, or Proto-Ionic, depending on style and place of origin of the design.

CAPITAL PUNISHMENT *See* CROSS; PUNISHMENT; STONING

CAPITALISM An economic system characterized by private and corporate ownership. *See* COMMUNISM

CAPPADOCIA *See* GEOGRAPHY OF THE HOLY LAND

CAPSTONE *See* CORNERSTONE

CAPTAIN An officer of some kind whose exact identity is not clear, attested by the fact that it is used to translate a large number of Hebrew and Greek words. This is the case since we know very little about army ranks in biblical times. Reference is made to "the captain of the temple guard" (Ac. 4:1; 5:24) who was second only to the high priest called "chief officer" in the OT (Jer. 20:1).

CAPTIVE Christ set the captive free (Lk. 4:18; Ro. 7:23). He gifted those set free (Eph. 4:8).

CAPTIVITY The Bible recognizes three dispersions, exiles, or captivities of Jews. One was the 400 years in Egypt from which they were led back by Moses and Joshua (Ge. 15:13-14). The second was seventy years in Babylon. From this they came back under Zerubbabel, Ezra, and Nehemiah (Jer. 25:11). The third is pictured as a worldwide diaspora. No specific time for return is associated with this diaspora, but it is clearly stated to be a regathering from all the countries of the world (Dt. 30:1-5; Eze. 36:24). As the word "captivity" is used, the usual thought is of the Assyrian and Babylonian one. The ten northern tribes were taken captive by the Assyrians in 722/721 B.C., while the two southern tribes, Judah and Benjamin, were taken by the Babylonians in a series of deportations spread over a number of years ending with the final one in 586 B.C. (2Ki. 25:1-4, 8-10). *See also* DIASPORA

CARAVAN *See* TRADE

CARBUNCLE(S) *See* PRECIOUS STONES AND METALS 5., *beryl* (Isa. 54:12, Carbuncles), *jewels* (NIV)

CARCAS A eunuch of the Persian king Xerxes (Est. 1:10). †

CARCASE, CARCASS *See* CORPSE

CARCHEMISH A strategic site located on the Euphrates Rivers at the place of

A Procession of Captives in Ancient Assyria

an important ford. It was the capital of the Hittite Empire in the E and guardian of the crossroads between Asia Minor and Mesopotamia and between the province of Palestine and Mesopotamia. In the days of Josiah, king of Judah, Pharaoh Neco of Egypt fought the Babylonians at Carchemish (2Ch. 35:20). However, a few years later the Babylonians under Nebuchadnezzar defeated the Egyptians there (Isa. 10:9; Jer. 46:2). †

CAREAH *See* KAREAH

CARITES Thought by some to be the same as the Kerethites (2Ki. 11:4, 19). †

CARMEL [orchard planted with vine and fruit-trees]
1. A mountain range in Palestine. *See* GEOGRAPHY OF THE HOLY LAND
2. A town (162-092) in the hill country of Judah (Jos. 15:55; 1Sa. 15:12; 2Sa. 23:35).

CARMELITE A person from the area of Carmel (1Sa. 30:5). *See* CARMEL

CARMI, CARMITE(S) [*possibly* (fruitful) vine, vineyard owner, IDB]
1. A son of Reuben (Ge. 46:9).
2. Father of the Achan who sinned at Ai (Jos. 7:1).

CARNAL [flesh, fleshly] A term that has come to us from the Latin Vulgate through the KJV, transliterated "carnal" in 1Co. 3:1 (*worldly* in the NIV). The word in many modern versions is "fleshly," which is the opposite of spiritual, and means to walk as mere men, not like Christ walked. A carnal Christian from the above context refers to one who engages in dissention and sectarianism—following one man over another. For the Christian, the consequences of promoting or being involved in divisions is found in 1Co. 3:10-14.

CARNELIAN *See* PRECIOUS STONES AND METALS

CARPENTER A worker in wood and timber. The best description of the art of the carpenter is found in Isa. 44:13-17. The Phoenicians seem to have been good carpenters (2Sa. 5:11). Jesus worked with his stepfather, Joseph, as a carpenter (Mt. 13:55; Mk. 6:3).

CARPUS [fruit] Paul's host at Troas where he left a cloak (2Ti. 4:13). †

CARSHENA A prince at the court of King Xerxes in Persia (Est. 1:14). †

CART Used for carrying persons or goods in civilian rather than military use (Ge. 45:19; 1Sa. 6:7-8). These were of wood with wooden wheels and drawn by a pair of oxen or cows (Nu. 7:3; 1Sa. 6:7). *See* LITTER

CASIPHIA An unidentified site in Babylonia (Ezr. 8:17). †

CASLUHIM, CASLUHITES An unidentified group of people (Ge. 10:14; 1Ch. 1:12). †

CASSIA *See* PLANTS, PERFUMES, AND SPICES

CASTANET *See* MUSIC

CASTLE(S) *See* FORT, FORTRESS, FORTIFICATION

CASTOR AND POLLUX *See* DEITIES 1.

CATAPULT *See* ARMS AND ARMOR

CATECHISM A systematic instruction of Christian beliefs.

CATERPILLAR(S) *See* BEASTS 6., *Grasshopper*

CATHOLIC EPISTLES These are the NT letters (epistles) not written by Paul; nor the books of Hebrews and Revelation.

CATTLE *See* BEASTS 4.

CATTLE FEED *See* FODDER

CAUDA A small island S of Crete (Ac. 27:16). †

CAUL KJV for the appendage above the liver of a sheep, goat, or ox. Caul is rendered as "covering" in the NIV and "fatty mass" in the JB. *See* SACRIFICES AND OFFERINGS, The Fellowship (Peace Offering)

CAUSEWAY KJV for a road (1Ch. 26:18).

CAVE From earliest times the caves in the soft limestone of Palestine served as homes (Ge. 19:30), temporary refuges (Jos. 10:16), and tombs (Ge. 23:9ff.). *See also* BURIAL; MOURN; MOURNING

CEDAR *See* TREES

CEDRON *See* KIDRON

CELLAR A storage place, though not under a house (1Ch. 27:27).

CENACLE *See* UPPER ROOM

CENCHREA(E) A seaport near Corinth visited by Paul, and the home of a Christian he commends to the church at Rome (Ac. 18:18; Ro. 16:1). †

CENSER A vessel usually of bronze but sometimes of gold for burning incense (Ex. 27:3; Lev. 10:1; 1Ki. 7:50). There is no biblical description, but archaeologists have found samples of small bowls with long handles.

CENSUS At Mt. Sinai two years after the start of the exodus from Egypt the first counting of the Israelites was made. The census was made of men twenty years old and over (Nu. 1:1-3), excluding Levites (1:47), the total of which was 603,550 (Nu. 1:45-46). The Levites were numbered separately, every male a month old or more, and totaled 22,000

(Nu. 3:39). The second census took place forty years later, just before the start of the conquest of Palestine, when those who were punished for their failure to believe God forty years earlier had died in the wilderness. There were 23,000 Levites and 601,730 other males (Nu. 14:20-24; 26:1-2, 51-62). King David took an unauthorized census during his reign for which he and the people were punished. It showed 800,000 men of fighting age in Israel and 500,000 in Judah (2Sa. 24:2, 9, 15). One census is noted in the NT, that of Caesar Augustus in the days when Quirinius was governor of Syria. It was at this time that Jesus was born in Bethlehem (Lk. 2:1-5).

CENTURION [ruler over 100]
1. *See* CORNELIUS and IMPERIAL REGIMENT.
2. A Roman officer in command of 100 foot soldiers. Those referred to in the Bible are mentioned in a good light (Mt. 8:8; Mk. 15:39; Ac. 10:1; 22:26; 27:43).

CEPHAS [rock] One of the names of the Apostle Peter (Jn. 1:42; 1Co. 1:12; 3:22; 9:5). †

CEREAL OFFERING *See* SACRIFICES AND OFFERINGS

CEREMONIAL LAW *See* LAW; SACRIFICES AND OFFERINGS

CERTIFICATE OF DIVORCE *See* DIVORCE; HILLEL

CHAFF Chaff can have metaphorical significance as something worthless and temporal (Ps. 1:4; Mt. 3:12; Lk. 3:17). *See* FARMING; WINNOWING

CHAINS
1. An ornamental chain. *See* ORNAMENTS
2. A device put on the hands or feet to secure people in prison (Ac. 12:7). The reference of two chains in Ac. 21:33 possibly meant a soldier on each side. Paul was not ashamed of his chains (2Ti. 1:16). He made mention of them in his letters (Eph. 6:20). He referred to them as "bonds." These chains increased his witness and encouragement to the

brothers (Php. 1:7, 13-14; Col.4:3, 18; Phm. 10, 13). *See* FETTERS

CHALCEDONY *See* PRECIOUS STONES AND METALS 1.

CHALCOL KJV in 1Ki. 4:31 and "Calcol" in 1Ch. 2:6. *See* CALCOL

CHALDEA, CHALD(A)EANS A region in and/or the inhabitants of southern Babylonia. They were a tribal people (warriors Eze. 23:15) and not a part of the city-dwelling Babylonians. Their living together was upset when the Assyrians invaded the S. Out of this struggle the Chaldeans came to be masters in the area. What is sometimes called the neo-Babylonian period was in actuality Chaldean, from Nabopolassar to Nabonidus when the Persians conquered the area in 538 B.C. The wise men of this group then went into other parts of the world as magicians and astrologers (Da. 2:10). Abraham left Ur of the Chaldeans to emigrate to Canaan (Ge. 11:28). Chaldeans are called Babylonians in Jeremiah 37. *See* BABYLON, BABYLONIA; DIVINATION

CHALDEAN ASTROLOGERS *See* WISE MEN

CHALDEES *See* CHALDEA, CHALD(A)EANS

CHAMBERING *See* ADULTERY; FORNICATION

CHAMBERLAIN
1. *See* EUNUCH.
2. The one in charge of the bed chamber of a king. The NIV translates the sense of the words and calls him a trusted personal servant, for anyone in that sphere of service must have been highly trusted (Ac. 12:20).

CHAMELEON *See* BEASTS 6.

CHAMOIS *See* BEASTS 2., *Mountain Sheep*

CHAMPAIGN KJV for "Arabah" (Dt. 11:30). *See* GEOGRAPHY OF THE HOLY LAND

CHANAAN *See* CANAAN

CHANCELLOR KJV for "commanding officer" (Ezr. 4:8-9, 17).

CHANGERS OF MONEY *See* MONEY CHANGER

CHANT *See* MUSIC

CHAPEL KJV for "sanctuary" (Am. 7:13). *See* SANCTUARY; TABERNACLE; TEMPLE

CHAPITER(S) *See* CAPITAL

CHAPMAN *See* TRADE

CHARASHIM *See* GE HARASHIM 2.

CHARCHEMISH *See* CARCHEMISH

CHARIOT A two-wheeled vehicle like the cart but used in battle rather than for carrying burdens. They were introduced to the Middle East, at some time before the eighteenth century, from the E and introduced to the Egyptians by the Canaanites later. They were made of iron or wood covered with metal plates. They carried two or three persons: the driver of the horse, an archer or spearman, and a shield-bearer (2Ch. 18:33; 1Ki. 22:34; Jos. 17:16). King Solomon was the first Israelite to make extensive use of the military chariot (1Ki. 10:26). An Assyrian record indicates that King Ahab of Israel had a great army of chariots. There is a debate among archaeologists as to whether the great stables at Megiddo were Solomonic or from the time of Ahab.

CHARISMATIC GIFTS *See* GIFTS; SPIRITUAL GIFTS

CHARISMATIC MOVEMENT A loosely-structured movement that highlights the charismatic gifts and especially the supernatural manifestations. Though this is a general name for many divergent beliefs, generally this movement emphasizes the unity of the Spirit (as distinguished from doctrinal emphasis, which could cause differences) among all who name Christ. This unity is based on those miracles, tongues, and revelations.

Cherub

Ancient Assyrian Chariot

CHARISMATICS Those who accept and practice the charismatic gifts.

CHARITY *See* LOVE

CHARMER *See* DIVINATION

CHARMS Small objects, amulets, usually pierced and worn around the neck, which were intended to give protection or ward off evil spirits. Some were worn by women, a kind of banding or wristlet (Isa. 3:20; Eze. 13:18, 20).

CHARRAN *See* HARAN

CHASTE, CHASTITY *See* PURIFICATION

CHASTISEMENT *See* DISCIPLINE, CHURCH

CHEBAR *See* KEBAR

CHECKER WORK KJV for "interwoven chains" in 1Ki. 7:17. This was ornamentation on the top of some of the columns of the temple. *See* TEMPLE

CHEDORLAOMER *See* KEDOR-LAOMER

CHEESE In the ancient Middle East cheese was made from the milk of goats, sheep, cows, and camels. Because of lack of refrigeration and the abundance of milk at the same time the cheese of milk was a staple part of the diet (2Sa. 17:29; Job 10:10).

CHELAL *See* KELAL

CHELLUH *See* KELUHI

CHELUB *See* KELUB

CHELUBAI *See* CALEB; KELUBAI

CHEMARIM KJV for "pagan" (Zep. 1:4).

CHEMOSH *See* DEITIES

CHENAANAH *See* KENAANAH

CHENANI *See* KENANI

CHENANIAH *See* KENANIAH

CHEPHAR-HAMMONAI *See* KEPHAR AMMONI

CHEPHIRAH *See* KEPHIRAH

CHERAN *See* KERAN

CHERETHIMS, CHERETHITES *See* KERETHITES

CHERITH *See* KERITH

CHERUB
1. They are represented in art and statuary as winged human-animal forms with various types of animal or even human faces (Eze. 1:5-12; 10:8, 14; cf. *living creatures*, Rev. 4:6-9). They guarded the entrance to Eden after Adam and Eve were expelled. A likeness in pure gold of two of them was on either side of the mercy seat on top of the Ark of Testimony. They were embroidered on the curtains of the tabernacle and on the veil of the temple (Ge. 3:24; Ex. 25:22; 26:1;

2Ch. 3:14). King Solomon had gold covered wooden ones placed in the temple (1Ki. 6:23-28). *See* KERUB

2. A place (Ezr. 2:59).

CHESALON *See* KESALON

CHESED *See* KESED

CHESIL *See* KESIL

CHEST *See* ARK 3.

CHES(T)NUT TREE *See* TREES, Other Trees, *Plane*

CHESULLOTH {loins or flanks (of Mt. Tabor), BDB; *possibly* sluggish (of Tabor), KB} *See* KESULLOTH

CHEZIB *See* KEZIB

CHIASMUS *See* POETRY

CHICKEN *See* BIRDS 2.

CHIDON *See* KIDON; NACON

CHIEF The leader of a family, clan, or tribe (Ge. 36:15; Zec. 12:5).

CHIEF PRIESTS Most often in the plural, this was a class of people that denotes members of the Sanhedrin who belonged to high priestly families. This included the high priests that were ruling, those deposed from office, and adult male members of the most prominent priestly members. These were an aristocratic and generally wealthy class. There were five distinct offices that chief priests could hold, each with its own pay and status. They were the executive branch of temple affairs (Mt. 2:4; 16:21; 20:18; 21:15; 26:3; 27:1-12).

CHILD, CHILDREN *See* BAR; BEN; PARENTING; SON, SONSHIP

CHILDBEARING *See* PARENTING

CHILDLESS *See* BARREN

CHILDREN OF GOD *See* BAR; SALVATION, APPLICATION OF

CHILDREN OF ISRAEL *See* ISRAEL

CHILEAB *See* KILEAB

CHILIASM *See* MILLENNIALISM

CHILION *See* KILION

CHILMAD *See* KILMAD

CHIMHAM *See* GERUTH KIMHAM; KIMHAM

CHINNERETH, CHINNEROTH *See* KINNERETH

CHIOS *See* KIOS

CHISLEU, CHISLEV *See* CALENDAR, *Kislev*

CHISLON *See* KISLON

CHISLOTH-TABOR *See* KISLOTH TABOR; KESULLOTH

CHITLISH *See* KITLISH

CHITTIM *See* KITTIM

CHIUN KJV for "pedestal" in Am. 5:26.

CHLOE {tender shoot} A woman from whose household some reported to Paul on the quarreling among the members of the church at Corinth (1Co. 1:11). †

CHOIR *See* MUSIC

CHOIRMASTER *See* PSALMS, TITLES OF 1.

CHOOSE *See* ELECT, ELECTION

CHORASHAN 1Sa. 30:30. *See* BOR ASHAN

CHORAZIN *See* KORAZIN

CHOSEN PEOPLE God has an "eternal purpose, according to the counsel of His will, whereby, for His own glory, He hath foreordained whatsoever comes to pass" (Westminster Shorter Catechism). In implementing this eternal purpose, God chooses individuals or groups out of the masses in order to achieve his goals. (*See* ELECT, ELECTION for a discussion of his choice of individuals.) The concept in the OT is that the Israelites were God's chosen people. He chose Abraham while he was in Ur and brought him to Canaan and there made an everlasting covenant with him and his descendants after him. This covenant included two parts: God's promise to bless the world through Abraham's seed; and to give the land of Canaan as an everlasting possession to him and his seed after him—the land from the River of Egypt to the great river, the Euphrates (Ge. 12:3; 15:18; 17:19; 18:10; Gal. 3:16). God chose the seed of Abraham when he brought them out of the bondage in Egypt and gave them their way of life in the law. This he did at Sinai. The victory over the peoples of Palestine was his gift so that they would have their national home as promised to Abraham (Ex. 3:6-10; Dt. 6:21-25; Isa. 43:1; 51:2; Ac. 13:17). God's spiritual purpose in this choice or election of a people was that he would have a people to be holy to himself, to be his witnesses in the world, and to bring his blessings of salvation to all peoples through the Messiah who was to be descended from them (Dt. 7:6; Isa. 43:10-12; 42:17; Mt. 12:15-21; Ro. 11:17-24; Eph. 2:11-13). *See* ELECT, ELECTION

CHOZEBA [flatterer, liar] *See* COZEBA

CHRIST, LIFE AND TEACHINGS OF [the Anointed One]

1. Who is Christ?
2. The nature of the Gospels
3. The six stages of Christ's life
   a. Christ's birth and childhood
   b. Christ's baptism and temptation
   c. Christ's Judean ministry
   d. Christ's Galilean ministry
   e. Christ's preparation for the end
   f. The last week of Christ
4. Why did Christ come?
5. What did Christ teach?
6. What did others think of Christ?

1. *Who is Christ?* Jesus Christ is the central figure in Christianity. His importance cannot be exaggerated either in the religious or secular sense. The calendar of the Western world revolves around his birth. Many secular institutions have been influenced by his teaching. The importance of Christ can be best understood by considering a number of questions about him.

To answer the question, *"Who is he?"* we cannot do better than note some of the names used of him, or used by him. In a Hebrew setting the name represented the nature, and the meaning of names was more important than in Western culture. The name by which he is most generally known is Jesus Christ. The first of these means "Savior," which shows him to be one who came in some sense to deliver his people from bondage. The other name, Christ, is really a title meaning "the Anointed One" (Messiah) and came to be used in the Jewish world for the coming deliverer who would introduce a new era. The main idea current at the time was that Messiah would rid his people of the Roman tyrants, but this was far from the purpose of Jesus. When the title was applied to him, it was used in a spiritual sense of a deliverer from moral bondage. The name Jesus Christ therefore puts in a nutshell what Jesus came to do.

Jesus avoided the use of the title Messiah since it would have been misunderstood. He was no revolutionary in a political sense, although his teaching contained many revolutionary ideas. He chose to speak of himself as the Son of Man. There has been much discussion over what he meant by it, but it seems most likely that he used it to represent all that the Jewish prophets and other teachers had predicted about the hoped-for deliverer, without implicating himself in current political ideas about the Messiah. It also focused attention upon Jesus as a true man. Another title was Son of God. He spoke in such a way that it is clear that he had a special relationship with God as Father. This colored his whole ministry.

Jesus used many metaphors to describe himself. He referred to himself as the Shepherd of the sheep, as the Door to the sheepfold, as the Light of the world, as the Life of men. These claims are astounding, but he made them without any apology. He stated them as facts. These are the terms on which his life and message must be considered.

2. *The nature of the Gospels.* When considering the biography of any person, one's first concern is for reliable

sources. In the case of the life of Jesus Christ, we have only the four accounts in our Gospels. Outside these books there is very little mention of Jesus by the secular historians of the time. Tacitus says that Christ was executed in the reign of Tiberius by the procurator Pontius Pilate. Suetonius refers to uprisings in Rome over one Chrestus, who may be identified as Christ, but says no more about him. The fact is that the pagan world passed him by with no more than the scantiest references. Even the Jewish historian Josephus makes only slight passing reference to him. Our sources, therefore, are almost wholly written by Christians.

The four Gospels are not biographies. They are Gospels, which means simply Good News. What they tell about Jesus Christ is with a definite purpose in view. John, who wrote one of them, said quite specifically that he wrote to encourage people to believe that Jesus was the Messiah and Son of God. If we want a bare record of facts, we shall not find it in any of these Gospels. But this does not mean that we can know no facts about the life of Jesus. Although the writers were men who had come to believe in Jesus in a certain way, they were nevertheless concerned to present a true account of him.

The question naturally arises: Where did they obtain their information? It seems certain that our Gospels were written either by eyewitnesses or else by those in close touch with eyewitnesses. This is important since otherwise we could have no confidence in the Gospels as sources of historical information. Some of the writers may have used other sources which were themselves based on eyewitnesses; but if so, this would not affect the reliability of the Gospels. It is widely believed, for instance, that Matthew and Luke were based on Mark and that both of them drew from another source which has not been preserved. Any attempt to find out at this stage exactly how the Gospel writers collected their information must in the nature of the case be largely speculative. Some

scholars have tried to maintain that much of the material used gives what the Christians thought happened rather than what actually did happen. But the early Christians would not have been prepared to suffer and even die for the creations of their own imaginations. We may proceed to outline main events in the life of Jesus with confidence.

3. *The six stages of Christ's life.* There were six main stages in the story of Jesus as far as it can be reconstructed.

a. From his birth to the beginning of his public work occupied about thirty years. The Gospels were not interested in this period, except for some details of his birth and one incident of his childhood. Something will be said about his birth or incarnation in the next section dealing with the question of why he came.

b. The second stage was the period of preparation, which is more particularly concerned with the way in which the coming of Jesus was announced by John the Baptist, who appeared in the garb of an ancient prophet and proclaimed judgment and the need for repentance. He used the rite of baptism as a symbol of repentance. He preached the coming of the kingdom. He, in fact, set the stage for the public ministry of Jesus.

The second stage is composed of two events. First, Christ's baptism by John in the Jordan River. This was not because Jesus needed to repent, but because he wished to identify himself with the needy people around him. One special feature of the baptism of Jesus which marked it out from all others was the descent of the Spirit of God upon him. The writers speak of the Spirit in the shape of a dove in order to make clear that something visible descended. Moreover, a voice was heard, at least by John the Baptist, which gave God's approval to the ministry of Jesus. John himself seemed to have had special insight into the coming mission of Jesus, for he pointed him out as the Lamb of God who was to take away the world's sin. The other important happening of a preparatory character was the temptation of Jesus. Matthew and Luke both record the same sample of temptations which Jesus faced at the beginning of his ministry and which may have recurred at times throughout. He was tempted to use supernatural power or spectacular methods to achieve his ends rather than following the path of God's will.

c. The third stage of the story was set in Judea. This is reported briefly by John, who concentrated on certain important features. The first disciples were called to follow Jesus, although it was not until later that they left their normal occupations to assist in his ministry. Among other features were two remarkable conversations which Jesus had, one with a Jewish teacher and the other with a Samaritan woman. In both cases Jesus made a deep impression on the minds of his hearers. Of special note is the fact that Jesus was not prepared to allow Jewish nationalist prejudice to prevent him from conversation with a Samaritan. The most notable aspect of his early Judean ministry was the spiritual emphasis in the teaching of Jesus. It may be said to set the tone for the whole ministry.

d. The fourth stage may be called the Galilean ministry. A wide variety of events are related which took place mainly in the vicinity of the Sea of Galilee, particularly in and around Capernaum. The whole of this period may be conveniently divided into three sections. The earliest period is marked by the gathering together of the twelve disciples whom Jesus specially called to share his mission with him. These were the men drawn from various walks of life, many of them fishermen, but at least one a professional man, a tax collector. They were sent out on a preaching tour and given specific instruction as to their behavior and message. Jesus was training these men to carry on his work later. His own preaching was being warmly acclaimed, but there were already rumblings of opposition from the Pharisees, who soon detected that Jesus was unorthodox.

The next period of the Galilean ministry was at the time when Jesus withdrew from northern Galilee. As in the first period, there were miracles of healing and controversies, notably about the Sabbath. With regard to the many healings which Jesus performed, in most cases there was some act of faith on the part of the person to be healed, which shows that Jesus did not perform miracles for their own sake. He was not a wonder-worker in the common sense of the term. The Pharisees developed their opposition. They even accused Jesus of casting out demons by the prince of the demons. He reserved until later a scathing denunciation of their abuses. But it was not only the Pharisees who rejected him. The people of Nazareth where he had been brought up refused to believe in him. Yet the common people were still favorable to him, particularly as a result of a miracle of mass feeding. Some of them even tried to make him king, but this was not part of his mission.

In the third period, which ended with the departure of Jesus from Galilee, the most significant event was Peter's confession at Caesarea Philippi. Jesus drew out of the disciples their own idea of who he was, which led Peter to declare him to be the Messiah, the Son of God. This was a turning point in the ministry, after which Jesus turned his attention more specifically to the twelve. Although he accepted the testimony of his disciples, he did not want them to publish it, no doubt because he knew it would be misunderstood. It was at this stage that he told Peter and the others about his church. Immediately after this, three of the disciples had an extraordinary experience of seeing Jesus transformed before their very eyes on a mountain. This experience shows the supernatural side of the nature of Jesus. Yet it was linked with the first of a threefold prediction that Jesus was to die a violent death, a fact which none of the disciples could grasp.

e. The fifth stage of the ministry of Jesus may be loosely described as the movement from the activity in the N towards the final events in Jerusalem. It was a period of further activity and teaching, the latter mainly in the form of parables. Such well-known parables as the Good Samaritan and the Prodigal Son are set in this period. Once again that religious hostility, which was to reach its climax in the crucifixion of Jesus, was much in evidence. During the same period must be set some incidents and teaching in Jerusalem recorded by John but not by the other Gospel writers. Jesus drew spiritual lessons from common things, such as the shepherd and his sheep, and through this means taught men the things of God. All the time he was preparing his own disciples for the time when he would no longer be with them. At length he drew near to Jerusalem for the last time, spending a brief period E of the Jordan in a district known as Perea. The real climax of this period was reached when he raised Lazarus from the dead in the village of Bethany just outside of Jerusalem. This not only caused amazement but hardened the determination of the religious leaders to do away with Jesus because they feared he might undermine their position.

f. The events of the sixth stage—the last week of Jesus' life—are told by all four writers in considerable detail, which shows the importance that each attached to them. It is almost as if they were more interested in his death than in his life. The entry of Jesus into Jerusalem on a donkey while being acclaimed by a large crowd of people must have appeared to some like the inauguration of his kingship, but events were to show that his kingdom was not of this world. One side of the story which is illuminating is the weeping of Jesus over the city, for its coming doom was more evident to him than to his contemporaries. His action in clearing the money changers out of the temple in a commanding gesture of religious indignation was too much for the authorities, who, after several vain attempts to trap him in his teaching, trumped up false charges against him.

With the assistance of Judas Iscariot, one of the twelve, they arranged to arrest him at night, away from the popular clamor. That same evening Jesus instituted in the presence of the disciples the Supper which was to remind them of him and to explain the meaning of his death as a sacrificial offering. Having arrested him, his enemies proceeded to put him on trial, if it could be called such. The Jewish Council condemned him but needed the ratification of their sentence by the Roman governor. The latter repeatedly declared that he found no fault in Jesus; but the priestly party stirred the crowds to demand crucifixion, the cruelest method of execution, used widely by the Romans in their dealings with the Jews. The disciples of Jesus had all scattered like sheep when Jesus their Shepherd was taken (Mt. 26:31). Peter had denied that he even knew him.

It seemed that the mission of Jesus had ended in disaster, but all this was changed when he rose from the dead on the third day as he said he would. The tragedy became a triumph. The fearful disciples became bold men with a message of hope. On the Day of Pentecost they began preaching this message, for it was then that they were filled with the Spirit of God. Henceforth, men were to find a deeper meaning in Jesus than his own disciples had ever suspected during his lifetime.

4. *Why did Christ come?* It is only when we stand back and look at the life of Jesus that we realize some of the deep questions it poses. It is clear that he was no ordinary man. His own claims and the confessions of others show him to be the Son of God in a special sense. When writing his Gospel, John made the profound statement that the Son called "the Word" was with God and was God (Jn. 1:1), and that he became flesh (Jn. 1:14). This sums up what is meant by the Incarnation. Although possessing the nature of God, he became man. Moreover, John clearly gave one of the answers to the question why he came. It was to give authority to all who believed in him to become children of God. He came, therefore, to make possible a new relationship with God as Father in a new way. He came moreover to fulfill the Jewish mes-

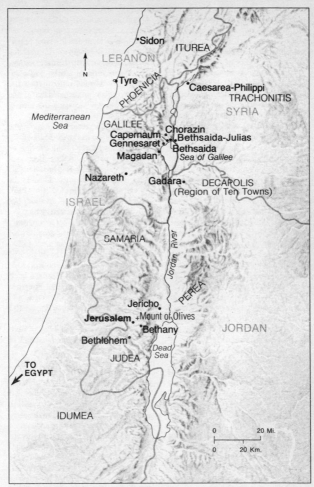

IMPORTANT PLACES IN THE LIFE AND MINISTRY OF JESUS CHRIST

sianic hopes in a new way, in a spiritual rather than a materialistic sense. He came to be a perfect man in order to be a perfect representative for man before God. (For a fuller discussion of why he

came, *See* CHRIST, WORK OF.)

5. *What did Christ teach?* As much importance must be attached to the teaching of Jesus as to his actions. A considerable proportion of the Gospels is

concerned with what he said. As a teacher, he was distinguished from the Jewish teachers of his day by the authority with which he spoke. He even claimed superiority over Moses in the content of his teaching.

The teaching may be summarized in two parts, one doctrinal, the other ethical, yet both closely related to each other. He taught new truths about God, especially in the realm of Fatherhood, which while not unknown to Jewish minds was never the intimate family relationship of which Jesus spoke. The teaching of Jesus about himself has already been referred to when mentioning his names in the first section. There is no doubt that he intended men to regard him as unique and to recognize that their own destiny was affected by their relation to him. When speaking of the kingdom, Jesus sometimes spoke of it as present in the hearts of believers and sometimes as an event which belongs to the end of the present age. It is therefore a present reality and a future hope. Another aspect of the teaching of Jesus was his promises about the coming Spirit of Truth, or Counselor, who was to make Jesus real to all who have come to believe in him. He drew a clear distinction between believers and unbelievers. Faith alone entitled men entry into the kingdom.

The ethical demands of Jesus were exacting. In the Sermon on the Mount, the fullest account of his ethical teaching, he frequently exhorted his listeners to actions which went beyond what might normally be expected, such as turning the other cheek to the one who strikes you and even loving your enemies. For this reason some have considered the ethics of Jesus to be too idealistic to be practical, but it is because he came to establish a new and higher order of living that his demands are so high. He never expected anyone to adhere to a higher or a lower moral standard than he adopted himself, and he knew that only through him could they achieve it.

6. *What did others think of Christ?* Two main sources enable us to reconstruct what the earliest Christians

thought about Jesus Christ. The book of Acts gives samples of speeches made by apostles, which set out the central message. It is evident that the most important theme is the death and resurrection of Jesus. These men had come to see how the resurrection of Christ had completely transformed things. They saw Jesus as the one predicted in the OT and were constantly stressing the idea of promise and fulfillment. It was the risen Christ who was preached. Moreover, he was proclaimed as Savior and Lord.

The other source of information on men's view of Christ is the collection of Epistles. The Apostle Paul had an exalted view of him. He described him as the "image of the invisible God"(Col. 1:15). He was the firstborn of all creation. Not only were all things created by him, but for him all things exist. Moreover, Paul's whole theology revolved around what Jesus Christ had done for men. Christians could now be said to be "in Christ." The other NT writers had no less an exalted view of him. In Hebrews he is presented as the great High Priest; in 1 Peter he is Lord, Shepherd, and Guardian; in the Johannine Epistles (1-3 Jn.) Jesus Christ is the Righteous, the advocate with the Father and Son of God; in the Revelation he is the slain Lamb of God now exalted on the throne.

These Christians were more interested in relating what Jesus had become to them than what he did and said while living among men. Yet the very fact that four records of his doings and sayings were written and treasured in the early church shows that they were not without deep interest in the historical Jesus.

Jesus Christ has never lost his relevance. In the vastly changed world of the twentieth century, his message and importance remain unchanged because he met the fundamental needs of mankind and not merely those of his own age. There is a sense, therefore, in which the life of Christ still continues in the life of the people of God. (D.G.)

CHRIST, WORK OF An expression frequently encountered in Christian theology is "the person and work of Christ." It designates the subject matter of Christology, which might be stated as, Jesus Christ, who he was and what he came to do. No understanding of the work of Jesus Christ is possible apart from an understanding of both who he was and is.

The centrality of Jesus Christ's person and work in Christian belief is indicated in the "Apostles' Creed," the earliest of the "ecumenical" creeds, which has had continuous use in the church for over 1,700 years. It is still today used in public worship, baptismal confession, and instruction of the young in most of the branches of Christendom in all parts of the world. In English translation it reads: "I believe in God the Father almighty, maker of heaven and earth; and in Jesus Christ His only Son, our Lord, who was conceived by the Holy Spirit; born of the virgin Mary; suffered under Pontius Pilate; was crucified, dead and buried; *He descended into hell* [a later addition]; the third day He rose again from the dead, He ascended into heaven, and sits on the right hand of God the Father almighty; from there He shall come to judge the quick and the dead. I believe in the Holy Spirit, the holy catholic church, the communion of saints, the forgiveness of sins, the resurrection of the body, and the life everlasting. Amen."

There are 109 words in this creed; 69 of them relate to Jesus Christ directly, and of these, 21 relate to his person while 48 relate to his work. This proportion is an accurate representation of the emphases given in true Christianity.

The work (creation) of the Lord (God, the Father almighty) may not be separated from the God-man (Jesus, his only Son) who performed it. Noteworthy also is the fact that not one word suggests that the significance of Jesus was that of the teacher of a new religion (or even the best teacher of an old one), nor an example of ethical integrity, nor a revelation of the highest humanity, as modern religionists frequently misrepresent his significance. Christians will readily acknowledge many of these compliments to their

Lord, but will still insist that they miss the point, for "the Father has sent his Son to be the Savior of the world" (1Jn. 4:14). Thus the *doing* was part of *being;* his work was not to tell us what to do but to do something for us.

The ancient creed cited is little more than a brief selection from and summary of the NT Scriptures. In these Scriptures there is constant focus on the fact that Jesus was destined, indeed, predestined, to accomplish his work by dying for the sins of men. Jesus did not say much about it, for he did not come to talk about dying, but rather to die. Yet he did make himself plain: " . . . the Son of Man did not come to be served, but to serve, and to give his life as a ransom for many" (Mt. 20:28). Immediately after his announcement of purpose to build his church (Mt. 16:13-18), it is reported, "From that time on Jesus began to explain to his disciples that he must go to Jerusalem and suffer many things at the hands of the elders, chief priests and teachers of the law, and that he must be killed and on the third day be raised to life" (Mt. 16:21). To Peter, Jesus' crucifixion was by "God's set purpose and foreknowledge" (Ac. 2:23), and his sacrifice was "of a lamb . . . chosen before the foundation of the world" (1Pe. 1:19-20), and to John the revelator he is "the Lamb that was slain from the creation of the world" (Rev. 13:8). So central is a proper understanding of the death of Christ to biblical Christianity that the Apostle Paul could write to the churches where he preached, "I resolved to know nothing while I was with you except Jesus Christ and him crucified" (1Co. 2:2). In keeping with this emphasis, the cross has been almost the only universal symbol of the Christian faith.

Explanation of the emphasis on the death of Christ in apostolic ministry is found, in part, in the leading place it has in the Christian gospel. Christianity is a missionary faith; it has a message to proclaim. Any program of human betterment is secondary. That message (gospel, proclamation, Gr. *kerygma)* is what, when received of men, saves them: "God was pleased through the foolishness of what was preached to save those who believe" (1Co. 1:21). The gospel pertains to Christ's person and work—who he was and his career (Ac. 10:36-43; 1Co. 15:1-4).

The distinctively Christian value of the OT is found in the predictions therein of the Savior, especially of his redeeming death. It also furnishes the categories for interpretation of the Savior's career. At several junctures in the Gospel narratives of the Lord's last days before Calvary, the ruling force of OT prophecies in shaping those events of passion and death is introduced. When, at the time of his seizure by Jewish authorities, Peter thought to defend Jesus with a sword, Mt. 26:53 records that Jesus said, "Do you think I cannot call on my Father, and he will at once put at my disposal more than twelve legions of angels? But how then would the Scriptures be fulfilled that say it must happen in this way?" (See also Mt. 27:9; Mk. 14:27; Lk. 22:37; Jn. 12:37-41; 15:25; 17:12; 19:24, 28, 36-37.) During the forty days before the ascension of Jesus he frequently interpreted the events just past as fulfilling Scripture; he even scolded his disciples for failing to see this (Lk. 24:25-27, 44-46). After the ascension, during the early period when the apostolic church remained near Jerusalem, Peter preached several sermons in which he connected the betrayal, passion, death, and resurrection with specific OT prophecies (Ac. 2:23-36), and even went so far as to say that "all the prophets" foretold of the death of Christ (Ac. 3:17-18, 24). Many years later, addressing a synagogue, Paul startled his audience by declaring, "The people of Jerusalem and their rulers did not recognize Jesus, yet in condemning him they fulfilled the words of the prophets that are read every Sabbath" (Ac. 13:27; see also 13:28-41). In fact, the invariable argument used by the apostles in appealing to Jews was based on the OT prophesies of the passion, death, and resurrection of Jesus.

Furthermore, as indicated above, the Lord himself and his apostles held that

the OT prophecy, ritual, and history interpreted the meaning of the Crucifixion and related events. Isa. 52:13 – 53:12, a comprehensive prophecy of the Lord's suffering and dying servant, lies in the background of interpretation of Jesus throughout the NT, from the words of the Father at the beginning of Jesus' ministry (Mt. 3:17; cf. Isa. 52:13), the comments of Matthew on his preaching and healing ministry (Mt. 8:14-17; cf. Isa. 53:4; Mt. 12:15-21; cf. Isa. 52:13; 42:1ff.), to his suffering and death (1Pe. 2:22; cf. Isa. 53:9 and 2Co. 5:21; 1Pe. 2:23; cf. Isa. 53:7; Heb. 12:3; 1Pe. 2:24; cf. Isa. 53:4, 11; 1Co. 15:3; Heb. 9:28; 1Pe. 2:24; cf. Isa. 53:5; 1Pe. 2:25; cf. Isa. 53:6). Millions of Bible-reading Christians have read the Gospels and then later read Isaiah 53 only to say, Isaiah has drawn a picture of our Savior's death in our place.

The OT figures in another very important fashion in interpreting the "work" of Christ, especially with respect to his threefold office of *prophet, priest,* and *king.* As the Christ, "the Anointed One," Jesus was the anointed prophet, priest, and king. Though "Christ" came later to be used as a name for Jesus, it first appears as his title as the predicted Messiah of the OT. The nation of Israel observed the custom of inducting official persons connected with their commonwealth into office by the ceremony of anointing with oil. This first is mentioned in Scripture in connection with Aaronic priests (Ex. 28:41). It is mentioned also in connection with induction into office of Israel's first king (1Sa. 9:15; 10:1). Though the practice is seldom mentioned in that connection, prophets were also sometimes so inducted into office (1Ki. 19:16; cf. Ge. 20:7; Ps. 105:15). The Hebrew word "to anoint with oil" is *masah;* the derived adjective *masiah,* anointed, becomes in the Greek a translation of the OT, *Messias,* whence the English word *Messiah.* A step further, the Greek translation of this word is *Christos* (derived from *Chrio,* to pour oil). This is transferred to Latin as *Christus* and from Latin to English as *Christ.* Hence the title *Christ* points directly to his threefold office: prophet, priest, and king.

The function of a prophet is to convey a written or spoken message from God to men, i.e., he was to teach with divine authority. Jesus did just that. In his person, words, and deeds he revealed the Father (Jn. 8:26; 14:9; 17:8), and he taught the people (Mt. 5–7). He was declared to be a prophet and was said to have done a prophet's work (Ac. 3:22; Mt. 13:57; Lk. 13:33; Jn. 6:14). In keeping with the requirements for a prophet (Dt. 18:14ff.), he produced the signs of a prophet—miracles and fulfilled predictions. There can be no doubt that Jesus' work as Messiah, the Christ of God, included his office of prophet.

Jesus also fulfilled the office of anointed priest. The biblical function of a priest was to mediate religiously between God and man in two ways: to offer sacrifices (especially blood sacrifices at the brazen altar) and to make intercession. Of these two, in the Mosaic ritual system, offering sacrifices was exclusively the priest's duty and right. The priest was mediator in a sense the prophet and king were not—it being his role to represent God to the people in the functions at the altar and likewise to represent them to God in prayer.

That Jesus fulfilled both these functions and did so as a divinely appointed priest is explicitly stated in Heb. 7:24-28. In connection with a "priesthood," which he holds "permanently," he "always lives to intercede for them" and "once for all when he offered himself." Jesus was both victim and sacrificing priest. This is the work of redemption to which, in a sense, all other "work" is subordinate and supplemental.

The third aspect of his office work is that of king. So Nathanael could confess, "You are the King of Israel" (Jn. 1:49); Jesus could speak of his kingship (Jn. 18:36), and when Pilate declared, "You are a King, then!" (Jn. 18:37), Jesus could answer, "You are right in saying I am a king" (Jn. 18:37), or as Luke put his affirmative answer, "Yes, it is as you say" (Lk. 23:3). In the great prophecy of Ps.

2:6, the LORD God says of him, "I have installed my king on Zion, my holy hill." Likewise, in Psalm 110 (containing a prophecy which Jesus appropriated for himself as Messiah), God proclaims, "Rule in the midst of your enemies" (v. 2). This messianic rule, though it began before his ascension among the disciples, was formally inaugurated at the enthronement at God's right hand (Php. 1:19-23). That reign focuses, in the present age, on the church, a kingdom of grace and spiritual power. It will expand to a visible kingdom, when at his second coming, he will assume the throne of David over Israel (Ps. 72), and from that throne rule all the nations as King of kings and Lord of lords (1Ti. 6:15; Rev. 19).

This OT background of the title of office "Christ" explains the confession of Peter (Mt. 16:16), and of Mary in Jn. 11:27. The former "You are the Christ, the Son of the living God" and the latter, "You are the Christ, the Son of God, who was to come into the world" were made by pious Jews steeped in the OT religious outlook. They could hardly have understood the title in any other way than that of designating one or all aspects of the threefold office. The NT clearly indicated that Jesus fulfilled all three designations of the title.

Having seen something of the full scope of his work, let the field of inquiry now focus on the stages of his work rather than the aspects of his work. These as related to our subject are Jesus' sinless life, his suffering (passion), death for sinners, burial, resurrection and post-resurrection ministry (for forty days), his ascension, his enthronement at the Father's right hand, present ministry in heaven, and his Second Advent.

1. *Jesus' Sinless Life.* More than once during his life with his disciples, Jesus called attention to his perfect moral integrity. It is a striking thing that men so intimately acquainted with a man, as Jesus' disciples were, would guilelessly and without refutation, irony, or embarrassment pass on reports of such a claim. John 8 for example, reports a bitter con-

troversy with the Jews over purity and fatherhood—possibly with overtones of his own mother's claim to a virginal conception of her son (Jn. 8:25, 33, 39, 41, 48). Jesus, on the other hand, most pointedly accused all his hearers of various sins and challenged his audience with these words, "Can any of you prove me guilty of sin? If I am telling the truth, why don't you believe me?" (Jn. 8:46).

Others, not among his own supporters, gave striking testimony to his innocence. Judas in remorseful terror cried out that he had betrayed "innocent blood" (Mt. 27:4), and we read how Pilate's wife intervened in the trial proceedings with the warning, "Don't have anything to do with that innocent man" (Mt. 27:19). Pilate could find nothing deserving of punishment in him and three times pronounced him innocent (Lk. 23:14-15, 22), even citing Herod in confirmation (v. 15). The overwhelmed centurion pronounced him a *righteous man* (Lk. 23:47), while one of the thieves, admitting his own guilt, testified that Jesus had "done nothing wrong" (Lk. 23:41).

One of his apostles was so impressed by Jesus' holy life that over thirty years later he wrote that his life was "an example, that you should follow in his steps. He committed no sin, and no deceit was found in his mouth" (1Pe. 2:21-22).

The sinlessness of Jesus is introduced in the NT record, not just to show that his condemnation was unjust, but to show that he who was slain by "wicked hands" was God's authentic sacrifice for sin—in the language of sin offering and Passover sacrifice employed by John the Baptist, "Look, the Lamb of God, who takes away the sin of the world!" (Jn. 1:29). The Lamb of the Passover had to be without blemish. The same was true of the sin offering (Ex. 12:5; Lev. 22:18-20; cf. 1Pe. 1:19; Heb. 9:14). This, his active obedience (as the theologians have called it) to the law of God, qualified him to be the perfect and sufficient sacrifice for all human sin. He being an infinite person thus qualified himself later. To use Paul's striking language in 2Co. 5:21, "God made him who knew no

sin to be sin for us, so that in him we might become the righteousness of God."

2. *Jesus' Passion.* Question 37 of the Heidelberg Catechism (1563): "What doest thou understand by the word suffered (in the Apostles' Creed)?" Answer: "That all the time He lived on earth, but especially at the end of His life, He bore in body and soul, the wrath of God against sin of the whole human race, in order that by His passion, as the only atoning sacrifice He might redeem our body and soul from everlasting damnation and obtain for us the grace of God, righteousness, and eternal life."

This venerable affirmation testifies that the passion of Christ has no importance to Christians apart from its culmination in his death. Christians witness to this by their frequent use of the expression "the suffering and death" of Jesus.

This suffering had its beginning in the treatment he received from his own household and neighbors. Long before the "passion week" his own brothers rejected him (Jn. 7:5). At a point very early in his ministry the men of his home village, when they heard him speaking in the local synagogue, "got up, drove him out of the town" and, except that he escaped them, would have killed him by throwing him over a nearby cliff (Lk. 4:28-30).

For a while he gained a sympathetic hearing, but for various reasons he lost support. Early in his ministry "he began to teach them that the Son of Man must suffer many things and be rejected by the elders, chief priests, and teachers of the law, and that he must be killed" (Mk. 8:31). Though all the elements of the martyrdom seeker were absent from him, he always understood that it was "written that the Son of Man must suffer much things and be rejected" (Mk. 9:12). He explained to his disciples: "The Son of Man is going to be betrayed into the hands of men. They will kill him" (Mk. 9:31). While walking toward Jerusalem for the last time, he took the Twelve aside and told them what was going to happen to him: "We are going up to Jerusalem . . . and the Son of Man will be betrayed to the chief priests and teachers of the law. They will condemn him to death and will hand him over to the Gentiles, who will mock him and spit on him, flog him and kill him" (Mk. 10:32-34).

Finally, even his disciples "all forsook him and fled." Of his immediate circle only a few women supporters and a boy (the youngest apostle) showed up for the Crucifixion, even while "a large number of others followed him" to the cross (Lk. 23:27).

Three things made the suffering most acute: it was inflicted by those whom he loved and whom he had come to save; it was endured alone; the final blow was dealt by his Father: "It was the LORD'S will to crush him and cause him to suffer" (Isa. 53:10).

All Christians accept a great deal of unfathomable mystery in this. The mystery is simply the mystery of the government of God over all in an intensified form. They glory in it. They know that existence would hold no mystery, only very obvious hopelessness, without it. They see the power of God ruling and overruling, making the wrath of man to praise him. They see Christ as "the stone that builders rejected"; nevertheless, by God's providence, it "has become the capstone" (1Pe. 2:7). And though not excusing wicked men for their violent deed, Christians nevertheless proclaim, "the LORD has done this, and it is marvelous in our eyes" (Ps. 118:22-23).

3. *The Death of Jesus.* As indicated above, though the Gospels justify us in finding some distinction between the Lord's suffering and death, they lead us, as they did the authors of the Confession cited, to discern the consummation of our Lord's suffering in his atoning death. In fact, though all life long he was "a man of sorrows, and familiar with suffering" (Isa. 53:3), when his cross was less than eighteen hours away he spoke of his suffering as still ahead: "I have eagerly desired to eat this Passover with you before I suffer" (Lk. 22:15). The suffering was consummated in and found its

meaning and purpose in his death.

The nature of the death Jesus experienced is no problem. Once a fully biblical view is taken of his person — incarnate God, fully God, fully man, as the ecumenical creeds also state — it can be understood. Death is three things: physical death, spiritual death, and the "second death" (Rev. 20:14), involving eternal exclusion from the presence of God. That physical death took place in Jesus' case has never been doubted except by a few ancient heretics. He bowed his head and commended his spirit to God (Lk. 23:46). Shortly thereafter a spear was thrust into his side, and blood and water gushed out, evidence that a separation of vital fluids in the heart region had taken place. The centurion testified to Pilate early in the evening that Jesus had already died (Mk. 15:42-45). Shortly thereafter, Joseph and Nicodemus buried him (Mk. 15:46; Jn. 19:38-42).

Spiritual death, that alienation from God which is the invariable effect of sin, also took place. This alone, as has always been generally understood, accounts for Jesus' agony in the Garden and his many remarks about revulsion from his "cup." The pitiful efforts of certain recent commentators to show that Jesus' agony arose simply out of fear of nonexistence (contrast with Socrates' last hours is noted) is shortsighted, unbiblical, and disrespectful of what the Bible says about the nature of man. The idea that the agony in the Garden was caused by resistance to efforts of Satan to kill him prematurely is bizarre.

Spiritual death was the immediate consequence of sin in the first pair. It is the state into which all men are now naturally born (Eph. 2:1-3; 4:17-19). This alienation, which took place in those moments when he took upon himself our guilt and penalty, is described in prophecy as making "his life a guilt offering" (Isa. 53:10), and God's making him "sin for us" (2Co. 5:21), is expressed in the Savior's heartbroken cry, "My God, my God, why have you forsaken me?" (Mt. 27:46). No other godly man has ever been forsaken by God at the time of death (Ps. 23:4).

The Heidelberg Catechism, in question 39, reads: "Is there something more in His having been crucified than if He had died some other death? Yes, for by this I am assured that He took upon Himself the curse which lay upon me, because the death of the cross was cursed by God (Gal. 3:13). Christ redeemed us from the curse of the law, having become a curse for us—for it is written, 'Cursed is everyone who hangs on a tree' " (cf. Dt. 21:23).

Did Jesus experience the "second death" also? Was it "eternal?" If it was a substitutionary death (and it was), and if that is the destiny of unrepentant men (and according to the Bible it is), then his death was in some sense "eternal," or as might better be said, of infinite value in the remission of sin. As Anselm *(Cur Deus Home)* argued and as orthodox interpreters usually agree, since he was an infinite being as second person of the Godhead he could suffer that eternal punishment in moments. Many have interpreted the "He descended into hell" clause of the creed in this manner, excluding any reference to a spatial journey.

Many different expressions are used in the Bible to interpret the Lord's death "for us," "for all," "for many," "for the whole world," etc. Most of the expressions are drawn from the OT sacrificial ritual *(see* SACRIFICES AND OFFERINGS). The Book of Hebrews explains that these sacrifices were insufficient in themselves to "take away sin" and had a typical value as foreshadowing God's own sufficient sacrifice at Calvary. The death of Christ is interpreted as:

a. *A sacrifice (or offering) for sins* (Heb. 10:10-12). This text and context (10:1-9) show that Jesus' death did what no other sacrifice had ever done. It removed completely and forever all guilt for the sin of those for whom it was offered. It leaves the conscience of the offerers free.

b. *A ransom* (Mt. 20:28; ITi. 2:5). The idea is not a payment to the devil, or

even to God, but a price paid to release or deliver. The figure is the release of captives. The NT Greek word *lutron* gets its meaning from the Greek OT which uses it at such places as Lev. 19:20.

c. *Redemption* (Php. 1:7). This word in the original is closely related in form and meaning to ransom. It refers to the deliverance secured by the price paid. The Greek OT uses the same word at Ex. 21:8.

d. *A fragrant offering* (Lev. 1:9; Eph. 5:2). The pleasing of God by voluntary, uncoerced sacrifice is the emphasis.

e. *A sin offering* (Lev. 5:17-19; Isa. 53:10; Ro. 8:3; 2Co. 5:21). In the Mosaic ritual this was a required sacrifice and had special reference to the removal of guilt for sins.

f. *Atoning sacrifice (propitiation or expiation in other versions)*. This word is the usual translation of the Greek words involved in ancient Greek literature and has reference to a satisfaction rendered to the persons and laws. Though it never appears in the KJV, *expiate* and *expiation* appear in the RSV ("atonement" in NIV) NT wherever the KJV has *propitiate* and *propitiation*. It is a word relating to the offended party. It is related to offense and offender. It is generally acknowledged that in Greek literature outside the NT *propitiate* and *propitiation* are the correct rendering. The texts involved are 1Jn. 2:2; 4:10; and Ro. 3:25.

g. *Reconciliation* (Ro. 5:10-11; 11:15; 2Co. 5:19; Eph. 2:16; Col. 1:20). This indicates that the death of Christ effected a reconciliation between man the sinner and his offended Creator. Since this is represented as a finished work, those interpreters who relate it to propitiation and removal of wrath through the execution of divine penalties on the sinners' substitute are correct. We live in a world that has been potentially reconciled. God has done all he as God can do. As Paul points out in 2Co. 5:19, it remains for sinners to accept it. Scripture teaches that those who die in rejection of God's reconciling sacrifice have no further expectation except renewal of God's fiery wrath (Heb. 10:26-31). This is a stern doctrine yet it is the NT teaching.

Readers of the KJV are accustomed to find *atonement* in the sense of a-tone-ment = reconciliation at Ro. 5:11. The NIV and RSV have *reconciliation*. Elsewhere, in the OT, *atone* and *atonement* appear dozens of times in connection with the sacrifices, which are said to *atone* or *make atonement*. In most cases the words so translated mean "to pacify," "to cover over," "appease," all relating to positive correction of the problem of sin as offense toward God. It seems likely that these numerous OT occurrences have brought about wide usage of "the atonement" as the comprehensive name for the work of Christ, for the OT sacrificial atonements were as we have seen, typical of Christ's final work of atonement – reconciliation

h. *A substitutionary sacrifice.* It is not possible merely to cite a few texts connected with this aspect of interpretation of Jesus' death. It is involved in all of the above. The idea of substitution of the life of the sacrificial victim for the life of the offerer was implicit in the act of laying the offerer's hand on the beast about to be slain in the several blood sacrifices (*see* SACRIFICES AND OFFERINGS), and it was nearly explicit in the action of the priest in confessing the people's sins over the beast in the case of the sin offerings on the Great Day of Atonement (Lev. 16:20-22; 4:22-26). These sacrifices were typical of Christ's (Heb. 10:1ff.). The typical significance of OT sacrifice points directly to a substitutionary atonement for human sin in Jesus' sacrifice.

It is taught directly in many texts. No one who believes that Jesus' work of atonement is the subject of Isa. 53:4-6 can doubt this. More than one famous commentator has written to the effect that if these verses do not describe vicarious (substitutionary) sacrifice, then it is impossible for human language to convey the idea. Elsewhere it is written: "For Christ died for sins once for all, the righteous for the unrighteous, to bring you to God" (1Pe. 3:18); he became "a

curse for us" (Gal. 3:13); "He himself bore our sins in his body on the tree, so that we might die to sins and live for righteousness; by his wounds you have been healed" (1Pe. 2:24).

The Bible is inexplicable without this feature, and they do injustice to that book who seek to remove that meaning from it. How, for example, can one explain why "it was the LORD'S will to crush him" (Isa. 53:10) or why the Father abandoned the Son (Mt. 27:46), on any other grounds? On what other grounds can the conscience of men be "set free?" This doctrine moves not through Scripture like a thread but like an irresistible avalanche sweeping all before it.

4. *The Burial of Christ.* The Apostles' Creed makes special mention of it. Paul's recital of the main elements of the gospel includes "that he was buried" (1Co. 15:4). This event is important for a number of reasons. In the first place it was the beginning of a new epoch in his work. Being abused by the ungodly came to an end with the thrust of the soldier's spear. After that, the hands of wicked men never touched him again. He was buried by righteous men in a rich man's tomb (Mt. 27:57-60; Jn. 19:38-42). In this perspective, death on the cross must be viewed as the end of humiliation and his burial the beginning of the change to exaltation. Yet from the fact that his death and burial are so frequently associated in Scripture it has association with his humiliation too. Many have observed that Jesus' burial proved that he was truly dead. The Roman watch was in part to ensure that public impression. Furthermore, Scripture speaks of union with him in his death as being "buried with him," of which baptism is a figure. One must not neglect to note that he made his burial in earth for a short period of time and his emerging alive a proof of his messiahship (Mt. 12:40; Jn. 2:18ff.).

5. *The Resurrection of Christ.* Five chapters in the four Gospels as well as part of the first chapter of Acts are devoted to narrative of Jesus' resurrection. No one can even explain Jesus' resurrection. It is a miracle which if

explicable would not be a miracle. Miracles are by definition inexplicable by natural causes. To discuss its significance fully is not possible. Eight propositions summarizing the NT's own interpretation of it will summarize its significance.

a. The Resurrection of Christ was *a fulfillment of prophecy*. Though less is made of this than in the case of Jesus' death, there is considerable attention to it. Jesus, of course, prophesied it to his disciples several times (Mt. 16:21; 17:23), and obliquely hinted at it to his enemies (Mt. 12:40; Jn. 2:19). After this event he declared that it was a matter of OT prophecy (Lk. 24:44-45). The apostles insisted it occurred "according to the Scriptures" (1Co. 15:4), and they preached many sermons on this subject. They cited Ps. 16 in Ac. 2:25-28 and 13:35, and Ps. 2 in Ac. 13:33, among other passages. This is a recurring theme in apostolic preaching. They never sought to prove the Resurrection took place. They simply reported that they had seen him in the same body in which he suffered and died. And they knew his appearances were not subjective visions or even spiritual experiences (Lk. 24:35-43). They claimed that their own witness, buttressed by prophetic Scripture, was sufficient to establish the fact.

b. The Resurrection *declared his deity:* "who through the Spirit of holiness was declared with power to be the Son of God by his resurrection from the dead: Jesus Christ our Lord" (Ro. 1:4). This is the declaration that rang clear to doubting Thomas and led him to exclaim, "My Lord and my God."

c. The Resurrection *certified his messiahship*. Men should have acknowledged him as the Christ by the many credentials he presented, but nevertheless this was to crown the divine certification (Mt. 12:38-40; Jn. 2:13-22).

d. The Resurrection *completed his victory over sin* and its penalty. "God raised him from the dead, freeing him from the agony of death, because it was impossible for death to keep its hold on

him" (Ac. 2:24; cf. 1Co. 15:1-11).

e. The Resurrection *enabled him to share his own righteousness* (by justification) with us: "God will credit righteousness—for us who believe in him who raised Jesus our Lord from the dead. He was delivered over to death for our sins and was raised to life for our justification" (Ro. 4:22-25). *See* IMPUTE

f. The Resurrection also *enables him to share with us his own eternal life*, thus providing a basis for the many biblical promises of eternal life *now* to those who believe in Christ (Jn. 5:24; Ro. 6:3-4).

g. The Resurrection of Christ *assures believers of their own future glorious resurrection* (see all of 1Co. 15, esp. vv. 12-20).

h. Of inestimable value to Christians of all generations is the resurrection of Jesus as the *ground of Christian evidences*, proof that our faith is founded on the rock of factuality. So Peter argued before Jews (Ac. 2:22-36; 3:12-26). So Paul argued before Gentiles (Ac. 17:16-34). So faithful apologists and evangelists declare to the present day.

6. *The Ascension of Christ*. This event, though described only in Lk. 24:50-51 and Ac. 1:11 is referred to many times in the NT (Mk. 16:19; Lk. 9:51; Jn. 13:3; 14:2, 28; 16:7-10; 1Ti. 3:16). It marked the end of his earthly ministry. Jesus put it in that perspective (Jn. 16:28). It prepared for the coming of the Holy Spirit and the inauguration of the church (Jn. 16:7; 1Co. 12:13). The present age, between the ascension and second coming of Christ, is sometimes designated "the dispensation of the Holy Spirit." The giving of the church's gifts of leadership and ministry are likewise connected with this event (Eph. 4:7-16). Christians see in this consummation of the Son of God's career by an ascension to heaven a strong assurance of a similar destiny for themselves. This assurance becomes for them an "anchor of the soul" (Heb. 6:18-20), cast into heaven wherein their "forerunner" has entered before them.

7. *Christ's Enthronement at God's*

Right Hand. The nature of this event prevents any "this-worldly" eyewitness report. Yet the NT provides by revelation both the fact itself and the meaning of it.

With reference to the fact, Jesus predicted it (Mt. 26:64) during his trials before Caiaphas. Peter in the first Christian sermon announced that Jesus had been exalted to the right hand of God (Ac. 2:24). Stephen in his dying moments saw Jesus at the "right hand of God," risen from his throne to receive to glory the first Christian martyr (Ac. 7:56). Through the NT the event is related to Christian doctrine, comfort, and admonition.

From the viewpoint of redemption, the enthronement at the Father's right hand was a signal that redemption was a finished work. By one sacrifice — once and for all — he had finished his work (Heb. 10:11-14). Thus the seated Savior is a ground of assurance of full forgiveness for the Christian. It completes the matter of setting the conscience free (Heb. 1:3; 12:2).

As in the case of other aspects of Messiah's work, the session is regarded as predicted in prophecy, prophecy which shaped the very language by which the whole subject is treated in the NT. That prophecy, to which this essay has before given attention, is Psalm 110: "The LORD says to my Lord: 'Sit at my right hand until I make your enemies a footstool for your feet.' . . . rule in the midst of your enemies . . . The Lord is at your right hand; he will crush kings on the day of his wrath." This phrasing is clearly recognizable in NT references to the session. Here at the fountain are the elements of Christ's kingly reign, a beginning in which he is declared king and a reign which takes place at first "in the midst of . . . enemies" but which will later triumph openly over all other sovereignties.

The appropriation by Christ of his kingly power, won by death and resurrection, took place at his enthronement at the right hand of the Father, and it is this which gives it great significance. It marks the beginning of the reign of Christ. This is the meaning assigned: "Jesus Christ . . . who has gone into heaven and is at God's right hand — with angels, authorities and powers in submission to him" (1Pe. 3:21-22). This reign, as Psalm 110 says, is "in the midst" of enemies and will progress until all of them are "under his feet" (Ps. 110:1-2, 5; Ps. 8:4-6; Heb. 2:6-9). That reign, presently invisible and acknowledged on earth only by Christians, will become visible at his second coming as King of kings and Lord of lords (Rev. 5:6-14; 11:15; 19:11-21). At that time will occur the resurrection of the righteous dead (Rev. 20:1-5), to be followed by Christ's millennial reign (Rev. 20:4-6). Then ensue the resurrection and judgment of "the rest of the dead" and their final judgment (Rev. 20:7-15), including presumably also all wicked angels, demons, and Satan. This will be succeeded (who knows how long?) by a merging of the reign of Christ with that of his Father, "for he must reign until he has put all his enemies under his feet" (1Co. 15:23-25; cf. Php. 2:9-11). The church's present share in and relation to the reign of Christ from the Father's right hand is mentioned at Eph. 1:20-23; 4:15; 5:23; Col. 1:18-20. It has been observed that the Christian confession, "Jesus Christ is Lord," is an acknowledgment of this reign.

8. *Christ's Present Ministry in Heaven.* There is other work besides redemption for the Son of God in heaven. He there intercedes for believers in the presence of the Father as their great High Priest (Heb. 7:23 — 8:7). He also is the believers' "advocate" with the Father in heaven (1Jn. 2:1). This is connected with the development of personal holiness, growth in grace, of all Christians on earth.

9. *Christ's Second Advent.* This will complete the span of the church age, or "age of the Holy Spirit." At the ascension, the apostles were visited by divine messengers who said, "This same Jesus, who has been taken from you into heaven, will come back in the same way you have seen him go into heaven" (Ac. 1:11).

His work will then be to complete the Christian's salvation by complete sanctification (1Th. 3:13; 5:23), the resurrection of dead believers (Php. 3:20-21), and the transformation of all believers' bodies according to the pattern of Christ's own resurrection body (1Co. 15:51-58; 1Th. 4:13-18). *See also* FUTURE LIFE (R.D.C.)

CHRISTIAN [follower of Christ] The term was first used at Antioch in Syria to refer to the NT disciples in the earliest days of the church (Ac. 11:26). Peter referred to "suffering as a Christian" (1Pe. 4:16). It was used by King Agrippa who asked Paul, "Do you think in such a short time you can persuade me to be a Christian?" (Ac. 26:28). Paul described the basis of the Christian gospel, the basis of the faith of the Christian, in these words: "Christ died for our sins according to the Scriptures, that he was buried, that he was raised on the third day according to the Scriptures" (1Co. 15:3-4). The faith that makes a Christian is personal trust, apart from any deeds or works, in Jesus as Lord and as the one who "was delivered over to death for our sins and was raised to life for our justification" (Ro. 4:24-25).

CHRISTIANITY The beliefs and practices of the followers of Christ, founded on the life and teachings of Jesus Christ. Christianity is unique because it is not merely a philosophy (solely in the world of ideas, cf. Ac. 17:19), but claims the resurrection of Jesus as a historical fact. If this claimed fact is true, then Christ and his teachings have great claims on our lives.

CHRISTMAS [Christ's mass] A day commemorating the birth of Christ, December 25th. The Eastern Orthodox church commemorates his birth on January 6th. The exact day of his birth is not known.

CHRISTOLOGY *See* SYSTEMATIC THEOLOGY

CHRONICLES, THE BOOKS OF *See* KINGS, BOOKS OF

CHRONOLOGY *See* ASSYRIA; BABYLON, BABYLONIA; EGYPT; HASMONEANS; HERODS, THE; ISRAEL; JUDGES; KINGS OF JUDAH AND ISRAEL; MACCABEES; PERSIA; ROMANS; SELEUCIDS. The study that measures historical time is called chronology. It divides the total lapse of time into units, primarily of numbered years; and it assigns events to their proper points in this sequence. Like all real history, the biblical events have a chronology in time, just as they have a geography in space. Such a chronology serves to clarify the record, by indicating the sequence and relative position of the incidents of Scripture, both with respect to each other and to the happenings of the ancient empires that surrounded God's people, Israel. It also serves to authenticate the record by emphasizing how the biblical events fit in with known history and are not just "stories" (see Ac. 26:26 or 2Pe. 1:16). God has, moreover, providentially preserved within the Bible enough information so that most of its major events may be dated with considerable accuracy (*see* CALENDAR).

Yet except for the wilderness period (Exodus through Deuteronomy) and a few times later (as in Jos. 4:19; 5:6 or 1Ki. 6:1), when events were dated in terms of Israel's exodus from Egypt (Ex. 40:17; Nu. 10:11; Dt. 1:3), the Bible used no one fixed point of reference for its dates. It used instead only a "relative" chronology, for example, in the first, second, third, etc. year of the life of a certain patriarch or reign of a king. Recourse must therefore be had to the nearby, but non-Israelite, pagan cultures that do furnish the information necessary for building up a system of absolute, B.C. and A.D. dates.

The years of Babylonia's rulers from 747 B.C. down to the second Christian century were accurately recorded in *The Canon* of Ptolemy, a Greek geographer and astronomer of Egypt who died about A.D. 161. Ptolemy also recorded and dated by reign over eighty verifiable astronomical phenomena, such as the eclipses of the moon on March 17, 721, and July 16, 523 B.C. Similarly, the neighboring Assyrians maintained "eponym" (a person for whom something is named) lists, in which each year was assigned the name of an important official. Since the "eponym" lists also include an eclipse of the sun on June 15, 763, the whole can be dated from 892 to 648 B.C. Prior to 892, Assyrian king lists carry us back to about 2000 (*see* ASSYRIA) and became fairly reliable from about 1700 B.C. onward, with a margin of error of less than ten years after 1400. Other king lists from Egypt, which can be cross-checked with the Assyrian and with other astronomical observations, produce dates of about 2133-1990 for Dynasty XI, when Abram entered Egypt (Ge. 12:10-20), of 1990-1786 for Dynasty XII (Middle Kingdom) with only a negligible margin of error, when Joseph

and then his whole family entered Egypt (Ge. 37—50), and of 1570-1095 for XVIII-XX (New Empire; *see* EGYPT), from the final century of Israel's Egyptian oppression to near the end of Israel's judges.

Biblical events may then be assigned absolute dates whenever they are mentioned in these other datable records. Thus the Babylonian Nebuchadnezzar's capture of Jerusalem in his eighth year (2Ki. 24:12), can be dated precisely to March 16, 597. Again, the Assyrian Shalmaneser III's contacts with kings Ahab and Jehu can be dated 853 and 841 respectively; and, while neither contact is discussed in the Bible, the fact that between Ahab and Jehu appear two other kings that occupy exactly twelve years proves that 853 must have been the last year of Ahab and 841 the first of Jehu.

Event	Reference Point	Biblical Basis	Date
Nehemiah's wall	Twentieth yr. of Artaxerxes I of Persia	Neh. 2:1	444 B.C.
Return decreed	First yr. of Cyrus II of Persia over Babylon	Ezra 1:1	538
Fall of Jerusalem	Nineteenth yr. of Nebuchadnezzar II of Babylon	2 Kgs. 25:8	586
Fall of Samaria	Last yr. of Shalmaneser V of Assyria	2 Kgs. 17:3	722
Division of Kingdom	Seventy-seven yrs. before sixth yr. of Shalmaneser III	(see para. above)	930
Temple founded	Fourth yr. of Solomon	1 Kgs. 11:42; 6:1	966
Exodus from Egypt	480th yr. before temple's founding	1 Kgs. 6:1	1446
Descent into Egypt	Inaugurating a 430 yr. sojourn there (but 397 there, plus 33 in Canaan, for "the sons of Israel," according to Gk.	Ex. 12:40	(Hebrew text, 1876)
			Gk/Heb Text
Jacob born	130 yrs. before	Gen. 47:9	1973 (2006)
Isaac born	60 yrs. before	Gen. 25:26	2033 (2066)
Abraham born	100 yrs. before	Gen. 26:5	2133 (2166)

Counting backward from these dates, one establishes Solomon's death and the division of the kingdom in 930 B.C. and the Exodus in 1446 (1Ki. 6:1). Among the more significant of the OT's absolute dates are shown on page 143.

Prior to Abraham, biblical chronology becomes indefinite. Usher's famous date of 4004 B.C. for the creation of Adam assumed that the twenty pre-Abrahamic patriarchs (Ge. 5 and 11: 10-26) overlapped, without gap. But the ancients often counted long periods by successive lifetimes, not by overlapping generations. Thus in Genesis 15, Israel's four centuries in Egypt (v. 13), which actually covered some ten generations (1Ch. 7:25-27), is said to entail only four such lifetime generations (v. 16). Applied to Genesis 5, this counting by "successive" patriarchs would mean, for example, that while Adam begat (an ancestor of) Seth when he was 130 (v. 3), the Seth of verse 68 actually arose as Scripture's next prominent figure only after Adam's full life of 930 years (v. 4). Adam would then date about 15,000 B.C., or a millennium before the famous Lascaux (in SE France) cave paintings.

Further, the two sets of ten patriarchs before and after the Flood may compare with the three sets, each of fourteen ancestors, in the genealogy of Christ (Mt. 1:1-17); and, just as the latter could omit three generations in verse 8 ("Joram begat [an ancestor of] Uzziah"), so Genesis may have omitted a number of links as well.

NT chronology covers but a single century: from the birth of Christ in about 5 B.C. (shortly before the death of Herod the Great in 4 B.C.), through his ministry covering four Passovers (Jn. 2:13; 5:1; 6:4; 12:1), from A.D. 26 to 30, to Jerusalem's fall to Rome in 70 and John's last Epistles some 25 years later. (J.B.P.)

CHRYSOLITE, CHRYSOLYTE *See* PRECIOUS STONES AND METALS, Precious Stones 6.

CHRYSOPRASE, CHRYSOPRASUS *See* PRECIOUS STONES AND METALS, Precious Stones 1.

CHRYSOSTOM, JOHN A commentator and preacher who lived from about A.D. 347 to 407.

CHUB *See* LIBYA

CHUN *See* CUN

CHURCH {assembly} A word that is used to translate the Greek *ekklesia*,

NEW TESTAMENT EVENTS	
6/5 B.C.	Christ's birth
A.D. 6/7	Jesus in the temple
26	John the Baptist begins his ministry
26/27	Christ is baptized, begins his ministry
30	Christ is crucified, resurrected, and enthroned
30	Pentecost
34/35	Paul's conversion
44	James, the apostle, is martyred
46-48	Paul's first missionary journey
49/50	Jerusalem council
50-52	Paul's second missionary journey
53-57	Paul's third missionary journey
59-62	Paul's imprisonment in Rome
67	Paul's second imprisonment
65-67	Peter martyred
68	Paul martyred
70	Jerusalem falls
90-95	John exiled
c. 100	John dies

which has the idea of an assembly and is thus translated in Ac. 19:32, 41. The Hebrew equivalent was *qahal* which in a religious sense referred to Israel as a religious body. The early church carried this religious sense over to *ekklesia* and considered itself to be a part of the true Israel of God, those who from any background had the faith of Abraham (Ro. 4:16-18; 9:6-8; Gal. 3:14, 29). The early believers began to organize themselves in groups or churches with various officers. Thus, it is clear that the early church thought of itself as a visible organization as well as an "invisible" one—namely, a body of all those in space and time who had come to believe in Jesus Christ (1Co. 12:13; Col. 1:24). *See* BODY OF CHRIST; SYNAGOGUE

CHURCH DISCIPLINE *See* DISCIPLINE, CHURCH

CHURCH FATHERS Christian authors after the first century. Clement, Ignatius, and Polycarp are three.

CHUSHAN RISHATHAIM *See* CUSHAN-RISHATHAIM

CHUZA, CHUZA *See* CUZA

CILICIA *See* GEOGRAPHY OF THE HOLY LAND; KUE

CINNAMON *See* PLANTS, PERFUMES, AND SPICES

CINNEROTH *See* KINNERETH

CIRCUMCISION The ceremonial cutting off of the foreskin of male children on the eighth day after birth. It was practiced by Israel's neighbors with the exception of the Philistines. For the Israelites it was a sign of the covenant between God and Israel (Ge. 17:9-14). Israelite slaves and any stranger who wished to keep the Passover also were required to be circumcised (Ge. 17:13; Ex. 12:48-49). Presumably all the early Christians, being Jews, were circumcised. The practice continued in the early church for converts from Judaism. Paul had Timothy circumcised, for he had a Jewish mother (Ac. 16:3). Before the practice was dropped for converts

from among the Gentiles, there was a vigorous controversy among the early Christians. Paul refused to let Titus be circumcised (Gal. 2:3). A council of the church was called for in Jerusalem to discuss whether it was necessary to be circumcised according to the custom taught by Moses in order to be saved. The decision was negative; and the practice gradually died out in the church (Ac. 15:1-31).

CIRCUMCISION OF THE HEART A figure of speech referring to internalized obedience and faith to the LORD (Dt. 30:6). To circumcise the heart was to be no longer obstinate to God's commands (Dt. 10:16).

CIS *See* KISH 1.

CISTERN A natural or man-made reservoir for storing water. In Palestine, with its abundance of limestone hills, there were many. Those made in other ways had their walls lined with waterproof lime plaster. These were both communally owned and each man could have his own (2Ki. 18:31). The winter rains were collected in them for later use, but springs for "living" (fresh) water, were vitally necessary as well as for the maintenance of a population. *See* FOUNTAIN; POOL; SPRING; WATER; WELL

CITADEL Translation of a Hebrew word that is frequently rendered "fort." In archaeological terms it is sometimes referred to as "tower," a part of a fortification (2Ch. 17:12; Ne. 7:2; Pr. 18:19).

CITES OF THE PLAIN Five cities listed in Ge. 13:10-12; 14.8.

CITY OF DAVID *See* DAVID, TOWN OF

CITY OF GOD The heavenly Jerusalem (Heb. 11:10, 16; 12:22; Rev. 21:2).

CITY OFFICIAL A NIV rendering in Ac. 17:6.

CITY OF REFUGE Among the forty-eight cities assigned to the Levites scattered throughout all of Israel, six were chosen to be places of refuge for the person who killed another. The avenger of blood could not touch the manslayer while he remained in the city of refuge. A trial for the manslayer was required, and only if found guilty could he be turned over to the avenger of blood and executed. If the killing was found to be accidental, the manslayer could stay in the city and be safe from this form of reprisal. Only after the death of the current high priest could he return to his home and be safe. Three of these cities were on each side of the Jordan. Later three more were added W of the Jordan (Nu. 35:6-32; Jos. 20:2-3; 21:13-38).

CITY OF SALT An unidentified town in the desert near En Gedi (Jos. 15:62). †

CITY OF THE SUN *See* HELIOPOLIS

CITY, TOWN The normal pattern of settlement in the biblical world was that of a cluster of unwalled villages around a central fortified town or city (Jos. 17:11). Prime requisites for the establishment of such a complex were availability of water, farmland, proximity to trade routes, and considerations of defense. The gate or gates of a city were of great importance, as they would be the weakest part in the circumvallation (surrounding) wall. Here too the elders and judges sat to hear cases and to give advice. Here important proclamations were made (Ru. 4:1-11; 1Ki. 22:10; Ne. 8:1). The cities had their own markets within, and merchants or manufacturers tended to live together in the same area of the city with others of the same trade. Apart from these natural groupings, there is little evidence of city planning. In most cases the population of each city or town is not given. Thus it is not possible always to distinguish between the two, and the English words are used interchangeably in the text of this dictionary, as well as in most versions of the Bible.

CLASPS Fastenings made of gold or bronze which held together the linen curtains or other hangings of the tabernacle (Ex. 35:11; 36:13, 18).

CLAUDA *See* CAUDA

CLAUDIA [*possibly* lame] A Christian lady in Rome who sent greetings to Timothy (2Ti. 4:21). †

CLAUDIUS
1. The fourth Roman emperor (A.D. 41 to 54), in whose days there was a severe famine (Ac. 11:28). He expelled the Jews from Rome (Ac. 18:2). †
2. One whose original name was Lysias, an officer in charge of the Roman garrison in Jerusalem in the days of Paul, who had purchased his Roman citizenship with great price (Ac. 22:28; 23:26). On two occasions he rescued Paul and on the second started him on his long journey to Rome (Ac. 21:31-40; 22:24-29; 23:10-33). †

CLAY *See* BRICK

CLAY TABLETS *See* WRITING

CLEAN AND UNCLEAN These terms referred to ritual and not physical cleanliness, ritual purity, or defilement. Certain things were declared "clean" by the law. Some things were never clean, such as the unclean animals. Other things had to be purified or cleansed ritually when they became unclean (Lev. 7:21; Nu. 19:11, 13; Dt. 14:3-20). The ritual for cleansing is spelled out in a number of cases; for example, that for the "leper" is recorded in Lev. 14:1-9. Paul stated that the law was to lead men to Christ, to bring men to see their need for purity and deliverance, and that once a man by faith had his sins forgiven he no longer needed this function of the law. The law had its place, but that place was not for salvation (Gal. 3:23-29). Legislation is very easily capable of legalism. Men can follow the letter of the law and are capable of legalism. Men can follow the letter of the law and sidestep the spirit of it. This accounts for the controversies between Jesus and the Pharisees (Mt. 9:10-13; Lk. 11:37-52). While Jesus himself did not himself abandon the ritual purity laws (Mt. 8:2-4), his emphasis on inward (spiritual) cleanliness rather than outward (physical) cleanliness (Mt. 15:18) soon caused the Christians to abandon the OT laws of purity.

CLEMENT {mild} A colaborer with Paul at Philippi (Php. 4:3). †

CLEOPAS [renowned father] One of the two disciples with whom Jesus walked and conversed on the way to Emmaus on the day of the Resurrection (Lk. 24:18). †

CLEOPHAS *See* CLOPAS

CLERGY In many religious spheres, those who have been consecrated for sacred service, as distinct from the laity.

CLOAK *See* DRESS

CLOPAS The husband of one of the Marys who stood at the foot of the cross (Jn. 19:25). †

CLOSET KJV for "room." *See* ROOM 1.

CLOTH, CLOTHES, CLOTHING *See* DRESS; WEAVING AND SPINNING

CLOTH, FOR THE FACE *See* HANDKERCHIEF; NAPKIN

CLOUD, BRIGHT *See* GLORY OF THE LORD (SHEKINAH)

CLOUD, PILLAR OF *See* PILLAR

CLOUDS These were the source of life-giving rain. They veiled the presence of God from human sight (Ex. 19:9; Jdg. 5:4). God is described as one who rides in the heavens or rides on the clouds. Daniel's "one like a son of man" comes riding on the clouds of heaven, as does the Son of Man, and the Christians are at the end of days to be caught up into heaven in the clouds to meet the Lord in the air (Ps. 68:4, 33; Da. 7:13; Mt. 26:64; 1Th. 4:17).

CLOUTS KJV for "old clothes" or "old rags" (Jer. 38:11-12).

CLUB *See* ARMS AND ARMOR; WAR

CNIDUS [age] A city of Asia Minor past which Paul's ship sailed on its way to Rome (Ac. 27:7). †

COAL As used in the Bible this does not refer to mineral coal but rather to charcoal, which is made by burning wood (Ps. 120:4; Isa. 54:16).

COAST *See* GEOGRAPHY OF THE HOLY LAND

COAT *See* DRESS

COAT OF MAIL *See* ARMS AND ARMOR

COBRA *See* BEASTS 1.

COCK *See* BIRDS 2.

COCKATRICE KJV for "viper." *See* BEASTS 1.

COCKCROWING KJV for the last watch of the night, 3:00-6:00 A.M. (Mk. 13:35). *See* WATCH 1.

COCKLE KJV for "weed" (Job 31:40).

CODEX A leaf form of a book having a spine. *See* BOOK

COFFER *See* ARK 3.

COFFIN These were not in general use among the Israelites. One only is mentioned in the Bible, that of Joseph, in which his body was transported from Egypt to Canaan (Ge. 50:26). *See* ARK 4.; BIER

COHABITATION *See* MARRIAGE

COHORT *See* BAND

COIN *See* MONEY

COL-HOZEH [every seer] A descendant of Judah whose son repaired the Fountain Gate after the return from the Babylonian captivity (Ne. 3:15; 11:5). †

COLLAR *See* CLOAK; DRESS; MANTLE; ROBE

COLLECTION, THE *See* GIVING

COLLECTOR, TAX *See* TAXES, TAXING; TRIBUTE; ZACCHAEUS

COLLEGE KJV for "Second District" (2Ki. 22:14; 2Ch. 34:22).

COLLOP KJV for "bulge of fat" (Job 15:27).

COLONY A settlement of Romans somewhere within that empire, usually for soldiers and their families (Ac. 16:12). †

COLORS The basic natural colors noted in the Bible include white, black, red, and green. They were seen in nature in the snow, milk, and wool, in the hair and ravens, in blood and wine, in plants and grasses (Ex. 4:6; Ge. 49:12; Rev. 1:14; Lev. 13:31; SS. 5:11; 2Ki. 3:22; Ex. 10:15). Gray was the color of old men's hair (Ps. 71:18). The striped, speckled, spotted, and mottled (blotched) were of course mixtures of various colors (Ge. 30:32; 31:10). Some colors or dyes were extracted from mollusks, insects, copper, or iron ore. These were variously rendered as blue, red, purple, or scarlet (Ex. 26:1, 31; Eze. 23:14).

COLOSS(A)E [punishment] A city in Asia Minor mentioned only once in the Bible, but about which we may learn from Paul's letter to the church there (Col. 1:2). Along with Laodicea and Hierapolis the area was visited by early evangelists, but not Paul. A church was started there (Col. 2:1; 4:13). †

COLOSSIANS, BOOK OF *See* PAULINE EPISTLES

COLT Used in the NT for a young donkey. *See* BEASTS 4.

COMBAT *See* ARMS AND ARMOR; WAR

COMFORT, COMFORTER
1. This word is similar to exhortation. Christian's faith can be a comfort to other Christians (1Th. 3:7; Phm. 7). To await the Lord's "catching up" is to be a comfort (1Th. 4:18). The Lord Jesus himself is our comfort (1Th. 2:17). *See* EXHORTATION
2. A title of the Holy Spirit in many versions, "Counselor" in the NIV (Jn. 14:16, 26; 15:26; 16:7). *See* GOD, NAMES OF, GODHEAD 6.

COMING OF CHRIST *See* CHRIST, WORK OF, *second advent*; *see also* ESCHATOLOGY

COMMANDER, FIELD *See* RABSHAKEH

COMMANDMENTS *See* LAW

COMMISSION, GREAT Christ's command to make disciples of all peoples in all places as they are going out, to baptize in the name of the triune God, and teach obedience to Christ's commands (Mt. 28:19-20). The main verb in the original is to "make disciples."

COMMUNION *See* LORD'S SUPPER

COMMUNION, VIEWS OF Different views exist concerning what Christ meant when he ordered the observance of the Lord's Table. There are four major views.

Transubstantiation is a view accepted by Roman Catholicism that the elements (bread and wine) are transformed into the actual body and blood of Christ, by a priest's ceremony. The bread and wine only has the appearance of elements. This view takes into strictest literalism the word "is" in Mk. 14:22, 24, "This *is* my body." This view sees Communion as a sacrament, which increases sanctifying grace and is a part of spiritual life.

Consubstantiation is a view that is held by the Lutheran church. This view holds that the elements (bread and wine) do not become the actual body and blood of Christ. The body and blood of Christ coexists "in, with, and under" the elements. The transformation is made by the Word of God, not a priest's pronouncement. This view also sees Communion as a sacrament.

Memorial is a view that sees the word *is* in the Catholic view as a figure of speech. They would ask, "If Christ was proclaiming the elements in his hand as his actual body and blood, then who was making the statement?" This view emphasizes the word "remembrance" in 1Co. 11:24. This view normally does not view this practice as a sacrament but an ordinance. This is held by most Baptists and affiliated groups.

Spiritual Remembrance is a view that does not see any use of elements in any physical form. This view would say that the Lord's Table was intended to have "only a spiritual meaning." The Old Covenant, they say, has ceremony and symbol and the New Covenant does away with all physical remembrance. This is held by the Friends Church (Quakers) and affiliated groups. (J.A.S.)

COMMUNISM A social and economic system in which the means of production are owned by the government, not by private parties. In its ideal form it is a classless and stateless society. Some see communism in Ac. 2:45; but it is not, because property was given *according to the need*. Furthermore, this assumed that the property was the believers to give. Communism assumes no such right, for the state owns all property.

COMMUNITY In the OT two Hebrew words are used to convey the idea of "community," "assembly," or "the Lord's people," and are thus translated in Ex. 12:3; Jos. 8:35; Nu. 31:16. In the NT the concept is sometimes rendered by the word "congregation," *ekklesia*, "the church," or "assembly" (Ac. 13:43).

COMPANY OF SOLDIERS *See* BAND

COMPASSION Synonym of mercy and pity in Scripture. Since this was the characteristic of God, he expected his people to show the same to their brethren and even to strangers in their midst (Zec. 7:9-10; Isa. 1:17; Mt. 18:33). This was a very prominent characteristic in the life, ministry, and teaching of Jesus (Mt. 9:36; 15:32).

CONANIAH [Yahweh sustains]
1. A Levite who was the chief officer in charge of the contributions, tithes, and offerings under King Hezekiah (2Ch. 31:12-13). †
2. A chief among the Levites who in the reign of Josiah gave lambs for the Passover to the other Levites (2Ch. 35:9). †

CONCEIT *See* PRIDE

CONCISION KJV for "circumcision" or "mutilators of the flesh" (Php. 3:2).

CONCORDANCE, ENGLISH BIBLE An alphabetical listing of Bible words, usually according to a particular version.

CONCUBINE A secondary wife usually taken from servants, slaves, or as booty in war, often because the principal wife was barren, as in the case of Abraham, with Sarah and Hagar (Ge. 16:1-2). This practice was regulated by law in the world of the time outside the Bible area (Code of Hammurabi, Nuzi Laws, for example), and it appears so also in the Bible (Dt. 21:15-17). Polygamy was practiced in OT times: Esau, Jacob, Gideon, David, and Solomon (Ge. 26:34; 29:29; 1Ki. 11:3), but to what extent among the common people is not clear.

CONCUPISCENCE KJV for "covetous desire," "evil desires" and "lust" respectively in the NIV in Ro. 7:8; Col. 3:5; and 1Th. 4:5. *See* LUST

CONDEMNATION *See* DEAD, ABODE OF THE; PUNISHMENT

CONDUIT *See* AQUEDUCT

CONEY *See* BEASTS 5.

CONFECTION KJV for perfume or medicine (Ex. 30:35). *See* PLANTS, PERFUMES, AND SPICES, Perfumes, Scents, Ointments, Drugs

CONFECTIONARY One who makes perfumes or medicines (1Sa. 8:13). *See* CONFECTION

CONFECTIONER KJV for a female maker of perfumes or medicines (1Sa. 8:13). *See* CONFECTION

CONFESSION
1. In both Testaments the basic idea is acknowledgment, whether of sin, of Jesus as Lord unto salvation, as a witness, or in praise (Lev. 5:5; 1Ki. 8:33; Mt. 3:6; Ro. 10:9; 14:11-12; 1Ti. 6:13;

Heb. 13:15). Confession can be private to God only (IJn. 1:9), or public to others in the church (Jas. 5:16), in behalf of a people (Da. 9:4ff.).

2. A creed or confession is a set of statements of what is believed. In church history there have been many formal statements of what the church believed about their faith, such as the Apostles' Creed, the Nicene Creed, the Athanasian Creed. For those who make the Bible their final authority, a study of the creeds can be profitable to the Christian, comparing Scripture with those creeds. The Reformers also formulated many creeds. *See* CREED

CONGREGATION *See* COMMUNITY

CONGREGATIONAL FORM OF CHURCH GOVERNMENT Church government which features the autonomy, self-government, and authority of the local church.

CONIAH {Yahweh sustains} Son and successor of King Jehoiakim in Judah, usually called Jehoiachin and sometimes Jeconiah (2Ki. 24:6; 1Ch. 3:16; Jer. 22:24). See the footnotes in the NIV. *See also* JEHOIACHIN and KINGS OF JUDAH AND ISRAEL

CONIES, CONEYS *See* BEASTS 5., *Rock Badger*

CONONIAH *See* CONIAH; CONANIAH 1.

CONQUEST OF CANAAN Led by Joshua, the Israelites conquered Canaan at the end of their years of wandering in the wilderness after their exodus from Egypt. Many archaeologists have concluded that it took place late in the thirteenth century B.C., on what they say is the evidence from excavated sites. 1Ki. 6:1, on the other hand, as the text stands, would put it in the fifteenth century. Lines are sharply drawn on this point between "liberal" and "conservative" scholars, and the arguments of each may be found in many volumes.

CONSCIENCE Conscience is a moral sense in man to do right and elude wrong. Those with the Law of God know when they have broken it, and can feel remorse and long for a "clean heart" (Ps. 51:1-12).

Gentiles who did not have God's law also have a kind of law written on their hearts, their conscience interacting with their thoughts (Ro. 2:14-15). The Christian is to account for his actions not only for his conscience but also others' (1Co. 10:29). The Christian is exhorted to live with a clear conscience (Ro. 13:5; Ac. 23:1; 1Ti. 1:5; 3:9; 2Ti. 1:3). Christ has set our conscience free with his atonement. *See* CHRIST, WORK OF, 3. a., *sacrifice* and h.; *also* 7. ¶ 3.

CONSECRATION Dedicating or setting a person or thing apart for the service of God. Animals, tithes and offerings, persons, or groups of persons, could be and were consecrated to God, the animals for sacrificial purposes (2Ch. 29:33; 31:6; 29:5, 31). In the NT the word "sanctifying" carries the same meaning (2Th. 2:13; 1Pe. 1:2). The Greek word also is rendered "holiness" or "holy" (1Co. 1:30; 1Th. 4:3).

CONSTANTINE The first Christian Emperor of Rome. (about A.D. 274/280-337)

Coin of Constantine Commemorating the First Official Recognition of Christianity

CONSTELLATION *See* STAR, STARS

CONSUBSTANTIATION *See* COMMUNION, VIEWS OF

CONTEST *See* ATHLETE

CONVERSION In Christianity, the act of turning from other religions (or no religion) to Christ (1Th. 1:9). *See*

CHRIST, WORK OF; SALVATION, APPLICATION OF

CONVERT *See* PROSELYTE

CONVICTION *See* BELIEVE; FAITH, FAITHFUL

CONVOCATION KJV for a religious assembly or festival (Ex. 12:16).

COOK *See* OVEN

COOS *See* COS

COPPER *See* BRONZE

COPPERSMITH KJV for "metalworker" (2Ti. 4:14).

COPTIC CHURCH The Christian Church in Egypt, established in the fifth century.

COR *See* WEIGHTS AND MEASURES

CORAL *See* PRECIOUS STONES AND METALS Precious Stones 7.

CORBAN {gift} A general term for all kinds of offerings. A gift vowed to God, in Mk. 7:11. *See* SACRIFICES AND OFFERINGS

CORD *See* ROPE

CORE KJV in Jude 11. *See* KORAH 5.

CORIANDER *See* PLANTS, PERFUMES, AND SPICES

CORINTH {decoration} A city and great commercial port center of Greece on the isthmus between the mainland and the Peloponnese on one of the most important E-W trade routes. Paul spent eighteen months there working as a tentmaker and established a church (Ac. 18:3, 11). Here Paul was tried and released by the Romans (Ac. 18:12-16). Troubles developed in the church after Paul left, and this accounts for his epistles to them. *See also* PAULINE EPISTLES and PAUL, LIFE AND TEACHINGS OF

CORINTHIANS, BOOKS OF *See* PAULINE EPISTLES

CORMORANT *See* BIRDS 3.

CORN *See* PLANTS, PERFUMES, SPICES, Plants for Food 1., *grain*

CORNFLOOR KJV for "threshing floor" (Hos. 9:1).

CORNELIUS {of a horn} A Roman centurion commanding the Italian Regiment who was converted to Christianity and baptized by Peter (Ac. 10:1, 3, 17-48). †
See GOD-FEARER

CORNERSTONE A large stone at the corner of a wall to bind the two walls together. In the OT it usually means a foundation stone and is a symbol of stability (Job 38:6; Ps. 118:22; Isa. 28:16). In the NT references are quotations or reflections of the reference in Ps. 118:22, where the NIV renders it "capstone" (Eph. 2:20; 1Pe. 2:6).

CORNET A "ram's horn" (*shofar*) or sometimes "horn" (*keren*), not a metallic trumpet. *See* MUSIC, MUSICAL INSTRUMENTS 2. (2) *wind instruments*

CORPSE A carcass in the NIV is the body of a dead animal, the touching of which makes a person unclean ceremonially (Lev. 11:26). The touching of a corpse could make a priest unclean; he must then go through a ceremony to be clean (Lev. 22:4). The "dead body" is another way to express "a corpse" (Nu. 5:2; 6:6; 9:7). *See also* CLEAN AND UNCLEAN; SOUL

CORRECTION *See* DISCIPLE, CHURCH; EXHORTATION

COS {summit} An island off the coast of Asia Minor, Paul's ship passed it on the way to Rhodes on his final recorded voyage to Rome (Ac. 21:1). †

COSAM {diviner} An ancestor of Jesus in Luke's genealogy (Lk. 3:28). †

COSMETICS There were cosmetics in the ancient world, for the eyes (2Ki. 9:30); also perfumes and ointments (Pr. 7:17). In the NT Peter urges emphasis upon the inner person and not external looks (1Pe. 3:3-4). *See also* PAINT, PAINTING

COTES KJV for "pen" as in a sheep pen (2Ch. 32:28).

COTTON *See* LINEN

COUCH *See* FURNITURE

COULTER A plowshare. *See* FARMING

COUNCIL *See* SANHEDRIN

COUNCIL OF JERUSALEM A Christian Council discussing the question of how Gentiles were to relate to Mosaic Law (Ac. 15:1-29). The conclusions are found in Acts 15:28-29.

COUNSELLOR A member of the Council (Mk. 15:43; Lk. 23:50). *See* SANHEDRIN

COUNSELOR One who gives counsel or advice such as a parent, an elder, a prophet or wise man, and God himself (Pr. 1:8; Eze. 7:26; Jer. 18:18; Ps. 16:7). The revelation of God, the Bible, is itself a counselor, and God gave his Holy Spirit to be a counselor (Ps. 119:24; Jn. 14:16). In the OT there is an additional usage. This seems to have been a title for a very close adviser to kings (2Ch. 25:16; Da. 3:24).

COUNTER-REFORMATION *See* REFORMATION, COUNTER

COURSES *See* LEVITES, *divisions*

COURT OF THE GENTILES *See* MIDDLE WALL OF PARTITION

COVENANT [agreement, contract] A pact, agreement, or treaty between persons or nations, or (in the Bible) between God and man (Ge. 21:27; 1Sa. 18:3; 1Ki. 20:34; Ge. 9:9-11; 17:1-14). It was customary to seal the covenant by a sacrifice in one of several ways and the blood of the sacrificial animal might even be applied to the covenantors (Ex. 24:8; Ps. 50:5; Jer. 34:18). Several covenants of major significance between God and man are noted in the Bible: (1) with Noah after the Flood (Ge. 9:9ff.); (2) with Abraham when the sign of circumcision was given (Ge. 17:7-10); (3) with Abraham in connection with the land of Pales-tine and blessing to the world (Ge. 17:7-8); (4) with the Israelites at Sinai when they were leaving the captivity in Egypt (Ex. 6:4-8); (5) and (6) with Adam and with Christ the second Adam. (While the word "covenant" is not used in the case of God and Adam, all those involved in the making of a covenant are there: parties, agreements or conditions, and rewards.) In this case God, on the one hand, and Adam and those who descended from him, on the other, were the parties. The rewards and conditions were life if Adam proved faithful, and sin and death on all mankind if he did not. The Adamic Covenant and the covenant between God and the second Adam, Christ (sometimes called by theologians the covenant of grace or redemption), are brought together in Paul's discussion (Ro. 5:12, 18-19).

The covenant with Noah promised that God would never again destroy all mankind by a flood (*see* 1 above). God promised to make a great nation out of Abraham and to be his God. Circumcision was its sign (*see* 2 above). God promised the land of Palestine to Abraham and his seed forever and that in him and his progeny all the families of the earth would be blessed (*see* 3 above). God promised to deliver his people to Canaan and to be their God. This was the national covenant of Israel, and the Law given at Sinai was its charter and basis of operation. The covenant with Adam, when broken, brought sin into the world (*see* 5 above). Christ the second or last Adam (1Co. 15:45ff.) fulfilled all righteousness and then offered himself in his death as the sacrifice that redeems all who "come unto God by him" (Heb. 9:11-26). Those who appropriate the condition of this covenant (*see* 6 above), who exercise faith in Christ and obedience to him, receive the blessing promised, eternal life.

Other covenants should also be noted: (1) the covenant of peace or perpetual priesthood (Nu. 25:12-13); (2) that made with David and reaffirmed with Solomon that there would always be one to sit on his throne (2Sa. 23:5; 7:12-16); and,

(3) another covenant of peace that will bring utopia to earth prior to eternity (Isa. 11:1-9; Eze. 34:25-31). *See* TESTAMENT

COVENANTAL VIEW OF BAPTISM *See* BAPTISM, COVENANTAL VIEW OF

COVENANT, BOOK OF THE The phrase comes from Ex. 24:7, where Moses took this book and read it to all the people at Mt. Sinai. This was at least the Ten Commandments, but may have been more. Some refer the title to the portion in Ex. 20:22—23:33. In 2Ki. 23:2, 21 it refers to the entire Deuteronomic law, or perhaps even to the entire legal system of the Pentateuch.

COVENANT THEOLOGY Sometimes called Federal Theology, it views the relationship between God and humanity as a type of agreement between them. The whole of Scripture is covered by two covenants; the covenant of works or the covenant of grace. *See* DISPENSATIONALISM

COVERING THE HEAD A practice in the early church for women, because of the angels (1Co. 11:4-16). It is problematic as to what "because of the angels" means.

COVET To express avarice, greed, envy—desiring what another has. It is considered sinful and is legislated against in the Ten Commandments (Ex. 20:17). In the NT the noun form is "greed" and the picture is that he who loves "things" is in danger of not loving God fully and may even carry it to the extent that it can be called idolatry (Mk. 7:21-23; Ro. 1:29; Eph. 5:3; Col. 3:5).

COW *See* BEASTS 4.

COZ {thorn, thornbush} *See* KOZ

COZBI {deceitful, ISBE; the luxuriant, KB} A Midianite woman with whom an Israelite played the harlot and brought a plague on Israel (Nu. 25:5-9, 18). †

COZEBA {liar} A descendant of Judah (1Ch. 4:22). †

CRACKNEL KJV for "cakes" (1Ki. 14:3).

CRAFT, CRAFTSMAN A skilled worker in Ex. 26:1, 31; 28:6, 15; 36:8, 35 (designer); 39:8. The emphasis is one of the thought process and creativity involved in the work. A second word for craftsman also involves creativity, but has a slight emphasis of the hands-on work—engraving and cutting (Ex. 36:36; 2Sa. 5:11; 1Ki. 7:14; 2Ki. 24:14; 1Ch. 29:5).

CRAFTSMEN, VALLEY OF *See* GE HARASHIM 1.

CRANE KJV in Jer. 8:7; Isa. 38:14. *See* BIRDS 4., *Swift*

CRAWLING THINGS *See* CREEPING THING

CREATION, CREATURE The Bible presents the story of creation in the first two chapters of Genesis and clearly states it as a fact in other places (Heb. 11:3; Jn. 1:3, 10). In summary, the picture that the Bible presents is one of all matter having a beginning and having come into existence only through the will and word of the eternal God. While there are many problems connected with the interpretation of the Creation account, it is clear that the writers of Scripture accepted an *ex nihilo* beginning for matter. The idea of natural development by natural causes from one simple beginning is not supported by the author of Genesis. This is most especially true in the account of the creation of man, since that states that man was not animate before the creative act that made him man (Ge. 2:7). He became what the animals were, living only after the divine inbreathing into the inanimate thing formed from the dust.

Some hold that there are two accounts of creation in the first two chapters of the Bible. In the first chapter, however, we have a presentation of the creation of the universe as a whole, while in the second chapter we find a detailed account of man's creation. What some call the second account has nothing to say about many of the items found in the first chapter—the creation of matter, the heavenly bodies, light itself, plants, or animals, except for the simple notice that the creation of animals took place before the creation of man. Some allege that these two chapters contain different orders of the creation of things, but chapter two is primarily concerned with the creation of man and woman. Thus, the second chapter supplements and complements the information found in the first.

The Greek word *ktisis* in the NT means that which has been created whether that be matter or a living thing, creation or creature (Ro. 1:25; 8:39; Heb. 4:13). The new creation of 2Co. 5:17 refers to a man who has had a spiritual experience with God in Christ that has made him new in his thinking and in his relationship to God. Paul taught that the creation will be delivered from its bondage to corruption at the time that the creature will receive his adoption, his resurrection (Ro. 8:18-23).

CREATIONISM The idea that all the universe and life originated from the direct, designed action of God.

CREATURE, LIVING *See* CHERUB

CREED *See* CONFESSION 2.

CREEK KJV for "bay" (Ac. 27:39).

CREEPING THING KJV in Ge. 1:24ff. The NIV and other versions render this as "things that move along the ground." This Hebrew word is also used to note things that move in the water; hence, the best way to translate "creeping things" is "things that move." *See* BEASTS 1.

CRESCENS A Christian friend of Paul's in Rome who later went to Galatia (2Ti. 4:10). †

CRETAN, CRETES, CRETIANS People from the island of Crete (Ac. 2:11; Tit. 1:12).

CRETE *See* GEOGRAPHY OF THE HOLY LAND

CRIB *See* MANGER

CRICKET *See* BEASTS 6.

CRIME Used in the Bible in the same sense as it is used in normal speech, "wrongdoing." In addition, however, the Greek word so translated is also used in the sense of "accusation" or "charge" (Lk. 23:4; Jn. 19:6).

CRIMSON A red dye made from an insect. Translated "scarlet" in Isa. 1:18 and Jer. 4:30 in the NIV. *See* DYED, DYEING

CRIPPLE *See* HEALING, HEALTH; SICK, SICKNESS

CRISPUS [curled] A ruler of the synagogue at Corinth converted and baptized by Paul (Ac. 18:8; 1Co. 1:14). †

CRITIC A critic in the area of Bible study is not one who gives harsh judgments; it is one who engages reasoned analysis, often professional, in the area of the biblical study. To be a "textual critic" is not one who is necessarily "critical" of the text of the Bible.

CRITICISM, COMPARATIVE-RELIGIONS An explanation of the traditions of the Judeo-Christian faith in terms of models or patterns of development believed to be common to all religions. This approach sometimes minimizes the Judeo-Christian revelatory features that were contrary to its culture and environment (that is truly unique to biblical religion at that particular time in history), or sees them rigidly in the large revolutionary framework.

CRITICISM, FORM (FORMGESCHICHTE) A technique of biblical study which aspires to describe the formation history of the text. It seeks to evaluate and identify layers of information which were added to the life-setting during the period of spoken transmission.

CRITICISM, HIGHER A system of biblical interpretation which goes above the written text. It attempts to identify the author, date, literary form, and other discussions. It is sometimes called literary criticism. Lower criticism deals with questions of the text itself.

CRITICISM, HISTORICAL A technique evaluating historical evidence, particularly for the Scripture document. The final aim is to ascertain what actually occurred.

CRITICISM, LITERARY-SOURCE A technique of study which attempts to separate the (assumed) various written sources on which the present biblical text is based. Though this approach can be applied to any book or passage of the Bible, this approach finds diverse sources in the first five books of the Bible. *See* DOCUMENTARY HYPOTHESIS

CRITICISM, REDACTION (RE-DAKTIONSGESCHICHTE) A method of study that seeks to separate the writers of the Gospels from the sources they used. The method then seeks to discover the *Sitz im Leben* (life situation) in which each Gospel writer wrote, and his purpose for writing the Gospel. This kind of critic does not try to harmonize the synoptic Gospels. *See* LOGIA; Q.

CRITICISM, STRUCTURAL Criticism which attempts to find certain generic elements of human existence and experience within the Bible text. It is also termed "structural exegesis."

CRITICISM, TEXTUAL Critical study which attempts to identify the exact form of the original text. This criticism begins with analyzing "variants" (not assumed errors) between manuscripts to determine the most probable original wording.

CROSS History records that from as early as the times of the Assyrians men were impaled on upright posts as a means of execution. By the time of the crucifixion of Christ by the Romans, men were affixed by nailing or by tying or both to crossed beams of wood. These were of four forms: the shape usually associated with the event, where the upright beam extends above the crossbar;

one that was T-shaped; one where the four extensions were of equal length and at right angles; and a similar one except that the form was like the modern letter "X." Crucifixion was a painful death, which ended in heart failure accompanied by suffocation. The word is used in three senses in the Bible: its literal sense, a wooden form; crucifixion; and, as a symbol for redemption (Lk. 23:26; Heb.12:2; Php. 3:18). The cross was sometimes referred to as a tree in the NT (Ac. 5:30; 10:39; 13:29; Gal. 3:13; 1Pe. 2:24). Tree is a general word for "wood." The apostles used this word because it brought to mind the OT vocabulary in the LXX (Dt. 21:22-23; Jos. 10:26).

The cross is an integral part of Christian theology, for it was on the cross by which atonement was made to God for man the sinner, and reconciliation was achieved. In Christian theology there is no divine remission of sin without the shedding of blood by the death of a savior, and that redemption was achieved through Christ's cross. This is sometimes misunderstood as being an innocent victim who is made to die for the salvation of others. This must be understood to be true and not true at the same time if the theology of the cross is to be understood. Christ was an innocent sinless victim, and he was made to die for others. However, Christ was also God the Son who had taken to himself a human form (Php. 2:5-8), and therefore his death was within the Godhead itself rather than God picking some third party to make this atoning sacrifice (Eph. 2:13-17; Col. 1:19-20; 2:13-14). The Apostle Paul, a Jew and a Roman citizen, for whom the death on a cross was considered a curse and something to be scorned, could only be "not ashamed" because of his conviction that the One who died there was the Son of God, dying for man's redemption (Ro. 1:16; Gal. 2:20).

CROWD A general word for a throng, multitude, large number of people (Mk. 3:7), sometimes disorganized and capable of crushing (Mk. 3:9). Jesus ministered to crowds, small groups, and individuals.

CROWN The word has several symbolic uses in addition to its reference to a part of the body (the top of the head), and to something that literally encircles the head, whether of the victor, the priest, or the king (Dt. 28:35; Sa. 12:30; Pr. 4:9). References are made to crowns of glory, righteousness, and life and crowns symbolic of triumph in the Christian life (2Ti. 4:8; Jas. 1:12; 1Pe. 5:4). A good wife is declared to be the crown of her husband, and the hoary or white head is a crown of glory also (Pr. 12:4; 16:31). Normally a "crown" in the NT is a victor's wreath (*stephanos*) and not a crown often pictured with royal jeweled tiaras (*diadema*). Before his crucifixion, Christ was mockingly crowned with a crown (wreath, *stephanos*) of thorns by the Roman soldiers (Mt. 27:29). *See* DIADEM

CROWN OF THORNS *See* CROWN

CRUCIBLE *See* FINING-POT

CRUCIFIXION *See* CROSS

CRUSE KJV for "water jug" or "water jar" (1Sa. 26:11-12, 16; 1Ki. 14:3; 17:12, 14, 16; 19:6; 2Ki. 2:20). *See* VESSEL

CRY *See* WEEP; WEEPING AND GNASHING

CRYPT *See* BURIAL

CRYSTAL *See* PRECIOUS STONES AND METALS, Precious Stones 15.; *see also* GLASS

CUB *See* LIBYA

CUBIT *See* WEIGHTS AND MEASURES

CUCKOO Lev. 11:16; Dt. 14:15. *See* BIRDS 5., *Gull*

CUCUMBER *See* PLANTS, PERFUMES, AND SPICES, Plants for Food 5.

CULTS Organizations which are heretical in one or more important ways and which often practice strong social control over their members. Any group which departs from the norm, or is not orthodox in its teaching and practices can be a cult.

CUMI [stand up!] *See* KOUM

CUMMIN *See* PLANTS, PERFUMES, AND SPICES

CUN [chosen] Sometimes called Berothai, a Syrian town from which David took much bronze (1Ch. 18:8). † *See* BEROTHAI

CUNEIFORM *See* WRITING

CUP A vessel with many sizes and shapes usually made of baked clay but also of metal, even gold. In addition to its use for drinking it was also used for divining (Ge. 40:11; 44:5; Mk. 9:41). In the Scriptures it is a figure of the wrath of God (Isa. 51:17, 22; Rev. 16:10). It is synonymous with "lot" or "fate" (Mt. 26:39). It has several symbolic usages: cup of consolation, sending food and drink to the bereaved; cup of salvation; cup of blessing, or cup of the Lord, which refers to the ritual Communion cup (Ps. 116:13; 1Co. 10:16, 21). The cup is used in connection with drunkenness (Pr. 23:31), and we read of the cup of staggering, the cup of horror and desolation, and the cup of fury or anger (Eze. 23:33; Rev. 14:10; 16:19).

CUPBEARER An officer of very great importance at a royal court (1Ki. 10:5). Nehemiah was cupbearer to the King of Persia, and a lengthy account of the cupbearer of the Pharaoh in Egypt is recorded in the accounts of Joseph (Ge. 40:2; Ne. 1:11).

CURDS An important part of the diet of the poor or common man in the Middle East, where milk was plentiful but refrigeration was not available. Milk was placed in a goatskin and churned together with sour curds left over from the last churning (Ge. 18:8; Pr. 30:33).

CURE *See* HEALING, HEALTH

CURSE An interdict by God against man for sin, or an asking the deity to bring evil or harm to the object of the curse (Dt. 28:20; 27:15-26; Ps. 109:17; 35:4-8). It was forbidden to curse the king, a deaf man, one's parents (Ex. 21:17), or God. Death was the penalty (Lev. 24:14-16). In Scripture it is considered a virtue, is even commanded, to bless those who curse you (Ps. 109:28; Lk. 6:28).

Anathema is a Hellenistic Greek word representing the Hebrew idea for something cursed or devoted, to destruction (Ro. 9:3; 1Co. 12:3; 16:22; Gal. 1:8).

A curse in the Bible is not the uttering of profanity, but the invocation of an affliction, plague or vexation. This could be on another (Lk. 6:28) or yourself (Mt. 26:74). *See also* DEVOTE; OATH; RACA

CURTAIN The fabric from which tents were made—in the Bible particularly associated with the tabernacle and the temple (Ex. 26:2; Mt. 27:51). The rent curtain in the NT is a symbol of the rending of the curtain that separates man from God (Heb. 10:20).

CUSH
1. An unidentified country through which the river Gihon flowed, as found in the creation account (Ge. 2:13). Some equate one of the references to Cush with Ethiopia, others with an area in Asia.
2. The son of Ham, grandson of Noah, and also of Nimrod (Ge. 10:68; 1Ch. 1:8-10).
3. A Benjamite mentioned in the title of Psalm 7.

CUSHAN A land or people mentioned in connection with Midian. Perhaps the words are synonyms (Hab. 3:7). †

CUSHAN-RISHATHAIM {man of Cush, doubly guilty} A king of Mesopotamia in the days of the Judges of Israel whom they served for a time (Jdg. 3:8-10). †

CUSHI, CUSHITE
1. The father of the prophet Zephaniah (Zep. 1:1). †

2. An ancestor of a member of King Jehoiakim's court (Jer. 36:14). †
3. A member of the Cushite people. One of the notables was the wife of Moses (Nu. 12:1; 2Sa. 18:21).

CUSTOM *See* TAXES, TAXING

CUTH, CUTHAH A Babylonian city from which settlers were brought by the Babylonian king who settled them in Israel. They intermarried in Israel and the Samaritans were the result (2Ki. 17:24, 30). †

CUTTING *See* TATTOO

CUZA {little jug} A steward of King Herod whose wife helped to provide the needs of Jesus, his disciples, and those with them (Lk. 8:3). †

CYLINDER SEALS *See* ORNAMENTS

CYMBAL *See* MUSIC

CYPRESS *See* TREES

CYPRUS *See* GEOGRAPHY OF THE HOLY LAND

CYRENE, CYRENIANS The capital of Libya and a Greek colony where Jews also lived. These had a synagogue in Jerusalem in NT times (Mt. 27:32; Mk. 15:21; Lk. 23:26; Ac. 2:10; 11:20; 6:9; 13:1). †

CYRENIUS *See* QUIRINIUS

CYRUS THE GREAT The founder of the Persian Empire, who under Darius the Mede, his vice regent, took the city of Babylon and brought that empire to an end (Da. 5). He encouraged the Jews to return to their ancestral home and to rebuild their temple (2Ch. 36:22; Ezr. 1:1; Isa. 44:27-28). His tomb has been found at Pasargadae, as well as his clay cylinder noting his decree given after his capture of Babylon encouraging all peoples to take their gods and go home. *See* PERSIA

D

DABAREH *See* DABERATH

DABBESHETH [hump] A border town (164-230) in Zebulun, exact location unknown; perhaps Tell esh-Shammam (Jos. 19:11). †

DABERATH [pasture] Modern Dabburiya (185-233). A Levitical town in Issachar on the border with Zebulun (Jos. 19:12; 21:28; 1Ch. 6:72). †

DAGGER *See* ARMS AND ARMOR

DAGON [(god of) cereal grain, IDB; fish, ISBE] *See* DEITIES

DALAIAH *See* DELAIAH

DALE, THE KINGS *See* SHAVEH, VALLEY OF

DALMANUTHA Neither this place (Mk. 8:10), nor the location Magadan, with which it is associated in Mt. 15:39, are identifiable. Perhaps they are to be found on the western shore of the Sea of Galilee. †

DALMATIA [deceitful] The southern part of the Roman province of Illyricum (Ro. 15:19), E of the Adriatic (2Ti. 4:10). †

DALPHON [crafty, ISBE; sleepless, KB] One of Haman's ten sons (Est. 9:7). †

DAMARIS A lady convert of Paul at Athens (Ac. 17:34).

DAMASCUS An oasis located on a plateau some 2200 feet above sea level, between the Ante-Lebanon Mountains and the desert, NE of Mt. Hermon. Throughout history it has been famous for its gardens and orchards produced in the rich soil with abundant water from the rivers Barada and el-A'waj (biblical Abana and Pharpar, 2Ki. 5:12). From earliest times it has been an important center of commerce and religion, located where most important military and trade routes met, and the capital of both modern and ancient Syria (Aramea). It is mentioned in the Abraham narratives (Ge. 14:15). David captured and garrisoned in it (2Sa. 8:5-6). Rebels took control of it in David's time (1Ki. 11:23-25), and throughout Israel's history it was one of her chief sources of opposition (1Ki. 15:18; 20:34; 2Ki. 8:7ff.). Captured by the Assyrians (733-732 B.C.), it never again became prominent in biblical times. The Romans made it a Nabatean kingdom. In Paul's day its population included many Jews and Christians (Ac. 9:2; 22:5-6, 11-12; 26:12).

There was a street in Damascus called "Straight Street"(Ac. 9:11). Though normally this would refer to a "lane," here it is one of two main streets that cross at right angles—either the *decumanus* or the *cadre* in a Roman town. If it is the same street at the same level (which is unlikely), *Derb el-Mustaqim* is its name today. A chapel at the west end known traditionally as Judas's house is below street level.

DAMNATION *See* DEAD, ABODE OF; JUDGMENT; PUNISHMENT

DAMASCUS
Jesus appeared to Paul (Saul) while Paul was going to Damascus to persecute the Christians there.

DAN, DANITES [judge] The fifth son of Jacob, full brother to Naphtali, born of Rachel's maid, Bilhah (Ge. 30:1-6). Dan was the name of one of the twelve tribes of Israel and one of her cities. One of the most famous members of the tribe was Samson (Jdg. 13:2, 24). The Danite tribe settled in the low country W of Jerusalem; but later most of the tribe moved N, making their seat at Laish (called Leshem in Jos. 19:47), giving it the name Dan, modern Tell el-Qadi (211-294). This is the northern town in the reference "Dan to Beersheba" (Jos. 19:40-47; Jdg. 1:34; 18:1ff.; 18:29; 20:1).

DANCE In the OT dancing most frequently had a religious character. Except where pagan influence was present, the sexes danced separately with rhythmic, harmonious body movements expressing spiritual joy or devotion before God. Women engaged in it on occasions of national liberation, after military victories, and at religious festivals (Ex. 15:20; Jdg. 21:19-21; 1Sa. 18:6). It was accompanied by instrumental and vocal music (Jdg. 11:34). David danced before the Ark, and on other occasions so did men in groups in their praising the LORD (2Sa. 6:16; Ps. 149:3). In the NT there is a reference to children calling out to others and saying, "You did not dance when we played the flute for you" (Mt. 11:17). It was done on the occasion of the prodigal's homecoming and when Salome danced before Herod (Lk. 15:25; Mk. 6:21-22).

DANIEL [El is my judge]
1. Second son of King David; also called Kileab/Chileab (1Ch.3:1; 2Sa. 3:3).

2. A priest who came up with Ezra from Babylon and sealed the covenant with Nehemiah (Ezr. 8:2; Ne. 10:6).

3. A man noted for his righteousness and wisdom, also mentioned together with Noah and Job. Tradition identifies him with the prophet (4 below), some with the Ugaritic mythological "Daniel" (Eze. 14:14, 20; 28:3).

4. A man of royal or noble family, of the tribe of Judah, carried into captivity in Babylon in 605 B.C. and there trained for royal service (Da. 1:16). The book of the Bible bears his name. (The reliability of this date 605 B.C. and, in fact, of many of the historical items noted in the book that bears his name stand true, even though consistently attacked since the second century. See the parenthetical note in the article DARIUS.) He was given the name Belteshazzar in Babylon, where, because of his divinely given wisdom and good judgment, he held important posts under several Babylonian and Persian kings. He acquired special fame as an interpreter of dreams. Only traditions remain relative to his end. Jesus refers to a portion of his book in a manner that regards both the portion and the man as historical (Mt. 24:15).

DANIEL, BOOK OF Traditionally considered a sixth-century B.C. document written by Daniel the prophet. Many evangelicals support this, but other scholars assign to it the date of 165 B.C. and say the author is unknown. They say: (1) it contains historical inaccuracies; (2) if written in the sixth century much of it would have to be considered predictive — and forecasting the future is impossible; and (3) it would have no real purpose in the sixth century, while in the second it would serve to encourage the Jews in their revolt against the Seleucids. (On these and other critical matters *see* DARIUS.) Of the twelve chapters, seven are historical.

DANITES *See* DAN

DAN-JAAN 2Sa. 24:6.

DANNAH [stronghold] A Judean town (area of 152-095) in the hill-country district of Debir (Jos. 15:49). †

DARDA, DARA Descendant of Judah, a skilled musician, and second only to Solomon in his wisdom (1Ki. 4:31; 1Ch. 2:6). † The footnote in the NIV in Chronicles passage reads: "most Hebrew manuscripts read 'Dara.'"

DARIC *See* DRACHMA

DARIUS [*Old Persian* he who upholds the good] The name of several rulers of the Persian period after 538 B.C.

1. Darius the Mede, son of Xerxes (Hebrew Ahasuerus), ruled after Belshazzar, the last of the neo-Babylonian kings (Da. 5:30-31), being made king of the realm of the Babylonians (*see* CHALDEA) at the age of sixty-two (Da. 9:1; 5:31; 6:6, 9, 25, 28). He set up 120 governors (satraps) under three presidents, of whom Daniel was one (Da. 6:1-3), and ruled only very briefly contemporaneously with Cyrus, the founder of the Persian Empire (Da. 6:28). Thus, the data as presented in the *Book of Daniel*. (Some consider the OT account of his reign a merging of confused traditions and that this Darius never existed.) The historicity of the Book of Daniel, including the account of Darius, has long been a watershed between "conservative" and "liberal" scholars. The negative arguments may be found in numerous encyclopedias and commentaries. The following brief bibliography may be found helpful, however. It presents not only the arguments against historicity but in addition attempts both to evaluate those negative arguments and to support positively the presentation of the text of Daniel. *Darius the Mede*, J.C. Whitcomb, 1959; *Exposition of Daniel*, H.C. Leupold, 1949; *The Prophecy of Daniel*, E.J. Young, 1949; *Studies in the Book of Daniel*, Series I, 1917, Series II, 1938.

2. Darius the Great, called Hystaspos (522-486 B.C.) in secular history, was the most famous of this name, defeated by the Greeks at Marathon, and in biblical history noted for his enabling the returned Jews to rebuild the temple at Jerusalem (Ezr. 4:5ff.; Hag. 1:1; Zec. 1:1).

3. Darius, known as Nothus, son of Artaxerxes (423-404 B.C.; Ne. 12:22).

4. Darius Codomanus (336-330 B.C.), the last king of Persia defeated by the Greeks.

DARKNESS *See* LIGHT AND DARKNESS

DARKON One of Solomon's servants whose sons returned with Zerubbabel from the exile (Ezr. 2:56; Ne. 7:58). †

DARNEL *See* PLANTS, PERFUMES, AND SPICES, Miscellaneous Plants 14., *Tares*

DATE PALM *See* TREES

DATHAN [strong] *See* KORAH

DATING *See* MARRIAGE

DAVID [beloved one] The youngest son of Jesse, of the tribe of Judah, born in Bethlehem, second king of Israel (c. 1040-970 B.C.). The account of his life is found in 1Sa. 16—1Ki. 2, and 1Ch. 11—29. The Book of Ruth traces his Israelite and Moabite ancestry. Items from the more than seventy Psalms ascribed to David, as well as his other poems (2Sa. 1:17; 3:33; 23:1), give valuable insights into his character, personality, feelings, and beliefs. In the Bible this name is reserved for this one individual alone (some 800 times in the OT and 58 in the NT), indicating something of the place he held in both Jewish and Christian tradition. To Jews he became a religious symbol, and their messianic hope was attached to his descendants. They looked for a Messiah who should sit on the throne of David forever (Jer. 33:17). To the Christians, Jesus the Messiah came of the seed of David, according to the flesh, and was the King to sit on the throne of David forever (Ro. 1:3; Rev. 22:16; Mt. 22:42-45; Ac. 2:25-36). In addition to king, warrior, and writer of poetry he was also a skilled musician (1Sa. 16:23; 2Sa. 6:5; Ne. 12:36, 45-46; Am. 6:5). His history is one of the most colorful in all Scripture.

Reared a shepherd, he became musician and armor-bearer at an early age to King Saul, who soon became jealous of his heroic acts and popularity. When Saul tried on several occasions to kill him, he fled the court and became a fugitive and wandered until the death of the king. After Saul's death, David became a great king, laid the foundation for the nation, planned and made preparation for the building of the temple, and set up the organization of the temple staff (1Ch. 23–26). Many of the stories from his life are exceedingly colorful: his victory over the giant Goliath (1Sa. 17); the mutual love of David and Jonathan (1Sa. 18–20); his famous lament over the deaths of Saul and Jonathan (2Sa. 1); and, even the story of his sin with Bathsheba and the murder of her husband Uriah (2Sa. 11). His reign was turbulent. Four times the ten tribes were split away from Benjamin and Judah by palace or external rebellions. After some of the rebellions, the king had to become a fugitive. Through all of these experiences, God was preparing the man, the musician, the poet, and the prophet. *See also* KINGS OF JUDAH AND ISRAEL

DAVID, TOWN OF

1. *See* JERUSALEM.

2. In Lk. 2:11, Bethlehem, the birthplace and early home of David, is called "the town of David."

DAWN Hebrew *shahar*, the start of day and a poetic name for the place where the sun rises (Job 3:9; 38:12; 41:18). The phrase "O morning star, son of the dawn" of Isa. 14:12 is applied to the king of Babylon. In the KJV the "daystar" is rendered "Lucifer" (literally "lightbearer," day star) and because of the similarity with Lk. 10:18 and Rev. 9:1 the identifi-

cation is made by some to Satan instead of the king of Babylon. *See also* DEVIL

DAY

1. Denotes time from sunrise to sunset, the time of daylight (Ge. 1:5).

2. A space of time from sunrise to sunset or vice versa, twenty-four hours (Ge. 1:5; Ne. 13:19).

3. Time in general (Ps. 37:19).

4. It is also used figuratively in reference to the day of the LORD (Eze. 13:5; Joel 1:15). *See* DAY OF THE LORD

DAY-AGE THEORY The concept that the *Yom* or "days" of Genesis 1 are longer than a normal day, possibly aeons. *See* DAY 2.

DAY OF ATONEMENT *See* CALENDAR and FESTIVALS

DAY OF CHRIST *See* CHRIST, WORK OF 9., *Second Advent*

DAY OF THE LORD Any time when God intervenes to punish sin (Am. 5:16-20; Isa. 13:6, 9). The climax comes when God intervenes personally to show his anger on foes and to deliver his people (Zep. 1:7ff., 14ff.; 2:2-3). In the NT this day is the second coming of Christ (1Co. 1:8; 2Th. 2:2), and is accompanied with physical cataclysms on the earth (Lk. 21:7-33; 2Pe. 3:12ff.), and great social changes. It includes both the judgments preceding the millennium and the millennial utopia itself which follows (Rev. 4–19, 20; cf. Isa. 11:1-9; 65:17-25). This day will culminate in the new heaven and earth (Rev. 21:1ff.).

DAY OF WRATH *See* DAY OF THE LORD; ESCHATOLOGY

DAYSPRING

1. A KJV rendering in Job 38:12 as a name for the dawn or morning.

2. In Lk. 1:78 interpreted by many versions as a title of Christ (so capitalized in the NASB "Sunrise," NKJV "Dayspring," JB "Sun"). The NIV, NEB and RSV do not capitalize, possibly emphasizing the dawning of the age of Messiah. *See* MESSIAH

DAYSTAR *See* DAWN; DEVIL, *Lucifer*; MORNING STAR

DEACON, DEACONESS [serve] The basic meaning of the Greek word *diakonos* and its derivatives is "minister" or "servant." Out of some 100 occurrences in the NT, the Greek word is translated three times as "deacon" or "deacons." The lady Phoebe is called a servant of the church, but the footnote in the NIV says "deaconess" (Ro. 16:1; cf. Php. 1:1; 1Ti. 3:8, 12). It usually conveys the idea of servant, even table-service, and is rendered as such in the great miracle of Cana. As a church office the concept comes from Ac. 6:1-7. Opinions differ as to whether women regularly held the office of a deaconess in the early church. The weight of evidence seems in its favor. *See* ELDER; PASTORS; OVERSEER

DEAD, ABODE OF This place is designated in the Scriptures by a number of words. One that refers to the abode of both good and bad in the OT is *Sheol*. It is rendered by "the grave," whether it refers to its final abode of the wicked or of the good (Ps. 9:17; Ge. 37:35). It is found over sixty times in the OT and is usually translated simply as "grave" but is also rendered "Destruction" (Job 28:22; 31:12). It was inside the earth (Nu. 16:30-33). In some cases it was considered a place of severe punishment (Ps. 9:17; 116:3); in others this concept is missing (cf. Ps. 16:10; Ac. 2:27), as they refer to the body of Jesus. The translation there is "grave." In the NT the most frequent word for the abode of the wicked is *hell (Gehenna* in the Greek— Mt. 10:28; 18:9; Mk. 9:43; Jude 7). (Fire, "eternal," or "fiery lake of burning sulfur" (Rev. 21:8), or "fiery furnace" (Mt. 13:42, 50), are usually associated with retributive punishment. In the NIV, it is sometimes translated "depths" (Mt. 11:23; Lk. 10:15), with Hades in the footnote). The Greek *hades* is rendered in English for the words *hell, the grave,* and *Hades* itself (Lk. 16:23; Ac. 2:27, 31; Rev. 1:18; 6:8; 20:13-14). Along with death, Hades is a temporary state, for both are eventually to be cast into "the lake of fire which is the second death" (Rev. 20:13-14). The place of fires is also called the "Abyss" (Rev. 9:12; 20:13). The "angel" of the Abyss is called *Abaddon* in the Hebrew and *Apollyon* in the Greek (Rev. 9:11). Abaddon is also found in the Hebrew text of Job 31:12; 26:6; and 28:22. The NIV translates it as "Destruction" but places Abaddon in the footnotes in each case. The demons feared the Abyss (Lk. 8:31).

DEAD SEA *See* GEOGRAPHY OF THE HOLY LAND; SALT SEA

DEAD SEA SCROLLS *See* BIBLICAL MANUSCRIPTS

DEADLY WEAPON *See* ARMS AND ARMOR

DEAF *See* HEALING, HEALTH; SICK, SICKNESS

DEATH It is the opposite of life; the normal end of life which comes with the departure of the spirit from the body (Dt. 34:5, 7; Ecc. 12:7). It is the result of sin (Ge. 2:7, 17; Ro. 5:12; 6:23), which causes the disintegration of the physical body and leaves the spirit in an intermediate state until it returns to the resurrected body in the end of days. (On the intermediate state *See* DEAD, ABODE OF; and RESURRECTION.) In the concept of both Testaments some are resurrected to everlasting life, some to everlasting contempt (Da. 12:2; 2Th. 1:8-10; Jn. 3:36). A "second death" is noted in Rev. 2:11; 20:6, which is eternal separation from God in a lake of fire. *See also* DEATH; FUTURE LIFE; IMMORTAL; SOUL; SPIRIT

DEBAUCHERY *See* DRUNKENNESS; FORNICATION; SIN

DEBIAH An ancestor of some who came back from the captivity with Zerubbabel but were not able to prove their families were descendants from Israel (Ezr. 2:59-60); also called Delaiah in Ne. 7:62.

DEBIR [back room (of a shrine temple for oracle pronouncement)]

1. A king of Eglon, SW of Jerusalem (Jos. 10:3).

2. A town on the border between Judah and Benjamin, between Jerusalem and the Salt Sea (Jos. 15:7).

3. A town in the tribal area of Gilead E of the Jordan River (Jos. 13:26).

4. A Canaanite city in the hill country (Jos. 15:48-49), and not in the western hills as some formerly thought. It is located S of Hebron at modern Khirbet Rabud; also called Kiriath Sannah and Kiriath Sepher (Jos. 15:49-50).

Conquered by Joshua (Jos. 10:38-39), the area was given by him to Caleb (Jos. 15:13). Caleb's nephew, Othniel, was given Debir as a reward for having captured it (Jos. 15:13-19). It became a possession of the priestly family of Aaron (Jos. 21:15). It was formerly thought to be located at Tell Beit Mirsim farther to the West. The presence of Late Bronze Age pottery together with the upper and lower springs support the Rabud site (Jos. 15:18-19).

DEBORAH [hornet, wasp, wild honey bee]

1. Rebekah's nurse who came with her from Mesopotamia (Ge. 24:59; 35:8). †

2. A prophetess in Israel, also listed with the judges who roused the tribes of Israel under Barak to revolt against the Canaanites. Her story and her beautiful victory song are recorded in Judges 4–5. † *See* JUDGES OF ISRAEL

DEBT, DEBTOR In Mosaic Law special provisions were provided to protect the Jewish debtor. On matters of interest and pledges for loans *see* USURY. The law was ignored later and debtors were often cruelly treated (2Ki. 4:1ff.). In NT times these laws were not followed; debtors were thrown into prison (Mt. 18:25-30, 34).

DECALOGUE A term meaning "ten words," an exact translation of the Hebrew usually rendered the "Ten Commandments." Throughout the history of Western civilization and the Judeo-Christian ethic, the decalogue has been honored as the epitome of the righteous conduct God expects of humanity.

Jesus twice stated the greatest commandments as "Love the Lord your God" and "Love your neighbor as yourself" (Mt. 22:37-40; Mk. 12:29-31). The first four commandments of the decalogue relate to the greatest commandment; the latter six to the second greatest. From the principles contained in these ten, the rest of the commandments of the law logically follow.

The decalogue appears twice in the law of Moses, in Ex. 20:1-17 and Dt. 5:6-21. In both contexts, it functions as the summary of the covenant relationship between Yahweh and Israel, the Savior and his redeemed community. The commandments of the decalogue and the rest of the law were given to a saved people as God's gracious instruction for a righteous life-style that would honor and glorify him and result in long, happy, and peaceful existence (Lev. 26:1-13; Dt. 4:40; 5:33).

Jesus chose the sixth and seventh commandments to demonstrate that the law was to be kept from within, not simply by observing the outward form of the commands, when he equated murder with anger (Mt. 5:19-22) and adultery with lust (Mt. 5:27-28). He used the fifth commandment to show that the tradition of the elders, intended to help one keep the law more meticulously, actually allowed one to break the law (Mt. 15:1-6).

Nine of the Ten Commandments are repeated in the NT, explicitly or in principle, as part of the law of Christ. Observance of the Sabbath Day, an outward sign of the Old Covenant, is made a matter of individual conscience (Ro. 14:5-8) for which no one is specially rewarded or judged (Col. 2:16-17). *See* LAW (J.R.K.)

DECAPOLIS [(league of) ten cities] Ten cities SE of the Sea of Galilee, occupied by Greeks after the conquest of Alexander in the fourth century B.C., which formed a league after the Roman occupation of Palestine in the first century B.C. (Mt. 4:25; Mk. 5:20; 7:31). The footnote in the NIV in each reference reads "That is, the Ten Cities."

DECAY The decomposition of organic matter. In Scripture it is used in connection with the change and decay naturally associated with death. Christ did not suffer "corruption," decay (Ps. 16:10; Ac. 2:27; 13:34, 37). Man's body will decay and perish, but through resurrection it will be made imperishable (1Co. 15:42ff.).

DECEIVED See FALSE CHRIST

DECEIVER See DEVIL

DESCENDANT See SEED

DECISION, VALLEY OF The place of God's judgment on the nations in the end of days, sometimes called the Valley of Jehoshaphat (Joel 3:2, 12, 14). Tradition identifies it with the Kidron Valley, but this is not certain.

DECREES OF GOD The decisions of God which, made in eternity past, render all that transpires within time as inevitable.

DEDAN, DEDANIM, DEDANITES
1. Dedan was a descendant of Noah through Ham and Cush (Ge. 10:1, 6-7).
2. A grandson of Abraham by his concubine Keturah (Ge. 25:3).
3. A place in NW Arabia S of Edom, the home of the Dedanites, an important trading people according to Isa. 21:13 and extrabiblical sources.

DEDICATION See CONSECRATION; HOLINESS

DEDICATION, FEAST OF An annual feast of eight days duration, commencing on the twenty-fifth of Kislev, commemorating the rededication of the temple in December 165 B.C., after it had been desecrated by Antiochus Epiphanes three years earlier. It has been known as the Feast of Lights, and currently as Hanukkah (Jn. 10:22-23). *See also* CALENDAR and FESTIVALS

DEEP A translation of various Hebrew and Greek words which refers to the primeval chaos (Ge. 1:2), the Flood (Ge. 7:11), the waters of the Red Sea (Ex. 15:5), the ocean (Job 41:31), underground water (Dt. 33:13), and which sometimes carry a figurative meaning (Ps. 88:6). In the NT the reference is to the depth of the Sea of Galilee (Lk. 5:4).

DEER See BEASTS 2.

DEFILE, DEFILEMENT See CLEAN AND UNCLEAN

DEGREES, SONGS OF See SONGS OF ASCENT

DEHAVITES A KJV, NKJV, ASV transliteration in Ezr. 4:9. Many versions translate this as a logical connector word, *that is* or *in*, between "Susanchites" and "the Elamites." In the NIV, Dehavites is represented by the English preposition "of": "Elamites of Susa."

DEISM The idea that God created this universe but has no ongoing involvement with it.

DEITIES
1. Foreign gods, some of which were introduced in Israel.

Ammonite and Moabite deities *Chemosh, Milcom/Molech/Moloch.*

Chemosh was the god of the Moabites (Nu. 21:29), and in a passage which Jephthah addressed to the Ammonites (Jdg. 11:12-24, 28), *Molech, Milcom,* and *Moloch* would appear to be three variants of the same Ammonite deities (1Ki. 11:5; Lev. 18:21; Ac. 7:43). *Milcom* is noted in the NIV in the footnotes as *Molech*. There is some evidence that all of these names are but titles for the god *Athtar*, an astral deity, and not the actual name of deities themselves. As a part of the rites, the sacrifice of children was included (2Ki. 3:27; 23:10), in spite of the death penalty commanded by Moses for anyone offering his child to Molech (Lev. 20:2-5). Solomon built a high place for Chemosh and Molech, which Josiah later destroyed (1Ki. 11:5, 7; 2Ki. 23:13). The cult seems to have continued, however (Eze. 16:20-21). *Anat* or *Anath*, a Canaanite goddess of war and fertility, sister of Baal, is found in people and place names in the Bible. Assyrian and

Babylonian deities are *Nisroch, Bel, Marduk (Merodach), Nebo, Nergal, Succoth Benoth. Nisroch* (2Ki. 19:35-37; Isa. 37:36-38), a name not found elsewhere but in the Bible, is the Assyrian deity in whose temple Sennacherib was killed by his sons after his return from Judah and Jerusalem. *Bel* was one of the three primary gods of ancient Sumer and is mentioned in the Bible along with *Marduk* the chief god of Babylon. The Hebrew text is vocalized *Merodach* (Jer. 50:2). *Nebo* (Babylonian *Nabu)* was a god of all science who had a temple in all major cities of both Assyria and Babylonia (Isa. 46:1). *Fortune* and *Destiny* are *Gad* and *Meni* in Hebrew; these two are Semitic pagan gods of good fortune. In Isa. 65:11 they are Babylonian. *Nergal* was associated with wars and disaster and was worshiped throughout Assyria and Babylonia with his chief temple being at Cuthah. Exiles from Cuthah brought his cult to Samaria after the fall of the northern kingdom (2Ki. 17:30). The men of Babylon who were brought to Samaria after 722 B.C. made *Succoth-Benoth* their god (2Ki. 17:30).

The one deity of Egypt noted in the Bible is *Amon* of the city of Thebes (Na. 3:8), called *No Amon* in the footnote in the NIV. The doom of this city, once the most magnificent of Egypt's capitals, was foretold by Jeremiah (Jer. 46:25), as he describes God's punishment of its deity. Though no other Egyptian deities are found in the Bible, they can be found indirectly in people and place names. For example, Raamses (*Ra* or *Re,* a principal sun god created him), Pibeseth, temple of Bastet (pagan goddess). There are many other examples.

The gods of Greece are represented by four, *Artemis, Hermes, Zeus,* and the twin gods *Castor* and *Pollux. Artemis,* the Greek goddess of hunting, corresponds to the Roman *Diana,* whose temple at Ephesus was one of the seven wonders of the ancient world (Ac. 19: 23 — 20:1). *Hermes* was the deity of literature, commerce, and youth; he is noted in the Bible at Ac. 14:12, as is also *Zeus,* the Roman *Jupiter. Castor* and *Pollux*

(with power over wind and waves) were protectors of sailors. They were especially worshiped at Sparta in Greece (Ac. 28:11).

Hermes (or Mercury)

In Philistia the god was *Dagon* (Jdg. 16:23; 1Sa. 5:2-7; 1Ch. 10:10), a Semitic deity from at least 2500 B.C. onward; but in biblical times known in connection with the Philistines at Gaza, Beth-shan, and Ashdod where, we read, the Maccabees destroyed his temple. By such names as *Beth-Dagon* in the tribal area of Judah and Asher we know that he had shrines outside the Philistine area as well (Jos. 15:41; 19:27). A temple was built to him at Ras Shamra-Ugarit, N of the Bibleworld, that was the rival of Baal's. Current scholarship rules out his origin as a fish deity and suggests a grain deity. Ekron, one of the major Philistine cities, had its own deity, *Baal-Zebub* (2Ki. 1:2-3, 6, 16).

After the fall of the Israelite kingdom in 722 B.C., foreigners were brought to Samaria by the conquering king of Assyria. These peoples brought some of their gods with them—already noted with respect to the gods *Nergal* and *Succoth Benoth.* Other gods similarly brought to Samaria at that time were: *Ashima,* known only from this reference in the OT, who was brought from Hamath (2Ki. 17:30; Am. 8:14ff.); *Nib-*

haz and *Tartak*, who were brought by the Avvites from their homeland (2Ki. 17:31); and *Anammelech and Adrammelech*, who were brought to Samaria by the Sepharvites, who burned their children in the fire to these two gods—suggesting some relation to the gods of Moab and Ammon noted above.

Dagon, the Fish-god

2. Pagan gods, more commonly known in Israel. *Asherah, Asherim* (masculine plural) and *Asheroth* (feminine plural), words that refer both to the W Semitic goddess and to the cult object that represented her (translated incorrectly "groves" in earlier versions). The RSV and NIV do not distinguish in their translations between the goddess and the object, transliterating in both cases by "Asherah." In Ras Shamra-Ugarit *Athirat* is the mother-goddess and consort of a pagan god named *El*, but in the OT she is associated with *Baal* (Jdg. 3:7). She was widely worshiped throughout the ancient Eastern world. Four hundred of her prophets ate at Jezebel's table in the time of Elijah (1Ki. 18:19). King Manasseh put her image in the temple at Jerusalem (2Ki. 21:7). Josiah endeavored to stamp out her cult practices during his revival (2Ki. 23:4-7). The Israelites were forbidden to put her cult objects in the tabernacle and were told to cut them

down and burn them (Dt. 12:3; 16:21; Ex. 34:13).

Ashtoreth (Ashtaroth, the plural form), goddess of the Sidonians also worshiped by Solomon (1Ki. 11:5). Her center in Jerusalem was later destroyed by Josiah (2Ki. 23:13). She was the *Ishtar* of the Babylonians and the *Astarte* of the Greeks, closely associated with the idea of lifegiver. The Semitic word *Baal* means "lord" or "possessor." The lord or possessor of a given piece of property or area was its *Baal* and as such was worshiped. The *Baals* of individual localities were identified by the names of the localities as was the case with *Baal of Peor* or *Baal Zephon* (for examples *see* Nu. 25:3; 33:7). Later *Baal* came to be recognized as one god. His cult received a serious setback in the days of Elijah when 450 of his prophets were destroyed (1Ki. 18:19, 40). The cult was obliterated in the time of Jehu (1Ki. 18:17-40; 2Ki. 10:18-28; 11:18), but was revived and again partially destroyed in the reforms of Josiah. Even after these two destructions, it still had strength to revive itself, however (2Ki. 23:4-5). *Baal-Berith* was a god with a shrine at Shechem mentioned in Jdg. 8:33 and 9:4.

Beelzebub is found only in the NT. (For Baal-Zebub see above under Philistine gods.) In Mt. 12:24, 27 the footnote in the NIV reads "Greek, Beezeboul or Beelzeboul." Both Jesus and his opposition applied this term to the prince of demons, Satan (Mt. 12:24, 27; Lk. 11:18-19).

Kaiwan, Sakkuth, Stargods are found only in the NIV in the footnote to Am. 5:26. *Rephan* is the only one from Amos 5 found in the quote of that passage in Ac. 7:43. Scholars are divided as to whether the first two were deities.

3. Teraphim Images and Serpent. The "household gods" is a translation given to the Hebrew word *teraphim* (Ge. 31:19). In Ge. 31:30 Laban called them his *elohim*, gods. They were small enough to go in a camel saddle and for Rachel to hide them by sitting on them. Yet in 1Sa. 19:13-16, where the translators used the word "idol," they would

seem to be the size of a man. They are mentioned in every period of Israel's history from the time of the patriarchs to the fall of Israel and Judah (Ge. 31:19; Jdg. 18:14; 2Ki. 23:24; Eze. 21:21; Zec. 10:2). They would seem to have been used especially in divination; and from the archaeology of the Nuzi period, it is known that heirs considered them important. Whoever held them received estate rights upon the death of the parent. This explains Rachel's interest in taking them when she left her father Laban.

Idols, Images, Carved Images were representations in various forms (some animal, some human) which were used in pagan worship and by the Israelites in idolatrous worship. They were carved from wood or stone, or cast in copper, silver, or gold (Isa. 44:14-17; 1Ki. 14:9). They were condemned in the Ten Commandments (Ex. 20:4) and throughout all of Israelite history (Isa. 30:22; Jer. 8:19; Mic. 5:13).

Serpent. In the entire ancient world serpent deities were known. In the Bible it is sometimes the symbol of Satan (Rev. 12:9).

DEITY OF CHRIST *See* CHRIST, LIFE OF; GOD, NAMES OF, GODHEAD; I AM

DEKAR [javelin] *See* BEN-DEKER

DELAIAH [Yahweh draws up (like water in a bucket)]

1. A priest of the twenty-third order of those who would minister in the sanctuary as set up by David (1Ch. 24:18).

2. A descendant of the royal line of David after and through Zerubbabel (1Ch. 3:24).

3. An officer of King Jehoiakim (Jer. 36:12, 25).

4. Father of one of Nehemiah's close friends (Ne. 6:10).

5. One who returned with Zerubbabel (Ezr. 2:59-60; Ne. 7:62).

DELILAH [tease] The Philistine woman from the Sorek Valley near Beth Shemesh (147-128) who by seduction delivered Samson to bondage (Jdg. 16:4-18). †

DELIVER, DELIVERANCE *See* CHRIST, WORK OF

DELIVERER The references are to human deliverers or to God's deliverers (Jdg. 3:9, 15; 2Sa. 22:2; Ps. 70:5). Moses is called deliverer (Ac. 7:35). Also to be noted is the prophetic item: "The deliverer will come from Zion" (Ro. 11:26), cited by Paul from Isaiah where the word is "Redeemer." The reference according to Paul is to a future coming of the Messiah.

The main theme of the Bible is the work of God in delivering man from the power of sin and death through Christ, his Redeemer and Deliverer. *See* CHRIST, WORK OF

DELUGE *See* FLOOD

DEMAS [(common) folks] A fellow laborer with Paul who later deserted him "because he loved this world" (Col. 4:14; Phm. 24; 2Ti. 4:10). †

DEMETRIUS [of Demeter]

1. A well-spoken-of Christian, commended by John (3Jn. 12). †

2. An Ephesian silversmith who stirred up a riot against Paul (Ac. 19:23-27). †

DEMON, DEMONIAC In the OT the demon is considered a nondivine but supernatural being, an evil spirit, one who can exercise power and influence, mostly destructive. Demons are also called gods, to whom their sons and daughters were sacrificed (Dt. 32:17; Ps. 106:37). In the NT the demon is a spiritual being hostile to God and man, and the demoniac a demon-possessed individual. Demons are agents of Beelzebub (Mk. 3:22). When possessed, a man may be dumb (speechless), live in tombs, refuse to wear clothes, act like an epileptic, have abnormal strength, or a combination of these (Mt. 12:22-24, 43-45; Mk. 9:17-20; Lk. 8:27; 11:14). In Mt. 4:24 it is noted that possession by a demon is something different from sickness. In the NT most of the occurrences are associated with opposition to the ministry of Jesus. Exorcising these evil spirits was not easy. *See also* DEVIL; SATAN

DEMONOLOGY *See* SYSTEMATIC THEOLOGY

DENARIUS *See* MONEY

DEPORTATION *See* CAPTIVITY; EXILE

DEPRAVITY *See* SIN

DEPUTY A vice-regent (1Ki. 22:47).

DERBE A city in the southern part of Asia Minor, NW of Tarsus, which was visited by Paul on his missionary journeys and from which came his traveling companion Gaius (Ac. 14:6, 20; 16:1; 20:4). †

DESERT, DESERTS The translation of a number of Hebrew and Greek words which refer to wilderness, waste, and arid regions (Ge. 16:7; Isa. 48:21). Unlike the concept of a desert as a completely barren area, the biblical desert was usable for grazing flocks, contained many rich oases, and had soil that only needed water to make it fertile (Ge. 16:7; 1Sa. 17:28). One of these words (Arabah), when preceded by the definite article, refers to the Jordan Valley from N of the Salt Sea to the Gulf of Aqabah. In the NT the translation "solitary place" is also found (Mt. 14:13; Mk. 1:35).

Several major deserts are mentioned in the Bible. The Desert of Zin was just S of the Negev (Nu. 13:21). Kadesh Barnea (Nu. 32:8) was located in the Desert of Zin. The Desert of Shur is at the extreme W of the Sinai and opposite the Desert of Zin (Ex. 15:22). The location of the Desert of Zin is not certain, but the Israelites were there between their time in the Desert of Shur and the Desert of Sinai. Probably it was on the eastern seacoast of the Red Sea between Shur and Sinai (Ex. 15:27; 16:1). The great central part of the Sinai, from E until the Desert of Sin, is called the Desert of Paran (Nu. 10:12); and the Desert of Sinai is at the southern tip of the Sinai (Nu. 3:4, 14).

DESIRE *See* LUST

DESOLATION, SACRILEGE *See* ABOMINATION THAT CAUSES DESOLATION

DESTINY, A GOD *See* DEITIES 1., *Babylonian gods*

DESTROY, DO NOT *See* PSALMS, TITLES OF 3.

DETACHMENT OF SOLDIERS *See* BAND

DETERMINISM The idea that all that occurs is caused and fixed, with no variables. *See* FATALISM

DEUEL {known of El} The father of a leader of the tribe of Gad while they were in the wilderness during the exodus from Egypt (Nu. 1:14; 7:42, 47; 10:20). In some manuscripts he is called Reuel *(see* NIV's footnote to Nu. 2:14). †

DEUTEROCANONICAL *See* SCRIPTURE, *Apocryphal*

DEUTEROISAIAH *See* ISAIAH, BOOK OF

DEUTERONOMY, BOOK OF {second (giving) of the law} The last of the five Books of Moses, known variously as the Torah, the Pentateuch, the Law. Its first four chapters contain Moses' review of the events from Sinai to the time of his expected death. His review of the laws given by God at Sinai for the conduct of the life of the people (Dt. 30:19-20), together with his emphasis on their spirituality and his urgent plea that they be observed, follows in chapters 5 through 26. This section in chapter 5 includes a repetition of the Decalogue. Moses' final blessings, instructions, exhortations, and farewell song are recorded in chapters 27–33 and his death in 34.

No portion of the Bible, unless it be the Book of Daniel, has caused more difference of opinion among scholars than the Pentateuch – in its entirety or in each of its five parts. Some consider it a late compilation from other sources and Moses not its author. Most recent views tend to a more conservative position on its unity and are assigning its writing to earlier periods. It is stated in the book that Moses wrote this Law (Dt. 31:9, 22, 24-27). The implications of the rest of the OT and the NT support this view. Jesus affirmed the Mosaic authorship of the Law in his teachings (Mk. 10:5; 12:26; Jn. 5:46-47; 7:19, 23). According to biblical chronology, he lived at the end of the fifteenth century B.C. *See also* PENTATEUCH

DEVIL In the OT demons and evil spirits are mentioned more commonly than devils (*see* DEMON). In the OT the chief of the evil spirits is called "the Satan" (1Ch. 21:1; Job 1:6-9; 2:1-7; Zec. 3:1-2). In the NT the archenemy of God and man is the devil called Satan, ancient serpent, great dragon, Beelzebub, tempter, and a liar (Rev. 12:9; Mt. 4:1-11; Lk. 8:12; Jn. 8:44; 13:2; Mk. 3:22; Lk. 11:18-19; 1Pe. 5:8). He, or his angels or spirits, is able to possess men. Jesus healed such demon-possessed people (Ac. 10:38). The devil has many characterizations in the NT: "god of this age" (2Co. 4:4), "ruler of the kingdom of the air" (Eph. 2:2), "the accuser of our brethren" (Rev. 12:10), "the one who leads the world astray" (Rev. 12:9), and "the deceiver of men" (Rev. 20:7-8). The concept of adversary or accuser at court well describes one of his chief roles (Zec. 3:1; Rev. 12:10). His end is to be cast into eternal fire together with his angels (Mt. 25:41; Rev. 20:10).

Lucifer in the KJV, following the Vulgate, in Isa. 14:12 is translated as "Morning Star" or "Day Star" (i.e. *Venus*) in most versions. The LXX has "the evening Star" (the same meaning), referring apparently to its visibility at that time. The context makes clear that this refers to the King of Babylon and his pride, yet many say that this is also a reference to Satan and his fall. *See also* DAWN

DEVOTE, DEVOTED THING Denotes things forbidden forever to common use. No person or thing devoted could be spared or ransomed (Lev. 27:28). A person devoted to destruction (Heb. *herem*) could not be ransomed but

must be put to death (Lev. 27:29; 1Sa. 15:3). This is the "curse" that is to be removed from the heavenly Jerusalem (Rev. 22:3). Material things devoted to the LORD could become the property of the priests (Lev. 27:21). These differ from things to be sacrificed, which could be recalled at any time before the sacrifice was to be made. The devoted thing could never be taken back by its offerer. *See also* ANATHEMA; CURSE

DEW In Palestine where there was no rain during the six months of summer, dew (the condensation of the moisture in the air at night time) was vital to prevent a complete drought and consequent famine. It is very important to agriculture and is often linked with rain in Scripture (2 Sa. 1:21; 1Ki. 17:1), and like rain is used as a symbol of blessing (Dt. 33:13; Ps. 133:3).

DIADEM [tiara, royal circlet] Represents four Hebrew words and one Greek word; it is sometimes translated "turban" or "crown"; sometimes it was wound around the head and worn by priests and kings as a symbol of the right to rule (Zec. 3:5; Isa. 62:3; Rev. 12:3; 19:12). It differs from the Greek word *stephanos*, also translated "crown" — but actually a symbol (wreath) of the victor. *See also* CROWN

DIAL *See* TIME

DIAMOND *See* PRECIOUS STONES AND METALS, Precious Stones, *Emerald* or *Flint*, Jer. 17:1 (KJV)

DIANA *See* DEITIES, The gods of Greece, *Artemis*

DIASPORA [scattered (like) seed] A word which may refer in Scripture to the Jews when not in their own land, or to the foreign places in which they are living (Jn. 7:35; Jas. 1:1). In the NIV it is usually translated as "scattered." While there were small colonies of Jews living outside Palestine earlier, the first major dispersion began with the deportations to Assyria and Babylon in the eighth and sixth centuries B.C. Some of the Jews returned under Ezra and Nehemiah, but some remained in Babylon and became a large and influential community. Between the first century before and the first century after Christ, the Jewish colonies in Egypt became the most influential outside of Palestine itself. By the end of the first century A.D., Jews were widely settled in many settlements outside of Palestine (Ac. 2:9-11). Relations between the Jews and their neighbors in these places were not always good; persecution and riots frequently erupted, even as early as NT times (Ac. 18:1-2). From Palestine, Babylon, Egypt, and other centers, the Jews were driven from country to country about the world, with continuous persecution; after the first and second centuries A.D., the persecution became more frequent, until it culminated in the Nazi holocaust.

In NT times Paul started his ministries in foreign cities in their synagogues (Ac. 17:1-2, 10). The Jews abroad maintained close connections with those at home, frequently making at least one of the three annual pilgrimages. The communication was two-way, as we note from Jas. 1:1 and 1Pe. 1:1, where letters were addressed to the Jewish Christians who lived abroad and perhaps others too. It is interesting to note that the early Christians who had converted from Judaism considered themselves also to be in the *diaspora*, when not in Palestine. The Scriptures indicate a worldwide regathering from the Jewish diaspora to "their own land." Some think that the modern State of Israel is at least the forerunner of this (Eze. 11:17; 28:25; 36:24). *See also* CAPTIVITY; EXILE

DIBLAH, DIBLATH Eze. 6:14. † *See also* RIBLAH

DIBLAIM [lump of (two dried fig) cakes] Father-in-law of the prophet Hosea (Hos. 1:3). †

DIBON, DIBON GAD
1. A town in the tribal area of Judah settled by Jews after the exile (Ne. 11:25).
2. A town (224-101) in Moab E of the Jordan. The Israelites took it during their exodus wanderings and the tribe of Gad

settled there (Nu. 32:34). Mesha, King of Moab, rebelled about 900 B.C. but was beaten by the Israelites (2Ki. 3:4-27). He left a valuable contemporary record on stone, the Moabite Stone, found in the modern excavations of Dhiban.

DICHOTOMY The view that man's irreducible parts are two, body and spirit. This view sees two parts to man, material and immaterial. According to this view, soul and spirit are interchangeable (Lk. 1:47). *See* SOUL; SPIRIT; TRICHOTOMY

DIBRI [*possibly* speak] A Danite who was stoned for blasphemy, the son of a mixed marriage—Israelite and Egyptian (Lev. 24:10-16).

DIDACHE An early manual of teaching regarding the Christian life and church government. Some date it from the late first century.

DIDRACHMA [two DRACHMA] A coin. *See* MONEY

DIDYMUS [twin] The Greek name of the Apostle Thomas which means "twin." *See* APOSTLES

DIGNITARIES *See* ELDER

DIKLAH [(place of) date palms] A son of Joktan thought to have lived in Arabia (Ge. 10:27; 1Ch. 1:21). †

DILEAN [cucumber, ISBE; protrude, KB] An unidentified town in the western foothills of Judah (Jos. 15:38). †

DILL A kind of seed used for seasoning. *See* PLANTS, PERFUMES, AND SPICES, Plants for Seasoning

DIMNAH [manure] One of four Levitical towns in the allotment of Zebulun (Jos. 21:35). †

DIMON, DIMONAH
1. The name of a town in Isa. 15:9, according to most English versions. The JB, RSV (with a footnote) read "Dibon," based on some ancient versions and MSS. † *See* DIBON
2. A town in the S of Judah thought by

some to be the same as Dibon (Jos. 15:22). † *See* DIBON

DINAH [judgess] A daughter of Jacob by Leah (Ge. 30:21), over whose honor her brothers destroyed Shechem (Ge. 34:24-30; 46:15). †

DINAITE KJV for "judges" (Ezr. 4:9).

DINHABAH An unidentified city of Bela, king of Edom (Ge. 36:32; 1Ch. 1:43). †

DIONYSIUS [belonging to Dionysus] A member of the Areopagus group, converted through the ministry of Paul (Ac. 17:34). †

DIOSCURI [sons of Zeus] *See* DEITIES, The gods of Greece, *Castor and Pollux*

DIOTREPHES An early Christian unfavorably described as one who puts himself first (3Jn. 9). †

DIP *See* BAPTISM

DIPHATH *See* RIPHATH (1Ch. 1:6)

DISCERNMENT OF SPIRITS *See* GIFT, GIFTS; SPIRITUAL GIFTS

DISCIPLE [student] A pupil, one who follows some doctrine or teacher. In the OT the Hebrew word is rendered thus only once (Isa. 8:16). In the NT this is a specific designation of the Twelve and of all followers of Christ. In the Gospels and Acts it is used over 250 times and in at least 90 percent of the time it refers to followers of Christ in general (believers), later called Christians (Ac. 6:1; 9:38). Sometimes it means followers of others, such as John the Baptist, or Moses, for example (Mt. 9:14; Jn. 9:28).

DISCIPLINE, CHURCH A process of chastening a Christian who is in sin; by the assembly which is called Jesus' body. The goal in discipline is for the brother or sister to quit the practice of that sin, and to be restored to God and man. A definite process occurs at each of four steps; a positive response stops the process. 1. Determine from Scripture that the behavior is a sin; speak privately with

him or her. 2. Go with one or two Christians as witnesses and speak with him or her again. 3. "Tell it to the church." 4. Excommunicate, treat him or her as an outsider (Mt. 18:15-20). Jesus promises to be in our midst when in agreement of this action. This is not a coldhearted action, but one with love and restoration in mind, done by the spiritually-minded, watching themselves so they do not also fall (Gal. 6:1-2). Blatant sexual immorality was not to be tolerated. After an apparently long process of rebuke, expulsion from the assembly resulted (1Co. 5:1-12). With repentance comes full forgiveness and restoration (2Co. 2:5-10). *See also* PARENTING

DISEASE For the most part the diseases of the Bible are those that still prevail; diseases seen in the skin such as leprosy; internal diseases such as dysentery, plague, malaria, tuberculosis; diseases caused by intestinal and other worms; eye diseases; mental disorders, and the like. From the limited descriptions given in the Bible some are difficult, if not impossible, to identify in modern terms. *See also* SICK, SICKNESS; *See also* BLINDNESS; DROPSY; DYSENTERY; SCALL

DISH *See* BOWL, BASIN, BASON; LAVER; POTTERY

DISHAN [an edible, indefinable animal] A clan chief of the Horites in Edom (Ge. 36:21, 28, 30; 1Ch. 1:38, 42). †

DISHON [an edible, indefinable animal]
  1. Son of the Horite clan chief Anah (Ge. 36:25-26, 30; 1Ch. 1:38, 41). †
  2. Son of the Horite clan chief Seir (Ge. 36:21). (A possibility exists linguistically that Dishon may be the place name of the clan; therefore, we could read in 36:30, "the chief of Dishon." †

DISOBEDIENCE *See* OBEDIENCE, OBEY

DISPENSATIONALISM A method of biblical interpretation and of theology which divides God's working into distinct ages. He administers these ages different ways. It involves a historical and grammatical interpretation of Scripture, a distinction between Israel and the church, with a premillennial and generally pretribulational view of eschatology. *See* COVENANT THEOLOGY

DISPENSATIONALISM, ULTRA Called *ultra* because it goes beyond the normal scheme of dispensationalism. According to this view, many portions of the NT are exclusively for certain eras and/or certain groups of people (such as Jews and Gentiles).

DISPERSION *See* DIASPORA

DIVIDED KINGDOM *See* KINGS OF JUDAH AND ISRAEL

DIVINATION, DIVINE Predicting the future by inspiration or efforts to discern the future by a special means known to certain classes of persons through the use of readings or the interpretation of omens. The practice was almost entirely limited to the OT, though it was certainly known in the Greek and Roman cultures of NT times. OT prophecy was a form of inspirational divination, when God revealed certain future events to his prophets, or seers (1Sa. 9:9).

One NT passage contains a case of fortune-telling. Paul considered the fortune-teller to be possessed by an evil spirit, which he exorcised (Ac. 16:16-18); *see* PYTHON. *See also* Ac. 13:8-11 for another NT incident. In the Bible the following terms are used:

1. *Astrologers*, those who receive information from the stars (Isa. 47:13; Da. 2:5, 10).

2. *Enchanters, magicians, sorcerers*, those who use spells, charms, omens, or magic to achieve their magical effects (Dt. 18:11; Da. 2:2, 27; 5:7; Ac. 13:8; 19:19).

3. *Mediums, witchcraft*, those acquainted with the secrets of the unseen world and/or in touch with the dead (Dt. 18:10-11, 14; 1Sa. 28:7; 2Ch. 23:6).

4. *Seers*, those who see above (Dt. 18:10; Eze. 21:21). Divination, except for illumination to a prophet, was prohibited

by God as a sin as evil as idolatry (Lev. 19:31; 20:6; 1Sa. 15:23). In spite of this, however, Israel was full of diviners in the days of the prophets. They used many different means: dreams or trances, visions, wood or arrows, teraphim, livers, necromancy or the consultation of the dead through a medium, and astrology (Eze. 21:21; Zec. 10:2; 1Sa. 28:7, 11). Diviners and those who consult the dead are all condemned (Dt. 18:10, 11, 14; 2Ch. 33:6). *See also* WISE MEN

DIVINER'S OAK *See* MEONENIM

DIVISIONS There were divisions occurring in the church at Corinth (1Co. 1:10-13). These schisms resulted in worldly practices of jealousy and strife. Divisions were the mark of a fleshly church (1Co. 3:3). Dissensions and factions are the mark of the flesh (Gal. 5:19; 1Ti. 6:4). Divisions are against the nature of the body of Christ—a unified whole. *See* BODY OF CHRIST 3.; CARNAL

DIVORCE The legal dissolution of the marriage bond between husband and wife. In the OT this was largely at the instigation of the husband and on the grounds that he found "something indecent" about his wife. It was consummated by his writing a bill of divorce putting it in her hand, and sending her from his house with the formula, "She is not my wife, and I am not her husband" (Dt. 24:1; Hos. 2:2). The "indecency" was usually interpreted as unchastity. They could not be remarried (Dt. 24:2-4).

In NT times to divorce a wife except on the ground of marital unfaithfulness was to make her commit adultery, and anyone who married a woman so divorced committed adultery. A man who divorces his wife except for marital unfaithfulness and marries another commits adultery. If a woman divorces her husband and marries another man, she commits adultery (Mt. 5:32; 19:9; Mk. 10:11-12; Lk. 16:18). In the NT an unbelieving partner who wishes to separate may do so, but the separation is not encouraged. Regulations concerning a husband or wife who separate for such a reason are carefully spelled out in 1Co. 7:10-16.

A married woman is released from the law of marriage after her husband dies and may then remarry without being guilty of adultery (Ro. 7:2-3; 1Co. 7:39). Heated debates are frequently conducted among clergymen over the question of the right of the "innocent party" in a divorce to remarry without committing adultery. Some argue that the one who committed the adultery that led to the divorce and then married another, is considered dead; thus, the bond is broken and the "innocent party" then may remarry. There is no specific Scripture on the point. *See also* ADULTERY; HILLEL 2.

DIZAHAB [that which has gold] One of the unidentified places, E of Jordan, where Moses gave his farewell addresses to Israel (Dt. 1:1). †

DO NOT DESTROY *See* PSALMS, TITLES OF 3.

DOCTOR *See* RABBI, RABBONI; SCRIBE; TEACHER; *see also* PHYSICIAN; SICK, SICKNESS

DOCTRINE A word that means teaching or instruction.

DOCUMENTARY HYPOTHESIS Known also as "J.E.D.P.," it is a theory which was given its classic expression by Julius Wellhausen (1844-1918). He speculated that the first five books of the Bible were written by different sources. The Scripture states plainly that Moses personally wrote down God's words. *See* PENTATEUCH

DODAI [beloved] One of David's captains or mighty men (2 Sa. 23:9; 1Ch. 11:12; 27:4). † *See also* DODO 2.

DODANIM *See* RODANIM 1.

DODAVAH, DODAVAHU [beloved of Yahweh] Father of the prophet who prophesied against King Jehoshaphat (2Ch. 20:37). †

DODO [beloved]
1. Grandfather of one of Israel's minor judges (Jdg. 10:1).
2. Some equate with Dodai, but in any case the father of David's mighty men (2Sa. 23:9; 1Ch. 11:26).
3. A Bethlehemite, father of another of David's mighty men (2Sa. 23:24).

DOE *See* BEASTS 2.

DOE OF THE MORNING *See* PSALMS, TITLES OF 4.

DOEG [anxious] An Edomite in Saul's employment who executed eighty-five priests of Nob and slew all who lived there (except Ahimelech's son who escaped and went to David) — men, women, and cattle, because Ahimelech of Nob had helped David (1Sa. 21:1-9; 22:19-23). †

DOG *See also* BEASTS 8. Occasionally in the ancient Near East this word was applied to sodomites, male homosexuals (Dt. 23:18, NIV footnote; Php. 3:2).

DOMINION To be master of, to rule, to have power over, to have authority. Ultimate and eternal rule belongs to God. He permits men to rule over nature and nations. In the end of days dominion will be given to the saints, the people of the Most High (Ps. 22:28; Da. 7:27). In the NT this dominion ascribed to God is ascribed to Christ a number of times, thus equating Father and Son as God (Mt. 28:18; Rev. 1:5).

DONKEY *See* BEASTS 4.

DOOR *See* HOUSE

DOPHKAH [drive (sheep)] One of the stopping places of the Israelites during their exodus from Egypt, the first after leaving the Desert of Sin — in other versions called the Wilderness of Zin (Nu. 33:12-13). †

DOR An ancient coastal town on the Mediterranean N of Caesarea (142-224). Founded after 1500 B.C., its king defeated by Joshua, visited by the Egyptian Wen-Amon in the eleventh century, located in the tribal area of Manasseh, it was still an important town in Roman days (Jdg. 1:27). Naphoth Dor probably refers to the same town (Jos. 11:2; 12:23; 1Ki. 4:11).

DORCAS [gazelle] The Greek name of a charitable Christian woman of Joppa whose Semitic name was Tabitha, whom Peter raised from the dead (Ac. 9:36-40). Dorcas societies are named after this charitable woman. †

DOT JB for "jot." *See* JOT

DOTHAN A city (172-202) where Joseph found his brothers and from which he was sold into slavery in Egypt (Ge. 37:17ff.). Here, too, God protected Elisha from the armies of Syria nearly 1000 years later (2Ki. 6:13ff.). The Joseph P. Free excavations indicate continuous occupancy of the site from 3000 to 700 B.C., with a small Hellenistic occupation later. †

DOTHAN
Joseph went from Hebron to Dothan to search for his brothers. At Dothan, which lay along the trade route to Egypt, Joseph's brothers sold him into slavery.

DOUBLE PREDESTINATION The doctrine that God has chosen some to be saved and also chosen others to be lost. Mankind's choice does not matter. *See also* ELECT, ELECTION; SALVATION

DOUBLE SHARE *See* FIRSTBORN

DOUGH *See* YEAST

DOVE *See* BIRDS 4.

DOVE ON FAR-OFF TEREBINTHS *See* PSALMS, TITLES OF, 5.

DOVE'S DUNG Found in 2Ki. 6:25, this could literally be "bird manure." In periods of siege Josephus tells of cattle manure being used for food (Jos. *Wars* 5:13.7). Some have tried to soften this repulsion by identifying it as a plant name—"seed pods" (NIV). This is unlikely or unnecessary for two reasons: (1) In time of siege there was no opportunity to gather herbs (see Josephus's reference above); (2) Context shows even more repulsive measures were occurring (2Ki. 6:28-29).

DOWN PAYMENT *See* SEAL

DOWRY *See* MARRIAGE

DOXOLOGY Proclamation giving glory or praise to God. In some churches this is a set form of liturgy. *See* MUSIC; PSALMS; SONG

DRACHMA A Persian gold coin of 8.424 grams, used in Palestine after the return from Babylon (Ezr. 2:69; Ne. 7:70ff.). *See* MONEY

DRAGON *See* DEVIL and BEASTS 8., *Jackal* (Ne. 2:13, NIV); 9. *dragon; see also* BEAST, THE; SATAN

DRAM KJV for *Daric* in 1Ch. 29:7 and Ezr. 8:27. *Drachmas*, Ezr. 2:69. *See* MONEY

DRAUGHT HOUSE KJV for latrine (2Ki. 10:27).

DRAWER OF WATER *See* GIBEONITES

DREAM A vision received usually at night while the recipient slept. In the OT, God was the source and often a special interpreter was necessary to determine its meaning. Joseph and Daniel were renowned for their interpretative powers. Dreams are not too frequently mentioned and play no significant part in the OT. The NT gives even less importance to them (Ge. 20:6; 37:5ff.; 41:1ff.; 1Ki. 3:5; Da. 2:3; 4:5; Mt. 1:20). Dreamers who tried to lure people from following

God were to be killed (Dt. 13:1-5). *See also* DIVINATION, DIVINE

DRESS Knowledge of the dress of the Bible times comes chiefly from ancient monuments and paintings in Egypt, Mesopotamia, and the land of the Hittites. Some Bible statements are relevant, and the traditions and usages of the modern Bedouin, who through the centuries resisted change in this area, are important. Apart from ornaments, belt, foot and headwear, the dress consisted of an outer garment (cloak, mantle, or robe), an undergarment (robe, coat, tunic, or similar garment), and a loincloth or waist cloth. The last was usually of linen and worn next to the body (Jdg. 14:12; Jer. 13:1; Mk. 14:51-52). Elijah wore one made of hair and a leather belt around it. John the Baptist wore one of camel's hair and also a leather belt (2Ki. 1:8; Mt. 3:4). *See also* Ex. 28:42; Lev. 6:10. The terms used for the outer and inner garments are general terms for clothing and in the translations they are often interchangeable. Worn next to the skin, made of linen or wool, draped over one shoulder and extending to the knees or ankles, with or without sleeves, was the *kuttonet* (Hebrew) or *chiton* (Greek). These words are translated as cloak, robe, tunic, garment (Ge. 37:3; 2Sa. 13:18-19; Ex. 28:4, 39; Job 30:18; Mt. 5:40; Lk. 6:29; Jn. 19:24). As a sign of mourning the robe was torn (Job 1:20). The *kuttonet* or *chiton* was also worn as the outer garment. When something was worn over it, it would be the *simlah* (Hebrew) and probably the Greek *himatia*, also translated coat, cloak, clothing, tunic, garment, mantle, or robe. This was a square or rectangular piece of cloth, thrown over one or both shoulders, with openings for the arms at the sides. It was not worn while working, and it was the garment used for a covering at night, thus it was not to be kept in pledge overnight by a creditor (Ex. 22:26-27; Dt. 22:3; Mt. 24:18). The "hem" is part of the outer garment (Ex. 39:24). These flowing robes were held in by a sash, girdle, or belt made of wool, leather, or linen and worn by both men and women (2Sa. 20:8; Isa. 3:24).

Headgear is not particularly mentioned in connection with men, except in connection with mourning or despair (2Sa. 15:30; Est. 6:12; Jer. 14:3). Turbans were worn by the three men cast into the fiery furnace (Da. 3:21). Women wore "headdresses" or turbans and veils with which they also covered the upper part of the body. Priests wore a head covering. In the NT while praying or prophesying, men were not permitted to wear a head covering and women were required to wear one (1Co. 11:4, 6).

Many of the special items worn by women are mentioned in Isa. 3:18-24. The poor usually went barefooted, but others wore sandals, made of leather or wood and held on with thongs, removed on entering a house (Am. 2:6; 8:6; Mk. 1:7). There is evidence of considerable variety in the quality of apparel, even though not in style, and the disparity between the rich and the poor is particularly notable.

A Bedouin in Full Dress

DRINK Water, beer, milk, wine, and vinegar were the chief liquids drunk in biblical times. The first came from cisterns or wells, and milk was usually goat's milk (Pr. 27:27). Wine could be sweet (the juice of the grape), sour (vinegar of wine), or fermented (Nu. 6:3; Ge. 9:21; 14:18). It was considered a food (Isa. 55:1). Beer is noted in Pr. 20:1. "Fermented drink," frequently in the Scriptures coupled with wine, was prepared by a formula from either wine or grain. It was forbidden to priests (Aaron and his sons) and Nazirites, and while not forbidden to others it was accompanied with warnings that it might pervert the judgment of its users (Lev. 10:9; Nu. 6:3-4; Dt. 14:26; Pr. 20:1; 31:4-5). Wine was not banned in Israel, nor even fermented drink, but drunkenness is always considered a disgrace and condemned (Ge. 19:31-36; Pr. 20:1; Jer. 13:13-14). An elder was not to be one that consumed too much wine (1Ti. 3:3; Tit. 1:7). The Christian was not to be drunk with wine but filled with the Spirit (Eph. 5:18).

DRINK OFFERING *See* SACRIFICES AND OFFERINGS, Grain (Meal) Offering

DROMEDARY *See* BEASTS 4., *Camels*

DROPSY A symptom rather than a disease. It manifests itself by an unnatural effusion of watery fluid in the tissues or some cavity of the body (Lk. 14:2). *See also* SICK, SICKNESS

DROSS The impurities of metals, used to describe something as worthless (Ps. 119:119; Isa. 1:22-25; Eze. 22:18-19).

DRUNKENNESS *See* DRINK

DRUSILLA The youngest daughter of Herod Agrippa I, who lived between the time of the death of Christ and that of Paul. She became the wife of the Judean procurator Felix after leaving her first husband. Paul made a defense before the couple (Ac. 24:24-25). †

DUALISM The belief that there are two irreducible and antagonistic forces, gods, or principles at work in the universe. The God of the Bible has no opposite equal; hence, the Bible is not essentially dualistic.

DUKE *See* CHIEF

DUMAH [silence, name of Underworld]
1. A son of Ishmael and ancestor of one of the Arabian tribes (Ge. 25:14; 1Ch. 1:30). †
2. A Judean town (148-093) in the hill country near Hebron (Jos. 15:52). †
3. An unidentified place in Edom (Isa. 21:11); *See* NIV footnote. †

DUNG *See* MANURE

DUNGEON *See* PRISON

DURA A plain near Babylon where Nebuchadnezzar's image was set up to be worshiped (Da. 3:1). †

DUST, SHAKE OFF THE A gesture that signified the breaking off of all association, and was equal to calling someone a heathen (Mt. 10:14; Mk. 6:11; Lk. 9:5; Ac. 13:51). This is what a Jew would do after leaving a heathen city.

DUTY *See* TAXES, TAXING

DWARF *See* PRIEST

DYED, DYEING Known and practiced from antiquity, it was used by the Israelites in the preparing of the skins for the covering of the tabernacle and in the temple (Ex. 26:1, 31; 2Ch. 3:14). The wealthy and the nobility used highly colored materials for their clothing (Pr. 31:22; Lk. 16:19). The Phoenicians had a near monopoly on this art but at Solomon's request taught it to his workmen (2Ch. 2:7). Dyeing vats have been discovered in a number of excavations.

DYSENTERY A disease of the lower bowel characterized by ulceration and hemorrhaging from which Paul healed the father of Publius on the island of Malta (Ac. 28:7-8). *See also* SICK, SICKNESS

E

EAGLE *See* BIRDS 5.

EAR *See* EMOTIONS; OBEDIENCE, OBEY

EARING KJV for "plowing" in Ge. 45:6 and Ex. 34:21. *See* FARMING

EARNEST *See* GOD, NAMES OF; GODHEAD 6., *Holy Spirit*; SALVATION; SEAL, *arrabon*

EARRING *See* ORNAMENTS

EARTH In the OT two words commonly rendered "earth" and "ground" have a wide range of meanings, some of which they have in common: material substance (Ge. 2:7); a territory or land (Ge. 28:15); the physical world in which man lives as opposed to the heavens (Ge. 1:1; Dt. 31:28; Ps. 68:8; Da. 6:27).

EARTHENWARE *See* POTTER, POTTERY

EARTHQUAKE Since Palestine lies within the active earthquake zone which records 20 percent of the earth's tremors, it is natural that the biblical writers should record such phenomena. While such trembling of the earth is caused sometimes by volcanic activity, the geological formation of the Jordan Valley and the fault lines which run into it from both E and W provide the necessary conditions for movements of the earth's surface, which more frequently than volcanic action produce earthquakes. Severe waves of vibration produce spectacular secondary effects which accompany the quakes, such as fissures in the earth (Nu. 16:32), thunder, rumblings, and flashes of lightning (Rev. 8:5). Earthquakes are recorded during the days of Moses (Ex. 19:18); Saul (1Sa. 14:15); Elijah (1Ki. 19:11); Uzziah (Am. 1:1; Zec. 14:5); and Paul and Silas (Ac. 16:26). In the excavations of Hazor evidence of the one in Uzziah's day was found. Josephus described a severe earthquake during the reign of Herod (Antiq. 15:5:2), of which archaeological evidence was found in the buildings of the Qumran community.

It is described as a feature of the LORD'S presence for revelation (Ex. 19:18), and for destructive judgment (Isa. 29:6). The earthquake is prophetically listed among the catastrophic elements of the last days (Mt. 24:7; Mk. 13:8; Lk. 21:11; Rev. 6:12; 8:5; 11:13, 19; 16:18).

EAST, DIRECTION OF *See* GEOGRAPHY OF THE HOLY LAND III., *Topography, Setting*

EAST (OR EASTERN) SEA *See* GEOGRAPHY OF THE HOLY LAND; SALT SEA

EAST WIND *See* WIND

EASTER {a pagan Teutonic goddess} Since the Council of Nicea in A.D. 325, the church celebrates the Resurrection of Jesus Christ on this day. There was no celebration of the resurrection in the New Testament. Later the Gentile Christians observed the day on Sunday, while the Jewish believers connected it with

Passover and celebrated it on the fourteenth of Nisan. Following the Council at Nicea, Easter has been observed on the first Sunday following the full moon after the vernal equinox, varying between March 22 and April 25. The KJV reference in Ac. 12:4 means "Passover."

EASTERN RELIGIONS *See* BUDDHISM; HINDUISM

EBAL

1. KJV for "Obal" (NIV in 1Ch. 1:22; cf. Ge. 10:28).

2. The third son of Shobal, a Horite clan chief in Edom (Ge. 36:23; 1Ch. 1:40).

3. A mountain just N of Nablus (Shechem), 3,077 feet high, *Jebel Eslamiyeh*, commands an extensive view over most of Galilee and Samaria. It is separated from Mt. Gerizim directly to the S by a very important E-W pass. Following their entry into the land of Canaan, the Israelites gathered here to confirm their covenant with the LORD and to recite the blessing and cursing (Dt. 27:4-26). Joshua built an altar on Mt. Ebal in accordance with Moses' earlier command (Jos. 8:30-35).

MOUNT EBAL

EBED [servant]

1. Father of Gaal, who unsuccessfully rebelled against Abimelech in Shechem (Jdg. 9:26-45). †

2. Son of a Jonathan, one of the fifty men of the family of Adin who returned from Babylon under Ezra (Ezr. 8:6). †

EBED-MELECH [servant of MELEK (king)] A Cushite (Ethiopian) whom the LORD promised safety and protection during the destruction of Jerusalem (Jer. 39:15-18), for his role in requesting the king's permission to have Jeremiah the prophet drawn from a dungeon (Jer. 38:7-13). †

EBENEZER [stone of help] A town near Aphek where the Israelites camped before being defeated and losing the Ark of God to the Philistines (1Sa. 4:1-22). Following a subsequent victory over the Philistines, Samuel set up a memorial stone calling it Ebenezer, "the stone of help" (1Sa. 7:12). †

EBER [(regions) beyond (the river), *or* eponym for Hebrew] Meaning "the other side," "across," from which (according to some scholars) the Gentile form "Hebrew" is derived and is explained as denoting those coming from the "other side of the river" (the Euphrates) — i.e., from Haran (Ge. 11:31), in Aram Naharaim, the home of Abraham and Nahor (Ge. 24:4, 7, 10). The name appears frequently:

1. A descendant of Shem. He was the son of Shelah, and the father of Peleg (in whose time the earth was divided) and Joktan (Ge. 10:21-25; 11:14-16; 1Ch. 1:19-25).

2. Head of a Gadite family (1Ch. 5:13).

3. Two Benjamite families (1Ch. 8:12-22).

4. The head of a priestly family in the days of Joiakim (Ne. 12:20).

5. Eber is also mentioned in the genealogy of Jesus as an ancestor of Abraham (Lk. 3:35).

EBEZ A town in Issachar whose location is unknown (Jos. 19:20). †

EBIASAPH [(my) father has gathered] 1Ch. 6:23, 37; 9:19. *See also* ABIASAPH

EBONY The highly prized, black core wood of the tree *Diospyrosebenum* imported into Palestine and Syria from South India, Ceylon, and Ethiopia for use in the manufacture of fine furniture, valuable turned vessels, scepters, and idols. It was highly prized by the Egyptians, Phoenicians, Babylonians, Greeks, and Romans, and is mentioned along with ivory tusks as a part of Tyre's trade with the men of Rhodes (Eze. 27:15).

EBRONAH *See* ABRONAH

ECBATANA Founded by the Median king, Deioces (Herodotus 1:96), and located at the foot of the Elvend Mountain, Ecbatana became the capital of Media. Following its capture by Cyrus the Great, it became a favorite summer residence of the Achaemenian kings. Ecbatana was where a copy of Cyrus's decree authorizing the rebuilding of the Jerusalem temple was found (Ezr. 6:2). The city remained famous for its luxury after its capture by Alexander the Great from the Persians in 330 B.C. and became a summer capital of the Parthian rulers. Though suffering a minor decline during Sassanian rule, the town was rebuilt following the Islamic conquest and continues to be one of the principal cities of Iran to the present time, known as Hamadan. †

ECCLESIASTES, BOOK OF The title, which comes to us through Jerome from the Septuagint, is a translation of the Hebrew word *Koheleth*, a word which means "teacher" or "preacher" (Ecc. 1:12), and which possibly means "one who participates in a popular assembly" or "one who assembles wise sayings for the purpose of teaching." Like Job, it is a fine example of OT wisdom literature.

ECCLESIOLOGY *See* SYSTEMATIC THEOLOGY

ECUMENICISM [the inhabited earth] The word emphasizes "worldwide" unity. In Christendom, ecumenicism is an endeavor to bring about solidarity among Christians. It may take the form of either collaboration between separate groups or actual integration into one organism.

ED [witness] KJV for "Altar of Witness" (Jos. 22:34).

EDAR [flock] *See* EDER

EDEN [paradise, delight, *possibly* flat land]
1. The environment in which God created an enclosed peaceful Garden which was Adam and Eve's residence until their expulsion because of sin. The location of this "garden" is said to be watered by four rivers (Ge. 2:11-14), two of which are identified as the Tigris and Euphrates. The most commonly held theory places the Garden somewhere in southern Mesopotamia, where the Pishon and Gihon were either canals or tributaries connecting the other two rivers. It has been suggested the Hebrew word translated "streams" in Ge. 2:6 may correspond to an Akkadian loanword from the Sumerian word for "river," indicating that the river overflowed the ground and provided natural irrigation. The delightful nature of the "paradise" of Eden became illustrative material for later Scripture writers (Isa. 51:3; Eze. 28:13; 31:9, 16, 18; 36:35; Joel 2:3). Though the idea of a primeval paradise seems well-developed in many ethnic religions (Persian, Indian), only indirect parallels to the Garden of Eden are found in the Sumerian "land of Dilmun" and the Babylonian "cedar forest of Irini" and "garden of Siduri."
2. A Gershonite who served under Kore in distributing the holy offerings during the time of Hezekiah (2Ch. 29:12; 31:15).

EDEN, PEOPLE OF An Aramaic city-state between the Euphrates and the Balikh River, identified with Bitadini in the Assyrian records, which blocked Assyrian expansion to N Syria. Its main city, Til Barsip (modern Tell Ahmar), on the east bank of the Euphrates, was taken by Shalmaneser III and became an Assyrian province in 855 B.C. The Bible mentions "the people of Eden who live in Tel Assar" taken together with Gozan, Haran, and Rezeph (2Ki. 19:12; Isa. 37:12), and predicts that its population of Beth Eden would be exiled to Kir (Am. 1:5). It was one of the places trading with Tyre (Eze. 27:23).

EDER

1. [flock] A sheepfold "tower" where Jacob camped following the death of Rachel, between Bethlehem and Hebron (Ge. 35:21). †

2. [*from Aramaic for* "helper"] A son of Mushi, the son of Merari. A Levite of David's time (1Ch. 23:23; 24:30). †

3. [*from Aramaic for* "helper"] A Benjamite family (1Ch. 8:15).

4. A place (Jos. 15:21). †

EDIFICATION, EDIFY, EDIFYING [*Latin* to build up] To build a believer up by speaking words of encouragement (Ro. 14:19; Eph. 4:29; 1Th. 5:11).

EDOM, DESERT OF *See* GEOGRAPHY OF THE HOLY LAND

EDOM, EDOMITES [red] *See* GEOGRAPHY OF THE HOLY LAND

EDREI

1. The royal city (253-224) of Og, King of Bashan (Dt. 1:4; Jos. 12:4), located at the extreme southern boundary of Bashan near the southern source of the Yarmuk River, about ten miles NE of Ramoth-Gilead, and about thirty miles E-SE of the Sea of Galilee. Og was defeated by the Israelites at Edrei (Nu. 21:33-35; Dt. 3:1-3); and the city was assigned to the half-tribe of Manasseh (Jos. 13:12, 31). In the temple of Ammon in Karnak, Edrei is listed among the cities which Thutmose III (1490-1436 B.C.) claimed to have conquered or dominated in Upper Retenu (Syria-Palestine).

2. A fortified city of Naphtali, near Kedesh (Jos. 19:37).

EDUTH [testimony]; SHUSHAN [lily] *See* PSALMS, TITLE OF, 10. (4)

EGLAH [heifer] The wife of David who was the mother of his sixth son, Ithream (2Sa. 3:5; 1Ch. 3:3). †

EGLAIM An unknown town on the border of Moab (Isa. 15:8). †

EGLATH SHELISHIYAH [*possibly* the third Eglath] A place mentioned in the oracles against Moab, location unknown (Isa. 15:5; Jer. 48:34). The KJV

translates as "an heifer of three years old." †

EGLON [circle, ISBE; young bull, KB]

1. A Canaanite royal city (124-106), probably to be identified with Tell el-Hesi, seven miles SW of Lachish at the edge of the foothills extending into the coastal plain of Philistia. One of the five-city Amorite coalition led by the King of Jerusalem against the Gibeonite confederacy, which was defeated by the Israelites under Joshua (Jos. 10:3ff.). Joshua captured the city, and it was later assigned to Judah (Jos. 15:39).

2. A King of Moab who invaded Israelite territory in the region of Jericho with the help of the Ammonites and Amalekites (Jdg. 3:12-13). The payment of annual tribute, required of Israel for eighteen years, provided the opportunity for Ehud's assassination of the obese monarch (Jdg. 3:20-25).

EGYPT The Egyptians are a Hamitic people descended through Mizraim (Ge. 10:6), Hebrew for "Egypt" (*see* GEOGRAPHY OF THE HOLY-LAND). A native priest named Manetho, writing in about 300 B.C., divided the history of his nation into thirty dynasties, a system that is still employed. There is also a predynastic period, extending from 4500 to 3000 B.C., with the dual kingdoms of upper Egypt to the South and Lower Egypt, the Nile delta to the North. They reunited under Menes, traditionally the first pharaoh, who inaugurated the protodynastic period of Dyn. I-II (3000-2600). While the Old Kingdom, Dyn. III-VI, with its capital at Memphis at the apex (the uppermost point) of the delta, was the age of the pyramid builders (*see* PYRAMIDS), the absolute power of the pharaoh suffered a decline in it. The First Intermediate Period, Dyn. VII-XI, was one of feudalism. This may account for the remarkable reception that the Hebrew patriarch Abraham received (Ge. 12:10-20).

Dyn. XII constitutes the Middle Kingdom, about 2000-1780 B.C. Wars created a standing army that broke the power of the feudal nobility, who were replaced by a bureaucracy. Under such conditions Joseph, who came to Egypt before 1850, was able to rise to power (Ge. 39-41; 45:8). This probably occurred under Senusert III, who conquered from Syria to the second cataract (waterfall) of the Nile. Joseph's brothers and their families then emigrated to Egypt (Ge. 46), where they multiplied (Ex. 1:7). During the succeeding centuries of the Second Intermediate Period, Dyn. XIII-XVII (1780-1580), the Israelites suffered oppression (Ge. 15:13), especially under the foreign Hyksos dynasties XV-XVI. A native dynasty, XVII, then arose at Thebes in the South and slowly drove back the hated Asiatics.

Egypt's New Empire, Dyn. XVIII-XX (1580-1100 B.C.) began with the expulsion of the Hyksos. The early XVIIIth Dyn. rulers, in fervent nationalism, intensified Israel's oppression (Ex. 1:13-22) and carried the antiforeign attack on into Syria. Thothmes III (1504-1450), the greatest of the pharaohs, fought seventeen campaigns, had fleets in the Aegean, and held from the fourth cataract to the Euphrates. He was probably the king from whom Moses fled but who died just prior to Israel's exodus in 1445 B.C. (Ex. 4:19; *see* CHRONOLOGY). His son Amenhotep II thus becomes the ill-fated monarch of the ten plagues and the Red Sea (Ex. 5-15). His grandson Amenhotep III abandoned Egypt's northeastern empire, opening the way for Joshua's conquest of Canaan (1406-1400). Amenhotep IV (Akhenaton), 1369-1353, was devoted to the sun god Aton, not the old god Amon. Whether it was true monotheism or devotion to one of the many gods (henotheism) is not certain. Egypt recovered parts of Syria under Rameses II (1304-1237), in the chaotic days of Israel's judges; but only the victory stela of his son Merneptah mentions defeating Israel.

Egypt's Dyn. XXI-XXX (1100-332 B.C.) constitutes the Period of Decline. It was, nevertheless, an honor when Solomon (970-930 B.C.) married a daughter of one of the last pharaohs of the XXIst Dyn. (1Ki. 3:1). Sheshonk I

(biblical Shishak), founder of Dyn. XXII, raided both Judah and Israel, exacting tribute from Solomon's son Rehoboam in 926 (1Ki. 14:25-26); but Zerah the Cushite, who may be associated with his son Osorkon I, was routed during a similar attempt in 895 by Asa of Judah (2Ch. 14:9-13). Later, Hebrew intrigues with "So king of Egypt" (2Ki. 17:4), perhaps Osorkon IV, and with Tirhakah of the XXVth or Cushite Dyn. (2Ki. 19:9), led respectively to the Assyrian destruction of Samaria and Israel in 722 and to the partial capture but miraculous deliverance of Judah and Jerusalem in 701. As the Assyrians said, Egypt was a "splintered reed of a staff, which pierces a man's hand and wounds him if he leans on it" (2Ki. 18:21; cf. Isa. 20; 30:1-7).

Egypt revived briefly under Neco II of the XXVth Dyn., who slew Josiah at Megiddo in 609 (2Ki. 23:29), and controlled Judah (2Ki. 23:32 35) until its loss to the Babylonians, following his defeat at Carchemish in 605 (2Ki. 24:7). It was again Egyptian intrigue, with Pharaoh Hophra (Jer. 37:5; 44:30; Eze. 17:15-17), that led to the Babylonian destruction of Jerusalem in 586. A number of Jews then fled to Egypt, despite Jeremiah, whom they took with them (Jer. 42-44). Years later, after Egypt's last (XXXth) Dyn. had been succeeded by the Macedonians and then the Romans, the baby Jesus and his family found refuge from Herod in this ancient land (Mt. 2:14, 19-21). (J.B.P.)

EGYPT, WADI OF The southern boundary of the land promised to Abram's descendants in Ge. 15:18, usually considered to be Wadi el-Arish, a streambed marking the SE boundary of the Egyptian province of Canaan with the boundary of the tribe of Judah (Nu. 34:5; Jos. 15:4, 47; 1Ki. 8:65; 2Ki. 24:7; 2Ch. 7:8; Isa. 27:12; Eze. 47:19; 48:28). With the northern boundary is the "entrance of Hamath," except in Isa. 27:12 where the Euphrates is mentioned. In other references to the S boundary of the territory yet to be taken in the days of

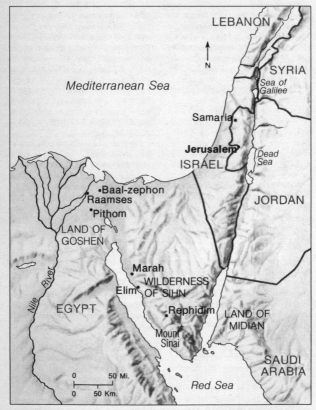

EGYPT AND ITS NEIGHBORING COUNTRIES

Joshua, the Shihor (Jos. 13:3; 1Ch. 13:5) and the Brook of the Arabah (Am. 6:14 NIV, *valley)* are named. These may all refer to Wadi el-Arish, originating in the middle of the Sinai Peninsula and flow-ing into the Mediterranean midway be-tween Gaza and Pelusium.

EGYPTIAN, THE An unnamed leader who started a revolt and led terrorists, whom the Roman commander of the fortress of Antonia, Claudius Lysias, mistook for Paul when he was mobbed in the temple precincts (Ac. 21:38). Josephus (*Antiq.* 20:8:6) mentions that this Egyptian with a band of rebels came to Jerusalem in A.D. 84 and persuaded a multitude of common people to follow him to the Mount of Olives, where he would demonstrate his powers as prophet in commanding the walls of Jerusalem to fall down. Roman soldiers took the initiative to disperse his followers, but the Egyptian escaped.

EHI {my brother (is exalted)} A son of Benjamin (Ge. 46:21). †

EHUD {united} *See* JUDGES OF ISRAEL

EISEGESIS Eisegesis is the procedure of reading one's own ideas *into* a biblical text, as opposed to the practice of exegesis – drawing *out* the meaning that is already there.

EKER {*possibly* offspring} A grandson of Jerahmeel and son of Ham (1Ch. 2:27). †

EKRON, EKRONITES *See* PHILISTINE CITIES

EL [God] *See* GOD, NAMES OF GOD 1.

ELA The father of Shimei, Solomon's commissary officer for the tribe of Benjamin (1Ki. 4:18). †

ELADAH *See* ELEADAH

ELAH {a species of a mighty tree}
1. A tribal chief in Edom descended from Esau, possibly of the district Elah (Elath?) (Ge. 36:41; 1Ch. 1:52).
2. The father of Hoshea, the last king of Israel (2Ki. 15:30; 17:1; 18:1, 9).
3. A son of Caleb (1Ch. 4:15).
4. A Benjamite residing in postexilic Jerusalem (1Ch. 9:8). *See also* KINGS OF JUDAH AND ISRAEL

ELAH, VALLEY OF The valley in which a confrontation occurred between the Israelites and the Philistines. It was there that David killed the Philistine

champion, Goliath (1Sa. 17:2, 19; 21:9). It is identified with the fertile Wadi es-Sunt ("Valley of the Acacia"), about fifteen miles W-SW of Bethlehem, the entrance of which was protected by the fortress of Azekah (Tell ez-Zakariya, 144-123).

ELAM, ELAMITES {highland}
1. A Son of Shem (Ge. 10:22; 1Ch. 1:17).
2. A son of Shashak, a descendant of Benjamin (1Ch. 8:24).
3. A Korahite son of one of the gatekeepers in the time of David (1Ch. 26:3).
4. The head of a family of 1,254 which returned with Zerubbabel (Ezr. 2:7; Ne. 7:12). Another "Elam" family is mentioned with the same number of members, called "the other Elam" (Ezr. 2:31; Ne. 7:34).
5. The father of two sons who returned from exile with Ezra (Ezr. 8:7).
6. A descendant of Elam who urged Ezra to take action against mixed marriages (Ezr. 10:2). Six of the same family put away their foreign wives (Ezr. 10:26).
7. A chief who sealed the covenant with Nehemiah (Ne. 10:14).
8. A priest who took part in the dedication of the rebuilt wall of Jerusalem (Ne. 12:42).
9. An area covering the territory of the Zagros Mountain range and of modern Luristan and Khuszistan with its capital at Susa. The language of the various tribes that made up its population, largely written in cuneiform, may well have continued centuries after Elam ceased to exist as an independent nation. Different from Sumerian, Semitic, and Indo-European, the script is largely undeciphered. The long history of the people, known through Mesopotamian documents and what is known from the Elamite tablets recovered mostly at Susa, beginning with urban communities and settlements as early as the end of the fourth millennium, was marked by alternating periods of ascendancy (domination) and suppression. Control of the

trade routes to the Iranian plateau, and to the SE, prompted regular attacks against Elam from the plains of Mesopotamia.

ELASAH {God has fashioned}

1. One whom King Zedekiah sent to Nebuchadnezzar carrying Jeremiah's letter of advice to the exiles in Babylon (Jer. 29:3).

2. One of the sons of Pashur who was guilty of marrying foreign wives (Ezr. 10:22).

ELATH {grove of large trees} A seaport town (150-882) located near biblical Ezion Geber in the area where modern Elat and Aqabah are situated at the head of the Red Sea. A stop in the Israelites' exodus from Egypt (Dt. 2:8). King Solomon later built ships and a fort there, the latter to guard his trade route (1Ki. 9:26). King Azariah (Uzziah) rebuilt and restored it to Judah, taking it back from the Edomites (2Ki. 14:22; 2Ch. 8:17; 26:2). Azariah is called by that name in the king's record and Uzziah in that of the Chronicles. Elam (the Syrians) took Elath later, only to be driven out, together with the Israelites, by the king of Edom (2Ki. 16:56). It served the Romans in NT times as a military post. †

EL-BERITH {a god of a covenant} A god worshiped at Shechem (Jdg. 9:46). †

EL BETHEL {God (El) of Bethel} The name which Jacob gave to the place of his vision on his way back from Paddan Aram (Ge. 35:7-9). † *See also* GOD, NAMES OF

ELDAAH {El is (my) desire} The last of the five sons of Midian, from the Abraham Keturah line (Ge. 25:4;˙1Ch. 1:33). †

ELDAD {beloved of El; *possibly* Dadi (pagan god) is god} One of the seventy elders appointed by Moses to assist him in the government of the Israelites during the wilderness sojourn, who together with Medad were not present at the door of the tabernacle to receive God's message and the gift of prophecy. In spite of their absence at the appointed place, El-

dad and Medad shared equally in the endowment where they were in the camp. When Joshua objected to the seemingly irregular display of divine power, Moses responded with the wish that all God's people were prophets (Nu. 11:24-29). †

ELDER Since in most civilizations authority has been committed to those best qualified to rule by reason of age or experience, it is natural that leaders in many ancient communities have had this title which comes from a root meaning "old age." Thus, references are made to dignitaries ("elders" in the Hebrew text) among the Egyptians (Ge. 50:7), the elders of the Moabites and Midianites (Nu. 22:7), and the Israelite elders (Ex. 3:16). The seventy elders of Moses' appointment (Ex. 24:1; Nu. 11:16) continued to function until after the wilderness period when according to Deuteronomic legislation every city seems to have had a ruling body of elders who also acted as judges. A constant feature of Israel's life from the days of Moses to those of Ezra, this national body exercised considerable influence, especially in civil matter under the monarchy.

In New Testament times each Jewish community had its council of elders, the most important of which was the Sanhedrin of Jerusalem, which served as a kind of "supreme court" for all Jewry. While they maintained the general administrative control over the Jewish communities and represented the Jews before Roman authorities, their main duty was their interpretation and maintenance of the law. Similarly, the Qumran community also recognized elders and a supreme council. The church quite naturally adopted the institution which functioned in ways comparable to the Jewish Sanhedrin. The Greek word is *presbuteros*, out of which comes "presbytery" (Ac. 11:30; 15:2, 4, 6, 22-23; 16:4; 21:18). These Christian elders exercised spiritual oversight in the congregations (Ro. 12:8; 1Th. 5:12-13; Jas. 5:14; 1Pe. 5:1-4).

ELEAD {El has testified} A descendant of Ephraim (1Ch. 7:21). †

ELEADAH [El has adorned] A descendant of the tribe of Ephraim killed by the men of the city of Gath (1Ch. 7:20). †

ELEALEH [El is high] A city W of the Jordan which was rebuilt by Reuben and later became a Moabite possession (Nu. 32:3, 37; Isa. 15:4; 16:9; Jer. 48:34), identified with el-Al (228-136), about two miles N-NE of Heshbon. †

ELEASAH [El has fashioned]
1. A member or family of the Jerahmeelites of the tribe of Judah (1Ch. 2:39-40). †
2. A Benjamite, descended from Saul (1Ch. 8:37; 9:43). †

ELEAZAR [El is a help]
1. The third son of Aaron and Elisheba (Ex. 6:23; Nu. 3:2). Following the death of his older brothers, Nadab and Abihu (Lev. 10:1-2), Eleazar was designated (Nu. 3:32) and later invested (clothed) by Moses as Aaron's successor (Nu. 20:25-28). As the chief priest, he assisted Moses in the numbering of the people (Nu. 26:1-2) and was responsible for dividing the spoils following a battle with the Midianites (Nu. 31: 25-54). He was appointed to help in the dividing of the Promised Land among the tribes (Nu. 34:17; Jos. 14:1; 19:51).
2. A son of Abinadab who was consecrated to care for the Ark after it was brought to his father's house at Kiriath Jearim from Beth Shemesh (1Sa. 6:19; 7:1).
3. A son of Dodai, one of David's thirty mighty men who gained special recognition in his battles with the Philistines (2Sa. 23:9-10; 1Ch. 11:12-14).
4. A Levite, in the time of David, a son of Mahli. Eleazar had only daughters, who then married their cousins (1Ch. 23:21-22; 24:28).
5. One of the Levite custodians of the temple treasures which were returned to Jerusalem by Ezra (Ezr. 8:33).
6. A descendant of Parosh, mentioned in a list of laymen who had married foreign women while in exile (Ezr. 10:25).
7. A Levite musician who participated in the dedication of the walls of Jerusalem (Ne. 12:42).
8. An ancestor of Joseph, the husband of Mary of whom was born Jesus (Mt. 1:15).

ELECT, ELECTION Since the fall of man (Ge. 2:15-17; 3:1-20), all men descended by natural generation from Adam are born in a state of sin and grow to rebel against the Creator. The redeeming grace of God is needed to deliver men from sin. The concept of election is that God, "out of his mere good pleasure, from all eternity, elected some to everlasting life, and did enter into a covenant of grace, to deliver them out of the estate of sin and misery, and to bring them into an estate of salvation by a Redeemer" (Westminster Shorter Catechism). This is the most restricted usage of the Greek word *ekloge* rendered in English by several words: elect, choose, and select (2Ti. 2:10; 1Pe. 1:1-2; Eph. 1:3-5, 11). There is no obligation upon God to bring into his presence any of those who are in sin or rebellion against him, and thus uninterested in any particular relationship with him. In his grace, however, through election, he sees that some, a vast multitude, will come to him. In the NT the concept is almost always in relation to individuals. In the OT one of its chief usages is of the choosing of Israel as a people because he loved them and had to keep the oath he swore to their fathers when he brought them out of Egypt. *See also* CHOSEN PEOPLE; PREDESTINATE; SAINT(S); SALVATION, APPLICATION OF

EL ELOHE ISRAEL [God, the God of Israel] The name of Jacob's altar erected near Shechem (Ge. 33:20). †

EL ELYON *See* GOD, NAMES OF 1.

ELEPH [ox] *See* HAELEPH

ELEPHANT *See* IVORY

ELEVEN, THE *See* APOSTLES

ELHANAN [El is gracious]
1. A son of Jair, who killed Lahmi, Goliath's brother (1Ch. 20:5). † (Jair is

called Jaare-Oregim in 2Sa. 21:19, but see the NIV footnote.)

2. One of David's thirty mighty men, a son of Dodo the Bethlehemite (2Sa. 23:24; 1Ch. 11:26). †

ELI [Yahweh is exalted, IDB; (El) is exalted, KB] A descendant of Ithamar, the fourth son of Aaron, high priest at Shiloh who judged Israel for forty years (1Sa. 1–3; 14:3; 1Ki. 2:27). The sinful conduct of Eli's sons (Phinehas and Hophni) and the failure of Eli's influence over them, culminated in the prophecy of the fall of the house of Eli (1Sa. 2:27-36), and its fulfillment in the Philistine capture of the Ark, the death of Phinehas and Hophni, the destruction of Shiloh, and finally the demise of Eli upon hearing of Israel's defeat (1Sa. 4:11-18). Eli was already old when Hannah brought the baby Samuel to give him to serve the LORD for his entire life (1Sa. 1:24-28). *See* ELOI; *see also* GOD, NAMES OF, GODHEAD 1., *El*

ELIAB [El is (my) father]

1. A son of Helon, a Zebulun tribal representative appointed to help Moses (Nu. 1:9; 2:7; 7:24, 29; 10:16).

2. A Reubenite whose sons Dathan and Abiram were involved in the rebellion of Korah against the leadership of Moses and Aaron (Nu. 16:1, 12; 26:8-10; Dt. 11:6).

3. An ancestor of Samuel the prophet (1Ch. 6:27); also called Elihu (1Sa. 1:1), and Eliel (1Ch. 6:34).

4. David's older brother (1Sa. 16:6; 17:13, 28), whom Samuel thought might be the LORD's appointed for kingship (1Sa. 16:6). While serving in Saul's army against the Philistines he was incensed at the suggestion that David, his youngest brother, would confront Goliath (1Sa. 17:28).

5. A Levitical musician of David's time (1Ch. 15:18, 20; 16:5).

6. A Gadite warrior who became an officer in David's army (1Ch. 12:8-9).

ELIADA(H) [El knows]

1. One of David's sons born to him in Jerusalem (2Sa. 5:16; 1Ch. 3:8). †

2. Father of Rezon, leader of a guerilla band against Solomon (1Ki. 11:23). †

3. Commander of a Benjamite military corps stationed at Jerusalem during Jehoshaphat's reign (2Ch. 17:17). †

ELIAH *See* ELIJAH 2.

ELIAHBA [El hides] A Shaalbonite, one of David's Thirty or mighty men (2Sa. 23:32; 1Ch. 11:33). †

ELIAKIM [El establishes]

1. A son of Hilkiah and successor of Shebna as King Hezekiah's palace administrator (2Ki. 18:18, 26, 37). He attempted to negotiate at Jerusalem with the representatives of Sennacherib (2Ki. 18:17-37; Isa. 36:1-22), and later headed a company directed to appeal for Isaiah's help (2Ki. 19:2; Isa. 37:2).

2. Pharaoh changed one by this name to Jehoiakim, and Neco made him the puppet king of Judah (2Ki. 23:34).

3. A priest at the dedication of the rebuilt wall of Jerusalem in Nehemiah's time (Ne. 12:41).

4. A grandson of Zerubbabel named in the genealogy of Jesus (Mt. 1:13).

5. A son of Melea in Jesus' genealogy (Lk. 3:30).

ELIAM [El is (my) kinsman]

1. The father of Bathsheba, the wife of Uriah the Hittite, whom David had killed so that he could have his wife (2Sa. 11:3; called Ammiel in 1Ch. 3:5). †

2. A son of Ahithophel and one of David's Thirty (2Sa. 23:34). †

ELIAS KJV for "Elijah." *See* ELIJAH

ELIASAPH [El has added]

1. Son of Deuel and tribal leader of Gad who assisted Moses in the census of Israel and with other duties in the Desert of Sinai (Nu. 1:14; 2:14; 7:42, 47; 10:20). †

2. Son of Lael and tribal leader of the Gershonites who cared for the tabernacle in the Desert of Sinai (Nu. 3:24). †

ELIASHIB [El restores]

1. A priest in the time of David (1Ch. 24:12).

2. A descendant of King David and of Zerubbabel (1Ch. 3:24).

3. A high priest in the time of Nehemiah, who directed the rebuilding of the Sheep Gate in the city wall (Ne. 3:1, 20-21).

4. A postexilic singer who had married a foreign wife (Ezr. 10:24).

5. Son of Zattu who had a foreign wife (Ezr. 10:27).

6. Son of Bani who also had a foreign wife (Ezr. 10:36).

7. Father of Johanan who assisted Ezra (Ezr. 10:6; Ne. 12:23).

ELIATHAH [El comes] A son of Heman the king's seer and grandson of Asaph, involved in the ministry of music in the temple in David's reign (1Ch. 25:4, 27). †

ELIDAD [El is (my) beloved] A Benjamite, one of those assigned the oversight of the division of Canaan to the nine and a half tribes to be settled W of the Jordan (Nu. 34:16-18, 21). †

ELIEHOENAI [my eyes (look) to Yahweh]

1. The eighth son of a gatekeeper from the family of Korah (1Ch. 26:3). †

2. Head of a family who returned to Jerusalem with Ezra (Ezr. 8:4). †

ELIEL [El is (my) God]

1. A chief or family head of the half of the tribe of Manasseh E of Jordan (1Ch. 5:24). †

2. A Levitical musician in the temple (1Ch. 6:34). †

3. Two chiefs or family heads of Benjamin (1Ch. 8:20, 22). †

4. Three of David's mighty men (1Ch. 11:46-47; 12:11). †

5. A Levite connected with bringing the Ark to Jerusalem (1Ch. 15:9, 11). †

6. A Levite of the time of Hezekiah (2Ch. 31:13). †

ELIENAI [my eyes (look) to Yahweh] A son of Shimhi and descendant of Benjamin (1Ch. 8:20). †

ELIEZER [El is (my) help]

1. Abraham's servant and heir until Ishmael was born (Ge. 15:2). He may

have been the unnamed servant sent to secure a bride for Isaac (Ge. 24). †

2. The second son of Moses and Zipporah (Ex. 18:4; 1Ch. 23:15, 17; 26:25). †

3. A grandson of Benjamin (1Ch. 7:8). †

4. A priest who blew a trumpet before the Ark as it was being returned to Jerusalem (1Ch. 15:24). †

5. A Reubenite chief in David's time (1Ch. 27:16). †

6. A prophet who rebuked Jehoshaphat for his military alliance with Ahaziah (2Ch. 20:37). †

7. A leader sent to encourage Israelites to return with Ezra (Ezr. 8:16-17). †

8. A priest and Levite, also a descendant of Harim who had married wives while in the exile (Ezr. 10:18, 23, 31). †

9. Mentioned in the genealogy of Jesus (Lk. 3:29). †

ELIHOENAI *See* ELIEHOENAI

ELIHOREPH A son of Shisha, a secretary and chief official in Solomon's court (1Ki. 4:3). †

ELIHU [Yahweh is (my) El]

1. The father of Jeroham and great-grandfather of Samuel (1Sa. 1:1); also called Eliel (1Ch. 6:34). †

2. A Manassite, who deserted Saul to join David in Ziklag (1Ch. 12:20). †

3. A Korahite gatekeeper in David's time (1Ch. 26:7). †

4. David's brother who became the officer over Judah (1Ch. 27:18). †

5. The youngest of Job's friends (Job 32:2-6; 34:1; 35:1; 36:1). †

ELIJAH [Yahweh is (my) El]

1. A ninth-century prophet from Tishbe of Gilead in the northern kingdom (1Ki. 17:1), who led in the struggle against the encroachment of Tyrian Baal worship (1Ki. 17). The struggle of the LORD against Baalism which was fostered by the marriage of Ahab to Jezebel centered in Elijah's denunciation of Ahab's compromise, false tolerance, and syncretism (mixing of paganism with Judaism) which were incompatible with the exclusive allegiance God required of

Israel (1Ki. 18). King Ahaziah also was denounced for inquiring of the Baal oracle of Ekron (1Ki. 18:17-19; 2Ki. 1:1-8). Elijah sent a letter to King Jehoram promising punishment for his apostasy (2Ch. 21:12-15). The impact of his words and acts ultimately claimed for him the role of harbinger (forerunner) of the eschatological age (Mal. 4:5-6). An expectation of Elijah's return is stated frequently in the NT (Mt. 11:14; 16:13-14; 17:10-13; Mk. 9:45, 13; Lk. 1:17; 9:30-33; Jn. 1:21, 25).

2. A Son of Jeroham (1Ch. 8:27).

3. A descendant of a priest, guilty of having married a foreign woman (Ezr. 10:21).

4. A descendant of a common man, guilty of marrying a foreign woman (Ezr. 10:26).

ELIKA A Harodite who belonged to David's Thirty (2Sa. 23:25). †

ELIM {big trees} An oasis marked by twelve fresh water springs and seventy palm trees, the fourth stop of the Israelites after crossing the Red Sea (Ex. 15:27; 16:1; Nu. 33:9-10). It has been identified with a site about sixty miles from Suez called Wadi Gharandel, where vegetation, palms, and water are plentiful even today. †

ELIM: The fourth stop before Rephidim and Mount Sinai

ELIMELECH {El is (my) king} An Ephrathite from Bethlehem, who with his wife Naomi and two sons, Mahlon and Kilion, migrated to Moab in the time of the Judges to escape a famine in Judah. He is remembered mainly because of the faithfulness of his daughter-in-law Ruth to Naomi following his death and the death of his sons (Ru. 1:2-3; 2:1, 3; 4:3, 9). †

ELIOENAI {my eyes (look) to Yahweh}

1. A postexilic descendant of David (1Ch. 3:23-24). †

2. A Simeonite clan head (1Ch. 4:36, 38). †

3. A grandson of Benjamin (1Ch. 7:8). †

4. A son of Pashur who had married a foreign wife in the exile (Ezr. 10:22). †

5. A son of Zattu who had married a foreign wife while in the exile (Ezr. 10:27). †

6. A postexilic priest involved in one of two choirs at the dedication of the rebuilt wall of Jerusalem (Ne. 12:41). †

ELIPHAL {(my) El sits in judgment} A member of David's mighty men (1Ch. 11:35). †

ELIPHALET {El is (my) deliverance} *See* ELIPHELET 1.

ELIPHAZ {El is fine gold *or* El crushes}

1. The eldest son of Esau and his Hittite wife, Adah, who married a Horite concubine, Timna, and became the ancestor of a number of Edomite tribes (Ge. 36:4, 10-11, 15; 1Ch. 1:35-36).

2. The first speaker in the dialogue against Job. Coming from Teman, he was perhaps known for his wisdom (Jer. 49:7). Eliphaz reasoned that Job's suffering was the natural outcome of his sin and that conversion was the only escape from God's continued retribution (Job 4, 5, 15, 22).

ELIPHELEH(U) {El, distinguish him!} A Levite harp player appointed by David to the musical ministry during the recovery of the Ark (1Ch. 15:18, 21). †

ELIPHELET {El is (my) deliverance}

1. A son of David born in Jerusalem (1Ch. 3:6, 8; 14:5).

2. One of David's Thirty (2Sa. 23:34).

3. A Benjamite and descendant of Saul (1Ch. 8:39).

4. An exile who returned with Ezra (Ezr. 8:13).

5. A son of Hashum who had married a foreign wife while in exile (Ezr. 10:33).

ELISABETH *See* ELIZABETH

ELISHA, ELISEUS [El is (my) salvation] The disciple and successor of Elijah who was a prophet during the reigns of Jehoram, Jehu, Jehoahaz, and Joash, kings of Israel (2Ki. 1–13). Continuing Elijah's battle against Baal worship, Elisha's ministry is marked by many miracles related to both relieving of private needs and affairs of state. As the recognized head of the prophetic schools, he enjoyed access to the royal courts because of his gifts of knowledge and foresight and capacity for miracle working. He endeavored to mold the nation's future by the prophetic proclamation of the LORD's will.

ELISHAH One of the descendants of Japheth in the "Table of Nations" (Ge. 10:4; 1Ch. 1:7), whose name was later applied to a maritime (coastal) region and its inhabitants who exported purple and blue-dyed products to Tyre (Eze. 27:7). It has been identified with Alashia, a part of Cyprus from which copper and other raw materials were exported. It is mentioned in cuneiform tablets from Mari, Alalakh, Ugarit, Tell el-Amarna and Khattushash, from the eighteenth to the thirteenth centuries B.C., and has been identified by C.F.A. Schaeffer with Enkomi on the E coast of Cyprus, where an important Late Bronze Age trading center has been excavated. †

ELISHAMA [El has heard]

1. An Ephraimite at the census in the Desert of Sinai, the grandfather of Joshua (Nu. 1:10; 2:18; 7:48, 53; 10:22; 1Ch. 7:26). †

2. One of David's sons born in Jerusalem (2Sa. 5:16; 1Ch. 3:6, 8; 14:7). †

3. The grandfather of Ishmael, a member of Judean royalty who killed Gedaliah at the time of the exile (2Ki. 25:25; Jer. 41:1). †

4. A descendant of Judah (1Ch. 2:41) †

5. A priest sent to teach Judeans the law (2Ch. 17:7-8). †

6. A secretary at Jehoiakim's court (Jer. 36:12, 20-21). †

ELISHAPHAT [El is (my) judge] A Judean commander of a unit of 100 who assisted Jehoiada the priest in the revolt that brought Joash to the throne (2Ch. 23:1-11). †

ELISHEBA [El is an oath, BDB; El is (my) fill, KB] The wife of Aaron (Ex. 6:23). †

ELISHUA [El is (my) salvation] A son of David born in Jerusalem (2Sa. 5:15; 1Ch. 3:6; 14:5; cf. 1Ch. 3:6). †

ELIUD [El is (my) grandeur] The father of Eleazar and ancestor of Jesus (Mt. 1:14-16). †

ELIZABETH [El is (my) oath] The wife of the priest Zachariah and mother of John the Baptist (Lk. 1:5-66). She was a woman of piety, faith, and spiritual gifts of the lineage of Aaron. Her barrenness was overcome in old age by the birth of the herald of the Messiah's coming. † (Cf. ELISHEBA)

ELIZAPHAN [El is (my) hiding]

1. The head of the Kohathites in the Desert of Sinai (Nu. 3:30; 1Ch. 15:8; 2Ch. 29:13). †

2. The Zebulun representative among the tribal leaders responsible for dividing the land of Canaan (Nu. 34:25). †

ELIZUR [El is (my) rock] The leader of the Reubenites who assisted Moses in taking a census of Israel in the Desert of Sinai (Nu. 1:5; 2:10; 7:30, 35; 10:18). †

ELKANAH [El has possessed]

1. A son of Korah, and leader of a Levite clan (Ex. 6:24; 1Ch. 6:25). †

2. The father of Samuel the prophet (1Sa. 1:1, 4, 8, 19, 21, 23; 2:11, 20; 1Ch. 6:34). †

3. An ambidextrous Benjamite warrior who left Saul to join David at Ziklag (1Ch. 12:2, 6). †

4. An official of the court of Ahaz

who was killed by Pekah when he invaded Judah (2Ch. 28:6-7). †

5. A name frequently used among the Levites, especially by the Kohathites; some were temple musicians (1Ch. 6:23, 25-26, 35-36; 9:16; 15:23). †

ELKOSH, ELKOSHITE The home of Nahum the prophet (Na. 1:1). Of a number of suggested locations, the chronological and circumstantial setting of the prophet's ministry is most in keeping with a Judean town. †

ELLASAR One of the city-state allies with Kedorlaomer, which invaded Palestine and fought against the cities of the plain in Abraham's time (Ge. 14:1, 9). It has been identified by some with the southern Babylonian kingdom of Larsa. †

ELM *See* TREES, *terebinth*

ELMADAM, ELMODAM An ancestor of Jesus (Lk. 3:28). †

ELNAAM [El is pleasantness] The father of Jeribai and Joshaviah, two of David's men (1Ch. 11:46). †

ELNATHAN [El has given]
1. Father of Nehushta, Jehoiachin's mother (2Ki. 24:8), who possibly was the one who led a party sent by King Jehoiakim to bring back the fugitive prophet Uriah from Egypt (Jer. 26:22-23; 36:12, 25). A reference from Lachish Ostracon III, which comes from this period, may record this action: "The commander of the host, Coniah son of Elnathan, has come down in order to go into Egypt." †
2. The name appears three times among those returning to Jerusalem from the exile (Ezr. 8:16). †

ELOHIM [a god, the God] *See* GOD, NAMES OF; GODHEAD

ELOI [my El (God)] An Aramaic transliteration in Mk. 15:34. A similar Hebrew transliteration is found in Mt. 27:46 (most versions) for the word "Eli." Both mean "my God." *See* next entry; *see also;* GOD, NAMES OF; GODHEAD 1. *El, Elohim*

ELOI, ELOI, LAMA SABACHTHANI A transliteration of the Hebrew-Aramaic expression recorded in Mt. 27:46 and Mk. 15:34, from Ps. 22:1, as the fourth utterance of Jesus' seven sayings while on the cross. The translation which the Gospels then give for the readers unfamiliar with either Hebrew or Aramaic, "My God, my God, why have you forsaken me?" had earlier in history been explained by Jesus in his discussion of the meaning of his death. The footnote to Mt. 27:46 in the NIV reads, "Some manuscripts Eli, Eli." †

ELON BETHHANAN [tree of BETHHANAN] A Danite village in Solomon's second administration district (1Ki. 4:9). †

ELON, ELONITES [a species of a mighty tree]
1. A son of Zebulun (Ge. 46:14; Nu. 26:26). †
2. The Hittite father of one of Esau's wives, Basemath (Ge. 26:34; 36:2). †
3. A minor judge from Zebulun (Jdg. 12:11-12). †
4. A village in the territory allotted to the tribe of Dan near Timnah (Jos. 19:43). Later the Danites moved N. Elon may possibly be identified with 'Alein, W of Beit Mahsir, or Khirbet Wadi 'Alin between Deir Aban and 'Ain Shems (Beth Shemesh). † *See* JUDGES OF ISRAEL

ELOTH *See* ELATH

ELPAAL [El creates] A Benjamite family (1Ch. 8:11-12, 18). †

ELPALET KJV in 1Ch. 14:4. *See* ELPELET

EL PARAN [tree of PARAN] The most southerly extent of Kedorlaomer's raid into Palestine (Ge. 14:6). †

ELPELET [El is deliverance] Elpelet is apparently a variant spelling of Eliphelet (1Ch. 3:6; cf. 14:5). *See* ELIPHELET 1. One of David's sons born to him in Jerusalem (2 Sa. 5:16; 1Ch. 14:5).

EL SHADDAI [god of mountains *or* god of breasts *or* (God who is) self-sufficient, KB] *See* GOD, NAMES OF 1.

ELTEKEH [meeting place] A Danite town assigned to the Levites which later fell into Philistine hands together with Timnah (Jos. 19:44; 21:23). A decisive victory by Sennacherib over the Egyptians at Eltekeh led to the capture of the city and Timnah and the ultimate invasion of Judah in 701 B.C. Eltekeh was N of Ekron (Khirbet el Muqanna) and has been identified with Tell Shalaf, (128-144). †

ELTEKON [El has arranged] A village of Judah in the district of Bethzur, possibly to be identified with Khirbet ed-Deir, about four miles W of Bethlehem (Jos. 15:59). †

ELTOLAD [generation, IDB; kindred of El, ISBE; El + place where children could be obtained, KB] An unidentified city of Simeon in the S of Judah, near Ezem and Hormah (Jos. 15:30; 19:4), called Tolad in 1Ch. 4:29. †

ELUL *See* CALENDAR

ELUZAI [El is my strength] A Benjamite warrior who defected to David at Ziklag (1Ch. 12:5). †

ELYMAS [*possibly* wise one, *hence* magician] *See* BAR-JESUS

ELYON *See* EL ELYON

ELZABAD [El has given]
1. A warrior from the tribe of Gad who defected to David at Ziklag (1Ch. 12:12). †
2. A Korahite doorkeeper (1Ch. 26:7). †

ELZAPHAN [El hides] A Kohathite Levite (Ex. 6:22; Lev. 10:4; Nu. 3:30; 1Ch. 15:8; 2Ch. 29:13). *See* ELIZAPHAN

EMANCIPATION *See* FREE MAN

EMBALMING *See* BURIAL

EMBROIDER Found chiefly in connection with the embroidery for the tabernacle (Ex. 26:36; 27:16; 28:39).

EMEK KEZIZ [valley of KEZIZ] A city in Benjamin (Jos. 18:21). †

EMERALD *See* PRECIOUS STONES AND METALS, Precious Stones 5.

EMERODS *See* TUMORS

EMIM, EMITES [frightening beings] Tall, powerful, inhabitants of Moab, associated with the area of Shaveh Kiriathaim (Ge. 14:5), who were later dispossessed by the Moabites (Dt. 2:10-11). A tribe similar to the Rephaim and Anakim. *See* REPHAIM

EMMANUEL [El with us] *See* IMMANUEL

EMMAUS [hot springs] A village about seven miles from Jerusalem to which two disciples were going when Jesus joined them in a postresurrection appearance (Lk. 24:13-35). At least four modern sites, Qaloniyeh (near modern Motza El-lit), El-Qubeibeh, Abu Ghosh, and Amwas, ranging from four to twenty miles from Jerusalem, have been proposed for NT Emmaus. The first, between the tribal area of Judah and Benjamin, seems most probable. †

EMMAUS
After his resurrection, Jesus accompanied two disciples on their way to Emmaus, but they did not recognize him. After he revealed himself to them, they returned to Jerusalem.

EMMOR [donkey] *See* HAMOR

EMOTIONS In the Bible the emotions are frequently referred to by a term which literally translated would mean a particular part of the body. There are also, of course, specific abstract terms. The most common parts of the body referred to as seats of emotions include: belly, stomach, ear, eye, heart, kidney, and liver. All have several translations and without checking in the Hebrew or Greek texts it is impossible to distinguish in most cases. *See* SOUL; SPIRIT.

1. *Belly, stomach,* and *inmost being* refer to the innermost part or soul of man, to the seat of his intellectual powers, to the seat of avarice and passion (Job 20:15, 23; Pr. 20:27, 30; Job 32:17-18).

2. *Ear,* almost the equivalent of the mind, expresses the entire faculty of understanding (Job 13:1, 17).

3. *Eye,* in addition to seeing and expressing sorrow and gladness, can speak of desire, lust, and understanding (Job 17:7; 1Sa. 14:27; Ecc. 4:8; 2Pe. 2:14; Jer. 5:21; 7:11 KJV).

4. *Heart.* Almost all the emotions are somewhere in the Bible attributed to the heart (Ps. 64:6), seat of the intellect or understanding, volition (choice), moral life, actions, psychic life, and compassion. It is even rendered "mind" in Job 12:3.

5. *Liver* in the Bible is usually mentioned in connection with the sacrifices. In other literature it is connected also with divination. It is also thought of as the seat of sorrow, exultation, glory, and honor. It is even rendered in Lamentations 2:11 and Ps. 16:9 as "heart." In Job 19:9 it is rendered "honor."

EMPEROR, EMPIRE The title, derived from the Latin *imperator* (lit. "commander"), was originally used to honor a general temporarily after a victory; but following the example of Julius Caesar who used the title permanently, it came to refer to the supreme military authority or the ruler of the Roman Empire. Augustus and his successors continued to use it in this way, while in theory the emperor ruled as princeps, "chief of state," rather than imperator.

Following both oriental and Hellenistic precedents, reverence was often paid to the Roman emperor, whether living or dead, as a divine being. Though unofficial enthusiasm recognized a degree of deity in some of the emperors while living (such as Julius Caesar and Augustus), officially Rome recognized the difference between the gods and the living emperor. Deity could only be recognized after the ruler's death by vote of the senate. It was felt that the approval of the Roman people, through the senate's vote, would recognize a divinity partially inherent in the emperor during his lifetime.

In the outlying areas of the Roman Empire, worship of a living emperor was encouraged by local authorities as an important symbol of solidarity during times of crisis. Thus in Pontus and Bithynia, Christians for a time were required to offer incense and wine before statues of the gods and the emperor Trajan. Those who rejected worship of the emperor were suspected of disloyalty. The word is used only in Ac. 25:21, 25. *See also* CAESAR

ENAIM, ENAM [two springs] One of the fourteen cities in the lowland of Judah and on the road to Timnah. It was in the area of Jarmuth, Azekah, Beth Shemesh, and Socoh (Ge. 38:14, 21; Jos. 15:34). †

ENAN [spring] The father of Ahira, the leader of the tribe of Naphtali in the Desert of Sinai (Nu. 1:15; 2:29; 7:78, 83; 10:27). †

ENCAMPMENT *See* CAMP

ENCHANTERS *See* CHARMS; DIVINATION, DIVINE

ENCOURAGEMENT *See* EXHORTATION

END *See* ESCHATOLOGY; FUTURE LIFE

END OF THE WORLD *See* DAY OF THE LORD; ESCHATOLOGY; FUTURE LIFE; MILLENNIALISM

ENDOR [spring of DOR] A village of Manasseh (Jos. 17:11-12) from which the Israelites were unable to drive out the Canaanites. Saul visited the local medium before his last battle with the

Philistines (1Sa. 28:7). Possibly located at Khirbet es-Safsafah, four miles S of Mt. Tabor. †

ENDURANCE Comes from the idea "to remain" (especially in the midst of pain and suffering). Those who endure will be saved (Mt. 10:22; 24:13; Mk. 4:17; 13:13; Lk. 21:19). Paul taught, practiced, and encouraged endurance (1Co. 4:12; 1Th. 1:4; 2Ti. 2:10-12; 3:11). Perseverance produces rewards (Jas. 1:12). *See* SALVATION, APPLICATION OF, *Perseverance; see also* APOSTASY

EN EGLAIM [spring of two calves] Mentioned together with En Gedi on the shores of the Dead Sea (Eze. 47:10). The probable location is Ain Feshka, about one and one-half miles S of Khirbet Qumran. † *See* AIN FESHKA

ENEMY An enemy is one who is at enmity with someone else. In the Old Covenant there were national enemies that were fought against and pursued (Lev. 26:7). But in the OT, the believers were to have no personal hatred of their neighbors (Lev. 19:18-19). Christians, as well, are to love their enemies (Mt. 5:43-48; Lk. 6:27-36; Ro. 12:20). The brother that needs admonishment is not to be regarded as an enemy (2Th. 3:15). For an explanation of the phrase "make your enemies a footstool," *see* STOOL.

EN FESHKA *See* SALT SEA

ENGAGED *See* BETROTH

EN GANNIM [spring of gardens]
1. A town (196-235) in the tribal area of Issachar, assigned to the Levites (Jos. 19:21; 21:29). †
2. A town of Judah in the western foothills, site unidentified (Jos. 15:34). †

EN GEDI [spring of young goat] An ancient oasis (187-096) in the tribal area of Judah in the desert near the Salt Sea (Dead Sea). It was occupied throughout biblical history. David hid there from Saul who sought his life (Jos. 15:62; 1Sa. 23:29; 24:1). In the mid-ninth century B.C., King Jehoshaphat won an important battle there; also called Hazezon Ta-

mar (Gen. 14:7; 2Ch. 20:2). It is prophesied that men will catch fish from En Gedi to En Eglaim in the end of days (Eze. 47:10; cf. SS. 1:14). †

ENGINE *See* ARMS AND ARMOR

ENGRAVER *See* CRAFTSMEN

EN HADDAH [spring of gladness] A town (196-232) in the tribal area of Issachar (Jos. 19:21). †

EN HAKKORE [spring of the partridge *or* spring of the caller] A spring from which Samson drank after a battle with Philistines (Jdg. 15:19). †

EN HAZOR [spring of HAZOR] An unidentified town in the tribal area of Naphtali (Jos. 19:37). †

EN MISHPAT [spring of judgment] An earlier name for a Kadesh in the Salt Sea area (Ge. 14:7). †

ENOCH [initiated, ISBE; follower, KB]
1 and 2. Cain's oldest son and a city built for the son by Cain (Ge. 4:17).
3. A descendant of Seth and the father of Methuselah. The record notes that he did not die but that "he was no more, because God took him away" (Ge. 5:18, 21, 24; Heb. 11:5).

ENOCH, BOOKS OF Attributed to the patriarch Enoch, this is a collection of exhortations, parables, prophecies, belonging to the category of apocalyptic literature.

ENOS, ENOSH [(mortal) man] Grandson of Adam, son of Seth (Ge. 4:26; 1Ch. 1:1).

EN RIMMON [spring of RIMMON] A city in the tribal area of Judah-Simeon occupied after the return from the exile in Babylon (Ne. 11:29).

EN ROGEL [spring of: the fuller *or* spy *or* wanderer] A spring in the Kidron Valley on the border between Benjamin and Judah S of Jerusalem, not to be confused with the spring of Gihon (Jos. 15:7; 18:16; 2Sa. 17:17; 1Ki. 1:9). †

EN SHEMESH [spring of (pagan god?) SHEMESH (sun)] A town (175-131) on the border between Benjamin and Judah just E of Bethany (Jos. 15:7; 18:17).

EN TAPPUAH {spring of apple} *See* TAPPUAH

ENVY Similar to strife, schisms, and jealousy, envy is deep in man's heart (Mk. 7:22). It is the state of mind of the reprobate (Ro. 1:29; Tit. 3:3); the fleshly mind (1Co. 3:3; 2Co. 12:20). It is in the vice list of the works of the flesh (Gal. 5:20-21). It shows up in earthly "wisdom" (Jas. 3:14). True love does not envy (1Co. 13:4). *See* JEALOUS; VIRTUE AND VICE LISTS

EPAENETUS {praised} *See* EPENE-TUS

EPAPHRAS {handsome} Called fellow servant and fellow prisoner by Paul. He was a native of Colosse and the founder of the church there (Col. 1:7; 4:10, 12; Phm. 23). †

EPAPHRODITUS {handsome} A fellow soldier and fellow worker of Paul's who brought Paul gifts from Philippi when he was in prison and carried back to his town the thanks of Paul (Php. 2:25, 30; 4:18). †

EPENETUS {praised} A Christian at Rome greeted by Paul (Ro. 16:5). †

EPHAH {darkness}
1. *See* WEIGHTS AND MEA-SURES.
2. A son of Abraham and Keturah (Ge. 25:4).
3. A concubine of Caleb (1Ch. 2:46).
4. A descendant of Judah (1Ch. 2:47).

EPHAI {my bird} His sons were among the leaders in Judah after the Babylonian captivity had begun and before the total exodus of 586 B.C. (Jer. 40:8). †

EPHER {(small) gazelle}
1. A grandson of Abraham by Keturah (Ge. 25:4; 1Ch. 1:33). †
2. A descendant of Judah (1Ch. 4:17). †
3. Head of a house in the part of the tribe of Manasseh that lived E of the Jordan (1Ch. 5:24). †

EPHES DAMMIM {border of DAM-MIM (blood)} Called Pas Dammim in 1Ch. 11:13; a place between Azekah and Socoh where the Philistines and the Israelites fought (1Sa. 17:1). †

EPHESIANS, BOOK OF *See* PAU-LINE EPISTLES

EPHESUS A seaport city (now silted in) of fame in Roman times where Paul lived and taught for nearly three years (Ac. 19:1, 8-10; 20:31). In Paul's day Artemis (the Diana of the Romans) was the goddess of the city (Ac. 19:25ff.). Massive results of archaeological work and remains are to be seen there and in a museum in East Berlin.

EPHLAL {judgment, arbitration} A descendant of Judah (1Ch. 2:37). †

EPHOD
1. A leader of the tribe of Manasseh, the son of Joseph (Nu. 34:23).
2. A garment originally worn by the priests but later by others as well — such as Samuel and David (Ex. 28:4; 2Sa. 6:14). The details of its construction are found in Ex. 28:4ff. and 39:2ff. While its full function is not clear it was used in part for seeking divine direction (1Sa. 23:12). Gideon and Micah misused an ephod (Jdg. 8:27; 18:18-20).

EPHPHATHA An Aramaic word uttered by Jesus as he was healing a deaf man (Mk. 7:34). It means "Be opened!" †

EPHRAIM {doubly fruitful} *See also* EPHRON
1. *See* GEOGRAPHY OF THE HOLY LAND.
2. A son of Joseph and the head of one of the twelve tribes, born of Asenath, the daughter of an Egyptian priest (Ge. 41:52). The word came later to designate Israel, the ten northern tribes (Hos. 4:16-17). The central hill country of Palestine was their tribal area (Jos. 16:5-10).
3. An unidentified village near the desert (Jn. 11:54).

EPHRAIM, FOREST OF The place in Gilead, E of the Jordan, where the forces

Escape

of David crushed the rebellion of Absalom (2Sa. 17:26; 18:6).

EPHRAIM, MOUNT *See* GEOGRAPHY OF THE HOLY LAND

EPHRAIMITE One from the tribe or clan of Ephraim. *See* EPHRAIM

EPHRAIN *See* EPHRON 3.

EPHRATAH, EPHRATH, EPHRATHAH

1. Rachel began to give birth to Benjamin at a place called "some distance from Ephrath." She was buried on the way to Ephrath, i.e., Bethlehem (Ge. 35:16-19).

2. A wife of Caleb (1Ch. 2:19, 24).

3. A former name of Bethlehem (Mic. 5:2). *See also* 1.

EPHRON [ganelle]

1. A Hittite from whom Abraham bought the cave of Machpelah for a burial place (Ge. 23:7-10).

2. A mountain ridge on the border between Judah and Benjamin (Jos. 15:9).

3. A city taken by Judah from Israel in the days of King Jeroboam (2Ch. 13:19).

EPICUREANS *See* SECTS

EPILEPSY *See* SICK, SICKNESS

EPIPHANY The *appearance* of Christ. It also is a festival of the Christian calendar (January 6th) in commemoration of the coming of the Magi as the first manifestation of Christ to the Gentiles.

EPISCOPACY From the Greek word for "overseer." It is the system of church government placing major authority in the office of the overseer (also called bishop). *See* OVERSEER; *see also* DEACON; ELDER; PASTORS

EPISTLE [letter] *See* PAULINE EPISTLES; for materials of ancient letters, *see* PAPYRUS; PARCHMENT; PEN; INK; for the process of dictation of an epistle, *see* TERTIUS.

EPONYM The person for whom something is named, used in the Bible for towns and tribes.

ER [watcher, watchful]

1. A son of Judah and husband of Tamar. The LORD put him to death because of his wickedness (Ge. 38:1-3, 6-7; 46:12; Nu. 26:19; 1Ch. 2:3). †

2. A descendant of Judah (1Ch. 4:21). †

3. One mentioned in the genealogy of Jesus (Lk. 3:28). †

ERAN, ERANITE(S) [watcher, watchful; *some MSS and ancient versions read* EDAN (delight)] A son of Ephraim (Nu. 26:36). †

ERASTUS [beloved] Friends of Paul having the same name (Ac. 19:22; Ro. 16:23; 2Ti. 4:20). †

ERECH An early Babylonian city, called by them Uruk and today Warka, N of Ur and 3 of Baghdad. After the Assyrian captivity of Israel, men from there were settled in Samaria. Their descendants were the Samaritans (Ge. 10:10; Ezr. 4:9-10). |

ERI, ERITE(S) [watcher] A descendant of Gad (Ge. 46:16), and his clan (Nu. 26:16). †

ERR, ERROR *See* SIN

ESAIAS *See* ISAIAH

ESARHADDON [Ashur has given a brother (for a lost son)] A son of Sennacherib who succeeded him on the Assyrian throne. He brought additional deportees to Samaria (2Ki. 19:37; Ezr. 4:2; Isa. 37:38). †

ESAU [hairy] Grandson of Abraham and twin brother of Jacob (Ge. 25:24-26). Although he was the older, he sold his birthright to the younger when he was hungry (Ge. 25:29-34). He married two Hittite wives and settled in the area of Mt. Seir (Ge. 26:34; 33:16). Paul used incidents from his life to show God's sovereign rights (Ro. 9:10-13).

ESCAPE God provides a way out or an escape to any temptation that the Christian cannot overcome (1Co. 10:13). The Christian can escape the corruption of the world (1Pe. 1:4). But to return to the world after escaping it and be overcome by corruption is to invite disaster (1Pe. 2:18-20).

ESCHATOLOGY {study of last events} The study (and theology) of last things, such as *death, resurrection, the afterlife, divine judgment, the end of the age,* and *the second coming (appearing) of Christ.* (The last two items only are discussed here. For the afterlife, heaven and hell *see* DEAD, ABODE OF. *See also* RESURRECTION; JUDGMENT; KINGDOM OF HEAVEN, KINGDOM OF GOD.)

Historically four major points of view have been held relative to the manner of the end of the age. One of these comprehends a wide range of views that are basically the same, held by followers of the schools of "Old Liberalism," "consistent eschatology," "realized eschatology," and "form criticism." Some of these views are almost mutually exclusive. In most of these views Jesus is human only, not God manifest in the flesh, and the Bible a human document, not "divinely inspired." Those who hold these views see the church as the kingdom of God and recognize Christ through the Spirit as now reigning, having given his kingdom powers to his followers who are carrying on his work in the kingdom. We are now in the "last times," Christ is present by his Spirit in the church at all times, and at the same time his "coming again" is "drawing nigh." (The two are, to all intents and purposes, one: his presence in the church and his coming in the church.)

Clearly over against all these views are three other views, differing the one from the other, yet having in common a regard for the Scriptures themselves. They present a physical, literal second coming of the same Jesus who was earlier here on earth to establish the church and to make provision for its salvation through his own life, death, and resurrection. "This same Jesus, who has been taken for you into heaven, will come back in the same way you saw him go into heaven," i.e., physically (Ac. 1:11). The

three do not differ as to the fact or manner of Christ's second coming, but they do differ as to the time of it in relation to his kingdom and as to the nature of the kingdom itself. The three agree that the same Jesus will return to earth in his divine glory at a literal point in time, somewhere between this present age and the beginning of eternity. This event will mark the "end of the age."

The chiliasts or millennarians expect this age to end with the physical coming of Christ, to be followed by 1000 years of his rule in his kingdom prior to the beginning of the eternal state, which will begin immediately thereafter. Another group, the amillennialists, do not believe in a literal millennium, or 1000-year reign of Christ on earth after his coming. In the early eighteenth century the third view, postmillennialism, arose. This view holds that the last 1000 years of this present age will be the utopia in which all the promises and prophecies of universal peace and righteousness on earth will be fulfilled in the kingdom, after which Christ will return and the eternal state begin. *See also* SYSTEMATIC THEOLOGY

ESDRAELON *See* JEZREEL 4.

ESDRAS, BOOKS OF *See* SCRIPTURE

ESEK {quarreling} The name given to a well dug by Isaac's men but contended for and taken by the men of Gerar (Ge. 26:20). †

ESHAN {support} An unidentified town in the Judean hill country (Jos. 15:52). †

ESH-BAAL {man of (pagan god) BAAL} A son of King Saul (1Ch. 8:33; 9:39). Because of objection to names associated with Baal, he is also called Ish-Bosheth (2Sa. 2—4). Abner tried to make him king of Israel after Saul's death, but Ish-Bosheth was murdered (2Sa. 3:8-10; 4:5-7). †

ESHBAN A descendant of Esau who lived in Edom (Ge. 36:26; 1Ch. 1:41).

ESHCOL [(grape) cluster]
1. An ally of Abram in his battle against the invading kings (Ge. 14:13, 24). †
2. A valley in the Judean hill country from which the twelve spies brought back the large cluster of grapes to Israel (Nu. 13:23-24; 32:9; Dt. 1:24). †

ESHEAN *See* ESHAN

ESHEK [oppressor] A descendant of King Saul, a Benjamite (1Ch. 8:39). †

ESHKALONITES *See* ASHKELON

ESHTAOL, ESHTAOLITES, ESH-TAULITES [(place of oracles) inquiry] A town (151-132) in the western foothills, first assigned to the tribe of Dan but which later came into Judean hands. Samson was born, lived, and was buried in the Eshtaol-Aphrah area (Jos. 15:33; 19:41; Jdg. 13:25; 16:31; 18:2, 8, 11; 1Ch. 2:53). †

ESHTARAH *See* BE ESHTARAH

ESHTEMOA, ESHTEMOH [(place where oracle is) heard]
1. A town (156-089) of Judah assigned to the Levites and a city of refuge (Jos. 21:9, 13-14); called Eshtemoh in Jos. 15:50.
2 and 3. Two descendants of Judah (1Ch. 4:17, 19).

ESHTON [*possibly* henpecked (husband) *or* effeminate] A descendant of Judah (1Ch. 4:11-12). †

ESLI [Yahweh sets apart] An ancestor of Christ (Lk. 3:25). †

ESROM *See* HEZRON 3.

ESSENES *See* SECTS, *Jewish*

ECSTATIC UTTERANCES *See* GIFTS; SPIRITUAL GIFTS; TONGUES

ESTHER [*Persian* star, *possibly* (Babylonian goddess) Ishtar] A Jewish orphan who became Queen of Persia. Her Hebrew name was Hadassah (Est. 2:7-9, 16-17). One of the famous lines of history comes from this story: "And who knows but that you have come to royal position [the kingdom] for such a time as this?" (4:14). She was instrumental in getting the Jews delivered from the evil scheme of Haman who wanted to kill them (8:58). This deliverance is still celebrated by Jews in the Feast of Purim. *See* HADASSAH

ESTHER, BOOK OF Written in the last part of the fifth century B.C. by an unknown author who never uses the name of God in his writing. Yet it is a book of the Hebrew Bible, the OT. From very early times apocryphal additions to the book existed; this may account for the debates about its canonicity at times in its history. It deals with an aspect of the history of the Jews remaining from the captivity in the Persian capital of Susa—how Haman desired their extermination, and how they were delivered through the Jewish orphan, who became Queen of Persia.

ETAM [*possibly* place of birds of prey]
1. A cave where Samson hid out from the Philistines (Jdg. 15:8, 11). †
2. A village of the sons of Simeon after the exile, unidentified (1Ch. 4:32). †
3. A city (167-121) in the hill country of Judah fortified by King Rehoboam (2Ch. 11:6). †
4. A descendant of Judah (1Ch. 4:3). †

ETERNAL LIFE *See* CHRIST, WORK OF 9., *Advent of Christ*; ESCHATOLOGY; ETERNITY; IMMORTAL; LIFE; TIME

ETERNAL PUNISHMENT The everlasting retribution sinners will encounter beyond this life.

ETERNITY Refers to an endless span of time, whether before the Creation or after the end of the present age. Called "forever," it is inhabited by God himself (Isa. 57:15). Several Hebrew words are used for perpetuity, meaning *ever, everlasting* and *forever.*

Eternal life is mentioned many times in the NT referring to the kind of life believers in Christ receive—for their enjoyment in this life and their reward for the life to come. Other things called eternal include: God (Dt. 33:27; Ro. 16:26); purpose of God (Eph. 3:11); dominion of God (1Ti. 6:16); the gospel (Rev. 14:6); God's covenant, salvation, redemption, judgment (Heb. 5:9; 6:2; 9:12; 13:20); God's inheritance for the believer (Heb. 9:15); eternal fire and punishment (Mt. 25:41, 46; Jude 6-7).

ETHAM An unidentified place on the desert route of the Israelites after they left Egypt and Succoth (Ex. 13:20; Nu. 33:58). †

ETHAN [long-lived, everflowing (streams)]
1. A wise man, possibly a contemporary of Solomon, called the Ezrahite (1Ki. 4:31).
2. A descendant of Judah (1Ch. 2:6).
3 and 4. Two temple musicians (1Ch. 6:42, 44).

ETHANIM [everflowing (streams)] *See* CALENDAR

ETHBAAL [with (him is) BAAL] A king of Sidon whose daughter Jezebel married King Ahab of Israel and brought pagan priests with her who corrupted Israel (1Ki. 16:31). †

ETHER
1. A village (138-113) in the western foothills of Judah (Jos.15:42). †
2. An unidentified village in the tribal area of Simeon (Jos. 19:7). †

ETHICS *See* SITUATIONAL ETHICS

ETHIOPIA *See* CUSH

ETHIOPIAN EUNUCH The treasurer of the Queen of Ethiopia who was reading the Book of Isaiah, to whom the Lord sent Philip to explain it. Upon declaring his faith, he was baptized (Ac. 8:26ff.).

ETH KAZIN An unidentified town in Zebulun (Jos. 19:13). †

ETHNAN [gift *or* hire] A descendant of Judah (1Ch. 4:7). †

ETHNARCH A governor (2Co. 11:32).

ETHNI [gift *or* hire] An ancestor of Asaph, David's head of the service of music in the Tent of Meeting (tabernacle) and later in Solomon's temple (1Ch. 6:41; cf. 1Ch. 6:21). †

EUBULUS [good counsel] A Christian who sent greetings to Timothy (2Ti. 4:21). †

EUCHARIST [thanksgiving] A Greek word for "thanksgiving," it refers to the Lord's Supper. *See* COMMUNION, VIEWS OF; LORD'S SUPPER

EUNICE [good victory] Timothy's mother, a Jewess married to a Greek, who was careful to bring up her son in the knowledge of the Scriptures (Ac. 16:1; 2Ti. 1:5; 3:15).

EUNUCH [one emasculated] A castrated male (2Ki. 9:32). Sometimes the word simply means an officer (Ge. 39:1; 2Ki. 23:11; Est. 2:21). It also is translated "trusted personal servant" (Ac. 12:20). Eunuchs could not be full members of the Jewish community (Lev. 21:16, 20; Dt. 23:1). "Eunuchs made eunuchs by men" (Mt. 19:12) are those who have given up reproduction in order to devote themselves to the service of God. *See also* CHAMBERLAIN

EUODIA(S) [good fragrance] A Christian woman in the church at Philippi with whom Paul pleaded that she live peaceably with Syntyche (Php. 4:2). †

EUPHRATES The largest river in western Asia. It rises in the mountains of Armenia, flows W until it turns S by the mountains of Lebanon and then runs 1,000 miles to the Persian Gulf. In ancient times it divided the empire of Assyria and the Hittite Empire. One of the great cities of antiquity, Carchemish, was on its bank. Here many important battles took place, some noted in the Bible (2Ki. 24:7; Jer. 46:2). Ultimately Israel's territory is to extend, by divine promise, to this river (Ge. 15:18), as it did in its great days under David and Solomon.

EURAQUILO, EUROCLYDON [SE (wind)] Euroclydon is a KJV, NKJV transliteration of a variant reading

THE EUPHRATES RIVER
Solomon's kingdom extended all the way north to the Euphrates River.

(Greek text) in Ac. 27:14. If translated it would mean "southeaster." The ASV and NASB transliterate another Greek reading "Euraquilo" (based on Latin renderings). The NEB, RSV, JB, NIV translate the reading of that same NASB Greek text as "Northeaster." Of the variant readings, "Northeaster" is the better one. It was a hurricane force (74 MPH or more) wind. *See also* WIND

EUTHANASIA [Greek for *easy death,*] An attempt to prevent the process of death from being excessive, painful, or prolonged. It may involve either the omission of treatment (passive euthanasia) or direct acts aimed at terminating life (active euthanasia). Active euthanasia is wrong because it sees man, not God, as the taker of life (Job 1:21; 38–41). Self-inflicted euthanasia is actually suicide, which the Bible does not approve or sanction as acceptable behavior.

EUTYCHUS [fortunate] A youth of Troas who, having fallen asleep, fell to the ground from a third-story window and died while Paul was preaching there. Paul restored him to life (Ac. 20:9-12). †

EVANGELICAL One whose focus is the gospel of pardon and regeneration through personal faith in Jesus Christ. Generally, this one has the conviction to share this gospel with others.

EVANGELISM The presentation of the gospel to someone with the purpose of bringing that one to have faith in Jesus Christ. *See also* GOSPEL

EVANGELIST [(a bringer of) good news] The word that describes one who conducts the activity of preaching the gospel, especially in areas where it had not been preached before; the founder of groups later cared for by the pastor. The use of the word to refer to the writer of a canonical book and to the reader of the lections in the liturgy is postbiblical. It is used only three times in the NT (Ac. 21:8; Eph. 4:11; 2Ti. 4:5). Currently the difference between a missionary and an evangelist would seem to be that the former opens up new territory where the gospel is not or is only little known, while the latter ministers in Christian areas and groups to stir them up to greater dedication to Christ and his service.

EVE [life] The first woman, the wife of Adam, created by divine action from Adam's side (Ge. 2:18-22; 4:1). Through disobedience to God on the part of Eve, followed by Adam, sin passed upon all mankind (Ro. 5:12). Her name is found twice in the NT (2Co. 11:3; 1Ti. 2:13). †

EVENING SACRIFICE *See* SACRIFICES AND OFFERINGS

EVERLASTING *See* ETERNITY

EVI [desire] A king of Midian killed by the Israelites in the time of Moses (Nu. 31:8; Jos. 13:21). †

EVIL *See* DEVIL; SIN

EVIL DESIRE *See* LUST

EVIL ONE *See* DEVIL

EVIL SPIRITS *See* DEMON, DE-MONIAC

EVIL-MERODACH {worshiper of Marduk(s) *changed in textual transmission to read* fool of "blessing"} A king of Babylon, the son of Nebuchadnezzar, who was murdered by his brother-in-law. He released King Jehoiachin of Judah from prison in Babylon and cared for him there (2Ki. 25:27-30; Jer. 52:31). †
See also BABYLON, BABYLONIA

EVOLUTION The assumed mechanism that develops one form into another. It is the biological assumption that all living forms have developed from simpler forms by a series of gradual stages. Evolution has been proposed as a grid for many or all forms of academic disciplines so as to be integrated in philosophy and religion, as well as in biology.

EVOLUTION, NATURALISTIC The concept that evolution has "proceeded" by means of physical laws of the universe; it is simply a matter of atomic motion, time, and chance — no God directs the process.

EVOLUTION, MACRO This is a name for large-scale evolution — change involving enormous and complex steps. *See* entry below.

EVOLUTION, MICRO The theory that there may have been some limited development of one form to another in minute variations. Belief in microevolution does not necessarily support macroevolution. *See* above entry.

EVOLUTION, THEISTIC The concept that God began the creation as a completely new deed and then worked from within the process of evolution to produce the desired results. He has intervened within the process to modify what was emerging.

EWE A female sheep. *See* BEASTS 4.

EXAMPLE Jesus taught service and humility by the example of his life (Jn. 13:1-15). Jesus is our model of response to suffering (1Pe. 2:21-23). Paul wanted his dedication to Christ to be followed by imitation (1Co. 11:1; Php. 3:17). Believers can become a model or "life-template" for other Christians (1Th. 1:7).

EXALTATION *See* PRAISE; WORSHIP

EXCOMMUNICATION *See* DISCIPLINE, CHURCH

EXECUTIONER *See* CAPTAIN

EXEGESIS *See* EISEGESIS

EXHORTATION The strengthening of a Christian through admonition, warning, counsel, or encouragement (1Th. 5:14; 2Th. 3:12; 2Ti. 4:2; Tit. 2:15; Heb. 3:13). The Scriptures of the OT encourage us (Ro. 15:4). Encouragement is a function of the NT prophet (1Co. 14:31). Paul constantly wanted the believers to be encouraged (Php. 2:1; Col. 2:2; 1Th. 5:11). *See also* COMFORT, COMFORTER 1.

EXILE *See* CAPTIVITY; CHRONOLOGY

EXISTENCE OF GOD The Bible always assumes the existence of God. Only a fool would say there is no God (Ps. 14:1). Concerning the resurrection of the dead, Paul assumes that if it were not true, then we would be false witnesses to God (1Co. 15:15-17), but never would the question enter his mind about his existence. Paul appeals to the Creation as a manifestation of God's character (Ro. 1:18-21). No doubt he received this assumption from the OT (Ps. 19:1).

A branch of Christian apologetics uses rational arguments to demonstrate God exists. Such arguments are cosmological (looking at the universe as an orderly system); teleological (design with purpose); anthropological (the complexity and character and destiny of man); moral (an appeal to values and conscience); and ontological (reasons of being).

These arguments can be profitable under some circumstances, yet in themselves could never bring one to salvation in Christ. The Christian faith is rooted and founded in revelation, i.e., the Scriptures, and Jesus Christ. (J.A.S.) *See* CHRIST; LOGOS; SCRIPTURE; THEOPHANY

EXISTENTIALISM A philosophy which accentuates existence over essence. Among the other themes of existentialism are human freedom and responsibility, subjectivity, and irrationality. There are many schools of this philosophy, some theistic and some atheistic.

EXODUS, BOOK OF *See* PENTATEUCH; PLAGUES OF EGYPT

EXORCISM, EXORCIST The expelling of evil spirits from persons or places by incantations or magic charms (Ac. 19:13). While the words are never used in the NT, the work of exorcism and the persons who do them, exorcists, are mentioned. Jesus cast out demons by the Spirit of God and passed this power on to his disciples who did it in his name (Mt. 12:28; Mk. 6:7; 9:25; Ac. 16:18).

EXPANSE A "firmament" is limited space (Eze. 1:22), or a vast heavenly expanse (Da. 12:3). It can refer as well to the sky (Ge. 1:6), where birds fly (Ge. 1:20). Because the word refers to an empty space, a firmament is not a prop holding up the sky.

EXPIATE, EXPIATION
1. *See* CHRIST, WORK OF, *atonement*.
2. Sin is both a failure to conform to the law of God and actual transgression against it; and two things are necessary to get rid of it. One is expiation and the other propitiation. The first requires satisfaction, the covering or blotting out of sin by a sacrifice. The second views this satisfaction as appeasing the wrath of God because of his anger against sin. Man's sin is expiated by the sacrifice of Christ on the cross, and God's wrath against sin is propitiated. Some consider

the idea of satisfaction, sacrifice, expiation, and propitiation as barbaric and out of keeping with a loving God. Such a God should not require the suffering of an innocent one for the guilty. What these fail to notice, however, is that it is God himself, God the Son, who does the suffering on the behalf of some third party (Ro. 3:25; Heb. 2:17-18; 1Jn. 2:2; 4:10). Similarly it is God propitiating himself through Christ's sacrifice. *See* PROPITIATION

EYE *See* EMOTIONS

EYE FOR AN EYE *See* LEX TALIONIS

EYES, PAINTING OF *See* COSMETICS

EYESALVE *See* SALVE

EZAR *See* EZER 1.

EZBAI The father of one of David's mighty men (1Ch. 11:37). †

EZBON
1. A descendant of Gad (Ge. 46:16). †
2. A grandson of Benjamin (1Ch. 7:7). †

EZEKIAS *See* HEZEKIAH

EZEKIEL [El strengthens] A Hebrew prophet and priest (Eze. 1:3). He was taken from Jerusalem into captivity to Babylon in the deportation of 598/597 B.C. In Babylon he lived with the other Jewish exiles in a place called Tel Aviv by the river Kebar (Eze. 3:15; 1:3). He was married (24:18), began prophesying in the fifth year of his captivity (1:2), and was still prophesying in the twenty-seventh year (29:17). Otherwise, we know very little about his personal life.

EZEKIEL, BOOK OF Two periods of history are reflected in this book. Up to chapter 24 the prophet spoke of the sin of Jerusalem and her coming punishment. After an eight-chapter interlude of judgments against foreign nations, he directs his attention to the coming Kingdom of God with a message of comfort for the people (chaps. 33—48). In the last section he notes that God will end the captivity, restore them to their land from all nations wherever they have been scattered (36:24), and give them a new heart to serve him (chaps. 34 – 36). The Gentile powers are to be defeated (chaps. 38 – 39), and a great new temple is to be built with all its holy services restored (chaps. 40 – 46).

EZEL A transliteration in many versions of a Hebrew word meaning "heap" or "mound" of stones (1Sa. 20:19). Some Hebrew specialists think that by switching two letters it would read "*that* stone" (NJB). †

EZEM {bone (strength)} An unidentified city in the tribal area of Simeon within the area of Judah (Jos. 15:29; 19:3; 1Ch. 4:29). †

EZER {help}
1. A descendant of Esau and Seir (Ge. 36:21).
2. A descendant of Judah (1Ch. 4:4).
3. A descendant of Ephraim (1Ch. 7:21).
4. A descendant of Gad who joined David at Ziklag (1Ch. 12:9).
5. One of those who worked on the wall with Nehemiah (Ne. 3:19).
6. A Levitical musician in the days of Nehemiah (Ne. 12:42).

EZIONGABER, EZION GEBER A city (147-884) on the Gulf of Aqabah near Elath where the children of Israel stopped just before going up to Kadesh for the second time (Nu. 33:35-36). It was a fortress of Solomon's guarding his sea trade route with Ophir. Solomon built ships there (1Ki. 9:26-28). Until recently it was thought that this city was an industrial one, where copper was smelted in Solomon's day. Archaeologists have now abandoned this idea. Some years later in the days of King Jehoshaphat and King Ahaziah, trading ships were built there, but they were destroyed before leaving the port (1Ki. 22:48-49).

EZNITE 2Sa. 23:8. *See* ADINO

EZRA {help}
1. A priest who came back from the Babylonian captivity with Zerubbabel; also called Azariah (Ne. 10:2; 12:1).
2. A Jewish scribe and priest, descended from the priestly line of Aaron, author and chief character in the book that bears his name, coworker with Nehemiah, and leader in the return from the Babylonian captivity. On his return he found many Jews married to foreign, heathen women and encouraged the annulment of those marriages. He kept a record of those who were thus married (chap. 10), reinstituted the reading of the Law and its observation, and the keeping of the festivals. The book that bears his name is almost an autobiography.

EZRA, BOOK OF Covers the history of the Jews from 536 to 432 B.C. from the return from the Babylonian captivity to the return of Ezra himself in 458 and then the rebuilding of the temple, and institution of service there. If the book was not written by Ezra, it bears that name because he is the principal character in it. Modern critics cast doubt on the historicity of Ezra himself and feel that this book, together with Nehemiah and 1 and 2 Chronicles, were one book written by a "chronicler" sometime in the fourth century B.C. Its right to a place in the canon and its own trustworthiness, however, are not related to the question of its authorship. The author, as a good historian, apparently made extensive use of existing written sources, and some think this accounts for the use of the two languages (Hebrew and Aramaic) in its writing, and for the differences of style that appear in the book.

The earlier historical books of the Bible (Kings and Chronicles) tell the history of Israel to the time of the destruction of Jerusalem by the Babylonians and the beginning of that captivity in 586 B.C. This book picks up that history fifty years later. Together with Nehemiah, Haggai, and Zechariah, we are given the history of the fifth century. Chapters 1–6 of Ezra give the account of the return of the Jews under Zerubbabel to the rebuilding of the temple. The last part of the book contains the history of the return of a second group with Ezra as its leader and of the religious reforms he instituted.

EZRAHITE 1Ki. 4:31; Pss. 88 and 89 titles. *See* ETHAN 1.; HEMAN 3.

EZRI {my help} King David's minister of agriculture (1Ch. 27:26). †

F

FABLE KJV for "myth" or "stories" in 1Ti. 1:4, 7; 2Ti. 4:4; Tit. 1:14; 2Pe. 1:16.

FABRIC *See* WEAVING AND SPINNING

FACE Used literally of the human or an animal face, and also figuratively in several senses. "To hide the face" is an idiom that expresses displeasure, "to set the face against" means opposition, "to make the face shine upon" means blessing and is found in the well-known blessing, "the LORD makes his face shine upon you" (Nu. 6:25).

FACECLOTH *See* NAPKIN

FADED, NOT FADED *See* PLANTS, Flowering Plants 8., *Amaranthine*

FAINT KJV for to "collapse" (from hunger) in Mt. 15:32; Mk. 8:3.

FAIR HAVENS A harbor on the South side of Crete where Paul stopped on his prison voyage to Rome (Ac. 27:8). †

FAITH, FAITHFULNESS These have the connotations of trust and trustworthiness. They may refer to the reliability of God (Ro. 3:3), but in the great majority of cases they refer to man's spiritual trust in something: in God; in his commandments; in the fact that Jesus is the Messiah; in Jesus himself. In Paul's teaching, faith is trust in the person of Jesus as God, in the truth of his teaching, that his death accomplished redemption from sin. In short, faith is a total submissive trust in Christ, his work, and his message (Ge. 15:6; Ps. 119:66; Jn. 11:27;

1Co. 15:1-3). To become a Christian one must believe, have faith, trust. To live as a practicing and active Christian one must show faithfulness. It is a part of that complex of attributes known as "the fruit of the Spirit" (Gal. 5:22). *See also* BE-LIEVE; CHRIST, LIFE AND TEACHINGS OF; HOPE; PAUL, LIFE AND TEACHING; SALVATION, APPLICATION OF

FAITH, GIFT OF *See* GIFTS; SPIRITUAL GIFTS

FAITH HEALING The practice of trusting God to supernaturally heal the sick or afflicted.

FALCON *See* BIRDS 5.

FALL, THE The term given to the incident in the life of Adam and Eve in which they disobeyed God and thus not only sinned but brought sin on all the race descended from them by natural generation. The account is in Genesis 3, and its implications in Ro. 5:12, 17-18.

FALL, SEASON OF *See* CALENDAR; TIME

FALLOW DEER KJV for "roe deer" (Dt. 14:5; 1Ki. 4:23). *See* BEASTS 2.

FALSE CHRIST A liar who falsely claims to be a messiah (Mt. 24:24; Mk. 13:6, 22; Lk. 21:8). He will deceive many.

FALSE PROPHET One who claims to be a prophet of God yet is not, or one who claims to speak for God and yet does not (Mt. 7:15; 24:11; Mk. 13:22; Lk. 6:26; Ac. 13:6; 2Pe. 2:1; 1Jn. 4:1). In the last times there will be a special false prophet, who eventually is thrown into the lake of fire (Rev. 16:13; 19:20; 20:10).

FALSE WITNESS *See* SLANDER; WITNESS

FAMILIAR SPIRIT KJV in many versions for "spirit of the dead" (Lev. 20:27), rendered in the NIV as "spiritist." *See* DIVINATION, DIVINE 3. and 4.

FAMILY *See* MARRIAGE; PARENTING

FAMINE Many are mentioned in the Bible (Ge. 41:56; Ru. 1:1; 2Sa. 21:1; 1Ki. 18:2; 2Ki. 6:25; Ac. 11:28). In Palestine they could be caused by lack of rain, rain at the wrong time, or hail, locusts and their caterpillars, or by military siege (*see* DOVE'S DUNG). They were sometimes caused by God as a judgment on his people. The word is also used in a figurative sense at a time when the words of God were not being heard (Am. 8:11).

FAN A wooden shovel or fork with two or more prongs. *See* THRESHING, THRESHING FLOOR

FARMING When Joshua had completed the conquest of Canaan, the land was divided among the tribes of Israel and carefully marked out with landmarks. It was forbidden in Israel to remove these "boundary stones" (Dt. 19:14). The land inheritance was not to pass from one tribe to another. If for any reason a person lost his land, it had to be returned in the Year of Jubilee, which

limited. The inhabitants depended on rainfall and dew, allowing the land to remain fallow every seventh year for an substitute for water and fertilizers, as well as for the foraging of animals (Ex. 23:10-11). The early rains came in December–February and the latter rains in March. Thus sowing time was around February and reaping time was between Passover and Pentecost. First came the barley harvest, then the wheat. The grain was placed on a hard flat area some twenty feet or more in diameter. Animals dragged something like sledges over it, and men turned it periodically until the kernels would be separated from the stalks. The floor was always placed where there would be a good wind so that the grain could be winnowed (*see* THRESHING; WINNOWING), a process of tossing the grain into the air and allowing the wind to blow the chaff (*see* CHAFF) away and the kernels to fall to the floor. This was sieved to remove impurities and then stored. The dangers to the crop could come from failure of the former rain's coming at the proper time to soften the soil for the primitive plowing, the failure of the latter rain to fill out the ears of grain, hot desert winds coming too near harvesttime, locusts, hail, or other natural causes coming while the grain was growing. *See also* WEIGHTS AND MEASURES, *Acre*; *see also* PLOW

FARTHING A KJV rendering in Mt. 5:26 and Mk. 12:42; *see* MONEY, *kodrantes*; also in Mt. 10:29 and Lk. 12:6; *see* MONEY, *Assarion*.

Ploughing the Field in Ancient Israel

occurred every fifty years (Lev. 25:28). Irrigation or means of fertilizing were

FAST, FASTING Abstinence from eating and drinking was for humbling oneself (Ps. 35:13). The fast on the Day of Atonement was the only one required in the Mosaic legislation, but individuals did fast for special reasons, or special fasts were sometimes called by the leaders for particular reasons (1Sa. 7:6; 2Sa. 12:16). Because of national calamities, regular fast days were set to commemorate them. Four in particular are noted. It is stated that they will ultimately be turned from days of sorrow to days of joy (Zec. 7:3-5; 8:19). Fasting was apparently quite common in the days of Jesus. He himself did it on occasion (Mt. 4:2; Lk. 2:37; 18:12). Jesus discussed fasting on two occasions, stressing the voluntary character required and that purity of heart and motives are integral to an acceptable fast (Mt. 6:16-17; 9:14-15). The NT perspective is that fasting is not condemned, but neither is it required. Fasting for personal or corporate reasons is voluntary and acceptable. *See also* FESTIVALS

FAT

1. The internal fat of the sacrificial animals was burned as a pleasing aroma to the LORD. It was forbidden to the Israelites to eat it (Lev. 3:3-5; 4:31; 7:23-25).

2. An expression of abundance, the best of something: land (Ge. 45:18); oil (Nu. 18:12).

3. KJV (*fats* or *winefat* in some KJV editions) for *vat* (Isa. 63:2; Joel 2:24).

FATALISM The idea that all that happens is fixed for all time by an impersonal force, and humans are powerless to change it. *See* DETERMINISM

FATHER, FATHERS Commonly the word refers to the immediate male or female progenitor (Ge. 2:24; 28:13). It is also used, however, in the sense of "ancestor." When parallel genealogies are compared and some names are not in one or the other, this meaning of "father" helps to explain the discrepancy.

FATHERHOOD OF GOD *See* GOD, NAMES OF; GODHEAD

FATHERLESS A very great emphasis is placed throughout the OT on the need for the care of the orphan, the fatherless (Dt. 10:18; Jer. 7:5-7). It is even mandatory for the people of God (Jas. 1:27).

FATHOM *See* WEIGHTS AND MEASURES, *Distance*

FATLING A fattened animal for sacrifice (2Sa. 6:13; Ps. 66:15). *See* FAT; SACRIFICES AND OFFERINGS

FEAR The word has two meanings in Scripture, in both Testaments: fear in the sense of being afraid, and fear in the sense of reverence. The latter, as used in the OT, is almost the equivalent of NT faith, which is reverential belief in and committal to (Pr. 9:10; Ecc. 12:13; Mal. 3:16).

FEAST Banqueting was a favorite form of eating and entertainment in antiquity (Est. 9:17; Job 1:5; Ecc. 7:2; Jer. 16:8). These were festive occasions at which the guests were robed, had their feet washed, and their heads anointed. There was often entertainment as well. Guests were seated or reclined at the banqueting benches, in assigned order of age or importance. It was not uncommon that food would be sent to others not able to attend (Ge. 43:34; Ne. 8:10; Lk. 14:10). On the religious feasts *see* CALENDAR and FESTIVALS.

FELIX [fortunate, lucky] The Roman governor at Caesarea to whom Paul was sent from Jerusalem, and before whom Paul was tried. He left Paul in prison for two years (Ac. 23:24-26; 24:2ff.; 25:14). †

FELLOWSHIP

1. For Fellowship Offering; *see* SACRIFICES AND OFFERINGS.

2. A NT word in verb and noun form used about 40 times, which means *association, communion, close relationship*. To have fellowship is to have partnership, participation, a share in something, like a fishing business (Lk. 5:10). Christians, by example, are to be in this association constantly (Ac. 2:42). To have fellowship is to give material

goods to believers in need and to be pleasing to God (Ro. 15:26; 2Co. 8:4; 9:13; Heb. 13:16—*contribution, share, partnership* in NIV).

To be given the right hand of fellowship is formally concluding an agreement, such as Paul and Barnabas did in Gal. 2:9.

Fellowship is often spiritual: with Jesus Christ (1Co. 1:9); with the Holy Spirit (2Co. 13:14; Php. 2:1); with the gospel (Php. 1:5); with the fellowship of Christ's sufferings (Php. 3:10). The act of Communion is fellowship (*participation*, NIV, 1Co. 10:16). Christians are not to be yoked with unbelievers, for there is no partnership between them (2Co. 6:14). A Christian cannot fellowship with God and yet not walk in his truth (1Jn. 1:3, 5). To walk in truth enables us to have fellowship with other Christians.

Biblical fellowship was much more than a social time of coffee and donuts. It was an association with Christians that sometimes meant digging deep into their wallets or purses. With God, it was to commune with him and walk in his Truth. (J.A.S.) *See* GIVING

FEMINIST THEOLOGY Theology which puts emphasis upon the standing and liberation of women. *See* LIBERATION THEOLOGY

FENCE *See* WALL

FENCED CITY *See* FORT, FORTRESS, FORTIFICATION

FERTILE CRESCENT *See* GEOGRAPHY OF THE HOLY LAND, PREFACE, *Mesopotamia*

FERTILITY *See* BARREN

FESTIVALS The festival-holy day calendar of biblical religion is summarized neatly in Ex. 23:10-17. It consisted of three annual festivals: one in late spring, another in early summer, a third in autumn harvest. The system is elaborated in Lev. 23, presenting a calendar of seven feasts and fasts grouped in relation to these three main feasts.

Some information on Jewish reckoning of time is necessary in order to understand this calendar. The *day* was counted as beginning at sunset (Lev. 23:32), possibly from the circumstance that the first day of the month could not be determined until the appearance of the new moon, after sunset. The *week* was a seven-day period loosely connected with the phases of the moon. The seven days were not named, but rather numbered from the first to the seventh, though the seventh was also called the Sabbath (rest); hence weeks were sometimes called Sabbaths (Lev. 23:15; Dt. 16:9). The *month* was approximately four weeks. The Jews early learned to calculate the day of the new moon (1Sa. 20:5). The year was of twelve lunar months: 354 days, 8 hours, 48 minutes, 38 seconds. An extra month was added to the year periodically to keep in fair conformity with the solar year. If no adjustment had been made, the feast would have made a complete cycle of the seasons every thirty-four years, impossible in a system geared to the agricultural cycle. Since the beginning of the year was counted from about the time of the spring equinox, four times every eleven years an *intercalary* or thirteenth month was added.

It is assumed by some that there came to be two calendars in use: a ritual-religious calendar beginning with Nisan (or Abib) our March—April. This was ordained by God to be the first month at the time of the Exodus (Ex. 12:2; cf. Josephus *Antiq.* 1:3:3). There appears to have been a civil year also in use. In Ex. 23:16 and 34:22 a seventh month is mentioned as the end of the year. Lev. 25:8-10 shows that the Year of Jubilee began in the seventh month of the ritual year. The months were named in later times (*see* CALENDAR for the names).

In this calendar there were six feasts, listed here in chronological order: Ex. 23:14-17; Lev. 23:1-44; Nu. 28:1—29:40; Dt. 16:1-17. At three of these times in the year all the men were required to appear before the LORD (in Jerusalem), at the Feast of Unleavened Bread, Feast of Harvest, and Feast of Ingathering or Tabernacles (Ex. 23:14-17; 34:23).

1. *The Passover.* The institution of Passover on the night of the exodus from Egypt is set forth in Ex. 12. It was the forepart of the Feast of Unleavened Bread, the first of the three when every male was to "appear before the Sovereign LORD," hence called one of the pilgrimages feasts (Ex. 23:14-17; Lev. 23:4-5). It was held at the end (evening) of the fourteenth day of the first month. It celebrated deliverance from condemnation and bondage in Egypt and beginning of new life.

2. *The Feast of Unleavened Bread.* Although the institution is found in Ex. 12:15-20, its place in the ritual year is in Lev. 23:6-8. It began on the fifteenth day (on sunset the previous day) and continued seven days, through the twenty-first day and continued seven days, through the twenty-first day. The Passover lamb, killed late afternoon of the fourteenth and eaten at "supper," really opened this festival. The chief feature was the eating of unleavened bread through the week, during which time every house was cleansed of leaven.

3. *The Feast of Weeks, Harvest, or Firstfruits.* The first is called *Shavuot* in Hebrew and occurs fifty days (seven weeks plus one day) after Passover (Greek Pentecost). On this day ancient Israel presented the firstfruits "of all that you produce" (Dt. 26:2). While this day was "firstfruits" (the occasion of the wheat harvest), the presentation of firstfruits could take place at any time between the Feast of Weeks and the Feast of Tabernacles (Ex. 23:9ff.; 34:22; Lev. 23:10-22; Nu. 28:26; Dt. 16:9-10; 26:1-11). The festival falls in the third month of the Hebrew calendar, Sivan, May or June in the non-Hebrew calendar. In the NT the name of this festival for the Christians was Pentecost (Ac. 2:6; 20:16; 1Co. 16:8).

4. *The Feast of Trumpets.* The Bible does not furnish much information about it. What little we know is drawn mainly from Lev. 23:23-25. It occurred the first day of the seventh month (the first of September of the modern calendar). It was followed on the tenth day of the same month by the great Day of Atonement (Lev. 23:26). The first day was announced by the blowing of trumpets; it was a special rest day. It was the beginning day of the civil year, as Passover was the religious one. This is Rosh Hashanah, the beginning of the year of present day Judaism.

5. *The Day of Atonement (Yom Kippur or Yom Hakippurim).* The institution, in detail, is to be found in Lev. 16; its place in the calendar in Lev. 23:26-32. The elaborate ritual, the symbolism of which underlies much of the NT discussion of the atonement of Christ, is too complex to discuss here. It was on this day only (the tenth day of the seventh month) that the high priest entered the holy of holies of the tabernacle (or temple) to sprinkle sacrificial blood on and before the atonement cover of the Ark (called "mercy seat" in many versions)—Lev. 16:14. A part of the ritual was the ceremony of the *azazel* (scapegoat). It differed from the others in having certain aspects of a fast day, it being required that the people had to "deny" themselves (Lev. 23:27). It was the high point of the ritual year, religiously speaking. *See* AZAZEL; SACRIFICES AND OFFERINGS

6. *The Feast of Tabernacles* (or booths). This was held at the end of the fall harvest—somewhat earlier in Palestine than in northern, western, central Europe and most of North America. It began on the fifteenth day of the seventh month and thus was just after the Day of Atonement and continued for a full week (Ex. 23:16; Lev. 23:33-43). The people spent the week camping out, as we would call it today. The weather is invariably good there in late September and early October. The heat of summer is over and the "early rains" are still several weeks away. The crops have been in process of harvest since the barley harvest in May, wheat some weeks later, then figs, olives, and grapes (wine). This was a week of family vacation, rest, recreation, and national rejoicing (Dt.

16:13-15). It was the end of the calendar of festivals.

During their history before the opening of NT times, the Jewish people added the feast of Purim (*see* PUR) and the feast of Dedication. The origin of the feast of Purim is found in Esther 9 and 10. It was not a pilgrim feast and, as observed, was more nationalistic than religious. Its observance (the fourteenth and fifteenth of Adar, the twelfth month, March) has attained great popularity in the new state of Israel. There is no mention of it in Scripture outside the book of Esther. *See* BOOTHS

The Feast of Dedication (also of Lights) celebrates the time when in 164 B.C. the temple, desecrated by Antiochus Epiphanes, was purified, restored to use, and rededicated to Jehovah. It began on the twenty-fifth of Kislev (December), the ninth month, and lasted eight days. Its origin is described in the Apocrypha (1Macc. 4:56-59 and 2Macc. 10:6ff.). Josephus (*Antiq.* 12:7:7) said it was called "Lights" from the first and described it as a joyful festival. It was a time of illuminating the temple area, and now it is a time when Jews illumine their homes with candles, lamps, and lanterns. Since it falls at the same season of the year as Christmas, scholars have supposed the Christian festival's date and many of its features were derived from it. It is mentioned only once in Scripture (Jn. 10:22). *See also* CALENDAR (R.D.C.)

FESTUS The successor of Felix as Roman governor at Caesarea, who also tried Paul. Paul appealed from this trial to Caesar at Rome (Ac. 24:27; 25:1-24, 26:24-32). †

FETTERS Chains or shackles (any of various fastening devices) usually for the feet (Jdg. 16:21; 2Sa. 3:34; Mk. 5:4). For chains on hands, *see* CHAINS

FEVER *See* SICK, SICKNESS

FIDEISM The reliance on faith and the inner witness of the Spirit as sufficient for accepting the truths of Christianity, rather than by proved reasons.

FIDELITY *See* FAITH, FAITH-FULNESS

FIELD *See* BOUNDARY STONE; FARMING

FIELD COMMANDER *See* RAB-SHAKEH

FIELD OF BLOOD *See* AKELDAMA

FIERY LAKE *See* DEAD, ABODE OF

FIFTIES A military unit as well as an administrative one in ancient Israel (Ex. 18:21, 25; 2Ki. 1:13).

FIG, FIG TREE *See* TREES

FIGHTING *See* ARMS AND ARMOR; WAR

FILIGREE Ornamental work with fine gold wire, usually as a setting for jewels. In the Bible it is mentioned in connection with the work of the priest's ephod and breastpiece (Ex. 28:11; 39:6, 13, 16, 18).

FILLETS KJV for "bands" (Ex. 38:10-19).

FINAL STATE *See* ESCHATOLOGY

FINGER *See* WEIGHTS AND MEASURES, *length*

FINING-POT KJV in Pr. 17:3 and 27:21. Both occurrences in the original are a noun form from the verb "refine, smelt, test" (as in metal work). "Crucible" is the translation in the NIV as a place where refining occurs or is a device used for refining.

FIR *See* TREES

FIRE Besides the normal uses of fire, it is pictured in the Bible with two special functions—punishment and purification. God uses it in both senses (Lev. 10:2; 1Co. 3:12-15). *See also* "lake of fire," "eternal fire," "fiery furnace" in DEAD, ABODE OF. *See also* BAPTISM OF FIRE

FIREPAN A vessel used for carrying live coals especially in connection with the burning of incense (Nu. 4:14). The Hebrew word is also rendered "censers" and "tray" (Lev. 10:1; Ex. 25:38).

FIRE, PILLAR OF *See* PILLAR

FIRKIN KJV for about eight to ten gallons (half a kilderkin); hence, Jn. 2:6 in the NIV, "twenty to thirty gallons." *See* WEIGHTS AND MEASURES, Liquid Measures, *Metretes*

FIRMAMENT KJV for "expanse" (Ge. 1:6ff.). *See* EXPANSE

FIRST-BEGOTTEN *See* FIRSTBORN

FIRST DAY OF THE WEEK *See* LORD'S DAY; SABBATH

FIRSTBORN The word refers to the firstborn of man and animals (Ex. 11:5). These had to be consecrated to God, the humans being redeemed and the animals sacrificed (Ex. 34:19-20; Nu. 3:41, 46-47). The firstborn was the heir who received a double portion of the inheritance. This was determined by the number of sons plus one. For example, if there were six sons, there were to be seven shares or portions in the inheritance. The firstborn was to receive two of these portions or shares, called a double share or portion. In a special usage Christ was the firstborn among many brethren, and so in the position of honor (Ro. 8:29; Col. 1:15, 18; Heb. 1:6; Rev. 1:5). *See also* INHERITANCE

FIRSTFRUITS *See* CALENDAR; FESTIVALS; SACRIFICES AND OFFERINGS

FIRSTLING *See* SACRIFICES AND OFFERINGS

FISH, FISHING In the many biblical references to fish, no clues are found to assist in their identification by species. They were important for food, caught by net or hook and line. Only fish with fins and scales were clean and could be eaten (Lev. 11:9-12; Mt. 17:27; Jn. 21:6). Even the proverbial whale that swallowed Jonah is called by the simple words "great fish" (Hebrew *daggadol*)—Jnh. 1:17.

FISH POOL *See* SONG OF SOLOMON, BOOK OF (SS. 7:4)

FISHHOOK *See* FISH, FISHING; HOOK

FITCH KJV in Isa. 28:25-27. *See* PLANTS, PERFUMES, AND SPICES, Plants for Seasoning, *Caraway*

FLAG KJV for "reed" in Job 8:11b. It is a synonym for papyrus, though bulrush, rush, or reed are all acceptable translations. *See* PLANTS, PERFUMES, AND SPICES, Flowering Plants 5. *See also* Miscellaneous Plants 3.

FLAGON *See* WEIGHTS AND MEASURES

FLASK Several different kinds of juglets or jars (2Ki. 9:1; Mt. 25:4; Lk. 7:37).

FLAX *See* PLANTS, PERFUMES, AND SPICES, Flowering Plants 3.

FLEA *See* BEASTS 6.

FLEECE The shorn wool of sheep, the first of which was a part of the tithe, the pay of the priests (Dt. 18:4). Gideon used a fleece to check on the revelation that God had given him (Jdg. 6:37-40).

FLESH The meaty part of the bodies of man and animals and by metonymy mankind (translation of Hebrew word for "flesh," Nu. 16:22, or "all living creatures" from the Hebrew of Ge. 6:19 which says: "from all living, from all flesh"). It also refers to the human as distinct from the spiritual part of man: "the spirit is willing but the body [literally flesh] is weak" (Mt. 26:41). A modification of the latter is human nature under the control of sin and not dominated by God's Spirit, translated in NIV as "worldly" and in other versions as "carnal" (1Co. 3:1-3). A further example is the NIV translation of "flesh" as sinful nature (Gal. 5:16-21), in contrast to the "fruit of the Spirit." *See* CARNAL; SOUL; SPIRIT

FLESHHOOK *See* HOOK

FLIES *See* BEASTS 6.

FLINT A very hard variety of the mineral quartz. When it is fractured it tends to leave sharp edges. Early man used flint for knives, axes, sickle blades, razors, and arrowheads. From it the knife used in circumcision was made (Ex. 4:25; Jos. 5:2). It was used as a symbol of hardness or determination (Isa. 50:7).

FLOCKS

1. Sheep or goats in a group (Lk. 2:8).

2. A figure for the LORD'S people (Zec. 13:7; Mt. 26:31; Lk. 12:32). Two flocks will be made into one (i.e., Israel and the Gentiles)—Jn. 10:16. Church leaders are to lead this flock (Ac. 20:28-29). The overseer of the church is subject to Christ, the Chief Shepherd (1Pe. 5:2-4). *See* SHEPHERD

FLOG *See* PUNISHMENT

FLOOD The Flood in the days of Noah has been much discussed and debated in both "liberal" and "conservative" Christian circles, especially its date and its pictured universality. Its story is told in Genesis 6–8. Jesus and Peter also spoke of it, implying its great scope (Mt. 24: 38-39; 2Pe. 2:5). Its reality cannot be questioned, then, even if its scope and area covered are debated. The biblical account is of a flood that covered "all the earth" and mountains to a depth of twenty feet, and lasted for about a year (Ge. 7:6; 8:13). The waters flooded the earth 150 days (Ge. 7:24), and killed everything that breathes through its nostrils, except for Noah and his immediate family, two of all kinds of animals, and seven pairs of the clean ones. The meaning of the word "all" is the point of debate, and some hold to a flood of limited scope, limited to the then inhabited area. Others believe it was a universal flood (Ge. 7:19).

FLOUR *See* FOOD; MEALS; MILL, MILLSTONE; Plants for Food 1.

FLOWERS *See* PLANTS, PERFUMES, AND SPICES

FLUTE *See* MUSIC

FLUX *See* DYSENTERY; SICK, SICKNESS

FLY *See* BEASTS 6.

FOAL A young donkey (Mt. 21:5, taken from Zec. 9:9). The prophecy shows that the LORD was mounted upon this to show his gentleness or meekness. The foal was unridden (not old and worn out) to show he was fit for a king. Except for walking, riding a donkey was probably the most common mode of travel at this time. *See* BEASTS 4.

FODDER Feed, or provender, for donkeys, oxen, cattle, camels, etc., consisting of a mixture of grains, hay (Ge. 24:25, 32; 43:24; Jdg. 19:19; Isa. 30:24; Job 6:5; 24:6; 1Co. 3:12).

FOLLOWER *See* BELIEVER; CHRISTIAN

FOLLY *See* FOOL; WISDOM

FOOD Little is known about the food consumed prior to the time of the Flood in the days of Noah. By that time man was eating meat as well as fruits and vegetables that grew with him. Clean and unclean animals went into the ark, those that could be eaten and those forbidden to eat (Ge. 7:23). Blood could not be eaten, as the concept was that it was lifeblood (other versions render "because its life is in the blood"). Cooking was very primitive, and was done in an earthenware pot over a small fire of thorns or brush. Wheat and barley were ground, from which bread was baked. Milk and *leben* (curdled milk) were abundant. Earlier men were food gatherers. Later people began to cultivate foods. *See also* BEASTS; BUTTER; CHEESE; CURDS; DRINKS; FISH; PLANTS, PERFUMES, AND SPICES, Plants for Food

FOOL The word is translated in the NIV as "fools," "lawless," "simple," "mockers," and "blind fools" (Ps. 14:1; Pr. 1:22; 19:29; 2Sa. 13:13; Mt. 23:17). A dozen Hebrew words are commonly used to convey the idea of scorners, scoffers, impious, and other like terms, some of which are also translated in the NIV as "fools."

FOOTMAN *See* ARMS AND ARMOR; ARMY; WAR

FOOTSTOOL *See* STOOL

FOOT WASHING A biblical custom of foot washing performed by a host to honor his guests. Jesus washed the disciples' feet (Jn. 13:1-17) as a symbol of humility and love. Some Christian groups practice foot washing to display Christ's example.

FORBEARANCE Long-suffering and patience sometimes convey the idea of forbearance (2Co. 6:6; 2Pe. 3:9, 15). Christians are to have this quality when relating to other Christians. It has the idea of enduring with someone, bearing with them. If one says, "I can't put up with him/her any more," then he is not being forbearing (Eph. 4:2; Col. 3:13). Forbearance with a gentle response, not weakness or sentimentality, is found in Php. 4:5.

FORD A shallow place in a river or other body of water where men and animals could cross on foot. These included the ford at the Jabbok River, the fords across the Jordan River that led to Moab, those of the Arnon River, and the fords in the desert—a reference to crossing of the Jordan (Ge. 32:22; Jdg. 3:28; Isa. 16:2; 2Sa. 17:16, 21).

FOREIGNER *See* BARBARIAN; STRANGER

FOREKNOWLEDGE *See* ELECT, ELECTION

FOREORDINATION KJV for "chosen" (1Pe. 1:20). *See* ELECT, ELECTION

FORESKIN *See* CIRCUMCISION

FOREST Land covered with trees, shrubs, or thickets. Various forests are mentioned in the Bible, including the forest of Lebanon from which came the cedars for the temple (1Ki. 10:17, 21). There was a forest of Hereth in the land of Judah, a forest of Ephraim, and even forest land in the Negev or semidesert area in the S (1Sa. 22:5; 2Sa. 18:6; Eze. 20:46-47).

FOREVER *See* ETERNITY; IMMORTAL; TIME

FORGIVENESS Pardon or remission usually based on one's repenting and being willing to make restitution or reparation. It results in the parties involved being returned to their former relationship. To restore God's favor to man after the Fall required him to forgive man. This in turn required the atonement provided in the death of Christ (Col. 1:14; 2:13-14). Man must repent of his sin and turn from it with a desire to make restitution by living a new life. Considerable emphasis is laid on the need of men to forgive one another just as God forgives men (Mt. 6:14-15; Lk. 6:37). There is only one sin for which there is no forgiveness—blaspheming the Holy Spirit (Mk. 3:28-29). *See* BLASPHEMY AGAINST THE HOLY SPIRIT

FORK *See* HOOK

FORMGESCHICHTE *See* CRITICISM, FORM

FORNICATION This is a broad word that can be used for a full spectrum of sexual sins (Lev. 18), though often understood to mean sexual intercourse outside of marriage. It is a symbol for idolatry, harlotry against God (Mt. 15:19; Rev. 17:4; 21:8). A distinction is made by some that fornication is sexual intercourse between unmarried people while adultery involves married people. Adultery and fornication are listed together in lists of sins, but the distinction does not stand up in Scripture. See Mt. 5:32 where "marital unfaithfulness" is a translation of the Greek word often rendered "fornication." *See also* ADULTERY; LUST; PROSTITUTE

FORT, FORTRESS, FORTIFICATION These consisted of a wall (often double or of the casemate variety) which surrounded all or part of a city and included the citadel.

Their construction differed at various times in history. For example, there were the Early Bronze Age massive mud walls, the Hyksos *glacis* (sloped fortification wall), and the casement wall of Solomon's time. At the turns of the wall it was customary to have towers which sometimes protruded for visibility for the defenders. The building material was usually stone (where that was available) or sundried mud bricks. *See* WALL

FORTUNATUS [fortunate] A Christian from Corinth who was with Paul at Ephesus (1Co. 16:8, 17). †

FORTUNE, (PAGAN GOD) *See* DEITIES, Foreign gods, *Gad*

FORTY While it has no religious or mysterious significance in its value, the number forty is widely used in Scripture as a round number expressing considerable duration. It is commonly considered to be the length of a separation. A man reached his prime at forty, double that was old age and triple was a life span (Ex. 2:11; Ac. 7:23; 2Sa. 19:34-35; Ge. 6:3; Dt. 34:7). Certain significant events took forty days and forty nights: it rained forty days and nights in the case of Noah's Flood; Moses was on the mount forty days and nights; Moses' spies were spying out the land of Canaan forty days; Elijah went forty days and nights in his flight to Horeb; Jesus fasted forty days and nights (Ge. 7:4; Ex. 24:18; Nu. 13:25; 1Ki. 19:8; Mt. 4:2). The Israelites were forty years in the desert, long enough for an entire generation to die; Eli led the people forty years, and many of the kings reigned a generation or forty years (Ex. 16:35; Nu. 32:13; 1Sa. 4:18; 2Sa. 5:4; 1Ki. 11:42; Jdg. 3:11).

FORUM OF APPIUS *See* APPIUS

FOUNDATION Usually refers to the base upon which a building stands, but has also many figurative uses, such as the foundation of the world, and Creation (Mt. 13:35). Jesus Christ is the foundation of the Christian faith (1Co. 3:11); Paul laid the foundation of a number of churches (1Co. 3:10); and the church is founded on the prophets and the apostles, as well as on Christ (Eph. 2:20).

FOUNTAIN A place where water springs forth from the ground or from the rocks. In a climate without rain for seven or eight months each year, these springs become strategically important both in times of peace and in times of siege. Towns and villages were built around such a source of water: En Gedi, En Eglaim, En Gannim, and En Rogel (SS. 1:14; Eze. 47:10; Jos. 21:29; 15:7). The word is also used figuratively of both good and evil sources (good sources: Ps. 36:9; Pr. 14:27; 16:22); evil source is rendered in the NIV as "polluted well" in Pr. 25:26. *See* AIN; CISTERN; POOL; SPRING; WATER; WELL

FOURSCORE KJV for four groups of twenty, hence "eighty."

FOWL *See* BIRDS

FOWLER A hunter and catcher of birds; figuratively used of those who trap or snare persons (Ps. 124:7; Jer. 5:26).

FOX *See* BEASTS 8.

FRANKINCENSE *See* PLANTS, PERFUMES, AND SPICES

FREE MAN, FREEDMAN The opposite of a slave, one who is free or who has been freed. Figuratively it refers to those who have been freed from the shackles of sin by the redemption of Christ (Jn. 8:34-36; Ro. 6:16-18, 22-23; 1Co. 7:22-23; Rev. 6:15).

FREE WILL The belief that man's choices are self-determined.

FREEWILL OFFERING *See* SACRIFICES AND OFFERINGS

FRIEND *See* BELOVED

FRINGES In the NIV the word is translated as "tassel" (Nu. 15:38-39; Dt. 22:12). A twisted cord ending in a sort of tassel sown at the four corners of the outer garment to remind the Israelite of his obligation to the commandments of God. They are worn by the "religious" Jew to this day. *See* PHYLACTERY

FROG *See* BEASTS 6.

FRONTLET *See* PHYLACTERY

FROST *See* SNOW

FRUIT

1. *See* TREES.

2. Figurative for childbirth, as in the OT phrase "fruit of the womb" (Lk. 1:42). *See* BARREN

3. Jesus uses the figure of productivity of the vine, resulting from abiding in Jesus (Jn. 15:5, 8, 16). The acts of men are the outward appearances (fruit) of their inner person (Mt. 7:16).

4. Fruit is the result, product or outcome (benefits) of the Spirit (Gal. 5:22).

5. The fruit (results) of righteousness (Eph. 5:9; Php. 1:11; Jas. 3:18).

FRUIT, FIRST *See* CALENDAR; SACRIFICES AND OFFERINGS

FRYING PAN *See* VESSEL

FUEL Fuel consisted of a number of varieties of dried vegetable matter used for making fires (Isa. 44:14-16; Eze. 15:1-6). Wood and its derivative charcoal, thorn bushes, dried grasses, and the dung of animals are used even today by the bedouin.

FULFILLED Completion or fulfillment are the basic meanings (2Ch. 36:21). The best definition of the word occurs in Jn. 19:28: "Later, knowing that all was now completed, and so that the Scriptures would be fulfilled . . . "

FULLER One who washed, cleaned, and bleached cloth. Because of the odor involved, this work was usually done outside the city. Where the fuller's field, called Washerman's Field in the NIV, of Kings and Isaiah was located is not known with certainty (2Ki. 18:17; Isa. 7:3; 36:2). The representative of the king of Assyria stood there and was able to be heard on the walls of old Jerusalem. Soap in the modern sense was unknown so that the "soap" mentioned in Mal. 3:2 refers to some alkali from ashes of certain plants. The Hebrew word is translated also "bleach" (Mal. 3:2). *See also* SOAP

FULLER'S FIELD *See* FULLER, *Washerman's field*

FULLER'S SOAP *See* SOAP

FULLNESS OR FULNESS Literally that which fills (Dt. 33:16). Jesus Christ bodily contains all the fullness of God (Col. 1:19; 2:9). When Paul spoke of "attaining to the whole measure of the fullness of Christ," he was speaking of corporate maturity of the Christian church in Christ (Eph. 4:13).

FUNDAMENTALISM A movement begun in the 1920s, its basic tenet that there are certain *fundamental* beliefs that cannot be compromised in the arena of theological debate. Today it is used generally of a theological conservative.

FUNERAL, FUNERAL PROCESSION *See* BURIAL; CAVE; MOURN, MOURNING

FURLONG *See* WEIGHTS AND MEASURES

FURNACE *See fiery furnace* under DEAD, ABODE OF and OVEN. The furnace must be distinguished from the oven. Furnaces were made of brick reinforced with stone, varied greatly in size, had a place for the fire, a chimney to assist with the draft, and a container where the bricks and other ceramics, including vessels, were to be fired (Pr. 17:3; Eze. 22:18; Rev. 1:15). Ore was smelted in such furnaces, and the smelted ore could be heated for forging or melted for casting. Archaeologists have found many examples. The word is also used figuratively in the phrase "furnace of affliction" (Isa. 48:10).

FURNITURE *See* BED; LAMP, LAMPSTAND; TABERNACLE, *The Articles of;* TABLE; TEMPLE, *The Articles of*

FURZE BUSH *See* JUNIPER

FUTURE LIFE *See* ESCHATOLOGY; ETERNITY; IMMORTAL; LIFE; TIME. *See also* CHRIST, WORK OF 9., *Christ's Second Advent*

G

GAAL {loathing} One who led and lost the revolt against Abimelech at Shechem (Jdg. 9:26-41). †

GAASH {rumble, quake} A hill in the mountains of Ephraim with ravines by the same name. Joshua was buried near there (Jos. 24:30; Jdg. 2:9; 2Sa. 23:30; 1Ch. 11:32). †

GABA {hill} *See* GEBA

GABBAI A descendant of Benjamin (Ne. 11:8). †

GABBATHA {*possibly* height, ridge} The Aramaic word for "pavement" (Jn. 19:13), where Pilate placed his judgment chair for the trial and judging of Jesus. There is very good reason to believe that this pavement may be seen today in the basement of the Ecce Homo Church in the Convent of Our Lady of Zion within the walled part of the city of Jerusalem. †

GABRIEL {(strong) man of El} Da. 8:16; 9:21; Lk. 1:19, 26. † *See* ANGEL

GAD, GADITES {fortune}
  1. The seventh son of Jacob and the father of one of the tribes of Israel (Ge. 30:9-11). At the time of the conquest the clan numbered 40,500, and since they were sheep and cattle raisers they settled E of the Jordan (Nu. 26:18; Jos. 18:7). Ultimately Assyria under her King Pul (Tiglath-Pileser) took them captive (1Ch. 5:26).
  2. A prophet to King David (1Sa. 22:5). God sent him with a message to David when David sinned in numbering the people (1Ch. 21:9-10). He kept a written chronicle of the affairs of King David, also of Samuel and Nathan (1Ch.

29:29). He was involved in arranging the musical service for David (2Ch. 29:25).
  3. A pagan deity. His name is seen in some of the compound names of the Bible such as Migdal Gad (Jos. 15:37; Isa. 65:11). *See* DEITIES, *Babylonian*

GADARENES Gadara was one of the cities of the Decapolis in NT times. In the Greek text there are variant readings: Gerasenes and Gergesenes (*see* the footnote to Mt. 8:28 and Lk. 8:26 in the NIV). The city of Gadara is identified with modern Umm Qeis some five miles SE of the Sea of Galilee. The total area of the Gadarenes apparently reached to the Yarmuk River and to the Sea of Galilee itself.

GADDI {my fortune} The spy who represented the tribe of Manasseh among those who went from Kadesh Barnea to spy out the land (Nu. 13:11). †

GADDIEL {El is my fortune, BDB; (pagan god) Gad is (my) god, KB} The Zebulunite spy, one of the twelve whom Moses sent to spy out the land (Nu. 13:10). †

GADI {my fortune} The father of Menahem who usurped the throne of Israel from his predecessor (2Ki. 15:14, 17). †

GAHAM {burning brightly} One of the sons of Abraham's brother Nahor by a concubine (Ge. 22:20-24). †

GAHAR, GAHER {(born in the) year of little rain} Some of his descendants were temple servants who came back from the captivity in Babylon with Zerubbabel (Ezr. 2:47; Ne. 7:49). †

GAIN To have the sum total of earthly

riches is not enough for the price of your soul (Mt. 16:26; Mk. 8:36; Lk. 9:25). Using similar words, Paul says that Christ is incomparably better than this life (Php. 1:11; 3:78). Dishonest gain by false teachers is of course condemned (Tit. 1:11; 1Pe. 5:2). *See* SOUL 8.

GAIUS

1. Paul's host at Corinth whom he also baptized (Ro. 16:23; 1Co. 1:14). †

2. A companion of Paul seized in the riot in Ephesus (Ac. 19:29). †

3. A Christian of Derbe who accompanied Paul (Ac. 20:4). †

4. The addressee of the Book of 3 John. Some of these may be the same person. The information is scant. †

GALAL [*possibly* tortoise, IDB; roll away, KB] Two Levites of postexilic times (1Ch. 9:15-16; Ne. 11:17). †

GALATIA *See* GEOGRAPHY OF THE HOLY LAND

GALATIANS, BOOK OF *See* PAULINE EPISTLES

GALBANUM *See* PLANTS, PERFUMES, AND SPICES

GALEED [heap of (stones that are a) witness] Jacob's name for the pile of stones raised by him and Laban (his father-in-law) as a sign of their covenant (Ge. 31:46-48). †

GALILAEAN, GALILEAN A resident from the region or district of Galilee. One who spoke from here, according to the Bible record, had a recognizable accent (Mk. 14:70).

GALILEE [ring, circle, *hence* region] *See* GEOGRAPHY OF THE HOLY LAND

GALILEE, SEA OF *See* GEOGRAPHY OF THE HOLY LAND

GALL A bitter and poisonous herb. It was mixed with wine and given to criminals before crucifixion to deaden pain. Jesus refused it (Mt. 27:34). It has a symbolic meaning also: bitterness (Ac. 8:23). *See also* POISON

GALLEY *See* SHIP

GALLIM [heaps] An unidentified site in Benjamin (1Sa. 25:44; Isa. 10:30). †

GALLIO The Roman proconsul of Achaia before whom Paul was tried and acquitted (Ac. 18:12-17). †

GALLOWS *See* HANGING; PUNISHMENT

GAMAD *See* GAMMAD

GAMALIEL [recompense of El]

1. A head of the tribe of Manasseh who was to help Moses (Nu. 1:10; 2:20; 7:54, 59; 10:23). †

2. A Pharisee, a highly honored teacher of the law, who was also Paul's teacher (Ac. 5:34; 22:3). He is the author of the widely known judgment: "Leave these men alone! Let them go! For if their purpose or activity is of human origin, it will fail. But if it is from God, you will not be able to stop these men; you will only find yourselves fighting against God" (Ac. 5:38-39). †

GAME, WILD Something hunted, wild animals (Ge. 25:28; 27:3ff.).

GAMES An athletic contest (1Co. 9:25).

GAMMAD, GAMMADIMS An unidentified place in Syria. Men from there were in the army of Tyre (Eze. 27:11). †

GAMUL [weaned] The head of one of the lots in the division of the priests after the return from the exile (1Ch. 24:17). †

GAP THEORY The theory that there is a time gap of aeons between Ge. 1:2 and 1:3. According to this theory, the scenario is as follows: (1:1) God created the universe; (1:2) then the earth *became* formless and void (a time gap); (1:3) then the earth was remade. In this gap, according to the theory, geological time must have developed.

GARDEN An area planted with trees, shrubs, and flowers and usually surrounded by a stone wall or a wall of thorny shrubs. When guarding would be needed, a watchman would man a tower (Pr. 24:30 31; Isa. 1:8; 5:5-6; Mk. 12:1). Several gardens are noted in Scripture, among them: the garden by the cave purchased by Abraham for burial place (Ge. 23:17); the Garden of Gethsemane noted for the incident in the life of Jesus on the eve of the Crucifixion (Mt. 26:36ff.); the first one, Eden (Ge. 2:8). The word is also used in an allegorical sense expressing spiritual prosperity if it is well watered and spiritual barrenness if it is not (Ps. 1:3; Isa. 1:30; 58:11).

GARDENER The risen Christ was mistaken as the gardener (Jn. 20:15). *See* GARDEN

GAREB
1. One of David's thirty mighty men (2Sa. 23:38; 1Ch. 11:40). †
2. An unidentified place near Jerusalem to which the LORD told Jeremiah the city would expand (Jer. 31:39). †

GARLIC(K) *See* PLANTS, PERFUMES, AND SPICES

GARMENT *See* DRESS

GARMITE [bone, bony] An unclear designation of the place Garm, the place of Keilah (1Ch. 4:19). †

GARNER KJV for "barn" or "storehouse" (Ps. 144:13; Joel 1:17).

GASHMU *See* GESHEM

GATAM A grandson of Esau (Ge. 36:11, 16; 1Ch. 1:36). †

GATE An opening in a wall, usually a city wall. As these were the weakest parts of the walls of a city they were usually protected by flanking towers. The approach road was sometimes perpendicular to the line of the gate, thus forcing the attackers to approach the gate with their sides exposed to the soldiers on the wall. A good city gate was made up of a series of gates or barriers, one inside the other through which the enemy would have to fight. This was where the elders and judges sat to hear cases and supply witnesses. The market was usually located there. The area inside a particular

gate would be called by the name of its gate (Dt. 21:18-19; Ru. 4:1; 2Ki. 7:1). (Some passages that deal with the gates are 1Ch. 26; Ne. 2–3; 8; 12; Eze. 40–48). *See* CITY, TOWN

GATH [winepress]
1. For the Philistine Gath, *see* PHILISTINE CITIES.
2. As there is a location in the Asher area and one in the Sharon area called in Arabic "Jett" (Hebrew "Gat"), it is assumed that there were additional towns by the name of Gath (172-264 and 154-200). It means simply "winepress," and there were many such presses—for example, Gath Hepher, and Gath Rimmon.

GATH HEPHER [winepress water pit] A bordertown (180-238) in Zebulun and the home of the prophet Jonah (Jos. 19:13; 2Ki. 14:25). †

GATH RIMMON [winepress of pomegranate]
1. A city (132-166) in the tribal area of Dan (Jos. 19:45). †
2. The suggestion has been made that Tell Jarisha beside the Yarkon River in Tel Aviv is the Danite Gath Rimmon (Jos. 21:24; 1Ch. 6:69). †
3. An unidentified city in Manasseh (Jos. 21:25). †

GAULANITIS A District E of the Sea of Galilee named after the town Golan. *See* GOLAN

GAZA, GAZATHITES, GAZITES *See* PHILISTINE CITIES

GAZELLE *See* BEASTS 2.

GAZER *See* GEZER

GAZEZ [*possibly* sheep shearer, IDB; *possibly* one born at the time of shearing, KB] A son and a grandson of Caleb (1Ch. 2:46). †

GAZZAM Ancestor of some temple servants who returned from the exile in Babylon (Ezr. 2:48; Ne. 7:51). †

GEBA Means "hill" in Hebrew. Since there are many hills in Palestine-Israel, it should not be unexpected that many towns and villages were called by that name.

1. Geba in Benjamin (175-140) is the one most frequently mentioned in the Bible. It was between Jerusalem and Bethel near the border with Judah (1Sa. 13:3; 14:5), E of Gibeon and just S of Michmash. It was a Levitical town (Jos. 21:17; 1Ki. 15:22).

2. Geba in North Benjamin (174-158), where Josiah upon his return broke down the shrines and gates and desecrated the pagan high place (2Ki. 23:8).

3. Geba in Samaria (171-192), located just four miles N of the city of Samaria, is mentioned in the Samaria ostraca. The name is in the ancient records but not in the Bible.

4. Geba-shemen (159-237) was NW of Megiddo about halfway to modern Akko. Pharaoh Amenhotep's records list the name. The site is not mentioned in the Bible.

5. Geba-carmel is likewise in ancient records but not found in the Bible, nor is its location known today.

GEBAL [*possibly* border, BDB; hill, KB]

1. A city (210-391) between Tripoli and Beirut, ancient Byblos (1Ki. 5:18; Eze. 27:9). †

2. An area in Edom in the mountains S of the Salt Sea (Ps. 83:7). †

GEBALITES A people of Gebal (Jos. 13:5). † *See* GEBAL 1.

GEBER [(strong young) man] One of King Solomon's chief administrators (1Ki. 4:19). †

GEBIM [ditches] An unidentified city in Benjamin on the predicted route to be taken by the invading Assyrian army (Isa. 10:31). †

GECKO *See* BEASTS 6.

GEDALIAH [great is Yahweh]

1. The last ruler of Judah, made a governor by Nebuchadnezzar after the fall of the southern kingdom (2Ki. 25:22ff.).

2. A temple musician in the time of David (1Ch. 25:3, 9).

3. A priest who had married a foreign wife during the time of the Babylonian captivity but put her away and for his guilt made a sacrifice (Ezr. 10:18-19).

4. One who urged the king to execute Jeremiah (Jer. 38:14).

5. Grandfather of the prophet Zephaniah (Zep. 1:1).

GEDEON *See* GIDEON

GEDER [wall (of stones)] An unidentified Canaanite city near Debir taken by Joshua (Jos. 12:13; cf. 1Ch. 27:28). †

GEDERAH [stone penfold, sheep corral] An unidentified town in the western foothills of Judah (Jos. 15:36).

GEDEROTH [stone penfolds, sheep corrals] An unidentified city in Judah in the Lachish region (Jos. 15:41; 2Ch. 28:18). †

GEDEROTHAIM [two stone penfolds, two sheep corrals] An unidentified village in Judah, distinct from Gederah and Gederoth (Jos. 15:36, RSV). †

GEDOR [wall, BDB; pockmarked, KB]

1. A city (158-115) in the hill country of Judah near Hebron (Jos. 15:58).

2. An unidentified town in Benjamin from which men came to David at Ziklag (1Ch. 12:7).

3. A descendant of Benjamin who lived at Gibeon (1Ch. 8:31).

GE HARASHIM

1. When translated, this word means "valley of the craftsman," and so it appears in Ne. 11:35.

2. Joab of Judah is "father," which in 1Ch. 4:14 means "founder" of the city (note the sentence which immediately follows it in 1Ch. 4:14). It was located somewhere on the southern border of the Plain of Sharon. †

GEHAZI [*possibly* valley of vision] The servant of the prophet Elisha. He is involved in the incidents of the raising of the Shunammite's son, in the restoration of the Shunammite's land, and also in the account of the healing of the leprosy of the Syrian captain Naaman (2Ki. 4:12ff.; 5:20ff.; 8:4ff.). †

GEHENNA [valley of Hinnom] *See* HINNOM, VALLEY OF

GELILOTH [region] The name of an unidentified place on the border between Judah and Benjamin. Some also equate it with the Gilgal in Jos. 15:7, not the one near Jericho (Jos. 18:17). Many versions translate as "border" in Jos. 22:10-11. †

GEMALLI [my reward, KB] Father of the representative of the tribe of Dan among the twelve whom Moses sent to spy out the land (Nu. 13:12). †

GEMARIAH [Yahweh has accomplished]
1. A messenger sent by King Zedekiah to the court of Nebuchadnezzar in Babylon with a letter written by Jeremiah for the exiles from Jerusalem (Jer. 29:3).
2. A prince who opposed the burning of Jeremiah's scroll (Jer. 36:25).

GENEALOGY [account of one's descent] A list of descendants or ancestors. These lists have their special functions. To make a list of every possible member is not one of them; frequently names are omitted. Major genealogical lists are found in Genesis 4 and 5, Numbers 1–3, 1 Chronicles 1–9, Ezra 2 and 8, Nehemiah 7, and those of Jesus in Matthew 1 and Luke 3.

Some of the major genealogical listings, including lists of place names and others, are found in the following books and chapters. The order of presentation is the order they are found in the Bible.

Table of nations (Ge. 10).
Adam to Abraham (1Ch. 1).
Esau's descendants, the Edomites (Ge. 36; 1Ch. 1).
Jacob's descendants, who went to Egypt (Ge. 40).
Family of Moses and Aaron (Ex. 6).
Census 1 and 2 taken by Moses (Nu. 1; 26).
Arrangement of the tribal camps around the Tent of Meeting (Nu. 2).
Israel's exodus wanderings (Nu. 33).
Kings defeated by Joshua (Jos. 12).
Allotment of the two and a half tribes E of the Jordan (Jos. 13).

Allotment of the rest of the tribes W of the Jordan (Jos. 14–19).
Descendants of the tribes (1Ch. 2–5; 7–9).
Cities of refuge, Levitical towns, Levite descendants, and David's singers, and treasury officials (Jos. 20–21; 1Ch. 6, 23–26).
David's thirty mighty men and other officials (2Sa. 23; 1Ch. 11–12; 27).
Solomon's officials (1Ki. 4).
Exiles who returned from Babylon (Ezr. 2; 8; Ne. 3; 11–12).
Returnees guilty of marrying foreign women (Ezr. 10).
Builders of Nehemiah's walls of Jerusalem (Ne. 3).
Those who sealed the covenant with Nehemiah (Ne. 10).
Jesus' genealogy, Abraham to Mary (Mt. 1).
Jesus' genealogy, Adam and Joseph, the father (so it was thought) of Jesus (Lk. 3).

GENEALOGY OF JESUS CHRIST *See* CHRIST, LIFE AND TEACHINGS OF; GENEALOGY

GENERATION In the OT a generation may refer to a period of time, or to the people living in a given period of time, and perhaps also to a place (Ps. 102:24; Ge. 7:1; Isa. 58:12, where the NIV translates it "age-old"). Its plural in the OT refers to genealogies. In the NT it has the meanings noted above as in the OT and also "race" or "nation" (Mt. 1:17; 11:16; 24:34; Ac. 13:36; 1Pe. 2:9).

GENESIS, BOOK OF [beginning] *See* PENTATEUCH

GENNESARET, LAKE OF, LAND OF *See* GEOGRAPHY OF THE HOLY LAND

GENRE A category of literary composition characterized by a certain form, content, or style. The Bible student must take into account the *genre* of a book to interpret it properly. For example, chaps. 4–22 in the Book of Revelation (apocalyptic form) cannot be interpreted the same way as the letters of Paul (epistolary form) because it has a different literary genre.

GENTILES A translation of the Hebrew word *goy*, plural *goyim*. Basically the word means "nation" and is so consistently translated in the NIV. It usually means a "non-Israelite people" but on occasion even Israel is called a *goy*, a nation (Ge. 12:2; Jos. 3:17; 4:1; Zep. 2:9). In many places the connotation is that of heathen nations and so the word is translated "heathen" in some versions. Jesus worked almost exclusively with the people, the Jews, not the nations or Gentiles; his work of atonement, however, was for all peoples. Paul, the apostle to the Gentiles (Ac. 9:15), taught that Jesus broke down the barrier between Jew and Gentile (Gal. 3:28; Eph. 2:11-22). *See* NATION

GENTILES, COURT OF THE *See* MIDDLE WALL OF PARTITION; TEMPLE

GENTLE, GENTLENESS *See* MEEK, MEEKNESS

GENUBATH [thief] A son of the Edomite Hadad by the sister of the Queen of Egypt (1Ki. 11:19-20). †

GEOGRAPHY OF THE HOLY LAND

I. PREFACE
Palestine of today is ruled by the State of Israel, inhabited mainly by Jews, who speak Hebrew, and Arabs, who speak Arabic. The capital is Jerusalem, which has also been known as Salem, Jebus, City of David, Zion, Yerushaliyim, Ariel, Aelia Capitolina, and El Kuds. Often places have numerous names in the Holy Land. Complexity in the naming of a country desired and controlled through the centuries by so many different peoples can be expected.

A few basic names can be briefly explained. The land Canaan may take its name from the expensive "royal purple" dye made from murex shells along the Mediterranean. (The name *Phoenicia* is not Semitic, but is apparently derived from the Greek word for "purple.") The term *Hebrew* was first applied to Abraham who "crossed over" the Euphrates River from *Mesopotamia* to a land known there as "Across the River." His grandson Jacob was renamed Israel after a confrontation with God. Jacob's son Judah was the father of a tribe who lived in Judah (*Judea* in Greek) and were known as "Jews." "Palestine" comes from the word *Philistine*, invaders from the sea, from *Crete* or *Cyprus*.

The lay of the land and the conditions it provides for human settlement are also extremely complex if one goes into detail.

II. INTRODUCTION
Geography is the study of the earth's surface as divided up into areas. This means, theoretically, that there are as many divisions to geography as there are kinds of forces acting to make distinctions between different parts of the earth.

III. TOPOGRAPHY
A. Setting
   The setting of Israel is water and rock. To the sunset is ocean; to the sunrise is desert. In other words, to the W is the Mediterranean (the Great Sea, the West Sea); to the E is Arabia (the wilderness, the desert). East is "before" and W is "behind" in the ancient world because one takes directions from the rising sun. So

ISRAEL AND ITS SURROUNDINGS
Shown during the time of the Babylonian Empire. Arrows show route of Judah's exiles.

the "West Sea" is our way of translating what the Bible literally calls the "Sea Behind." So the "East Country" (or East Sea, East Wind, or East Gate), is literally the "Country Before." Between the "before" and the "behind," the sunrise and the evening, is a long, narrow country of land largely fertile for cultivation, though often demanding arduous toil to terrace the hills or irrigate the oasis area within it. To the N and the S were the great powers of old. From the far N, out of the peninsulas of the Mediterranean, came the Greeks of Macedonia and the Romans of Italy. From the high mountain plateau around the Halys River of Asia Minor came the Hittites. From the great plains of the Tigris and Euphrates rivers of Mesopotamia came the Assyrians and Babylonians. From the mountains to the E of those rivers came the Persians. Small wonder then that "north" is "the hidden, the dark," the quarter from which all these invaders came, the quarter from which one does not know what to expect. These peoples all came down from the N — though spread from Italy to India — because the sea and the desert gave no other choice.

To the S, at least, there was always Egypt, but the pharaohs came too, and often, in both second and first millennia B.C. They came out of an even more narrow land because the Egyptians are confined almost entirely to the banks of one mighty river, the Nile. So it could be promised as regarding the Hebrew slaves in Egypt, I will "bring them up . . . into

a good and spacious land" (Ex. 3:8). The Promised Land was broad symbolically too, a land where the people would be freed from the oppression, the troubles of oppression in a foreign land (Ps. 107:6ff.; Zec. 10:11).

To reach Egypt to the SW one must first cross the Sinai peninsula, which is mostly desert. But between it and the fields of Canaan, the Promised Land, is the southern part of Canaan, a wide border area of pasturage and, in wet years, considerable grain. This border area is called the *Negev*, the "dry place" (Ge. 12:9; 20:1); but since it is to the S, it also very often refers to that direction, "the south" or "southward" (Ge. 13:14; 28:14). The Negev is where the patriarchs Abraham, Isaac, and Jacob lived. Their descendants became numerous during the year they were slaves in Egypt. Their descendants, the Israelites, returned eventually to occupy the entire Promised Land.

B. Formative Forces

1. *Geology.* Forces from within the earth have, it seems, raised and lowered the land many times throughout the centuries. What are now the hills of Israel were once plains submerged and raised, submerged and raised, again and again from the Great Sea to the W. This movement is evidenced by the many layers of sedimentary limestone and chalk rocks of which these hills are made. High up in the hills are found beautiful fossils of sea shells.

The Arabian plateau, or tableland to the E, was less affected. Its basis is a mighty platform of hard igneous granite rock from the depths of the earth. Above it is the red sandstone sometimes exposed by erosion. This sandstone is also sedimentary, but is formed above water in contrast to the limestones and chalks formed underwater. The sea did at times cover this plateau too, but the platform was high and hard and resisted change. This resistance was important at the time when the hills of Israel were formed.

Regardless of whether it really happened just this way, there is a helpful way to picture the process. Imagine a great force under the Western Sea which pushed a vast area of land eastward. But the land could not proceed because it came up against the hard granite platform, so it buckled. For the most part the buckling took place in one long wave, a long ridge running from N to S the entire length of Canaan. However, in the Negev area, in the southern part of Canaan, it rippled into five waves, each one a bit higher than the next, as it approached the platform. The final highest waves were more or less the continuation of the long wave to the N.

So then, the hills of Israel can be schematically represented as a long ridge running from N to S and fanning out, to the S and SW, into a number of smaller ridges which extend into the plains of the upper Sinai peninsula. Down at the tip of the peninsula, wild rugged mountains again appear. Among them is Mt. Sinai where Moses received the Law. But the land not only buckled and rippled—in some places it cracked and broke. One great break, in some places a double break, runs all the way from Asia Minor to the long slender lakes of Tanzania and Nyasaland of Western Africa. Along these breaks the earth's crust sank. The surface of the Salt Sea, lying in this rift valley, is 1,295 feet below sea level, the lowest spot on the face of the earth. Joshua and the Israelites came down off the platform and entered the Promised Land near Jericho (192-142) just N of the Salt Sea. Moses who had brought them

up out of Egypt was buried high up on the platform at Mt. Nebo (220-131). Many lesser cracks or faults in the earth's crust were exploited by runoff rainwater. Rushing down the sides of the central ridge, they eroded out the innumerable gullies and creek beds and often magnificent gorges of the hill country.

2. *Climate*. Forces of climate acting above on the surface of the land worked further on the crude topography formed from below. Water did the main work of carving out the valleys and creating alluvial (silted) plains with the earth it carried away. But its action is controlled by sun and wind.

In January, the sun is hot at 31 degrees 45' latitude (Jerusalem), so temperatures rarely fall below freezing even in January. Average temperatures in January in the *eastern plateau* are in the mid 40s F.; in the *central hills*, the upper 40s; at the *coast*, the mid 50s; and in the *rift valley*, warmest of all, the upper 50s. In August temperatures are: hills, mid 70s; coast and plateau, upper 70s; and the *rift valley*, around 90° F. These averages can be misleading till one takes note of the range of temperature, generally most extreme in the desert areas. A clue to range is the all-time low, recorded in *Galilee*, +8.6° F., and the all-time high, recorded in the rift valley, +129.2° F. But it is more helpful to note that in the winter there are occasional frosts even down in the valley (in the N) and snowfalls in the hills, and rather often in the summer temperatures are over 100° F.

The prevailing winds of the winter bear rain from the W. In summer local conditions take over. Since hot air rises from the eastern desert during the day, the cooler air over the Mediterranean Sea flows in toward the E. Since warm air rises above the sea at night, breezes from the more quickly cooling desert flow out to sea during the night and early morning, till the sun warms up the desert again and the flow reverses directions once more.

Scattered periods of oppressive heat last several days at a time during the summer, especially during the turning of the seasons. The first is at the beginning of the nearly absolutely dry summer in April-May, and the second is at the beginning of the rainy winter after September-October. At these times, for a day to several days, an E wind comes off the desert, blowing its dry heat all day, scarcely letting up at night.

Rain is carried in from the sea by the winter westerlies. As the winds push eastward, they force the warm moist air up over the mountain ranges, where the air cools and dumps its rain. The dry air then pushes eastward into the rift, quickly warms up again, and by the time it reaches sea-level altitudes again, it is all rained out—a system that has over many years produced the Arabian desert.

There is an E-to-W pattern of rainfall. Total rainfall on the west coast near Tel Aviv (Joppa) (126-162) is about twenty inches annually. This figure drops somewhat as the wind proceeds inland. But soon the land rises, cooling the air and forcing out water, so Jerusalem (172-131) gets even a bit more—twenty-two inches at her elevation of 2,600 feet at the top of the ridge. Farther E, down below sea level in the rain shadow, lies Jericho (192-142), getting only four inches. Jericho exists as a luxuriant spring-water oasis in the small but awesome, wild, rugged desert which lies along these back eastern slopes of the central hills. The nearby *Salt Sea* and the ruins of *Qumran* (193-127) (source of the Dead Sea Scrolls) get only about two inches. Climbing 4,300 feet to *Es-Salt* (218-161), 3,000 feet above sea level, the wind drops its last rain there—thirty inches annually.

The general rule as one crosses Palestine is that the weather gets hotter and drier the further E or S or downhill one goes. Even though the progression described was eastward (and one would expect the climate to be drier), the height of Es-Salt was so great that it overcompensated for this eastward progression. As one approaches the equator, the W winds come across the Sahara Desert and not the Mediterranean Sea. To the E the wind loses both its cooling power and

moisture as it leaves behind the Mediterranean, source of these two factors. And down in the *rift valley*, the air is the densest on earth (most capable of holding heat) as well as being in the rain shadow of the hills. There is also a N-to-S pattern of rainfall: from N to S, *Mt. Hermon* (225-305), 9,200 feet, on the edge of the plateau and towering above it, gets sixty inches; *Mt. Meron* (189-267) in the central hills gets forty-four inches; *Jerusalem* (172-131), twenty-two inches; *Beersheba* (134-072) in the *Negev*, ten inches; and *Elath* (150-882) on the Red Sea, one inch or less. Here, of course, the effect is exaggerated because of the downward as well as the southward trend. A final important point on climate is the irregularity of rainfall in the whole country, but especially in the great rift valley and the Negev. In these latter areas, rainfall can be as little as one-third of the annual average, or as much as twice the average amount. Rain also tends to come in concentrated doses—sudden, short-lived storms. Radical examples are 2.6 inches in *Beersheba* in twenty-four hours (1934), and 5.75 inches in a day in Sinai (1925). In general, Jerusalem (172-131) and London get roughly the same amount of rain, only the former in fifty days and the other in three hundred. The irregularity hurts most in the *Negev*. Here it is not just a matter of getting a poorer crop. If the early (fall) rains or the late (spring) rains do not come, one does not get any crop at all. The "aridity border" runs through this area. This is the line beyond which crops will surely fail with less than ten inches of rainfall annually. In fact, one has to consider a safe margin at fourteen inches because there are many below-average years. In this area wells are of life and death importance for the flocks. Numerous Bible stories tell of contests over water, especially in the area formerly inhabited by the patriarchs (Ge. 21:25-31; Ex.2; Jn. 4).

Dew provides some moisture even during the dry summer. More common in coastal areas than elsewhere, it is most heavy on Mt. Carmel, which rises out of the sea at *Haifa* (149-248). Here dew can appear 250 nights a year. About thirty miles to the E may be the setting of the story of Gideon's fleece (Jdg. 6).

C. The Results of the Formative Forces

1. *North-South Strips.* Four parallel strips run in a N-S direction. They are (a) the Mediterranean coastal plain; (b) inland to the E the central hill ridge of Galilee, Samaria and Judea; (c) the Jordan valley with the Sea of Galilee and the Salt Sea; and (d) the *plateau* E of the Jordan.

2. *East-West Interruptions and Resulting Divisions of the Strips.* These parallel N-S strips are interrupted in a few places by E-W features. The coastal plains of Galilee to the N (Asher, Zebulun, Acre, Haifa Bay—some other names for this area) are separated from the plains of Carmel by Mt. Carmel, a spur of land branching off from the central ridge out into the Mediterranean Sea. This ridge forms the bulge in the coastline at Haifa (149-248). The narrow Carmel coast is separated from the Sharon plains by the Crocodile River. Sharon and Philistia are separated by the Yarkon River which empties just N of Joppa (126-162).

The main interruption of the central hill ridge is a generally flat valley which extends all the way from Haifa (149-248) on the Mediterranean Sea, past Megiddo (167-221) to Jezreel (181-218), where it slopes downward to Beth Shan (197-212) below sea level in the Jordan Valley. Throughout the centuries this has been the major E-W pass. The Kishon River drains it to the sea, and the Harod drains the eastern section to the Jordan. This valley separates Galilee to the N from Samaria to the S. It is called Armageddon (or Jezreel, or Esdraelon).

3. The *Beersheba basin*, another major interruption of the hills, is just S of Judea. It is almost a complete interruption from the coast to the Jordan Valley. It begins up at *Arad* (162-076), perched up just W of the southern basin of the Salt Sea, and extends all along the southern

end of the hills of Judea, past Beersheba (134-072). It then flows into the Besor Brook, which empties into the sea S of Gaza (099-101) near the southern edge of the *Philistine plain*. It is the heart of the Negev. It too has been a pass since ancient times. In NT times the area was called "Idumea" because the Edomites were forced to come here from their homeland E of the Jordan.

No other equivalent E-W interruption exists. Judea (Judah) especially is well isolated as a unified hilly plateau area. Only near its northern border does the deep narrow Sorek Valley cut way back inland from the coastal plain. The Rephaim branch of the Sorek reaches to Jerusalem (172-131) itself, which perches on the water divide between the Mediterranean Sea and the Jordan Valley.

From Jerusalem, at a low point on the water divide, one proceeds northward up into the hills of *Samaria*. Samaria is not so well isolated because it is deeply penetrated by deep narrow branches of the Yarkon, which drains just N of Joppa (126-162). Such branches are the Ajalon, the Shiloh, and the Kanah. Just to the N of the latter and contrasting with these narrow winding valleys or wadis is the straight and wider Shechem (176-179) valley. This valley comes up from the Sharon plain and actually cleaves a low pass through the heart of the hills. Above this pass are Mt. Gerizim to the S and Mt. Ebal to the N of the town of Shechem (176-179) (Ge. 12), located at the top of the pass (modern Nablus). The pass continues down a magnificent narrow gorge to the NE into the neighborhood of present-day Tubas (182-188), called earlier Tirzah (1Ki. 15:33). There the route continues down to the SE through the wider straight Wadi Fari'ah to the Jordan Valley. The turbulence and early downfall of the northern kingdom of Israel might have been considerably influenced by the geographical openness of its home in these hills of Samaria, i.e., by the lack of easily defendable borders such as Judea had.

Southern or Lower Galilee is yet more open and was rarely, if ever, a major power center. Here we cannot even properly speak of a central hill ridge, because actually there are four small E-W hill ridges. Nestled up in the middle of the southernmost of them is Nazareth (178-234), mentioned in the NT (Mt. 2; Lk. 2). Nazareth overlooks the wide flat plains of Megiddo (167-221) (Armageddon, Kishon basin, Esdraelon plain, or Jezreel Valley—the latter referring in Scriptures to the eastern part drained by the Harod), which separate it from Samaria to the S. Rising separately above the plain to the SE of Nazareth (178-234) are Mt. Tabor (186-232) like a great inverted bowl, and the volcanic Hill of Moreh with Nain (183-226) on its northern slopes.

Beautiful, picturesque, flat little E-W valleys lie between these ridges of Lower Galilee. But the last valley to the N is bounded by the great scarp (i.e., a line of cliffs caused by erosion) of Upper Galilee which thrusts up into the wildest, most isolated area of the country. This area of rich vegetation is drained by several magnificent gorges. It is bounded on the N by the Litani (Leontes) River, which comes from the great rift valley N of the sources of the Jordan and cuts straight across out westward to the sea just N of Tyre (168-297).

The great rift valley continues practically uninterrupted from Mt. Hermon (225-305) (Ps. 29:6; 89:12) in the N to Elath (150-882) on the Red Sea in the S. Mt. Hermon (Dt. 3:9), towers over 9,000 feet to the NE just above the Huleh Valley, the northern section of the rift valley where the Jordan sources are located. In fact, its height allows it to catch sixty inches of rain annually, which it feeds out into the rich springs of Hasbani, Dan, and Hermon (Paneas). These join in the Huleh Valley into the new Jordan River channels which have now replaced the Huleh lake and swamps.

The *swamps* are a result of a lava outflow related to the volcanic cones of the Golan Heights to the E. The outflow dammed the Jordan River and lake, but this degenerated into swamps.

From the Sea of Galilee (nearly 700 feet below sea level), the Jordan River meanders more than seventy-five miles along a nearly flat slope to the Salt Sea (Sea of the Arabah) or Dead Sea about 1,300 feet below sea level. The riverbed of these meanderings is dwarfed by the immense floor of the rift valley down whose middle the river makes its way. This great valley floor, the Ghor, was not eroded out by the Jordan, but resulted from the sinking of the earth's crust along great N-S rifts. Near Jericho the floor is called the Plains of Jericho and just across the river to the E, the Plains of Moab (Nu. 36:13). The end of the Jordan is a deep sea with no outlet, the Salt Sea. Solid materials in its slimy solution measure between 25 and 30 percent of its total content.

South of the Salt Sea, the land rises in Arabah section of the rift valley. It rises gradually to over 650 feet above sea level and then subsides gradually to the Red Sea at Elath (150-882). In this great valley far to the N, across from the island of Cyprus, is its northern gate, the city of Hamath, which corresponds to Elath (150-882) in the S. Coming S up the Orontes River on which Hamath is located are high mountains on both sides, the Lebanon, ancient Phoenicia, to the W along the Mediterranean, and the Ante-Lebanon to the E on the fringe of the Arabian desert plateau, which ends at Mt. Hermon (225-305). Its foothills extend out into the rift valley just N of the Huleh basin and somewhat choke up the valley (the region of Ituraea). The valley route is difficult here. However, just N of Mt. Hermon (or Mt. Sirion; see Ps. 29:6) there is a pass across the Ante-Lebanon. This pass became important, especially since an oasis at its E end right on the desert fringe permitted the building of a great city, Damascus. This city was the home of the Aramean and later Syrian kingdoms, which gathered wealth from their position on the trade routes.

South of Damascus, and up E of the Huleh Valley begins the plateau E of the Jordan (the Transjordanian plateau), the last of the four N-S strips. The first E-W interruption of this strip is the canyon of the Yarmuk River, which empties into the Jordan just S of the Sea of Galilee. The territory between it and Mt. Hermon is Bashan (or Golan Heights). It gets sufficient rainfall for crops and rich pasturage for two reasons: Rainbearing winds off the Mediterranean get through the E-W valleys of Lower Galilee without being forced to lose much moisture, and the gradual slope of the Bashan plateau upward toward Mt. Hauran in the E forces the moisture out. Only beyond Hauran does the desert begin in earnest, but the rocky "torn" area (*Trachonitis*) just to the NW of Mt. Hauran is scarcely habitable either, except as a refuge.

South of the Yarmuk is the region of Gilead. Here and to the S the desert approaches ever closer to the edge of the plateau near the rift valley, both because the plateau tilts down toward the E, and because it gets higher and higher as one goes S. What water is left in the clouds after already being tossed over the Samarian and Judean hills gets forced out mostly at the steep rise of the edge, leaving none for the plateau slanting eastward. Through the middle of Gilead runs the Jabbok River in whose upper reaches dwelt the *Ammonites* at Rabbath Ammon (238-151) (see Ge. 19:38).

Along the E side of the Salt Sea was Moab (Nu. 21–24), home of the Moabites. Through it runs the fantastic Arnon gorge with cliffs 1,600 feet high over a canyon scarcely 100 feet wide.

At the southern end of the Salt Sea, the Zered flows out of its canyon. South of the Zered, along the rugged plateau edge called Mt. Seir, dwelt the *Edomites* (Nu. 20:14), with their center at Sela (Petra) (192-971). In Christ's day, the Nabateans lived here. The Edomites had been forced out across the rift into the Negev S of Judea. The Negev then became known as Idumea.

4. *Distribution of Water.* Even though the lay of the land is largely formed as a result of climatic forces, the topography in return affects the climate by increasing rainfall. For example, Mt. Carmel (155-238) gets thirty-six inches of rain though only 1,500 feet high because of

its steep slopes up above the sea. Mt. Meron (189-267), nearly 4,000 feet in Upper Galilee, is the highest W of the Jordan and gets the most rain, over forty inches. Across the Jordan, Mt. Hermon, over 9,000 feet, gets sixty inches. Bashan, because it is tilted up to the E, is watered far inland, whereas Edom, higher up, gets about the same amount of rain, twenty inches, even though it is much further S. Only a small area at the edge of the plateau is watered because it is tilted down toward the E.

Topography has also produced deserts. Eastward lie the Deserts of Edom and Moab and the vast Arabian desert. No moisture is left after the winds have been twice tossed high and cooled. To the S of Judea there is desert because there is little moisture in winds that have come across the Sahara Desert of Africa. The wild, rugged, barren little Desert of Judea (Jeshimon) is on the eastern slopes and cliffs of the Judean Hills as they drop down steeply below sea level to the Salt Sea (-1,300 feet). Only two inches of rain fall in this amazing "rainshadow." Here lay En Gedi (187-097), David's refuge from King Saul (1Sa. 24). Also here was the refuge of the Essenes who wrote the Dead Sea Scrolls at their Qumran (193-127) settlement. And here at Masada (184-081) was the tragic refuge of the last Jewish survivors of the Great Revolt against Rome (A.D. 66-73), where over 900 committed suicide rather than become Roman slaves. *See* MASADA.

Basically the general location of Israel makes it the meeting place of two major world climatic zones: seacoast (Mediterranean) and desert (Saharo-Sindian of Africa across to India). On examining the vegetational zone, it is evident that yet three more major climatic zones are represented: the sparsely watered mountain plateaus of Persia and Turkey are represented on the desert fringes; the tropics of Africa and India on tropical oases in the rift valley; and even the often snowbound areas of Europe and Siberia on the cool heights of Upper Galilee. Especially in the case of the latter two zones, it is obvious that topography is responsible for the cool heights and the sultry depths. But even in the case of the desert fringe it has provided an unusually expansive fringe in the Negev, the Beersheba basin. Plants adapted to suffer lack of water both from summer drought and also from winter cold are able to manage with the scanty rainfall here. This pattern provides a very great variety of plant species – up to 2,250 kinds, as over against 1,700 in wet England, or 1,500 in dry Egypt.

Topography is related not only to rainfall as mentioned, but also to the ground water supply. Springs are numerous in Israel, along the edges of the central hills and especially along the edges of the rift valley. Along such edges deep watertight strata are exposed which give back rain that fell years earlier up in the hills. Gradually it seeps down to gather in underground streams that in some places come literally gushing to the surface. So deep are some of the strata that in a number of places the water comes back as hot springs – the most famous since antiquity being those already then developed as resorts near the Sea of Galilee and the Salt Sea. There are even towns called Hammath (201-241) which are named after these "hot" springs (Jos. 19:35).

Often a stream erodes a valley until it cuts into a water-bearing layer; then the stream is reinforced by spring water as well. This is important in Israel because otherwise all of the wadis or streambeds would dry up in the summer – as so many of them do. Ancient Jerusalem, Jebus (172-131), owed its existence to such exposure of the Gihon spring. Thus some springs are found up in the hills as well, although they are not so mighty as those down at the edges.

The Yarkon, located inland from the old seaport of Joppa (126-162), is such a stream arising at Aphek (143-168), where the hills meet the plain; today it supplies not only the modern city of Tel Aviv and Jaffa, but its water is pumped up to Jerusalem as well.

The most impressive springs are the Dan (211-294) and the Banias (215-294)

in the Huleh Valley at the foot of Mt. Hermon (225-305); together with the Iyon and the Hasbani, they form the headwaters of the Jordan. Such drama in nature inspired primitive man as well. Semitic deities as well as the Greek god Pan, were worshiped at the spring of "Banias" (earlier, Paneas, from the pagan god Pan). In Jesus' day the town of Caesarea Philippi (215-294) was located here (Mt. 16). Near the Salt Sea it is only this precious spring water which makes possible such oasis towns as Jericho (192-142) and En Gedi (187-097).

Sometimes erosion has not lowered a valley floor or creek bed far enough to expose the underground streams, but has gotten close enough so man can dig a well to reach the water. Such is Jacob's Well at Sychar near Shechem (176-179). There Jesus revealed himself to the Samaritan woman as the Living (fresh) Water, the Messiah who can be worshiped any place in the world in spirit and in truth, and not at any specific cultic place alone (Jn. 4).

Such underground streams near the surface are extremely important in the Negev. Witness the frequent struggles over wells here in the period of the patriarchs and the very story of the name of Beersheba (134-072) itself (Ge. 21). Still further SW out in the desert, in the Desert of Paran, lay Kadesh Barnea (096-006) (Nu. 13:26; 20:22), the oasis whose springs and wells supported the Israelites for most of their forty years in the wilderness after the Exodus from slavery in Egypt.

IV. SETTLEMENT ON THE LAND
A. Determining Factors

Chief essential factors of any settlement, in order of priority, are: water, land, safety, and trade. The significance of topography is immediately apparent. Abundant water and usable agricultural land are generally located low in valley bottoms or out on plains. But safety in ancient times demanded a position that could be well fortified and easily defended. Usually this meant choosing some place high up on a hilltop, preferably with cliffs all around, such as Masada (184-081) or Petra (192-971), so no enemy could storm its walls. Fear drove people to such places, a burden on the everyday life of the farmer. How valuable water was, and how carefully it was used.

It is clear that fear and the need for safety hindered not only easy access to food and water but trade connections as well. Trade routes naturally follow the shortest and easiest lines and pass large towns where provisions can be obtained. Only when enemies controlled the better routes would the trade caravans be forced into mountains and along desert fringes to secondary markets or provision centers. For example, in periods of strong foreign control over the whole land the most important administrative centers were often down on the Sharon seacoast plain. Egyptian centers were at Gaza (099-101) and Gezer (142-140) in the Canaanite period, a Roman center was at Caesarea (140-212) in the time of Jesus, and an Arab center was at Ramle (138-148) throughout the early Middle Ages – in preference over Jerusalem (172-131), tucked way up on the water divide of the central hill range. Defensive needs also clarify passages which speak of a city with its villages (Jos. 19); in time of peace the villages were the farmer's homes, but the city was the fortified point where provisions could be stored and people could flee in times of attack and siege.

B. Ancient Route and Major Towns

Factors determining the location of the routes are: profit, safety, and ease of travel. The last factor requires routes that are comfortable, the shortest possible, well supplied with water, food, and resting inns. For example, those few valleys in the Carmel range which have chalky soil became the natural passes – at Jokneam (160-230), Megiddo (167-221), and Dothan (172-202) – both because such soil beats down into a smooth, hard-surfaced roadbed and also because erosion has made the general terrain in such areas much more gradual and

rounded than the surrounding rugged limestone areas. In fact, caravans proceeding northwards out of Shechem (176-179) in the hills of Samaria did not take the shortest line straight N but swung around to either the E past Tirzah (182-188) or to the W past Samaria (Heb. *Shomron*) (168-187) in order to follow the chalk valleys which allow the traveler to avoid the hard rock of Mt. Ebal.

Fear could easily keep caravans off the easiest routes. For example, the most gradual route from the coast to Jerusalem (172-131), the modern railroad route, is past Beth Shemesh (147-128) and on up the Sorek Valley and its Rephaim tributary. This may be the way the strong Philistines came up to attack David (2Sa. 5). But this valley is narrow and winding, and therefore very dangerous if suddenly a defender appears above on the steep sides around the next bend. Because of this, attacking armies have throughout history often preferred the Beth Horon (160-143) route (Jos. 10:10) which climbs up a ridge just N of the neighboring Ajalon Valley. Caravans, often armed for protection, were frequently forced to make such deliberations, to choose a less convenient route for safety's sake.

Routes play a large part in the location of many towns. After availability of water and land have established the location of major populated areas, and connections have sprung up between distant areas, then the connecting routes in turn influence the location of supply centers, especially the junctions of importance. The towns of the Carmel passes are good examples: Jokneam (160-230), Megiddo (167-221), Taanach (171-214), Dothan (172-202), and also rift valley towns like Jericho (192-142), Beth Shan (197-212), and Hazor (203-269). Extreme examples are desert towns like Avedat (128-022) and Shivtah (115-033), which lived only for trade, and whose inhabitants had to make clever, strenuous schemes to maintain some agriculture in the vicinity. David moved his capital from Hebron (159-103) to Jerusalem, (172-131) in a more dangerous area, in

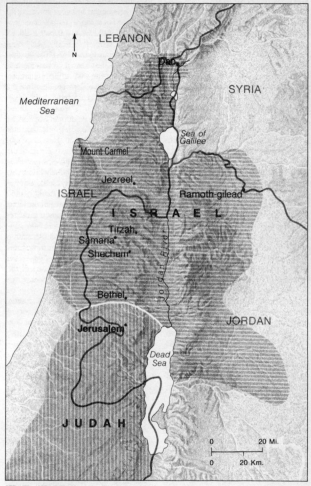

ISRAEL AND JUDAH

order to get near a better route as well as into a more central position for consolidating the tribes.

Once grown, a junction town not only supplied traffic but drew traffic to its own markets—or drew jealous armies. When Jerusalem was strong, it could impose customs even on caravans passing along the coast. The Egyptian Pharaoh himself with all his army could not pass safely down there (2Ki. 23). Even when Jerusalem was not strong enough to stop the coastal traffic, it was still feared; the Greek Seleucid generals of Syria on their way to Egypt secured the safety of their passing armies by first conquering Jerusalem before pushing on S.

1. *Major North-South Routes*. Of all ancient routes the most loaded with dramatic history is the "Way of the Sea." This was the main trail from Mesopotamia to Egypt. Century after century commercial and military expeditions were conducted between these two old power centers, and usually on this trail.

Angling SW from Mesopotamia toward the Mediterranean, the trail passed the Tadmor (Palmyra) and Damascus oases on the fringe of the desert and crossed Bashan down into the rift valley at Hazor (203-269) in the Huleh region. Going straight S, it reached the Sea of Galilee near Tiberias (201-242) and then started angling SW again up past the base of Mt. Tabor (186-232) across the valley plains of the Kishon Brook to the strategic city of Megiddo (167-221) at the opening of the chief pass across the Carmel range. This area is likely the most famous battleground of history, all the way from the contests of the ancient giant powers to the battles of this twentieth century. Known by several names, Megiddo, Jezreel, Esdraelon, Armageddon, the area reveals its importance in the last name, where it has come to stand for the climatic battle of the Judgment Day (Rev. 16:16).

Passing through the Carmel hills, the trail again heads more directly S along the coastal plains of Sharon. Nearby, Herod the Great built Caesarea (140-212), destined to be the administrative capital and leading seaport of the country (Ac. 10:23ff.). Farther S the route branched at Aphek (143-168), also known as Antipatris, near the Yarkon spring (1Sa. 4). One branch continues directly S past Gezer (142-140) and along the edges of the western foothills of Judea (Shephelah—"lowlands" when viewed from the higher range itself), until it swings out across the Philistine plain toward the sea S of Gaza (099-101) (Jdg. 16). The other branch goes immediately out to the sea at Joppa (126-162) and continues S just inside the beach dunes through Ashdod (117-129), Ashkelon (107-118), and Gaza (142-140), leading Philistine cities. Then it crosses the desert, passing the wadi of Egypt, and finally through the Desert of Shur into the Nile delta of Egypt itself.

Another route S from Mt. Tabor (186-232) continues straight S across the Kishon into the Samarian hills, and after passing Dothan (172-202) and Shechem (176-179) follows the water divide of the central hills past such venerable sites as Shiloh (177-162) (1Sa. 1), Bethel (172-148) (Ge. 28), Jerusalem (172-131), Bethlehem (169-123), Hebron (159-103), and then runs SW down to Beersheba (134-072) and on into the desert in the region of Kadesh Barnea (096-006). Finally it crosses westward from there into Egypt. The water-divide section of this route has later been called the "Way of the Patriarchs" because its towns are the settings for most of the stories about them.

There are two other notable NS routes, both of which run from Damascus down the whole length of the area E of the Jordan. The King's Highway (Nu. 20:17; 21:22) goes along the water divide at the edge of the plateau above the rift valley. "The Way of the Desert" of Moab (Dt. 2:8), or of Edom (2Ki. 3:8), skirts around the upper reaches of the canyons which cut back from the rift valley eastward into the desert fringe. This way avoids having to climb in and out of each of these canyons as the King's Highway must do, but the disadvantage is the lack of food and water, since there is scarcely a village so far out in the desert. The King's Highway in contrast went right through the heart of the populated areas. It passed through or near such towns as: Karnaim (247-249) and Ashteroth (243-244) in Bashan; Ramoth Gilead (244-210) and Rabbath Ammon (238-151) in Gilead; Heshbon (226-134) and Kir Hareseth (217-066) in Moab; and Bozrah (208-016) in Edom.

2. *Major East-West Routes*. There are several routes eastward out of Egypt across Sinai. It is not clear which one was used by the Israelites following the Exodus from oppression in Egypt. It is clear that they did not follow the Way of the Philistines, the line of forts along the shortest route across the northern Sinai peninsula. This is part of the famous Way of the Sea.

Farther S, the Way of Shur crossed the Desert of Shur (Ex. 15:22) just outside of Egypt and continued E to the area of the oasis of Kadesh Barnea (096-006). Its extension eastward was the way to the Arabah, the rift valley S of the Salt Sea.

Right across the middle of the Sinai, a vast area then called Mt. Paran in the Desert of Paran (Dt. 33:2), ran the Way to Seir (Edom). It crossed at the head of the Red Sea near Elath (150-882) and Ezion Geber (147-884). The southern-most route from Egypt dropped S along the Red Sea coast through the Desert of Sin (?) to the Desert of Sinai and Mt. Sinai (Ex. 19), traditionally located near the southern tip of the peninsula. Then it went up along the eastern branch of the Red Sea toward Seir (Edom).

The coastal Way of the Sea (Via Maris) and the King's Highway E of the Jordan finally met at Damascus, but from the Negev northward are a number of E-W trails connecting them. These routes are most easily named and identified by the junction towns, many right on the water divide of the central hills, which was a N-S route. Such junction towns are Beersheba (134-072) in the Negev, Hebron (159-103) near the high point of the Judean hills, and the Jerusalem (172-131) area where the routes passed from Joppa's seaport (126-162) (Ac. 10; Jn. 1:3; 2Ch. 2:16) to tropical Jericho (192-142). From Joppa came the Way of Beth Shemesh (147-128) up to the Sorek Valley, and the way of Beth Horon (160-143) came up a steep ridge N of the Ajalon Valley. The former crossed the divide at Jebus or Jerusalem (172-131), which is located on a small ridge below Mt. Moriah. The trail then dropped down the slopes of the Mt. of Olives by

way of the Pass of Adummim to Jericho (192-142) (Jos. 2; 15:7; 18:17). The latter crossed just N of Jerusalem and could descend to Jericho down the way of the Arabah past Ai on the slopes.

Further junction towns are Shiloh (177-162) — located in the hills of Ephraim; Shechem (176-179) on the comfortable pass cutting between Mt. Gerizim and Mt. Ebal and on down the Wadi Fari'a eastward to Adam (201-167) on the Jordan; and most famous of all, Megiddo (167-221) — not only controlling the most strategic Carmel pass just SW of it, but also on a second coast-to-valley route, the one proceeding SE down to the rift valley at Beth Shan (197-212), nestled just below Mt. Gilboa. Located at this junction between the Sharon Plain and the Huleh Valley, and also between the Galilean coastal plains and the Beth Shan Valley, Megiddo has been destroyed and rebuilt over twenty times. Today this one-time grand chariot city of King Solomon (1Ki. 9:15) and of King Ahab lies in ruins and by its name, Armageddon (Rev. 16:16), testifies to a final reckoning of God with the mighty and the proud of this world.

Akko (158-258), known also as Acre and Ptolemais (Ac. 21:7), must be mentioned as the strongest seaport of the country. From it routes crossed Lower Galilee and the rift valley to the King's Highway. One branch descended to the Plain of Gennesaret on the western shores of the Lake of Galilee and continued past Capernaum (204-254), Jesus' second home after Nazareth (178-234), and Bethsaida (208-255), up onto the Bashan plateau (Mt. 4:13; 11:23).

C. The Promised Land

This land is the Promised Land. It, or major parts of it, has been known by many names representing different languages and periods of history: Canaan, Land of the Habiru; Land of the Israelites; Israel and Judah; Palestine; Cis-Jordan and Transjordan; and the Holy Land.

This land was promised to Abraham's offspring.

Parts of God's revelation are more precisely understood in the light of certain climate and terrain in the Holy Land. For example, unless one works diligently, the stormy winter cloudbursts wash away the powdery soil pulverized by months of searing summer heat, and the land quickly turns to rocky wastes. But if worked, the fertile land gives abundant fruit. One does not learn only diligence and self-help from these conditions; the great irregularity of the winter rains in much of the country also keeps one amply aware of dependence on Providence for the success of one's crops. Topographical, climatic, and vegetational variety are immense. Snow-capped mountains and tropical valley, ocean coasts, and desert expanses exist almost side by side. A traveler from any part of the world can find something familiar, something easy and natural to understand. Since three continents meet here at this crossroad for the contact of their civilizations, it is no wonder that the caravans and the armies that have passed here are innumerable.

Just because these innumerable influences all converge on this land, one could suppose that its people would be overwhelmed by various and conflicting opinions, ideologies, philosophies, and religions. In fact, they often were overwhelmed.

But God had other plans. He chose and prepared this central location as "precisely the place" where his gospel message could be focused in explosive intensity. Here people would become so overwhelmed and emboldened by his love that they would reverse the incoming tides of influence and become themselves an influence aimed at reaching the ends of the earth.

God's style is hereby revealed. He chooses the *particular* (a man—Abraham; a nation—the Jews; his Son—Jesus . . . all in a specific location) in order to demonstrate and prove his love and faithfulness in a concrete, specific, believable way, but then the universal invitation goes out to join the particular

family he chose and is still gathering to himself. (H.R.T.R.)

GERA

1 and 2. A son and grandson of Benjamin (Ge. 46:21; 1Ch. 8:3).

3 and 4. Father of an Ehud, a Benjamite, and a descendant of Ehud, also a Benjamite (Jdg. 3:15; 1Ch. 8:7).

5. Father of the Shimei who cursed David (2Sa. 16:5).

GERAH *See* WEIGHTS AND MEASURES

GERAR A town (112-087) on an important caravan route near Gaza. Abraham and later Isaac sojourned there with King Abimelech. Here King Asa of Judah later defeated the Cushites (Ethiopians). The modern name of the site is Tell Abu Hureira (Ge. 20:12; 26:1ff.; 2Ch. 14:13-14).

GERASA, GERASENES, GERGESA *See* GADARENES

GERIZIM, MOUNT *See* GEOGRAPHY OF THE HOLY LAND

GERSHOM {traveler there}

1. One who returned from the Babylonian captivity with Ezra (Ezr. 8:2).

2. The first son of Moses, born in Midian (Ex. 2:22).

GERSHON, GERSHONITES The first son of Levi (Gen. 46:11; Ex. 6:16; 1Ch. 6:1). The Gershonite Levites were in charge of the tabernacle, the tent of meeting (Nu. 3:25-26). The family continued in the services of the temple in Solomon's time and later (1Ch. 26:21; 2Ch. 29:12).

GERUTH KIMHAM {lodging place of Kimham} An unidentified place near Bethlehem (Jer. 41:17). †

GESCHICHTE *Geschichte* is a German word in theology for "significant history," related to the subjective inner effect of an event in history on an individual. This is contrasted to *Historie*, which pertains to the objective facts of an historical ever.:. *See* HEILS-GESCHICHTE; HISTORIE

GESHAN, GESHAM A descendant of Caleb (1Ch. 2:47). †

GESHEM [rain shower] An Arab who tried to oppose the building of the walls by Nehemiah (Ne. 2:19; 6:1-6). †

GESHUR, GESHURI, GESHUR-ITES

1. A part of the area of Syria-Aram (2Sa. 15:8; Dt. 3:14). David married the daughter of one of their kings (2Sa. 3:3).

2. A people who lived in the S, the Negev, near the Philistines (Jos. 13:2).

GETHER A grandson of Shem (Ge. 10:23; 1Ch. 1:17). †

GETHSEMANE [olive oil press] The place in the Kidron Valley on the lower slopes of the Mount of Olives where Jesus prayed the evening when Judas betrayed him (Mt. 26:36; Mk. 14:32). †

GEUEL [grandeur of El] The representative of the tribe of Gad among the twelve sent by Moses to spy out the land of Canaan (Nu. 13:15). †

GEZER [*possibly* pieces] An important site (142-140) on the rise between the Aijalon and Sorek valleys guarding the most important road (the Beth Horon Road) up into the hill country of Judah. The Egyptians held it in the middle of the second millennium B.C., and the pharaoh gave it as a wedding gift to Solomon when he married a daughter of the pharaoh (Jos. 16:3; 1Ki. 9:15-17). David drove back the Philistines from Gibeon to Gezer (2Sa. 5:25). Solomon later rebuilt it.

GEZRITES *See* GIRZITES

GHOST A departed spirit or phantom (Mk. 6:49). In the KJV the word ghost means spirit. *See* SPIRIT

GIAH [bubbling spring] An unidenti-

THE GARDEN OF GETHSEMANE

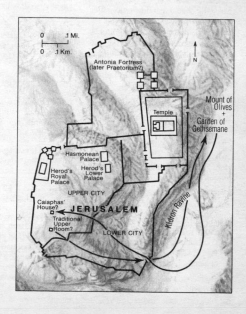

fied place near Gibeon where Joab pursued Abner (2Sa. 2:24). †

GIANTS *See* NEPHILIM

GIBBAR, GIBEON [(young vigorous) man, hero] Father of ninety-five persons who came back from the Babylonian captivity in Ezra's time. He is called Gibeon in the parallel account (Ezr. 2:20; Ne. 7:25).

GIBBETHON [mound, hill] A Levitical city (137-140) in the tribal area of Dan which the Philistines took and held for many years in spite of Israelite attempts to conquer it (Jos. 19:44; 21:23; 1Ki. 15:27; 16:15-17). †

GIBEA [mound, hill] A grandson of Caleb (1Ch. 2:49). †

GIBEAH [mound, hill]

1. A city of Benjamin (172-136) sometimes called also Gibeah of Saul, the king (Jdg. 19:12; 1Sa. 11:4). Here the concubine of the Levite was abused and murdered by the Benjamite inhabitants, leading to her dismemberment and the decimation of the men of Benjamin by the rest of Israel (Jdg. 19—20). Many important incidents in the lives of Saul and Jonathan took place here (1Sa. 10—15).

2. An unidentified town in the hill country of Judah (Jos. 15:57).

3. An unidentified town in the hill country of Ephraim where Eleazar was buried. He was one of Aaron's sons (Jos. 24:33).

GIBEAH OF GOD [hill of Elohim] An unidentified site of a Philistine outpost. Here Saul met a band of prophets and himself joined them (1Sa. 10:5).

GIBEATH [mound, hill] *See* GIBEAH 1.

GIBEATH HAARALOTH [hill of the foreskins] A hill where Joshua circumcised the Israelites after their entry into the land of Canaan from the forty years of wandering in the desert (Jos. 5:3). †

GIBEON [mound, hill] A city (167-139) in the tribal area of Benjamin. Its original inhabitants were Hivites (Jos. 9:3, 7).

Here took place the incident of the sun and moon standing still for the pursuit after the battle of Gibeon (Jos. 10). Here, too, took place the hand-to-hand fight between twelve men of Benjamin and twelve men of Judah under Abner and Joab. Since all of them died in the fight, it was a no-decision contest. A battle therefore followed (2Sa. 2:12-28). Joab slew Amasa at Gibeon, and David gave the Philistines a severe defeat there (2Sa. 20:8; 1Ch. 14:16). After the Babylonian captivity, men returned to Gibeon from Babylon and worked on the repair of Jerusalem's city wall (Ne. 3:7).

GIBEONITES [people from GIBEON] A people of the city of Gibeon, wood cutters and water carriers (Jos. 9:23). *See* GIBEON

GIBLITES *See* GEBALITES

GIDDALTI [I pronounce (God as) Great, ISBE; I reared up, KB] A temple musician in the time of David (1Ch. 25:4, 29). †

GIDDEL [big]

1 and 2. Ancestors of two groups who returned from the Babylonian captivity (Ezr. 2:47, 56; Ne. 7:49, 58). †

GIDEON [one who cuts, hacks] *See* JUDGES OF ISRAEL

GIDEONI [one who cuts, hews] The father of Abidan, the leader of the people of Benjamin (Nu. 1:11; 2:22; 7:60, 65; 10:24). †

GIDOM [a cutting off, stop pursuit] An unidentified site E of Gibeah (Jdg. 20:45). †

GIER EAGLE KJV for "osprey" (Lev. 11:18; Dt. 14:17). *See* BIRDS 5.

GIFT, GIFTS These may be natural gifts, men to men; or sacrifices, men to God; or spiritual endowments, God to men. The first may be gifts as we consider them or as it is sometimes translated as "present" or "tribute" or may even be a bribe (Ge. 33:11; 2Sa. 8:2; Pr. 18:16). The second type is the most frequently noted in the Bible (Lev. 1:10;

THE BATTLE FOR GIBEON

Five Amorite kings wanted to destroy the Gibeonites; Israel came to their aid and attacked the kings outside of Gibeon and chased them as far as Azekah and Makkedah.

17:4). People could even be referred to in this sense. The Levites were a gift to Aaron to help him (Nu. 8:19). In the third sense, God to men, the most basic gift was that of righteousness and eternal life through the life and death of Jesus Christ, his Son, given to men to be appropriated by faith (Ro. 5:15-17; 6:22-23). Beyond this, God has endowed all those in Christ with the indwelling presence of his Holy Spirit to lead, guide, and sanctify them (Ac. 2:38; 10:45). He also gives various spiritual gifts for special tasks to individuals of his choice (1Co. 12:11), such as the ability to speak in an unknown tongue, to drive out unclean spirits, to heal the sick, to prophesy, to preach, to have discernment and special knowledge (1Co. 12:8-11; Ro. 12:6; 1Co. 2:4). The presence and work of the Holy Spirit in a life is intended to produce a life that exemplifies love, joy, peace, patience, kindness, goodness, faithfulness, gentleness, and self-control (Gal. 5:22-23). *See also* GRACE; HELPS; TONGUES, GIFT OF

GIFTS, SPIRITUAL *See* GIFT, GIFTS

GIHON

1. One of the four rivers in Eden, possibly in SE Mesopotamia (Ge. 2:13). †

2. A spring in the Kidron Valley in Jerusalem. Solomon was anointed to be king here. King Hezekiah built his famous conduit here in order to get the water from the spring through the rock ridge into the city especially in time of siege (1Ki. 1:33-45; 2Ch. 32:30; 33:14).†

GILALAI A Levite musician (Ne. 12:36). †

GILBOA, MOUNT *See* GEOGRAPHY OF THE HOLY LAND

GILEAD

1. *See also* GEOGRAPHY OF THE HOLY LAND.

2. A descendant of Manasseh whose name passed over to the tribal area (Nu. 26:29-30).

3. The father of the judge Jephthah. *See* JUDGES OF ISRAEL

4. A family of the territory of Gad (1Ch. 5:11, 14).

GILGAL [circle (of stones)] The first camp (193-143) of the Israelites in Canaan after their exodus from Egypt (Jos. 4:19-20). Here Saul was made the king over Israel (1Sa. 11:15), and later angered God by acting as a priest and making a sacrifice (1Sa. 13:9).

2. An unidentified site in the story of Elijah and Elisha (2Ki. 2:1; 4:38).

3. An unidentified site whose king was defeated by Joshua (Jos. 12:23).

4. An unidentified site noted in Dt. 11:30, located in the Arabah.

5. An unidentified site noted in Jos. 15:7, located in the tribal area of Judah.

GILOH, GILONITE An unidentified village in the hill country of Judah (Jos. 15:51; 2Sa. 15:12; 23:34). †

GIMZO [place of sycamore trees] A city (145-148) of Judah in the western foothills near Beth Shemesh (2Ch. 28:18). †

GILGAL: The first camp of Israelites in Canaan

GIN *See* SNARES

GINATH The father of the Tibni who tried to seize the Israelite throne (1Ki. 16:21-22). †

GINNETHO(N), GINNETHOI A priest who came back from the Babylonian captivity with Zerubbabel; called Ginnethon in the NIV (Ne. 10:6; 12:4, 16). †

GIRDLE *See* DRESS

GIRGASHITE(S), GIRGASITE A Canaanite tribe whom God said the Israelites would drive out (Ge. 10:16; Jos. 3:10).

GIRZITES [people from GEZER] An unknown people among those raided by David when he was living in Philistine territory (1Sa. 27:8). †

GIS(H)PA An officer over the temple servants who lived on the hill of Ophel in the time of Nehemiah (Ne. 11:21; cf. Ezr. 2:43). †

GITTAH-HEPHER *See* GATH HEPHER

GITTAIM [two winepresses] A town (140-145) in Benjamin to which the Beerothites fled from Saul (2Sa. 4:3). Returnees from the Babylonian captivity settled there (Ne. 11:33).

GITTITE A name for an inhabitant of Gath (Jos. 13:3). *See* PHILISTINE CITIES

GITTITH *See* PSALMS, TITLES OF 10. (5)

GIVING

1. *See* TITHE.

2. In the NT the first Christians gave generously, according to the need (Ac. 2:42-44). A collection was made by the other churches to give to the believers in Palestine (Ac. 11:28-30; Ro. 15:25-28; 1Co. 16:1). The second letter to the Corinthian church (chaps. 8—9) discusses the collection further. The collection was to be made according to certain principles: regularly (1Co. 16:2); according to one's bounty (2Co. 8:11); willingly (2Co. 9:7). The entire gift was then sent to brothers in need in another land (1Co. 16:3). The Book of Philippians (a Macedonian church) was apparently a thank you letter for the gift given to this collection.

3. The financial structure of the local church (derived from NT verses alone), apart from the collection, is not known in detail. However, we do know that elders received "double honor," which according to the context must signify financial reward (1Ti. 5:17). (J.A.S.)

GIZONITE A man from the unknown town of Gizon who was one of David's mighty men (1Ch. 11:34). †

GLADNESS This word can have the idea of worshiping God as in the OT Psalms (Ps. 35:27). The Christians went from house to house with glad hearts giving thanks (Ac. 2:46). A similar word is "rejoice" (2Co. 13:9; Php. 2:17-18; 1Pe. 4:13).

GLASS A substance well known as early as the third millennium B.C. in Egypt and a specialty of the Phoenicians later. It is not mentioned in the OT of the NIV. The NIV notes "mirrors," but in antiquity these were made of a polished reflecting metal (Job 37:18). In the NT the word is mentioned in Rev. 4:6 (sea of glass, clear as crystal); Rev. 15:2 (sea of glass); Rev. 21:18 (glass); Rev. 21:21 (transparent glass). Glass begins to appear commonly in the archaeological records only in Roman times. *See* MIRROR

GLAZE "Like a coating of glaze over earthenware" (Pr. 26:23). In antiquity paints were sometimes rubbed on earthen vessels, hand polished to brightness, and then baked a second time to give a shiny glaze. The NIV footnote to the Proverbs text reads "of silver dross."

GLEANING About half of the appearances of this word in the OT are in the Book of Ruth. The poor were allowed to follow the reapers and gather the gleanings, or what was left—a practice established by Mosaic Law (Lev. 19:9-10; 23:22). The practice is noted throughout Israelite history (Ru. 2:2; Isa. 24:13; Mic. 7:1). The word is also used figuratively to describe the total destruction of Israel (Jer. 6:9).

GLEDE *See* BIRDS 5., *Red Kite*

GLOOM In both Testaments reference is made to the gloom of darkness. In the OT it frequently refers to the Day of the LORD as a day of gloom and punishment (Joel 2:2; Zeph. 1:15). The NT refers to the nether region of gloom where the fallen angels and others are reserved until the final day of judgment (2Pe. 2:4, 17; Jude 6).

GLORIFICATION *See* SALVATION, APPLICATION OF

GLORY OF THE LORD (SHEKINAH) God came among his people on earth in various ways. He was in the pillar of cloud and fire that led the Israelites through the wilderness in the exodus from Egypt. The word "shekinah," from the Hebrew word "to dwell," is not found in the Bible; but it was used by the early rabbinic writers to refer to the appearing of God to his people, as in the pillar of cloud and fire. For an example, God spoke to Moses through the "shekinah" out of the burning bush. Allusions to this are found in the NT in such passages as Jn. 1:14 and Ro. 9:4. Glory is both literal and spiritual in the NT, seen both physically and spiritually (Lk. 2:9; Jn. 17:22). A bright cloud overshadowed Jesus and

the three disciples on a high mountain when Jesus was transfigured. The face of Jesus shone like the sun and his garments became white like light (Mt. 17:18).

GLOSSOLALIA *See* TONGUES, GIFT OF

GLOWING METAL Eze. 1:4. *See* AMBER

GNASH *See* WEEPING AND GNASHING

GNAT *See* BEASTS 6.

GNOSTICISM [knowledge] *See* SECTS

GOAD A long wooden stick tipped with a sharp point sometimes of metal used to clean the plow tip and also to prod the plow animals if they slowed down. A judge of Israel killed 600 Philistines with one. The word is also used to illustrate the futility of kicking against a superior power. The words of the wise can be a prod, or goad. (*See* 1Sa. 13:21; Ecc. 12:11; Ac. 26:14.)

GOAH Jer. 31:39. †

GOAT *See* AZAZEL; BEASTS 4.

GOATH *See* GOAH

GOB [cistern] An unidentified place where David fought twice with the Philistines (2Sa. 21:18-19; cf. 1Ch. 20:4). †

GOD, NAMES OF; GODHEAD
1. El, Elohim (God)
2. Yahweh (the LORD)
3. El-Shaddai (God Almighty)
4. Adonai
5. Ab (God the Father)
6. The Holy Spirit
7. Alpha and Omega
8. Messiah
9. Son of God
10. Son of Man
11. The Word

Throughout the Bible the existence of one true God is never questioned. The inspired writers had no need to argue proofs of God's existence (*see* EXIS-

TENCE OF GOD). They did not describe his nature in abstract theological definitions, because God is known by what he does and what he says. Yet the many names of God reveal the many aspects of his nature and his relationship to mankind and all creation. God is the eternal Person, the only and supreme Creator of the universe, perfect in wisdom, righteousness, power, and love. God is to be worshiped, obeyed, and loved by all people.

1. *El, Elohim.* Elohim is the plural of *El,* the form most often used in the OT, translated "God" in English. This is the oldest word for God, used without specifying any particular aspect of God. It usually refers to the God of Israel, but it can be used of other gods (Dt. 5:7); and heathen nations also described their gods by this word. In the OT the plural word "Elohim" is nearly always used with a singular verb when it means the true God, but when the writer means the gods of the nations, it has a plural verb or pronoun. Many explanations of this plural form have been given—that it indicated the greatness of God, or even the three Persons of the Trinity. But since this plural is found even in heathen writings, it probably points to the concentration in one Person of the several divine powers that constitute the sum total of Deity. "Elohim" is also used to describe lesser beings. In Ps. 8:5 the LXX and KJV render it "angels." The NIV renders it "heavenly beings." It can even mean human leaders (Ps. 82:6), such as judges (Ex. 21:6; Jn. 10:34).

The singular *El* is more often joined to a further descriptive title, such as *El Roi,* "God of seeing" (Ge. 16:13); *El-Shaddai,* "God Almighty" (Ge. 17:1; Ex. 6:3).

Another title for God is *El Elyon,* "God Most High" (Ge. 14:18-20, 22), or *Elyon,* "Most high" (Nu. 24:16; Dt. 32:8; Ps. 18:14; 9:3; 21:8; 46:5; 50:14; 73:11; 77:11; 78:17; 83:18; 87:5; 91:1, 9; 92:2; 107:11; Isa. 14:14; La. 3:35, 38). Unmistakably this same title is found in the NT—with the title *God Most High* in Mk. 5:7; Lk. 2:14; 8:28; Ac. 16:17; and Heb. 7:1; and *Most High* in Lk.

1:32, 35, 76; 6:35; and Ac. 7:48.

El is also used in names of people, such as *El-eazar,* "God is helper" (Ex. 6:25), *El-hanan,* "God is gracious" (1Ch. 20:5) and many others.

2. *Yahweh.* The KJV uses Jehovah, the RSV and NIV use LORD (the NJB uses *Yahweh).* The Hebrew gives only the four consonants JHVH (or YHWH). The vowels in Jehovah are taken from the Hebrew *Adonai,* "Lord," and those in Yahweh are a probable guess. In the NIV, KJV, and RSV Yahweh is usually rendered as "LORD," in capital letters. Yahweh is the distinctive title for God among the people of Israel. It is the name by which God revealed himself to them as being the God of the Covenant, the God who chose them to be his own special people. When God made the covenant with their first parent Abraham, he revealed himself by the name *El-Shaddai,* "God Almighty" (Ge. 17:1-2; 35:11, NIV footnote; *see* 3 below). But when the time came to establish the covenant relationship with the developed nation, he used the name Yahweh, "LORD" (Ex. 6:2-9). This does not mean that the name Yahweh was unknown to Abraham or even to his predecessors (Ge. 15:7), but to Abraham in his weakness God came as the God of power, and to the nation of Israel as the God of love, the eternal God who would be faithful to the covenant by which he bound himself to them. The exact significance of YHVH cannot be decided, but the idea of "being" is certainly at the root of the name. The same root word is found in Ex. 3:14, "I AM"; but here it is *EHYEH* in Hebrew, perhaps "I will be," indicating something of the content of the name Yahweh which is used in verse 15. This was the name by which God was to be remembered by every generation of Israelites, and it was in this name that God always called them back to true faith and obedience.

Another title for God is *Yahweh Tsebaoth,* "LORD Almighty" (translated "LORD of Hosts" in some versions). In its earlier use "Hosts/Almighty" may mean the armies of Israel or the spiritual forces used by God (1Sa. 17:45). But the full sense of the title as used by the prophets (282 times) reveals God as sovereign over all the powers of the universe (Isa. 6:5; Mal. 1:14).

3. *El-Shaddai.* The name *El-Shaddai,* "God-Almighty," seems to be one of the oldest names for God. Shaddai probably means "sovereign power." It is used some fifty-five times in the OT, thirty-one of them in Job where it is always in the simple form "the Almighty." The LXX translates Shaddai as *Pantokrator,* "The All-Powerful," and it is this word which is used in the NT—once by Paul (2Co. 6:18) and eight times in Revelation.

4. *Adonai.* The English "Lord" represents two different Hebrew words, *Adonai* and *Yahweh.* Adon is commonly used of men as a term of respect, "sir" or "master." The plural Adonai described God as the supreme Master, and is written "Lord" in English Bibles. Later generations of Jews developed a rather artificial respect for the divine name Yahweh and would not say it aloud but always read out Adonai instead, so the LXX translated it as *kurios,* "Lord," making it no different from their translation of Adonai. The English "LORD" represents Yahweh, and "Lord," Adonai. Sovereign LORD, found many times in the NIV, is the translation of Adonai YHVH or LORD (Eze. 36:22ff.). In the NT Jesus is called Lord, at first as a term of respect (Mk. 7:28), but when his divine glory was realized, the title Lord made him equal to Yahweh. Words spoken of Yahweh in the OT are even applied to Christ in the NT (Heb. 1:10-12).

5. *Ab* (God the Father). God's fatherly care for his people is revealed throughout the OT, but the idea of God being Father is used only to describe their dependence on God as their Creator and therefore their obligation to him and to one another, and God's covenant relation to his chosen people (Ex. 4:22-23; Hos. 11:1; Mal. 1:6). God is clearly the Creator and Lord of all the nations, but these passages in the OT give no ground for regarding God the Father of all men in the sense of a special

personal relationship. Each is written primarily concerning Israel. It is through Jesus that the fatherhood of God comes fully in the light. He frequently calls God "My Father" (Mt. 7:21) and to his disciples says, "your Father" (Mt. 6:6; Mk. 11:25; Jn. 20:17). Jesus' prayer was that of a son talking to his father (Lk. 10:21-22; Mk. 14:36; Lk. 23:46), and ours is to be the same (Mt. 6:6-9). The nature of God's fatherhood is seen in the Sermon on the Mount (Mt. 5:43-7:11), summed up in 6:32: "Your heavenly Father knows that you need them." It involves a believing and obedient response from his children (Mt. 7:21-23), and also discipline from the Father (Heb. 12:5-11). People prove that they are true children of the Father by behaving as he does (Mt. 5:43-48). The fact that God is kind to the unjust as well as to the just does not imply that God is the Father of all men. This relationship is made only by being born anew into God's family through faith in his only Son, Jesus Christ (Jn. 1:12-13; 3:6-8; Php. 2:15; 1Pe. 1:22-23).

6. *The Holy Spirit.* The word *spirit* speaks of living breath. An attribute or work of the Spirit of God is the living energy of God active in the world and among men. The Spirit of God brought order out of chaos at Creation (Ge. 1:2); he gave intelligence and skill (Ex. 31:3), strength (Jdg. 13:25; 14:6), ecstatic utterance (1Sa. 10:10; 16:13-14), prophetic ministry (Mic. 3:8). The outpouring of this Spirit was promised in the future for all God's people, no longer for specialized individuals (Joel 2:28-29), as fulfilled on the Day of Pentecost. The name Holy Spirit is found in Isa. 63:10-11 because God is the Holy One, and this is the Spirit of God. God's holiness is the totality of his unique divine attributes. Thus the title Holy Spirit indicates that the Spirit also is divine. Since God is the supreme Person, the activity of God's Spirit must also be personal, but the OT does not clearly show that the Holy Spirit is a distinct Person within the Godhead, within the Godhead, although there are some indications of this in Isa. 48:16 and 63:14. In the NT the activity of the Spirit

comes into prominence. At first the Spirit of Prophecy is seen as in the OT. John the Baptist, the last of the prophets, is filled with the Holy Spirit from birth (Lk. 1:15). By the Spirit Zacharias prophesied (Lk. 1:67). Jesus was conceived by the Holy Spirit (Lk. 1:35), and also equipped for his ministry (Lk. 3:22; 4:1, 18). Jesus was to baptize in the Holy Spirit (Mk. 1:8), and so he promised the Spirit to his disciples (Lk. 11:13; Ac. 1:4-5). In John's Gospel the function of the Holy Spirit was amply described. He is to create new life (Jn. 3:58; 7:38-39) and continue to provide the spiritual presence of Jesus after his return to the Father (Jn. 14:16-18, 26; 15:26; 16:7-15). From these passages it is clear that the Holy Spirit is divine and personal. He is "another Counselor" ("Comforter" in the KJV), Jesus being the *first* Comforter (Jn. 14:16). The Spirit would do for them what Jesus had already been doing, but he would now work within them (Jn. 14:17), revealing the truth concerning Jesus Christ and bringing conviction to the world. The Holy Spirit is the agent of rebirth and renewal (Tit. 3:5). By the Holy Spirit the disciples became effective witnesses of Jesus Christ (Ac. 1:8; 5:32; 1Co. 2:4-5) and in many ways demonstrated the power of God in their lives. That the Holy Spirit is a distinct Person within the one Godhead is confirmed by Ac. 5:3-5, where it is said by Peter that Ananias lied to the Holy Spirit, i.e., to God. The personal action of the Holy Spirit appears in his sending out Saul and Barnabas (Ac. 13:2-4) and directing their work (Ac. 16:6); also in his giving special powers to some people as he chooses to bestow them (1Co. 12:4-11). Divine qualities of character are produced in people by the Holy Spirit (Gal. 5:22-23).

7. *Alpha and Omega*. These are the first and last letters of the Greek alphabet. The name indicates that God is eternal: nothing comes before or after him; therefore, all is under his control. He is the Almighty. Both God the Father and Jesus claim this same title (Rev. 1:8; 21:6; 22:13, 16).

8. *Messiah*. The word "Messiah" in the English text occurs only in Jn. 1:41; 4:25 in the NIV. The Hebrew word is translated in the NIV in Daniel 9:25-26 as the "Anointed One." The Hebrew word means "anointed." By being anointed with oil, men were consecrated to a special ministry. This occurred with high priests (Lev. 21:12), kings (1Sa. 24:6, 10), and prophets (Ps. 105:15). In later times the title was applied to the great Deliverer whom for centuries God had been promising for the restoration and salvation of his people. These promises were fulfilled in Jesus, who was therefore called "the Christ" (Greek for "Messiah," Jn. 1:41). The OT gives indications that this person would have divine powers (Ps. 72:5-7; 110). Jesus, the God-man, perfectly accomplished the service of the anointed priest, prophet, and king. The apostles declared that this Jesus was the expected Christ, but also the Lord (Ac. 2:36; 17:3).

9. *Son of God*. Israel is called the first-born son (Ex. 4:22-23; Hos. 1:10; 11:1). Angelic beings were also called sons of God (Job 38:7, NIV footnote), and later in writings outside the OT it was a title for the expected Messiah (*see also* BAR; BEN). A special relationship to God is therefore indicated by this name, but when Peter said, "You are the Christ, the Son of the living God," he expressed a truth so high that only God could have revealed it to him (Mt. 16:16-17). This title signified more than it did in the OT. This was the eternal Son standing in a unique relationship to God, being himself divine. The union of the divine and human had been ensured by his unique birth, so the angel told Mary, "So the holy one to be born will be called the Son of God" (Lk. 1:35). The devil recognized Jesus' divine nature when he said, "If you are the Son of God, tell these stones to become bread" (Mt.4:3; *see* 8:29). The awed disciples used this title when they saw in Jesus the power of the Creator commanding wind and wave (Mt. 14:33). The purpose of John's Gospel was to create faith that "Jesus is the Christ, the Son of God" (Jn. 20:31).

Therefore, in this Gospel the deity of Jesus is most completely revealed. The title "one and only Son" ("only begotten Son" in the KJV, "only Son" in the RSV) assures us that as the Son of God, Jesus is truly divine (Jn. 1:14, 18; 3:16). The original word does not mean that the Son was produced by the Father, but that he was the unique, divine "Son of God." Jesus rarely used the title 'Son of God' himself, but accepted it from others (Mt. 16:16; 26:63-64). For the apostles it signified the one who was the object of their highest faith and worship and the source of eternal salvation (Ro. 1:3-4; Gal. 2:20).

10. *Son of Man*. This is the name by which Jesus most frequently referred to himself. It may come from Dn. 7:13-41 where "one like a son of man" is given universal and eternal sovereignty. Jesus did not call himself Messiah because the people expected the Messiah to be a conquering warrior-king. The name "Son of Man" possibly conveyed Messianic ideas (as in Daniel) but was not associated with the false expectations of the people. In Jesus' use of it, the name was associated with his coming suffering and resurrection (Mk. 8:31) and with his coming divine glory. The Son of Man has authority to forgive sins, which only God can do (Mk. 2:7-10); he is Lord of the Sabbath (Mk. 2:28); and he will return enthroned in glory (Mt. 16:27; 24:30; 25:31). The name combines the reality of his human life with the highest authority of his divine status.

11. *The Word*. The Greek word *logos*, translated "Word" in Jn. 1:114, signifies not only speech, but the context of speech, the reason and wisdom which are expressed in the uttered word. A man's words tell what is in his mind. His very personality is made known by his words, and by them his purposes are put into effect. When the Son of God came into the world in the person of Jesus, the personality of the unseen God was visibly made known, and his saving purposes were put into effect. Jesus is therefore rightly called "the Word." He is not a being halfway between God and

man. He is God yet not the same person as was God the Father, for "the Word was God," and yet at the same time "The Word was with God" (Jn. 1:1). By the word, God created the universe, for "by the word of the LORD were the heavens made, their starry host by the breath of his mouth" (Ps. 33:6, 9). Likewise, of the Word, John wrote, "Through him all things were made" (Jn. 1:3). Although Greek and Jewish philosophers also used this title *logos*, it was not from them that John gathered it. The origins of this title for the Son of God are rather to be seen in the OT as in Ps. 33 and Pr. 8, where wisdom is regarded almost as a person equal with God in his creative power. (J.C.C.)

GOD-FEARER A class of people found in the ancient world. These people were monotheists and subscribed to certain practices of Judaism and the synagogue. They were less committed than Jewish proselytes, for they were uncircumcised. Ancient literature has made multiple reference to them, and in 1976 an inscription was found in ancient Aphrodesia, thought by some to be a reference to this class of people (Ac. 10:2, 22; 13:16, 26, 43; 16:14; 17:4, 17; 18:7).

GODS, GODDESS *See* DEITIES; GOD, NAMES OF 1.

GODLINESS *See* HOLINESS; SALVATION, APPLICATION OF

GOG
1. A descendant of Reuben (1Ch. 5:4). †
2. The chief prince of Meshech and Tubal of the land of Magog. Gog is the leader of the hosts of evil against God and his people in the end of days, the nations which Satan will lead (Eze. 38; 39:1-11; Rev. 20:7-10). †

GOIIM {nations, Gentiles} A people whose king was Tidal and who were involved in the battle at Sodom in Abraham's day (Ge. 14:1, 9). † *See also* GENTILES; NATION

GOLAN A city (238-243) in Bashan in the tribal area of Manasseh E of the

Jordan in the N. It was a Levitical city of refuge (Dt.4:43; Jos. 20:8; 21:27; 1Ch. 6:71). †

GOLD *See* PRECIOUS STONES AND METALS, Metals 3.

GOLDEN CALF *See* IDOL

GOLDSMITH A craftsman in gold (Isa. 40:19; 41:7; 46:6; Jer. 10:9, 14; 51:17; Ne. 3:8, 31-32). †

GOLGOTHA {skull} The place of Christ's crucifixion, the anglicized version of an Aramaic and Greek word meaning "skull." The Latin word for the same is *calvarius*, from which comes our word *Calvary*. All refer to the same place outside the city wall of Jerusalem (Mt. 27:33; Mk. 15:22; Jn. 19:17). Two possible sites have been suggested in modern Jerusalem. †

GOLIATH A giant in the army of the Philistines who defied Israel to send out a single champion for a duel. David killed him by felling him with a slingshot and then cutting off his head (1Sa. 17: 4, 8, 23; 21:9; 22:10; 2Sa. 21:19; 1Ch. 20:5). †

GOMER {complete}

1. Eldest son of Japheth, grandson of Noah, whose name was passed on to a people, perhaps the Greeks named Cimmerians (Ge. 10:2-3; 1Ch. 1:5-6; Eze. 38:6). †

2. The wife of the prophet Hosea (Hos. 1:3, 6, 8). †

GOMORRHA, GOMORRAH {to overwhelm with water} One of the five cities of the plain at the southern end of the Salt Sea. Its site is not identified. God destroyed it because of the wickedness of its people, and it is held up in later biblical history as an example of depravity and subsequent judgment and destruction (Ge. 10:19; 13:10; Dt. 29:23; Isa. 13:19; Mt. 10:15; Jude 7).

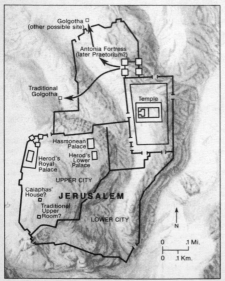

GOLGOTHA

Golgotha (other possible site)

Antonia Fortress (later Praetorium?)

Traditional Golgotha

Temple

Hasmonean Palace

Herod's Royal Palace

Herod's Lower Palace

UPPER CITY

Caiaphas' House?

JERUSALEM

Traditional Upper Room?

LOWER CITY

N

0 .1 Mi.

0 .1 Km.

GONG *See* MUSIC, MUSICAL INSTRUMENTS

GOODNESS Goodness is an attribute of God (1Ch. 16:34; Ps. 118:1). His kindness comes from that goodness. Its opposite is, of course, evil. The believer is to exhibit moral goodness, for it is a fruit of the Spirit (Gal. 5:22; cf. Ro. 15:14; Eph. 5:9). *See* VIRTUE AND VICE LISTS

GOOD NEWS *See* GOSPEL; NEWS, GOOD

GOPHER WOOD *See* TREES, Other Trees, *Cypress*

GOSHEN
1. A city (137-087) of Judah located in the hill country near Debir (Jos. 15:51).
2. A geographical area occupied by Joshua, somewhere in the southern part of Palestine, the Negev (Jos. 10:41; 11:16).
3. The "Land of Goshen" in Egypt, probably in the NE part of the delta, where the Israelites spent their 400 years in Egypt (Ge. 45:10; Ex. 9:26).

GOSPEL [good news] A word used in the NT, derived from an Anglo-Saxon word which means "good news." In current usage reference is either to the essence of Christianity or to the books in which are found the story of Christ's life and teaching. The good news was that Christ died according to the Scriptures to accomplish redemption (Mk. 1:1; Ro. 1:2; 1Co. 15:1-4). *See also* EVANGELISM; GOSPELS, THE FOUR

GOSPELS, THE FOUR The four Gospels form one pillar of the historical testimony concerning the origin of Christianity, the other pillar being the testimony of Paul, linked to the Book of Acts.

There is good reason for advocating the traditional authorship of the Gospels: two by apostles, Matthew and John; two by men closely associated with apostles, Mark with Peter and Luke with Paul. We are thus assured of the highest degree of historic truth from eyewitness sources (Lk. 1:1-4). If the apostolic link with

Christ and the beginnings of Christianity would be broken by denying the truthfulness of the Gospels, the church's own testimony to her origins is destroyed and nothing has been or can be devised to fill up the gap. It is good history and good sense to face the issue of the deity of Christ and the truths of his claims, for thus a reasonable explanation of the origin of the church is provided, and we can have a reasonable hope of the success of the church's mission in the world. If the church has grossly erred in its account of its own origin, what confidence can we have in the rest of its message?

The Gospels are not complete biographies of Jesus Christ. Rather, the emphasis falls on those parts of his life which are of decisive importance for human redemption. Hence, all four Gospels clearly regard Jesus as the Son of God, basing this conviction on his own revealed self-consciousness of who he was and is and his purpose in coming into the world. Proceeding from this unanimous perspective, each of the Gospels emphasizes certain features of Jesus' work and person that are relevant to basic human needs.

From a combined report of the four Gospels, we learn of Jesus' birth at Bethlehem in the time of Herod the Great (5 or 6 B.C.), when Augustus was Caesar. The early church, in calculating the year from the founding of Rome which they proposed to designate as the year 1, erred. When the error was discovered, so many dates had been fixed on this erroneous basis that the date of the birth of Christ was expressed as B.C. and is recognized as an anachronism. One scene from the Lord's youth is given in Luke 2, as he stands in the temple in the midst of the teachers, amazing them with his understanding and answers. The years intervening up to the time of the beginning of Jesus' ministry are passed over in silence by the Gospels, leaving us to infer that he must have been reared as a carpenter's son in Nazareth.

Highly significant events mark the beginning of Christ's work. His baptism, associated with the descent of the Spirit as a dove, explains his name and title as the Anointed One (Messiah, Christ). He, marked by the presence of the Holy Spirit as the eternal Son of God, has grace and power to bring many sons into glory by his redeeming work.

His temptation followed his baptism. In the biblical scheme of redemption it is clear that Christ as the Second Adam vindicated himself by successfully overcoming the tempter and temptations before Adam fell. He thus proceeded to accomplish the redemptive work laid out for him. It was fitting and proper that he, through whom and for whom all things are, in bringing many sons into glory, himself be made perfect through sufferings. Jesus established a residence in Capernaum and returned to Judea for a preliminary ministry. He and John the Baptist ministered concurrently until John was imprisoned. Jesus then moved to Galilee where he ministered about a year and a half. The Synoptic Gospels (Matthew, Mark, and Luke) have a very similar outline which gives much detail about this Galilean ministry. The whole narrative shows the plan and will of Christ leading toward a clearly defined goal.

Jesus' work in Galilee began with his appearance at Nazareth (Lk. 4) and his claim, in the words of Isaiah, that the Spirit of God was enabling him to preach and minister. He was rejected and proceeded to present himself in the synagogue at Capernaum, showing his power to heal, challenging the evil power of Satan. Part of Christ's plan was to establish a community in the world, and to that end he chose men whom he appointed as apostles and trained for that great and momentous task. The Synoptic Gospels list their names. The twelve are divided into three groups of four. The first name of each group is always the same; the order of others within the group may vary. Peter is always first; Philip always fifth; James of Alphaeus always ninth. The first group is the two pairs of brothers: Peter and Andrew, James and John. Philip and Bartholomew (Nathanael), Matthew and Thomas compose the second group. James of Alphaeus, Simon the Canaanaean, Judas of James, and Judas Iscariot complete the list.

The work of teaching, training, and healing progressed in the face of increasing opposition. After the Twelve were chosen, it was logical and necessary to lay before them the challenging outline of teaching which Jesus had in mind. This we find in the famous Sermon on the Mount, delivered in the spring or early summer probably at the Horns of Hattin, overlooking the Sea of Galilee. The sermon began with the Beatitudes, which analyzed the law which underlies them. It called men to seek the grace of God, assuring them that if they, being evil, knew how to give good gifts to their children, in infinitely greater degree would their heavenly Father give good gifts to those who seek him. Jesus' own claim to lordship dominated the discourse, and he presented himself as final Judge of the eternal destinies of man. The message concluded with the vivid pictures of the foolish and wise men building respectively on the sand or the rock of Jesus' teachings.

The work in Galilee continued. The servant of the centurion in Capernaum was healed; demons were cast out, occasioning the bitter taunt that he cast out demons by complicity with Beelzebub.

The increase of suspicion and opposition led to a new form of teaching, the parables spoken by the sea. Because of the simplicity and naiveté and charm of the parable, even the hostile and dull heard him and got the main point that men must choose for or against the grace of God. The best known parable, under the figure of the sower, shows four relations of men to the message of God. The seed has no effect on the hard-trodden path where the birds can take the seed away immediately. Shallow, stony soil induces a quick generation, but gives no depth for rootage and growth. Thorns and weeds in another person can prevent fruitful maturity of the seed. Few hearers would miss the lesson of the good ground where the seed produces a crop. The notable miracle of stilling the storm on Galilee falls in this period of Jesus' ministry.

As the Galilean work neared completion, Jesus sent out the Twelve in pairs to minister. They returned, exulting in the power and results — even the devils were subject to the name of Jesus. Their return from this period of labor culminated in retirement to the E of the Jordan in the territory of Bethsaida. The eager multitude followed and was miraculously fed. John 6 shows that Passover was near. This Passover was just a year from the Crucifixion.

The remainder of the time in Galilee was especially devoted to training the Twelve for their future work. A lengthy journey to Tyre and Sidon gave relief from the busy public ministry. The return journey followed a wide circuit through the Decapolis beyond the Jordan, ending in the miraculous feeding of four thousand probably on the SE shore of the lake. Who would fail to see the parallel between One who could create food for the hungry and One who gave manna in the wilderness? Jesus' journeys of retirement and instruction next led to Caesarea Philippi (Banias). Peter, speaking for all, confessed Jesus as Messiah, and on that fact was based Jesus' subsequent teaching and action. Thence forward, Jesus walked purposefully to the cross, and the fact and meaning of his death were made ever clearer.

The months between late summer of the year A.D. 29 and the Passover of the year 30 were devoted to Jesus' concluding ministry in all parts of the land. The fall and winter brought the notable visit to Jerusalem at Tabernacles (Jn. 7–10), a period of travel and teaching (Lk. 9–18), a visit to Jerusalem at Dedication (Hanukkah) (Jn. 10), and a brief visit from retirement beyond Jordan to the raising of Lazarus from death (Jn. 11). This miracle crystallized the opposition to Jesus and led to his retirement to the territory of Ephraim until the time came to make his final journey to Jerusalem.

The events of the Passover week are told in detail, occupying nearly half of the Gospel narratives. This literary fact corresponds to the emphasis the church later gave to the proclamation of Jesus' death and resurrection, in accordance with Jesus' own emphasis.

Jesus arrived in Bethany Sabbath eve, March 31 (8 Nisan), A.D. 30. At supper came Mary's beautiful act of devotion in anointing Jesus. Judas was present and Jesus' rebuke helped explain Judas' treachery (Jn. 12). On Sunday Jesus crossed the Mount of Olives at Bethphage, securing a donkey to ride to the city, thus clearly presenting himself in the manner of the ancient kings in what is traditionally known as the Triumphal Entry.

On Monday began a series of incidents which led to the cross. Jesus asserted his authority, casting out of the temple the money changers and tradesmen. When challenged, he answered with the question, "John's baptism, was it from heaven, or from men?" (Mt. 21:25).

Tuesday brought the lesson in prayer taught by the withered fig tree and a series of conversations with opponents who sought to catch Jesus in some utterance. With majestic wisdom and confidence Jesus subdued his questioners and then put forth his own question, "What do you think about the Christ? Whose son is he?" (Mt. 22:42). The day closed as Jesus and his apostles gathered on the Mount of Olives for the conference at which Jesus presented the scenario of the last things, known as the Olivet Discourse (Mt. 24). The central point of the discourse finds its parallel in the Book of Daniel. Jesus predicted in the last days the appearance of the abomination mentioned by Daniel (Da. 9), and he said that this event will be the sign of his return in the clouds of heaven.

Wednesday was spent in retirement. On Thursday, April 6, 14 Nisan, Jesus sent Peter and John to prepare the Passover, and that evening Jesus and the twelve celebrated it. In connection with the Passover meal, Jesus instituted the symbolic and memorial supper observed by the church ever since. (*See* LORD'S SUPPER.)

After the supper, with the help of Judas, Jesus' enemies arrested him in Gethsemane; and after early morning ecclesiastical trials sent Jesus to Pontius Pilate. Jesus died claiming he was the Messiah. Pilate, though admitting Jesus' innocence of any capital crime, delivered him over to be crucified. It is well that Jesus taught in advance of the event the true meaning of his death so that what seems so senseless and tragic is seen to be a triumphant act of divine grace: the Lamb of God bears the sin of the world. Jesus was crucified on Friday, 15 Nisan, April 7, A.D. 30, outside the city. The ancient rubric (statute) for the sin offering directed that the body of the Asham (sin offering) be deposited outside the city. Because the darkness was coming late on Preparation (Friday), Jesus was laid in a tomb nearby. His friends rested on the Sabbath, and early on the first day of the week, when they came with spices to prepare his body for proper burial, found the tomb empty. An angel announced that he had risen, and later that day on five occasions Jesus appeared to his friends.

On these simple facts rest the church and its testimony. The courage and conviction arising in the hearts of those who believed in Jesus led to the establishment of the church. The presence of a risen Savior with his church ever since is the only adequate explanation of its existence and persistence through history. (W.B.W.)

GOTHIC VERSIONS See BIBLE VERSIONS

GOUGE See BLINDNESS

GOURD See PLANTS, PERFUMES, AND SPICES, Miscellaneous Plants 6.

GOVERNMENTS KJV for "administration" in the sense of a spiritual gift (1Co. 12:28). See GIFTS; SPIRITUAL GIFTS

GOVERNOR One who rules an area, territory, or province on behalf of a supreme ruler to whom he is responsible. The Bible mentions both Jewish and non-Jewish governors: Joseph in Egypt, Daniel in Babylon, Gedaliah in Jerusalem appointed by a foreign ruler, Tattenai, and Nehemiah (Ge. 42:6; Da. 2:48; Jer. 40:5; Ezr. 5:3; Ne. 5:14).

GOYIM {nations, Gentiles}
1. An unidentified place in Gilgal (Jos. 12:23). † *See* GOIIM
2. *See also* HAROSHETH HAG-GOYIM.

GOZAN One of the cities in NE Mesopotamia through which the Habor River flowed and in which some of the Israelites were placed in captivity by the Assyrian king (2Ki. 17:6; 18:11; 19:12; 1Ch. 5:26; Isa. 37:12). †

GRACE The word "grace" is found very frequently in the NT, but relatively infrequently in the OT, and there the reference is almost always to God's grace. (In the OT the word that is rendered "grace" in the KJV is frequently rendered in the NIV as "kind favor.") Grace in the NT has a Christian theological meaning: God's free and unmerited love and favor for sinful man shown when he "did enter into a covenant of grace, to deliver them out of the estate of sin and misery, and to bring them into an estate of salvation by a Redeemer." The Redeemer is "the Lord Jesus Christ, who, being the eternal Son of God, became man, and so was, and continueth to be God and man in two distinct natures and one person forever." The redemption was achieved by Christ's "once offering up himself a sacrifice to divine justice, and reconciling us to God, and in making continual intercession for us." (The three quotations are from the Westminster Shorter Catechism.) This is the grace of the NT where God himself in the person of the Son sacrificed himself in the Crucifixion and thereby reconciled the sinner to God and made himself propitious to that sinner. This is free grace, not earned or earnable by man. The classical references in the NT are found in Eph. 2:1-22 and 3:1-7. *See also* EXPIATION; PROPITIATION; SALVATION, APPLICATION OF

GRAIN See PLANTS 1.

GRANARY See STOREHOUSE

GRAPE See PLANTS, PERFUMES, AND SPICES

GRASS See PLANTS, PERFUMES, AND SPICES

GRASSHOPPER See BEASTS 6.

GRATE, GRATING A copper piece that was used in the tabernacle in relation to the sacrifices. Rendered "network" in the NIV (Ex. 27:4; 35:16; 38:4-5).

GRAVE See DEAD, ABODE OF

GRAVE CLOTHES See BURIAL; CHRIST, WORK OF 4., *The Burial of Christ*

GRAVEN IMAGE {carved image} See DEITIES

GREAT LIZARD See BEASTS 6.

GREAT OWL See BIRDS 5.

GREAVES See ARMS AND ARMOR

GRECIA, GRECIANS, GREECE See GEOGRAPHY OF THE HOLY LAND; GREEK

GRECIAN JEWS Hellenists were Greek-speaking Jews (Ac. 6:1; 9:29). They were in contrast with the group of Christians that likely spoke Aramaic or possibly Hebrew. Since the word "Hellenists" was not used by any writer prior to Luke, the author of Acts, it is not known if Hellenists also practiced Greek customs and Greek practices.

GREED See COVET

GREEK In the NIV the word is used in three senses: Greek nationality, Greek language, and in the sense of non-Greek (sometimes Jew). The NT was written in the Greek language and the OT was translated into Greek in a version known as the Septuagint (LXX). This latter version was begun in Egypt, early in the third century B.C. The word is used only once in the OT where God was rebuking the Phoenicians and Philistines for sell-

ing the people of Judah and Jerusalem to the Greeks (Joel 3:6; Jn. 19:20). See BIBLICAL LANGUAGES; MACCABEES

GREYHOUND KJV, NKJV in Pr. 30:31. The RSV, NASB, NEB, JB, NIV renders this same word "rooster" based on the interpretation by ancient versions (the Vulgate and others) of this now obscure Hebrew word. See BIRDS 2.

GRIND See MILL, MILLSTONE

GROUND See EARTH

GROVE KJV for a pagan deity, *Asherah* or *Asherim*, in many places in the Old Testament. See DEITIES 2., *Pagan gods*

GUARANTEE A pledge or assurance that something will be done as specified. Used only in the NT and there in the sense that God has given his Holy Spirit to all believers as a guarantee of their ultimate resurrection and salvation (2Co. 1:22; 5:5; Eph. 1:14). In the OT the word "pledge" is in the Judah-Tamar account (Ge. 38:18). See SEAL

GUARD See WATCHMEN, WATCHTOWER

GUDGODAH A stop on the Israelite exodus from Egypt, in the deep S of the Negev (Dt. 10:7). †

GUEST CHAMBER An eating hall. See UPPER ROOM

GUILE KJV for "falseness, trickery, deceit" and similar ideas.

GUILT, GUILTINESS The words *guilty, guilt,* and *guiltless* are found many times in the Bible, most of them in the OT. This is to be expected since the OT makes so much more of law than does the NT. To be guilty is to be deserving of punishment for the breaking of a law or the failure to conform to it. As ignorance of the law is no excuse in modern society, so it was in the OT (Lev. 5:17). God set up that society so that there was collective guilt for law breaking (Jos. 22:20). In the NT Jesus placed a great emphasis on the importance of the attitude of the heart in law-keeping as over against mere outward conformity to law (Mt. 5:17-48). In Ro. 5:12-21 Paul taught that the guilt of Adam in his first sin was imputed to all his progeny (descendants). It is stated (v. 12) that all men sinned together with him in that sin, even though they were not yet born. *See* IMPUTE

GUILT OFFERING *See* SACRIFICES AND OFFERINGS

GULL *See* BIRDS 5.

GUNI, GUNITE(S) [spotted sand grouse]

1. A son of Naphtali, and his clan (Ge. 46:24; Nu. 26:48; 1Ch. 7:13). †
2. A man of Gad (1Ch. 5:15). †

GUR An elevated area N of Samaria where Jehu's men mortally wounded Ahaziah the king of Judah (2Ki. 9:27). †

GUR BAAL A city or town where some Arabs lived, against whom King Uzziah of Judah fought. Location is thought to be somewhere in Edom or in the southern Negev (2Ch. 26:7). †

GUTTER *See* AQUEDUCT

H

HAAHASHTARI {the Ahashtarites} A descendant of Judah (1Ch. 4:6). †

HABAIAH {Yahweh has hidden} *See* HOBAIAH

HABAKKUK, BOOK OF {garden plant, KB} *See* PROPHETS, BOOKS OF THE MINOR

HABAZINIAH, HABAZZINIAH {*possibly* exuberant in Yahweh} One of the family of the Recabites (Jer. 35:3). †

HABERGEON KJV for "coat of mail" and "armor" (2Ch. 26:14; Ne.4:16). *See* ARMS AND ARMOR; WAR

HABIRU An ancient Near Eastern name of an ethnic or social class of people. There is no certainty that these are the Hebrew people. *See* HEBREW

HABOR *See* GOZAN

HAC(H)ALIAH The father of Nehemiah (Ne. 1:1; 10:1). †

HACHILAH {dark} *See* HAKILAH

HAC(H)MONI, HAC(H)MONITE {wise} One from Hachmon who was one of David's mighty men (1Ch. 11:11; cf. 2Sa. 23:8). † Father of one of the men who attended David's sons (1Ch. 27:32). †

HADAD {thunderer (Semitic storm god); *(except 2.)*}
  1. *See* HADAD RIMMON.
  2. A son of Ishmael (Ge. 25:15); {sharp}.

3 and 4. Two kings of Edom (1Ch. 1:46, 50).
  5. A prince of Edom who fled to Egypt in David's days and returned when Solomon became king (1Ki. 11:14-19, 21-22). *See also* HADAR

HADADEZER {(pagan god) HADAD is a help} King of Zobah who ruled an area NE of Damascus and conquered all the way to the Upper Euphrates. David fought several battles with him and, after defeating him, put a garrison in Damascus and took tribute from him (2Sa. 8:3-8; 10:6-14, 15-18; 1Ch. 18:3-10).

HADAD RIMMON A combination of two names, Hadad and Rimmon. The first is the Amorite storm god, perhaps the god of thunder. The second is either another similar deity or a title for Hadad. A great mourning was made for this deity in the Valley of Megiddo (Zec. 12:11; cf. 2Ki. 5:18). †

HADAR {thunder, Semitic storm god} A variant of Hadad 3 (Ge. 36:39).

HADASHAH {new} A village in the tribal area of Judah in the western foothills (Jos. 15:37). †

HADASSAH {myrtle, BDB and KB; *possibly* myrtle *or* bride, IDB} A Jewish girl who became the queen of the Persian king Xerxes (Est. 2:7), who was instrumental in saving her people from their destruction planned by Haman. † *See* ESTHER

HADATTAH [new] *See* HAZOR HADATTAH

HADES [the underworld] *See* DEAD, ABODE OF

HADID [sharp] A village (145-152) in the tribal area of Benjamin at the NW corner of the western hill country, together with Lydda and Ono and others that were at the mouth of the Valley of Aijalon (Ezr. 2:33; Ne.7:37; 11:34), to which several hundred returned from the captivity in Babylon. †

HADLAI [resting, ISBE; fat, IDB; be stout, KB] Father of one of the chiefs of the Ephraimites (2Ch. 28:12). †

HADORAM [HADAD is exalted]
1. A descendant of Shem (Ge. 10:27; 1Ch. 1:21). †
2. Son of Tou, the king of Hamath, who was sent to congratulate David on his victory over the king of Zobah; also called Joram (2Sa. 8:9; 1Ch. 18:10). † *See* JORAM 3.
3. King Rehoboam's taskmaster over his labor force (2Ch. 10:18, NIV footnote). *See* ADONIRAM

HADRACH A town in the NW part of Lebanon (Zec. 9:1). †

HAELEPH A word whose meaning is not certain, found only in Jos. 18:28. Some suggest that it is to be joined with the preceding word as a proper noun, a name of an unidentified place. †

HAGAB [locust] The ancestor of a family that returned from the Babylonian captivity (Ezr. 2:46; cf. Ne. 7:48). †

HAGABA, HAGABAH [locust] Ancestor or ancestors of some who returned from the Babylonian captivity with Zerubbabel (Ezr. 2:45; Ne. 7:48). †

HAGAR, HAGARENES, HAGARITE(S), HAGERITE, HAGRITE
1. The Egyptian slave girl of Sarah, Abraham's wife, who was given to Abraham as a concubine. The son of this union was Ishmael who at Sarah's instigation was driven away. Ishmael became an ancestor of Arabs. His wife was

an Egyptian. Paul uses Sarah and Hagar figuratively for the difference between law and grace (Ge. 16:1, 4, 15; 21:14; Gal. 4:24-25).
2. A people descended from Hagar (1Ch. 5:10, 19-20; 27:31). †

HAGARENES, HAGARITE(S) *See* HAGRITE

HAGGAI, BOOK OF [festal, BDB; born on the feast day, KB] *See* PROPHETS, BOOKS OF THE MINOR

HAGGEDOLIM [the great ones] Father of one of the overseers in the time of Nehemiah after the return from the Babylonian captivity (Ne. 11:14). †

HAGGERI *See* HAGRI

HAGGI, HAGGITES [festal, BDB; born on the feast day, KB] A son of Gad (Ge. 46:16; Nu. 26:15). †

HAGGIAH [feast of Yahweh] A descendant of Levi (1Ch. 6:30). †

HAGGITH [festal, BDB; born on the feast day, KB] A wife of David and mother of Adonijah who tried to take the throne in place of Solomon to whom David had promised it (2Sa. 3:4; 1Ki. 1:5, 11; 2:13; 1Ch. 3:2). †

HAGIOGRAPHA *See* TANAKH, *Writings*

HAGRI Father of one of David's mighty men (2Sa. 23:36; 1Ch. 11:38). †

HAGRITE [*possibly* people from Hagar] A nomadic tribe living E of the Jordan in Moab, descendants of Hagar and enemies of Israel. The Reubenites conquered them (1Ch. 5:10, 19-20; Ps. 83:6). One of them was overseer of David's flocks (1Ch. 27:30).

HAHIROTH [mouth of the canals *or* temple of the Syrian goddess] The same as Pi Hahiroth (Nu. 33:8, NIV footnote).

HAI [the ruin] *See* AI

HAIL
1. A greeting used only in the Gospels (Jn. 19:3).
2. Hailstorms are recorded in the

Bible as doing much damage to crops and to life of men and animals. They are often accompanied with violent wind, rain, or snow (Ex. 9:18-34; Jos. 10:11; Eze. 38:22; Isa. 30:30; Ps. 148:8). This was a phenomenon of nature God often used to punish the people.

HAIR Nazirites — Samson, and others — were never allowed to cut their hair. It may be that long hair was preferred by Israelite men (Nu. 6:1, 5; Jdg. 13:5; 2Sa. 14:25-26). It was forbidden to the men of Israel to cut the corners of the beard, the hair above and to the face side of the ear (Lev. 19:27). Today the *pe'ot* or "prayer-locks" reflect this commandment. In the NT, however, long hair on men was considered a disgrace (1Co. 11:14). Hair turning white quickly on the body could be a sign of leprosy, but if there was no raw flesh, then the leprosy was considered healed. Thin yellow hair was a symptom of another disease — not leprosy but related to it (Lev. 13:9-17, 29-37; 14:9).

HAKELDAMA NASB for Akeldama. *See* AKELDAMA

HAKILAH A hill somewhere in the region of Hebron where David hid from King Saul (1Sa. 23:19; 26:1-3). † *See* KEILAH

HAKKATAN [the small one] A man that came up from the Babylonian captivity with Ezra (Ezr. 8:12). †

HAKKOZ [the thorn]
1. One of the priests mentioned in the divisions of the "sons of Aaron" (1Ch. 24:10).
2. One of the priests coming back after the exile in Babylon with Zerubbabel; he could not find his family record (Ezr. 2:61; Ne. 3:4, 21; 7:63). †

HAKUPHA [crooked] Ancestor of some temple servants who returned with Zerubbabel from the Babylonian captivity (Ezr. 2:51; Ne. 7:53). †

HALAH A town in Assyria on the Habor River where the Assyrian king ex-iled some of the Israelite captives (2Ki. 17.6; 18:11; 1Ch. 5:26). †

HALAK, MOUNT OF [bare, bald] The southern limit of the conquest of Joshua, a mountain ridge (Jos. 11:16-17; 12:7). †

HALHUL A town (160-109) in the hill country of Judah near Hebron (Jos. 15:58). †

HALI [adornment] A town (164-241) on the southern border of the tribe of Asher (Jos. 19:25). †

HALL A room hall or pillared porch (colonnade) for living or eating or an audience room for judgment (1Ki. 7:67; Da. 5:10; Ac. 25:23).

HALLEL [praise] One of the groups of psalms called the "Hallel" is Psalms 113 to 118. This Hallel was recited in the homes in celebration of the Passover. The latter part of this Hallel (Psalms 115-118), was sung at the end of the supper. Then possibly other psalms were sung, such as Psalms 120 to 136, especially 136 (See Mt. 26:30; Mk. 14:26). *See* SONGS OF ASCENT

HALLELUJAH A word used widely in the Bible and transliterated in basically this form into many languages; a Hebrew word consisting of two parts, *hallelu* meaning "You all praise!" and *ya*, a shortened form for the word LORD (Yahweh). *See* GOD, NAMES OF, GODHEAD 2.; PRAISE

HALLOHESH [the whisperer] Father of one who worked on Nehemiah's wall and perhaps the same as one who signed the covenant with Nehemiah (Ne. 3:12; 10:24). †

HALLOW, HALLOWED [to render as holy] *See* HOLINESS; CONSECRATION

HALOHESH *See* HALLOHESH

HAM
1. A son of Noah and father of Cush, Egypt, Put, and Canaan. See further on each of these four. While they may have all been dark skinned, they were not the

forefathers of the negroid races, but rather of peoples associated with Egypt in the N of the continent of Africa. The Egyptians thought of Canaan as one of their provinces even into very late times (Ge. 5:32; 10:6; Ps. 105:23, 27).

2. Another name for Egypt as in Ps. 105:23.

3. A city (226-213) of the Zuzim, situated on the King's Highway. Not related to the son of Noah (Ge. 14:5).

HAMAN The enemy of the Jews in the days of Esther who endeavored to have them all destroyed. He himself was hanged on the gallows he prepared for Mordecai, the uncle of Queen Esther (Est. 3:1—7:10).

HAMATH, HAMATHITE(S) [fortress]
1. *See* GEOGRAPHY OF THE HOLY LAND.
2. A very ancient and important town situated on the Orontes River in northern Syria. It was founded in neolithic times according to its excavators. The Israelite spies went that far N (Nu. 13:21), but the Israelites did not control it until the time of Jeroboam II of Israel who "recovered" it for Israel (2Ki. 14:28; 1Ch. 13:5; Am. 6:14).
3. A people from Hamath (Ge. 10:18; 1Ch. 1:16).

HAMATH ZOBAH [fortress of ZOBAH] An unidentified town known by this name, by the name Zobah, or even by the name of Hamath, belonging to the kingdom of Zobah—mentioned only once (2Ch. 8:3). †

HAMMATH [hot springs]
1. A city (201-241) in the tribal area of Naphtali located on the western shore of the Sea of Galilee (Jos. 19:35).
2. Archaeologists know of a Hammath in the Jordan valley S of Beth Shan (197-197).
3. A town or area from which came the Kenites who were descended from Caleb (1Ch. 2:55). *See* HAMMOTH DOR

HAMMEDATHA [given by the moon (god)] Father of the villain of the Book of Esther, Haman (Est. 3:1, 10; 8:5; 9:10, 24). †

HAMMELECH [the king] KJV transliteration in Jer. 36:26; 38:6; translated "the king" in most versions. *See* KING, KINGSHIP

HAMMER These were of two types, the hammer proper or the mallet for driving tent pegs. Both are called hammers in the NIV. Figuratively the hammer is the instrument God on occasion uses in punishment (Jdg. 4:21; Jer. 23:29), called "war club" in Jer. 51:20.

HAMMOLECHETH, HAMMO-LEKETH [the queen] Sister of Gilead and ancestress of several groups in the tribe of Manasseh (1Ch. 7:18). †

HAMMON [hot spring]
1. A place (164-281) in the tribal area of Asher S of Tyre (Jos.19:28). †
2. A Levitical city in Naphtali of unidentified location (1Ch. 6:76). †

HAMMOTH DOR [hot spring of DOR] An unidentified city of Naphtali (Jos. 21:32). †

HAMMUEL [El (god) of Ham, KB] A descendant of Simeon (1Ch. 4:26). †

HAMMURABI, CODE OF *See* BABYLON, BABYLONIA, ¶ 2.

HAMONAH [multitude] An unidentified city where the hosts of Gog are to be destroyed after an unsuccessful attack on Israel (Eze. 39:16). †

HAMON GOG [multitude of GOG] A valley which is to be set aside for the burial of the dead after the battle of Gog against Israel (Eze. 39:11, 15). †

HAMOR [male donkey] The father of the Shechem who violated Dinah, Jacob's daughter. Abraham bought there a burial plot from his sons (Ge. 33:19; 34:2-26; Jos. 24:32; Jdg. 9:28; Ac. 7:16). †

HAMRAN *See* HEMDAN

HAMSTRING HORSES To cripple by cutting the tendon of an ox or horse. It was a military act intended to disable one's enemy (Jos. 11:6; 2Sa. 8:4; 1Ch. 18:4). Simeon and Levi hamstrung oxen, and were later blamed for their cruelty by Jacob (Gen. 34:25-29; 49:6).

HAMUEL *See* HAMMUEL

HAMUL, HAMULITES {pitied} A descendant of Judah through Perez and his clan (Ge. 46:12; Nu. 26:21; 1Ch. 2:5). †

HAMUTAL {my husband's father is like dew} The mother of King Jehoahaz of Judah (2Ki. 23:31; 24:18; Jer. 52:1). †

HANAME(E)L {El is gracious} A cousin of the prophet Jeremiah (Jer. 32:7-12). †

HANAN {gracious}
1. A descendant of Benjamin (1Ch. 8:23).
2. A later descendant of Benjamin through Saul (1Ch. 8:38).
3. One of David's mighty men (1Ch. 11:43).
4. A man of God who lived in the temple (Jer. 35:4).
5. An ancestor of some temple servants who came back from the Babylonian captivity (Ezr. 2:46).
6. A Levite who helped others to understand the law (Ne. 8:7).
7, 8, and 9. Levites who signed the covenant with Nehemiah (Ne. 10:10, 22, 26).
10. An assistant to one of Nehemiah's treasurers (Ne. 13:13).

HANANE(E)L, TOWER OF {El is gracious} A tower on the N wall of Jerusalem (Ne. 3:1). Both Jeremiah and Zechariah predicted it would be rebuilt (Jer. 31:38; Zec. 14:10).

HANANI {gracious}
1. Father of the prophet Jehu who rebuked both Baasha and Asa king of Judah. Asa put him in prison for it (1Ki. 16:1-7; 2Ch. 16:7, 10).
2. A Levite musician in David's day (1Ch. 25:4).
3. A musician in Nehemiah's day (Ne. 12:36).

4. A brother of Nehemiah who brought him news to Babylon and was later made a ruler in Jerusalem (Ne. 1:2; 7:2).

HANANIAH {Yahweh is gracious}
1. A priest denounced by Jeremiah for falsely prophesying and whose death he predicted (Jer. 28:1-17).
2. Father of an official by the name of Zedekiah in Jeremiah's day (Jer. 36:12).
3. Grandfather of the captain of the guard Irijah who seized the prophet Jeremiah (Jer. 37:13).
4. One of Daniel's three friends to whom the Babylonians gave the name Shadrach (Da. 1:6-7).
5. A descendant of Benjamin (1Ch. 8:24).
6. A Levite musician in David's day (1Ch. 25:4).
7. One of King Uzziah's royal officials (2Ch. 26:11).
8. A son of Zerubbabel who was in the royal line (1Ch. 3:19).
9. One who returned from the captivity (Ezr. 10:28).
10 and 11. Two who helped Nehemiah build the wall of Jerusalem (Ne. 3:30; 7:2, NIV footnote).
12. A leader who signed the covenant with Nehemiah (Ne. 10:23).
13. Head of a priestly family in the days of Joiakim (Ne. 12:12).
14. A priest who was present at Nehemiah's dedication of the walls of Jerusalem (Ne. 12:41).

HANDS, IMPOSITION OF, LAYING ON OF *See* AZAZEL; LAYING ON OF HANDS; ORDAIN

HANDBREADTH *See* WEIGHTS AND MEASURES

HANDKERCHIEF A *face cloth* for wiping perspiration (Ac. 19:12). A burial cloth for the face (Lk. 19:20; Jn. 11:44; 20:7). *See also* NAPKIN

HANDLE A door handle, with a lock (SS. 5:5). *See also* HOUSE

HANDMAID, HANDMAIDEN A female slave or servant. *See* SERVANT; SLAVE

HANDSTAFF KJV for "war club" in Eze. 39:9. *See* ARMS AND ARMOR

HANES A city of Egypt (Isa. 30:4). †

HANGING Capital punishment, death by strangulation, is not taught in the Scriptures. The custom in those times was to give additional degradation to a criminal by hanging his corpse over specially erected posts or from a tree. Pharaoh's servant was killed and then hanged (Ge. 40:19). The same is reflected in the Deuteronomic law (Dt. 21:22-23). Ahithophel and Judas Iscariot committed suicide by hanging themselves (2Sa. 17:23; Mt. 27:5). *See* PUNISHMENT

HANGINGS Curtains in the tabernacle (Ex. 26:1-14; 27:9-19). *See* TABERNACLE

HANIEL *See* HANNIEL

HANNAH [favor] The mother of the prophet Samuel (1Sa. 1:2-22; 2:1, 21). †

HANNATHON A city (174-243) on the northern border of Zebulun (Jos. 19:14). †

HANNIEL [favor of El]
  1. A descendant of Asher, Jacob's son (1Ch. 7:39). †
  2. The representative from the tribe of Manasseh involved in the dividing of the land among the tribes (Nu. 34:23). †

HANOCH, HANOCHITE(S)
  1. A grandson of Abraham by Keturah (Ge. 25:4; 1Ch. 1:33).
  2. A son of Reuben, Jacob's first son (Ge. 46:9).
  3. A clan from Hanoch (Nu. 26:5).

HANUKKAH [dedication] *See* DEDICATION, FEAST OF

HANUN [favored]
  1. An Ammonite king who insulted King David's messengers and so brought war on himself (2Sa. 10:1-17).
  2 and 3. Two who repaired the wall of Jerusalem with Nehemiah (Ne. 3:13, 30).

HAPHARAIM, HAPHRAIM [place of two trenches] A city (192-223) in Issachar (Jos. 19:19). †

HAPIRU *See* HABIRU

HAPPIZZEZ A descendant of Aaron and the name of one responsible for duties as a temple priest (1Ch. 24:15). †

HAPPY *See* BEATITUDES; BLESS

HARA [hill, highland] An unidentified place to which some of the Israelite captives were taken by the Assyrians (1Ch. 5:26). †

HARADAH [place of fear] An unidentified stop en route from Egypt (Nu. 33:24-25). †

HARAN
  1. Abraham's brother and father of Lot (Ge. 11:26-32).
  2. A son of Caleb (1Ch. 2:46).
  3. A Levite who lived in the days of David and Solomon (1Ch. 23:9).
  4. A city in N Mesopotamia to which Abraham's family moved and from which Abraham himself emigrated to Canaan after his father's death. Both Isaac and Jacob got their wives from a family that remained in Haran (Ge. 11:31; 24:4; 27:43; 29:4-5; Ac. 7:2-4).

HARARITE [mountain dweller] Three of the mighty men of David had fathers who were Hararites. This was either the name of a tribe or an area (2Sa. 23:11; 1Ch. 11:34-35).

HARBONA(H) A eunuch of the Persian king Xerxes who suggested the hanging of Haman (Est. 1:10; 7:9). †

HARDEN *See* HEART, HARDEN THE

HARE *See* BEASTS 5., *Rabbit*

HAREM A word used only in Esther referring to the abode of the women at the court of the Persian king (Est. 2:3-14).

HAREPH [autumn *or* sharp, IDB; scornful, ISBE] A descendant of Caleb and Hur (1Ch. 2:51). †

HARETH *See* HERETH

HARHAIAH The father of a goldsmith who worked with Nehemiah to rebuild the walls of Jerusalem (Ne. 3:8). †

HARHAS Grandfather of the husband of the prophetess Huldah; also called Hasrah (2Ki. 22:14; 2Ch. 34:22). †

HARHUR [*possibly* fever, BDB; *possibly* raven, IDB; one born during a fever of his mother, KB] Ancestor of some of the temple servants who returned from the Babylonian captivity with Zerubbabel (Ezr. 2:51; Ne. 7:53). †

HARIM [consecrated (to Yahweh)]
1. Head of a priestly division in David's time (1Ch. 24:8).
2. Some men who returned with Zerubbabel from the Babylonian captivity came from this town. They had foreign wives (Ezr. 2:32; 10:31).
3. Ancestor of some priests in the same condition as the men of 2 above (Ezr. 2:39; 10:21). A descendant was a head of a priestly family in the days of Joiakim (Ne. 12:15).
4 and 5. Two who signed the covenant with Nehemiah (Ne. 10:5, 27).

HARIPH [one born at harvesttime]
1. His descendants came back from the Babylonian captivity with Zerubbabel (Ne. 7:24); also called Jorah (Ezr. 2:18). †
2. One who signed the covenant with Nehemiah (Ne. 10:19). †

HARLOT *See* PROSTITUTE

HARMON An unidentified place (Am. 4:3, NIV footnote).

HARNEPHER [(pagan god) Horus is merciful] A descendant of Asher (1Ch. 7:36). †

HAROD, HARODITE [trembling]
1. A spring at the foot of Mt. Gilboa where God selected 300 from Gideon's fighting men (Jdg. 7:1-7). †
2. Either the clan or more probably the place from which came two of David's mighty men (2Sa. 23:25; 1Ch. 11:27). In the Chronicles passage he is called the Harodite. †

HAROEH [the seer] A descendant of Judah (1Ch. 2:52). †

HARORITE *See* HAROD 2.

HAROSHETH HAGGOYIM [HAROSHETH of the nations] An unidentified site from which came Sisera, Jabin's army captain (Jdg. 4:2, 13, 16). †

HARP *See* MUSIC, MUSICAL INSTRUMENTS

HARROW A farming practice in the ancient world, the nature of which is not exactly known but it is connected with breaking up the soil (Isa. 28:24). *See* FARMING; PLOW; *see also* PICK

HARSHA [deaf] Ancestor of some temple servants who returned from the Babylonian captivity with Zerubbabel (Ezr. 2:52; Ne. 7:54). †

HART *See* BEASTS 2.

HARUM [consecrated] Father of a clan leader in Judah (1Ch. 4:8). †

HARUMAPH [disfigured nose] The father of one who helped Nehemiah rebuild the wall of Jerusalem (Ne. 3:10). †

HARUPHITE [sharp *or* autumn] The designation of one of the men who joined David at Ziklag (1Ch. 12:5). He came either from the clan or place Haruph. †

HARUZ The grandfather of King Amon of Judah (2Ki. 21:19). †

HARVEST *See* THRESHING, THRESHING FLOOR

HARVEST, FEAST OF *See* CALENDAR and FESTIVALS

HASADIAH [Yahweh is faithful] A son of Zerubbabel in the royal line (1Ch. 3:20). †

HASENUAH *See* HASSENUAH

HASHABIAH [Yahweh has reckoned] A common name particularly for priests and Levites; so much is this so that it is possible that there is some duplication in the names that follow.
1. The ancestor of Ethan whom David made a temple singer (1Ch. 25:3).

2. Another musician, son of Jeduthun in David's time (1Ch. 25:3).

3. One of the officers in charge of the temple treasure in David's time. He was from Hebron (1Ch. 26:30).

4. One of David's officers over the tribe of Levi (1Ch. 27:17).

5. A Levite official in the time of King Josiah (2Ch. 35:9).

6. A Levite who returned with Ezra from the Babylonian captivity (Ezr. 8:19).

7. The ancestor of a Levite who came back from the Babylonian captivity (1Ch. 9:14).

8. One worked on the wall of Jerusalem with Nehemiah next to some Levites (Ne. 3:17).

9. A Levite who signed the covenant with Nehemiah (Ne. 10:11).

10. The grandfather of a gatekeeper among the new servants of Jerusalem in the days of Nehemiah (Ne. 11:22).

11. A head of a priestly family in the days of Joiakim (Ne. 12:21).

12. A leader of the Levites in Nehemiah's day (Ne. 12:24).

HASHABNAH One who signed the covenant with Nehemiah (Ne. 10:25).

HASHABNEIAH, HASHABNIAH

1. The father of one who repaired the walls of Jerusalem with Nehemiah (Ne. 3:10).

2. A Levite who commanded the people to praise God (Ne. 9:5).

HASHBADANA, HASHBADDANA One who stood with Ezra when the law was read to the people (Ne. 8:4).

HASHEM The father of some of David's mighty men (1Ch. 11:34); also called Jashen (2Sa. 23:32). †

HASHMONAH An unidentified stop of the exodus from Egypt (Nu. 33:29-30). †

HASHUB *See* HASSHUB

HASHUBAH {consideration} A son of Zerubbabel (1Ch. 3:20). †

HASHUM

1. Ancestor of some who returned

from the Babylonian captivity with Zerubbabel who had married a foreign wife (Ezr. 2:19; 10:33; Ne. 7:22). †

2. One who stood with Ezra when the law was read (Ne. 8:4). †

3. One who signed the covenant with Nehemiah (Ne. 10:18). †

HASHUPHA *See* HASUPHA

HASMONEANS *See also* CHRONOLOGY; MACCABEES and SELEUCIDS. In 168 B.C., when Antiochus IV of Syria outlawed Jewish religious practices and attempted to substitute a Hellenistic culture in Israel (*see* SELEUCIDS), an elderly priest named Mattathias, of the Hasmonean family, revolted in the Jewish village of Modin (1Macc. 2:1). He refused pagan sacrifice and slew a Jew who yielded. The death of the officiating Syrian followed, and Mattathias issued his ringing declaration of war, "Let everyone who has any zeal for Law and takes his stand on the covenant come out and follow me." (1Macc. 2:27, NJB). He roused the pious in Israel to guerilla attack against both Syrians and apostate Jews. Mattathias died in 167, but he appointed his son Judas as leader, who succeeded, at the end of two years, in driving back the pagans and cleansing the temple in Jerusalem from its abominations (*see* MACCABEES). After Judas had fallen in battle in 161, the remaining Hasmonean brothers fought on to achieve a corresponding political independence.

Jonathan (161-143 B.C., 1Macc. 9:23 – 12:53) followed Judas as the guerilla leader and began to regain power. Three years later, in 158, the Greek general Bacchides, who had crushed Judas, answered the appeal of the Jewish Hellenizers and returned to Israel. But he could not break Jonathan, who was able to gain a truce. Thus, left alone, Jonathan proceeded to destroy the Greek sympathizers from among the Jews (1Macc. 9:58-73). In 153, Alexander Balas, who was a contender for the Syrian throne, sought to gain the support of Jonathan by appointing him to be high priest of Israel (10:166). Later, another contender, Tryphon, treacherously captured Jonathan and put him to death. But the struggle was continued by Simon, the last of the sons of Mattathias. In 143 B.C., Tryphon's rival Demetrius II granted to Simon the national sovereignty that was the goal of the Hasmoneans (1Macc. 13:36-43).

As an independent high priest, Simon (in 142) minted coins, starved out the Syrian garrison that still remained in the citadel at Jerusalem, and built up Judea (1Macc. 13:51). He was confirmed in his position by the Romans (14:16-24). In 135 both Simon and his sons Judas and Mattathias were murdered by his son-in-law Ptolemy.

John Hyrcanus I (135-105 B.C.), the surviving son of Simon, drove out Ptolemy, but was temporarily subdued by Antiochus VII of Syria (for the political relationships of this period, *see* SELEUCIDS). Having recovered his position, Hyrcanus I established it by a treaty with Rome, on the strength of which he conquered the land E of the Jordan, Idumea, and Samaria. He destroyed the Samaritan temple on Mt. Gerizim in 128.

Aristobulus I (105-104), son of Hyrcanus I, shared the rule with his brother, Antigonus I, but soon murdered him. Though Hyrcanus I may have sought the title of king, it is Aristobulus I who is first known to have assumed it. Despite cruelties and Hellenistic sympathy, he ruled well and added Galilee, which he compelled to Judaize. Strict Jews opposed his kingship as non-Davidic.

Alexander Jannaeus (104-78 B.C.), another brother of Aristobulus I, was designated king by the latter's widow, Alexandra, whom he proceeded to marry. By constant warfare he enlarged the kingdom even further, but was personally unfit to be high priest and faced wide opposition.

In 95 B.C. the rising nation of the Nabatean Arabs under Aretas III extended their power to Damascus and defeated Alexander, who had to make concessions. The geographical expansion of the Hasmoneans was at an end.

Seven years later Alexandra (78-69), his widow, succeeded as regent, though their son Hyrcanus II acted as high priest. The party of the Pharisees, through their domination of the Sanhedrin, held the actual rule.

Upon the death of Alexandra, Aristobulus II (69-63) displaced the rightful succession of his brother Hyrcanus II. But Antipater, a governor in Idumea, stirred up Hyrcanus II to make an alliance with Aretas and attack Aristobulus II. When the Roman general Pompey intervened, Aristobulus II resisted. The Romans took the citadel in Jerusalem after a three-month siege, and in 63 B.C. Hasmonean independence came to an end. Judea was reduced in size. Hyrcanus II was retained only as high priest and "ethnarch" under the province of Syria, and many Jews were taken captive to Rome. Antipater continued as the power behind the mild Hyrcanus II.

But then Antigonus II, a son of Aristobulus II, took Jerusalem with Parthian (Persian) help and deposed Hyrcanus II. Antipater's son Herod, who had married a granddaughter of Hyrcanus, fled to Rome to promote the cause of his young brother-in-law Aristobulus III, but was himself appointed king. Backed by Roman troops, Herod recaptured Jerusalem in 37, and Antigonus II was executed. Aristobulus III served briefly as high priest; but with his murder at the hands of the suspicious Herod, the Hasmonean dynasty came to an end. (J.B.P.)

HASRAH *See* HARHAS

HASSENAAH Father of those who built the Fish Gate in the days of Nehemiah (Ne. 3:3) (cf. SENAAH). †

HASSENUAH [the hated women] An ancestor of the Benjamites who returned from the Babylonian captivity (1Ch. 9:7; Ne. 11:9).

HASSHUB [considerate]

1 and 2. Two who helped Nehemiah in the repair of the wall of Jerusalem (Ne. 3:11, 23).

3. One who signed the covenant with Nehemiah (Ne. 10:23).

HASMONEAN PRIEST-KINGS				
		Mattathias (167-166)		
John	Simon (143-135)	Judas (167-161)	Eleazar	Jonathan (161-144)
Judas	John Hyrcanus I (135-105)	Mattathias		Daughter married Ptolemy
	Aristobulus I (105-104)	Antigonus I (105)		Alexander Jannaeus (104-78) married Alexandra (78-69)
	Hyrcanus II (63-40) Alexandra married Alexander (daughter of Hyrcanus II) (son of Aristobulus II)		Aristobulus II (69-63) Antigonus II (40-37)	
		Mariamne, married Herod the Great	Aristobulus III (36-35)	
End of Hasmonean Dynasty				

4. Father of a Levite who lived in Jerusalem after the return from the captivity (Ne. 11:15).

HASSOPHERETH [the scribes] Descendant of some of Solomon's servants who returned from the Babylonian captivity with Zerubbabel; also called Sophereth (Ezr. 2:55; Ne. 7:57). †

HASUPHA Ancestor of some temple servants who returned from the Babylonian captivity with Zerubbabel (Ezr. 2:43; Ne. 7:46). †

HAT *See* DRESS, *headgear*

HATACH *See* HATHACH

HATE
1. The opposite of love. It is a mark of one who walks in spiritual darkness (IJn. 2:9, 11). *See* LOVE
2. A figure for comparison between two opposites with no shades of meaning between them. To hate one wife over another wife is to have the second "to be

loved less" (Ge. 29:31, KJV; Dt. 21:15, KJV). The same is true for one's child (Pr. 13:24, NIV). In the NT comparing two texts one can see this at work (Lk. 14:26; cf. Mt. 10:37).

HATHACH [good] A eunuch who waited on the Persian queen Esther (Est. 4:59). †

HATHATH [*possibly* terror, BDB and KB; *possibly* weakness, IDB] A descendant of Judah and David (1Ch. 4:13). †

HATIPHA [taken captive] Ancestor of a temple servant who returned with Zerubbabel from Babylon (Ezr. 2:54; Ne. 7:56). †

HATITA Ancestor of a gatekeeper who returned from the Babylonian captivity with Zerubbabel (Ezr. 2:42; Ne. 7:45). †

HATTIL [talkative] Ancestor of one of Solomon's servants who returned from the Babylonian captivity with Zerubbabel (Ezr. 2:57; Ne. 7:59). †

HATTIN, HORNS OF *See* GOSPELS, THE FOUR; SERMON ON THE MOUNT

HATTUSH
1. A descendant of David who came back from the Babylonian captivity with Ezra (Ezr. 8:2; 1Ch. 3:22). †
2. One who helped Nehemiah repair the wall of Jerusalem (Ne.3:10). †
3. One who signed the covenant with Nehemiah (Ne. 10:4). †
4. A priest who returned with Zerubbabel from the captivity (Ne. 12:2). Probably the same as 3. †

HAURAN *See* GEOGRAPHY OF THE HOLY LAND

HAVENS {harbor} *See* FAIR HAVENS

HAVILAH {stretch of sand}
1. A descendant of Noah, Ham, and Cush (Ge. 10:7).
2. A descendant of Shem (Ge. 10:29).
3. An unidentified land where there was gold and around which the unidentified river Pishon flowed (Ge. 2:11).
4. The Ishmaelites lived in a land by this name located "from Havilah to Shur, near the border of Egypt or toward Asshur" (Ge. 25:18).

HAV(V)OTH JAIR {villages of JAIR} A cluster of villages that were taken by Jair the son of Manassehin Gilead, i.e., Bashan (Nu. 32:41; Dt. 3:14; Jdg. 10:4; 1Ch. 2:23).†

HAWK *See* BIRDS 5.

HAY *See* FODDER

HAZAEL {El sees} When Ben-Hadad the king of Syria was sick, he sent his servant Hazael to the prophet Elisha who told Hazael that Ben-Hadad would die and that he would be the next king of Syria (2Ki. 8:7-8, 13). After ascending the throne Hazael attacked the two-and-a-half tribes of Israel E of the Jordan, and then Judah itself (2Ki. 10:32; 12:17-18).

HAZAIAH {Yahweh sees} A descendant of Judah who lived in Jerusalem after the return from the Babylonian captivity (Ne. 11:5). †

HAZAR Meaning "settlement" or "village," Hazar is used in combination with other names to produce the name of a town, city, or village—e.g., "Hazar Addar." See next entry.

HAZAR ADDAR {settlement of ADDAR} A city (100-999) on the southern border of the tribal area of Judah (Nu. 34:4); also called Addar (Jos. 15:3). † *See* ADDAR

HAZAR ENAN (ENON) {settlement of ENAN}
1. A village on the northern border of Israel (Nu. 34:9-10). †
2. A place on the northern boundary of Damascus with the border of Hamath to the N (Eze. 47:17; 48:1). †

HAZAR GADDAH {settlement of (pagan god) GAD} An unidentified southern town in the tribal area of Judah (Jos. 15:27). †

HAZAR HATTICON, HAZER-HATTICON A town (Eze. 47:16). †

HAZARMAVETH {village of (pagan god) MAVETH} A descendant of Shem (Ge. 10:26; 1Ch. 1:20). †

HAZAR SHUAL {settlement of SHUAL (jackal)} An unidentified town in the tribal area of Judah (Jos. 15:28; 19:3; 1Ch. 4:28; Ne. 11:27). †

HAZAR SUSAH, HAZAR SUSIM {settlement of SUSAH (horse)} An unidentified town in the tribal area of Judah which was given later to Simeon (Jos. 19:5); also called Hazar Susim (1Ch. 4:31). †

HAZAZON TAMAR {HAZAZON of the palm trees} A city (173-024) in the Wadi Arabah S of the Salt Sea, formerly thought to be on the western shore of the Sea itself (Ge. 14:7; 2Ch. 20:2). †

HAZEL TREE KJV for "almond tree" in Ge. 30:37. *See* TREES, Fruit Trees, *Almond*

HAZELELPONI *See* HAZZELELPONI

HAZER HATTICON [place of HAT-TICON] A place on the border in his vision of the future Israel (Eze. 47:16). †

HAZERIM [unwalled settlements] KJV for "villages" in Dt. 2:23. *See* CITY; HAZAR; VILLAGES

HAZEROTH [settlements] A stopping place of the Israelites on their exodus from Egypt. Aaron and Miriam rebelled against Moses here (Nu. 11:35; 12:1-16; 33:17-18; Dt. 1:1). †

HAZEZON TAMAR *See* HAZAZON TAMAR

HAZIEL [vision of El] A Levite who served David in his latter years (1Ch. 23:1, 9). †

HAZO An uncle of Rebekah (Ge. 22:22). †

HAZOR [an enclosure]
   1. A Canaanite royal city (203-269) and the head of all the kingdoms of that area in the time of Joshua, conquered and sacked by the Israelites (Jos. 11:10-13; 12:19). Later, King Jabin who reigned in Hazor was defeated by Deborah and Barak (Jdg. 4:1-17). King Solomon rebuilt it as a grain storage center, and it remained in Israelite hands until taken by the Assyrians in 732 B.C. (1Ki. 9:15; 2Ki. 15:29). Archaeologists have discovered twenty-one strata going back to Chalcolithic times, a fine example of a Solomonic gate, and several temples of importance, together with a massive and unusual water system within the acropolis area itself.
   2. A town in the Negev in the tribal area of Judah; also called Kirioth Hezron (Jos. 15:23, 25). *See* KERIOTH HEZRON
   3. An unidentified town N of Jerusalem occupied by Benjamin after the return from the Babylonian captivity (Ne. 11:33).
   4. An unidentified place attacked by Nebuchadnezzar, King of Babylon (Jer. 49:28-33).

HAZOR HADATTAH [new HAZOR] An unidentified site in the southernmost

THE BATTLE FOR HAZOR
Hazor, the largest Canaanite center in Galilee, was destroyed by Joshua.

part of the tribal area of Judah (Jos. 15:25). †

HAZZELELPONI A woman descended from Judah (1Ch. 4:3). †

HAZZOBEBAH A descendant of Judah (1Ch. 4:8). †

HEAD
   1. Just as the head is an essential part of a human body, so the head represents a superior rank (but not of kind) in the relationship of husband and wife (1Co. 11:3; Eph. 5:23). Christ is the head over the church and the universe (Eph. 1:22; 4:15; 5:23; Col. 1:18; 2:10). "Headship" is a closer, personal term of relationship than simply "ruler."
   2. In the OT the "head" of a hill is the top of a hill or an extremity of a geographical area.

HEAD OF THE CHURCH *See* BODY OF CHRIST; HEAD

HEADBAND, HEADDRESS, HEADGEAR *See* DRESS, *headgear*

HEADSTONE *See* CORNERSTONE

HEALING, HEALTH Some six or more Hebrew and Greek words are used in the Bible to refer to health with the basic idea of being whole or complete, or of well-being, safety, and peace. One of the words in each Testament is translated in some cases as "salvation." That word in the OT has the same root as the prope names "Joshua" and "Jesus." It is frequently rendered "deliver," "deliverance," or "rescue" (Ps. 3:8; Php. 1:19; Ac. 7:25). Its uses to refer to physical salvation and deliverance, which would include deliverance to health, are many (1Sa. 2:1; Isa. 25:9; 33:2; Jnh 2:9). Words or concepts rendered "health" are also used figuratively or in the sense of spiritual health and healing (Jer. 30:17; 1Pe. 2:24; Mt. 13:15). For a description of the diseases noted in the Bible *see* SICK, SICKNESS. These are in the body, including lameness, demon possession, or mental problems.

Healing may be the restoration to normalcy of these organic or psychological disorders. Probably in the great majority of cases healing was by natural means because of lack of scientific knowledge of the causes of disease, and of medicine or therapy. There are, however, many cases in both Testaments of miraculous healings, where the healing is attributed to the direct intervention of God or one of his servants (Nu. 12:9-16; 2Ki. 4:32-37; Lk. 4:40; 7:11-15; Ac. 3:1-8, 16; 9:36-40; 28:8). These were not just cases of healing for the sake of healing. They were for the purpose of attestation of the healer, of his relationship to God, and of the power of God. With the close of the period during which God spoke to the world through prophets, and with the close of the period of the writing of Scripture, this phenomenon was much less frequent, even though it has not ceased to this day.

One part of the health question that should not be overlooked is the matter of hygiene and sanitation. The first five books of the Bible show a wealth of information about selection and inspection of clean and unclean foods, methods of slaughter, control of certain infectious diseases, disposal of sewage and even corpses, water supply, bathing, personal and public hygiene (Lev. 11–26). One may even find suggestions which, if followed, would lead to good mental health and the prevention of bad mental health by such means as thoughtful care of the more needy and healthy intra-family attitudes.

HEAR *See* OBEDIENCE

HEART The word occurs hundreds of times in the Bible but almost exclusively in a figurative sense (Ps. 4:4; 119:2; Mt. 15:19; Lk. 2:19). The heart is the seat of almost all of the emotions: sadness and gladness, fearfulness and confidence, loving and hating, good and bad desires (Ne. 2:2; Isa. 35:4; 2Ch. 17:6; Ps. 105:25; Ac. 14:17; Ro. 1:24; 10:1). It is translated in the NIV also as "mind" and "idea" (Isa. 46:8; Nu. 16:28). *See* EMOTIONS; MIND; SOUL

HEART, HARDNESS OF An obstinacy, stubbornness, or coldness of thought and response to God (Dt. 9:27; Mt. 19:8; Mk. 10:5). It is characterized by an unrepentant heart (Ro. 2:5). A similar idea is to be stiff-necked (Ac. 7:51). To have an uncircumcised heart is to be hardhearted (Dt. 10:16; Jer. 4:4; Ac. 7:51).

HEARTH *See* ALTAR

HEATH *See* PLANTS, PERFUMES, AND SPICES, Miscellaneous Plants 13., *Aroer*

HEATHEN *See* GENTILES; GOIIM; NATION

HEAVE OFFERING *See* SACRIFICES AND OFFERINGS, The Fellowship (Peace) Offering, *Ritual* (Wave and Heave offering).

HEAVEN *See* DEAD, ABODE OF; KINGDOM OF GOD

HEAVING AND WAVING *See* SACRIFICES AND OFFERINGS

HEBER, HEBERITE(S) [associate]
1. Grandson of Aher and his clan (Ge. 46:17; Nu. 26:45).
2. The husband of the Jael who killed Sisera (Jdg. 4:11).
3. A descendant of Judah and Caleb (1Ch. 4:18).
4. A descendant of Benjamin (1Ch. 8:17).

HEBREW A term used by Israelites and foreigners alike in reference to the descendants of Abraham (Ge. 14:13;

39:17; Jer. 34:9). Whether they originate with Eber (Ge. 10:21), or with Abraham is debated. Their language is that of the OT, a dialect of NW Semitic and particularly of Canaanite. Their religion is, of course, that presented in the OT. *See also* BIBLICAL LANGUAGES; HABIRU; ISRAELITE; JEW

HEBREW OF THE HEBREWS *See* PAUL, LIFE AND TEACHINGS OF

HEBREWS, BOOK OF Hebrews does not tell us the name of the author nor the location of the recipients. However, the identity of the writer seems well known to his reader (13:19, 22-23). The ancient tradition of Pauline authorship is early and not to be ignored, though other persons have been suggested throughout church history. Pauline influence and material are recognized in the book, and recent critical estimates of its date (about A.D. 63) bring it within the range of Paul's life.

The letter must have been written before the fall of the temple in A.D. 70. The language of 8:4, 9:6, and 10:1 seems to contemplate the temple ritual as going on.

The epistle is written to a group of people who know their OT and who seem to have had intimate knowledge of Christian beginnings but whose faith was wavering and who needed encouragement to faith and patience. The exact situation they faced is not revealed in detail, but the argument of Hebrews seems to be directed against the doctrine of salvation by Levitical priesthood and sacrifice. The categorical statement of 10:4 and 10:11 that the blood of bulls and goats cannot take away sins would imply that the idea was in the minds of the readers. Hebrews 7:11-12, by the phrasing as a contrary-to-fact condition, sharply negates the idea that there was "perfection" (salvation) by the Levitical priesthood.

Assuming this basic problem in the mind of the readers leads to a helpful analysis of the contents of the book. There is apparently an eager interest in pointing out the gospel in the OT, and it

is assumed that the readers would accept the identification of Jesus as the Son of God, "the same yesterday and today and forever" (13:8). The key argument of Hebrews is that if Jesus and the gospel were known to OT believers, then it is a misinterpretation of the OT to expect "perfection" or salvation by Levitical priesthood and sacrifice.

The main argument of Hebrews runs from 1:1 through 10:18 and the remainder is a powerful exhortation. The argument alternates with a series of warnings and pleas. The series of argumentative portions are: 1:1-14; 2:5–3:6; 4:14–5:10; 7:1–10:18. Christ, the eternal Son of God, is the true and proper High Priest of his people, who took flesh and blood that he might bring many sons into glory through sufferings. He is the Son over God's house, whose house we are, the word "we" including believers of all ages.

He is qualified as High Priest by divine appointment based on sonship. Though the language of chapter 7 is subtle and allusive, the divine attribute of eternal being seems to be given to Melchizedek, and hence he has been regarded by some to have been the Son of God in a preincarnation Christophany—though others see him as simply a type of the eternal Christ. If this eternal priest received tithes from Abraham and gave blessing to Abraham, then Abraham's descendants, the Levitical priests, must themselves be dependent on Melchizedek for salvation and cannot by their offerings bring eternal salvation to others. Christ then is the minister and assurance of the everlasting covenant, serving in the greater and more perfect heavenly tabernacle, and offering the better sacrifice, even the sacrifice of himself. Having willingly offered this one sacrifice for sins forever, he has resumed his place at the right hand of God and "waits for his enemies to be made his footstool" (10:13).

There follows the moving exhortation to accept the salvation of this great High Priest, drawing near to God in the way opened by the death of Christ, and living a life of faith. So great is the work of our High Priest and so great the reward before us, "So do not throw away your confidence; it will be richly rewarded. You need to persevere so that when you have done the will of God, you will receive what he promised" (10:35-36). The citation of the great text from Habakkuk, "The righteous will live by his faith" (Hab. 2:4), leads to the uniquely great display of men of faith (Heb. 11) with the ensuing application: "Therefore, since we are surrounded by such a great cloud of witnesses, let us throw off everything that hinders and the sin which so easily entangles, and let us run with perseverance the race marked out for us." (12:1). Christ's example is presented for endurance and encouragement in discipline and trials. These great principles lead to the detailed ethical applications of chapter 13 in life and worship. The epistle concludes with the picture of Christ, the Great Shepherd of the sheep, brought again from the dead through the blood of the eternal covenant, equipping his people to do the will of God. (W.B.W.)

HEBREW POETRY *See* POETRY; PSALMS

HEBRON [association]

1. A city (159-103) SW of Jerusalem favored by nature with a good altitude, plenty of farmable land, and an abundance of water. With such an endowment it doubtless has a very much older occupation than the written sources give it. Its earliest known name was Kiriath Arba, named for Arba who was the greatest man among the Anakites (Jos. 14:15). Its earlier archaeological record is unknown but the biblical account refers to its "founding" seven years before Zoan in Egypt, thus giving the founding date of about 1700 B.C. (Ge. 23:2; Nu. 13:22). Abraham tented in the vicinity and bought a burial place for Sarah his wife from a Hittite who lived there (Ge. 13:18; 23:2-20). The tradition of the burial of the patriarchs here is preserved to the present in the great mosque built over a cove in the city called by the Arabs today *el-Khalil*, the friend. The reference

is to Abraham as the friend of the Merciful One, the friend of God, a tradition well preserved in the Bible itself (Isa.41:8; 2Ch. 20:7; Jas. 2:23). At the time of the conquest under Joshua the city was taken by the Israelites and given to Caleb (Jos. 15:13-14). Here too David was anointed to be king of Judah and Israel (2Sa. 2:4; 5:3). It became one of the important fortified cities of Judah in the days following King Solomon and was still occupied by the men of Judah after their return from the captivity in Babylon (2Ch. 11:10; Ne. 11:25). In postbiblical times it became the fourth most sacred place of the Muslim, was taken by the Crusaders, and later retaken by the Muslim.

2. A son of Kohath and an uncle of Moses and Aaron. He had the oversight of Israel W of the Jordan River in the days of King David (Ex. 6:18; 1Ch. 26:30).

3. A descendant of Judah and of Caleb, but not the Caleb who was one of the twelve spies and the inheritor of Hebron above (1Ch. 2:42-43).

JACOB'S JOURNEY BACK TO HEBRON

HEDGE *See* WALL

HEDGEHOG *See* BEASTS 10.

HEDONISM The belief that pleasure is the only or chief end of life.

HEGAI The king of Persia's eunuch in charge of all the women (Est. 2:3, 8, 15). †

HEGLAM [deport] Transliterated as a name in RSV (with footnote). All other major versions translate it, "he deported them"—or in similar words (1Ch. 8:7).

HEIFER *See* BEASTS 4.; RED HEIFER

HEILSGESCHICHTE German for *Salvation History*. According to some theologians, this is the basic message of the Bible, i.e., God's history of redemption. *See* GESCHICHTE

HEIR The son of an owner of property. According to the NT picture presented in Galatians, sons were treated like slaves, under guardians until set at liberty by the father. Paul uses this to illustrate the relationship of men prior to their spiritual salvation, under bondage to law until set free by adoption as sons (Gal. 4:17). *See also* FIRSTBORN

HELAH [necklace, IDB; rust, KB] A wife of Ashhur of a clan of Judah (1Ch. 4:57). †

HELAM An unidentified site in Syria where David defeated their king Hadadezer (2Sa. 10:15-19). †

HELBAH An unidentified town in Asher (Jdg. 1:31). †

HELBON An unidentified site in the Damascus area mentioned for its wine (Eze. 27:18). †

HELDAI
1. David's military commander of the twelfth month (1Ch. 27:15). †
2. One who brought silver and gold to the prophet Zechariah to make a crown for the high priest Joshua (Zec. 6:10-14). †

HELEB Some think he is the same as Heldai in 1 above (2Sa. 23:29ff.).

HELECH Possibly an area in SE Asia Minor (Eze. 27:11). †

HELED Heldai (1Ch. 27:15), a Netophathite. Heled is one of David's mighty men (2Sa. 23:29).

HELEK, HELEKITE(S) [portion, lot] A descendant of Manasseh, and his clan (Nu. 26:30; Jos. 17:2). †

HELEM
1. 1Ch. 7:32, 35. *See* HOTHAM 1.
2. KJV *See* HELDAI 2.

HELEPH [*possibly* sharp, cutting] A town (189-236) on the border of Naphtali (Jos. 19:33). †

HELEZ [vigour, BDB]
1. One of David's Thirty (2Sa. 23:26; 1Ch. 11:27; 27:10). †
2. A name in a genealogy (1Ch. 2:39). †

HELI [ascent (to God)] The father of Joseph, the husband of Mary, of whom Jesus was born (Lk. 3:23). †

HELIOPOLIS, ON [sun (god) city] The capital of an Egyptian province located near the place where Cairo is located today. As it was called *iwnw* by the Egyptians it came over into Hebrew as *on*. Called "the temple of the sun" in the text of the NIV, but see also the NIV footnote to Jer. 43:13.

HELKAI [Yahweh is (my) portion] A priest in the days of Joiakim (Ne. 12:15). †

HELKATH [portion] A Levitical town (160-232) on the border of the tribal area of Asher (Jos. 19:25; 21:31); also called Hukok (1Ch. 6:75). †

HELKATH HAZZURIM [*possibly* portion (field) of rock, *or* swords, IDB; portion (field) of snare, KB] A place in Gibeon where twelve of the young men of Abner met in a hand-to-hand fight with twelve of those of Joab. All were killed (2Sa. 2:16). †

HELL *See* DEAD, ABODE OF; PUNISHMENT

HELLENISTS *See* GRECIAN JEWS

HELMET *See* ARMS AND ARMOR

HELON The father of the head of the census for the tribe of Zebulun which was taken after leaving Egypt (Nu. 1:9; 7:24-29).

HELPER SUITABLE *See* EVE; WOMAN, *helper fit for.*

HELPMEET *See* EVE; WOMAN, *helper fit for.*

HELPS A spiritual gift in 1Co. 12:28. The original has the idea of "helpful deeds" and the verb form of this word means to "come to one's aid." For more on the gifts, *see* GIFTS; SPIRITUAL GIFTS

HEM OF A GARMENT *See* FRINGES

HEMAM *See* HOMAM, HEMAN

HEMAN [faithful]
1. A man whose wisdom was exceeded by that of Solomon (1Ki. 4:31).
2. A son of Zerah descended from Judah (1Ch. 2:6).
3. A descendant of Levi; also called "the Ezrahite" in the title of Psalm 88, who was assigned to the ministry of music (1Ch. 6:33; 15:17; 2Ch. 5:12).

HEMATH *See* HAMATH or HAMMATH (1Ch. 2:55)

HEMDAN [desirable] A descendant of Abraham through Ishmael's line (Ge. 36:26); also called Hamran in the NIV footnote at 1Ch. 1:41. †

HEMLOCK KJV for a poisonous plant (Hos. 10:4; Am. 6:12).

HEN [gracious]
1. A person (Zec. 6:14). †
2. A mother chicken (Mt. 23:37; Lk. 13:34). † *See* BIRDS 2.

HENA [(pagan god) ANAT] A city on the Euphrates N of Babylon (2Ki. 18:34; 19:13; Isa. 37:13).

HENADAD [favor of HADAD (pagan god)] Father of some Levites who came back from the Babylonian captivity and helped in the rebuilding of the temple and walls of Jerusalem. They also signed the covenant with Nehemiah (Ezr. 3:9; Ne. 3:18, 24; 10:9). †

HENNA *See* PLANTS, PERFUMES, AND SPICES

HENOCH *See* ENOCH; HANOCH 1.

HENOTHEISM Polytheism that holds one god above all others. Monotheism is the belief that there is only one God.

HEPHER, HEPHERITE(S)
1. A city (141-197) conquered by Joshua on the W side of the Jordan River (Jos. 12:17; 1Ki. 4:10).
2. A descendant of Manasseh through Gilead, and his clan (Nu. 26:32).
3. A descendant of Judah (1Ch. 4:6).
4. One of David's mighty men (1Ch. 11:36).

HEPHZIBAH [my pleasure is in her]
1. Mother of Manasseh, King of Judah (2Ki. 21:1). †
2. A new name for Zion (Isa. 62:4). †

HERB *See* PLANTS, PERFUMES, SPICES

HERDS *See* BEASTS 4.

HERES [sun] An unidentified pass E of the Jordan from which Gideon turned back from his pursuit of the Midianites (Jdg. 1:35; 8:13). †

HERESH [deaf, silent] A descendant of Levi (1Ch. 9:15). †

HERESY Mentioned only once in the NIV and that time in the plural. A philosophy or sect the opposite of orthodoxy (2Pe. 2:1). The Greek word, however, is several times rendered "sect" or "party." Sometimes it is used in Acts with reference to the early Christian church as being a "sect" of Judaism. (Ac. 5:17; 24:5, 14; 28:22).

HERETH A forest (1Sa. 22:5). †

HERITAGE *See* INHERITANCE

HERMAS A Christian at Rome to whom Paul sent greetings (Ro. 16:14). †

HERMENEUTICS From the Greek word for "interpretation," this pertains to the method explaining the Bible. Usually there are set principles in any hermeneutical system. The Bible has been interpreted allegorically, literally, liberally, and existentially. *See* CRITICISM; INSPIRATION

Those who use an allegorical approach see deeper or hidden spiritual meanings beyond the normal sense. Paul uses an allegory in Gal. 4:24. Many of the church fathers were allegorists, in various degrees. Some Catholics are allegorists.

Those who make literal interpretations see the normal sense of Scripture as the only interpretation. They also recognize figures of speech and literary forms. Some Protestants interpret literally.

Those who make liberal interpretation see the Bible as strictly a historical document. Generally they view the religion of the Bible in an evolutionary grid. They have a low view of the integrity of the Bible in its present form, and they often use comparative religion to study the Bible.

The existentialists see that the main emphasis of interpreting Scripture is what it means to the individual as he reads it. This does not mean they do not use the tools of Bible study (often from the liberals). However, the only "meaningful meaning" is God's Word as it is experienced. This experience authenticates their faith. Neo-orthodox is sometimes a name for this approach. *See* NEO-ORTHODOXY (J.A.S.)

HERMES

1. A god (Ac. 14:12). *See* DEITIES
2. A Christian (Ro. 16:14). †

HERMOGENES {born of HERMES} A professed Christian who deserted Paul (2Ti. 1:15). †

HERMON, MOUNT {consecrated place} Called by the Sidonians "Sirion" and by the Amorites "Senir" (Dt. 3:9; 1Ch. 5:23; Eze. 27:5). The Hebrew text once calls it "Siyon" (Dt. 4:48). *See* GEOGRAPHY OF THE HOLY LAND

HERODS, THE Antipater of Idumea was the power behind the weak Jewish high priest Hyrcanus II (63-40 B.C.); *see* HASMONEANS. Having assisted Julius Caesar at a crucial point in a war against Egypt, Antipater was rewarded with the official procuratorship (oversight) of Israel in 47 B.C. He appointed his sons, Phasael and Herod, as governors of Jerusalem and Galilee respectively. When Antigonus II (40-37) took Jerusalem and deposed his uncle Hyrcanus II, Phasael committed suicide, but Herod escaped to Rome, where he received appointment as king over Israel.

With the backing of Rome, this man now known as Herod the Great (37-4 B.C.) recaptured Jerusalem. After the decisive battle of Actium in 31, Herod managed to win the friendship of Augustus Caesar and was confirmed in his kingship. Through suspicion and jealousy Herod had murdered his uncle Joseph and a number of other relatives. In 29 B.C. he put his wife, Mariamne, to death, and later her mother, Alexandra. Herod's oldest son, Antipater, slandered Herod's two sons by Mariamne and caused the execution of both in 7 B.C., Antipater himself was caught attempting to poison Herod and was executed in the last days of his father's reign in 4B.C.

Herod's Idumea (Edomite) ancestry created popular Jewish opposition from the start; and this increased with his ruthless suppression of all enemies. He oppressed the people to bribe his Roman masters; he was a strong Hellenist, without biblical religion. He erected many Greek buildings, even establishing the Greek cities of Caesarea and Sebaste (Samaria). Yet he sought to pacify his Jewish subjects by reconstructing the Jerusalem temple on magnificent lines, starting in 20 B.C. (cf. Jn. 2:20, to be dated A.D. 27). Herod kept peace and order; but his increasing cruelty and suspicion were climaxed at the close of his life by his attempt to kill Christ in the slaughter of the Bethlehem innocents (Mt. 2).

Upon the death of Herod the Great in 4 B.C., the rule was divided among three of his sons (Lk. 3:1). Archelaus was appointed ethnarch (ruler of the people) of Judea (4 B.C.–A.D. 6). At the first he killed 3,000 Jews in a Passover riot; and when he went to Rome for the kingship, the people opposed him (as in Jesus' parable in Lk. 19:12-27) and the title was not granted. Joseph and Mary went to Nazareth to avoid him (Mt. 2:22). He was deposed and sent to Gaul for his cruelties and in his place were appointed Roman procurators from A.D. 6-41, including Pontius Pilate (26-36).

Herod Antipas (4 B.C.—A.D. 39), the most capable of the brothers, was made tetrarch (ruler of a fourth part) of Galilee and built his capital, Tiberias, on the Sea of Galilee. He divorced a daughter of Aretas IV of Arabia to marry his niece Herodias who had deserted her husband, Herod Philip, another of the brothers but not a tetrarch. For this he was condemned by John the Baptist (Mt. 14:4-12), whom Herod killed. He was defeated by Aretas in 36, so that he had to appeal to Rome for help. He thought that Jesus was John risen from the dead (Mt. 14:2). Christ called him "that fox" (Lk. 13:31-32), and he participated in Pilate's trial of Christ (Lk. 23:7-12). The third brother, Philip (4 B.C.—A.D.34), tetrarch of Trachonitis and other areas toward Damascus, is noted chiefly for his enlarging of Paneas, which he named Caesarea Philippi (Mt. 16:13).

Herod Agrippa I was a grandson of Herod the Great and Mariamne, who went to Rome, became a personal friend of Caesar Caligula, and supported his rise to emperor. Caligula rewarded Agrippa with the tetrarchy of Trachonitis, vacant since Philip's death in 34, with the added title of king three years later. Herodias in envy incited her husband Antipas to seek kingly status, too, over Galilee. But Agrippa anticipated the rivalry, had Antipas banished to Gaul, and himself received Galilee in A.D. 39. Being in Rome at the time of Caligula's murder in 41, he encouraged Claudius to take the throne and was rewarded with Judea and Samaria. He was now king over all the land once held by Herod the Great. Herod Agrippa I was careful to observe the law and conciliate the Jews; but part of this policy involved his murder of James the apostle, brother of John, and his attempted murder of Peter (Ac.

12:1-19). God smote him in A.D. 44 for accepting divine honors (Ac. 12:20-23; cf. Josephus *Antiq.* 18:6:7; 19:8:2).

Herod Agrippa I, with the Greek Inscription Meaning, "King Agrippa the Great, Lover of Caesar"

His son, Herod Agrippa II, was to have been made king, but because of his youth (age seventeen) the procuratorship was reinstituted. After the death of his uncle Herod, king of Chalcis in Lebanon, Agrippa II was given the latter's kingdom in A.D. 48. Two years later he was transferred to Trachonitis, to which parts of Galilee were added in 55. He was made guardian of the Jerusalem temple and, with his immoral sister-mistress, Bernice, heard Paul's defense before the procurator Festus (Ac. 25—26). Agrippa supported the Romans in the Jewish wars of 66-70 and maintained a corrupt life in Rome for thirty years thereafter. (J.B.P.)

HERODIANS *See* SECTS

HERODIAS [fem. of HEROD] The adulterous granddaughter of Herod the Great who was instrumental in getting John the Baptist beheaded (Mk. 6:17-19).

HERODION A Christian at Rome and fellow countryman of Paul to whom he sent greetings (Ro. 16:11). †

HERON *See* BIRDS 5.

HESED [loyal love] *See* BEN-HESED, *person*; *see also* COMPASSION

HESHBON A city (226-134) of the Moabites E of the Jordan which was taken by Sihon the Amorite king. The Israelites took it from the Amorites and it became the tribal area of the Reubenites (Nu. 21:21-31; Jos. 13:15-17). The city and surrounding area changed hands between Israel and the Moabites several times. The Moabite inscription adds details to the biblical account (Jdg. 11:26; 1Sa. 12:9, 11).

HESHMON An unidentified town in the tribal area of Judah (Jos. 15:27). †

HETH Descendant of Noah, Ham, and Canaan, and the ancestor of the Hittites (Ge. 10:15, NIV, "Hittites"). One of the great peoples of biblical times.

HETHLON An unidentified place in Syria on the northern boundary of Israel described in the final vision of the prophet Ezekiel (Eze. 47:15; 48:1). †

HEXATEUCH [six books] A recent designation for a literary unit of the first six books of the Bible.

HEZEKI See HIZKI

HEZEKIAH [Yahweh is (my) strength]
1. See KINGS OF JUDAH AND ISRAEL.
2. An ancestor of the prophet Zephaniah (Zep. 1:1).
3. The ancestor of some who returned from the Babylonian captivity with Zerubbabel (Ezr. 2:16).
4. A leader of the people who signed the covenant with Nehemiah (Ne. 10:17).

HEZEKIAH'S TUNNEL See AQUEDUCT; GIHON; SILOAM, POOL OF

HEZION [vision, BDB; one with floppy ears, IDB] Grandfather of Ben-Hadad, king of Syria (1Ki. 15:18). †

HEZIR [boar]
1. The head of one of the divisions of the priests (1Ch. 24:15). †
2. One who signed the covenant with Nehemiah (Ne. 10:20). †

HEZRAI, HEZRO One of David's thirty men (2Sa. 23:35; 1Ch. 11:37). †

HEZRON, HEZRONITE(S) [enclosure]
1. An unidentified place on the southern border of Judah (Jos. 15:3).

2. A son of Reuben and his clan (Ge. 46:9; Nu. 26:6, 21).
3. A descendant of Judah (Ge. 46:12), whose name also appears in both the genealogies of Jesus (Mt. 1:3; Lk. 3:33).

HIDDAI One of David's thirty men; also called Hurai (2Sa. 23:30; 1Ch. 11:32). †

HIDDEKEL See TIGRIS

HIEL [El lives] One from Bethel who rebuilt Jericho in the time of King Ahab and upon whom Joshua's curse fell (1Ki. 16:34; Jos. 6:26). †

HIERAPOLIS [(pagan) sacred city] A city in Asia in the territory of Phrygia in which Epaphras had labored, mentioned to the Colossians by Paul (Col. 4:12-13). †

HIEROGLYPHICS [sacred carving] A system of writing using pictures (pictographs) to stand for ideas. See WRITING

HIGGAION A NIV transliteration in Ps. 9:16 in the instructions for the performance of the psalm. In Ps. 92:3 it is translated "harp." One would then conclude that the meaning in 9:16 has to do with harp sounds. A related word in Ps. 19:14 is translated "meditation." Thus it is difficult to give a precise meaning for the word. See MUSIC, MUSICAL INSTRUMENTS, *Harp*

HIGH PLACES Elevated places associated with the worship of pagan deities in particular association with Canaanite worship. The Israelites were commanded by the Lord through Moses to destroy all the high places after they entered the land W of the Jordan (Nu. 33:52), and their failure to do this caused them to adopt idolatrous worship which ultimately resulted in their punishment by God and their being sent into foreign captivity. During intermittent times of revival under certain judges and kings they, as a part of their reforms, destroyed high places (1Ki. 12:32-33; 2 Ki. 23; 2Ch. 31:1; 33:3). Prior to the building of the temple in Jerusalem, the Israelites on occasion also made their sacrifices on high places, but to the LORD their God (1Ki. 3:25).

HIGH PRIESTS *See* CHIEF PRIESTS; PRIESTS

HIGHER CRITICISM *See* CRITICISM, HIGHER

HILEN *See* HOLON 1.

HILKIAH [Yahweh is (my) portion]
1. The father of Eliakim who was King Hezekiah's palace administrator (2Ki. 18:18).
2. The high priest during the reign of King Josiah who found the Book of the Law and was sent by the king to the prophetess Huldah to inquire of the LORD. He was an ancestor of Ezra (2Ki. 22; Ezr. 7:1).
3. An ancestor of Levi, musician in the temple (1Ch. 6:45).
4. A grandson of Hosah who was among the capable men in David's day (1Ch. 26:11).
5. One who stood beside Ezra as he read the law to the people (Ne. 8:4).
6. A leader of the priest who returned with Zerubbabel from the captivity in Babylon (Ne. 12:7).
7. Father of Jeremiah the prophet (Jer. 1:1).
8. Father of one of the men that King Zedekiah sent with a letter to Nebuchadnezzar in Babylon (Jer. 29:3).

HILL *See* MOUNT, MOUNTAIN, HILL

HILL COUNTRY *See* GEOGRAPHY OF THE HOLY LAND

HILLEL [he has praises]
1. Father of Abdon, one of the judges of Israel (Jdg. 12:13; 15). †
2. A contemporary of Herod the Great. A learned Pharisee, he favored a broad interpretation of the law. He lived from 30 B.C. to A.D. 10. He is not mentioned in the Bible by name. He and his followers favored a broad understanding of when one could divorce a wife (when she "found no favor in his eyes"—Dt. 24:1; Mt. 19:1-11). The school of Sham-

mai (contemporary to Hillel) took a narrower view that only for "shameful conduct" could divorce take place. The Lord clarifies that no divorce is to take place "except for fornication." The Lord was thus leaning toward the school of Shammai, yet his appeal was to Scripture and not traditions. *See* DIVORCE

HIN *See* WEIGHTS AND MEASURES

HIND *See* BEASTS 2., *Doe*

HINDUISM A religion which teaches reincarnation, karma, nirvana. They believe there are cycles of death and rebirth until the person is one with (or absorbed into) the whole of reality. The person is then released out of the phenomenal (i.e., the seen) world. For the Christian, the Scriptures clearly teach that it is destined for man to die once and then face judgment (Heb. 9:27).

HINGE The Hebrew word rendered "hinges" in Pr. 26:14 occurs only once in the Bible; hence, its meaning is not certain. From its context it is assumed that it is some sort of "hinge." As we know from archaeologists, doors turned on parts that protruded from the top and bottom and fitted into sockets, but not on metal hinges as we know them today. The NIV renders other Hebrew words for "hinge" by "socket" (1Ki. 7:50).

HINNOM, VALLEY OF A literal translation of the text in some places would read "valley of the son of Hinnom." In the NIV it appears as Valley of Ben Hinnom (son of Hinnom, Ben being the Hebrew word for "son"). Nothing is known about this man except that he gave his name to the valley that runs S on the W side of the ridge on which is located today the ancient walled city of Jerusalem. The Hinnom runs S for about a half mile and then turns sharply E, cutting off the ridge entirely, joins the Kidron Valley, and together they run S. This valley separated the tribal area of Judah, on the S of it, from that of Benjamin on the N (Jos. 15:8; Ne. 11:30). Here pagan cults burned their children to their gods in a part that came to be known as Topheth (2Ki. 23:10; Jer. 7:31; 32:35). Even some Israelites were drawn into this pagan rite (2Ch. 28:1-3). In the reforms of King Josiah the place was defiled by him and the burning of children was stopped (2Ki. 23:10).

The Hebrew words for this valley, *ge hinnom* or *ge benhinnom*, were transliterated into Greek as *gehenna*, and because of the fires that continually burned there, the latter word was used to convey the concept of eternal hell fire in the teaching of Jesus. Usually rendered "the fire of hell!" which elsewhere is called eternal (Mt. 5:22; 18:9; 25:41). *See* BENHINNOM

HIP AND THIGH A KJV, NKJV, RSV, ASV, NEB formal translation in Jdg. 15:8. The phrase is interpreted functionally as "ruthlessly" (NASB), "for all he was worth" (JB), and "viciously" (NIV).

HIPPOPOTAMUS *See* BEASTS 9.

HIRAH A friend of Judah who lived at Adullam (Ge. 38:1, 12). †

HIRAM [(my) brother is elevated]
1. A king of Tyre, a Phoenician, who helped David and Solomon with cedar and pine logs and laborers for the building of their palaces and the temple (2Sa. 5:11; 1Ki. 5:8-12). Solomon built ships at Ezion Geber, and Hiram sent sailors who knew the sea to serve on Solomon's trading ships (2Ch. 9:21). Solomon supplied Hiram with produce (1Ki. 5:10-11) and gave him twenty cities, which Hiram did not like; also called Huram (2Ch. 2:3, NIV footnote).
2. A man whose father was Phoenician and his mother Jewish, who was a craftsman skilled in bronze work. King Solomon brought him to Jerusalem to work on the temple (1Ki. 7:13ff.); also called Huram (1Ki. 7:13ff.; 2Ch. 4:11; 2:13).

HIRELING One hired as a laborer. The regulations concerning them were spelled out and reflected in the Bible, especially the prophets (Ex. 12:43-45; Job 7:2; Mic. 3:5; Isa. 21:16).

HISTORIE German for mundane, factual, normal history. Geschichte is subjective, *significant history*. *See* GESCHICHTE

HISTORY *See* ASSYRIA; BABYLONIA; CALENDAR; CHRONOLOGY; EGYPT; FESTIVALS; GEOGRAPHY OF THE HOLY LAND; HASMONEANS; HERODS, THE; JUDGES OF ISRAEL; KINGS OF JUDAH AND ISRAEL; PERSIA; ROME, ROMANS; SELEUCIDS

HITTITES [descendants of HETH] One of the great powers of the ancient world at the time of Assyrian and Babylonian power (2Ki. 7:6; Jos. 1:4). During Bible times from Abraham on they were a prominent people throughout the land of Israel (Ge. 23:10; Ex. 23:23, 28; 2Sa. 11:3-24; Ne. 9:8). Joshua overwhelmed them in his conquest of Palestine at the "waters of Merom" (Jos. 11:19). There was considerable intermarriage between the Israelites and the Hittites which the prophet condemned (Eze. 16:3, 45). Some Hittites served under King David, and Solomon made them slaves (1Sa. 26:6; 1Ki. 9:20-21). Their empire ended with the fall of Carchemish to the Assyrians in 717 B.C., which is also reflected in the biblical record of King Hezekiah (2Ki. 19:13, Hamath). Within the lifetime of modern biblical scholars the Hittites were written off by most with the words, "a people known only from the references to them in the Bible." Many even doubted their existence until the excavations of Hugo Winckler in 1906-07. Today we know more about them from extrabiblical sources than we do from the Bible, and that is quite considerable.

HIVITES A people whose identity is yet unknown. They were descended from Canaan and together with a number of other groups inhabited early Palestine (Ge. 10:17). The center of their population appears to have been in the area of Mt. Hermon in Lebanon (Jdg. 3:3; Jos. 11:3). King Solomon enslaved them together with the related groups (1Ki. 9:20-21). Some equate the Hivites with the Horites and the Hittites. The problem is not yet resolved.

HIZKI {Yahweh is (my) strength, *or* my strength} A descendant of Benjamin (1Ch. 8:17) †

HIZKIAH {Yahweh is (my) strength} A descendant of David and Solomon (1Ch. 3:23). † In the KJV in Zep. 1:1; *see* HEZEKIAH 2.

HIZKIJAH *See* HEZEKIAH 4.

HOBAB {beloved, *possibly* deceit} Jethro was the father-in-law of Moses (Ex. 18:1). The Nu. 10:29 (see also Jdg. 4:11) passage is not sufficiently clear to let it be known whether Hobab or Reuel were other names for Jethro. One of them was called Moses' father-in-law in that text. †

HOBAH An unidentified place N of Damascus to which Abraham pursued the captors of Lot (Ge. 14:15). †

HOBAIAH {Yahweh has hidden} One whose descendants could not find the family records after the return from the captivity in Babylon and so was excluded from the priesthood (Ezr. 2:61-62; Ne. 7:63). †

HOD {grandeur} A descendant of Asher (1Ch. 7:37). †

HODAIAH, HODAVIAH {give thanks to Yahweh}

1, 2, and 3. Descendants of Manasseh, Benjamin, and David (1Ch. 5:24; 9:7; 3:24).

4. Ancestor of some Levites who returned from the Babylonian captivity with Zerubbabel (Ezr. 2:40; Ne. 7:43).

HODESH {new moon} Wife of a descendant of Benjamin (1Ch. 8:9). †

HODEVAH {give thanks to Yahweh *or* grandeur is Yahweh} *See* HODAIAH 4.

HODIAH, HODIJAH {grandeur of Yahweh}

1. A descendant of Judah (1Ch. 4:19).
2. A Levite who helped to explain the

Book of the Law of Moses, as Ezra read it (Ne. 8:7).

3, 4, and 5. Three who signed the covenant with Nehemiah (Ne. 10:10, 13, 18).

HOGLAH {partridge} The daughter of a descendant of Manasseh who had no sons; for whom, therefore, a special inheritance law was made (Nu. 26:33; 27:5-7). *See also* BETH-HOGLA, BETH HOGLAH

HOHAM A king of Hebron, one of the five who allied themselves against Joshua and the Israelites and lost his life because of it (Jos. 10:3, 22-26). †

HOLINESS, HOLY The basic concept in the words *holy, holiness, hallow, sanctify,* and *sanctification* is separation and uniqueness from pagan culture. In the Bible it is separation from sin and evil and separation unto God and his ways. Holiness is intended to be the character of the life of the man who has entered into a personal relationship to God through faith (Lev. 18:1-4; Eph. 2:19-22). It also may refer to things separated to God for worship. From Ex. 3:5 to Rev. 22:19 the words "holy," "holiness," "sanctify," and their derivatives occur hundreds of times. God is holy as is his name and word, his Son and his Spirit (Ex. 15:11; Lev. 20:3; Jer. 23:9; Mk. 1:24; Isa. 63:10-11). He has consecrated or hallowed his tent of meeting (the tabernacle), his temple, his altar, and the sacrifices, his city Jerusalem, and Zion (Ex. 40:6-9; 2Ch. 29:5-7; Nu. 18:17-19; Ne. 11:1, 18; Ob. 17). In the NT considerable emphasis is placed on the need for holiness in the believer (the temple of God) and on the holiness of the church itself (1Co. 3:16-17; Eph. 2:19-22; 1Pe. 1:13-16). Some of the Pauline Epistles commence with a doctrinal section which is followed with an extended section describing holy living, as Ro. 1—11 and 12—16. Christ died for the church in order to make it holy, and thus its individual members are called "saints" (holy) (1Co. 1:2; Eph. 5:25-27; Ro. 1:7; Eph. 1:1; Php. 1:1; Col. 1:2). *See also*

ATTRIBUTES OF GOD; CHRIST, WORK OF and SALVATION, APPLICATION OF

HOLM RSV, ASV for "cypress" in KJV, NASB, NKJV, NIV. The NEB has "Ilex" in Isa. 44:14. *See* TREES, Other Trees, *Cypress*

HOLOCAUST A burnt offering (Lev. 1:13-17).

HOLON
1. An unidentified city in the hill country of Judah (Jos. 15:51; 21:15); also called Hilen (1Ch. 6:58). †
2. An unidentified site in Moab (Jer. 48:21). †

HOLY GHOST *See* GOD, NAMES OF, GODHEAD 6., *Holy Spirit*

HOLY OF HOLIES *See* TABERNACLE and TEMPLE

HOLY PLACE *See* TABERNACLE and TEMPLE

HOLY SPIRIT *See* GOD, NAMES OF, GODHEAD 6.

HOMAM, HEMAN A grandson of Seir the Horite; also called Heman (Ge. 36:22; 1Ch. 1:39). In a NIV footnote to the Genesis passage he is called Hemam. †

HOMER [the load a donkey can carry] *See* WEIGHTS AND MEASURES

HOMOLEGOMENA Accepted books of the NT canon that needed no discussion before recognition. *Antilegomenon* are books that were disputed.

HOMOSEXUALITY Sexual activity among people of the same sex. The practice is forbidden in Lev. 18:22. It is condemned as an act of the natural man in Ro. 1:27. Because of salvation, Christians are assumed to no longer be practicing this sin nor the other sins of 1Co. 6:9-11.

HONEY The product of the bee, first wild and later domesticated (Jdg. 14:8; 2Ch. 31:5; Ps. 81:16). The word may also refer to a sort of thick syrup made from grapes, a favorite of the Arabs. It was an important item for both food and export (Ge. 43:11; Pr. 24:13). Honey and honeycomb figuratively refer to sweet and pleasant things (Pr. 16:24).

HONOR When referring to God, the translation of this word and the word glory is usually "majesty" or "splendor." In the OT the reference is usually to man, and the translation is "honor." It conveys the idea of respect and esteem for or from other persons. It is a gift from God and consists of physical and spiritual blessings. It may be forfeited if man sins against God. In both Testaments great emphasis is placed on the showing of honor to one's parents. It is one of the Ten Commandments (Ex. 20:12; Mt. 15:4; Eph. 6:13). Jesus has been crowned with honor as the result of his having suffered death to redeem mankind, and in due time to him every knee will bow and every tongue confess (1Ti. 1:17; 6:16; 2Pe. 1:16-21; Rev. 4:9; 5:9-12; 7:12).

HOOD *See* DRESS

HOOK The English translation of many Hebrew words and one Greek word which refer to such items as: hooks that support the curtains of the tabernacle by fastening them to the pillars or cross rods; hooks put in animals or captives by which to lead them; hooks for fishing; hooks for picking up hot meat called forks (Ex. 26:31-33; 1Sa. 2:13-14; Eze. 19:9; 2Ki. 19:28; Am. 4:2; Job 41:1; Ex. 27:3).

HOOPOE *See* BIRDS 5.

HOPE In the Bible this word is used in the usual sense of expecting and trusting, without any particular theological meaning (Ru. 1:12). It has in addition a very distinct theological connotation, closely tied with faith. In the OT God is the hope of Israel (Jer. 14:7-8; Ps. 62:5). The Greek word in the NT is *elpis* and carries the idea of hope, trust, and faith, as may be seen from the contexts of Heb. 10:23 and Eph. 1:12. It is clearly expressed elsewhere (Ro. 5:2; Gal. 5:5; Eph. 1:11-14). NT hope is also the hope of eternal life (1Co. 15:19-26ff.). Paul presents a concept of deliverance for this physical universe as well (Ro. 8:19-25), associated with man's final redemption. The apostle also tied together the hope of the Christian with the hope of Israel (Ac. 26:6-8; 28:20). *See* FAITH

HOPHNI [tadpole] *See* PHINEAS

HOPHRA [(pagan god) RA endures, IDB] A Pharaoh of the time of Jeremiah whose doom he predicted (Jer. 44:30). †

HOR
1. The mountain in the Negev, near the border of Edom (104-017), where Aaron died (Nu. 20:22-29).
2. A mountain in Lebanon on the N border of the land given to Israel (Nu. 34:7-8).

HOR HAGGIDGAD [cavern of the GIDGAD] A stop on the exodus route of the Israelites from Egypt; also called Gudgodah (Nu. 33:32-33; Dt. 10:7). †

HORAM [height, ISBE] A king of Gezer defeated by Joshua (Jos. 10:33). †

HOREB [dry, desolate] A synonym of Mt. Sinai (Ex. 3:1; Dt. 1:2, 6, 19). *See* SINAI

HOREM [consecrated] An unidentified site in the tribal area of Naphtali (Jos. 19:38). †

HORESH [wooded place, forest] The underlying Hebrew text in the LXX apparently read HODESH which was translated "new." An unidentified place in the Desert of Ziph where David hid from Saul and Jonathan covenanted with David (1Sa. 23:15-18). In the KJV the word is translated "word."

HORI, HORIMS, HORITES
1. The firstborn son of Lotan (Ge. 36:22; 1Ch. 1:39).
2. The father of Shaphat, tribe of Simeon (Nu. 13:5).
3. A tribe from Hori (1.). They lived in the area of Seir (Ge. 14:6). The Edomites replace them in Seir (Dt. 2:12, 22).

HORMAH [consecration] A city (146-069) in the tribal area of Judah and Simeon (Jos. 15:30; 19:4; Jdg. 1:17).

Earlier the Israelites tried unsuccessfully to take the area by force after God had decreed judgment upon them for the "bad report" that the twelve spies brought back from Canaan (Nu. 14:39-45).

HORN A container made from the horn of an animal for holding liquids. It is sometimes translated "writing kit" in the NIV (1Sa. 16:1; Eze. 9:2). Symbolically horns represent force (1Ki. 22:11; Zec. 1:18-21). *See* ALTAR; MUSIC

HORNS OF THE ALTAR *See* ALTAR

HORNET *See* BEASTS 6.

HORONAIM [twin hollows, twin caves] A place (211-055) in Moab (2Sa. 13:34; Isa. 15:5; Jer. 48:3, 5, 34). †

HORONITE A designation of Sanballat perhaps referring to his place of origin (Ne. 2:10, 19; 13:28). †

HORSE *See* BEASTS 4.

HORSE LEECH KJV in Pr. 30:15. *See* BEASTS 6., *leech*

HOSAH [refuge]
1. A town (perhaps 170-293), on the northern border of Asher, near Tyre (Jos. 19:29). †
2. A gatekeeper before the Ark of the Covenant in David's day (1Ch. 16:38; 26:10-11, 16). †

HOSANNA A word which if literally translated would mean "save us, please!" but which was and is used as an exclamation of praise (Mt. 21:9).

HOSEA [salvation] One of the prophets, who was commanded to marry Gomer, and love her even though she was unfaithful. Through this experience he learned something of God's love for his people, for they too had been unfaithful (Hos. 1:1, 3; 3:1).

HOSEA, BOOK OF *See* PROPHETS, BOOKS OF THE MINOR

HOSHAIAH [Yahweh has saved]
1. One of the leaders of the dedication procession after the rebuilding of the wall of Jerusalem by Nehemiah (Ne. 12:32). †

2. Father of one of the commanders who opposed Jeremiah (Jer. 42:1; 43:2ff.). †

HOSHAMA {Yahweh has heard} A descendant of David and Solomon (1Ch. 3:18). †

HOSHEA {salvation}
1. *See* KINGS OF JUDAH AND ISRAEL.
2. The name of Joshua prior to the time that Moses changed it (Nu. 13:16).
3. A leader of the tribe of Ephraim in the days of David (1Ch. 27:20).
4. One who signed the covenant with Nehemiah (Ne. 10:23).

HOSPITALITY The practice of welcoming strangers and giving lodging. This was found in the OT (Ge. 18:18). The NT encourages it (Ro. 12:13; Heb. 13:2; 1Pe. 4:9). It is a requirement of church leaders (1Ti. 3:2; Tit. 1:8) and widows on the list (1Ti. 5:10).

HOST {army} *See* ARMY; GOD, NAMES OF, GODHEAD 4., *Yahweh Tsebaoth*

HOTHAM {signet ring, seal}
1. A descendant of Asher (1Ch. 7:32, 35). †
2. The father of two of David's mighty men (1Ch. 11:44). †

HOTHAN *See* HOTHAM

HOTHIR {one who remains} One of the sons of a seer of David (1Ch. 25:4, 28). †

HOUGH *See* HAMSTRING HORSES

HOUR
1. A time of the day (Mk. 11:11).
2. A (short) unit of time. The 12th part of a day, the duration of daylight (Ac. 5:7). This word can mean "a moment" (Gal. 2:5).
3. A numbered hour that is reckoned differently than modern time (Ac. 2:15). The third hour is 9:00 A.M.
4. A general, indefinite word for "that time" (Mt. 10:19). It can refer to the end times (Rev. 3:3; 14:7). *See* TIME

HOUSE An abode for humans from the simplest types for peasants to palaces for nobles or royalty, including temples for deities. In the hill country of Palestine the lower parts of houses were made of field or dressed stone while the upper part might be of mud or mud bricks dried in the sun. Where stone was a scarce commodity, the entire structure was made of mud bricks. Wood was used for the roof support and sometimes for the superstructure as well. On the wooden support would be laid brushwood with mud plaster on top of that. Roofs were usually flat and had a multiplicity of uses. It was the duty of a good son to keep the mud roof properly plastered during the rainy season.

From the street one usually entered a courtyard off of which were the doors to the several rooms. The floors of the room might be of beaten earth or earth packed over a layer of rough stones. In better homes stone slab floors were used, and some even were plastered with lime and earth mixtures. Wooden doors were used in some cases with locks and keys. Windows were treated as small doors usually high in the walls. Hearths for fire existed, but rarely was there a chimney. The smoke escaped through the doors and windows. Modern archaeologists have learned much about the floor plans and structures of houses in antiquity. Almost any archaeological report will show plans. *See also* BETH 2.; BRICKS

HOUSEHOLD GODS *See* DEITIES 3.

HOZAI "the seer" (see NIV footnote to 2Ch. 33:19). †

HUBBAH A descendant of Asher (1Ch. 7:34). In the KJV the name appears as Jehubbah. †

HUKKOK A town (175-252) in the tribal area of Naphtali by the waters of Merom (Jos. 19:34). †

HUKOK *See* HELKATH

HUL A descendant of Noah and Shem (Ge. 10:23; 1Ch. 1:17). †

HULDAH {weasel} A prophetess in the days of King Josiah (2Ki. 22:14; 2Ch. 34:22). †

HUMAN *See* MAN, MANKIND

HUMAN NATURE The universal makeup of a human being.

HUMANISM This word is a general word that can refer to interest in the studies of the literary humanities. This word in Christian circles can refer to the idea that mankind is to focus all its attention and energy to itself and not look for help or salvation from any deity. Mankind is elevated to a majestic status without God. Christians respond that man has majesty indeed, but only because of the source of his being, God the Creator. The Creator therefore has priority in everything. To know God and enjoy him is the purpose of life.

HUMANITY OF CHRIST *See* CHRIST, LIFE AND TEACHINGS OF

HUMBLE, HUMILITY Humility can imply lower status on the economic and social scale. Humility has a positive sense with respect to one's not thinking too highly of one's self and his/her social standing. God pours out his favor on humble persons. Humility is a requirement for heavenly reward (Mt. 18:4; 23:12; Lk. 14:11; 18:14). Christ exhibited humility in his sacrifice (Ac. 8:32-33). Paul served with humility of mind (Ac. 20:19). The Christian is to relate in humility to others (Php. 2:3, 5-11; 1Pe. 3:8). A similar word is gentleness. The opposite of humility is pride (Jas. 4:6). *See* PRIDE

HUMTAH {an (unclean) reptile} An unidentified site in the hill country of Judah (Jos. 15:54). †

HUNDREDS The name of a military unit (Ex. 18:21; Nu. 31:14).

HUNDRED, TOWER OF *See* MEAH

HUNGER This word can be used two ways: literally to be physically hungry; figuratively to want eagerly (Dt. 28:48; Mt. 5:6). *See* SOUL 5.

HUNTING Pursuing wild animals for food or pleasure or, for safety from dangerous ones. Weapons, snares, or nets, dogs and falcons were commonly used. The blood of game animals had to be poured out on the ground and covered with earth according to the Levitical dietary laws (Lev. 17:13). Among the weapons used were the bow and arrow, the spear, the sword, or even the club (Ge. 27:3; Mic. 7:2; 1Sa. 17:40).

HUPHAM, HUPHAMITES A descendant of Benjamin; perhaps also called Huppim and even Huram (Nu. 26:39; Ge. 46:21; 1Ch. 8:5). †

HUPPAH {canopy, *hence* protection} Head of one of the priestly divisions (1Ch. 24:13).

HUPPIM *See* HUPHAM

HUR
   1. A man who with Aaron held up the hands of Moses during a battle with the Amalekites and later assisted Aaron in the administration of the Israelites (Ex. 17:10, 12; 24:14).
   2. Grandson of Bezalel of the tribe of Judah who was both a skilled artist and craftsman in the work of the tabernacle and also gifted by God to teach others (Ex. 31:25; 35:30-34).
   3. A descendant of Judah and son of Caleb, founder of Bethlehem (1Ch. 2:19; 4:1, 4).
   4. A king of Midian (Nu. 31:8).
   5. Father of one Rephaiah who worked on the wall of Jerusalem with Nehemiah (Ne. 3:9).

HURAI *See* HIDDAI

HURAM *See* HIRAM and HUPHAM

HURAM-ABI *See* HIRAM

HURI {linen weaver, ISBE} A descendant of Gad (1Ch. 5:14). †

HURRIANS *See* HORI, HORITES

HUSBAND *See* MARRIAGE

HUSBANDMAN, HUSBANDRY A tiller of the ground, mostly of vineyards but also of farmlands. *See* FARMING; GARDENER; VINE, VINEYARD

HUSHAH, HUSHATHITE A descendant of Judah (1Ch. 4:4). Sibbecai

(Mebunnai), one of David's mighty men, was from this village (2Sa. 21:18; 23:27; 1Ch. 11:29; 20:4; 27:11). †

HUSHAI The friend of David who stayed in Jerusalem in order to counter the advice of Ahithophel when David had to flee (2Sa. 15:32-37; 17:5-15).

HUSHAM A king of Edom who reigned there before Israel had a king (Ge. 36:34-35; 1Ch. 1:45-46). †

HUSHATHITE *See* HUSHAH, HUSHATHITE

HUSHIM, HUSHITES
 1. A son of Dan probably also the one called Shuham (Ge. 46:23; Nu. 26:42-43). †
 2. Descendants of Benjamin (1Ch. 7:12). †
 3. One of the two wives of a descendant of Benjamin (1Ch. 8:8, 11). †

HUSKS KJV for "skins" (of a grape) (Nu. 6:4), and "carob pods" (Lk. 15:16). *See* TREES, Other Trees, *Carob*

HUZ *See* UZ 2.

HUZZAB KJV takes this as a proper name; other versions think it is the verb *to establish, determine, or decree.* NIV translates this as "decreed" (Na. 2:7).

HYACINTH *See* PRECIOUS STONES AND METALS, Precious Stones 6., *Jacinth*

HYENA *See* BEASTS 8.

HYKSOS *See* EGYPT

HYMENAEUS {of (pagan god) HYMEN} One who had adopted heresies for which he was excommunicated by Paul (1Ti. 1:19-20; 2Ti. 2:17-18). †

HYMN {song} *See* HALLEL; MUSIC

HYPOCRISY, HYPOCRITE {pretender, pretentious} In the NIV used only in NT. Where the KJV uses these translations in the OT, the NIV usually uses "godless" or "ungodly" (Isa. 33:14; Job 8:13). These words are transliterations into English of Greek words which meant to act a part in a play or to pretend. Hence in English these words carry the negative connotation of feigning to be what one is not. Some scholars think that this is what is meant in NT usage, while others think strongly that the NT meaning is more like that of the OT—namely, opposition to God and thus the godlessness of the one who opposes him.

HYSSOP *See* PLANTS, PERFUMES, AND SPICES, Miscellaneous Plants 7.

I

I AM

1. Ex. 3:14; *see* GOD, NAMES OF, GODHEAD, *Yahweh*.

2. Jesus Christ gave seven titles of who he was:

Jn. 6:35	I am the Bread of Life.
Jn. 8:12	I am the Light of the World.
Jn. 10:7	I am the Door of the sheep.
Jn. 10:11	I am the Good Shepherd.
Jn. 11:25	I am the Resurrection and the Life.
Jn. 14:6	I am the Way, the Truth and the Life.
Jn. 15:1	I am the true Vine.

3. It is axiomatic that the deity of Christ is taught in Scripture (Jn. 1:1). Some think that because Jesus in the Gospel of John used a phrase "I am" (*ego eimi*) that this is a reference to Ex. 3:14 and the divine personal name of God (*see* 1 above). But in John it is usually not the divine name. Normally the Greek idea is a rather bland construction that means simply "it is me." Possibly instead of invoking the divine name, Jesus was stating his eternality in Jn. 8:58. The full divine name in Ex.3:14 in the Septuagint is *ego eimi ho on*, sometimes shortened, as in Rev. 1:8, to just *ho on* "who is" (BD sect. 143); cf. 22:13. In this verse "the Lord God" is also the common OT designation of "I AM," *Yahweh* (the divine name) and *Elohim*. (J.A.S.)

IBEX *See* BEASTS 2.

IBHAR {he chooses} One of the sons of David, born in Jerusalem (2Sa. 5:15; 1Ch. 3:6; 14:5). †

IBIS RSV for "Great Owl" in Lev. 11:17. Most other versions have "Screech Owl." *See* BIRDS 5.

IBLEAM A town (177-205) in Asher which was assigned to Manasseh (Jos. 17:11; Jdg. 1:27; 2Ki. 9:27). †

IBNEIAH, IBNIJAH {Yahweh built} Descendant of Benjamin (1Ch. 9:8). †

IBRI {Hebrew} A descendant of Levi (1Ch. 24:27). †

IBSAM {fragrance} A grandson of Issachar (1Ch. 7:2). In the KJV the name appears as Jibsam. †

IBZAN {swift} *See* JUDGES OF ISRAEL

ICE *See* SNOW; *see also* PRECIOUS STONES AND METALS, Precious Stones 15., *Crystal*

ICHABOD {where is the glory?} Grandson of Eli. His mother died during his birth and gave him this name when she was told that the glory of God had departed from Israel. The words *i* and *chabod* mean "no glory" (1Sa. 4:19-22). †

ICONIUM A city in Asia Minor visited by Paul on his missionary journey where he endured persecutions (Ac. 13:51; 14:1, 19-21; 16:2; 2Ti. 3:11). †

ICONOCLAST One who breaks icons or images or one opposed to their worship. A controversy emerged between the state (wanting to remove icons) and church (wanting to keep icons) from A.D. 717 to 843.

IDALAH An unidentified site in the tribal area of Zebulun (Jos. 19:15). †

IDBASH {honey} A descendant of Judah (1Ch. 4:3). †

IDDO

1. Father of one of Solomon's twelve officers in charge of providing his food (1Ki. 4:14).

2. A descendant of Levi (1Ch. 6:21).

3. An officer over part of the tribe of Manasseh in the time of David (1Ch. 27:21).

4. A prophet who wrote some of the history of King Solomon and his son and grandson (2Ch. 9:29; 12:15; 13:22).

5. The grandfather of the prophet Zechariah (Zec. 1:1, 7).

6. The head of some temple servants from Casiphia who sent men to help Ezra after the Babylonian captivity (Ezr. 8:17).

7. Father of a priest in the days of Joiakim (Ne. 12:16).

IDLENESS *See* LAZY

IDOL, IDOLATRY {image} This was the worship of false gods, usually by means of images. Whenever images were involved, the Israelites were commanded to "destroy them out" of their land. After the LORD had made a covenant not to make any graven image (Ex. 20:4), the insecure people needing a god to go before them constructed a golden calf (Ex. 32:1ff.). Their idolatry eventually led them into the punishment of foreign captivity (Ex. 23:23-24; Dt. 7:5; 1Ki. 14:22-24; 16:30-33). In the NT, the OT concept is carried over and made even more stringent in that it is considered idolatry to put anything ahead of God (Eph. 5:5; Col. 3:5). *See also* DEITIES 3., *Images*

IDUMEA {(land of) EDOM} *See* GEOGRAPHY OF THE HOLY LAND

IEZER, IEZERITE {my (father) is help} A descendant of Manasseh (Jeezer in the KJV) and his clan; also called Abiezer (Nu. 26:30; Jos. 17:2). †

IGAL, IGEAL {he redeems}

1. The spy that represented the tribe of Issachar (Nu. 13:7). †

2. One of David's mighty men, son of Nathan (2Sa. 23:36). †

3. A descendant of David (1Ch. 3:22), spelled Igeal in the KJV. †

IGDALIAH {Yahweh is great} "A man of God" in Jeremiah's time (Jer. 35:4). †

IGEAL {he redeems} *See* IGAL 3.

IIM {heaps, ruins} An unidentified site in Judah (Jos. 15:29). †

IJE-ABARIM *See* IYE ABARIM

IJON {place of heaps (of stone)} A town (205-308) in the tribal area of Naphtali, early captured by the Syrian king Ben-Hadad and later by the king of Assyria, Tiglath-Pileser III (1Ki. 15:20; 2Ki. 15:29; 2Ch. 16:4). †

IKKESH {crooked, perverted} Father of Ira, one of David's Thirty (2Sa. 23:26; 1Ch. 11:28; 27:9). †

ILAI One of David's mighty men; also called Zalmon (1Ch. 11:29; 2Sa. 23:28). †

ILEX *See* HOLM; TREES

ILLNESS *See* HEALING, HEALTH; SICK, SICKNESS

ILLYRICUM *See* DALMATIA

IMAGE, IMAGES *See* DEITIES 3.; IDOL, IDOLATRY

IMAGE OF GOD That which differentiates mankind from the rest of creation (Ge. 1:26). *See* ADAM

IMAGE WORSHIP *See* IDOL, IDOLATRY

IMAGO DEI Latin for "image of God."

IMLA(H) {fullness} The father of the prophet Micaiah who lived in the days of King Ahab (1Ki. 22:8-28; 2Ch. 7-8). †

IMMACULATE CONCEPTION The Roman Catholic teaching that Mary,

Jesus' mother, was preserved from original sin. However, she experienced the temporal penalties of Adam's sin: bodily limits, sorrow, and bodily death.

IMMANENCE The indwelling and activity of God in the universe and in human history. The counterpart of this word is "transcendence."

IMMANUEL, EMMANUEL [with us (is) El] The name given by Isaiah to the child whose special birth he predicted, applied to Jesus in the NT (Isa. 7:14; 8:8; Mt. 1:23), which means "God with us." *See* MAID; VIRGIN BIRTH

IMMER [lamb, KB]
1. Head of one of the priestly divisions in the days of David (1Ch. 24:14).

2, 3, 4, and 5. Priests by this name are mentioned in Ezra and Nehemiah, some of whom may be descendants of the Immer above. One is noted among those who returned with Zerubbabel from Babylon; another as one who married a foreign wife in that period; another was the father of one who helped Nehemiah repair the wall of Jerusalem; and another as an ancestor of some who lived in Jerusalem after the return (Ezr. 2:37; 10:20; Ne. 3:29; 11:13).

6. Father of the priest who beat Jeremiah the prophet and put him in the stocks (Jer. 20:1-2).

7. One of the places in Babylonia where Jewish captives were kept (Ezr. 2:59).

IMMERSION *See* BAPTISM

IMMORAL *See* FORNICATION

IMMORTAL, IMMORTALITY The NT concept of immortality is that of eternal life of the whole person, spirit and body. At death the nonmaterial part of man goes either to paradise or to a place which is described as one where the inhabitant is "in agony in this flame" (Lk. 23:43; 16:24). The material part, or body, goes to the grave (Ps. 88:5). According to the Bible, there is to be a resurrection in which the bodies, restored in the nature of the case, come out of the graves, are reinhabited by their spirits, and commence the eternal form of their existence to either live in heaven or to be condemned to hell (Da. 12:2; Isa. 26:19; Ps. 16:9-11; Isa 19:25-27; Ps. 16:9-11; Isa. 26:19; Da. 12:2; Jn. 5:28-29; 1Co. 15:12-54; 1Th. 4:16). The NT presents the picture of all the resurrected gathered before God for separation. They are to be judged on the basis of what they did in life, and those whose names are not found in the "book of life" will be "thrown into the lake of fire." The basis of the separation for the two aspects of eternal life is as to whether those judged are considered by Christ as "my sheep" or not, those for whom he made the atonement when he laid down his life (Jn. 10:7-11, 27-30). Eternal life for the believer is not an inactive endless existence but rather freedom from all the evils of this present world and active service of worshiping God in fellowship with his Son their Savior. *See* DEAD, ABODE OF; *See also* DEATH; FUTURE LIFE; SOUL; SPIRIT

IMMUTABILITY [not changeable] *See* ATTRIBUTES OF GOD 5.

IMNA [*possibly* he is withheld, BDB; luck, fortune, IDB] A descendant of Asher (1Ch. 7:35). †

IMNAH, IMNITE [good fortune]
1. A son of Asher and his clan (Ge. 46:17; Nu. 26:44; 1Ch. 7:30). In the KJV the name appears as Jimnah. †

2. A Levite who lived in the days of King Hezekiah (2Ch. 31:14). †

IMPERISHABLE Something that is not subject to rust, moths, old age, or decay. Therefore, the word has the idea of timelessness. God has this characteristic (Ro. 1:23; 1Ti. 1:17). The resurrection body will have this quality (1Co. 15:52). Unlike the earthly victor's wreath (*stephanos*) that withers and shrivels, the heavenly victor's wreath is not perishable (1Co. 9:25). A woman's looks and clothing and jewelry will fade, but the spiritual qualities will endure (1Pe. 3:4).

IMPERIAL REGIMENT The name of the segment of Roman soldiers whose centurion was responsible for bringing Paul to Rome (Ac. 27:1).

IMPOSITION OF HANDS *See* LAYING ON OF HANDS

IMPRECATORY PSALMS *See* PSALMS, BOOK OF (4)

IMPRISON *See* CAPTIVITY; PRISON

IMPURE *See* CLEAN AND UNCLEAN

IMPURITY *See* CLEAN AND UNCLEAN; FORNICATION

IMPUTE, IMPUTATION The transfer as a charge or credit of one's sin or righteousness to another. The biblical image is of reckoning or keeping accounts as in a ledger book. Romans 5:18-19 is a good summary verse of the concept of imputation in both the positive and negative sense. Through Adam's transgression, sin was imputed to all men, resulting in condemnation. Through Jesus Christ's act of sacrifice, imputation of righteousness is made to all men. The means to this reckoning of righteousness for a person is found in Ro. 4:3-5. Paul argues here that righteousness is reckoned through faith not works. The Christian is urged to acknowledge this fact and respond to his new life in Christ by no longer letting sin rule in his mortal body, but presenting himself alive to God as an instrument of righteousness (Ro. 6:1-14). *See* SALVATION

IMRAH [he rebels] A descendant of Asher (1Ch. 7:36). †

IMRI {Yahweh spoke}
1. A descendant of Judah who returned from captivity (1Ch. 9:4). †
2. Father of one of the men who built the wall of Jerusalem with Nehemiah (Ne. 3:2). †

INCANTATION
See DIVINATION

INCARNATION [taking on flesh] *See* CHRIST, LIFE OF

INCENSE Incense which was burned to make a pleasant odor was used in either religious worship or to honor a distinguished individual. The prescription for making incense for the worship of God was regulated in the law, and this type was not allowed to be used for other purposes (Ex. 30:34-38). There was an altar of incense overlaid with pure gold placed in the temple itself just in front of the veil that separated the holy place from the outer part of the temple. Here Aaron, and later the high priest in Israel, burned incense daily; and on the Day of Atonement he carried incense within the veiled area itself (Ex. 30:1-9; Lev. 16:11-14ff.).

INCEST Sexual relations between family members and in-laws, forbidden and outlined in great detail in Lev. 18:1-30.

INCORRUPTIBLE *See* IMMORTAL, IMMORTALITY; IMPERISHABLE

INDIA The Persian king Xerxes reigned from India to Ethiopia (Cush), the only references to India in the Bible (Est. 1:1, 8:9).

INERRANCY The belief that the Bible has no error (not even in history or science), normally ascribed to the original documents. This term has a broad range of qualifications by various theologians. *See* SCRIPTURE

INFALLIBILITY
The belief that God's Word will not fail in its purpose. The exact nature of its "purpose" lies at the heart of debate on inerrancy and inspiration.

INFANT BAPTISM *See* BAPTISM, INFANT

INFANTRY *See* ARMS AND ARMOR; ARMY; WAR

INFIRMITY *See* SICK, SICKNESS; WEAKNESS

INFLAMMATION *See* SICK, SICKNESS

INGATHERING, FEAST OF *See* CALENDAR and FESTIVALS

INHERITANCE Inheritance was fully and carefully regulated by law in ancient Israel. This referred to the land owned by a family as well as to items of personal property. The land had to stay within the family. The estate was divided into so many portions, according to the number of the sons, plus one. The heir, the first-born, then received two of these portions, called a double portion, and the other sons shared equally the remainder. If there were no sons, then the estate could go to a daughter; but it was necessary for her to marry within the tribe as the land was never allowed to leave it. If there were no daughter, it still had to stay within the family or tribe, and this too was under legislation (Nu. 27:8-11; 36:6-9; Dt. 21:17). The heir cared for the women, but if there was no heir, then the next of kin on the husband's side was required to marry her and raise up seed for the deceased relative (Ru. 3:8-13). *See* MARRIAGE, *Levirate Marriage.*

The word *inheritance* is used in symbolic senses in the Bible. It refers to such items as: the land of Canaan promised by God as an inheritance to Abraham and his seed after him; Israel as God's inheritance; Christ being God's heir; those who believe in Christ as being adopted by God and thus fellow heirs with Christ (Nu. 34:2; 1Ki. 8:36; Ge. 17:7-8; Dt. 32:9; Jer. 10:16; Heb. 1:2; 9:14-15; Ro. 8:17). The inheritance of the believer is the blessing of God in this present life, and the blessings of an eternal state free from evil and wickedness in the future life (Mt. 25:34; 1Co. 6:9-11; 1Pe. 1:3-5). *See also* BIRTHRIGHT; FIRSTBORN

INIQUITIES *See* SIN

INK A mixture of lampblack or vegetable soot and gum arabic (i.e., the sap of an acacia tree) moistened with water (Jer. 36:18; 2Jn. 12).

INN In the NIV the word is used only in the account of the birth of Jesus and in the story told by Jesus of the Samaritan who cared for the injured traveler found on the Jericho road (Lk. 2:7; 10:34). References to "lodging places" are found.

Inns were not like our concept of hotels or lodging places. They were more frequently than not merely an enclosure where a person could spend the night, either in the open courtyard, or in a stall around its edges, or in a cave opening off of the courtyard. Since these lacked comfort and since the keeper often had a bad reputation, it became customary for travelers to seek the hospitality of friends (2Ki. 4:8; Heb. 13:2).

INNOCENT, INNOCENT BLOOD

1. Innocent can mean to be righteous, having no reason for punishment (Mt. 23:35; Lk. 23:47). To be "clean" is to be innocent (Ac. 20:26).

2. The phrase "innocent blood" is an OT phrase found in Dt. 19:10; 27:25 ("blood" not translated). Blood is a figure representing the whole person or life of the person. Innocent blood refers to a guiltless person (Mt. 27:4, 24). *See* BLOOD

I.N.R.I. Latin initials: *I,* Jesus of; *N,* Nazareth; *R,* King of; *I,* Jews.

INSECTS *See* BEASTS 6.

INSIGHT *See* UNDERSTANDING

INSPIRATION God's breath actively producing, and having ultimate control over, the Scripture (2Ti. 3:16; 2Pe. 1:19-21). *See* HERMENEUTICS; SCRIPTURE

INSPIRATION, DICTATION The belief that God dictated the actual words of Scripture to the writer's literary style and personality.

INSPIRATION, DYNAMIC The belief that God gave the writers of Scripture the thoughts to write but not the choice of words.

INSPIRATION, ILLUMINATION The belief that God heightened the regular abilities of the writers of Scripture but gave no direct guidance.

INSPIRATION, PLENARY, VERBAL Plenary inspiration involves the belief that all portions of all books in the canon are fully inspired by God. Verbal means specific guidance was given by God to use the exact words he wanted. This view does not normally deny the personality of the author to write according to his/her style.

INSTRUCTION *See* DISCIPLE; TEACHER

INSULT *See* BLASPHEMY; CURSE; OATH; SLANDER

INTERCESSION *See* PRAYER

INTEREST *See* DEBT

INTERMEDIATE STATE *See* RESURRECTION; DEAD, ABODE OF; RAPTURE

INTERPRETATION *See* HERMENEUTICS

INTERTESTAMENTAL PERIOD *See* ALEXANDER 1.; HASMONEANS; MACCABEES; PTOLEMY; SELEUCIDS

INVOKE To call on someone for help or to call down a curse or a blessing upon oneself or another (2Sa. 14:11; Mt. 26:74). *See* CURSE

IOB *See* JASHUB, JASHUBITE(S)

IOTA The smallest Greek letter. *See* JOT

IPHEDEIAH, IPHDEIAH {Yahweh redeems} A descendant of Benjamin (1Ch. 8:25). †

IPHTAH {he opens} An unidentified site in the western foothills of Judah (Jos. 15:43). In the KJV the name appears as JIPHTAH. †

IPHTAH EL {El opens} An unidentified valley between the tribal areas of Asher and Zebulun (Jos. 19:14, 27). †

IR {*possibly* stallion donkey} A descendant of Benjamin (1Ch. 7:12; cf. 7:7). †

IRA {*possibly* stallion donkey}
1. A priest in the time of David (2Sa. 20:26).
2 and 3. Two of David's Thirty (2Sa. 23:26, 38).

IRAD A grandson of Cain (Ge. 4:18). †

IRAM One of the chiefs of Edom descended from Esau (Ge. 36:43; 1Ch. 1:54). †

IRAN *See* PARTHIANS; PERSIA

IRI A Benjamite (1Ch. 7:7). †

IRIJAH {Yahweh sees} The captain of the guard who seized Jeremiah (Jer. 37:13-14). †

IR NAHASH {city of NAHASH} A site (191-010) in the tribal area of Judah (1Ch. 4:12). †

IRON
1. Iron did not come into general use until the time of the Hittites in the middle of the second millennium B.C. Prior to that, some beads of meteoric iron were found in predynastic Egypt, plus one mass of iron from Sixth Dynasty times. There is one early reference to iron in the Bible probably of the meteoric variety (Ge. 4:22). Israel had trouble driving out the Canaanites since they had iron while Israel did not (Jdg. 1:19; Jos. 17:18). The Philistines controlled the ability to sharpen iron instruments (1Sa. 13:19-20). Later the Phoenician craftsmen taught the Israelites this art, after which it spread rapidly to all sorts of uses in Israel: for instruments of war, for farming, and for building (2Ch. 2:11-14; Job 20:24; 2Sa. 12:31; 1Ch. 22:14). The iron yoke was a symbol of slavery and captivity, and iron symbolized strength for both security and destruction (Job 40:16-18; Ps. 107:10-11; Jer. 28:13; Da. 7:7). *See* PRECIOUS STONES AND METALS, Metals 4., *Iron*
2. *See* YIRON

IRPEEL {El heals} An unidentified site in the tribal area of Benjamin (Jos. 18:27). †

IRRIGATION *See* AQUEDUCT; FARMING

IR SHEMESH {city of SHEMESH} An unidentified site in the tribal area of Dan (Jos. 19:41). †

IRU A son of Caleb (1Ch. 4:15). †

ISAAC [he laughs, he will laugh, *some contexts* mock; *other contexts* El (God) laughs] The son of Abraham and Sarah, husband of Rebekah, and father of Esau and Jacob (Ge. 21:3; 22:7; 24:67; 25:21, 25-26). In obedience to the command of God, Abraham went to Moriah to offer his son as a sacrifice; but God prevented it and provided a substitute instead (Ge. 22:2, 12-13). He had many of the same troubles that his father did in Gerar and Beersheba (Ge. 26). His mother conspired with Jacob and stole the ancestral blessing from Esau. Isaac died in Hebron (Ge. 27:1-10; 35:27-29).

ISAIAH, ISAIAS [Yahweh saves] One of the major writing prophets, son of Amoz, who lived and prophesied in the days of the kings of Judah—Uzziah, Jotham, Ahaz, Hezekiah, and perhaps also Manasseh (Isa. 1:1). In the OT we learn a few details of his life from his relations with King Hezekiah (2Ki. 19—20; 2Ch. 32:20-32), otherwise only from the book that bears his name. In the NT twenty of his prophecies are cited in connection with fulfillments, more than those of any other single prophet, five of them in Romans and the rest in the Gospels and Acts. Besides the quotations in the NT there is the incident of the Ethiopian eunuch who was reading Isaiah to whom an angel of the Lord sent Philip as an expositor (Ac. 8:26-35).

ISAIAH, BOOK OF The first of the Major Prophets, the Book of Isaiah consists of sixty-six chapters, representing a prophetic ministry of nearly sixty years (c. 739-683 B.C.), and covering a wide variety of themes. Because of the wealth of predictions concerning Christ, Isaiah has been called "the evangelical prophet." The unity of the authorship of the entire book is clearly attested by the NT evangelists and apostles (Mt. 3:3; 12:17-18; Ac. 8:34; Ro. 10:16, 20; note esp. Jn. 12:38-41, which definitely asserts the same author for Isa. 6:9-10 and Isa. 53:1.) The truthfulness of Christ and his apostles is therefore at issue in the question of Isaiah's authorship of chapters 40—66.

Nevertheless, because of a rationalistic dislike of the possibility of supernatural revelation and fulfilled prophecy, higher criticism since Johann Doederlein (1789) has argued for a later authorship ("Deutero-Isaiah") for chapters 40—66. The argument is that the writer of Isaiah must have written shortly before the fall of Babylon in 539 since he foresaw the conquest of Babylon by Cyrus of Persia. Nineteenth-century higher critics have sought to prove even later authorship for chapters 56—66. The objective evidence of the text itself cannot, however, be reconciled with postexilic authorship. (1) It is inconceivable that the true name of the author of the admittedly sublimest passages in all Hebrew prophetic literature could have been totally forgotten, when even the two-page prophecy of Obadiah still bears the author's name. (2) The eighth-century prophet Isaiah evidently knew about the coming Babylonian captivity (cf. 13:1, "An oracle concerning Babylon that Isaiah son of Amoz saw"). He even knew of the restoration from exile (cf. 6:13), which states that after the complete devastation, depopulation, and exile of Judah, a remnant, a "tenth" shall return to the land, a promise which Isaiah evidently claimed when he in 7:3 named his firstborn son Shear-Jashub, which meant "a remnant shall return". (3) Isaiah 40—66 refers to idolatry as a gross and prevalent evil in contemporary Judah (cf. 57:4-5, with its reference to infant sacrifice practiced most commonly in the reign of Manasseh). Isa. 57:7 indicates idolatrous worship upon the high places; Isa. 65:2-4 and 66:17 refer to the abominable pagan rites in temple gardens. All responsible modern authorities agree that no idolatry was practiced in postexilic Judah, and the testimony of Ezra, Zechariah, Nehemiah, and Malachi (which protest against all the current evils and abuses of this period) by their silence about idolatry conclusively confirm this. (4) The extreme degeneracy and moral breakdown deplored in chapters 58 and 59 correspond most closely with conditions known to exist in Judah under Manasseh (696-641 B.C.). (5) Stylistic similarities are unmistakable between the supposed Isaiah I and Isaiah II (cf.14:27 and 43:13; 35:10 and 51:11; 11:12 and 56:8; 34:8 and 61:2; 11:6-9 and 65:25; 35:6 and 41:18; 11:2 and 61:1; 1:11, 14 and 43:24; 28:5 and 63:3; and many others).

The remarkable correspondence and allusions linking together all parts of the book in artistic unity have convinced even such liberal scholars as W.H. Brownlee that Isaiah is indeed a literary unit although (according to him) composed in the postexilic period (because of the elements of fulfilled prophecy, explainable to him only as prophecy after the fulfillment).

The text of Isaiah may be divided into eight main sections.

I. Volume of Rebuke and Promise (chaps. 1—6) admonishing the backslidden nation to turn back to the LORD (Yahweh) in repentance, lest they be visited with invasion, devastation, and exile.

II. Volume of Immanuel (chaps. 7—12) predicts the coming Messiah as God incarnate (9:6) and the downfall of Damascus and Samaria within the next few years, and ultimately Assyria as well. Messiah will be descended from David and unite Jewish and Gentile believers under his rule (ch. 11).

III. Volume of Burdens upon the Nations (chaps. 13—23)—Babylon, Philistia, Moab, Damascus, Samaria, Ethiopia, Egypt, Edom, Arabia, Tyre, and even Jerusalem itself.

IV. General Judgment and Promise (chaps. 24—27), speaking of punishment for oppressors and the preservation of God's true believers.

V. Volume of Woes upon Believers in Israel (chaps. 28—33)—doom predicted for drunkards and scoffers both in Israel and in Judah, but a Foundation Stone will be laid in Zion for the believers. Confidence in God is opposed to confidence in pagan allies such as Egypt.

VI. Second Volume of General Judgment and Promise (chaps. 34—35)—total destruction of Gentile world power;

the highway of holiness is opened up for the redeemed.

VII. Volume of Hezekiah (chaps. 36—39). The deadly anger of Sennacherib's invasion is miraculously averted in response to the prayer of faith. Chapter 38 tells of Hezekiah's near-fatal illness and miraculous healing—giving him ten more years to live, which ultimately led to his boastful display of his treasures to the Babylonian envoys.

VIII. The Volume of Comfort (chaps. 40—66) is subdivided into three sections: A. the Purpose of Peace (40—48); B. the Prince of Peace (49—57); C. the Program of Peace (58—66).

Some of the sublimest passages on the transcendence and sovereignty of God are found here—as are the proof of scriptural inspiration through fulfilled prophecy (41:21-26; 42:9, 23; 44:78). Most notable are the passages on the LORD's (Yahweh's) Servant, a term including both spiritual Israel as God's covenant nation, and the personal Messianic Servant, who is Christ himself; thus, the clearest and most moving description of the Crucifixion and its meaning are found in chap. 53 (which sets forth Christ as a vicarious substitutionary atonement for truly believing Israel, and thus precludes the notion that Israel itself could be the Servant of the LORD intended here). His gospel is clearly set forth in 61:14, and the ultimate triumph and glory of true Israel are proclaimed in the clearest and most encouraging terms. (G.L.A.)

ISCAH A niece of Abraham, daughter of Haran (Ge. 11:29). †

ISCARIOT, JUDAS [Judah man of KERIOTH *or* of the assassins] *See* APOSTLES

ISHBAH [he boasts, congratulates] A descendant of Judah (1Ch. 4:17). †

ISHBAK A son of Abraham by Keturah (Ge. 25:2; 1Ch. 1:32). †

ISHBI-BENOB A Philistine giant who was killed while trying to kill David (2Sa. 21:16-17). †

ISH-BOSHETH [man of shame] *See*
ESH-BAAL

ISHHOD [man of grandeur] A descendant of Manasseh (1Ch. 7:18).

ISHI
1 and 2. Two descendants of Judah
(1Ch. 2:31; 4:20). †
3. Father of the leaders of the
Simeonites who defeated the Amalekites
(1Ch. 4:42). †
4. A descendant of Manasseh (1Ch.
5:24). †
5. KJV for "my husband" (Hos. 2:16).

ISHIAH *See* ISSHIAH

ISHIJAH [Yahweh forget] One who
married a foreign wife during the
Babylonian captivity (Ezr. 10:31). †

ISHMA [desolate, ISBE; (EI) he heard,
KB] A descendant of Judah (1Ch. 4:3). †

ISHMAEL [EI he heard]
1. The son of Abraham by Hagar and
thus half-brother to Isaac. Because of the
jealousy of Sarah, he and his mother
were driven out into the desert where he
grew up as an expert hunter with the bow
(Ge. 16:3, 15; 21:9-10, 17-21). He was the
ancestor of the Ishmaelites, married an
Egyptian wife, and died at the age of 137
(Ge. 21:21; 25:12-18).
2. A descendant of Saul and Jonathan
(1Ch. 8:38).
3. The father of Zebadiah who was
over the house of Judah in the days of
King Jehoshaphat (2Ch. 19:11).
4. A military officer who supported
the priest Jehoiada and helped him bring
the young Josiah to the throne (2Ch.
23:1ff.).
5. A member of the royal family of
Judah who organized and carried out the
assassination of Gedaliah, whom Nebuchadnezzar of Babylon had made governor of Judah after he had captured
Jerusalem (2Ki. 25:23-25; Jer.
40:8–41:18).
6. A priest who married a foreign
wife during the Babylon captivity (Ezr.
10:22).

ISHMAELITE, ISHMEELITE(S)
[one from ISHMAEL] *See* ISHMAEL

ISHMAIAH [Yahweh heard]
1. A Gibeonite who joined David at
Ziklag, and one of David's mighty men
among the Thirty (1Ch. 12:4). †
2. David's commander from the tribe
of Zebulun (1Ch. 27:19). †

ISHMEELITE *See* ISHMAELITE

ISHMERAI [Yahweh guards] A descendant of Benjamin (1Ch. 8:18). †

ISHOD *See* ISHHOD

ISHPAH [he judged] A descendant of
Benjamin (1Ch. 8:16). †

ISHPAN A descendant of Benjamin
(1Ch. 8:22). †

ISHTAR *See* DEITIES 2., *Ashtoreth*

ISHTOB [man of TOB] KJV, NKJV for
"men of Tob" in 2Sa. 10:68. *See* TOB

ISHVAH A son of Asher (Ge. 46:17;
1Ch. 7:30). †

ISHUAI *See* ISHUI, ISHVI

ISHUI, ISHVI, ISHVITE
1. A son of Asher, and his clan (Ge.
46:17; Nu. 26:44).
2. A son of King Saul (1Sa. 14:49).

ISLAM Arabic for *obedience*, it is the
religion of Muhammad (A.D. 570-632)
based on teachings in the Koran. Two
sects of Islam today are the Sunni (meaning *accepted practice*) and Shiite (meaning *party*). They disagree over the basic
question of leadership. The Sunni Mus-
lims adhere to the orthodox traditions
and acknowledge the first four caliphs
(successors) as the rightful successors of
the founder Muhammad. The Shiá sect
believes Ali and the Imams (leaders from
the line of Ali [Muhammad's cousin]) are
the only rightful, infallible successors of
Muhammad.

ISLAND, ISLE There are a number of
islands mentioned by name in the Bible.
Those that are named are found only in
the NT, in connection with Paul's travels
(Ac. 27:16; 28:1) or John's imprisonment

(Rev. 1:9). The word is used in the OT (Isa. 24:15; 41:5; Eze. 26:18), but is translated often as "coast" (Isa. 20:6).

ISMACHIAH, ISMAKIAH [Yahweh sustains] A Levite in the days of King Hezekiah (2Ch. 31:13). †

ISMAIAH *See* ISHMAIAH 1.

ISPAH *See* ISHPAH

ISRAEL [he struggles with El] The name given by the angel to Abraham's grandson and Isaac's son Jacob, and that which the Israelites were and are called (Ge. 32:28; 35:10). At times in Israel's history the term applied to all the twelve tribes and at other times to the northern confederacy of ten tribes as distinct from Judah. For Israel's history *see* CALENDAR; CHRONOLOGY; JUDGES OF ISRAEL; KINGS OF JUDAH AND ISRAEL. For Israel's religion *see* FESTIVALS; SACRIFICES AND OFFERINGS; TEMPLE.

ISRAELITE [one from ISRAEL] People (formally "sons") from the clan of Israel, son of Isaac. *See* HEBREW; ISRAEL; JEW

ISSACHAR [there is reward — Ge. 30:18; may (God) show mercy, IDB; hired hand, KB] The son of Jacob who gave his name to a tribe (Ge. 30:18; 35:23).

ISSHIAH

1. A descendant of Issachar (1Ch. 7:3). †

2. One who joined David at Ziklag (1Ch. 12:6). †

3. At the end of David's reign he organized the priests for service. One of these was Isshiah (1Ch. 23:20; 24:25). †

4. Another Levite of David's days (1Ch. 24:21). †

ISSHIJAH *See* ISHIJAH

ISSUE *See* SICK, SICKNESS

ISUAH *See* ISHVAH

ISUI *See* ISHUI

ITALIAN REGIMENT *See* CORNELIUS

ITALY *See* GEOGRAPHY OF THE HOLY LAND; ROME

ITCH *See* SCALL; SICK, SICKNESS

ITHAI One of David's mighty men (2Sa. 23:29; 1Ch. 11:31). †

ITHAMAR [*possibly* (is) land of palms, BDB; (father) of TAMAR, KB] One of the four sons of Aaron by Elisheba (Ex. 6:23). Though a priest, he was on one occasion rebuked by Moses for not following the prescribed ritual (Lev. 10:16-18). From his descendants came some of the men who conducted the priestly divisions (1Ch. 24:3-4). A descendant of his, Daniel, returned from the Babylonian captivity with Ezra (Ezr. 8:2).

ITHIEL [El is with me]

1. One of the two to whom Proverbs 30 was addressed (Pr. 30:1). †

2. A descendant of Benjamin (Ne. 11:7). †

ITHLAH [hanging, lofty place] An unidentified site in the tribal area of Dan (Jos. 19:42). In the KJV the word appears as Jethlah. †

ITHMAH [fatherless, KB; purity, ISBE] One of David's mighty men, a Moabite (1Ch. 11:46). †

ITHNAN An unidentified site in the S of the tribal area of Judah (Jos. 15:23). †

ITHRA [abundance, BDB; what remained, KB] *See* JETHER

ITHRAN [what is over, profit, KB; excellent, ISBE]

1. A descendant of Seir, a Horite (Ge. 36:26; 1Ch. 1:41). †

2. A descendant of Asher (1Ch. 7:37). †

ITHREAM [remainder of the people] A son of David born at Hebron (2Sa. 3:5; 1Ch. 3:3).

ITHRITE [excellence, *or* preeminence, ISBE; remainder, KB] A clan that lived at Kiriath Jearim from which came two of David's mighty men (1Ch. 2:53; 11:40; 2Sa. 23:38). †

ITTAH-KAZIN *See* ETH KAZIN

ITTAI [*possibly* with me, BDB] A Philistine from Gath who fought with David and became commander over one-third of David's army. In Absalom's rebellion he followed David into exile and returned with him (2Sa. 15:18-23; 18:2-12). † *See* ITHAI

ITURAEA, ITUREA *See* GEOGRAPHY OF THE HOLY LAND

IVAH *See* AVVA; IVVAH

IVORY Ivory was imported from India and used chiefly for inlay and decoration. Solomon's great throne was of ivory overlaid with gold (1Ki. 10:18). King Ahab built a palace overlaid with ivory (1Ki. 22:39). It was a mark of luxury; as such, its abuse was denounced by the prophet Amos (Am. 3:15; 6:4).

IVVAH An unidentified site, perhaps in Syria, but captured by the armies of the Assyrian king Sennacherib (2Ki. 18:34; 19:13; Isa. 37:13). †

IYE ABARIM [heaps of ABARIM (regions beyond)] An unidentified stopping place along the wilderness route of the Israelites in their exodus from Egypt (Nu. 21:11; 33:44).

IZCHAR *See* IZEHAR

IZEHAR, IZEHARITES, IZHAR [gleam (of oil)] A descendant of Levi and head of a clan (Ex. 6:18; Nu. 3:27; 1Ch. 6:2).

IZLIAH [long living, eternal, IDB; Yahweh delivers, ISBE] A descendant of Benjamin (1Ch. 8:18). †

IZRAHIAH [Yahweh, he shines] A descendant of Issachar (1Ch. 7:3). †

IZRAHITE [shining] A man belonging to an unidentified family or town called Izrah. One Izrahite was the captain of the fifth army division that served the king (1Ch. 27:8). †

IZRI [Yahweh designs] A musician in David's time (1Ch. 25:11). †

IZZIAH [may Yahweh sprinkle (in atonement), BDB; Yahwehunites, ISBE] One who married a foreign wife during the Babylonian exile (Ezr. 10:25). In the KJV the name appears as Jeziah. †

J

JAAKAN *See* AKAN

JAAKOBAH [may (deity) protect, IDB] A descendant of Simeon (1Ch. 4:36). †

JAALA, JAALAH Descendant of some of Solomon's servants who returned from the exile with Zerubbabel; also called Jaalah (Ezr. 2:56; Ne. 7:58). †

JAALAM *See* JALAM

JAANAI *See* JANAI

JAAR [timberland] An unidentified site mentioned in connection with Ephrathah (Ps. 132:6; see NIV footnote). †

JAARE-OREGIM Since he is called Jair in the parallel account and since the word *oregim* (Hebrew for "weaver") also appears in the next line, it is generally felt that the name of this individual is only Jair (2Sa. 21:19, see NIV footnote; 1Ch. 20:5). †

JAARESHIAH [Yahweh plants] A descendant of Benjamin (1Ch. 8:27). †

JAASIEL [El does]
1. One of David's mighty men (1Ch. 11:47). †
2. One who was over the Benjamites in David's day (1Ch. 27:21). †

JAASU, JAASAU One who married a foreign wife during the Babylonian captivity (Ezr. 10:37). †

JAAZANIAH [Yahweh listens]
1. One of the leaders who called on Gedaliah after he had been made governor of Jerusalem by Nebuchadnezzar;

also called Jezaniahin 2Ki. 25:23; Jer. 40:8; (see NIV footnote). †
2. One of the Rechabites in the days of Jeremiah (Jer. 35:3). †
3. An idolatrous elder of Israel in the days of Ezekiel (Eze. 8:11). †
4. A prince of Israel who was giving wicked counsel in the days of Ezekiel (Eze. 11:1-4). †

JAAZER *See* JAZER

JAAZIAH [may Yahweh nourish, IDB] The father of Beno and descendant of Levi in David's time (1Ch. 24:26-27). †

JAAZIEL [El strengthens, ISBE] A Levite and temple musician in David's time; also called Aziel (1Ch. 15:18, 20). †

JABAL A son of Lamech and descendant of Cain (Ge. 4:20). †

JABBOK A principal tributary of the Jordan River on the E side about midway between the Sea of Galilee and the Salt Sea. Its banks housed many towns and settlements in antiquity. It arises near Amman and flows N for a distance before it turns westward. East of the S-N portion lived the Ammonites (Nu. 21:24). The E-W part was the border between the Amorites with their king Sihon on the S and Og the king of Bashan on the N (Jdg. 11:22; Jos. 12:5). Later it divided N and S Gilead where the two halves of the tribe of Gilead, were settled (Jos. 12:2-6). It was at a ford on this river that Jacob wrestled with the man who changed his name from Jacob to Israel (Ge. 32:22-38).

THE JABBOK RIVER
Near a ford on the Jabbok River, Jacob wrestled with an angel. From there his journey took him eventually to Hebron.

JABESH [dry]

1. Father of the Shallum who murdered the king of Israel and reigned in his stead only one month (2Ki. 15:10, 13).

2. A short name for Jabesh Gilead.

JABESH GILEAD [dry GILEAD] A city (214-201) a night's march E of the Jordan River; also called Jabesh (1Sa. 11:1). It is located in the tribal area of half the tribe of Manasseh (Nu. 32:33). The people of the city, except 400 virgins, were killed by the rest of Israel for not coming to Mizpeh to help in the action against Benjamin, and the 400 were given to Benjamites as wives (Jdg. 20:1; 21:8 and context). Saul delivered the city from the Ammonites and then was made king of all Israel. The men of Jabesh Gilead much later rescued Saul's corpse from the walls of Beth Shan (1Sa. 11:1-15; 31:11-13).

JABEZ

1. A descendant of Judah (1Ch. 4:9-10). †

2. An unidentified site in Judah (1Ch. 2:55). †

JABIN [perceptive]

1. King of Hazor in Galilee whom Joshua defeated and killed (Jos. 11:1-11). †

2. Another Canaanite king of Hazor whose forces under Sisera were defeated by Deborah and Barak in the period of the Judges (Jdg. 4:2-24; Ps. 83:9). †

JABNEEL [El will build]

1. A town (126-141) in the tribal area of Judah on its border with Dan near Joppa; also called Jabneh (Jamnia) (Jos. 15:11; 2Ch. 26:6). It became the center of the Sanhedrin after the expulsion of the Jews from Jerusalem by the Romans and its history continues to the present. †

2. A town (198-235) in the tribal area of Naphtali (Jos. 19:33). †

JABNEH *See* JABNEEL

JACAN, JACHAN A descendant of Gad (1Ch. 5:13). †

JACHIN, JACHINITES [he will establish] *See* JAKIN; *see also* BOAZ

JACINTH *See* PRECIOUS STONES AND METALS

JACKAL *See* BEASTS 8.

JACOB [follower, replacer, one who follows the heel]

1. The father of Joseph the husband of Mary (Mt. 1:15).

2. Also called Israel after his wrestling all night with the angel at the river Jabbok (Ge. 32:28). He was the son of Isaac and Rebekah and grandson of Abraham and Sarah, brother of Esau, husband of Leah and Rachel, and father of the twelve sons who became head of the tribes of Israel (Ge. 25:21-26; 29:31–30:24; 25:23-26). He bought the birthright from his twin brother Esau and stole the paternal blessing by deceiving his father (Ge. 25:29-34; 27:1ff.). For these actions he had to flee from Palestine. In Paddan Aram he served Laban for his two wives, their maids, who became his concubines, and a great wealth of cattle and sheep (Ge. 28:1–31:21). After fleeing again, he was overtaken by Laban; he made a treaty with the angel and had his name changed. He became reconciled with his brother on his return to Palestine and dwelt at Shechem (Ge. 31:22–33:20). Later he moved farther S where he continued until famine forced the entire family down to Egypt to the land of Goshen where he died. He was buried in Hebron (Ge. 35:27; 42:1-4;

46:1-7; 49:33; 50:13). His famous blessing of his sons is recorded in Genesis 49.

JACOB'S LADDER A ladder or stairway in Jacob's dream (Ge. 28:12) alluded to in Jn. 1:51.

JADA [shrewd one, BDB; (God) has cared, IDB] A descendant of Judah, a Jerahmeelite (1Ch. 2:28, 32). †

JADAH A descendant of Saul; also called Jehoaddah (1Ch. 9:42; 8:36). Jarah is suggested in the NIV footnote at 1Ch. 9:42. †

JADDAI One who married a foreign wife during the time of the Babylonian captivity (Ezr. 10:43). †

JADDUA [one known]
1. One who signed the covenant with Nehemiah (Ne. 10:21). †
2. A priest who lived into the reign of Darius the Persian (Ne. 12:11, 22). †

JADON [*possibly* frail one *or* Yahweh rules, IDB] One who helped repair the wall of Jerusalem in the time of Nehemiah (Ne. 3:7). †

JAEL [mountain goat] Wife of Heber the Kenite who acquired fame in Israel for having killed Sisera, the leader of the army opposing Deborah and Barak (Jdg. 4:17-22; 5:6, 24). †

JAGUR An unidentified site in the southern part of the tribal area of Judah (Jos. 15:21). †

JAH *See* GOD, NAMES OF, GODHEAD 2.

JAHATH [snatch up]
1. A descendant of Judah (1Ch. 4:2).
2, 3, and 4. Three Levites (1Ch. 6:20, 43; 23:10-11; 24:22).
5. A Levite in the time of King Josiah who was an overseer of temple repairs (2Ch. 34:12).

JAHAZ, JAHAZA, JAHAZAH A Levitical city (236-110) E of the Jordan in the tribal area of Reuben, also later called a city of Moab (Nu. 21:23; Jos. 13:15, 18; 21:36; Jer. 48:34).

JAHAZIAH *See* JAHZEIAH

JAHAZIEL [El will see]
1. A Benjamite who joined David at Ziklag (1Ch. 12:4). †
2. A priest in David's time who accompanied the Ark to Jerusalem (1Ch. 16:6). †
3. A Levite appointed to service by David in his later years (1Ch. 23:19; 24:23). †
4. A Levite who prophesied in the time of King Jehoshaphat of Judah (2Ch. 20:14). †
5. The father of one who came back from the Babylonian captivity with Ezra (Ezr. 8:5). †

JAHDAI [Yahweh lead] A descendant of Judah related to Caleb (1Ch. 2:47). †

JAHDIEL [El gives joy] A head of a family of Manasseh (1Ch. 5:24). †

JAHDO [(El) gives joy] A descendant of Gad (1Ch. 5:14). †

JAHIEL A man in charge of David's treasury (1Ch. 29:8). † *See* JEHIEL

JAHLEEL, JAHLEELITE(S) [wait for El (God), BDB; *possibly* may El show himself friendly, IDB] A son of Zebulun and his clan (Ge. 46:14; Nu. 26:26). †

JAHMAI [protect] A grandson of Issachar (1Ch. 7:2). †

JAHWEH *See* GOD, NAMES OF GOD; GODHEAD 2.

JAHZAH A Levitical town in the tribal area of Reuben (1Ch. 6:78). Later, when it had been taken by the Moabites the judgment of God fell on it (Jer. 48:21). †

JAHZEIAH [Yahweh sees] One of the four who opposed Ezra on his decision about mixed marriages (Ezr. 10:15). †

JAHZERAH A priest; perhaps also called Azarel (1Ch. 9:12; cf. Ne. 11:13). †

JAHZIEL, JAHZEEL(ITES) [El apportions] A son of Naphtali (Ge. 46:24; 1Ch. 7:13) and his clan (Nu. 26:48). †

JAIR, JAIRITE [he gives light]
1. *See also* JUDGES OF ISRAEL and JAARE-OREGIM.

2. A descendant of Manasseh (Nu. 32:41; Dt. 3:14).

3. Father of Mordecai and grand-uncle of Queen Esther (Est. 2:5).

4. One Ira, a Jairite, was a priest of David (2Sa. 20:26).

JAIRUS [he gives light] A synagogue ruler whose daughter Jesus raised from the dead (Mk. 5:22, 35; Lk. 8:41, 49-51). †

JAKAN *See* JAAKAN

JAKEH The father of the Agur who wrote Proverbs 30 (Pr. 30:1). †

JAKIM [he will establish]

1. A descendant of Benjamin (1Ch. 8:19). †

2. The head of one of the priestly divisions in the days of David (1Ch. 24:12). †

JAKIN, JAKINITE [he establishes]

1. A son of Simeon; also called Jarib (Ge. 46:10; 1Ch. 4:24) and his clan (Nu. 26:12).

2. Leader of the twenty-first division of priests in David's days (1Ch. 24:17).

3. A priest living in Jerusalem in the time of Nehemiah (Ne. 11:10).

4. The name of the S pillar in the porch of Solomon's temple made of cast bronze by Huram of Tyre (1Ki. 7:13-22).

JALAM A son of Esau (Ge. 36:5, 14, 18; 1Ch. 1:35). †

JALON A descendant of Judah and Caleb (1Ch. 4:17). †

JAMBRES One who together with Jannes opposed Moses; mentioned only in the NT (2Ti. 3:8). †

JAMBS Structural parts of a gate, decorative in the vision of Eze. 40:9; 41:3.

JAMES [Gr. for Jacob]

1. Son of Zebedee, one of the Twelve; *see* APOSTLES.

2. Son of Alphaeus, one of the Twelve; *see* APOSTLES.

3. A brother of Jesus who was unbelieving during the life of Jesus but who saw Jesus in one of the resurrection appearances (Mt. 13:55; Jn. 7:5; 1Co. 15:7) and then became a believer. He became the leader of the Jerusalem church and presided at its first council (Ac. 15:6, 13; 21:17-18; Gal. 1:19). He is most probably also the author of the book that bears this name and brother of Jude the author of another book (Jas. 1:1; Jude 1).

4. Father of one of the apostles by the name of Judas, not Iscariot (Lk. 6:16).

5. One of whom a Mary is called mother and identified by some with number 2 above (Mt. 27:56).

JAMES, EPISTLE OF One of the books of the NT and ascribed by tradition to James the brother of the Lord. *See* JAMES 3. "The twelve tribes scattered among the nations," to whom the book was addressed, could not be the Jews of the Diaspora. The belief that the epistle was written to Jewish Christians or to Christians who considered themselves the new Israel is inconclusive. It is perhaps better to think of its having been written directly to Jewish Christians in the first instance because of the presence of Jewish legal references (2:2; 4:2, 11; 5:12) and the absence of things against which Paul so often warns the Gentile Christians, and in the second instance to all the people of God, as with the other books of the NT. The message is not a treatise upon a single theme but rather remarks on a number of miscellaneous items of significance to the Christians: trials and temptations; doing and not merely hearing the Word of God; loving all without partiality towards rich or poor; controlling the tongue; coveting and speaking evil of one another; enduring patiently under suffering; and others. The section 2:14-26 stresses the other side of the coin from the one which Paul emphasized as well. Faith and works supplement one another, for saving faith (Paul) is to manifest itself in good works (James); and if the latter is not visible, one may question the genuineness of the former.

JAMES, SON OF ALPHAEUS *See* APOSTLES 2.

JAMES, SON OF ZEBEDEE *See* APOSTLES 1.

JAMES THE LESSER (i.e., the younger) *See* APOSTLES; JAMES 2.

JAMIN, JAMINITE(S) [*possibly* right hand, BDB; south—an indication of (good) fortune, KB]

1. A son of Simeon and his clan (Ge. 46:10; Nu. 26:12).

2. A descendant of Judah, Caleb, and Jerahmeel (1Ch. 2:27).

3. A Levite who helped to explain the law, as Ezra read it (Ne. 8:7).

JAMLECH [he will reign] A descendant of Simeon (1Ch. 4:34). †

JANAI, JAANAI [he will answer] A descendant of Gad (1Ch. 5:12). †

JANIM An unidentified town of Judah in the hill country (Jos. 15:53). †

JANNA, JANNAI [he will answer] An ancestor of Joseph, husband of Mary of whom Jesus was born (Lk. 3:24). †

JANNES *See* JAMBRES

JANOAH, JANOHAH [resting place]

1. A town (173-265) in the tribal area of Naphtali noted as being captured by Tiglath-Pileser of Assyria (2Ki. 15:29). †

2. A town (184-173) on the borders of Ephraim (Jos. 16:67). In the KJV it is spelled Janohah. †

JANUM *See* JANIM

JAPHETH [enlarge] A son of Noah and, according to the names of his sons, the ancestor of the Indo-European peoples from the S coasts of Europe to Persia (Ge. 5:32; 10:25).

JAPHIA

1. A town (176-232) on the eastern border of the tribal area of Zebulun (Jos. 19:12). †

2. A king of Lachish who fought against Joshua, lost and was killed (Jos. 10:3, 22, 26). †

3. A son of David (2Sa. 5:15; 1Ch. 3:7; 14:6). †

JAPHLET [he delivers, IDB; *possibly*

he escapes, ISBE] A descendant of Asher (1Ch. 7:32-33). †

JAPHLETI, JAPHLETITES [of JAPHLET] A clan on the border of the allotment to the descendant of Joseph (Jos. 16:1-3). †

JAPHO *See* JOPPA

JAR *See* POTTER, POTTERY; VESSEL

JARAH [honeycomb] *See* JADAH

JAREB [fearful, great] KJV, NKJV, ASV takes this as a proper name. The rest of the major versions translate this from the common Hebrew word for "great, feared, respected" in Hos. 5:13; 10:6. †

JARED [servant, KB] The father of Enoch and listed in the genealogy of Jesus (Ge. 5:15-20; 1Ch. 1:2; Lk. 3:37). †

JARESIAH *See* JAARESHIAH

JARHA An Egyptian slave who was allowed to marry the daughter of Sheshana Jerahmeelite (1Ch. 2:34-35). †

JARIB [Yahweh contends]

1. A son of Simeon; also called Jakin (Gen. 46:10; 1Ch. 4:24). †

2. One who was sent by Ezra to Iddo asking that some ministers for the house of God be sent to Jerusalem (Ezr. 8:16). †

3. A priest who married a foreign wife during the Babylonian captivity but agreed to put her away on his return (Ezr. 10:18). †

JARMUTH [height]

1. A city (147-124) in the western foothills in the tribal area of Judah (Jos. 15:35).

2. A Levitical city (199-221) in the tribal area of Issachar; also called Remeth and Ramoth (Jos. 19:21; 21:29; 1Ch. 6:73).

JAROAH [soft, delicate] A descendant of Gad (1Ch. 5:14). †

JASHAR (JASHER), BOOK OF [upright, straight] A book not now in existence and known only from its quotations found in the Bible (Jos. 10:13; 2Sa. 1:18).

In the Septuagint of 3 Kings 8:53 (1Ki. Hebrew text), it is known as "Book of the Song."

JASHEN *[possibly* asleep*]* Father of some of David's mighty men; also called Hashem (2Sa. 23:32; 1Ch. 11:34). †

JASHOBEAM One of David's mighty men; also called Josheb Basshebeth (1Ch. 11:11; 2Sa. 23:8). He was one who joined David at Ziklag (1Ch. 12:6).

JASHUB, JASHUBITE(S) *[he returns]*
  1. A son of Issachar and his clan (Ge. 46:13; Nu. 26:24); also called "Iob" in the NIV footnote to Ge. 46:13.
  2. One who married a foreign wife during the captivity in Babylon, (Ezr. 10:29).

JASHUBI LEHEM *[(they) returned to* LEHEM*]* An unidentified place in Judah (1Ch. 4:22). †

JASIEL *See* JAASIEL 1.

JASON Paul's host at Thessalonica who also sent greetings to the church at Rome (Ac. 17:59; Ro. 16:21). †

JASPER *See* PRECIOUS STONES AND METALS

JATHNIEL *[El* hires, BDB; El is forever, KB*]* A Levite and gatekeeper in David's time (1Ch. 26:2). †

JATTIR *[possibly* preeminence, IDB*]* A Levitical town (151-084) in the hill country of Judah (Jos. 15:20, 48; 1Ch. 6:57).

JAVAN A son of Japheth and grandson of Noah whose name passed on to the Ionians (Greeks) (Ge. 10:2, 4; 1Ch. 1:5, 7); also an OT name for Greek (Eze. 27:19). †

JAVELIN *See* ARMS AND ARMOR

JAZER *[he helps]* A town in Gilead E of the Jordan in the tribal area of Gad which became a Levitical city (Nu. 21:24-32; 32:34-35; Jos. 21:39).

JAZIZ One who was over David's flocks (1Ch. 27:31). †

JEALOUS, JEALOUSY In the Bible both men and God show this attitude. It may be a negative jealousy or it may be zeal for something, i.e., jealousy of something or jealousy for something which later is often called zeal. Rachel was jealous of Leah's ability to bear children, and the young man who reported to Moses was jealous for Moses (Ge. 30:1; Nu. 11:26-29). Both kinds of jealousy are also well attested in the NT but rendered as "envy" or "zeal" or "desire" (Isa. 9:7; Zec. 1:14-17; 8:23; Ro. 1:29). *See* ENVY

JEALOUSY, WATER OF *See* WATER ¶ 2.

JEARIM *[timberlands]* A hill on the border of the tribal area of Judah; also called Kesalon (Jos. 15:10). †

JEAT(H)ERAI A descendant of Levi (1Ch. 6:21). †

JEBERECHIAH, JEBEREKIAH *[Yahweh blesses]* The father of one of the witnesses to what Isaiah wrote on a scroll (Isa. 8:2). †

JEBUS *See* JERUSALEM

JEBUSI, JEBUSITES *[of JEBUS]* A clan first mentioned in Ge. 10:16 as descending from Canaan and living in the hill country before Israel conquered it (Ge. 15:17-21; Jos. 3:10). They lived on in Jebus (Jerusalem) until David finally conquered and drove them out (Jdg. 19:11; 2Sa. 5:69). The threshing floor of Araunah was purchased by David from a Jebusite and later became the site of Solomon's temple (2Sa. 24:16-18).

JECAMIAH *[Yahweh establishes]* *See* JEKAMIAH 2.

JECHONIAH *See* KINGS OF JUDAH AND ISRAEL, *Jehoiachin*

JEC(H)OLIAH *[Yahweh is able]* The mother of King Azariah of Judah (2Ki. 15:2; 2Ch. 26:3). †

JECONIAH, JECHONIAS The name of Jehoiachin found in a number of places (1Ch. 3:16; Mt. 1:11-12). *See* KINGS OF JUDAH AND ISRAEL, *Jehoiachin*

JEDAIAH

1. {Yahweh has favored, IDB}. A descendant of Simeon (1Ch. 4:37).

2. {Yahweh knows}. Head of the second priestly division as arranged by David in his latter years (1Ch. 24:7).

3. A Jerusalem priest who returned from the Babylonian exile (1Ch. 9:10).

4. Ancestor of some priests who came back from the exile with Zerubbabel (Ezr. 2:36).

5 and 6. Two other priests who returned with Zerubbabel (Ne. 12:6-7).

7. One who worked with Nehemiah to repair the wall of Jerusalem (Ne. 3:10).

8. An exile who came back from Babylon to Jerusalem and gave silver and gold for the rebuilding of the temple (Zec. 6:10, 14).

JEDIAEL {known of El}

1. A son of Benjamin (1Ch. 7:6, 10-11). †

2. A mighty man of David (1Ch. 11:45; 12:20). †

3. One of David's gatekeepers (1Ch. 26:2). †

JEDIDAH {beloved, BDB; lovely, beloved, KB} The mother of King Josiah (2Ki. 22:1). †

JEDIDIAH {beloved of Yahweh} The name given by the prophet Nathan to the baby Solomon (2Sa. 12:25). †

J.E.D.P. *See* DOCUMENTARY HYPOTHESIS

JEDUTHUN

1. One of the Levites that David put over the ministry of music in the temple (1Ch. 25:1-6). One of his sons was a gatekeeper before the Ark of the Covenant (1Ch. 16:38).

2. The name is found in the titles of a number of Psalms (such as Pss. 39, 62, and 77). *See* PSALMS, TITLES OF 1. and 6.

JEEZER, JEEZERITE(S) {my (father) is help} *See* ABIEZER; IEZER

JEGAR SAHADUTHA {witness heap} The stone set up as a pillar of witness between Laban and Jacob. So called by Laban in Aramaic. Jacob called it in Hebrew "Galeed" (Ge. 31:47). †

JEHALLELEL, JEHALELEEL, JEHALELEL {he shall praise El, BDB; Elshines forth, IDB}

1. A descendant of Judah (1Ch. 4:16)

2. Father of one of the Levites who helped King Hezekiah cleanse the temple (2Ch. 29:12).

JEHDEIAH {Yahweh rejoices (in his works)}

1. A Levite who served in David's day (1Ch. 24:20). †

2. David's servant in charge of the donkeys (1Ch. 27:30). †

JEHEZEKEL, JEHEZKEL {El gives strength} Head of the twentieth priestly division in David's time (1Ch. 24:16). †

JEHIAH {Yahweh lives} A Levite doorkeeper who guarded the Ark in David's day (1Ch. 15:24). †

JEHIEL {El lives}

1. A Levite musician in David's time and also in charge of the treasure (1Ch. 15:18, 20; 23:8).

2. A tutor for the sons of David (1Ch. 27:32).

3. A son of King Jehoshaphat of Judah (2Ch. 21:2).

4. A Levite appointed by King Hezekiah of Judah to help with the repair of the temple storerooms (2Ch. 31:13).

5. A chief officer in the temple in the days of King Josiah (2Ch. 35:8).

6. The father of one of those who returned with Ezra from the Babylonian captivity (Ezr. 8:9).

7. Father of one who married a foreign wife during the captivity (Ezr. 10:2).

8 and 9. Two who married foreign wives during the captivity (Ezr. 10:21, 26).

JEHIELI {of JEHIEL} The same as JEHIEL 1., above (1Ch. 26:21-22). †

JEHIZKIAH {Yahweh gives strength} A chief of the tribe of Ephraim who stood against enslaving the men and women of

Judah in the days of King Ahaz of Judah (2Ch. 28:12-13). †

JEHOA(D)DAH *See* JADAH

JEHOADDAN, JEHOADDIN The mother of King Amaziah of Judah (2Ki. 14:2; 2Ch. 25:1). The second name is a variant of the first (see NIV footnote at 2Ki. 14:2). †

JEHOAHAZ [Yahweh holds] There are three kings by this name. *See* KINGS OF JUDAH AND ISRAEL

JEHOASH [Yahweh bestows, ISBE; man of Yahweh, KB] There are two kings by this name. *See* KINGS OF JUDAH AND ISRAEL

JEHOHANAN [Yahweh has been gracious]
1. A Levite gatekeeper in the temple in David's day (1Ch. 26:3, 12).
2. A military commander in the army of King Jehoshaphat (2Ch. 17:15).
3. Father of a military commander of hundreds when Joash was made king (2Ch. 23:1).
4. Head of a priestly family after the return from Babylon (Ne. 12:13).
5. One who married a foreign wife during the time of the Babylonian captivity (Ezr. 10:10, 28).
6. Son of the Tobiah who corresponded with others in an attempt to make Nehemiah afraid to continue the work (Ne. 6:17-19).
7. A priest who was with Nehemiah at the dedication of the wall of Jerusalem (Ne. 12:42).

JEHOIACHIN [Yahweh supports] *See* KINGS OF JUDAH AND ISRAEL

JEHOIADA [Yahweh has known]
1. Father of one of David's valiant military commanders (2Sa. 8:18; 23:20).
2. One of David's counselors and grandson of Jehoiada 1 (1Ch. 27:34).
3. The priest who helped to enthrone the only royal son that Athaliah was not able to kill. He ultimately was able to get Jehoash (Joash) on the throne and have

Athaliah herself killed (2Ki. 11:1-4, 12, 18, 20-21).
4. One who led a group to David at Hebron. Perhaps the same as number 1 above (1Ch. 12:27).

JEHOIAKIM [Yahweh lifts up, establishes] *See* KINGS OF JUDAH AND ISRAEL

JEHOIARIB [Yahweh argues (for me)]
1. A priest who came back from the exile in Babylon; also called Joiarib (1Ch. 9:10; Ne. 11:10). †
2. The head of one of the priestly divisions in the days of King David (1Ch. 24:7). †

JEHONADAB [Yahweh is generous, noble] *See* JONADAB 2.

JEHONATHAN [Yahweh has given]
1. A Levite sent by the king of Judah, Jehoshaphat, to teach the law to his people (2Ch. 17:8). †
2. A priest in the days of Joiakim (Ne. 12:18). †

JEHORAM [Yahweh exalts] There are two kings by this name. *See* KINGS OF JUDAH AND ISRAEL

JEHOSHABEATH [Yahweh is an oath, ISBE; Yahweh gives plenty, satisfies, KB] *See* JEHOSHEBA

JEHOSHAPHAT [Yahweh has judged]
1. *See* KINGS OF JUDAH AND ISRAEL.
2. Father of the Jehu who became a king of Israel (2Ki. 9:2, 14).
3. The recorder in the time of David and Solomon (2Sa. 8:16; 1Ki. 4:3).
4. Solomon's man in Issachar responsible for getting the food for the king's household (1Ki. 4:17).

JEHOSHAPHAT, VALLEY OF [valley of Yahweh's judgment] An unidentified valley into which God is to bring the nations of the world for judgment (Joel 3:2, 12). Many have identified it with the lower parts of the Kidron Valley, but there seems to be no substantial reason for accepting this identification.

JEHOSHEBA [Yahweh is an oath, ISBE; Yahweh gives plenty, satisfies, KB] The daughter of King Jehoram of Judah; also called Jehoshabeath. She saved the life of Jehoash (Joash) and hid him until her husband was able to get him enthroned (2Ki. 11:2ff.; 2Ch. 22:11). †

JEHOSHUA, JEHOSHUAH *See* JOSHUA

JEHOVAH [*written as* YHWH] An artificial form for the personal name of God. The consonants "J" and "Y" represent *yodh* and "V" is *waw*. The consonant "H" is the Hebrew letter *he*. The vowels are from another Hebrew word for "master." Strictly speaking, the name is not "Jehovah," but YAHWEH or YAHWAH. Most versions (dating back to antiquity) translate these four letters as "the LORD." While no mystical quality exists in saying the sounds of these four consonants, reading a version with the personal Name can remind Christians of the personal nature of their God and his beneficial care for them (Ex. 3:14). *See also* GOD, NAMES OF, GODHEAD 2.; *see also* BIBLE VERSIONS, English Versions, 2., *Jerusalem Bible*

JEHOVAH-JIREH [Yahweh sees] KJV in Ge. 22:14. *See* GOD, NAMES OF, GODHEAD 2.

JEHOVAH-NISSI [Yahweh is my banner] KJV in Ex. 17:15. *See* GOD, NAMES OF, GODHEAD 2.

JEHOVAH-RO'IY [Yahweh is my Shepherd] Ps. 23:1.

JEHOVAH-SHALOM [Yahweh is peace] KJV in Jdg. 6:24. *See* GOD, NAMES OF, GODHEAD 2.

JEHOVAH-SHAMMAH [Yahweh is there] Name of the city of God in Eze. 48:35, NEB. *See* GOD, NAMES OF, GODHEAD 2.

JEHOVAH-TSIDKENU [Yahweh is our righteousness] Jer. 23:6; 33:16 *See* GOD, NAMES OF, GODHEAD 2.

JEHOZABAD [Yahweh endows]
1. One of the assassins of King Josiah of Judah (2Ki. 12:19-21; 2Ch. 24:26). †
2. A Levite whom David appointed as one of the gatekeepers for the temple (1Ch. 26:4). †
3. A descendant of Benjamin who served King Jehoshaphat (2Ch. 17:18). †

JEHOZADAK [Yahweh is just] One who was taken into captivity by the Babylonians. The father of the high priest Joshua at the time of the return from the captivity (1Ch. 6:14-15; Ezr. 3:2; Ne. 12:26; Hag. 1:1, 12, 14; 2:2, 4; Zec. 6:11). Spelled also Josedech, Jozadak. †

JEHU [Yahweh is he]
1. *See* KINGS OF JUDAH AND ISRAEL.
2. A prophet who prophesied against King Baasha of Israel and also Jehoshaphat of Judah. He wrote a set of annals (1Ki. 16:1; 2Ch. 19:1-3; 20:34).
3. A descendant of Judah (1Ch. 2:38).
4. A descendant of Simeon (1Ch. 4:35).
5. A descendant of Benjamin who joined David at Ziklag (1Ch. 12:3).

JEHUBBAH *See* HUBBAH

JEHUCAL [Yahweh is capable] One sent by King Zedekiah to the prophet Jeremiah requesting prayer; also called Jucal (Jer. 37:3; 38:1). He was among the princes who recommended the death of the prophet. In the NIV footnote at Jer. 38:1 the Hebrew text reads "Jucal." †

JEHUD [declare] A town (139-159) in the tribal area of Dan (Jos. 19:45). †

JEHUDI [Jew] An officer of King Jehoiakim, sent to Baruch to hear what was in the scroll which the prophet Jeremiah had dictated (Jer. 36:14-23). †

JEHUDIJAH [Jewish] KJV and NKJV for "Judean" or similar words in most other versions (1Ch. 4:18).

JEHUSH *See* JEUSH

JEIEL [El has preserved, IDB; *possibly* El sweeps up, KB]

1. A descendant of Reuben (1Ch. 5:7).

2. A descendant of Benjamin and ancestor of Saul (1Ch. 8:29). The name is not in the Hebrew text.

3, 4, and 5. One of David's mighty men, a Levitical member of a choir for bringing up the Ark and a Levitical harpist (1Ch. 11:44; 15:18, 21).

6. Ancestor of Jahaziel who prophesied in the days of King Jehoshaphat (2Ch. 20:14).

7. A secretary in the army of King Uzziah (2Ch. 26:11).

8. A Levite chief who contributed to the great public Passover in the days of King Josiah (2Ch. 35:9).

9. One who married a foreign wife during the Babylonian captivity (Ezr. 10:43).

JEKABZEEL {El gathers} A town (148-071) inhabited by some of the returnees from the Babylonian captivity (Ne. 11:25). †

JEKAMEAM {(my) kinsman establishes} A descendant of Levi in the days of David (1Ch. 23:19; 24:23). †

JEKAMIAH {Yahweh will establish}
1. A descendant of Judah through Jerahmeel (1Ch. 2:41). †
2. One of the sons of King Jehoiachin (Jeconiah) (1Ch. 3:18). †

JEKUTHIEL {El will nourish} A descendant of Judah (1Ch. 4:18). †

JEMIMA(H) {dove} A daughter of Job (Job 42:14). †

JEMUEL A son of Simeon; also called Nemuel (Ge. 46:10; Ex. 6:15; Nu. 26:12). †

JEPHTHAH, JEPHTHAE {Yahweh opens, frees} *See* JUDGES OF ISRAEL

JEPHUNNEH
1. The father of Caleb, one of the twelve spies sent to Canaan by Moses (Nu. 13:6).
2. A descendant of Asher (1Ch. 7:38).

JERAH {moon (god?)} A descendant of Shem and son of Joktan, father of a number of eastern clans (Ge. 10:26; 1Ch. 1:20). †

JERAHMEEL(ITE) {El will have compassion}
1. A descendant of Judah and brother of Caleb with whom David had contact when he was at Ziklag (1Ch. 2:9, 25-42; 1Sa. 27:10; 30:29).
2. A son of Caleb (1Ch. 2:42).
3. A son of King Jehoiakim sent to arrest the prophet Jeremiah (Jer. 36:26).

JERED {rose, IDB; servant, KB} A descendant of Judah (1Ch. 4:18). †

JEREMAI {possibly fat} One who married a foreign wife during the Babylonian captivity (Ezr. 10:33). †

JEREMIAH, JEREMIAS {Yahweh loosens (the womb), BDB; Yahweh lifts up, IDB; possibly Yahweh shoots, establishes, KB}
1. Jeremiah of Libnah was the father of Hamutal, the mother of kings Jehoahaz and Zedekiah of Judah (2Ki. 23:31; 24:18).
2. A descendant of Manasseh (1Ch. 5:24).
3, 4, and 5. A descendant of Benjamin who joined David at Ziklag, and two descendants of Gad who joined David at the stronghold in the wilderness (1Ch. 12:4, 10, 13).
6. A priest who signed the covenant with Nehemiah (Ne. 10:2).
7. A priest who returned with Zerubbabel from the Babylonian captivity, father of the head of a priestly family in the days of Joiakim (Ne. 12:1, 12).
8. Father of Jaazaniah, a Recabite whom Jeremiah took to the house of the LORD (Jer. 35:3-4).
9. One who participated with Nehemiah in the dedication of the wall of Jerusalem (Ne. 12:34).
10. The writing prophet, son of Hilkiah, from Anathoth, who prophesied to Judah from the days of King Josiah to the very end of the Kingdom of Judah, even after their being taken into captivity to Babylon. He was then taken into Egypt (Jer. 1:1-2; 39:1-8, 11-14; 43:5-7). His life was a tumultuous one;

he was often in trouble with the other Israelites because of his prophecies of doom (Jer. 25:1ff.; 36:20ff., 37:11ff.; 43:6). He was the author of two books, one bearing his own name and the other, "Lamentations."

JEREMIAH, BOOK OF, AND THE LAMENTATIONS OF These two works are from the pen of Jeremiah (10 above), who lived and wrote during the declining days of the Kingdom of Judah just prior to their Babylonian captivity. The Book of Jeremiah has a logical rather than a chronological order for the presentation of its material. Through chap. 25 the prophet is primarily concerned with the sins of Jerusalem and Judah and the impending captivity as a punishment from God for their sins (Jer. 3:6-13; 7:15). In the middle section (26–45) the prophet becomes autobiographical and recounts his evil treatment by the king and populace for his prophecies of impending doom. He discusses the last days of Jerusalem prior to the Babylonian captivity and his being carried to Egypt. He is threatened with death (26:11), imprisoned (38:6), and under constant threat by the establishment. In this section he prophesied an end to the captivity, return from it, and that ultimately a New Covenant would be established by God with them when he would have regathered them from a far greater diaspora than the one to Babylon, from a worldwide diaspora. This New Covenant is tied in to the New Covenant of the NT by the writer of the Book of Hebrews (Jer. 30:1-3; 31:31-34; 32:37-44; Heb. 8:8-12). Israel and Judah, regathered from all the countries of the diaspora and not merely Babylon, will share in the New Covenant which the church had been enjoying for some two thousand years. The final section of the book deals with prophecies against specific cities and countries: Egypt, Moab, Edom, Damascus, Babylon, among others (Jer. 46–52).

The Lamentations of Jeremiah are five elegies or lamentations wrung from the prophet at the thought of the fall of

Jerusalem. Their structure deserves a note. The first four are acrostics, i.e., the successive verses begin with the letters of the Hebrew alphabet in order. There are twenty-two verses (corresponding to the twenty-two letters of that alphabet) in chaps. 1, 2, and 4. Chapter 3 has sixty-six verses and is a triple acrostic, three verses, to each letter of the alphabet in order. While chap. 5 has twenty-two verses, it is not an acrostic at all. This style is quite atypical as far as Hebrew poetry (in general) is concerned and thus is of special interest.

JEREMOTH, JERIMOTH

1 and 2. Two descendants of Benjamin (1Ch. 7:8; 8:14). †

3. A Levite assigned to the work of the house of the LORD by David; also called Jerimoth (1Ch. 23:23; 24:30; 25:4, 22).†

4. David's officer over the tribe of Naphtali (1Ch. 27:19). †

5, 6, and 7. Three who married foreign wives during the Babylonian captivity (Ezr. 10:26-27, 29). †

JEREMY *See* JEREMIAH

JERIAH [Yahweh founds] A descendant of Moses; also called Jerijah (1Ch. 23:19; 24:23; 26:31-32). †

JERIBAI One of David's mighty men (1Ch. 11:46). †

JERICHO A green oasis (192-142) with an abundant water supply located where the central mountain ridge of Palestine tapers off before the desert that stretches to where the Jordan River begins. The water supply, its winter climate, its location near an important ford of the Jordan, and its defense capabilities all contribute to its long history. This history goes back to pre-pottery neolithic times and makes it probably among the oldest post-Flood cities in the Middle East. As the Israelites were encamped opposite it in the plains of Moab, the elders of Moab and Midian hired Balaam to curse them. This failed but turned into a promise of blessing (Nu. 22–24). Later we read that two spies searched out the city's defenses for

Joshua (Jos. 2:1). The city was taken by Israel in a spectacular manner and destroyed under the leadership of Joshua (Jos. 6), and not rebuilt for centuries, until the time of King Ahab of Israel (1Ki. 16:34). It then became again an important city and so remained through the time of the monarchy, the time of Ezra and Nehemiah, and the time of Christ. Nearby was built what is called NT Jericho (2Ki. 2:18; 25:5; Ezr. 2:34; Mk. 10:46).

JERICHO
The first major city in Canaan that the Israelites set out to conquer was Jericho.

JERICHO, PLAINS OF *See* GEOGRAPHY OF THE HOLY LAND

JERIEL [founded of El, BDB; El will see, IDB] A grandson of Issachar (1Ch. 7:2). †

JERIJAH [Yahweh founds] *See* JERIAH

JERIMOTH
1. A grandson of Benjamin (1Ch. 7:7).
2. Another descendant of Benjamin who joined David at Ziklag (1Ch. 12:5).
3. *See* JEREMOTH 3.
4. The father-in-law of King Rehoboam (2Ch. 11:18), and a son of David.
5. A Levite in the days of King Hezekiah of Judah (2Ch. 31:13).

JERIOTH [tents] A wife of Caleb (1Ch. 2:18). †

JEROBOAM [the people increase, BDB] There were two kings by this name. *See* KINGS OF JUDAH AND ISRAEL

JEROHAM [he will be compassionate]
1. Grandfather of the prophet Samuel (1Sa. 1:1).
2 and 3. Fathers of three different Benjamites, two of whom joined David at Ziklag (Joelah and Zebadiah) and one who returned from the Babylonian captivity (1Ch. 9:8; 12:7).
4. Father of a priest who returned with Zerubbabel from the Babylonian captivity (1Ch. 9:12; Ne. 11:12).
5. Father of the leader of the tribe of Dan in David's day (1Ch. 27:22).
6. Father of a commander of a hundred in the days of King Josiah, whom Jehoiada used to help enthrone this king (2Ch. 23:1).

JERUB-BAAL [BAAL contends] Another name for Gideon. *See* JUDGES OF ISRAEL

JERUB-BESHETH [SHAME (BAAL) contends] Another name for Gideon (2Sa. 11:21). † *See* JERUB-BAAL

JERUEL [El is a foundation] An unidentified area, the Desert of Jeruel, in the tribal area of Judah (2Ch. 20:16). †

JERUSALEM [foundation of Shalem (peace)]
1. Topography
2. Names
3. Excavations
4. The Pre-Davidic and United Monarchy Periods
5. The Divided Kingdom
6. The Intertestamental Period
7. Herod the Great
8. Jesus Christ
9. Acts of the Apostles
10. Jewish War of A.D. 66-70
11. Bar Cochba Revolt (132-135)

1. *Topography.* Jerusalem is located at an elevation of 2,460 feet above sea level in the hills of Judea. The original settlement was on a ridge above the year-round Gihon spring (the Virgin's Fountain). There is another spring to the S,

En-Rogel (Job's Well), which is not in as advantageous a position as Gihon.

The ridge above Gihon was easily defended, bounded on the E by the Kidron Valley, and on the W by the central valley called the Tyropeon (Cheesemaker's) by Josephus. The shape of the latter is today obscured by about fifty feet of fill. The hill to the W of the Tyropeon, which is today called "Mount Zion," is bounded on the W by the Hinnom (Gehenna) Valley, which curves to the E to meet the other two valleys.

The Jebusite city captured by David was restricted to the eastern ridge and was less than ten acres in size. Solomon built the temple to the N. The extent and exact direction of later expansion under the Judean kings is uncertain. It is now known that the western hill, "Mount Zion," was not incorporated until the time of Agrippa I (A.D. 40-44), in whose time the city had expanded to a size of 310 acres.

2. *Names.* The earliest extrabiblical reference to Jerusalem is in newly discovered texts from Ebla (twenty-third century B.C.), followed by those in the execration texts (i.e., texts of curses) of the nineteenth to eighteenth centuries B.C. from Egypt. The fourteenth century B.C. Amarna letters from Egypt mention *Urusalim,* and its king, Abdi-Heba (a Hurrian name). The name of Jerusalem, *Yeru-Shalem,* appears to mean "foundation of [the god] Shalem." The abbreviated form, Salem (Heb. *Shalem*), first occurs in Genesis 14, when Abraham offered a tithe to Melchizedek, its king. Moriah, where Abraham offered his son Isaac (Ge. 22:2), has been interpreted as Jerusalem (2Ch. 3:1).

In the period of the Judges, the city was called Jebus, after its inhabitants the Jebusites, who are probably related to the Hurrians (Jdg. 19:10). With the capture of the Jebusite stronghold by David, it is called the City of David, Zion, possibly "stronghold of water." By the time of Josephus the name "Zion" had been transferred to the western hill. The term *Ophel,* strictly speaking, applies to the northern part of the eastern ridge toward

the temple area, but is commonly used of the entire eastern ridge. A cryptic term, *Ariel,* which may mean "hearth of God," or less probably "lion of God," is used in Isa. 29:1-2.

3. *Excavations.* Archaeologists have been faced with formidable problems in the excavation of Jerusalem. Since the city is still inhabited, very few areas are free for excavations. Extensive quarrying has taken place on Ophel, removing traces of early occupations. The huge Herodian temple platform has irrevocably buried any remains in that area from the OT period. Nonetheless, the efforts of a century of work have yielded important data. The first important efforts were the tunnels and shafts dug by a British army engineer, Charles Warren, in 1867-70. Most important are the excavations which have been conducted by Kathleen Kenyon primarily at Ophel from 1961-67. Excavations begun by Benjamin Mazar in 1968 S of the temple, those begun by Nahman Avigad in the Jewish Quarter in 1969, and those begun by Y. Shiloh in the Ophel area since 1978, have added immensely to our knowledge of Jerusalem, especially in the Herodian period.

4. *The Pre-Davidic and United Monarchy Periods.* Some traces of habitation from the third millennium B.C. have been found. The earliest structure on Ophel is a massive "Jebusite" wall discovered by Kenyon just above the Gihon spring. It was built about 1900 B.C. and was used until about 800 B.C. by the Israelites. Joshua defeated Adoni-Zedek, the king of Jerusalem, and his allies (Jos. 10), but Jerusalem was not liberated from the Jebusites until the time of David.

After having made Hebron (to the S of Jerusalem), his capital, David and his men moved against the Jebusites at Jerusalem (2Sa. 5; 1Ch. 11). It is possible that the *tsinnor* by which Joab led the attack is a "water shaft" (2Sa. 5:8), which led from the waters of Gihon inside the Jebusite walls discovered by Warren in 1867. David built himself a palace (2Sa. 5:11), and having brought back the Ark of the LORD (2Sa. 6), desired to build a temple for it. To that end he purchased the threshing floor of Araunah the Jebusite (2Sa. 24:18-25), but the building of the temple was to be accomplished by his son Solomon and not himself. In excavations in the southern part of Ophel (in 1913-14), Weill discovered curious tunnel-like structures, which he interpreted as the tombs of David and other kings. This is very doubtful.

David (2Sa. 5:9) and Solomon (1Ki. 9:15) are both said to have repaired the "terraces" (Heb. *millo*). Kenyon interprets this to mean the massive platforms on the eastern edge of Ophel, which needed constant repair.

With the help of Phoenician craftsmen sent to him by Hiram, king of Tyre, Solomon spent thirteen years building his own palace (1Ki. 7:1) and seven years building the first temple (1Ki. 6:38). The only possible traces of a Solomonic building to be found are a Proto-Ionic column and a segment of a casemate wall found by Kenyon in the northern part of Ophel. Traces of Solomon's temple must lie buried under the temple platform built by Herod. The so-called "Stables of Solomon," however, in the SE part of the platform are simply the supports built by Herod and later rebuilt by the Crusaders.

5. *The Divided Kingdom*. The present city walls of Jerusalem are largely the work of Suleiman the Magnificent (sixteenth century A.D.), resting on earlier foundations. The walls form a square, enclosing the temple area in the southeastern quarter. Both "Mount Zion" and Ophel are outside the walls to the S.

The Iron Age settlement in Jerusalem has been clarified by recent discoveries. Mazar has found near the SW corner of the temple platform tombs (eighth century B.C.), which he suggests may represent a royal cemetery. To the W Avigad has uncovered a massive "Broad Wall" (see Ne. 3:8) which probably enclosed the *Misneh* or "second quarter" (2Ki. 22:14; Zep. 1:10). He suggests that the wall was probably built by Hezekiah.

In preparation for the siege by the forces of the Assyrian king Sennacherib, in 701 B.C., Hezekiah built a tunnel from the Gihon spring to the site of Siloam, 1,000 feet to the SW. The actual course of the tunnel, which may still be traversed today by taking an S-shaped course, covers about 1,800 feet. In 1880 an inscription of Hezekiah was found in the tunnel. This described in vivid term the meeting of the teams who had worked from both ends. The Assyrian general who taunted the inhabitants of Jerusalem stood "at the aqueduct of the upper pool on the road to the Washerman's Field" (Isa. 36:2). He was probably standing on the southern end of the western ridge, facing Siloam. Assyrian records confirm the biblical account of the failure of the Assyrians to capture Jerusalem.

In 597 B.C., however, Nebuchadnezzar, the king of Babylon, captured Jerusalem, and in 587-86 he destroyed the temple. Mass burials with decapitated bodies found by Weill in Orphel may date to this attack. In 1975 Avigad found arrowheads which had been shot by the Scythian archers of the Babylonians.

After the capture of Babylon by the Persians in 539 B.C., the Jews were allowed by Cyrus to return to Jerusalem. After some delay, the temple was rebuilt in 516. When Nehemiah visited Jerusalem in 445, however, the city walls were still unrepaired. In Ne. 2:14 we read that "there was not enough room for my mount to get through." The vast tumble uncovered by Kenyon illustrates this verse. The postexilic walls were constructed for the reduced size of the population. Now that we know that the circuit was only 8,530 feet (since the western ridge was not settled until later), Nehemiah's claim that the walls were repaired within fifty-two days (Ne. 6:15) is that much more credible.

6. *The Intertestamental Period*. In the late fourth century B.C. the Persian Empire was overrun by the Macedonian army of Alexander the Great. There is a legend that Alexander visited Jerusalem. For about a century Palestine was con-

JUDAH EXILED
The Babylonian army marched into Jerusalem, burned the temple, tore down the city's walls, and carried away the Jews into captivity.

THE JOURNEY HOME TO JERUSALEM
A group of Jewish exiles made the long journey home from Babylon to Jerusalem.

tested by the Seleucids of Syria and the Ptolemies of Egypt. In 198 B.C. the Seleucids gained control. Antiochus IV imposed a forced policy of Hellenization upon the Jews, desecrating the temple by the sacrifice of swine in 168. He also erected a gymnasium and installed a Syrian garrison on the Akra, overlooking the temple area. The Akra was possibly located on the site of the Citadel. The archaeologist Johns found in the Citadel a Seleucid coin of the second century. The Maccabees rededicated the temple in 165, but succeeded in liberating the Akra only in 142. There are signs of Hasmonean construction in the Citadel area. It is possible that Josephus' first N wall which runs from the Citadel to the temple area, directly W-E, S of the present David Street, dates from this time.

Two structures dated by earlier excavators to the Jebusite period are now to be dated to the Hellenistic period. The so-called "Jebusite tower" and "Jebusite ramp" excavated by MacAlister and Duncan in 1923-25 on the brow of Ophel have been shown by Kenyon to be Hellenistic. A massive gate on the W side of Ophel, excavated by Crowfoot and Fitzgerald in 1927-28, is also thought by Kenyon to be Hellenistic. In the Kidron Valley below the SE corner of the temple area are the so-called Tomb of the Bene Hezir and Tomb of Zechariah—both Hellenistic.

7. *Herod the Great.* In 63 B.C. Pompey made Syria a Roman province. In Palestine he intervened on behalf of the high priest Hyrcanus against his brother Aristobulus. Some of the latter's followers established themselves in the temple area which Pompey forcibly seized. Entering the Holy of Holies, Pompey was surprised to find it bare.

Hyrcanus was advised by Antipater, an Idumaean. One of Antipater's sons,

Phasael, was made prefect of Jerusalem, and another, Herod, prefect of Galilee. In 40 B.C. Parthians attacked Jerusalem, carrying off Phasael and later killing him. Herod fled to Rome, where he was proclaimed king of the Jews. In 37 B.C., after a five-month siege, he captured Jerusalem with the aid of Roman troops.

Herod, an admirer of Hellenistic culture, provided Jerusalem with a stadium, a theatre, and a hippodrome. He built himself a sumptuous palace in the area S of the Citadel. To the N of the palace he erected three massive towers, named Phasael, Hippicus (after a friend), and Mariamne (after his wife). Phasael, the tallest, towered 148 feet high. The base of Phasael has been incorporated in the NE tower of the Citadel, popularly called "David's Tower."

Northwest of the temple area Herod built a fortress, named Antonia, after his friend Marc Anthony. The court of the Antonia with its huge flagstones, some inscribed with Roman names, has been uncovered in the basement of the Sisters of Zion building. This calls to mind the "pavement" mentioned in Jn. 19:13, where Jesus was tried before Pilate. Other scholars believe that the place of judgment before Pilate was in Herod's palace.

Herod's supreme accomplishment was the rebuilding of the second temple, a project begun in 20 B.C. and not finally completed until A.D. 64, just a few years before its utter destruction. The huge platform, 2,575 feet by 985 feet, is known today as the *Haram* or "Sanctuary," and comprises about one-sixth of the area of the present walled city. Mazar has determined that Robinson's Arch at the SW corner of the temple platform supported a monumental staircase rather than a bridge across the upper Tyropeon Valley as in the case of Wilson's Arch further N. Herod would have used the former. The common people ascended to the temple mount through the Huddah Gates in the S, remains of which may be seen today, the Double Gate under the alAksa Mosque, and the Triple Gate. The so-called "Golden Gate," was the gate through which Jesus entered the temple area on Palm Sunday. The present structure is a late reconstruction, resting, however, on earlier remains.

The large, beautifully drafted Herodian masonry may be seen at both the southeastern and the southwestern corners of the Haram. At the former point it extends 52 feet above the surface, and (from information from Warren's shaft) 78 feet below the surface. In 1968 Mazar exposed Herodian pavement S of the southwestern corner. The famous Western or Wailing Wall is a portion of Herodian masonry on the W, a focal point of Jewish devotion up until 1948, and now once again since 1967.

8. *Jesus Christ.* Two of the scenes of Jesus' acts of healing have been identified with certainty. The pool of Bethesda, with its five porches (Jn. 5:2), has been excavated on the property of the Church of St. Anne, just N of the Haram. The actual site of the miracle may have been in a cave to the East. The pool of Siloam (Jn. 9:7), where Hezekiah's tunnel ends, is also well known. Other sites are not as certainly identified.

The tradition of the *Cenaculum* (Latin for "upper room"), site of the Last Supper, shown on Mt. Zion, does not go back before the fourth century A.D. On the traditional site of the House of Caiaphas, M. Broshi in 1971-72, uncovered unique frescoes of birds. The Jewish Quarter of the walled city contains the remains of the Upper City where the wealthy high priests lived. Avigad found there a stone weight with the name Bar Kathros, one of the priestly families in the Talmud accused of exploiting the people. He found also, among many interesting things, extensive remains of a massive basilica from the seventh century A.D., the Nea Church.

Great controversy has surrounded the question of the place of Lord's crucifixion and of his burial. Dissatisfied by the appearance of the traditional site of the Church of the Holy Sepulchre, some Protestants have favored a rocky knoll N of the Damascus Gate. This is called Gordon's Calvary, after General Charles

Gordon who popularized the site in 1883. The hill has two cavities which give it the appearance of a skull, but these cavities are probably recent. Nearby is the so-called Garden Tomb pointed out as the site of Christ's burial. The tomb, however, is not earlier than A.D. 300.

The site of Calvary was covered by the forum and temple of Venus of Hadrian's pagan city of Aelia Capitolina. Helena, the mother of Constantine, in the fourth century A.D. "rediscovered" the site, and the Church of the Holy Sepulcher was rebuilt over Calvary and the supposed tomb of Christ. To be authentic the site must lie outside the second northern wall described by Josephus. Unfortunately, the description that he gives is not clear. But there is every reason to believe that the tradition for Calvary is sound. Kenyon's excavations in the Muristan area S of the Church of the Holy Sepulchre has demonstrated that this area was outside the walls until the second century A.D. Quarrying between A.D. 30-68,

however, may have demolished the authentic tomb.

9. *Acts of the Apostles.* The Greek inscription of Theodotus found by Weill on Ophel may refer to the synagogue of the freedmen, mentioned in Ac. 6:9. Agrippa I, grandson of Herod the Great, became king over Judea in A.D. 40 after having ruled in other areas earlier. His sudden death in A.D. 44 is recorded in Ac. 12:23. It was he who killed James, the son of Zebedee (Ac. 12:2), and imprisoned Peter. In his short four years over Judea, Agrippa proved himself to be a vigorous builder.

Josephus says that Agrippa began the building of the third N wall, which was not completed until just before the war with Rome (see below). Kenyon's recent excavations now reveal that it was he who was responsible for the incorporation of the western hill, "Mount Zion." On the Bishop Gobat School on Mt. Zion, Maudslay in 1975 traced remains of towers and cisterns. Bliss and Dickie

JERUSALEM AND GOLGOTHA

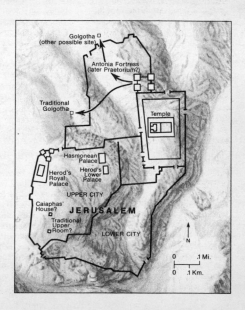

in 1894-97 uncovered a magnificent paved street in the Tyropeon Valley, which Kenyon dated to Agrippa's time.

On Paul's final visit to Jerusalem a riot suddenly erupted because the Jews thought that Paul had taken a Gentile into the inner temple area (Ac. 21). Two copies of the Greek inscription warning Gentiles not to go beyond the Court of the Gentiles upon penalty of death have been recovered (*see* MIDDLE WALL OF PARTITION).

10. *Jewish War of A.D. 66-70.* To quell the revolt which began under Nero in 66, Titus with an army of 65,000 men besieged Jerusalem in 70. Agrippa's third N wall was hastily finished by the Jewish defenders. The exact line of this wall has been one of the most controversial problems. Robinson in 1838 first noticed traces of a massive wall N of the present wall. In 1925-27 Sukenik and Mayer excavated considerable portions of this wall; in 1940 further sections were uncovered. The exposed portions form a line about 1,230 feet long. Sukenik claimed that this was the third wall.

Vincent, however, claimed that this wall did not fit the enthusiastic description of Josephus, and suggested that the third wall should lie under the present N wall. Excavations by Henessey at the Damascus Gate convinced him and Kenyon that Vincent's proposal was correct. These British excavators suggest that the Sukenic-Mayer wall was set up by Titus as a circumvallation (i.e., surrounding fortification) wall.

In 1972 additional sections along the Sukenik-Mayer line, including two towers projecting outward, were uncovered. This new discovery supports the view that this was the third wall.

After the destruction of the third wall, Titus' troops took the Antonia in July, burned the temple in August, and finally seized the Upper City in September. Titus left the three towers of Herod as a monument and installed the Tenth Legion in a camp to the S of the Citadel. In 1947 and in 1968 Avi-Yonah excavated remains of an installation of the Tenth

Legion at Givat Ram, a western suburb of Jerusalem.

Evidences of the Roman siege of Jerusalem include thick layers of ash found by Mazar and Aviga, Roman catapult balls from below the Convent of the Sisters of Zion, and the skeletal remains of a woman from a house in the Upper City.

11. *Bar Cochba Revolt.* From the evidence of some coins it now appears that Hadrian's decision to rebuild Jerusalem as a pagan city, Aelia Capitolina, was the cause and not the result of the Bar Cochba revolt in A.D. 132-35. After the defeat of the rebels, Hadrian forbade the entrance into Jerusalem of Jews and of Christians of Jewish extraction. The famous Ecce Homo arch at the beginning of the Via Dolorosa is actually part of a triple arch set up by Hadrian. Kenyon has found remains of Aelia's southern wall just S of the Haram area. Much of the present walls probably are shaped by the walls of Aelia. The Roman sewer down the N-S depression of the walled city is still the main sewer of this area.

Professor Mazar's excavations S and E of the Haram coupled with those of Professor Avigad inside the city wall in the Jewish Quarter of the city have made herculean contributions to unraveling the history of Jerusalem. Excavations continuing in the Ophel will produce many additions. (E.M.Y.)

JERUSALEM, NEW A new city of God to go with the new heaven and earth (Rev. 3:12; 21:1-5). *See* REVELATION

JERUSHA(H) [possession] Mother of King Jotham of Judah (2Ki. 15:33; 2Ch. 27:1). †

JESAIAH *See* JESHAIAH 1. and 6.

JES(H)ARELAH A son of Asaph; also called Asarelah (1Ch. 25:2, 14). †

JESHAIAH [Yahweh will save]
1. A grandson of Zerubbabel in the royal line after the return from the Babylonian captivity (1Ch. 3:21). †
2. A musician in David's day who

prophesied using the harp (1Ch. 25:3, 15). †

3. One of those in charge of the treasuries of the house of the LORD in David's day (1Ch. 26:25). †

4. A family head who returned with Ezra from the Babylonian captivity (Ezr. 8:7). †

5. One sent to help Ezra from the place Casiphia (Ezr. 8:1719). †

6. An ancestor of Sallu or descendant of Benjamin in the return from the captivity in Babylon (Ne. 11:7). †

JESHANAH [old]

1. A town (174-156) in the tribal area of Ephraim taken from Israel by King Abijah of Judah (2Ch. 13:19). †

2. NIV for a gate (Ne. 3:6; 12:39). †

JESHEBEAB [father lives] Head of the fourteenth priestly division in the time of David (1Ch. 24:13). †

JESHER A son of Caleb (1Ch. 2.18). |

JESHIMON A word which means "desert" and is sometimes translated that way or as "wasteland" (Dt. 32:10; Nu. 21:20). When used as a proper noun, it refers to the desert area SE of Hebron near the Salt Sea, in which place David hid from Saul (1Sa. 23:19, 24).

JESHISHAI [aged] The ancestor of a family of Gadites (1Ch. 5:14). †

JESHOHAIAH An ancestor of a Simeonite (1Ch. 4:36). †

JESHUA(H) [Yahweh saves]

1. Also called Joshua, the son of Nun (Ex. 17:9; Ne. 8:17).

2. Head of a priestly division in David's time, who assisted in the distribution of gifts (1Ch. 24:11).

3. A Levite in the days of King Hezekiah (2Ch. 31:15).

4. Ancestor of some who returned with Zerubbabel from the Babylonian captivity (Ezr. 2:6).

5. The high priest in the days of Zerubbabel; also called Joshua (Ezr. 3:2; Zec. 3:3, 8). He played a prominent role in postexilic days. See especially the books of Haggai and Zechariah.

6 and 7. Ancestor of some priests, and some Levites, who returned from Babylon with Zerubbabel (Ezr. 2:36, 40).

8. Father of a Levite in Ezra's days (Ezr. 8:33).

9. Father of one who worked on the reparation of the wall of Jerusalem with Nehemiah (Ne. 3:19).

10. A Levite who helped to explain the law as Ezra read it (Ne. 8:7).

11. A Levite who signed the covenant with Nehemiah (Ne. 10:9).

12. A town (149-076) occupied by returnees from the captivity in Babylon (Ne. 11:26).

JESHURUN [upright] A name of the land of Israel, used in poetry (Dt. 32:15; 33:5, 26; Isa. 44:2). †

JESIAH *See* ISSHIAH 3.

JESIMIEL [El will establish] A descendant of Simeon (1Ch. 4:36). |

JESSE A descendant of Boaz and Ruth, and father of King David (Ru. 4:18, 22; 1Sa. 17:12).

JESUI, JESUITES *See* ISHUI, ISHVI, ISHVITE 1.

JESURUN *See* JESHURUN

JESUS [*Gr. for* JOSHUA]

1. *See* CHRIST, LIFE AND TEACHINGS OF and CHRIST, WORK OF.

2. Jesus who is called Justus, who sent greetings to the church of Colosse (Col. 4:11). *See also* JUSTUS 3.

3. One in the genealogy of Christ in the ASV (Lk. 3:29). *See* JOSHUA 4.

JESUS CHRIST [Yahweh Saves, Anointed One] *See* CHRIST, LIFE AND TEACHINGS OF *and* CHRIST, WORK OF; GOD, NAMES OF; GODHEAD; SALVATION, APPLICATION OF; VIRGIN BIRTH

JETHER [abundance]

1. A son of Gideon, the judge of Israel (Jdg. 8:20).

2. Father of the Amasa whom Joab murdered; also called Ithra (1Ki. 2:5;

2Sa. 17:25, NIV footnote).

3. A descendant of Judah and Jerahmeel (1Ch. 2:32).

4. Another descendant of Judah (1Ch. 4:17).

5. A descendant of Asher; also called Ithran (1Ch. 7:38).

JETHETH A chief of Edom descended from Esau (Ge. 36:40; 1Ch. 1:51). †

JETHLAH *See* ITHLAH

JETHRO {remainder, KB}
The father-in-law of Moses; also called Reuel (Ex. 3:1; 2:18). Hobab is the son of Jethro (Reuel), therefore an in-law of Moses (Nu. 10:29). It was Jethro who advised Moses on how to set up his administration through appointed assistants (Ex. 18:13-27).

JETUR A son of Ishmael (Ge. 25:15; 1Ch. 1:31; 5:19). †

JEUEL {El has preserved}
1. A descendant of Judah who returned from the Babylonian captivity (1Ch. 9:6). †

2. A family head who came back from Babylon with Ezra (Ezr. 8:13). In the KJV his name appears as Jeiel. †

JEUSH, JEHUSH
1. A son of Esau (Ge. 36:4).

2. A descendant of Benjamin (1Ch. 7:10).

3. Another descendant of Benjamin and of Saul (1Ch. 8:39).

4. A Levite in the days of David (1Ch. 23:10-11).

5. A son of King Rehoboam of Judah (2Ch. 11:19).

JEUZ {he comes to help, BDB; *possibly* encouraged, IDB} A descendant of Benjamin (1Ch. 8:10). †

JEW {from JUDAH} The word used to refer to the men of Judah as from the times of Jeremiah. There are many instances of its use, especially in the plural, in the books of Jeremiah, Ezra, Nehemiah, and Esther, and of course in the NT where the greater number of uses occur. Prior to the sixth century B.C., these people were called "men of Judah"

(2Ki. 16:6). At first the word *Jew* was used of the men of Judah, but since the majority of those who returned from the captivity in Babylon belonged to this tribe or came from the former Kingdom of Judah it came to refer to any descendant of Abraham, any Israelite in the larger sense (Est. 2:5). In the NT the word *Jew* comes to be used as the opposite of Gentile in a very general sense (Ac. 14:1-2, 5; 1Co. 1:23; Gal. 2:14-15).

The term *Jew* has often been used as a derogatory term by much of the Christian church. Anti-Semitism has been excused because the Jewish leadership of that day handed over Christ to the Roman government of that time. Crucifixion then became the mode of the Savior's atonement for the whole world. To project to all Jews of all time the responsibility for Christ's death is outside the Scripture's views of responsibility.

The Bible also teaches that: (1) The Jews were the first to receive the gospel (Ro. 1:16). (2) The Gentiles were like a grafted branch (Ro. 11:11ff.), of which the Jews were the nourishing base. (3) Paul exhorts the Gentiles not to be arrogant, but appreciative of their reconciliation to God because of the unbelief of the Jews. (4) This unbelief happened "in part until the full number of Gentiles has come in" (Ro. 11:25).

Though anti-Semitism has been found throughout church history, it is not in the spirit of the Scriptures, which is to love all people.

The NT does not permit discrimination of the Jewish people because of the delivery of Christ to the cross. Rather, Christians should take the attitude of Paul the Apostle, a "Hebrew of Hebrews" (Php. 3:5), to make it their hearts' desire and prayer to God that the Israelites may be saved (Ro. 10:1). *See* HEBREW; ISRAELITE

JEWEL, JEWELRY *See* ORNAMENTS; PRECIOUS STONES AND METALS

JEWRY KJV in Da. 5:13; Lk. 23:5; Jn. 7:1. *See* JUDAH, JUDEA

JEZANIAH {Yahweh gives ear} *See* JAAZANIAH

JEZEBEL *[possibly* unexalted, unhusbanded, BDB] Jezebel's name might be associated with Baal, the consonants of this name *zbl* are found as a title for Baal. (Her father's name was Eth-Baal; he was a protector of the Baal cult.

1. Daughter of the king of Sidon, queen of King Ahab of Israel, and mother of the Athaliah, who married the king of Judah and introduced the pagan worship of Baal into both Israel and Judah (1Ki. 16:30-32; 2Ki. 8:16-18, 25-26). Jezebel fed 450 prophets of Baal and 400 prophets of Asherah at her table and killed any prophet of the LORD she could find (1Ki. 18:4, 13, 19; 2Ki.9:7). The story of her running battle with the prophet Elijah, that of the slaughter of the entire house of Ahab, and of Jezebel's own tragic death is one of the great classics of OT history. This began with her opposition to the God of Israel and was triggered in particular by her murder of Naboth in order to seize his vineyard at Jezreel (1Ki. 21:1-22:40; 2Ki. 1:17; 9:1-10:11).

2. In the NT city, Thyatira, there was a "woman Jezebel, who calls herself a prophetess" who misled the people (Rev. 2:18-20).

JEZER, JEZERITE(S) {formed, fashioned} A son of Naphtali and his clan (Ge. 46:24; Nu. 26:49; 1Ch. 7:13). †

JEZIAH *See* IZZIAH

JEZIEL A Benjamite who joined David at Ziklag (1Ch. 12:3). †

JEZLIAH *See* IZLIAH

JEZOAR *See* ZOHAR

JEZRAHIAH A leader of the temple choirs at the time of the dedication of the wall of Jerusalem rebuilt by Nehemiah (Ne. 12:42). † See the same name (in Hebrew) but transliterated *Izrahiah* and referring to a different individual in 1Ch. 7:3.

JEZREEL, JEZREELITESS {El will sow}

1. A descendant of Judah (1Ch. 4:3).
2. A son of the prophet Hosea (Hos. 1:45).
3. The site, unidentified, from which David got his wife Ahinoam (1Sa. 25:43; 27:3).
4. A city (181-218) W of the base of Mt. Gilboa in the tribal area of Issachar (Jos. 19:17-18). King Ahab of Israel had a palace there (1Ki. 21:1). *See* JEZEBEL 1., for the chief incidents that took place in the town. The valley below the city is known as the Valley of Jezreel and is to be distinguished from the Plain of Esdraelon (the Greek form of the word "Jezreel") which is the same as the Plain of Megiddo, the larger valley to the W of Jezreel. *See also* GEOGRAPHY OF THE HOLY LAND

JIBSAM *See* IBSAM

JIDLAPH {he weeps} Son of Nahor and nephew of Abraham (Ge. 22:22). †

JIMNA(H), JIMNITES *See* IMNAH, IMNITE

JIPHTAH *See* IPHTAH

JIPHTHAH-EL *See* IPHTAH EL

JOAB {Yahweh is father}

1. A descendant of Judah (1Ch. 4:14).
2. One whose descendants came back from the Babylonian captivity with Zerubbabel (Ezr. 2:6).
3. A son of David's sister Zeruiah (1Ch. 2:15-16) and commander-in-chief of David's armies (2Sa. 2:18; 8:16). He led David's men against the rebellions created by descendants of Saul and by David's own sons (2Sa. 2:12ff.; 18:2, 14). He was ruthless in battle or with anyone who opposed him or the king. In the end he supported the wrong son of David for the succession and for it lost his life (1Ki. 1:5-7, 13; 2:19, 25, 28-34).

JOAH {Yahweh is brother}

1. A recorder in the days of King Hezekiah of Judah (2Ki. 18:18).
2. A descendant of Levi in the time of King Hezekiah (2Ch. 29:12).
3. A Levite among the divisions of the

gatekeepers in the days of King David (1Ch. 26:4).

4. A recorder in the days of King Josiah (2Ch. 34:8).

JOAHAZ {Yahweh grips} *See* KINGS OF JUDAH AND ISRAEL

JOANAN An ancestor of Joseph, the father (so it was thought) of Jesus, according to Luke's genealogy (Lk. 3:27). †

JOANNA The wife of Herod's steward Cuza. She had been healed by Jesus and then helped to provide for his means (Lk. 8:13). She was one of the women at the tomb the morning of Jesus' resurrection (Lk. 24:10). †

JOASH {Yahweh has bestowed}
1. There are two of these kings; both also called Jehoash. *See* KINGS OF JUDAH AND ISRAEL

2. The father of Gideon, the judge of Israel (Jdg. 6:11).

3. A son of King Ahab (1Ki. 22:26).

4. A descendant of the royal line after the exile (1Ch. 4:22).

5. A grandson of Benjamin (1Ch. 7:8).

6. A Benjamite who joined David at Ziklag (1Ch. 12:3).

7. One who was over the stores of oil of King David (1Ch. 27:28).

JOATHAM KJV in Mt. 1:9. *See* JOTHAM 1.

JOB, BOOK OF His name is associated with one of the major wisdom literature books of the OT. His locality was "the land of Uz," but there seems to be little agreement among scholars as to his date or the location of Uz. Some think that the book is pre-Mosaic and reflects only a patriarchal background. Others think that such reflections can come from a backward, relatively isolated area where Canaanite contacts and customs from earlier times were still known. Such, for example, could be the area of Edom (Jer. 25:20; La. 4:21). Solomonic times would fit well in view of the fact that in the land of the Bible that was an era of wisdom literature. The book has the structure of the Code of Hammurabi

(reversed): a poetic section sandwiched in between two prose sections. It is also similar to the Krt legend from Ugarit in style and structure, a Canaanite epic from the time of the Judges of Israel.

In chaps. 1–2 we are told of Job's great calamities and losses, which he bemoans in chap. 34. Chapters 4–37 is the running debate between Job and Eliphaz, Bildad, and Zophar and finally the argument with the younger Elihu. They were trying to prove him selfrighteous, and he was maintaining his innocence. Then God appeared in controversy with Job (chaps. 38–42), in which God pointed out the right and the power of the Almighty to do as he thinks best with his creatures – to establish his own interests in their lives and through their witness. Job learned the lesson, and his vision of God greatly increased. He then repented in dust and ashes for his former failure to understand (Job 42:1-6).

JOBAB
1. A descendant of Shem (Ge. 10:29).

2. A king of Edom (Ge. 36:33).

3. A king of Madon who allied himself with Jabin of Hazor and was defeated by Joshua at the battle of the Waters of Merom (Jos. 11:1-9.

JOCHEBED {Yahweh is glorious} The descendant of Levi who married Amram and became the mother of Aaron, Moses, and Miriam (Ex. 6:20; Nu. 26:59). †

JODA, JUDA An ancestor of Jesus in Joseph's line (Lk. 3:26). †

JOED {Yahweh is witness} A descendant of Benjamin (Ne. 11:7). †

JOEL {Yahweh is El}
1. Son of Pethuel and author of one of the Minor Prophets (Joel 1:1).

2. An ancestor of the prophet Samuel (1Ch. 6:36); also called Shaul (1Ch. 6:24).

3. A son of the prophet Samuel (1Sa. 8:2; 1Ch. 6:33).

4, 5, 6, and 7. Descendants of

Simeon, Reuben, Gad, and Issachar (1Ch. 4:35, 5.4, 12, 7.3).

8, 9, and 10. Three men in 1Ch.: one of David's mighty men; a Levite of David's time who helped before the tent of meeting and helped with the temple treasury; and David's officer over the tribe of Manasseh (1Ch. 11:38; 23:8; 26:22; 27:20).

11. A Levite in the time of King Hezekiah of Judah (2Ch. 29:12).

12. One whose descendants married a foreign wife during the time of the Babylonian captivity (Ezr. 10:43).

13. An overseer of Nehemiah's time, a Benjamite (Ne. 11:9).

JOEL, BOOK OF *See* PROPHETS, BOOKS OF THE MINOR

JOELAH A descendant of Benjamin who joined David at Ziklag (1Ch. 12:7). †

JOEZER [Yahweh is help] A descendant of Benjamin who joined David at Ziklag (1Ch. 12:6). †

JOGBEHAH [height] A site on the route Gideon took when he defeated the two kings of Midian (Nu. 32:35; Jdg. 8:11). †

JOGLI Father of the Benjamite Bukki of the tribe of Dan who was in charge of the division of the land under Moses (Nu. 34:22). †

JOHA
1. A descendant of Benjamin (1Ch. 8:16). †
2. One of David's mighty men (1Ch. 11:45). †

JOHANAN [Yahweh is gracious]
1. A military leader of the remnant of Judah after the Babylonian captivity had begun and Gedaliah had been made the governor. Johanan rescued those taken captive by Ishmael of the royal house who rebelled against the Babylonians. Taking Jeremiah and others with him, he went down to Egypt to escape Babylonian reaction (2Ki. 25:23; Jer. 40:15; 41:11–43:7).
2. A son of King Josiah (1Ch. 3:15).

3. A descendant of King David in the royal line (1Ch. 3:24).
4. A priest who served in the temple (1Ch. 6:9-10).
5 and 6. Two who joined David at Ziklag, one from Benjamin and one from Gad (1Ch. 12:4, 12).
7. Father of a leader in Ephraim in the days of King Ahaz of Judah (2Ch. 28:12).
8. One who returned from the Babylonian captivity with Ezra (Ezr. 8:12).
9. *See* JEHOHANAN 4.

JOHANNINE THEOLOGY A term for those doctrines or ideas that are unique to John's writings. When some use this term, they are assuming there are different theologies taught in the NT.

JOHN [*Gr. for* Yahweh is gracious]
1. *See* JOHN THE BAPTIST.
2. *See* APOSTLES.
3. John Mark, *see* MARK
4. The father of the Apostle Peter (Jn. 1:42).
5. A member of the high priestly family (Ac. 4:6).

JOHN, THE APOSTLE *See* JOHN 2.

JOHN THE BAPTIST The son of Zechariah and Elizabeth, the forerunner and baptizer of Jesus (Lk. 1:5-25, 57-60; Mt. 3:1-3, 13-17). John was beheaded for rebuking Herod the Tetrarch for having married his brother Philip's wife (Mt. 14:3-4). *See* BAPTISM

JOHN, EPISTLES OF Differences of opinion exist among scholars as to whether the Gospel of John, the three Epistles of John, and the Book of Revelation were all written by the same John, by several, by a Johannine school, or by several and edited by one. The early church considered that the Gospel and the first Epistle were both written by the apostle. The style and ideas of the second and third Epistle indicate a very strong probability that the author is also John the Apostle. All four of these documents, the Gospel and the three Epistles, have many similarities in thought, in language, and in style.

There is no recognizable plan for the five chapters of the first Epistle. In these, however, heresies are attacked and admonitions given. False teachers are called antichrists and liars. The author states that the true doctrine is that Jesus is the Christ, the Son of God come in the flesh, and that to deny this is to be antichrist and a liar (1Jn. 4:2-3, 15; 2:22). One of the strong emphases of the first Epistle is that the disciples are to love one another, for love is of God. One who does not love does not know God, for he is love. In the second and third Epistles the opening and closing thoughts are the same, while the second was written to "the chosen lady and her children" and the third to "Gaius." In the second Epistle the author emphasizes again the thoughts of the first: be wary of false teachers, especially those that deny that Jesus Christ has come in the flesh; keep the commandments but particularly the one to love one another. Half of the third Epistle is commendatory of Gaius and perhaps others for their hospitality shown to visiting brethren, and the other half is concerned with one called Diotrephes, whose conduct was harmful to the church.

JOHN, GOSPEL OF *See* GOSPELS, THE FOUR

JOHN MARK *See* JOHN 3.

JOIADA [Yahweh knows]

1. One who worked on the wall of Jerusalem with Nehemiah (Ne. 3:6), called also Jehoiada.

2. A son of the priest Eliashib. One of his sons married the daughter of Nehemiah's opponent Sanballat the Horonite, and for that Nehemiah "drove him away" (Ne. 12:10; 13:28).

JOIAKIM [Yahweh lifts up] The father of the high priest Eliashib in the days of Nehemiah (Ne. 12:10, 12, 26; cf. 13:28). †

JOIARIB [Yahweh contends, pleads (your case)]

1. *See* JEHOIARIB 1.

2. One sent to find some Levites by Ezra when he noticed that none of the sons of Levi had volunteered for service in the temple at Jerusalem (Ezr. 8:15-16).

3. Descendants of Judah who settled in Jerusalem after the exile (Ne. 11:35).

4. A priest in Nehemiah's day (Ne. 11:10; 12:6).

JOKDEAM An unidentified site in the hill country of Judah (Jos. 15:56). †

JOKIM [Yahweh lifts up] A descendant of Judah (1Ch. 4:22). †

JOKMEAM A Levitical town (196-170) in the tribal area of Ephraim (1Ki. 4:12; 1Ch. 6:68). † *See* KIBZAIM

JOKNEAM A Levitical town (160-230) on the S edge of the Plain of Megiddo guarding one of the major passes through the Carmel range (Jos. 12:22; 19:11; 21:34; 1Ch. 6:77). †

JOKSHAN A son of Abraham by Keturah (Ge. 25:23; 1Ch. 1:32). †

JOKTAN [smaller] A descendant of Noah and Shem (Ge. 10:22-29; 1Ch. 1:19-23). †

JOKTHEEL

1. An unidentified site in the western foothills of Judah (Jos. 15:33, 38). †

2. The name given to the Edomite place (205-020), called by them Sela, after King Amaziah of Judah conquered it (2Ki. 14:7). †

JONA KJV, NKJV in Jn. 1:42 (cf. Mt. 16:17), "Simon, the son of Jona." This is based on a Greek text not used by most modern translations. The RSV, NIV, ASV, NEB, JB, NASB (with footnote), all translate it from other Greek manuscripts as "John." *See* JOHN 4.

JONADAB [Yahweh is generous, noble]

1. The nephew of David who planned the rape of Absalom's sister Tamar by Amnon, the son of David (2Sa. 13:1ff.).

2. Also called Jehonadab, son of Recab (2Ki. 10:15, 23). He commanded his descendants that they should not drink wine or even engage in the growing of grapes (Jer. 35:6-10).

JONAH {dove} One of the writing prophets, son of one Amittai (2Ki. 14:25). He was sent by God to Nineveh to prophesy but fled in a ship for Tarshish, was shipwrecked, rescued by a great fish, vomited up on the shore, and then went to Nineveh. The city "repented," but other than this statement there is no knowledge of just what happened (Jnh. 1:1-7; 2:10; 3:3, 10; 4:11).

JONAH, BOOK OF *See* PROPHETS, BOOKS OF THE MINOR

JONAN, JONAM An ancestor of Joseph, the father (so it was thought) of Jesus (Lk. 3:30). The KJV has "Jonan" based on a different reading in certain Greek manuscripts. †

JONAS A KJV transliteration of "Jonah" in the NT. *See* JONAH

JONATHAN {gift of Yahweh} A very popular name in ancient Israel meaning "God has given."

1. A grandson of Moses (NIV) and priest in Dan. The Hebrew text reads "Manasseh" (Jdg. 18:30).

2. A son of Saul and perhaps the best known of the Jonathans; a very close personal friend of David, defeater of the Philistines, and yet in the end defeated and killed by them (1Sa. 13:16; 14:13-15; 18:1-3; 31:8). David's lament on Saul and Jonathan is one of the beautiful poems in the Bible (2Sa. 1:19, 27).

3, 4, and 5. A nephew, an uncle, and one of David's Thirty (2Sa. 21:21; 1Ch. 27:32; 2Sa. 23:32).

6. A son of Abiathar, a priest descended from Eli. The son was a close ally of David (2Sa. 15:24-30; 17:17-20).

7. A descendant of Judah and Jerahmeel (1Ch. 2:32-33).

8. One in charge of some of David's storehouses (1Ch. 27:25).

9. The father of the head of one of the houses, of Judah which returned from the Babylonian captivity (Ezr. 8:6).

10. One who opposed Ezra's policy on mixed marriages made during the Babylonian captivity (Ezr. 10:15).

11. A Levite descendant of Joshua in Nehemiah's time (Ne. 12:11).

12. A priest, head of a priestly family in the time of Nehemiah (Ne. 12:14).

13. The father of Zechariah who was a member of one of the musical groups at the dedication of the rebuilt wall of Jerusalem (Ne. 12:35).

14. A secretary whose house had been made a prison in which Jeremiah the prophet was incarcerated (Jer. 37:15, 20).

15. A number of important people in intertestamental times.

JONATH ELEM RECHOKIM {dove} *See* PSALMS, TITLES OF 10. (3)

JOPPA {beautiful } A very ancient and important city (126-162) on the Palestine seacoast, the port for the city of Jerusalem. It was in the tribal area of Dan, but they apparently never conquered it. It was the most important city of the northern part of the Philistine Plain. Egyptians had shops here for the repair of their war chariots. From Solomon's time

JOPPA

Peter traveled to Lydda where he healed Aeneas; then he went on to Joppa because the brothers there had sent for him after a godly woman died, whom Peter then brought back to life. After this, Peter received a vision that led him to Caesarea, where he brought the gospel to Cornelius, a Gentile.

it was under Israelite control until Seleucid and then Roman times. The Maccabees burned it in part, and the Romans destroyed it. Lumber for both the first and second temples came in through this port. It was involved in the Jonah story and in several incidents in the ministry of the Apostle Peter (Jos. 19:46; 2Ch. 2:16; Ezr. 3:7; Jnh. 1:3; Ac. 9:36-43; 10:58; 11:5-13). †

JORAH [one born during harvest] *See* HARIPH 1.

JORAI [*possibly* Yahweh sees, IDB; whom Yahweh teaches, ISBE] A descendant of Gad (1Ch. 5:13). †

JORAM [Yahweh is exalted]
1 and 2. *See* KINGS OF JUDAH AND ISRAEL. There were two by this name; also called Jehoram.
3. The son of Toi, king of Hamath; also called Toi in the Hebrew text, was sent to congratulate David. Joram is also called Hadoram (2Sa. 8:10; 1Ch. 18:10).
4. A descendant of Levi (1Ch. 26:25).

JORDAN OF JERICHO Possibly an early name for the Jordan River (Jos. 20:8, NIV footnote).

JORDAN, VALLEY OF, PLAINS OF, RIVER OF [river of descent] *See* GEOGRAPHY OF THE HOLY LAND

JORIM An ancestor of Joseph, the father (so it was thought) of Jesus (Lk.3:29). †

JORKEAM, JORKOAM A descendant of Judah and Caleb (1Ch. 2:44). †

JOSABAD *See* JOZABAD 1.

JOSAPHAT *See* JEHOSHAPHAT

JOSE The KJV, NKJV rendering for the name found in Lk. 3:29, based on a Greek text which has the reading "Jose." Other versions (ASV) use a Greek text reading "Jesus" and this same reading is translated in the NIV, RSV, NEB, NASB, and JB as Joshua. *See* JOSHUA 4.

JOSECH An ancestor of Joseph, the father (so it was thought) of Jesus (Lk. 3:26). †

JOSEDECH *See* JEHOZADAK

JOSEPH [he will add]
1. The son of Jacob and Rachel. His dream incurred the wrath of his brothers who sold him into slavery in Egypt (Ge. 30:24; 37:5-11, 19-28). In Egypt he became next to the pharaoh and was the savior of his own people who had come to live in Egypt in the land of Goshen because of the famine in their own land. He died at the age of 110, and his bones were taken by Moses at the time of the exodus of the Israelites and ultimately buried in Shechem (Ge. 41:37-44; 50:26; Ex. 13:19; Jos. 24:32). The beautiful stories of Joseph's treatment of his brothers in return for their evil treatment of him are recorded in Genesis 42 – 50. His rise to fame and power in Egypt are in chapters 40 – 41. *See* ZAPHENATH-PA(A)NEAH
2. Father of Igal who was the spy representing the tribe of Issachar when Moses sent the twelve to spy out the land (Nu. 13:7).
3. A son of Asaph in the time of David, a musician for the temple (1Ch. 25:2).
4. One who married a foreign wife during the time of the Babylonian captivity (Ezr. 10:42).
5. Head of a priestly family in the days of Joiakim who came up from the Babylonian captivity with Zerubbabel (Ne. 12:14).
6 and 7. Two ancestors of Joseph, the father (so it was thought) of Jesus (Lk. 3:24, 30).
8. The husband of Mary the mother of Jesus, a carpenter who lived in Nazareth of the seed of David (Mt. 1:16; 13:55; Lk. 2:4). The relationship of Mary, Joseph, and Jesus is clearly explained in Mt. 1:18-25. *See* VIRGIN
9. A brother of Jesus; also called Joses (Mt. 13:55; 27:56; Mk. 6:3; 15:40).
10. Joseph of Arimathea, a disciple of Jesus who buried Jesus' body in his own tomb (Mt. 27:57-60).
11. Joseph called Barsabbas, the one (of the two) not chosen in the casting of the lot for the successor to Judas Iscariot (Ac. 1:23).
12. Joseph, called Barnabas by the apostles, a Levite from Cyprus who sold

a field and brought the proceeds to the apostles (Ac. 4:36 37).

JOSEPH BARSABAS *See* BAR-SABBAS 1.

JOSEPH OF ARIMATHEA *See* JOSEPH 10.

JOSEPHUS A Jewish historian (37-98 A.D.). His voluminous writings include *The Jewish War*, *Jewish Antiquities*, *Against Apion*, and *The Life*. Generally, the detail he furnished has great historical value.

JOSES *See* JOSEPH 9.

JOSHAH {gift of Yahweh} A descendant of Simeon (1Ch. 4:34). †

JOSHAPHAT {Yahweh judges}
1. One of David's mighty men (1Ch. 11:43). †
2. A priest who was to blow a trumpet before the Ark when David was returning it to Jerusalem (1Ch. 15:24). Spelled Jehoshaphat in the KJV. †

JOSHAVIAH {Yahweh places} One of David's mighty men (1Ch. 11:46). †

JOSHBEKASHAH, JOSHBAKAS-HAH {one sitting in request (prayer?)} A Levite musician in the time of David (1Ch. 25:4, 24). †

JOSHEB-BASSHEBETH {one sitting in the seat} *See* JASHOBEAM

JOSHIBIAH {Yahweh places} A descendant of Simeon (1Ch. 4:35). †

JOSHUA {Yahweh saves}
1. The son of Nun, successor of Moses and leader of the Israelites in their conquest of Canaan (Ex. 33:11; Nu. 27:12-23; Jos. 1:13). He was one of the two of the twelve spies who brought back a report that the Israelites should go up and take the land; forty years later he led them in (Nu. 13:8; 14:6-10; Jos. 1:1ff.). He was successful in conquering the land and then having it divided between the tribes (Jos. 7 and 14); also called Hoshea (Nu. 13:8, 16).
2. A man in whose field in Beth Shemesh the Ark stopped on is way back

from the Philistines (1Sa. 6:14, 18).n3. The governor of Jerusalem in the days of King Josiah (2Ki. 23:8).
4. An ancestor of Joseph, the father (as it was thought) of Jesus (Lk. 3:29).

JOSHUA, BOOK OF The author of the book about Joshua's conquest and settlement of the land of Canaan is not known. The evidence points to a time of writing before David, since he did not know of the temple (Jos. 9:27), but after the rise of the Judges of Israel since he refers to Othniel and also to the migration N of the tribe of Dan (Jos. 15:17; 19:47). His references to Sidon rather than Tyre indicate a date earlier than 1200 B.C. (Jos. 11:8; 13:46). There is considerable evidence of an author who was an actual eyewitness, living early in the fourteenth century. Chapters 1—12 describe the conquest, and 13—22 the settlement of the tribes. The two final chapters contain the great leader's final addresses.

JOSIAS, JOSIAH
1. *See* KINGS OF JUDAH AND ISRAEL.
2. A son of Zephaniah who gave gold and silver for the crown of the high priest in postexilic times (Zec. 6:10-11).

JOSIBIAH *See* JOSHIBIAH

JOSIPHIAH {Yahweh will add} Father of some who returned from the Babylonian captivity with Ezra (Ezr. 8:10). †

JOT Smallest letter in the Hebrew alphabet. *See* TITTLE

JOTBAH {good, pleasant} A Levitical city (176-248) in the tribal area of Judah and the home of the king of Judah's mother; also called Juttah (2Ki. 21:19; Jos. 15:55). †

JOTBATH, JOTBATHAH {good, pleasant} A stopping place for the children of Israel on their exodus route from Egypt (Nu. 33:33-34; Dt. 10:7). †

JOTHAM {Yahweh will complete}
1. *See* KINGS OF JUDAH AND ISRAEL.
2. The youngest son of Jerub-Baal, or Gideon (Jdg. 7:1; 9:5), and the only one

of his sons to escape the murders of Abimelech his brother.

3. A descendant of Judah and Caleb (1Ch. 2:47).

JOURNEY, SABBATH DAY'S The distance one could legally travel on the Sabbath. Later extra-biblical references place the distance somewhere between two and four thousand cubits. See a NIV footnote to Ac. 1:12, which reads "about 3/4 of a mile."

JOY A part of the complex called "fruit of the Spirit" and thus also a part of the character of God (Gal. 5:22-23; Ps. 104:31). Joy and rejoicing is not dependant on our circumstances, as Paul models for us (2Cor. 6:3-10). *See* VIRTUE AND VICE LISTS

JOZABAD [Yahweh bestowed]

1, 2, and 3. Three who joined David at Ziklag, one from Benjamin and two from Manasseh (1Ch. 12:4, 20).

4. A Levite overseer in the house of the LORD in the time of King Hezekiah of Judah (2Ch. 31:13).

5. A leader of the Levites in the days of King Josiah (2Ch. 35:9).

6. One of the assassins of King Jehoash (Joash); also called Zabad (2Ki. 12:21; 2Ch. 24:26).

7. A Levite treasurer in the temple of Ezra (Ezr. 8:33).

8 and 9. A priest and a Levite who married foreign wives during the captivity (Ezr. 10:22-23).

10. Levite who explained the law as Ezra read it (Ne. 8:7).

11. A Levite chief in Jerusalem after the return from the Babylonian captivity (Ne. 11:16).

JOZACHAR [Yahweh remembered] *See* JEHOZABAD 1. and JOZABAD 6.

JOZADAK [Yahweh is righteous] *See* JEHOZADAK

JUBAL A descendant of Noah and Cain, sons of Lamech, "the father of those who play the harp and flute" (Ge. 4:21). †

JUBILE(E) The Jubilee year in ancient Israel was every fiftieth year. In it all Israelites who had come under bondage to another Israelite had to be set free, all ancestral lands had to be returned to their original owners, and the land had to have rest from agriculture (Lev. 25:10-54ff.). *See* CALENDAR and FESTIVALS; RELEASE, YEAR OF

JUBILEES, BOOK OF This is an OT apocryphal book. The book is a history of the world from the beginning to Moses' time, in increments of a Jubilee (i.e., every fifty years).

JUCAL *See* JEHUCAL

JUDA *See* JUDAH and JUDE

JUDAEA [land of the Judahites, Jews] *See* JUDEA

JUDAH [praised]

1. A son of Jacob and Leah and head of one of the twelve tribes from which came the royal line and eventually Jesus. In the Joseph incidents he was the spokesman to his brethren, to his father, and to Joseph in Egypt later (Ge. 29:35; 43:3; 44:15ff.) Not only did his name come to be associated with a tribe but also with the Kingdom of Judah, i.e., the two tribes in the S. (1Ki. 14:21). *See also* JEW

2. Ancestor of some Levites who returned from the Babylonian captivity with Zerubbabel, called in NIV, Hodaviah. See the NIV footnote to Ezr. 3:9 which reads, "Hebrew, *Yehudah*, probably a variant of *Hodaviah.*"

3. A Levite who married a foreign wife during the captivity (Ezr. 10:23).

4. An overseer in Jerusalem after the return from the captivity. A descendant of Benjamin (Ne. 11:9).

5. A Levite who returned from the captivity with Zerubbabel (Ne. 12:8).

6. A leader of Judah who was involved with Nehemiah in the dedication of the restored wall of Jerusalem (Ne. 12:34).

7. A musician who had a part in the dedication of the wall of Jerusalem (Ne. 12:36).

8. One of the ancestors of Joseph, the father (so it was thought) of Jesus (Lk. 3:30).

JUDAH, JUDEA AND MOUNTAINS OF, WILDERNESS OF *See* GEOGRAPHY OF THE HOLY LAND

JUDAH, KINGDOM OF *See* KINGS OF JUDAH AND ISRAEL

JUDAISM The religion and society of the Jewish people.

JUDAS [*Gr. for* Judah] A very popular name in Maccabean times and then later in the NT.

1 and 2. Two of the twelve apostles.

3. A brother of Jesus (Mt. 13:55; Mk. 6:3).

4. A Jew of Galilee who raised an insurrection in ancient Israel shortly after the birth of Jesus (Ac. 5:37).

5. Paul's host in Damascus where Ananias met him (Ac. 9:11).

6. Judah Barsabbas, who gave a report to the church in Antioch on the Jerusalem Council (Ac. 15:22ff.).

JUDAS BARSABAS [Judah son of Sabas] *See* JUDAS 6.

JUDAS OF GALILEE *See* JUDAS 4.

JUDAS ISCARIOT [Judah man of KERIOTH *or* of the assassins] *See* APOSTLES

JUDE, EPISTLE OF [Judah] The author of this Epistle is considered to have been a brother of Jesus, *see* JUDAS 3. above. The principal thrust of this little letter is against false teaching in the church (v. 4). He developed elaborately his condemnation of them (5-16), and instructed his readers as to their duty in such case (17-23). It is not clear as to whether he quoted from the actual Book of Enoch or whether he was quoting, from an unnamed source, something that tradition ascribed to Enoch. The dating of the Book of Enoch is not certain.

JUDEA, MOUNTAINS OF, WILDERNESS OF *See* GEOGRAPHY OF THE HOLY LAND

JUDGE A civil magistrate. The administration of Moses was suggested by his father-in-law, Jethro, and judges were set up over groups from a size of ten to a size of thousands (Ex. 18:13-26). After the establishment of the monarchy, the system was continued, even though the king himself also heard cases directly (1Ki. 3:28; 1Ch. 23:4). These persons apparently abused their offices since the prophets found many occasions for rebuking them (Mic. 3:11; Am. 5:12). In the NT there are many references to this office, but God himself is the chief judge of all (Heb. 13:4; Rev. 18:8). And the Father has committed judgment to the Son (Jn. 5:22-24; Ac. 10:42; 17:30-31).

JUDGES, BOOK OF The seventh book of the OT containing the accounts of the judges of Israel from the time of the conquest of Palestine to the time of Samuel (Jdg. 2:16). On the judges themselves, their chronology, and therefore the context of this book itself, see the next entry and the article CHRONOLOGY. The Book of Ruth is usually associated with the Book of Judges since it is set in the same time. In this "postscript" to Judges we have the story of Ruth and Boaz and the early ancestry of King David and hence also the early ancestry of Jesus. In neither Judges nor Ruth do we have any claim as to authorship.

It is quite generally assumed that the author of the Book of Judges wrote from existing sources in the very early days of the monarchy under Saul and that it reflects much earlier material. The period of time in which the events recorded took place is also difficult to determine since there is so much difference among scholars as to the date of the conquest of Israel, all the way from about 1380 B.C. to 1220 B.C., both dates being held by leading conservative scholars. Secular and liberal scholars quite uniformly hold the latter date.

Chapters 3–16 of Judges recount the events from Othniel to Samson. The first two chaps. bridge the historical gap from Joshua and recount the partial success only of driving out the pagans. The concluding chapters recount some special events that took place in the general period: the Levite who worked privately for anyone's pay; the migration northward of the tribe of Dan; and the brutal treatment of the concubine of the Levite, which resulted in the decimation of the men of Benjamin (Jdg. 17–18, 19–21).

JUDGES OF ISRAEL, THE The biblical "judge" was a leader of Israel, divinely appointed to deliver and lead his people. Judicial capacity was only one aspect of his activity and was often slight (but see Jdg. 4:5; 1Sa. 7:15-17).

Twelve such people are described in the Book of Judges in addition to Eli and Samuel who also judged Israel (1Sa. 4:18; 7:15).

The chronology of the judges depends upon the following principles: (a) Their period reaches from the first oppression after the death of Joshua to the establishment of the kingdom in Israel. (b) Since the date of the death of Joshua is unknown, one must work backward from 1043 B.C., the probable date of the accession of Saul (*see* KINGS OF JUDAH AND ISRAEL). Then if the period in 1Sa. 7:2 of "twenty years" and Israel's "lamenting after the LORD" is equated with the length of Samuel's leadership as the last judge, 1063 must mark the overthrow of the Philistine oppressions that preceded Samuel (1Sa. 7:7-14); and this, in turn, provides a basis for the tentative dating of the rest of the events of the period. (c) Certain sections of Judges record events that had only local significance and that overlap events in other areas. For example, while the Philistines were overwhelming Israel on the W, the Ammonites were simultaneously oppressing the tribes E of the Jordan (Jdg. 10:7). The terms therefore of Jephthah, who fought Ammon, and of Ibzan, Elon, Abdon, the three minor judges that followed (10:17–12:15), must have run concurrently with the forty-year Philistine oppression. (d) A given period of oppression or deliverance may embrace more than one judge. Ehud's eighty-year

peace (3:30), for example, included the period of Shamgar ("He too saved Israel," 3:31). Similarly, the twenty-three years of Tola seem to embrace the twenty-two of Jair (10:13), since only the former is said to have "saved Israel." Again, much of Eli's judgeship, together with all of Samson's (16:31), belong under the forty years of Philistine oppression. Samson, in reality, accomplished no deliverance at all but simply "led Israel for twenty years in the days of the Philistines" (15:20).

Tabulation, therefore, of the dated oppressions and subsequent saving of Israel results in the following outline:

The total period is thus 339 years (compare the 300 years down to Jephthah in Jdg. 11:26-29).

During these almost three-and-a-half centuries of the judges, biblical history demonstrates a repeated cycle of sin by the Israelites, servitude to their enemies as a result, their supplication to God, and his salvation that followed. Chapter 2 of Judges serves as a summary and presents these basic propositions: God's wrath at sin (2:11, 14), God's mercy upon repentance (2:16), but man's depravity (2:19). Under the judges, when "everyone did as he saw fit" (17:6; 21:25), individual responsibility proved a failure; man on his own inevitably goes wrong. (J.B.P.)

JUDGMENT An opinion passed down by men, or as is more often the case, a sentence or an actual calamity sent by God for punishment. More notable among the latter are: the Fall, the Flood, the confounding of tongues at the Tower of Babel, the Babylonian captivity, and the subsequent worldwide diaspora, the deliverance of believers by the judgment placed on Christ, and the final judgment of those who fail to accept that deliverance worked out by Christ (Ge. 3:1ff.; 11:1-8; Dt. 28:15, 25; 28:58-68; Mt. 25:31ff.; Jn. 3:16-19; 2Th. 1:5-10; 2Pe. 3:8-13).

JUDGMENT, DAY OF *See* ESCHATOLOGY; JUDGMENT

	Years	Dates (B.C.)
Samuel's judgeship (1 Sam. 7:2), including his sons at the end (8:1)	20	1063-1043
Philistine oppression (Judg. 10:7; 13.1) (including Ammonite, etc. in the east)	40	1103-1063
Tola's deliverance (10:2, NIV footnote), including Jair	23	1126-1103
Abimelech's misrule (9:22ff.)	3	1129-1126
Gideon, judge (8:28)	40	1169-1129
Midianite oppression (6:1)	7	1176-1169
Deborah and Barak (5:31)	40	1216-1176
Canaanite oppression by Jabin (4:3)	20	1236-1216
Ehud (3:30), including Shamgar	80	1316-1236
Moabite oppression by Eglon (3:14)	18	1334-1316
Othniel (3:11)	40	1374-1334
Mesopotamian oppression by Cushan-Rishathaim (3:8)	8	1382-1374

JUDGMENT, THE LAST *See* ESCHATOLOGY; JUDGMENT

JUDGMENT HALL *See* PRAETORIAN GUARD, PRAETORIUM

JUDGMENTS OF GOD *See* ESCHATOLOGY; JUDGMENT

JUDGMENTS OF REVELATION *See* ESCHATOLOGY; JUDGMENT; REVELATION, *chaps. 15—19*

JUDGMENT SEAT OF CHRIST *See* SEAT, JUDGMENT

JUDITH [(fem. of) "Jew" or "Judahite"] A wife of Esau (Ge. 26:34). †

JULIA [of Julian (the family of Julius Caesar)] A Christian lady in Rome to whom Paul sent greetings (Ro. 16:15). †

JULIUS [of Julian (the family of Julius Caesar)] A Roman centurion in whose charge Paul was sent to Rome when he appealed to Caesar (Ac. 27:1-3). †

JUNIA(S) A Christian in Rome to whom Paul sent greetings (Ro. 16:7). †

JUNIPER KJV, ASV (with footnote) for "broom tree" in 1Ki. 19:4-5; Job 30:4; and Ps. 120:4 in many versions. The JB renders as "furze bush." *See* PLANTS, PERFUMES, AND SPICES, Miscellaneous Plants 2. and 13.

JUPITER [Latin for (pagan god) Zeus] *See* DEITIES 1., *The gods of Greece*

JUSHAB-HESED [loyal love will be returned] A son of the Zerubbabel who brought Israelites back from the Babylonian captivity (1Ch. 3:20). †

JUST *See* RIGHTEOUSNESS

JUSTIFICATION *See* CHRIST, WORK OF; SALVATION, APPLICATION OF

JUSTIN MARTYR An early Christian convert (about A.D. 100-165). At the age of thirty-two, he came to faith in Christ from pagan philosophies. This background and his zeal made him a leading apologist at this early time in church history.

JUSTUS
1. The surname of Joseph Barsabbas (Ac. 1:23). † *See* JOSEPH 12.

2. A host of Paul at Corinth, called Titius Justus (Ac. 18:7). †

3. The surname of the Jesus who was Paul's comforter in his imprisonment in Rome (Col. 4:11). †

JUTTAH *See* JOTBAH

K

KAB *See* WEIGHTS AND MEASURES, Liquid Measures

KABZEEL {El collects} A city (148-071) on the border of Judah with Edom. One of David's mighty men came from there (Jos. 15:21; 2Sa. 23:20).

KADESH, KADESH BARNEA {sacred place of BARNEA}
1. Kadesh Barnea (096-006); also called Meribah Kadesh in the Desert of Zin (Dt. 32:51; Eze. 47:19), and earlier known as En Mishpat (Ge. 14:7). Here the children of Israel encamped after leaving Mt. Sinai, and from here Moses sent out the twelve to spy out the land of Canaan. After the forty years of wandering, they returned here and began their final journey that was to lead them into the Promised Land (Nu. 33:37; Dt. 2:14; 9:23; Jos. 10:41; 14:7; Jdg. 11:17).
2. Kadesh on the Orontes (291-444),

where the famous battle took place between the Egyptians under Pharaoh Ramses II and the Hittites in 1288 B.C. Not noted in the Bible.

KADMIEL {(stand) before El} Two postexilic Levites who returned from the Babylonian captivity with Zerubbabel and Ezra and one who signed the covenant with Nehemiah (Ezr. 2:40; 3:9; Ne. 9:4; 10:9).

KADMONITES {easterners} A nomadic people who lived between Syria and the Euphrates River (Ge. 15:19). †

KAIN A city (164-100) in the hill country of the tribal area of Judah (Jos. 15:57). †

KAIWAN *See* DEITIES

KALLAI A priest in the days of Nehemiah (Ne. 12:20). †

KAMON A town (218-221) in Gilead where the judge Jair was buried (Jdg. 10:5). †

KANAH {reed}
1. A ravine that was a part of the border between the tribal areas of Ephraim and Manasseh (Jos. 16:8; 17:9). †
2. A location (178-290) on the N border of the tribal area of Asher, E of Tyre (Jos. 19:28). †
3. *See* CANA, the NT town, not to be confused with 2 above.

KAREAH {bald head} The father of Johanan (2Ki. 25:23; and mentioned thirteen times in Jer. 40:8−43:5.

KADESH BARNEA

KARKA, KARKAA [floor, ground] A place (089-007) on the southern border of the tribal area of Judah (Jos. 15:3). †

KARKOR An unidentified site where Gideon destroyed the army of the Midianites under Zebah and Zalmunna (Jdg. 8:10). †

KARNAIM, PROVINCE OF [two horns (mt. peaks)] (Am. 6:13). † *See* GEOGRAPHY OF THE HOLY LAND

KARTAH An unidentified city in the tribal area of Zebulun (Jos. 21:34; 1Ch. 6:77, NIV). †

KARTAN An unidentified Levitical site in the tribal area of Naphtali (Jos. 21:32). †

KATTATH An unidentified site in the tribal area of Zebulun (Jos. 19:15). † *See* KITRON

KATYDID *See* BEASTS 6.

KEBAR A river in Mesopotamia or perhaps a large canal beside which the exiles from Palestine lived during the Babylonian captivity (Eze. 1:1, 3).

dan River in the tribal area of Reuben (Dt. 2:26; Jos. 13:18; 21:37; 1Ch. 6:79). †

KEDESH [sacred place]
1. An unidentified site in the tribal area of Issachar (1Ch. 6:72, 76). Mentioned in connection with Daberath (foot of Mt. Tabor).
2. An unidentified site in the tribal area of Judah (Jos. 15:23).
3. Kedesh in Naphtali (202-237) SW of the Sea of Galilee (Jos. 12:22; 19:37). The town figures in the battles of Deborah and Barak and was later captured by the Assyrians (Jdg. 4:6-11; 2 Ki. 15:29).
4. Kedesh in Galilee (200-279) usually thought to be farther N than 3 and yet in the area of that tribe, a city of refuge (Jos. 20:7; 21:32).

KEDESH NAPHTALI [sacred place of Naphtali] *See* KEDESH 3.; NAPHTALI

KEDORLAOMER A king of Elam who fought with a coalition of kings at Sodom and Gomorrah (Ge. 14:1, 4-5, 9, 17). †

KEDRON *See* KIDRON

RIVER KEBAR
Ezekiel served the Lord among the exiles in various colonies near the Kebar (Chebar) River in Babylonia.

KEDAR [mighty] A son of Ishmael and grandson of Abraham, the founder of a nomadic tribe (Ge. 25:13; Eze. 27:21).

KEDEMAH [east] A son of Ishmael and founder of a nomadic tribe (Ge. 25:15; 1Ch. 1:31). †

KEDEMOTH [east (pl.)] A site (233-104) in the desert area E of the Jor-

KEEP *See* OBEDIENCE, OBEY

KEHELATHAH [assembly] A place mentioned in Nu. 33:22-23. †

KEILAH
1. A city (150-113) in the western foothills of Judah which David rescued from the Philistines but then had to abandon (Jos. 15:44; 1Sa. 23:1-13).

2. A descendant of Judah and Caleb (1Ch. 4:19).

KELAIAH A Levite who married a foreign wife during the Babylonian captivity; also called Kelita (Ezr. 10:23). †

KELAL [perfection, completeness] A man who married a foreign woman during the time of the Babylonian captivity (Ezr. 10:30). †

KELITA [dwarfed, crippled]
1. *See* KELAIAH.
2. One who explained the law as Ezra read it (Ne. 8:7).
3. One who signed the covenant with Nehemiah, perhaps the same person as 2 above (Ne. 10:10).

KELUB [basket]
1. A descendant of Judah (1Ch. 4:11). †
2. Father of one of David's officers (1Ch. 27:26). †

KELUBAI [dog, BDB] A descendant of Judah. In Hebrew *Kelubai* is a variant of Caleb (1Ch. 2:9, NIV footnote). *See also* CALEB

KELUHI One who married a foreign woman during the Babylonian captivity (Ezr. 10:35). †

KEMUEL [El's mound, ISBE]
1. A nephew of Abraham (Ge. 22:21). †
2. The representative of the tribe of Ephraim in the division of the land (Nu. 34:24). †
3. The father of the man who was over the tribe of Levi in David's day (1Ch. 27:17). †

KENAANAH [toward Canaan]
1. A descendant of Benjamin (1Ch. 7:10).
2. Father of the false prophet Zedekiah who prophesied in the days of Ahab (1Ki. 22:11, 24).

KENAN A near descendant of Adam (Ge. 5:9-14; 1Ch. 1:2). †

KENANI [Yahweh strengthens] A Levite in the time of Ezra (Ne. 9:4). †

KENANIAH [Yahweh strengthens]
1. A Levite director of singing in the time of David (1Ch. 15:22).
2. An official and judge during the days of David (1Ch. 26.29).

KENATH A city (302-241) E of the Jordan in Bashan. Its conqueror changed its name to Nobah (Nu. 32:42; 1Ch. 2:23). †

KENAZ
1. A grandson of Esau. *See also* KENIZZITE (Ge. 36:11, 15).
2. Father of Othniel and nephew of Caleb (Jos. 15:17; Jdg. 1:13).
3. A grandson of Caleb (1Ch. 4:15).

KENEZITE *See* KENIZZITE

KENITES [of the (copper) smiths] A tribal group descended from Hobab were in the land by the time of Abraham and were still there at the time of Joshua's conquest of it (Ge. 15:19; Jdg 4:11; Nu 24:21-22). In Moses's time Heber the Kenite was living among the Midianites. He was the brother-in-law of Moses (Jdg. 4:11). They moved with the Israelites to Canaan and maintained a close relationship with them at least through the time of King David (Jdg. 4:11; 5:24; 1Sa. 15:6; 30:26-29).

KENIZZITE [of KENAZ] A tribe or group in the land as early as Abraham (Ge. 15:19). Caleb of the tribe Judah is called the son of a Kenizzite (Nu. 32:12; Jos. 14:6, 14). It is not known from which Kenaz this group is descended.

KENOSIS The Greek word meaning *empty*. The doctrine of kenosis pertains to Christ's emptying of himself and taking upon himself humanity and the position of a servant (Php. 2:7).

KEPHAR AMMONI [village of Ammonites] An unidentified site in Benjamin (Jos. 18:24). †

KEPHIRAH [village] A Gibeonite city (160-137) assigned to Benjamin still occupied after the return from the Babylonian captivity (Jos. 9:17; 18:26; Ezr. 2:25; Ne. 7:29). †

KERAN A descendant of Esau (Ge. 36:1, 26; 1Ch. 1:41). †

KERCHIEFS KJV for "veil" in Eze. 13:18, 21 (in most other versions). *See* DRESS, *headgear*

KEREN-HAPPUCH [horn of (cosmetic) eyeshadow; *i.e.*, cosmetic case] A daughter of Job (Job 42:14). †

KERETHITES [*possibly* Cretans, BDB and KB; executioners, ISBE] Perhaps originally from Crete, a people who lived in the S of the tribal area of Judah Simeon (1Sa. 30:14; 2Sa. 8:18; Eze. 25:16; Zep. 2:5).

KERIOTH [burg, town] A city (215-105) E of the Jordan in Moab which is pictured by the prophet Jeremiah as ruined under God's judgment (Jer. 48:24; Am. 2:2). †

KERIOTH HEZRON [town of HEZRON] A city (161-083) in the tribal area of Judah; also called Hazor (Jos. 15:25). †

KERITH [cut off, perish] An unidentified ravine E of the Jordan where Elijah hid from King Ahab and was fed by the ravens (1Ki. 17:3, 5). Some think it was in Gilead. †

KEROS Ancestor of some who returned from the Babylonian captivity with Zerubbabel (Ezr. 2:44; Ne. 7:47). †

KERUB An unidentified site in Babylonia from which some returned to Palestine after the captivity but who were unable to prove their Israelite descent (Ezr. 2:59; Ne. 7:61). †

KERYGMA Greek for preaching or proclamation of a message.

KESALON A village (154-132) on the northern border of Judah near Mt. Jearim (Jos. 15:10). †

KESED [Chaldean (Babylonian)] A nephew of Abraham (Ge. 22:22). †

KESIL An unidentified town in the S of Judah (Jos. 15:30). †

KESULLOTH A town (180-232) on the border between the tribal areas of Zebulun and Issachar (Jos. 19:18). †

KETTLE *See* POT

KETURAH [incense, scented one] The wife of Abraham after the death of Sarah, also called his concubine. From their sons many of the tribes of desert people originated (Ge. 25:1ff.; 1Ch. 1:32ff.). †

KEVEH *See* KUE

KEY, KEY OF THE KINGDOM Literally, a key opens or locks doors or gates. In antiquity they were usually massive in size and made of metal or of wood with metal or wooden pegs (Jdg. 3:25). The symbolic use in Scripture is, however, the more important one. It represents authority, power, and control, usually delegated by God. The prophet speaks of the key of the house of David, which appears again in the Revelation as the key of David, speaking of the power of David's descendant, the Messiah, to admit or exclude men from his kingdom (Isa. 22:22; Rev. 3:7). The key given to Peter and through him to the church has the same significance. Belief in the confession Peter made, "You are the Christ, the Son of the living God" is the key to admittance to the church. Believing or rejecting this message given to Peter for proclamation is the key to salvation and Peter, knowing it was the key, realized it had to be passed on to others (Mt. 16:15-19). And there are keys for the Abyss and Hades (Rev. 1:18; 20:1).

KEZIAH, KEZIA [cassia (cinnamon)] A daughter of Job (Job 42:14). † *See* PLANTS, PERFUMES, AND SPICES, Perfumes, Scents, Ointments, *cassia*

KEZIB [deceit] An unidentified place where Judah's wife bore him a son (Ge. 38:5). †

KEZIZ *See* EMEK KEZIZ

KIBROTH HATTAAVAH [graves of lust, greed] The stop on the wilderness journey of the Israelites where they craved for meat, and God gave them quail to eat — but many of them died for their lust and rebellion (Nu. 11:34-35; 33:16-17; Dt.9:22). †

KIBZAIM An unidentified site in the tribal area of Ephraim (Jos. 21:22). † *See* JOKMEAM

KID *See* BEASTS 4.

KIDNEY *See* EMOTIONS and SACRIFICES AND OFFERINGS

KIDON The name of the threshing floor, or of its owner, where Uzzah died for touching the Ark (1Ch. 13:9). †

KIDRON Called a valley and brook, but actually only a wadi immediately E of the city of Jerusalem and its eastern border. Important incidents in the life of Jesus took place there on the last night before his crucifixion. These included his prayers in Gethsemane and his arrest (Jn. 18:1ff.).

KILEAB The second son of David; also called Daniel (2Sa. 3:3; 1Ch. 3:1). †

KILION {annihilation} A son of Naomi and brother-in-law to Ruth the Moabitess (Ru. 1:25; 4:9). †

KILL *See* MANSLAYER

KILMAD An unidentified place that traded with the city of Tyre (Eze. 27:23). †

KIMHAM A Gileadite who went with King David on David's return after the rebellion of Absalom (2Sa. 19:37-40; 1Ki. 2:7). †

KINAH {lament, dirge} An unidentified site in the southern area of the tribe of Judah (Jos. 15:21-22). †

KINE *See* BEASTS 4., *Cow*

KING, KINGSHIP In the extrabiblical ancient world, the king was considered a divine being. In earliest time each city had its own king. The idea of empire grew up later. In the Bible, a king was merely considered to have been appointed by God and was not divine in his own right. As early as the time of Abraham and before the Israelite monarchy, there were many city kings and local area

kings in Canaan (Ge. 14:1-2; 20:2; Jos. 12:7-24). Earlier God had intimated that Israel too would have a king (Ge. 17:6; Dt. 17:14-20). The stories of the KINGS OF JUDAH AND ISRAEL begin with Saul and end with the Babylonian captivity. In the NT Jesus Christ is presented as God's King and Ruler (1Co. 15:24; Rev. 1:5; 15:3; 17:14). *See also* HERODS, THE; MACCABEES

KING'S DALE *See* SHAVEH

KING'S GARDEN *See* SILOAM, POOL OF

KING'S HIGHWAY *See* GEOGRAPHY OF THE HOLY LAND, *Major N-S Routes*

KINGDOM OF GOD, KINGDOM OF HEAVEN The former would seem to be the more general of the two phrases as it appears throughout the NT, while the latter is limited to Matthew. For this reason some contrast the two and state that the latter is messianic only, the establishment of the kingdom of God on earth, while the former is universal, entered only by the new birth. According to some interpretations, the two have almost all things in common. The two phrases are considered by very many as virtually synonymous. This latter position is held also by many premillennarians, and thus the distinction is not a necessary one for the maintaining of that position. God's kingdom is here now in the hearts of men and will be established literally on the earth for a time before it becomes eternal (Mt. 12:28; Jn. 3:3, 5-7; 1Co. 15:24-26).

KING JAMES VERSION *See* AUTHORIZED VERSION; BIBLE VERSIONS

KINGS *See* KINGS OF JUDAH AND ISRAEL

KINGS, BOOKS OF The Books of 1 and 2 Kings contain the history of Judah and Israel from the end of David's reign to the fall of Jerusalem to the beginning of Babylonian captivity. The history of the KINGS OF JUDAH AND

ISRAEL is the content of these two works by an unknown author who used written source material (1Ki. 11:41; 14:19, 29; 2Ch. 32:32).

The books of 1 and 2 Chronicles, also by an unknown author, would seem to have been written around the time of Ezra as the end of 2 Chronicles is the beginning of Ezra. Thus 2 Chronicles carries the history of Israel beyond that of 2 Kings. Furthermore, the entire emphasis of 1 and 2 Chronicles is different. First Chronicles starts with genealogies that enable Jews living in the time of Ezra to carry their ancestral records back to the beginnings (chaps. 1–9). The two books also carry a full version of the history of David and Solomon to the building of the first temple (1Ch. 10–2Ch. 9), apparently for the information of those interested in building the second temple, the temple of Ezra. From chaps. 10–35, the historical emphasis is on the southern kingdom, Judah, and in particular the reforms of King Josiah.

KINGS OF JUDAH AND ISRAEL

When Samuel the judge grew old and his sons proved corrupt and took bribes (1Sa. 8:3; *see* JUDGES OF ISRAEL), the Israelites came to him requesting that he institute a kingship. Their motivation was twofold: (1) they wanted to be "like the nations" (1Sa. 8:5), forgetting that God had chosen them to be holy and separate (Lev. 20:26); and (2) they wanted a leader in battle (1Sa. 8:12; 12:12), forgetting that it was their own unfaithfulness and their demands for a king that were the cause of their defeats. Yet even in their sinful request, Israel was accomplishing God's original purpose, namely, to prepare a kingdom for his Son, Jesus Christ who would someday appear and rule (Ge. 49:10; Ps. 2:6-7; Lk. 1:32-33). So the basic idea of the kingdom was a right one, even though Israel's particular motives in seeking it were wrong. God therefore directed Samuel to anoint a king (1Sa. 8:7, 22) which he did: Saul, of the tribe of Benjamin (1Sa. 10:1, 24; 11:15). Yet this very answer to Israel's request proved in itself to be their punish-

ment. Saul, it is true, won a series of victories (1Sa. 14:47-48) but ended up wasting his nation's resources in the fruitless pursuit of his rival David (1Sa. 19–26), and then falling in an overwhelming defeat before the Philistines (1Sa. 31). God then established as king the man after his own heart (1Sa. 13:14), David, of the tribe of Judah (1Sa. 16:13; cf. Ge. 49:10); initially in Hebron over Judah alone (2Sa. 2:4), and seven and a half years later in Jerusalem over all the twelve tribes of Israel (2Sa. 5:7). This was the dynasty that ruled the united kingdom of Israel during the seventy-three years until its division into Israel in the N and Judah in the S. It continued in Judah throughout its existence and has now attained its imperishable goal in the kingdom of Jesus Christ (Mt. 1:6-16).

Dating for the kings of Judah and Israel is determined by their correlations with other clearly datable events of ancient history. The two earliest are the termination of Ahab's reign over Israel in 853 B.C. and the commencement of Jehu's in 841. A counting backwards and forwards from those dates then produces the following overall outline for the kings:

The united kingdom under David and Solomon (1003-930 B.C.) marked the high point in the ancient state of Israel. David enlarged his borders on all sides (2Sa. 8:1-14) so that his son, Solomon, inherited an empire in which he "ruled over all the kingdoms from the River [Euphrates] to the land of the Philistines, as far as the border of Egypt" and "Judah and Israel were as numerous as the sand on the seashore" (1Ki. 4:20-21). This marked the fulfillment of God's territorial promises to the founding Hebrew patriarchs (Ge. 15:18; 22:17). David is also noted for making Jerusalem a religious as well as a political capital. He brought into it the sacred Ark of God's presence (2Sa. 6), established the Levitical singers and the services of worship about it (1Ch. 15–16), and made preparations for God's temple (1Ch. 22; 28-29), which Solomon was able to construct between the years 966 and 960 B.C. (1Ki. 6:1, 38). Above all, God renewed to David his ancient covenant, specifying that out of the line of David he would raise up his "anointed" (Hebrew, Messiah; Greek, Christ), the Son of God, with salvation for his people (2Sa. 7:14; 23:5).

But Solomon in his later years lapsed into idolatry (1Ki. 11:1-13), with the result that upon his death in 930 God divided the kingdom, leaving only the southern tribes of Judah and Benjamin under the Davidic Dynasty in Jerusalem (1Ki. 11:31; 12:1-20, 21-24). The ten northern tribes, however, were led away by their new king Jeroboam I into even worse apostasy, identifying two golden calves (in their substitute sanctuaries of Dan and Bethel) as Jehovah the God who had brought them out of the land of Egypt (1Ki. 12:26-33).

The founder of the northern kingdom was henceforth spoken of as "Jeroboam son of Nebat and his sin which he had caused Israel to commit." His action became the cause for the downfall both of his own dynasty and of the entire kingdom of Israel (1Ki. 13:34; 2Ki. 17:16-23). For over two centuries the kingdoms of Judah and Israel lived in interaction, the S under the one line of Davidic kings, and the N (which lacked Judah's divine sanction upon the ruling family), through an unstable sequence of twenty kings representing ten different dynasties (*see* Hos. 8:4). More generally, however, the relations of the two states may be traced through a series of seven stages:

(1) *Conflict, 930-865 B.C.* Solomon's son, Rehoboam, raised armies to subdue Jeroboam in Israel, but God forbad it (1Ki. 12:21ff.). It was best, in preparing for the coming of God's Son, that the more sinful N be allowed to go its own way. Still, hostilities continued (1Ki. 14:30), even after Judah was humbled before God by the invasion of Shishak in 926 (2Ch. 12:6-8; *see* EGYPT). Abijah of Judah continued the war and won a great victory through faith (2Ch. 13:18). Baasha, founder of the Second Dynasty

in Israel, pressed the conflict and built up Ramah, only a few miles N of Jerusalem. Asa of Judah hired Ben-Hadad I of Damascus to divert Baasha, which gave temporary relief; but God rebuked Asa's reliance upon foreign mercenaries rather than upon himself (2Ch. 16:7). Omri, who established Israel's fifth dynasty, proved to be a strong monarch, founding Samaria as the northern capital and making an alliance with Phoenicia through the marriage of his son Ahab to the pagan Sidonian princess Jezebel. But this produced disastrous effects, not only in the N as Jezebel sought to establish Phoenician Baalism and persecuted those who remained faithful to Israel's God Yahweh, but also in the S. For though Judah had trusted God up to this point and prospered (2Ch. 16:9), its reforming king Jehoshaphat (see 2Ch. 17:6-9; 20:12, 20; 17:2-5) yet weakened. This brought about a new period.

(2) *Alliance, 865-841 B.C.* Specifically, Jehoshaphat married his son Jehoram to Athaliah, the daughter of Ahab and Jezebel in the N (datable prior to the birth of their son Ahaziah in 863) (2Ki. 8:26). Yet the alliance was lost in war when Ahab was killed by a stray arrow at Ramoth Gilead in 853 (1Ki. 22:29-35) and when Moab, Edom, and other formerly dependent territories revolted (2Ki. 1:1; 3:27; 8:20-22). When the prophets Elijah and Elisha, as a part of their general reform, anointed Jehu to wipe out the dynasty of Omri in the N (841 B.C.), Jehu slew Ahaziah of Judah as well (2Ki. 9); and the government was left in the hands of his Baal-worshiping mother, Athaliah. So, ironically, at the very moment that Jehu was wiping out Baalism in Samaria, Athaliah was sponsoring it in Jerusalem. Compromise and sin had brought national failure to Judah (2Ch. 21:10).

(3) *Mutual oppression, 841-790 B.C.* There followed a period of domination by the Arameans of Damascus over both of the Hebrew kingdoms (2Ki. 10:32-33; 12:17-18; 13:3, 7). The boy-king Joash was returned to the throne of Judah in place of his grandmother Athaliah (2Ki.

DIVIDED KINGDOM

ISRAEL	Ref	Yrs	B.C.	JUDAH	Ref	Yrs
Jeroboam I	1 Kgs. 14:20	22 yrs.	930	Rehoboam	1 Kgs. 14:21	17 yrs.
			913	Abijah	1 Kgs. 15:1-2	3 yrs.
			910	Asa	1 Kgs. 15:9	41 yrs.
Nadab	1 Kgs. 15:25	2 yrs.	909			
Baasha	1 Kgs. 15:33	24 yrs.	886			
Elah	1 Kgs. 16:8	2 yrs.	885			
Zimri	1 Kgs. 16:15	7 days	885			
Omri (with Libni)	1 Kgs. 16:23	12 yrs.				
Ahab	1 Kgs. 16:29	22 yrs.	874			
			869	Jehoshaphat	1 Kgs. 22:42; cf. 2 Chron. 16:12 and 2 Kgs. 8:16 with 2 Kgs. 3:1	25 yrs.
Ahaziah (son of Ahab)	1 Kgs. 22:51	2 yrs.	853	Jehoram (coregent in 853 and full power)	2 Kgs. 17:1-17	8 yrs.
Joram (son of Ahab)	2 Kgs. 3:1	12 yrs.	852		2 Kgs. 8:16-7	
Jehu	2 Kgs. 10:36	28 yrs.	841	Ahaziah	2 Kgs. 8:25-26	1 yr.
			840	Athaliah	2 Kgs. 11:3	7 yrs.
			835	Joash	2 Kgs. 12:1	40 yrs.
Jehoahaz	2 Kgs. 13:1	17 yrs.	814			
Jehoash	2 Kgs. 13:10	16 yrs.	798			
			796	Amaziah	2 Kgs. 14:1-2	29 yrs.

Israel	Reference	Reign	Date	Judah	Reference	Reign
Jeroboam II (coregencies were involved)	2 Kgs. 15:1-2 14:2, 17; 13:10	41 yrs.	793 767	Azariah (also called Uzziah; coregencies involved)	2 Kgs. 15:1-2	52 yrs.
Zechariah	2 Kgs. 15:8	6 mos.	753			
Shallum	2 Kgs. 15:13	1 mo.	752			
Menahem	2 Kgs. 15:17	10 yrs.	752			
Pekahiah	2 Kgs. 15:23		742			
Pekah	2 Kgs. 15:25, 27, 32 (full power in 740)	20 yrs.	740			
			739	Jotham 32-33-coregent but full power only in 739	2 Kgs. 15:5, 32-33	16 yrs.
			736	Ahaz 32-33-coregent but full power in 736	2 Kgs. 16:1-2	16 yrs.
Hoshea	2 Kgs. 17:1	9 yrs.	732 726	Hezekiah (coregent but full power in 726)	2 Kgs. 18:1-2	29 yrs.
FALL OF SAMARIA			722			
			697	Manasseh	2 Kgs. 21:1	55 yrs.
			642	Amon	2 Kgs. 21:19	2 yrs.
			640	Josiah	2 Kgs. 22:1	31 yrs.
			609	Jehoahaz	2 Kgs. 23:31	3 mos.
			609	Jehoiakim	2 Kgs. 23:36	11 yrs.
			598	Jehoiachin	2 Kgs. 24:8	3 mos.
			597	Zedekiah	2 Kgs. 24:18	11 yrs.
			586	FALL OF JERUSALEM	2 Kgs. 25:8	

11:12), and he was able to restore the temple through his well-known money chest (2Ki. 12:4-16). But later he fell into sin and slew Zechariah the priest who tried to correct him (2Ch. 24:17-22). In 803 Adadnirari III of Assyria subdued Damascus (2Ki. 13:5), and Jehoash of Israel, encouraged by Elisha, succeeded in recovering his people's losses to Aram in three great battles (2Ki. 13:14-25).

The mutual relations of Judah and Israel now entered their next stage:

(4) *Domination of the S by the N, 790-782 B.C.* Amaziah of Judah had reconquered Edom; but his successes had led him to a foolish challenge of Jehoash in the N despite the warning in the form of a fable of the latter (2Ki. 14:9-10). In the ensuing battle, Amaziah was defeated, and a part of the wall of Jerusalem was broken down. The domination seems to have lasted until the death of Jehoash in 782.

(5) *Mutual prosperity, 782-752 B.C.* The long reigns of Jeroboam II in the N and Azariah (Uzziah) in the S were marked by mutual recognition and expansion. The former, aided by the prophet Jonah, controlled land from Hamath in the N to the Salt Sea in the S (2Ki. 14:25); the latter conquered Ammon and the Arabs to the E and Philistia to the W (2Ch. 26). But while Uzziah, except for his last days, was marked by piety, Samaria's luxuries were leading to moral and spiritual decay (see the prophecies of Hosea or Amos).

(6) *Domination of the N by the S, 752-743 B.C.* In the twenty years beginning with 752 Israel lapsed into chaos, marked by five different dynasties. Under such circumstances Azariah, almost upon the default of the N, took over the leadership in foreign affairs, particularly against Assyria, and came to control southward down to Elath on the Red Sea (2Ch. 26:2). Tiglath-Pileser III, however, marched against Azariah. In 743 Hamath fell, and Rezin of Damascus, Hiram II of Tyre, and Menahem of Israel were forced to pay heavy tribute (2Ki. 15:19). The Assyrians turned back, and

Azariah was left untouched. Jotham ruled well as regent during his father Azariah's leprosy (2Ki. 15:5).

(7) *Conflict, 743-722 B.C.* Suffering in the N from Assyria seems to have provoked the final stage in the relations of the two kingdoms, one of hostility in which the N attempted revenge. Pekah of Israel, with Rezin, king of Syria, attacked Judah's new, weak, and thoroughly corrupt king, Ahaz (1Ki. 16:15), and took Elath (1Ki. 16:6). Ahaz disregarded the prophecies of Isaiah, who predicted the imminent fall of both Samaria and Damascus, and called upon Assyria for his help against Pekah and Rezin (2Ki. 16:7) in 734 B.C. The Assyrians destroyed Damascus and took part of Israel captive (2Ki. 15:29). Hoshea murdered Pekah to become the last king of Israel from 732 to 722 (2Ki. 15:30). Hezekiah assumed the regency in Judah in 728, a year or two before the deaths of both Tiglath-Pileser and Ahaz (Isa. 14:28-29), and Shalmaneser V and Sargon II proceeded to take captive the remaining tribes of the N in 722 (2Ki. 17:36).

For almost another century and a half, Judah was able to maintain its independent existence. Some time after his first official year in 726 (cf. 2Ch. 29:3 and 30:12, which could not have been in the same year), Hezekiah instituted sweeping national reforms and in 701 was able to reassert his independence from Assyria, despite serious losses (2Ki. 18:13-16; 19:35-36). His long-lived but generally evil son, Manasseh (697-642), forfeited both the spiritual and political achievements of his father (2Ki. 21:1-16; *see also* ASSYRIA) and became the cause of Judah's ultimate downfall (2Ki. 21:11; 23:26; 24:3). Only Josiah, with his three stages of reformation in 632, 628, and 622 (the greatest of all based upon the rediscovered law book of Moses— 2Ch. 34:3, 8, 14-21), was able to prepare God's people spiritually and strengthen their faith in God and the promises of his Word (*see* 2Ki. 23:25) for the days of exile and temptation ahead (*see* Isa. 7:14; 9:67; 11:15). Three of Josiah's sons occupied the throne between 609 and 597; all were evil. The four deportations by Nebuchadnezzar brought the Kingdom of Judah to an end (*see* BABYLONIA). (J.B.P.)

KINNERETH [zithers, lyres]
1. The Sea of Galilee. *See* GEOGRAPHY OF THE HOLY LAND.
2. A fortified city (200-252) in the tribal area of Naphtali on the NW of the Sea of Galilee (Jos. 19:35).
3. The region around Kinnereth which included what later came to be called the plain of Gennesaret (1Ki. 15:20; Mt. 14:34).

KINSMAN-REDEEMER *See* MARRIAGE

KIOS An island in the Aegean Sea opposite which Paul's ship anchored for a night on his final trip to Jerusalem (Ac. 20:15). †

KIR [walled enclosure]
1. A place in Mesopotamia from which Arameans had emigrated to Syria (Am. 9:7), and to which the Assyrians later exiled them (Am. 1:5).
2. A city (217-066) of Moab (Isa. 15:1); also called Kir Hareseth (2Ki. 3:25; Isa. 16:7, 11; Jer. 48:36).

KIR-HARASETH, -HARESETH, -HARESH, -HERES [walled (city) of pottery fragments] *See* KIR 2.

KIR OF MOAB *See* KIR 2.

KIRIATH ARBA [city of four] *See* HEBRON

KIRIATH ARIM [city of timberlands] *See* Ezr. 2:25, NIV footnote. Considered to be the same as Kiriath Jearim.

KIRIATH BAAL [city of BAAL] *See* BAALAH and KIRIATH JEARIM

KIRIATH HUZOTH [city of HUZOTH (outside spaces)] An unidentified place in Moab in the Balaam stories (Nu. 22:39). †

KIRIATH JEARIM [city of timberlands] A town in the tribal area of Judah later given to Benjamin; also called Baalah and Kirjath Baal (Jos. 15:9, 60; 18:14, 28). When the Philistines returned the Ark of God, it was brought here by the men of Beth Shemesh before being taken to Jerusalem by David twenty years later (1Sa. 6:21–7:2; 1Ch. 13:5-6).

KIRIATH SANNAH [city of SANNAH] *See* DEBIR

KIRIATH SEPHER [city of scribe] *See* DEBIR

KIRIATHAIM [two cities]
1. A city (220-128) in Moab given by Moses to the tribe of Reuben (Nu. 32:37; Jos. 13:15-19; Jer. 48:1, 23).
2. An unidentified Levitical site in the tribal area of Naphtali (1Ch. 6:76). *See also* KARTAN

KIRIOTH *See* KERIOTH

KIRJATH *See* KIRIATH, *et. al*

KIRJATHAIM *See* KIRIATHAIM 1. and 2.

KIRJATH-ARBA *See* KIRIATH ARBA

KIRJATH-ARIM *See* KIRIATH ARIM

KIRJATH-BAAL *See* KIRIATH BAAL

KIRJATH-HUZOTH *See* KIRIATH HUZOTH

KIRJATH-JEARIM *See* KIRIATH JEARIM

KIRJATH-SANNAH *See* KIRIATH SANNAH

KIRJATH-SEPHER *See* KIRIATH SEPHER

KISH
1. The Father of King Saul (1Sa. 9:13).
2. A descendant of Benjamin (1Ch. 8:30).
3. Father of some men who married the daughters of Eleazar who had no sons at his death (1Ch. 23:21-22).

4. A Levite in the time of King Hezekiah (2Ch. 29:12).

5. An ancestor of the uncle of Queen Esther, Mordecai (Est. 2:5).

KISHI [*possibly* gift, IDB; snarer, ISBE] The father of a Levitical musician appointed by David; also called Kushaiah (1Ch. 6:44; 15:17). †

KISHION A Levitical city (187-229) in the tribal area of Issachar (Jos. 19:20; 21:28). †

KISHON A river whose source is in Mt. Tabor and Mt. Gilboa and which flows westward through the Plain of Megiddo to empty into the Mediterranean. Here Deborah and Barak defeated the Canaanite coalition under Sisera, and here too the false prophets of Jezebel were killed after Elijah's victory on Mt. Carmel (Jdg. 4:7, 13; 5:21; Ps. 83:9; 1Ki. 18:40).

KISLEV *See* CALENDAR

KISLON [slow, IDB; strength, ISBE] The father of the representative of the tribe of Benjamin involved in the division of the land of Canaan among the tribes (Nu. 34:21). †

KISLOTH TABOR Jos. 19:12, probably identical with Kesulloth.

KISON *See* KISHON

KISS Besides being the usual greeting between friends and relatives, a kiss was used in the worship of pagan deities or as a means of identifying one's master

whom he wished to betray to the authorities (1Ki. 19:18-20; Ps. 2:12; Mt. 26:48-49). In early church times there was a "holy kiss," a special type of greeting (Ro. 16:16; 1Co. 16:20) – also called "kiss of love" (1Pe. 5:14).

KITE *See* BIRDS 5.

KIT(H)LISH A site in Judah in the western foothills (Jos. 15:40). †

KITRON [incense, (sacrificial) smoke] An unidentified site in the tribal area of Zebulun (Jdg. 1:30). † *See* KATTATH

KITTIM The Hebrew name for Cyprus which was inhabited originally by people descended from Javan, Greeks (Ge. 10:4; 1Ch. 1:7). It is translated "Cyprus" on a number of occasions (Isa. 23:1, NIV footnote). The ships of Kittim (Da. 11:30, NIV footnote) were most probably ships of Grecian design. The NIV calls them "ships of the western coastlands."

KNEADING TROUGH These, also called kneading bowls, were used in the making of bread. On the night of the LORD's passing through at the first Passover, the Israelites took their dough before the yeast was added and carried it in kneading troughs bound in their clothing (Ex. 8:3; 12:34; Dt. 28:5, 17).

KNEE, BOW THE *See* WORSHIP

KNIFE A sharp instrument of flint (for circumcision, shaving, or making a sickle) or of metal used as a sword, a razor, for killing a sacrifice, or for normal cutting (Jos. 5:23; 1Ki. 18:28; Eze. 5:1; Ge. 22:6, 10; Pr. 23:2).

KNOCK Christ, as a friend, stands knocking, asking to once again have fellowship with his people (Rev. 3:20).

KNOW *See* UNDERSTANDING

KOA A site E of Mesopotamia listed among those whose people were about to invade Judah (Eze. 23:23). †

KOHATH, KOHATHITE A son of Levi (Ge. 46:11), and the name of his descendants (Nu. 3:17-20, 27-31).

KOINE Greek for "common." Biblical Greek (*Koine* Greek) was the common dialect of NT times. *See* BIBLICAL LANGUAGES

KOINONIA *See* FELLOWSHIP

KOLAIAH {Yahweh's voice}
1. The father of the false prophet Ahab in the days of Jeremiah (Jer. 29:21). †
2. A descendant of Benjamin after the return from the Babylonian captivity (Ne. 11:7). †

KORAH, KORA(T)HITE, KOR-HITES {shaven, bald}
1 and 2. A son and a grandson of Esau (Ge. 36:5, 14-18).
3. A descendant of Judah and Caleb (1Ch. 2:43).
4. A Levite from whom descended the Korahite clans who were the doorkeepers and musicians of the tabernacle and the temple (Ex. 6:21, 24; Nu. 26:58;

1Ch. 26:1; 2Ch. 20:19). The sons of Korah are named in the titles of Psalms 42, 44–49, 84–85, 87–88.
5. One who led a revolt against Moses and lost his life, and that of the others involved with him, by being swallowed up by the earth (Nu. 16).

KORAN The sacred book of Islam. Also transliterated *Qur'an*, thought to be revealed by the angel Gabriel, written by Mohammed. It consists of 114 chapters of various subjects. In this book Jesus is called the son of Mary, but is only a prophet, not God. *See* ISLAM

KORAZIN A site just N of the Sea of Galilee denounced by Jesus at the same time he denounced Bethsaida and Capernaum (Mt. 11:21; Lk. 10:13). †

KORE {proclaimer}
1. A Korahite gatekeeper of the temple (1Ch. 26:1).
2. A Levite over the offerings in the days of King Hezekiah (2Ch. 31:14).

KOUM {rise!} An Aramaic word meaning "arise," used by Jesus in raising the daughter of the ruler (Mk. 5:41). †

KOZ {thorn} A descendant of Judah (1Ch. 4:8). † *See also* HAKKOZ 2.

KUE A place mentioned in 1Ki. 10:28 and 2Ch. 1:16 (NIV). Probably Cilicia in Asia Minor. This is translated "linen yarn" in the KJV. †

KUKOK *See* HELKATH

KUSHAIAH *See* KISHI

L

LAADAH A descendant of Judah (1Ch. 4:21). †

LAADAN *See* LADAN

LABAN {white} The brother of Rebekah and father of Jacob's two wives Leah and Rachel who covenanted with Jacob in Gilead (Ge. 24:29; 29:16, 25-30; 31:24ff.).

LABOR, LABORER There was work and labor before the fall of Adam (Ge. 2:15). In this pre-Fall state work was honorable and God-given. After the Fall, Adam was to care for the Garden but in a fallen state. The work was to be painful, the garden full of weeds (Ge. 3:15). To refuse to work is to be a sluggard (Pr. 21:25). Diligence brings prosperity (Pr. 10:4). Laborers were to be treated fairly (Dt. 24:14-18; cf. Col. 4:1). Though Christians are to expect the Lord's return at any time, they are to live quiet lives and work (1Th. 4:11).

LACHISH At first a royal city (135-108) of the Canaanites and then a Judean border fortress guarding one of the important approaches from the western foothills into the hill country west of Hebron (Jos. 10:3, 31-32; 15:39). Its burning in about 1230 B.C. is ascribed to the Israelite conquest by some, but by others to a later Egyptian raid. King Rehoboam of Judah made it a fortified city (2Ch. 11:9). It was taken by the Assyrian king Sennacherib as a preface to the surrender of Hezekiah of Judah (2Ki. 18:14, 17; 2Ch. 32:9). It was resettled after the return from the Babylonian captivity (Ne. 11:30). Here was found the famous cache of twenty-one inscribed ostraca called "the Lachish Letters."

LADAN, LAADAN
1. An ancestor of Moses' successor, Joshua (1Ch. 7:26).
2. A Levite son of Gershom; also called Libni (1Ch. 23:7; Ex. 6:17).

LADDER *See* JACOB'S LADDER

LAEL {(belonging) to El} The father of Eliasaph, a Levite leader of the families (Nu. 3:24). †

LAHAD A descendant of Judah (1Ch. 4:2). †

LAHAI-ROI *See* BEER LAHAI ROI

LAHMAM, LAHMAS An unidentified site in the western foothills of Judah (Jos. 15:40). †

LAHMI A brother of the giant Goliath (1Ch. 20:5). †

LAISH
1. A city (211-294) near the headwaters of the Jordan River which was conquered by the Danites and renamed Dan (Jdg. 18:7-29); also called Leshem (Jos. 19:47). † *See also* LAISHAH
2. The father of the man to whom Saul gave his daughter Michal, David's wife (1Sa. 25:44; 2Sa. 3:15). †

LAISHAH {lion} A site in the tribal area of Benjamin (Isa. 10:30). †

LAITY A Greek word for "people." It has come to mean those not ordained to

THE TRIBE OF DAN MOVES NORTH TO LAISH
Some men from the tribe of Dan traveled from Zorah and Eshtaol into Ephraim, where they persuaded Micah's priest to join them. They continued north to Laish, where they murdered its citizens. The city was renamed "Dan."

sacred work. Some have questioned this distinction for the NT church.

LAKE *See* SEA

LAKE OF FIRE *See* DEAD, ABODE OF

LAKKUM, LAKUM An unidentified site in Naphtali (Jos. 19:33). †

LAMA {why?} *See* ELOI, ELOI LAMA SABACHTHANI

LAMB The young of the sheep and even of the goat, a delicacy for food and milk, and used as a sacrificial animal (Dt. 32:14; Ge. 22:7). Lambs were sacrificed on all the holidays in the tabernacle and temple, but they were especially important at Passover. The lamb was to be totally eaten on the Passover night or else it was to be burned the next morning (Ex. 12:1-3). *See also* LAMB OF GOD

LAMB OF GOD The name given to Jesus by John the Baptist (Jn. 1:29, 36). It signifies the redemptive character of the death of Christ and places it in the context of the Passover sacrifices of the OT, which in time came to be the picture of redemption from sin (1Co. 5:7).

LAME *See* SICK, SICKNESS

LAMECH Son of Methushael; also called Methuselah (Ge. 5:25-31). He was a descendant of Cain (Ge. 4:18ff.; 1Ch. 1:3; Lk. 3:36). †

LAMENTATIONS, BOOK OF *See* JEREMIAH, BOOK OF

LAMP, LAMPSTAND A vessel for giving light and its stand, often just a niche in a wall. While no description of a lamp is found in the Bible, archaeology has given us a full picture. A lamp consisted of a hollow saucer or bowl of clay in which the oil would be placed. A pinch was made in the lip where the wick could be laid. So well known is their stylistic development that lamps are used as one of the criteria for the dating of archaeological strata.

An Ancient Lamp

Lampstands are usually mentioned in connection with the golden candlestick (lampstand) in the tabernacle and temple (Ex. 25:31, 37; 2Ch. 4:19-20). It is only natural that the lighted lamp would have symbolic meaning, speaking to man of the light of God; his Word, his salvation, his guidance (Ps. 119:105; 2Pe. 1:19; Isa. 62:1; Ps. 18:28).

The Golden Lampstand (or Candlestick)

LANCE *See* ARMS AND ARMOR

LANDMARK *See* BOUNDARY STONES

LANE An alley way (Lk. 14:21). This is narrower than a street (Greek, *plateia*). *See* STREET

LANGUAGES *See* BIBLICAL LANGUAGES

LAODICEA, CHURCH AT A city in Asia Minor and seat of an important church in post-NT times. It is mentioned a number of times by Paul in his letter to the church at Colosse and is the recipient of one of the letters of John, the writer of the Book of Revelation (Col. 2:1; 4:13-16; Rev. 1:11; 3:14). †

LAODICEANS, EPISTLE TO In Col. 4:16 a reference is made to a letter from Paul to the Laodiceans that was to be read by the Colossian Christians. This letter may have been lost, though many identify it as the letter to the Ephesians. Those who see the Ephesian Epistle as this letter cite evidence that the phrase "in Ephesus" in Eph. 1:1 is missing from the earliest manuscripts. And the letter itself seems to be a general letter that could have been passed from church to church (as an encyclical). *See* PAULINE EPISTLES, THE 4., *Ephesians*

LAPIS-LAZULI *See* PRECIOUS STONES AND METALS, Precious Stones 11., *Sapphire*

LAPPIDOTH, LAPIDOTH {flames} The husband of the prophetess Deborah (Jdg. 4:4). †

LAPWING A Hoopoe bird, unclean to eat (Lev. 11:19; Dt. 14:18). *See* BIRDS 5.

LASEA A seaport town in Crete mentioned in connection with Paul's travels (Ac. 27:8).

LASH, LASHING *See* PUNISHMENT; SCOURGE, SCOURGING; STRIPES

LASHA An unidentified site on the eastern side of the Canaanite clans (Ge. 10:19). †

LASHARON {(belonging to) SHARON} An unidentified site taken by Joshua (Jos. 12:18). †

LAST DAYS *See* ESCHATOLOGY

LAST SUPPER Though this combination of words is not found in the Bible, it refers to the supper on the evening before the crucifixion of Jesus when he sat down to a Passover supper and converted it into what the church considers the first Communion or eucharistic service (Mt. 26:17-29). *See* COMMUNION, VIEWS OF; LORD'S SUPPER

LATCHET *See* DRESS, *sandal-thong*, last ¶

LATIN The language of ancient Rome and Israel and one of the three languages in which the inscription was written that was placed above the cross of Jesus (Jn. 19:20).

LATTICE A construction made by crossing laths or other material to cover an opening for privacy, ventilation, or adornment (Jdg. 5:28; Pr. 7:6).

LAVER {basin} A large vessel containing water which was in the courtyard between the tent of meeting and the altar. It was used for the washing of the feet and hands of the priest who served there (Ex. 30:18-28).

LAW The key word for law in the OT, *torah*, means "instruction" or "guidance." Only rarely (12 of 220 occurrences) is *torah* in the plural, indicating individual laws or regulations (Lev. 26:46; Isa. 24:5). As singular, "the law," it usually refers to the sum total of gracious covenant relation between Yahweh and Israel.

Several other terms are used of general categories of law. *Mitsvah* is usually a direct command (Ex. 15:26; Dt. 6:25); *mishpat* is often a rule that results from a judicial decision, a "judgment" or *requirement* (Nu. 27:11). *Dabar*, the normal word for "word," emphasizes law as a direct revelation from God, as in the case of the Ten Commandments: "Ten Words" in Hebrew (*see also* DECALOGUE). *Hoq* and *huqqah*, related to the word "engraving," point to an established law, an *ordinance* (Ex. 12:14). *Edut*, "testimony," testifies to God's dealing with his people; the tablets of the Ten Commandments (Ex. 32:15), the Ark (Ex. 40: 22), and the tabernacle (Nu. 1:50) were often associated with this word.

God revealed his law to a redeemed community as gracious instruction for a righteous life-style that would honor and glorify him and result in a long, happy, and peaceful existence (Lev. 26:1-13; Dt. 4:40; 5:33). It was not intended as a means of salvation but as an expression of love and devotion (Dt. 6:49). "Do this and live" (Lev. 18:5; Ro. 10:5) did not mean that one gained eternal life by keeping the law, but that (positively) the one who obeyed God's law out of love and reverence lived long and lived well, and that (negatively) he was not killed for his disobedience (Lev. 26). As Jesus summarized, the heart of the law is "Love the Lord your God" and "Love your neighbor as yourself" (Mt. 22:37-40; Mk. 12:29-31). In the OT as in the NT, keeping this law is not too difficult for the one who loves God (Dt. 30:11-16; 1Jn. 5:13).

In the NT there is one major word for law, *nomos*, but it has a wide variety of usage. Law can refer to the OT in whole or in part (Lk. 16:16-17). Law often refers to the Old Covenant (Ro. 5:13) and those within this covenant are "under law" (1Co. 9:20). Law can also mean any aspect of God's will, so that even those not in the Old Covenant are still "under law" (1Co. 9:21). A third and negative meaning of "under law" is used of those who look to law as a means of salvation or gaining favor with God (Ro. 6:14-15; cf. 9:30—10:4). Law is also used of a general principle, such as the "law of sin" (Ro. 7:21-25).

The law as contained in the Old Covenant is never condemned in the New; it is "holy, righteous and good" (Ro. 7:12); "put in charge to lead us to Christ" (Gal. 3:24). But keeping the law cannot save (Ro. 3:28; 8:3); law apart from faith can only condemn (Ro. 7:7-11). Legalism, at-

tempting to gain favor or salvation by keeping the law, is strongly condemned and is an impossible route to eternal life (Gal. 3:10-12; 5:4).

The Christian is under God's law, Christ's law (1Co. 9:21). Jesus said, "If you love me, you will obey what I command" (Jo. 14:15, 23). Again, this obedience is motivated by love and reverence, not by legalistic obligation. Some elements of OT law are repeated in the NT (Mt. 5:21-48; Eph. 6:1). Others, such as the priesthood, temple, and sacrificial system, are clearly done away with (Heb. 7—10). Some are made a matter of personal conscience, such as diet and holy days (Ro. 14; Col. 2:16-23). What is clearly commanded in the NT, Christians are to obey because of their love for Jesus. What is clearly done away with, Christians should not practice. What is not clear should be carefully evaluated to see if its observance promotes love for God and fellow believers (Ro. 14:22-23). *See also* DECALOGUE. (J.R.K.)

LAW OF CHRIST 1Co. 9:21; Gal. 6:2. *See* LAW

LAW OF MOSES *See* LAW; MOSES

LAW OF SIN A "law" mentioned in Ro. 7:23, 25; 8:2 is apparently a principle or rule of action, not a codified law in the legal sense.

LAWGIVER The Scriptures confirm that there is only one ultimate Lawgiver and Judge, God himself (Jas. 4:12). In the Old Covenant, Moses, though a key figure, was merely the vehicle for God to give his covenant. In contrast, Jesus Christ emanated grace and truth (Jn. 1:17). *See* DECALOGUE; LAW; MOSES

LAWLESS ONE The Antichrist (2Th. 2:8).

LAWYER A term in the Bible that denoted a class of men especially trained to understand the OT law, to teach it to the next generation of lawyers, and to decide on specific questions of law for those who wanted advice (Lk. 7:30; 11:45; 14:3). *See* SCRIBE

LAYING ON OF HANDS In both Testaments this act could signify the giving of a blessing, benediction, or parental inheritance, or the bestowal of the gifts and rights of an office (Ge. 48:14-20; Dt. 34:9; Mt. 19:13-15; Ac. 13:3). In the OT sacrificial system it also symbolized the transfer of sin from an individual or people to the sacrificial animal (Lev. 16:21). In the NT it was the external symbol of the giving of the Holy Spirit to an individual (Ac. 19:6). By extension, from 1Ti. 4:14 and 2Ti. 1:6, it became for the church a part of the procedure for the ordination of one of its leaders.

LAZARUS
1. The brother of Martha and Mary who was raised from the dead by Jesus (Jn. 11:5, 43ff.).
2. The poor man in the parable of the rich man and Lazarus told by Jesus (Lk. 16:19ff.).

LAZY Laziness is to be disinclined to do work. It is part of a fool's folly. Sloth or sluggard are synonyms. The opposite is the diligent person (Pr. 10:4; 12:24, 27; 19:15; 26:15; Mt. 25:26; Tit. 1:12).

LEAD One of the important metals in antiquity (Nu. 31:22). It was used in the reduction of silver (Jer. 6:27-30). Tarshish traded with Tyre for her lead (Eze. 27:12). It had many commercial uses: weights, sinkers for fishnets, and for plumblines.

LEAGUE KJV for "Treaty." *See* COVENANT

LEAH {*possibly* wild cow, BDB; wild cow, gazelle, IDB; cow, KB; cf. Rachel = ewe} Elder daughter of Laban and one of Jacob's wives, mother of some of the founders of the tribes of Israel (Ge. 29:16, 23, 31ff.).

LEANNOTH, MAHALATH {the suffering of affliction, NIV; sickness or suffering poem, JB} Ps. 88 title. † *See* PSALMS (I)

LEASING KJV for "falsehood" and "lies" (Ps. 4:2; 5:6).

LEAST STROKE *See* TITTLE

LEATHER(N) *See* DRESS; SKIN; TANNER; WINESKIN

LEAVEN *See* YEAST; UNLEAVENED BREAD

LEBANA, LEBANAH {white} An ancestor of some sons who were temple servants in the second temple in the days of Ezra and Nehemiah (Ezr. 2:45; Ne. 7:48). † There are two spellings of the name of the same man.

LEBANON {white, snow} *See* GEOGRAPHY OF THE HOLY LAND

LEBAOTH *See* BETH LEBAOTH

LEBBAEUS {(one near to) my heart} *See* APOSTLES, *Thaddaeus*

LEBEN *See* FOOD; MILK

LEBONAH A town (173-164) between Shiloh and Shechem (Jdg. 21:19). †

LEBO HAMATH *See* HAMATH 2.

LECAH {to you} A descendant of Judah (1Ch. 4:21). †

LEEKS *See* PLANTS, PERFUMES, AND SPICES, Plants for Food 3.

LEGION {military company} The chief and largest unit of the Roman army but never used in that sense in the Bible. There it is used only in a figurative sense, of numerical largeness (Mt. 26:53; Mk. 5:9, 13; Lk. 8:30).

LEHABITES, LEHABIM Descendants of Ham who occupied the N coast of Africa W of Egypt, thought to be the ancestors of the Libyans (Ge. 10:13; 1Ch. 1:11). † *See also* LIBYA

LEHEM *See* JASHUBI LEHEM

LEHI {jawbone,} An unidentified site in the tribal area of Judah where Samson killed 1,000 Philistines with a jawbone, and for that reason it is also called Ramath Lehi ("the place of the jawbone") (Jdg. 15:9-19). †

LEMUEL [(belonging) to El] An unknown king whose mother taught him the proverbs (Pr. 31:19). †

LENTIL(E)S *See* PLANTS, PERFUMES, AND SPICES

LEOPARD *See* BEASTS 8.

LEPER, LEPROSY *See* SICK, SICKNESS

LEPTON *See* MONEY

LESBIANISM *See* HOMOSEXUALITY

LESHEM [lion] *See* DAN, DANITES and LAISH 1.

LETTER *See* EPISTLE

LETTER OF PAUL *See* PAULINE EPISTLES

LETUSHIM, LETUSHITES The descendants of a grandson of Abraham by Keturah (Ge. 25:3). †

LEUMMIM, LEUMMITES The descendants of a grandson of Abraham by Keturah (Ge. 25:3). †

LEVANT A wind which comes from the direction of the sunrise (E) in the Mediterranean area, known to be hot and dry. Levant often is used as a synonym of the Near East, the Eastern Mediterranean area. *See* WIND

LEVI
1. A son of Jacob by Leah and founder of one of the tribes of Israel, the one that served in Israel's religion (Ge. 29:34; 34:25ff.; Nu. 3:5-9).

2 and 3. Two ancestors of Joseph, who was the husband of Mary and the father (as it was thought) of Jesus (Lk. 3:24, 29).

4. A tax collector who became one of Jesus' disciples (Mk. 2:14); also called Matthew (Mt. 9:9).

LEVIATHAN [coiled one (like a serpent)] *See* BEASTS 9.

LEVIRATE MARRIAGE *See* MARRIAGE, *Levirate Marriage*

LEVITES [of LEVI] The descendants of Levi who by their loyalty to Moses and to God at the time Aaron built the golden calf were set aside for the service of God (Ge. 35:23; Ex. 32:2-7, 25-29). These were the priests and other officers of God in the service of the tent of meeting and later the temple, the treasury, the music and song (Nu. 3:5-13, 38; 1Ch. 6:31, 33ff.; 2Ch. 17:8-9; Ezr. 8:15ff.; Ne. 7:43). In the NT it is stated that since perfection could not be brought by man, not even by the Levitical priesthood, it was necessary for another priest, from a different tribe and order, to come to do the work of atonement and sanctification, namely Jesus, a priest after the order of Melchizedek, who antedated the Levitical system. The service priests and Levites were divided into twenty-four groups, called divisions (or courses). Each had its own head and its own function, and each served for a week in rotation (1Ch. 24–25; Lk. 1:8).

LEVITICAL CITY *See* CITY OF REFUGE

LEVITICUS, BOOK OF *See* PENTATEUCH

LEVY *See* TAXES, TAXING; TRIBUTE

LEX TALIONIS The principle of retaliation, in the OT (Ex. 21:24). This is not found in the NT (Mt. 5:38; Ro. 12:19-21).

LIAR *See* DEVIL

LIBATION [pour (as an offering)] *See* SACRIFICES AND OFFERINGS, *The Grain (Meal) Offering*

LIBERALISM Any movement that seeks to change the conventional or traditional teachings. A general movement in Protestantism that stresses intellectual free thinking, stressing individual faith apart from orthodox teachings. A cornerstone of liberalism is the nature and value of the Bible. *See* HERMENEUTICS

LIBERATION THEOLOGY An umbrella phrase for several theological movements. Third world, Feminist, and Black theologies are some of the movements. It stresses redemption from the bondage of this world in social, political, and economic terms, as opposed to stressing personal redemption from sin through Christ's atonement. *See also* FEMINIST THEOLOGY

LIBERTINES KJV for "Freedmen" (Ac. 6:9).

LIBERTY *See* FREE MAN, FREEDMAN; JUBILE(E)

LIBNAH [white]
   1. A city (145-116) in the western foothills of Judah captured by Joshua and designated as one of the Levitical cities (Jos. 10:29-32; 21:13). It was one of the cities besieged by King Sennacherib of Assyria (2Ki. 19:8). The wife of King Josiah and mother of two of Judah's kings came from Libnah (2Ki. 23:31; 24:18).
   2. An unidentified stop on the Israelite exodus route from Egypt (Nu. 33:20-21).

LIBNI, LIBNITES [(descendant of) LIBNI *or* white]
   1. A descendant of Levi (1Ch. 6:17).
   2. A Levite son of Gershon; also called Ladan. *See also* LADAN 2.

LIBYA A part of North Africa W of Egypt. It was the country of the Lehabites. Cyrene was one of its cities (Eze. 30:5; Da. 11:43; Ac. 2:10). *See also* LEHABITES; LUBIM

LICE *See* BEASTS 6., *Gnat*

LICENTIOUSNESS A lacking of moral, especially sexual, restraints. *See* FORNICATION

LIE *See* WITNESS, *False Witness*

LIEUTENANT *See* SATRAP

LIFE The term life may refer either to the animate part of man or animal, physical or natural life, or it may refer to that part of man's "life" after death, spiritual or eternal life (*see* SOUL; SPIRIT). That is, it may refer to two parts of man's existence: the period of his earthly existence, his lifetime, or to his eternal existence into which he enters through death. Both are presented as gifts of God to his creatures. Physical life was given in the acts of Creation. In the case of man, his body was formed from the dust of the ground, and he became animate when God breathed into his nostrils the breath of life. At this point man became a living being. All animals before him already were "living creatures" (Ge. 1:20-25; 2:7). The words rendered "living creatures" in Ge. 1:24 are the same as "living being" in 2:7. According to the NT, eternal life is also the gift of God, emanating from the divine life, the life of God (Eph. 4:18). Eternal life is given to all believers in Christ as a present possession and a future guarantee of everlasting life (Jn. 3:36; 5:24; Ro. 5:10; Eph. 2:18; 1Jn. 5:11-12). *See also* BLOOD; IMMORTAL and FUTURE LIFE; SEAL; SOUL

LIFE, LAMB'S BOOK OF, AND TREE OF These expressions are found only in Revelation (Rev. 3:5; 13:8; 17:8; 20:12, 15; 21:27), except for the references to the latter which occur in Genesis and in Revelation (Ge. 2:9; 3:22, 24; Rev. 22:2, 14, 19). The book contains a record of those who inherit eternal life. The "tree" found originally in the Garden of Eden turns up again in the account of eternal life in Revelation.

LIGHT AND DARKNESS The former is the symbol of purity and holiness, while the latter is the symbol of sin and the outer darkness reserved for the devil and his angels. Light has many symbolic meanings: God is light (1Jn. 1:5); believers dwell in light (Eph. 5:8-9); Jesus is the light of the world (Jn. 8:12); God's written revelation is called light (Ps. 119:105); and believers or special emissaries of God are light (Jn. 5:35; Php. 2:15).

LIGHTNING *See* THUNDER

LIGHTS, FEAST OF *See* CALENDAR and FESTIVALS

LIGN-ALOES *See* PLANTS, PERFUMES, AND SPICES, Perfumes,

Scents, Ointments, Drugs (Nu. 24:6), *aloes*

LIGURE *See* PRECIOUS STONES AND METALS, Precious Stones 9., *Jacinth*

LIKENESS *See* IDOL, IDOLATRY

LIKHI {take, marry} A descendant of Manasseh (1Ch. 7:19). †

LILIES *See* PSALMS, TITLES OF 2., *Shoshannim*

LILY *See* PLANTS, PERFUMES, AND SPICES, Flowering Plants 4.

LIMITED ATONEMENT *See* ATONEMENT, LIMITED

LINE *See* WEIGHTS AND MEASURES, Measures of Length

LINEN A product of the flax plant. Its fibers were woven usually by women in an art learned in Egypt (Ex. 35:25; Pr. 31:13, 19). The plant itself was grown in the Jericho area and perhaps also in the low area around Beth Shan (Jos. 2:3, 6). It was used for all kinds of clothing and cloths for many other purposes as well. *See also* KUE; PLANTS, PERFUMES, AND SPICES, Flowering Plants 3.

LINTEL The horizontal cross piece (a "header") at the top of a door frame to restrain what is above it (Ex. 12:22-23).

LINUS A Christian with Paul at Rome who sent greetings to Timothy (2Ti.4:21). †

LION *See* BEASTS 8.

LISTEN *See* OBEDIENCE

LITTER A rendering in Isa. 66:20 in most versions for "wagon" (NIV, NEB). *See* CART

LITTLE OWL *See* BIRDS 5.

LITURGY A set form of a worship service.

LIVE *See* WALK

LIVER *See* EMOTIONS

LIVING ANIMALS, BEASTS, CREATURES *See* CHERUB

LIVING SACRIFICE This is a paradoxical phrase for service and worship to God (Ro. 12:1).

LIZARD *See* BEASTS 6.

LO-AMMI {not my people} A Hebrew transliteration in Hos. 1:9-10; 2:23. It is translated as "not my people" in some versions.

LO DEBAR {no pasture} A town (207-219) E of the Jordan, in Gilead, the home of Mephibosheth, Saul's grandson, and of Makir, a helper of David (2Sa. 9:46; 17:27; Am. 6:13). † *See* DEBIR

LOAF *See* BREAD

LOAN *See* DEBT; USURY

LOCK *See* HOUSE

LOCUST *See* BEASTS 6.

LOD The Lydda (140-151) of the NT, a town in the western foothills of Judah near Joppa (1Ch. 8:12; Ezr. 2:33; Ne. 7:37; 11:35; Ac. 9:32, 35, 38). †

LYDDA
Peter traveled to Lydda, where he healed Aeneas. From there he went to Joppa and then to Caesarea.

LODGE *See* HOSPITALITY; INN

LOG *See* WEIGHTS AND MEASURES

LOGIA This usually refers to a collection of the sayings of Jesus. Sometimes this is referred to as the *Q* (source) document, thought by some to underlie the sayings found in Matthew and Luke which are not found in Mark. *See* CRITICISM, REDACTION

LOGOS [word, The Word] A title of Christ in Jn. 1:1. In this verse it relates to the creative act of God (cf. Ge. 1:3ff., "and God said"). The Word of Jn. 1:1 has the same essence as God, not Godlikeness. *See* GOD, NAMES OF, GODHEAD 11., *The Word*

LOINCLOTH *See* DRESS

LOIS The grandmother of Timothy (2Ti. 1:5). †

LONELY PLACE *See* DESERT

LONG-SUFFERING *See* PATIENCE

LOOKING GLASS *See* MIRROR

LOOM *See* WEAVING AND SPINNING

LOOPS The coverings of the tabernacle were held together by the clasps which went through the loops of goat's hair or other material (Ex. 26:4-11).

LOOSING *See* BINDING AND LOOSING

LORD The English translation of a number of Hebrew and Greek words used of both God and men to express the recognition of respect or authority. As applied to God *see* GOD, NAMES OF. As applied to men it shows respect (as to a master) or ownership and nobility (Ge. 23:11; 1Ki. 1:31; Mt. 20:25). When the reference is to a human, it is spelled in lower case letters without capitals. In the OT when the reference is to God, it is written LORD. In the overwhelming number of cases in the NT the reference is to Jesus, and sometimes to God the Father.

LORD OF HOSTS [Yahweh of armies] *See* GOD, NAMES OF

LORD'S DAY [day belonging to the master (Jesus)] A day consecrated to the Lord Jesus Christ for rest and worship, on the first of the week, as a memorial to his resurrection which took place on that day (Rev. 1:10). It was sharply contrasted with the sixth day or the Sabbath as far as observance of the day was concerned. One could consider any day sacred since, as far as salvation was concerned, all days were alike (Ro. 14:5-6). It became customary for Christians to assemble on that day and to break bread together (Ac. 20:7). *See* SABBATH

LORD'S PRAYER The title given to the prayer which Jesus taught his disciples to pray (Mt. 6:9-13; Lk. 11:24), commonly called in many languages the "Our Father."

LORD'S SUPPER The name commonly given to the meal that Jesus ate with his disciples the night before he was crucified, the supper which started as a Passover meal but which Jesus changed as a memorial service to be kept by the church until his return (Mt. 26:17, 26-28; 1Co. 10:16; 11:17-32). *See* COMMUNION, VIEWS OF

LO-RUHAMAH [no compassion] A Hebrew transliteration in Hos. 1:6, 8. It is translated in Hos. 2:23 "not my loved one." An adequate rendering is "no compassion." *See* COMPASSION

LOST *See* PERISH

LOT
1. The nephew of Abraham who emigrated with him to Canaan but left him there to go down to Sodom and Gomorrah. Here he was captured by foreign kings, rescued by Abraham, escaped the destruction of the cities, and became the ancestor of the Moabites and the Ammonites (Ge. 11:27, 31; 13:8-12; 14:12ff.; 19:1-30).
2. A portion or a share of something that one receives, i.e., a piece of land or a position in service (Jos. 15:1).
3. Like dice to be cast on the ground, or other devices to be drawn from a receptacle. This was a very common method to help make decisions in the ancient world and in Bible times (Est. 3:7; Jh. 1:7; Mt. 27:35; Ac. 1:24-26).

LOT, SHARE, PORTION *See* IN-
HERITANCE; LOT 2.

LOTAN [of LOT] The first son of Seir
and founder of the Horite clan in Edom
(Ge. 36:20, 22, 29; 1Ch. 1:38-39). †

LOTUS *See* PLANTS, PERFUMES,
AND SPICES, Flowering Plants 4.

LOVE An inner emotion or drive which
both initiates and maintains relationships
between human beings or between men
and God, whether it be friendship, loyalty, kindness, or even mercy and pity.
The Bible in the OT speaks of love in the
human society, love within the family,
sexual love, the love of man for God, and
the electing covenant love of God for his
people (2Sa. 1:26; Ru. 4:15; 2Sa. 13:1,
15; Dt. 6:5; 7:6-9). In the NT, while the
above nuances are also found, the main
thrust is different. God is love by nature,
and man's chief end is to love God
supremely and to glorify him by keeping his commandments. There is emphasis also upon the need for man to love his
fellowman (1Jn. 4:7-12, 16, 19-21). Involved in this is the keeping of the commandments of God (Mt. 22:36-40; 1Jn.
5:2-3). God's love for men includes his
redeeming them, supplying all their
needs, and securing for them a place in
his presence throughout eternity (Ro.
5:8; Php. 4:19; Ro. 8:28-39; Eph.
2:4-8).

LOVE FEAST [AGAPE feast] While
the term is found only once in the Bible
(Jude 12), the concept grew up in the
early church from a communal meal apparently eaten in connection with the observance of the Lord's Supper. Abuses
soon entered, and the Apostle Paul
warned the church against them (1Co.
11:20-29, 33-34).

LOVING-KINDNESS Related terms
are mercy; loyal, unfailing, steadfast
love; "chesed" in Hebrew.

LOWLY *See* HUMBLE; POOR

LUBIM KJV for a people, translated
"Libyans" in 2Ch. 12:3; 16:8; Na. 3:9.
See LIBYA

LUCAS [Luke] *See* LUKE

LUCIFER [morning star, Venus] *See*
DEVIL; SATAN

LUCIUS
 1. A man from Cyrene who was a
Christian in Antioch (Ac. 13:1). †
 2. One associated with Paul who sent
greetings to the Christians at Rome (Ro.
16:21). †

LUCRE KJV for "money" or "dishonest
gain" in the NIV.

LUD, LUDIM, LUDITES
 1. Lud, a son of Shem (Ge. 10:22).
 2. The Ludites were descended from
Ham, another son of Noah who became
the father of the Ludites, perhaps the ancient Lydians (Ge. 10:13). Some scholars
think that the Ludites were North Afri-
can people. If so, they are not now identifiable.

LUHITH An unidentified town in Moab
(Isa. 15:5).

LUKE The writer of the third Gospel
and of the Book of Acts, apparently both
a physician and a historian (Lk. 1:15; Ac.
1:13; Col. 4:14). The "we" sections of the
Book of Acts (16:10-17; 20:5-15; 21:18;
27:1—28:16) indicate that he traveled
with Paul extensively. Except for two
other references (2Ti. 4:11; Phm. 24), we
know nothing more about this unusual
man, though there is much speculation
in the form of tradition. †

LUKE, GOSPEL ACCORDING TO
See GOSPELS, THE FOUR

LUNATIC, LUNATICK [moon struck]
See SICK, SICKNESS

LUST Several Hebrew and Greek words
are thus translated and carry the ideas of
delight in, desires for the things of the
world, passionate desire, as well as sexual desire (Ps. 68:30; Pr. 11:6; Mt. 5:28;
Ro. 1:24; Eph. 4:22; 1Th. 4:5; 1Jn.
2:16-17). *See* FORNICATION

LUTE *See* MUSIC

LUTHER, MARTIN An early
reformer in Germany (A.D. 1483-1546).

He began to question the relationship of tradition and Scripture and the way of personal salvation through faith, not works. These questions and others led to a dramatic break with the Roman Catholic church and the eventual formation of the Lutheran church. *See* CALVIN; COUNTER-REFORMATION; REFORMATION; PROTESTANT

LUZ [almond tree]

1. A site on the N border of the tribal area of Benjamin. Here Jacob had his dream in which he saw angels ascending and descending a ladder. He changed its name to Bethel (Gen. 28:19; Jos. 18:13).

2. A city in the land of the Hittites (Jdg. 1:26).

LXX This is an abbreviation for the Septuagint. *See* BIBLE VERSIONS, Ancient Versions

LYCAONIA(N) A district in Asia N of the Taurus mountain range whose cities Lystra and Derbe were visited by the Christians who were escaping the persecution in Iconium (Ac. 14:1, 56). †

LYCIA Ac. 27:5. † *See* GEOGRAPHY OF THE HOLY LAND

LYDDA *See* LOD

LYDIA

1. A lady from the city of Thyatira who sold purple goods in Philippi. She became a convert by Paul's witness, and groups of believers met in her house (Ac. 16:14-15, 40).

2. A site or area mentioned in a message about Egypt in association with Cush (Upper Egypt) and Put (Jer. 46:9), and also with all Arabia and Libya (Eze. 30:5), and in lament for Tyre in connection with Persia and Put (Eze. 27:10). *See* PUT

LYING *See* WITNESS

LYRE *See* MUSIC

LYSANIAS The tetrarch of Abilene, a small region in Lebanon (Lk. 3:1). †

LYSIAS Claudius Lysias, a Roman officer who arrested Paul and later sent him to Caesarea to be judged (Ac. 21:32ff.; 23:26ff.; 24:22). †

LYSTRA A site in Lycaonia (central Turkey) to which some persecuted Christians fled (Ac. 14:1, 5-6). Caesar had one of his military strongholds there. Paul healed a man whose feet were crippled from birth, with a resultant uproar in the city (Ac. 14:8-18). Here, too, Paul was stoned and left for dead (Ac. 14:19). In spite of it all, a church was established which Paul visited again on a later missionary journey (Ac. 16:1-2). †

LYSTRA IN LYCAONIA

M

MAACAH, MAACATH, MAAC-HAH, MAACHATHI AND MAAC-ATHITES

1. A son of Nahor and nephew of Abraham (Ge. 22:24).

2. A wife of David and the mother of Absalom (2Sa. 3:3).

3. The father of Achish, the king of Gath (1Ki. 2:39-40).

4. The wife of King Rehoboam of Judah and mother of his successor, Abijah. Her grandson, King Asa, deposed her from her place of influence in the kingdom because of her idolatry (1Ki. 14:31; 15:2, 10, 13). The relationship between Maacah, Abijah, and Absalom (Abishalom) is not clear (see 2Ch. 11:22; 13:2).

5. A concubine of Caleb (1Ch. 2:48).

6. The wife of Makir, a descendant of Manasseh (1Ch. 7:16).

7. The wife of Jeiel the father of Gibeon (1Ch. 8:29).

8. The father of one of David's mighty men (1Ch. 11:43).

9. The father of the head of the Simeonites in David's service (1Ch. 27:16).

10. A small kingdom on the western border of Bashan N of Gilead whose people, the Maacathites, fought with the Ammonites against David, and on being defeated became his servants (Dt. 3:14; Jos. 12:5; 2Sa. 10:6-19). The Israelites did not expel them but dwelt among them, and some of their descendants later assisted David and others in Israel (Jos. 13:13; 2Sa. 23:34; 2Ki. 25:23).

MAADAI
One who married a foreign wife during the Babylonian captivity (Ezr. 10:34). †

MAADIAH, MOADIAH
A family from whom came a head of a priestly family after the return with Zerubbabel from the Babylonian captivity (Ne. 12:5, 17). †

MAAI
One who helped with the musical instruments in the dedication of the rebuilt wall of Jerusalem (Ne. 12:36). †

MAALEH-ACRABBIM
[ascent of Akrabbim (scorpions)] See SCORPION PASS

MAARATH
[barren] An unidentified site in the tribal area of Judah (Jos. 15:59). †

MAASAI, MAASIAI
[work of Yahweh] A priest in postexilic times (1Ch. 9:12). †

MAASEIAH
[work of Yahweh]

1. A Levite gatekeeper in David's time (1Ch. 15:18, 20).

2. One of the military officers who helped the priest Jehoiada to put the young Jehoash (Joash) on the throne of Judah (2Ch. 23:1ff.).

3. An officer of King Uzziah of Judah (2Ch. 26:11).

4. A son of King Ahaz of Judah (2Ch. 28:7).

5. The governor of Jerusalem in the days of King Josiah sent to help repair the temple (2Ch. 34:8).

6, 7, 8, and 9. Four who married foreign wives during the Babylonian captivity (Ezr. 10:18, 21-22, 30).

10. The father of one of those who built a portion of the wall of Jerusalem in Nehemiah's time (Ne. 3:23).

11 and 12. Two who stood with Ezra as he read the law to the people in Jerusalem (Ne. 8:4, 7). One of them instructed the people in the law.

13. One who signed the covenant with Nehemiah (Ne. 10:25).

14 and 15. Descendants of Judah and of Benjamin who returned from the Babylonian captivity (Ne. 11:5, 7).

16 and 17. Two priests who were involved in the musical part of the program of dedication of the rebuilt wall of Jerusalem (Ne. 12:41-42).

18. The father of a priest that the king sent to inquire of the prophet Jeremiah (Jer. 21:1; 29:25).

19. The father of the false prophet Zedekiah in the days of Jeremiah (Jer. 29:21).

20. Keeper of the door of the temple in the days of Jeremiah (Jer. 35:4).

21. *See also* BAASEIAH.

MAATH An ancestor of Joseph, the father (so it was thought) of Jesus (Lk. 3:26). †

MAAZ A descendant of Judah and Jerahmeel (1Ch. 2:27). †

MAAZIAH {Yahweh is a refuge}

1. Head of the twenty-fourth priestly division in the service of the tabernacle as arranged by David (1Ch. 24:18). †

2. One who signed the covenant with Nehemiah (Ne. 10:8). †

MACBANNAI A descendant of Gad who joined David (1Ch. 12:13). †

MACBENAH A descendant of Caleb (1Ch. 2:49). †

MACCABEES {hammer} Judas, son of the priest Mattathias, was called the Maccabee, from the Hebrew or Aramaic *maqqaba*, which means "hammer." It may have arisen from the crushing blows that Judas, as hero of Israel's revolt against Antiochus IV, inflicted upon his

people's oppressors (*see* SELEUCIDS). The term *Maccabean* is sometimes applied to his party or, less accurately, to his family's entire dynasty (*see* HASMONEAN and the family chart there).

At his death in 167 B.C. Mattathias appointed Judas to be the continuing leader against Antiochus, his Syrian armies, and his policy of Hellenization. By strategy, courage, and the grace of God, Judas Maccabeus won four victories: over Apollonius, near Samaria (1Macc. 3:10-12); over Seron, at Beth Horon (1Macc. 3:23-24); over Ptolemy, Nicanor, and Gorgias, at Emmaus, 166 B.C. (1Macc. 4:12-22); and over the viceroy Lysias, at Bethsura, 165 (1Macc. 4:33, 34). As Judas affirmed, "For victory in war does not depend on the size of the fighting force: Heaven accords the strength. They are coming to us in full-blown insolence and lawlessness to destroy us, our wives and children, and to plunder us; but we are fighting for our lives and our laws, and he will crush them before our eyes;" (1Macc. 3:19-21, NJB). In December 165 Judas cleansed the Jerusalem temple and reestablished the daily sacrifice. This event continued to be observed as the Feast of Dedication or "Lights" (Jn. 10:22; *see* CALENDAR).

Judas went on to subdue the surrounding areas of Idumea, the area E of the Jordan, and Philistia (1Macc. 5). Lysias and the young Antiochus V (164-162) defeated Judas at Bethzacharias, 163 (1Macc. 6:31-47); but revolt in Antioch caused them to withdraw. Judas was granted religious liberty (1Macc. 6:57-60). Demetrius I (162-150), however, appointed Alcimus, a corrupt Hellenizer, as high priest, whom Judas opposed and drove out (1Macc. 7:15). Judas destroyed a supporting Syrian army of Nicanor at Adasa, March 161, and is supposed to have concluded a treaty with the Romans (1Macc. 8). But in April, at Elasa before an even larger Syrian army under Bacchides, with most of his forces having fled, Judas Maccabeus died in battle (1Macc. 9:1-22), leaving his brothers to carry on the struggle to its ultimately successful conclusion.

The books of 1 and 2 Maccabees, also identify two of the intertestamental writings of the Apocrypha that describe the career of Judas and accompanying events. First Maccabees is a historical work of great value. It exhibits a pious spirit (as in 3:51) but makes no claim of miracles; it is patriotic and pro-Hasmonean. Second Maccabees is an inartistic abbreviation of a lost history of Jason of Cyrene (2Macc. 2:23), emphasizing the theology of Pharisaism (2Macc. 7:9), stressing the miraculous (2Macc. 3:23-24), and making reference to purgatory and prayers for the dead (2Macc. 12:44-45). It more readily grants the imperfections of the Hasmoneans (as in 2Macc. 10:20). (J.B.P.) *See also* INTERTESTAMENTAL PERIOD; SCRIPTURE, *Apocrypha*

MACEDONIA *See* GEOGRAPHY OF THE HOLY LAND

MACEDONIAN The area of northern Greece: Thessalonians, Bereans, and Philippians were Macedonians (Ac. 19:29; 27:2; 2Co. 9:4).

MACEDONIA (Arrows show travels of Paul and co-workers.)

MACHBANAI *See* MACBANNAI

MACHBENAH *See* MACBENAH

MACHI [bought] *See* MAKI

MACHINE *See* ARMS AND ARMOR

MACHIR, MACHIRITES *See* MAKIR, MAKIRITES

MACHNADEBAI *See* MACNADEBAI

MACHPELAH [double (cave)] A field and cave near Hebron which Abraham bought from Ephron the Hittite for a burial ground. The patriarchs are buried here under a great Muslim mosque today (Ge. 23:9-19; 25:9; 49:30; 50:13). †

THE CAVE OF MACHPELAH

MACNADEBAI One who married a foreign wife during the Babylonian captivity (Ezr. 10:40). †

MACROEVOLUTION *See* EVOLUTION, MACRO

MADAI [Medes] A son of Japheth and grandson of Noah, ancestor of the Medes (Ge. 10:2; 1Ch. 1:5). †

MADIAN *See* MIDIAN

MADMANNAH [dung place] A town (143-084) in southern Judah founded by a descendant of Caleb (Jos. 15:31; 1Ch. 2:49). †

MADMEN A town (217-077) in Moab noted in the dirge of Jeremiah (Jer. 48:2). †

MADMENAH An unidentified site in the tribal area of Benjamin (Isa. 10:31). †

MADNESS *See* SICK, SICKNESS

MADON An unidentified site NW of the city of Tiberias whose king was

defeated by Joshua (Jos. 11:1; 12:19).
†

MAGADAN *See* DALMANUTHA

MAGBISH An unidentified site from which some came back with Zerubbabel from the Babylonian captivity (Ezr. 2:30). †

MAGDALA *See* DALMANUTHA, *Magadan*

MAGDALENE {of Magdala} *See* MARY

MAGDIEL {choice gift of El} A chief of the Edomites (Ge. 36:43; 1Ch. 1:54). †

MAGGOTS *See* BEASTS 6.

MAGI *See* WISE MEN

MAGIC, MAGICIAN *See* DIVINATION

MAGNIFICAT A nonbiblical word for Mary's song of praise (Lk. 1:46-55).

MAGOG A son of Japheth and grandson of Noah; the land from which Gog is to come. This attack is noted in the prophets (Ge. 10:2; 1Ch. 1:5; Eze. 38-39; Rev. 20:8). Early historians identify the area as that from which the Scythians came in the sixth century B.C. The places associated with Magog in Genesis and 1 Chronicles are located in Asia Minor (Turkey) and not in the area of modern Russia as some students of prophecy believe. † *See also* MESHECH

MAGOR-MISSABIB {terror on every side} A name given to Pashhur (Jer. 20:3). †

MAGPIASH One who signed the covenant with Nehemiah (Ne. 10:20). †

MAGUS, SIMON *See* SIMON 8.

MAHALAH *See* MAHLAH 2.

MAHALALEEL, MAHALALEL {praise of El}
1. A descendant of Seth and Noah called Mahalaleel in the genealogy of Joseph, the father (so it was thought) of Jesus (Ge. 5:12; Lk. 3:37).

2. A descendant of Judah after the return from Babylon (Ne. 11:4).

MAHALATH
1. A daughter of Ishmael and wife of Esau; also called Basemath (Ge. 28:9; 36:3).
2. A wife of King Rehoboam of Judah, granddaughter of David (2Ch. 11:18).

MAHALATH LEANNOTH {the suffering of affliction, NIV; sickness or suffering poem, JB} Ps. 88 title. † *See* PSALMS (1)

MAHALI *See* MAHLI(TE) 1.

MAHANAIM {double camp} A Levitical town (214-177) and city of refuge on the border between Gad and Manasseh E of the Jordan in Gilead (Jos. 13:26, 30; 21:38). It was so named by Jacob after angels met him there on his return from Paddan-aram (Ge. 32:2). It was briefly the capital of Israel, and David stayed there while waiting out the rebellion of his son Absalom (2Sa. 2:8; 15:10; 19:32).

MAHANAIM
When Absalom crowned himself king in Hebron, David fled from Jerusalem, crossed the Jordan River, and went to Mahanaim.

MAHANEH DAN {camp of Dan} An unidentified site between Beth Shemesh and Kiriath Jearim, where God's Spirit first began to stir in Samson; a camping place of the tribe of Dan as they were en route to take Laish (Jdg. 13:25; 18:12). †

MAHARAI {impetuous, ISBE} One of David's thirty mighty men (2Sa. 23:28; 1Ch. 11:30; 27:13). †

MAHATH
1. A Levite appointed by David to serve with the temple musicians in the time of David (1Ch. 6:35). †
2. A Levite who served in the time of King Hezekiah to help purify the temple (2Ch. 29:12; 31:13). †

MAHAVITE {villagers} The family name of one of David's mighty men (1Ch. 11:46). †

MAHAZIOTH {visions} One assigned by David to praise God in song and music in the temple (1Ch. 25:4, 30). †

MAHER-SHALAL-HASH-BAZ {quick to the plunder, swift to the spoil} Symbolic name given to a son of the prophet Isaiah. The symbolism pointed to the destruction of Syria and Ephraim (Isa. 8:1-3). †

MAHLAH, MAHALAH
1. The eldest daughter of a man of Manasseh who had no son and who therefore inherited the father's land (Nu. 26:33; 27:1; 36:11; Jos. 17:3). †
2. A descendant of Manasseh. It is not stated whether this person is a man or a woman (1Ch. 7:18). †

MAHLI(TE)
1. A descendant of Levi and son of one Merari in the time of Moses (Ex. 6:19; Nu. 3:20).
2. Another descendant of Levi, son of Mushi, in the time of David (1Ch. 6:47; 23:21).

MAHLON Ruth's first husband, son of Naomi (Ru. 1:2, 5; 4:9-10). †

MAHOL {place of round-dancing} The father of some wise men referred to in connection with the wisdom of Solomon (1Ki. 4:31). †

MAHSEIAH, MAASEIAH {Yahweh is a refuge} Grandfather of the staff officer Seraiah to whom Jeremiah gave a message when he entered into the Babylonian captivity (Jer. 32:12; 51:59). †

MAID, MAIDEN, WOMENSERVANTS, AND SLAVE GIRLS The translation of a number of words used many times in the OT but only a few in the NT. Some of these words refer to girls as the property of owners (slave girls), handmaids or maidservants (Lev. 19:20; Lk. 12:45). Another refers to a young unmarried girl who could also be a womanservant (2Ki. 5:2; Est. 2:4). Yet another refers to a young girl of marriageable age, but never, as far as known context is concerned, having been married or known a man. This is the word translated "virgin" and found in the much discussed "virgin birth" prophecy of Isa. 7:14 (also translated "maidens"; *see* Ge. 24:43 and Ps. 68:25). It is the word rendered "virgin" from the Greek of the Isaiah passage in Mt. 1:23. The word translated "virgin," "virginity" in many cases in the OT is the Hebrew word *bethulah* (Ge. 24:16; Lev. 21:14; Dt. 22:19; 1Co. 7:28). This word refers to a girl who is, in most cases, secluded and therefore has not known a man. However, there are in the literature references to a *bethulah* who had been married, and therefore presumably had known a man (Joel 1:8). The Aramaic incantation literature has other cases. It was for this reason that Isaiah could not use this normal word for a virgin (*bethulah*) but instead chose the one of which no case of cohabitation with a man is known. *See* VIRGIN; VIRGIN BIRTH

MAIL, COAT OF *See* ARMS AND ARMOR, ¶ 1.

MAIMED NIV in Lev. 22:22; Mt. 18:8; Mk. 9:43. *See* HEALING, HEALTH; SICK, SICKNESS

MAJESTY A word of greatness ascribed to Christ and God (Lk. 9:43; Heb. 1:3; 8:1; 2Pe. 1:16-17; Jude 25).

MAKAZ An unidentified site near Beth Shemesh (1Ki. 4:9). †

MAKHELOTH {assemblies} An unidentified stop on the Israelite exodus from Egypt (Nu. 33:25-26). †

MAKI The father of the representative of the twelve spies from the tribe of Gad (Nu. 13:15). †

MAKIR, MAKIRITE
1. A son of Manasseh and his clan. He was the father of Gilead after the conquest (Nu. 26:29; 32:39-40).
2. The protector of Saul's grandson Mephibosheth and helper of King David (2Sa. 9:45; 2Sa. 17:27ff.).

MAKKEDAH [locality of shepherds] An unidentified site in the western foothills of the tribal area of Judah conquered by Joshua (Jos. 10:10-29; 12:16; 15:41). †

MAKTESH [mortar] KJV for "Market district" in Zep. 1:11.

MALACHI, BOOK OF [my messenger *or* messenger of Yahweh] *See* PROPHETS, BOOKS OF THE MINOR

MALCAM, MALCHAM [their king, ISBE and KB; *or* (servant of) MALK (pagan god)] A descendant of Benjamin (1Ch. 8:89). †

MALCHIAH, MALCHIJAH [Yahweh is king] *See* MALKIJAH

MALCHIEL, MALCHIELITES *See* MALKIEL, MALKIELITE

MALCHIRAM [(my) king is lauded] *See* MALKIRAM

MALCHI-SHUA, MALKI-SHUA, MELCHISHUA [(my) king saves] A son of Saul (1Sa. 14:49).

MALCHUS [king] The servant of the high priest whose ear Peter cut off on the night before Christ's crucifixion (Jn. 18:10). †

MALE AND FEMALE *See* ADAM; CREATION

MALEDICTION *See* CURSE

MALEFACTOR [evil doer] KJV for "criminal" in the NIV.

MALELEEL *See* MAHALALEEL

MALICE A general term for badness or evil. Christians are to put it away (Eph. 4:31; Col. 3:8; 1Pe. 2:1).

MALKIEL, MALKIELITE [El is (my) king] A grandson of Asher (Ge. 46:17).

MALKIJAH, MALCHIJAH, MALCHIAH [Yahweh is (my) king]
1. A descendant of the Levite Kohath whom David put in charge of the service of song in the temple service (1Ch. 6:40).
2. Head of one of David's priestly divisions (1Ch. 24:9).
3 and 4. Two who married foreign wives during the Babylonian captivity (Ezr. 10:25, 31).
5, 6, and 7. Three who worked on the repairing of the wall of Jerusalem with Nehemiah (Ne. 3:11, 14, 31).
8. One who stood with Ezra as he read the law to the people (Ne. 8:4).
9. A priest who signed the covenant with Nehemiah (Ne. 10:3).
10. A priest involved in the dedication ceremony of Nehemiah's restored wall of Jerusalem (Ne. 12:42).
11. The father of one who was sent to Jeremiah by King Zedekiah (1Ch. 9:12; Jer. 21:1; 38:1ff.).
12. A son of King Zedekiah who had a cistern in which Jeremiah was imprisoned (Jer. 38:6).

MALKIRAM [(my) king is exalted] A descendant of King Jehoiachin who was in the captivity in Babylon (1Ch. 3:18). †

MALLOTHI, MALOTHI [my expression] A musician appointed with others, by David to serve in the temple (1Ch. 25:4, 26). †

MALLOW A rendering in most versions of a plant (Job 30:4); "salt herb" in the NIV for other plants. The NEB, ASV renders here as "saltwort." *See* PLANTS, PERFUMES, AND SPICES, Miscellaneous Plants 10., *Salt Herb*

MALLUCH(I) [counsellor, ISBE; king, KB]
1. A descendant of Levi (1Ch. 6:44).
2 and 3. Two who married foreign wives during the Babylonian captivity (Ezr. 10:29, 32).

4 and 5. Two who signed the covenant with Nehemiah (Ne. 10:4, 27).

6. One from the priests and Levites who returned from the Babylonian captivity with Zerubbabel (Ne. 12:2, 14).

MALTA An island S of Sicily where Paul was shipwrecked on his voyage to Rome (Ac. 28:1). †

MALTA

MAMMON {wealth} *See* MONEY

MAMRE An Amorite living in Abraham's days beside some great trees, "the great trees of Mamre," which came to identify a place where Abraham later lived (Ge. 14:13, 24; 18:1; 23:17, 19).

MAN, MANKIND *See* ADAM; CREATION; SALVATION, *Regeneration, Adoption, Sanctification*

MAN OF SIN *See* ANTICHRIST

MAN, SON OF *See* GOD, NAMES OF, GODHEAD

MANAEN {comforter} A Christian of Antioch who had been brought up with Herod the tetrarch (Ac. 13:1). †

MANAHATH {resting place}

1. A town (167-129) in Edom to which some descendants of Benjamin were deported (1Ch. 8:6).

2. A descendant of Esau and of Seir the Horite (Ge. 36:23).

3. Descendants of Caleb (1Ch. 2:52, 54).

MANAHATHITES, MANAHETHITES {of MANAHATH} *See* MANAHATH 3.

MANASSE(A)S, KING *See* MANASSEH 2.

MANASSEH {one that makes to forget}

1. A son of Joseph who became the head of one of the tribes of Israel (Ge. 41:51; 48:1).

2. *See* KINGS OF JUDAH AND ISRAEL.

MANASSITES A people of the tribe or clan of Manasseh. *See* MANASSEH 1.

MANDRAKE *See* PLANTS, PERFUMES, AND SPICES, Miscellaneous Plants 8.

MANEH *See* WEIGHTS AND MEASURES, Measures of Weights, *Minah*

MANGER A trough, box, or stall used for feeding cattle, and translated in the NIV also as manger or stall (1Kg. 4:26; Isa. 1:3). Luke states that at the birth of Jesus he was placed in a manger (Lk. 2:7, 12, 16). *See also* FODDER

MANNA {What is it?; *possibly* food} A special food provided by God for the Israelites during their wilderness wanderings. It was called "bread," it came at night, and was white. It was like coriander seed, looked like resin, tasted like wafers made with honey and olive oil, and the people had to grind it in a handmill or crush it in a mortar, then cook it in a pot or make it into cakes. The description indicates that it was not a natural phenomenon, but rather supernatural. It stopped when the Israelites no longer had need of it for food (Ex. 16:31-35; Nu. 11:6-9; Jos. 5:12; Ps. 78:24; Jn. 6:31).

MANOAH {rest} Father of Samson (Jdg. 13:2-21; 16:31). †

MANSION A dwelling place, room, or place to live (Jn. 14:2, KJV). The NIV renders it "rooms." A large rambling mansion like on an old Southern plantation is not what the Greek word conveys.

MANSLAYER Anyone who killed another human being deliberately was a murderer and had to be put to death. The accidental killer of an individual was called a manslayer. The assembly was required to judge between the manslayer and the avenger of blood. In the meantime the manslayer was required to find asylum in a city of refuge and could stay there until the death of the high priest. He was then free to return to his own city (Ex. 21:14; Nu. 35:6-28).

MANTLE *See* DRESS

MANURE Manure is the excretion from man or animal. Animal dung was used for fuel (1Ki. 14:10), although human dung apparently could be used as well (Eze. 4:15). It could be food in times of siege (2Ki. 6:25 — *see* DOVE'S DUNG). This is used figuratively as mere refuse, something worthless and dishonored (2Ki. 9:37; Jer. 8:2). Paul considered his past life rubbish (dung) in order to gain Christ (Php. 3:8).

MANUSCRIPTS, DEAD SEA *See* BIBLICAL MANUSCRIPTS; SCROLLS, DEAD SEA

MAOCH Father of Achish king of Gath (1Sa. 27:2). †

MAON [dwelling]
1. A town (162-090) in the western foothills of the tribal area of Judah (Jos. 15:55). David hid from Saul in the Desert of Maon (1Sa. 23:25). It was the home of Nabal and Abigail, the latter of whom later became one of David's wives.
2. A descendant of Caleb (1Ch. 2:42-45).

MAONITES People from the clan of Maon (Jdg. 10:12). The relationship between the Maonites and the city of Maon is not clear. Some identify this people with the Meunim (1Ch. 4:41), but this is not certain. *See* MAON; *see also* MEUNIM, MEHUNIM

MARA [bitter] The name Naomi gave herself after the death of her husband and sons (Ru. 1:20). † *See* MARAH

MARAH [bitter] An unidentified watering place for the Israelites in their desert wanderings on their exodus from Egypt. The water was bitter and Moses sweetened it (Ex. 15:23; Nu. 33:8-9). †

MARALAH A border site belonging to Zebulun, N of Megiddo (Jos. 19:11). †

MARAN-ATHA [our Lord has come *or* our Lord, come!] Aramaic in 1Co. 16:22.

MARBLE *See* PRECIOUS STONES AND METALS, Precious Stones 2.

MARCUS *See* MARK, JOHN

MARDUK *See* DEITIES

MAREAL *See* MARALAH

MARESHAH
1 and 2. Descendants of Judah and Caleb (1Ch. 2:42; 4:21).
3. A city (140-111) in the western foothills of the tribal area of Judah which King Rehoboam fortified and where King Asa defeated the Ethiopian (Cushite) army. It was the home of the prophet Eliezer who spoke against the alliance of Jehoshaphat of Judah with the wicked King Ahaziah of Israel (Jos. 15:44; 2Ch. 11:5-12; 14:9-15; 20:35-37).

MARISHES KJV for "marshes" (Eze. 47:11).

MARK, GOSPEL ACCORDING TO *See* GOSPELS, THE FOUR

MARK, JOHN [Mark = *Latin* a large hammer; John = *Semitic* gracious] The son of Mary of Jerusalem in whose home Christians stayed while Peter was in prison; a companion of Paul and Barnabas on the first missionary journey. Because Paul refused to take him on the second journey, he went with Barnabas to Cyprus. Later Paul speaks of him lovingly. The tradition of the very early church is that he is the author of the Gospel that bears his name, and the content of his book is believed to be what he learned from Peter (Ac. 12:12, 25; 13:4; 15:37, 39; Col. 4:10; 2Ti. 4:11). Peter called him "son."

MARK OF THE BEAST *See* TATTOO

MARKET, MARKETPLACE In the Book of Acts (Ac. 16:19; 17:17), the markets are typical Greek marketplaces, the centers of public life, the *agora*. Temples, public buildings, the courts, and judges were located there. In the OT and in the four Gospels, the marketplaces were the typical oriental streets of small shops in front of which children played, men stood around and visited or worked, and the sick were often laid for the pity of the passersby (Ps. 55:11; Pr. 7:12; Mt. 11:16). In such places many of Jesus' miracles of healing took place (Mk. 6:56).

MAROTH {bitterness} An unidentified site in the tribal area of Judah whose inhabitants were still expecting good when God had prophesied the opposite (Mic. 1:12). †

MARRIAGE The union of a man and a woman first consummated in the Garden of Eden between Adam and Eve. This union became the pattern for all others to follow (Ge. 2:24; Mt. 19:46). The father of the man made the selection of the girl, and the father of the girl gave his daughter to the husband to be (Ge. 24:4; 29:23, 28; 34:8; Jos. 15:16); dating per se was not practiced. A purchase price, called a bride price, was paid to the father of the bride (Ge. 31:15; Ex. 22:17; 1Sa. 18:25). The father of the bride usually gave her a gift called the "dowry," which might be property or a maid. This was her own money and property, and from it she had to supply her husband with a concubine, sometimes her own maid, if she herself was unable to present him with a male heir later. This is reflected in the Abraham, Sarah, Hagar account (Ge. 16:13) as well as in Assyrian archives discovered in ancient Nuzi. Other examples of dowries are recorded (Jos. 15:18-19; 1Ki. 9:16). The first step after the agreements was the betrothal or "pledge to marry," but was not the same as the actual marriage itself which came later (Dt. 20:7). In the matter of adultery a betrothed woman was considered as if she were married (Dt. 22:23-24, 28-29). This explains the actions of Joseph the husband of Mary the mother of Jesus (Mt. 1:18-20). At the time of the actual

marriage a legal contract was drawn up and witnessed, as is known again not only from the Nuzi documents but also reflected in the Bible. Other practices still seen in the Orient today were a part of the actual wedding itself: beautiful clothes, ornaments, the veil worn by the bride, the feast and procession of the bridegroom and his friends, and on occasion a bridal procession to the place of the ceremony (SS. 3:11; Isa. 61:10; Ge. 24:65; Jdg. 14:10-11; Ps. 45:14). Music accompanied the processions and was a prelude to the wedding banquet (Jdg. 14:10-11; Jer. 7:34).

The function of a marriage was more than to enable two people to love and live together. It was to produce a progeny and to supervise the raising of the children to be an object lesson of the relation of God to his people. In this the role of the parents is particularly important and is very clear both in the OT and NT (Isa. 54:56; Eph. 5:21—6:4).

Levirate marriage, or the duty of a brother-in-law, is described in Dt. 25:5-10, the marriage that is required when a brother dies without a son. In such a case the husband's brother is required to marry the widow and raise up a family in the name of the deceased (Ru. 2:20; 4:10). He is called the kinsman-redeemer. If the brother refuses to marry the woman, she spits in his face, slaps his face with one of his own sandals, and his line is known thereafter as the family of the unsandaled.

Polygamy in the OT resulted from: not knowing or understanding God's model in the first marriage (in the Garden), i.e., one man—one woman—one flesh; the desire for male heirs; and international treaties involving marriage between two groups. In the NT it is always assumed that marriage is to be between one man and one woman only. Marriage after divorce, except under certain carefully regulated circumstances, is considered adultery (Mt. 19:9).

1Co. 7:3 refers to the marriage bed and mutual submission in sexual relationships for the benefit of the partner. The deprivation of marital rights is to occur only under certain conditions (1Co. 7:5). *See also* DIVORCE; PARENTING; SEXUAL RELATIONS,

MARS HILL KJV from the Greek *Areopagus*, which means "Hill of Ares." Ares was the Greek god of war, and the Romans called this god "Mars," hence "Mars Hill." Most versions transliterate the word from the Greek rather than translate because the council, not the physical hill, is in mind. *See* AREOPAGUS

MARSENA A prince of Persia and Media who had special access to the Persian king Xerxes (Est. 1:1, 14). †

MARSH *See* GEOGRAPHY OF THE HOLY LAND, THE RESULTS OF FORMATIVE FORCES, *swamps*

MARTHA {a lady, (female) lord} The sister of Mary and Lazarus (Lk. 10:38-39; Jn. 11:2, 20).

MARTYR {witness} One who gave his life as a witness for Christ (Ac. 22:20). †

MARY {Gr. for MIRIAM}
1. The virgin mother of Jesus. Her song, known today as the Magnificat, came in reaction to the announcement made to her by the angel Gabriel (Mt. 1:18, 23; Lk. 1:26ff., 46ff.). She was with her son at the performance of some of his miracles and at the Crucifixion where Jesus commended her to John (Jn. 2:1; 19:25ff.; 21:24).
2. The mother of James and Joseph, and perhaps the wife of Clopas. She was present both at the Crucifixion and the Resurrection (Mt. 27:56; Mk. 15:40, 47; 16:1; Jn. 19:25).
3. The sister of Martha and Lazarus, the Mary who anointed the feet of Jesus (Lk. 10:38; Jn. 11:2, 20, 32; 12:3).
4. Mary Magdalene from whom seven demons were cast out; one of the women who accompanied Jesus to minister to him (Lk. 8:12). She too was present at the Crucifixion and at the empty tomb (Mt. 27:56, 61; 28:1).
5. The mother of John Mark (Ac. 12:12).

6. One to whom Paul sends greetings at Rome (Ro. 16:6).

MARY, THE VIRGIN *See* MARY 1.

MASADA The site of an ancient fortress overlooking the Dead Sea. Herod used it as a safe place in 40 B.C. Zealots in A.D. 70 held this place in rebellion against the Roman army until May 2, 73. Upon taking the fortress, the Romans found only seven alive of the 960 who preferred self-inflicted death over Roman subjection.

MASH *See* MESHECH

MASHAL *See* MISHAL, MISHEAL

MASKIL *See* PSALMS, TITLES OF 7.

MASON Several Hebrew words have been translated as "mason" in the NIV: one who builds walls (2Ki. 22:6); *craftsman* (1Ch. 22:15); one who hews stones (2Ch. 24:12; Ezr. 3:7). The KJV uses the same range of Hebrew words, but in different contexts.

MASREKAH An unidentified royal site in Edom before Israel had a king (Ge. 36:36; 1Ch. 1:47). †

MASS A Roman Catholic term for the Eucharist. Since the fourth century A.D., it has referred to the whole of the worship service.

MASSA {burden, oracle} A son of Ishmael (Ge. 25:14; 1Ch. 1:30). †

MASSAH {test, try} An unidentified site in Horeb where Moses drew water from a rock (Ex. 17:7; Dt. 6:16; 9:22; 33:8; Ps. 95:8). † *See* MERIBAH

MASTER *See* GOD, NAMES OF; GODHEAD; LORD; RABBI; TEACHER

MATHUSALA *See* METHUSELAH

MATRED Mother of a wife of the king of Edom (Ge. 36:39; 1Ch. 1:50). †

MATRI, MATRITES {rainy} A family of Benjamites to which King Saul belonged (1Sa. 10:21). †

MATTAN {gift}

1. A priest of Baal in the time of wicked Queen Athaliah who was killed in Jehoiada's reform (2Ki. 11:18; 2Ch. 23:17). †

2. The father of one who recommended the death of Jeremiah (Jer. 38:1). †

MATTANAH {gift} An unidentified stop on the Israelite exodus route (Nu. 21:18-19). †

MATTANIAH {gift of Yahweh}

1, 2, and 3. Three Levites, one in the time of David, an ancestor of one in the time of King Jehoshaphat of Judah, and one in the time of King Hezekiah of Judah (1Ch. 25:4; 2Ch. 20:14; 29:13).

4, 5, 6, and 7. Four who married foreign wives during the time of the Babylonian captivity (Ezr. 10:26-27, 30, 37).

8. The original name of the last king of Judah, Zedekiah (2Ki. 24:17).

9, 10, 11. Three Levites in postexilic times, one of them a musician with Zerubbabel (1Ch. 9:15; Ne. 11:17; 12:8, 25).

12. Ancestor of a priest who shared in the dedication of the walls of Jerusalem as rebuilt in Nehemiah's time (Ne. 12:35).

13. Ancestor of one of the keepers of Nehemiah's storerooms (Ne. 13:13).

MATTATHA An ancestor of Joseph, the father (so it was thought) of Jesus (Lk. 3:31). †

MATTATHIAS {gift of Yahweh}

1 and 2. Two of the ancestors of Joseph, the father (so it was thought) of Jesus (Lk. 3:25-26).

3. *See Maccabees* under HASMONEANS.

MATTATTAH, MATTATHAH { gift}
One who married a foreign wife during the time of the Babylonian captivity (Ezr. 10:33). *See also* MATTITHIAH

MATTENAI {gift}

1 and 2. Two who married foreign wives during the time of the Babylonian captivity (Ezr. 10:33, 37). †

3. The head of the priestly family in

the days of Joiakim and Nehemiah (Ne. 12:19). †

MATTHAN An ancestor of Jesus through his mother's line (Mt. 1:15).

MATTHAT

1 and 2. Two ancestors of Joseph, the father (so it was thought) of Jesus (Lk. 3:24, 29).

MATTHEW {gift of Yahweh} *See* APOSTLES

MATTHEW, GOSPEL ACCORDING TO *See* GOSPELS, THE FOUR

MATTHIAS {gift of Yahweh} The disciple chosen by lot to replace Judas Iscariot (Ac. 1:24ff.).

MATTITHIAH {gift of Yahweh}

1. A Levite musician in the time of David (1Ch. 15:18, 21).

2. A Levite chosen by David to minister before the tabernacle (1Ch. 16:5).

3. A descendant of Levi in postexilic times who was in charge of baking the offering bread (1Ch. 9:31).

4. One who married a foreign wife during the time of the Babylonian captivity (Ezr. 10:43).

5. One who stood at the right hand of Ezra as he read the law to the people (Ne. 8:4).

MATTOCK A special type of pickaxe with a point at one end and a blade for grubbing at the other. It needed frequent sharpening, which was difficult for the Israelites since the Philistines had a monopoly on sharpening tools and weapons (1Sa. 13:20-21).

MAUL *See* HAMMER

MAW KJV for "inner parts" or "stomach" (Dt. 18:3).

MAZZAROTH KJV for "constellation" (Job 38:32).

MEADOW *See* ABEL 2.

MEAH {hundred} KJV for "Tower of the Hundred" (Ne. 3:1; 12:39). †

MEAL *See* FOOD *Meal; see also* SACRIFICES AND OFFERINGS, The

Grain (Meal) Offering; *see also* MEALS

MEAL OFFERING *See* SACRIFICES AND OFFERINGS, The Grain (Meal) Offering

MEALS The words *breakfast, dinner,* and *supper* are used in Scripture. The first is found only in connection with the postresurrection appearance of Jesus at the seashore (Jn. 21:12). The references to supper, except for one (Lk. 17:8), are either in connection with the Lord's Supper or an eschatological supper (Lk. 22:20; 1Co. 11:20-25; Rev. 19:9, 17). There are also several references to dinner (Mt. 22:4; Jn. 12:2). These three words are not to be confused with their modern counterparts as to time or content. As is still the custom today in the more primitive parts of the Orient, the first meal comes late in the morning, the men leaving for work without eating at all or just taking a piece of bread or cheese. At sometime between ten and twelve in the morning a principal meal is eaten, called dinner. This meal is often eaten at work and therefore consists of things that can either be taken by the workman to his work or brought there later by wife or children. When the day's work is done, which today is between two and four in the afternoon, the supper is eaten, unless that supper is to be a festive meal on the order of a banquet.

Bread, in the shape of a patty or modern pancake (pita), was the staple item and was usually eaten with meat gravy, sour wine, or certain seeds ground up into a paste with a little oil. Fruits and grains were usually in good supply and great variety. The meat came from sheep, goats, lambs, kids, fatted calves, and from wild game as it was available. Fish was available everywhere. Milk and particularly cheese made from curdled milk and kept in skins were an integral part of the diet.

The meal was eaten while seated on the floor in earlier times. After the return from the Babylonian captivity, it became the custom in Palestine to eat the evening meal reclining on couches around a table, banquet style (Jn. 21:20). The hands, not knives, forks, and spoons, were used for eating. There was a profusion of different types of bowls and plates, about which we are learning more with the progress of modern archaeology. From such stories as the Egyptian record of Sinuhe's travels in Palestine we learn additional information about foods and family conditions in that land at that time. *See* FOOD

MEARAH *See* ARAH

MEASURE *See* WEIGHTS AND MEASURES, *Metretes*

MEAT *See* FLESH; FOOD; MEALS

MEAT FORK, MEAT HOOK *See* HOOK

MEAT OFFERING KJV for "Grain Offering." *See* SACRIFICES AND OFFERINGS, Grain Offerings

MEBUNNAI One of David's thirty mighty men; also called Sibbecai (2Sa. 23:27; 1Ch. 11:29). † *See also* SIBBEC(H)AI

MECHERATHITE *See* MAACAH; MEKERATHITE

MECONAH [foundation] An unidentified place in the western foothills of Judah inhabited by those who returned from the captivity with Zerubbabel (Ne. 11:28). †

MEDAD [beloved] One who prophesied in the Israelite camp in the desert days of Moses (Nu. 11:26-27). †

MEDAN [dissension] A son of Abraham by Keturah (Ge. 25:2; 1Ch. 1:32). †

MEDEBA A city (225-124) E of the Jordan in Moab that was initially in the tribal area of Reuben. David fought there. The city is currently noted because of the ancient mosaic map of Palestine, the remains of which are to be found in the floor of the fifth century church there (Nu. 21:30; Jos. 13:9; 1Ch. 19:7ff.).

MEDES, MEDIA *See* GEOGRAPHY OF THE HOLY LAND

MEDIATION, MEDIATOR 1Ti. 2:5; Heb. 8:6; 9:15; 12:24. *See* CHRIST, LIFE AND TEACHINGS OF, Work of Christ, 7. and 8.

MEDICINE *See* SICK, SICKNESS

MEDITATION Unlike Eastern meditation which has a focus on a single word or locution (which can produce an altered state of awareness that is irrational), meditation in the Bible denotes concentrated thought and reflection. The word has the idea of "muse, mutter, or utter." It is a thought process, deep and studious, related to God's gracious law (Jos. 1:8; Ps. 1:2; Ps. 119:15ff.).

MEDITATION, TRANSCENDENTAL (TM) An Eastern meditative practice. Founded by Mahesh Yogi, the practice was popularized by the music group The Beatles in the 1960s. Though it is touted as a relaxation response technique, it has many vestiges of Hinduism, according to many. Unlike TM, biblical meditation always involves a thought process, usually pondering the Scriptures (Ps. 1:2).

MEDITERRANEAN SEA *See* GEOGRAPHY OF THE HOLY LAND, III. *Topography*

MEDIUM *See* DIVINATION

MEEK, MEEKNESS The word is perhaps best defined by the variety of ways the Greek and Hebrew words are translated: gentle, humble, downtrodden, oppressed. It is set forth as the proper attitude toward God (one of humble dependence) and the proper attitude toward others. It is the opposite of rich, arrogant, defiant toward God, which show complete reliance on one's own abilities, might, and power (Ps. 10:17; 37:11; Isa. 29:19; Mt. 5:5; Eph. 4:2; Col. 3:12; Jas. 3:13). Moses is described as the meekest of men (Nu. 12:3). In the complex of characteristics called the fruit of the Spirit, it is listed as "gentleness" (Gal. 5:22-23).

MEGIDDO, PLAINS OF *See* GEOGRAPHY OF THE HOLY LAND; *see also* ARMAGEDDON

MEGIDDON *See* MEGIDDO

MEHETABEL, MEHETABEEL {El does good}
1. The wife of an Edomite king (Ge. 36:39; 1Ch. 1:50). †
2. The grandparent of one hired by Sanballat and Tobiah to discourage Nehemiah (Ne. 6:10). †

MEHIDA The ancestor of some temple servants who returned from the Babylonian captivity with Zerubbabel (Ezr. 2:52; Ne. 7:54). †

MEHIR {hired hand} A descendant of Judah (1Ch. 4:11). †

MEHOLAH, MEHOLATHITE The man to whom King Saul gave one of his daughters as wife (1Sa. 18:19), and the unidentified place from which he came.

MEHUJAEL A descendant of Adam through Cain (Ge. 4:18). †

MEHUMAN One of the eunuchs of the Persian king Xerxes (Est. 1:10). †

MEHUNIM(S) *See* MEUNIM, MEUNITES

ME JARKON {waters of Jarkon (greenish?)} An unidentified place in the original tribal area of Dan, perhaps near Joppa (Jos. 19:46). †

MEKERATHITE, MECHERATHITE {one of MEKERATH} Added to the name of one of David's mighty men, perhaps a place or area, Mekerath, from which he came (1Ch. 11:36; cf. 2Sa. 23:34).

MEKONAH *See* MECONAH

MELATIAH {Yahweh sets free} One who worked on the repair of the walls of Jerusalem with Nehemiah (Ne. 3:7). †

MELCHI *See* MELKI

MELCHIAH {(my) king is Yahweh} *See* MALKIJAH 11.

MELCHIAS *See* MALKIJAH 3 and 4.

MELCHISEDEC *See* MELCHIZEDEK

MELCHISHUA [(my) king is salvation]
See MALCHI-SHUA

MELCHIZEDEK [(my) king is ZE-DEK (just)] A king of Salem and priest of the Most High God. Abraham paid tithes to him and was blessed in turn by this Melchizedek. There was also a priestly order of Melchizedek which was long before the Aaronic priesthood (Ge. 14:18-20; Ps. 110:4). It should be noted in addition, however, that this priest was also a king, which was not the case with the Aaronic priesthood. All other reference to this man and to his priesthood are in the Book of Hebrews. Here we are told that he was a high priest and that his ancestry is shrouded in mystery since it is not known. He was king of Salem, i.e., king of peace, and the translation of his name is "king of righteousness" (Heb. 7:14). Salem is usually identified as Jerusalem (Ps. 76:2). The thrust of the NT references all in the one book is that Christ is superior to all creatures and men, and specifically in this Melchizedek connection, that Christ's royal priesthood is of a kind that precedes the Aaronic and that continues after it even forever (Heb. 7:23 – 10:18). *See* HEBREWS, BOOK OF; PRIEST

MELEA An ancestor of Joseph, the father (so it was thought) of Jesus (Lk. 3:31). †

MELECH [king] A descendant of Benjamin, Saul, and Jonathan who returned from the Babylonian captivity (1Ch. 8:34-35; 9:40-41). †

MELICU *See* MALLUCH(I) 6.

MELITA *See* MALTA

MELKI [my king]

1 and 2. Two ancestors of Jesus, the father (so it was thought) of Jesus (Lk. 3:24, 28). †

MELODY *See* MUSIC

MELON *See* PLANTS, PERFUMES, AND SPICES, Plants for Food 4.

MELZAR [steward] KJV for "guard" in Da. 1:11, 16. †

MEMBERS

1. Parts of a human body (Mt. 5:29-30). A struggle with sin occurs there (Ro. 6:13; 7:5, 23). A Christian's body is part of Christ (1Co. 6:15).

2. The church is like parts (members) of a body working together (Ro. 12:5; 1Co. 12:12-27; Eph. 4:25; 5:30).

MEMORIAL *See* COMMUNION, VIEWS OF

MEMPHIS The first capital of united Egypt (before 3000 B.C.), often mentioned in secular sources but in the Bible only in the prophetic writings. When the Jews fled Jerusalem after the revolt at the time of Gedaliah (about 580 B.C.), they went to Memphis (Jer. 41:16-18; 44:1 – Noph in Hebrew text). The prophet Jeremiah predicted that Memphis would become a ruin (Jer. 46:13-19). Ezekiel also predicted its difficulties (Eze. 30:13-16). Apparently the earlier prediction of Hosea was fulfilled in this descent of Jews to Egypt (Hos. 9:6).

MEMUCAN One of the legal experts consulted by the Persian king Xerxes (Est. 1:14, 16, 21). †

MENAHEM [comforter] *See* KINGS OF JUDAH AND ISRAEL

MENAN *See* MENNA

MENE, MENE, TEKEL, AND PARSIN This Aramaic expression is found only in Da. 5:25 accompanied with an explanation in Da. 5:26-28. Daniel noted that *Mene* meant that God had numbered the days of the kingdom of Belshazzar and brought it to an end; *Tekel* that the king was weighed on the scales and found wanting; and *Peres* that his kingdom was given to the Medes and Persians. All of this took place that very night. Literally these three words refer to weights: *mene* is the Hebrew mina, *tekel* is the Hebrew shekel, and *peres* is the Hebrew half-mina.

MENI *See* DEITIES, *Babylonian*

MENNA An ancestor of Joseph, the father (so it was thought) of Jesus (Lk. 3:31). †

MENORAH *See* LAMP, LAMP-STAND

MEONENIM {diviner} KJV for "soothsayer's" in Jdg. 9:37.

MEONOTHAI {my dwellings} A descendant of Judah, Caleb, and Othniel (1Ch. 4:13-14). †

MEPHAATH A Levitical town (239-140) in the tribal area of Reuben in Moab (Jos. 13:18; 21:37; 1Ch. 6:79; Jer. 48:21). †

MEPHIBOSHETH {from the mouth of shame (a derogative term for BAAL)}
1. A son of Saul by Aiah's daughter, Rizpah (2Sa. 21:8-9).
2. Son of Jonathan and grandson of Saul; also called Merib-Baal. He was only a child when his father was killed. A friend, Makir, reared him until David finally took over the provision for him (2Sa. 4:4; 2Sa. 9:4-7; 1Ch. 8:34).

MERAB {abundant} The daughter of King Saul promised to David but given to another (1Sa. 14:49; 18:17-19; 2Sa. 21:8). †

MERAIAH {loved by Yahweh} Head of a priestly family in the days of Nehemiah (Ne. 12:12). †

MERAIOTH {rebellious}
1. An ancestor of Ezra (Ezr. 7:3).
2. Ancestor of some priests who returned from the Babylonian captivity (1Ch. 9:11; Ne. 11:11).

MERARI(TE) {bitter} A son of Levi and ancestor of the Merarites (Ge. 46:11; Jos. 21:40; 1Ch. 6:1; Ezr. 8:19).

MERATHAIM {double rebellion} Jeremiah's symbolic name for Babylon in his oracle against that city and nation (Jer. 50:21). †

MERCHANDISE, MERCHANT *See* MONEY CHANGER; TRADE

MERCIFUL, MERCY *See* COMPASSION

MERCURY, MERCURIUS *See* DEITIES 1., The gods of Greece, *Hermes*

MERCYSEAT *See* TABERNACLE

MERED {rebel} A descendant of Judah (1Ch. 4:17-18). †

MEREMOTH
1. A priest who acted as a treasurer of the second temple, who also helped Nehemiah in the rebuilding of the wall of Jerusalem (Ezr. 8:33; Ne. 3:4, 21).
2. One who married a foreign wife during the days of the Babylonian captivity (Ezr. 10:36).
3. One who signed the covenant with Nehemiah (Ne. 10:5).
4. The head of a priestly house in the days of Nehemiah (Ne. 12:3, 15).

MERES An expert in matters of law and justice to King Xerxes in Persia (Est. 1:14). †

MERIBAH, MERIBATH KADESH
1 and 2. Two different unidentified stops of the Israelites in their wanderings during the exodus from Egypt. In one of them Moses struck the rock at a place called Horeb in Rephidim; in the other near Kadesh Barnea he was commanded to speak to the rock but struck it instead (Ex. 17:1-7; Nu. 20:1-13). For this failure to do as God told Moses, he lost his right to enter the Promised Land (Dt. 32:51). *See* KADESH BARNEA; MASSAH

MERIB-BAAL {BAAL contends} The son of Jonathan; also called MEPHIBOSHETH.

MERODACH {(pagan Bab. god) MARDUK} KJV in Jer. 50:2. † *See* DEITIES 1.

MERODACH-BALADAN {Marduk has given a son} A king of Babylon (2Ki. 20:12; Isa. 39:1). † *See* BABYLON

MEROM, THE WATERS OF Until recently thought to be the same as the marshes of the Huleh Lake of the Sea of Galilee. Recent research, however, places it (190-275) in the center of the mountains of Upper Galilee near Mt. Merom. A great battle of Joshua's northern campaign was conducted here (Jos. 11:5-7). †

MERONOTHITE A resident of an unidentified area called Meronoth in the tribal area of Naphtali (1Ch. 27:30; Ne. 3:7).

MEROZ An unidentified place in Galilee whose inhabitants were cursed because they refused to heed the call for help from Deborah and Barak (Jdg. 5:23). †

MESECH *See* MESHECH

MESHA

1. A descendant of Benjamin (1Ch. 8:9).
2. A king of Moab who recorded his deeds on the famous "Moabite Stone." He threw off the yoke of Israel in the days of King Jehoram of Israel (2Ki. 3:4-5). The Scripture states he sacrificed one of his sons to his god (2Ki. 3:26-27).
3. A place in the territory where the Joktanites lived, between Mesha and Sephar (Ge. 10:30).
4. A son of Caleb, the brother of Jerahmeel (1Ch. 2:42).

MESHACH *See* SHADRACH

MESHECH

1. A grandson of Noah and son of Shem (1Ch. 1:17) called Mash in the Hebrew text of Ge. 10:23 (see the NIV footnote).
2. A son of Japheth and grandson of Noah (Ge. 10:2).

MESHELEMIAH {Yahweh repays} The father of the Zechariah who was a gatekeeper in the time of the return from the Babylonian captivity; also called Shelemiah and perhaps even Shallum (1Ch. 9:17, 21; 26:14).

MESHEZABEL, MESHEZABEEL {El delivers}

1. An ancestor of one who worked with Nehemiah on the repair of the wall of Jerusalem (Ne. 3:4). †
2. One who signed the covenant with Nehemiah (Ne. 10:21). †
3. Father of an important official in Jerusalem after the return from the Babylonian captivity (Ne. 11:24). †

MESHILLEMITH, MESHILLE-MOTH {restitution}

1. Ancestor of a priest in Nehemiah's day; also called Meshillemoth (1Ch. 9:12; Ne. 11:13). †
2. A descendant of Ephraim in the days of King Ahaz (2Ch. 28:12). †

MESHOBAB A descendant of Simeon (1Ch. 4:34). †

MESHULLAM {restitution, KB}

1. The grandfather of one sent by King Josiah to the temple to inquire of the high priest (2Ki. 22:3).
2. A son of Zerubbabel of the royal line after the return from Babylon (1Ch. 3:19).
3, 4, 5, and 6. A descendant of Gad and three of Benjamin (1Ch. 5:13; 8:17; 9:7-8).
7 and 8. Two priests, one the father of Hilkiah and the other the son of Meshillemith (1Ch. 9:11-12).
9. A Levite who helped in the repair of the first temple, in the days of King Josiah (2Ch. 34:12).
10. One sent by Ezra to Iddo to bring Levites from Casiphia (Ezr. 8:16).
11. One who was against Ezra on his ideas of mixed marriages (Ezr. 10:15).
12. One who married a foreign wife in the days of the Babylonian captivity (Ezr. 10:29).
13 and 14. Two who worked on the repair of the walls and gates of Jerusalem in the days of Nehemiah (Ne. 3:4, 6).
15. One who stood with Ezra as he read the law to the people (Ne. 8:4).
16 and 17. Two who signed the covenant with Nehemiah (Ne. 10:7, 20).
18, 19, and 20. Two priests and a gatekeeper in the days of Joiakim and Nehemiah (Ne. 12:13, 16, 25).
21. One involved with Nehemiah in the dedication of the rebuilt wall of Jerusalem (Ne. 12:33). Perhaps the same as number 18.

MESHULLEMETH {restitution} The wife of King Manasseh (2Ki. 21:19). †

MESOBAITE *See* MEZOBAITE

MESOPOTAMIA {(land) between rivers} *See* GEOGRAPHY OF THE HOLY LAND, III. Topography

MESS A portion of food at a meal. *See* MEAL

MESSENGER *See* ANGEL; APOSTLES; PROPHET

MESSIAH {anointed (royally or priestly)} *See* ANOINT; CHRIST, LIFE AND TEACHINGS OF; *see also* GOD, NAMES OF, GODHEAD 8.

MESSIAS *See* CHRIST, LIFE AND TEACHINGS OF; *see also* GOD, NAMES OF; GODHEAD 8., *Messiah*

METAL WORKER *See* COPPERSMITH

METALS *See* PRECIOUS STONES AND METALS

METEYARD KJV FOR "measures of length" (Lev. 19:35).

METHEG HAMMAH, METHEG AMMAH An unidentified site that David took from the Philistines (2Sa. 8:1). †

METHUSAEL *See* METHUSHAEL

METHUSELAH {man of the javelin} A descendant of Noah and Seth and father of Lamech, who is recorded as living longer than any other individual in the Bible (Ge. 5:21-27; 1Ch. 1:3). His name is included in the genealogy of Joseph, the father (so it was thought) of Jesus (Lk. 3:37).

METHUSHAEL A descendant of Adam and Cain and father of a Lamech, other than the descendant of Methuselah above (Ge. 4:18). †

MEUNIM, MEUNITES
1. Ancestor of some temple servants who returned with Zerubbabel from the Babylonian captivity (Ezr. 2:50). †
2. A people Uzziah fought against (2Ch. 26:7). †

ME-ZAHAB, MEZAHAB {waters of gold} The grandfather of the wife of Hadad, king of Edom (Ge. 36:39; 1Ch. 1:50).

MEZOBAITE, MESOBAITE The place or area from which one of David's mighty men came—Mezoba, or perhaps a title (1Ch. 11:47). †

MIAMIN *See* MIJAMIN

MIBHAR One of David's mighty men (1Ch. 11:38). †

MIBSAM
1. A son of Ishmael and grandson of Abraham (Ge. 25:13; 1Ch. 1:29).
2. A descendant of Simeon (1Ch. 4:25).

MIBZAR {bastion} A chief of Edom, descendant from Esau (Ge. 36:42; 1Ch. 1:53).

MICA, MICAH, MICHA, MICHAIAH {who is like Yahweh?}
1. A son of Mephibosheth and great-grandson of King Saul; also called Micah (2Sa. 9:12; 1Ch. 8:34).
2. A Levite active after the return from the Babylonian captivity; also called Micaiah (1Ch. 9:15; Ne. 12:35).
3. One who signed the covenant with Nehemiah (Ne. 10:11).

MICAH {who is like Yahweh?}
1. An Ephraimite who made an idol and then later got a priest for himself and his idol. The idol and priest were later taken by the Danites to their new town of Dan in the N. (Jdg. 17:1-13; 18:2-27, 30).
2. A descendant of Reuben (1Ch. 5:5).
3. Son of Mephibosheth. *See* MICAH 1.
4. A Levite of David's days (1Ch. 23:20).
5. The father of one sent by King Josiah to inquire of the LORD for him; also called Michaiah (2Ch. 34:20; 2Ki. 22:12).
6. One of the "minor" prophets. *See* PROPHETS, BOOKS OF THE MINOR

MICAH, BOOK OF *See* PROPHETS, BOOKS OF THE MINOR

MICAIAH, MICHAIAH [who is like Yahweh?]

1. The only prophet who foretold the defeat of King Ahab at Ramoth Gilead, an act for which he was imprisoned (1Ki. 22:8-28).

2. The mother of King Abijah of Judah. In the Hebrew text it is Maacah (1Ki. 15:2; 2Ch. 13:2).

3. One sent by King Jehoshaphat of Judah to teach throughout the cities of Judah (2Ch. 18:8).

4. One who was with Nehemiah when the walls of Jerusalem were dedicated (Ne. 12:41).

5. A son of Gemariah who reported the existence of Jeremiah's scroll in the days of King Jehoiakim (Jer. 36:11, 13).

6. *See* MICAH 2. and 5.

MICHA [who is like Yahweh?] *See* MICA

MICHAEL [who is like El?]

1. The father of one of the twelve spies in the time of Moses. The representative of the tribe of Asher (Nu. 13:13).

2, 3, 4, 5 and 6. Descendants of the following: two of Gad, one of Levi, one of Issachar, and one of Benjamin (1Ch. 5:13-14; 6:40; 7:3; 8:16).

7. A descendant of Manasseh who defected to David at Ziklag before he was king (1Ch. 12:20).

8. The father of one of David's officers from the tribe of Issachar (1Ch. 27:18).

9. A son of King Jehoshaphat of Judah (2Ch. 21:2-4).

10. The father of Zebadiah who was a leader in the return from the Babylonian captivity (Ezr. 8:8).

11. The great prince in the visions of Daniel, who stands for his people, Israel (Da. 10:13, 21; 12:1), called "the archangel" in the NT (Jude 9; Rev. 12:7).

MICHAH [who is like Yahweh?] *See* MICAH 4.

MICHAIAH [who is like Yahweh?] *See* MICAIAH

MICHAL [who is like (El)?] The daughter of Saul whom David married. She saved David's life but was taken from him by the king and given to another. Later, she was offended by David's conduct when he was bringing the Ark up to Jerusalem (1Sa. 14:49; 18:20; 19:11-17; 25:44; 2Sa. 6:16-23).

MICHTAM *See* PSALMS, TITLES OF 8.

MICMASH, MICHMAS(H) A city (176-142) in the tribal area of Benjamin that guarded one of the important passes up into the hill country from Jericho. Here Jonathan started a battle that won a great victory over the Philistines (1Sa. 13–14), and here too the British under General Allenby made an important breakthrough against the Turks in 1918. The Assyrians left their baggage here (Isa. 10:28). Men returned to this place from the Babylonian captivity (Ezr. 2:27; Ne. 7:31; 11:31).

MICMETHATH, MICHMETHAH A place (175-176) on the border between the tribal areas of Manasseh and Ephraim (Jos. 16:6; 17:7). †

MICRI, MICHRI A descendant in the tribe of Benjamin (1Ch. 9:8). †

MICROEVOLUTION *See* EVOLUTION, MICRO

MIDDIN A town (188-127) in the southern desert of the tribal area of Judah (Jos. 15:61). †

MIDDLE WALL OF PARTITION KJV for "the dividing wall of hostility" (Eph. 2:14). Some see this partition both as figurative, a cultural hostility being broken down, and an image of an actual wall that divided the Gentile Court (Outer Court) from the Jewish Court in the temple. Josephus (*Antiq.* 15:11:5) gives a description of this stone wall, and an inscription found by Clermont-Ganneau in 1871, now in Istanbul, states the death penalty for a Gentile passing beyond this partition wall. This explains why the charge of having a Gentile go beyond the wall meant the death penalty for Paul (Acts 21:28). *See also* TEMPLE

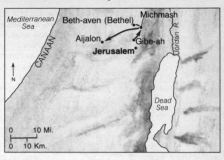

MICHMASH
Having entered Mich-
mash, Jonathan chased
the Philistines as far as
Aijalon.

MIDIAN, MIDIANITES, MIDI-ANITISH The first was a son of Abraham by Keturah and the second a people descended from him who lived in a land that bore his name (Ge. 25:1-3; 37:28, 36). Their land was both E and W of the Jordan rift, the Arabah, and S of Palestine proper. Moses spent forty years here before he began to lead the Exodus. His wife came from the area (Ex. 2:15—3:1). Because of later developments, God had to command the Israelites to smite the Midianites who apparently had allied themselves with the sins of Moab (Nu. 25:17). Gideon, the judge, delivered the Israelites from the oppression of the Midianites (Jdg. 6:1—9:17). Later references in the Bible all refer back to these times and these events.

MIDNIGHT The end of the second Roman watch of the night (12:00 A.M.). *See* WATCH

MIDTRIBULATIONALISM The view that halfway through the Great Tribulation in Revelation the church will be raptured. *See* RAPTURE; TRIBULATION

MIGDAL EDER [tower of flock] *See* EDER

MIGDAL EL [tower of El] An unidentified site in the tribal area of Naphtali (Jos. 19:38). †

MIGDAL GAD [tower of Gad] A city (140-105) in the western foothills of the tribal area of Judah (Jos. 15:37). †

MIGDOL [tower]
1. The Israelites encamped between Migdol and the sea just before crossing the Red Sea (Ex. 14:2). But the site is unknown.
2. An unidentified site in northern Egypt where the Jews settled in the days when Jeremiah was taken there (Jer. 44:1; 46:14).
3. A place, unidentified, in northern Egypt which God says he will destroy when he destroys all Egypt. Perhaps 2 and 3 are the same (Eze. 29:10; 30:6, NIV).

MIGRON An unidentified place in the tribal area of Benjamin. King Saul was here with his troops, and the Assyrian conqueror also passed that way (1Sa. 14:2; Isa. 10:28). †

MIJAMIN, MIAMIN, MINIAMIN
1. Head of a priestly division in David's days (1Ch. 24:9).
2. One who married a foreign wife in the days of the Babylonian captivity, (Ezr. 10:25).
3. One who signed the covenant with Nehemiah (Ne. 10:7).
4. A priest who returned from the Babylonian captivity with Zerubbabel (Ne. 12:5).
5. A Levite who assisted Nehemiah with music in the dedication of the rebuilt walls of Jerusalem (Ne. 12:41). *See* MINIAMIN

MIKLOTH

1. A descendant of Benjamin (1Ch. 8:32).

2. The chief officer under Dodai (1Ch. 27:4, in most versions).

MIKNEIAH [Yahweh acquires] A Levite musician in David's day (1Ch. 15:18, 21). †

MIKTAM *See* PSALMS, TITLES OF 8.

MILALAI One who was with Nehemiah in the dedication of the rebuilt wall of Jerusalem (Ne. 12:36). †

MILCAH [queen]

1. The wife of Abraham's brother Nahor and grandfather of Rebekah, wife of Isaac (Ge. 11:29; 24:15).

2. One of the daughters of the Zelophehad who died without leaving a son as heir (Nu. 26:33).

MILCOM *See* DEITIES

MILE *See* WEIGHTS AND MEASURES, *Stadion*

MILETUS, MILETUM A seaport city in Asia visited by Paul on one of his missionary journeys (Ac. 20:15-17; 2Ti. 4:20). †

MILETUS
Paul traveled from Troas to Miletus, where he summoned the elders of the church in Ephesus.

MILK *See* FOOD

MILL, MILLSTONE An apparatus used to grind grain into flour. It consisted of flat or slightly concave-convex upper and lower stones. The upper stone was turned by hand with a stick placed in a hole on its upper surface. Some larger stones were of a different type, with the lower stone conical at the top fitting into a conversely shaped upper stone which had holes on the outside for the insertion of beams, which were then pushed or pulled by men or animals for its rotation (Dt. 24:6; 2Sa. 11:21; Isa. 47:2; Mt. 18:6).

MILLENNIALISM, MILLENARIANISM Latin from the Greek *chilioi* for "1,000." The view that there will be a rule of God on earth for a thousand years. *See* AMILLENNIALISM; POSTMILLENNIALISM; PREMILLENNIALISM

MILLENNIUM [thousand] A thousand years. *See* ESCHATOLOGY

MILLET *See* PLANTS, PERFUMES, AND SPICES, Plants for Food 1.

MILLO [solid] *See* BETH MILLO

MINA *See* WEIGHTS AND MEASURES

MIND The translation of a number of Greek and Hebrew words which involve both the reflective thinking of the brain and the emotional thinking associated with the heart. For example, one of the words translated "mind" is the Hebrew word *leb* or "heart" (Isa. 46:8; 65:17; Jer. 3:16; 19:5). The heart was considered the center of the entire personality and as such a natural rendering would be "mind." For Paul's difference between flesh and mind and spirit, *see* PAUL, LIFE AND TEACHINGS OF. *See also* HEART; MEDITATE; UNDERSTANDING; WISDOM

MINERALS OF THE BIBLE *See* PRECIOUS STONES AND METALS

MINES, MINING Israel had the ability to hew rock as Hezekiah's tunnel shows. Mines are mentioned with vertical or semivertical shafts in Job 28:4.

Gold, silver, copper, tin, iron, and lead were of such quantities that mining had to be a large industry. There is a reference to an ironsmelting furnace in Dt. 4:20. But the Bible speaks little about mining directly.

MINGLED PEOPLE *See* STRANGER

MINIAMIN {from the right, good fortune}

1. A Levite in the days of King Hezekiah who was one of the distributors of the gifts given to the LORD (2Ch. 31:15).

2. A priest who helped Nehemiah in the dedication of the rebuilt wall of Jerusalem (Ne. 12:41). *See* MIJAMIN

MINISTER, MINISTRY {servant} In both Testaments, one who serves or assists. The minister may be either free or bond, but if the latter, he is more than a simple bond servant. Joshua was Moses' assistant but not his servant (Jos.1:1). Epaphroditus took care of Paul's needs but was not the servant of either the minister or his congregation (Php. 2:25). The basic idea in the Bible is service, even though the nature of the service is not always spelled out (Ex. 30:20; Isa. 56:4-6; Mt. 25:44; Col. 4:7; 2Ti. 1:18). The majority of uses in the OT are connected with service in the tabernacle or temple (Ex. 28:43; 2Ch. 29:11). In the NT the word at first had a nontechnical use, but even there the beginnings of the concept of ministers as minor officers in the church is clear, and some of the requirements for a holder of this office are spelled out (Ac. 6:4; Ro. 15:16; 2Co. 5:8; Eph. 4:11-12; 1Ti. 3:12; 4:6; 5:17). Those who ministered in NT times were called elders (presbyters), pastors, bishops, deacons, and deaconesses. The gradual development of these various offices into the positions they hold today in various denominations is postbiblical for the most part, a development through need, and not a development of exegesis of Scripture. *See also* DEACON; LAITY; SERVANT

MINJAMIN, MINIAMIN {from the right, good fortune} Head of a priestly family in the days of Nehemiah (Ne. 12:17).

MINNI A people and an area in the mountain region NE of Mesopotamia (Jer. 51:27). †

MINNITH An Ammonite city E of the Jordan in the tribal area of Reuben which Judge Jephthah conquered in order to free Israel from their yoke (Jdg. 11:32-33; Eze. 27:17). †

MINOR PROPHETS *See* PROPHETS, BOOKS OF THE MINOR

MINSTREL *See* MUSIC, MUSICAL INSTRUMENTS

MINT *See* PLANTS, PERFUMES, AND SPICES, Plants for Seasoning

MIRACLES, MIRACULOUS The word "miracle" is used in the OT only in Ex. 7:8, but the concept is noted in the NIV under such terms as "wonders" or "miraculous signs" (Ex. 4:21; Ps. 78:43). In the NT these words are used chiefly in connection with the promise that the followers of Jesus would do supernatural things (Ac. 1:8; 1Co. 12:10, 28-29), extraordinary events not capable of explanation by natural causes but requiring supernatural power and coming to pass to serve as a sign. The common rendering in the NIV for this kind of phenomenon is "sign" or "miraculous sign" (Ex. 7:3; Dt. 13:1; Isa. 8:18; Mt. 12:38-39; Ac. 2:43).

MIRIAM

1. The sister of Moses (Nu. 26:59; Ex. 2:4ff.; Nu. 12:1ff.; 20:1).

2. A descendant of Judah and Caleb (1Ch. 4:17).

MIRMAH, MIRMA {deceit} A descendant of Benjamin (1Ch. 8:10). †

MIRROR The early looking glasses were of smoothed metals, primarily polished bronze, and not as functional as modern ones of glass; hence, Paul's reference in 1Co. 13:12 of seeing in a mirror dimly (see also Job 37:18; Jas. 1:23).

Ancient Bronze Mirrors

MISGAB [height] A KJV, ASV, NEB transliteration as a proper name in Jer. 48:1, translated "stronghold" in NIV, NASB and "fortress" in the RSV, JB. *See* FORT, FORTRESS, FORTIFICATION

MISHAEL [who belongs to El?]
1. A Levite cousin of Moses and Aaron who helped to carry the bodies of Nadab and Abihu out of the camp (Lev. 10:4-5).
2. One who stood with Ezra as he read the law to the people (Ne. 8:4).
3. *See* SHADRACH.

MISHAL, MISHEAL A Levitical city (164-253) in the tribal area of Asher; also called Mashal (Jos. 19:26; 21:30; 1Ch. 6:74).

MISHAM A descendant of Benjamin (1Ch. 8:12). †

MISHEAL *See* MISHAL

MISHMA [rumor]
1. A son of Ishmael (Ge. 25:14; 1Ch. 1:30).
2. A descendant of Simeon (1Ch. 4:25-26).

MISHMANNAH [fatness] A descendant of Gad who defected to David (1Ch. 12:10). †

MISHRAITES A clan of Kiriath Jearim descended from Judah (1Ch. 2:53). †

MISPAR, MIZPAR [number] One who returned from the Babylonian captivity with Zerubbabel; also called Mispereth (Ezr. 2:2; Ne. 7:7). †

MISPERETH *See* MISPAR

MISREPHOTH MAIM [waters of MISREPHOTH (lime burning)] A region or city in Phoenicia near Sidon to which place Joshua pursued his enemies after the battle of the Waters of Meron (Jos. 11:8; 13:6). †

MISSIOLOGY The study of missions.

MISSIONARY JOURNEYS *See* ACTS, *mission career*

MIST *See* ABEL (person); VAIN

MITE Small copper coins known as *lepton*. *See* MONEY, last ¶

MITER, MITRE *See* DRESS, *turban*

MITHCAH, MITHKAH [sweetness] One of the desert stops of the Israelites in their exodus from Egypt (Nu. 33:28-29). †

MITHNITE The family name or place from which came Joshaphat, one of David's mighty men (1Ch. 11:43). †

MITHREDATH [gift to (pagan deity) MITHRA]
1. A Persian treasurer (Ezr. 1:8). †
2. A Persian officer involved in the attempt to stop the building of the walls of Jerusalem in the days of Nehemiah (Ezr. 4:7, 12). †

MITHRAISM *See* MYSTERY RELIGIONS

MITYLENE A seaport on the island of Lesbos, SE of Asia Minor, where Paul stopped on his third missionary journey (Ac. 20:14). †

MIZAR [small] Mt. Mizar would seem to be a part of the Hermon range, unidentified (Ps. 42:6). †

MIZPAH [lookout point]
1. As a common noun *mizpeh* (Hebrew, *mitspeh*; English, *mizpah*) refers to a lookout point or a watchtower (2Ch. 20:24 [NIV *overlooks*]; Isa. 21:8). The word is associated with at least five other place names to indicate local sites, high spots.
2. Mizpah of Benjamin (170-143) is a

MIZPAH, A CITY OF BENJAMIN

city of Benjamin on the border between the kingdoms of Israel and Judah, not far N of Jerusalem. It has not only been located with Tell en-Nasbeh, but also with a modern place called Nebi Samwil (Jos. 18:26). It was involved in the wars between Judah and Israel (1Ki. 15:22, and the account which precedes it). In the time of the prophet Samuel, it was the center of worship for all the Israelites (1Sa. 7:5-16; 10:17ff.).

3. Mizpah of Gilead, an unidentified site E of the Jordan N of the Jabbok River where Laban and Jacob covenanted (Ge. 31:49). Under Judge Jephthah the Israelites encamped there before fighting the Ammonites (Jdg. 10:17; 11:11, 29, 34).

4. Mizpah of Judah, an unidentified site in the western foothills of the tribe of Judah (Jos. 15:38).

5. Mizpah of Moab, an unidentified site in Moab where David left his parents during part of the time of his military troubles (1Sa. 22:3).

6. The region of Mizpah or the Valley of Mizpeh, an area into which Joshua pursued the defeated enemy after the battle of the Waters of Merom (Jos. 11:3, 8).

7. Ramath Mizpah (223-169), a site in the tribal area of Gad, by some equated with 3 above (Jos. 13:26).

MIZPAR *See* MISPAR

MIZPEH *See* MIZPAH

MIZRAIM, MITSRAIM A son of Ham (1Ch. 1:8, 11). A normal rendering for the "land of Mizraim" is Egypt. *See* EGYPT

MIZZAH An Edomite descendant of Esau (Ge. 36:13, 17; 1Ch. 1:37). †

MNASON A resident of Jerusalem from Cyprus; a Christian who hosted Paul after his third missionary journey (Ac. 21:16). †

MOAB, PLAIN OF, DESERT OF *See* GEOGRAPHY OF THE HOLY LAND

MOABITE STONE, THE An inscription on stone found in 1868. It tells of the worship of the Moab god Chemosh and has given us an extrabiblical look at the revolt of Moab (2Ki. 1:1). There are many names, places, religious allusions to the biblical time of Omri, Ahab, and Ahaziah. It also gives one a look at a related language to biblical Hebrew of this period. S.R. Driver has a very detailed article in "Notes on the Hebrew Text of Samuel." *See* AROER; DEITIES; DIBON 2.; HESHBON; MESHA

MOADIAH *See* MAADIAH

MOHAMMED *See* ISLAM; KORAN

MOLADAH {generation} A town (142-074) in the southern part of the tribal area of Judah. Since Simeon's area overlapped with that of Judah, it is also listed in the tribal area of Simeon (Jos. 15:26; 19:2; 1Ch. 4:28; Ne. 11:26). †

MOLE KJV for an unclean animal translated "chameleon" in all the major versions (Lev. 11:30). The NJB transliterates it as "tinshameth." *See* BEASTS 6.

The Moabite Stone The whole stone measures 3 feet, 7 inches by 1 foot, 11 inches.

MOLECH [(pagan god) MALK, Shameful King—from the consonants of Hebrew "king" and vowels from the Hebrew word for "shame"] *See* DEITIES

MOLID [descendant] A descendant of Judah (1Ch. 2:29).

MOLOCH *See* MOLECH; *see also* DEITIES

MOLTON IMAGE *See* IDOL, IDOLATRY

MOLTON SEA *See* SEA, MOLTON; TEMPLE

MONEY Coined money was not introduced into Palestine until the reign of Darius I, under the Persian Empire. Prior to that time, payments in silver and gold (or bronze) were made in the form of bullion ingots weighed out in the scales, and calculated as gerah (1/20 shekel), bekahs (1/2 shekel) shekels (c. 4/10 oz.), or even as manehs (a maneh varied from 50 or 60 to 100 shekels). Even the unit referred to as *kesitah* in the NIV footnotes of Ge. 33:19, Jos. 24:32, and Job 42:11 was an uncoined measure of weight, possibly amounting to 1430 grams (judging from Arabic *quistun*). It may have borne a merchant's stamp on it, but it was not a government-guaranteed coin, stamped with an official device.

The first regularly minted money was coined in the Kingdom of Lydia in Asia Minor around 700 B.C. and consisted of gold staters (sometimes of electrum, a mixture of three parts of gold to one of silver) and (later on) silver sigloi. These bore the forepart of a lion facing the forepart of bull; the reverse of the coin was simply a crude punch of no particular shape (as was true of the imperial Persian currency right down to the fourth century B.C.). The earliest pure silver coinage was minted on the Greek island of Aegina S of Attica; it bore a sea tortoise on its front side, and dated from about 650 B.C. Persian gold darics (with a kneeling figure of the robed king as an archer) and silver sigloi, more or less

identical in size and shape, appeared in large numbers by the time of Darius I (521—485 B.C.). The '*adarkon* of 1Ch. 29:7 probably refers to the gold daric (at least as a unit of weight), and the silver drachma (a Greek denomination) in Ezr. 2:69. Silver tetradrachms (i.e., four-drachma pieces) from Athens, with the head of Athena on the front side and an owl on the reverse, have been discovered in excavations of the fifth century level in Palestine. After the Alexandrian conquest in 334 B.C., Macedonian and Greek currency replaced the Persian in the entire Near and Middle East. The silver coinage of Alexander bore the handsome head of Heracles in lion's-mane headdress and the enthroned Zeus on the reverse. The gold staters (weighing two gold drachmas) had the head of Athena in a Corinthian helmet, with the goddess Nike on the reverse. After Alexander's death, Palestine came under the rule of the Ptolemaic Dynasty in Egypt, until the Seleucid emperor Antiochus III wrested it away from them (about 200 B.C.). Thus the Seleucid and Ptolemaic issues dominated Judean finance until the Maccabean revolt in 168 B.C. But even under the Hasmonean Jewish dynasty the native mintage seems to have been confined to bronze lepta, beginning with John Hyrcanus I (135-105); the silver shekels and subdivisions of shekel formerly attributed to the Hasmoneans have been shown by more recent archeology to have been from the First Revolt (A.D. 68-70). Thus the Jews must have used Hellenistic silver issues, despite their pagan coin imprints. Of particular importance was the Tyrian tetradrachma (or shekel) bearing the head of Heracles Baal Melqart, and a strutting eagle on the reverse, probably the predominating type of silver piece in the payment which Judas Iscariot received as the price of betraying Christ. With the rise of Herod the Great, the Hasmonean bronze lepta were replaced by Herodian lepta, while the silver coins were still provided by the Hellenistic drachms, didrachms, and tetradrachmas (all of which are mentioned in the NT) and by Roman denarii, with all their pagan images. This latter coin, about the size and value of a drachma, almost invariably bore "the image and superscription of Caesar" (i.e., the reigning emperor, whether Augustus, Tiberius, Claudius, or Nero) on its front side (Mt. 22:20-21). The bronze coins mentioned in the NT include: the *assarion* (translated "penny" in the NIV) or Roman *as* (Mt. 10:29; Lk. 12:6), worth 1/16 of a denarius; the *kodrantes* or Roman *quadrans* (also translated "penny" in the NIV) (Mt. 5:26; Mk. 12:42), worth 1/4 *as*; and the *lepton*, or smallest bronze of all (translated "copper coins" in the NIV(Mk. 12:42; Lk. 12:59). These last were usually the old Hasmonean issue, or the Herodian bronzes, or else the mintages of the various Roman procurators, such as Pontius Pilate (who issued two types: either with an augur's wand or a *simpulum* [ladle] as the picture on the front side). If the widow who Christ observed (Mk. 12:42) was using the most recently minted "mites," these would have been the kind she cast into the offering box. But more likely she would have used the old Hasmonean lepta, free of pagan images. See also table of weights and measures in the NIV.

The word "mammon" is found in Mt. 6:24 and Lk. 16:9, 11, 13. This is a transliteration that has come down to us in the translations (the Vulgate, KJV, ASV and others). Mammon is a Aramaic word for "wealth" or "property." The NIV translates this word as "money" or "wealth." In the context of Mt. 6:19-24, spiritual and earthly treasures are contrasted. (G.L.A.)

MONEY CHANGER Three feasts a year required mandatory attendance (Ex. 23:14-17) (*see* FESTIVALS). There were sacrifices required to give to the Lord at these feasts. In order to purchase a sacrificial animal and pay the temple tax, the foreign money had to be converted into Jewish money. A money changer would do this, probably for a handling fee. This function and others had turned the Outer Court area of the temple into an emporium (Mt. 21:12; Mk. 11:15; Lk. 19:45-48; Jn. 2:15).

MONOGAMY The practice of being married only once in a lifetime, or married to one partner at a time. *See* DIVORCE; MARRIAGE

MONOTHEISM {one God} Belief in only one God, distinguished from henotheism, polytheism, or atheism.

MONSTER OF THE DEEP *See* BEASTS 9.

MONTHS, NAMES OF *See* CALENDAR

MOON, NEW MOON, FEAST OF The luminary for the night, given with the sun "to mark seasons, and days, and years" (Ge. 1:14). The new moon, marking the start of a new month, was like the Sabbath in that special prayers and rituals were performed as prescribed by the law (Nu. 10:10; 28:11-15; 29:6; 2Ki. 4:23; Ps. 81:3). It is well known that the worship of the moon was a common practice of the extrabiblical world of antiquity and may even have intruded into false worship in Israel, but there is no evidence of it as an extensive practice. *See* CALENDAR and FESTIVALS

MORALS Relating to right and wrong actions.

MORASTHITE {of MORESHETH} *See* MORESHETH, MORESHETH GATH

MORDECAI {pagan Bab. god MARDUK}
1. Esther's cousin who had reared her. He saved the life of King Xerxes and later thwarted the plan of Haman to exterminate the Jews of Persia (Est. 2:7, 21ff.; 4:7ff.).
2. One who returned from the Babylonian captivity with Zerubbabel (Ezr. 2:2).

MOREH {(place) instructor}
1. An unidentified hill near which the Midianites were encamped against the

Israelites before Gideon defeated them. Probably near the Valley of Jezreel (Jdg. 7:1). †

2. An unidentified place near Shechem where Abraham camped and erected an altar to God (Ge. 12:67; *see also* Dt. 11:30). †

MORESHETH, MORESHETH GATH [possession of Gath] A city (141-115) in the tribal area of Judah from which the prophet Micah came (Jer. 26:18; Mic. 1:1, 14). †

MORIAH, MOUNT *See* GEOGRAPHY OF THE HOLY LAND

MORNING In the NT the fourth watch of the night, 3:00 to 6:00 A.M. *See* WATCH

MORNING SACRIFICE *See* SACRIFICES AND OFFERINGS

MORNING STAR *See* DEVIL, *Lucifer*

MORSEL *See* FOOD; MEALS

MORTAL, MORTALITY *See* DEAD, ABODE OF; IMMORTAL; LIFE

MORTAL BODY The part of man that dies (Ro. 8:11). *See* IMMORTAL, IMMORTALITY

MORTAR *See* BRICK

MOSERA, MOSERAH, MOSEROTH [possession] An unidentified stop of the children of Israel in their wanderings during their exodus from Egypt (Dt. 10:6; Nu. 33:30-31).

MOSES [drawn out, Ex. 2:10; technically Egyptian for "is born;" related to the names of pagan Egyptian gods as in AMMON-MOSE, KB] The Levite son of Amram and Jochebed, rescued at his birth by the daughter of the pharaoh and reared in that court (Ex. 6:20; 2:1-10). As an adult he killed an Egyptian and fled to Midian where he met and married Zipporah the daughter of Jethro (Ex. 2:11-22). After the death of the pharaoh, forty years after Moses's flight, he returned and led the Israelites out of Egypt to the borders of the Promised Land of Canaan. His history of miracle working and leadership is interwoven with all the laws given by God through him for the life of the people after their entry into the land of Canaan (Ex. 20 through Dt.; note especially Lev. 18: 4-5). Before his death on Mt. Nebo at the age of 120 (Dt. 34:7), he had led his people in the conquest of the area E of the Jordan and in the settlement of some of the tribes there (Nu. 21:21ff.; Dt. 2:26ff.; 3:1ff.). It is the name of Moses that has always been associated with the law of Israel, the foundation of life and practice for Israel and the Jews to this day, and the foundation of the faith of the church as well. *See also* BURNING BUSH

MOSES, ASSUMPTION OF An OT apocryphal book, which apparently Jude (verse 9) alludes to.

MOSES, LAW OF *See* DECALOGUE; LAW

MOST HIGH *See* GOD, NAMES OF, GODHEAD 1., *El Elyon*

MOST HOLY PLACE *See* HOLY OF HOLIES

MOTE KJV for "speck of sawdust" in Mt. 7:35; Lk. 6:41-42.

MOTH *See* BEASTS 6.

MOTHER *See* MARRIAGE

MOUNT, MOUNTAIN, HILL, MOUNT Compared to major mountain chains of the world (e.g., the Rocky Mountains) the mountains of the Bible are hills. *See* GEOGRAPHY OF THE HOLY LAND

MOUNT OF BEATITUDES *See* SERMON ON THE MOUNT

MOUNT EPHRAIM *See* GEOGRAPHY OF THE HOLY LAND

MOUNT OF OLIVES *See* OLIVES, MOUNT OF

MOUNT ZION *See* GEOGRAPHY OF THE HOLY LAND and JERUSALEM

MOURN, MOURNING *See* BURIAL; CAVE

MOUSE *See* BEASTS 5., *Rat*

MOWING *See* FARMING; SICKLE

MOZA
1. A descendant of Benjamin and King Saul (1Ch. 8:36-37).
2. A descendant of Judah and Caleb (1Ch. 2:46).

MOZAH An unidentified site (165-134) in the tribal area of Benjamin (Jos.18:26). †

MUFFLER KJV for "veil" (Isa. 3:19). *See* DRESS, *headgear*

MULBERRY TREE *See* PLANTS, PERFUMES, AND SPICES, Miscellaneous Plants 12., *Balsam tree*

MULE A cross breed of a donkey and horse. Cross breeding was forbidden in the law, yet was either practiced or quietly endorsed by the nation of Israel. The mule was a beast of burden as well as an animal ridden by a king (2Sa. 18:9; 1Ki. 1:33, 38; 2Ki. 5:17). *See* BEASTS 4.

MULTITUDES *See* CROWD

MUMMIFICATION *See* BURIAL

MUPPIM A son of Benjamin (Ge. 46:21); also called Shephuphan and Shupham (1Ch. 8:5; Nu. 26:39), and his clans either Shuppites or Shuphamites (1Ch. 7:12; cf. 7:7; Nu. 26:39). †

MURATORIAN CANON A fragment found by L.A. Muratori, published in 1740. It is a fragmentary register of accepted NT books in about A.D. 200.

MURDERER *See* MANSLAYER

MURMUR KJV for "grumble."

MURRAIN *See* SICK, SICKNESS 3., *Plague*, Ex. 9:3

MUSHI, MUSHITES A descendant of Levi and the clan he founded (Ex. 6:19; Nu. 3:33).

MUSIC, MUSICAL INSTRUMENTS
1. Music has one reference in the Bible prior to the Flood, with respect to the harp and flute, and where we note that Jubal was the father of all those who play these instruments (Ge. 4:21). Nothing further is added in the Scriptures about music in this very ancient time. In post-Flood times, music was associated with social merrymaking, with summons to battle, in battle, and with worship (Ge. 31:27; Jdg. 7:20-22; 1Sa. 13:3-4; Jos. 6:4ff.; 1Ch. 25:1). There is no record that music as an organized art with choirs and orchestras was in use in Israel prior to the time of the great musician, King David. David was a brilliant poet, musical instrumentalist, and organizer of musicians (2Ch. 7:6; 1Ch. 15:27-28; 16:5-6; 6:31; 16:37, 42). There are many references in the Bible to psalms, songs, hymns, chants, and music (Ps. 47:7; Eph. 5:19; Ex. 15:1; Eze. 32:16; 1Sa. 18:6). There are many references to dances and dancing in connection with the praise of God with music, song, and choirs (Jdg. 11:34; Ps. 150:4). An interesting item is the "lament of the bow" (2Sa. 1:17, NIV). It appears that men were trained in the use of shooting the bow to a cadence of the rhythm of poems. *See* PSALMS, TITLES OF and SELAH
2. Musical instruments may be summarized under three headings: (a) percussion, (b) wind instruments, and (c) stringed instruments.
(a) Percussion instruments did not have variable pitch and so were used as noisemakers and for rhythm indicators. For the most part, they were held in the hand and struck by the hand. Those mentioned include the *tambourine,* used like the modern triangle or drum (Ge. 31:27; 2Sa. 6:5; Ps. 81:2; 149:3; Isa. 30:32). The *cymbal* was in form and use much like its modern counterpart by the same name (1Ch. 16:42; 25:1; Ps. 150). The *sistrum* is purely a noisemaker like a rattle or castanet (2Sa. 6:5); the *gong*

is mentioned in connection with the cymbal (1Co. 13:1), and *bells* are mentioned in connection with the robes of the priests and the harness of horses, apparently for the purpose of calling attention to their passing (Ex. 28:33; Zec. 14:20). Several of these instruments were not used in worship but were used by the women, for the most part to add din to the jubilation.

(b) The most frequently mentioned wind instrument is the *horn* or *trumpet* (Heb. *shofar*). It was usually the horn of a ram but later included that of other animals as well. It could even be of metal. It is most frequently rendered as "trumpet" or "rams' horns" (Lev. 25:9; Jos. 6:4, 8, 13; 2Sa. 6:15). Its most common uses were in connection with battle and with special religious events and festivals (Jdg. 3:27-28; Ps. 81:3). In the NT the word is used in connection with the trumpet to be sounded by God at the end of time (1Co. 15:52; 1Th. 4:16; Rev. 8:7ff.). It was not an orchestral instrument. *Flutes* were apparently shrill in sound and often coarse. If they were used in orchestras for worship in the temple, it was apparently not a common use. They were used in joyous or ecstatic times (1Sa. 10:5; Job 21:12; 1Co. 14:7).

(c) There were several stringed instruments in the general family of the harp: the *harp* itself, the *lyre*, and the *lute*. These were the instruments especially used in religious worship and orchestration. David was a specialist (1Ch. 13:8; 15:16, 20, 28; Ps. 33:2; 71:22; 150:3). *See*

related terms HIGGAION; PSALMS, TITLES OF. The major difference between these three would seem to be in the number of strings and in the shape of the part that held the strings. The *zither* is mentioned in Daniel 3:7.

MUSLIM Arabic for "one surrendered to God." *See* ISLAM; KORAN

MUSTARD *See* PLANTS, PERFUMES, AND SPICES, Plants for Seasoning

MUTHLABBEN {death of son} A transliteration for the title of Ps. 9. It is translated "[to the tune of] death of a Son" in the NIV. It is problematic as to its meaning. *See* PSALMS, TITLES OF

MUZZLE A device to prevent animals from eating (Dt. 25:4). The one muzzled did not receive material compensation for labor. This quotation of Scripture (Paul also quotes Lk. 10:7 as Scripture!) show material goods should be provided to the elders. This verse explains what "honor" is in the prior verse (1Ti. 5:17-18).

MYRA A southern port of Lycia in Asia Minor where Paul stopped on his voyage to Rome as a prisoner (Ac. 27:2-5). †

MYRRH *See* PLANTS, PERFUMES, AND SPICES

MYRTLE *See* PLANTS, PERFUMES, AND SPICES

MYSIA A district in the NW part of Asia Minor visited by Paul on his second missionary journey (Ac. 16:7-8). †

MYSIA
Paul's second missionary journey went through Mysia to Macedonia.

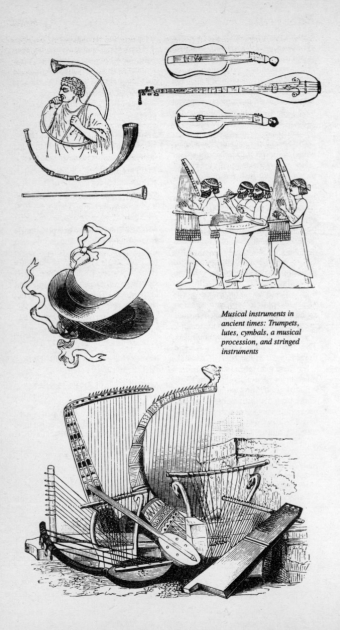

Musical instruments in ancient times: Trumpets, lutes, cymbals, a musical procession, and stringed instruments

MYSTERY [secret] The transliteration of a Greek word, *mysterion*, used frequently by Paul and otherwise found four times in Rev. (1:20; 10:7; 17:5, 7). In the Gospels it is translated by the word "secret" (Mt. 13:11; Mk. 4:11; Lk. 8:10). In Paul's writings, however, it had a particular usage meaning. As the word *mysterion* came into the Bible by way of Greek paganism, we must find its meaning both from that source and from its NT contexts. It is a secret passed on only to the initiated and unknown until it is revealed. In its specialized adaption in Pauline theology it is a synonym for the gospel message: " . . . by my gospel and the proclamation of Jesus Christ, according to the revelation of the mystery hidden for long ages past, but now revealed and made known through the prophetic writings by the command of the eternal God, so that all nations might believe and obey him" (Ro. 16:25-26; see 1Ti. 3:16).

The mystery includes: Christ himself who is our life (Col. 1:26-28; 2:23; 4:3); that the Gentiles are now also joint-heirs of God with Jewish believers (Eph. 3:3-12); and that this is to be made known through the church, even though it was in the eternal purpose of God from the beginning (Eph. 3:9-11); and, eventually, the consolidation of all things in Christ (Eph. 1:9-10). As with the Greek concept of *mysterion*, which required initiation into the group in order that the mystery could be understood, so it is with the gospel. It requires the "new birth" of the individual in order to understand the salvation which is in Christ (Jn. 3:3, 7, 16-17).

MYSTERY RELIGIONS A large umbrella term for many cults from the Middle East. *Dionysus*, *Cybele*, *Isis*, and *Mithra* are four major ones. They had secret symbols and rites.

MYSTICAL PRESENCE *See* COMMUNION, VIEWS OF

MYTHS Myths are stories, tales, and legends. They are to be ignored by the Christian (1Ti. 1:4; 4:7; 2Ti. 4:4; Tit. 1:14). The gospel is no myth (2Pe. 1:16).

N

NAAM [pleasant] A son of Caleb of the tribe of Judah (1Ch. 4:15). †

NAAMAH [pleasant]
1. The sister of Tubal-Cain (Ge. 4:22).
2. The mother of Judah's king Rehoboam, a wife of Solomon, an Ammonite (1Ki. 14:21, 31).

NAAMAN, NAAMITE(S) [pleasantness]
1, 2, and 3. A son, a grandson, and a great-grandson of Benjamin (Ge. 46:21; Nu. 26:40; 1Ch. 8:7). They were called Naamites.
4. The Syrian officer cured of leprosy by the prophet Elisha after dipping seven times in the Jordan (2Ki. 5:1-27; Lk. 4:27).

NAAMATHITE [of Naamath] One of Job's friends, Zohar, was from this unidentified area of Naamah in NW Arabia and therefore a Naamathite (Job 2:11; 42:9).

NAARAH [(young) woman]
1. One of the wives of Shur, a descendant of Judah (1Ch. 4:5-6). †
2. A city (190-144) near Jericho in the tribal area of Ephraim (Jos. 16:7). Perhaps also the Naaran of 1Ch. 7:28 on the border of Benjamin and Ephraim. †

NAARAI [young man of Yahweh] One of David's mighty men; also called Paarai (1Ch. 11:37; 2Sa. 23:35). †

NAARAN See NAARAH 1.

NAARATH See NAARAH 2.

NAASHON, NAASSON See NAHSHON

NABAL [fool] The wealthy herder who refused David's request for help. When he realized the implications of what he had done, he took sick and died. David married his widow (1Sa. 25:2-42).

NABATEA, NABATEANS A kingdom E of Palestine which ran from the Red Sea to Damascus. Its capital city was Petra. In A.D. 106 it became a Roman province.

NABONIDAS, NABONIDUS [(pagan god) Nabu is wonderful] See BABYLON, BABYLONIA, *Nabunaids*

NABOPOLASSAR [(pagan god) Nabu protect the son!] See BABYLON, BABYLONIA (626-605 B.C.)

NABOTH [a sprout] The owner of the vineyard in Jezreel that King Ahab coveted which Queen Jezebel got for him by having Naboth murdered (1Ki. 21:1-16; 2Ki. 9:21-26). † See JEZEBEL

NACHON'S See NACON

NACHOR See NAHOR

NACON [established] Owner of the threshing floor where Uzzah died for touching the Ark and where the Ark remained some time before David again tried to bring it to Jerusalem (2Sa. 6:6ff.); also called Kidon (1Ch. 13:9). †

NADAB [volunteer, free will offering]
1. A son of Aaron and a priest; killed for offering strange (i.e., unauthorized)

fire before the LORD (Ex. 6:23; 28:1; Lev. 10:1-2).

2. *See* KINGS OF JUDAH AND IS-RAEL, a King of Israel.

3. A Jerahmeelite (1Ch. 2:28).

4. A descendant of Benjamin (1Ch. 8:30).

NAGGAI, NAGGE An ancestor of Joseph, the father (so it was thought) of Jesus (Lk. 3:25). †

NAG HAMMADI LIBRARY A village in Upper Egypt where thirteen books from the fourth century A.D. were found. The writings are all pseudepigraphal.

NAHALAL, NAHALLAL [watering place] An unidentified site in the tribal area of Zebulun; also called Nahalol (Jos. 19:15; 21:35; Jdg. 1:30). †

NAHALIEL [wadi of El] An unidentified site or valley perhaps where the Israelites stopped E of Jordan at the end of their exodus wanderings (Nu. 21:19). †

NAHALOL *See* NAHALAL

NAHAM [repent, console] The brother-in-law of Hodiah and thus brought into the line of Judah (1Ch. 4:19). †

NAHAMANI [Yahweh has consoled] One who returned from the Babylonian captivity with Zerubbabel (Ne.7:7). †

NAHARAI, NAHARI One of David's thirty mighty men (2Sa. 23:37; 1Ch. 11:39). †

NAHASH [viper *or* copper]

1. A king of the Ammonites from whom Saul took Jabesh Gilead and who became a supporter of David (1Sa. 11:1ff.; 2Sa. 10:1-2).

2. The father of Abigail (2Sa. 17:25).

NAHATH [descent; *possibly* rest]

1. A descendant of Esau (Ge. 36:13; 1Ch. 1:37).

2. A Levite (1Ch. 6:26).

3. An overseer in Hezekiah's time (2Ch. 31:13).

NAHBI The representative from Naphtali among the twelve spies sent out by Moses (Nu. 13:14). †

NAHOR

1 and 2. A grandfather of Abraham and a brother of Abraham (Ge. 11:22-27).

NAHSHON [small viper] A descendant of Judah who was assigned to assist Moses; a brother-in-law of Aaron, and an ancestor of David and Joseph, the father (so it was thought) of Jesus (Nu. 1:7; Ex. 6:23; Ru. 4:20; Lk. 3:32).

NAHUM [comfort]

1. One of the minor prophets who came from Elkosh (Na. 1:1). †

2. An ancestor of Joseph, the father (so it was thought) of Jesus (Lk. 3:25). †

NAHUM, BOOK OF *See* PROPHETS, BOOKS OF THE MINOR

NAIL, NAILING The translation of several Hebrew and Greek words (rendered "nails," "pegs," "tent pegs"). Nails or pegs were first made of stone chips, wood or bone, and later of metal. The fingernails and the tent peg are among the translations (Dt. 21:12; Da. 4:33; Jdg. 4:21-22; Zec. 10:4). The nail of the general kind known today was also driven by a hammer at that time (1Ch. 22:3; Jer. 10:4). One NT reference is found to the nails used to fasten Jesus to the cross (Jn. 20:25). The word "nailing" is used once also by Paul where he talks of God's nailing to the cross the legal demands against man (Col. 2:14).

NAIN A village in Galilee near Mt. Tabor where Jesus raised a widow's son from the dead (Lk. 7:11-17). †

NAIOTH [dwellings] An unidentified place near Jerusalem where David stayed with Samuel on one of his flights from the jealousy of King Saul (1Sa. 19:18−20:1). †

NAKEDNESS This may mean without any clothing at all, or merely poorly clothed (Ge. 2:25; Jas. 2:15; Jn. 21:7).

NAME *See* GOD, NAMES OF, GODHEAD

NAME, GIVING OF A name in the Bible given to someone (or some place) can have significance and even help us understand the passage. An example of this is the name "Jesus" and his title "Christ" (Lk. 2:11; Mt. 1:21-22). An example for a place is "Achor" (Jos. 7:26). The person of Abel (*see* ABEL) is yet another more subtle play on words, or Nabal (fool) (*see* NABAL). It lends insight into the interaction of characters in a passage.

But the careful Bible student will use this definition of the name wisely. For example, in a list of names in Chronicles or places in Joshua and Judges the name will be just a name, unless there is something in the context to demand a comment on the name's meaning.

The naming of someone shows the authority over another. So God named Adam (Ge. 1:26); man named his counterpart, woman (Ge. 2:23); Adam named the animals (Ge. 2:19); woman her children (Ge. 4:1). God gave Jesus' name, sent through the word of the angel (Mt. 1:21). Likewise John the Baptist was named by God through an angel (Lk. 1:13).

NAOMI {my joy} The wife of Elimelech and mother-in-law of Ruth who helped her to find Boaz that he might perform the role of the next of kin in the case of the deceased relative and husband (Ru. 1:2, 4; 2:20-22; 4:13).

NAPATH, NAPHATH {coastland} *See* DOR

NAPHISH {refreshed} A son of Ishmael and grandson of Abraham (Ge. 25:15; 1Ch. 1:31; 5:19).

NAPHTALI {wrestling} The son of Jacob and one of his concubines who gave his name to one of the twelve tribes of Israel. The tribal area was just W of the Sea of Galilee (Ge. 30:7-8; Jos. 20:7).

NAPHTUHIM, NAPHTUHITES A people of Egypt descended from Ham. Much conjecture exists as to their location and relationships (Ge. 10:13; 1Ch. 1:11).

NAPKIN KJV for "piece of cloth" (Lk.

19:20), "cloth" (Jn. 11:44), "burial cloth" (Jn. 20:7). There is no relationship with the modern day napkin.

NARCISSUS Greetings were sent by Paul from Rome to those in his household (Ro. 16:11). †

NARD *See* PLANTS, PERFUMES, AND SPICES, Miscellaneous Plants 9.

NATHAN {gift}
1. A son of David, one in the genealogy of Joseph, the father (so it was thought) of Jesus (2Sa. 5:14; Lk. 3:31).
2. A prophet in David's time who prevented him from building the temple, who rebuked him for his murder of the Hittite and his adultery with Bathsheba, and who supported Solomon for the throne. He wrote a record of the times of both David and Solomon (2Sa. 7:4, 8-13; 12:1-14; 1Ki. 1:38; 1Ch. 29:29; 2Ch. 9:29).
3. The father of Igal, one of David's Thirty (2Sa. 23:36).
4. One sent by Ezra to Casiphia to bring back some Levites after the end of the Babylonian captivity (Ezr. 8:16-17).
5. One who married a foreign wife during the Babylonian captivity (Ezr. 10:39).
6. A Jerahmeelite (1Ch. 2:36).

NATHAN-MELECH {gift of king *or* gift of MELEK, MOLECH, MALK (pagan god)} An official who had a room near the entrance to the house of the LORD (2Ki. 23:11). †

NATHANAEL {gift of El} *See* APOSTLES

NATION This is one English translation for the Hebrew *goy* and the Greek *ethnos*, both meaning nation. While Israel is also called a *goy*, one among the many nations, this word usually refers to non-Israelite nations. Another rare translation in NIV is "pagans" (1Co. 12:2). *See* GENTILES; GOIIM

NATURAL MAN *See* SALVATION, *Election*; SCRIPTURE, last ¶; SIN

NAUGHTINESS *See* SIN

NAUM *See* NAHUM 2.

NAVE KJV for "hub" (1Ki. 7:33). *See also* WHEEL

NAVEL KJV for "muscles" (Job 40:16); "bones" (Pr. 3:8); "(umbilical) cord" (Eze. 16:4); and "navel" (SS. 7:2) in the NIV.

NAVY A fleet of ships. *See* SHIP

NAZARETH, NAZARENE [*possibly* sprout, branch *or* watchtower] A town in lower Galilee in the tribal area of Zebulun. It is never mentioned in the OT, but because of its association with Mary and Jesus, it is many times noted in the NT. A Nazarene, one from that town, was a term often applied to Jesus by himself and by others (Mt. 2:23; 21:11; Mk. 14:67; Ac. 2:22; 22:8). The followers are once referred to as the sect of the Nazarene (Ac. 24:5).

NAZARETH IN GALILEE (Arrows show route of Jesus' early ministry.)

NAZARETH DECREE Discovered in 1878, this is a decree dating from about A.D. 50, which states the death sentence be given to anyone disturbing a tomb, as the apostles were accused of (Mt. 28:11-13). Many argue that this was the emperor's response to the Resurrection event.

NAZARITE, NAZIRITE(S) [one under sacred vow] These were people in Israel who renounced grapes and all grape products (including wine), who renounced the use of the razor, and who could never come in touch with a dead body. The laws relative to them are found in Nu. 6:1-23 (*see also* Jdg. 13:5). John the Baptist was probably a Nazirite from birth (Lk. 1:15). Nazirite vows generally were permanent; they could also be temporal to fulfill some special need of the one taking upon himself or herself the vow (Ac. 21:23-27). One should note that though spelled similarly, Nazarene and Nazirite are two separate ideas in the original text.

NEAH An unidentified site in the tribal area of Zebulun (Jos. 19:13). †

NEAPOLIS [new city] The seaport of Philippi in ancient Macedonia which was visited by Paul on his second missionary journey (Ac. 16:11). †

NEARIAH [(young) man of Yahweh]
1. A descendant of Judah and David in the royal line (1Ch. 3:22-23). †
2. A descendant of Simeon (1Ch. 4:42). †

NEBAI [thrive] One who signed the covenant with Nehemiah (Ne. 10:19). †

NEBAIOTH, NEBAJOTH A son of Ishmael and grandson of Abraham (Ge. 25:13).

NEBALLAT A town (146-154) in the tribal area of Benjamin mentioned with Lod and Ono (Ne. 11:34). †

NEBAT [look to, regard (approvingly)] The father of Jeroboam the first king of the northern kingdom, Israel (1Ki. 11:26).

NEBO, MOUNT [height *or* Mt. of NABU (NEBO)] *See also* DEITIES 1., and GEOGRAPHY OF THE HOLY LAND

NEBO-SARSEKIM The name or title of one of the princes of Babylon involved in the final taking of Jerusalem (Jer. 39:3). This is the NIV rendering; in the other versions the "Nebo" goes with the prior word. † *See* SAMGAR-NEBO

NEBUCHADNEZZAR, NEBUCHA-DREZZAR [NEBO protect my boundary stone, BDB and IDB; NEBO protect my son!, KB] A king of Babylon, often mentioned in the Bible, who lived in the beginning of the sixth century B.C. The latter form of the name is found in NIV only in the footnotes to "Nebuchadnezzar" in Jeremiah and Ezekiel. He was the son and successor of the founder of the Neo-Babylonian Empire and the victor over the Egyptians at Carchemish on the Euphrates (2Ch. 35:20; Jer. 46:2). This important victory put the entire area, including Palestine, under his control (2Ki. 24:1). Several kings of Judah, Jehoiakim, Jehoiachin, Zedekiah, and governor Gedaliah were his tools and puppets. See BABYLON and KINGS OF JUDAH AND ISRAEL

NEBUSHASBAN, NEBUSHAZBAN [NEBO (Nabu) save me!] An officer of King Nebuchadnezzar of Babylon in the siege of Jerusalem (Jer. 39:11-14).

NEBUZARADAN [NEBO (Nabu) has given seed (offspring)] A commanding officer of Nebuchadnezzar at the destruction of the temple and the city of Jerusalem who was ordered to take care of Jeremiah (2Ki. 25:8-10; Jer. 39:11).

NECHO See NECO

NECKLACE A chain worn around the neck for ornaments or rings (SS. 4:9).

NECO The Pharaoh of Egypt who assisted the Assyrians in their last days, removed Jehoahaz from Judah's throne and placed Jehoiakim upon it, killed King Josiah in battle, and then marched to Carchemish to fight the Babylonians where he was defeated by Nebuchadnezzar (2Ki. 23:29-35; 2Ch. 35:20−36:4; Jer. 46:2).

NECROMANCER [mantic conjurer of dead] See DIVINATION

NEDABIAH [Yahweh volunteers] A descendant of King Jehoiachin (1Ch. 3:18). †

NEEDLE, EYE OF The phrase is found only in one statement by Jesus in Mt. 19:24 and its parallels in Mark and Luke. He was teaching how impossible it is for one bound up in his riches to enter the kingdom of God. There seems to be no support for the idea of the eye of a needle being a small gate within a larger one.

NEEDLEWORK See EMBROIDER

NEESING KJV for "sneezing" (Job 41:18).

NEGEV, NEGEB [dry (land), *hence* south country] See GEOGRAPHY OF THE HOLY LAND

NEGINAH See PSALMS, TITLES OF 10. (7)

NEHELAM, NEHELAMITE An unidentified place from which came the false prophet who opposed Jeremiah (Jer. 29:24-32).

NEHEMIAH [Yahweh has comforted]
  1. One who returned from the Babylonian captivity with Zerubbabel (Ezr. 2:2).
  2. One who was the son of Azbuk and who helped in the repair of the walls of Jerusalem (Ne. 3:16).
  3. The cupbearer to the Persian king Artaxerxes (Ne. 1:11), who returned to Jerusalem with the blessing of the king in order to hasten the finishing of the rebuilding of the city and wall. He returned to Babylon but soon came back to Jerusalem to deal with irregularities there. Details are scattered throughout the book that bears his name.

NEHEMIAH, BOOK OF The book that records the rebuilding of Jerusalem and the reforms instituted by Nehemiah in the worship of God in the restored temple. It covers the final history of Israel to be recorded in the OT from about 445-420 B.C. Chapters one and two record his return to Jerusalem, followed by an account of the rebuilding under great difficulties caused by some who did not wish to see the city rebuilt (3:1−7:4). Genealogies of those who returned from the captivity in Babylon are recorded (7:5-73). The spiritual revival and signing of a covenant are found in three chapters (8−10). Prior to the dedication of the completed walls and final reforms, some additional genealogies are recorded (11–13).

NEHUM {comfort} One who returned from the Babylonian captivity with Zerubbabel (Ne. 7:7). † *See* REHUM

NEHUSHTA {(strong as *or* color of) bronze} The wife of Judah's King Jehoiachin (2Ki. 24:8). †

NEHUSHTAN {*combination of* bronze *and* viper} *See* SERPENT OF BRONZE

NEIEL A town (171-255) on the border between Asher and Zebulun (Jos. 19:27). †

NEIGHBOR
1. In the OT a neighbor was a fellow member of the community of Israel (Lev. 19:16-18; Dt. 5:20-21).
2. In the NT a neighbor is a person who extends himself to do kind acts to all mankind, even despised mankind (Lk. 10:25-37—the story of the Good Samaritan). The good neighbor in the story of the Good Samaritan was the man who had compassion.

NEKEB {passage, tunnel} *See* ADAMI NEKEB

NEKODA
1. Ancestor of some temple servants who returned from the Babylonian captivity with Zerubbabel (Ezr. 2:48).
2. Ancestor of some who returned with Zerubbabel but could not prove their Israelite ancestry (Ezr. 2:60).

NEMUEL, NEMUELITE(S)
1. A son of Simeon (Nu. 26:12); also called Jemuel and his clan (Ge. 46:10).
2. A descendant of Reuben (Nu. 26:9).

NEOORTHODOXY This theology is associated with Karl Barth, Emil Brunner, Reinhold Niebuhr, and many others. It was a reaction against liberalism. It was an attempt to recover biblical perspectives. Stress is given to the transcendence of God, reality of sin and guilt, personal responsibility, the uniqueness of Christ as mediator of revelation and grace, and a personal subjective encoun-

ter with God. The neoorthodox position accepts higher criticism. In this system, the Bible is (becomes a witness to) the Word of God as you encounter it. *See* HERMENEUTICS, *existential*

NEO-PENTECOSTAL *See* CHARISMATIC MOVEMENT

NEPHEG
1. A descendant of Levi (Ex. 6:21). †
2. A son of David (2Sa. 5:15; 1Ch. 3:7; 14:6). †

NEPHILIM {ones falling (upon), *hence* violent ones, *possibly* giants} Although translated "giants" in the KJV, the meaning of the word is not clear and hence the Hebrew word is simply transliterated in the NIV. They were probably not angelic fallen beings. They are called also "sons of Anak," a reference which is of little value in determining who or what they were (Ge. 6:4; Nu. 13:33).

NEPHISH *See* NAPHISH

NEPHISHESIM *See* NEPHUSIM

NEPHTHALIM, NEPTHALIM *See* NAPHTALI

NEPHTOAH, WATERS OF A spring (168-133) on the border between Judah and Benjamin (Jos. 15:9; 18:15). The Egyptian word for water was *mer*. Thus this site in Egyptian was *mer nephtah*, the name of one of their kings. †

NEPHUSIM, NEPHUSSIM Ancestors of some temple servants who returned from the Babylonian captivity with Zerubbabel (Ezr. 2:50; Ne. 7:52). †

NER {lamp} The father of Abner, the commander of Saul's army (1Sa. 14:50-51).

NEREUS {pagan Gr. deity} A Christian in Rome to whom Paul sent greetings (Ro. 16:15). †

NERGAL {pagan deity} 2Ki. 17:30. † *See* DEITIES 1.

NERGAL-SHAREZER {Nergal protect the prince!} The officer of Nebuchadnezzar who released the prophet Jeremiah from prison (Jer. 39:3, 13-14). †

NERI {lamp of Yahweh} Ancestor of Joseph, the father (so it was thought) of Jesus (Lk. 3:27). †

NERIAH {lamp of Yahweh} Father of Baruch, the scribe of Jeremiah (Jer. 32:12).

NERIGLISSAR *See* NERGAL-SHAREZER

NERO {family name} *See* EMPEROR, EMPIRE; ROME, ROMAN CITIZEN

NESTORIAN A theologian of the fifth century A.D. who said that the nature of Jesus Christ was actually two distinct persons—one human, one divine. This view was condemned at the Council of Ephesus in A.D. 431, reaffirming the Nicene Creed.

NET String or cord woven into mesh and used for the catching of birds, fish, or animals. In the NT the word is used only in the literal sense. In the OT it is used figuratively of chastisement of a people or a person, or of snares that might entrap them (Job 19:6; Ps. 10:9).

Ancient Egyptians Fishing with a Dragnet

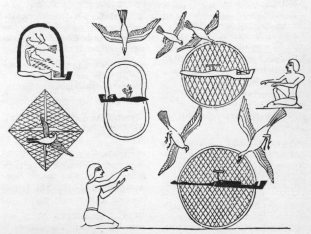

Ancient Egyptian Bird-traps

NETAIM {plantings} An unidentified site in the tribal area of Judah, where some potters lived (1Ch. 4:23). †

NETHANEL, NETHANEEL {El has given}
1. The representative of the tribe of Issachar chosen to assist Moses (Nu. 1:8; 7:18, 23).
2. A brother of King David (1Ch. 2:14).
3. A priest in the time of David whose duty was to blow the trumpet before the Ark (1Ch. 15:24).
4 and 5. A Levite and a gatekeeper in David's day (1Ch. 24:6; 26:4).
6. One sent by King Jehoshaphat to the towns to teach his people (2Ch. 17:7).
7. A Levite in the days of King Josiah of Judah (2Ch. 35:9).
8. A priest who married a foreign wife during the time of the Babylonian captivity (Ezr. 10:22).
9. The head of a priestly family in the days of Joiakim and Nehemiah (Ne. 12:21).
10. A priest who was with Nehemiah at the dedication of the rebuilt walls of Jerusalem (Ne. 12:36).

NETHANIAH {Yahweh has given}
1. The father of one by the name of Ishmael in the last days of Judah. Ishmael assassinated Gedaliah (2Ki. 25:23, 25).
2. A son of Asaph the seer in David's day (1Ch. 25:2, 12).
3. One of the Levites sent out by Jehoshaphat to teach (2Ch. 17:8).
4. The father of one sent to remonstrate with Baruch, Jeremiah's scribe (Jer. 36:14).

NETHERWORLD *See* DEAD, ABODE OF

NETHINIM {(those) given (to service)} KJV for "temple servants" (Ezr. 2:43).

NETOPHAH, NETOPHATHI, NETOPHATHITES {trickle, drip} Netophah was a town (171-119) in the hill country of Judah near Bethlehem (2Sa. 23:28-29; Ezr. 2:22; 1Ch. 9:16).

NETTLE *See* PLANTS, PERFUMES, AND SPICES, Spiny Plants

NETWORK *See* GRATE, GRATING

NEW JERUSALEM A new holy city where God himself will dwell (Rev. 3:12; 21:2).

NEW MOON, FEAST OF *See* CALENDAR and FESTIVALS

NEW TESTAMENT *See* ACTS, BOOK OF; CANON; CHRONOLOGY; GOSPELS, THE FOUR; HEBREWS, BOOK OF; JAMES, EPISTLE OF; JOHN, EPISTLES OF; JUDE, EPISTLE OF; PAUL, LIFE AND TEACHINGS OF; PAULINE EPISTLES; PETER, EPISTLES OF; REVELATION, BOOK OF; SCRIPTURE; TESTAMENT

NEW YEAR *See* FESTIVALS 4., *Feast of Trumpets*

NEWS, GOOD Besides its use to refer to news in general, the words are used together with others, such as "good news about Jesus" (Ac. 8:35), "good news of the kingdom of God" (Lk. 4:43), "the good news is preached to the poor" (Mt. 11:5). In these and similar cases it is the gospel news about the person and work of Christ relative to salvation that is the point of reference. *See* GOSPEL

NEZIAH {director (of worship)} Ancestor of some temple servants who returned from the Babylonian captivity with Zerubbabel (Ezr. 2:54; Ne. 7:56). †

NEZIB {pillar, garrison} A village (151-110) in the western foothills of the tribal area of Judah (Jos. 15:43). †

NIBHAZ *See* DEITIES 1.

NIBSHAN A town (186-123) in the desert of the tribal area of Judah (Jos. 15:62). †

NICANOR {victor} One of the first seven chosen to assist the Twelve in the temporal affairs of the church; called deacons in the KJV (Ac. 6:5). †

NICENE CREED *See* CONFESSION 2.

NICODEMUS {victor over people} A member of the council who came to enquire of Jesus by night with the result that Jesus gave him the most famous reference to the new birth (Jn. 3:3-8, 16). The entire account appears in John 3. He also spoke for Jesus to the leaders of his day and later brought spices for the burial of Jesus and assisted Joseph of Arimathea in the entombment (Jn. 7:45-50; 19:39). †

NICOLAITANS, NICOLAITANES {follower of NICOLAS} *See* SECTS

NICOLA(U)S {victor over people} One of the groups of seven chosen to assist in the temporal affairs of the church, called deacons in the KJV (Ac. 6:5). †

NICOPOLIS {victory city} A city on the W coast of Greece where Paul determined to winter on one occasion (Tit. 3:12). †

NIGER {black} A prophet or teacher in the church at Antioch. He is referred to as "Simeon called Niger" (Ac. 13:1). †

NIGHT *See* TIME; WATCH

NIGHTHAWK *See* BIRDS 5.

NILE The main river of Egypt, starting on the equator, flowing 2,500 miles to the Mediterranean. The Hebrew text uses the word for a stream with the definite article preceding it. *The* stream in Egypt is, of course, the Nile. Hence the NIV renders, "the stream" in Hebrew by "Nile" in English (Ge. 41:1; Ex. 4:9; Isa. 19:5-6). No reference to it is found in the NT.

NIMRAH {spotted leopard, BDB; basin of limpid (clear) water, KB} An unidentified site in Gilead assigned to the tribal area of Gad (Nu. 32:3).

NIMRIM, WATERS OF {limpid (clear) waters, KB; wholesome waters, BDB; *possibly* waters of leopards, IDB} An unidentified source of water in Moab which the prophets said were "desolate" (Isa. 15:6; Jer. 48:34). †

NIMROD A grandson of Ham and described as a mighty hunter and founder of an area called the land of

THE NILE RIVER IN EGYPT

Nimrod (Ge. 10:9; 1Ch. 1:10—see NIV footnote; Mic. 5:6).

NIMRUD *See* CALNEH

NIMSHI Father or perhaps grandfather of King Jehu of Israel (1Ki. 19:16; 2Ki. 9:2, 14, 20; 2Ch. 22:7). †

NINEVE(H) A city founded by Nimrod, the great-grandson of Noah. It was important throughout all the history of the Middle East until the fall of the Assyrian Empire to Babylon in 612 B.C. It is located on the Tigris opposite modern Mosul. *See also* ASSYRIA and NIMROD

NIRVANA The aspiration of the Hindu. To have attained this state of being is to have ended the cycles of reincarnation. *See* BUDDHISM; HINDUISM

NISAN *See* CALENDAR

NISROCH *See* DEITIES 1.

NITER {carbonate of soda, lye} *See* SOAP

NO *See* THEBES

NO BE NO *See* YES BE YES

NOAMMON *See* THEBES

NOADIAH {meet with Yahweh}
1. A Levite treasurer in the temple (Ezr. 8:33).
2. A prophetess opposed to Nehemiah (Ne. 6:14). †

JONAH'S JOURNEY TO NINEVEH
Jonah began in Joppa (in a ship heading to Tarshish), returned back to Israel, and went on to Nineveh, the capital of the Assyrian Empire.

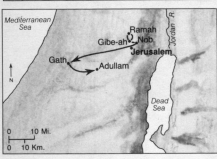

DAVID'S ESCAPE TO NOB
When David learned of Saul's plans to kill him, he fled to Samuel at Ramah, returned to Gibeah to say farewell to Jonathan, then escaped to Nob where he received food and Goliath's sword from the priest. He then fled to Gath and on to a cave near Adullam.

NOAH {rest, comfort}

1. A daughter of Zelophehad who had no sons (Nu. 26:33).

2. The maker of the ark that saved people and animals in the great Flood, and the father of Shem, Ham, and Japheth. The rainbow was given to him by God as a sign of his covenant never again to destroy the earth by a flood. (Ge. 6; 9:8, 13-17). *See* ARK 1.; FLOOD

NOB A town (173-134) in the tribal area of Benjamin. The incident with Doeg the Edomite against the priests (because they had helped David) took place here (1Sa. 21:1; 22:9-19; Ne. 11:32; Isa. 10:32). †

NOBAH

1. A descendant of Manasseh who conquered the town of Kenath (302-241) and named it after himself (Nu. 32:42). †

2. An unidentified site near which judge Gideon defeated the Midianites (Jdg. 8:11). †

NOBAI {fruitful one of Yahweh} *See* NEBAI

NOD {wandering} An unidentified district E of Eden to which Cain went (Ge. 4:16). †

NODAB An unidentified site E of Judah against which Israel made war (1Ch. 5:19). †

NOE *See* NOAH

NOGAH {joy, splendor} A son of David (1Ch. 3:7; 14:6). †

NOHAH {rest} A son of Benjamin (1Ch. 8:2; cf. Ge. 46:21). †

NON *See* NUN

NOON In the NT this was the sixth hour, the middle of the day.

NOPH *See* MEMPHIS

NOPHAH A town of Moab (Nu. 21:30). †

NORTH, DIRECTION OF See GE-OGRAPHY OF THE HOLY LAND, III. *Topography, Setting*

NORTHEASTER, WIND See EU-ROCLYDON

NOSE JEWEL KJV for "nose ring" (Isa. 3:19). *See* DRESS

NOSE, NOSTRILS, NOSE RING The nose is the normal organ of breathing, but as the nostrils quiver when one is angry (a "hot nose"), one word serves in Hebrew both for the organ itself and for the emotion "anger" (Ge. 27:45; Ex. 4:14; 11:8). For the Hebrew word "nose" the NIV translators used "organ" and "face" as well as "nose" (Ge. 19:1). Ps. 10:4 in Hebrew reads literally "the height of his nose." It is translated "in his pride." The phrase "slow to anger" is an interesting case in point (Ex. 34:6; Ne. 9:17), literally, slow of nostrils. Rings for adornment were sometimes placed in the nose as also was the ring or hook of captivity (Ge. 24:47; Isa. 37:29).

NOVICE KJV for "recent convert" (1Ti. 3:6). †

NUMBERED (CENSUS) See CENSUS

NUMBERS, BOOK OF See PEN-TATEUCH

NUMBERS, SIGNIFICANCE OF From early times the Hebrews used the decimal system in counting, as is clear from the emphasis on the tens and hundreds. The numbers were first spelled out as words, then the letters of the alphabet in sequence stood for the numbers, *aleph* for one, *beth* for two, *gimel* for three, etc. There was also a system of strokes, but of its origin and development not too much is yet known. This came in some time after the return from Babylon. Numbers were also used symbolically throughout the ancient world and in the Bible as well. Considerable caution must be exercised in interpreting numbers symbolically since much subjectivity is involved. Each number stands for many things, and thus

there is not, nor can be, complete agreement as to just exactly what a given number symbolized. For an example, the number three may be taken by some to be the symbol of the Trinity. Obviously it does not mean that in the interpretation of Jews. To some, three means emphasis, or even completeness (but so does seven). There were to be three festivals per year, daily prayers were to be three times in the day, there was a taboo on the fruit of a tree for its first three years, ritual baths were to be on the third as well as the seventh day (Ex. 23:14; Da. 6:10; Lev. 19:23; Nu. 19:11-12). Some numbers seem to have been used, in some cases at least, as round numbers. Such is forty for a generation and seventy for the number of sons a famous man is supposed to have. Nor is it always possible to be certain that a small number does not merely represent "a few" and not an exact number. This would be an idiomatic and not a symbolic use, as in Isa. 17:6 and Jer. 36:23. A further idiomatic use would be the fairly numerous use in poetry of the three-four or four-five motif (Pr. 30:15, 18, 29). Of even the number seven, by all considered to be the most symbolic, one may only state that its symbolic uses are so many and varied that it is virtually impossible to summarize them briefly. Among the more common would be completeness, finality or consummation, perfection, or infamy (Pr. 6:16-19). Seven days make a full week and seven years a cycle. Caution is thus advised in making too much of numbers in biblical interpretation. See *also* FORTY

NUN [fish *hence* fertile, productive] The father of Joshua (Ex. 33:11). Nothing more is known about him.

NURSE The word has three usages in the Bible, none corresponding to the concept of nurse in modern medical terms. One is the maid; another the wet-nurse who supplied milk for a baby when the mother for any reason was not able; third is the man or woman who cared for the small children in a family (Ge. 24:59; Ex. 2:7; 2Ki. 11:2; 2Sa. 4:4). The word *nurse* is also used in a figurative sense (Nu. 11:12; Isa. 49:23).

NUTS *See* PLANTS, PERFUMES, AND SPICES, Plants for Food 6.

NYMPHA(S) The Christian lady of Colosse in whose home the early church of Colosse met (Col. 4:15). †

O

OAK *See* TREES

OAK, DIVINER'S *See* MEONENIM

OAK, MAMRE *See* MAMRE

OARSMAN *See* SHIP

OATH This was an appeal to God to be a witness of the truth of some statement, or of the binding character of some promise or agreement (Ge. 21:24; 24:41-53; 2Ch. 15:12-14). In addition to swearing by God "as surely as the LORD lives," swearing was done by the name of the other person, by one's own head, by the life of the king, by the temple, by Jerusalem, but never by a strange god (1Sa. 14:39; 1:26; Mt. 23:16; 1Sa. 17:55; Jos. 23:7). Jesus forbade swearing by heaven, by earth, or by Jerusalem, and gives his reasons in Mt. 5:34-36. This indicates that others used those terms in oaths.

OBADIAH [servant (worshiper) of Yahweh]

1. A descendant of Gad who defeated David's forces (1Ch. 12:9).

2. The father of the representative of the tribe of Zebulun in David's administration (1Ch. 27:19).

3. The steward of King Ahab who feared God and hid his prophets from Jezebel who determined their death (1Ki. 18:3ff.).

4. One of the men whom King Jehoshaphat sent to teach his people (2Ch. 17:7).

5. A Levite overseer in the days of the reforms of King Josiah of Judah (2Ch. 34:12).

6. A descendant of David who lived after the return from the Babylonian captivity (1Ch. 3:21).

7. A descendant of Issachar (1Ch. 7:3).

8. A descendant of King Saul (1Ch. 8:38).

9. A Levite of postexilic times; also called Abda (1Ch. 9:16; Ne. 11:17).

10. The head of a family who returned from the Babylonian captivity with Ezra (Ezr. 8:9).

11. One who signed the covenant with Nehemiah (Ne. 10:5).

12. A gatekeeper in the days of Joiakim and Nehemiah (Ne. 12:25).

13. One of the "minor" prophets known only by his book, one chapter in length. *See* PROPHETS, BOOKS OF THE MINOR

OBADIAH, BOOK OF *See* PROPHETS, BOOKS OF THE MINOR

OBAL *See* EBAL 2.

OBED [servant (worshiper)]

1. An ancestor of Joseph, the father (so it was thought) of Jesus (Lk. 3:32), and the son of Boaz and Ruth (Ru. 4:17-21).

2. A descendant of Judah and Jerahmeel (1Ch. 2:37).

3. One of David's mighty men (1Ch. 11:47).

4. A gatekeeper of the tabernacle in David's day (1Ch. 26:7).

5. Father of one who helped Jehoiada put the youthful Joash on the throne (2Ch. 23:1).

OBED-EDOM {servant (worshiper) of EDOM}

1. The name of the man in whose house David left the Ark after the death of Uzzah, who died because he touched it (2Sa. 6:10-11).

2. A gatekeeper before the Ark in David's time (1Ch. 15:18; 16:38).

3. A keeper of the temple gold, silver and vessels in the days of King Amaziah (2Ch. 25:24).

OBEDIENCE, OBEY In both Testaments the words for obey carry also the idea of hearing. The two concepts are inseparable. The Hebrew *shama* means both "to listen to" and "obey," as does also the Greek word *hupakouo*. The biblical concept is, then, of a hearing that takes place and the need to comply with what is heard. The child hears and obeys his parents, the pupil his teachers, the employee his employer, all mankind hears God and is expected to obey (Ex. 19:5; Col. 3:20, 22 – in both cases the Hebrew and Greek is the usual word for "to hear"). Obedience to God's laws and statutes was the expected way of living for the Israelite (Lev. 18:4-5). Disobedience would bring severe punishment, even *diaspora* (Dt. 28:58-59, 64). Obedience is the supreme test of faith in God (1Sa. 15:22-24), or, as the NT puts it, "Faith without works is dead" (Jas. 2:14-26). Thus obedience and faith are always very closely linked in the Bible. The most illuminating illustration to be found is in the treatment of the incidents in the life of Abraham in the NT (Ro. 4:1-3; Jas. 2:21-26).

Another Hebrew word is also translated in the NIV as "obey." Its basic meaning is "to guard." Thus the language of the OT has the two: obey equals "hear" and obey equals "guard" (Ps. 119:8, 17, 34; Ex. 34:11).

OBEISANCE See WORSHIP

OBEY See OBEDIENCE

OBIL {camel driver} An Ishmaelite who was in charge of the camels of David (1Ch. 27:30). †

OBLATION See SACRIFICES AND OFFERINGS

OBOTH An unidentified stopping place on the Israelites' journey to Moab during their desert wanderings (Nu. 21:10-11; 33:43-44). †

OBSERVE See OBEDIENCE

OCCULT Latin for something secret or concealed. See DIVINATION

OCCUPATIONS AND PROFESSIONS See BARBER'S; BLACKSMITH; BRASS; BRASSWORKER; CARPENTER; CONFECTIONARY (PERFUMER); COPPERSMITH (METAL WORKER); CRAFTSMEN; ENGRAVER; GARDENER; GOLDSMITH; HUSBANDMAN; MASON; SILVERSMITH; SMITH; TENTMAKER

OC(H)RAN {trouble} The father of the man from the tribe of Asher who assisted Moses in the taking of the census (Nu. 1:13; 2:27; 7:72, 77; 10:26). †

ODED {restorer}

1. The father of the prophet who spoke for God to King Asa (2Ch. 15:1, 8ff.). †

2. A prophet who opposed the attempts of King Pekah of Israel to enslave men and women from the tribe of Judah (2Ch. 28:9ff.). †

ODOR See AROMA

OFFERING See SACRIFICES AND OFFERINGS

OFFICIALS OF THE PROVINCE, THE See ASIARCHS

OG The king of Bashan who was defeated by the Israelites under Moses and his territory given to the tribe of Manasseh. He was a man of gigantic proportions needing an oversized bed (Nu. 21:33ff.; Dt. 3:11; Jos. 13:29-30).

OHAD A son of Simeon (Ge. 46:10; Ex. 6:15). †

OHEL [(skin) tent] A son of Zerubbabel in the royal line after the exile (1Ch. 3:20). †

OHOLAH [she who has a tent] In the parable concerning Judah and Israel in Eze. 23:4-44, she is called a prostitute. Her sister, symbolizing the Kingdom of Judah, is called Oholibah. Oh:olah (Samaria), according to her symbolic name, had a "tent" which was Samaria's own sanctuary. Oholibah (Judah) had Yahweh's sanctuary (tent), hence the name "My tent is in her." With the first he predicts the Assyrian captivity and with the second the Babylonian. †

OHOLIAB [tent of (my) Father] An assistant of Bezalel the craftsman who assisted in the detail work of the tent of meeting (the tabernacle), the Ark of the Testimony, and the other furnishings (Ex. 31:6; 35:34; 36:1-2; 38:23). †

OHOLIBAH [my tent is in her] See OHOLAH

OHOLIBAMAH [(my) tent is a high-place]
1. A wife of Esau (Ge. 36:2).
2. A chief of Edom descended from Esau (Ge. 36:41).

OIL In the Bible "oil" almost always signifies olive oil, which was used for food, cooking, medication, and lamp oil, in addition to its use in ceremonial anointing (Ex. 29:2; 25:6; 29:7; Lk. 10:34). Olive oil was made by smashing or beating the olives in a mortar or rock carved press. The process was similar to that involving the grape press (*see* WINE). The crushed olives were strained by draining and the remainder was the "pure" or "clear" oil (Ex. 27:20; Lev. 24:2). This oil was the best oil, what a cook today would call "virgin oil." The remaining pulp was then heated, pressed under pressure, and the oil skimmed off the top as the sediment settled. *See also* ANOINT

OIL TREE *See* PLANTS, PERFUMES, AND SPICES, Flowering Plants 6., *olive tree*

OINTMENT *See* PLANTS, PERFUMES, AND SPICES

OLD TESTAMENT *See* CHRONOLOGY; DECALOGUE; ELDER; KINGS OF JUDAH AND ISRAEL; LAW; PROPHETS, BOOKS OF THE MINOR; PENTATEUCH; PROMISE; PROPHETS; PSALMS; SABBATH; SACRIFICES AND OFFERINGS; SCRIPTURE; TABERNACLE; TEMPLE; TRIBES

OLIVE *See* TREES

OLIVES, MOUNT OF, OLIVET *See* GEOGRAPHY OF THE HOLY LAND

OLIVEYARD KJV for "olive grove."

OLYMPAS A Roman Christian to whom Paul sent greetings (Ro. 16:15). †

OMAR [speaker] An Edomite, a grandson of Esau (Ge. 36:11, 15; 1Ch. 1:36).

OMEGA The last letter of the Greek alphabet, used as a title of Christ in Revelation (1:8; 21:6; 22:13). † *See* GOD, NAMES OF, GODHEAD 7.

OMEN *See* DIVINATION

OMER *See* WEIGHTS AND MEASURES

OMNIPOTENCE [all power] *See* ATTRIBUTES OF GOD

OMNIPRESENCE [all presence] *See* ATTRIBUTES OF GOD

OMNISCIENCE [all knowing] *See* ATTRIBUTES OF GOD

OMRI [worshiper of Yahweh]
1. *See* KINGS OF JUDAH AND ISRAEL.
2 and 3. Descendants of Judah and Benamin (1Ch. 7:8; 9:4).
4. David's officer over the tribe of Issachar (1Ch. 27:18).

ON
1. A descendant of Reuben (Nu. 16:1).
2. *See also* HELIOPOLIS.

ONAM [intense, strong]
1. A grandson of Seir, a Horite, and

descendant of Esau (Ge. 36:23; 1Ch. 1:40). †

2. A descendant of Judah, a Jerahmeelite (1Ch. 2:26, 28). †

ONAN {powerful, intense} A son of Judah who refused to do his duty as a brother-in-law, for which God put him to death (Ge. 38:4, 10). *See* MARRIAGE

ONE ANOTHER The Greek word for one another (*allelon*) has the idea of mutuality and reciprocity. It is a beautiful and edifying concept pertaining to Christian interpersonal relationships. Jesus commands that Christians are to love one another (Jn. 13:34-35; 15:12, 17). The NT writers give the church varied exhortations to promote a rich church life (*see* Ro. 12:10, 16; 13:8; 14:13, 19; 15:5, 7, 14; 16:16; 1Co. 11:33; 12:25; Gal. 5:13, 15, 26; 6:2; Eph. 4:2, 25, 32; 5:21; Php. 2:3; Col. 3:9, 13; 1Th. 3:12; 4:9, 18; 5:11, 15; Heb. 10:24; Jas. 4:11; 5:9, 16; 1Pe. 1:22; 4:9; 5:5; 1 Jn. 3:11).

ONESIMUS {useful} The slave of Philemon who ran away from his master. He became a Christian, and Paul sent him back to his master with the request that he be freed (Col. 4:9; Phm. 1:8ff.). †

ONESIPHORUS {one bringing usefulness} One whose household was commended by Paul because its head (Onesiphorus) had often been kind to Paul during his imprisonment in Rome (2Ti. 1:16-18; 4:19). †

ONION *See* PLANTS, PERFUMES, AND SPICES, Plants for Food 3.

ONLY BEGOTTEN A Greek word for "unique." In the writings of John only used of Jesus (Jn. 1:14; 3:16; 1Jn. 4:9). In certain cases it is analogous to "firstborn."

ONO A town (137-159) in the coastal plain in the tribal area of Benjamin (1Ch. 8:12). After the return from the Babylonian captivity, many settled there (Ezr. 2:33; Ne. 6:2; 7:37; 11:35).

ONYCHA *See* PLANTS, PERFUMES, AND SPICES

ONYX *See* PRECIOUS STONES AND METALS

OPHEL {mound, hill} *See* JERUSALEM

OPHIR

1. A descendant of Shem (Ge. 10:29).

2. The unidentified land occupied by the descendants of Ophir, 1. It was an area where there was much gold. It required sailing to get there (1Ki. 9:28; 10:11; 2Ch. 9:10; Isa. 13:12). Much was brought from there to Israel by Solomon and Hiram of Tyre.

OPHNI An unidentified site in the tribal area of Benjamin (Jos. 18:24). †

OPHRAH {young gazelle}

1. A descendant of Judah and Othniel (1Ch. 4:14).

2. A town (178-151) in the tribal area of Benjamin modern et Taiyiba (Jos. 18:23).

3. A town (177-223) in the tribal area of Manasseh that belonged to the Abiezrites where the angel of the LORD commissioned Gideon as judge of Israel (Jdg. 6:11, 15, 24; 8:27, 32).

OPHRAH
The angel of the Lord appeared to Gideon at Ophrah.

ORACLE {speak} The word is used of the introductory formula to a message usually given by God directly to a prophet but may also be of human origin (Nu. 24:22-24; Pr. 30:1; 31:1; Isa. 15:1; 17:1; 19:1; 21:1, 11). The word itself is not used in the NIV but "words of God" replace it. The reference is to God's revelation, the Bible itself. *See* DIVINATION; PROPHET

ORAL TRANSMISSION Passing on of traditions or teachings by a spoken form, as opposed to a written form.

ORATOR *See* (for OT) DIVINATION; (for NT) DIVINATION 2., *Enchanter*; LAWYER

ORCHESTRA *See* MUSIC, MUSICAL INSTRUMENTS

ORDAIN In the OT the English translation of a number of Greek and Hebrew words which carry the idea of instituting how to do something in the prescribed manner and setting apart someone or something for a special duty or office, with or without a ceremony (1Ki. 12:33; 1Ch. 15:13; Ex. 29:9, 29, 33-35). In the NT hands were laid on officers of the church for certain work, yet though there is no instruction that it be done or perpetuated (1Ti. 4:14; 2Ti. 1:6). The practice was extended in post-NT times. *See* LAITY

ORDINANCE A practice carried out in obedience to Christ. It is distinguished from a sacrament which is believed to merit grace or even salvation. An ordinance is seen as a memorial or simple act of obedience and does not merit grace or salvation.

ORDINATION The practice of setting a person apart for ministry. Some believe it gives special powers for ministry. Others believe it a public recognition that the one ordained has God's approval. *See also* LAYING ON OF HANDS

OREB {raven} A leader of Midian captured and killed in Gideon's victory over Midian (Jdg. 7:25; 8:3; Ps. 83:11; Isa. 10:26). †

OREB, ROCK OF The place where Oreb was killed. *See* OREB; *see also* ZEEB

OREN {fir or cedar, BDB and IDB; lau-

rel, KB} A Jerahmeelite descendant of Judah (1Ch. 2:25). †

ORGAN *See* MUSIC, MUSICAL INSTRUMENTS, *Flute*

ORIENT *See* EAST, DIRECTION OF

ORIGEN A theologian and textual critic who lived in Egypt (A.D. 185 to 254).

ORIGINAL SIN Adam's sin is imputed to all men. *See* IMPUTE

ORION A heavenly constellation mentioned in connection with others, namely the Bear and Pleiades (Job 9:9; 38:31-32; Am. 5:8). †

ORNAMENTS Objects of adornment whether on human or beast (Ge. 24:53; Jdg. 8:26; Pr. 25:12; Isa. 3:16-23; Jer. 2:32). These were also worn by men (Ex. 33:4-6). Crowns, bracelets, pendants, gems, jewels, and crescents (for camels) are all ornaments mentioned in the OT. Ornaments could be a symbol of rulership (Ge. 41:42; Da. 5:7, 16, 29). The following passages also speak of ornaments: 1Ti. 2:9; Jas. 2:2; 1Pe. 3:3-4.

Certain kinds of signet rings were not merely ornamental. They were used to sign documents and prove one's identity. Judah, for example, left the equivalent of his personal identification card in his exchange with Tamar (Ge. 38:18, 25). Similar devices were seals, cylinder seals, and scarabs. *See also* BRACELET; SEAL

ORNAN *See* ARAUNAH

ORONTES *See* ANTIOCH 1.

ORPAH The daughter-in-law of Naomi who did not go with Naomi and Ruth when they returned from Moab to Naomi's country, Israel (Ru. 1:3-4, 14). †

ORPHAN The fatherless. The Bible expresses great concern for them and often enjoins God's people to care for them (Ex. 22:22; Ps. 10:14; Mal. 3:5; Jas. 1:27).

ORTHODOX Conformity to the standard doctrines of the church. The word has also been used in names like the

Eastern Orthodox Church and the Russian Orthodox Church.

OSEE *See* HOSEA

OSHEA *See* JOSHUA

OSNAPPAR A RSV, NASB, NKJV, and ASV Aramaic transliteration in Ezr. 4:10. The KJV and NEB spell it as "Asnapper" with the same meaning. This name means "Ashurbanipal," and is so rendered in the JB and NIV. *See* ASSYRIA last ¶

OSPRAY, OSPREY *See* BIRDS 5., *Black Vulture*

OSSIFRAGE *See* BIRDS 5., *Vulture*

OSTRICH *See* BIRDS 6.

OTHNI A Levitical gatekeeper in the days of David (1Ch. 26:7) †

OTHNIEL *See* JUDGES OF ISRAEL

OUTER COURT *See* MIDDLE WALL OF PARTITION

OVEN The oven for baking in antiquity did not differ greatly from the oven used in modern times by the Bedouin or other primitive peoples of the Middle East. Many ancient ovens have been found in modern excavations. They were, and are, cylindrical structures of clay two or three feet in diameter and two or three feet high. They are usually built on the floor and often inside the house. A quick hot fire was built inside the oven, then the ashes were removed, and the moist flat cakes of dough were stuck on the hot insides of the oven. When dry the dough would fall from the wall and the "bread" would be removed from the oven. Ovens were also made with stone. Grass, thorns, shrubs, and even dung or a mixture of such were used as fuel (Lev. 2:4). In the NT translated as "the fire" (Mt. 6:30, NIV). *See* BREAD; FURNACE

OVERCOME *See* VICTORY

OVERSEER A word used for an office in the NT church. Overseers are frequently designated as "bishops" in various translations (Ac. 20:28; Php. 1:1; 1Ti. 3:1-2; Tit. 1:7). The hierarchical distinction we know today did not begin until after the first century A.D. In 1Pe. 2:25 Jesus is called "Overseer."

OWE *See* DEBT, DEBTOR; USURY

OWL *See* BIRDS 5. and Isa. 34:15.

OX *See* BEASTS 4.

OXGOAD *See* GOAD

OZEM
1. A brother of David (1Ch. 2:15). †
2. A Jerahmeelite and descendant of Caleb (1Ch. 2:25). †

OZIAS *See* UZZIAH 1.

OZNI, OZNITE(S) {my ear, my hearing} A descendant of Gad and his clan (Nu. 26:16); also called Ezbon (Ge. 46:16). †

P

PAARAI *See* NAARAI

PAD(D)AN, PAD(D)AN ARAM {plain of ARAM} *See* ARAM

PADON {ransom} Ancestor of some temple servants who came back from the Babylonian captivity with Zerubbabel (Ezr. 2:44; Ne. 7:47). †

PAGAN *See* GENTILES; GOIIM; NATION

PAGIEL {pleading of El} The representative of the tribe of Asher both when the census was taken in the days of the desert wanderings and later (Nu. 1:13; 2:27; 7:72, 77; 10:26). †

PAHATH-MOAB {supervisor of Moab}
1. The ancestor of some who returned from the Babylonian captivity with Zerubbabel (Ezr. 2:6; 8:4; 10:30; Ne. 7:11). †
2. Father of one who worked on the rebuilding of the wall of Jerusalem in the days of Nehemiah (Ne. 3:11). †
3. One who signed the covenant with Nehemiah (Ne. 10:14). †

PAI *See* PAU

PAINT, PAINTING Paint was used both for persons and things. In the former case it might be eye paint or other cosmetics and in the latter it was liquid color applied to walls, buildings, pottery, carvings, and, in the nonbiblical world, idols. Colors used were blue, green, red, yellow, black, white, and those produced by mixing certain of these. The words themselves are used only a few times in

the Bible and half are in connection with the eyes. The hands, feet, nails, and hair were often stained with henna and produced the characteristic orange-red color. The color, but not its use, is noted twice in the Bible (SS. 1:14; 4:13). For eye paint the special colors were the green copper ore malachite and the dark gray ore of lead galena which were made into a paste and then drawn around the eye to produce an oblong shape, added to the eyebrow to extend it, and sometimes placed under the eye as well (2Ki. 9:30; Jer. 4:30; Eze. 23:40). The son of King Josiah painted his palace with red produced from hematite, or iron ore, a color mentioned again only in connection with the idolatrous drawings of the Assyrians (Jer. 22:14; Eze. 23:14). Much of the painted pottery being found by the archaeologists was also decorated with red hematite, which when baked took on more of a reddish-brown color.

PAINTING THE EYES *See* COSMETICS; PAINT, PAINTING

PALACE The residence of a king or a high dignitary such as the high priest (Mt. 26:3). The first to be noted in the Bible is in the time of David and Solomon (1Ki. 4:6; 1Ch. 28:2). The palace of Ahab follows (1Ki. 22:39; 2Ki. 10:5). Palaces are mentioned several times in the Bible (sometimes fortresses) of: the kings of Babylon, Egypt, Ben-Hadad of Syria (called "fortresses" in Jer. 49:27, NIV), the multiple palaces of Jerusalem, and that of Pilate the Roman procurator are to name a few (Da. 4:29; Jer. 43:9; Est. 2:8; Jer. 17:27; Mk. 15:16). The house of Solomon ("fortress") contained both stone locally cut and much wood supplied by his friend Hiram, king of Tyre (2Ch. 2:1-3, 8-9). Ahab's, on the other hand, was called a house of ivory and contained much decorative ivory and white marble. Perhaps even entire walls were faced with ivory (1Ki. 22:39). While the archaeologists have discovered the locations of many palaces, for the most part they have only the floor plans. It should be remembered that the ravages of time or destruction by ancient conquerors have left nothing but paltry remains except for a few such as the palace of Nebuchadnezzar of Babylon. Some of the literary sources, however, such as those of Josephus, supply valuable descriptions.

PALAL [he has judged] One who worked on the repair of the walls of Jerusalem in the days of Nehemiah (Ne. 3:25). †

PALESTINA KJV for "Philistia" (Ex. 15:14) and "Philistine" (Isa. 14:29, 31).

PALESTINE *See* PHILISTIA

PALLU, PALLUITE(S) [wonderful] A son of Reuben and his clan (Ge. 46:9; Nu. 26:5).

PALM SUNDAY The week before Easter, Christ's entry into Jerusalem (Mt. 21).

PALM TREE *See* TREES

PALMER WORM KJV for a type of locust that cannot be precisely identified (Joel 2:25). *See* BEASTS 6.

PALMYRA *See* TADMOR

PALSY *See* SICK, SICKNESS, *Paralytic, Paralyzed*

PALTI [(El) is (my) deliverance] The representative of the tribe of Benjamin among the twelve spies sent into Canaan by Moses (Nu. 13:9).

PALTIEL [El is (my) deliverance]
1. The representative of the tribe of Issachar in the dividing of the land among the tribes (Nu. 34:26).
2. The man to whom Saul gave his daughter Michal, David's wife, after he had taken her away from David; also called Palti (1Sa. 25:44, and NIV footnote to 2Sa. 3:15).

PALTITE The designation of a man in 2Sa. 23:26; also called a Pelonite. *See* PELONITE

PAMPHYLIA *See* GEOGRAPHY OF THE HOLY LAND

PANNAG Likely some kind of food, this is a transliteration of a Heb. word in some versions. Translated "confections" in Eze. 27:17 (NIV). †

PANTHEISM The belief that God is in the entire physical universe, and the entire physical universe is in God. Thus, God = The Universe. In this concept, God is totally and completely immanent. He is not a god who is a "person."

PAPER *See* PAPYRUS

PAPHOS A city on the island of Cyprus visited by Paul on his first missionary journey where the blinding of the false prophet at the word of Paul led to the conversion of the Roman proconsul Sergius Paulus (Ac. 13:6-14). †

PAPYRUS [reed plant] A reedlike plant growing to heights of over ten feet in aquatic areas, particularly in ancient Egypt, but to some extent in Palestine also. The ancients wove it into mats, used it thus for tents, made baskets and even boats from it. Paper (our word comes from "papyrus") was made by drying together thin strips of the inner pith to a material of the consistency of modern heavy wrapping paper (Job 8:11; Isa. 18:2; 2Jn. 12). It soon becomes brittle and decays easily in damp climates. However, many papyri were well preserved under the sands of Egypt, some of which (when discovered) display significant portions of the New Testament

PAPHOS: Paul went to Paphos on his first missionary journey.

text. *See* BIBLICAL MANUSCRIPTS, *NT Papyri*

PARABLE Used infrequently in the OT (Ps. 78:2; Pr. 26:7, 9; Eze. 17:2; 24:3; Hos. 12:10) and often by Jesus in the Gospels (*see* NT verses below). It is a brief narrative intended to illustrate a single idea. The parable is different from the fable or myth, from the allegory and from the proverb, in that it does not mix the natural and the symbolic. It is a story with a point. But for the few cases noted in the OT, all the other occurrences are those used by Jesus in his teaching ministry. He stated that it was an effective method for revealing truth to the spiritually illuminated while keeping it hid from others (Mt. 13:10-16). A list of the better known parables would include: those of the sower and the seed; the workers in the vineyard; the ten virgins; the talents; the Good Samaritan; the Prodigal Son; and the Pharisee and the tax-collector (Mt. 13:1-23; 20:1-16; 25:1-13; 25:14-30; Lk. 10:30-37; 15:11-32; 18:9-14).

PARACLETE {comforter, exhorter} *See*

GOD, NAMES OF; GODHEAD 6., *Holy Spirit*

PARADISE {park *or* garden} *See* DEAD, ABODE OF

PARADOX An apparent contradiction in which two opposing ideas are held in tension to each other. *See* ANTINOMY

PARAH {cow} An unidentified site in the tribal area of Benjamin (Jos. 18:23).

PARALLELISM *See* POETRY

PARALYSIS {lame} *See* SICK, SICKNESS

PARALYTIC {lame} *See* SICK, SICKNESS

PARAMOUR An illicit lover (Eze. 23:20). A male prostitute (NEB). *See* CONCUBINE

PARAN, MOUNT PARAN, DESERT OF PARAN {plain} SW of Elath (Ezion Geber). Paran is a site in the Sinai. *See* DESERT and GEOGRAPHY OF THE HOLY LAND

PARAPET A protective wall, elevation, or barrier required in the law to be constructed at the edge of a roof (Dt. 22:8).

PARBAR KJV for "court" (1Ch. 26:18).

PARCHED, PARCHED GRAIN In general the word indicates something dried up (Jer. 17:6; 48:18; Hos. 13:15). With respect to grain it means roasted. In the KJV it is called parched "corn," an archaic word referring to a grain. In the NIV what is called "parched corn" in the KJV is called "roasted grain" in some references and "roasted corn" in others (Lev. 23:14; Ru. 2:14). Corn as known today was unknown in antiquity. What is translated "corn" was some kind of grain. It was parched by roasting in a pan or even by holding some stalks near the coals of a fire. Either way, it was a food staple used as one of the most common items of the diet of all the people (Lev. 2:14; 23:14; Jos. 5:11).

PARCHMENT {vellum} One of the ancient writing materials, made from the skins of animals and thus more durable than papyrus. It is different from leather in that it is not tanned. The form called vellum is a better quality, made from the skins of calves or kids (2Ti. 4:13). *See also* PAPYRUS

PARDON *See* FORGIVENESS

PARENTAL BLESSINGS *See* BLESS, BLESSING; FIRSTBORN

PARENTING The raising of children in the Bible is in the responsibility of both the mother and the father. Training a child includes the idea of impressing on the child, continuously, the Word of God, (Dt. 6:49). Though not a promise, it is generally true that this training will be lifelong in the child (Pr. 22:6). The pattern of training is set by God himself in his relationship to his "son" Israel (Hos. 11:1-2). In the New Covenant similarly God is called our "Father" (Mt. 6:9). The parent is therefore to strive to first be godly before attending to methods of discipline and training (Ex. 34:6-7) (*see also* ATTRIBUTES OF GOD, moral attributes).

Fathers are encouraged not to provoke (irritate, make angry) their children but instead to bring them up in the Lord's instruction (Eph. 6:4).

Corporeal punishment is taught in the Scriptures (Pr. 13:24; 22:15; 29:15-17) and should only be done by one in control of his temper (Pr. 16:32). Women also are to be agents of discipline and training (Pr. 1:8). (J.A.S.) *See also* NAME, GIVING OF; WOMAN

PARENTS *See* MARRIAGE

PARMASHTA One of the ten sons of Haman, all of whom lost their lives in the abortive attempt to destroy the Jews of Susa in the days of Esther (Est. 9:9). †

PARMENAS {steady, reliable} One of the seven chosen by early Christians to minister to the temporal needs of the church; called deacons in the KJV (Ac. 6:5). †

PARNACH The father of the representative of the tribe of Zebulun in the dividing of the land among the tribes (Nu. 34:25). †

PAROSH {flea}

1. Ancestor of some who returned from the Babylonian captivity with Zerubbabel and Ezra (Ezr. 2:3; 8:3; 10:25).

2. The father or ancestor of one who worked on the repair of the walls of Jerusalem in the days of Nehemiah, perhaps the same as 1 above (Ne. 3:25).

3. One who signed the covenant with Nehemiah (Ne. 10:14).

PAROUSIA {presence, coming} *See* CHRIST, LIFE AND TEACHINGS OF, *Work of Christ 9.*, "Second Advent"; ESCHATOLOGY

PARSHANDATHA One of the sons of Haman (Est. 9:7). † *See* PARMASHTA

PARSIN *See* MENE, MENE, TEKEL AND PARSIN

PARTHIANS {Iranian tribal group} Noted in the Bible only in Ac. 2:9, where Jews from this area were in Jerusalem in the time of the first Christian Pentecost. Parthia was a small country NW of the old Persia, within the area of modern Iran. They were an independent kingdom (248 B.C. to A.D. 224) constantly at war with the Romans.

PARTITION *See* MIDDLE WALL OF PARTITION

PARTNER, PARTNERSHIP *See* FELLOWSHIP

PARTRIDGE *See* BIRDS 4.

PARTY *See* HERESY

PARUAH {blooming, ISBE; cheerful, KB} The father of one of King Solomon's chief food-gathering officers, from the tribe of Issachar (1Ki. 4:17). †

PARVAIM An unidentified place from which Solomon received a certain type of gold (2Ch. 3:6). †

PASACH A descendant of Asher (1Ch. 7:33). †

PASCHAL [Passover] Refers to Passover celebration. *See* CALENDAR and FESTIVALS

PAS DAMMIM *See* EPHES DAMMIM

PASEAH [hobbling one]
1. A descendant of Judah (1Ch. 4:12). †
2. The ancestor of some who returned with Zerubbabel from the Babylonian captivity (Ezr. 2:49; Ne. 7:51). †
3. The father of Joiada in the days of Nehemiah (Ne. 3:6). †

PASHHUR, PASHUR
1. A priest who beat Jeremiah the prophet and then put him in stocks (Jer. 20:1-6).
2. The father of Gedaliah, the governor of Jerusalem after the last king had been deported (Jer. 38:1).
3. One who urged Judah's last king to imprison Jeremiah and execute him for making the people afraid (Jer. 38:1-4).
4. The ancestor of some priests who returned from the Babylonian captivity with Zerubbabel (Ezr. 2:38; 10:22).
5. One who signed the covenant with Nehemiah (Ne. 10:3).

PASSION *See* LUST

PASSION OF CHRIST *See* CHRIST, LIFE AND TEACHINGS OF, Work of Christ 2., *Jesus' Passion*

PASSOVER [pass over, spare] *See* CALENDAR and FESTIVALS

PASTORAL EPISTLES *See* PAULINE EPISTLES

PASTORS [one who gives pasture to sheep] The pastor is the religious shepherd or leader of a people. The word is used in the NIV only in Eph. 4:11 but found frequently in the Hebrew and Greek texts, and usually translated here as "shepherd." Christ is the "Good Shepherd" (Jn. 10:11-14; Heb. 13:20; 1Pe. 2:25; 5:4). Quite naturally the word is used of those who herd sheep (Lk. 2:8). Israel's leaders were called shepherds of Israel (Jer. 3:15; 17:16; 23:1-2; Eze. 34:1-16).

PASTURE LANDS OF SHARON *See* GEOGRAPHY OF THE HOLY LAND

PATARA An important port of Lycia located in SW Asia Minor where Paul stopped on his final journey to Jerusalem (Ac. 21:1). †

PATHROS [south land, Upper Egypt] The name of a land in Upper Egypt, southern Egypt, mentioned in the Bible only in the prophets in some most interesting references. God is to destroy it and then return the Egyptians to it after forty years (Eze. 30:14; 29:14). Many Jews were there after the fall of Jerusalem to the Babylonians (Jer. 44:1, 15; Isa. 11:11), and it is one of the places from which the Jews will be brought back to Palestine in the last days. †

PATHRUSIM, PATHRUSITES [of PATHROS] The people from the area of Pathros in Upper Egypt (Ge. 10:14; 1Ch.1:12).

PATIENCE The translation of two Greek words, one of which signifies endurance under affliction or trials, rendered sometimes by "perseverance" in the NIV, and the other "long-suffering" (Ro. 12:12; Eph. 4:2; 2Ti. 4:2; Jas. 1:3-4; 5:10). It is listed as one of the ingredients in the "fruit of the Spirit" (Gal. 5:22). It is used only six times in the RSV (Job 6:11; Pr. 14:17; 25:15; Ps. 37:7; 40:1; Ecc. 7:8), but it is related to the Hebrew word "long" and is found in combination with other words, the combination of which indicated the concept of patience (Pr. 14:29; 19:11, "slow to anger," for an example).

PATMOS A small island of some twenty-five square miles with a rocky coastline, one of those used by the Romans for the banishment of prisoners. It was located in the Aegean Sea SW of Asia Minor. John found himself imprisoned here because of his Christian testimony (Rev. 1:9). †

PATMOS

PATRIARCH [first father (of a nation, tribe)] While this English word is found in the NIV only eight times, the idea behind it is common ("father, fathers of old, forefathers") and refers to the founders of the Hebrew people and their religion, specifically to Abraham, Jacob, and his twelve sons, and to David (Ac. 7:8-9; Heb. 7:4).

PATROBAS [father of existence] A Christian at Rome to whom Paul sent greetings (Ro. 16:14). †

PAU, PAI The unidentified capital city of King Hadar of Edom, called by both names (Ge. 36:39; 1Ch. 1:50).

PAUL, LIFE AND TEACHINGS OF "A Hebrew born of Hebrews," Saul, who is also called Paul, was raised from earliest youth in the strict traditions of Pharisaism, first in his home at Tarsus, and then at Jerusalem under the instruction of Gamaliel I (Php. 3:5; 2Co. 11:22; Ac. 22:3). As one zealous for the law and eager to keep Israel united in its commitment in days of approaching Messianic blessing, Saul early directed his efforts against Jewish believers in Jesus of Nazareth; for, as he saw it, their leader had been discredited by crucifixion and their schismatic preaching could only further delay Israel's promised Messianic age. Thus we first read of Saul as officiating at the martyrdom of Stephen, imprisoning Christians in Jerusalem,

and taking the initiative in returning believers who had fled for safety to areas outside of Palestine (Ac. 7:58–8:3; 9:1-2; Php. 3:6). But, though undoubtedly earnest and motivated by a desire to do God's will as he understood it, he was actually, as he later came to realized, opposing God "ignorantly in unbelief" (1Ti. 1:13).

While traveling to Damascus to extradite Christians, Saul was confronted by the risen and glorified Christ who asked: "Saul, Saul, why do you persecute me?" (Ac. 9:22, 26). It was then that the young rabbi came to see that Jesus was and is Israel's long-awaited Messiah whose person and work had been vindicated by God. And in commitment to this risen Lord, Saul found (1) the ancient tension of his people, that of divine promise and awaited fulfillment, brought to consummation; (2) true righteousness and intimate fellowship with God; and (3) the understanding that redemption in Jesus has universal significance, being intended for Gentiles as well as Jews. It was this encounter on the road to Damascus that transformed Saul's thought and life; though, of course, the implications of this meeting and of his commitment were later more fully explained by the ministry of Ananias in Damascus, a three-year period of meditation in Arabia, and certain situations providentially controlled during his succeeding ministry.

The preaching of the converted young Pharisee began almost immediately in Damascus, where he proclaimed Jesus, whom he had persecuted, as indeed "the Christ (Messiah)" and "the Son of God" (Ac. 9:19-22, KJV). Then after three years in Arabia, he took up the ministry among Hellenistic Jews in Jerusalem that had lain dormant since Stephen's death; but he faced the same opposition which once he himself had led, and was forced to leave for Caesarea and from there to Tarsus (Ac. 9:26-30; Gal. 1:18-24). Probably he continued to witness in Tarsus, his hometown, where he resided for an additional ten years—though we hear nothing of his work during these years from either Luke in Acts or Paul in his letters, unless the recollection of his many afflictions in 2 Corinthians 11:23-27 included experiences from this time. It was Barnabas who sought him out in Tarsus and involved him in the ministry at Antioch of Syria, where he ministered for at least a year preaching Christ to many and taking a leading part in the collection for famine-stricken believers in Jerusalem (Ac. 11:25-30).

While at Antioch, the Holy Spirit called Paul, together with Barnabas, to minister more widely in the Roman Empire; and the Book of Acts records three journeys undertaken in carrying out this mandate. The first was with Barnabas, accompanied by John Mark, to cities of Cyprus and southern Asia Minor (Ac. 13–14). On this journey God led Paul to testify directly to Gentiles, apart from any necessary relation to the synagogue or to Judaism. It is at this point in the record where he begins to be called by his Roman name, Paul, rather than his Jewish name, Saul (Ac. 13:9). Here was a new and somewhat revolutionary aspect in the Christian mission, about which many Jewish Christians were uncertain. But matters were clarified at the Jerusalem Council, where the Jerusalem apostles concluded that, while they could hardly join in a direct ministry to Gentiles themselves, they could not stand in opposition to God's evident working through Paul in such an enterprise (Ac. 15). The second and third missionary journeys were with Silas, a prominent Jerusalemite Christian, with Timothy

from Lystra serving as their principal aide. After revisiting believers in Asia Minor, Paul pushed on by divine direction to evangelize Macedonia and Achaia (Greece) on the second journey (Ac. 15:26–18:22). And on the third, together with strengthening churches in areas traversed before, the apostle centered his activities at Ephesus (Ac. 18:23–20:38). Following his recorded ministry in the eastern part of the empire, the apostle went to Jerusalem with representatives from the major centers of Gentile Christianity to present a gift of money to the impoverished believers there. While in Jerusalem, he was accused of attacking the Jewish religion and disturbing the peace of Rome, and as a result, was confined to prison at Caesarea for two years. On appeal to Caesar, he was transferred to Rome and there imprisoned for another two years (Ac. 21–28). From references and allusions in the Prison and Pastoral Epistles, it may be inferred that Paul was released from this first Roman imprisonment and carried on a further ministry in lands surrounding the Aegean Sea. Clement of Rome, writing in A.D. 95, speaks of the apostle preaching as far west as Spain and tells of his martyrdom at Rome (1 Clem. 5:6) probably in A.D. 67 under Emperor Nero and sometime during the later sixties or early seventies of his life.

The basic message of Paul is briefly stated in such passages as Ro. 3:21-31; Gal. 4:4-5; 2Co. 5:17-21; Gal. 4:4-5; Php. 2:6-11; and Col. 1:15-23; and may be summarized in five points: (1) The law and the prophets were meant to witness to the righteousness of God and to prepare men for the coming of the Messiah, not to be an end in and of themselves. (2) Jesus of Nazareth is God's Messiah, come at the appropriate time in history, who in his person and work has made redemption available for all men. (3) Man needs to respond to Jesus by faith, apart from any thought of human merit, in order to experience forgiveness and reconciliation with God. (4) This message of gratuitous salvation must be preached to

Gentile and Jew alike, and on the same basis, for there is ultimately no distinction before God. (5) On the basis of new life "in Christ," the Christian is called upon to live a new life in this world, a life that reflects Christ's attitudes, imitates Christ's actions, and proclaims Christ's redemptive message. For Paul, in fact, a Christian's entire life was encompassed and controlled by the relationship of being "in Christ." (R.N.L.)

PAULINE EPISTLES, THE

1. Galatians
2. 1 and 2 Thessalonians
3. 1 and 2 Corinthians, Romans
4. Colossians, Philemon, Ephesians, and Philippians
5. 1 and 2 Timothy, Titus

The letters of Paul can appropriately be grouped according to the missionary journeys or imprisonments of the apostle.

1. Probably the earliest is the Letter to the *Galatians*, written about A.D. 49, just prior to the Jerusalem Council of Acts 15, to converts of southern Galatia won to Christ during Paul's first missionary journey and from Antioch in Syria (or on the way from Antioch to Jerusalem); though others, stressing the affinities between Galatians and Romans, view it as composed during the third missionary journey, from Ephesus or the region of Macedonia, sometime between A.D. 53 and 57, and addressed to converts of northern Galatia won on the second journey. The Judaizers who followed Paul into Asia Minor taught fidelity to the Mosaic Law as a precondition to full acceptance by God, and they argued against the legitimacy of a direct approach to Gentiles in the Christian mission. Evidently they also depreciated Paul's apostolic qualifications and represented themselves as bringing a truer form of the gospel. Paul's response to such a threat was this emotionally laden letter, alternately stern and tender, in defense of the liberty of the Christian. Galatians has been aptly called "the charter of Christian liberty," and throughout the whole epistle the note of grace reverberates. The letter may be outlined as follows: (1) salutation and occasion for writing (1:1-9); (2) Paul's apostolic authority and the authenticity of his message (1:10—2:20); (3) exposition on liberty in Christ (3:1—4:31); (4) exhortations to liberty in Christ (5:1—6:10); and (5) postscript on sacrificial living (6:11-18).

2. Written from Corinth on the second missionary journey, probably about A.D. 50-51, are the two letters addressed to the Thessalonians. The church at Thessalonica had been founded by Paul on his second journey (Ac. 17). Arriving in Athens, the apostle sent Timothy back to Thessalonica (1Th. 3:13). Timothy later returned to Paul, reporting on conditions at Thessalonica. *First Thessalonians* is in response to that report. In it are interwoven (1) commendation for growth, zeal, and fidelity; (2) encouragement in face of local persecution; (3) defense of the apostle's motives against pagan attack; (4) teaching regarding holiness of life; (5) instruction regarding the coming of the Lord; and (6) exhortation to steadfastness and patience. Evidently the Thessalonian believers misunderstood this first letter, for the apostle had to write *Second Thessalonians* a few months later to correct their false notions regarding the return of Christ and the ethical disorders resulting therefrom. While the Christian lives in eager expectation of his Lord's return, Paul had to insist that immanency must not be construed to mean immediacy; rather, it is the basis for steadfastness and dogged persistence. Few today doubt the Pauline authorship of 1 Thessalonians. The authenticity of 2 Thessalonians, however, has been suspicioned in many quarters, chiefly because the eschatological section of 2:1-12 is either too crassly Jewish or too different from 1 Thessalonians to be by Paul. But with the realization that though early Christians found fulfillment in Jesus they still shared with Judaism expectations regarding the future, much of the objection to the Jewish character of Paul's eschatology disappears; and though the two letters differ in tone and temper, this is largely

a reflection of the situation addressed.

3. On his third missionary journey, Paul wrote *1* and *2 Corinthians* and *Romans. First Corinthians* was composed during the apostle's extended ministry at Ephesus (1Co. 16:8, 19), probably about A.D. 55 or 56, in response to disquieting reports brought to his attention concerning the church at Corinth. Paul had written the Corinthians earlier (1Co. 5:9-10), but that letter was misinterpreted. In the meantime, some in the church wrote him seeking his guidance on certain matters. In his reply, Paul included: (1) salutation (1:1-9); (2) disorders (divisions and strife) reported by the family of Chloe (1:10—4:21); (3) disorders widely rumored (immorality, pride, lawsuits) (5:1—6:20); (4) matters concerning which the church wrote— marriage, food offered to idols, decorum of women in worship, observance of the Lord's Supper, spiritual gifts (7:1— 14:40); (5) the resurrection (15:1-58); and (6) the collection and conclusion (16:1-24). On all these matters Paul wrote in strong pastoral tones; and while he instructed as to specific situations, he also gave principles which can be applied to similar circumstances today. In A.D. 95, Clement of Rome wrote in a similar vein to the church at Corinth, citing Paul's admonitions in 1 Corinthians in support. That attestation is the earliest for any of Paul's letters, and coupled with internal evidence, has silenced any doubts regarding the authenticity of the first epistle.

Written from Macedonia (Philippi?), probably between A.D. 55 and 57, *Second Corinthians* is the apostle's earnest response to the triumphs and continuing difficulties in the Corinthian church. Its content may be outlined as follows: (1) salutation and thanksgiving (1:1-11); (2) Paul's answer to his critics (1:12—7:16;) (3) the collection for the poor of Jerusalem (8:1—9:15); (4) Paul's vindication of his apostolic authority (10:1—13:10); and (5) conclusion (13:11-14). Stylistically, the letter is noted for its breaks and changes of tone. Two self-contained units have often been identified: (1) chapter 1—9, ending with a brief doxology and expressing a conciliatory tone, and (2) chapters 10—13, ending with another doxology and speaking in tones of severity and warning. Many also consider 6:14—7:1 a unit detached from its context, suggestion that perhaps it is part of the "lost" letter of 1Co. 5:9. Various answers have been proposed to explain these divisions and arrangements, but in none of them is Pauline authorship denied.

The Pauline authorship of the Letter to the *Romans* is so well attested by external and internal evidence that few have challenged it. Written from Corinth at the close of the apostle's recorded missionary journeys and before his final trip to Jerusalem (Ro. 15:17-33), the letter can be dated about A.D. 57 or 58. The Greek world in the eastern part of the Roman Empire had been evangelized (15:19, 23). The flame had been kindled and the fire was spreading, and Paul desired to transfer his ministry to the Latin world, going as far W as Spain (15:24). Evidently he expected to use Rome as his base of operations, much as Antioch of Syria had served previously. He earlier had hoped to go directly to Rome from Achaia, but his presence was essential at Jerusalem in the presentation of the Gentile contribution to impoverished Jewish Christians there (15:22ff.). Therefore, in place of a visit, in preparation for his future coming to them, and to declare the righteousness of God, Paul sent this formal letter to the Christians of Rome.

The longest and most systematic of Paul's writings, Romans is more a comprehensive exposition of the gospel than a letter as such. Some have suggested, in fact, that the body of the work may have been composed by the apostle early in his ministry and was circulated among his Gentile churches as something of a missionary tractate giving a resume of the apostle's message; and when directed to Rome, received its personal elements of chapters 15 and 16. Such a view would go far toward explaining the uncertainties within the early church as to the relation of chapters 15 and 16 to the rest of the writing, the absence of "in Rome" at 1:7 and 1:15, in some minor manuscripts, and the presence of two doxologies at 15:33 and 16:27.

Romans may be divided into five sections: introduction (1:1-17); doctrinal exposition (1:18 – 8:39); Israel and the church (9:1 – 11:36); practical exhortations (12:1 – 15:13); and conclusion (15:14 – 16:27). In the "doctrinal exposition" (1:18 – 8:39), Paul asserts the equality of Jew and Gentile before God and that true righteousness is based only upon the justifying work of Jesus Christ, to which and to whom man responds by faith. While recognizing certain advantages given to Israel by God historically, the apostle insisted that ultimately both Jew and Gentile stand equally before God in condemnation and equally in need of the righteousness which only God can impart. And in contrast to the human desire to gain acceptance before God by works, the apostle insisted that God's one requirement is faith: a loving and thankful response, as exemplified by Abraham and as needs to characterize the Christian life continually. In his discussion of the relation of "Israel and the church" (9:1 – 11:36) Paul made the distinction between spiritual and national Israel, spoke of Christians as in continuity with spiritual Israel, yet declared God's future restoration of the nation. In his "practical exhortations" (12:1 – 15:13), he urged that these theological truths be expressed as living realities in his addressees' corporate and individual lives; and in the process, his words often echoed teachings of Jesus.

The church at Rome was of mixed racial background. Evidently, at first, Jewish Christians were in the majority; but after the edict of the emperor Claudius in A.D. 49, temporarily banishing Jews from Rome, Gentile Christians were predominant. The Letter to the Romans spoke to both elements. It speaks to both today.

4. The letters to the *Colossians*, *Philemon*, the *Ephesians* and the *Philippians* were written during Paul's two-year imprisonment in Rome, probably during A.D. 61-63. In *Colossians* the apostle was countering a syncretistic and dualistic type of religious philosophy which taught that since the world of matter is defiled and intrinsically opposed to God, man must seek true knowledge and union with Deity in some higher sphere of the nonmaterial. On such a view, the incarnation of our Lord and his work on the cross are either rejected or considered an inferior first step toward reconciliation with God.

Paul, in his answer, did not minimize the humanity and sacrifice of Christ; rather, he gloried in the Incarnation and the cross, for by them God effected man's redemption (Col. 1:20-22). To the specific objections of the heresy confronted, however, the apostle proclaimed the cosmic Christ in whom all fulness dwells and in whom the believer finds complete fulfillment (Col. 1:15ff.; 2:9ff.).

The Letter to *Philemon* was addressed to one of Paul's converts living in Colosse, whose slave Onesimus had robbed his master and fled to Rome. Brought to Christ by Paul, Onesimus had proven helpful to the apostle while in prison. Now Paul wrote on his behalf, urging Philemon to receive him back as a "beloved brother in the Lord." From the references to Tychicus and Onesimus in Col. 4:7-9 and the greetings of Col. 4:10-17 and Phm. 23-24, it can be deduced that the two letters were written and sent at the same time, probably about A.D. 61 or 62.

Ephesians reflects no specific local situation, and its tone, together with the omission of "in Ephesus" in the leading ancient manuscripts, has led many to view it as something of a circular letter sent widely to churches in Asia Minor. Prominent doctrines include the church as the body of Christ, the foundational nature of the apostles and prophets, predestination, the believer's relation "in Christ," and the demolishing of the distinction between Jew and Gentile. It also was delivered by Tychicus (Eph. 6:21), very likely written shortly after Colossians.

In *Philippians* Paul wrote to thank believers for their financial aid (Php. 4:10-19) and to commend Epaphroditus, their messenger to him in prison, against any possible criticism that he had not completed his task (Php. 2:25-30). He also took the occasion to explain regarding his present circumstances, to exhort to steadfastness, unity, and humility, and to warn regarding the Judaizers. In that Paul alluded to an approaching trial (Php. 1:20ff.) and expressed his hope to visit Philippi shortly (Php. 2:24), the letter may be taken to have been written toward the end of his first Roman imprisonment, about A.D. 63.

5. Assuming a release at his first trial, a further ministry in lands surrounding the Aegean, and a second trial at which capital punishment was imposed, Paul wrote *First Timothy* and *Titus* during the period of release in A.D. 64-66 and *Second Timothy* just prior to his death in A.D. 67. In his first letter to Timothy, the apostle sought to encourage his young colleague in his pastoral responsibilities at Ephesus. He exhorted Timothy to deal decisively with certain false teachers, and he gave instruction regarding the qualifications for leaders and the treatment of various members in the church. In his letter to *Titus,* the minister of the church in Crete, Paul again admonished as to pastoral duties, dealing with (1) qualifications for leaders in the church; (2) the need to oppose false doctrine; (3) treatment of various classes of members in the church; and (4) proper attitudes for believers in a pagan society.

Second Timothy is chronologically later than the other Pastoral Epistles, and breathes a different atmosphere. Whereas in 1 Timothy and Titus the apostle was free to make plans and move about at will, in 2 Timothy he was a prisoner, and the end was rapidly approaching. Apparently written from Rome while awaiting execution, Paul was anxious for Timothy to come to him before winter. But more than this, he was concerned that Timothy be exemplary in his life and faithful to the ministry to which he had been called. This final letter of the

great apostle is rich and varied. Interwoven are touching appeals, ringing charges, and the note of triumph in face of imminent death. It is, in fact, the great apostle's last will and testament; which, after many years of service for Christ, he closed with repeated shouts of victory (2Ti. 4:6-8, 16-18). (R.N.L.) *See also* ACTS; EPISTLE

PAULUS *See* SERGIUS PAULUS

PAVEMENT *See* GABBATHA

PAVILION KJV for a dwelling place (Ps. 27:5; 31:20).

PEACE Used in the Bible as in modern times, both as a greeting and to indicate calm as between men, or as between men and God, or of a man within himself (2Ki. 9:17-31; Mk. 4:39; Lk. 10:5; Jos. 9:15; Job 22:21; Isa. 57:21; Nu. 6:26). Paul indicated that our peace with God is made through Jesus Christ (Ro. 5:1; Col. 1:19-20). Peace in the world is predicted for eschatological days (Isa. 9:6-7; 11:6-9; Mic. 4:1-4).

PEACE OFFERING *See* SACRIFICES AND OFFERINGS

PEACOCK KJV for "baboon" (1Ki. 10:22; 2Ch. 9:21); and "ostrich" (Job 39:13, NIV). *See* BEASTS 3. and BIRDS 7.

PEARL *See* PRECIOUS STONES AND METALS, Precious Stones 10.

PEDAHEL [El emancipates] The representative of the tribe of Naphtali in the division of the land among the tribes of Israel (Nu. 34:28). †

PEDAHZUR [the Rock emancipates] The father of Gamaliel who represented the tribe of Manasseh in the census taking of Moses (Nu. 1:10; 2:20; 7:54, 59; 10:23). †

PEDAIAH [Yahweh emancipates]
1. The father of King Jehoiakim's mother (2Ki. 23:36).
2. A son of King Jehoiachin and either the father or nephew of the Zerubbabel who brought back some of the

captives from the Babylonian captivity (1Ch. 3:18-19).

3. The father of one of David's officers (1Ch. 27:20).

4. One who helped to repair the walls of Jerusalem in the days of Nehemiah (Ne. 3:25).

5. One who stood with Ezra as he read the law to the people (Ne. 8:4).

6. A descendant of Benjamin (Ne. 11:7).

7. A Levite appointed as treasurer by Nehemiah (Ne. 13:13).

PEKAH {he has opened} *See* KINGS OF JUDAH AND ISRAEL

PEKAHIAH {Yahweh opens} *See* KINGS OF JUDAH AND ISRAEL

PEKOD A small Aramean tribe living on the Lower Tigris River in the days of Jeremiah and Ezekiel (Jer. 50:21; Eze. 23:23). †

PELAIAH {Yahweh is spectacular}

1. A descendant of King Solomon (1Ch. 3:24). †

2. One who helped to explain the law after Ezra read it to the people (Ne. 8:7). †

3. One who signed the covenant with Nehemiah (Ne. 10:10). †

PELALIAH {Yahweh intercedes in arbitration} A priest who served in the days of Nehemiah (Ne. 11:12). †

PELATIAH {Yahweh rescues}

1. A descendant of Zerubbabel (1Ch. 3:21). †

2. A descendant of Simeon (1Ch. 4:42). †

3. One who signed the covenant with Nehemiah (Ne. 10:22). †

4. A son of Benaiah and an evil prince against whom Ezekiel gave one of his oracles (Eze. 11:1-13). †

PELEG {water canal} A descendant of Shem in whose days "the earth was divided." A possible reference to the confounding of the languages of the peoples (Ge. 10:25; 11:16-19; 1Ch. 1:19, 25; Lk. 3:35). †

PELET {rescue}

1. A descendant of Judah and Caleb (1Ch. 2:47). †

2. A descendant of Benjamin who joined David at Ziklag (1Ch. 12:3). †

PELETH

1. Descendant of Reuben who was a part of the rebellion against the leadership of Moses (Nu. 16:1).

2. A descendant of Judah and Jerahmeel (1Ch. 2:33).

PELETHITES An unidentified group who along with the Kerethites comprised the bodyguard of King David (2Sa. 8:18; 15:18; 1Ki. 1:38, 44).

PELICAN A common rendering in many versions (Lev. 11:18; Dt. 14:17; Ps. 102:6) for an unclean, inedible bird. Rendered "desert owl" in the NIV, and "jackdaw" in the NKJV. *See* BIRDS 5.

PELLA One of the ten cities in Decapolis. *See* DECAPOLIS

PELONITE An unidentified title or place from which two of David's mighty men came (1Ch. 11:27, 36; 27:10).

PELUSIUM An Egyptian fortress town on their NE frontier called "the stronghold of Egypt" (Eze. 30:15-16). †

PEN, PENKNIFE An iron stylus or a reed pen for writing (Job 19:24; Ps. 45:1; 3Jn. 13). *See* WRITING, *reed*

PENANCE This word has the idea of "to repent" (with a notion of punishment). It implies confession and practices of austerity.

PENCE *See* MONEY, *Denarii*

PENIEL, PENUEL {face of El} A place, (215-176) E of the Jordan River where Jacob wrestled all night with the man who subsequently blessed him (Ge. 32:22-31). Gideon destroyed the town, and Jeroboam I of Israel later rebuilt it (Jdg. 8:8-17; 1Ki. 12:25).

PENINNAH {*possibly* pearls, coral branches, BDB; woman with rich hair, KB} One of the wives of Elkanah, the father of Samuel (1Sa. 1:24). †

PENNY *See* MONEY

PENTATEUCH [five books, *i.e.*, the *torah* or law] This term (lit. "five in a case"—i.e., five books in one volume) refers to the first five books of the OT, commonly called "The Five Books of Moses." Exodus 17:14 and 24:4 affirm that Moses personally wrote down God's words, and Ex. 24:7 that he read these words to the Israelite people. Deuteronomy 31:9 states that Moses had a complete written copy of the Law delivered to the priests. Joshua was bidden by God (Jos. 1:8) to study faithfully the written Pentateuch daily; King David referred to this written law when he bade Solomon to study and to obey it (1Ki. 2:3). In Mt. 19:8 Jesus referred to Moses as the personal author of Dt. 24:1, and then of the Messianic prophecies in the Torah (Jn. 5:46-47). Paul quoted Moses as author of Dt. 18:15 (*see* Ac. 3:22), and also of Lev. 18:5 (*see* Ro. 10:5). There is no reason to doubt that Christ and the apostles regarded Moses as the author of the Pentateuch. This is confirmed by the internal evidence of the text. Its author must have been originally a resident of Egypt, for he referred to Egyptian seasons and weather conditions rather than to Palestinian (Ex. 9:31-32) and employed a larger number of Egyptian names and loan-words than in any other part of the OT. He compared the lush green of the Jordan plain to a locality in Egypt (Ge. 13:10), which would be meaningful only to a reading public familiar with Egypt but unfamiliar with Palestine. Likewise he dated the founding of Kirjath-arba (the ancient name of Hebron) by reference to the building of Zoan in Egypt (Nu. 13:22), and he described Shechem in Canaan as "a city of Shechem which is in the land of Canaan" (Ge. 33:18). He referred to Jerusalem only once, as "Shalem" in Ge. 14:18, which would be an unthinkable omission if at the time of composition of the Pentateuch, Jerusalem had been the royal capital for several centuries (as many OT scholars allege). Among all the detailed injunctions concerning worship in Exo-

dus and Leviticus, there is not the slightest mention of a guild of Levitical singers or of the use of musical instruments, even though these became very prominent elements in Israelite worship from 1000 B.C. onward. The predominant type of legislation in Exodus, Leviticus, and Numbers is nomadic or agricultural; even in Deuteronomy there is very little special reference to urban conditions or the problems of a mercantile society, such as obtained from the time of David onward. Thus it is fair to say that the objective data bearing upon the Pentateuch point to its composition prior to the Hebrew conquest of Canaan. Moses was raised as an adopted son of the royal house in Egypt, enjoying the finest opportunities of education among a highly literate people, at a time when even Semitic slaves at the Egyptian mines at Serabit el-Khadim (Sinai Peninsula) were writing their records in alphabetic letters; hence, any arguments based upon Moses' alleged illiteracy must be totally abandoned. Moses had every incentive to commit to writing the constitution of the new theocracy to be set up in the land of Canaan, and he had forty years in which to finish it. Since the numerous references to God's covenant with the patriarchs in Exodus through Deuteronomy point to a prior record of the establishment of this covenant, a book like Genesis, which contained this record, was absolutely indispensable to make Exodus through Deuteronomy intelligible. This confirms the NT indications that Moses was the author of Genesis also, as well as of the other four.

Genesis, then, sets forth the beginnings of the human race and the preservation of a godly remnant through the time of the Flood (chaps. 1-11). Next it relates the career of Abraham (12-25) and then the life of Isaac and his family (25-26). The career of Jacob and the birth of his twelve sons (27-36) is followed by the adventures of Joseph (37-50), who prepared the way for his family to increase to a great nation during the 430 years of their residence in Egypt.

Exodus resumes the narrative with the birth of Moses at a time when Israel had become a nation of oppressed slaves. His training for leadership and his call to lead Israel out of bondage are set forth in chaps. 1–4. The contest with Pharaoh, the ten plagues, and the Red Sea (Heb. *suph*, "reed") crossing are covered by 5–18. The confrontation between the nation and Yahweh at Sinai and the giving of the law (beginning with the Ten Commandments) are dealt with in 19–23. Provisions for priesthood, worship, and sacrifice are given in 24–31. Chapters 32–33 relate the apostasy connected with the worship of the golden calf. Chapters 34–40 resume instruction concerning worship, with warnings against idolatry and provisions for claiming God's forgiveness and grace; it closes with the solemn dedication of the tabernacle to God's service.

Leviticus contains a manual of special instruction for the priests and Levites in their spiritual service to the nation, as well as for all the Israelites. Regulations concerning the various types of sacrifice (1–7) are followed by a record of the consecration of Aaron and his sons to the priesthood (8–10). Laws of purification and separation from defilement (unclean foods, leprosy, etc.) come next (11–15), followed by the ordinances of the Day of Atonement, Yom Kippur, (16), and the sanctity of the altar and the atoning blood (17). Laws against unchastity, uncleanness, and idolatry (18–20) lead to a discussion of priestly holiness and priestly duties (21–22). The religious calendar with all the seven feasts (23) leads to the symbols of consecration and the penalties for desecration (24), followed by the laws concerning the sabbatical year and the Year of Jubilee (25). Chapter 26 outlines the blessings of obedience and the curses upon disobedience (with such remarkable foreknowledge of the future exile and restoration of Israel as to compel the anti-supernaturalist to resort to some theory of postexilic date of authorship to explain it away). The payment of tithes and vows is discussed in the final chapter.

Numbers resumes the narrative of Israel's journey through the wilderness. After a census of the troops of the twelve tribes (1–4), laws aimed at excluding defilement from the camp (5) lead up to the establishment of the Nazirite order, closing with the Aaronic benediction (6). The twelve tribes dedicate treasures to the tabernacle (7) and witness the installation of the priests in their service of the tabernacle (8). The first annual Passover and the rules concerning the following of the pillar of cloud take up chap. 9. The journey from Sinai to Kadesh Barnea (10–14) is marked by rebellions against Moses' authority, culminating in Israel's refusal at Kadesh Barnea to trust God for conquest of Canaan. For this they are condemned to die off in the wilderness during the next forty years. Chapter 15 gives rules concerning certain types of sacrifice and the punishment for blasphemy. The abortive rebellion of Korah leads to renewed confirmation of the Aaronic priesthood (16–17) and an explanation of the service role of Levites toward the priests (18). After a second smiting of the rock at Kadesh and a repulse by the Edomites, the Israelites arrive at Moab and crush Sihon and Og of Transjordan (20–21). After the encounter with King Balak and the prophet Balaam (22–25), arrangements are drawn up for the coming conquest of Canaan, the apportionment of its territories, and the crushing of the Midianites (26–36).

Deuteronomy contains a final restatement of the Law delivered by the aged Moses as his parting charge to Israel to remain a holy commonwealth, walking in love toward God, obedience to his will, and abhorrence toward all the idolatries of Canaan. Chapters 1–4 contain a historical review of God's gracious dealings with his covenant people (the insertion of this type of historical survey characterized second millennium king-vassal [servant] treaties, but not those of the first millennium). Chapters 5–26 contain the stipulations in God's "treaty" with Israel, the laws by which the holy commonwealth is to live. Basic commandments (5— 11), statues of worship and of a holy life (12—16), and judgments concerning specific offenses, relationships, and duties (17—26) make up this section. Chapter 17 has rules to govern future kings; chapter 18 concerns future prophets and the Messianic Prophet; 27—33 contain warning and prediction (some of which point to the fall of Jerusalem to Titus in A.D. 70), and set before every Israelite the alternatives of blessing and of curse. The Song of Moses sets forth the nation's responsibility to keep God's covenant with an earnest warning against apostasy. Chapter 33 contains a prediction and blessing for each of the twelve tribes, and chap. 34 presents an obituary notice and eulogy, doubtless added soon after Moses' death. (G.L.A.)

PENTECOST [fiftieth (day)] *See* CALENDAR and FESTIVALS

PENTECOSTALISM A movement that gives doctrinal emphasis on the baptism of the Holy Spirit as a second blessing. This movement also emphasizes certain spiritual gifts like speaking in tongues and healing. *See* CHARISMATIC MOVEMENT; GIFTS; SPIRITUAL GIFTS

PENUEL [face of El]
1. A descendant of Judah (1Ch. 4:4).
2. A descendant of Benjamin (1Ch. 8:25).

PEOPLE OF GOD A phrase which indicates the children of Israel in the OT and the same people or the church in the NT (Nu. 11:29; Jdg. 5:11; 1Sa. 2:24; Mal. 3:16-17; Ro. 11:1-2; 2Co. 6:14-18; 1Pe. 2:9-10).

PEOR [opening]
1. A place (164-119) put in the tribal area of Judah in the LXX of Jos. 15:59.
2. The name of a high mountain peak in Moab from which Balaam was supposed to curse Israel (Nu. 23:28).
3. A short form of Baal-peor. *See* DEITIES

MOUNT PEOR

PERAEA [beyond (the Jordan River)] A distinct region E of the Jordan River (Isa. 9:1; Mt. 4:25; Mk. 3:7-8), commonly referred to as *Beyond* the Jordan (KJV), or *region across* the Jordan (NIV) or *Transjordan* (JB, NEB). For other regions, *see* GEOGRAPHY OF THE HOLY LAND

PEREA

PERAZIM [breaking out] *See* BAAL PERAZIM

PERDITION [ruin, destruction] In Rev. 17:8, 11 the reference is to the final state of the wicked, the common meaning of the word in our day. King David in his twice-recorded poem spoke of the torrents of perdition engulfing him, but went on to note how God saved him from them (2Sa. 22:5; Ps. 18:4). The only other references are by Jesus speaking of Judas Iscariot and by Paul speaking of "the man of lawlessness" (2Th. 2:3), the Antichrist who is also called "son of perdition" (Jn. 17:12, KJV).

PERDITION, SON OF *See* BAR; BEN; PERDITION; SON

PEREA *See* PERAEA

PERES *See* MENE, MENE, TEKEL, AND PARSIN

PERESH [offal eviscerated, BDB; dung, ISBE; contents of stomach (not intestine), KB] A descendant of Manasseh (1Ch. 7:16). †

PEREZ, PEREZITE, PHAREZ [breaking out]

1. A son of Judah by Tamar, one in the genealogy of Jesus (Ge. 38:29; Ru. 4:12, 18; Lk. 3:33).

2. One from the tribe or clan of Perez (Nu. 26:20).

PEREZ UZZA(H) [breaking out of UZZAH] The name given by David to the place where God killed Uzzah for putting out his hand to touch the Ark, even though he thought he was doing it to protect the Ark from falling (2Sa. 6:8; 1Ch. 13:11). †

PERFECT, PERFECTION The rendering of two Hebrew and one Greek word meaning "end," "finished," "completed." The words do not mean final and/or ultimate completion and perfection but a completed state as of a given time. Job was twice declared by God to be perfect (the Hebrew word is translated "blameless" in the NIV), yet he had much to learn so that in the end he was more "perfect" (Job 1:8; 2:3). The man of God is being completed, but his final completion awaits his resurrection (Php. 3:12; Jas. 3:2). The term is a relative one, showing relationship between time and the absolute state of completeness, perfection.

PERFECTIONISM The belief that a believer in this life can achieve a sinless state.

PERFUMERS *See* CONFECTIONARY

PERGA The chief city of ancient Pamphylia in SE Asia Minor visited by Paul on his first missionary journey (Ac. 13:13-25). †

PERGAMOS, PERGAMUM A city in Mysia in W Asia Minor to which one of the seven letters found in the Revelation was written (Rev. 1:11; 2:12). †

PERICOPE A passage within a collection of literature which, when *cut off* (i.e., isolated), can stand alone. For example, Jn. 8:1-11 is a pericope.

PERIDA [single, unique] Ancestor of some of Solomon's servants who returned with Zerubbabel from the Babylonian captivity (Ne. 7:57); also called Peruda (Ezr. 2:55). †

PERISH To be lost or destroyed in either the physical or spiritual sense (Ge. 41:36; Dt. 8:20; Jn. 3:16; 2Pe. 3:9).

PERIZZITE(S) [villager] An ethnic group in the land of Palestine when Abraham, and later the Israelites after the years in Egypt, dwelt there. They are mentioned along with groups known to have existed (based in nonbiblical sources) — Canaanites, Hittites, Horites — and with others whose identity is not currently known, except in the Bible (Ge. 13:7; 15:20; Ex. 3:8; Jos. 3:10; Ne. 9:8).

PERSECUTION In the Old Covenant, to be pursued or persecuted was a sign of the cursings for disobedience (Lev. 26:33; Pr. 16:7). In the New Covenant, one is blessed (not cursed) if men persecute him (Mt. 5:10-12). The Christian is to pray for the persecutor (Mt. 5:44-48). As Jesus was persecuted, so are his followers (Jn. 15:20). Saul of Tarsus was a persecutor (Ac. 9:4; 22:4; 1Co. 15:9; Gal. 1:13; Php. 3:6). The persecution resulted in the gospel being spread to other lands (Ac. 11:19).

PERSEPOLIS *See* PERSIA

PERSEVERANCE *See* SALVATION, APPLICATION OF, second to last ¶

PERSIA One of the sons of Japheth was Madai (Ge. 10:2), the ancestor of the Medes and of a related, Indo-European speaking people, the Persians. Both set-

PERGA
Paul, Barnabas, and John Mark left Paphos and landed at Perga in Pamphylia. From there they went to Antioch.

tled in the mountains E of Mesopotamia. In about 650 B.C. the ancient Persian dynasty was founded by Achaimenes. The fourth of his line married a daughter of Astyages the Mede; and from this union came Cyrus II (the Great), who reigned from 558 to 529. Cyrus overcame Astyages in 550 and incorporated the Median Empire into his own, fulfilling Daniel's prediction of a dual empire: the bear that was raised up on one side (Persia over Media (Da. 7:5; cf. 2:32, 39) and the ram with two horns, of which the latter was the higher (Da. 8:3-4, 20). By 546 Cyrus had defeated the Lydians in the West and by 539 the Bactrians of Afghanistan, so that he held from the Aegean to the borders of India. In October of 539 the Babylonians under Belshazzar were defeated by his general, Gobryas, perhaps to be equated with "Darius the Mede" who received the Kingdom of Babylon (Da. 5:31), though only for a short period (cf. Da. 9:1 and 11:1). Cyrus himself then assumed control over the former Babylonian Empire, including Judah in the West.

Under his general policy of being friendly toward conquered peoples, Cyrus issued an edict to the Jews in 538, authorizing their return from exile and reinstitution of temple worship in Jerusalem (2Ch. 36:22-23; Ezr. 1:1-4), as had been specifically predicted by Isaiah over a century and a half before (Isa. 44:28; 45:1). Samaritan opposition was able to stop the temple's reconstruction (Ezr. 4:1-5, 24) until after the death of

Cyrus's son and successor, Cambyses (529-522), possibly because of the latter's wish to avoid trouble near the border of Egypt, which he conquered in 525.

Darius I (522-485) succeeded to the throne of Persia only after lengthy conflicts with rivals and insubordinate governors. He accordingly reorganized the empire into twenty-one satrapies (i.e., provinces or counties), in a system that combined local autonomy, central power, and an efficient system of checks and balances. His reasonableness is illustrated by his handling of the report of Tattenai, satrap of the fifth (Syrian) province (Ezr. 6:1-12), with respect to the rebuilding of the temple between 520 and 515. By 512 he had conquered the Punjab in India and Thrace in Europe, though Athens escaped at Marathon in 490 B.C. Under his reign (521), Persepolis was begun by Darius. Many wonderfully preserved ruins are there today.

His son Xerxes I (485-465) was weak and thoroughly corrupt, as indicated all too clearly by the events in the Book of Esther in 483 B.C. (Est. 1:3) and 479-474 (Est. 2:16; 3:7). Between these two periods Xerxes (Ahasuerus) was engaged in mounting a massive attack on Greece (as predicted in Da. 11:2). His forces, however, were routed at Salamis harbor on Sept. 20, 480, and European culture was saved. Harem intrigues then controlled Persia until his murder and replacement by Artaxerxes I (465-424). Under Artaxerxes Judah prospered. In 458 he granted Ezra the authority by which he led back a second return of the Jews from Babylon (Ezr. 7—8) and instituted reforms (9—10), while only a renewed Samaritan opposition stopped the rebuilding of the city walls of Jerusalem (Ezr. 4:7-23; 9:9). Even this was achieved in 444 when Artaxerxes granted special authority as governor to his Jewish cupbearer, Nehemiah (Ne. 2:5-8; 6:15).

The OT comes to a close, chronologically, with the Book of Nehemiah, the last ruler that he mentioned being Darius II, the Persian (423-404) (Ne. 12:22; cf. 13:6-7). Among Persia's later monarchs, Artaxerxes II suffered an invasion in 401 by Greek professional soldiers; but it was Darius III in 331 who finally fell before the Greek troops of Alexander the Great, as predicted by Daniel long before (Da. 8:5-7, 21; 11:13). (J.B.P.)

PERSIS {female Persian} A Christian at Rome to whom Paul sent greetings (Ro. 16:12). †

PERUDA {single, unique} *See* PERIDA

PESHITTA {simple, *i.e.*, no marginal notes} *See* BIBLE, ANCIENT VERSIONS

PESTILENCE *See* SICK, SICKNESS

PESTLE The wooden or stone instrument held in the hand with which to grind or crush the material in a mortar (Pr. 27:22).

PETER, EPISTLES OF Internal evidence reflects clearly in the first epistle the mind and life of the Apostle Peter.

This, with the unanimous testimony of the early fathers going back to about A.D. 125, gives us the assurance of Petrine authorship. The second epistle purports to have been written by Peter (2Pe. 1:1), but has the least external attestation of any NT book. All that exists comes from a very late period, mid-third century. Internal evidence and tradition (late) make it feasible to accept a Petrine authorship, however. While some date the first epistle around A.D. 100 and the second even later, a good case can be made for dates between A.D. 65 and 70.

In the first epistle the author is concerned to make clear the Christian message of salvation (1Pe. 1:3-12) and the moral and ethical obligations for the Christian resulting from that salvation. As he led up to a discussion of proper conduct under suffering (4:12—5:11), it is assumed that those to whom he wrote were in need of encouragement to help them to endure their then present lot. In the second epistle the author was concerned to point out the presence, nature, and perils of turning away from the truth of the gospel and the written Word of God (2Pe. 2:1-22). He urged patient endurance and conformity to the truth in view of the coming Day of the Lord with all that it will mean in judgment for the wicked and blessing for the believers (2Pe. 3:8-18).

PETER, SIMON {(masc.) rock, stone} *See* APOSTLES

PETHAHIAH {Yahweh opens}

THE MEDO-PERSIAN EMPIRE
(Arrow shows route of returned exiles.)

1. The head of a priestly division in David's time (1Ch. 24:16). †

2. A priest who married a foreign wife during the time of the Babylonian captivity (Ezr. 10:23). †

3. A Levite in the time of Ezra (Ne. 9:5). †

4. A Levite overseer in the time of Nehemiah (Ne. 11:24). †

PETHOR A place in Mesopotamia, the home of Balaam who was called in by Balak to curse Israel (Nu. 22:5; Dt. 23:4). †

PETHUEL The father of the prophet Joel (Joel 1:1). †

PETRA {(fem.) rock, cliff, rock grotto} *See* SELA

PEULLETHAI, PEULTHAI {worker, wage earner} A Levite gatekeeper of the tabernacle in David's days (1Ch. 26:5). †

PHALEC *See* PELEG

PHALLU *See* PALLU

PHALTI *See* PALTI, PHALTIEL 2.

PHALTIEL *See* PALTIEL

PHANUEL {face of El} The father of the prophetess Anna when Christ was born (Lk. 2:36). *See* PENUEL, PENIEL

PHARAOH {the great house} A title meaning "the great house" or a title used as a name for a king of Egypt. The great majority of the occurrences of this word are in the Pentateuch and secondly elsewhere in the OT. There are only five occurrences in the NT (Ac. 7:10-21; Ro. 9:17; Heb. 11:24). From before 3000 B.C. to the time of the Persian conquest (525 B.C.) there were some twenty-six dynasties, perhaps more, in view of the silent Hyksos period. Abraham had contact with a Pharaoh (Ge. 12:15ff.). So too did Joseph, his brothers, and his father, Jacob (Ge. 39—50). This latter period was concluded with the conflict of Moses and Aaron with the Pharaoh that led to the exodus of the Israelites (Ex. 1—14). There were important contacts between King Solomon and the Pharaohs, Solomon marrying one of the

daughters of a Pharaoh (1Ki. 3:1; 9:16). Among the others that are mentioned, but very occasionally, is Pharaoh Neco, who defeated and killed King Josiah of Judah (2Ki. 23:29-35).

PHARAOH-HOPHRA Jer. 44:30. *See* HOPHRA

PHARES, PHAREZ {breech, breaking out} *See* PEREZ, PEREZITE

PHARISEES {separate ones} *See* SECTS

PHAROSH *See* PAROSH

PHARPAR *See* DAMASCUS

PHARZITE {of PEREZ} *See* PEREZ, PEREZITE

PHASEAH {hobbling one} *See* PASEAH 2.

PHEBE *See* PHOEBE

PHENICE, PHENICIA *See* PHOENIX (Ac. 27:12, KJV); PHOENICIA (Ac. 11:19; 15:3, KJV).

PHI-BESETH *See* PI BESETH

PHIC(H)OL Captain of the armies of King Abimelech of Gerar in the days of Abraham (Ge. 21:22, 32; 26:26). †

PHILADELPHIA {love of brother, sister} A city in W Asia Minor in the province of Lydia which was one of the early strongholds of Christianity (Rev. 1:11; 3:7). The city suffered from many severe earthquakes as of A.D. 17. †

PHILEMON {beloved} The owner of a slave by the name of Onesimus (Phm. 1). Paul pleaded with the owner to take the runaway back and to treat him as a brother. *See also* PAULINE EPISTLES

PHILEMON, BOOK OF *See* PAULINE EPISTLES

PHILETUS {beloved} One of the false teachers condemned by Paul (2Ti. 2:17). †

PHILIP {horse lover}

1. *See* APOSTLES.

2. One of the first deacons of the church, called also an evangelist

(Ac. 6:5). He was God's messenger at the conversion of the Ethiopian eunuch and Paul's host in Caesarea (Ac. 8:26ff.; 21:8-9). He had four unmarried daughters who prophesied.

3. A Tetrarch (Lk. 3:1), *see* HERODS, THE.

4. The husband of Herodias (Mt. 14:3; Mk. 6:17). *See* HERODS, THE

PHILIP THE APOSTLE *See* PHILIP 1.

PHILIP THE EVANGELIST *See* PHILIP 2.

PHILIPPI Named after Philip II of Macedon, Philippi is a city in E Macedonia about ten miles up river from the Aegean Sea, not to be confused with Caesarea Philippi in Palestine. *See* CAESAREA PHILIPPI. Paul visited it on his second missionary journey and later wrote an epistle to them. It was the first city of Europe to hear his message. Here he met Lydia, the seller of purple dye, and established a church in her home, and here he was jailed by owners of a slave out of whom he drove an evil spirit (Ac. 16:12-40; 20:6; Php. 1:1; 1Th. 2:2).

PHILIPPIANS, BOOK OF *See* PAULINE EPISTLES

PHILISTIA Another word for "Palestine." Palestine is found four times in KJV; in the NIV it is rendered Philistia or Philistines, appearing the same four times and five others (Ex. 15:14; Isa. 14:29, 31; Joel 3:4; Ps. 60:8; Zec. 9:6). The reference is to the coastal strip S of Joppa and W of the Shephelah, an area inhabited by the Philistines from whom the area derived its name. *See* GEOGRAPHY OF THE HOLY LAND and PHILISTINE CITIES

PHILISTIM KJV for "Philistines."

PHILISTINE CITIES *See also* GEOGRAPHY OF THE HOLY LAND, Ancient routes and major towns, *Relationships, Major North-South Routes, Major East-West Routes*

PHILO OF ALEXANDRIA A Jewish philosopher (13 B.C. to A.D. 45-50). He was also known as Philo Judaeus. His writings mixed Greek philosophy and Hebrew religion. Some terms he uses are also used in the NT, i.e., *logos, paraclete,* and others.

PHILOLOGUS [lover of words (education)] A Christian lady in Rome to whom Paul sent greetings (Ro. 16:15). †

PHILOSOPHY [lover of discernment, lover of wisdom] Reflection on the major questions of life. Logic, aesthetics, ethics, metaphysics, and epistemology are some of the concerns of modern philosophy. The Scriptures identify wisdom as beginning with the fear of *Yahweh* (Pr. 9:10). *See* PROVERBS, BOOK OF; WISDOM

PHINEAS, PHINEHAS [the Negro]
1. A son of Eli and brother of Hophni. *See* HOPHNI

2. Father of a priest in the time of Ezra (Ezr. 8:33).

3. A grandson of Aaron who settled at Gibeah after the conquest and ministered at Bethel (Ex. 6:25; Nu. 25:7ff.; Jos. 24:33; Jdg. 20:26-28).

PHLEGON [burning] A Christian at Rome to whom Paul sent greetings (Ro. 16:14). †

PHOEBE [radiant] A deaconess of the church at Cenchrea who was commended to the Christians at Rome by Paul (Ro. 16:1). †

PHOENICIA [land of purple (dye for trading), *possibly* land of date palms] cf. CANAANITE; *See* GEOGRAPHY OF THE HOLY LAND

PHOENIX [date palm *or* mythological bird of Egypt] A harbor on the S side of the island of Crete which Paul hoped to reach on his journey to Rome. The wind drove them past it (Ac. 27:12). †

PHRYGIA *See* GEOGRAPHY OF THE HOLY LAND

PHURAH *See* PURA

PHUT *See* PUT 1.

PHUVAH, PUA *See* PUAH

PHYGEL(L)US [fugitive] One who deserted Paul (2Ti. 1:15). †

PHYLACTERY [safeguard, means of protection] Mentioned only in Mt. 23:5, a small receptacle which contained some verses from the Bible that were bound on the arm and forehead by long leather thongs during prayer. The verses may have been Ex. 13:1-10; Dt. 6:4-9; 11:13-21. *See* FRINGES

PHYSICIAN Originally one who rendered first-aid to the wounded, a healer in that sense (2Ch. 16:12; Jer. 8:22; Lk. 5:31). *See* SICK, SICKNESS. Luke, the writer of Acts and the third Gospel, was a physician (Col. 4:14).

PI BESETH [temple (house) of Bastet (pagan goddess)] A city in the delta region of Egypt occupied over a long period of time but mentioned in the Bible only in connection with Ezekiel's prophecy against Egypt (*see* Eze. 30:17, NIV footnote).

PICK A sharp instrument of iron mentioned only in connection with saws and iron axes with which the Ammonites were either tortured or made to work by King David (2Sa. 12:31; 1Ch. 20:3).

PIETISM Christianity that emphasizes personal experience, personal study, and holiness.

PIETY *See* GODLINESS

PIG *See* BEASTS 10.

PIGEON *See* BIRDS 4.

PI HAHIROTH [temple (house) of Hathor (pagan goddess); *possibly* mouth of canals] An unidentified town or place in N Egypt where the Israelites last encamped before crossing the Red Sea (Ex. 14:2, 9; Nu. 33:7-8). †

PILATE [family name] The procurator or Roman governmental representative in Palestine at the time of the crucifixion of Christ. Pontius was his family name (Lk. 3:1; 23:1-25, 52; Jn. 18:29—19:38). Pilate delivered Jesus, after the trial, to be crucified and saw that the execution was carried out. His name has been found on an inscription in the excavations at Caesarea.

PILDASH [steely, ISBE; spider, KB] A son of Nahor and therefore nephew to Abraham (Ge. 22:22). †

PILEHA *See* PILHA

PILGRIM KJV for "alien," "stranger," or "sojourner." *See* STRANGER

PILGRIMAGE

1. A journey of the faithful to a holy site. Three times a year the Jewish male traveled to Jerusalem: Passover, Pentecost, Booths (Ex. 34:23). *See* CALENDAR

2. A figure for a man's journey through life, Christians are aliens and strangers to this world (1Pe. 2:11).

PILHA [millstone, IDB; ploughman, ISBE; harelip, KB] One who signed the covenant with Nehemiah (Ne. 10:24). †

PILLAR A stone monument set up as a memorial or an object of worship, called a *massebah* in Hebrew (Ge. 35:20; Ex. 23:24; 24:4). There were other stone memorials as well as the pillars (Jos. 4:19-24). Stone pillars or columns were also used in buildings both for structural reasons and for beauty. Stone pillars have been found standing alone in excavations for which no satisfactory explanation exists (IKi. 7:6; 15:22).

God's provision and guidance were manifested through the pillar or column of fire and cloud (Ex. 13:21-22). *See also* THEOPHANY

PILLOW *See* BED

PILOT KJV for "seamen" (sailors) (Eze. 27:8, 27-29). Also rendered "helmsman" (Jas. 3:4).

PILTAI [Yahweh rescues] A priest in the days of Nehemiah and the high priest Joiakim (Ne. 12:17). †

PIM A weight equal to about two-thirds of a shekel, which the Philistines charged the Israelites for sharpening a plowshare or mattock (1Sa. 13:21). †

PIN KJV for a tent peg (Jdg. 4:21).

PINE TREE *See* TREES

PINNACLE A Greek word for "wing" (Mt. 4:5); it describes the extremity of a building. The exact location is unknown. Many refer to the SE corner of the temple outer wall or possibly along the eastern wall facing the Kidron Valley. Josephus (*Antiq.* 15:11:5 and 20:9:7) said the SE corner was so high one who stood on the top of it could not see the bottom—and it "makes one dizzy." Along the eastern wall the valley floor was 600 feet below.

PINON [darkness, ISBE; *name related to* famous coppermines, KB] An Edomite chief and descendant of Seir (Ge. 36:41; 1Ch. 1:52). †

PINT *See* WEIGHTS AND MEASURES

PIPE *See* MUSIC, MUSICAL INSTRUMENTS

PIRAM [*possibly* wild ass, IDB; indomitable, ISBE; *possibly* zebra, KB] The king of the city of Jarmuth who joined an alliance against Joshua, was defeated and killed (Jos. 10:3ff.). †

PIRATHON, PIRATHONITE A town (165-177) in the hill country of Ephraim from which one of the minor judges and one of David's mighty men came (Jdg. 12:13-15; 2Sa. 23:30; 1Ch. 11:31; 27:14). †

PISGAH A mountain peak in Transjordan just NW of Mt. Nebo from which one could look down on the Israelite encampment and from which Balak tried to get Balaam to curse Israel (Nu. 21:20; 23:14). From this altitude God showed Moses the Promised Land into which he would not be allowed to go (Dt. 3:27; 34:1).

MOUNT PISGAH

PISHON An unidentified river that flowed out of the Garden of Eden (Ge. 2:11). †

PISIDIA *See* GEOGRAPHY OF THE HOLY LAND

PISON *See* PISHON

PISPAH A descendant of Asher (1Ch. 7:38). †

PISTACHIO *See* PLANTS, PERFUMES, AND SPICES, Plants for Food 6.

PIT *See* DEAD, ABODE OF

PITCH An inflammable (Isa. 34:9), viscous (sticky), or semiliquid mineral substance found in the area of the Dead Sea and Mesopotamia. The ark of Noah and the basket of bulrushes of the baby Moses were caulked with it (Ge. 6:14; Ex. 2:3). It was used instead of cement in building with bricks in Mesopotamia (Ge. 11:3).

PITCHER An earthenware jar fired in a kiln and used for storing grain or other material (Ecc. 12:6; Jer. 35:5). Much is known about these as the result of modern archaeological work. *See* POTTER, POTTERY

PITHOM {temple (house) of (pagan god) Atum} An unidentified city in Egypt which along with Rameses was built for the Pharaoh by the captive Israelites prior to their exodus (Ex. 1:11). †

PITHON A descendant of Saul (1Ch. 8:35; 9:41). †

PITY *See* COMPASSION

PLAGUE *See* SICK, SICKNESS

PLAGUES OF EGYPT These were the evil happenings to the Egyptians which God used to induce the Pharaoh to let the Israelites leave Egypt. Some, endeavoring to circumvent miracles, try to find naturalistic explanations for all of these. This is not satisfactory, especially when the timing of the events is taken into consideration. The water of Egypt *became* blood (not *like* blood), frogs covered the land as did lice and flies, and a plague of some sort hit all the livestock. This plague was followed by boils on man and beast. Then there came hail which destroyed crops and animals in the open to be followed by a plague of locusts. Darkness came suddenly on the land, and finally the firstborn of man and animal (where the angel did not see the atoning blood) died suddenly in one night. Throughout biblical history these incidents are used as warnings for God's people (Ex. 7:14–12:36).

PLAGUES OF REVELATION A transliteration of a word that means "a

blow" or "misfortune sent by God": three plagues of fire (Rev. 9:18, 20); seven last plagues (Rev. 15:1, 6, 8); heaven's people come out of plagues (Rev. 18:4); Babylon will receive the plagues (Rev. 18:8). The exact interpretation of these plagues is debated.

PLAINS *See* GEOGRAPHY OF THE HOLY LAND

PLAISTER *See* PLASTER

PLAITING KJV for "braided" hair (1Pe. 3:3).

PLAN OF GOD *See* WILL OF GOD

PLANE TREE *See* TREES, Other Trees, *Plane Tree*

PLANTS, PERFUMES, AND SPICES Some seventy items are discussed in this article and another two dozen under trees. (*See also* TREES.) Due to the fact that the references to many of these items in the Bible are so few, a measure of uncertainty exists in every effort to define them in modern terms. These more difficult areas are noted below. Scientific names are left, with but a few exceptions, for more complete treatments which may be found in multi-volume encyclopedias.

PLANTS FOR FOOD
1. *Wheat, barley, spelt*, and *millet* were the ancient and common staples, annual grasses sown with the early winter rains and reaped in May-June. The first two in their modern varieties are well known generally. Spelt is a form of *triticum* (wheat) (Ex. 9:32; Isa. 28:25; Eze. 4:9). Millet (Eze. 4:9) may be either *panicum miliaceum* or one of the sorghums. "Roasted grains," "new grain," and "roasted corn" usually refer to wheat (Dt. 8:8; 1Sa. 25:18; Lev. 2:14; Ex. 9:31; Nu. 5:15).
2. *Beans* and *lentils* are well-known staple items of the ancient diet. The former is the common broad bean and the latter, identified through its modern Arabic name is *lens esculenta* commonly used in pottage (Ge. 25:34; 2Sa. 17:28; 23:11; Eze. 4:9).
3. *Onions, garlic*, and *leeks* are

three bulbous members of the *allium* (lily) family of which some seventy or more varieties are known. The first two are well known even today in the Western world. The third looks like an elongated onion, is usually eaten raw, and quite evidently was an item of Israelite diet loved by them while enslaved in Egypt (Nu. 11:5). All were well-known staples in the ancient diet. It should be noted that the Hebrew word rendered "leeks" in the passage above is many times translated "grass" elsewhere in all the versions.

Melon

Leeks

4. *Cucumbers* and *melons* (Nu. 11:5; Isa. 1:8; Jer.10:5). The second is a variety of our commonly known watermelon, red inside. The first is much more likely to have been a muskmelon (cantaloupe), known in the Middle East from earliest times—a sweet melon and not our modern cucumber.

5. *Grapes* and *raisins*, the latter a dried form of the former (1Sa. 25:18). The former for wine (and its leaves as a vegetable) is so well known as to need no special description. The fruit of the vine is as much a staple in Palestine of antiquity as wheat, milk, or honey. The number of references to grapes, milk, and honey are about equal, and those to bread only slightly outnumber wine.

6. *Nuts* were of the *pistachio* and al-

mond variety and perhaps also the *walnut*. There is only one reference to the pistachio (Ge. 43:11), but there are many references to the almond nut, tree and flower taken together (Ge. 43:11; Ex. 25:33; Ecc. 12:5). See also below. There is also a reference to "a grove of nut trees" (SS. 6:11). *See also* PULSE.

FLOWERING PLANTS (including trees)

As noted in the general introduction above, nearly 100 flora species are mentioned in the Bible, but only a few are noted in connection with their flowers, and the identification of some of these is not certain. (A question mark after a flower indicates the uncertainty of the identification of the Hebrew word involved.)

1. *Almond*. Its flower is mentioned in connection with Aaron's rod which put forth buds and blossoms (Nu. 17:8). And on the golden lampstand of the tabernacle were patterned almond flowers (Ex. 25:33; 37:19).

2. *Chabazzelet* is rendered *"rose"* (of Sharon) (?), *"crocus"* (?) and it may even have been a *narcissus* (SS. 2:1; Isa. 35:1).

3. *Flax* and *henna* were flowering and noted as such in the Bible. The first was grown for fiber and seeds, the second

Almond Branch

Papyrus

for a reddish-brown dye (Ex. 9:31; SS. 1:14; 4:13).

4. The *lily* and *lotus* are both mentioned in connection with flowers, but the exact identity of either is unknown (1Ki. 7:26; Job 40:21-22).

5. *Reed* or *papyrus* and *vines* are noted as bearing flowers (Job 8:11-12; SS. 2:13; Isa. 18:5).

6. Among the trees, all of which have a flower, of course, the *olive* and the *pomegranate* are specifically mentioned with their flowers (SS. 2:13; Job 15:33; SS. 6:11).

7. The *grass* of the field is noted with its flower more often than any other single plant, and especially in connection with teaching the transitory character of life (Isa. 40:6-8; 1Pe. 1:24).

8. *Amaranthine*, a type of straw flower that does not wither when picked. This is used as a description of our unfading (i.e., eternal) inheritance and reward (1Pe. 1:4; 5:4).

SPINY PLANTS

There are some 100 plants in this category in Palestine and some fourteen Hebrew words refer to the spiny shrubs of one or more of the 100 kinds. The identification or equation of these words with an exact English botanical equivalent is virtually impossible. They include: *brambles, briars, nettles, thistles, thorns, thornbush* (Jdg. 9:14-15; Lk. 6:44; Isa. 55:13; 5:6; Isa. 34:13; Hos. 9:6; 2Ki. 14:9; Hos. 10:8; Mk. 15:17; Isa. 7:19).

PLANTS FOR SEASONING

Eight are noted in the NIV: *caraway, coriander, cummin, dill, mint, mustard, rue, saffron. Coriander sativum* is a known annual from whose seed a medicine and a condiment (seasoning) are made (Ex. 16:31; Nu. 11:7). The manna was like coriander seed and looked like resin (Nu. 11:7). *Cummin* is an aromatic seed somewhat like *caraway* (Isa. 28:27), and not used greatly in modern times (Isa. 28:25-27; Mt. 23:23). *Dill* is sometimes rendered *"anise"* in the KJV (Mt. 23:23), even though a true anise is not grown in Palestine. Dill is used in pickling and an oil from the seed is medicinal as well (Isa. 28:25-27). Three species of the aromatic *mint* leaf and flower grow in Palestine and are used for their aroma and flavor (Mt. 23:23; Lk. 11:42). *Mustard* is a common weed in modern Palestine, growing to tree height. Oil from its small seeds was used as a condiment, *brassica nigra* (Mt. 13:31). In the NT its small seed was used as an illustration for faith. *Rue,* one of the *Rutas,* was used as a medicine and condiment. It is used only in Lk. 11:42 where the parallel is dill. *Saffron* is the pollen of a crocus used both to dye food and in medicine—found only in SS. 4:14.

PERFUMES, SCENTS, OINTMENTS, DRUGS

Here again we deal with a number of names used but rarely in the text of the Bible, some well known because of the continuity of their use and some not easy to identify. Except in Nu. 24:6 and SS. 4:14 where *aloes* seems to be a tree (perhaps incorrectly translated "oak") it refers to a plant somewhat like the century plant. As used in the Bible, however, it would seem more probably that the reference is to some aromatic wood (Ps. 45:8; Jn. 19:39). *Balm* is a spice that appears to be a medicinal resin or gum from a mastic tree of the sumac family (Ge. 37:25). *Henna* is a shrub from whose dried leaves a reddish dye is secured that is used as a cosmetic and a hair coloring today. It is not clear how extensively it was used as such in biblical times (SS. 1:14). *Cane, sweet cane, calamus,* and *sweet calamus* are grasses that yield sweet volatile oils (i.e., vaporous, aromatic) such as *citronella* (Ex. 30:23; Isa. 43:24; Jer. 6:20). *Cinnamon* was an import into Palestine and not a native plant (Ex. 30:23; SS. 4:14; Rev. 18:13). *Cassia* is a translation of two Hebrew words whose meaning is not clear. One might be a tree of the cinnamon type and the other an aromatic shrub. Both would be imports to Palestine (Ex. 30:24; Ps. 45:8). *Myrrh* is a resin or gum exuded from a tree from which both a drug and

a perfume were made. It was used in embalming and, like cassia, cinnamon, aloes, and others, in making the holy oil of the temple used for anointing (Ex. 30:23; Pr. 7:17; Jn. 19:39). *Nard* is a perennial herb with a strongly aromatic root used in perfume and was an import to Palestine from E. India. Mary poured this expensive perfume on Jesus' head and feet (SS. 4:14; Mk. 14:3; Jn 12:3). *Frankincense* was made from a gum resin of several trees of the genus *boswellia* and was an import to Palestine (Ex. 30:34ff.). *Galbanum* is both an incense and a medicine derived from a plant of the same family as the carrot. It was used in the tabernacle incense (Ex. 30:34). Another ingredient of perfumes was *onycha,* found in the Bible only in Ex. 30:34. Its origin is not clear. *Myrtle* is a many-branched shrub used in perfumery and one of the "four kinds" required in the Feast of Booths, *myrtus communis* (Ne. 8:15; Isa. 41:19; Zec. 1:8-11).

Myrhh

MISCELLANEOUS PLANTS

Many of these plants are only rarely mentioned in the Bible and not enough information is given for identifications that are sure.

1. *Bitter herbs.* An unidentified herb used in the Passover meal (Ex. 12:8; Nu. 9:11).

2. *Broom tree,* a shrub that can grow high enough to make shade for animals

Myrtle

Hyssop

under it, *retama raetam* (1Ki. 19:4-5). Its roots were used for food (Job 30:4).

3. *Papyrus*, a reed that grows near water from which baskets and boats were made. From its pith, paper (papyrus) was made (Ex. 2:3; Job 8:11; Isa. 18:2).

4. *Linen*, a well-known modern plant, but noted only twice in the Bible (Est. 1:6; Isa. 19:9).

5. *Flax* was used in the textile industry. Linen was made from its fibers and its seeds were used both for food and paint oil (Ex. 9:31).

6. *Gourd*. Several varieties existed. One was poisonous but used for medicinal purposes (2Ki. 4:39-41); also called the vine of Sodom (Dt. 32:32).

7. *Hyssop*. It was used for the sprinkling of the sacrificial blood (Ex. 12:22; Lev. 14:4). Jesus was offered vinegar on a hyssop while he was dying on the cross (Jn. 19:29). Its buds and seed pods are used to make capers (relish or jam).

8. *Mandrake*, found only in Ge. 30:14-16 and SS. 7:13, refers to the druglike fruit of the plant, but it is not an aphrodisiac as legend would have it.

9. *Salt herb, saltwort*. This plant is rendered by most versions as *Mallow* (Job 30:4). The original idea of "salt" in its root; hence, a plant that grows in the salt marshes. It was a food eaten by the poor.

10. *Purslane* (Job 6:6, RSV) is translated "tasteless food" in the NIV and most versions as a figure of something loathsome.

11. *Balsam tree* (2Sa. 5:23-24; 1Ch. 14:14-15) is translated in KJV as "mulberry tree."

12. *Aroer* is a plant in Jer. 17:6 and 48:6; translated "heath" in KJV, "bush" in the NIV. Some Hebrew dictionaries define as "juniper." For KJV "juniper," *see* Misc. 2. Broom Tree. *See also* JUNIPER.

13. *Tares* are mentioned in the KJV (Mt. 13:25ff.). This is translated as "weeds" in the NIV, "darnel" in many

versions. A troublesome weed that resembles wheat.

PLASTER Used only in three contexts in the NIV, all in connection with plastering of walls (Lev. 14:41-48; Dt. 27:2-4; Da. 5:5). The plaster might be a mixture of clay and straw, of gypsum and ashes, or of slaked lime and sand.

PLEASURES *See* LUST

PLEDGE *See* DEBT; SEAL

PLEIADES [heap, group (of stars)] A grouping of stars known by the same name today (Job 9:9; 38:31; Am. 5:8). †

PLINY THE YOUNGER Pliny wrote Emperor Trajan a famous message (A.D. 112) supplying information about early Christian worship. He declared Christians spoke their songs to Christ as if he were a god. Pliny the Elder (author of *Natural History*) was his uncle. He became governor of Pontus/Bithynia (in modern Turkey) in about A.D. 110.

PLOW, PLOUGH, PLOWSHARE A plowshare, crude by today's standards, was used to turn the soil. The iron could be transformed into a weapon (Joel 3:10) and vice versa (Isa. 2:4). When a team plowed, it was not to be yoked with two different animals (Lev. 26:12; Dt. 22:10). This is alluded to in 2Co. 6:14. The Christian here is encouraged to also practice purity in a range of relationships with unbelievers, including business and premarital. See also 1Sa. 13:20-21; Mic. 4:3. *See* FARMING; WEIGHTS AND MEASURES, *Acre*

PLUMB LINE A measuring line for vertical accuracy used in connection with destruction (2Ki. 21:13; Isa. 28:17); a cord with a weight of tin or lead or stone was used for straight walls (Isa. 34:11; Am. 7:7-8; Zec. 4:10).

PLUNDER When an enemy was defeated, the victor took the plunder or booty—property and people as the prize of war. In some cases in ancient Israel the enemy and the property were called "condemned things" (Dt. 13:17) and/or "devoted" to the LORD (Jos.

6:17-19). When this was the case, the goods went to the temple treasurer and the persons were killed.

PNEUMATOLOGY *See* SYSTEMATIC THEOLOGY

POCHERETH *See* POKERETH-HAZZEBAIM

POETRY In the NT the easily recognized poems are all to be found in the Gospels connected with the birth narratives of John and Jesus. We know them today as the Magnificat of Mary, the prophecy of Zacharias, the Gloria in Excelsis of the angels, and the *Nunc Dimittis* (named after the first two words of the Latin version) of Simeon (Lk. 1:46ff.; 1:68ff.; 2:14; 2:29ff.). These are in the Hebrew poetic style recited by Jews originally. Elsewhere in the NT it is a matter of elevated, lyrical language or eloquence that creates the feeling of poetry, not a certain form, in spite of the fact that the language is Greek. Classical Greek poetry secured its poetic form by careful attention to a form built around syllabic feet and vowel length (i.e., counting the sounds in a line, consistently, so as to produce a rhythm or meter). This poetry is totally unknown in the OT, and since the writers of the NT were Jews of the OT tradition, Greek poetry only peeks through a few elevated passages of the NT: Ro. 11:33−12:2; 1Co. 13; Eph. 5:24; 1Ti. 3:16; 6:16. The Hebraic style comes through very clearly in the longer quotations of poetic portions of the OT: Ro. 3:10-18; 10:18-20; 11:9-10.

As we have noted, Greek poetry secured its poetic style by a rhythm or meter. Our English poetry traditionally secured its rhythm by a rhythm of accents (i.e., raising and lowering the tone in words and phrases). The poetry of the OT used neither method. Its rhythm is one of thoughts and ideas repeated, contrasted, or advanced in parallel or successive lines of the poem. Illustrations will help the reader to understand. The *synonymous* or repeated style in its simplest form develops its thought in alternate lines with the in-between lines being the ones that repeat the thoughts.

"The earth is the LORD'S, and the fulness thereof;
the world, and they that dwell therein;
For he hath founded it up the seas,
and established it upon the floods.
Who shall ascend into the hill of the LORD?
or who shall stand in his holy place?"
(Ps. 24:13, KJV).

The *contrasted* (antithetic) style is found abundantly, but especially in the Proverbs. The thought of the second line is in contrast with that of the first:

"A wise son maketh a glad father:
but a foolish son is the heaviness of his mother.
Treasures of wickedness profit nothing:
but righteousness delivereth from death.
The LORD will not suffer the soul of the righteous to famish:
but he casteth away the substance of the wicked" (Pr. 10:1-3, KJV).

The advanced style is usually referred to as *synthetic* parallelism. While it is not parallelism in the strictest sense of that word, the technique is used so frequently that there is agreement among all scholars that this was a deliberate poetic device. The second line advances the thought of the first.

"He is like a tree planted by streams of water,
which yields its fruit in season and whose leaf does not wither. . . .

Not so, the wicked!
They are chaff that the wind blows away" (Ps. 1:3-4).

In all three basic types there are interesting variations and minor stylistic features. There is no poem altogether made up of one form of parallelism. Extra lines are here and there thrown in also. No extended portion resembles Greek or English poetic style with syllabic or accentual rhythm. Strophes (i.e., a poetic stanza) and epistrophes

(i.e., repetitions of words or phrases) and acrostics (*see* ACROSTIC) do appear but are rare, certainly only incidental features. The poetic rhythm comes from the repetition of ideas with the various forms intermingled quite casually within any given poem.

It is estimated that about one-third of the OT is poetry. It is easily identified. Whenever one or more of the three parallelisms or repetitions noted above appear, there is poetry.

Another biblical poetic device in both Testaments is a chiasmus, which is an inverted relationship between the syntactic (structural) elements of parallel phrases, often with a central line that is an emphasis or pivot. It is actually as much thought-form as a conscious poetic device, though at times both are true. They are found in: lists (Ge. 12:16); prophecies (Isa. 60:13; Am. 5:4b-6a); and in the NT.

Examples are:
Mk. 2:27
(a) The Sabbath
(b) was made for *man,*
(b) not *man*
(a) for the Sabbath.

or helpful for interpretation:

Mt. 7:6
(a) Do not give dogs what is sacred;
(b) do not throw your pearls to pigs.
(b) If you do, they *[the pigs]* may trample them under their feet,
(a) and then *[the dogs]* turn and tear you to pieces.

Bible students should be sensitive to poetry and rhythm in the Bible.

POETS, PAGAN, QUOTATIONS FROM *See* SCRIPTURE, *ancient writers*

POISON This came either from reptiles or certain plants. An evil tongue of a human is referred to as full of poison (Dt. 29:18; Job 20:16; Ps. 140:3; Hos. 10:4; Jas. 3:8).

POKERETH-HAZZEBAIM, POCHERETH OF ZEBAIM [pitfall of

gazelles, *i.e.*, gazelle hunter} The ancestor of some who returned with Zerubbabel from the Babylonian captivity (Ezr. 2:57; Ne. 7:59). †

POLE *See* BANNER

POLL *See* CENSUS

POLLUTION *See* CLEAN AND UNCLEAN

POLLUX *See* DEITIES 1., The gods of Greece, *Castor and Pollux*

POLYGAMY {many marriages} The practice of having more than one wife at a time. *See* CONCUBINE; MARRIAGE

POLYTHEISM Belief in or worship of more than one god. *See also* HENOTHEISM; MONOTHEISM

POMEGRANATE *See* TREES

POMMEL KJV for "bowel" or "bowl shaped" (2Ch. 4:12-13, most versions). The JB has "moldings." *See* CAPITAL; TEMPLE

PONTIUS PILATE *See* PILATE

PONTUS *See* GEOGRAPHY OF THE HOLY LAND

POOL, POOLS Natural or artificial reservoirs for holding water. In a country totally devoid of rainfall for seven to nine months of every year, these become very important for survival. Among the interesting ones noted in the Bible for some special event that took place beside the pool are those at Gibeon, Hebron, Samaria, Hezekiah's upper, lower, and old pools (2Sa. 2:13ff.; 4:12; 1Ki. 22:38; 2Ki. 18:17; 20:20; Isa. 22:9, 11). *See* AIN; CISTERN; FOUNTAIN; SPRING; WATER; WELL

POOR The translation of several Hebrew and Greek words meaning "poor" in a material sense, "weak," "unfortunate," or "afflicted." The Mosaic Law was very specific on care for the poor and gave considerable space to the subject. Because Israel became careless in this matter, the prophets took up the theme in extended passages (Ex. 22:25;

23: 3-11; Lev. 19:9-15; 25:25-30, 39-54; Dt. 24:10-22; Isa. 10:1; 2; Am. 2:6; 5:7; Mal. 3:5). Jesus associated himself with the poor and showed great concern for them, although his major emphasis was on the spiritually poor (Mt. 5:3; cf. Lk. 6:20). The NT gives considerable evidence of concern among the members of the early church for the poor in their midst, even to the appointing of special officers (deacons) for their care (Lk. 6:20-26; 2Co. 6:10; Ac. 6:1-6; Gal. 2:10; Jas. 2:3-6).

POPE The head of the Roman Catholic church.

POPLAR *See* TREES

PORATHA One of the sons of Haman, the opponent of the Jews in the Persian court in the time of Esther (Est. 9:8). †

PORCH The entrance room of a building or courtyard, frequently roofed. The RSV usually renders it "vestibule." Important buildings such as King Solomon's palace and the temple (NIV "portico") had elaborate vestibules, while even relatively simple buildings had such entryways. The later is now well known from various excavations (1Ki. 6:3; 7:6ff.; Eze. 40:7ff.; Mt. 26:71; Jn. 5:2).

PORCIUS *See* FESTUS

PORNOGRAPHY Written or visual materials that promote fornication in the broadest sense. To look upon a woman with lust is a serious sin (Mt. 5:28).

PORPHYRY *See* PRECIOUS STONES AND METALS

PORTENT *See* MIRACLES

PORTICO *See* PORCH

PORTION, LOT, SHARE, POSSESSION *See* LOT 2.; *see also* INHERITANCE

POSSESSION Besides the usual meaning of this word in the sense of ownership, it is used to refer to possession of an individual by a demon. *See* DEMON, DEMONIAC

POST These refer to doorposts or gateposts. One of the words used is rendered in the RSV as "threshold" (Ex. 12:7; 2Ch. 3:7; Eze. 45:19). The word is also used in the sense of a place of duty. The priests stood at their posts (2Ch. 7:6).

POSTMILLENNIALISM A belief that in the end times Christ will return at the end of the Millennium. Those of this view see Christ reigning through his church during the Millennium, and not physically or bodily.

POT The English translation for more than a dozen Hebrew and Greek words for ceramic and metal vessels. *See* POTTER, POTTERY; VESSEL

POTENTATE KJV for "ruler" (1Ti. 6:15). The Greek word can also be rendered as "sovereign" and comes from the word for powerful or mighty.

POTIPHAR [he whom (pagan god) Ra gives] The officer of Pharaoh to whom Joseph was sold (Ge. 37:36; 39:1ff.). †

POTIPHERA(H) [he whom (pagan god) Ra gives] The priest of On in Egypt and the father-in-law of Joseph (Ge. 41:45, 50; 46:20). †

POTSHERD A piece of broken pottery, also called a sherd or shard. Job used them to scrape himself, and he described the underparts of leviathan as like potsherds with their rough edges (Job 2:8; 41:30). One of the gates of the city of Jerusalem was called the "Potshed Gate," presumably near the quarter of the potters and where they dumped their broken material (Jer. 19:2).

POTTAGE A thick vegetable soup or stew with meat added occasionally (Ge. 25:29-34; 2Ki. 4:38-40).

POTTER, POTTERY Pottery was the ancient ceramic, used for many things besides dishes and other vessels. Clay was worked and then baked at high temperatures in an oven with a resulting product of a stone-like character. In the latter end of the neolithic times, after about 5000 B.C., man discovered the art of pottery making. At first it was very crudely done. Later the wheel came into use, and vessels of finer shape and greater variety resulted. Painting on pottery was known from very early times, and much of it was from iron ore and thus reddish or reddish-brown in color. Simple geometric designs and later more or nate drawings of birds and animals were used. Polishing to a high gloss was also known from at least 2500 B.C. The potter's wheel at first was a very simple and small affair consisting of two stones. The lower had a hole in its flat upper surface and the upper stone had the nipple in its flat undersurface to fit that hole. This stone, flat also on the upper surface, was turned while the potter made his vessel upon it. Some of these were only inches in diameter. Bowls, platters, jugs, juglets, storage jars of massive proportions, strainer jars, lamps, cooking pots, and other vessels were made. The styles of all of these vessels varied through the centuries, and that development is well known to all archaeologists—so much so that it is by the style of the pottery that they date the various strata of their excavations. In various periods there were beautiful imports; for example the Mycenaean ware of the Late Bronze period (Isa. 41:25; 45:9; Jer. 18:2-6). *See also* BRICK; VESSEL

POTTER'S FIELD The piece of ground bought for the burial of strangers by the priests with the money with which Judas Iscariot betrayed Jesus. The place is called "Akeldama," which translated means "field of blood" (Mt. 27:7, 10). *See also* AKELDAMA

POUND *See* WEIGHTS AND MEASURES

PRAETORIUM, PRAETORIAN GUARD [residence of the Praetor (leader)] The praetorium was originally the name of the tent of a Roman general. Later it came to be the name of the residence of an important Roman official or even any important house, villa, or "palace" and is usually so rendered in the NIV. The praetorian guard, used in the RSV only in Philippians 1:13, might refer to a bodyguard or to the military or imperial court in a praetorium. In the NT the praetorium was the judgment hall (Mt. 27:27; Mk. 15:16; Jn. 18:28, 33; Ac. 23:35).

PRAISE The giving of thanks, blessing or glory to living or inanimate things, and especially to men or God (Ge. 29:35; 1Ch. 16:4; Ps. 146:1; Lk. 19:37; Eph. 1:6-14). Praises often take the form of poems or songs (1Ch. 16:9; 2Ch. 29:30). A prominent theme of the NT is the praise of God for spiritual redemption (Eph. 1:5-7).

PRAYER In its most simple form prayer is conversation and intercession with God. One may address a prayer, a request or petition, to a man or men, but here we are concerned with prayers to Deity. These may be the recitation or reading of liturgical prayers or they may be spontaneous creations of the heart and mind. Prayer can include petition and intercession, thanks and praise, adoration, and meditation. The Bible does not lay down laws relative to the time and place for prayer, nor does it require any particular attitude or position to be assumed by the one who is praying. The word "pray" and its related forms are used scores of times in the NIV. These do not include cognate words such as "ask," or "petition." Ez. 9–10; Ne. 1; Ps. 17; 86; 90; 102; 142; Dan. 9; Mt. 6; Php. 1:9-11 provide examples of prayer in the Bible.

PREACH, PREACHER, PREACHING This is to herald or proclaim (forthtell) a message committed to one by another. The prophet was a preacher. He passed on the messages given to him by God. In the NIV these words are found only nine times in the OT but scores of times in the NT where the role of the OT prophet no longer existed. Modern preaching consists of disseminating the message of the Bible, the Word of God, in any of several different ways.

PRECIOUS STONES AND METALS In the case of the precious stones it is often difficult to make accurate and specific identifications in terms of stones known today. This is frequently true in view of the fact that a small number of references to them in the Bible does not give enough data for positive identification. Of the precious stones, twelve were found in the breastplate of the high priest, starting with Aaron (Ex. 28:19), and in the walls of the New Jerusalem (Rev. 21:19-20). Some are in both.

PRECIOUS STONES

1. *Agate, carnelian, chalcedony, chrysoprase, jasper, onyx, sardonyx, ruby* are varying forms of quartz or chalcedony, a kind of colored quartz with the lustre of wax. Carnelian is red. Chalcedony is often milky or grayish. Chrysoprase is apple-green. The ruby is also red and may be the same as the carnelian or sardius. The sardonyx is a form of onyx and is used only in Ge. 2:12; Ex. 25:7; 28:17, 19; 39:10; Eze. 28:13; Rev. 21:10, 19-20. Some of these are found as only onyx in the Bible and no one of them more than twelve times.

2. *Alabaster, marble.* Marble is a recrystallized limestone, a form of calcite or calcium carbonate. Alabaster is another of this group much used in making perfume jars or bottles. There are only three occurrences of the first and five of the second noted in the NIV (1Ch. 29:2; SS. 5:15; Mt. 26:7).

3. *Amethyst,* a purple quartz, one that adorned the high priest's breastplate (Ex. 28:19; 39:12; *see also* Rev. 21:20).

4. *Basalt,* not really a precious stone but one of great importance since, because of its hardness, it was used in grinding. Vessels of various types were made from it. It is a black volcanic rock common in Palestine, even if not mentioned in the Bible.

5. *Beryl, emerald, turquoise.* The emerald is a green precious stone of some kind, green beryl, feldspar or turquoise. Beryl is perhaps a "poor man's" emerald, a green feldspar (Ex. 28:17, 20; Rev. 21:19-20). The carbuncle may be a green beryl (Ex. 28:17; 39:10; Eze. 28:13).

6. *Chrysolite,* in modern times a

golden-yellow topaz; one of the high priest's stones in the breastplate (Ex. 28:20; Eze. 1:16; 28:13; Rev. 21:20).

7. *Coral*, the hard calcareous (i.e., containing calcium) skeleton of certain types of marine animals, pinkish or red in color (Job 28:18; Eze. 27:16).

8. *Flint*, an impure form of quartz, a very hard stone. From it were made some of man's first implements (Ex. 4:25; Jos. 5:2; Jer. 17:1).

9. *Jacinth*, one of the stones in the high priest's breastplate and in the walls of the New Jerusalem. Its identity is not certain (Ex. 28:19; Rev. 21:20).

10. *Pearl*, not a stone but usually listed with them because it was and is an important jewel (Mt. 7:6; 13:45; Rev. 21:21).

11. *Sapphire*, considered by some as a fine form of corundum, while others think that in antiquity the Hebrew word behind it referred to lapis lazuli (Ex. 24:10, Eze. 1:26; Rev. 21:19).

12. *Lapis lazuli, see* the NIV footnote to Ex. 24:10. It was blue in color (Ex. 24:10; Rev. 21:19).

13. *Topaz*, probably a form of quartz. There were various varieties as far as color is concerned but the yellow was the most prized (Ex. 28:17; 39:10; Rev. 21:20).

14. *Resin, see* Ge. 2:12; Nu. 11:7; transliterated "Bdellium" in the KJV.

15. *Crystal*, in Rev. 4:6; 21:11; 22:1 probably a type of rock crystal, but possibly it could be translated "ice" (Eze. 1:22, LXX) due to the context of describing water with the crystalline appearance. *See also* GLASS

METALS

1. *Copper* and *bronze* are translations of the one Hebrew word *nechosheth*. The first is a pure metal. Bronze is an alloy of copper and tin, while brass, used in the KJV, means "bronze." Copper was gold and metallic iron and the earliest metal used by man. From the middle of the fourth millennium B.C. (with the exception of the unexplained reference in Ge. 4:22 to Tubal-Cain who worked with both copper and iron prior to the

time of the Flood of Noah's day), man began to use copper tools and implements of many types to replace those of stone he had been using before (Dt. 8:9; Job 28:2; Lk. 21:2). Copper was usually hammered, while bronze was cast.

2. *Bronze, iron, lead, silver*, and *tin* are mentioned in connection with being melted in a furnace or forged (Isa. 44:12; Eze. 22:18-20; bellows are noted in Jer. 6:29). These had to be refined or even extracted by heat from ores which contained them in combination with other chemicals. What some refer to as "mercury" or "quicksilver" is the dross resulting from this refining. Dross was used as a slip on pottery or other objects and in a figurative sense of wicked people (Ps. 119:119; Pr. 25:4; Isa.1:22, 25; Eze. 22:18-19).

3. *Gold* was one of the earliest natural minerals or metals used in ornaments and for decorating (Ge. 2:11-12, and many others). Goldsmiths, images covered with gold, cloth woven with gold are noted in the Bible (Isa. 40:19; 30:22; Ps. 45:13).

4. *Iron* was smelted from an oxide and carbonate. The ore, hematite, was early used as a paint for pottery (Ge. 4:22; Nu. 31:22). There is one reference to a blacksmith (Isa. 44:12). Its use in the Bible before the Flood is interesting from the point of view of the archaeologist who puts the "iron age" not before 1202 B.C. Perhaps the Gen. reference is to meteoric iron.

5. *Lead* is extracted from galena, lead sulphide. Metallic lead is very rare (Nu. 31:22; Eze. 22:18, 20).

6. *Silver* in earliest times was more costly than gold. This changed only as late as the middle of the first millennium B.C. when the quantity of available refined silver had greatly increased. Silver was used for jewelry and for vessels in palaces, the tabernacle, and the temple (Ge. 13:2; Nu. 7:13). There are references to a silversmith and silver overlay (Jdg. 17:4; Ac. 19:24; Isa. 30:22).

7. *Tin* was extracted from an ore, found at first in streambeds, and mined

in Roman times (Nu. 31:22; Eze. 22:18, 20; 27:12).

PREDESTINATE, PREDESTINED The word is defined in Ac. 4:28 as that which God predetermined in his plan. In Ro. 8:28-29 Paul made the point that God calls according to his purpose those whom he predetermined would be conformed to the image of his Son. God predestines both events and persons, both individuals and groups. This is otherwise called his election and those thus affected are called the elect. *See also* ELECT, ELECTION

PREDICT To foretell or prophesy. "The new moons predict what shall befall" (Isa. 47:13). The prophets of the OT frequently spoke about future events. They predicted or foretold what God had revealed to them was to come to pass later (Ro. 9:29; 1Pe. 1:11). The apostles of the NT also foretold future events but much more rarely (Jude 17). *See also* PROPHET, PROPHECY

PREMILLENNIALISM The belief that Christ will come to earth for 1,000 years and rule on the earth.

PREFECT Used only in Daniel of some appointed to a position of authority (Da. 2:48; 3:2-3, 27; 6:7).

PREPARATION DAY Friday, the day of preparation for the Sabbath or Passover (Mt. 27:62; Mk. 15:42; Lk. 23:54; Jn. 19:14, 31, 42).

PRESBYTERY {old man, Elder} KJV for "Elders." *See* ELDER; OVERSEER; PASTORS

PRESIDENTS Like "prefect" above, a word appearing only in Da. 6:27 (KJV), referring to top administrators in the realm of the Persian king Darius. There were three, of which Daniel was one.

PRESS FAT KJV for "wine vat" (Hag. 2:16). *See* OIL; WINE

PRESS OIL *See* OIL; WINE

PRESSING *See* CROWD

PRETRIBULATIONALISM The belief that Christ will remove the church from earth before the Great Tribulation.

PRICK KJV for what is called "barb" (Nu. 33:55, NIV) and "goad" (Ac. 26:14, NIV). *See* GOAD

PRIDE Pride is a character flaw according to the Scripture. Arrogance, loftiness, boasting (verbalized pride), haughtiness are all ample synonyms. Often the rich are characterized as proud. Pride and boasting can turn one into a person without substance, a windbag (Pr. 25:14). The LORD will be against the proud (Pr. 15:25; Isa. 2:11; Am. 6:8). And pride is part of the world's system (1Jn. 2:16). Therefore, Christians are to clothe themselves with humility (1Pe. 5:5). In the context of spiritual gifts, Christians are not to think higher or lower of themselves than they ought to, but to think with clear judgment (Ro. 12:3). *See* HUMBLE

PRIESTS, PRIESTHOOD The priest is a minister of religion whether pagan, Jewish, or Christian (Ge. 41:45; Ex. 31:10; 1Pe. 2:4-5). During the time of the wilderness wanderings after the exodus from Egypt, God gave to the Israelites the instructions concerning the founding and procedure for the priestly order in Israel. There, too, he chose the tribe of Levi to be the priestly tribe (Ex. 28–29; Lev. 8; Nu. 3).

Numbers 8:14-19 is a key section in respect to the call and role of the Levites in the service of God and his people. There were many restrictions as to who could be a priest. First he had to be a son of Aaron (Lev. 21:1), and then he had to be of good health with no physical handicaps (Lev. 21:16-21). He could marry only a virgin (Lev. 21:13). These requirements were to emphasize that the people of Yahweh and his priests were to be holy (i.e., unique and special) in keeping with the theme of the Book of Leviticus.

In ancient Israel there was a high priest (or chief priest), Levites who were priests, and Levites who were not priests but served God and his people in other capacities. That is, all priests were Levites, but not all Levites were priests. (On the pre-Mosaic priest, *see* MELCHIZEDEK. On Christ as priest, *see* CHRIST, WORK OF.) The Book of Hebrews treats this latter subject at considerable length (Heb. 1:3; 2:9; 6:10–7:17; 8:5; 7:27; 9:26). In the NT in particular, but not exclusively, there is a priesthood of believers (1Pe. 2:5-9). As the believer takes the message of God to men he executes the function of a priest (Rev. 1:5-6). *See* CHIEF PRIESTS

PRIESTHOOD OF ALL BELIEVERS A Christian has direct access to God through Christ. In the NT each believer is part of a royal priesthood (1Pe. 2:9). *See* PRIESTS

PRINCE, PRINCESS While the princess is the wife or daughter of a king or a chief, the prince may be any person of prominence who has authority. There were princes of nations and princes of cities; even important merchants were called princes (Ge. 34:2; Eze. 28:2; Isa. 23:8). Messiah is called prince, and so are important demons as well as their leaders (Da. 9:25; Isa. 9:6; Lk. 11:15). The NIV frequently translates it "ruler" (Mt. 2:6; Rev. 1:5).

PRINCIPALITIES These are powerful angels or demons as organized against God and his people (Eph. 3:10; 6:12; Col. 2:15).

PRINT KJV in Lev. 19:28 for "tattoo," translated "mark" in Job 13:27 and Jn. 20:25 (NIV).

PRISCA, PRISCILLA The wife of Aquila who with her husband left Rome and joined Paul after the persecutions in Rome; also called Prisca (Ac. 18:2; Ro. 16:3).

PRISON A place of incarceration, be it under custody or guard only or in a place of confinement, even a dungeon (Lev. 24:12; 1Ki. 22:27; Jer. 37:16). Two special cases of imprisonment are noted, that of former disobedient spirits now,

and that of Satan to come (1Pe. 3:19-20; Rev. 20:7). *See* SPIRITS 2.

PRIZE *See* REWARDS

PROC(H)ORUS One of the seven first deacons of the church (Ac. 6:5). †

PROCONSUL A Roman official of high rank in both the military and civil spheres. Paul converted one and was tried before another (Ac. 13:7-12; 18:12).

PROCURATORS *See* PILATE

PROFANE To defile or desecrate by doing the forbidden at a holy place or with the holy things (Ex. 20:25; Lev. 18:21; 19:29; Nu. 18:32). In the NT to be godless was to be profane (1Ti. 1:8-11).

PROFIT *See* REWARDS

PROMISE This word and those related to it occur nearly 100 times in the OT of the NIV, even while there is no Hebrew word that specifically means "to promise." When God is the subject of the verbs that normally mean "to say," "to speak," or "to swear," and when his people are the recipients of the message, the translators rendered these three words "to promise." "And I have promised to bring you up out of your misery in Egypt" (Ex. 3:17, NIV). And also, " . . . so that the LORD will bring about for Abraham what he has promised him" (Ge. 18:19, NIV). As God does not change, his word is his promise. Great OT promises were made to or about individuals: to those in the Garden of Eden, which included the protoevangelium, the first promise of redemption from sin (Ge. 3:14-19); to Abraham, reaffirmed in his son and grandson and later to Moses at the time of the constitution of the theocracy—that God would make of him and his seed a great nation through whom all the families of the earth would be blessed, a promise that included both the coming of Messiah for spiritual blessing and redemption and the promise that the land of "Palestine" would perpetually be Israel's (Ge. 15:18; 17:6-8; 18:19; 26:1-5; Jn. 8:56; Gal. 3:16); to King David—that his throne would be established forever, never lacking one to sit upon it, a promise Christians see fulfilled in the Messiah Jesus (2Sa. 7:16; Ps. 89:20, 29-37; Lk. 1:31-33; Ac. 2:29-32); and to all Israel — that they would be gathered from any part of the world into which they might be driven and brought back to the land of their forefathers and there be made again into a great nation prior to the great Day of the LORD in the end of days (Jer. 23:5-8; Eze. 11:17; 28:25-26; 36:24-28; 37:24-28). In the opinion of the Jewish Christians in post-NT times this promise to Israel had not at that time been fulfilled. It was, in their opinion, not to come to pass until after the time known as the time when God will have "visited the Gentiles, to take out of them a people for his name" (Ac. 15:14-16).

In the NT three words related in form convey the idea of promise. Here too it is God in relation to his people. Foremost among NT promises is the one in which God shows his intention to visit his people in the person of his Son to redeem them from sin. Paul indicates that all God's promises are focused in this particular promise (2Co. 1:19-20; Eph. 3:4-6), and that the promise to Abraham included both the circumcision (Israel according to the flesh) and those who have the faith of Abraham (Gentiles who become related to God through Christ) (Ro. 4:11, 13, 16; Gal. 3:6-9, 13-14). Important NT promises include the coming again of Christ and eternal life for the believer (Heb. 6:15; Jas. 1:12; 2Pe. 3:9).

PROOF TEXT A passage of Scripture that is used to support a teaching. Without a clear inductive use of the context, a proof text is more of a weapon than a tool for Bible study. It is worth noting that "a proof text without a context is a pretext."

PROPHET, PROPHETESS, PROPHECY [speak before] Two basic concepts underlie these three words: forthtelling and foretelling. The first is the more basic and frequent. It means that one person becomes the "mouthpiece" for another, often consoling or correcting. This is the Hebrew word *nabi*. Aaron

played this role for his brother, Moses (Ex. 7:1). Prior to the time of Samuel, a prophet was called a "seer" in Israel, *ro' eh* (1Sa. 9:9). Later there were "schools" (i.e., a member of a class, order, or guild) of prophets and those in them were "sons of the prophets" (2Ki. 4:38; 2:3-15). In earliest times there were many prophets who did not write but spoke only; Gad, Nathan, Ahijah, Jehu, Elijah, and Elisha being but some of them (1Sa. 22:5; 1Ki. 1:23; 14:2; 16:7; 18:36; 2Ki. 9:1). We do not know the names of the authors of the biblical books of Joshua, Judges, Kings, and Samuel, but they are commonly known as the former prophets. Their message is one of forthtelling primarily. The writing prophets, in which there is also much foretelling or predictive material in addition to the parts which are delivering other messages from God (forthtell), are Isaiah, Jeremiah, Ezekiel, and those called the twelve "minor" prophets, Hosea to Malachi in the commonly-known English Bible order. In all the rest of the OT, and in fact in all the rest of the Bible, everything is foretelling and in that sense prophetic. Scattered through all these other parts of predictive material foretelling is also to be found. It should not be thought that because a given book is found in the third section of the Hebrew canon it is not prophetic. All of these books meet the requirement of forthtelling, and many of them contain sections of foretelling as well. One in each Testament (Daniel and Revelation) is even put in the apocalyptic class, where the foretelling is by way of visions and strange symbolisms.

The message of the prophets, whether nonwriting or writing, is very generally the same. First comes a rebuke from God for sin and for departure from God's ways. The second part tells of God's judgment that will come upon the person or people under condemnation. The third part, pertaining usually to a nation, tells of God's love for his people and the great blessing he will bring upon them after they have learned their lessons in the chastisement and have turned back to

God. Such a cycle may be seen in Deuteronomy 28–30.

The prophetess may be only the wife of a prophet or she may be an actual prophet (Ex. 15:20; 2Ki. 22:14; Isa. 8:3; Lk. 2:36).

For examples of predictive prophecy *see* PROMISE. *See also* DIVINATION; PREACH

PROPHETS, BOOKS OF THE MINOR The dating of the writing of these twelve books by some is uncertain and often debated. There is a tendency on the part of some scholars to lower the dates to exilic or even postexilic times. (They are called "minor" because they are shorter than the larger books–Isaiah, Jeremiah, Ezekiel–not because they have less value or authority.) After six of the twelve it is quite generally agreed that a question mark should be placed: Joel, Obadiah, Nahum, Habakkuk, Zephaniah, and Malachi. These do not state in their introductions the name(s) of the kings of their days, nor are there sufficient historical allusions in the text of the books to be of much value in dating them. Traditionally they are all called prophets to the southern kingdom, Judah, and, with question marks in respect of their dates, are put at about 800, 650, 640, 630, 550 and 430 B.C. respectively. Micah dated himself in the reigns of Jotham, Ahaz, and Hezekiah, a prophet to Judah (Mic. 1:1). This would be from about 740 to 700. Zechariah and Haggai are exactly datable to the second year of Darius (520 B.C.). They prophesied to Judah after the exile (Hag. 1:1; Zec. 1:1). The prophets to the northern kingdom, Israel, were Jonah, Amos, and Hosea. The first is variously dated between about 750 and the beginning of the sixth century B.C. Amos stated that he saw the vision in the days of Uzziah of Judah and Jeroboam of Israel, two years before an earthquake (Am. 1:1). The reigns of these two kings overlapped between about 780 and 740 B.C. Hosea noted that the word of the LORD came to him in the days of Uzziah, Jotham, Ahaz, and Hezekiah of Judah and Jeroboam of Israel (Hos. 1:1). This would give a date of about the same time as Amos.

Some notes on content should be appended. These are in order of the books themselves in the Bible.

Hosea. The book begins with the account of the prophet's marriage, which was an illustration of God's dealing with his people, both the married wife, Israel, and the "bride," the church (Hos. 1–3; Ro. 9:25-26). The rest of the book is concerned with noting the sin of God's people, impending judgment, exhortations to repentance, and God's love–the last in chapter 11.

Joel. A plague of locusts is portrayed and used as the basis for urging the people to repent and to give a promise of blessing if they will. In the second cycle we are told about God's judging the nations and of judgment being followed by the blessing of deliverance for Israel.

Amos. This is the third book in the section called the twelve, or more commonly, the Minor Prophets. He was a shepherd from Tekoa, in Judea, in the time of Uzziah (Am. 1:1). He calls for judgment against surrounding nations and Israel. Amos tells of present personal sin and social injustice, defined by the standards of the Old Covenant (Ex. 20–24; Lev. 17–26; Dt. 5–26; cf. Am. 3:1). The LORD sent cursings based on his faithfulness to keep his promise in the conditional blessings for obedience and cursings for disobedience in that Mosaic Covenant (Lev. 26; Dt. 27–28; cf. Am. 2:48). In customary prophetic form, Amos calls for repentance (5:1). Yet he predicts a future time of Israel's destruction, and ultimately Israel's restoration.

Obadiah was a prophecy on Edom's judgment by God and subsequent blessing.

Jonah contains the famous incidents connected with this prophet's running away from God, his return, and trip to Nineveh to deliver God's message there.

Micah predicted God's judgment on Samaria and Jerusalem, the return from the captivity, and God's ultimate blessings on his people in the end of days. One of the well-known predictions on the birth of Christ is found in 5:2.

Nahum predicted the destruction of Nineveh.

Habakkuk concerned himself in the beginning with the righteousness of God in punishing people, follows it with a message of doom on the Chaldeans, and ends with the beautiful prayer of chapter 3.

Zephaniah concerned himself with God's judgment on a number of peoples and God's promise to send great deliverance through the Messianic Age later.

Haggai urged the people on in their rebuilding of the postexilic temple.

Zechariah commenced with six chapters of visions, some of them highly symbolic. Chapters 7 and 8 are concerned with the keeping of the fasts now that the people are back in Jerusalem, the fact that the fasts will become feasts, and that all nations will receive the blessings (8:20-23). The final six chapters are concerned with God's judgment on the nations and his mercy on his people when the Prince of Peace will come.

Malachi described God's love for his people but complained about the negligence of people and priests and called them back to the Law. The book ends with a prophecy that Elijah is to return before the Day of the LORD.

PROPITIATION KJV for "atoning sacrifice" (Ro. 3:25; 1Jn. 2:2; 4:10). *See* CHRIST, WORK OF 3. (f) *Propitiation*; EXPIATE; SALVATION, APPLICATION OF

PROSELYTE The concept is much earlier than the only occurrences of the word in the NT would indicate (Mt. 23:15; Ac. 2:10; 6:5). In these cases the reference is to Gentile proselytes to Judaism in pre-Christian times. The Greek word used in these three cases is the word the LXX uses to translate the Hebrew word *ger*, which means "sojourner," one for some reason taking refuge with a foreign people. At some time before the NT,

the word changed in meaning from immigrant sojourner to proselyte.

PROSTITUTE Several Hebrew and Greek words are thus rendered in the NIV. Religious prostitution was practiced at pagan shrines by male and female prostitutes and this is noted in the Bible (Dt. 23:17; 1Ki. 14:24). The law of Israel forbade parents to force their daughters into this practice, its priest to marry them, or their wages to be brought into the house of God (Lev. 19:29; 21:7; Dt. 23:18). Prostitutes could be punished by being burned or stoned to death. Promiscuity was forbidden both men and women. The penalty was death (Lev. 21:9; Dt. 22:20-29). The word "dog" is used of male prostitutes and sodomites in other passages as well. *See also* ADULTERY and FORNICATION

PROVENDER *See* FODDER

PROVERB A saying, often very short but not necessarily so, pithy and colorful, expressing a commonly observed fact or piece of wisdom. Doubtless as long as man has lived, wisdom was passed on in this way, but samples in writing become numerous only with the beginning of the second millennium B.C. In the Bible such sayings are widely scattered but an important collection is, of course, the Book of Proverbs. A proverb is: "capsulated wisdom." (IDB).

PROVERBS, BOOK OF In Pr. 1:1; 10:1; and 25:1 the words "the proverbs of Solomon" appear. In the third of the references there is added "copied by the men of Hezekiah king of Judah." At the head of chap. 30 we find "the saying of Agur" and at the head of chap. 31 "the sayings of King Lemuel." At 22:17 and 24:23 we find "the sayings of the wise," which are believed to cover some eighty-two verses, or a little less than two and a half chapters out of the book of thirty-one chapters. It is suggested that these seven headings indicate that the Book of Proverbs is a collection of various sets of proverbs, collections attributed or ascribed to the various persons mentioned, and that these persons are not themselves the authors. Those who take this point of view usually suggest that the compiling into the present form of the collection took place at the earliest around 685 B.C., even though some of the individual proverbs may have been collected or even composed by Solomon himself after 950 B.C. The more traditional view is that while we do not know who Agur or Lemuel were, and even "the wise," yet "the proverbs of Solomon" do indicate authorship, and that there is not sufficient objective evidence to deny it. There was, obviously, later collecting and perhaps even editing, but the basic work is the collecting or composing or some of both by King Solomon who prayed for and was given by God a wise and discerning mind (1Ki. 3:9-12).

In the first nine chapters there are found longer and shorter treatments of the theme which contrasts sin and righteousness. Here in an extended passage wisdom is personified as a righteous woman and sin as a harlot. The section from 10:1 to 22:16 is a collection of one-verse proverbs. Here in addition to synonymous parallelism, as in the poetic style, we find an abundance of antithetic parallelism. See POETRY. In 22:17–29:27 there are again proverbs of varying lengths, but the basic message is the same. It is in this part that we find the proverbs so much like those in Egyptian writing. Finally we find the chapters with the words of Agur and Lemuel in some respects like what precedes as far as content is concerned, but with an interesting stylistic form scattered through the first and the extolling of a good wife in the second (Pr. 30:18-19, 21-23; 31:10-31).

PROVIDENCE The Westminster Assembly defined God's works of providence as his "most holy, wise, and powerful preserving and governing all his creatures and all their actions."

PROVINCE A word appearing almost exclusively in the postexilic books of Ezra, Nehemiah, Esther, and Daniel to refer to Babylonian or Persian adminstration districts. It is found in the NT in the same sense of district (Ac. 23:34; 25:1). In the NT the word *district* is used in the normal broad English sense of area. See PERSIA; SATRAP

PROVOCATION See WRATH

PRUNING HOOK A blade of iron attached to a handle and used for cutting off unwanted branches or shoots from a vine (Lev. 25:3-4; Isa. 2:4; Joel 3:10).

PSALMODY See MUSIC; PSALMS

PSALMS, BOOK OF On poetic style, see POETRY. On the titles, see next entry and SONGS OF ASCENT. In the titles of many of the psalms, names of individuals are found. Traditionally these have been considered the authors of those psalms, and the Hebrew particle *le* in front of the names has been called the *lamed* of authorship, after the name of the Hebrew letter. The name of David appears at the head of seventy-three. Two psalms, which do not have that name, or any other, at their head are ascribed to David in the NT: Ps. 2 in Ac. 4:25 and Ps. 95 in Heb. 4:7. Four that do carry his name in the title are authenticated as Davidic in the NT: Ps. 16 (according to Ac. 2:25), Ps. 32 (according to Ro. 4:6), Ps. 69 (according to Ac.1:16 and Ro. 11:1-10), and Ps. 110 (according to Lk. 20:42 and Ac.2:34). Furthermore, no psalm bearing any other name in the title or containing any late historical allusion is ascribed to David or associated with him in the NT. These several lines of evidence, together with our knowledge of the man himself as a musician and poet, point to Davidic authorship for these particular psalms. Other names appearing in the titles are: Asaph (50, 73–83); Solomon (72, 127); Heman (88); Ethan (89); Moses (90); the sons of Korah (42–49, 84–85, 87).

The collection of 150 psalms is divided into five books, each separated from the other by a short doxology at the end: "Blessed be the LORD, the God of Israel, from everlasting to everlasting! Amen and Amen!" being one of the forms (Ps. 1–41; 42–72; 73–89; 90–106;

107–150). Book I consists of personal and individual prayers, all but the first of which are ascribed to David by either the heading, the NT, or the LXX. Books II and III are anonymous. Books IV and V are largely liturgical psalms. While some of these are ascribed to David the majority are anonymous.

Numerous attempts to classify the psalms as to content and use have been made. These will be found by comparing the various encyclopedias and commentaries. In brief summary here we may note among the various types the following: (1) prayers for blessing, protection or actual help in various types of adversity, and for the needs of others (21, 67, 86, 88, 102); (2) penitential prayers, requesting forgiveness (not confessions as such) and psalms of praise for blessings received (6, 32, 145, 104); (3) psalms in which the author confesses his beliefs in various items of doctrine including God's sovereignty, or those in which he expresses his worship (97, 136, 145, 147); (4) a special class called imprecatory in which the writer calls on God to punish his enemies (59, 109); (5) psalms extolling God's revelation, his Word, his Law (1, 19, 119); (6) psalms of the wisdom literature type (37, 49, 78). One special category should be mentioned in addition; the messianic. The NT declares David to be a prophet and that not only in the sense of forthtelling, as in all of his psalms, but also predicting (*see* PROPHET) (Ps. 16; 110; Ac. 2:29-31, 34-35). That others of his psalms are also predictive is evidenced by the use of excerpts from them in the NT where the predictive meaning is pointed out (Ps. 2; cf. Ac. 4:24-30; Ps. 22; cf. Jn. 19:23-24).

PSALMS, TITLES OF In the titles of the psalms there are some seventeen words whose exact meaning is debated or unclear. Twelve of these are transliterated because of the uncertainty as to just what they do signify. Three can be translated but teach us nothing that is helpful with any degree of certainty. Two cannot

be translated. *See also* MUTHLAB-BEN; SHOSHANNIM

In the Hebrew Bible the titles in the psalms are numbered as verse one. Whether or not these titles are part of the inspired text is debated, but they may be helpful to see the context in which a psalm is written (or was believed to be written). All major versions include the titles in the translation of a psalm, except the NEB.

1. *Choirmaster*, Hebrew *menazzeah*, is found at the head of fifty-five psalms (for example, see Ps. 4–6; 39). Some suggest these belong to a "Director's collection." Others think the word refers to the character of these psalms: God's blessing or victory is indicated by them; or they are triumph songs. Perhaps it is most probable that the word refers to the head of the musicians or to the master of the religious ceremonies where they were used. This last is inferred from Ps. 39:1 where Jeduthun may be the name of one such.

2. *Lilies*.

3. *Do not destroy. See* number 10b below.

4. *Doe of the morning*.

5. *Dove on Far-off Terebinths. See* number 10c below.

6. *Jeduthun. See* last sentence of number 1 above. Some suggest another alternative, namely that the word is a reference to some expression of confession or penitence (Ps. 39).

7. *Maskil*. It is suggested that psalms so indicated are either meditations or teaching psalms (Ps. 74–79).

8. *Miktam*. Some suggest "meaning unknown." Others note that they all seem to be laments and suggest they were connected with atonement rituals (Ps. 16; 56–60).

9. *Shiggaion*. Some suggest that the reference is to a religious or cultic practice, the nature of which is unknown. Others suggest a choral song of a wild, vehement character, usually irregular in form (Ps. 7).

10. *"Cue Words."* With the three exceptions noted above (numbers 3–5), all these are transliterated only from the

Hebrew. One theory is that they are names of ancient melodies to which the particular psalm might be sung. Others think they are musical instructions of some unknown kind. In some cases (below), a third alternative is suggested.

(a) *Alamoth*. The third alternative suggested is that the music is to be rendered "flutingly" or perhaps with a high tone (Ps. 5).

(b) *Do not destroy*, Number 3 above (Ps. 57–59; 75).

(c) *Dove on Far-off Terebinths*, Number 5 above. One suggests also the possibility of some connection with the dove sacrifices (Ps. 56).

(d) *Eduth*.

(e) *Gittith*. Ps. 8; 81.

(f) *Doe of the Morning*, Number 4 above. Also possibly connected with some sacrifice (Ps. 22).

(g) *Neginah*. A Hebrew transliteration in Psalm titles, Ps. 54–55; 61; 67; 76. It means with "stringed instrument."

(h) *Sheminith*. Ps. 6 and 12 in the titles.

PSALTER *See* MUSIC 2. (3) *Lyre*; *see also* PSALMS

PSALTERY *See* MUSIC 2. (3) *Lyre*; *see also* PSALMS

PSEUDEPIGRAPHA [false writing] *see* SCRIPTURE

PTOLEMAIS *See* ACC(H)O

PTOLEMY After the death of Alexander the Great in 323, the Macedonian kingdom was split into four major areas. One of his generals, Ptolemy, received the Egyptian area, which was ruled by his dynasty from 323 to 30 B.C. Israel was a buffer zone between a rival area of the Seleucid dynasty in the area of Syria. *See* MACCABEES; SELEUCIDS

PUA *See* PUAH 2.

PUAH

1. A Hebrew midwife in Egypt at the time of the birth of Moses (Ex. 1:15).

2. A son of Issachar (1Ch. 7:1); also called Puvah (Ge. 46:13).

3. One of the minor judges of Israel (Jdg. 10:1).

PUBLIC PLACE *See* MARKET, MARKETPLACE

PUBLICAN *See* OCCUPATIONS AND PROFESSIONS; *see also* TAXES, TAXING; TRIBUTE; ZACCHAEUS

PUBLIUS [first] A Roman official in Malta in Paul's visit there (Ac. 28:7ff.). †

PUDENS A Christian who sent greetings to Timothy by Paul's letter (2Ti. 4:21). †

PUHITES *See* PUTHITES

PUITE This is an alternate reading in the NIV and NEB in Nu. 26:23, based on strong evidence of certain MSS and ancient versions (also cf. 1Ch. 7:1). Most other major versions translate the Hebrew text "Puah [or Puvah] of the Punites"; except the JB chose the reading "Puvite" which conforms to the Hebrew text but is apparently not supported by any evidence. *See also* PUNITES

PUL An alternate name for Tiglath-Pileser, king of Assyria (2Ki. 15:19; 1Ch. 5:26). †

PULSE KJV and ASV for "vegetable" ("herb" in NIV footnote) in most major versions (Da. 1:12, 16). For other plants, *see* PLANTS, Plants for Food

PUNISHMENT Several types of punishment are noted in the Bible. The most frequently mentioned are death for: idolatry, adultery, blasphemy, witchcraft, kidnapping, reviling a parent, and other offenses. This could be by stoning, burning, the sword, decapitation, or being sawn in two. As additional disgrace or curse, the dead body could be hung until the setting of the sun of the day of the execution (Ex. 22:18; 21:15-17; 32:25-28; Lev. 20:2, 10, 14; 24:16; Dt.22:23-24; Mt. 14:10; Heb. 11:37). Other forms of punishment short of death included: stripes or lashes, being cut with metal, being punished in kind by fine or by restitution (Ex. 21:23-25, 30; Dt. 22:18-19; 25:2; 2Co. 11:24; 2Sa. 12:31;). Punishment was usually meted out by the courts and their appointees or by the avenger of blood after the courts had declared the person guilty. God frequently meted out punishment directly (Ge. 4:9-16). Eternal fire, destruction, punishment are noted in the NT for those who reject God's love in Christ (Mt. 25:31-46; Jn. 3:16-19). *See* DEAD, ABODE OF; STOCKS; STONING

PUNISHMENT, EVERLASTING *See* ETERNITY; PUNISHMENT; WRATH

PUNITES *See also* PUITE

PUNON A stopping place (197-004) in the Israelites' wilderness wandering after their leaving Sinai (Nu. 33:42-43). †

PUR A foreign word meaning "lot." Lots were cast in order to obtain oracles. This was done in Persia to determine the most favorable times for the murder of the Jews there by Haman in the days of Queen Esther (Est. 3:7; 9:24-26). Today Purim (the plural in the Hebrew form) is the Jewish festival held each spring to commemorate the deliverance of the Jews by Mordecai and Esther. †

PURA, PURAH {branch, ISBE; imposing, KB} A servant of Judge Gideon (Jdg. 7:10-11). †

PURE *See* CLEAN AND UNCLEAN

PURGATORY In Roman Catholic theology, purgatory is an intermediate state of purification and punishment for those who die in God's grace yet have to completely atone for their sins.

PURIFICATION The law of Moses required ceremonial purification after contact with the dead, after childbirth, and after having had certain diseases (Nu. 19:11-19; Lev. 12:1-8, 13-14). Mark 7:3-4 gives a good picture of the attitude of the time. The NT also emphasized the need for purity but gives a greater emphasis upon inner purity, purity of thought and motive (Mt. 5:27ff.; 1Co. 5:9-13; 6:18-20). Ritual washing, bathing or baptizing were considered important. *See* BAPTISM and CLEAN AND UNCLEAN

PURIM {lots} *See* CALENDAR; FESTIVALS; PUR

PURITY *See* CLEAN AND UNCLEAN and PURIFICATION

PURLOINING KJV for "stealing" (Tit. 2:10).

PURPLE *See* COLORS

PURSE Baglike containers of leather or woven material drawn together at the neck by a cord or a leather thong and used for a receptacle for money or its equivalent (Pr. 1:14; Isa. 46:6; Lk. 22:35-36).

PURSLANE *See* PLANTS, PERFUMES, AND SPICES, Miscellaneous Plants 11.

PUT
1. The third son of Ham (Ge. 10:6).
2. A geographical area thought to be in Libya (Jer. 46:9; Na.3:9).

PUTEOLI {*Latin* rotten (sulphur) smell *or* well, spring} The Italian seaport near Naples where Paul landed on his imprisonment journey to Rome (Ac. 28:13). †

PUTEOLI
Paul passed through Puteoli on his way to Rome.

PUTHITES A family descended from Judah (1Ch. 2:53). †

PUTIEL {he whom El gives} The father-in-law of Eleazar, son of Aaron (Ex. 6:25). †

PUVAH *See* PUAH

PYGARG KJV and ASV for "ibex" in many versions (Dt. 14:5). *See* BEASTS 2.

PYRAMIDS [*possibly* pointed (like a flame tongue, or a wheat tip)] A true pyramid's shape was to resemble the shape of a sacred stone of the sun god Ra in Heliopolis, near modern Cairo (biblical "On"). They were built at many times in Egyptian ancient history, some nearly a millennium before the reign of Joseph (III-IV Dynasty); they were often tombs for the dead, especially royalty. Joseph, assuming he had gone by there, would have seen the Great Pyramids of Khufu, Khafra and Menkaure (less the haze from the industrial age) much as we do today in scenic pictures. *See also* EGYPT

PYRRHUS [fiery-red] A man of Berea whose son accompanied Paul as he left Greece (Ac. 20:4). †

PYTHON A spirit dragon of divination that in mythology guarded the entrance to the Delphian oracle (Ac. 16:16).

Q. The first letter of the German word *Quelle.* It means "source." *See* LOGIA

QOHELETH The Hebrew pronunciation of the "Preacher" (Ecc. 1:1).

QUAIL *See* BIRDS 4.

QUART *See* WEIGHTS AND MEASURES

QUARTUS {fourth (born)} A Christian who sent greetings by Paul's letter to the church in Rome (Ro. 16:23). †

QUATERNION {four} KJV, ASV, NASB (in a footnote) for "a squad of four soldiers" in Ac. 12:4 in the NIV, NEB, JB. The NKJV, RSV, are the least complete in capturing the thought in the original because the idea is clear that each of the four squads present consisted of a unit of four, totaling sixteen soldiers. Four soldiers would be watching the prisoner at each of the four watches of the night, making escape humanly improbable, if not impossible, in the mind of the one who arrested Peter. *See* SQUADS

QUEEN Three types are of note in the Bible: the wife of a king, the mother of a king, and one who rules in her own person. In the latter category are the well-known Queen of Sheba of Solomon's day, the Queen of the Ethiopians in early Christian times, and Athaliah who ruled Judah after the death of her husband (1Ki. 10:1, 4, 10-13; Ac. 8:27; 2Ki. 11:1,

3). Among the better-known wives of kings are Vashti and Esther of Persia (Est. 1:9; 2:22). Since the mother of the king is mentioned so frequently in the Bible, we cannot but conclude that she extended great influence over the reigning monarchs (1Ki. 2:19; 14:21; 15:2).

QUEEN OF HEAVEN A female deity and object of worship mentioned as one to whom the Hebrew women of the time of Jeremiah made offerings. Some identify her with Ashtoreth, Ishtar, and Venus, goddesses of love and fertility in Canaan, Babylon, and Rome (Jer. 7:18; 13:18; 29:2; 44:17-25).

QUICK KJV for "living" or "alive."

QUICKEN KJV for "to make alive" or "give life" (Ro. 8:11).

QUICKSANDS *See* SYRTIS

QUIRINIUS The governor of Syria at the time of the birth of Jesus (Lk. 2:2). *See* CENSUS

QUIVER *See* ARMS AND ARMOR

QUMRAN, KHIRBET *See* SCROLLS, DEAD SEA

QUOTATIONS FROM PAGAN POETS *See* SCRIPTURE 2.

QUR 'AN *See* KORAN

QURUN HATTIN *See* SERMON ON THE MOUNT, *Horns of Hattin*

R

RA [pagan sun god of Egypt] *See* DEITIES 1.

RAAMA, RAAMAH The grandson of Ham (Ge. 10:7; 1Ch. 1:9; Eze. 27:22). †

RAAMIAH One who returned from the Babylonian captivity with Zerubbabel (Ne. 7:7); also called Reelaiah (Ezr. 2:2). †

RAAMSES *See* EGYPT, *Rameses*

RABBAH, RABBATH [chief, capital (city)]
1. A city (238-151) of the Ammonites, modern Amman in Jordan, and before that Philadelphia. The iron bedstead of King Og of Bashan, measuring 13½ feet long by 6 feet wide, was kept there (Dt. 3:11). David conquered it and later the prophets have much to say about it (1Ch. 20:1; Jer. 49:2-3; Eze. 25:5; Am. 1:14).
2. Rabbah in Judah is the Rubute of the Amarna Letters which was formerly thought to be another name for Beth Shemesh but now is identified with a tell (ancient mound) between Gezer and the entrance to the valley ("the corridor") leading to Jerusalem (Jos. 15:60).

RABBAT AMMON [chief city of AMMON] *See* GEOGRAPHY OF THE HOLY LAND

RABBI, RABBONI [(my) great one, (my) master] In OT times these were names for teachers, particularly teachers of the law. In the NT they were used as titles of honor, in addition. Translated they mean "my master" or "teacher"

(Mt.23:7-8; Jn. 1:38; 9:2; 20:16). *See also* TEACHER

RABBAH, CONQUERED BY DAVID
(Arrows show David's military ventures.)

RABBIT *See* BEASTS 5.

RABBITH [great] An unidentified town in the tribal area of Issachar thought by some to be the same as Daberath (Jos. 19:20). †

RABMAG [chief official, commander of troops, KJV in Jer. 39:3, 13.] The ASV, NASB, NKJV also transliterate but note in the margins that it is a title. The RSV keeps the name, but gives it as a title "*the* Rabmag." The NIV, NEB, JB translate it as indicating an official title of Nergal-Sharezer, i.e., a high official or troop commander. *See* NERGAL-SHAREZER

RABSARIS [he who stands by the king, *i.e.*, court official] The title of an unidentified type of Assyrian official, but thought by some to be a designation for eunuchs at the court (2Ki. 18:17; Jer. 39:3, 13).

RABSHAKEH [chief cupbearer] The title for a type of administrative court official in the Assyrian and Babylonian court (2Ki. 18:17—19:8; Isa. 36:2—37:8).

RACA [empty (headed)] A rare Aramaic word for an "airhead" or a man devoid of morals (Mt. 5:22). † *See also* CURSE

RACAL [trade] An unidentified city in the tribal area of Judah to which David sent captured Amalekite booty (1Sa. 30:29). †

RACE *See* GENTILES

RACHAB *See* RAHAB 2.

RACHAL [trade] *See* RACAL

RACHEL [ewe] The younger sister of Leah and second wife of Jacob for whom Jacob served a total of fourteen years and mother of Joseph and Benjamin (Ge. 29:1–30:23ff.; 35:16ff.). She died in childbirth and was buried near Bethlehem (Ge. 35:19-20). As a mother in Israel she is pictured in Jeremiah as rising from the dead to weep for her children going into captivity (Jer. 31:15). It is this that the NT considers prophetic of the slaughter of the children in Bethlehem by Herod at the time of the birth of Jesus (Mt. 2:18). *See* RAMA

RADDAI [*possibly* beating down, ISBE; Yahweh rules, KB] A brother of David (1Ch. 2:14). †

RAGAU *See* REU

RAGE *See* WRATH

RAGUEL [friend of El] *See* REUEL 2.

RAHAB [spacious, broad]
  1. A prostitute *(see also* the NIV footnote) of Jericho who protected the two Israelite spies in the days of Joshua (Jos. 2:1ff.; 6:17ff.; Heb. 11:31; Jas. 2:25).
  2. The mother of Boaz and mentioned in the genealogy of Jesus (Mt. 1:5).

3. *See also* BEASTS 9.; DEITIES.

RAHAM [compassion] A descendant of Caleb (1Ch. 2:44). †

RAHEL *See* RACHEL

RAIMENT A general Middle English word for "clothing," "garment," or "dress." *See* DRESS

RAIN This varies from thirty-plus inches per year in the hill country of Palestine-Syria to zero to four inches in the southern part of Palestine, the modern Negev, the Sinai peninsula and Egypt, and in the desert area to the E of the Jordan Rift and S of Syria. The heavy rains come in late November through early March. Before and after this period come the usually lighter early and latter rains respectively, the former coming in October-November and the latter in March-April. The early rains soften the sunbaked hard ground and prepare it for plowing, while the lighter latter rains bring the crop to maturity (Dt. 11:14; Jer. 5:24; Joel 2:23). The absence of rain produced famine because a country was so completely dependent upon it, and its withholding by God was a terrible punishment (Dt. 28:22-24). God used drought in the punishment of Ahab, Jezebel, and the false prophets (1Ki. 17:1; Jas. 5:17-18). *See* GEOGRAPHY OF THE HOLY LAND, B.2., *Climate*

RAINBOW God used the rainbow after Noah, his family, and the animals came out of the ark as a sign that he would never again destroy the whole earth with a flood (Ge. 9:8-17). Ezekiel likens the glory of God to the beauty of a rainbow, and John on Patmos saw God's throne encircled by one (Eze. 1:28; Rev. 4:3; 10:1). †

RAISING CHILDREN *See* PARENTING

RAISINS *See* PLANTS, PERFUMES, AND SPICES, Plants for Food 5.

RAKEM [weaver, embroider] A descendant of Manasseh (1Ch. 7:16). †

RAKKATH [narrow place] A city (199-245) in the tribal area of Naphtali probably under or near modern Tiberias (Jos. 19:35). †

RAKKON {narrow place} An unidentified town in the tribal area of Dan (Jos. 19:46). †

RAM {high, exalted, *(numbers 1-3)*}
1. An ancestor of David and Jesus (Ru. 4:19; Mt. 1:3-4; Lk. 3:33).
2. The son of Jerahmeel of Judah and nephew of number 1 above (1Ch. 2:9, 25, 27).
3. The name of the family from which Elihu, one of Job's friends, came (Job 32:2).
4. The male of the sheep, a sacrificial animal (Lev. 5:15; 6:6).
5. On battering ram, *see* ARMS AND ARMOR.

RAM'S SKINS See TABERNACLE

RAMA, RAMAH {elevated spot}
1. An unidentified town in the tribal area of Asher (Jos. 19:29).
2. A town (172-140) in the tribal area of Benjamin just N of Jerusalem, frequently mentioned in the accounts of Samuel, David, Saul, Asa, and postexilic groups (1Sa. 15:34; 19:18; 2Ch. 16:1ff.; Ne. 7:30). Rachel's weeping for her children lost in the captivity was heard in Ramah (Jer. 31:15; Mt. 2:18). *See* RAMATHAIM ZUPHIM
3. A fortified city (187-259) in the tribal area of Naphtali in the hills of lower Galilee (Jos. 19:36).
4. An unidentified town of Simeon in the tribal area of Judah; also called Ramoth (Jos. 19:8; 1Sa. 30:27).

RAMATH LEHI {height (hill) of LEHI} Jdg. 15:17. † *See* LEHI

RAMATH MIZPAH {height (hill) of MIZPAH (watchtower)} Jos. 13:26. † *See* MIZPAH

RAMATH OF THE SOUTH *See* RAMA 4.

RAMATHAIM ZUPHIM, RAMATHAIM-ZOPHIM {two heights of ZOPHIM} A place in the hill country of Ephraim where Samuel the prophet was born (1Sa. 1:1). In all other references to

Samuel in the NIV his city is called Ramah. It is puzzling that his parents leave their home in Ramathaim Zuphim (1Sa. 1:1) but return to their home in Ramah (1Sa. 1:19). *See* RAMA 2. The NIV, JB, NEB gives an alternate translation of the word "Zuphim," and understand it to describe the man as from the clan of Zuph.

RAMATHITE {of RAMA} A person from the town of Ramah. *See* RAMA

RAMESES {Ra (pagan sun god) created him} *See* EGYPT

RAMIAH {Yahweh is exalted} One who married a foreign wife during the exilic times (Ezr. 10:25). †

RAMOTH A Levitical town (199-222) in the tribal area of Issachar (1Ch. 6:73); also called Jarmuth and Remeth (Jos. 21:29; 19:21). The Crusaders Belvoir was built here; called today Kaukab el-Hawa (recently excavated).

RAMOTH GILEAD {heights in Gilead} A fortified town (244-210) in Gilead in Transjordan, a city of refuge for the Israelites (1Ki. 4:13; 22:3; 2Ki. 8:28).

RAMOTH NEGEV 1Sa. 30:27.

RAM'S HORN *See* HORN; *see also* MUSIC, MUSICAL INSTRUMENTS 2. (2), *Shofar*

RANSOM The price for the redemption of a slave or reparation for damages (Ex. 21:30; Lev. 19:20; 1Sa. 14:45). In the NIV the word is connected with the work of Christ in his life and death by which he redeemed his people and gave them salvation (Mt. 20:28; 1Ti. 2:6; Rev. 5:9). *See* REDEEM

RAPHA {*possibly* one healed} A son of Benjamin (1Ch. 8:2).

RAPHAH {*possibly* one healed} A descendant of Saul; also called Rephaiah (1Ch. 8:37; 9:43). †

RAPHU The father of the representative from Benjamin among the twelve spies (Nu. 13:9). †

RAPTURE A Latin term that means "to catch up" (1Th. 4:17). It is the removal of the church from earth. There are primarily four views; see below.

RAPTURE, MIDTRIBULATIONAL The view that Christ will rapture all the church halfway through the seven years of tribulation.

RAPTURE, PARTIAL The belief that not all the church is raptured at the same time, based on readiness.

RAPTURE, POSTTRIBULATIONAL The view that all the church will go through the Great Tribulation and then be raptured.

RAPTURE, PRETRIBULATIONAL The belief that Christ will rapture the entire church before the Great Tribulation.

RAS SHAMRA {fennel mound} The ancient name of this mound is Ugarit. Discovered in 1928 by a farmer plowing on the Mediterranean coast of Syria. It is about 300 air miles N of Jerusalem. From the extensive texts found there, one learns much about Baal worship; e.g., that "to boil a kid in its mother's milk" (Ex. 23:19), was a practice in pagan festival worship and hence forbidden in Scripture. The study of this language has been helpful in understanding other passages of the OT.

RAT See BEASTS 5.

RAVEN See BIRDS 8.

RAVINE See BROOK; WADI

RAZOR A shaving instrument, first made of flint, then of bronze and finally of iron. A Nazirite, as long as his vow was on him, was not allowed to let a razor come on him; and the priests could not shave the corners of their beards (Lev. 21:5; Nu. 6:5). The word is also used symbolically: of the tongue as a sharp razor, and of punishment by a foreign power (Ps. 52:2; Isa. 7:20).

RE, RA {RA (pagan sun god} See DEITIES 1., *Raamses*

REAIA(H) {Yahweh has seen}
1. A descendant of Judah; also called Haroeh (1Ch. 2:52; 4:2). †
2. A descendant of Reuben (1Ch. 5:5). †
3. The ancestor of some temple servants who came back from the Babylonian captivity with Zerubbabel (Ezr. 2:47; Ne. 7:50). †

REAPING See FARMING; THRESHING, THRESHING FLOOR

REBA {fourth part} A king of Midian who was killed by the Israelites in Moses' time (Nu. 31:8; Jos. 13:21). †

REBECCA, REBEKAH {*possibly* choice calf] The wife of Isaac and mother of Esau and Jacob (Ge. 22:23; 24:15-30ff.; Ro. 9:10-12).

REBIRTH See REGENERATION

RECAB, RECABITE
1. One of the two murderers of Ishbosheth (2Sa. 4:2, 5, 9).
2. The founder of the order known as Rechabites (2Ki. 10:15; Jer. 35:6ff.).

RECAH An unidentified place in the tribal area of Judah (1Ch. 4:12). †

RECHAB, RECHABITES See RECAB 1. and 2.

RECHAH See RECAH

RECKON, RECKONED See IMPUTE

RECOMPENSE See PUNISHMENT

RECONCILIATION See CHRIST, WORK OF

RECORDER A high-ranking official in the royal courts of Israel, more than just a royal scribe (2Sa. 8:16; 2Ki. 18:18; Isa. 36:22).

RED See COLORS

RED HEIFER The ashes of a red heifer were used in the ceremonial cleansing of one defiled by contact with the dead (Nu. 19:2, 9, 20-21).

RED SEA See SEA, RED

REDACTION CRITICISM See CRITICISM, REDACTION

REDEEMER, REDEMPTION *See* CHRIST, WORK OF; RANSOM

REDEEMING THE TIME KJV for "making the most of every opportunity" (Eph. 5:16; Col. 4:5). This same phrase is found in Da. 2:8 in the LXX and Theodotion Greek Versions. The word in the Semitic text is a Aramaic word that has the idea "to buy." Most versions render as *gain time*.

In Daniel to "buy the time" was to stall, to selectively talk in an evasive manner, which may be the sense in the NT passages. Writing from prison, Paul is urging caution in when and where to speak. This interpretation would then have the sense "to be careful" (wise, i.e., shrewd) in how one talks to outsiders so as not to bring undue persecution. This would not negate boldness in Christian witness.

REDEMPTION OF LAND This is the act of purchasing back land that was sold due to financial problems. The land could be bought back on a prorated scale by a relative or seller. Every Jubilee (fiftieth) year the land reverts back to the original owner, as a reminder that the LORD was the true owner (Lev. 25:23-34). *See* JUBILE(E); RELEASE, YEAR OF

REEDS

1. *See* PLANTS, PERFUMES, AND SPICES, Flowering Plants 5.

2. The stalk of a reed was used as a measuring rod, and was six cubits in length (Eze. 42:16-19).

REELAIAH One who returned from the Babylonian captivity with Zerubbabel; also called Raamiah (Ezr. 2:2; Ne. 7:7). †

REFINING Refers to two different processes in the Bible. One is the filtering or straining of liquids, such as wine (Isa. 25:6), and the other is the process of liquefying a metal and removing the sludge or dross (Ps. 12:6). It is also used of the purifying of a people (Mal. 3:3).

REFORMATION, PROTESTANT A movement to reform the Roman Catholic church in about 1500. Martin Luther is a key figure in the Reformation, beginning with the nailing of the *Ninety-five Theses* pertaining to the nature of penance. Eventually it led to a split from the Catholic church.

REFORMATION, COUNTER-REFORMATION A reform movement in the Roman Catholic church in the 1600s endeavoring to purify and strengthen it.

REFRESHING, TIMES OF Noted only in Ac. 3:19 and referring to a spiritual time of blessing coming from the Lord when people turn to the Messiah.

REFUGE, CITIES OF Three cities on either side of the Jordan River which were set aside as places to which the accidental killer of a human being could flee for refuge from the avenger of blood until his case could be heard by the courts. These were: Bezer, Ramoth Gilead, and Golan to the E and Kedesh, Shechem, and Hebron to the W (Jos. 20:7-8).

CITIES OF REFUGE

REFUSE *See* MANURE

REGEM [friend] A descendant of Caleb (1Ch. 2:47). †

REGEM-MELECH [friend of king, *possibly* chief of troops of the king] One of those sent by the people of Bethel to inquire of the LORD about keeping the fasts (Zec. 7:2). †

REGENERATION *See* CHRIST, WORK OF; SALVATION, APPLICATION OF

REGIMENT OF SOLDIERS *See* BAND

REHABIAH {Yahweh has enlarged} A grandson of Moses and a Levite (1Ch. 23:17; 24:21; 26:25). †

REHOB {broad, wide (place, market)}
1. A town (177-280) in Galilee, the northernmost place to which the twelve spies penetrated, near Dan, the same as Beth Rehob (Nu. 13:21; 2Sa. 10:6-8).
2. A town (166-256) in the tribal area of Asher (Jos. 19:28-30).
3. The father of a king of Zobah (2Sa. 8:3, 12).
4. One who signed the covenant with Nehemiah (Ne. 10:11).

REHOBOAM {(my) people will enlarge, expand} There are two; *see* KINGS OF JUDAH AND ISRAEL.

REHOBOTH {broad, wide (places, markets)}
1. An unidentified city in Edom and the home of one of their kings by the name of Saul (Ge. 36:37; 1Ch. 1:48). †
2. An unidentified place near Beersheba where Isaac dug a well after he left Abimelech of Gerar (Ge. 26:7-22). †

REHOBOTH IR {city of open spaces *or* the open spaces of the city (i.e., Nineveh)} A city in Assyria (Ge. 10:11). †

REHUM {(he) is compassionate}
1. One who came back from the Babylonian captivity with Zerubbabel; also called Nehum (Ezr. 2:2; Ne. 7:7).
2. A commander in Jerusalem in the time of Ezra who wrote a letter against Jerusalem to the Persian king Artaxerxes (Ezr. 4:8-9).
3. One who helped to repair the walls of Jerusalem in the days of Nehemiah (Ne. 3:17).
4. One who signed the covenant with Nehemiah (Ne. 10:25).
5. A priest who returned from the Babylonian captivity with Zerubbabel (Ne. 12:3).

REI {friendly *or* (my) friend} One who backed Solomon for the throne against Adonijah (1Ki. 1:8). †

REIGN *See* CHRIST, WORK OF, Threefold office, 7., *Christ's session at God's right hand. See also* KINGS, BOOK OF; KINGS, KINGSHIP

REINCARNATION The belief of some Eastern religions that a soul is reborn in a new body after death in the previous life (cf. Heb. 9:27). *See* BUDDHISM; HINDUISM

REINS KJV for "kidneys" or "hearts" or "mind" (Job 16:13; Ps. 7:9; 26:2). *See* EMOTIONS; HEART

REJOICE *See* GLADNESS

REKEM {friendship}
1. A city (192-971) in Edom.
2. A king of Midian killed by the Israelites in the time of Moses (Nu. 31:8).
3. A descendant of Caleb (1Ch. 2:43-44).
4. An unidentified city in the tribal area of Benjamin (Jos. 18:27).

RELEASE, YEAR OF This was the Year of Jubilee, the year when the Israelites proclaimed liberty throughout the land to all the inhabitants. It recurred every fifty years (Lev. 25:10; Eze. 46:17). In this year a Jew held as a slave by another Jew, or property held temporarily by a Jew who was not the original owner, was set free or returned. Some, apparently based on an early erroneous translation, consider the seventh or sabbatical year one of release also. But that was merely a year of remission of debts (Dt. 15:13). *See* JUBILE(E); REDEMPTION OF LAND

RELIGION Service or worship to God or a higher power, often with a set of personal or institutional teachings. Though the word "religion" is found in the Bible (Jas. 1:26), Christ often states that personal belief in him is the only way to God (Jn. 14:6). *See* BUDDHISM; CHRISTIANITY; CULTS; HINDUISM; IS-

LAM; MYSTERY RELIGIONS; SECTS

REMAIN To abide with Christ is to have a close relationship with Christ. To remain in him will make one fruitful, make him one with Christ's desires. To obey his commands is to remain in Christ's love (Jn. 15:4-9).

REMALIAH {Yahweh has adorned} The father of King Pekah of Israel (2Ki. 15:25-30).

REMEMBRANCE, BOOK OF Books to contain reminders, records, were kept in antiquity, especially at the royal courts (Ex. 17:14; Est. 3:1), and there was a set of officers called "recorders." But one book is of special importance: God's book of remembrance noted in Mal. 3:16. In this book were recorded the names of those who feared (believed) the LORD and thought on his name. Some think this is a roster of believers analogous to "the book of life" in the NT. *See also* RECORDER

REMETH {heights} *See* JARMUTH 2.; RAMOTH

REMISSION OF SINS *See* CHRIST, WORK OF; FORGIVENESS

REMMON *See* RIMMON

REMMON METHOAR *See* RIMMON 3.

REMNANT Something that is left over. In the Bible it frequently refers to the remnant of a community of people, the remainder upon whom the hope of future rebuilding and growth depend (Ge. 45:7; 2Ki. 19:29-31; Isa. 10:20-22). One of the major eschatological themes of the OT is that God will regather his remnant from all countries where they have been scattered and bring them back to the land of their fathers and there again make them into a great nation, a spiritual people who will be a witness to the world (Mic. 2:12; Zec. 8:11-13). *See also* PROPHET, PROPHETESS, PROPHECY. Paul referred to Christian converts from Judaism in his day as a "remnant, chosen by grace" (Ro. 11:5).

REMPHAN *See* DEITIES 2., *Rephan*

REND, OF CLOTHES This was a sign of mourning, sorrow, or repentance practiced to this day by members of the Jewish community (2Sa. 3:31; Jer. 36:24). Under certain circumstances priests were not allowed to show this sign of mourning (Lev. 10:6; 21:10). The prophet invited the people to return to God by rending their hearts and not their clothes (Joel 2:13).

REPENTANCE *See* CHRIST, WORK OF; SALVATION, APPLICATION OF

REPHAEL {El heals} A Levite gatekeeper in the days of David (1Ch. 26:7). †

REPHAH {*possibly* rich, IDB; easy (life), KB} A descendant of Ephraim (1Ch. 7:25). †

REPHAIAH {Yahweh heals}
1, 2, and 3. Descendants of Judah, Simeon, and Issachar, respectively (1Ch. 3:21, 4:42, 7:2).
4. *See* RAPHAH.
5. One who helped to repair the wall of Jerusalem in the days of Nehemiah (Ne. 3:9).

REPHAIM, VALLEY OF REPHAIM {sunken, powerless ones (giants), BDB; *possibly* shades, ghosts of the dead (giants), KB}
1. A Hebrew word sometimes translated "the dead" or "shades." With the exception of the reference in Isa. 26:19 their case would seem to be a hopeless one (Ps. 88:10; Pr. 9:18; Isa. 14:9; 26:14).
2. An ethnic term referring to the pre-Israelite inhabitants of Palestine and sometimes in both the KJV and the RSV translated "giants" (Dt. 2:11; 1Ch. 20:4-8).
3. The Valley of the Rephaim (sometimes called the Valley of the Giants) is a fine agricultural area near Jerusalem on the SW side. The Philistines frequently tried to take it from Israel (Jos. 15:8; 18:16; 2Sa. 5:18-22; Isa. 17:5).

REPHAIMS *See* REPHAIM 2.

REPHAN *See* DEITIES 2.

REPHIDIM [*possibly* supports, rests, BDB; resting place, KB] A stopping place for the Israelites on their exodus route from Egypt, not identified with certainty. Here Moses struck the rock and secured water, the Israelites defeated the Amalekites, and possibly it is also here that Jethro met and counseled Moses (Ex. 17:1-8; 18:5).

REPHIDIM
A possible location of Rephidim.

REPROBATE KJV for "depraved," "to fail" or be "unfit" (Ro. 1:28; 2Co. 13:5-7; 2Ti. 3:8; Tit. 1:16).

REPTILE [creeping, crawling] *See* BEASTS 1.

REQUITE Positively to repay for a service and negatively to repay for a wrong (Dt. 32:41; 2Sa. 3:39; Ps. 62:12). An interesting case of requiting good for evil is the messianic reference in Ps. 41:10; cf. Jn. 3:18.

RESEN An unidentified city in Assyria (Ge. 10:12). †

RESERVOIR *See* CISTERN; FOUNTAIN; POOL, POOLS; WATER; WELL

RESHEPH [flame, flash of fire] A descendant of Ephraim (1Ch. 7:25). †

REST A word with many references in the Bible: God rested from his work of creating; the seventh day was to be a day of rest; the land was to have rest from farming every seventh year; the Israelites

were promised rest in the land of Canaan; Christ promised a spiritual rest of soul for those who believe in him; and Christ has a rest for the people of God yet future (Ge. 2:2; Ex. 16:23; Lev. 25:4; Dt. 12:9; Mt. 11:28; Heb. 4:1-11). *See* LORD'S DAY; SABBATH

RESURRECTION In this article we speak only of rising from the dead. In the biblical concept man in a disembodied state is incomplete. The departed soul is waiting for the redemption of the body. At the resurrection of the body the two are joined again for eternity (Ro. 8:23; 2Co. 5:3ff.). The only clear reference to resurrection in the OT is in Da. 12:2: "Multitudes who sleep in the dust of the earth will awake: some to everlasting life, others to shame and everlasting contempt." There are a few other OT passages which point in this direction, but on the whole the OT is silent on this particular subject (Job 19:25-27; Ps. 16:10ff. –
cf. Ac. 2:25ff.; Ps. 49:14ff.). The resurrection of Christ is the capstone of all his ministry and his teaching. It is by that fact that he is declared to be the Son of God with power (Ro. 1:4). His resurrection was the necessary complement to his atoning death (Ro. 4:24-25). *See* CHRIST, LIFE OF; CHRIST, WORK OF 5.; and NAZARETH DECREE; PAUL, LIFE AND TEACHINGS OF

In the NT one of the simplest statements is "there will be a resurrection of both the righteous and the wicked" (Ac. 24:15). In fact, these two resurrections are described separated in time by 1000 years (Rev. 20:4-15; cf. 1Th. 4:16; 1Co. 15:23-24). The certainty of resurrection and the nature of it are described by Paul at great length in 1Co. 15:12-54. Our resurrection bodies will be like our Lord's after his resurrection (Php. 3:20, 21; 1Jn. 3:2).

RESURRECTION OF THE DEAD *See* CHRIST, LIFE AND TEACHINGS OF, Work of Christ 9., *Christ's Second Advent*; *see also* ESCHATOLOGY; SALVATION, APPLICATION OF, *Glorification*

RESURRECTION OF JESUS CHRIST *See* CHRIST, LIFE AND TEACHINGS OF, Work of Christ 5.

RETURN FROM EXILE AND CAPTIVITY *See* CHRONOLOGY; EZRA, BOOK OF; NEHEMIAH, BOOK OF; PERSIA

REU [friend of (El)] A descendant of Shem (Ge. 11:18-21), one in the genealogy of Jesus (Lk. 3:35).

REUBEN [see, a son! — Ge. 29:32; substitute a son, IDB] The eldest son of Jacob (Ge. 29:32). He saved Joseph when some of his other brothers wished to kill him and later offered his own sons as security that he would bring Benjamin safely back from Egypt (Ge. 37:19-22; 42:37). The tribe settled in Transjordan after the exodus from Egypt (Nu. 32:1-5, 33).

REUBENITES [of Reuben] People of the tribe or clan of Reuben. *See* REUBEN

REUEL [friend of El]
  1. A son of Esau (Ge. 36:4-17).
  2. The father-in-law of Moses. *See* JETHRO and HOBAB (Ex. 2:18).
  3. The father of the leader of the people of Gad during the wilderness wanderings (Nu. 2:14).
  4. A descendant of Benjamin (1Ch. 9:8).

REUMAH The concubine of Nahor, the brother of Abraham (Ge. 22:24). †

REVEAL, REVELATION The making known of truth. God makes himself known to man (1) in nature, (2) in the person and work of his Son, Jesus Christ, and (3) by his Spirit speaking to holy men of old who recorded what was revealed to them in a historical document that became known as the Scriptures or the Bible (Ps. 19:1ff.; Jn. 14:8-9; 2Co. 5:19; Col. 1:15; 1Ti. 5:18; 2Ti. 3:16; Heb. 1:12; 2Pe. 1:20-21; 3:15-16). *See also* SCRIPTURE

REVELATION, BOOK OF The last book of the Bible. Indications in the book itself and in early Christian tradition show that it was written by the Apostle John on the island of Patmos on the coast of Asia Minor after the fall of Jerusalem in A.D. 70. The book records a series of visions which Jesus Christ gave to John through an angel. The book is both a revelation *from* Jesus Christ and a revelation *of* Jesus Christ. The major divisions and ideas of the book are:

Chapter 1. Heading of the book; John's greeting to the seven churches of Asia; the initial vision of the majestic coming again of Jesus Christ.

Chapters 2–3. Seven letters from Christ to the churches of the Roman province of Asia Minor. These were churches established during Paul's ministry about the years 50-56 when all Asia heard the gospel (Ac. 19:10) (*see* ASIA). Paul's work, followed by John's ministry after the fall of Jerusalem, established these strong churches and helps us to understand the church history of the following centuries. The early church councils took place in Asia Minor, and some of the best recorded events of early church history are linked to people and places of Asia Minor; Papias of Hierapolis and Polycarp of Smyrna appear in the first age following the apostles.

Chapters 4–5. John had a vision of the throne of God in heaven, with Jesus crucified, yet living and standing before the throne, about to receive an important document.

Chapters 6–7. The seals of the document Jesus received are opened by him. The events which follow the breaking of the seven seals are possibly meant to portray the history of the church in the centuries between the close of the apostolic age and the time of the end when Christ comes again.

Chapters 8–11. John saw the events which follow, as seven successive trumpets were sounded. This period is probably 3½ years, the time of the work of the two witnesses of chapter 11. This period ends with the seventh trumpet which is the time of the resurrection of dead believers of all time and the instant transformation of those still living.

Chapters 12–14. John introduced a series of pictorial events which probably coincide with events already narrated, or which are to follow in chapters 15–19. They would serve as illustrative and confirmatory material. Among the most significant of these is the famous picture of the birth of a male child (chap. 12). This is often taken to portray Christ, but on reflection this is seen to be very unlikely. Christ was not caught up to heaven as soon as he was born, nor can we imagine him being about to be devoured by Satan. The same Greek word is used ("caught up") as is used of the resurrection of believers (1Th. 4:17). A more likely interpretation is that the resurrection of believers is intended and that the figure of a male child who is to rule shows the reign of the resurrected and glorified believers with Christ over a world which has been delivered from the bondage of corruption and brought into the glorious liberty of the sons of God as Romans 8 indicates.

Chapters 15–19. The events of this section are portrayed by another series of seven: the seven bowls of wrath. Since a central part of prophecy of the last times is the seventieth *seven* of Daniel, and this seven is seven years long, it is obvious that John is orienting his book to Daniel's prophecy. The seven trumpets concern the first 3½ years, culminating in the resurrection of the church; the last half of the *seven* is concerned with the dreadful judgments God will bring on earth, culminating in the destruction of a great complex of religious and political evil called Babylon. Chapters 17 and 18 show in detail the cosmic importance and dreadfulness of the destruction of a society in rebellion against its Creator and Redeemer.

In the vision of *chapter 20,* John saw the result of the coming of Christ from heaven with his glorified believers. Satan is bound for a thousand years. Believers who came to life 3½ years before serve as priests and reign as kings under Christ for the thousand years of blessedness. This is in a world where the will of Christ is done and the nations have beaten their swords into plowshares and their spears into pruning hooks, and are not learning war anymore. At the conclusion of the period, Satan is released, deceives the nations, and then is cast with the wicked into eternal punishment, the lake of fire.

Chapters 21–22. This section begins with the complete dissolution of the present universe and the introduction of a new creation, a new heaven and earth, the eternal habitation of glorified believers. The beauty and perfection of their state is described in terms of a community in which Christ dwells in radiance and splendor. Evil is forever banished; Christ's people serve him and see his face (i.e., have an intimate relationship with him).

The book concludes with a series of communications parallel to the opening paragraphs of the book. The angel messenger of the beginning appears again (22:8–11); Christ speaks directly again (vv. 12-20) words of encouragement and warning. John echoes the longing of believers of all ages: "Amen. Come, Lord Jesus!"

The value of the book arises from the relevance of predictive prophecy to the progress of the work of redemption. Redemptive deed and redemptive word are both necessary. In the case of future events, both the deeds and explanation are given in advance. The ultimate value of the book arises from a serious commitment to its truth as a genuine divine revelation, relating to actual historical events. If really true, men may find encouragement or warning and act accordingly. (W.B.W.)

REVELLING KJV for "excessive feasting"; it is used as a characteristic of pagan pleasure, which behavior the Scripture wants us to put aside for godly living (Gal. 5:21; 1Pe. 4:3). *See* DRINK

REVERENCE *See* FEAR

REVISED VERSIONS *See* BIBLE VERSIONS, ENGLISH VERSIONS

REWARDS *See* CROWN

REZEPH [heated stones, live coals] An important town in Assyria on one of the caravan routes between Assyria and Palestine (2Ki. 19:12; Isa. 37:12). †

REZIA *See* RIZIA

REZIN
1. A king of Damascus and an ally of Pekah, king of Israel, against Ahaz of Judah (2Ki. 15:37-38).
2. Ancestor of some temple servants who returned from the Babylonian captivity with Zerubbabel (Ezr. 2:48).

REZON [prince, IDB; high official, KB] A Syrian leader who opposed Solomon (1Ki. 11:23-25). †

RHEGIUM A town in southern Italy (modern Reggio) where Paul stopped on his journey to Rome (Ac. 28:13). †

RHEGIUM

RHESA The son of Zerubbabel and an ancestor of Jesus (Lk. 3:27). †

RHODA [rose] A maid in the house of Mary, the mother of John Mark (Ac. 12:13). †

RHODES A large island between Crete and the mainland of Asia Minor to the NE, where Paul stopped on his journey from Troas to Caesarea and then to Jerusalem for the last time (Ac. 21:1). †

RIBAI [opponent] A Benjamite and father of one of David's thirty mighty men (2Sa. 23:29; 1Ch. 11:31). †

RIBLAH An ancient Syrian town near the head waters of the river Orontes situated at the meeting point of the Egyptian and Mesopotamian military highways. King Jehoahaz of Judah was put in bonds there by Pharaoh Neco, and later King Zedekiah was captured by the Babylonians and brought there where he saw his sons killed before his own eyes before they were put out. Other captive Judeans were also killed there at the same time (2Ki. 23:33; 25:6-7, 20-21).

RICHES The rich Christian can fall into temptation and foolish lust that leads to destruction (1Ti. 6:9-10). The rich are to be humble minded, not trusting in their riches, but God. They are to be rich in good works and generous (1Ti. 6:17-19). *See* WEALTH

RIDDLE A puzzling saying or question whose hidden meaning takes imagination or ingenuity to discover. The best example in the OT is found in the story of Samson (Jdg. 14:12-19). The queen of Sheba tested the wisdom of Solomon with her hard questions (riddles) (1Ki. 10:1). They are also found in the poetic books, especially the wisdom literature (Ps. 49:1-4; Pr. 1:5-6; Eze. 17:2). They are even found in the prophets who also used them on occasion.

RIE *See* PLANTS, PERFUMES, AND SPICES, Plants for Food 1., *Spelt*; RYE

RIGHTEOUSNESS The basic concept in the word is rightness or justness in respect of the norm indicated in the particular context—whether in matters of weights and measures, or in matters of judges, rulers, and kings and their attention to law and government, or rightness in speech or ethnics (Dt. 25:15; Lev. 19:15; Dt. 1:16; Isa. 58:2; Pr. 8:8; 1:3; 2:9). Man in and of himself or through his own efforts is incapable of making himself righteous in God's sight; that is why the NT presents the concept of righteousness coming through the atoning work of Christ imputed to the believer (Ro. 3:19-26). *See* CHRIST, WORK OF and PAUL, HIS LIFE AND TEACHING

RIMMON [pomegranate, *or* Rimmon (pagan thunder, storm god)]

1. The father of the men who killed Ishbosheth, Saul's son (2Sa. 4:2-9).

2. A Syrian god worshiped in Damascus (2Ki. 5:18).

3. A city (179-243) in the tribal area of Zebulun, a Levitical city (Jos. 19:13); also called Rimmono (1Ch. 6:77).

4. An unidentified town in the tribal area of Judah-Simeon in the S; perhaps more properly called En Rimmon (Jos. 15:32; 1Ch. 4:32). It was resettled after the return from the Babylonian captivity (Ne. 11:29).

5. The Rock of Rimmon was near Gibeah; it was the place to which the Benjamites fled when being attacked by the rest of Israel in punishment for their treatment of the Levite and his concubine (Jdg. 20:45-47; 21:13).

RIMMON PAREZ [pomegranate pass (breach)] *See* RIMMON PEREZ

RIMMON PEREZ [pomegranate pass (breach)] An unidentified stopping place of the Israelites on their exodus journey from Egypt (Nu. 33:19-20). †

RIMMON, ROCK OF [pomegranate rock] *See* RIMMON 5.

RIMMON-METHOAR [Rimmon which turns or stretches] *See* RIMMON 3.

RIMMONO [pomegranate] *See* DIMNAH and RIMMON

RING The English translation of a number of Hebrew and Greek words referring to signet or seal rings, nose rings, and earrings, rings for the staves and curtains of the tabernacle and temple and their vessels when needing transportation. They were symbols of wealth, dignity, and authority (Ge. 24:30, 47; 35:4; 41:42; Ex. 25:12-27; Est. 8:2-10; Lk. 15:22; Jas. 2:2). *See also* ORNAMENTS

RING-STR(E)AKED KJV for "streaked."

RINNAH [ringing cry (of joy) to Yahweh] A descendant of Judah (1Ch. 4:20). †

RIPHATH A descendant of Noah through Japheth (Ge. 10:3; 1Ch. 1:6). †

RISSAH [dew, ISBE] An unidentified stop of the Israelites on their exodus route from Egypt (Nu. 33:21-22). †

RITHMAH [(place of) broom plants] An unidentified stop of the Israelites on their exodus route from Egypt (Nu. 33:18-19). †

RIVER In the OT the common words for river are two, the *nahar* (Greek *potamos*) and the *nahal*. The first is the word for river as usually understood in our Western terminology. Those mentioned in the Bible include: Tigris, Euphrates, Jordan, Abana, Pharpar, Chebar, Gozan, Kishon, River of Egypt (Wadi el-Arish), Jabbok. The Nile, and once the Tigris, is called a *ye'or*. The *nahal*, on the other hand, usually refers to a torrent that appears only after a rain. The rest of the time the river bed is dry. This is commonly called in the Middle East a wadi and in the English translations, because of the normal dryness of the bed, a "valley," a "brook," or a "ravine" (1Ki. 17:47; 1Sa. 17:40; Dt. 21:4-6; Job 30:6). *See* BROOK; WADI

RIVER OF EGYPT *See* EGYPT, WADI OF; *see also* RIVER

RIZIA [*possibly* pleasant one, KB] A descendant of Asher (1Ch. 7:39). †

RIZPAH [heated stones, live coals] A concubine of Saul whose two sons, along with the five sons of Merab-Michal, were killed by the Gibeonites with David's consent. Because of her mourning, David gave Saul and Jonathan and the seven sons of Saul proper burial (2Sa. 3:7ff.; 21:1-14). †

ROADS, BIBLICAL *See* GEOGRAPHY OF THE HOLY LAND

ROBBERY *See* STEALING

ROBE *See* DRESS

ROBOAM *See* KINGS OF JUDAH AND ISRAEL, *Rehoboam*

ROCK The translation of two Hebrew words, *sela* and *tsur* and the Greek word *petra*. The most important usages in the Bible are the symbolic. God is Israel's rock and fortress, *sela* (2Sa. 22:2) and *tsur* (Ps. 31:3). In the NT the figurative meaning is noted when believers in Christ are called living stones in a spiritual house, and when Christ calls his disciple "Simon, *petros*" because Simon Peter's confession is the foundation stone of truth on which Christ's church was to be built: "You are the Christ, the Son of the living God" (Mt. 16:13-18; cf. 1Pe. 2:5). *See* PETER; PRECIOUS STONES AND METALS; SELA; STONE

ROCK BADGER *See* BEASTS 5.

ROD *See* WEIGHTS AND MEASURES

ROD, ROD OF AARON, ROD OF MOSES A stick cut from the branch of a tree or a rod made from iron and used for various purposes which would include beating an individual or individuals in punishment, or merely as a cane or staff (Ge. 32:10; Pr. 22:15; 23:13-14; Isa. 30:31; Rev. 12:5; 19:15). Aaron's rod was his staff with which God performed some of the miracles in the incidents that led up to Pharaoh's letting the Israelites leave Egypt. It was often referred to as Aaron's rod that budded and was later placed in the Ark (Ex. 7:8-20; 8:16-17; Heb. 9:4). Moses' rod was also used in many miracles connected with the Exodus and the wilderness wanderings (Ex. 4:17-20; 9:23; 14:16; 17:5-7; Nu. 20:8-11).

ROD, WEAVERS *See* BEAM

RODANIM [people of Rhodes]
1. One of the grandsons of Japheth, son of Noah (Ge. 10:4; 1Ch. 1:7). †
2. A tribe descended from Javan, the Rhodians from the island of Rhodes; perhaps the word *Dodanim* refers to the same people.

ROEBUCK, ROE DEER *See* BEASTS 2., *Gazelle*

ROGELIM [(place of) treaders, fullers (one who cleans clothes by kneading with no soap)] A city (223-215) in Gilead and the home of Barzillai who was a friend of David (2Sa. 17:27; 19:31). †

ROHGAH A descendant of Asher (1Ch. 7:34). †

ROLL *See* PAPYRUS; PARCHMENT; SCROLL; WRITING

ROMAMTI-EZER [(he is my) highest help] A Levitical musician in the time of King David (1Ch. 25:4, 31). †

ROMAN *See* ROME, CITIZEN OF ROME, ROMAN

ROMAN CATHOLICISM A body of Christians that follow the Pope in Rome; generally they believe that he is the infallible interpreter of church doctrine. There is a hierarchy of bishops and priests as the ruling class in the Catholic church. Their worship is liturgical, and their dogma (i.e., teachings) developed over the centuries. This dogma is a product of Scripture and traditions of the Catholic church. Today it is in contrast to the Protestants.

ROMAN EMPIRE *See* ROME, CITIZEN OF ROME, ROMAN

ROMANS, EPISTLE OF *See* PAULINE EPISTLES, THE

ROME, CITIZEN OF ROME, ROMAN The city-state of Rome was founded, traditionally, in 753 B.C., when certain villages on the Tiber River, composed of Latin and Oscan peoples, united on the "seven hills" (Rev. 17:9) for protection against the Etruscans. Republican government replaced kings in 509. During the next two centuries the common citizens, or plebeians, gained increasing rights against the patrician nobility; and Roman domination came to extend over the surrounding lands. By 265 B.C. Rome had conquered the Greeks of southern Italy and gained control of the peninsula. Conquered territories were amalgamated (merged) into Rome by implanted colonies, while allowing for local self-government. Roman citizenship spread which, together with the Roman location, discipline, and faithfulness to treaties, contributed to the city's success.

Rome's foreign expansion began as a result of the Punic Wars: in 241 Rome took Sicily from Carthage, and later Spain. The first appearance of the Roman Empire proper emerged when Sicily was assigned an imperial governor and not brought into alliance with Rome. Roman expansion into the E had been predicted long before by Balaam (Nu. 24:24) and by the prophet Daniel (Da. 11:30) under the phrase "ships of Kittim" (Cyprus), for Rome did indeed enter the Near East from the Mediterranean. Soon after 200 B.C. Rome began to move against the kingdoms of the Macedonian generals who had succeeded Alexander the Great. In 190 Antiochus III of Syria was checked at Magnesia in what is now Turkey, as predicted by Daniel (11:18); and his son Antiochus IV, in Egypt in 168 (Dan. 11:30; *see* SELEUCIDS). Simon, the brother of Judas Maccabeus, was confirmed as an independent ruler in Judah in 143 (1Macc. 14:16-19, 24; cf. 8:17 and 12:1), under the Roman policy of keeping their rivals weak through a balance of power.

Up to this point Rome's approach to the E had been one of preventing aggression, not of effecting it. But imperialism arose in the second century B.C. Rome's last colony was founded in 184 and assimilation slowed down. Treaty obligations were increasingly neglected; and mistreatment arose as Greek greed, self-expression, and love of luxury infected Rome. During the Mithridatic War of 74-63 B.C., the Roman senate gave its general Pompey extraordinary powers over the Near East. He converted Syria into a Roman province in 64 and the following year intervened in the politics of the Jews, capturing Jerusalem and ending the kingdom of the Hasmoneans. After a period of Persian invasions, Palestine was converted into a client kingdom of Rome under Herod the Idumean (37-4 B.C.); and Herod was able to maintain his position when Augustus

Caesar in 30 B.C. became Rome's emperor.

While Augustus chose to govern his frontier provinces directly, pacified provinces were generally under the senate with annually appointed proconsuls as governors (Ac. 13:7). A standing army maintained the *pax Romana* (Roman peace); emperor worship arose in the provinces. Palestine came under the general supervision of the Syrian legate. Quirinius conducted the census for taxation which took Joseph and Mary to Bethlehem (Lk. 2:1-2) in about 5 B.C. Judas of Galilee led a revolt against such a census in A.D. 68 (Ac. 5:37). Upon the death of Herod in 4 B.C., his son Archelaus went to Rome seeking the kingship, but he was opposed by a delegation of the Jews (cf. Lk. 19:12-27) and his kingship was not granted. Instead, Augustus divided the area among Herod's sons as tetrarchs (see Lk. 3:1); and Joseph and Mary, with the child Jesus, deliberately avoided the Judean territory of Archelaus (Mt. 2:22). In A.D. 6 he was deposed for cruelty, and in his place were appointed Roman procurators. It was under the fifth of these, Pontius Pilate (A.D. 26-36) that Christ was crucified; (see Ac. 24:27 on the later governors Felix and Festus).

Rome is protrayed in Daniel as "the legs of iron" in the image that represented the world's successive empires (Da. 2:33), and the powerful beast with the great iron teeth (7:7), "forasmuch as iron breaketh in pieces and subdueth all things" (2:40, KJV). Yet the *pax Romana* permitted travel and communication in ways better than ever before or for 1500 years after (see Acts 27; Rev. 18:11-19), making possible the rapid spread of Christianity. Roman law was rough, but generally effective in protecting the Christians from their first enemies, the Jews. An enterprising man could become a "Roman" by effort or by purchase (Ac. 22:25-28); and Paul's Roman citizenship saved him more than once, as it restrained lawlessness.

Jews from Rome were among the first converts to Christ at Pentecost (Ac.

2:10), and a Gentile church developed at Rome before any apostle arrived. Paul wrote his epistle to these Romans in about A.D. 52 and was brought as a prisoner to Rome in 60, when he could speak even of "saints in Caesar's household" (Php. 4:22). Though released in 62, Paul seems subsequently to have lost his life in Rome, as did also Peter (see 2Ti. 4:6, 16; 2Pe. 1:14).

Because of their refusal to worship the emperor, the church suffered persecution that reached an initial peak under Nero, who died in A.D. 68.

ROME (Arrows show last part of Paul's trip to Rome.)

The Book of Revelation describes Rome in its ruthlessness as a harlot, "drunken with the blood of the martyrs of Jesus" (Rev. 17:1-7, 18). Yet it served, indeed, to punish the Jews for their rejection of Christ (Mt. 21:41; 23:39; cf. 27:25). General Titus destroyed Jerusalem in A.D. 70 (just as Jesus and the prophets had predicted—Lk. 21:20-24; cf. Zec. 11:15-16). But Rome itself was then destined to be consumed by others (Zec. 11:17; Rev. 14:9-11; 17:16; 18:2-8), fulfilled historically in the fall of Rome in A.D. 476 in the west, and of Constantinople in 1453, capital of the Roman Empire in the east. (J.B.P.) *See also* EMPEROR, EMPIRE

ROOF In biblical times the roof was flat and made of or covered with mud. In the dry hot weather this mud baked in the sun. In the rainy season it had to be continually watched and patched with additional mud plaster. One mark of a good son at Ras Shamra Ugarit was that he plastered his father's roof in rain. The family spent much time on this roof-patio and often slept there in hot weather (1Sa. 9:25ff.; Ecc. 10:18; Lk. 5:19; Ac. 10:9).

ROOM
1. A partitioned part of a building (Ac. 1:13). *See also* UPPER ROOM
2. A KJV term in Mt. 23:6; Lk. 14:7, 8; 20:46 which is obsolete. The NKJV translates this "best places," and many versions "places of honor."

ROOT OF DAVID, JESSE The word root is usually used in a figurative sense as we use the phrase "root of the matter," or in the sense of source or place of origin (Dt. 29:18; Job 19:28; Jer. 12:2). The Root of David and the Root of Jesse are taken as references to Christ the Messiah (Isa. 11:1-10; cf. Ro. 15:2; Rev. 5:5; 22:16).

ROPE A rope or cord was used in warfare (2Sa. 17:13) and shipping (Isa. 33:20). To wear it was a sign of poverty (Isa. 3:24). To wear a rope around your neck was a sign of submission (1Ki. 20:31). "Cords of sheol" is figurative for death (Ps. 18:5).

ROSE, ROSE OF SHARON *See* PLANTS, PERFUMES, AND SPICES, Flowering Plants 2.

ROSH [head, leader] Mentioned only in Ge. 46:21 as a son of Benjamin. He is not mentioned in either of the other two places that the sons of Benjamin are mentioned (Nu. 26:38-39; 1Ch. 8:1-5). The NIV translates it "chief prince" (Eze. 38:2-3; 39:1).

ROSH HASHANAH *See* FESTIVALS 4., *The Feast of Trumpets*

ROW, ROWERS *See* SHIP, *Oars*

ROYAL LAW These two words are used together only in Jas. 2:8 and refer to the Law: "Keep the royal Law in Scripture, 'You shall love your neighbor as yourself.'"

RUBBISH *See* MANURE

RUBY *See* PRECIOUS STONES AND METALS, Precious Stones 1.

RUDDY From the Hebrew word "red," the word is possibly similar to our expression "rosy-cheeked"–i.e., fair-skinned and healthy (1Sa. 16:12). *See* COLORS

RUE *See* PLANTS, PERFUMES, AND SPICES, Plants for Seasoning

RUFUS {red haired}
1. The father of the man from Cyrene who carried the cross of Jesus (Mk. 15:21). †
2. A Christian to whom Paul sent greetings in his letter to Rome. He is thought by some to be the same as number 1 above (Ro. 16:13).

RUHAMAH {pitied} KJV for "loved one" (Hos. 2:1).

RULE, RULER The translation of several Hebrew and Greek words which are also translated in a number of other ways. A ruler may refer to a king, overseer, leader, deputy, magistrate, head of a synagogue (Mk. 5:38), mayor of a city (Ac. 17:6-8), and even to "the powers of

this dark world and against the spiritual forces of evil in the heavenly realms" (Eph. 6:12, NIV). *See also* POTENTATE

RUMAH {height} The home (177-243) of the mother of King Jehoiakim (2Ki. 23:36). †

RUN *See* ATHLETE; PERSECUTION

RUNNELS Watering troughs for flocks (Ge. 30:38-41).

RUSH, RUSHES A reed-like plant usually found in marshes or near rivers.

RUTH {friendship, BDB; refreshed (as with water), IDB; *possibly* comrade, companion, ISBE} The Moabitess wife of one of the sons of Naomi who left her native Moab and went with her mother-in-law back to Bethlehem after the death of Naomi's two sons and husband. Ruth married Boaz and became an ancestress of David and Jesus (Ru. 1:2; 4:10-22; Mt. 1:15).

RUTH, BOOK OF *See* JUDGES, BOOK OF

RYE *See* PLANTS, PERFUMES, AND SPICES 1., *Spelt*

S

SABACHTHANI [left me] *See* ELOI, ELOI, LAMA SABACHTHANI

SABAOTH, THE LORD OF [Yahweh of (angelic) armies] *See* ARMY; GOD, NAMES OF, GODHEAD 4., *Yahweh Tsebaoth*

SABBATH [cease, rest] The last day of a seven-day week. Following the precedent found in the creation story where God finished all his work in six days and then rested on the seventh, the seventh day has become the weekly day of rest and prayer and worship for the Jews (Ge. 2:13; Ex. 16:23-29; 20:8-11). The prophets frequently reminded the people of their obligation to keep the Sabbath; in fact, to break it was punishable by death (Nu. 15:32-36; Isa. 56:2-5; Jer. 17:21-27). The codification of things prohibited on the Sabbath was made during the years between the end of the writing of the OT and the beginning of the Christian era. While it was Jesus' custom to go into the synagogue on the Sabbath Day, his attitude of opposition to the rigidity of that codification was clear. He taught that their observance of the Sabbath was more rigid than God intended, for God made the Sabbath for man's benefit and not vice versa (Mk. 2:27). It was not wrong to do good or to heal or even to pick off the heads of wheat on the Sabbath if one needed food on that day (Mk. 2:23-28). At first the Christians, all being Jews, continued the Sabbath as a day of rest, study, and prayer, while at the same time worshiping on the first day of the week, the day commemorating the Resurrection (Ac. 2:1; 1Co. 16:1-2). *See* LORD'S DAY; REST

SABBATH DAY'S JOURNEY *See* WEIGHTS AND MEASURES, *Measures of Length*

SABBATICAL YEAR This was the final year in the cycle of seven. In it the land was to lie fallow (Lev. 25:2-5). *See also* CALENDAR and FESTIVALS

SABEANS A Semitic people resident in the SW part of the Arabian Peninsula who were well known as traders (Job 1:15; Isa. 45:14; Joel 3:8). They lived in the fertile area known as the Yemen and carried on extensive trade to the N and W, having colonies even in N Africa (Ge. 10:7; 28; 25:3; Eze. 38:13). One of their queens visited King Solomon to test his wisdom with hard questions, and probably with an interest to do trade in gold, precious stones, and spices (Ps. 72:15; Isa. 60:6; Eze. 27:22). *Sabeans* is found in the NIV only four times: Job 1:15; Isa. 45:14; Eze. 23:42; Joel 3:8. †

SABELLIANISM An explanation that the three persons of the Trinity are actually three modes (manifestations) of one God. This explanation makes the Son and Holy Spirit temporary appearances of the Father. This explanation attempts to explain the unity of God (*see* ATTRIBUTES OF GOD, *Unity*) but at the expense of the diversity (three "personhood") of God. *See* GOD, NAMES OF 1.

SABTAH, SABTA The third son of Cush who, in turn, was the grandson of Noah. This name was applied to a tribe descended from him, which most scholars locate in an unidentified area in SW Arabia (Ge. 10:7; 1Ch. 1:9). †

SABTEC(H)A(H) A son of Cush and, like the word above, the name of an unidentified locality probably in Arabia (Ge. 10:7; 1Ch. 1:9). †

SACAR [reward (given by God), *possibly* hired hand]
1. The father of one of David's mighty men (1Ch. 11:35); also called Sharar (2Sa. 23:33). †
2. A Levite gatekeeper in the days of David (1Ch. 26:4). †

SACHIA *See* SAKIA

SACKBUT KJV for "lyre" (Da. 3:5ff.). *See* MUSIC, MUSICAL INSTRUMENTS 2.(3)

SACKCLOTH A rough garment of cloth made from goat's or camel's hair. There is some difference of opinion as to whether it was a full garment or a smaller one like a loincloth, but there is no evidence that it was used primarily because of its qualities of physical discomfort since it was the ordinary garment of the shepherd and the poor. It had a well-known symbolic meaning from very early times. It was a symbol of mourning, and it was also used by entire groups in time of national emergencies (2Sa. 3:31; 2Ki. 6:30; 19:1-2; Ne. 9:1).

SACRAMENT [something obligated (to do)] A sacred ceremony which is regarded as a cause or a sign of grace.

SACRED A translation of a word that is more frequently rendered by "holy" or "sanctified." The basic idea is separation from profane to divine use (Ex. 30:25; Jos. 6:19; Zep. 3:4). *See* SECULAR

SACRIFICE, CHRIST'S *See* CHRIST, WORK OF

SACRIFICES AND OFFERINGS

Though there are prescriptions and formulas regarding sacrifices and offerings of the Mosaic system scattered through the last three books of the Pentateuch, the basic materials are in chaps. 1 to 7 of Leviticus. All were to be presented at the national sanctuary (tabernacle, temple) in connection with the rituals at the brazen altar. So after describing the details of construction of the building and its furnishings and their dedication, the narrative continues with detailed instructions concerning the five types of sacrifices to be presented at the altar (Lev. 1–7). This is followed by narrative (Lev. 8–10). The instruction came to Moses from the LORD who "spoke to him from the tent of meeting."

Both priests and sacrifices existed from the earliest times. The first sacrifices are mentioned in connection with the initial offspring of our first parents (Ge. 4), and Hebrew priests are mentioned among the nation before the giving of the Law (Ex. 19:22, 24). Sacrifices were a part of the culture. In the laws of the Pentateuch (note the manner of their introduction at Lev. 1:1-2, "When any of you brings an offering to the LORD" etc.), they were initiated and regulated by and for the LORD, rather than invented by Moses.

There were five distinct kinds of Mosaic sacrifices (*see* below), each with its own special ritual. The immediate purpose of the offerings was religious symbolism. We do not learn much of that symbolism from the Pentateuch, but the rest of the OT, especially the Prophets, tells us much concerning its immediate meaning in OT times. The NT, specifically relating it (as type to antitype) to the redemptive work of Jesus (*see* CHRIST, WORK OF), finds the many aspects of Christian salvation foreshadowed in it. This is in addition to complex social significance as part of the calendar of feasts and festivals (*see* FESTIVALS). The burnt offering symbolized self-dedication. The meal and peace offerings were eucharistic, in that they were expressions of love and devotion to God and visible "means of grace" whereby Communion at "the Lord's Table" was enacted. The sin and trespass offerings were expiatory, i.e, for sins' atonement.

We must remember that the OT followers of Mosaic religion did not have at hand the books of Galatians and Romans to tell them that the Law (of Moses) was a "pedagogue" [tutor] to lead them to Christ (Gal. 3:24, KJV) and to give knowledge of sin (Ro. 3:10), nor the Book of Hebrews to tell them the sacrificial rituals were types (predictive symbols) of Christ's sacrifice (Heb. 9:6-10). Yet, they did know that sacrifice was the divinely appointed means for them to receive forgiveness of sin (Lev. 4:31, 33-35; Nu. 15:26, 28). "Without the shedding of blood there is no forgiveness" was primarily an OT revelation (Lev. 17:11; cf. Heb. 9:18-22). Yet the reason *why* shed blood effected forgiveness is a NT revelation, even though some OT saints might have connected it with the Messiah's death on the basis of Isaiah 53. Essentially their faith rested in the truthfulness of God's word, not on their understanding of *how* God was going to make the system work.

It is instructive in this connection to observe something of the *order* of the offerings. In the description of Leviticus 1-7 they are in the order of burnt offering, grain offering, fellowship offering, sin offering, and guilt offering. This appears to be because the primeval offerings were the first two and possibly the third. Atonement for sin is a less conspicuous element in these. But in actual observance, the sin offering, having to do primarily with atonement for sin, was always first. The sacrifices of devotion, being acts performed by forgiven sinners, appropriately followed those which provided the appointed bases for forgiveness. The sacrifices for forgiveness of sins had two aspects. On the one hand they secured atonement for fractures of the national law, whenever the offense was one of human frailty through ignorance, error, or neglect (Nu. 15). There was no remission of temporal punishment in cases of obstinate, willful law-

breaking (Nu. 15:27-31; cf. Heb. 10:26ff.). On the other hand, the prophetic writings show there was a distinct spiritual significance, as a means of expressing repentance and receiving forgiveness, which could have belonged to it only as a type of the great atonement (i.e., Christ's sacrifice).

Any treatment of the sacrifices which stops short of the typical significance of them—so far as it can be determined by NT study and by principles derived by comparisons of all Scripture—is less than Christian interpretation. Reserve and humility must be observed in stating the specific typical significance apart from specific NT statements, but those statements are clear that the typology is more extensive than the NT authors specifically delineate. Thus, reverent research and preaching on typology of a sort presently not popular is biblically justified and will inevitably recur in the churches.

The comprehensive Hebrew word for all offerings of every sort was *qorban*, derived from a verb which in the causative stem means "to bring near." This word was understood in NT times to mean "presented," "given," "dedicated" (Mk. 7:11-12).

So, it indicated simply that the "offerings" (KJV, RSV) or "oblations" (RV, ASV) were simply things dedicated to God for his use and disposal. This word is used for all offerings collectively (Lev. 1:2; 7:37-38), of the burnt offering (Lev. 1:3), grain offering (Lev. 2:1), fellowship offering (Lev.3:1), sin offering (Lev. 4:23), and of the guilt offering (Nu. 5:5-10). It is also used of Aaron's consecration offering (Lev. 6:20), the Nazirite consecration offering (Nu. 6:14, 21) the Passover sacrifice (Nu. 9:7, 13), oxen and wagons dedicated for the Levites to use (Nu. 7:3-4), gifts at the dedication of the tabernacle, booty given to God (Nu. 31:50), and even wood for the altar fires is a related word (Ne. 10:35; 13:31). So anything dedicated by men for official use or consumption in the tabernacle ceremonies, whether a slain sacrifice or not, was *qorban*. The word does not seem to have been used in the case of dedicated persons.

In addition, while all offerings were *holy*, those either wholly burned or eaten officially by priests were "most holy" (Lev. 2:3). And those, such as the fellowship offering, which were expressions of devotion, were called *"sweet savour"* (KJV) or *"pleasing odor"* offering.

The animal sacrifices were all of domesticated varieties (including birds) and were also, according to dietary laws, clean for food (Lev. 1:2, 14). The probable reason was that as life-providers (food), they were fit symbols, and when cooked could be eaten as the rituals required. Also, as having cost the offerers something they were true "sacrifices." The fact that edible game was not admitted supported this supposition.

THE BURNT OFFERING (Lev. 1:1-17; 6:8-13) *Name*.

The Hebrew *olah* means simply "an ascent" (Eze. 40:26). The idea of burning is not inherent in the word. The idea emphasized was that the entire carcass *ascended* to God (in the smoke and vapors). *"Holocaust"* (all-burned) is less used but preferable.

Varieties. A male of the herd (oxen) (Lev. 1:3); of the flock, a male sheep or goat (Lev. 1:10); fowl, dove, or pigeon (Lev. 1:14). The specimen was to be without visible blemish. Ritual was the same in each case except for fowl, which were allowed only in cases of extreme poverty of offerers (cf. Lk. 2:22-24; 2Co. 8:9).

Ritual. The (a) unblemished animal was led to the door of the "tent" of meeting, where (b) the offerer laid his hand upon the animal's head and then (c) killed it. Thereupon the officiating priest (d) caught some of the blood, made an act of presentation to God, sprinkled some about the altar and perhaps poured out the excess into some channel which carried it away. The priest next (e) flayed the animal and cut it in pieces. Then (f) a fire of wood was ignited on the altar and (g) the parts of the animal, including head and fat, washed legs, and entrails were placed on the fire where they were completely consumed.

Subsequent to the ceremony the ashes were carried away to a clean place "outside the camp." The skin of the animal became the property of the officiating priest and was his "fee" (Lev. 7:8), a very valuable item in that day.

There were complementary offerings of meal (see meal offerings) and wine (Lev. 23:18), with the burnt offering (Nu. 28–29; Jdg. 13:19). Though not special "offerings," both salt (Lev. 2:13; cf. Mk. 9:49) and oil (Nu. 28:11) might be added at some point in the ritual.

THE GRAIN (MEAL) OFFERING (Lev. 2; 6:14-18) *Name*.

Derived from the fact that grain, usually ground to flour, was the basic element. The Hebrew word *minhah* really means "gift, present, tribute."

Varieties. It might be uncooked, fine flour cakes baked in an oven or in a pan, or it might be fried in a pan. It could even be parched green ears of grain. Probably only wheat was used.

Added Materials. Both oil and frankincense were added, as well as salt.

Excluded Materials. Honey (very sweet) and leaven (very sour) (Lev. 2:11).

Ritual. It was much more simple than that of the burnt offering since no slaughter of an animal was involved. The cereal was (a) presented to the LORD by bringing it to the priest at the door of the tabernacle, after the offerer himself first anointed it with oil. From the mixture (b) the officiating priest took a handful and (c) put frankincense on it, brought to the altar by the offerer as part of his "gift." Then (d) the priest put the portion, thus treated, on the altar where it would be burnt with one of the animal sacrifices. (e) Evidently as part of the sacrifice and not merely to help the priest with his personal maintenance, the priest ate the rest of the meal offering in the tabernacle precincts (cf. 6:16).

Apparently, the meal offering was always accompanied with a portion of wine as a drink offering (libation)—*see* Ex. 29:40; Lev. 23:13; Nu. 15:5, 10. The

Law gives regulations for the disposal of it.

The grain offering seems never to have been offered apart from the fellowship offering or burnt offering (Ex. 29:38-40; Nu. 15:1-13).

FELLOWSHIP (PEACE) OFFERING

(Lev. 3; 7:11-21, 28-34) *Name*. The word is always in plural in this connection, indicating superlative degree: lit. "slaughtered sacrifice of peaces," to be interpreted loosely as "slain animal sacrifice celebrating fullness of welfare, blessedness," etc. (In the Septuagint "sacrifice of salvation" is an accurate translation.)

Varieties. Male or female specimens (unblemished) of oxen or sheep or goats.

Occasion. This is bound up with the significance of it. It was brought as an (a) expression of thanks to God (Lev. 7:11-15), in which case both leavened and unleavened bread were brought with it; (b) for fulfillment of a vow, i.e., as a votive offering (Lev. 7:16-18;); (c) as a freewill expression of devotion (Lev. 7:16-18). (d) On the basis of texts such as Jdg. 20:26; 21:4; 1Sa. 13:9; 2Sa. 24:25, it is held that it might also accompany special prayer.

Ritual. The first four stages are the same as for burnt offering, but after the ritual with the blood, the ceremony continued with opening of the carcass and removal of all the abdominal fat, including that of kidneys and entrails. This together with the "caul" of the liver and the two kidneys were burned on the altar (in the case of the sheep also the fat tail). Then the carcass was divided. The breast (brisket) was given to the priests officiating at the temple for a "wave offering" (i.e., presented to God by moving it right and left), who then cooked and ate it (Lev. 7:15-17). The right shoulder was given to the individual priest officiating. Before he and his family ate it, it was "heaved" — i.e., moved up and down (heave offering), before the LORD (Lev. 7:32-33). The rest of the carcass was returned to the offerer to be used for festive purposes. For regulations regarding eating it, *see* Lev. 7:13-21; 22:29-30; Dt. 12:5-12.

THE SIN OFFERING (Lev. 4; 5:1-13; 6:24-30)

There is a problem of interpretation, too technical for discussion in this limited space, over whether 5:1-13 applies to sin offering or trespass offering. We follow several leading authorities in applying it to the sin offering.

Name. The word *hatta'th* may be rendered "sin" (as in Lev. 4:3) or "sin offering" as well as "punishment for sin" (La. 4:22). It is derived from the verb *to fail, miss*, or as in the moral realm, *to sin*. It is so named because its occasion was specific acts of sin against God's law.

Varieties. About the same varieties of animals as the *shelem* or peace offering. In addition, the red heifer of Numbers 19 and the two goats of the Great Day of Atonement were sin offerings.

Occasions. Reading of the sections of Leviticus indicated and Nu. 15:22-31 will show that when one personally committed some breach of the law of God (through ignorance, weakness, or rashness), and it came to his attention and weighed on his conscience, this offering was appointed as the means of forgiveness. Likewise national sin offerings were prescribed.

Ritual. In general it was the same as for burnt and peace offerings down to disposal of the carcass. Following that, it was different from either. In certain cases the blood was sprinkled seven times before the veil of the sanctuary (Lev. 4:6-7); sometimes blood was placed on the horns of the altar of incense (Lev. 4:6-7); sometimes blood was placed on the horns of the brazen altar. The same inner parts as in the case of the peace offering were burnt on the altar. In the case of an offering for the sin of a priest or the whole congregation, the carcass, together with entrails, legs, dung, and skin, was burnt outside the camp (Lev. 4:12, 21). In other cases it was officially eaten by the priests (Lev. 6:24-26).

THE GUILT (TRESPASS) OFFERING

(Lev. 5:14 – 6:7; 7:15). The word "trespass offering" is rendered in the NIV very accurately as "guilt offering."

The ritual of this offering was in almost all respects the same as that of the sin offering, with two exceptions. It usually consisted of a ram to which was added a fifth of the value of the ram (according to the priest's evaluation) in money and presented to the priest. This indicates that the "guilt offering" was an offering for sin in which the offense given admitted of some sort of human estimation and recompense, so that in addition to the atonement required there might also be the payment of a restitution.

An examination of the passages (Lev. 5:14–6:7; 7:1-7; Nu. 5:5-8) shows that the sins in view in the trespass offering were those in which the offender had made a false oath in some dealing with other men. The breaking of an oath made the act not only a wrong against man but a sin against God. Thus, a part of the ritual was restitution of the value of loss involved to man plus a fifth part, and this was necessary before the offering could be accepted at God's altar. It is blessed to read in the prophecy of Isa. 53:10 that Christ became our guilt offering. (R.D.C.)

SACRILEGE [stealing—*hence*, profaning something sacred] Making the sacred unclean or profaning it. In the LXX this Greek word is used to translate the Hebrew word which the NIV renders "abomination" (Da. 9:27; 11:31; 12:11).

SADDUCEES [followers of ZADOK; *possibly* righteous] *See* SECTS

SADNESS *See* JOY

SADOC *See* ZADOK 9.

SAFFRON *See* PLANTS, PERFUMES, AND SPICES, Plants for Seasoning

SAIL *See* SHIP

SAINT(S) [unique, consecrated, holy ones] A translation of words which basically mean "holy," "sanctified," or "set apart" from the profane to the sacred. In the OT the reference is usually to those

consecrated to God's service or to Israel as God's people (Dt. 7:6; Ps. 50:5; 89:5; 132:9). In the NT, while the word would have the usages just noted, it came to have a more frequent reference to those who were "in Christ," to Christians (Eph. 1:1; 3:8, 18; Php. 1:1; 1Ti. 5:10).

SAKIA [*possibly* one who looks to Yahweh, KB] A descendant of Benjamin (1Ch. 8:10). †

SAKKUTH *See* DEITIES 2.

SALA [missile *or* petition, ISBE; *possibly* javelin, KB] An ancestor of Jesus; also called Salmon and Salma (Ru. 4:20-21; 1Ch. 2:11; Mt. 1:4-5; Lk. 3:32).

SALAH [missile *or* petition, ISBE; *possibly* missile, javelin, KB] *See* SHELAH 1.

SALAMIS One of the main cities of Cyprus, visited by Paul on his first missionary journey (Ac. 13:5). †

SALAMIS

SALATHIEL [*possibly* I have asked of El, KB; *possibly* El is a shield *or* El is a victor, IDB] *See* SHEALTIEL

SALCAH, SALCHAH, SALECAH A city (311-212) in the eastern part of Bashan assigned to the tribal area of Gad; also called Salcah, Salchah (Dt. 3:10; Jos. 13:11; 1Ch. 5:11).

SALEM [peace] A city or area over which Melchizedek was king and because of Ps. 76:2 identified with Jerusalem (Ge. 14:18; Heb. 7:1-2). *See also* JERUSALEM

SALIM While the exact location is not known, most agree that it is to be found in the area some seven to eight miles S of Bethshan in the Jordan Valley. John baptized at Aenon near Salim (Jn. 3:23). †

SALLAI
1. A descendant of Benjamin in Nehemiah's days (Ne. 11:8). †
2. A priest in the days of Nehemiah; also called Sallu (Ne. 12:7, 20). †

SALLU [*possibly* he restores]
1. A descendant of Benjamin who lived in Jerusalem after the return from the Babylonian captivity (1Ch. 9:7; Ne. 11:7; 12:7). †
2. *See* SALLAI 2.

SALMA [little spark, KB]
1. The father of Boaz, the husband of Ruth; also called Salmon and Sala (Ru. 4:20-21; 1Ch. 2:11; Mt. 1:4-5; Lk. 3:32).
2. A Calebite founder of Bethlehem (1Ch. 2:51-54).

SALMAI *See* SHALMAI

SALMON [little spark, KB] *See* SALMA 1.

SALMONE One of the points or capes of the island of Crete which figures in the shipwreck voyage of Paul (Ac. 27:7). †

SALOME [peaceful, prosperous one]
1. The daughter of Herodias who danced before Herod. At her mother's request she asked for the beheading of John the Baptist. Her name does not appear in the Bible, but she is referred to in Mt. 14:6ff. and in Mk. 6:22ff.
2. A woman present at both the Crucifixion and the empty tomb of Jesus (Mk. 15:40; 16:1). †

SALT Israelite salt came either from the Phoenicians in the N or from the region at the SW of the Dead Sea, where there is a hill or mountain of rock salt (Zep. 2:9). This Dead Sea salt was of a poor quality, and the outer part of the salt cakes or chunks soon lost its salty flavor. Jesus used this in his teaching that his disciples were the "salt" of the earth (Mt. 5:13; Mk. 9:50). In the OT newborn babies were rubbed with salt (Eze. 16:4); salt was also required to be used with certain sacrifices (Lev. 2:13). The reference to the "covenant of salt" (Nu. 18:19), meaning a permanent covenant, probably arose from the preservative quality of salt. Salt was also a symbol of desolation, as when Abimelech, having destroyed Shechem, sowed it with salt (Jdg. 9:45).

SALT, CITY OF A Judean city N of Engedi and probably to be identified with Qumran where an Iron Age city was discovered below the Hellenistic one (Jos. 15:62).

SALT, COVENANT OF *See* SALT

SALT, VALLEY OF An unidentified valley; some place it in the tribal area of Judah, while others put it in Edom, where the Israelites and the Edomites fought periodically (2Sa. 8:13-14; 2Ki. 14:7).

SALT HERB *See* PLANTS, PERFUMES, AND SPICES, Miscellaneous Plants 10., *Salt herb*

SALT SEA A salt lake at the southern exit of the Jordan River sometimes called "Eastern Sea" or "Sea of the Arabah" (Dt. 3:17; Zec. 14:8). It lies between the Judean hills and mountains of Moab, from map grid 130 N to 50 S and 185 W to 203 E. Often called the lowest spot on earth, its surface is nearly 1300 feet below sea level, and its depth runs from a few feet to about 1300. Its area is approximately 390 square miles in a geological rift that runs from the Caucasus mountains in the N to the heart of Africa in the S. Because of its high salinity (averaging 30 percent), no life is found in it. It is exceedingly rich in minerals, which are being mined currently. A fertile valley in Abraham's day, it became a waste shortly thereafter (Ge. 13:10). Oases made livable areas around its shores; the one at En Gedi (187-096) has a long history and was often frequented by King David (1Sa. 24:1). One at En Feshka (192-126) supplied water to the Qumran or Dead Sea Scroll community. The prophet predicted a freshening of the waters of the Salt Sea with the production of rich life (Eze. 47:8-10). Two of Herod's "impregnable" fortresses were located in this desolate area, at Masada and Machaerus, the former becoming the place of the last stand of the Jewish Zealots in A.D. 70. *See also* DEAD SEA; GEOGRAPHY OF THE HOLY LAND; MASADA

SALTWORT *See* MALLOW

SALU [restored, IDB] The father of the Israelite who was killed for bringing a Midianite woman into the camp of Israel (Nu. 25:14). †

SALUTATIONS In biblical usage "to salute" meant "to greet." It could be the simple greetings between people meeting on the street, formal greetings between ordinary people and rulers, or the greetings expressed at the beginnings or ends of letters (1Sa. 25:6; Da. 2:4-5; Lk. 10:5; 1Co. 1:13; Eph. 6:23-24).

SALVATION, APPLICATION OF The first interpretation of the person and redemptive work of Jesus Christ in the NT was given by an angel to Joseph, the husband of the virgin: "You are to give him the name Jesus, because he will save his people from their sins" (Mt. 1:21, NIV). Thus is introduced to the NT the concept of save, salvation, Savior. The OT word for salvation is embodied in the name Jesus, a rendering into the Greek of the Hebrew name Joshua, "Jehovah saves." The word "to save" (Hebrew *yashau*) meant "to be wide and roomy" and came to mean "prosperous and free; by extension to save, help, rescue, be in good health."

An understanding of the biblical doctrine of salvation presupposes an understanding of what man is—fallen, lost, and under condemnation. Salvation is the renewal and restoration of man from all he lost in the Fall. It is not only escape from the wrath of God, but deliverance from all the effects of sin, including also the spiritual blessings which come in Christ.

It is thus both a positive and a negative idea. Two texts will show the two sides. First Thessalonians 5:9 says, "God did not appoint us to suffer wrath, but to receive salvation through our Lord Jesus Christ." This is the negative side—escape from wrath. Second Peter 1:3 states that, "His divine power has given us everything we need for life and godliness," which is the positive side.

This salvation is comprehensive as to time. For it is not only a past act (2Ti. 1:9) and a future goal (Ro. 13:11), but also a present process (1Co. 1:18). It is, however, very frequently presented as completely finished, the present possession of all who believe in Christ (Ro. 8:29-30), and absolutely certain as to its final issue (1Th. 5:24).

The Bible states plainly that the Triune God is in every respect the sole author of salvation (Mt. 1:21; Tit. 3:4-6; Jas. 1:17; 1Jn. 4:4). Jesus Christ, the Second Person of the Godhead, is the special mediator of this salvation (Jn. 14:6) and apart from him there is no salvation (Ac. 4:12).

Two problems have arisen among those who accept the foregoing statements. This is to say simply that Christians have differed on these two questions. The first may be put in this manner: Granting that God only is the author of salvation, how is it conveyed to man? That is, how, specifically, does God bring this benefit to an individual man? There have been those who said it comes through mystical experience, imparted directly through the Holy Spirit, quite apart from any means whatsoever. At the opposite extreme there have been those who said it is conveyed through divinely appointed church ordinances varying from two in most Protestant systems (baptism and the Lord's Supper) to seven: (1) Baptism (of an infant by effusion [pouring] or sprinkling); (2) Confirmation (an adolescent making public confession); (3) the Eucharist (Communion by transubstantiation); (4) Penance (also called Reconciliation); (5) Sacrament of the Sick (also known as Last Rites); (6) Matrimony; and (7) Holy Orders (ordination). Matrimony and ordination among the so-called sacraments do not directly relate to salvation in Catholic systems. Evangelical Christianity affirms that while there is a proper place for mystical experience and the observance of sacraments (ordinances), neither is a usual, invariable, or necessary means of bringing the salvation to men. Rather, salvation is conveyed simply through the instrumentality of a message. The NT name for this message is "Good News" or "gospel." This message is from God regarding his Son and his redemptive work; the message is recorded in Scripture, preached by various messengers, and applied by the Holy Spirit. The Bible itself speaks very plainly on this point. Paul declares, "God was pleased through the foolishness of what was preached to save . . ." (1Co. 1:21) and "you have known the holy Scriptures which are able to make you wise for salvation" (2Ti. 3:15, NIV). In another place Paul stated that the gospel is the power of God to salvation (Ro. 1:16). The Scriptures declare that there is a "message" ("words," KJV) that has power to save (Ac. 11:14), and that it is the implanted Word which produces new birth (1Pe. 1:23), without which no one can enter God's heavenly kingdom (Jn. 3:1-16).

The second question relates to the method by which men receive salvation. John 1:12 and 13 raises the question and settles it. It is not by some biological inheritance ("not of blood"); nor is it by self-determination, i.e., legalistic words ("nor of the will of the flesh"); nor by the efforts of others for us ("nor of the will of man"). The same text states, "To all who received him [Christ], to those who believed in his name, he gave the right to become children of God." Thus we learn that faith is the means by which men receive salvation. Innumerable texts amplify this statement. They are the very texts that changed the lives of the Protestant Reformers of the sixteenth cen-

tury—Luther, Zwingli, Calvin, and others—and gave the world that breath of spiritual revival called the Reformation. Appropriately these men called themselves "evangelical," i.e., believers in and preachers of the gospel. To quote all these texts of Scripture and comment on them would be to turn this article into an evangelistic tract. Among the most striking are: Jn. 3:16; 5:24; Ac. 16:30-31; Ro. 10:9-10; Eph. 2:8-9.

Any preaching of this divine truth inevitably calls forth a large number of biblical and theological terms. Some of these terms have self-evident meanings, but most require biblical explanation. An arrangement of them frequently used by the author of this article follows on page 472.

This outline indicates that all of salvation, from election and calling to final glorification, are by God's grace and in union with Jesus Christ. It is beyond the scope of this article fully to demonstrate this statement. A reading of the following texts will be convincing, to the persevering reader who looks them up, as regarding the comprehensive basis of all aspects of salvation in divine grace: Ac. 18:27; 20:24; Ro. 5:2, 15, 20-21; 11:5; 1Co. 15:10; 2Co. 12:8-9; Gal. 1:15; Eph. 1:7; 2:8; 1Th. 2:16; 2Ti. 2:1; Tit. 3:5; Heb. 12:28; and 1Pe. 3:18. Among the passages which support the statement that all of Christian salvation takes place in union with Jesus Christ are: Ro. 6:1-11; 7:4; 8:1; 1Co. 1:4-5; 10:16-18; Eph. 1:4-7; 2: 5-6, 10, 13; Col. 2:12; 2Ti. 1:9. The above outline also distinguishes three things as to the character of each of the eleven events or processes involved in Christian salvation. Some are God's act *for* man while others are God's work *in* man. An act is here distinguished from a work. We think of such an event as a divine appointment or thought, such as is involved in the forgiveness of sin as an act. A work on the other hand is an event that produces objective effects—as, for example, God's call by which he reaches the heart of man and draws him to himself. Three of them are designated as man's act. Faith, for example, is some-

Election	God's act for man	Previous to man's decision
Calling	God's work for man	
Repentance	Man's act	At the time of man's decision
Faith	Man's act	
Conversion	Man's act	
Justification	God's act for man	
Regeneration	God's work for man	
Adoption	God's act for man	
Sanctification	God's work in man	Subsequent to man's decision in this life
Perseverance	God's work in man	
Glorification	God's work in man	Subsequent to man's decision, subsequent to this life, at the coming of Christ.

thing man himself does. God does not and cannot do it for him, though he may enable him to do it. It is not called a work, for works are meritorious. To assign merit to any of these acts of man would be to deny grace (Ro. 4:1-5; 11:6). Hence, these three distinctions are very important to an accurate understanding of a Christian's salvation.

Grace is the favor of God extended toward sinful men, unmerited by them, and in spite of their demerit. Every aspect of salvation, including even those aspects which involve man's acts—repentance, faith, and conversion—are by God's grace. The first Jerusalem church acknowledged this in saying "God has even granted the Gentiles repentance unto life" (Ac. 11:18). Paul declared it true of faith (as all aspects of salvation): "For it is by grace you have been saved, through faith—and this is not from yourselves, it is the gift of God" (Eph. 2:8). See below on conversion.

Union with Christ is the vital spiritual connection with the Godhead, through the Second Person by virtue of which life is imparted to all believers. This union begins in eternity with our election—"He chose us in him before the creation of the world" (Eph. 1:4)—continues through all stages of salvation and is consummated by our final glorification (Ro. 8:11, 18-25). This union is symbolized in the ordinances of baptism (Ro. 6:1ff.) and the Lord's Supper (1Co. 11:23-26). It is the theme of many of Jesus' discourses (Jn. 6—15) and of many other passages in the NT (Eph. 1; Ro. 6).

Election is the name the Bible gives to God's choice of all who believe unto salvation and effectuation of the same. In spite of all the problems and objections to this doctrine, the Bible everywhere boldly traces all the initiative in salvation to God; none at all to man. Whether we can explain it or not (and it is not inexplicable, for God has explained why it is necessary in the doctrine of sin) it is man's duty to believe it. Some clear texts are Ac. 13:48 and Eph. 1:1, 4-5, 11. The first text reads, " . . . and all who were appointed for eternal life believed."

Calling is of two sorts. God genuinely invites all men to accept his gospel, receive his Son, and thus be saved (Jn. 3:16-18; Ro. 10:13). But if God did no more than simply sound forth the message, none would be saved, for because of sin and the Fall "the message of the cross is foolishness to those who are perishing" (1Co. 1:18), and "the man without the Spirit does not accept the things that come from the Spirit of God, for they are foolishness to him and he cannot understand them, because they are spiritually discerned" (1Co. 2:14). This is to say, man is "depraved," without power to turn to God without God's enabling. Thus, though faith is wholly man's act, God enlightens his soul invariably, enabling the elect to believe (1Co. 12:3; cf. Jn. 6:27, 44, 65). The going forth of a divine power in enablement, working in the heart a desire for things of God is known as a "special calling." It is a work of God in man by which he brings man to Christ. Reference to this effective or special call is made at Ro. 8:30 and 1Co. 1:24. In the first passage the connection between election and calling appears.

Repentance and *faith* are two aspects of one act of man which together are called *conversion*. To turn from sin is repentance; to turn toward God is faith; viewed together they are conversion. In the Bible saving faith is that act of the whole man (Ro. 10:9-10) whereby, giving up the whole project of pleasing God by his own effort, the sinner throws himself on the mercy of God, trusting God's grace working through redemption (*see* CHRIST, WORK OF) to save him from death, the wages of sin, and to give him without charge the gift of eternal life. "For the wages of sin is death, but the gift of God is eternal life in Christ Jesus our Lord" (Ro. 6:23). "Now when a man works, his wages are not credited to him as a gift, but as an obligation. However, to the man who does not work but trusts God who justifies the wicked, his faith is credited as righteousness" (Ro. 4:4-5); "And without faith it is impossible to please God, because anyone who comes to him must believe that he exists and that he rewards those who earnestly seek him" (Heb. 11:6; see also Jn. 6:27-29; Ro. 3:21-26 and Php. 3:4-9). Such a trust in God will always be accompanied (and preceded) by that regret for sin, disgust with it, and turning from it that the

the Bible calls repentance (Ac. 2:37-38; 17:30-34). Whole-souled faith is represented in Scripture as invariably leading to obedience. Hence many texts use the words almost interchangeably (Heb. 11:8). It should be added that biblical faith is a far more rugged product than mere quiet expectation that somehow everything will "come out right." Indeed repentance takes place only as it is acknowledged that all will *not* come out right unless a change is made. Nor does saving faith occur without evidence (Ro. 10:19). It does not base itself on sight; rather on the testimony of God concerning his Son given in the Scriptures. *Conversion* is seldom found by that name in Scripture. More often terms such as "turn" and "return" are used. These are indistinguishable from repentance in most texts, especially in the OT where the words appear hundreds of times, especially in the Prophets.

Justification is the act of God whereby he declares the sinner righteous and treats him as righteous. This he does for the sake of Christ and on the basis of his redemptive work. As used in connection with salvation, justification is always of undeserving persons. That is to say, the subjects of this justification (exoneration, acquittal) are called "ungodly" (Ro. 4:5) and "sinners" (Ro. 3:19-24). The entire doctrine of justification is summarized in Ro. 3:24-25: "and are justified freely by his grace through the redemption that came by Christ Jesus. God presented him as a sacrifice of atonement, through faith in his blood. He did this to demonstrate his justice, because in his forbearance he had left the sins committed beforehand unpunished—" (1) The *subjects* are sinful men—"they," referring to the preceding verse, "all have sinned." There is no other kind of man. If God justifies any man whatsoever, that man will be a sinner. There is no other kind of man on earth. (2) The *fact* is that man is "being justified." It is important to remember that this does not mean "to make righteous" but "to declare righteous" and "to treat as righteous." It is a forensic act which, while changing a sinner's status before God, the judge of all, leaves the sinner's character as sinner unaffected. Change of character is related to regeneration and sanctification (see below). (3) The *method* is "by . . . grace." In the law courts, from which the term *justify* comes, justification is supposed to be only of the truly innocent; the offenders are properly convicted, or declared guilty. The glory of divine grace is to justify those who deserve condemnation. (4) The *manner* is "as a gift." The more usual translation is "freely," meaning "without payment of any price whatsoever" (Isa. 55:1). Salvation of man must be in this manner, for nothing an unbeliever does pleases God (Jn. 6:28-29; Heb. 11:6). How can a man in open rejection of the Son please the Father with tithes, donations, pilgrimages or acts of devotion? (5) The *basis* is "through the redemption which is in Christ Jesus." For God to declare a sinner righteous as an act of omnipotence would be a misuse of power. No human judge would be approved for such a lawless act toward a lawbreaker. For God to do so would bring God under the condemnation of his own rules and bring him under the woe he has denounced upon others (Isa. 5:20). That basis is called "redemption" in Ro. 3:24 (KJV) and is in the next verse represented as a "propitiation" of God's wrath.

"Expiation" is not as good a rendering as "propitiation" for the Greek *hilasterion*. The Greek word has the invariable sense of appeasement or propitiation of wrath throughout ancient Greek literature. The NIV translates this Greek word as "atoning sacrifice." Since, in the Bible, any atonement clearly implied satisfaction of God's wrath, this is an adequate rendering.

Expiation (which is indeed treated in other contexts) has reference to sins; *propitiation* has reference to the wrath (penalty) involved in broken laws and offended persons. See CHRIST, WORK OF; EXPIATE; PROPITIATION; *see also* "faith" above.

Regeneration is generally understood today as that work of God in man whereby his heart and spirit (his moral and spiritual faculties) are renewed by the very presence of the Holy Spirit in the believing sinner's own body. He is given a love of God and of his Word. He receives spiritual discernment to know and respond to spiritual things, whereas before he was "dead in . . . transgressions and sins" (Eph. 2:1; cf. 4:17-19). Paul connected this with the believer's union with Christ: "Therefore, if anyone is in Christ, he is a new creation; the old has gone, the new has come" (2Co. 5:17). It is also described as a "washing of rebirth and renewal by the Holy Spirit" (Tit. 3:5). Jesus declared it to be indispensable for salvation (Jn. 3:1-10).

Adoption is not a work of God external to himself, but rather an act of God's reckoning, as is also justification. Those in whom God works regeneration (i.e., another birth) are counted by God as having all rights and privileges as members of God's family. This doctrine is peculiar to the portions of the NT written by Paul (see Gal. 3:23—4:7). Paul used the word "adoption" in connection with the believers' future resurrection as well (Ro. 8:23).

Sanctification is a work of God in believers whereby their moral character is refined so that it truly corresponds with and equals their official standing before God as justified and adopted. If God is going to justify ungodly sinners, such a work is necessary. The important thing to see, and this is basically what the Protestant Reformation was all about, is that God justifies us while we are still sinners, in response to our faith. Then he begins to purify us inwardly. He gives us eternal life when we do not deserve it, when we could not possibly merit it. Then he finishes his work progressively by purifying our lives through his Spirit and Word, both working through Providence, consummating this work ultimately when our bodies are raised from the dead, though certainly purifying the soul completely when at death we go to be with him in "the Glory." Some passages on which this doctrine rests are

Ro. 6; Eph. 5:25-27; 1Th. 3:11-13; 5:23-24; Heb. 12:1-17; and 1Jn. 3:13. The Bible also makes mention (chiefly several times in the Book of Hebrews) of a positional holiness or sanification. This is the act of God in setting us aside for himself and is related to the idea of the holiness of consecrated things used only for God's service, as the OT tabernacle, its vessels and furniture. It is by virtue of this sanctification that all Christians are called saints, holy, sanctified men (Ro. 1:7; 1Co. 1:2; Eph. 1:1; Php. 1:1; Col. 1:2).

Perseverance is closely related to sanctification. It is, from the standpoint of the believer's own experience, a name given to the permanence of the believing sinner's striving toward perfection throughout life, in spite of slips, falls, and failures. From the point of view of God's work in us, perseverance is the perfection of God's work of saving us. He whom God effectually calls, who believes on Christ truly and sincerely, will persevere in faith until the end of life on earth. There may be lapses, but there will also be renewals. Judas, the traitor, who apostatized and never returned and who was a "son of perdition" (Jn. 17:12), is cited frequently as an example of a professed believer who did not persevere because he was a hypocrite all the time. Peter, who denied the Lord but shortly wept bitter tears of genuine repentance, afterwards lived a life of faithful service to Christ as an example of a genuine believer who, though he slipped for a brief time, did not fall forever (Lk. 22:31-32). Passages frequently cited in support of this doctrine are: Ro. 8:28-29; 11:28-29; Php. 1:6; 2Th. 3:3; 2Ti. 1:12; and 1Pe. 1:5.

Glorification is that future event when all the saved shall be raised from the dead (or translated if still alive on earth) in glorified bodies, like Christ's body, free from sin and all its effects, prepared to dwell forever in the presence of the risen glorified Christ, of all the holy angels, and of one another forever. It is the consummation of sanctification and perseverance. Some of the passages which speak of this are Ro. 5:2; 8:19, 30; 1Co. 15:43; Php. 3:20-21; and Col. 1:27. (R.D.C.) *See also* IMPUTE, IMPUTATION

SALVE An unidentified compound of medicinal value for the eyes (Rev. 3:18). †

SAMARIA [belonging to clan of SHEMER—1Ki. 16:24 (BDB)] *See* GEOGRAPHY OF THE HOLY LAND

SAMARITANS [of Samaria] One tradition has it that when the leaders of Samaria and its environs (surrounding areas) were deported by the Assyrians, the leaders of other communities were brought in to replace them. The intermarriage of the people produced the Samaritans. Because of this intermarriage, the Samaritans came to be disliked by the Jews. The Samaritans themselves, however, hold that not all of them were deported, that those who went into exile returned, and that they are the true descendants of the original Israelites. The matter of the double deportation is a matter of history (2Ki. 17:24). There is, however, no evidence of Assyrian or other foreign elements in the practice of these people or in their religion, a fact that goes against the concept of assimilation. The word itself is found in the OT only in 2Ki. 17:29, but appears much more frequently in the NT and in the extrabiblical literature of that later period (Jn. 4:9; Ac. 8:25). The Samaritans have a long tradition going back to the early times of the kings of Judah and Israel. They rejected all of the OT except the five books of Moses and believed that Mt. Gerizim, not Jerusalem, was where God intended he be served.

SAMGAR-NEBO An officer or a title of an officer, of the Babylonian king Nebuchadnezzar who was present and involved in the taking of Jerusalem (Jer. 39:3). Some versions place the "Nebo" with the next word. *See* NEBO-SARSEKIM

SAMLAH A king of Edom (Ge. 36:36-37; 1Ch. 1:47-48). †

SAMOS

SAMOS [heights, lofty place] An island in the Aegean. Paul sailed past it at the end of his third missionary journey (Ac. 20:15). †

SAMOTHRACE, SAMOTHRACIA [Thracian Samos] An island in the Aegean on the route of Paul's second missionary journey (Ac. 16:11). †

SAMSON [little one of SHEMESH (pagan solar god) *or* sunny, IDB and KB; strong, *Josephus Antiq.* 5:8:4] *See* JUDGES OF ISRAEL

SAMUEL [his name is El, BDB, IDB, and ISBE; heard of El, KD (1Sa. 1:20); the unnamed god is El, KB] A judge, a priest, and a prophet in the eleventh to tenth century B.C. Israel (1Sa. 7:69; 9:9; Ac. 13:20). He was born in answer to his mother's special prayers and given to God for his service at the tabernacle at Shiloh (1Sa. 1:11, 19-20; 2:11). He was God's messenger to anoint both Saul and

later David as kings (1Sa. 10:1; 16:13). One of the better known stories about him is the attempt by Saul to consult him through the necromancer (i.e., a witch that summons the dead) at Endor (1Sa. 28:8-19).

SAMUEL, BOOKS OF The biblical tradition as to the authorship of the books 1 and 2 Samuel comes from 1Ch. 29:29 where the Chronicles of Samuel, Nathan, and Gad are mentioned, together with the statement of 1Sa. 10:25, where Samuel is said to have written in a book the rights and duties of kingship. It is therefore most probable that several authors were involved, Samuel providing the material or the copy of the part that involved his own life. The story of the birth of Samuel, his call to the priesthood, the stealing of the Ark by the Philistines and its return are told in 1Sa. 1—6.

Chapter 7 contains the prophet's challenge to Israel and the defeat of the Philistines. The relations of Saul and Samuel are found in 1Sa. 8—15, and of David and Samuel in 1Sa. 16—25. The account of the life of David continues to the end of the book and through all of 2 Samuel.

SANBALLAT [Sin (pagan moon god) has given life] The governor of Samaria and Nehemiah's most bitter opponent who, in a time of Nehemiah's absence from Jerusalem, got his daughter married to the son of the high priest. Nehemiah ejected him from the temple

SAMOTHRACE

upon his return (Ne. 2:10, 19; 4:1-8; 6:1-14; 13:28). †

SANCTIFY, SANCTIFICATION The position and process of uniqueness, set-apartness. *See* CHRIST, WORK OF; HOLINESS; SALVATION, APPLICATION OF

SANCTUARY *See* TABERNACLE and TEMPLE

SAND ON THE SHORE A figure of speech for vastness (Ge. 22:17; Jer. 33:22; Ro. 9:27; Heb. 11:12).

SANDAL *See* DRESS

SANDAL-THONG *See* DRESS

SANHEDRIN [sit together] This council, called *sunedrion* in Greek—from which it came into Hebrew as a loan word *sanhedrin*, was the supreme tribunal of the Jews after the return from the Babylonian captivity through NT times. It is also found in reference to lesser councils as well. In Roman times (after 63 B.C.) the council was given important powers over Jews in the area, powers that were recognized even by Jews living abroad (Ac. 22:5; cf. Ac. 26:12). But these began to wane in A.D. 70, and the organization itself is lost to history by the fourth century A.D. Even during the period A.D. 70 to 400, its real powers were taken over by the Beth Din (the house of the judge, i.e., court) which met in various places from Jabneh (Jamnia) to Tiberias.

SANNAH *See* DEBIR

SANSANNAH A town (140-083) in the tribal area of Judah near Ziklag (Jos. 15:31). †

SAPH A Philistine descendant of the giant who was killed at Gob; also called Sippai (2Sa. 21:18; 1Ch. 20:4). †

SAPHIR *See* SHAPHIR

SAPPHIRA [beautiful] The wife of Ananias and member of the early church in Jerusalem. They lost their lives for lying to God (Ac. 5:1-10). †

SAPPHIRE *See* PRECIOUS STONES AND METALS, Precious Stones 11.

SARA, SARAH, SARAI [princess] The wife of Abraham; also called Sarai at the first (Ge. 11:29; 17:15). She was the mother of Isaac, died at the age of 127, and was buried in the cave of the Hittite of Machpelah in Hebron (Ge. 21:1-7; 23:1, 12-19). Before the birth of Isaac, Sarah gave her handmaid to Abraham as a concubine, and the resultant son was called Ishmael, who with his mother was driven out into the wilderness (Ge. 21:8ff.).

SARAI [princess] The earlier name of Sarah above.

SARAPH [burning one, serpent] A descendant of Judah (1Ch. 4:22). †

SARDINE, SARDIUS
1. Sardine is a transliteration of a stone in many versions (Rev. 4:3). Translated as "carnelian" in the NIV and RSV, "cornelian" in NEB and "ruby" in JB.
2. In the KJV sardius is translated as "ruby" (Ex. 28:17; 39:10; Eze. 28:13). *See* PRECIOUS STONES AND METALS, Precious Stones 1.

SARDIS One of the cities in Asia Minor to which a letter was directed by the author of the Book of Revelation (Rev. 1:11; 3:14). †

SARDITE *See* SERED, SEREDITE

SARDONYX *See* PRECIOUS STONES AND METALS

SAREPTA *See* ZAREPHATH

SARGON [firm, faithful king, BDB; the king is legitimate, IDB] The Assyrian king who finally took Samaria (his father had begun the siege) and who is named as the attacker of Ashdod (2Ki. 17:3ff.; Isa. 20:1). † *See* ASSYRIA

SARID A town (172-229) in the tribal area of Zebulun (Jos. 19:10-12). †

SARON *See* SHARON, PLAINS OF

SARSECHIM, SARSEKIM [possibly chief of the slaves] *See* NEBO-SARSEKIM

SARUCH *See* SERUG

SASHES A part of the dress bound around the waist translated "headband" in Isa. 3:20, KJV.

SATAN [hostile opponent] *See* DEVIL

SATRAP [protector of the land] Viceroys or governors of provinces having considerable power. In the KJV they are called lieutenants or princes. Darius of Persia organized his empire into twenty satrapies (Ezr. 8:36; Est. 9:3; Da. 6:1-7). *See* PERSIA; PROVINCE

SATYR [hairy (goat form)] A demon whose character and appearance are not defined exactly. The idea in the Hebrew word is "hairy one." Sacrifices were made to them, and they are mentioned as dancing on the ruins of Babylon (Lev. 17:7; Isa. 13:21; 34:14). The NIV translates as wild goat.

SAUL [asked, *possibly* dedicated to God]
1. *See* KINGS OF JUDAH AND ISRAEL.
2. *See* SHAUL 1.
3. The Hebrew name of Paul (Ac. 13:21). *See* PAUL

SAVED *See* CHRIST, WORK OF

SAVIOR *See* CHRIST, WORK OF

SAVOR, SAVOUR KJV for "Aroma" (Lev. 1:9).

SAW A knife with a notched blade used for cutting wood, stone, or even in the torture of humans (2Sa. 12:31; 1Ki. 7:9; Isa. 10:15; Heb. 11:37).

SAWDUST *See* MOTE

SAYINGS OF JESUS *See* LOGIA

SCAB *See* SICK, SICKNESS

SCALES
1. An instrument or a part of an instrument used in weighing (Isa. 40:12), sometimes called a balance (Pr. 16:11).
2. The scales of a fish. Only fish having both scales and fins were considered ceremonially clean (Lev. 11:9-12). Something like scales fell off Paul's eyes when

his sight was restored to him—possibly a symbolic or figurative use (Ac. 9:18). *See also* SCALL

SCALL KJV, NKJV, ASV for "sore" in the NIV, "itch" RSV, "scale" NASB, "scurf" NEB, "tinea" JB in Lev. 13:30ff. *See* SICK, SICKNESS 1., *Skin diseases*

SCANDAL *See* STUMBLING BLOCK

SCAPEGOAT A NIV rendering in Lev. 16:7ff. *See* AZAZEL

SCARLET A red dye for fabrics and leather obtained from the bodies of certain insects. The thread and cloth made from it was highly prized in ancient Israel (Ex. 25:4; 28:5; 38:23; Lev. 14:49; Mt. 27:28).

SCATTERING, THE *See* DIASPORA

SCENT *See* PLANTS, PERFUMES, AND SPICES

SCEPTER [royal staff] The staff or baton of a king (sometimes held by a lesser poser) which symbolized his power and authority (Ge. 49:10; Est. 5:2; Isa. 14:5).

SCEVA A Jewish high priest whose sons in Ephesus were trying to exorcise evil spirits in the name of Jesus (Ac. 19:13-16). †

SCHOOL *See* PROPHET

SCORPION *See* BEASTS 6.

SCORPION PASS A pass S of the Salt Sea (Dead Sea) on the SE border of Judah, between Judah and the Amorites (Nu. 34:4; Jos. 15:3; Jdg. 1:36).

SCOURGE, SCOURGING, STRIPES Beating with a rod or a hide whip for the purpose of discipline for slaves, children, and fools. Forty strokes or stripes were the maximum allowed under biblical law, and thirty-nine were usually given to allow for an error in counting (Pr. 13:24; 26:3; 1Ki. 12:11; Dt. 25:1-3). Scourging was done in the synagogues and came to be applied for infraction of many of the laws for whose breaking no particular penalty was laid down in the Bible (Mt. 23:34). Pilate had Jesus scourged, but Paul being a Roman citizen could not be scourged (Jn. 19:1; Ac. 22:24-29). There is one reference to the tongue as a scourge (Job 5:21). This word may also be used in a much broader sense, that of an evil or a plague happening to an individual (Jos. 23:13; Ps. 91:10).

SCREECH OWL *See* BIRDS 5.

SCREEN Three screens or veils are mentioned in connection with the tabernacle. One was at the gate of the outer court, one at the entrance to the tabernacle itself, and the third separated the innermost part of the tabernacle, which contained the Ark, from the rest of the tabernacle. This screen was called the "veil of the screen," two words for the same thing being used (Ex. 38:18; 39:38; 40:21). These are not specifically mentioned in connection with the temple, but it may be assumed that they existed, as the latter was patterned after the former, and in the account of the day of Christ's crucifixion it is recorded that the "curtain" of the temple was torn in two (Mt. 27:51).

SCRIBE [write, copy] At first the scribe was a sort of secretary, an official in charge of documents, but the term took on a special meaning to refer to a professional student and teacher of the law (Ezr. 4:8; 7:6, 12; 2Ki. 22:3-8; Mt. 2:4). Since Jesus' view of additions to the written law, whether by interpretative manipulation or by extensions, differed from that of the scribes of his day, the NT has many references to this class of professions (Mt. 12:28-38; 15:1). *See* LAWYER

SCRIP KJV for "bag" (Mt. 10:10; Mk. 6:8; Lk. 9:3; 10:4; 22:35-36). *See* DRESS

SCRIPT [write] Many scripts (methods of writing) were known throughout the period of history covered by the Bible, but this word is used in the NIV in connection with the story of Esther where we read that the king sent letters to all the provinces in the script of each particular province (Est. 1:22; 3:12; 8:9).

SCRIPTURE [writing]
  1. Definition and Scope of Scripture
  2. The Reliability of the Bible
  3. The Teaching of the Bible about Itself
     a. God of the Bible
     b. The Preparation of Men Who Wrote the Bible
     c. The Prophets' and Apostles' Authority
  4. Apocrypha and Pseudepigrapha
  5. Revelation and Inspiration

1. *Definition and Scope of Scripture.* The name "Bible" does not appear in the book referred to by that name. The most comprehensive name, employed by the book itself in a comprehensive way, is "Scripture" with the variations "the Scripture," and "holy Scriptures" (2Ti. 3:16; cf. 3:15; Jas. 4:5; Mt. 26:54). It is a book of two main parts, an OT of thirty-nine books composed before the birth of Jesus and a NT of twenty-seven books composed in the first decades after the death and resurrection of Jesus. Information in the OT itself, coupled with modern knowledge of ancient, chronology indicates that the first portions of the OT were written by Moses about 1400 B.C. and the last portions about 400 B.C. The NT books came into existence between about the years A.D. 45 and as late as A.D. 95.

2. *The Reliability of the Bible.* The confidence that Christian people have always placed in this book they call "the Bible" is indicated in the attitude of Jesus himself, and that circle of first followers called apostles. These men had the books of the OT already and were themselves soon to be engaged in the production of the NT (Jn. 14:25-27). Jesus said, "Scriptures cannot be broken" (Jn. 10:35); he rebuked the Jews of his time, saying they were wrong in their opinions because of ignorance of the Scriptures (Mt. 22:29). On one occasion he went so far as to say that even a resurrected saint's message could have no higher authority than that of Moses and the OT prophets (Lk. 16:29-31). Paul, author of over a dozen NT books, declared in one

of them that even an angel of heaven could have no authority to correct or modify the message of his (Paul's) book (Gal. 1:8), and in other writings the same Apostle Paul cited the OT writings as the highest possible divine authority (Ro. 4:3; cf. 9:17; 10:10-11; 11:2). His characteristic answer to questions of belief is, "What does the Scripture say?" (Ro. 4:3). Similar expressions are to be found in all parts of the NT. Paul sometimes quoted ancient writers, whose words are found in the Scriptures: "For we are his offspring" (Ac. 17:28), from Cleanthes or Aratus; "In whom we live and move and exist" (Ac. 17:28), from Epimenides; "Bad company corrupts good character" (1Co. 15:33), from Menander; "Cretans are always liars, evil brutes, lazy gluttons" (Tit. 1:12), from Epimenides. Paul used these writers in a very selective sense and was not giving his endorsement of their entire works or worldview.

This confidence in Scripture was characteristic of the official creeds of the church even in ages when ignorance and overemphasis on forms and ceremonies caused the Bible to fall into disuse. Denial of the inspiration and authority of the Bible has been a heresy in all periods of church history.

When the Reformation of the sixteenth century took place, the leaders, who thought of themselves as the restorers of original Apostolic Christianity, took as their basic principle that the Scriptures of the OT and NT are the only source of Christian doctrines, entirely sufficient in themselves as a guide to salvation and the good life. (*See* in other reference works Lutheran, Reformed Presbyterian, Anglican, Congregational, Baptist, and Methodist statements; and Philip Schaff's, *The Creeds of Christendom,* Vol. III, pp. 93-97, 832, 362, 381-389, 489-492, 600-606, 742, 935).

The evangelical sons and daughters of the Reformation have these same opinions regarding the Bible. They find the Bible making claim to divine authority and ultimate truth; their reading of it does not convince them that the Bible fails to support its claims in its state-

ments about reality, in whatever realm it speaks. Of course, the Bible does not speak on many questions. There is, for example, no specific word in the Bible on calculus or quantum physics. In matters concerning technical science, the Bible does not speak in a technical manner, but in a "phenomenal" manner, i.e., in language of appearance, as people of all ages have done. Thus the universe is not described in the creation narrative of Genesis 1 in scientific language, but rather as it appears to men, as "the heaven and earth." The heaven is further analyzed as sun, moon, and stars.

3. The teaching of the Bible about itself may systematically be arranged as follows:

a. God of the Bible.

The Bible never defines God or attempts to prove him. But this book which starts with "In the beginning God" soon provides sufficient *data* about this God. He is "that infinite and eternal Spirit in whom all things have their source, support, and end." The reader soon realizes that the God of the Bible, through providence (government of the world), is in general charge of things, that nothing ever happens, from the fall of a raindrop to the fall of an empire, which is outside his control. Convinced that God is not only big but infinitely so, not only wise and powerful, but infinitely so, he has no difficulty in accepting a book as written by special divine power and guidance. *See* ATTRIBUTES OF GOD

b. The preparation of men who wrote the Bible. We know the names of many of the authors of various books of the Bible; for example, Paul wrote the Epistle to the Romans, and Jeremiah wrote the first fifty-one of the fifty-two chapters of the large book which bears his name. Some sections of Scripture are anonymous, for example the latter parts of Proverbs, many Psalms and the books of Kings and Chronicles. It is not important who they were. It is important that they were prepared by God for their task as authors of Scripture. One of them says God "set me apart before I was born . . . called me by his grace" (Gal. 1:15) for his special work as revealer of God. Another says about the same in language which suggests preparation both by heredity and experience (Jer. 1:4ff.). Though each, in a sense, was prepared to speak to his own generation (Ac. 13:36), there was also a timelessness about their work, for being in touch with true reality they could speak enduring timeless truth (Mt. 5:17-20; Jn. 10:35).

c. *The prophets' and apostles' authority.* One thinks of Nabal's words, "Many servants are breaking away from their masters these days" (1Sa. 25:10). So there are and were many seemingly nice people who claim to speak for God yet are either self-deceived or liars. Out of the clamor of claims and counterclaims in religion how can one know what is right?

The answer to this question is crucial. If the people of Bible times had no basis other than popularity, education, or glamor upon which to judge a prophet's truth claim, then it is hard to accept their judgments as correct. Why were certain authors and their books rejected and others received? To answer this scripturally is to provide the principle of *canonicity,* as it is called *(see* ANTILEGOMENA; CANON). The biblical teaching is that God fully certified each of these men to his own generation as a man with authority to speak (or write) for God. The best place to begin is with certain words of Moses in Deuteronomy chapters 13 and 18. After forty years as their leader, Moses, the aged man of God, knew his death was near and that divine guidance for his people in Canaan was indispensable. First, he strictly prohibited any relationship whatsoever with Canaanite religious institutions and practices, especially those connected with attempts to forecast the future. His exact words, containing a remarkable list of pagan practices (some still observed in civilized modern dress), are to be found in Deuteronomy. At the same time Moses announced the establishment of the office of prophet, to furnish a continuing line of accredited divine messengers. Their authority to speak for

God was to be no less than that of Moses, himself, and they were to be believed and obeyed (Dt. 18:15-19; *see* PROPHET).

At this juncture the basis for infallible recognition of the authentic messenger or detection of the imposter was announced. That basis was fivefold: (1) The messenger must be a Hebrew, "from among you, from your brothers," not a foreigner but an indigenous (native) minister. This principle is confirmed in the NT (Ro. 3:1-2). (2) The messenger would always speak in the name of Yahweh, the Hebrew proper name of the one true God of all the earth. Thus monotheism was insured (Dt. 18:15, 18, 22; cf. 13:1-18). (3) Special supernatural verification was to be furnished by ability to accurately predict the near future (Dt. 18:21-22; cf. Ge. 15:14-16; 18:10-14; 21:1-2; Ex. 3:11-12). Many chapters of the OT and NT furnish examples of this test in operation. A very striking one is Jeremiah 28. (4) Ability to perform miracles was a fourth sign (Dt. 13:1ff.; cf. Ac. 2:33; Heb. 2:1-5). Moses and Aaron had used this extensively in connection with the exodus from Egypt. There was finally (5) the requirement that the messenger in each case would present a message consistent with that of Moses and other previous prophets. He would in no case begin a new religion (Dt. 13).

A very striking case where all these five marks are seen in impressive display is in the case of Elijah (1Ki. 17–18). Another is that of Jesus himself.

It is important to see that no church meeting or convention of ecclesiastics (i.e., church leaders) conferred authority, i.e., "canonized" any biblical book. The books carried from their human authors the marks of authentic messages from God. The people received them as such long before churchmen got around to discussing or listing them.

By applying these texts, when the OT period came to an end, the Jewish people knew exactly which books belonged to the canon of Scripture. Josephus, a first-century Jewish historian, is very emphatic on this point (*Against Apion*, Book 1:8). The evidence on the NT and the Masoretic text (official Hebrew biblical text) is to the same effect. These books are the thirty-nine of the Hebrew Bible, also of Protestant affirmation.

4. *Apocrypha and pseudepigrapha.* There are other books of religious interest, some springing from pre-Christian times, others from post-Christian times, often called *pseudepigrapha*, that were anciently read by Christians or Jews. Books so called are generally not regarded by any religious body as inspired Scriptures. These were Gospels, Epistles, Acts, Apocalypses – the major ones more than seventy in number. Normally ascribed to be written by an apostle, their teachings are regarded as heresy. The infancy Gospels try to fill in details of Jesus' early years. The *Infancy Gospel of Thomas* has almost amusing details of the apocryphal Jesus' precociousness. Certain others, mainly composed originally in Greek, usually by English-speaking Protestants, called the *Apocrypha*, are received by the Roman Catholic church as Scripture; though considered by many theologians as of lesser authority than the books of the Hebrew canon, they are sometimes called deuterocanonical. The books, usually referred to as the Apocrypha, are fourteen in number as published under Protestant guidelines. (a) *I Esdras.* This book of nine fairly long chapters goes over the history of the canonical books of Ezra and Nehemiah; also called III Esdras. (b) *II Esdras.* This book of sixteen chapters relates mainly to alleged visions and revelations received by Salathiel during the Babylonian captivity. It is highly fanciful and falls far short of credibility. (c) *Tobit.* An unhistorical tale of fourteen chapters teaching Jewish piety. (d) *Judith.* A fictitious patriotic tale of sixteen chapters with "Judith," a beautiful Jewish widow as heroine, and Halofernes, a general of "Nebuchodonosor" as villain. (e) *Additions to Esther*, sixteen chapters. (f) *Wisdom of Solomon.* Nineteen chapters in imitation of the biblical Proverbs. (g) *Ecclesiasticus* (also called Wisdom of Sirach). Fifty-one chapters, much of

religious value in the style of the biblical books of wisdom. (h) *Baruch* with the *Epistle of Jeremy.* Supposed supplement to the canonical book of Jeremiah by the prophet's amanuensis (secretary) and letter of Jeremiah. (i) *The Song of the Three Holy Children.* An attempt to supplement the story of the "fiery furnace" incident; inserted after Da. 3:23, sixty-eight verses. (j) *History of Susanna.* Sixty-four verses of pious detective story about protection of a young wife's virtue, partly through the wisdom of Daniel. (k) *Bel and the Dragon.* An interesting story of idolatry and a dragon in the days of Daniel and King Cyrus; forty-two verses. (l) *The Prayer of Manasses.* An attempt to report the penitential prayer of evil King Manasseh mentioned at 2Ch. 33:13, only a few lines in length. (m) *1 Maccabees.* This book of sixteen chapters gives a generally trustworthy report of events in Palestine from about 175 to 135 B.C. (n) *2 Maccabees.* Enlarges on certain details of 1 Maccabees. Not generally regarded as reliable a history as 1 Maccabees.

Though St. Jerome, official translator of the Roman Latin Vulgate Bible, rejected all fourteen books of the Apocrypha, the Council of Trent (1546) and the First Vatican Council (1870) declared all except *I* and *II Esdras* and *The Prayer of Manasses* "sacred and canonical."

Although Protestants have always regarded the fourteen books as noncanonical, they have been many times published with the Bible as useful and conducive to piety. Luther's German Bible (1534) included the Apocrypha as an appendix, and all editions of the King James Version of the Bible carried them up to 1827. They are now published separately. *See* AUTHORIZED VERSION; BIBLE VERSIONS

5. *Revelation and inspiration.* A pair of verses in the NT will summarize the fact that the content of the biblical books has God as its ultimate source, i.e., *it is divine revelation:* "In the past God spoke to our forefathers through the prophets at many times and in various ways, but in these last days he has spoken to us by

Book	Approx. Date	Orig. Lang.	Type of Lit.	Contents	Purpose
1 Esdras	200 B.C.	Aram.	Fiction	The Bible, plus	On rebuilding the temple
2 Esdras	A.D. 100	Aram.	Apocalypse	Prophecies	To encourage oppressed Jews
Tobit	175 B.C.	Aram.	Fiction	Tobias's trip	To enforce Pharisaism
Judith	150 B.C.	Heb.	Fiction	Jerusalem saved	Nationalistic Judaism
Rest of Esther	125 B.C.	Greek	Fiction	Additions	To make Esther religious
Wisdom of Solomon	A.D. 40	Greek	Philosophy	Didactic poetry	For Pharisaism's faith
Ecclesiasticus	180 B.C.	Heb.	Wisdom	Didactic poetry	Toward Sadduceeism
Baruch	200–100 B.C.	Heb.	Legend	Letter to exile	For Jews in trouble
Jeremy	125 B.C.	Aram.	Polemic	Letter to exile	Against idolators
Song of the Three Holy Children	150 B.C.	Aram.	Fictional add. to Daniel	Prayer and hymn	Independent praises
Susanna	150 B.C.	Aram.	Fictional add. to Daniel	Woman rescued	To teach morality
Bel	150 B.C.	Aram.	Fictional add. to Daniel	Daniel vs. idols	Against idolatry
Prayer of Manasses	50 B.C.	Heb.	Lyric	Penitent prayer	For repentance
1 Maccabees	75 B.C.	Heb.	History	Judah 175–135	To glorify Hasmoneans
2 Maccabees	50 B.C.	Greek	Legend	Judah 187–160	To enforce Pharisaism

his Son, whom he appointed heir of all things, and through whom he made the universe." (Heb. 1:1-2, NIV). These verses tell us that actual information was conveyed from God to man, facts and data that could be formed into propositions and organized into a creed or catechism—plus, of course, much of indescribable personal experience (Ex. 3:1ff.; Isa. 6:1ff.; 2Co. 12:1-4). The idea of "revelations" is neither pure factual datum nor pure experience or "event." It is both and more besides.

We understand that the "many and various ways" by which God spoke to prophets in OT times include such revelations as the visions of Isaiah, the dreams of Daniel, Moses' tablets of stone inscribed by supernatural means, the inner voice of the Spirit when David sang psalms, the researches of Kings and Chronicles under the power of God's Spirit, or the personal experiences of Matthew in his Gospel. All were methods of revelation in the meaning of Heb. 1:1. The NT revelation came not from a mere human prophet but from "a Son" of God, the Second Person of the Godhead supernaturally incarnate as Jesus of Nazareth. All the NT is directly or indirectly from him. Shortly before his death he announced that his apostles would complete the revelation he was leaving unfinished (Jn. 14—16), but it would be *his* revelation nonetheless.

Thus, while acting freely as individuals (Paul, for example was never more fully Paul than when writing 2 Corinthians, an intensely personal letter), what these men wrote was divine revelation as to its matter. *See* INERRANCY; INSPIRATION

The word "inspired" essentially means the same as the expression "Word of God." If the president or prime minister sends a letter, makes a speech, signs his name to a note typed by his secretary, or even confirms a telephone message of his wife, it is his word. He stands behind it. It bears the force of his authority. When Paul preached in Thessalonica on his second great missionary journey he preached the message he distinctly said was given him "through a revelation" (Gal. 1:11-12). So later Paul could write to the Thessalonians (1Th. 2:13). "When you received the word of God, which you heard from us, you accepted it not as the word of men, but as it actually is, the word of God." When Paul said, "All Scripture is inspired by God" (2Ti. 3:16, RSV), he did not mean anything less than that it was produced by God, created by him. A better translation than *in*spired would be *out*spired. The NIV correctly renders this verse, "All Scripture is God-breathed." Just as the breath of the wind makes a cloud of dust, so the breath of God creates Scripture, mediately, of course, by human writers. The breath of God is an anthropomorphism in the Bible for his creativity: "By the word of the LORD were the heavens made, their starry host by the breath of his mouth" (Ps. 33:6; cf. Ge. 1:3, 6, 9, 14, 20, 24, 26; Heb. 11:1).

Holding as they do such a high view of their Holy Scriptures, it is not surprising that Christians attach a great deal of importance to understanding the meaning of the Bible. They believe that understanding sufficient for salvation is not attained except through the illumination of the soul of man by the God who inspired the Bible. Man as he exists apart from the special saving power of God is "dead in trespasses and sins" (Eph. 2:1). "The man without the Spirit does not accept the things that come from the Spirit of God, for they are foolishness to him and he cannot understand them, because they are spiritually discerned" (1Co. 2:14, NIV). And of men's rational faculties it is written that they have "the understanding darkened, being alienated from the life of God through the ignorance that is in them" (Eph. 4:18, KJV). Hence the Spirit of God is active in leading sinners, through the Scriptures, to see that Christ is Lord (1Co. 12:13), and growth in spiritual understanding of the Bible will come only in response to humble, prayerful search. (R.D.C.)

SCROLL A papyrus or parchment

(leather) roll, usually with writing on it. This was the "book" of biblical times (Jer. 36:2-32; Rev. 5:19).

SCURF *See* SCALL

SCURVY KJV, ASV; for "festering sore" in the NIV; "itching disease" in the RSV; "eczema" in the NKJV, NASB; and "scab" NEB. This skin disease was of some kind of drying and scaling. Those who had it were not fit for service because they were to be holy (unique and fit) representatives of the holy God (Lev. 21:20; 22:22). *See* SICK, SICKNESS 1.

SCYTHIANS Horse-riding fighters, nomads, who came into the world of the fertile crescent in the late eighth century from W Siberia. The word is used in the Bible only in Col. 3:11. Some think that the Ashkenaz were Scythians. † *See* ASHKENAZ

SEA A sea is generally understood to be a great body of water that covers much of the earth. Relatively speaking, the seas of the Bible are not large. The Mediterranean Sea is small and more or less landlocked. The Sea of Galilee is a small lake compared to many of the world. The Hebrew term in 1Ki. 7:23ff. is translated "sea," and it is the same word as the bodies of water mentioned above, but is to be understood as simply a basin which held liquid. See the articles below for more information.

SEA, ADRIATIC Ac. 27:27ff.

SEA, AEGEAN The body of water between Asia Minor and the E coast of Greece. Not mentioned by name in Ac. 17:14.

SEA, ARABAH *See* SALT SEA

SEA, BRAZEN *See* SEA, MOLTEN

SEA, CHINNERETH *See* SEA OF GALILEE

SEACOW *See* BEASTS 5.

SEA, DEAD *See* DEAD SEA and GEOGRAPHY OF THE HOLY LAND; SALT SEA

SEA, EASTERN *See* DEAD SEA; SALT SEA

SEA, EGYPTIAN A term for the Sea of Reeds (Red Sea) which the Israelites crossed when they left Egypt. Used only in Isa. 11:15.

SEA OF GALILEE *See* GEOGRAPHY OF THE HOLY LAND

SEA (LAKE) OF GENNESARET Lk. 5:1. *See* SEA OF GALILEE

SEA OF GLASS John in his Revelation twice refers to "what looked like a sea of glass, clear as crystal" being before the throne of God. No additional detail is known (Rev. 4:6; 15:2).

SEA, THE GREAT *See* GEOGRAPHY OF THE HOLY LAND

SEA OF JAZER An unknown body of water in Jer. 48:32 (KJV, NIV, ASV, NASB). The RSV, NEB, JB omit "sea" as a textual corruption. In agreement with acceptable Hebrew use of language, Keil thinks a relatively small lake (pond?) could have been in this area and called a "sea."

SEA, MOLTEN Called the brazen or bronze sea in the KJV, this was a very large vessel of bronze, cast by Hiram, king of Tyre, and placed somewhere in the temple precincts (1Ch. 18:8). It stood five cubits high and had a diameter of ten cubits (1Ki. 7:23-26). It was broken up when Jerusalem fell and was taken in pieces as booty to Babylon (2Ki. 25:13, 16).

SEA MONSTER *See* BEASTS 9.

SEA, RED Literally, "sea of reeds," *yam suph*. The word "red" in the words "red sea" came by way of the Greek translation and the Latin, but where they got it is unknown. Possibly it was named after a king *Erythras* (Greek for *red*; *see* Pliny's *Natural History*, Book VI, section xxviii). Originally it would seem to have applied to the Egyptian "Papyrus Lake" near Baal-zephon but later apparently spread to include the entire Persian Gulf and even the Indian Ocean (Ex. 13:18; 15:22; Ps. 136:13-15). God miraculously took the Israelites through it, but the army of Egypt was drowned in it. Elath, where Solomon built his trading fleet and Ezion Geber were on the "Red Sea" (1Ki. 9:26). But this was obviously a different place from that crossed earlier by the Israelites in their exodus from Egypt.

One should note it is merely coincidence that "Red" and "Reed" are similarly spelled. There is no connection in the original language, nor, for that matter, in the English. *See also* GEOGRAPHY OF THE HOLY LAND; RED SEA

SEA, REED *See* SEA, RED

SEA, THE SALT *See* DEAD SEA; SALT SEA

SEA OF TIBERIAS Jn. 6:1; 21:1. *See* SEA OF GALILEE

SEA, THE WAY OF *See* GEOGRAPHY OF THE HOLY LAND

SEAH *See* WEIGHTS AND MEASURES

SEAL An engraved stamp, ring, or cylinder for making an impression which would be proof of authenticity, either the substitute for or the authenticating of a signature. Stamp seals were first used in the fourth millennium B.C., and the engraved cylinder came a little later. These were either impressed or rolled on soft clay in earliest times and in later times on wax. The Egyptian scarab was such a seal. From the Palestinian excavations have come many stamped jar handles, indicating not content but ownership. In both Testaments the word is used literally and figuratively—as well as metaphorically. In the OT God seals up the sins of men (Dt. 32:34; Job 14:17; 33:16). In the NT Paul's converts are God's seal on Paul's ministry (1Co. 9:2), and believers are said to be sealed with the promised Holy Spirit and sealed for the day of redemption (Eph. 1:13; 4:30). The NT sealing of the believer is called the *arrabon* in Greek, a word transliterated from the Hebrew *'errabon* and used in clear OT contexts which show its meaning to be "a pledge." See the story in Ge. 38:12-26. The gift of the Spirit is the pledge, token, seal, earnest, that the one engifted will ultimately be fully redeemed. *See* ORNAMENTS; TATTOO

SEASON *See* TIME

SEAT, CHIEF *See* ROOM 2.; THRONE

SEAT, JUDGMENT A tribunal platform where judgment was made (Mt. 27:19; Jn. 19:13; Ac. 18:12, 16); mentioned also in connection with the final judgment of mankind by God (Ro. 14:10; 2Co. 5:10).

SEAT, MERCY A seat built on top of the Ark of the Covenant where God met with the high priest and his people (Ex. 25:17; Lev. 16:2-15; Heb. 9:5).

SEAT, MOSES' In Mt. 23:2 (the only reference in the Bible to Moses' seat), Jesus said that the scribes and Pharisees sit on Moses' seat. In later tradition we learn that this was a seat allegedly made for Moses to sit upon as the giver of the Law, or a place where the Law itself was placed on occasion. One was found in the excavation of Chorazin.

SEBA The son of Cush who gave his name to the Sabeans (Ge. 10:7).

SEBAM *See* SIBMAH

SEBAT *See* CALENDAR, *Shebat*

SECACAH [thicket, cover] A town (187-125) in the tribal area of Judah (Jos. 15:61). †

SECHEM *See* SHECHEM

SECHU *See* SECU

SECOND COMING OF CHRIST *See* CHRIST, LIFE AND TEACHINGS OF; CHRIST, WORK OF 9.

SECOND DEATH *See* DEATH

SECOND DISTRICT, QUARTER *See* COLLEGE

SECRET *See* MYSTERY

SECRETARY *See* SCRIBE

SECT *See* HERESY

SECTS The religious and political groups or sects noted in the NT are placed in three groups: those more particularly Greek in origin or approach; those distinctly Jewish; and a few of lesser significance or of which little is really known.

GREEK

Epicureans, mentioned in the Bible only in Ac. 17:18, were Greeks who held a philosophy that happiness could be achieved by serenity and detachment. They had no fear of divine intervention in this life or of punishment after death or of resurrection. The concept of the pursuit of pleasure to bring happiness is a later doctrine of this group.

Stoics, also mentioned only in Ac. 17:18 in the Bible, were other Greeks whom Paul met in Athens. A Stoic sought virtue by aligning himself with the will of the universe, taking and accepting things as they are.

Gnostics are not mentioned in the Bible by name. They were a heretical sect of the first two Christian centuries. Some of the statements of the NT reflect a conscious opposition to their teachings. Their views diminished the importance of the historicity of the facts about Jesus' life, death, resurrection, and ascension. Their teachings brought opposition from the NT writers. The dualistic views of Gnosticism and their concept of man's salvation — being merely the release of the soul of man from its imprisonment in the body and its ultimate absorption into its source — ran into heavy opposition in the church. *See* NAG HAMMADI LIBRARY

JEWISH

Of these the Scribes, Sadducees, and Pharisees are the most frequently mentioned in the NT. The words are not found in the OT since their origins are in post-OT times. One Zealot is mentioned in the NT, and the Essenes not at all.

Scribes. See also SCRIBE. These were men who preserved the law and the manuscripts. They were the "doctors" (intense scholars) of the law, the teachers of the law, and those who were prepared and able to act like "lawyers" with respect to this law. Their clashes with Jesus usually came because he taught with authority, an authority which did not always conform to the law as they saw it. In spite of this, the NT tells us that some of them believed in him (Mt. 7:29; 8:19; Mk. 12:38). Some of them sided with Paul on the doctrine of the resurrection as against the Sadducees (Ac. 23:9).

Sadducees. Their origin is not clear and is much debated. They had little following among the common people but were generally from the most wealthy and powerful families. In Herodian and Roman times their influence was at its height in the powerful Sanhedrin, but this died out after the fall of Jerusalem in A.D. 70. As against the Pharisees they accepted only the written law and rejected the idea of the immortality of the soul and that of bodily resurrection (Mt. 16:1-12; 22:23; Ac. 23:6-8).

Pharisees. Called *Hasidim*, this movement arose during the early second century B.C. in reaction to secularization trends when the military leaders also took on the role of high priest.

Unlike the Sadducees they believed in the immortality of the soul, in life after death, in resurrection, in a future judgment day, and in the coming of Messiah. Also, unlike the Sadducees, they did not believe in a rigidly fixed law but believed it could be adapted to changing conditions after careful study. A majority vote would make the decision binding on all. In other words, they felt that the oral law was a vital factor as well as the Scriptures, the written law. Some were deeply involved in temple and state affairs; they were trying to have the law applied in these spheres, even working with the Romans if need be. Others, a minority of them, withdrew from such contacts to pursue a more specifically religious way of life. As they were very rigorous and strict interpreters and appliers of the law, it was only inevitable that they would clash with Jesus, who pointed out that one's righteousness had to exceed that of theirs if he would enter the kingdom of heaven (Mt. 5:20). (The reason for this latter position was that entrance into the kingdom of heaven was not by works, or legal obedience, but by faith in God's promised deliverance through a Messiah and through atonement based on shed blood.) Since the majority of the NT references to this group are concerned with law-keeping and righteousness, the majority of the references found there are therefore negative. This has created a picture of Pharisees in the churches that is not fully in conformity with the facts relative to their beliefs, zeal, and points of agreement with Jesus and Paul.

Zealots. The Zealots formed a political party in late Hellenistic times, the end of the first century B.C. They were strongly opposed to the Roman rule over Israel and to all those who accepted it. Their activity was greatest in post-NT times. Rather than their being forced to bow to Rome and her paganism, they committed mass suicide on Masada in A.D. 73. The word is found only twice in the Bible and both of these refer to one of Jesus' disciples, Simon the Zealot (Lk. 6:15; Ac. 1:13).

Essenes. A religious sect among the Jews in the last century B.C., much like the Pharisees in faith, but with their own distinctive view as well. They did not, for example, believe in physical resurrection. They rejected the concept of private property and led a communal life, mostly on farms scattered widely in the Palestine world of their day. If the Qumran community was an Essene one, then we have much more information about them than existed formerly, but this equation is still debated. They are not mentioned by name in the Bible.

MISCELLANEOUS About the *Nicolaitans* little is known. Were they followers of the Nicolas of Ac. 6:5? Was it their purpose to introduce certain pagan practices into the church to make it easier to get proselytes? They are noted only negatively (Rev. 2:6, 15).

The *Herodians* are noted only in the NT and there as opponents of Jesus (Mt. 22:16; Mk. 3:6; 12:13). Little is known of them. Were they propagandists for the hated Herod?

The *Hellenists* and the *Hebrews* are two mutually exclusive groups in NT times. They are referred to in only a very limited number of passages. The latter were apparently Jews who were not influenced by the Hellenization tendencies of their day. Paul was one of them (Ac. 6:1; 2Co. 11:22; Php. 3:5). The Hellenists or Grecians were the Greek-speaking persons of any race, the opposite of "barbarians" or illiterate ones. They included Jews (Ac. 6:1; 9:29; 11:20; Ro. 1:14). A Hellene, on the other hand, was a non-Jew, a Greek, and the term was virtually a synonym for Gentile (Ro. 1:16). *See* GRECIAN JEWS

SECU {lookout point} An unidentified site in the tribal area of Benjamin (1Sa. 19:22). †

SECULAR From the word for "age," it is anything that is not religious. Secular relates to the temporal concerns of this age, not the eternal or spirit. *See* SACRED

SECUNDUS A traveling companion of Paul whose home was in Thessalonica (Ac. 20:4). †

SECURITY *See* SALVATION, APPLICATION OF

SEED
1. Plant seed is mentioned in the Bible (Nu. 24:7; Dt. 28:38; Mt. 13:32; Mk. 4:31; 1Co. 15:38).
2. Male semen (Nu. 5:28).
3. A figure for a descendant or offspring (Ge. 3:15; 13:15; Lk. 1:55; Ac. 7:5-6).
4. A word other than "seed" is used in a technical way, to beget or become the father of. It means to cause someone to be born or come into existence (1Ch. 1:13, 20, 34; 2:10; Mt. 1:2ff.).

SEEDTIME *See* FARMING, *sowing time*

SEER *See* DIVINATION and PROPHETS

SEGUB {exalted}

1. A descendant of Judah (1Ch. 2:21-22). †

2. The son of the Hiel who lost his life when Jericho was rebuilt as Joshua had predicted many years earlier (1Ki. 16:34). †

SEIR {hairy, shaggy, covered with trees, BDB and IDB; *possibly* the place of the goats *or* the place of Esau—Ge. 25:25, (BDB); small forest, rich forest, KB}

1. The home of Esau and his descendants (Ge. 32:3).

2. A mountain forming part of Judah's N border (Jos. 15:10). *See* JEARIM

SEIR, MOUNT, WAY OF *See* GEOGRAPHY OF THE HOLY LAND, *Edom;* SEIR

SEIRAH, SEIRATH {place of the goats, BDB; *possibly* woody hills, IDB and KB; shaggy forest, ISBE} Either a city or an area in Ephraim to which Ehud, the judge, escaped after killing the king of Moab (Jdg. 3:26). †

SELA {rocky crags, cliffs}

1. A place (205-020) in Edom which was conquered by King Ahaziah of Judah; often called Petra today.

2. An unidentified place on the border between Judah and the Amorites (Jdg. 1:36).

3. An unidentified place in Moab (Isa. 16:1).

SELAH A term of unknown meaning used three times in Hab. and seventy-one times in Psalms. Some suggest it was a direction for the conductor; others that it had some liturgical function (for examples, see Ps. 3:4, 8; 4:2, 4; Hab. 3:3). *See* PSALMS

2. A former name of Joktheel (2Ki. 14:7). *See* JOKTHEEL

SELA-HAMMAHLEKOTH {slippery rock, BDB} Translated as "rock of escape" (RSV) and "rock of parting" (NIV) in 1Sa. 23:28. †

SELED {jump for joy} A descendant of Judah and Jerahmeel (1Ch. 2:30). †

SELEUCIA *See* GEOGRAPHY OF THE HOLY LAND

SELEUCIDS Upon the death of Alexander the Great in 323 B.C., his empire passed, not to his young son, but, as Daniel had long before predicted, to his leading commanders, the Diadochi, or "successors" (Da. 11:4; cf. 8:8, 22). Ptolemy took over Egypt; but his chief general was Seleucus, who became an independent king in Babylon in 311 and had conquered to the Indus by 302. He took Syria, where he established Antioch as the capital of what became the Seleucid dynasty (Da. 11:5). Its earlier members were forecasted in Daniel's prophecies, while the later Seleucids played a major part in the histories of the Maccabees and Hasmoneans.

The son of Seleucus, Antiochus I, and his grandson Antiochus II fought with Ptolemy II in 275-271 and 261-252 respectively; but a truce was sealed by the marriage of Ptolemy's daughter Berenice to Antiochus II, who put away his wife Laodice. The latter, however, took revenge by murdering both Berenice and Antiochus (Da. 11:6). Ptolemy III avenged the death of his sister and took Antioch (Da. 11:7-8). Laodice's son Seleucus II later attempted to invade Egypt but was defeated (Da. 11:9).

Of the two sons of Seleucus II (Da. 11:10), the elder, Seleucus III, had only a brief reign; but the younger, Antiochus III, the Great, pressed the war with Egypt. He conquered as far as Transjordan and Gaza; but Ptolemy IV met and defeated him at Raphia, 217, though he failed to follow up his advantage (Da. 11:11-12). Antiochus III spent 212-204 conquering to the Caspian Sea and India. He resumed the attack upon Egypt in 202; the general of young Ptolemy V was ultimately defeated at Paneas in northern Palestine; and in 198 B.C. Jerusalem welcomed Antiochus and Syrian rule (Da. 11:13, 16). A Seleucid princess was later married to Ptolemy (Da. 11:17). Antiochus lost out, however, to the Romans at Magnesia in what is now Turkey, in

190 B.C. (Da. 11:18) and died three years later (Da. 11:19). Seleucus IV represented a loss of power and attempted to rob the Jerusalem temple (Da. 11:20).

Upon the death of Seleucus, his brother Antiochus IV usurped the throne (Da. 11:21). He had two wars with Ptolemy VII, winning the first (Da. 11:25-28) in 170-169, but being repulsed from Egypt by Rome in the second (Da. 11:29-30) in 168. He determined to unify his empire under Hellenistic culture (Da. 11:39; 1 Macc. 1:41ff.). When he was opposed by the Jews, he wreaked havoc in Jerusalem, slaughtered the pious, and set up the "abomination of desolation," an altar of Zeus, in the temple (Da. 11:31; 12:11), in December 168. He prohibited all Jewish customs. Some of the Jews submitted, others fled, but many resisted (1 Macc. 1:62-64; 2 Macc. 7:1ff.), and finally retook and cleansed the temple in December 165 (*see* MACCABEES). Antiochus IV died in 164, about three and a half years after the abomination had been set up (Da. 12:11).

After two years, Demetrius I murdered his young cousin, Antiochus V, but he could not break Jonathan, the brother of Judas Maccabeus, in Judah (1 Macc. 9:58-73; 2 Macc. 13:1-8). Alexander I, Balas, who was held to be another son of Antiochus IV, defeated and killed Demetrius I in 150, but the latter's son Demetrius II appeared in 147 and two years later killed Alexander I. To gain the favor of Jonathan, Demetrius II granted him certain districts in Samaria (1 Macc. 11:28-37). The infant son of Alexander, Antiochus VI, was not put in power by the general Trypho, who later took the crown for himself and put Antiochus to death. In his struggles with Trypho, Demetrius II in 143 B.C. granted Simon, the last of the brothers of Judas, the political independence for which the Jews had so long fought (1 Macc. 13:36-43).

After the capture of Demetrius II by the Parthians (Persians), his brother Antiochus VII overcame Trypho; but when Antiochus attempted to reimpose the Seleucid yoke on the Jews, Simon's troops defeated him decisively (1 Macc. 16:8-10). Antiochus was able to subdue Simon's son, John Hyrcanus I; but after the death of Antiochus VII in 129 and the reassumption of the Syrian throne by his brother Demetrius II who had been released by the Parthians, the latter found himself too occupied with attacks by Alexander II, Zabinas (said to be the son of Alexander I, Balas), to pursue further aggression against the Jews. In 109 Hyrcanus fought off Antiochus IX, a nephew of Demetrius, and took Jezreel. The sons of Hyrcanus, Aristobulus I (105-104) and Alexander Jannaeus (104-78) continued to enlarge Israel while Antiochus IX fought with his resurgent cousin, Antiochus VIII. Of the latter's sons, Demetrius III sought to stir up civil revolt against Alexander Jannaeus in 88, but Antiochus XII was defeated by the rising nation of the Nabatean Arabs in 85, who extended their power to Damascus. The last of the Seleucids was a grandson of Antiochus IX, Antiochus XIII; he was deposed after a five-year reign when the general Pompey converted Syria into a province of Rome in 64 B.C. (J.B.P.) *See also* MACCABEES; PTOLEMY

SELF-RIGHTEOUSNESS A belief that one has lived up to a code without an intermediary. According to the Bible, this is an illusion. Righteousness comes through the mediation of Jesus Christ. *See* SALVATION, APPLICATION OF; *See also* CHRIST, WORK OF

SEM *See* SHEM

SEMACHIAH, SEMAKIAH [Yahweh sustains, consecrates] A gatekeeper in David's day (1Ch. 26:7). †

SEMEI, SEMEIN [Yahweh has heard] An ancestor of Jesus (Lk. 3:26).

SEMITES [of Shem] A group of peoples now represented chiefly by Jews and Arabs, but in ancient times also by the Babylonians, Assyrians, Arameans, Canaanites, and Phoenicians (Ge. 10:21-31).

SENAAH The ancestor of some who returned from the Babylonian captivity with Zerubbabel (Ezr. 2:35; Ne. 7:38). †

SENATE Mentioned only in Ac. 5:21 and probably the same as the Sanhedrin. *See* SANHEDRIN

SENATE, SENATOR KJV for "elders" (Ps. 105:22; Ac. 5:21).

SENEH {thorny, BDB; *possibly* (cliff shaped like) a tooth, IDB} The southern of two peaks at the pass of Micmash. The other was Bozez (1Sa. 14:4). †

SENIR, SHENIR The Amorite name of Mt. Hermon (Dt. 3:9; 1Ch. 5:23; SS. 4:8; Eze. 27:5). † *See* HERMON, MOUNT

SENNACHERIB {(pagan moon god) Sin has increased the brothers, BDB and ISBE; Sin replaced the (lost) brothers, IDB} A king of Assyria in the time of Hezekiah of Judah. *See* ASSYRIA

SENUAH {sons of the hated (rejected) woman, i.e., the poor class, BDB} *See* HASSENUAH

SEORIM {one born at the time of the barley (harvest)} The head of one of the priestly divisions as David set them up (1Ch. 24:8). †

SEPARATE *See* HOLINESS

SEPHAR The eastern limits of the settlement of the sons of Joktan (Ge. 10:30). †

SEPHARAD {Sardis} An unidentified place to which some of the people of Jerusalem were taken captive (Ob. 20). †

SEPHARVAIM An unidentified place in Syria or Mesopotamia from which the Assyrians brought captives to be settled in Samaria (2Ki. 17:24-31; 18:34).

SEPTUAGINT {seventy} *See* BIBLE VERSIONS

Sennacherib on the Throne

SEPULCHRE *See* BURIAL

SERAH [one who explains, opens, extends, IDB; abundance, ISBE and KB] A daughter of Asher (Ge. 46:17; Nu. 26:46; 1Ch. 7:30). †

SERAIAH [Yahweh persists, BDB and ISBE; Yahweh is prince, IDB; Yahweh contends, KB]

1. David's scribe or secretary; also called Shavsha, Sheva, and perhaps Shisha (2Sa. 8:17; 1Ch. 18:16; 2Sa. 20:25; 1Ki. 4:3).

2. The chief priest executed by Nebuchadnezzar at the time of the fall of Jerusalem (2Ki. 25:18-21; Jer. 52:24-27); also an ancestor of Ezra (Ezr. 7:1).

3. One who joined Gedaliah, the governor of Judah, at Mizpah after the fall of Jerusalem (2Ki. 25:23).

4 and 5. Descendants of Judah and Simeon (1Ch. 4:13-14, 35).

6. One who returned from the Babylonian captivity with Zerubbabel (Ezr. 2:2).

7. One who signed the covenant with Nehemiah (Ne. 10:2).

8. A priest in the days of Nehemiah (Ne. 11:11).

9. One sent by King Jehoiakim to arrest Jeremiah (Jer. 36:26).

10. The quartermaster of King Zedekiah to whom Jeremiah gave a message for the king as he was being taken into captivity (Jer. 51:59).

SERAPHS, SERAPHIM(S) [burning ones, (winged) serpents] They were heavenly beings with human forms but each with six wings. All we know about their persons and roles is to be found in these two verses. Some think they were winged serpents (Isa. 6:2-6). †

SERED, SEREDITE A son of Zebulun and his clan (Ge. 46:14; Nu. 26:26). †

SERGIUS PAULUS The proconsul of Cyprus who became a Christian through the ministry of Paul (Ac. 13:7, 12). †

SERMON ON THE MOUNT The teaching of Jesus recorded in Matthew 5—7. Some place the site where these teachings were given in the hills above Capernaum, and others place it near the Horns of Hattin between Nazareth and the southern end of the Sea of Galilee. In this section of the teachings of Jesus there are to be found: the Beatitudes (5:3-10); some details Jesus adds to older and well-known laws (5:17-48); and miscellaneous teachings about proper living and conduct (6:1—7:29).

SERPENT *See* BEASTS 1.; DEITIES 3.; DEVIL

SERPENT OF BRONZE; SERPENTS, FIERY God sent fiery serpents among the Israelites in the wilderness as a punishment. Their fatal poison worked quickly, which may be an explanation of the word "fiery." God told Moses to set up Nehushtan, a bronze figure of a serpent on a pole, and instructed those bitten by the fiery serpents to look at this bronze replica and then he would heal them (Nu. 21:4-9). This is the imagery behind the account found in Jn. 3:14-16.

SERUG [descendant *i.e.*, younger branch, BDB] A descendant of Shem (Ge. 11:20-23; 1Ch. 1:26; Lk. 3:35). †

SERVANT One, male or female, under the service of another. These might be domestic, governmental, or even free ministers or officials of God or a king (Ex. 12:45; 14:31; 2Ki. 19:6). *See also* DEACON; MINISTER; SLAVE

SERVANT OF THE LORD A term applied many times to Moses (Jos. 13:8; 22:2-5; 1Ch. 6:49; 2Ch. 24:6, 9; Ne. 1:7-8; Mal. 4:4). While Moses is the servant *par excellence*, a number of other persons are occasionally also called God's servants: Abraham, Caleb, David, Israel (Ge. 26:24; Nu. 14:24; 2Sa. 3:18; Lk. 1:54). In the NT several who serve Christ are called servants of God: Paul, James, Jude, Peter, John (Tit. 1:1; Jas. 1:1; Jude 1; Rev. 1:1). Moses predicted that God would raise up later a prophet like himself (Dt. 18:15). Peter decided that this prophet was Christ (Ac. 3:22-23). In the Book of Isaiah two servants are noted. One is God's witnessing servant (Isa. 41:8-10; 43:10-13, 22; 44:12; 41:8-10), and the other is the one to bring light to the Gentiles (Isa. 42:1-4; Mt. 12:15-21; Isa. 49:5-6; Lk. 2:26-32; Ac. 26:22-23). The latter servant, the one whose work is described in detail in Isa. 52:13—53:12, has always been considered by Christians to be Christ himself.

SERVICE *See* DEACON, DEACONESS; MINISTER; SERVANT; SLAVE

SETH {determined, granted—Ge. 4:25; restitution, KB} One of the sons of Adam (Ge. 4:25-26). He is listed in the genealogy of Jesus (Lk. 3:38).

SETHUR {concealed (by Deity), IDB} The representative of the tribe of Asher in the twelve spies sent to spy out Canaan by Moses (Nu. 13:13). †

SEVEN, SEVENTY *See* NUMBERS, SIGNIFICANCE OF

SEVENEH KJV, ASV transliteration for "Aswan" in the NIV and "Syene" in other versions (Eze. 29:10; 30:6). *See* SYENE

SEXUAL IMMORALITY *See* ADULTERY; CHAMBERING; FORNICATION

SHAALABBIN, SHAALBIM {site of foxes} A city (148-141) in the tribal area of Dan; also called Shaalabbin (Jos. 19:42). At the first it was occupied by Amorites, but the Israelites finally subjugated them (Jdg. 1:35; 1Ki. 4:9). †

SHAALBONITE One from Shaalbim (2Sa. 23:32; 1Ch. 11:33). † *See* SHAALBIM

SHAALIM, SHALIM {possibly (land of) hollow depth, KB} An unidentified area through which Saul went looking for his father's donkeys (1Sa. 9:4). †

SHAAPH Two descendants of Caleb (1Ch. 2:47, 49). †

SHAARAIM {double gates}
1. An unidentified city in the tribal area of Judah (Jos. 15:36; 1Sa. 17:52). †
2. A city in the tribal area of Simeon

called Sharuhen in the parallel list and therefore located at (093-097) (Jos. 19:6; 1Ch. 4:31). Sharuhen is a well-known city of Egyptian records and the times of the Hyksos. †

SHAASHGAZ A eunuch in charge of King Ahasuerus's concubines (Est. 2:14). †

SHABBETHAI {one born at Sabbath, ISBE and KB} Levites in the days of Ezra and Nehemiah (Ezr. 10:15; Ne. 8:7; 11:16). †

SHACHIA *See* SAKIA

SHADDAI {the Mountain One, IDB; *other suggestions*; 1. mountain; 2. maternal goddess of many breasts; 3. self-sufficient; 4. an Accadian spirit, Shad; 5. all-mighty, omnipotent, KB} *See* GOD, NAMES OF; GODHEAD 1., *El Shaddai*

SHADOW The sun dial was a device for measuring time and is noted in the Bible only in connection with King Ahaz (2Ki. 20:9-11; Isa. 38:8). In this case some think that the "dial" was a stairway whose steps (a formal rendering of the Hebrew *ma'alot* here translated "shadow") marked the time of day as the shadow passed over them.

SHADRACH {servant of (pagan moon god) AKU} One of the three companions of Daniel, along with Meshach and Abednego. These were the names given to Hananiah, Mishael, and Azariah by the eunuch of the king of Babylon. They were cast into the fiery furnace for refusing to bow to the image of the Babylonian king (Da. 1:7; 3:20ff.).

SHAFT *See* MINES, MINING

SHAGE(E) {wanderer, meanderer (like feeding sheep)} The father of one of David's mighty men (1Ch. 11:34). †

SHAHARAIM {one born at early (reddish) dawn, KB} A descendant of Benjamin (1Ch. 8:8). †

SHAHAZIMAH, SHAHAZUMAH {elevated place} An unidentified town in the tribal area of Issachar (Jos. 19:22). †

SHALIM *See* SHAALIM

SHALISHA An unidentified area through which Saul passed while looking for his father's lost donkeys (1Sa. 9:4; cf. 2Ki. 4:42). †

SHALLECHETH, SHALLEKETH [*possibly* (gate of) sending forth, BDB] A gate in the W part of the enclosure of the temple (1Ch. 26:16). †

SHALLUM [peace, well-being, prosperity]
1. The assassin of King Zechariah of Israel; *see* KINGS OF JUDAH AND ISRAEL.
2. One of the alternate names of King Jehoahaz of Judah, *see* KINGS OF JUDAH AND ISRAEL.
3. The husband of the prophetess Huldah (2Ki. 22:14).
4. A descendant of Jerahmeel (1Ch. 2:40-41).
5. A descendant of Simeon (1Ch. 4:25).
6. A priest and one of the ancestors of Ezra (1Ch. 6:12-13; Ezr. 7:2).
7. A son of Naphtali (Ge. 46:24; Nu. 26:49); also called Shillem (1Ch. 7:13).
8. One who returned from the Babylonian captivity with Zerubbabel; a gatekeeper (Ezr. 2:42).
9. A descendant of Levi, a gatekeeper after the return from exile (1Ch. 9:17).
10. Father of one who refused to let the men of Israel bring captives of the Judeans into Ephraim (2Ch. 28:12).
11 and 12. Two who married foreign wives during the time of the Babylonian captivity (Ezr. 10:24, 42).
13 and 14. Two who worked with Nehemiah on the repair of the walls of Jerusalem (Ne. 3:12, 15).
15. An uncle of the prophet Jeremiah (Jer. 32:7).
16. The father of the keeper of the threshold in the days of Jeremiah (Jer. 35:4).

SHALLUN Ne. 3:15. *See* SHALLUM 13. and 14.

SHALMAI The ancestor of some temple servants who returned from the Babylonian captivity with Zerubbabel (Ezr. 2:46; Ne. 7:48); also called Shamlai. †

SHALMAN [*abbreviation of* SHALMANESER, IDB and ISBE] An unidentified foreign king (Hos. 10:14). †

SHALMANESER *See* ASSYRIA

SHAMA [one obedient (to Yahweh)] One of David's mighty men (1Ch. 11:44). †

SHAMARIAH KJV in 2Ch. 11:19. *See* SHEMARIAH

SHAMBLES KJV, ASV for "meat market" in most major versions (1Co. 10:25). The JB has "butcher shops." *See* MARKET, MARKETPLACE

SHAMED *See* SHEMED

SHAMER *See* SHEMER, SHOMER 2.

SHAMGAR [(the pagan Hurrian god); Shimke gave (a son), IDB] *See* JUDGES OF ISRAEL

SHAMHUTH [*possibly* one born at a time of a horrible event, KB] One of David's mighty men, possibly the same as Shammoth (1Ch. 7:8; 11:27). †

SHAMIR [*possibly* thorny *or* emery (flint)]
1. A Levite in David's day (1Ch. 24:24).
2. A village of Judah (Jos. 15:48). †
3. A village in Ephraim (Jdg. 10:1-2). †

SHAMLAI *See* SHALMAI

SHAMMA A descendant of Asher (1Ch. 7:37). †

SHAMMAH
1. An Edomite descendant of Esau (Ge. 36:13).
2. A brother of King David; also called Shimeah, Shimea, Shimma, and Shimei (1Sa. 16:9; 2Sa. 13:3; 21:21; 1Ch. 2:13).
3. One of David's mighty men (2Sa. 23:11-12).
4. Another of David's mighty men;

also called Shammoth and Shamhuth (2Sa. 23:25; 1Ch. 11:27; 27:8).

SHAMMAI

1, 2, and 3. Three descendants of Judah (1Ch. 2:28, 44-45).

4. A rabbi, a contemporary of Hillel (2.). *See* HILLEL

SHAMMOTH *See* SHAMMAH 4.

SHAMMUA(H) [*possibly* (Yahweh) hears, KB; rumor, ZPEB]

1. The representative of the tribe of Reuben among the twelve spies sent to Canaan by Moses (Nu. 13:4).

2. A son of David; also called Shimea (2Sa. 5:14; 1Ch. 3:5).

3 and 4. A Levite and a priest in Nehemiah's day (Ne. 11:17; 12:18).

SHAMSHERAI [*a combination of* SHEMESH (pagan sun god) and SHAMAR (guard)] A descendant of Benjamin (1Ch. 8:26). †

SHAPHAM A descendant of Gad (1Ch. 5:12). †

SHAPHAN [rock badger]

1. A secretary of King Josiah (2Ki. 22:3ff.).

2. The father of one of the idolatrous elders of the house of Israel (Eze. 8:11).

SHAPHAT [he judges]

1. The representative of the tribe of Simeon among the twelve spies sent by Moses to spy out the land of Canaan (Nu. 13:5).

2. The father of the prophet Elisha (1Ki. 19:16).

3 and 4. A descendant of David and a descendant of Gad (1Ch. 3:22; 5:12).

5. One of David's herdsmen (1Ch. 27:29).

SHAPHER *See* SHEPHER

SHAPHIR, SAPHIR [lovely] An unidentified place (Micah 1:11). †

SHARAI One of those who married a foreign wife during the Babylonian captivity (Ezr. 10:40). †

SHARAIM *See* SHAARAIM 1.

SHARAR *See* SACAR 1.

SHARD *See* POTSHERD

SHARE, SHARING, LOT, PORTION *See* FELLOWSHIP; INHERITANCE

SHAREZER [(pagan god) protect the king!]

1. A son of Sennacherib (2Ki. 19:37; Isa. 37:38). † *See* ASSYRIA

2. One who came from Bethel to inquire of the LORD in the days of King Darius (Zec. 7:2). †

SHARON, PLAINS OF [plain, level country] The maritime or coastal plain from Joppa N to the Plain of Dor, S of Mt. Carmel. *See* GEOGRAPHY OF THE HOLY LAND

SHARONITE One from the Plain of Sharon (1Ch. 27:29). *See* SHARON, PLAIN OF

SHARUHEN *See* SHAARAIM 2.

SHASHAI One who married a foreign wife during the Babylonian captivity (Ezr. 10:40). †

SHASHAK A descendant of Benjamin (1Ch. 8:14, 25). †

SHAUL, SHAULITE(S) [asked, *possibly* dedicated to God]

1. An Edomite king descended from Esau (Ge. 36:37-38).

2. A descendant of Simeon and his clan (Ge. 46:10; Nu. 26:13).

3. An ancestor of Samuel the prophet (1Ch. 6:24).

4. *See also* JOEL 2.

SHAVEH, VALLEY OF [level valley] The valley where Abraham met Melchizedek; also called the King's Valley (Ge. 14:17; 2Sa. 18:18). It is suggested that this is another name for the Kidron Valley in Jerusalem, or a part of the Hinnom Valley. †

SHAVEH KIRIATHAIM [level plain of two towns] An unidentified place in Transjordan where the Emites were defeated (Ge. 14:5). †

SHAVING *See* HAIR; NAZARITE, NAZIRITES

SHAVSHA *See* SERAIAH 1.

SHEAF A bundle of grain heads and the shafts brought in from the field to the threshing floor (Mic. 4:12). A forgotten sheaf was to be left for the poor (Dt. 24:19).

SHEAL One who married a foreign wife during the time of the Babylonian captivity (Ezr. 10:29). †

SHEALTIEL, SALATHIEL [I have asked (him) of God (El), BDB, ISBE, and KB; *possibly* El is a shield, El is a victor, IDB] The father of Zerubbabel (Ezr. 3:2), and listed in both of the genealogies of Christ in the NT (Mt. 1:12; Lk. 3:27).

SHEARIAH [*possibly* Yahweh breaks] A descendant of King Saul (1Ch. 8:38; 9:44). †

SHEARING HOUSE OF THE SHEPHERDS A KJV, ASV, NEB (with footnote *Beth Eker*) translation (2Ki. 10:12-14). The NIV, JB, NASB (with footnote *house of binding*) transliterates this as the proper name "Beth Eked." *See* BETH EKED

SHEAR-JASHUB [a remnant will return] The symbolic name given by Isaiah to one of his sons (Isa. 7:3). †

SHEBA [seven *or* oath]
1. *See* SABEANS.
2. One who rebelled against David and was later beheaded for it (2Sa. 20:1ff.).
3. A descendant of Gad (1Ch. 5:13).
4. A son of Joktan in the line of Seth (Ge. 10:28).
5. A place from which a queen came to visit Solomon, the Queen of Sheba.

SHEBAH [oath or gifted, NIV] *See* SHIBAH

SHEBAM Num 32:3. *See* SEBAM

SHEBANIAH
1. A priest in the days of David (1Ch. 15:24).
2. A Levite who stood with Ezra at the reading of the Law (Ne. 9:4-5).

3, 4, and 5. A priest and two Levites who signed the covenant with Nehemiah (Ne. 10:4, 10, 12). *See also* SHEC(H)-ANIAH

SHEBARIM [quarry] An unidentified place between Ai and Jericho to which the men of Ai chased the Israelites (Jos. 7:5). The NIV translates this place as the "quarry." †

SHEBAT [(the month of) destroying (rain)] *See* CALENDAR

SHEBER [*possibly* lion, IDB; *possibly* breaking, crushing *or* roughly broken grain, KB] A descendant of Caleb (1Ch. 2:48). †

SHEBNA, SHEBNAH [(Yahweh) return now, IDB] A steward and secretary of King Hezekiah. Isaiah denounced him (2Ki. 18:18, 26, 37; Isa. 22:15ff.).

SHEBUEL [*possibly* captive of El *or* El restores] *See* SHUBAEL

SHEC(H)ANIAH [Yahweh has taken up his abode]
1. A descendant of Zerubbabel (1Ch. 3:21-22).
2. The head of one of the priestly divisions in David's day (1Ch. 24:11).
3. A priest in the days of King Hezekiah (2Ch. 31:15).
4. One who returned from the Babylonian captivity with Ezra (Ezr. 8:5).
5. The father-in-law of the Tobiah who opposed Nehemiah (Ne. 6:18).
6. One who married a foreign wife during the Babylonian captivity (Ezr. 10:2).
7. A priest who returned from the Babylonian captivity with Zerubbabel (Ne. 12:3).

SHECHEM, SHECHEMITE(S) [*possibly* shoulder (saddle of a hill), BDB; shoulders (and upper part of the back), KB]
1. The son of Hamor, the man from whom Jacob bought land on which to erect his tent (Ge. 33:19; Jdg. 9:28).
2. The man who violated Dinah, Jacob's daughter and brought about the

slaughter of all of Hamor's sons (Ge. 34).

3. One from the tribe of Manasseh and his clan listed in the census after the plague (Nu. 26:31; Jos. 17:2).

4. A Canaanite city (176-179) in the hill country of Ephraim which became important as an Israelite political and religious center (Jos. 20:7; 24:1; Jdg. 9:1-7; 1Ki. 12:1; Ac. 7:16).

SHECHEM

SHEDEUR The father of the representative of the tribe of Reuben in the census that Moses took (Nu. 1:5; 2:10; 7:30, 35; 10:18). †

SHEEP *See* BEASTS 2.

SHEEPMASTER KJV for one who "raises sheep" (2Ki. 3:4, NIV), not to be confused with the concept of the "Chief Shepherd" (1Pe. 5:1-4). *See* SHEPHERD

SHEERAH, SHERAH [blood relationship *or* female relative, IDB; remainder, KB] The daughter of Ephraim who built Upper and Lower Beth Horon (1Ch. 7:24). †

SHEHARIAH [he seeks Yahweh] A descendant of Benjamin (1Ch. 8:26). †

SHEKEL [weight] *See* MONEY and WEIGHTS AND MEASURES

SHEKINAH [that which resides] *See* GLORY OF THE LORD (SHEKINAH)

SHELAH, SHELANITE(S) [missile (a weapon), sprout, ISBE]

1. A descendant of Shem, son of Noah (Ge. 10:24).

2. A son of Judah and his clan (Ge. 38:5, 11; Nu. 26:20).

3. *See also* MESHELEMIAH.

4. A pool (Ne. 3:15). *See* SILOAM

SHELEMIAH [Yahweh pays back, *possibly* restores peace offering of Yahweh]

1. One of the gatekeepers in David's administration; also called Meshelemiah and perhaps even Shallum (1Ch. 9:21, 31; 26:1-2, 9-14).

2 and 3. Two who married foreign wives during the Babylonian captivity (Ezr. 10:39, 41).

4. The father of one who worked on the wall of Jerusalem with Nehemiah (Ne. 3:30).

5. A priest whom Nehemiah made treasurer (Ne. 13:13).

6. The ancestor of one sent by the princes to fetch Baruch to read his scroll (Jer. 36:14).

7. The father of one sent by King Zedekiah to Jeremiah requesting prayer (Jer. 37:3).

8. The father of one sent to arrest Jeremiah (Jer. 37:13).

SHELEPH [one plucked out, drawn out] A son of Joktan and descendant of Shem (Ge. 10:26; 1Ch. 1:20). †

SHELESH [triplet, KB; *possibly* obedient *or* gentle, IDB] A descendant of Asher (1Ch. 7:35). †

SHELOMI [at peace] The father of the representative of the tribe of Asher in the division of the land of Canaan between the tribes (Nu. 34:27). †

SHELOMITH [at peace]

1. The mother of one who was stoned for blaspheming (Lev. 24:11).

2. A daughter of Zerubbabel (1Ch. 3:19).

3. A Levite; also called Shelomoth (1Ch. 23:18; 24:22).

4. A son of King Rehoboam of Judah (2Ch. 11:20).

5. One who returned from the Babylonian captivity with Ezra (Ezr. 8:10).

SHELOMOTH {at peace}

1. A Levite of the time of David (1Ch. 23:9).

2. Another Levite of David's time; also called Shelomith (1Ch. 23:18; 24:22).

3. A descendant of Moses who lived in David's time (1Ch. 26:25-26, 28).

SHELTER *See* BOOTH; TABERNACLE; TENTMAKER

SHELUMIEL {El is (my) peace} The representative of the tribe of Simeon in the census Moses took in the wilderness (Nu. 1:6).

SHEM One of the sons of Noah (Ge. 5:32; 9:23), also listed in the genealogy of Jesus (Lk. 3:36).

SHEMA {he hears}

1 and 2. Descendants of Caleb and Reuben (1Ch. 2:43-44; 5:8).

3. A descendant of Benjamin; also called Shimei (1Ch. 8:13, 21).

4. One who stood with Ezra when he read the Law to the people (Ne. 8:4).

5. A town, *see* SHEBA.

SHEMAAH {*possibly* Yahweh hears} A descendant of Benjamin (1Ch. 12:3). †

SHEMAIAH {Yahweh hears}

1, 2, and 3. Descendants of Zerubbabel, Simeon, and Reuben respectively (1Ch. 3:22; 4:37; 5:4).

4. A prophet to King Rehoboam and a scribe of his time (2Ch. 11:2ff.; 12:15).

5 and 6. A Levite and father of another one in postexilic times (1Ch. 9:14, 16).

7, 8, and 9. Three Levites in David's day: one helped to bring the Ark up, one was a scribe, and the third a gatekeeper (1Ch.15:8, 11; 24:6; 26:4).

10. One who helped King Jehoshaphat in the teaching of the Law (2Ch. 17:8).

11 and 12. Two Levites in the time of King Hezekiah (2Ch. 29:14; 31:15).

13. A Levite in the time of King Josiah of Judah (2Ch. 35:9).

14 and 15. Two who assisted Ezra: one came back from the captivity in Babylon with him; the other also returned, but Ezra sent him to Casiphia to bring back some Levites (Ezr. 8:13, 16).

16 and 17. Two who married foreign wives during the time of the Babylonian captivity (Ezr. 10:21, 31).

18. One who helped Nehemiah with the repair of the wall of the city of Jerusalem (Ne. 3:29).

19. A prophet hired by Sanballat the Horonite to frighten Nehemiah and to try to get him to stop the repairs of Jerusalem (Ne. 6:10-11).

20. A priest who signed the covenant with Nehemiah (Ne. 10:8).

21. A priest who returned from the Babylonian captivity with Zerubbabel (Ne. 12:6).

22. A prince of Judah who was present at the dedication of the rebuilt wall of Jerusalem (Ne. 12:34).

23 and 24. Two musicians who were present at the dedication of the rebuilt wall of Jerusalem (Ne. 12:36, 42).

25. The father of a prophet in the days of King Jehoiakim (Jer. 26:20).

26. A prophet already in the captivity in Babylon who was opposing Jeremiah (Jer. 29:24).

27. The father of a prince in Judah who commanded Baruch to read to them the content of his scroll (Jer. 36:12).

SHEMARIAH {Yahweh guards, preserves}

1. A descendant of Benjamin who joined David at Ziklag (1Ch. 12:5).

2. A son of King Rehoboam of Judah (2Ch. 11:19).

3 and 4. Two who married foreign women during the time of the Babylonian captivity (Ezr. 10:32, 41).

SHEMEBER The king of Zeboiim defeated in the battle with Kedorlaomer and his coalition of kings (Ge. 14:2ff.). †

SHEMED, SHAMED {destruction} A descendant of Benjamin (1Ch. 8:12). †

SHEMER, SHAMER {*possibly* watch, IDB; *possibly* sediment of wine from which clear wine is made, KB}

1. The man who owned the hill of Samaria (1Ki. 16:24).

2. A descendant of Levi (1Ch. 6:46).

3. A descendant of Asher; also called Shomer (1Ch. 7:32, 34).

SHEMIDA, SHEMIDAH, SHEMI-DAITE(S) [*possibly* the name known, BDB and KB; *possibly* (pagan god) Eshmun has known, IDB] A descendant of Manasseh and his clan (Nu. 26:32; Jos. 17:2)

SHEMINITH [eight (strings)] *See also* PSALMS, TITLES OF 10. (8)

SHEMIRAMOTH [heights, heavens, BDB; *possibly* proper name of a pagan goddess, KB]
1. A Levite musician in the time of King David (1Ch. 15:18, 20;16:5). †
2. A Levite who taught the Law in the revival in the days of King Jehoshaphat of Judah (2Ch. 17:8). †

SHEMUEL [*possibly* his name is El, BDB, IDB, and ISBE; the unnamed god is El, KB; heard of El, KD]
1. The representative of the tribe of Simeon in the division of the land of Canaan among the tribes (Nu. 34:20).
2. A descendant of Issachar (1Ch. 7:2).
3. KJV in 1Ch. 6:33, *see* SAMUEL.

SHEN [tooth, crag (of rock)] 1Sa. 7:12. *See* JESHANAH

SHENAZAR, SHENAZZAR [may (the pagan moon god named) SIN protect] A son of King Jehoiachin of Judah (1Ch. 3:18). †

SHENIR *See* SENIR

SHEOL [*possibly* place of inquiry (of the dead), BDB; desolate place, nocountry underworld, KB] *See* DEAD, ABODE OF

SHEPHAM An unidentified place on the Upper Orontes River (Nu. 34:10-11). †

SHEPHAT(H)IAH [Yahweh has judged]
1. A son of King David (2Sa. 3:4).
2, 3, and 4. Two descendants of Benjamin and one of Simeon (1Ch. 9:8; 12:5; 27:16).

5. A son of King Jehoshaphat of Judah (2Ch. 21:2).

6 and 7. The ancestor of two groups who came back from the Babylonian captivity with Zerubbabel (Ezr. 2:4; 2:57; 8:8).

8. A descendant of Judah in the days of Nehemiah (Ne. 11:4).

9. One who encouraged King Zedekiah to kill Jeremiah the prophet (Jer. 38:1ff.).

SHEPHELAH [lowland] *See* GEOGRAPHY OF THE HOLY LAND, *Ancient Routes and Major Towns*

SHEPHER An unidentified stopping place on the wilderness route of the Israelites (Nu. 33:23-24). †

SHEPHERD Literally, of course, the tender of sheep. Figuratively, one divine or human, who cares for human beings. God is called the Shepherd of Israel (Ge. 49:24; Ps. 80:1; Jer. 31:10). Both Moses and Cyrus, the king of Persia, are called God's shepherds (Isa. 63:11; 44:28). In the NT Christ is called Shepherd (Heb. 13:20; 1Pe. 2:25; 5:4). Jesus' discourse on the shepherd is found in John 10. The leaders of the people of God in both Testaments are also called shepherds. *See also* PASTORS; SHEEPMASTER

SHEPHI, SHEPHO [*possibly* track—bare ways formed without human work by the traffic caravans, KB] A Horite, son of Seir (Ge. 36:23; 1Ch. 1:40). †

SHEPHUPHAM, SHEPHUPHAN *See* MUPPIM

SHERAH *See* SHEERAH

SHERD *See* POTSHERD

SHEREBIAH [*possibly* Yahweh has sent burning heat, BDB]
1. A Levite in the days of Ezra who was one of the twelve to whom Ezra entrusted the offerings for the rebuilding of the temple. He also was one of the instructors in the Law (Ezr. 8:18-25; Ne. 8:7; 9:4-5).
2. One who signed the covenant with Nehemiah (Ne. 10:12).
3 and 4. Two Levites in Nehemiah's

day, one of whom returned from the Babylonian captivity with Zerubbabel (Ne. 12:8, 24).

SHERESH {root, rootstock, sucker (of a plant)} A descendant of Manasseh (1Ch. 7:16). †

SHEREZER *See* SHAREZER 2.

SHESHACH {*cryptogram for* Babel (Babylon)} Possibly a hidden reference to Babylon in Jer. 25:26; 51:41. † *See* BABYLON, BABYLONIA

SHESHAI {*possibly* sixth (child)} One of the descendants of the Anakim driven out of Hebron by Caleb (Nu. 13:22; Jos. 15:14; Jdg. 1:10). †

SHESHAN A descendant of Judah and Jerahmeel (1Ch. 2:31-35). †

SHESHBAZZAR {may (the pagan moon god named) SIN protect (the father)} The prince of Judah who was made governor of the Jerusalem area and given the sacred vessels to take back from Babylon (Ezr. 1:8-11; 5:14). He laid the foundation for the second temple (Ezr. 5:16). †

SHETH A name connected with the name Moab in the prophecy of Balaam, otherwise unknown (Nu. 24:17). †

SHETHAR A prince of Media and Persia who served with King Ahasuerus (Est. 1:14). †

SHETHAR-BOZENAI, SHETHAR-BOZNAI One of the opponents of Ezra in his attempt to rebuild the temple (Ezr. 5:3, 6; 6:6, 13). †

SHEVA {vanity, emptiness, IDB; one who will emulate, IDB and KB}
1. A descendant of Judah and Caleb (1Ch. 2:49).
2. The secretary of King David. *See* SERAIAH 1.

SHEWBREAD *See* SHOWBREAD

SHIBAH {*possibly* seven, BDB and ISBE; *possibly* oath, BDB and IDB; plenty, KB} The name of one of the wells dug by the servants of Isaac in the Beersheba area (Ge. 26:33). †

SHIBBOLETH, SIBBOLETH {flowing stream, BDB and KB; *or* ear of grain, IDB} Two ways of pronouncing the same Hebrew word meaning "an ear of grain," a dialectal difference in pronunciation. By it the judge Jephthah was able to tell whether the speaker was an Ephraimite or not (Jdg. 12:6). †

SHIBMAH *See* SIBMAH

SHICRON *See* SHIKKERON

SHIELD *See* ARMS AND ARMOR

SHIGGAION, SHIGIONOTH {go astray, wander (i.e., a wild, passionate song, with rapid changes in rhythm), BDB; *possibly Akkadian for* dirge, KB} A title in Hab. 3:1 in the plural, singular in Ps. 7. *See* PSALMS, TITLES OF 9.

SHIHON *See* SHION

SHIHOR LIBNATH An unidentified place or river in the tribal area of Asher (Jos. 19:26). †

SHIHOR, SIHOR {*possibly* black water, BDB; *Egyptian* Canal of (pagan god) Horus, KB} An unidentified body of water in NE Egypt (Jos. 13:3; 1Ch. 13:5; Isa. 23:3).

SHIKKERON, SHICRON {*possibly* drunkenness, IDB; hog bean plant, IDB} An unidentified town in the tribal area of Judah (Jos. 15:11). †

SHILHI {*possibly* (my) javelin (thrower?), IDB and KB} The father-in-law of Asa, the king of Judah (1Ki. 22:42; 2Ch. 20:31). †

SHILHIM An unidentified town in the S of the tribal area of Judah (Jos. 15:32; cf. 1Ch. 4:31). †

SHILLEM, SHILLEMITE(S) {recompense, BDB and IDB; *possibly* whole, healthy, complete, KB} *See* SHALLUM 7.

SHILOAH *See* SILOAM

SHILOH The tabernacle was first set up in Shiloh (177-162) after the conquest of the land by Joshua (Jos. 18:1, 8-10). During the time of the Judges and the time of

Samuel it was the sanctuary of Israel (Jdg. 18:31; 21:12-21; 1Ki. 14:3). In one passage the house of the LORD there was even called a temple (1Sa.1:9).

SHILOH
Samuel, born in Ramah, lived in Shiloh.

SHILONI *See* SHELAH (Ne. 11:5, KJV).

SHILONITE [of SHILOH] A man from the town of Shiloh above (1Ki. 11:29; Ne. 11:5).

SHILSHAH [*possibly* obedient *or* gentle, IDB; third (part, child?), triplet, KB] A descendant of Asher (1Ch. 7:37). †

SHIMEA, SHIMEAH [he has heard *or* he is obedient]
1. A brother of King David; also called Shammah, Shimeah, Shimma, and Shimei (1Ch. 2:13; 20:7).
2. A son of King David; also called Shammua (1Ch. 3:5).
3 and 4. Two descendants of Levi (1Ch. 6:30, 39).
5. A descendant of Benjamin; also called Shimeam (1Ch. 8:32; 9:38).

SHIMEAM *See* SHIMEA 5.

SHIMEATH The father of one of the murderers of King Joash of Israel (2Ki. 12:21). *See* SHIMRITH

SHIMEATHITES 1Ch. 2:55. *See* SHIMEATH

SHIMEAH, SHIMEI, SHEMI, SHIMHI [Yahweh hears *or* obedient one]
1. A grandson of Levi (Ex. 6:17).

2. A descendant of Benjamin, related to King Saul, who cursed David as he was fleeing from the rebellion under Absalom. David forgave him but later suggested that Solomon should execute him (2Sa. 16:5ff.; 19:22-23; 1Ki. 2:6-36).
3. A brother of King David (2Sa. 21:21).
4. King Solomon's officer in the tribal area of Benjamin (1Ki. 1:8; 4:18).
5. A brother of Zerubbabel (1Ch. 3:19).
6, 7, and 8. Descendants of Simeon, Reuben, and Levi respectively (1Ch. 4:26-27; 5:4; 6:29).
9. A great-grandson of Levi (1Ch. 6:42).
10. A descendant of Benjamin who routed the Gittites; also called Shema (1Ch. 8:13).
11. The head of one of the divisions of the Levites in David's day (1Ch. 25:17).
12. The keeper of King David's vineyards (1Ch. 27:27).
13. A Levite in the time of King Hezekiah (2Ch. 29:14).
14, 15, and 16. Three who married foreign women during the time of the Babylonian captivity (Ezr. 10:23, 33, 38).
17. An ancestor of Queen Esther's cousin, Mordecai (Est. 2:5).

SHIMEON [*possibly* offspring of hyena and wolf, BDB and KB] One who married a foreign wife during the time of the Babylonian captivity (Ezr. 10:31). †

SHIMHI *See* SHEMA 3.

SHIMI *See* SHIMEAH

SHIMITE, SHIMEITES *See* SHIMEAH

SHIMMA *See* SHIMEA (1Ch. 2:13, KJV), or SHAMMAH 2.

SHIMON A descendant of Judah (1Ch. 4:20). †

SHIMRATH [guardian, watchman] A descendant of Benjamin (1Ch. 8:21). †

SHIMRI {Yahweh guards, preserves}
1. A descendant of Simeon (1Ch. 4:37). †
2. The father of one of David's mighty men (1Ch. 11:45). †
3. A Levite gatekeeper in David's day (1Ch. 26:10). †
4. A Levite in the time of King Hezekiah of Judah (2Ch. 29:13). †

SHIMRITH, SHIMEATH {guardianess, watch woman} The mother of one of the murderers of King Joash of Judah (2Ch. 24:26); also called Shomer (2Ki. 12:21).

SHIMROM, SHIMRON, SHIM-RONITE(S) {guardian, watchman}
1. A son of Issachar and his clan (Ge. 46:13; Nu. 26:24).
2. A town (170-234) whose king fought against Joshua and was later in the tribal area of Zebulun (Jos. 11:1; 19:15).

SHIMRON MERON An unidentified Canaanite town defeated by Joshua (Jos. 12:20). †

SHIMSHAI {one given to (pagan sun god) SHEMESH} The scribe who wrote to Artaxerxes against Zerubbabel and Ezra (Ezr. 4:8-9, 17, 23). †

SHINAB {(pagan god) SIN is his father} The king of Admah defeated by Kedorlaomer (Ge. 14:2ff.). †

SHINAR A name for Babylonia (Ge. 10:10; 14:1, 9; Isa. 11:11; Zec. 5:11). †

SHION, SHIHON An unidentified town in the tribal area of Issachar (Jos. 19:19). †

SHIP Before the times of the kings of Judah and Israel there are only four references to ships: Ge. 49:13; Nu. 24:24; Dt. 28:68; Jdg. 5:17. In antiquity the peoples who lived on rivers and oceans developed the idea of floats and ships. Inasmuch as the Hebrews were nomadic and agrarian, we do not find many references to ships and sailing prior to the days of Solomon who started vast trading with many parts of the world. Even in his day the help of the Phoenician expert Hiram, king of Tyre, was needed for the floating of the timber for both the temple and palace from Phoenicia to Jaffa, and the building of his fleet of "Ships of Tarshish." (Perhaps their name originally referred to ships trading with Tarsus and then came to be used for all ships of that type.) Some early Phoenician boats or ships had but one sail and one bank of oars. They had high poops and sterns but were in reality low overall. They may have had a crow's nest for a lookout (Pr. 23:34; Eze. 27:6-7). In Isa. 33:21 one of the ships mentioned is the galley. A later king, Jehoshaphat, also tried to build a trading fleet on the Red Sea, but a storm destroyed the vessels before they could put out to sea (1Ki. 22:48). Two of the best descriptions of seagoing in the OT are to be found in Ezekiel 27 and the Book of Jonah, while in the NT one is found in Acts 27-28. Sailing on the Sea of Galilee is prominent in the NT. These boats had a single sail, were equipped with oars also (Lk. 8:23; cf. Jn. 6:19), and had anchors (Ac. 27:29-30, 40). Through archaeological discoveries we are beginning to learn something of the great size possible for some of the early ships and of their Atlantic (and around the cape of Africa) seagoing possibilities.

SHIPHI {flowing abundance} A descendant of Simeon (1Ch. 4:37). †

SHIPHMITE *See* ZABDI 3.

SHIPHRAH {beautiful, fair} One of the Hebrew midwives in Egypt when Moses was born (Ex.1:15). †

SHIPHTAN {he has judged} The father of the representative of the tribe of Ephraim in the dividing of the land of Canaan among the tribes (Nu. 34:24). †

SHISHA *See* SERAIAH 1.

SHISHAK The Egyptian Pharaoh who gave asylum to Jeroboam, the son of Nebat. He attacked Jerusalem in the days of King Rehoboam (1Ki. 11:40; 2Ch. 12:2ff.).

SHITRAI {scribe, officer} One of King David's herdmen (1Ch. 27:29). †

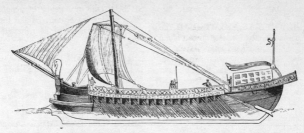

Ancient Ship of the Largest Size

SHITTAH TREE {acacia tree} KJV for "acacia tree" in most other versions (Isa. 41:19). *See* TREES, Other Trees, *Acacia*

SHITTIM {acacia trees} ABEL SHITTIM occurs once in this form. The latter is the full name and the former an abbreviation of the place in Moab where the Israelites encamped before they crossed into Canaan (Nu. 33:49; 25:1; Jos. 3:1; Mic. 6:5).

2. The wood from the Shittah tree, *see* TREES.

SHIZA The father of one of David's mighty men (1Ch. 11:42). †

SHOA An unidentified people (Eze. 23:23). †

SHOBAB {one who turns back, repents}
1 and 2. A son of David and a son of Caleb (2Sa. 5:14; 1Ch. 2:18).

SHOBACH The commander of the Syrian king Hadadezer who lost his life in a battle with the Israelites under David; also called Shophach (2Sa. 10:16-18; 1Ch. 19:16, 18). †

SHOBAI {*possibly* captive *or* Yahweh returns} The ancestor of some of the gatekeepers who returned from the Babylonian captivity with Zerubbabel (Ezr. 2:42; Ne. 7:45). †

SHOBAL
1. A son of Seir the Horite (Ge. 36:20).
2. A descendant of Caleb (1Ch. 2:50).

SHOBEK {victor, IDB} One who signed the covenant with Nehemiah (Ne. 10:24). †

SHOBI {*possibly* captive *or* Yahweh returns} One who assisted David when he was fleeing from the rebellion instigated by his son Absalom (2Sa. 17:27ff.; 1Ch. 19:1-2). †

SHOCHOH *See* SOCOH

SHOCO *See* SOCO

SHOE *See* DRESS

SHOE LATCHET *See* DRESS, *thong*

SHOFAR {ram horn} *See* MUSIC, MUSICAL INSTRUMENTS 2. (2), *Shofar*

SHOHAM {carnelian (precious stone)} A descendant of Levi who lived in the time of David (1Ch. 24:27). †

SHOMER {guardian, watchman}
1. *See* SHIMRITH.
2. A descendant of Asher; also called Shemer (1Ch. 7:32, 34).

SHOPHACH *See* SHOBACH

SHOPHAN *See* ATROTH SHOPHAN

SHOPHAR {ram horn} *See* MUSIC, MUSICAL INSTRUMENTS 2., (2), *Shofar*

SHOSHANNIM {big flower, lily} A KJV, ASV, NASB transliteration in the titles of Pss. 45, 69, 80 that has to do in some way with "lilies." The other major versions translate the word. *See* PSALMS, TITLES OF 2., *lilies*

SHOWBREAD, SHEWBREAD The Hebrew can be rendered "bread of the face," i.e., the bread which was put before God in the tabernacle and temple. It is also found in the NIV as "bread of the Presence." This bread consisted of twelve pancake-like bread cakes which had to be replaced each Sabbath Day with new bread. The old bread was eaten by the priests. It was this which one of them gave to David when he was hungry (Ex. 25:30; Lev. 24:5-9; 1Sa. 21:1-6; 1Ch. 9:32; 23:29; 2Ch. 29:18).

SHROUD A sheet of linen in which the dead were wrapped (Mk. 15:46).

SHRUB *See* PLANTS

SHUA {prosperity, ISBE}
1. The father of the Canaanite woman who became Judah's wife; also called Bathshua (Ge. 38:2; 1Ch. 2:3). †
2. A woman descended from the tribe of Asher (1Ch. 7:32). †

SHUAH {depression, lowland (an Aramean land on the Euphrates River)} A son of Abraham by Keturah (Ge. 25:2; 1Ch. 1:32). *See* SHUHAH

SHUAL {fox *or* jackal}
1. A region (1Sa. 13:17). †
2. A descendant of Asher (1Ch. 7:36). †

SHUBAEL {*possibly* captive of El, *or* El restores}
1. One of the division chiefs in David's administration called (1Ch. 23:16; 26:24 [KJV and other versions, Shebuel]; 24:20).
2. A Levitical musician in David's day; also called Shubael (1Ch. 25:4), [KJV and other versions, Shebuel]; 25:20).

SHUHAH, SHUAH {pit, depression} A descendant of Judah (1Ch. 4:11).

SHUHAM, SHUHAMITE(S) A descendant of Dan and his clan (Nu. 26:42-43). *See* HUSHIM

SHUHITE {one from the land of SHUAH} One of a group of people descended from Shuah. Bildad the friend of Job was one of them (Job 8:1; 18:1; 42:9).

SHULAMITE, SHULAMMITE A title or name of a young woman (SS. 6:13). †

SHUMATHITES A family descended from Caleb (1Ch. 2:53). †

SHUNEM, SHUNAMMITE A place (181-223) in the tribal area of Issachar and one of a group of people from that place (Jos. 19:18; 1Ki. 2:17-22; 2Ki. 4:8, 12-36).

SHUNI, SHUNITE(S) A son of Gad and his clan (Ge. 46:16; Nu. 26:15). †

SHUPHAM, SHUPHAMITE(S) A son of Benjamin and founder of the group called Shuphamites (Nu. 26:39). *See also* MUPPIM

SHUPPIM 1Ch. 26:16. † *See* MUPPIM

SHUR, WAY OF, WILDERNESS OF *See* GEOGRAPHY OF THE HOLY LAND

SHUSHAN *See* SUSA

SHUSHAN EDUTH {lily of testimony} *See* PSALMS, TITLES OF 2. and 10., (4)

SHUTHELAH, SHUTHELAHITE, SHUTHALHITES
1 and 2. Both a son of Ephraim and a descendant of Ephraim and his clan (Nu. 26:35-36; 1Ch. 7:20-21).

SHUTTLE *See* WEAVING AND SPINNING

SIA, SIAHA Two names of the same person, an ancestor of some temple servants who came back from the Babylonian captivity with Zerubbabel (Ezr. 2:44; Ne. 7:47). †

SIBBEC(H)AI One of David's mighty men; also called Mebunnai (2Sa. 21:18; 23:27).

SIBBOLETH *See* SHIBBOLETH

SIBMAH The name of a special variety of grape that came from Sebam, Sibmah (Isa. 16:8-9; Jer. 48:32), and the name of the place itself in Transjordan (Nu. 32:38).

SIBRAIM An unidentified place on the N border of Canaan (Eze. 47:16). †

SICHEM *See* SHECHEM

SICILY *See* SYRACUSE

SICK, SICKNESS The equating of diseases mentioned in the Bible with a modern variety is not easy because of the very limited contexts in which some of them are described there.

1. Various types of *skin disease* were mentioned fairly frequently: *Boil, itch, leprosy, scab, tetter, ulcer.* The *tetter* (mentioned only in Lev. 13:39) is unknown. The *scab* is noted only three times and would appear to be on the order of a ringworm (Lev. 21:20; 22:22; Isa. 3:17). The *ulcer* another skin disease (rather than in the digestive tract), is found only in Dt. 28:27. The *itch* was a "leprosy" or a form of ringworm of the head and neck. It is found in the chapter which refers most frequently to the disease of leprosy (Lev. 13:30-37). The *boil* is found in the same chapter (Lev. 13:18-23), as well as elsewhere. It was one of the plagues of Egypt (Ex. 9:9-11). A cure suggested was to lay a fig poultice on it (Isa. 38:21). *Leprosy* was apparently not what we know today as Hansen's disease but a skin disease of some other sort. Extended passages discuss it: Lev. 13:8-52; 14:7, 44-57. Miriam, Uzziah, and Simon had it (Nu. 12:10; 2Ch. 26:21; Mk. 14:3).

2. *Dropsy, epilepsy, palsy, dysentery* are noted in specific cases only once each (Lk. 14:2; Mt. 17:15; Ac. 8:7; 28:8).

3. *Pestilence* and *plague* may refer to more than one disease each. The former is noted in connection with military sieges and thus may have something to do with cholera or a fever, while the latter is generally thought to be a bubonic outbreak (Lev. 26:25; Dt. 28:21-22; Ex. 9:3; 11:1). The *tumors* of 1Sa. 5:6-12

and 6:4-17 are considered to be a form of bubonic plague.

4. The *fever* may be one of several types: undulant, malarial, or that which might accompany a number of other diseases (Lev. 26:16; Mt. 8:14-15; Ac. 28:8).

5. *Madness* is used more often in a general sense of anger rather than that of insanity. The latter meaning is found, however, in Dt. 28:28.

6. *Medicine* is found one time and *physician* six. "A cheerful heart is good medicine" and they "used many medicines in vain" (Pr. 17:22; Jer. 46:11). One of the functions of the physician in Egypt was that of embalming (Ge. 50:2); and the writer of two of the books of the NT was a physician, Luke (Col. 4:14). *See* HEALING, HEALTH; *see also* BLINDNESS; TOUCH OF JESUS

SICKLE An instrument for cutting standing grain made at first from pieces of flint set in a curved horn or piece of wood. Later, they were made of metal (Dt. 16:9; Joel 3:13; Mk. 4:29).

SIDDIM, VALLEY OF [*possibly* valley of furrows, valley of demons, BDB; valley of bordering furrows, KB] A valley in the vicinity of the S end of the Dead Sea where the five kings of the area fought with Kedorlaomer and his allies (Ge. 14:3-10). †

SIDON *See* GEOGRAPHY OF THE HOLY LAND

SIEGE A means by which all communication in and out of a city was cut off by an enemy in an attempt to conquer it. Then large earthen mounds were built against the city wall so that the siege machines could be rolled up to the wall to batter it down or for the bowmen or infantry attacks over it. On occasion, tunnels were dug under the walls or other methods were used to break into the city (Jos. 10:31; Isa. 23:13; 37:33; Eze. 4:2; 21:22).

SIEGEWORKS A barrier constructed for defense, used both literally and figuratively (Jer. 50:15; Isa. 26:1); sometimes translated "ramparts" (Ps. 48:13).

SIGN *See* MIRACLES, MIRACULOUS; TATTOO

SIGNET *See* SEAL

SIHON The Amorite king of Heshbon, NE of the Dead Sea, who had many contacts with the Israelites through the time of the Judges (Nu. 21:21-34; Dt. 2:24-32; Jos. 13:10-27; Jdg. 11:19-21).

SIHOR *See* SHIHOR

SILAS {asked, *possibly* dedicated to God, SILVANUS,} A Roman citizen and an active member of the young church in Jerusalem. With Paul and Barnabas he carried the message of the Jerusalem Council to Antioch (Ac. 15:22-23, 32; 16:37). He was with Paul on parts of his missionary journeys as may be inferred from the references in the epistles of Paul (2Co. 1:19; 1Th. and 2Th. 1:1).

SILK Silk from the silkworm was known in the Far East from very early times and in the Near East by the first millennium B.C. (Eze. 16:10-13; Rev. 18:12).

SILLA An unidentified part of the city of Jerusalem (2Ki. 12:20). †

SILOAH, SHILOAH *See* SILOAM

SILOAM, POOL OF {sent, Jn. 9:7; "water sender," *i.e.*, aqueduct} A pool in Jerusalem near the joining of the Kidron, Tyropeon, and Hinnom valleys. The water from the Gihon spring was brought to it through the conduit built by King Hezekiah (Lk. 13:4; Jn. 9:7-11). The King's Garden was found in this area (Ne. 3:15). † *See* GIHON

SILOAM, TOWER OF A tower somewhere near the pool of Siloam (Lk. 13:4). *See* SILOAM; TOWER

SILVANUS *See* SILAS

SILVER *See* PRECIOUS STONES AND METALS

SILVERSMITH A worker in silver. An idol maker (Jdg. 17:4; Pr. 25:4; Ac. 19:24).

SIMEON {he has heard *or* obedient one}
1. One of the sons of Jacob who gave his name to one of the tribes of Israel (Ge. 29:33).
2. The devout man who blessed the baby Jesus as he was presented in the temple (Lk. 2:25ff.).
3. An ancestor of Jesus (Lk. 3:30).
4. *See* SYMEON.

SIMEONITE {of Simeon} One from the tribe or clan of Simeon. *See* SIMEON

SIMON {he has heard *or* obedient one}
1. Simon Peter, one of the twelve apostles, *see* APOSTLES.
2. Simon the Zealot, another of Jesus' apostles.
3. A brother of Jesus (Mt. 13:55; Mk. 6:3).
4. A leper and the host of Jesus at Bethany (Mt. 26:6; Mk.14:3).
5. A Pharisee who hosted Jesus (Lk. 7:37-40).
6. The father of Judas Iscariot (Jn. 6:71; 13:2, 26).
7. The man from Cyrene who carried Jesus' cross (Mt. 27:32; Mk. 15:21).
8. Simon Magus who tried to buy the power to confer the Holy Spirit but was rebuked by Peter (Ac. 8:9ff.).
9. A tanner at Joppa and host of Peter (Ac. 9:43).
10. *See* SYMEON.

SIMON MAGUS *See* SIMON 8.

SIMON PETER *See* APOSTLES

SIMON THE CANANAEAN, THE ZEALOT *See* APOSTLES

SIMRI *See* SHIMRI 3.

SIN Scripture does not reveal the origin of evil, although it is clear that God is not the author. When God made all things, he pronounced them "good" (Ge. 1:31). There are two kinds of evil — physical or natural evil, which we find in the world in general, and moral evil, or sin, which exists in all men's hearts. Although evil did not exist in the world at the beginning, it soon made its presence felt when man rebelled against God. The essence of sin is willful disobedience to the declared will of God. When sin entered the world, it brought in its aftermath sorrow, suffering, and death. Sin became and still remains the great curse of human life. It describes the evil course which man has deliberately chosen to follow and which carries untold misery with it. The term "total depravity" is sometimes used to describe the state of fallen man. This does not mean that every man is as bad as he possibly could be or that he has entirely lost every trace of the divine image which was originally his. It does mean, however, that sin has affected man's whole being, his will, his thoughts, his emotions, his appetites. Because of sin, man's will is perverted, his understanding darkened, his conscience defiled, and his affections depraved (Eph. 4:18).

Adam's defiance of God's will not only meant that he himself thereby forfeited his original intimate relationship with God and became alienated from him, but the whole human race was also affected. Man is therefore a "fallen creature," born with a bias toward sin, which is sometimes referred to as "the law of sin" (Ro. 5:12-15; Ro. 7:23; 8:2).

"Sin" basically means failure to meet the divine requirements. The Bible gives a number of words which highlight different aspects of sin. Sin in general is regarded as "missing the mark" — failing to measure up to God's standards. It may also be defined as "transgression" — a deliberate act of rebellion, the crossing of a boundary which God has set. Paul distinguished transgression, such as the sin of Adam, from sin, which is the wider term (Ro. 5:14).

Sin is essentially a moral evil, and the words used to designate it take this into account. The word "iniquity" conveys the idea of perversion of heart. Three different words are used in Ps. 32:1-2: transgression (rebellion), sin (missing the mark), and iniquity (perversion of heart).

The words *err* and *error* convey the notion of straying away from the right path (1Ti. 6:10, 21). Thus false teaching is described as error, but so also is departure from right conduct (2Ti. 2:18). Error, while serious, is not so grievous as heresy, which represents a more deliberate departure from the true faith coupled with the propagation of false teaching (Jude 11).

The Bible gives us many more words which illustrate ways in which man's sinful disposition expresses itself. We could sum up the situation by stating that sin is a coming short of God's standard through an act of will, which leads to an attitude of mind and heart that deliberately chooses to disobey and displease God. John uses the word "lawlessness" to describe this innate human desire to be independent of God (1Jn. 3:4).

The word *wicked (wickedness)* is used in the English Bible to translate a dozen or more Hebrew words and several Greek words. The wicked are contrasted with the righteous (Ps. 73). Wickedness is pictured as an active, destructive principle at work in the world (Pr. 21:10; 29:16).

The Apostle Paul portrayed sin as something external and objective, a sort of king ruling as a tyrant over men (Ro. 7). Sin for him was an alien power attacking men from without, bringing all men under its dominion (Ro. 3:23; 5:12; 11:32).

A distinction is often drawn between sin and sins. Sin, the principle of lawlessness, is found in all men, but sins vary considerably according to heredity, environments, disposition, and circumstances. Sin might be described as the tree, whereas sins are the fruit. Sin is in our very nature, and it expresses itself in various ways. Sin is a matter not only of the act but of the attitude. Such sins as pride, jealousy, greed, impurity, and self-will may be hidden within a man's heart and only occasionally reveal themselves in outward acts (Mk. 7:21-23).

Sin is consistently represented as something which God hates (Jer. 44:4), against which his holy nature must revolt (Hab. 1:13). It leads inevitably to spiritual death (Ro. 6:23; Jas. 1:15). Since man is a moral being, when he sins he is guilty in the sight of God, and this guilt incurs the divine wrath. Since men are guilty of having sinned, all stand condemned (Ro. 3:19-23). Although a distinction is drawn between "sins of ignorance" and "sins of presumption," and the extent of guilt is related to the degree of light given, sin as such is inexcusable and must always be regarded as an affront to God (Nu. 15; Ps. 51:4). Any deviation from God's moral law must be punished since the claims of that law must be vindicated. The glory of the Christian gospel is that, while taking full account of the seriousness of sin, it points to One who has grappled with the problem on man's behalf and in man's stead. The simplest expression of that gospel is found in the words, " Christ died for our sins" (1Co. 15:3). *See also* SALVATION, APPLICATION OF (G.W.K.)

SIN, CITY OF *See* PELUSIUM

SIN, STRONGHOLD OF EGYPT *See* PELUSIUM

SIN, UNPARDONABLE *See* BLASPHEMY AGAINST THE HOLY SPIRIT

SIN, WILDERNESS OF [desert of clay *or possibly* desert of SIN (pagan moon god)] *See* GEOGRAPHY OF THE HOLY LAND

SIN OFFERING *See* SACRIFICES AND OFFERINGS

SINA *See* SINAI

SINAI, MOUNT, WILDERNESS OF [SIN (pagan moon god); glare (from white chalk), ISBE] *See* GEOGRAPHY OF THE HOLY LAND

SINEW KJV for "tendon" (Ge. 32:32; Isa. 48:4).

SINGING *See* PRAISE; PSALMS; SONGS

SINGLE EYE KJV for "sound," "healthy," or "good" vision (Mt. 6:22; Lk. 11:34). It could have the idea of not having "double vision" (i.e., single vision). The context argues that this is the opposite of "bad" (*poneros*) and hence is similar to the general word "good" (*kalos*).

SINIM *See* SYENE

SINITES An unidentified group of Canaanites (Ge. 10:17; 1Ch. 1:15). †

SINNER *See* SIN

SION, MOUNT *See* HERMON, MOUNT; JERUSALEM; ZION

SIPHMOTH An unidentified village in the tribal area of Judah (1Sa. 30:28). †

SIPPAI *See* SAPH

SIRACH, WISDOM OF A wisdom writing probably composed in Greek (possibly Hebrew) about 180 B.C. by Jesus Ben Sira. This work is not unlike the Book of Proverbs. It is deuterocanonical, with the name Ecclesiasticus. *See* SCRIPTURE, Apocrypha, *Ecclesiasticus*

SIRAH A cistern in an unidentified place involved in the account of the murder of Abner by Joab (2Sa. 3:26). †

SIRION Dt. 3:9; Ps. 29:6. † *See* HERMON, MOUNT

SISAMAI *See* SISMAI

SISERA
1. The leader of the Canaanite kings against whom Deborah and Barak were victorious. He was killed by Jael, who drove a tent peg through his head while he slept (Jdg. 4:2ff.; 5:24).
2. The ancestor of some temple servants who came back from the Babylonian captivity with Zerubbabel (Ezr. 2:53).

SISMAI [*possibly* belonging to SISAM (pagan god)] A Jerahmeelite descendant of Judah (1Ch. 2:40). †

SISTER, BROTHER
1. A normal sense of a blood family member, female sibling (Jn. 11:1). This can be used for a half sister (Ge. 20:12).
2. A figure for a member of the believing community (Ro. 16:1). This is the same use as Christian "brother" (1Co. 7:15, KJV).

SISTRUM *See* MUSIC, MUSICAL INSTRUMENTS

SITHRI [*possibly* Yahweh is my hiding place] A Levite in the days of Moses (Ex. 6:22). †

SITNAH [hostility] The name of a well dug by the servants of Isaac near Gerar (Ge. 26:21). †

SITUATION ETHICS A form of ethics which says that one's behavior is only governed by love. There are no absolutes in behavior; if it is done in *love,* then it is "correct." Even murder and adultery are in some settings. It all depends on the situation. This "love" is not defined by the Bible's confines of love: To do what is good and right is to keep the LORD'S commands (Dt. 6:17-18). To love Christ is to obey his commands (Jn. 14:15). To do the loving thing is to do what pleases God. What pleases God is in conformity to his character and will. His character and will are explained in his word. *See* WILL OF GOD

SITZ IM LEBEN German for "life setting."

SIVAN *See* CALENDAR

SIYON *See* HERMON, MOUNT

SKIN The substance of a man or animal that covers the body. The animal skin was sometimes burned in the offering (Lev. 8:21). Human skin can have disease (Lev. 13:2ff.). A skin could be a bottle to hold water (Ge. 21:14), or wine (*see* WINESKIN). Some skins were dyed for the Temple (Ex. 25:5).

SKINK *See* BEASTS 6.

SKIRT *See* DRESS

SKULL *See* GOLGOTHA

SLANDER False statements which harm or malign a person's reputation. If it is against God, it is called blasphemy. The ninth commandment concerns the bearing of a false witness (Ex. 20:16; Lev. 19:16; 2Sa. 19:24-30; Mt. 15:19). It is many times condemned in the NT by the apostles (2Co. 12:20; Eph. 4:31; 1Pe. 2:1). *See* WITNESS

SLAVE A human being who is owned by another. Their treatment in Israel was more human than in the neighboring countries for two reasons: the divine laws given about them, and the fact that the Hebrew and Greek words in so many cases refer to servants and not slaves in the modern sense. The latter is seen in the KJV renderings where the word "slave" is found only twice and the word "slavery" not at all. Slaves or servants could be acquired as booty in war or by abduction, by purchase, or default on debts, by birth, or by one's voluntarily selling himself (Jdg. 5:30; 2Ki. 5:2-3; Dt. 24:7; Lev. 25:44-46; Ge. 15:3). Hebrew slaves could gain their freedom and could not be permanently enslaved (Ex. 21:2ff.; Lev. 25:25ff.; Dt. 15:12ff.). In NT times slavery is known also. Paul sent the slave of Philemon back to him (Phm. 1:16). In Christ there is neither bond nor free (1Co. 7:21; Gal. 3:28). All Christians are to consider themselves servants or slaves to their Lord, to Christ himself (Ro. 6:16-22). In the passages concerning proper human relations in the family, the relationships of slaves and masters is also included (Eph. 6:5ff.; Col. 3:22ff.). *See* SERVANT

SLAY *See* MANSLAYER

SLEEP
1. An altered state of awareness, natural sleep (Mt. 1:24).
2. An euphemism for physical death (Jn. 11:11-13; 1Co. 15:51; Eph. 5:14; 1Th. 5:10).
3. A figure for not being attentive (1Th. 5:67).

SLING *See* ARMS AND ARMOR

SLOPES *See* GEOGRAPHY OF THE HOLY LAND

SLOTHFUL *See* LAZY

SLUG *See* BEASTS 6.

SLUGGARD *See* LAZY

SMALLEST LETTER *See* JOT

SMELTING *See* MINES, MINING

SMITE KJV for to "strike" or "kill." *See* MANSLAYER

SMITH Before Noah the Bible refers to one Tubal-Cain who was a worker in both bronze and iron (Ge. 4:22). This is considered by some as a historical impossibility, but others think that the reference is to the cold forging of native copper and meteoric iron. The matter is not clear. Until recently it was felt that at Tell el-Kheleifeh (Ezion Geber) there was an example of an early smelting furnace and the literature has extensive descriptions. More recently, however, it has been determined that this is not the case and that the installation there is merely a typical example of an Iron Age fort. In Iron I (1200-900 B.C.) smelting was done in the hills to the W and N of Elath-Ezion Geber, where we find that the ore was burned in open pits. In the days of the prophet Samuel there was no smith in Israel, but by the times of the Kings the situation had changed (1Sa. 13:19; 2Ki. 24:14-16).

SMYRNA A city on the Aegean coast of Asia Minor; a church to which one of the seven epistles in the Book of Revelation was addressed (Rev. 1:11; 2:8). †

SNARES Literally, snares were used in the hunting of both birds and animals (Ps. 124:7; Hos. 9:8). Figuratively, a number of things are called snares: riches, false gods or prophets, a slanderer (Dt. 7:16; Hos. 9:8; 1Ti. 3:7; 6:9). The child of God is warned against the wiles and snares set by the devil for his entrapment (2Ti. 2:26).

SNOW While snow is relatively rare in Palestine, and when it does come it very rarely outlasts the heat of one sunny day, it is noted in the Bible. It is particularly used as a symbol of whiteness or purity (Ex. 4:6; Nu. 12:10; Ps. 51:7; Isa. 1:18). It is used figuratively in connection with the vision of God in Da. 7:9 and Rev. 1:14 and of the angel who stood by the empty tomb on the first resurrection morning (Mt. 28:3).

SNUFFERS Golden or bronze implements used in tending the light of the tabernacle and temple. Based on the derivation of the Hebrew word it is felt that these were not tongs but rather like scissors used for trimming the wicks (2Ki. 12:13; 25:14-15).

SOAP This is mentioned only in Mal. 3:2 and Jer. 2:22 in the Bible and not too frequently in other ancient literature. The inference would seem to be that other materials were used for cleansing the body. The connection with the word "lye" would seem to point to the direction that the "soap" referred to was some potash dissolved in water or oil. In Job 9:30 (NIV) the word is normally translated "snow." *See also* FULLER

SOCHO, SOCHOH *See* SOCO

SOCKET *See* TABERNACLE

SOCO, SOCOH {*possibly* thorny place, IDB}
1. A town (153-194) on the E edge of the Sharon Plain, N and W of Samaria (1Ki. 4:10), at modern Shuweikeh.
2. A town (147-121) on the E side of the Shephelah between Adullam and Azekah near the Vale of Elah (Jos. 15:35; 1Sa. 17:1).
3. A town (150-090) in the hill country of Judah near Debir, S of Hebron (Jos. 15:48).

SODI {Yahweh confides} The father of the representative of the tribe of Zebulun among the twelve spies which Moses sent to spy out the land (Nu. 13:10). †

SODOM, SODOMA Along with Gomorrah, a city held up as an example of wickedness which had to be destroyed by God. It was located in some unidentified location around the southern end of the Dead Sea, perhaps now under its waters. Its destruction is frequently pointed out in Scripture as a warning of judgment against sin (Ge. 19:24-28; Isa. 13:19; Jer. 50:40; Lk. 10:12; 17:29; Jude 7). Jerusalem is once called Sodom (Rev. 11:8).

SODOMITE {of SODOM} *See* DOG

SODOMY *See* HOMOSEXUALITY; SEXUAL IMMORALITY

SOJOURNER *See* STRANGER

SODOM AND GOMORRAH
Possible location of Sodom and Gomorrah

SOLDIER See ARMS AND ARMOR; ARMY; WAR

SOLOMON [peace, well-being] *See* KINGS OF JUDAH AND ISRAEL

SOLOMON, SONG OF *See* SONG OF SOLOMON

SOLOMON'S PORTICO *See* PORCH

SOLOMON'S SERVANTS The Bible gives a list of Solomon's servants, i.e., his princes and officers, in 1Ki. 4:1-19. Besides these Solomon made extensive use of the forced draft of the remnants of the conquered people such as the Amorites and Hittites, who were still to be found in Canaan (1Ki. 9:15-22). There is no doubt but that he also thus drafted the Israelites as well, which may be inferred from the reaction of the people to Rehoboam after the death of his father, Solomon (1Ki. 12:1-11). The sons of Solomon's servants are noted among those who returned from the Babylonian captivity with Ezra and Zerubbabel (Ezr. 2:55-58; Ne. 7:57-60).

SOLOMON'S TEMPLE *See* TEMPLE

SON *See* BAR; NAME, GIVING OF

SON, SONSHIP In OT usage, unlike English usage, a son may be the direct heir or any subsequent descendant. Jesus is called the son of David, the son of Abraham (Mt. 1:1). It is translated in the NIV as "children," reflecting the known usage that would cover both sexes (Ge. 3:16). Both Testaments recognize the fact that believers are called "sons of God" (Dt. 14:1; Ro. 8:14; Gal. 3:26). Sonship means membership in a group, as is clear in 2Ki. 2:3-5. Thus reference may be made to the divine sonship of Christ, one with the Father and the Holy Spirit, and the sonship of all believers as being members of the family of God (Ro. 8:15; 9:4). *See also* BAR; BEN

SON OF DAVID A messianic title of Christ (Ps. 2:7; 110:1ff.; Mt. 9:27; Ro.1:3). He is the son of David, but also the Lord of David (Mt. 22:42-44). *See* CHRIST, *throne of David; see also* BAR

SON OF GOD *See* BAR; GOD, NAMES OF, GODHEAD

SON OF MAN *See* BAR; GOD, NAMES OF, GODHEAD

SONG *See* MUSIC

SONG OF DEGREES *See* SONGS OF ASCENT

SONG OF SOLOMON, BOOK OF The author has been held to be Solomon because of the references to him by name in the book (1:5; 3:7, 9, 11; 8:11), as well as to many allusions that fit him well. Some put the book much later and some speak of later redactions (i.e., editorial revisions) of the text because of the Aramaisms and Greek words found in it. In general these perceived differences stem from varying views held as to the origin of the Bible as a whole. Tradition puts it in Solomonic times. There is a great amount of variation in the interpretation of the book and the personages in it: a literal story of Solomon; a literal story of someone in Solomon's times; an allegory only; or a poem with typological meanings. While there may be such differences of opinion, the basic message is clear; namely that love is sacred and an emotion to be cherished. "Do not arouse or awaken love until it so desires" (2:7; 3:5; 8:4).

SONG OF SONGS *See* SONG OF SOLOMON, BOOK OF

SONG OF THE THREE HEBREW CHILDREN *See* SCRIPTURE, *Apocrypha*

SONGS OF ASCENT The translation of the titles of Psalms 120–134; also called "the Songs of Degrees." It is believed that these songs were sung on the steps (degrees) going up from the women's to the men's court in the temple. Others believe that they were songs sung by pilgrims on their ascent to the temple. *See* HALLEL

SONS OF GOD *See* SON, SONSHIP

SONS OF THE PROPHETS *See* PROPHETS, PROPHECY

SOOTHSAYER *See* DIVINATION

SOP, A MORSEL OF BREAD KJV for "piece or bit of bread" (Jn. 13:26). *See* FOOD; MEALS

SOPATER [saving one's father] A man from Berea who went with Paul on his final trip to Jerusalem (Ac. 20:4). †

SOPE *See* SOAP

SOPHERETH [scribe] *See* HAS-SOPHERETH

SORCERY, SORCERER *See* DIVINATION

SORE *See* SCALL; SICK, SICKNESS

SOREK, VALLEY OF [(blood red grapes); *hence*, choice vines] A valley near and W of Beth Shemesh occupied by the Philistines where Samson's mistress Delilah lived (Jdg. 16:4).

SOSIPATER [saving one's father] One who sent greetings to the church at Rome (Ro. 16:21; cf. Ac. 20:4). †

SOSTHENES
1. A ruler of the synagogue at Corinth in Paul's day. He was beaten by the Corinthians (Ac. 18:17).
2. An associate of Paul at the time of his writing the first epistle to Corinth (1Co. 1:1).

SOTAI The ancestor of some of Solomon's servants who returned from the Babylonian captivity with Zerubbabel (Ezr. 2:55; Ne. 7:57). †

SOTERIOLOGY *See* SYSTEMATIC THEOLOGY

SOUL The idea of "soul" is used in both Testaments: about 750 times in the OT and 100 times in the NT. It has a broad range of meanings and is translated by many English words and ideas. Generally a soul is something that you cannot see (though note usage numbers 1 and 7). Because it is the immaterial part of man, it is similar to spirit (*see* number 10). Usage numbers 2, 3, and 4 are the most common utilizations in both OT and NT. Physical animate life is most often in mind, yet the NT gives some new perspectives. Usage numbers 5 and 6 show some of the psychological aspects of the biblical use of "soul"; these are often what is thought to be the major biblical use of soul, when it is simply one element of many. Numbers 8 and 10 give NT perspectives related to the eternal aspects of soul.

VALLEY OF SOREK

To discover what a word means one must discover how it is used. To discover what a word means in a given passage one must study the context carefully. For example, the Greek word for "soul" in Ac. 15:24 is translated "mind" (most versions), yet two verses later it is translated "life."

1. Soul can refer to the *throat* or *neck* (Jnh. 2:5, NJB, NIV footnote; Ps. 69:2; Ps. 124:4).

2. Soul can refer to *self* or the *person*. It usually in this meaning is translated by a pronoun (*I, me, you, yourself, himself, anyone, everyone, etc.*); only occasionally translated *soul* (Ps. 16:10 and Ac. 2:27; Ps. 30:4; 49:15; 86:13; 89:48; Pr. 23:14). The NT has the same usage (Lu. 12:19; Ac. 2:27, 41; 7:14; 2Co. 12:15; 1Pe. 1:22; 3:20).

3. Soul can refer to *life*—blood is the seat of the "soul" (Dt. 12:23). It is used in Isa. 10:18 with flesh to show the totality of destruction, translated in the NIV as "completely destroy" (lit. "from the soul to the flesh"). It is used with another word for "body" in Ps. 31:10 and is translated as "oneself" in Pr. 11:17. When the soul leaves the body, death follows (Ge. 35:18; Jer.15:9). If the soul (life) comes back to a corpse, then he comes back to a living condition (1Ki. 17:21). The NT has a similar usage in the following verses: opposite of death (Mk. 3:4; Lk. 6:9; Ac. 20:10); of a child (Mt. 2:20); related to food and drink (Mt. 6:25; Lk. 12:22-23); able to find rest (Mt. 11:39); able to be well pleased (Mt. 12:18); physical life to be taken (Lk. 12:20); by patience you will gain your lives (Lk. 21:19); a shepherd for his sheep (Jn. 10:11, 15, 17); risked for Jesus' sake (Ac. 15:26; Ac. 20:24); lose life in a ship wreck (Ac. 27:10; 27:22); God as a witness upon my life (2Co. 1:23); risked his physical life (illness) (Php. 2:30; 1Jn. 3:16); not just words but our very lives (1Th. 2:8); anchor for the soul (Heb. 6:19); leaders watch over it (Heb. 13:17); unstable lives (2Pe. 2:14); lives sacrificed (Rev. 6:9); Christ gave his "life" in redemption (Mt. 20:28; Mk. 10:45; Jn. 12:27; Jn. 15:13; 1Jn. 3:16).

4. Soul can be a *living being*—man (Ge. 2:7; 1Co. 15:45) or beast (Ge. 1:20, 24, 30; 2:19; Rev. 8:9; 16:3). Here "soul" refers simply to animate life.

5. A soul can be the seat of the *physical cravings* (also as a figure of speech of desire for God); hunger and thirst (Eze. 7:19). In Ps. 107:9, though, "soul" is not translated in the NIV literally: "He satisfies the throat [soul] of the one thirsting and fills the throat [soul] of the one hungering." It is translated "appetite" in Isa. 56:11, that which can be satisfied with food and drink (*see also* Ps. 63:5; Pr. 13:25 "heart"; Jer. 50:11).

6. A soul is a seat of the *heart, mind, emotions, desires*, or *will*; the extent of rulership, "all your heart (soul) desires" (2Sa. 3:21; 1Ki. 11:37). God does what he pleases, "what his soul desires" (Job 23:13). The desires (soul) of the diligent are satisfied (Pr. 13:4). The man (soul) that is wicked craves evil (Pr. 21:10) and boasts of the cravings of his heart (soul) (Ps. 10:3). The righteous heart (soul) desires the LORD (Isa. 26:8). The NT also has this meaning: the seat of grief or emotion (Mt. 26:38; Mk. 14:34; Heb. 12:3); seat of thoughts or mind (Lk. 2:35; Ac. 4:32; 14:2; 15:24). It can be tormented (2Pe. 2:8); it can prosper (3Jn. 2). It is the seat of sincerity and volition (the heart) (Eph. 6:6; Col. 3:23; 1Pe. 2:11; 4:19).

7. A soul can be a *dead body* (Lev. 21:1; 22:4; Nu. 6:11; 9:7)

8. The NT gives some unique perspectives on the *eternal aspects* of the soul: a soul is beyond the body, yet the soul (with the body) is able to be cast into hell or be saved (Mt. 10:28; 16:26; Mk. 8:36; Heb. 10:38-39; Ja. 1:21; 1Pe. 1:20; Rev. 18:13; 20:4)—and to lose the soul is to find it (Mt. 10:39; 16:25; Mk. 8:35; Lk. 9:24; 17:33; Jn. 12:25; Rev. 12:11).

9. Soul can be used in phrases to show the *whole life* or *totality of life*: as when it's used to love God (Dt. 6:4; Mt. 22:37; Mk. 12:30; Lk. 10:27); and used with body and spirit (1Th. 5:23).

10. Soul and spirit are both compared and contrasted. Soul is used synonymously with "spirit" in Lu. 1:46. Simi-

larly soul is used as a synonym of "spirit" to show unity of purpose and struggle for the gospel (Php. 1:27). Soul and spirit are distinguished in Heb. 4:12. *See also* SPIRIT (J.A.S.)

SOUTH, DIRECTION OF *See* GE-OGRAPHY OF THE HOLY LAND, III. *Topography, Setting*

SOVEREIGNTY OF GOD *See* AT-TRIBUTES OF GOD

SOWER, SOWING *See* FARMING

SPAIN A country in SW Europe that Paul hoped he might be able to visit (Ro. 15:24, 28). †

SPAN *See* WEIGHTS AND MEA-SURES

SPANKING *See* PARENTING

SPARROW *See* BIRDS 9.

SPEAR *See* ARMS AND ARMOR

SPICE, SPICES *See* PLANTS, PER-FUMES, AND SPICES

SPIDER *See* BEASTS 6.

SPIKENARD *See* PLANTS, PER-FUMES, AND SPICES, Perfumes, Scents, Ointments, Drugs, *Nard*

SPINDLE *See* WEAVING AND SPINNING

SPINNING *See* WEAVING AND SPINNING

SPIRIT The Hebrew and Aramaic for "spirit" (*ruach*) occurs 389 times in the OT; the Greek *pneuma* occurs 379 times in the NT. More than 120 of these refer to the Holy Spirit or Spirit of God (*see* HOLY SPIRIT). The words are also translated "wind" and "breath."

In both OT and NT "spirit" has a variety of usage. As "wind" it is an invisible and powerful force (Ge. 8:1; 1Ki. 19:11; Jnh. 4:8; Jn. 3:8). As "breath" it pictures both man and animal as possessing life (Ge. 6:16; 7:15, 22; Ecc. 3:19-21). The distinction between definitions is not always clear and often overlaps (cf. Ge. 1:2 and 8:1; Jn. 3:58).

With reference to mankind, "spirit" is often used in conjunction with "soul" to represent man's inmost being or essential existence (Job 7:11; Isa. 26:9; Lk. 1:46-47; *see also* SOUL). Spirit sometimes refers to a higher level of human nature than does soul (1Co 1:14-15; 15:45; Jude 18-19). Spirit is often contrasted to the material part of man, "flesh" or "body" (Mt. 26:41; Jn. 6:63; Rom. 8). Both body and spirit can be devoted to God (1Co. 7:34), and both contaminated by the world (2Co. 7:1).

God is spirit, and must be worshiped in spirit and truth (Jn. 4:24). Angels and demons are good spirits and evil spirits, respectively (1Ki. 22:21; Job 4:15; Ac. 23:8; Heb. 1:14). Such spirits can influence or possess people (1Sa. 16:14-15; Eph.2:2), thus spirits must be tested to see if they are from God (1Jn. 4:1). The spirit of man is separated from the body at death (Lk. 8:55; Jas. 2:26). Between death and glorification, humans are referred to as spirits (Heb. 12:23; 1Pe. 3:19), but the final state of mankind is spirit united with a glorified body (2Co. 5:1-5). *See also* SOUL (J.R.K.)

SPIRIT FILLED To be controlled by the Spirit. Used in some Christian circles to refer to the believers who manifest certain spiritual gifts.

SPIRIT OF GOD, HOLY SPIRIT *See* GOD, NAMES OF, GODHEAD 6.

SPIRITS
1. Distinguishing between spirits. Paul lists this as one of the spiritual gifts (1Co. 12:10). Since many false prophets were in the world, it was necessary to use judgment to see which speaker, prophet, or message was of God (1Jn. 4:1). The test was conformity to the revelation of God, his law, and testimony (Isa. 8:20, NIV) in the Scripture.
2. Spirits in prison (1Pe. 3:18-20). This passage is one of the most controversial of the Book of First Peter. What Peter means is problematic. Did Christ preach in his pre-incarnation? Is Noah the person making proclamation to those in prison? Did Christ preach to the lost in Hades just before the Resur-

rection, alluded to in Ac. 2:27? If either of last two are true, did Christ preach to one group only (in the "days of Noah"), or is it generalized to all who die (a second chance)? The best one can say for the last option is that it is a foolish man who would reject Christ for the slim hope that a second chance would be his. It also contradicts Heb. 9:27.

SPIRITS IN PRISON *See* PRISON; SPIRITS 2.; *see also* DEAD, ABODE OF

SPIRITUAL GIFTS As used in the NT, these words refer to certain extraordinary gifts given to Christians by the Holy Spirit to equip them for ministry, whether preaching or other service. Several lists of them are given: Ro. 12:6-8; 1Co. 12:1-11, 28-30; Eph. 4:7-12. The chief gift to be desired was to be able to prophesy—i.e., to forthtell or preach the Word of the living God effectively (1Co. 14:1). Some believe that this could also be a gift of foretelling the future (Ac. 11:28). *See also* GIFTS; HELPS

SPOIL *See* PLUNDER

SPOKES *See* TEMPLE ¶ 2., "each mounted on four wheels"

SPORTS *See* ATHLETE

SPOUSE *See* MARRIAGE

SPREAD, SPREADING *See* DIASPORA

SPRING *See* AIN; CISTERN; FOUNTAIN; POOL; WELL; WATER

SPRING, SEASON OF *See* CALENDAR; TIME

SPRINKLE As a part of the ceremony of sanctifying or cleansing persons or things, the priest was required to dip hyssop or his finger (Ex. 12:22; Lev. 16:14) in the blood of a sacrificial animal, in oil, or in pure water, and sprinkle the blood, the oil, or water on that which was to be set apart to God or cleansed. If the finger of the priest was used, the symbolic liquid was either sprinkled or directly applied (Ex. 29:21; Lev. 14:15-18; Nu. 8:6ff.; 19:14-22). In the NT Christ is the

sacrifice for man's sin, and reference is made to the sprinkling of his blood (in symbol) on man for his cleansing (Heb. 10:19-22; 12:24; 1Pe. 1:2). In the prophetic description of the sacrifice of the Servant of God (Isa. 52:14 15), who is Christ in Christian interpretation, Isaiah noted that the "marring of the servant" will result in the "sprinkling" and thus the cleansing of many from sin. The OT symbolism is thus carried through in this passage. The RSV renders "startle" (NIV and most versions, "sprinkle") and says of the Hebrew word in a note: "The meaning of the Hebrew word is uncertain." This would seem to be for theological and not philological reasons. It might have been better to have said, "The meaning of the Hebrew word at this point is uncertain for us," for they render the word, even in the very same form, in other contexts as "sprinkle" (*see* Lev. 16:14; Nu. 19:21 in the RSV).

SQUADS *See* QUATERNION

STABLE *See* MANGER

STACHYS [head of grain] A Roman Christian to whom Paul sent greetings (Ro. 16:9).

STACTE *See* PLANTS, PERFUMES, AND SPICES, *gum resin*

STADIA, STADION *See* WEIGHTS AND MEASURES

STAFF, STAVES *See* ROD, ROD OF AARON, ROD OF MOSES

STALL *See* MANGER

STAR OF THE WISE MEN *See* STAR, STARS

STAR, STARS As used in the Bible these words refer to any luminous nonterrestrial body other than the sun and moon. Scientific "astronomy" was not a concern of the Bible, but certain identifiable constellations are mentioned: Arcturus (the Bear), Orion, Pleiades (Job 9:9; 38:31-32). A number of explanations have been offered for the "star of Bethlehem" (Mt. 2:2), none of which are particularly satisfactory. *See also* DEVIL, *Lucifer*

STAR-GOD *See* DEITIES

STATER *See* MONEY

STATUTES *See* LAW

STAY *See* REMAIN

STEADFAST LOVE Steadfastness conveys the ideas of constancy, fidelity, and patient enduring. The two words "steadfast love" as used in the RSV ("kindness" NIV) are the translation of the Hebrew word *hesed* (for examples, see Ge. 24:12; Ps. 36:5-10). On the exact meaning of this Hebrew word there is a very great body of literature. The KJV usually renders it "mercy" but in a limited number of cases by "kindness." The lexicographers suggest kindness, loving-kindness, loyal love, and mercy. In the NT it is related to the concept of grace.

STEALING Stealing is to take property from another. It is forbidden and condemned in Scripture (Ex. 20:15; Mt. 19:18). This can be by threat of force, robbery or mugging, often ambushing (Mal. 3:8; Lk. 10:30).

STEEL KJV for "bronze" in most major versions. The ASV rendering of "brass" is not correct (2Sa. 22:35; Job 20:24; Ps. 18:34; Jer. 15:12). *See* BRONZE

STEPHANAS [victor's wreath] A Christian of Corinth, the members of whose house were the first converts of Achaia (1Co. 16:15-18).

STEPHEN [victor's wreath] One of the seven first deacons of the early church in Jerusalem. His speeches angered the religious authorities and they stoned him, making him the first Christian martyr (Ac. 6:5-12).

STEPPE The more frequent translation of the Hebrew is "desert" or "wilderness" (1Ch. 6:78; Job 39:6).

STERILITY *See* BARREN

STEW *See* POTTAGE

STEWARD The word ordinarily applied to a servant who oversees the affairs of his master's household (Ge. 43:16; Da.

1:16). In the NT it has the same usage (Lk. 16:1-8), but there a religious stewardship becomes prominent. Overseers are God's stewards, as are, in a sense, all Christians. Christians are expected to use their time, abilities, and possessions in God's service (1Co. 4:1-2; Eph. 3:2; Tit. 1:7; 1Pe. 4:10).

STIFF-NECKED Stiff-necked means to be obstinate and unresponsive. A similar figure is "hard-hearted" (Ac. 7:51). *See also* Ex. 32:9; 33:3, 5; 34:9; Dt. 9:6; 9:13; 10:16; 31:27. *See* HEART, HARDEN THE

STOCKS An instrument of punishment. The hands and feet were locked in a frame which was capable of being used also to stretch the legs of the prisoner painfully. As used in the Bible the word also is a substitute for "prison" (2Ch. 16:10; Job 13:27; Ac. 16:24). *See* PUNISHMENT

STOICS, STOICKS [(learners on the painted) porch] *See* SECTS

STONE Palestine is a very stony country with bedrock being just under the surface in most places and often outcropping over large areas. Thus stone was a common item for instruments, building, weapons, and monuments. A common use was as a landmark (Dt. 27:2; Jos. 4:1-9; 2Sa. 20:8). Another use was in the construction of altars from unhewn stones (Dt. 27:5-8). Among the figurative uses is the "stony heart" which God will replace with a "heart of flesh," namely a heart of faith and trust, a new spirit (Eze. 11:19-21). God is "Israel's Rock" (Ge. 49:24). Simon the disciple is given the name Peter (little stone), and Christ is presented as the cornerstone of a building of God, a temple made from living stones (believers) (Eph. 2:20-22; 1Pe. 2:5-8). *See also* PRECIOUS STONES AND METALS; ROCK

STONE, PRECIOUS *See* PRECIOUS STONES AND METALS

STONE QUARRY *See* SHEBARIM

STONING Certain offenses against the law of God were punishable by stoning to death. These included blasphemy, idolatry, adultery, involvement in human sacrifice, Sabbath desecration (Lev. 24:16; Dt. 13:6-10; Lev. 20:2; Nu. 15:32ff.). *See* PUNISHMENT

STOOL As used in the NIV the reference is only to God's making the enemies of Christ a stool (footstool) for his feet (Lk. 20:43; Ac. 2:35; Heb. 1:13; 10:13). The delivery stool (Ex. 1:16) was a special stool on which women sat during labor. The Hebrew word *kise* is usually rendered in the RSV and NIV by "chair" (2Ki. 4:10).

STOREHOUSE Known as a barn in some versions (Hag. 2:19; Mt. 3:12; 6:26; 13:30). It was a storage place (granary or warehouse) for threshed grain, after being winnowed on the threshing-floor. It was a sign of blessing for obedience, to have a full barn, in OT times (Dt. 28:8; Pr. 3:10). When no grain would be available to put in the barn, it was a curse for disobedience (Dt. 28:22; Joel 1:17).

STORK *See* BIRDS 5.

STOVE *See* OVEN

STRAIGHT STREET *See* DAMASCUS

STRANGER The translation of a Hebrew word which would be better translated as "sojourner" (Ex. 12:48-49; Heb. 11:13; 1Pe. 2:11). In Lev. 19:33-34 it conveys clearly the concept of "foreigner."

STRANGLE To choke to death and not drain the blood from the animal carcass was forbidden (Lev. 17:12; Ac. 15:20; cf. Ge. 9:4).

STRAW The stalk of wheat or barley, but unlike the Western use of the whole stalk the reference is to the chopped stalk after the threshing process has taken place. It was used for food as well as for bedding (Ge. 24:32; Isa. 11:7). In Egypt it was mixed with clay in brick making. An enzyme resulting from straw in wa-

ter made the working of the clay easier (Ex. 5:7-18). *See also* FODDER

STREAM OF EGYPT *See* EGYPT, WADI OF

STREET In addition to the normal use of this word it could refer to a piazza-like opening in a road or street or even to the bazaar held in a street (Jos. 2:19; Pr. 7:12; Jer. 37:21).

STREET CALLED STRAIGHT *See* DAMASCUS

STRIKER, A PUGNACIOUS PERSON KJV, ASV, and NASB in 1Ti. 3:3; Tit. 1:7; not to be a striker or a pugnacious person is a qualification for an elder. The NIV, RSV, and NKJV have "not violent." *See* ELDER

STRINGED INSTRUMENTS *See* MUSIC, MUSICAL INSTRUMENTS 3.

STRIPES *See* PUNISHMENT; SCOURGE, SCOURGING; STRIPES

STROKE *See* TITTLE

STRONG DRINK *See* DRINK

STRUGGLE *See* ATHLETE

STUBBLE *See* STRAW

STUDY KJV for "diligence," "zeal," "eagerness" in 2Ti. 2:15. The NIV says, "Do your best."

STUMBLING BLOCK A snare set in a pathway which would cause one to fall. This word can be an enticement to sin (Rev. 2:14). It also has the idea of an obstacle or hindrance. The cross of Christ was a hindrance to the belief of the Jews (1Co. 1:23).

SUAH [*possibly* offal, dung, viscera] A descendant of Asher (1Ch. 7:36). †

SUCATHITES A family of scribes in Judah (1Ch. 2:55). †

SUCCOTH [booths]
  1. A city (208-178) in the tribal area of Gad in Transjordan (Jos. 13:27). Jacob stopped there on his return from Haran and later Gideon punished its inhabitants

for not assisting his effort to expel the Midianites (Ge. 33:17; Jdg. 8:5-16).

2. An unidentified stop of the Israelites on their journey after leaving Rameses (Ex. 12:37; Nu. 33:5).

SUCCOTH

SUCCOTH BENOTH 2Ki. 17:30. *See* DEITIES 1.

SUCHATHITES *See* SUCATHITES

SUFFERINGS OF BELIEVERS Christ is the Christian's example of how to respond to suffering (1Pe. 2:21-23). Suffering actually can have spiritual benefits (1Pe. 4:1, 13). Suffering is a part of the Christian life (Php. 1:29). *See* PERSECUTION

SUFFERINGS OF CHRIST *See* CHRIST, WORK OF

SUICIDE The deliberate act of taking one's own life. The Bible does not call this the unpardonable sin. Yet, those who have practiced it were in utter remorse or despondency, not seeking God's perfect will (1Sa. 31:1-13; Mt. 27:1-9). Suicide rejects the biblical view that God is the giver and taker of life. Suicide has been rightly called by some as the ultimate act of selfishness, not thinking of its influence on others, including family and friends and associates. Those plagued by these thoughts should seek qualified Christian counselors.

SUITABLE HELPER *See* EVE; WOMAN

SUKKIIM(S), SUKKITES A contingent in the troops of Pharaoh Shishak in his campaign against Jerusalem in the days of Rehoboam (2Ch. 12:3). †

SUKKOTH [booths] *See* FESTIVALS 6.; SUCCOTH

SULPHUR *See* BRIMSTONE

SUMER *See* BABYLON, BABYLONIA

SUMMER *See* CALENDAR; TIME

SUN The sun divides night and day and its rising indicates the E as its setting indicates the W (Ge. 1:14; Ps. 50:1; Isa. 45:6). It is used in Scripture as a symbol of faithfulness and constancy (Jer. 31:35-36).

SUNDAY *See* LORD'S DAY; SABBATH

SUPERNATURAL All events and phenomena that are not natural. For example, a normal birth is wonderful, but not supernatural. A virgin birth is above and beyond how births naturally occur—hence, supernatural.

SUPERSCRIPTION *See* MONEY, *Roman Denarii*

SUPH [reeds, rushes] An unidentified place in Transjordan where Moses delivered an address to Israel (Dt. 1:1). †

SUPHAH An unidentified place, perhaps in Moab (Nu. 21:14). †

SUPPER *See* MEALS and LORD'S SUPPER

SUPPER, LORD'S *See* LORD'S SUPPER

SUPPLICATION *See* PRAYER

SUPREME COMMANDER *See* TARTAN

SURETY One who assumes responsibility for a debt or the fulfillment of an engagement by another. Judah became surety to his father for the safety of Benjamin (Ge. 43:9; 44:32). Jesus is the surety of the New Covenant (Heb. 7:22). The word carries the idea of certainty and guarantee (Ge. 15:13; Ac. 12:11). *See* DEBT; USURY

SURFEITING KJV, ASV for "dissipation" in the RSV and NIV and "carousing" in the NKJV (Lk. 21:34). Synonyms associated with this word are: dizziness, staggering, and hangover. *See* DRINK

SUSA, SHUSHAN The capital of Elam in SW Iran, ancient Persia (Ne. 1:1; Est. 1:2-5; Da. 8:2).

SUSANCHITES A KJV, ASV transliteration in Ezr. 4:9 rendered in most versions as "people *of Susa*, which are the Elamites." *See* SUSA, SHUSHAN

SUSANNA [lily]
1. One of the women who served Jesus (Lk. 8:3). †
2. *See* SCRIPTURE, (4) *History of Susanna*.

SUSI [(my) horse] A descendant of Manasseh (Nu. 13:11). †

SWADDLING CLOTHES An action word that means "to wrap" (in swaddling cloth) (Lk. 2:7, 12; cf. Eze. 16:4). To swaddle is to wrap, bind, or swathe an infant in bands of cloth.

SWALLOW *See* BIRDS 4.

SWAMPS *See* GEOGRAPHY OF THE HOLY LAND, III. C., The Results of Formative Forces, *Swamps*

SWAN KJV for the "white owl" (Lev. 11:18; Dt. 14:16). *See* BIRDS 5.

SWEARING *See* OATH

SWEAT *See* LABOR

SWIFT *See* BIRDS 4.

SWINE *See* BEASTS 10., *Pigs*

SWORD *See* ARMS AND ARMOR

SYCAMINE TREE KJV for "mulberry" tree (Lk. 17:6, most versions). *See* TREES

SYCAMORES, SYCAMORE-FIG *See* TREES, Fruit Trees

SYCHAR A village of Samaria located somewhere near Jacob's well. Jesus met the Samaritan woman there (Jn. 4:5). †

SYCHAR

SYCHEM KJV spelling for Shechem (Ac. 7:16). *See* SHECHEM

SYCOMORE *See* SYCAMORE-FIG

SYENE A village in Egypt called Assuan today (Isa. 49:12; Eze. 30:6). A strange prophecy of the destruction of Egypt from Assuan to the sea is found in Eze. 29:10. The expression "Syene to Migdol" expresses the totality of the land of Egypt in the same way "Dan to Beersheba" does for Israel.

SYMBOLS *See* NUMBERS, SIGNIFICANCE OF; *see also* COLORS

SYMEON, SIMON [he has heard *or* obedient one]
1. A Christian from Antioch; also called Niger (Ac. 13:1).
2. The name of the Apostle Peter (Ac. 15:14).

SYNAGOGUE [place of congregating] A word found some sixty-eight times in the NT of the NIV. In the NIV it is absent in the OT. In the KJV, however, it is used once in the OT also (Ps. 74:8), where the NIV renders it "place of worship." The ancient Greek translation of the OT known as the Septuagint frequently uses the Greek word *synagoge* in reference to the assembly of Israel. The basic concept is that of a gathering of people, and from this the word came to refer to the place where they met (Lk. 12:11; 21:12; Jn. 16:2; 18:20). After the destruction of the first temple in 586 B.C., and thus during the time of the Babylonian captivity and the restoration after it, *synagogue* referred to a group of people meeting together for biblical instruction, study, and prayer. From that time to this day the synagogue has been the center of the religious life of the Jews. The early post-NT literature has descriptions of the buildings and the activities conducted in them. Archaeology is finding in Israel the ruins of synagogues that go back to the first and second centuries A.D. – Masada, Korazin, Capernaum, and others. *See* CHURCH

SYRACUSE: *A resting stop on Paul's journey to Rome*

SYNCRETISM The fusing together of differing beliefs or practices.

SYNOD In the Roman Catholic church a synod is a governing body that helps make legislation or apply canon law. In some Protestant denominations it is an association or maybe governing body that is above the local bishops, pastors, or elders. The converse is the local autonomous church structure that does not answer to another ecclesiastical body in the legal sense.

SYNOPTIC GOSPELS The Gospels of Matthew, Mark, and Luke. *See* GOSPELS, THE FOUR

SYNTYCHE [coincidence, success] A Christian woman of the city of Philippi whom Paul exhorted to be reconciled to Euodia there (Php. 4:2-3). †

SYRACUSE A city on the E coast of the island of Sicily. Paul's ship stayed there several days on his imprisonment journey to Rome (Ac. 28:12). †

SYRIA *See* GEOGRAPHY OF THE HOLY LAND

SYRIA-DAMASCUS KJV for "Aramean Damascus" (1Ch. 18:6).

SYRIAC, SYRIACK KJV for "Aramaic." *See* BIBLICAL LANGUAGES

SYRIAC VERSIONS *See* BIBLE VERSIONS, Ancient Versions

SYRIAN MAACHAH *See* MAACAH, MAACATH, MAACATHITES 10.

SYRIAN PHOENICIA *See* SYROPHENICIAN

SYROPHENICIAN One who lived in the area between Tyre and Sidon. In the NT there is recorded the incident of a Greek woman of the area who won from Jesus the healing of her daughter. So important is this example of persistent asking, persistent prayer, that this incident finds a place in Scripture (Mk. 7:26).

SYRTIS The name of two sandbars on the N coast of Africa where it was easy for ships to run aground; thus, they were feared by the ancient sailors (Ac. 27:17). †

SYSTEMATIC THEOLOGY Systematic theology is an orderly arrangement of truth about God and his work. It can be a useful tool to help us understand the truth about Scripture. It can test our interpretations of any single text and give us a fuller view of a topic of Scripture. Systematic theology should be based on sound biblical interpretation and organize truth inductively. It should, to some degree, glean information from other sources, including church history. The student should be reverent and careful when he comes to the Scriptures. A danger for those involved in systematic theology is that they can discount or re-interpret certain passages of Scripture if they do not fit into one's own system.

The major areas of systematic theology are:

Bibliology (the study or doctrine of the Bible)

Theology Proper (the study or doctrine of God)

Christology (the study or doctrine of the Christ)

Pneumatology (the study or doctrine of the Holy Spirit)

Soteriology (the study or doctrine of Salvation)

Ecclesiology (the study or doctrine of the Church)

Anthropology (the study or doctrine of Man)

Eschatology (the study or doctrine of Last Things)

Angelology (the study or doctrine of [good] Angels)

Demonology (the study or doctrine of Satan and Demons) (J.A.S.)

SYZYGUS _See_ YOKEFELLOW

T

TAANACH An important Canaanite city (170-214) near one of the major passes through the Carmel range, not conquered by Israel at the first but in the tribal area of Manasseh, near Megiddo. An important town in the days of David and Solomon—recently excavated (Jos. 12:21; 17:11; 1Ki. 4:12).

TAANATH SHILOH [*possibly* approach to Shiloh, IDB] A town (185-175) in N Ephraim (Jos. 16:6). †

TABALIAH A gatekeeper of the temple in David's day (1Ch. 26:11). †

TABBAOTH [(ornamental or signet) ring] A family of temple servants who returned from the Babylonian captivity with Zerubbabel (Ezr. 2:43; Ne. 7:46). †

TABBATH [*possibly* good] An unidentified place mentioned in the route by which the Midianites were chased by Gideon (Jdg. 7:22). †

TABEEL, TABEAL [El is good]
1. An officer of King Artaxerxes of Persia (Ezr. 4:7). †
2. The father of a man that Rezin, king of Syria, and Pekah, king of Israel, wanted to make king of Judah (Isa. 7:6). †

TABERAH [burning] An unidentified place on the exodus route from Egypt where the fire of God consumed some of the people as an act of God's punishment (Nu. 11:3; Dt. 9:22). †

TABERNACLE *Tabernaculum* is the Latin word for "tent," which was used to translated the Hebrew *ohel* ("tent"); usually the fuller form *ohel, moed* ("the Tent of Meeting") is used in the Pentateuch, or else *ohel haedut* ("the Tent of the Testimony"). Another common designation was *hammikan* ("the dwellingplace"). This was the portable shrine provided for the worship of God during the period of wandering in the wilderness, while the Israelites of the Exodus were making their way to Canaan. It also served their needs after the conquest until the time of King David; it was replaced in the reign of Solomon by his splendid temple around 960 B.C.

The tabernacle consisted of a large tent measuring 30 cubits by 10 cubits, surrounded by a court 100 cubits by 50. (The cubit measured between eighteen and twenty inches.) The court was enclosed by large curtains or drapes hanging from poles supported by twenty pillars on each long side and ten on each short side. At the east end was a separate hanging at the entrance. Between the entrance gate and the entrance at the E end of the tabernacle itself was: (a) a large altar for blood sacrifice, measuring 5 cubits by 5, and 3 cubits high; it consisted of a hollow box of acacia wood overlaid with bronze; (b) a large basin or laver (*kiyyor*) of bronze, containing water for washing the hands and feet of priests who were about to enter the tent itself. Inside the tent was the "Holy Place" (*qodesh*), measuring 20 cubits by 10 cubits and containing: (c) on the N side a gold-overlaid "table of shewbread" (*sulhan welehem panim*, "table and bread of the Presence"), two cubits by one cubit, one and a half cubits tall—it was intended to hold twelve loaves made from fine flour, representing the twelve tribes; (d) on the S side a seven-branched lampstand (*menorah*) of beaten gold, holding seven lamps, which were to be daily trimmed and cared for by the priests; (e) right in front of the curtain leading into the inner sanctum a small golden altar for incense, one cubit square and two cubits tall; it consisted of an acacia box overlaid with gold. The separating curtain in front of it was so constructed as to permit the smoke of incense to enter and pervade the inner sanctum. This sanctum was called "the Holy of Holies (*qodes qodasim*, i.e., most holy place), or the "oracle" (*debir*— "rear room"), measuring ten cubits square, and containing only the Ark of the Covenant (*'ron berit*) or Ark of the Testimony (*rom ha'edut*, so called because it contained the two tablets of the Law—the Decalogue). It consisted of a chest made of acacia, heavily overlaid with gold and covered with a solid gold lid called "the propitiary" (*hakkapporet*, AV "mercyseat"), fashioned into two facing cherubim with outstretched wings touching each other. Upon this the high priest was to sprinkle the atoning blood each yearly Day of Atonement (*yom kippur*). After being skillfully constructed under Spirit-empowered master-craftsmen, Bezalel and Oholiab (Ex. 35:30, 34), it was solemnly dedicated to God's service on the first month of the second year after the Exodus (Ex. 40:17) and sanctified by the presence of his Shekinah glory. (G.L.A.) *See* CALENDAR and FESTIVALS

TABITHA [gazelle] A Christian woman of Joppa whom Peter raised from the dead; also called Dorcas (Ac. 9:36-40). †

TABLE The translation of many different Hebrew and Greek words, tables for eating, writing, money changers and for ritual vessels being among them. Two special tables should be noted: the tables of the Law and the Table of the Lord. The former were the two stone tablets upon which the Ten Commandments were written, and the latter refers to both the altar of burnt offering and the Christian Communion table (Mal. 1:7, 12; 1Co. 10:21).

TABLE OF SHEWBREAD *See* SHOWBREAD

TABLES OF THE LAW *See* DECALOGUE; LAW

TABLET KJV in Ex. 35:22; Nu. 31:50 for "ornament"; in Isa. 3:20 for "bottle of perfume." *See* DRESS

TABOR
1. On Mt. Tabor and the plain of Tabor, *see* GEOGRAPHY OF THE HOLY LAND.
2. An unidentified Levitical town in the tribal area of Zebulun (1Ch. 6:77); perhaps to be identified with Daberath.

TABRET *See* MUSIC, MUSICAL INSTRUMENTS 2., *Tambourine*

TABRI(M)MON [(pagan god) RIMMON is good] The father of Ben Hadad, king of Syria (1Ki. 15:18). †

TACHE KJV for "clasp" (Ex. 26:6, 11; 35:11; 36:13, 18; 39:33). They were used to fasten the curtains of the tabernacle together. *See* TABERNACLE

The Tabernacle

TACHEMONITE, TACHMONITE *See* TAHKEMONITE

TADMOR An important spot on one of the main trade routes between Egypt, Palestine and Mesopotamia (NE of Damascus in the desert). As such it would have great antiquity, but it came into prominence when Solomon built it up and later when the Romans made a great city, Palmyra, there (1Ki. 9:18; 2Ch. 8:4). †

TAHAN, TAHANITE(S) [*possibly* grace, favor]
1. A son of Ephraim and the founder of the Tahanites (Nu. 26:35). †
2. A later descendant of Ephraim (1Ch. 7:25). †

TAHAPANES *See* TAHPANHES

TAHASH [a species of dolphin] A son of Nahor and thus nephew of Abraham (Ge. 22:24). †

TAHATH [compensation]
1, 2, and 3. A Levite and two descendants of Ephraim (1Ch. 6:24; 7:20).

TAHKEMONITE, TAHCHEMON-ITE The family of the chief of David's three mighty men (2Sa. 23:8).

TAHPANHES [the fortress of Penhase (the Black Man)] A city of ancient Egypt by an important road between Egypt and Palestine in the NE part of the Delta (Jer. 2:16; 43:7-9; 46:14). *See* TE-HAPHNEHES

TAHPENES [*title* wife of the king] The queen of Egypt whose sister married the Edomite prince Hadad (1Ki. 11:19-20). †

TAHREA [*possibly* clever one, BDB] A descendant of Saul through Mephibosheth; also called Tarea (1Ch. 8:35; 9:41). †

TAHTIM HODSHI 2Sa. 24:6. † The RSV, JB, NEB conjectures based on ancient versions, and in some versions' footnotes, "to Kadesh land of the Hittites."

TALE *See* MYTHS

TALENT *See* MONEY; WEIGHTS AND MEASURES

TALITHA CUMI [little lamb, rise] Aramaic words which Jesus spoke when he raised Jairus's daughter, "Little girl, I say to you, get up" (Mk. 5:41).

TALMAI [*possibly* (my) furrow maker]
1. A descendant of Anak at Hebron whom Caleb drove out (Nu. 13:22; Jos. 15:14).
2. The king of Geshur whose daughter was one of David's wives (2Sa. 3:3; 1Ch. 3:2).

TALMON A family of temple gatekeepers, some of whom returned from the Babylonian captivity and resumed the same occupation in the time of Nehemiah (Ezr. 2:42; Ne. 11:19).

TALMUD [education, instruction] Consisting of two similar bodies of tradition, the Palestine and Babylon Talmud. The Babylonian is the authoritative body of tradition in the Jewish religion consisting of the Mishna (codified oral law now written down) and the Gemera (commentary on the Mishna). *See* TRADITION

TAMAH *See* TEMAH

TAMAR [date palm]
1. A Canaanite woman who married Er, then Onan, and then bore Perez and Zerah to her father-in-law Judah. These were in the ancestry of Jesus (Ge. 38:6-9, 12ff.; Ru. 4:12; Mt. 1:3).
2 and 3. A sister and a daughter of Absalom (2Sa. 13:1ff.; 14:27).
4. A city (173-024) in the SE part of Judah in the Arabah S of the Dead Sea (Eze. 47:18-19; 48:28).

TAMARISK *See* TREES

TAMBOURINE *See* MUSIC

TAMIR *See* TADMOR

TANACH *See* TAANACH

TANAKH A word that is an abbreviation for what the Christians call the Hebrew OT; (T) Hebrew for "Law"; (N) Hebrew for "Prophets"; (K) Hebrew for

"Writings." These three sections comprise the canon of the Christian OT, Genesis to Malachi, but in different order and in slightly different configurations (Lk. 24:44 – the Book of Psalms heads the "Writings" section).

TANHUMETH [comfort] The father of one who joined Governor Gedaliah (2Ki. 25:23; Jer.40:8). †

TANIS *See* ZOAR

TANNER One who prepared skins by treating them with lime from the bark or leaves of certain trees or the juice of certain plants (Ex. 25:5; 35:7, 23; Ac. 10:6).

TAPHATH [*possibly (fem.) for* little child] A daughter of King Solomon (1Ki. 4:11). †

TAPPUAH [apple]
1. An unidentified city in the Shephelah of Judah (Jos. 15:34).
2. A city (172-168) on the border between Ephraim and Manasseh conquered by Joshua. Its spring was called Entappuah (Jos. 12:17; 16:8; 17:7-8).
3. A son or descendant of Hebron and Caleb (1Ch. 2:43).

TARAH *See* TERAH

TARALAH An unidentified town in the tribal area of Benjamin (Jos. 18:27). †

TAREA *See* TAHREA

TARES *See* PLANTS, PERFUMES, AND SPICES, Miscellaneous Plants 14., *Weeds*

TARPELITES [officials] KJV for "men from Tripolis" (Ezr. 4:9).

TARSHISH, SHIPS OF TARSHISH [*possibly* (precious stone) yellow jasper, BDB; *possibly* greedy one, IDB; foundry, refinery, KB]
1. A descendant of Noah (Ge. 10:4), associated with others related to Javan, the probable ancestor of the Greeks in the Aegean area.
2. An unidentified port perhaps somewhere in the western Mediterranean with which important trade was conducted. It may have been as far away

as western Spain. Jonah took a ship for there in his running from the LORD (Jnh. 1:3). At first the trade was with this place, and then later the ships which used that route came to be called "ships of Tarshish." This type of ship then even put out from Ezion Geber in the Red Sea (1Ki. 10:22; Isa. 23:14).
3. A descendant of Benjamin (1Ch. 7:10).
4. One of the seven eunuchs of the Persian king Ahasuerus (Est. 1:14).

TARSUS A city in Cilicia in Asia Minor (peninsula, not Roman province), the hometown of the Apostle Paul (Ac. 9:11, 30; 11:25; 21:39; 22:3). †

PAUL'S RETURN TO TARSUS
After time alone in Arabia, Paul returned to Damascus and then to Jerusalem. The apostles found it hard to believe that this former persecutor could be a Christian. He went to Caesarea where he boarded a ship bound for Tarsus.

TARTAK *See* DEITIES 1.

TARTAN [*title* field marshall, BDB; second in command, KB] Not a proper name but rather a title of a top military officer in the Assyrian army (2Ki. 18:17).

TASSEL *See* FRINGES

TASTE A figure for experiential knowledge (Ps. 34:8; Mt. 16:28; Jn. 8:52; 1Pe. 2:3).

TATNAI, TATTENAI The Persian governor W of the Jordan River who was ordered by the Persian king to help the

Jews in their rebuilding of the temple in the days of Ezra, after he had tried to stop it (Ezr. 5:3-6; 6:6-13). †

TATTOO Several words in the original are at work here. One was a cutting of the body, forbidden in Scripture. Though clearly a pagan practice, it is unclear if this included putting pigment in the cut (Lev. 19:28). The most common idea of a sign or distinguishing mark on a person is the same word as that of a miracle "sign." This mark (seal) can protect the person (Ge. 4:15; Eze. 9:4; Rev. 7:3). A phylactery was a sign (Ex. 13:9; Dt. 6:8). The Beast's mark has the idea of a cutting, etching, engraving or branding and also may pertain to ownership and submission (Rev. 13:16-18; 14:9, 11; 19:20; 20:4).

TAVERNS, THREE The place where the Christians of Rome met Paul to accompany him to Rome, just over thirty miles SE of Rome (Ac. 28:15). Taverns were shops or huts.

TAX COLLECTOR *See* TAXES, TAXING; TRIBUTE; ZACCHAEUS

TAXES, TAXING In earliest times gifts were given to rulers and other governing persons in return for protection and other favors. Later, forced labor and money were required. The tribute charged by conquering monarchs was forced tax (Ex. 30:13; Jos. 16:10; 2Ki. 17:3; Mk. 2:14; Lk. 19:2).

TEACHER A word frequently interchanged with *master* in the translations and many times applied to Jesus in the NT (Mt. 8:19; Lk. 9:38). A leader in the church must be able to teach, and teaching is one of the gifts of the Spirit (Eph. 4:11; 1Ti. 3:2; 2Ti. 2:24). *See* GOD, NAMES OF; GODHEAD; LORD; RABBI

TEBAH [*possibly* one born at the time or place of slaughtering, KB and IDB]
1. A Syrian city from which David took much spoil (2Sa. 8:8).
2. A son of Nahor and nephew of Abraham (Ge. 22:24).

TEBALIAH [Yahweh has dipped (*i.e.*, ceremonial purity)] *See* TABALIAH

TEBETH *See* CALENDAR

TEHAPHNEHES [the fortress of Penhase (the Black Man)] An alternate form of Tahpanhes (Eze. 30:18, KJV and RSV). *See also* TAHPANHES

TEHINNAH [supplication for favor] A descendant of Judah (1Ch. 4:12). †

TEIL TREE *See* TREES, Other Trees, *Oak and Terebinth*

TEKEL *See* MENE, MENE, TEKEL, AND PARSIN

TEKOA(H), TEKOITE A city (170-115) of Judah S of Jerusalem. It was one of the towns that Rehoboam fortified and the hometown of the prophet Amos (2Sa. 14:2-9; 2Ch. 11:6; Am. 1:1).

TEL *See* TELL

TEL ASSAR [ruined city mound of ASSAR] An unidentified place, whose gods, according to the Rabshakeh of Assyria, were not able to deliver their people from the Assyrians (2Ki. 19:12; Isa. 37:12). †

TEL AVIV, TEL-ABIB [mound of barley, ISBE; *Akkadian* mound of storm tide, KB; mound of flood, IDB] A place in Babylonia where Ezekiel visited Jewish exiles in the days of the Babylonian captivity (Eze. 3:15). †

TEL HARSHA, TEL-HARESHA An unidentified place in Babylonia from which some captives returned to Israel with Zerubbabel (Ezr. 2:59; Ne. 7:61). †

TEL MELAH, TEL-MELAH [ruined city and mound of salt] A city in the same category as Tel Harsha above (Ezr. 2:59; Ne. 7:61; cf. Jdg. 9:45). †

TELAH [fissure, split, fracture] A descendant of Ephraim (1Ch. 7:25). †

TELAIM [lambs] An unidentified place, probably in Judah, where Saul mustered his army to go against the Amalekites (1Sa. 15:4). †

TELEM

1. An unidentified city of Judah (Jos. 15:24). †

2. One who married a foreign wife during the Babylonian captivity (Ezr. 10:24). †

TELL A mound in which are buried the ruins of ancient cities, one upon the other. Such cities were usually walled and in this way distinguished from other ancient town or city ruins, called Khirbets. The Hebrew word *tel* is sometimes translated "mound of ruins" (Dt. 13:16; Jer. 49:2; 30:18).

TEMA {on the right side, *hence* south country} One of the twelve sons of Ishmael and founder of a tribe that lived in the area of the Arabian desert by that name (Ge. 25:12-16; Job 6:19; Jer. 25:23).

TEMAH The ancestor of some temple servants who returned from the Babylonian captivity with Zerubbabel (Ezr. 2:53; Ne. 7:55).

TEMAN {on the right side, *hence* south country}

1. A city (197-971) in Edom where the Temanites lived (Jer.49:7). One of the most mentioned is Job's friend Eliphaz (Job 2:11; 4:1).

2. A grandson of Esau and an Edomite chief, probably the one who gave the name to the area noted above (Ge. 36:11, 15).

TEMANI, TEMANITES An inhabitant from the city of Teman. *See* TEMAN 1.

TEMENI {one from the right, *hence* southerner (palestine)} A descendant of Judah (1Ch. 4:6). †

TEMPLE, THE In the fourth year of Solomon's reign (c. 965 B.C.), construction was begun on the national temple of Israel in Jerusalem (1Ki. 6:1). Its dimensions were double those of the tabernacle: sixty cubits by twenty cubits (the cubit being eighteen to twenty inches long); and it was thirty cubits in height. These would appear to have been the inside measurements, not including the chambers, arranged in three stories, which flanked the N and S walls, and were intended for storage purposes and living quarters for officiating priests. In front of the entrance porch at the eastern end stood two pillars of cast bronze named Jachin and Boaz (possibly pet names for "*yakin* Yahweh" ("Jehovah will establish") and "*boaz hammelek*" ("In him the king is strong"). These were each eighteen cubits high and twelve cubits in circumference (1Ki. 7:15), surmounted by lily-shaped capitals five cubits in height. The temple walls were constructed of hewn stone, paneled with cedar overlaid with gold, and adorned with carved cherubim, palms, garlands, and flowers (1Ki. 6:18). The ceiling was flat, consisting of cedar beams with gold overlay, and roofed over the marble. The inner sanctum measured twenty cubits by twenty cubits and contained the Mosaic Ark of the Covenant, set between two standing cherubim ten cubits tall, with outstretched wings five cubits wide, touching the wingtip of each other with one wing, and the wall of the sanctum with the other. The entrance to the sanctum consisted of a door with hinges (1Ki. 7:50), rather than the veil or curtain of the tabernacle and of Herod's temple (Mt. 27:51). Inside the "Holy Place," measuring forty cubits by twenty were placed: (a) a golden altar of incense with a cedar frame, presumably larger than that of the tabernacle (possibly two cubits square and four cubits tall); (b) ten golden lampstands of seven branches each, five on the N side and five on the S; (c) ten gold-overlaid tables of shewbread, likewise five on each side. The entrance to the Holy Place or "house" had a gold-plated door like that into the sanctum sanctorum (i.e., Holy of Holies).

In the court of the Solomonic temple was a huge round basin of bronze, ten cubits in diameter (1Ki. 7:23), mounted upon twelve bronze oxen that stood back to back facing toward the four compass directions. There were also ten smaller basins four cubits in diameter, each mounted upon smaller basins four cubits in diameter, mounted upon four wheels, presumably for ceremonial cleansing of the priests, but possibly also for washing portions of sacrifices to be burnt on the altar The altar of burnt offering was twenty cubits square and ten cubits high (2Ch. 4:1), which must have required some sort of ramp or platform to be usable by the officiating priest. Apparently the blood of the sacrifices was carried off by a large pipe bored through a hole in the celebrated rock, which is now surmounted by the Dome of the Rock; the drain system carried the flow out to a spout emptying into the Kidron Valley.

The inner court of the temple was of unspecified dimensions but built upon a higher level than the outer court (Jer. 36:10) and surrounded by a wall composed of three layers of stone surmounted by cedar beams. The "great court" (2Ch. 4:9) was intended for the lay public and was probably enclosed by another wall. This entire temple precinct was situated on Mt. Moriah, along with various palaces and audience halls erected on the northern sector for governmental purposes.

The second temple, erected by Zerubbabel and finally completed about 516 B.C. after two decades of frustration and delay, was apparently erected on the foundations of Solomon's temple and was therefore of the same dimensions, although of far less expensive materials and workmanship. It seems to have contained no Ark of the Covenant, since the original Ark was lost during the exile. It may have had only one lampstand in the Holy Place, since Antiochus Epiphanes found only one to carry off as spoil in 168 B.C. In December 165 the desecrated temple was cleansed and rededicated by Judas Maccabeus. Around 19 B.C. Herod the Great undertook a major renovation and enlargement, which was not finally completed until A.D. 64. He built a new porch 100 cubits wide and 100 cubits high, and a gate measuring twenty cubits by forty. An empty room above the holy place raised it another sixty cubits to a total height of 100 cubits. The size

of the courts was greatly enlarged; the foundations of two of the S gates have been found under the present el-Aqsa Mosque. The entire structure was leveled to the ground by the Romans under Titus in A.D. 70, and it has never been rebuilt since that time. (G.L.A.)

TEMPTATION An attempt to entice to do evil. It may be the exact opposite of testing, which, if surmounted, brings spiritual strength and good. One is inspired by Satan (Eph. 6:11), the other by God (Dt. 8:16; Job 23:10; 1Pe. 1:7). The record of the attempts of Satan to tempt Christ is found in Mt. 4:1-11. Christ, the second Adam, was victorious in his temptation, while the first Adam failed in his (Ge. 3:1-7). *See* TRIAL

TEMPTER *See* DEVIL

TEN COMMANDMENTS *See* LAW

TENDONS *See* SINEW

TENS In addition to its meaning as a number, a "ten" was a military unit of troops (Ex. 18:21; Dt. 1:15). *See* NUMBERS, SIGNIFICANCE OF

TENTS, FEAST OF *See* BOOTH; TABERNACLE

TENT OF MEETING, TENT OF THE CONGREGATION *See* TABERNACLE

TENTMAKER As was common among many rabbis, Paul worked with his hands. His craft was leather working. Tents were made of both leather or goat hair cloth. Prisca and Aquila were also of the same craft (Ac. 18:3).

TERAH The father of Abraham (Ge. 11:24-28, 31-32; Nu. 33:27-28; Jos. 24:2; 1Ch. 1:26). He is mentioned in the genealogy of Jesus (Lk. 3:34). †

TERAPHIM *See* DEITIES 3.; DIVINATION

TEREBINTH *See* TREES

TEREBINTH, DOVE OF FAR-OFF *See* PSALMS, TITLES OF 10., (3)

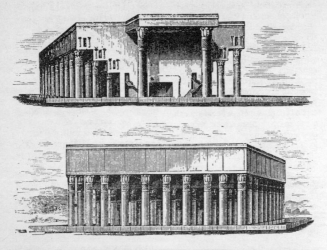

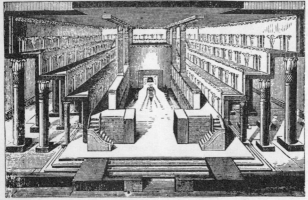

Solomon's Temple

TERESH A eunuch of the Persian king Ahasuerus (Est. 2:21; 6:2). †

TERROR *See* FEAR

TERTIUS [third] Paul's amanuensis (one who takes dictation) in the writing of the Book of Romans, who added his own greeting at the end (Ro. 16:22). †

TERTULLUS [third] One of those who brought accusation against Paul before Felix (Ac. 24:1ff.).

TEST *See* TEMPTATION

TESTAMENT A written document by which a person disposes of his estate after his death, usually known today as a "will." The word *testament* is not found in the NIV, where the Greek word *diatheke* is rather rendered by "covenant" (1Co. 11:25; Heb. 9:15-20). *See* COVENANT

TESTAMENTS OF THE XII PROPHETS *See* SCRIPTURE, *apocrypha*

TESTIFY *See* WITNESS

TESTIMONIES, TESTIMONY A synonym of commandments, statutes, and ordinances, the laws God gave his people by which he intended them to live and conduct themselves (Dt. 4:45; Ps. 99:7; 119:24). The word in the singular often refers to that which was placed in the Ark of the Covenant, also called the Ark of the Testimony (Ex. 40:3), the Ten Commandments, and other testimonial items which were to remind the people of their deliverance from Egypt and their preservation in the wilderness wanderings (Ex. 25:16; 31:18). In the NT God bears witness (testimony) to his Son; and this is the testimony that God gave us — eternal life — and this life is in the Son (1Jn. 5:9-12).

TETRAGRAMMATON *See* YHWH

TETRARCH {ruler of a fourth part} The title of a petty ruler in the Roman Empire even though such a ruler was sometimes called a king (Mt. 14:1; Mk. 6:14, 26; Lk. 3:1; Ac. 13:1). It seems probably that the three titles — king, ethnarch, and tetrarch — were somewhat interchangeable. Their roles are not exactly definable.

TETTER *See* SICK, SICKNESS 1., *Leprosy*

TEXTS AND VERSIONS *See* BIBLE VERSIONS, ANCIENT VERSIONS

TEXTUAL CRITICISM *See* CRITICISM, TEXTUAL

TEXTUS RECEPTUS *Latin* for "received text." The generally accepted body of literature. The Textus Receptus is also a name for the Greek NT published by the Elzevir brothers in the early seventeenth century.

THADDAEUS {*possibly* breast nipple} *See* APOSTLES

THAHASH *See* TAHASH

THAMAH *See* TEMAH

THAMAR *See* TAMAR 1.

THANK OFFERING *See* SACRIFICES AND OFFERINGS

THANKSGIVING *See* EUCHARIST; LORD'S SUPPER; PRAISE

THARA *See* TERAH

THARSHISH *See* TARSHISH (1Ch. 7:10), "trading ship" (1Ki. 10:22, NIV).

THEATER A structure which apparently did not exist in OT times but came into use in Greece in the middle of the first millennium B.C. and which is mentioned twice in the NT (Ac. 19:29, 31). The ancients made use of semicircular seating arrangements in natural hollows in hillsides conducive for an audience to watch a dramatic presentation or hear a lecture.

THEBES The capital of Egypt during the Eighteenth Dynasty, now known as Karnak and Luxor, where the ancient ruins are still standing after more than 3,000 years. God pronounced judgment upon Thebes by the prophets (Jer. 46:25; Eze. 30:14-16).

THEBEZ A town in the tribal area of Ephraim NE of Shechem. Gideon's son took it but was also killed there when a woman dropped a millstone on his head (Jdg. 9:50; 2Sa. 11:21). †

THEISM Belief in deity in the most general sense. *See* HENOTHEISM; MONOTHEISM; POLYTHEISM

THEISTIC EVOLUTION *See* EVOLUTION, THEISTIC

THELASAR *See* TEL ASSAR

THEOCRACY {rule of God} The rule of a nation by God.

THEOLOGY The study of God and his relation to his creation and how he reveals himself. *See* SYSTEMATIC THEOLOGY

THEBEZ

THEOLOGY OF LIBERATION *See* LIBERATION THEOLOGY

THEOLOGY PROPER *See* SYSTEMATIC THEOLOGY

THEOPHANY [appearance of God] Manifestation of God, usually to his people—by voice (Ge. 3:8; Mt. 17:5); by the burning bush (Ex. 3:2-6); by the pillar and cloud; by thunder, lightning, dark black smoke (Ex. 19:16); by the Angel of the LORD (*see* ANGEL).

Jesus Christ was not only an appearance of God, but God himself (Jn. 1:1). God became flesh and lived among mankind (Jn. 1:14). The one seeing Jesus has seen the Father (Jn. 14:9).

THEOPHILUS [friend of God] Luke addressed both of his books to a person by this name (Lk. 1:3; Ac. 1:1). †

THEOSOPHY A mystical religion originating in the U.S. in 1875. Followers believe in pantheism and evolutionary reincarnation, much as a Buddhist does.

THESSALONIANS, BOOKS OF *See* PAULINE EPISTLES

THESSALONICA Named after the sister of Alexander the Great, Thessalonica is a city in Macedonia visited by Paul on his missionary journeys (Ac. 17:1, 11, 13; Php. 4:16).

THEUDAS [gift of God] A Jewish leader who raised a political uprising some time before the ministry of Christ

began, to which Gamaliel referred (Ac. 5:36). †

THIEF, THIEVES *See* STEALING

THIGH *See* HIP AND THIGH

THIMNATHAH *See* TIMNAH 1.

THIRST In the Western culture where water is usually not more than a water tap away, today's Bible student has a hard time experiencing deep-down thirst.

1. Thirst is often referred to literally (Ex. 17:3). Christians are to give water to the thirsty enemy (Ro. 12:20).

2. Thirst for God is an intense figure of longing for God (Ps. 42:1-2; 63:1; 143:6; Rev. 22:17). *See* SOUL 5.; WATER

THISTLE *See* PLANTS, PERFUMES, AND SPICES, Spiny Plants

THOMAS [twin] *See* APOSTLES

THOMAS, GOSPEL OF *See* SCRIPTURE, *Pseudepigrapha*

THORN IN THE FLESH Paul's ailment mentioned in 2Co. 12:7. Varied suggestions have been offered as to his malady, none really certain. The figure of pain and irritation that comes from a thorn-inflamed sore is certainly vivid enough for empathy toward Paul.

THORNS *See* PLANTS, PERFUMES, AND SPICES, Spiny Plants

THOUSAND YEARS *See* ESCHATOLOGY; MILLENNIUM

THOUSANDS The designation of a military unit in addition to its literal numerical value (Nu. 31:14, 52, 54; 2Ch. 25:5). *See* NUMBERS, SIGNIFICANCE OF

THREE HOLY CHILDREN, SONG OF *See* SCRIPTURE, *Apocrypha*

THREE TAVERNS *See* TAVERNS, THREE

THRESHING, THRESHING FLOOR The latter is a flat place on very hard soil or better on rock where grain was threshed in one of several ways: by beating with a flail or by oxen who drew wooden sleds with notched bottoms over the grain. When the kernels were loosened from the stalks, wooden shovels or forks were used to toss the grain and chaff so that a strong wind would blow the chaff away and the kernels would fall below and be collected (Dt. 25:4; Isa. 28:27; 30:24; 1Ti. 5:18). *See* WINNOWING

THRONE A symbol of majesty and authority on which kings, governors, judges, and high priests would sit (Ge. 41:40; Ps. 9:7). God is pictured as seated on a throne (Isa. 6:1-3; Da. 7:9; Rev. 4:2-11). In the end of days the Messiah and the twelve apostles will be seated on thrones (Mt. 25:31).

THUMMIM *See* URIM AND THUMMIM

THUNDER Thunder and lightning are not everyday occurrences in Palestine. In fact, they are rather rare and usually limited to short periods in either the spring or fall. In the Bible they are interpreted frequently as a manifestation of divine power and are a part of the imagery with which the throne of God in heaven is described (Dt. 32:41; Job 26:14; 28:26; Eze. 1:24; Rev. 4:5). It is interesting to note the references to these storms coming from the E, as they do frequently (Jdg. 5:4-5; Mt. 24:27).

THUNDER, SONS OF *See* BOANERGES

THUTMOSE [(Egyptian god) Thoth is born] *See* EGYPT, Dyn. XVIII-XX, Thothmes III

THYATIRA An important commercial center in the province of Asia in Paul's day. When Paul was in Philippi, he met a seller of purple goods from Thyatira by the name of Lydia (Ac. 16:12-15). One of the letters to the seven churches of Asia Minor found in the Book of Revelation was written to the church at Thyatira (Rev. 1:11; 2:18, 24). †

THYINE *See* PLANTS, PERFUMES, AND SPICES, *Citronella* (Ex. 30:23)

TIBERIAS A city on the W side of the Sea of Galilee (201-242) founded by Herod Antipas between A.D. 2025 and named in honor of Tiberius Caesar who reigned in Rome from A.D. 14-37. Even as early as NT times the Sea of Galilee was also called by that name (Jn. 6:1, 23), and the city itself is once mentioned.

TIBERIAS, SEA OF *See* SEA OF GALILEE; *See also* TIBERIAS

TIBERIUS The reigning Roman emperor at the time of the crucifixion of Christ. The baptism of Jesus took place in his fifteenth year. He reigned from A.D. 14 to 37 (Lk. 3:1). †

TIBHATH A city in Syria which David captured and whose riches he took to Jerusalem (1Ch. 18:8).

TIBNI *See* KINGS OF JUDAH AND ISRAEL

TIDAL The king of Goiim (KJV "Nations"), one of those aligned against the confederacy at the southern end of the Dead Sea in Abraham's time (Ge. 14:1, 9). †

TIGLATH-PILESER, TILGATH-PILNESER [my trust is in the son of (the temple) Esharra] A famous name among Assyrian kings. *See* ASSYRIA

TIGRIS The KJV transliterates the Hebrew word "Hiddekel" in Ge. 2:14; Da. 10:4 for the name of a river. The NIV has "Tigris River." †

TIKVAH {hope}
1. The father-in-law of the prophetess Huldah; also called Tokhath (2Ki. 22:14; 2Ch. 34:22). †
2. The father of one who opposed the plan for dealing with those who had taken foreign wives during the Babylonian captivity (Ezr. 10:15). †

TIKVATH *See* TIKVAH

TILES A word found only in Lk. 5:19 in the account of the lowering of the paralytic through the roof in order to get him into the presence of Jesus. Tiles were not a common roof material in NT times. Mark refers to "removing the roof."

Some suggest that Luke is using the expression "through the tiles" in an idiomatic sense.

TILON A descendant of Judah (1Ch. 4:20). †

TIMAEUS [precious, valuable] The father of the blind Bartimaeus at Jericho whose sight was restored by Jesus (Mk. 10:46).

TIMBREL *See* MUSIC, *Tambourine*

TIME On the division of time into periods *see* CALENDAR. Time in the sense of knowing how many years a king reigned or that it was 480 years from the Exodus to the building of the temple was known and used in ancient Israel, of course. But time is something abstract. The idea of the abstract continuity of time is foreign to biblical concept. Time in the Bible is rather the concept of a particular moment of history. They referred to events such as the Exodus, the Babylonian captivity, the earthquake (Am. 1:1), and not to time as a continuum when they used the words we render into English as "time." The Bible lays the emphasis on "times" as points at which God himself does certain things on the earth and in his universe. When we read, "My times are in your [God's] hands" the picture is not that of the x number of years that my life will run but rather of the events that will be happening to me (Ps. 31:15). When we read of "eternity" or "forever," the concept is not the continuity of the time but rather the events of that particular period. The Hebrew has no clear word for eternity. The words *ad* and *olam* usually translated as "eternity" refer to periods of time of which the coming end is not known or determined. For example, Samuel was to be left at the tabernacle "for ever" (KJV), that is for the full duration of his life, for an example (1Sa. 1:22). *See also* FUTURE LIFE

TIMES, OBSERVER OF *See* DIVINATION, DIVINE

TIMEUS [precious, valuable] *See* TIMAEUS

TIMNA [lot, portion]
1. A concubine of the son of Esau (Ge. 36:12).
2. A grandson of Esau (1Ch. 1:36).
3. A daughter of Seir and Horite (Ge. 36:22; 1Ch. 1:39).
4. A chief of Esau, that is Edom (Ge. 36:40).

TIMNAH, TIMNATH [lot, portion]
1. A town (141-132) near Beth Shemesh that is perhaps best known from the Samson incidents. It was in the tribal area of Dan. Uzziah took it from the Philistines and Sennacherib conquered it later (Jdg. 14:5; Jos. 15:10; 19:43).
2. An unidentified town in the hill country of Judah (Jos. 15:57).

TIMNATH HERES, TIMNATH SERAH [place of the sun (worship)] Joshua's inheritance (160-157) in the tribal area of Ephraim, where he was also buried (Jdg. 2:9; Jos. 19:50; 24:30). There are a number of suggestions, none of them altogether satisfactory, as to the reason for the two forms of the name.

TIMNITE A person from the town or village of Timnah. *See* TIMNAH 1.

TIMON [precious, valuable] One of the seven early deacons of the church (Ac. 6:5). †

TIMOTHEUS [precious one of God] *See* TIMOTHY

TIMOTHY [precious one of God] A young man who came to know Christ through Paul and then went on to be his close friend and traveling companion (Php. 2:19-22; 1Ti. 1:2). He had a devout Jewish mother from whom he learned the Scriptures from infancy (2Ti. 1:5; 3:15), factors which made him the man he was.

TIMOTHY, BOOKS OF *See* PAULINE EPISTLES

TIN *See* PRECIOUS STONES AND METALS, Metals 2.

TINEA *See* SCALL

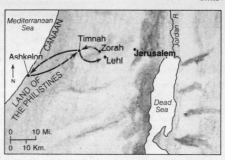

TIMNAH Samson, of Zorah, wanted to marry a Philistine woman of Timnah. Having been tricked at his marriage feast, he went to Ashkelon, killed some Philistines, and brought their coats to pay off a debt. Then he went to Lehi where he killed 1,000 men.

TINKLING KJV for "clanging" (1Co. 13:2).

TINSHAMETH *See* BEASTS 6.; MOLE

TIPHSAH

1. A town on the trade route between Palestine and Mesopotamia on the Euphrates River, the northernmost point of Solomon's realm (1Ki. 4:24). †

2. An unidentified town in the tribal area of Ephraim or Manasseh, N of Jerusalem (2Ki. 15:16). †

TIRAS One of the sons of Japheth (Ge. 10:2; 1Ch. 1:5). †

TIRATHITES A family of scribes that lived at Jabez (1Ch. 2:55). †

TIRE *See* DRESS, *headgear* or *turban*

TIRHAKAH A king of Ethiopia, about 689 B.C., who became the king of Egypt also, in the Twenty-fifth Dynasty (2Ki. 19:9; Isa. 37:9). †

TIRHANAH A son of Caleb (1Ch. 2:48). †

TIRIA A descendant of Judah (1Ch. 4:16). †

TIRSHATHA KJV for "governor" (Ezr. 2:63; Ne. 7:65, 70; 8:9; 10:1). †

TIRZAH [pleasant one *or* compensation]

1. The youngest daughter of Zelophehad who had no sons and so requested that his daughters be given land in the division under Joshua (Nu. 26:33; 27:1; Jos. 17:3).

2. The capital (182-188) of the northern tribes for forty years until Omri built Samaria, known today as Tell el-Far'ah (Jos. 12:24; 1Ki. 14:17; 15:21; 16:6-23).

TISHBE, TISHBITE An unidentified city in Gilead, the home of the prophet Elijah (1Ki. 17:1; 21:17; 2Ki. 1:3, 8; 9:36).

TITHE, TITHES [a tenth] The principle of a 10 percent tax is ancient and not limited to the Bible. Abraham was accustomed to it at the beginning of the second millennium B.C. (Heb. 7:59). Jacob promised it to God (Ge. 28:22). The tithe (10 percent) of everything (Ge. 14:18-20) was the LORD's, and he gave it as an inheritance to the Levites (Lev. 27:30-32; Nu. 18:21-26). The laws of tithing were spelled out in Dt. 12:6-17 and 14:22-28. The economy in Roman times made tithing a difficulty, but it was still observed by the faithful (Mt. 23:23; Lk. 18:12). While tithing is not required as such in the NT, proportionate giving is (1Co. 16:2; 2Co. 8—9). *See* GIVING

TITTLE KJV for "smallest stroke," a projecting point, or hook (Gr. *horn*) on a letter. For example, the difference between a minuscule *t* and a majuscule *T* is the small projecting point above the horizontal line of that letter (Mt. 5:18). *See also* JOT

TITUS A Gentile convert to Christianity and helper of Paul. A significant event in his life was Paul's refusing to allow his circumcision in Jerusalem on the grounds that he was a Gentile and that circumcision was not necessary to salvation or membership in the church (Gal. 2:3). He served Paul in both Corinth and Crete (2Co. 2:13; 7:6-14; 8:6-23; 12:18). Paul wrote one of his epistles to him.

TITUS, BOOK OF *See* PAULINE EPISTLES

TITUS JUSTUS *See* JUSTUS

TIZITE A designation of one of David's mighty men (1Ch. 11:45). †

TOAH A descendant of Levi (1Ch. 6:34). †

TOB {good} A city and the surrounding area in Transjordan, et Taiyibeh, but not the one in modern Israel. Jephthah, the judge of Israel, fled to Tob and was later called back to deliver Israel from the Ammonites (Jdg. 11:3-5). Joab defeated men of Tob in his day (2Sa. 10:68).

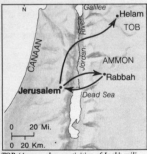

TOB (Arrows show activities of Joab's military ventures.)

TOB-ADONIJAH {good is (my) lord Yahweh} A Levite who taught the Law during the revival in the days of Jehoshaphat (2Ch. 17:8). †

TOBIAH {Yahweh is good}
1. The ancestor of some who returned from the Babylonian captivity but could not prove his Israelite descent (Ezr. 2:60).
2. An Ammonite who opposed Nehemiah in his rebuilding of Jerusalem. Nehemiah ejected him from the place he was occupying in the temple (Ne. 2:10, 19; 4:3, 7; 6:1-19; 13:4-8).

TOBIJAH {Yahweh is good}
1. A Levite who taught the law in the days of revival under Jehoshaphat of Judah (2Ch. 17:8).
2. One who brought gifts for the second temple (Zec. 6:10, 14).

TOBIT, BOOK OF {Yahweh is good} *See* SCRIPTURE, *Apocrypha*

TOCHEN *See* TOKEN

TOGARMAH, BETH TOGARMAH An unidentified place somewhere N of Palestine. Some put it between the Euphrates River and the Antitaurus mountains, but others feel it should be farther from Palestine. Togarmah was a descendant of Japheth (Ge. 10:3; Eze. 27:14; 38:6).

TOHU A descendant of Ephraim and ancestor of Samuel (1Sa. 1:1).

TOI The king of Hamath who congratulated David on his Syrian victory (2Sa. 8:9-10; also called Tou (1Ch. 18:9-10).

TOKEN {measure} An unidentified town in the tribal area of Simeon (1Ch. 4:32). †

TOKEN, A SIGN KJV for "sign."

TOKHATH *See* TIKVAH 1.

TOLA, TOLAITE(S) {worm of scarlet} A son of Puah of the tribe of Issachar and his clan (Nu. 26:23). *See* JUDGES OF ISRAEL

TOLAD An unidentified city in the tribal area of Simeon (1Ch. 4:29).

TOMB *See* BURIAL

TONGUE A word used in many senses in the Bible: an organ of the body and of speech, a language (literally *tongue)* or dialect, or a people with a common language (Dt. 28:49; Jdg. 7:5; Isa. 66:18; Mk. 7:35). Figuratively speaking, the tongue is called a sharp sword, a smiting instrument, or even soft (gentle) (Ps. 57:4; Jer. 18:18; Pr. 25:15).

TONGUES AS OF FIRE The phenomenon that took place on the Day of Pentecost when small flames of fire like tongues rested on the heads of the believers as they were all filled with the Holy Spirit and began to speak in tongues foreign to them (Ac. 2:3-4).

TONGUES, CONFUSION OF The confusion of the languages of men which took place in the days after Noah (Ge. 11:1ff.; cf. Ac. 2:1-13). *See* BABEL, TOWER OF

TONGUES (GLOSSOLALIA) Speaking in tongues is a genre of prophecy when the speaker speaks prophetically, ecstatically, and miraculously in a language he has not learned.

The Greek word (*glossa*) is used in this sense twenty-four times in the NT and perhaps once in the OT (Isa. 28:11). These occur in four (or five?) contexts in the NT (Ac. 2:1ff.; 10:46; 19:6; 1Co. 12–14). There might be other veiled references (Eph. 5:18 and 1Th. 5:19). It is generic for various "kinds" of tongues (1Co. 12:28).

The fifth appearance of speaking in tongues in Mark 16:17 is part of the long ending of Mark (16:9-20), which the great majority of textual scholars believe was not part of the original Mark but was a later addition.

Two kinds may be differentiated: *Pentecostal* and *Corinthian*. They are significantly different. Pentecostal embraced the hearer who, out of the din, could miraculously hear the message in his native language. *No one* understands Corinthian tongues unless a second miracle occurs, the gift of translation, to translate the tongues. If the tongues of Caesarea and Ephesus are the Pentecostal kind, Pentecostal tongues are initiatory. Corinthian tongues are an on-going integral part of Christians' weekly worship service (1 Co. 14:26). Everybody spoke in Pentecostal tongues and all at the same time (Ac. 2:4), but the Corinthian tongues are limited to two or, at the most, three per worship service and one following the other.

The contemporary theology of speaking in tongues teaches that just as the sinner experiences salvation, he must later experience the baptism with the Holy Spirit (Ac. 1:5) to receive power (Ac. 1:8). It is believed the sign that indicates he has experienced this second work of grace is his speaking in tongues. Christians are then classified into two groups, the empowered and the powerless. However, it is clear from 1Cor. 12:11 that spiritual gifts are distributed by the will of God to serve the needs of the body, not as signs of spiritual power. (E.W.G.) *See* GIFTS; TONGUES AS OF FIRE

TONGUE, UNKNOWN KJV in 1Co. 14:2ff. for the common word for "tongue" or "language." The word "unknown" is not explicit in the original and must be extrapolated from the context. The KJV translation committee may have felt justified to call it an *unknown* tongue because this tongue speaks mysteries (*musteria*). This seems to be different than the tongues in Acts 2, where they were called dialects (*dialektos*, Ac. 2:6). In the latter passage only known languages can be derived from the context.

TOPAZ *See* PRECIOUS STONES AND METALS, Precious Stones 13.

TOPHEL An unidentified place in the wilderness wanderings of the Israelites after their exodus from Egypt. It was in the area where Moses gave his first address recorded in the Book of Deuteronomy (Dt. 1:1). †

TOPHET, TOPHETH *See* HINNOM, VALLEY OF

TORAH {instructor, teacher} *See* DECALOGUE; LAW; PENTATEUCH

TORTOISE *See* BEASTS 6., *Great Lizard*

TOTAL DEPRAVITY *See* SIN

TOU *See* TOI

TOUCH OF JESUS The confirmed leper was considered unclean. No contact was to be made (Lev. 13:45). A person who touched the leper would also be unclean. But Jesus' healing touch, instead of producing uncleanness in Christ, produced cleanness in the leper. Jesus often touched those he healed (Mt. 8:3; 20:34; Mk. 1:41; Lk. 5:13). Sometimes people touched him or even his garment and were healed (Mt. 9:20; 14:36; Mk. 3:10; 5:27-28; 6:56; 8:22; Lk. 6:19; 8:44-47). *See* SICK, SICKNESS

TOWEL *See* DRESS; LINEN

TOWER Connected with a city gate in antiquity for defense. Some were large enough to be used as citadels or fortresses in time of attack. At strategic points around a city wall, especially at points where the wall turned, towers were erected for observation by the defending forces. In the vineyards and fields smaller ones were built for watching the ripening crops even as they are to this day (2Ch. 26:9-10; 27:4; Isa. 23:13; Zep. 1:16; Mt. 21:33). Towers were made of stone blocks or rough fieldstone, or even of sun-dried mud bricks at varying times in the history of fortifications.

A famous tower in Jerusalem was the Tower of Antonia, rebuilt by Herod, named after the emperor Mark Antony. This tower kept a cohort (about 600) of soldiers to keep peace during the feasts of the temple, located directly N ("at the corner of two cloisters of the temple") of the temple area. The historian Josephus records this Tower by name (*Wars* 5:5:4). Acts 21:31-32 records the soldiers running out to restore order in the temple and to save Paul's life, though the tower is not mentioned by name there.

TOWER OF BABEL *See* BABEL, TOWER OF

TOWER OF HUNDRED *See* MEAH

TOWN *See* CITY; VILLAGES

TOWN CLERK Only in Ac. 19:35 in the NIV is the Greek word thus translated; elsewhere in the NT the reference is to a Jewish scribe. In the Greek world,

as at Ephesus, this man was an important official, even the ruler of the city, as well as the keeper of the records.

TRACONITIS *See* GEOGRAPHY OF THE HOLY LAND

TRADE Our knowledge of trade in the ancient world comes from literary sources for the most part, but also to some extent from ancient art and artifacts. The literary sources are the Bible, ancient contracts mostly in cuneiform tablets, and sometimes, as at Nuzi and Mari, in massive archives. From the excavations of the ancient cities, evidence of trade is found in the artifacts of one area being found in the cities of another. A case of the latter would be the Cypriot or the Mycenaean ware, excellent potteries made abroad and imported into the area of Palestine. Ancient trade routes were well established and widely known and used. Among these were the "Way of the Sea," the "King's Highway," and the later Nabatean routes across the Negev of Palestine. *See* GEOGRAPHY OF THE HOLY LAND. Along these routes great cities grew up for defense and for services to the traders. While the concept of trade is clear, and abundant evidence of its taking place is clear in the Bible, the word itself is found infrequently. Abraham was a trader at Gerar, called a "sojourner," but the first use of the word "trade" in the NIV is not until Jacob's return from Haran (Ge. 34:10, 21; 42:34). Trading is mentioned in the Prophets, fourteen times in Ezekiel alone (Eze. 27:13-24; 28:5-18), and in a number of passages in the NT. Jesus accused the people of making God's house a house of trade when it should have been a house of prayer and worship (Jn. 2:16). The word was also used in the sense of an occupation. Paul and Aquila were tentmakers by trade (Ac. 18:3).

TRADITION From the word for "something that has been handed down," a tradition can be a distortion of God's Word, as in the tradition of the elders (Mt. 15:26; Mk. 7:3-13); the Colossian heresy (Col. 2:8); or rabbinic tradition

(Gal. 1:14). From the Christian perspective some traditions are good, as in the apostles' traditions handed (1Co. 11:2; 2Th. 2:15; 3:6; Jude 3). *See also* TALMUD

TRAIN *See* DRESS, "Skirt of a robe"; *See also* PARENTING, "Train up a child"; *See* DISCIPLINE, "To discipline"

TRAJAN *See* EMPEROR, EMPIRE

TRANCE *See* VISIONS

TRANSCENDENTAL MEDITATION (TM) *See* MEDITATION, TRANSCENDENTAL

TRANSFIGURATION The event in the life of Christ when his appearance was transformed so that his face shone like the sun and his clothes became dazzling white. This came from within and was not a reflection of some light from without. For a few moments his body was transformed into the likeness of what his resurrection body was to become in the glorified state. All three of the Synoptic Gospels carry the story (Mt. 17:2; Mk. 9:2; Lk. 9:28ff.).

TRANSGRESSION *See* SIN

TRANSJORDAN, TRANS-JORDAN {beyond (East of) the Jordan} *See* GEOGRAPHY OF THE HOLY LAND; PERAEA

TRANSLATE, TAKE AWAY *See* ENOCH 3.

TRANSLATION The process of rendering words and meaning from one language to another. *See* BIBLE VERSIONS; TRANSLITERATION

TRANSLATIONS OF THE BIBLE *See* BIBLE VERSIONS, Ancient Versions

TRANSLITERATION Transliteration is the process of spelling or representing the characters from one language to another. In the Bible some Hebrew, Aramaic, and Greek names of people, places, or concepts go through this process. For example, the word *baptize* is not translated but transliterated from the Greek word *baptizo*. Ezra 4:9 is a good example of getting different renderings based on whether or not one transliterates (as did the KJV) or translates (as did the NIV). Transliteration often occurs when a translator encounters a person, place name, or technical term (like *baptize*) that cannot be rendered clearly in the translation, or if the translator is not sure what the meaning is, as probably is the case in Ezr. 4:9 in the KJV. (For specific examples of the differences between transliteration and translation: *See* APHARSAKITES; APHARSATHCHITES, APHARSITES; ARCHEVITES; DEHAVITES; ERECH; SUSANCHITES; TARPELITES.)

TRANSPORTATION *See* TRADE

TRANSUBSTANTIATION *See* COMMUNION, VIEWS OF

TRAP *See* SNARES

TRAVEL *See* TRADE

TREASURE This word has the idea of something that is stored. It is used for something valuable—valuable cloth or precious metal. The Christian is not to hoard earthly treasures (Mt. 6:19-21; 19:21; Mk. 10:21; Lk. 12:33-34; 18:22). In Christ are all treasures of knowledge and wisdom (Col. 2:3). *See* RICHES

TREE OF CHRIST *See* CROSS

TREE OF KNOWLEDGE OF GOOD AND EVIL Like the tree of life, a miraculous tree in Eden, real but unidentifiable. Sin came not from tasting this fruit, but from disobeying God who told Adam and Eve not to eat of it. Theologians speculate as to what is meant by the knowledge of good and evil.

TREE OF LIFE A special, miraculous, and therefore unidentifiable tree that appears only in the Garden of Eden (Ge. 2:9) and in the New Jerusalem (Rev. 22:2). Adam and Eve were driven from Eden to prevent their eating of the fruit of this tree and thus acquiring immortality.

TREES These were of two kinds, fruit trees and those not producing food. In biblical times some twenty-five different types of trees were known, and the area of Palestine was much more wooded than at present. As late as Crusader times they hunted game in the Sharon Forest. In Turkish times the situation was changed, and Palestine lost its forest. Only since the arrival of the Jews in the area has the situation begun to change through the planting of millions of evergreen trees on the hills and the growing of many citrus and other fruit trees.

FRUIT TREES *Almond, pistachio, nut* While the third tree is surmised only from the one reference to "nut trees" in SS. 6:11, the other two are specifically noted by name and their identity is sure (Ge. 30:37; 43:11).

Branch of an Olive Tree

The *fig, olive,* and *palm* produced some important food crops (Ge. 8:11; Nu. 13:23; Dt. 34:3; Jer. 11:16; SS. 7:7; Joel 1:12; Mt. 7:16). While the palm is mentioned a number of times the word "date" in connection with it does not appear. It is certain, however, from extrabiblical sources that dates were produced and eaten in the area.

Branch of a Fig Tree

The *pomegranate* and *apple* are both well-attested food trees of biblical times (Nu. 20:5; Dt. 8:8; SS. 2:3; Joel 1:12).

Sycamore and *balsam*. The sycamore was a type of fig tree, important to the economy of Palestine as judged by the

Date-palm Tree

fact that David had an officer in charge of them (1Ch. 27:28). Various suggestions including the mulberry, poplar, or even that it is not a tree at all have been given about the balsam (2Sa. 5:23-24; 1Ch. 14:14-15).

OTHER TREES

The *acacia* is well known and attested. It was abundant in the Sinai and in the Jordan Valley. The Ark of the Covenant was made of this hard, durable wood (Ex. 25:10-28; Dt. 10:3). *See* SHITTIM

The *cedar*, so well known in Lebanon (*cedrus libani*), is perhaps the most frequently mentioned specific tree in the Bible. Large amounts of cedar wood were brought to Palestine by David and Solomon for the building of their palaces and the temple (1Ki. 5-7).

The *cypress* is not specifically identified. It is sometimes translated as "pine logs" (Isa. 41:19; 44:14; 60:13) and "gopher wood" (Ge. 6:14). It is noted in reference with the cedar on a number of occasions (1Ki. 5:8-10).

The Hebrew words translated "fir" are not yet identifiable. It may refer to one of the juniper species. There are only a few uses in the Bible (Isa. 60:13). The *plane (platanus orientalis)* is noted in Ge. 30:37 and elsewhere (Isa. 41:19).

The *pine* is literally translated from the Hebrew "oil tree," not known unless it is one of the pines so rendered in Isa. 60:13 (NIV).

The *oak* and the *terebinth* are very much alike in the Hebrew but are distinct trees as is clear from Isa. 6:13 and Hos. 4:13. The former is the tree *quercus* of which two species are known in Palestine. The latter is *pistacia palaestina*.

The *poplar* (Ge. 30:37; Hos. 4:13) would be better translated "storax" as judged from the type of area in which it grows (*styrax*).

The *tamarisk* is definitely identifiable. It is a fast-growing tree in the desert areas of Palestine as well as on river banks (*tamarix*) (Ge. 21:33; 1Sa. 22:6; 31:13).

The *willow* is of two types: the *salix acmophylla* of the Jordan River area of Palestine and the *populus euphratica* of Babylonia, rendered "poplar" in the NIV (Lev. 23:40; Ps. 137:2).

Algum, or almug, are not able to be

identified. In each use the NIV footnote gives the other translation. They were commonly called "costly woods" (1Ki. 10:11-12; 2Ch. 2:8; 9:10-11).

Ebony noted in Eze. 27:15 was an import from Rhodes (Dedan in the Hebrew text).

Carob (ceratonia siliqua), a Mediterranean evergreen, its fruit a long sickle-like and sweet pod. The pods contain small seed kernels, food for pigs (Lk. 15:16).

Citron wood was a pleasant-scented wood. The tree produced a lemon or lime type of fruit from North Africa (Rev. 18:12).

TRENCH *See* SIEGE

TRESPASS *See* SIN

TRESPASS OFFERING *See* SACRIFICES AND OFFERINGS

TRIAL The word is used in the Bible in the same two senses in which we use it today—a test and a court trial (Jas. 1:12; Ac. 26:6). The most famous of the latter is the trial of Jesus; *see* CHRIST, LIFE OF. The word "trial" is not used in connection with the court cases in which Jesus' case was heard. *See* TEMPTATION

TRIBES A word used many times in the Bible and in the overwhelming number of cases of the twelve tribes of Israel, or of one or several of them. Occasionally, as in Rev. 14:6, the reference is to all people in general. The twelve sons of Jacob were: Reuben, Simeon, Levi, Judah, Zebulun, Issachar, Dan, Gad, Asher, Naphtali, Joseph, and Benjamin. God withdrew Levi from the list of tribes, for he wished to use them in the transport and care of the tabernacle and its service (Nu. 1:47-53). Why Joseph was dropped from the tribal list (Nu. 1:32) we are not told, but his two sons, Ephraim and Manasseh, were selected to make up the number of twelve. Some suggest it was an expression of the double portion of inheritance to a firstborn son, showing that Joseph's dream was in fact true.

Before and after the conquest of the Promised Land, the tribes of Reuben, Gad, and a-half of Manasseh were settled in Transjordan (Nu. 32:33). The settlement of the nine and a half tribes W of the Jordan is recorded in Joshua 15 – 19. In the case of Benjamin and Zebulun the borders are pretty thoroughly defined. In the case of the other tribes many of the cities, but not the borders, are noted. Benjamin, Judah and Simeon were in the S, as was Dan at the first before moving to the N. Ephraim and one-half of Manasseh were located in the hill country N of Benjamin, which in turn was N of Judah. The other four were N of the Jezreel Valley, with Asher on the coast and Naphtali by the Sea of Galilee.

The tribes were one kingdom through the reign of Solomon, in spite of several attempts to disrupt them. After Solomon the permanent division came, with ten tribes headquartered in Tirzah and then Samaria, and the two others with their capital at Jerusalem.

TRIBULATION In both Testaments the word refers to trouble, of a general sort, but sometimes as a punishment from God. The NT refers in a few cases to a great tribulation (Mt. 24:21, 29; Mk. 13:19, 24; Rev. 2:22; 7:14). It will be a period of unparalleled suffering in the end of days.

TRIBUNE A Roman military officer over a cohort (Ac. 21:13-37; 22:24-29). *See* BAND

TRIBUTE A compulsory contribution taken from an inferior by a superior, whether by a state or by a powerful individual (Dt. 16:10; Est. 1:1; Lk. 20:22). *See* TAX

TRICHOTOMY This is the view that man's irreducible parts are three: body, soul, and spirit (1Th. 5:23). *See* DICHOTOMY

TRIGON An ancient harp. *See* MUSIC, MUSICAL INSTRUMENTS 2., (3)

TRINITY {triad, union of three} *See* ATTRIBUTES OF GOD, *Unity*; GOD, NAMES OF 1.

TRITHEISM Three Gods. A view of the Trinity that discounts the unity of God (Dt. 6:4). *See* ATTRIBUTES OF GOD, *unity*

TROAS The name of a city and a region located in NW Asia Minor visited by Paul on his missionary journeys. He left a cloak, books and parchments there and asked Timothy to bring them to him (Ac. 16:8-11; 20:5-6; 2Ti. 4:13).

TROGYLLIUM A place mentioned in Ac. 20:15, according to some manuscripts, and found in some translations (KJV, NKJV, JB). But the word does not appear in several of the earliest manuscripts and therefore is not included in the RSV, NEB, NIV and NASB, which all consider this an insertion in the Greek text.

TROPHIMUS {nourished (child)} A Christian from Ephesus who went with Paul to Jerusalem on his final journey to that city. Misunderstanding about him led to a riot, which in turn led to Paul's arrest. Trophimus was later ill in Miletus (Ac. 20:4; 21:29ff.; 2Ti. 4:20). †

TRUMPET *See* MUSIC, MUSICAL INSTRUMENTS

TRUMPETS, FEAST OF *See* CALENDAR *and* FESTIVALS

TRUST *See* FAITH

TRUTH This word may refer either to facts themselves (that which conforms to reality) or to the relation of a statement to the reality. The first refers to the real state of affairs in itself. The second is relational. Christ is *the truth*, in himself as the embodiment of reality (Jn. 1:14; 14:6). "Knowing the truth will make a person free" (Jn. 8:32) is an illustration of the second usage. Relationship to Christ must be based on both aspects of "truth."

TRYPH(A)ENA {dainty} A Christian at Rome to whom Paul sent greetings in his epistle to that church (Ro. 16:12). †

TRYPHOSA {delicate} A Roman Christian, a woman, to whom Paul sent greetings (Ro. 16:12). †

TROAS
From Troas Paul went to Philippi in Macedonia.

TUBAL A son of Japheth and grandson of Noah (Ge. 10:2).

TUBAL-CAIN A descendant of Cain; he was a forger of bronze and iron (Ge. 4:22). †

TUMORS *See* SICK, SICKNESS

TUNIC *See* DRESS

TUNNEL *See* AQUEDUCT

TURBAN *See* DRESS

TURTLE, TURTLEDOVE *See* BIRDS 4., *Dove, Turtledove*

TWELVE, THE *See* APOSTLES

TWIN BROTHER *See* DEITIES 1., *Castor and Pollux*

TWIN, THE *See* APOSTLES

TYCHICUS [good fortune] An Asian who went with Paul to Jerusalem on his last visit to that city. Paul refers to him as a beloved brother and helper. He is mentioned in connection with carrying two of Paul's Epistles (Ac. 20:4; Eph. 6:21-22; Col. 4:7-8; 2Ti. 4:12; Tit.3:12). †

TYPE Greek for "figure, form, example." *See* EXAMPLE

TYRANNUS [ruler] The owner of a hall in which Paul argued daily at Ephesus (Ac. 19:9). †

TYRE [rocky place] A Phoenician coastal city (168-297) and the people of a city, mentioned seventy times in the Bible. The first mention in the Bible of this already much older city is Joshua's assigning it to the tribal area of Asher (Jos. 19:29). It became a great trading center and one of its kings, Hiram, a great friend of David and Solomon, supplied them with lumber and skilled craftsmen for the building of their palaces, the temple, and also Solomon's fleet (1Ki. 7:13-14; 9:11-12; 2Ch. 2:3, 11). Oracles on Tyre are found in Isaiah 23 and Ezekiel 26—28. Jesus visited the area, and he referred to it in his rebuke of Korazin and Bethsaida (Lk. 6:17; 10:13-14). On his final journey to Jerusalem, Paul's ship landed at Tyre (Ac. 21:3-7). *See also* GEOGRAPHY OF THE HOLY LAND

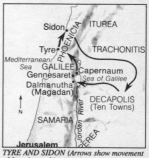

TYRE AND SIDON (Arrows show movement of Jesus' preaching tour.)

TYROPEON VALLEY [valley of the cheese makers] *See* JERUSALEM, ¶ 2., *Tyropeon*

TYRUS *See* TYRE

U

UCAL {*possibly* I am consumed, *or* I cease} One of the two to whom Agur's words were addressed (Pr. 30:1). †

UEL {*possibly* will of El (God), BDB and KB} One of those who married a foreign wife during the Babylonian captivity (Ezr. 10:34).

UGARIT *See* RAS SHAMRA

UKNAZ {and Kenaz} *See* KENAZ 3.

ULAI A river or canal in Elam that flowed through Susa the capital (Da. 8:2, 16). †

ULAM {fist, leader}
   1. A person of the tribe of Manasseh (1Ch. 7:16-17). †
   2. A person of the tribe of Benjamin (1Ch. 8:39-40). †

ULCERS *See* SICK, SICKNESS

ULLA A descendant of Asher (1Ch. 7:39).

ULTRADISPENSATIONALISM *See* DISPENSATIONALISM, ULTRA

UMMAH *See* ACC(H)O

UNBELIEF To refuse to believe, to be faithless. The qualities opposite of true faith and belief. *See* FAITH

UNCHASTITY *See* FORNICATION; PROSTITUTE

UNCIRCUMCISED A word for "foreskin of the penis." It most often has the idea of heathenism, thinking or acting like a Gentile, being a Gentile (Col.

3:11). *See* CIRCUMCISION; CIRCUMCISION OF THE HEART

UNCLEAN *See* CLEAN AND UNCLEAN

UNCTION An anointing. *See* ANOINT, ANOINTED

UNDEFILED *See* CLEAN AND UNCLEAN

UNDERSTANDING Many words, often overlapping, translate this idea. To *know* can be the idea of understanding as a normal thought process. This idea sometimes comes from the word "to see," other times the word for "mind" or "knowledge." To know can also suggest intimacy (Jn. 10:14ff.; 2Ti. 2:19), even sexual relations (Lk. 1:34, KJV). To *understand* can be simply "to perceive," but it can be a spiritual kind of insight (Lk. 24:45; Eph. 5:17).

Wisdom, knowledge, and understanding in this special sense come from Christ (Col. 2:3). The Book of Proverbs can also bring wisdom and understanding. The student has to watch the context carefully to comprehend if "understanding" is mundane or special insight from the LORD.

UNDERWORLD *See* DEAD, ABODE OF

UNFADING GLORY *See* PLANTS, FLOWERING PLANTS 8., *Amaranthine*

UNICORN {one horn} KJV for "wild ox" (Nu. 23:22). There is absolutely no connection with the beast of mythology, nor, likely, was any intended.

UNION WITH CHRIST *See* SALVATION, APPLICATION OF

UNITY *See* ATTRIBUTES OF GOD; BODY OF CHRIST; CARNAL; CHURCH; SPIRITUAL GIFTS

UNIVERSAL CHURCH *See* CHURCH, *invisible*

UNIVERSE *See* WORLD

UNKNOWN GOD Ac. 17:23.

UNKNOWN TONGUE *See* TONGUE, UNKNOWN

UNLEAVENED BREAD When used literally, this refers to bread made without any fermented dough. It was required to be used during Passover (Ex. 12:8-30). When used in a figurative sense the thought is "unmixed" (1Co. 5:7-8). *See* YEAST

UNLEAVENED BREAD, FEAST OF *See* CALENDAR and FESTIVALS

UNLIMITED ATONEMENT The belief that Christ's atonement was for all humanity, not just for the elect.

UNNI {Yahweh has answered}
1. A Levite musician in the time of David (1Ch. 15:18-20).
2. A Levite in postexilic times (Ne. 12:9); called Unno in some versions. †

UNNO {Yahweh has answered} A Levite who returned from the Babylonian captivity with Zerubbabel (Ne. 12:9).

UNPARDONABLE SIN *See* BLASPHEMY AGAINST THE HOLY SPIRIT; SUICIDE

UNRIGHTEOUSNESS *See* RIGHTEOUSNESS

UPHARSIN This means "and parsin." *See* MENE, MENE, TEKEL, AND PARSIN

UPHAZ An unidentified place from which gold was procured (Jer. 10:9; Da. 10:5). Translated "waist" in the NIV in Daniel. †

UPPER EGYPT *See* PATHROS

UPPER ROOM The place of the last meal of Jesus with his disciples. Tradition puts it somewhere on the western ridge of ancient Jerusalem (Mk. 14:15; Lk. 22:12). Here Jesus started with a Passover meal and converted it into the first "Lord's Supper" for the church. *See* JERUSALEM 8.; LORD'S SUPPER

UPRIGHT *See* RIGHTEOUSNESS

UR {flame, light} The father of one of David's mighty men (1Ch. 11:35). †

UR OF THE CHALDEES The original home of Abraham in southern Mesopotamia from which God called him to go to Palestine. The city has been extensively excavated (Ge. 11:28-31; 15:7; Ne. 9:7). *See* CHALDEA, CHALDEANS

URBANUS {refined, elegant} A Christian at Rome to whom Paul sent his greetings (Ro. 16:9). †

URI {Yahweh is (my) flame, light}
1. The father of the artist and artisan Bezalel who did the work on the tabernacle (Ex. 31:2ff.).
2. The father of the officer of Solomon in the land of Gilead (1Ki. 4:19).
3. A gatekeeper in the days of Ezra who married a foreign wife during the Babylonian captivity (Ezr. 10:24).

URIAH, URIAS, URIJAH {Yahweh is (my) flame, light}
1. A Hittite, first husband of Bathsheba, one of David's mighty men (2Sa. 11:3ff.; 23:39; 1Ki. 15:5; 1Ch. 11:41; 2Sa. 12:9-10; Mt. 1:6).
2. A Priest (Isa. 8:2).
3. Chief priest in Ahaz's time (2Ki. 16:10, 15-16).
4. A prophet, son of Shemaiah (Jer. 26:20-23).
5. Father of Meremoth (Ezr. 8:33; Ne. 3:4, 21).
6. A man present at the reading of the Law (Ne. 8:4).

URIEL {El is (my) flame, light}
1. A descendant of Levi (1Ch. 6:24).

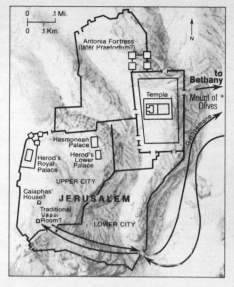

UPPER ROOM AND GETHSEMANE
Jesus and the disciples ate the traditional Passover meal, celebrated the New Covenant in an upper room in Jerusalem, and then went into the Garden called Gethsemane.

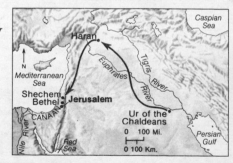

UR OF THE CHALDEANS
Abram traveled from Ur of the Chaldeans to Canaan by way of Haran.

2. The father of King Abijah's mother (2Ch. 13:2).

URIJAH [Yahweh is (my) flame, light] *See* URIAH

URIM AND THUMMIM [lights and perfections] A way of finding God's will, used through the priests. There is no agreement as to what they were or how they were used. This does not appear to be spoken revelation, so probably a yes or no question would have to be asked. The following passages refer to them: Ex. 28:30; Lev. 8:8; Nu. 27:21; Dt. 33:8; 1Sa. 28:6; Ezr. 2:63; Ne. 7:65.

USURY The lending of money at interest. Forbidden in the Old Covenant for transactions between Yahweh's people, it was to be practiced only with foreigners (Ex. 22:25; Dt. 23:19-20).

The NT does not directly speak to the issue in a codified form. Jesus gives inference that to make a profit is acceptable in parabolic form (Mt. 25:27), but that is only secondary to the point, and not a clear binding teaching. Paul in Ro. 13:8 says to "owe no man anything," but this debt may or may not be including material debt.

The Christian may profit, though not be bound, to explore the idea of not charging interest to a Christian brother or sister. Also, the Christian may profit, though not be bound, to explore the idea of not borrowing so as to have no "outstanding claims against him." (J.A.S.)
See also DEBT, DEBTOR

UTHAI {*possibly* superiority of Yahweh, IDB; *possibly* (my) restoration, KB}
1. A descendant of Judah (1Ch. 9:4).
2. One who came back from the Babylonian captivity with Ezra (Ezr. 8:14).

UZ
1. A grandson of Shem (Ge. 10:22-23).
2. A son of Nahor and nephew of Abraham (Ge. 22:21).
3. A Horite descendant of Seir (Ge. 36:28).
4. A land in which Job lived. Incidents in Job's book and elsewhere indicate it to have been a good pastureland; there was an important city there (Job sat in the gate); one of his friends came from Teman; and Chaldeans attacked it. These may indicate a place E of Petra. Others think it was in the land of Bashan E of the Sea of Galilee (Job 1:1, 15, 17; Jer. 25:20).

UZAI {Yahweh has given ear, listened} Father of Palal who worked on Nehemiah's wall (Ne. 3:25). †

UZAL A descendant of Shem, the son of Noah (Ge. 10:27).

UZZA
1. The owner of the garden in which King Manasseh of Judah was buried (2Ki. 21:18, 26).

2 and 3. Descendant of Levi and Benjamin (1Ch. 6:29; 8:7).
4. Ancestor of some temple servants who returned from the Babylonian captivity with Zerubbabel (Ezr. 2:49).

UZZA, GARDEN OF *See* UZZA 1.

UZZAH {strong, fierce one} One of the sons of Abinadab who assisted in bringing up the ark but died because he touched it (2Sa. 6:3ff.).

UZZEN SHEERAH, UZZEN-SHERAH One of the towns built by a lady, Sheerah, daughter of Ephraim (1Ch. 7:24).

UZZI {Yahweh is (my) strength}
1, 2, 3, and 4. A descendant of Aaron, a grandson of Issachar and of Benjamin, and another descendant of Benjamin (1Ch. 6:5-6; 7:2-3; 7:7; 9:8).
5. A Levite overseer in the days of Nehemiah (Ne. 11:22).
6. A priest in the high priesthood of Joiakim (Ne. 12:19).

UZZIA {(my) strength *or* Yahweh is (my) strength} One of David's mighty men (1Ch. 11:44). †

UZZIAH {Yahweh is (my) strength}
1. One of the kings of Judah; also called Azariah. *See* KINGS OF JUDAH AND ISRAEL
2. A descendant of Levi; also called Azariah (1Ch. 6:24, 36).
3. Father of one of David's treasurers (1Ch. 27:25).
4. A priest who married a foreign wife during the Babylonian captivity (Ezr. 10:21).
5. A descendant of Judah who lived in Jerusalem after the return from the Babylonian captivity (Ne. 11:4).

UZZIEL(ITE) {El is (my) strength}
1. A son of Kohath and grandson of Levi (Ex. 6:18).
2. A descendant of Simeon (1Ch. 4:42).
3. A grandson of Benjamin (1Ch. 7:7).

4. A musician in the days of King David (1Ch. 25:4, 18); also called Azarel.

5. A Levite in the days of Hezekiah, king of Judah (2Ch. 29:14).

6. One who worked with Nehemiah on the repair of the walls of Jerusalem (Ne. 3:8).

V

VAGABOND KJV for "wanderer" (Ge. 4:12, 14).

VAHEB *See* WAHEB

VAIL *See* VEIL

VAIN The translation of a number of Hebrew and Greek words all carrying the general idea of transient and unreliable, something light and vaporous. Even taking the name of Yahweh your God in vain is to treat it lightly, like vapor (Ex. 20:7; Ps. 2:1; 33:17; Isa. 49:4; Ro. 13:4; Gal. 4:11).

VAIZATHA {*possibly* given of the best one, BDB} One of the sons of the Haman who tried to kill the Jews but was killed himself instead (Est. 9:9). †

VAJEZATHA *See* VAIZATHA

VALE, VALLEY *See* BROOK; RIVER

VALE OF SIDDIM *See* SIDDIM

VALLEY OF CRAFTSMEN *See* GE HARASHIM 1.

VANIAH {*possibly* worthy of love, IDB} One who married a foreign wife during the Babylonian captivity (Ezr. 10:36). †

VASHNI {and the second} KJV for "second" (1Ch. 6:28). †

VASHTI {one beautiful, desired} A queen of King Ahasuerus of Persia just before Esther (Est. 1:9-19; 2:1-17). †

VAT *See* OIL; WINE

VEIL *See* DRESS; TABERNACLE; TEMPLE

VENGEANCE Retributive punishment for correction but not for revenge. In the NT it is reserved for God (Ro. 12:19). In the OT also the reference is frequently to God's coming day of punishment on the wicked for their sins (Jer. 46:10; Eze. 25:12-17).

VENISON KJV for something hunted—i.e., wild game. This is not restricted to the deer family. *See* GAME, WILD

VERBUM Latin for *logos* (word) in John's Gospel (1:1).

VERMILION *See* COLORS, *red*

VERSIONS OF THE SCRIPTURES *See* BIBLE VERSIONS

VESSEL *See* CUP; IDOL, IDOLATRY; POT; POTTER, POTTERY; SHIP; TABERNACLE, ARTICLES OF; TEMPLE, ARTICLES OF

VESTIBULE *See* PORCH

VESTURE An archaic English word that means "robe," "clothing," "cloak," "garment," "apparel," etc. *See* DRESS

VIAL *See* BOWL; FLASK

VICE LIST *See* VIRTUE AND VICE LISTS

VICTORY This word often is used in a military battle or athletic contest. Christ has success over everything opposed to God—i.e., the world (Jn. 16:33). The Christian can overcome evil with good (Ro. 12:21). The Resurrection has given believers the victory over death (1Co. 15:54; 1Jn. 2:14; 4:4; 5:4-5).

VICTUAL *See* FOOD

VIGILANCE *See* WATCH 3.

VILLAGES Smaller settlements, mostly for farming, grouped around a central town which was the economic and defense center for the area (Nu. 21:15; Jos. 15:32; 19:39; Ne. 11:25). *See* CITY

VINE, VINEYARD The grape is one of the most common plants mentioned in the Bible. It is mentioned in connection with an immediate post-Flood event (Ge. 9:20-21), where drunkenness is also noted. Grapes were a major item of the diet in antiquity; they were a source of sugar, were eaten as raisins, and were preserved as pressed raisin cakes. From the grapevine came a sweet juice drink (wine is mentioned as a food along with milk) and a fermented one also; and, soured, the juice was used both as vinegar, a condiment, or diluted with water—a popular drink (Dt. 23:24; Ru. 2:14; 2Sa. 16:1; Ps. 69:21; Isa. 55:1; Hos. 3:1; Eph. 5:18). The Bible speaks of the culture, pruning and harvesting of the grape and of its preparation for the foods above (Nu. 22:24; Ps. 80:8-13; SS. 2:15; Isa. 5:1-2, 10; Jer. 31:5; Mt. 20:1-16). Winepresses and collection vats and the storage of the wine in skins are noted (Isa. 16:10; Mt. 9:17; 21:33-41). The gleanings were to be left for the poor, and in the seventh year the fruit was not to be picked (Lev. 19:10; 25:3). Pruning of the vine is also noted, and the pruned branches were gathered and burned (Jn. 15:16). One of the important usages of the words "vine" and "vineyard" is symbolic. Israel was God's vine brought from Egypt and planted in the Promised Land; but she turned out to be a wild vine, and for this had to be punished—cut off. However, then she would grow again and produce fruit fit for the vinedresser (Ps. 80:89; Isa. 5:1-7; 65:8-9; Jer. 2:21; Hos. 2:12, 14-16). In the NT Jesus calls himself the "true vine" and God his Father the "vinedresser" and his followers the

"branches" which must abide in this vine in order to be fruitful (Jn. 15:1-11).

The Grape Vine

VINE OF SIBMAH A special grape from the town of Sibmah. *See* SIBMAH

VINE OF SODOM A vine with clusters of poisonous grapes, to which Moses compared Israel (Dt. 32:32).

VINEGAR *See* VINE, VINEYARD

VINEYARDS, PLAIN OF THE *See* ABEL KERAMIM

VIPER *See* BEASTS 1.

VIRGIN, VIRGINITY While the words "virgin birth" are not found in the Bible, the concept of virgin birth is. *See* VIRGIN BIRTH; *See also* MAID

VIRGIN BIRTH The miraculous work that Jesus Christ was born of Mary without being conceived through sexual intercourse. The non-material Holy Spirit was the source of conception (Mt. 1:18). Aside from the question of the meaning of "virgin" in Isa. 7:14, in Lk. 1:34 it is plainly stated by Mary, "How can this be since I am a virgin?" The KJV is closer to the Hebrew idiom (formal equivalence) "I know not a man." Here context demands (and scholars agree) that "to know" is a euphemism for sexual relations (cf. Ge. 4:1). Context in the Gospels clearly show that *parthenos* means "virginity" in the sense of "chaste." *See* MAID

VIRTUE AND VICE LISTS A designation for an inventory list of vices or virtues.

1. Vices: Mt. 15:19; Mk. 7:21-22; Ro. 1:29-32; 1Co. 6:9-10; Gal. 5:19-21.

2. Virtues: 1Ch. 13:13; Gal. 5:22-23; 1Pe. 1:5-8.

VISIONS These are means by which God transfers to men information which otherwise would not be available to them. Sometimes the vision is described and then its interpretation given. In most cases there is only the simple statement "the vision that" so and so had. Then only the message itself is given (Isa. 1:1; Da. 7:2; Ob.1:1; Ac. 10:9-16, 17-23). *See* REVELATION, REVEAL

VISIT, VISITATION When God comes to his people in either reward and honor or punishment and disaster. Usually the latter is meant when used in the expression "the day of visitation" (Jer.

8:12; 10:15; 11:23; 23:12; 46:21; 48:44; 50:27; 51:18; Hos. 9:7). *See* DAY OF THE LORD

VOICE, LISTEN TO THE A Hebrew phrase that means "to hearken or obey" the LORD or man. *See* OBEY

VOPHSI The father of the representative of the tribe of Naphtali among the twelve sent by Moses to spy out the land of Canaan (Nu. 13:14). †

VOW(S) Voluntary promises to God to do certain things, usually but not exclusively in return for some desired favor. Illustrations of both are clear (Ge. 28:20-22; Ps. 132:1-5). In the Mosaic legislation are found sections which regulate the making and implementing of vows, sometimes called dedications (Lev. 22:17-25; 27:1ff.; Nu. 15:1-10). Numbers 6 is related to the special Nazirite vow.

VULGATE {general, common} *See* BIBLE VERSIONS

VULTURE *See* BIRDS 5.

WADI [ravine, valley] *See* BROOK; RIVER

WAFERS A form of bread, often beaten thin before baking. The ordinary variety was baked with honey or oil (Ex. 16:31; Nu. 11:8). Usually the wafer appears in Scripture in connection with one of the offerings (Ex. 29:2; Lev. 7:12).

WAGES Basically this is pay for services rendered. The words are sometimes translated by "hire" or "reward." In early times paid laborers were not as common as today, in view of the fact that each worked his own farm or worked for another for his keep and some extra reward in kind (Ge. 29:15; 31:7). There were not fixed wage scales. This matter was settled between the parties. The law did, however, have some protection in it for the hired one (Lev. 19:13; Dt. 24:14-15). In the NT, a *denarii* was about one day's wage for the common worker.

WAGON *See* CART

WAHEB Noted only in Nu. 21:14. If it is a proper noun, it would be an unidentified place in Moab; and it would also be the only proper noun commencing with the Hebrew letter *w* in the Bible. †

WAIL *See* MOURN, MOURNING

WAISTCLOTH *See* DRESS

WALK
1. A word describing motion. To walk is to go from one place to another (Mt. 2:20; Mk. 2:9).
2. A word describing life-style. To

walk is how one lives his life. It relates to one's conduct in life. Christians are to walk worthy of their calling (Eph. 4:1; Php. 3:17-18; Col. 1:10; 1Th. 2:12). This figurative use is also found in Jn. 8:12; 1Pe. 4:3. The NIV often translates these passages "live," while the KJV uses the more formal "walk."

WALL Fields and vineyards, houses and cities had walls made of sun-dried mud bricks or of stone. In ordinary buildings the stone would be unhewn fieldstone. City walls often had partly-hewn stone, while the more ornate palaces had well-cut and finished stones. Mud was used for mortar or else nothing was used, and the upper tiers, especially in certain periods or situations, were of the mud brick variety. City walls were often massive and carefully built, since protection from attack was one of their chief functions. *See* FORT

WALLED CITY *See* FORT, FORTRESS, FORTIFICATION

WALLET *See* PURSE

WANDER AWAY *See* APOSTASY; APOSTATE

WANDERINGS IN THE WILDERNESS *See* EXODUS

WAR Peace was a scarce commodity in OT times. Nations, peoples, and tribes were constantly at war with one another over land or booty. During the period of Israel's judges there were oppressions by foreign powers, wars of liberation, and then a new cycle of the same. Israel's kings David and Solomon extended Israel's border by war. After the divided monarchy, Israel was attacked again and again by some foreign power until finally both of her kingdoms were taken into captivity. Jesus predicted that there would be wars and rumors of wars to the end of days, and in the last book of the Bible we read of terrible ones connected with the last days themselves (Jdg. 5:8; 11:4; 2Ki. 8:28; Mt. 24:6; Rev. 13:7; 17:14). The Christian life is called a warfare (1Ti. 1:18; 2Ti. 2:3), and the Christian's armor is described in Eph. 6:10-20. *See also* CAMP 2.

WAREHOUSE *See* STOREHOUSE

WARNING *See* EXHORTATION

WARP KJV for "woven" (as opposed to knitted) (Lev. 13:48ff). *See* WEAVING AND SPINNING

WARRIOR *See* ARMS AND ARMOR; ARMY; WAR

WASHERMAN'S FIELD *See* FULLER

WASHING *See* BAPTISM; BATH, BATHING; CLEAN AND UNCLEAN; PURIFICATION

WASHPOT KJV for "washbasin" (Ps. 60:8; 108:9). *See* BOWL; LAVER; SACRIFICES AND OFFERINGS

WATCH
1. In OT times the night was divided into three watches of four hours each (Jdg. 7:19). In NT times the Roman order was apparently followed, four watches each of three hours (Mk. 6:48).
2. What the KJV calls a "watch" the NIV calls an "guard," a group of soldiers, or others who do guard duty (Mt. 27:65-66).
3. To beware, be on guard, take care (Mt. 24:4).

WATCHER An unidentified type of heavenly being used frequently in post-OT literature but only three times in the Bible (Da. 4:13, 17, 23).

WATCHMEN, WATCHTOWER
These towers were for two purposes: to guard the cattle or produce in the field, or to guard entrance to cities or key spots around a city wall. Archaeologists have discovered remaining foundations of numerous such towers at city entrances and around their walls (2Ki. 18:8; Isa. 5:2). The watchmen were those who manned such towers, or simply guards used for other purposes (2Sa. 18:24-27; Isa. 62:6; Hos. 9:8).

WATER, BITTER WATER, WATER OF CLEANSING In a climate such as that in Palestine, where there is no rain whatsoever from late March to late November, water becomes a crucially important commodity. Extensive use is made of cisterns which are filled during the rainy season. These are not sufficient, however, and so a determining factor in the planting of an ancient city was the presence of a perennial spring, or well. This has additional importance in Palestine where there are so few permanently running streams. Water was used not only for drinking and cooking but played an important role in various types of ceremonial washings. Symbolically these washings speak of purification from sin (Lev. 11:32; 16:4; Eze. 36:25; Heb. 10:22).

The *water of bitterness,* the water that brings the curse, was water mixed with dust from the tabernacle floor which a woman suspected of adultery was required to drink. It was a kind of trial by ordeal (Nu. 5:12-31).

The *water of cleansing* (KJV, "separation") is the water for the removal of impurity, the removal of sin (Nu. 19:9; 31:23). This water was usually sprinkled on the person or thing to be cleansed (Nu. 19:21). *See* AIN; CISTERN; FOUNTAIN; POOL; SPRING; THIRST; WELL

WATER OF JEALOUSY *See* WATER ¶ 2.

WATER OF SEPARATION *See* WATER ¶ 3.

WATERING TROUGHS See RUN-NELS

WATERPOT KJV for "water jar" (Jn. 4:28). *See* VESSEL

WAVE OFFERING *See* SACRIFICES AND OFFERINGS

WAY *See* WALK

WAY OF THE SEA *See* GEOGRA-PHY OF THE HOLY LAND, IV. B., ANCIENT ROUTES AND MAJOR TOWNS

WAYFARING MAN *See* STRANGER

WEAKNESS The Christian is to help the weak (1Th. 5:14). We have a high priest who knows our weaknesses (KJV, "infirmities") (Heb. 4:15). *See* FLESH; SICK, SICKNESS

WEALTH In Bible times this meant an abundance of property which in turn consisted of land and buildings, slaves, farm stock, commodities, and metals (Jos. 22:8). It was God who controlled this wealth, whether to give, to withhold, or even to take away (Dt. 8:17; Job 1:9-12). The possession of wealth brings with it special dangers, either to forget God or to covet, which are sinful (Ex. 20:17; Dt. 8:17-18). He who has it is expected to be generous, and its wise use brings God's blessings (2Co. 8:15; 9:10-15; 1Ti. 6:9-10). *See* RICHES

WEAPONS *See* ARMS AND ARMOR

WEASEL *See* BEASTS 8.

WEATHER *See* GEOGRAPHY OF THE HOLY LAND, III. B., FORMA-TIVE FORCES, *Climate*

WEAVING AND SPINNING The latter is the making of thread from small fibers of flax (linen), cotton, or the hair of sheep, goats, or camels. The spindle and distaff are both noted in the Bible (Lev. 13:47; Ex. 35-36; Pr. 31:19; Mt. 3:4). It was forbidden the Israelites to weave from mixed yarns (Lev. 19:19). The finished thread of yarn was woven, usually (but not exclusively) by women, into cloth. The Bible mentions both warp and woof, the two series of threads which were at right angles to each other (Ex. 35:25, 35). The Bible also mentions the weaver's beam, the shuttle, the loom, the pin, and the web (Jdg. 16:14; 1Sa. 17:7; Job 7:6).

WEDDING *See* MARRIAGE

WEEDS *See* PLANTS, PERFUMES, AND SPICES, Plants for Seasoning, *Mustard*; or Miscellaneous Plants 14., *Tares*

WEEK A period of time, usually seven days long. It is also used in the sense of a grouping of seven (Da. 9:24-27). *See* CALENDAR; TIME

WEEKS, FEAST OF *See* CALENDAR and FESTIVALS

WEEKS OF YEARS *See* WEEK

WEEP *See* BURIAL; CAVE

WEEPING AND GNASHING A figure of speech for torment caused by punishment (Mt. 8:12; 13:42, 50; 22:13; 24:51; 25:30; Lk. 13:28). The weeping is not of repentance but loss. The gnashing (grinding or shivering) of teeth is possibly from despair or the cold. This is a figure of speech depicting utter despair, and the reality may be much worse.

WEIGHTS AND MEASURES It is generally agreed that weights and measures in biblical times were not sufficiently fixed and established to enable us to give the exact metric equivalents of today. Futhermore, the standards between the various ancient countries were not fixed and it was also true that within any one country two standards might prevail—for example, royal or common, light or heavy, short or long, common or of the sanctuary. From the existing evidence it is possible, nevertheless, to make rather good approximations.

The description below endeavors to show relationships within the weights or measures themselves, not to discuss in detail the modern equivalents. The NIV footnotes in each case endeavor to give its modern equivalent.

LIQUID MEASURES

Log. Mentioned only in Lev. 14:10, 12ff., equal to one-quarter of a *kab* (two-thirds of a pint).

Hin. One-sixth of a bath and so about one gallon (Ex. 30:24; Nu. 28:14).

Bath. A liquid measure equal to the ephah, about five and one-half gallons (Eze. 45:11, 14).

Cor. Equals ten baths and equal to an homer (1Ki. 5:11; Eze. 45:14).

Metretes. A liquid measure found in Jn. 2:6. Equal in volume to about nine gallons. The NIV, RSV, NASB, JB, and NEB all translate this "twenty to thirty gallons."

DRY MEASURES

Cab. Only in 2Ki. 6:25, possibly one-eighteenth of an ephah.

Omer. One-tenth of an ephah or about two quarts (Ex. 16:13-26).

Seah. Supposedly is one-third of an ephah (Ge. 18:6; 1Ki. 18:32).

Ephah. A dry measure equal to the bath (Eze. 45:11, 14), about one-half of a bushel and one-tenth of a homer (Eze. 45:11).

Homer. Equals ten ephahs and is the same as a cor (1Ki. 4:22; 5:11; Eze. 45:14).

MEASURES OF LENGTH

Finger. Mentioned only in Jer. 52:21, one-quarter of a handbreadth.

Fathom. About six feet (Ac. 27:28).

Handbreadth. The width of the hand at the base of the fingers and thus equal to four fingers, or one-third of a span (Ex. 25:25; Eze. 40:5).

Span. The distance between the extended thumb and little finger and equal to one-half of a cubit (Eze. 43:13).

Cubit. The length of the forearm from elbow to fingertips. These vary with individuals, of course. If one follows the lead of the Siloam inscription in Hezekiah's tunnel, one could estimate the cubit as about seventeen and a half inches.

Rod. The measuring rod of Eze. 40:5ff. was given as six cubits.

Line or *length.* A measuring cord of unspecified length (2Sa. 8:2; Am. 7:17;

Mic. 2:5). *See also* Ps. 78:55 (KJV, *cast a cord*).

MEASURES OF WEIGHTS

Gerah. One-twentieth of a shekel (Ex. 30:13; Eze. 45:12).

Beka. One-half of a shekel (Ex. 38:26).

Shekel. A weight that varied considerably from time to time and in different areas as well. There were royal shekels (known only in Babylonia, apparently), common shekels and temple shekels (2Sa. 14:26; 1Sa. 17:5; Ex. 30:13). These varied from ten grams to thirteen grams.

Mina. Equal to fifty shekels, the common mina is in some cases sixty (Eze. 45:12; Ezr. 2:69). In the NT the unit of money used in Jesus' parable of the ten minas (talents in KJV).

Talent. 3,000 shekels; also, a generic term indicating a large sum.

MISCELLANEOUS MEASURES

Day's Journey. Its length is variously estimated (Ge. 30:36; Ex. 3:18). Regarding a Sabbath day's journey, there also is difference of opinion. Some put it at 2,000 cubits (Ac. 1:12).

Furlong. Not used in the NIV, where the Greek word is rendered as "a considerable distance," equal to about 220 yards. This is a translation of the Greek *stadion* found in the NIV as "stadia" (Rev. 14:20; 21:16; in NIV footnotes to Lk. 24:13, and Jn. 6:19, where the meaning is also stadia). In both of these gospel references the NIV translates it as *miles*.

Pint. Mary anointed Jesus at Bethany with a pint of nard (Jn. 12:3; cf. 19:39).

Pound. Used in the NT, a weight of twelve ounces.

Acre. The amount of area a pair of oxen could plow in one day (1Sa. 14:14; Isa. 5:10).

WELL Wells and springs are of vital importance in the dry Palestine climate. The most common Hebrew word for a well is *be'er* and is found in many place names, such as Beersheba, Beerelim, Beeroth. *See* AIN; CISTERN; FOUNTAIN; POOL; SPRING; WATER

WELLHAUSEN'S THEORY *See* DOCUMENTARY HYPOTHESIS

WEN KJV for "wart" (Lev. 22:22). *See also* SICK, SICKNESS

WEST, DIRECTION OF *See* GEOGRAPHY OF THE HOLY LAND, III. A. TOPOGRAPHY, Setting

WHALE *See* BEASTS 9.

WHEAT *See* PLANTS

WHEEL At first probably just a thin section of a round log, but by about 2000 B.C. the spoked wheel was well known. With the coming of the chariot, the rumbling of wheels meant the coming of an enemy (Jer. 47:3). *See also* POTTER, POTTERY, *potter's wheel*

WHELP KJV for "cub" (of a lion or bear).

WHIP *See* PUNISHMENT; SCOURGE, SCOURGING; STRIPES

WHIRLWIND Any violent wind, but not particularly, if at all, a tornado or whirling wind of that type. It was a strong wind that would bring destruction. The Hebrew word is often translated by "tempest" or just by "storm" (Job 27:20; Isa. 29:6; Na. 1:3).

WHORE, WHOREDOM, WHORE-MONGER *See* FORNICATION; PROSTITUTE

WICKEDNESS *See* SIN

WIDOW Concern for the lot of the widow in the OT is very marked. Along with the orphan and the stranger, God requires that they be well cared for (Ex. 22:21-24; Dt. 24:19-21). *See also* MARRIAGE and specifically *Levirate marriage*. In the NT the early church also gave them special consideration (Ac. 6:1; 1Ti. 5:13-16; Jas. 1:27).

WIELDED HIS SWORD *See* ADINO

WIFE, WIVES *See* CONCUBINE; MARRIAGE

WILD VINE OR GRAPE *See* PLANTS, PERFUMES, AND SPICES, Plants for Food 5., *Grapes*

WILDERNESS *See* DESERT and GEOGRAPHY OF THE HOLY LAND III, C. 3.

WILL *See* TESTAMENT

WILL OF GOD This involves God's wishes, resolves, wants, and desires. God's exact will for the Christian life includes his desires made known in his Word. His *will* will not take one outside of the commands and principles of his Word, as some modern philosophies expound (*see* SITUATION ETHICS). Wisdom is not found in the same confines as modern philosophy (*see* PHILOSOPHY). The Christian is to search for opportunities and make the most of them for God's purposes (Eph. 5:15-16). The will of God includes: not being conformed to the world as a prerequisite to finding out his will (Ro. 12:2); to be set apart by abstaining from fornication (1Th. 4:3); to be joyful, pray, and give thanks in everything continually (1Th. 5:16-18); and to do good (1Pe. 2:15).

WILLOW KJV for "poplar tree." *See* TREES, *Willow, Poplar*

WILLOWS, BROOK OF THE KJV for "Ravine of the Poplars" (Isa. 15:7).

WILLS *See* COVENANT; TESTAMENT

WIND God creates them and controls them for his purposes. They come from the four corners of the earth. The N wind brings cold. The S wind and the E wind bring the dry, hot desert air that sometimes kills. The W wind brings the rain and the moderate breezes. This, of course, is a general characterization only. Gales come from the NW and the NE winds drive rain away (1Ki. 18:44-45; Eze. 37:9; Hos. 13:15; Am. 4:13). The moving of the Spirit of God is likened to the movements of the wind (Jn. 3:8). *See also* Ac. 27:14; EUROCLYDON; LEVANT

WINDOW In biblical times a rectangular opening in the wall of a house. Some had latticework in them and some were recessed (1Ki. 6:4; 7:4). One of the references is to "the windows of heaven," a way of speaking of the place from which rain came (Ge. 7:11; 8:2; Isa. 24:18).

WINE This has always been one of the chief products of Palestine—both when fermented and unfermented. When wine sours to vinegar it is a condiment; mixed with water a favorite drink; and mixed with a drug it was given as a sedative potion to those being executed (Ge. 14:18; 27:28; Lev. 23:13; Pr. 31:45; Mk. 15:23). Priests were forbidden to drink wine while serving, and Nazirites were not even allowed to touch grapes while their vows were on them (Lev. 10:9; Nu. 6:1-4). Grapes were pressed by being trodden underfoot in a press usually made of stone. The juice would run out through a hole near one end into a collecting vat. The juice was put in large jars or sacks made from the skins of animals. *See also* VINE, VINEYARD

WINEBIBBER KJV for "drunkard" (Mt. 11:19; Lk. 7:34).

WINEFAT *See* FAT 3.

WINEPRESS, WINE VAT *See* WINE

WINESKIN A leather pouch made from goat- or sheepskins that held liquid (Jos. 9:4; Mt. 9:17; Mk. 2:22; Lk. 5:37). The animal was skinned in one piece and the cord tied on the appendages; the neck served as the funnel for pouring. An old wineskin did not have enough elastic quality to withstand stretching by new (still fermenting) wine. This image was used by Jesus to indicate that Christianity would not be simply an offshoot of Pharisaism, but a whole new thing (Mt. 9:17).

WING OF TEMPLE *See* PINNACLE

WINNOWING A process in which the chopped stalks and heads of the grain were tossed by a fork or fan into the air so that the wind could blow the chaff away and allow the kernels of grain to fall back onto the threshing floor. At first a wooden fork, like a hay fork, was used, and then later a shovel (Isa. 41:16; 30:24; Mt. 3:12). *See* THRESHING

WINTER *See* CALENDAR; TIME

WISDOM An attribute of God, and a quality of the mind of man which makes him wise and skilled (Dt. 34:9; Jer. 10:9; Ro. 11:33-36). The fear of the LORD is declared to be the beginning of wisdom (Job 28:28; Ps. 111:10; Pr. 9:10). In an extended passage, wisdom is personified (Pr. 8:2ff.). The Bible contains three books in the class of "wisdom literature," what the wise men taught and wrote, and it also includes a number of the Psalms (Pss. 19; 37; 104). The books are Job, Proverbs and Ecclesiastes. In the NT Christ is called the wisdom of God and the source of our wisdom (1Co. 1:24, 30). This wisdom he passes on to men through his Spirit and his Word (the Bible), making it clear and meaningful to men (Col. 3:16; cf. Eph. 6:18). *See* PROVERBS, BOOK OF

WISDOM OF SIRACH *See* SCRIPTURE, *Apocryphal Literature*

WISDOM OF SOLOMON *See* SCRIPTURE, *Apocryphal Literature*

WISE MEN The word is most frequently used to refer to men and women of understanding (Dt. 1:13; Pr. 1:2-6), or those with special skills (Ex. 31:2-5).

In the NT wise men or astrologers (properly *magoi*) from the East came to worship the new King of the Jews (Mt. 2:1, 7, 16). The number coming into Jerusalem, three, is legendary. More likely there would be a notable caravan with dozens or maybe a hundred coming into Jerusalem with pomp. *See also* DIVINATION; ZOROASTRIANISM

WITCH, WITCHCRAFT *See* DIVINATION

WITHERED HAND *See* SICK, SICKNESS

WITNESS One who is called upon to bear witness or to testify concerning what he knows firsthand concerning a fact or an event. It is not used in the Bible in the sense of watching something. Things may also be a witness or a testimony to an event: a heap of stone, an altar, the Ten Commandments, the Law. The Law required at least two or three witnesses to validate the truth (Dt. 17:6; 19:15; Mt. 18:16ff.) The one who bears a false witness is to be punished as for the crime to which he gave the false witness (Dt. 19:16-21). In the NT the witness may be one who bears testimony to truths about God or one who tells what he knows, saw, or heard about Jesus (Jn. 3:11, 32-34; Ac. 1:8; 10:41; 1Jn. 1:1-3).

WITNESS OF THE SPIRIT *See* GOD, NAMES OF, GODHEAD 6., *Holy Spirit*

WIZARD *See* DIVINATION, *spiritist*

WOLF *See* BEASTS 8.

WOMAN Eve was especially created as a "helper fit for" Adam. As a pair they were given dominion over all the creatures, and it was intended by God that they would live together "as one flesh" (Ge. 2:18-25). As a wife she had the particular role of looking after her husband's needs and being a partner with him in procreation. As a mother, a woman is responsible for the care and development of the children (Ge. 24:11; 27:9; Ti. 2:4-5). Respect for mother was mandatory, and disrespect was punishable (Dt. 27:16). As a member of the total society she was deeply involved in the socioeconomic and religious life of the community. She was even involved in the political and military life of the group, as we know from the involvement of the queens and queen mothers, female judges, and deliverers: Miriam, Deborah, Athaliah, Jezebel (Dt. 16:13-14; Jdg. 4:45; 1Ki. 19:1ff.; 2Ki. 22:14; Pr. 31:16-24; Jer. 9:17; Ac. 16:14; 18:2-3). Consistent with the above was the often recounted equality between the men and the women. For example, both parents are to be revered by the children (Dt. 5:16). In spite of this, however, there were areas in which the woman had an inferior status (Lev. 27:1-7). In the NT, women also played leading roles, women such as Elizabeth, Anna, Martha, and the several Marys. After the crucifixion, resurrection, and ascension of Jesus,

the disciples met in Mary's home; there was an early church in Lydia's home; Phoebe was a deaconess (Ac. 12:12; 16;13-15; Ro. 16:1). In the beautiful picture of the family in Eph. 5:21-33 the role of the woman is likened to the bride of Christ, a phrase referring to the church.

WOMAN, YOUNG *See* MAID

WOMB *See* BARREN

WONDERS *See* MIRACLES

WOOF KJV for "knitted" (as opposed to woven) (Lev. 13:48ff.). *See* WEAVING AND SPINNING

WOOL The fleece of sheep or goats, an important product of Palestine. The law forbad wearing garments of mixed linen and wool; and, in a country where snow is relatively rare, wool became a symbol of whiteness and so of purity (Dt. 22:11; Isa. 1:18).

WORD OF GOD *See* SCRIPTURE

WORD, THE LOGOS *See* GOD, NAMES OF, GODHEAD 11.

WORK *See* LABOR

WORKS, SALVATION BY *See* GRACE; SALVATION, APPLICATION OF

WORLD A word with many denotations: the inhabited universe (Lk. 21:26), the universe as a whole (Ac. 4:24), the planet earth (Ac. 17:24), the world of people (Jn. 16:20), the world that is at enmity with God – having different ideas than those of God (Jas. 1:27; 4:4), the place where God's revelation was given and his redemption worked out (Jn. 3:16; 2Co. 5:19). Concerning the origin of this world there is no distinct *ex nihilo* statement to be found in the Bible in just those terms, but the concept is clear and theologically required in such a statement as: "Through him all things were made; without him nothing was made that had been made" (Jn. 1:1-3, NIV). As the world had a beginning, so too its end is pictured. First there is to be removed from it the curse that came on it with man's sin. This takes place at the same time as the revealing of the sons of God in their resurrection bodies (Ro. 8:18-23). After this the Scripture speaks of the passing away (in fire) of the heavens that now are and the establishment of a new heavens and a new earth (2Pe. 3:10-13).

WORM *See* BEASTS 6.

WORMWOOD A plant with a bitter taste, used metaphorically to describe sorrow and bitterness (Pr. 5:4; La. 3:15, 19). In Rev. 8:11, a star by the name of Wormwood is seen falling from heaven and turning a third of the waters on earth to wormwood so that men die from drinking it.

WORSHIP In the OT the two words most frequently used would be literally translated "work/service" and "prostrate oneself." These give the twin ideas of worship/service and homage. These can be rendered to man or God, but here we are concerned with divine worship. In the earliest biblical period, that of Abraham, worship was an individual or family affair. Where there was a theophany, an altar was erected, sacrifices made, and gifts given (Ge. 22:5; 24:26, 48). When the Israelites left Egypt and during their wanderings in the wilderness, God gave the pattern of the tabernacle and the full system of worship through personal and group sacrificing. After the conquest of Palestine, the tabernacle was set up at Shiloh and institutional worship was begun. This was later replaced with the grander temple and developed ritual that included orchestras and choirs. There were added harvest festivals and, with all of them, sacrifices and offerings (Ex. 23:14-19). With the fall of Jerusalem and the destruction of the temple, new systems of worship were developed in Judaism; and with the rise of Christianity, worship took a new route. Private worship took on new importance and the church developed its own liturgies that commemorate the great events in the life of Christ, particularly his atoning death and resur-

rection. The Lord's Supper was the most important of these (1Co. 11:23-26).

WRATH, WRATH OF GOD There are illustrations of the anger and fury of man in the biblical narratives, but they are few (Ge. 49:7; Ps. 76:10; Pr. 15:1; 20:2; Eph. 4:31; Col. 3:8) as compared to the references to the wrath of God. His justice cannot permit some to obey and others to disobey without an expression of displeasure. His holiness cannot accept sin and evil in his subjects without a reaction of negation and an attempt to correct thereby. As justice and holiness are among the infinite, eternal, and unchangeable parts of his being, so must be his wrath. God's reaction to man's sin is expressed in the Westminster Shorter Catechism thus: "All mankind, by their fall, lost communion with God, are under his wrath and curse, and so made liable to all the miseries of this life, to death itself, and to the pains of hell for ever." This is of necessity and by revelation one attribute of the God of the Bible. The other, and perhaps the one that mankind is more ready to accept, is that "God . . . from all eternity . . . elected . . . to deliver them out of the estate of sin and misery, and to bring them into an estate of salvation by a Redeemer." That Redeemer, being God himself, the Son, became man by taking to himself a true body in his birth by the virgin Mary, and in that body he satisfied all the requirements of justice and holiness so that wrath could justly be removed and God's holiness be no longer offended (Ro. 1:18-32; Ro. 4:15; 5:9; Eph. 2:3).

WRESTLE *See* ATHLETE

WRITING PAPYRUS and PARCHMENT. Besides these two writing materials, people wrote on a wide variety of other things: stone, metal, and clay, which was usually baked for preservation. Broken pieces of pots and dishes, called *sherds* (the result is called an *ostracon),* wood, and linen cloth were used. On some the writing had to be done with a reed stylus and ink; on some by a stylus which could make dents in the clay while it was still soft; and on others by incising in rock. The art of writing began with picture writing in Mesopotamia around 3200 B.C. The picture of an object soon came to stand also for related ideas, so that the picture of a bird could also mean "flying." Pictographic (i.e., picture writing) writing thus developed to logographic (i.e., word symbol) and from that to phonetic writing (i.e., symbols relating to sounds) and finally to full alphabetic writing (i.e., a set of symbols relating to specific sounds). In Mesopotamia the pictures became highly stylized with the transfer from simple line drawing to impressing on clay with a triangular headed stylus, so much so that it is virtually impossible to recognize the original item being depicted. That writing is called "cuneiform."

In Egypt the picture writing did not change appreciably during the several millennia in which it was used. Egyptians had many uniconsonantal signs; so they were able to spell out words, and an alphabetic system was easily developed. A cursive and simplified script developed in parallel with the retained picture writing. The Hittites of Asia Minor at some time after 2000 B.C. adapted the Semitic cuneiform system to write their Indo-European language. It was in Palestine, the crossroads of the world, that the first true alphabetic writing originated. At Ras Shamra (ancient Ugarit) in N Syria there was discovered in 1929 a large collection of clay tablets with a writing in cuneiform symbols on them. This turned out to be a genuine alphabet. Another, linear (i.e., drawing with lines)

and not cuneiform (i.e., imprinting wedges in clay), which was developed in the Sinai peninsula, is thought by some to be the first true alphabetic writing. From this there developed in Phoenicia the script that has come to be known as Phoenician. By a gradual process of development this produced the forms of Hebrew writing known today, Greek and Roman writing, and through them our English alphabet as well.

Long before the events of biblical history took place in Mesopotamia, Egypt, and Palestine—well over a thousand years before these events—man knew how to read and write and to record the events of his days for posterity. In the Palestine of Moses' day many different scripts were used, and the scribes of the day recorded the historic occurrences of their times. While many feel that the early books of the Bible are compilations made much later from these sources and from oral tradition *(see* for an example, PENTATEUCH), there is no reason as far as the knowledge and use of writing is concerned not to believe that they were written at the time they indicate and by the people ascribed to them as authors (Ex. 17:14; 24:4; 34:27; Dt. 28:58; 31:9, 24; Jos. 8:32; Mk. 12:19, 26; Lk. 20:28; Ro. 10:5). *See also* HIEROGLYPHICS

WRONGDOING *See* SIN

WYCLIFFE, JOHN John was called the "morning star of the Reformation" (A.D. 1329-1384). He attacked the papacy and the doctrine of the common view of the Lord's Table. He instigated the translation of the Vulgate into English. *See* BIBLE VERSIONS, English Versions

XERXES A king of Persia whose Greek name was Xerxes; ruled Persia from 486 to 465 B.C. He was the husband of Esther, a Jewess, and was known as a cruel despot (Est. 1:2; 2:16-17 and Ezr. 4:6). *See also* AHASUERUS and PERSIA

XENOPHILE One friendly or attracted to foreign persons or things.

YAH An abbreviation of YAHWEH. *See* GOD, NAMES OF, GODHEAD 2.; YHWH

YAHWEH *See* GOD, NAMES OF, GODHEAD 2.

YARKON RIVER *See* GEOGRAPHY OF THE HOLY LAND

YARMUK RIVER *See* GEOGRAPHY OF THE HOLY LAND

YARN *See* KUE

YEAR *See* CALENDAR

YEAST The NIV usually translates the word "unleavened" as "without yeast." It is a substance added to bread dough or liquids to produce fermentation. The yeast used in ancient bread making was a piece of a former batch of dough with this element in it. It is used to illustrate several negative principles: bad influence in Gal. 5:9; the hard-to-understand saying in Mk. 8:15; the doctrine of the Pharisees and Sadducees in Mt. 16:6; and hypocrisy in Lk. 12:1. As seen from the above examples, there is not just one static, unchanging definition of the concept of *leaven* in the Bible. *See* UNLEAVENED BREAD

YES BE YES A wordplay in Greek that stresses that an oath should be unnecessary because there is complete dependability in what one says without any embellishment (Mt. 5:37; Jas. 5:12). When children cross their fingers behind their backs they are not letting their "yes

be yes." If adults have to "swear on a stack of Bibles" in order to establish the truth of a situation, they are not letting their "yes be yes."

YHWH The tetragrammaton (four letters) which come from the Hebrew text for the name of the LORD. When certain vowels are added, either the name *Jehovah* or *Yahweh* can be pronounced. *See* GOD, NAMES OF, GODHEAD 2., *Yahweh*

YIRON A town (189-276) in the tribal area of Naphtali (Jos. 19:38); "Iron" in the NIV and KJV.

YODH The smallest Hebrew letter. *See* JOT

YOKE A wooden frame placed on or over the necks of draft animals which would be attached by various means to the vehicle to be drawn (Dt. 21:3; 1Sa. 6:7). In Scripture the word is much more frequently used of being put in a yoke to be tied to other individuals when being taken into captivity—the yoke of slavery. This then is used figuratively for subjection and servitude, whether to a foreign power or even to God (Ge. 27:40; 1Ki. 12:4-14; Jer. 27:8-12; Mt. 11:29-30; Gal. 5:1). *See also* PLOW

YOKEFELLOW "Yokefellow" is a formal translation of the Greek in Php. 4:3. Functionally, it is a familial term that is endearing—a brother and loyal comrade. The JB transliterates the Greek word as a proper name, "Syzygus." Other versions give this name a footnote. There is not one example of this as a name in all of outside literature, and the adjective ("genuine") that modifies Syzygus makes it awkward to render it as a personal name.

YOM KIPPUR {day of atonement} *See* FESTIVALS 5.

YOUNG WOMAN *See* MAID; VIRGIN BIRTH; WOMAN

Z

ZAANAIM *See* ZAANANNIM

ZAANAN An unidentified place, probably in Judah; possibly the same as Zenan (Micah 1:11). †

ZAANANNIM An unidentified site in the tribal area of Naphtali (Jos. 19:33; Jdg. 4:11).

ZAAVAN [*possibly* trembling, terror] A descendant of Seir, a Horite (Ge. 36:27; 1Ch. 1:42). †

ZABAD [he bestows]
1 and 2. A Jerahmeelite and an Ephraimite (1Ch. 2:36-37; 7:21).
3. One of David's mighty men (1Ch. 11:41).
4. One of the assassins of King Jehoash of Judah (2Ch. 24:26). *See also* JOZABAD
5, 6, and 7. Three who married foreign wives during the Babylonian captivity (Ezr. 10:27, 33, 43).

ZABBAI
1. One who married a foreign wife during the Babylonian captivity (Ezr. 10:28). †
2. The father of one of the men who worked on the repair of the walls of Jerusalem in Nehemiah's day (Ne. 3:20). †

ZABBUD *See* ZACCUR 5.

ZABDI [Yahweh bestows]
1. The father of Achan who took some of the things at Ai that were supposed to have been destroyed (Jos. 7:1, 17-18). *See* ZIMRI

2. A descendant of Benjamin (1Ch. 8:19).
3. One of David's officers who was in charge of the vineyards (1Ch. 27:27).
4. A Levite in the days of Nehemiah; also called Zicri (Ne. 11:17; 1Ch. 9:15).

ZABDIEL [El bestows]
1. The father of David's man who was in charge of his affairs for the first month of each year (1Ch. 27:2). †
2. A priest in the time of Nehemiah (Ne. 11:14). †

ZABUD [(he has) bestowed upon] The father of Solomon's officer over the officers (1Ki. 4:5). †

ZABULON *See* ZEBULUN 2.

ZACCAI The ancestor of some who returned from the Babylonian captivity with Zerubbabel (Ezr. 2:9; Ne. 7:14). †

ZACCHAEUS [righteous, pure one] A tax collector who was one of Jesus' hosts (Lk. 19:28). †

ZACCHUR *See* ZACCUR

ZACCUR, ZAKKUR [remembering]
1. The father of the representative of the tribe of Reuben among the twelve spies (Nu. 13:4).
2. A descendant of Simeon (1Ch. 4:26).
3 and 4. A Merarite and an Asaphite in religious service in David's day (1Ch. 24:27; 25:2).
5. The ancestor of some who returned from the Babylonian captivity

with Ezra. KJV has Zabbud, a variant in the Hebrew text (Ezr. 8:14).

6. One who helped Nehemiah repair the wall of Jerusalem (Ne. 3:2).

7. One who signed the covenant with Nehemiah (Ne. 10:12).

8. Father of one of Nehemiah's treasurers (Ne. 13:13).

ZACHARIAH *See* ZECHARIAH 1.

ZACHARIAS *See* ZECHARIAH 33. (Mt. 23:35), or ZECHARIAH 32 (Lk. 1:5ff.)

ZACHER *See* ZECHER

ZADOK {righteous one}

1. A priest and descendant of Aaron through Eleazar (2Sa. 8:17; 1Ch. 6:8ff.). He was a close associate of David as was his son after him, and in Solomon's day he became the head of the priesthood in Jerusalem (2Sa. 15:24ff.; 1Ki. 2:26ff.).

2. The father of Jerusha, the mother of King Jotham (2Ki. 15:33).

3. A priest and descendant of Zadok 1. (1Ch. 6:12).

4. A military man of valor who joined David at Hebron (1Ch. 12:28).

5 and 6. Two who helped in the repair of the wall of Jerusalem in the time of Nehemiah (Ne. 3:4, 29).

7. One who signed the covenant with Nehemiah (Ne. 10:21).

8. One appointed treasurer by Nehemiah (Ne. 13:13).

9. An ancestor of Jesus (Mt. 1:14).

ZAHAM {putrid, loathsome} A son of King Rehoboam (2Ch. 11:19). †

ZAIR {small, insignificant, *hence* narrow pass} An unidentified city where King Jehoram of Judah fought the Edomites (2Ki. 8:21). †

ZALAPH {low, prickly shrub (caper plant)} The father of one who helped repair the walls of Jerusalem in the days of Nehemiah (Ne. 3:30). †

ZALMON

1. {in his image, a copy}One of David's mighty men (2Sa. 23:28).

2. {black hill} A mountain in the area of Shechem (Jdg. 9:48).

3. {black hill} A region or mountain in Bashan mentioned only once and then in connection with a snowfall (Ps. 68:14).

ZALMONAH {dark, gloomy, shaded place} The first stop (188-021) of the Israelites after they left Mt. Hor (Nu. 33:41-42).

ZALMUNNA {protection refused} A Midianite king killed by Gideon (Jdg. 8:5-21; Ps. 83:11).

ZAMZUMMIMS, ZAMZUM-MITES {babbling ones} A race of "giants" who lived E of the Jordan, whose land was taken over by the Ammonites (Dt. 2:20-21).

ZANOAH

1. A town (150-125) of Judah in the Shephelah (low country) (Jos. 15:34).

2. An unidentified town in the hill country of Judah (Jos. 15:56).

3. Either a personal name or the way of referring to the founder of the town of Zanoah (1Ch. 4:18).

ZAPHENATH-PA(A)NEAH {the (pagan) god speaks and he (*i.e.*, the newborn) lives} The Egyptian name given to Joseph by the Pharaoh (Ge. 41:45).

ZAPHON {*possibly* North *or* (proper name of a god) ZEPHON} A city (204-186) in the tribal area of Gad (Jos. 13:27; Jdg. 12:1; Ps. 48:2).

ZARA, ZARAH *See* ZERAH 3.

ZAREAH, ZAREATH, ZAREATH-ITE(S) *See* ZORAH, ZORATHITES

ZARED *See* ZERED, VALLEY OF

ZAREDA *See* ZARET(H)AN

ZAREPHATH {*possibly* smelting place, BDB; place of pigmenting, staining, KB} A seacoast town (176-316) between Tyre and Sidon to which Elijah was sent (1Ki. 17:9-10; Ob. 20; Lk. 4:26). †

ZARET(H)AN A place (205-172) mentioned in connection with the Israelite crossing of the Jordan River when Joshua was their leader (Jos. 3:16; 1Ki. 4:12).

ZAREPHATH
After being in Samaria, Elijah left Cherith Brook and went to Zarephath, where a widow and her son fed him and gave him lodging.

ZARETH SHAHAR *See* ZERETH SHAHAR

ZARHITES *See* ZERAH, ZERAHITE 4.

ZARTANAH *See* ZARET(H)AN

ZARTHAN *See* ZARET(H)AN

ZATT(H)U
1. The ancestor of some who returned from the Babylonian captivity with Zerubbabel and Ezra. Some of them had married foreign wives (Ezr. 2:8; 8:5; 10:27; Ne. 7:13). †
2. One who signed the covenant with Nehemiah (Ne. 10:14). †

ZAVAN *See* ZAAVAN

ZAZA [a form of a shortened nickname; term of endearment] A Jerahmeelite (1Ch. 2:33). †

ZEALOT, SIMON THE *See* APOSTLES

ZEALOTS [radicals, fanatics] *See* SECTS

ZEALOUS
1. In a good sense, *fervor, ardor, enthusiasm* (2Co. 9:2; Ro. 10:2; Jn. 2:17).
2. In a bad sense, *jealousy* (Ro. 13:13; 1Co. 3:3; Gal. 5:20). *See* JEALOUS, JEALOUSY

ZEBADIAH [Yahweh bestows]
1 and 2. Two descendants of Benjamin (1Ch. 8:15, 17).
3. One who joined David at Ziklag (1Ch. 12:7).
4. A Levite gatekeeper in David's day (1Ch. 26:2).
5. One of the monthly officers of King David (1Ch. 27:7).
6. One of the Levites sent by King Jehoshaphat of Judah to teach the Law (2Ch. 17:8).
7. The governor of the house of Judah in the days of King Jehoshaphat (2Ch. 19:11).
8. One who returned from the Babylonian captivity with Ezra (Ezr. 8:8).
9. A priest who married a foreign wife during the Babylonian captivity (Ezr. 10:20).

ZEBAH [sacrifice] One of the Midianite kings killed by Gideon (Jdg. 8:5ff.).

ZEBAIM *See* POKERETH-HAZ-ZEBAIM

ZEBEDEE [Yahweh bestows] The father of the apostles James and John (Mt. 4:21).

ZEBIDAH The mother of King Jehoiakim of Judah (2Ki. 23:36). †

ZEBINA [one bought, purchased] One who married a foreign wife during the days of the Babylonian captivity (Ezr. 10:43). †

ZEBOIIM One of the cities of the Arabah destroyed along with Sodom and Gomorrah (Ge. 10:19; 14:2, 8; Dt. 29:23).

ZEBOIM [hyenas]
1. An unidentified town occupied by Benjamites after the Babylonian captivity (Ne. 11:34). †
2. A valley in the tribal area of Benjamin (1Sa. 13:18). †

ZEBOIM, VALLEY [Hyena Valley] *See* ZEBOIIM, ZEBOIM

ZEBUDAH *See* ZEBIDAH

ZEBUL [elevation, height, lofty (temple)] The governor of the city of Shechem under the judge Abimelech (Jdg. 9:28-41). †

ZEBULONITE *See* ZEBULUNITE

ZEBULUN [honor—Ge. 30:20, ISBE]
1. One of the twelve sons of Jacob (Ge. 30:20), the founder of one of the tribes of Israel (Rev. 7:8).
2. A territory named after 1. (Eze. 48:27; Mt. 4:13, 15).

ZEBULUNITE A descendant of Zebulun (Jdg. 12:11-12). *See* ZEBULUN

ZECHARIAH [Yahweh remembers] Perhaps the most popular personal name in the Bible, at least a name given to more individuals than any other.
1. One of the kings of Israel. *See* KINGS OF JUDAH AND ISRAEL (2Ki. 14:29; 15:10).
2. The grandfather on the maternal side of King Hezekiah of Judah (2Ki. 18:2).
3. A descendant of Reuben (1Ch. 5:7).
4. A great-uncle of King Saul; also called Zecher (1Ch. 9:37).
5. A Levite musician in David's day (1Ch. 15:18).
6. A priest who took part with David in bringing the Ark up to Jerusalem (1Ch. 15:24).
7 and 8. Two Levites in the time of David (1Ch. 24:25; 26:11).
9. The father of Iddo who was over the tribe of Manasseh in David's service (1Ch. 27:21).
10. One of the men sent by King Jehoshaphat to teach the law to the people (2Ch. 17:7).
11. The father of one who prophesied to King Jehoshaphat of Judah (2Ch. 20:14).
12. One of the sons of King Jehoshaphat (2Ch. 21:2).
13. The son of the priest Jehoiada who prophesied in the days of King Joash of Judah and was ordered by the king to be stoned for it (2Ch. 24:20ff.).
14. One of King Uzziah's spiritual instructors (2Ch. 26:5).

15. One of the Levites who helped to cleanse the temple in the days of the revival under King Hezekiah (2Ch. 29:13).
16. One who helped to repair the temple in the days of King Josiah of Judah (2Ch. 34:12).
17. A chief officer of the temple in the days of King Josiah (2Ch. 35:8).
18. One of the two witnesses whom Isaiah the prophet called upon (Isa. 8:2).
19. A gatekeeper who came back from the Babylonian captivity (1Ch. 9:21).
20 and 21. Two who returned from the Babylonian captivity with Ezra (Ezr. 8:3, 11).
22. One of those sent by Ezra to Casiphia to bring some Levites back to Jerusalem (Ezr. 8:16).
23. One who married a foreign wife during the time of the Babylonian captivity (Ezr. 10:26).
24. One who stood with Ezra while he read the Law to the people (Ne. 8:4).
25 and 26. Two descendants of Judah who came back from the Babylonian captivity (Ne. 11:4-5).
27. A priest in the days of Nehemiah (Ne. 11:12).
28. A priest when Joiakim was the high priest in the days of Nehemiah (Ne. 12:16).
29 and 30. A priest and a Levite who were present at the dedication of the wall of Jerusalem in the days of Nehemiah (Ne. 12:35, 41).
31. One of the twelve minor prophets who by his prophecy and writing encouraged the people in Ezra's days to finish the building of the temple (Ezr. 5:1; 6:14-15).
32. The father of John the Baptist (Lk. 1:5ff.).
33. A martyr mentioned by Jesus, possibly the same as 13 (Mt. 23:35; Lk. 11:51).

ZECHARIAH, BOOK OF *See* PROPHETS, BOOKS OF THE MINOR

ZECHER [(Yahweh) remembers] *See* ZECHARIAH 4.

ZEDAD A city on the N border of Palestine (Nu. 34:8; Eze. 47:15). †

ZEDEKIAH [Yahweh is (my) righteousness]

1. *See* KINGS OF JUDAH AND ISRAEL, Judah's last king.

2. A prophet of God in the days of King Ahab of Israel (1Ki. 22:11ff.).

3. One who signed the covenant with Nehemiah (Ne. 10:1).

4. A false prophet in the days of Jeremiah (Jer. 29:21ff.).

5. One of the princes of King Zedekiah who listened as Baruch read Jeremiah's scroll (Jer. 36:12).

ZEEB [wolf] A prince of Midian killed by Gideon's men (Jdg. 7:25; 8:3; Ps. 83:11). †

ZELAH, ZELA [side, slope]
An unidentified town in the tribal area of Benjamin, where David reburied the remains of King Saul and his son Jonathan (Jos. 18:28; 2Sa. 21:14).

ZELEK [cry aloud, KB] One of David's mighty men (2Sa. 23:37; 1Ch. 11:39). †

ZELOPHEHAD [shadow of dread, terror (*i.e.*, protection from dread and terror) A Manassite who died without a male heir and whose daughters, therefore, were given inheritances in the division of the land in the days of Joshua (Nu. 26:33; 27:1, 7; Jos. 17:3).

ZELOTES [fanatic] *See* ZEALOT, SIMON THE

ZELZAH An unidentified town near Rachel's tomb on the border of Judah (1Sa. 10:2). †

ZEMARAIM [*possibly* double peak, KB]

1. A city (170-146) near the N border of Benjamin (Jos. 18:22). †

2. A mountain in the hill country of Ephraim N of Jerusalem (2Ch. 13:4). †

ZEMARITES [(snow, wool) white; *possibly* peak, height] A Canaanite group that lived N of Lebanon (Ge. 10:18; 1Ch. 1:16). †

ZEMER The unidentified place where the Zemarites lived. *See* ZEMARITES

ZEMIRAH [*possibly* song (with instrumental accompaniment), KB; *possibly* (South Arabic) Yahweh has helped, IDB] A descendant of Benjamin (1Ch. 7:8). †

ZENAN [place of flocks] An unidentified village in the low country of Judah (Jos. 15:37). †

ZENAS [gift of Zeus] A lawyer whom Paul asked Titus to send to him from Crete (Tit. 3:13). †

ZEPHANIAH [Yahweh has hidden (to shelter) *or* Yahweh has hidden (as a treasure)]

1. A descendant of Levi (1Ch. 6:36).

2. A priest in the days of King Zedekiah, taken in one of the captivities and killed (Jer. 21:1; 37:3; 52:24ff.).

3. One of the minor prophets. *See* PROPHETS, BOOKS OF THE MINOR

4. The father of a Josiah from whom they took gold and silver to make a crown for the high priest (Zec. 6:10, 14).

ZEPHANIAH, BOOK OF *See* PROPHETS, BOOKS OF THE MINOR

ZEPHATH [watchtower, IDB] An unidentified town in the tribal area of Judah (Jdg. 1:17). †

ZEPHATHAH [watchtower, IDB] An unidentified valley SW of Jerusalem where the Ethiopians were defeated by King Asa (2Ch. 14:10). †

ZEPHI, ZEPHO [*possibly* gaze, BDB and ISBE; *Assyrian* personal name, KB and IDB] A grandson of Esau (Ge. 36:11; 1Ch. 1:36).

ZEPHON [*possibly* gaze, BDB; *possibly* lookout (tower), watch, KB] A descendant of Gad; also called Ziphion (Nu. 26:15; Ge. 46:16).

ZEPHONITES A descendant of Zephon (Nu. 26:15). *See* ZEPHON

ZER An unidentified town in the tribal area of Naphtali (Jos. 19:35). †

ZERAH, ZERAHITE [dawning, shining *or* flashing (red or scarlet) light, KB]

1 and 2. Two descendants of Esau (Ge. 36:13, 33).

3. A son of Judah by Tamar and the twin brother of Perez (Ge. 38:30).

4. A descendant of Simeon (Nu. 26:13).

5. A descendant of Levi (1Ch. 6:21).

6. An Ethiopian (Cushite) who invaded Judah but was repulsed by King Asa (2Ch. 14:9ff.).

ZERAHIAH [Yahweh shines brightly (red or scarlet); Yahweh has risen (like the sun), BDB]

1. An ancestor of Ezra (Ezr. 7:4).

2. The father of one who returned with Ezra from the Babylonian captivity (Ezr. 8:4).

ZERED, VALLEY OF, BROOK OF [valley of (some kind of) plant] A valley and a brook that divided Edom and Moab and whose waters run into the Dead Sea. The Israelites encamped there before crossing into Canaan (Nu. 21:12; Dt. 2:13-14).

ZEREDA(H) The birthplace (159-161) of the Jeroboam who became the first king of Israel in distinction to Judah (1Ki. 11:26; 2Ch. 4:17). †

ZEREDATHAH *See* ZARET(H)AN

ZERERAH, ZERERATH An unidentified place in the direction in which Gideon's army pursued the Midianites after their defeat (Jdg. 7:22).

ZERESH [possibly (pagan goddess) Kirisha, BDB and IDB; gold, ISBE; mop-head, KB] The wife of the Haman in the Persian court who wished to destroy the Jews (Est. 5:10, 14; 6:13). †

ZERETH A descendant of Judah (1Ch. 4:7). †

ZERETH SHAHAR A city (203-111) in Moab assigned to the tribe of Reuben (Jos. 13:19). †

ZERI [balsam, IDB] A Levitical musician in David's day (1Ch. 25:3). †

ZEROR [money bag, pouch *or possibly* pebbles, KB] An ancestor of King Saul (1Sa. 9:1). †

ZERUAH [one with skin disease] The mother of Jeroboam I, son of Nebat, the first king of Israel after the final schism (1Ki. 11:26). †

ZERUBBABEL [offspring (seed) of Babylon, BDB, ISBE and KB; scion (*i.e.*, one grafted into the "plant") of Babylon, IDB] The grandson of King Jehoiachin who brought a group of captives back to Palestine at the end of the Babylonian captivity (1Ch. 3:19; Ezr. 2:2; Hag. 1:1), and then became governor of Jerusalem.

ZERUIAH [perfumed resin, IDB and KB] A sister of David and the mother of three of David's important military people: Joab, Abishai, and Asahel (2Sa. 2:18; 1Ch. 2:16).

ZETHAM [*possibly* olive tree] A descendant of Levi, living in David's day (1Ch. 23:8; 26:22). †

ZETHAN [olive tree *or* one who deals in olives] A descendant of Benjamin (1Ch. 7:10). †

ZETHAR [*possibly* conqueror, BDB; slayer, KB] One of the eunuchs of the Persian King Ahasuerus (Est. 1:10). †

ZEUS [shine, bright] Ac. 14:12-13. † *See* DEITIES 1., *gods of Greece*

ZIA [*possibly* trembler, IDB] A descendant of Gad (1Ch. 5:13). †

ZIBA [gazelle] A servant of King Saul who was given the role of looking after his lame son (2Sa. 9:1ff.; 16:1.; 19:26ff.).

ZIBEON [hyena] A descendant of Seir, a Horite (Ge. 36:2).

ZIBIA [gazelle] A descendant of Benjamin (1Ch. 8:9). †

ZIBIAH [gazelle] The mother of Jehoash, King of Judah (2Ki. 12:1; 2Ch. 24:1). †

ZICRI, ZICHRI [Yahweh remembers, IDB]

1. A descendant of Levi (Ex. 6:21).

2, 3, and 4. Three descendants of Benjamin (1Ch. 8:19, 23, 27).

5 and 6. Two descendants of Levi (1Ch. 8:27; 9:15).

7. A descendant of Reuben (1Ch. 27:16).

8. A descendant of Judah (2Ch. 17:16).

9. The father of one of the military officers who helped to put the young Joash on the throne of Judah (2Ch. 23:1).

10. One of King Pekah's men involved in the plot that put Pekah on the throne of Israel (2Ch. 28:7).

11. A descendant of Benjamin in the days of Nehemiah (Ne. 11:9).

12. A priest when Joiakim was high priest in Nehemiah's day (Ne. 12:17).

ZIDDIM [place on the sides or flanks (of the hill)] An unidentified town in the tribal area of Naphtali (Jos. 19:35). †

ZIDKIJAH *See* ZEDEKIAH 3.

ZIDON *See* SIDON

ZIDONIANS People from Sidon, Sidonians. *See* SIDON

ZIF *See* CALENDAR, *Ziv, May*

ZIHA
1. The ancestor of some temple servants who returned from the Babylonian captivity with Zerubbabel (Ezr. 2:43; Ne. 7:46).
2. An overseer (Ne. 11:21). †

ZIKLAG A city (119-088) first in the tribal area of Simeon and then in that of Judah which was taken and held by the Philistines until the time of David when Achish the Philistine king of Gath gave it to him (Jos. 15:31; 19:5; 1Sa. 27:6; 30:1-26; 2Sa. 1:1; 4:10). After the return from the Babylonian captivity, it was again occupied by Jews (Ne. 11:28).

ZIKRI *See* ZICRI

ZILLAH [(God is my) shadow (*i.e.*, protection)] One of the wives of Lamech (Ge. 4:19-23). †

ZILLETHAI [Yahweh is (my) shadow (*i.e.*, protection)]
1. A descendant of Benjamin (1Ch. 8:20). †

ZIKLAG. (Arrows show David's military ventures.)

2. A descendant of Manasseh who joined David at Ziklag (1Ch. 12:20). †

ZILPAH [short-nosed person, KB] Leah's slave and Jacob's concubine, the mother of Gad and Asher (Ge. 29:24; 30:9ff.).

ZILTHAI *See* ZILLETHAI 1. and 2.

ZIMMAH [consider, plan, ISBE]
1 and 2. Two descendants of Levi (1Ch. 6:20, 42).

ZIMRAN [wild goats, sheep, ISBE] A son of Abraham by Keturah (Ge. 25:2; 1Ch. 1:32). †

ZIMRI [wild goats, sheep, ISBE; *possibly* awe of Yahweh, IDB]
1. A king of Israel for seven days who murdered his predecessor and then killed himself (1Ki. 16:8ff.).
2. A descendant of Simeon killed by Aaron's grandson for bringing a Midianite woman into the camp of Israel (Nu. 25:6ff.).
3. A descendant of Benjamin (1Ch. 8:36).
4. An ancestor of the Achan who brought trouble on Israel at Ai (Jos. 7:1, 17-18; 1Ch. 2:6).
5. *See also* KINGS OF JUDAH AND ISRAEL.

ZIN *See* GEOGRAPHY OF THE HOLY LAND

ZINA [*possibly* dry place] A descendant of Levi; also called Ziza (1Ch. 23:10-11).

ZION *See* JERUSALEM

ZIOR [small, insignificant] An unidentified city in Judah (Jos. 15:54). †

ZIPH, ZIPHITES

1. A descendant of Caleb (1Ch. 2:42).

2. A descendant of Judah, son of Jehallelel (1Ch. 4:16). Some relate him to 1.

3. A town, an inheritance of Judah, in the Negev, probably related to 1 (Jos. 15:24). Not currently identified.

4. A town, an inheritance of Judah, in the hill country (Jos. 15:55; 2Ch. 11:8). Identified as Tell Ziph (162-098).

5. A desert that was the place where David sought refuge from Saul. The Ziphites were apparently inhabitants of this region. This is related to 4 (1Sa. 23:14-23; 26:1-5; Ps. 54, title).

ZIPHAH A descendant of Judah and brother of Ziph 2. (1Ch. 4:16).

ZIPHIMS *See* ZIPH 5.

ZIPHION [*possibly* gaze, BDB and ISBE; *possibly* place of the lookout, tower, KB] *See* ZEPHON

ZIPHITES *See* ZIPH

ZIPHRON A place on the N border of Canaan (Nu. 34:9). †

ZIPPOR [bird, swallow] The father of the Balak who brought Balaam to curse Israel (Nu. 22:2, 4, 10).

ZIPPORAH [bird, swallow] The wife of Moses (Ex. 2:21-22; 4:24ff.; 18:2). †

ZITHER *See* MUSIC, MUSICAL INSTRUMENTS, (3), *Stringed Instruments*

ZITHRI *See* SITHRI

ZIV [bright (as in colorful flowers)] *See* CALENDAR

ZIZ [*possibly* ascent where the flowers grow] A mountain pass in SE Judah near En Gedi (2Ch. 20:16). †

ZIZA, ZIZAH [a childish reduplicated abbreviation, as a name of endearment, IDB and ISBE]

1. A descendant of Simeon (1Ch. 4:37).

2. A son of Judah's King Rehoboam (2Ch. 11:20).

3. *See* ZINA.

ZOAN A city in NE Egypt; also called Avaris. It was the Hyksos capital. Later it was called Per-Raamses and even later Tanis, from which the Hebrew name Zoan is derived (Nu. 13:22; Ps. 78:12, 43; Isa. 19:11, 13; Eze. 30:14).

ZOAR [small, insignificant] A city (194-049) connected with Sodom and Gomorrah in the attack of the kings and in the overthrow of the area by God (Ge. 13:10; 14:2-8; 19:22-30).

ZOBA(H) A town (162-132) and kingdom N of Palestine. Saul and David fought against it (1Sa. 14:47; 2Sa. 8:3-12; 10:6-8; 1Ch. 18:35).

ZOBEBAH [one who slithers (like a lizard), *or* one born in a covered wagon] *See* HAZZOBEBAH

ZIPH
From the forest of Hereth, David attacked the Philistines at Keilah. Saul came from Gibe-ah to attack David, but David escaped into the wilderness of Ziph. Having met Jonathan at Horesh, David then fled to the caves of Engedi.

Mediterranean
Sea

CANAAN

valley
of Sorek •Eshtaol
•Zorah •Jerusalem

Jordan R.

N

Hebron•

•Gaza

Dead
Sea

0   10 Mi.
0   10 Km.

ZODIAC *See* DIVINATION, DIVINE, *Astrology*

ZOHAR [one yellowish red, tawny]
1. The father of the Hittite from whom Abraham bought the burial cave for his wife and family (Ge. 23:8; 25:9).
2. A son of Simeon (Ge. 46:10; Ex. 6:15); also called Zerah.
3. A son of Helah (1Ch. 4:7).

ZOHELETH [serpent] A marker stone (1Ki. 1:9). †

ZOHETH [proud] A descendant of Judah (1Ch. 4:20). †

ZOPHAH [bellied jug] A descendant of Asher (1Ch. 7:35-36). †

ZOPHAI [(dripping, full) honeycomb] An ancestor of Samuel; also called Zuph (1Sa. 1:1; 1Ch. 6:26). †

ZOPHAR [*possibly* peep, twitter (as a bird), KB] One of the three friends of Job (Job 2:11; 11:1; 20:1; 42:9). †

ZOPHIM [watchers, lookouts] An unidentified height to which Balak took Balaam when he wanted him to curse Israel (Nu. 23:14). †

ZORAH, ZORATHITES A city (148-131) that first belonged to Dan and then went to Judah (Jos. 19:41; 15:33). The city is found in the Samson accounts (Jdg. 13:2, 25; 16:31). The Danites sent their spies up N from this city (Jdg. 18:11).

ZOREAH *See* ZORAH

ZORITES 1Ch. 2:54.

ZOROASTRIANISM A religion founded in Iran by Zoroaster (*Iranian, Zarathustra*) in the sixth century B.C. He taught an ethical religion founded in the folk religion of Iran. He promoted the worship of one spirit, *Ahura-Mazda*. According to Herodotus, its priestly class was known as *Magi*. It is reasonable that the Persians came into contact with Jewish exiles from the time of Daniel on, which could perhaps explain how the *Magi* knew about the one born King of the Jews. *See* WISE MEN

ZOROBABEL *See* ZERUBBABEL

ZUAR [little one] The father of Nethanel, the representative of the tribe of Issachar in the census of Moses (Nu. 1:8; 2:5; 7:18, 23; 10:15). †

ZUPH [honeycomb] *See* ZOPHAR

ZUR [rock]
1. The daughter of the Midianite chief, who was killed, along with her father, by Aaron's son when she was brought into the camp of Israel (Nu. 25:15; 31:8).
2. A descendant of Benjamin (1Ch. 8:30; 9:36).

ZURIEL [El is (my) rock] A descendant of Levi (Nu. 3:35). †

ZURISHADDAI [Shaddai is (my) rock] The father of the representative of the tribe of Simeon in the census taken by Moses (Nu. 1:6).

ZUZIM, ZUZITES [strong nations, ISBE; babblers, KB] The name of a people, not identified, who lived in the days of Abraham in an unidentified place called Ham (Ge. 14:5). †

ZWINGLI, HULDRYCH A Swiss Reformer (A.D. 1484-1531). His break with the Roman church was more radical than Luther's on the questions of the sacraments and past traditions. In the last years of his life, he became politically active.